JOHN OF IBELIN

THE MEDIEVAL MEDITERRANEAN

PEOPLES, ECONOMIES AND CULTURES, 400-1500

VOLUME 50

JOHN OF IBELIN

Le Livre des Assises

EDITED BY

PETER W. EDBURY

BRILL
LEIDEN · BOSTON
2003

Cover illustration: Godfrey of Bouillon presents the laws to the people in Jerusalem. Venice: Bib. Marciana: MS fr. App. 20 (= 265) fo. 1r: reproduced with permission.

This book is printed on acid-free paper.

Library of Congress Cataloging-in-Publication Data

The Library of Congress Cataloging-in-Publication Data is available on http://catalog.loc.gov

ISSN 0928–5520
ISBN 90 04 13179 5

PRINTED IN THE NETHERLANDS

To my colleagues in the School of History and Archaeology, Cardiff University

CONTENTS

PREFACE

All historians rely to a greater or lesser extent on texts edited by their predecessors, and to these men and women we owe a tremendous debt and one that can never be repaid. We can, however, follow in their footsteps, and in a sense therefore this edition is an expression of gratitude to all those whose editorial labours in the past have facilitated my own research as well as being something that it is hoped will be of value to scholars in the future. It has taken several years, and during that time many people have been generous with their advice, expertise and support. I want to thank all those, both in Cardiff and elsewhere, who have allowed me to use them as a sounding board for my ideas. In particular I should like to mention Jonathan Riley-Smith, who first introduced me to John of Ibelin and his *magnum opus* as long ago as 1969; Wolfgang van Emden for his advice on Old French; and Jaroslav Folda, John France, Michael Metcalf, Catherine Otten-Froux and Jean Richard for answering particular questions. In Cardiff my colleagues, Denys Pringle, Helen Nicholson, Peter Coss and Bill Aird, have been a constant source of help and encouragement, and it is to them and our other colleagues that this work is dedicated.

Progress on this project was helped immensely by the award of a British Academy/Leverhulme Trust Senior Research Fellowship for the academic year 1999–2000, and it is a particular pleasure for me to record my thanks to these bodies. Thanks are also due to the A.G. Leventis Foundation and the late Mr Constantine Leventis for a grant to purchase microfilm of the principal manuscripts.

Finally I should also like to thank Julian Deahl, Marcella Mulder and their colleagues at Brill Academic Publishers for their patience and unfailing courtesy throughout.

Peter Edbury
January 2003

INTRODUCTION

1. The Author and his work

John of Ibelin, count of Jaffa and Ascalon and lord of Ramla, was one of the foremost aristocrats in the Latin East in the mid-thirteenth century. In the thirty years before his death at the end of 1266 he was a member of a small group of closely related nobles who dominated the politics of the truncated kingdom of Jerusalem and who at the same time had powerful interests in the kingdom of Cyprus. John's father, Philip of Ibelin, had been regent of Cyprus from 1218, and, until his death in 1236, his uncle and namesake, John of Ibelin lord of Beirut, had led the opposition in the East to the Hohenstaufen emperor, Frederick II. The family had been in the East since early in the twelfth century, and by the time of John's birth in c. 1216 the Ibelins were already closely related to the royal families of both Jerusalem and Cyprus. In 1232–33 John was just old enough to participate in the closing stages of the war against the emperor's partisans. Their success left his kinsmen in control of most of the kingdom of Jerusalem and the dominant force in Cyprus where the youthful king, Henry I, relied heavily on their counsel. John and Henry were each to marry a sister of King Hethum I of Cilician Armenia (1226–69), and it may have been his proximity to the throne that resulted in Henry giving John the town and lordship of Jaffa and reviving the title of count that had lain dormant since the late twelfth century. This grant can be dated to 1246 or 1247, and henceforth John had the onerous responsibility of defending the southern frontier of the kingdom of Jerusalem. His subsequent career is reasonably well-documented. He was briefly regent in Acre in the mid-1250s, and in 1258 he intervened decisively in the War of Saint Sabas, fought between the Genoese and Venetians in and around Acre, by bringing the authorities there firmly over to the side of the Venetians who were then winning. John clearly behaved in a manner typical of the high nobility of his age. John of Joinville singled him out for the conspicuous display of his arms during the crusade of King Louis IX, and Pope Urban IV was later to censure him for his illicit relationship with Plaisance of Antioch, the widowed queen of Cyprus.

Jaffa itself fell to the Muslims in 1268, little over a year after John's death. His heirs, now based in Cyprus where they had substantial estates, continued to style themselves 'counts of Jaffa and Ascalon' until the extinction of the line around the middle of the fourteenth century.[1]

John was the author of two extant works: the legal treatise, and a short discourse on the regency, or *bailliage*, of the kingdom of Jerusalem which is edited below as appendix 8.[2] The history of the regency is highly tendentious and sets out to justify the Ibelin dominance in Acre to 1258. John was writing his legal treatise, or at least was putting the finishing touches to it, between 1264 and his death two years later. This, as Maurice Grandclaude established in the 1920s, we learn from a chance remark in which John referred to his brother-in-law, the Cilician Armenian nobleman Oshin of Gorighos, as deceased.[3] Oshin was a brother of King Hethum I, and the Armenian sources record his death as having occurred in December 1264.[4] The manuscripts do not give a title for the work, but the rubric to the prologue in the earliest versions would indicate *Le livre des assises et des usages et des plais de la haute cort dou reiaume de Jerusalem*. Later manuscripts suggest, *Le livre des assises et des bons usages dou roiaume de Iherusalem*, but the earlier alternative, with its mention of the High Court and the reference to pleading which is given ample attention in the text, seems preferable.

2. The *Livre des Assises*

At almost 160,000 words, John's legal treatise is by far the longest of the vernacular legal writings from the Latin East. Despite, or perhaps because of its size, it acquired a reputation as the best work on its subject, with the result that later redactors sought to improve it by adding material drawn from other sources or by writing new

[1] For a detailed treatment of his career, P.W. Edbury, *John of Ibelin and the Kingdom of Jerusalem* (Woodbridge, 1997), chapter 3.

[2] Previous published as 'Documents relatifs à la successibilité au trône et à la régence', *R[ecueil des] H[istoriens des] C[roisades]. Lois*, 2, cap. 2, pp. 397–401.

[3] Cap. 131. M. Grandclaude, *Étude critique sur les Livres des Assises de Jérusalem* (Paris, 1923), p. 88.

[4] *La Chronique attribuée au Connétable Smbat*, trans. G. Dédéyan, Documents relatifs à l'histoire des croisades 13 (Paris, 1980), p. 116 and n. 13.

sections so that in the end, in the version assembled in Cyprus in 1369 that was intended as an official work of reference in the Cypriot High Court, the book had come to exceed 200,000 words. It is fortunate that one of the extant medieval manuscripts, MS V, is a copy of the 1369 version. The fact that it was still being revised and copied in Cyprus over a century after John's death is testimony to its reputation. Even more remarkable is the fact that in the 1530s the Venetian authorities in Cyprus had it and other legal texts translated into Italian.[5] On that occasion, however, they chose not to translate the 1369 revision—maybe the official copy had been lost—but instead decided to use the manuscript here designated as MS A which had belonged to John de Nores, a member of the commission charged with making the translation. Indeed, it was as a direct result of this decision that the manuscript was taken to Venice, eventually to find its way into the Marciana Library.[6]

In the seventeenth century John's treatise became the subject of antiquarian interest. In 1626 Nicolas-Claude Fabri de Peiresc (1580–1637) arranged for the Vatican manuscript (MS V) to be copied, and at least six manuscripts, all dating from the seventeenth century, survive that are derived from this copy. Peiresc's copy was defective—the copyist clearly cheated his patron by omitting passages from many of the longer chapters—but it was from a manuscript descended from Peiresc's that the first printed edition of the French text was made. This was work of G. Thaumas de La Thaumassière and was published in Bourges in 1690.[7] Also in the seventeenth century the English jurist and antiquarian, John Selden (1584–1654),

[5] Edited in *L'Alta Corte, le Assise, et buone usanze del Reame de Hyerusalem* (Venice, 1535), fols 1–74^{v}; P. Canciani (ed.), *Barbarorum leges antiquae* (Venice, 1792), 5, pp. 133–296. The fullest modern discussion of the sixteenth-century Italians translation is G. Grivaud, Ὁ πνευματικός βίος και η γραμματολογία κατά την περίοδο τησ Φραγκρατίας, in *Ιστορία της Κύπρου*, ed Th. Papadopoullos, vol. 5 (Nicosia, 1996), pp. 1133–9.

[6] For annotations made to the manuscript in the 1530s, see *RHC Lois*, 1, p. 21 note 1.

[7] G. Thaumas de La Thaumassière, *Coustumes de Beauvoisis, par Messire Philippes de Beaumanoir Bailly de Clermont en Beauvoisis. Assises et bons usages du royaume de Jerusalem, par Messire Jean d'Ibelin comte de Japhe et d'Ascalon, sire de Rames et de Baruth. Et autres anciennes coutumes le tout tiré des Manucripts* (Bourges, 1690); M. Grandclaude, 'Classement sommaire des manuscrits des principaux livres des assises de Jérusalem', *Revue historique de droit français et étranger* ser. 4, 5 (1926), pp. 450–2, 471–5; P.W. Edbury, 'The Disputed Regency of the Kingdom of Jerusalem, 1264/6 and 1268', *Camden Miscellany*, 27 (= Camden Fourth Series, 22, 1979), pp. 1–3.

acquired the manuscript (MS O) which in the fifteenth century had belonged to Francesco Attar, another member of the commission established in Cyprus by the Venetians in 1531 to translate the work into Italian. This manuscript, along with Selden's other books, subsequently passed into the possession of the Bodleian Library in Oxford. Similarly, the two medieval manuscripts that eventually found their way into the Bibliothèque Nationale in Paris (MSS B and C) are known to have been in the possession of French *érudits* at the same period, and excerpts from John's text are also to be found in a seventeenth-century manuscript evidently copied in Lorraine and now in Munich.[8]

The edition on which historians have hitherto had to rely appeared in 1841 edited by Count A. Beugnot in the first volume of the *Lois* in the new series sponsored by the Académie des Inscriptions et Belles-Lettres: the *Recueil des Historiens de Croisades*.[9] Although Beugnot's edition has the appearance of being based on a critical analysis of the manuscripts, in fact he only used those that were located in Paris, and he totally failed to appreciate the nature of the manuscript tradition. Probably influenced by the fact that the Venice manuscript had served as the base for the sixteenth-century Italian translation, he chose to base his edition on an eighteenth-century copy of that manuscript (now BN fr. 12206) which he designated MS A. He did make use of two medieval manuscripts (MSS B and C) as well as two of the seventeenth-century manuscripts derived from Peiresc's copy (Beugnot's MSS D and E) and the La Thaumassière edition. In the 1920s Maurice Grandclaude pointed out the shortcomings of Beugnot's edition, and, together with Georges Recoura, he made major progress in locating the principal manuscripts and constructing a *stemma*.[10] But although the inadequacies of Beugnot's edition have frequently been lamented, it is only now that a new critical edition has been made.

---

[8] Grandclaude, 'Classement sommaire', pp. 455–8, 459–60, 467–71.

[9] *RHC Lois*, 1, pp. 1–432.

[10] Grandclaude, *Étude critique*, pp. 81–8; idem, 'Classement sommaire', pp. 440–53, 455–8, 459–63, 475; G. Recoura, 'Notes sur six manuscrits inédits ou peu connus des Assises de Jérusalem', *Mélanges d'archéologie et d'histoire de l'École française de Rome*, 42 (1925), pp. 147–51.

3. The Manuscripts

No autograph has survived. What we have are five manuscripts from the medieval centuries from which all later copies are derived, and it is on a examination of these five that this edition has been prepared. In the order in which they will be considered they are:

- MS C: Paris Bibliothèque Nationale: MS fr. 19025 (= Beugnot's MS C)
- MS O: Oxford Bodleian: MS Selden 3457 (otherwise MS Selden Supra 69) (unknown to Beugnot)
- MS A: Venice Marciana: Ms fr. App. 20 (= 265) (not used by Beugnot who used an eighteenth-century copy as his MS A)
- MS B: Paris Bibliothèque Nationale: MS fr. 19026 (= Beugnot's MS B)
- MS V: Rome Vatican: Codex Vaticanus latinus 4789 (not used by Beugnot who used corrupt seventeenth-century derivatives as his MSS D and E)

MS C: Paris BN: MS fr. 19025

Provenance: Acre c. 1280—comprising 220 folios numbered 2–221 (i.e. the end-paper is counted as fol. 1).

Contents: solely John of Ibelin's treatise with no table of contents. Chapter numbers in roman numerals (i–ccxxv) added after the manuscript was written.

Bibliography: J. Folda and P.W. Edbury, 'Two Thirteenth-Century Manuscripts of Crusader Legal Texts from Saint-Jean d'Acre', *Journal of the Warburg and Courtauld Institutes*, 57 (1994), pp. 243, 249–50, 253–4 (with references to earlier literature).

Illustration: Folda and Edbury, 'Two Thirteenth-Century Manuscripts', plate 32 (fol. 2^{r}).

MS O: Oxford Bodleian: MS Selden 3457

Provenance: Cyprus early fourteenth century (fols 1–310) with additions of the fifteenth and sixteenth centuries (fols i–xiv and 311–13)—comprising 326 folios numbered i–xiv and 1–313. Lacks fol. 196 and an unnumbered folio from between fols 306 and 307. Owned in the early sixteenth century by the Cypriot Francesco Attar (cf. fols iii^{r}, 1^{r}).

Contents:

(i) Rubrics to John of Ibelin's treatise, not taken from the recension which forms the bulk of this manuscript but from the version preserved in MS A, added in a fifteenth-century hand. Fols iii^{r}–xiii^{r}. (These rubrics have not been utilised in this edition.)

(ii) Ordinance of King James I of Cyprus dated January 1396 (n.s.). Fols xiii^{v}–xiv^{v}. Edited J. Richard, 'Freedom and Servitude in Cyprus and Rhodes: An Assize Dating from 1396', in *Intercultural Contacts in the Medieval Mediterranean*, ed. B. Arbel (= *Mediterranean Historical Review*, 10) (London, 1995), pp. 272–9.

(iii) John of Ibelin's treatise. Fols 1^{r}–310^{v}. The chapters were originally unnumbered, but numbers in roman numerals have been supplied in a sixteenth century hand (that of Francesco Attar?) from MS A. The same person has also made marginal notes noting chapters present in MS A but missing from this manuscript and indicating that they have been added on additional folios at the end.

(iv) Sixteenth-century copy from MS A of chapters missing from the text. Fols 311^{r}–313^{v}. There was originally more of this material, and it is clear that one or more signatures have been lost. According to marginalia at fol. xiii^{r}, the last chapter (MS A chapter 273 = appendix 3.13 of this edition) began at fol. 326. (The text of the surviving folios has not been utilised in this edition.)

Bibliography: G. Recoura, 'Notes sur six manuscrits inédits ou peu connus des Assises de Jérusalem', *Mélanges d'archéologie et d'histoire de l'École française de Rome*, 42 (1925), pp. 147–8; M. Grandclaude, 'Classement sommaire des manuscrits des principaux livres des assises de Jérusalem', *Revue historique de droit français et étranger*, ser. 4, 5 (1926), pp. 456–8.

Illustration: D. and I. Hunt (eds.), *Caterina Cornaro: Queen of Cyprus* (London, 1989), p. 20 (fol. 52^{r}).

MS A: Venice Marciana: Ms fr. App. 20 (= 265)

This comprise two distinct manuscripts bound together. Owned in the mid-fifteenth century by the Cypriot nobleman John of Nores (cf. fol. ccclxiv^{v}), and in the sixteenth by his descendant and namesake, John of Nores count of Tripoli (cf. fol. i^{r}) in whose time it was taken to Venice.

PROVENANCE:
(a) Acre c. 1290 with later additions (see (iv) below). Fols 1–10 and i–cciv.
(b) Cyprus, mid-fourteenth century (after 1346 with additions dating to after 1355—see (xiv) below). Fols ccv–ccclxiv.

CONTENTS:
(A) ACRE SECTION

(i) Rubrics to John of Ibelin's treatise. Fols 1r–9v. (Fol. 10r–v blank)
(ii) John of Ibelin's treatise in 273 chapters. Fols ir–clxxivv. Fol. ir has a double column headpiece miniature and an illuminated initial.
(iii) John of Ibelin's discourse on the regency. Fols clxxivv–clxxviir. Edited below as appendix 8.
(iv) Summary index of chapter headings to John of Ibelin's treatise. Fol. clxxviir–v. (Fol. clxxviir is in a distinct, later (?) fourteenth-century hand and fol. clxxviiv in another later (?) fifteenth-century hand.) Edited below as appendix 4.3.
(v) Geoffrey Le Tor's treatise, version A. Fols clxxviiir–clxxxiir. (Fol. clxxxiiv blank). Edited *RHC Lois*, 1, pp. 435–43.
(vi) James of Ibelin's treatise. Fols clxxxiiir–cxcir. Edited *RHC Lois*, 1, pp. 453–68.
(vii) *Les Lignages d'Outremer* (earlier recension). Fols cxcir–cxcviiv. Edited *RHC Lois*, 2, pp. 441–3, 444–5, 446–7, 450–9, 466–7, caps 1, 3, 5–6, 9–20, 31.
(viii) *De la bataille por murtre*. Fols cxcviiir–ccr. Edited *RHC Lois*, 2, pp. 327, 329, 331, 333, 335.
(ix) *Document relatif au service militaire*. Fols ccv–ccivv. Edited *RHC Lois*, 2, pp. 427–34.

(B) CYPRUS SECTION

(x) Philip of Novara's treatise. Fols ccvr–cclxv. Edited *RHC Lois*, 1, pp. 471–571.
(xi) *Le clef des assises*. Fols cclxir–cclxxviiiv. Edited *RHC Lois*, 1, pp. 575–600.
(xii) *Abrégé du livre des assises de la cour des bourgeois*. Fols cclxxixr–ccclviiv. Edited *RHC Lois*, 2, pp. 233–352.

(xiii) *Formules*. Fols ccclviii^{r}–ccclxi^{v}. Edited *RHC Lois*, 2, pp. 383–9.
(xiv) *Assise* of May 1355. Fols ccclxii^{r}–ccclxiv^{v} (in later (?) cursive script). Edited *RHC Lois*, 2, pp. 373–8.

Bibliography: Folda and Edbury, 'Two Thirteenth-Century Manuscripts', pp. 244–9, 250–3 (with references to earlier literature).
Illustration: Folda and Edbury, 'Two Thirteenth-Century Manuscripts', plate 31 (fol. 1^{r}). J. Folda, 'The Hospitaller Master in Paris and Acre: Some Reconsiderations in Light of New Evidence', *Journal of the Walters Art Gallery*, 54 (1996), p. 272 plate 5 (fol. 1^{r} detail of miniature—colour)

MS B: Paris Bibliothèque Nationale: MS fr. 19026
Provenance: Cyprus (?), mid fourteenth century—comprising 277 folios numbered in arabic numerals. Fols 1–16 appear not to have formed part of the original manuscript.

Contents:
(i) *Livre des Assises de la cour des Bourgeois* (ending with the chapter edited by Beugnot as cap. 83). *RHC Lois*, 2, pp. 19–65. Fols 1–16. (Blank unnumbered folio follows fol. 16.)
(ii) Rubrics to all the works that follow with the exception of James of Ibelin's treatise. Fols 17^{r}–32^{r}. (The rubrics to John of Ibelin's treatise occupy fols 17^{r}–28^{v}.) (Fol. 32^{v} blank.)
(iii) John of Ibelin's treatise in 284 chapters. Fols 33^{r}–214^{v}. In a substantial number of instances spaces have been left for rubrics that were not copied into the text (although the table of rubrics is complete). Also there are many blank spaces for unexecuted initials. On fol. 33^{r} there is space for a headpiece miniature.
(iv) *Les Lignages d'Outremer* (earlier recension). Fols 214^{v}–221^{r}. Edited *RHC Lois*, 2, pp. 441–3, 444–5, 446–7, 450–9, 466–7, caps 1, 3, 5–6, 9–20, 31. This text follows John of Ibelin's treatise without a break. The chapter numbers in both the table of rubrics and the text continue sequentially with the *Lignages* chapters numbered 285–301.
(v) James of Ibelin's treatise. Fols 221^{r}–230^{v}. Edited *RHC Lois*, 1, pp. 453–68.
(vi) Geoffrey Le Tor's treatise, version B. Fols 230^{v}–235^{r}. Edited *RHC Lois*, 1, pp. 444–50.

(vii) Philip of Novara's treatise. Fols 235^{v}–264^{v}. Edited *RHC Lois*, 1, pp. 471–571.

(viii) *Le Livre au Roi*. Fols 265^{r}–276^{r}. (Fol. 276^{v} blank.) Edited *RHC Lois*, 1, pp. 601–44; ed. M. Greilsammer, Documents relatifs à l'histoire des croisades 17 (Paris, 1995).

BIBLIOGRAPHY: Grandclaude, 'Classement sommaire' pp. 459–60; *Livre au Roi*, ed Greilsammer, pp. 31–3.
ILLUSTRATION: Folda and Edbury, 'Two Thirteenth-Century Manuscripts', plate 33 (fol. 17^{r}).

MS V: ROME VATICAN: CODEX VATICANUS LATINUS 4789
PROVENANCE: Cyprus, early fifteenth century—comprising 320 folios numbered 1–24[11] and i–ccxcvi plus four unnumbered folios at the end. Owned in the mid-fifteenth century by the Cypriot aristocrat James of Fleury, count of Jaffa (died 1463), and his son-in-law, Hugh Boussat.

CONTENTS:

(i) Notes in Greek (written in Latin characters) and in Italian relating to the affairs of the mid-fifteenth-century owners. Fol. 1^{v}. (Fol. 1^{r} blank)

(ii) Beginning of the *tomos synodikos* of the Council of 1351. Fol. 2r.

(iii) Large monogram of the Cantacuzenos family; the text of a *horismos* of Matthew Cantacuzenos; notes in Greek including one at the bottom of the page in Latin characters. Fol. 2^{v}.

(iv) Rubrics to John of Ibelin's treatise and the *Lignages d'Outremer*. Fols 3^{r}–18^{v}.

(v) Prologue to the 1369 recension of John of Ibelin's treatise. Fols 19^{r}–22^{r}. Edited below as appendix 7.1

(vi) Four full page paintings of coats of arms:
Fol. 22^{v}: Hugh Boussat
Fol. 23^{r}: Charlotte Cantacuzène de Fleury (Hugh's wife)

[11] The numbering of the early folios has been added since the publication of E. Brayer, P. Lemerle and V. Laurent, 'Le Vaticanus latinus 4789. Histoire et alliances des Cantacuzènes aux XIVe–XVe siècles', *Revue des Etudes byzantines*, 9 (1951), pp. 47–105. The foliation given by these authors differs from that given here.

Fol. 23v: Queen Charlotte of Cyprus (died 1487) with inescutcheon of the Arms of Savoy and the insignia of the Order of the Sword

Fol. 24r: Cardinal Ascanio-Maria Sforza (died 1505) (Fol. 24v blank)

(vii) John of Ibelin's treatise in 330 chapters. Fols ir–cclxxvv.

(viii) *Les Lignages d'Outremer* (later recension). Fols cclxxvv–ccxcviv. Edited *RHC Lois*, 2, pp. 441–3, 445–7, 448–9, 455–7, 460–6, 467–74, caps 1, 2, 4, 5, 7, 8, 17–19, 22–30, 32–42. Note that the chapter numbers in both the table of rubrics and the text continue sequentially from John of Ibelin's treatise so that the *Lignages* chapters are numbered 331–61 (332–62 in the table of rubrics due to a copyist's error).

(ix) Various notes mostly in Greek (some written in Latin characters) relating to the affairs of the fifteenth-century owners on four unnumbered folios (published and discussed together with (i)–(iii) above in the articles by Brayer *et al.* and Richard cited below).

BIBLIOGRAPHY: Grandclaude, 'Classement sommaire' pp. 462–3; E. Brayer, P. Lemerle and V. Laurent, 'Le Vaticanus latinus 4789. Histoire et alliances des Cantacuzènes aux XIVe–XVe siècles', *Revue des Etudes byzantines*, 9 (1951), pp. 47–105; J. Richard, *Chypre sous les Lusignans: Documents chypriotes des archives du Vatican (XIVe et XVe siècles)* (Paris, 1962), pp. 123–32.

ILLUSTRATION: Brayer *et al.*, 'Le Vaticanus latinus', p. 53 (fol. 22v, fol. 23r: arms of Hugh Boussat and Charlotte Cantacuzène de Fleury); W.-H. Rüdt de Collenberg, 'L'Heraldique de Chypre', *Cahiers d'Heraldique*, 3 (1977), fig. 7 (fol. 22v: arms of Hugh Boussat); fig. 8 (fol. 23r: arms of Charlotte Cantacuzène de Fleury); D. and I. Hunt, *Caterina Cornaro*, following p. 72 (fol. 23r: arms of Queen Charlotte—colour); J. Charles-Gaffiot (ed.), *La France aux portes de l'Orient; Chypre XIIème–XVème siècle* (Paris, 1991), p. 74 (fol. 23r: arms of Queen Charlotte—colour), p. 75 (fol. ir—colour).

4. The Transmission and development of the text

Grandclaude was the first to propose that MS C in conjunction with MS O should be used as the basis for any future new edition,[12] and my own investigations strongly endorse his view. MS C contains only John's text, and it was evidently copied in the Acre scriptorium. Jaroslav Folda and I have previously suggested that it dates to the early 1280s, largely on the basis of the similarities of the calligraphic decoration and general codicological characteristics to the Old French Bible (Paris BN: MS nouv. acq. fr. 1404) of c. 1280.[13] It would thus appear to be the oldest surviving manuscript, and, I would argue, the one that comes closest to preserving the treatise as John originally composed it. MS O, which is thought to date to the early fourteenth century and was almost certainly copied in Cyprus,[14] follows it closely in both content and detailed readings. But there are significant differences between them, sufficient to dispel any possibility that either of these manuscripts is derived directly from the other. MS O contains one chapter drawn from the treatise by Philip of Novara which is not to be found in MS C nor indeed in any of the other John of Jaffa manuscripts,[15] while MS C contains two passages not in O or in any of the others.

These two unique passages in MS C are of particular interest. One is a short section inserted towards the end of chapter 53.[16] It illustrates a feature of Latin Syrian succession law applicable when property is recovered from Muslim occupation, and explains how it was that Margaret of Ibelin, the widowed lady of Caesarea, acquired the lordship of Ibelin when it was ceded to the Christians in 1241 in preference to her nephew, Balian lord of Beirut (1236–47). Margaret received Ibelin because she was the daughter of Balian of Ibelin (died c. 1193) who had been the last in seisin before Saladin's conquest of 1187, whereas Balian's namesake and grandson was a more

[12] Grandclaude, *Étude critique*, p. 88; idem, 'Classement sommaire', pp. 448, 458.

[13] J. Folda and P.W. Edbury, 'Two Thirteenth-Century Manuscripts of Crusader Legal Texts from Saint-Jean d'Acre', *Journal of the Warburg and Courtauld Institutes* 57 (1994), p. 250.

[14] Recoura, 'Notes sur six manuscrits', pp. 147–8; Grandclaude, 'Classement sommaire', pp. 456–8.

[15] Below, appendix 2. See Philip of Novara, 'Livre de forme de plait', *RHC Lois*, 1, pp. 523–4.

[16] Below, appendix 1.1.

distant kinsman, even though he was the descendant of Balian's eldest child and in the male line. The bulk of this chapter is present in all the manuscripts and describes the legal principle known as 'Fors de Turs ne tolt seisin' ('Forcible occupation by the Turks does not affect [rights to] seisin'), and gives what appears to be a fictive illustrative example—John uses the word 'senblance'—relating to the succession to Daron. In the sentence immediately before the insertion, MS C twice speaks of 'le fis et la fille' instead of simply 'le fis', thereby allowing for the circumstance in which the claimant would be a woman and so preparing the reader for Margaret of Caesarea's successful assertion of her rights. The presence of this alteration argues strongly against the possibility that the passage in question had been in the original text and had then been omitted from the ancestor of all the other manuscripts. The important point about this insertion is that it is decidedly autobiographical: Margaret is named as the author's aunt, and Balian of Ibelin as the author's grandfather. In other words, it was the work of John of Jaffa himself.

The same conclusion—that John was responsible for the addition—is clear from the other unique passage. Directly after cap. 129 is a chapter lifted from Philip of Novara's treatise.[17] In Philip's version of this passage there is mention of John of Jaffa, and in MS C the phrase concerned is recast into the first person, reading 'je meismes m'en entremis moult' for 'moult s'en entremist le conte de Jaffe'. Autobiographical references in John's treatise are relatively uncommon, and so it is all the more remarkable that both these interpolations should contain them. They leave no doubt that after John had produced his treatise and had allowed members of his circle to make copies of it, he was still tinkering with his text. That in itself is not particularly unusual or surprising, but it does have an important corollary: everything else that MS C contains—and everything else in C is also present in the other four manuscripts—was therefore in John's own copy of his work, and so represents what John himself, and not some later editor, wrote or chose to include.

The significance of this conclusion comes into focus when we turn to the other three manuscripts (A, B and V), all of which contain extensive later interpolations. As already mentioned, both C and O

[17] Below, appendix 1.2. This chapter consists of about three-quarters of Philip of Novara, cap. 73 (pp. 543–4).

include chapters taken from the law book by John's older contemporary, Philip of Novara. Philip was writing in the 1250s or early 1260s,[18] and his work was to have an appreciable influence on John's treatise and on the subsequent emendations to John's text. There is one other chapter adapted from Philip of Novara present in all the extant manuscripts of John's treatise, and it must therefore have been put there by John.[19] MS A is another product of the Acre scriptorium, and has been dated to c. 1290, not long before the city's destruction in 1291,[20] while MS B evidently dates from the fourteenth century and is likely to have been of Cypriot provenance.[21] Both these manuscripts share a number of characteristics which distinguish them from C and O. They have additional chapters in common; existing chapters are divided or combined; and in a few cases chapters are placed in a different sequence. I have counted twenty-one extra chapters, of which eleven are lifted or adapted from Philip of Novara,[22] while nine have not been identified as coming from any extant source.[23] The twenty-first chapter, which in MS A serves as the conclusion to the whole treatise, contains some material from Philip of Novara,[24] and, in addition, in both MS A and MS B there is a passage describing *Les Letres dou Sepulcre*, also taken from Philip's treatise, interpolated into the prologue. There are countless instances of MSS A and B sharing detailed readings which differ from those to be found in C and O, and sometimes the reading in A and B is self-evidently preferable.[25] The seven instances in which some of the longer chapters in CO are split into two and the two instances in which two chapters in CO are combined into one in AB are of less

[18] P.W. Edbury, 'Philip of Novara and the *Livre de forme de plait*', in *Πρακτικά του Τρίτου Διεθνούς Κυπρολογικού Συνεδρίου (Λευκωσία, 16–20 Απρίλιου 1996)*, vol. 2, ed. A. Papageorgiou (Nicosia, 2001), pp. 555–69.

[19] Cap. 141. Taken from Philip of Novara, cap. 29 (pp. 503–6).

[20] Folda and Edbury, 'Two Thirteenth-Century Manuscripts', pp. 243–9.

[21] Grandclaude, 'Classement sommaire', pp. 459–60.

[22] Below, appendices 3.2 (cf. Philip of Novara cap. 11, pp. 484–5); 3.3 (cf. Novara cap. 30, p. 507); 3.5 (cf. Novara caps 20–2, pp. 494–5); 3.7 (cf. Novara cap. 51, pp. 526–7); 3.8.1 (cf. Novara cap. 37, p. 514); 3.8.2 (cf. Novara cap. 39, p. 516); 3.10.1 (cf. Novara cap. 35, pp. 512–13); 3.10.2 (cf. Novara cap. 38, pp. 515–16); and 3.11 (cf. Novara cap. 62, pp. 532–4).

[23] Below, appendices 3.4, 3.6, 3.9, 3.12.

[24] Below, appendix 3.13 (from Philip of Novara cap. 94, pp. 569–70).

[25] For example, in cap. 172, where AB list surrendering one's city or fortress ('chastiau') to the enemy as something meriting confiscation and disinheritance, CO speak of surrendering one's city or horse ('cheval').

intrinsic significance. It has to be said that some of these changes are clumsy in the extreme.[26] Nowhere is this more apparent than in the prologue. In CO the prologue comprises a well-rounded survey of the history of the legal system ending with a prayer and pious exhortations. In AB this material is broken up into five chapters, with the result that the sense of unity is lost, while the passage relating to *Les Letres dou Sepulcre* is awkwardly inserted into the section dealing with the legal provision for the Syrian community in the kingdom.[27] Directly after the prologue MSS A and B have an extensively revised version of the two chapters describing the coronation of the kings of Jerusalem, repositioned from their more logical place at the end of the treatise.[28] These chapters also break up the natural flow of the argument from the prologue to the opening chapter of the treatise as found in MSS C and O.

These common features that distinguish A and B from C and O show that, at some point between John's composition of the version of his treatise from which C and O are both derived and the making of MS A in about 1290, a substantially revised recension of the text came into being. Grandclaude in his stemma labelled this recension '*z*'.[29] It is worth asking whether how far John himself may have been responsible for these revisions. In one of the chapters adapted from Philip of Novara there is a reference to John of Jaffa's uncle and namesake, John of Ibelin lord of Beirut, who is described as 'mon seignor mon oncle le vieill seignor de Baruth'.[30] John himself certainly used the phrase when mentioning his uncle in the context of his opposition to the Emperor Frederick II and his representatives in the late 1220s and 1230s.[31] Similar phrases—'mon seignor mon oncle le vieill sire de Baruth' and 'mon seignor mon oncle'—appear in another chapter taken from Philip of Novara which is present in both A and V but not in B or CO, and in a second chapter, which cannot be identified as coming from any extant source, found only in MS V.[32] The allusions to his uncle strongly suggest that John himself either wrote or adapted these chapters, although it is always

[26] A good example is represented by the interpolation that forms appendix 3.2.
[27] Below, appendix 3.1.1 (from Philip of Novara, cap. 47, pp. 521–2).
[28] Cap. 219–20.
[29] Grandclaude, 'Classement sommaire', p. 475, cf. pp. 445–9.
[30] Below, appendix 3.10.2.
[31] Cap. 178.
[32] Below, appendices 4.1, 7.2.

possible that they were introduced later by someone trying to pass them off as John's authentic work.

Another chapter found in AB and V but not in C and O and which would appear to be John's work is the description of the oath that the *bailli* (or regent) of the kingdom had to swear on taking up office.[33] Here the essential clue is provided by John's other extant writing, his discourse on the regency which is preserved only in MS A where it follows directly at the end of John's treatise.[34] That text speaks of the 'sairement avant dit' that the *bailli* swears to the liege men, and the only place anywhere in John's treatise that the oath is described is this chapter.

So it might appear that John was associated in some way with at least two of the additional chapters incorporated into the '*z*' recension. Nevertheless, I am reluctant to assume on the basis of this evidence that he himself was responsible for all the changes indicated, if only because it is unlikely that he himself would have repositioned the chapters describing the coronation so clumsily. It is more likely that more than one person was involved and that the revisions were carried out over an extended period.[35]

MS A is really two manuscripts bound together—one from the Acre scriptorium and dated c. 1290 and one of mid-fourteenth-century Cypriot provenance—comprising legal texts from the Latin East. Besides the text of John of Jaffa's treatise, the Acre section of the manuscript contains various shorter works including the only copy of John's discourse on the regency of Jerusalem and three items that are all securely datable to the 1270s: the treatise by James of Ibelin, the earlier recension of the *Lignages d'Outremer*, and the text published with the title 'Document relatif au service militaire'.[36] James of Ibelin, who was the son of John of Jaffa, is said to have composed his treatise on his death-bed, in 1276.[37] He was also one of the protagonists in the 1271 arguments over military service.[38] Furthermore, as Marie-Adélaïde Nielen-Vandevoorde has demonstrated, the earlier

---

33 Below, appendix 3.6.2.

34 Below, appendix 8.1.

35 It should be noted that whoever added appendix 3.6.1 was aware that the chapters relating to the coronation were now located near the beginning of the book and not at the end.

36 Folda and Edbury, 'Two Thirteenth-Century Manuscripts', pp. 250–3.

37 James of Ibelin, 'Livre', *RHC Lois*, 1, p. 453 n. 2.

38 *RHC Lois*, 2, pp. 427–34.

recension of the *Lignages*, which cannot have been completed before 1268 and could be several years later, was also composed in Ibelin circles.[39] It might therefore be suggested that the changes to John of Jaffa's treatise evidenced by MSS A and B were also made in the 1270s by or for the same people who wanted these other texts grouped together in the same manuscript.

Although MSS A and B share a number of features that set them apart from MSS C and O, it is also true that there are significant differences between them. There are plenty of textual variants that are unique to one or the other. MS A contains two chapters lacking in B,[40] whilst B has eleven chapters not found in A as well as some other distinctive features. It is therefore clear that both manuscripts represent further developments of the text from the recension that Grandclaude in his stemma designated as '*z*'. Of the eleven additional chapters in B, one is taken from the *Livre des Assises de la Cour des Bourgeois*,[41] two are adapted from Philip of Novara,[42] one is a chapter that appears in the writings of both Geoffrey Le Tor and James of Ibelin,[43] and two are taken from Brunetto Latini's *Li Livres dou Tresor*.[44] The other five are not identified as coming from any extant source.[45] B, however, does contain the chapter that in A forms the conclusion to the whole work. It consists of a summary history of the kings of Jerusalem, giving a version of the epitaph on the tomb of King Baldwin I, followed by an account of how King Aimery tried unsuccessfully to persuade Ralph of Tiberias to make a written record of the *assises* of the kingdom—this part is adapted from Philip of Novara's treatise—and the chapter is then rounded off with a request that the readers pray for those mentioned and for the author. In A this chapter bears the rubric: 'Ce est le dereain chapitle de cest livre', and the request for prayer at the end adds weight to

---

[39] M.-A. Nielen-Vandevoorde, 'Un livre méconnu des *Assises de Jérusalem*: Les *Lignages d'Outremer*', *Bibliothèque de l'Ecole des chartes*, 153 (1995), pp. 110–13, 118–19.

[40] Below, appendices 4.1 (from Philip of Novara cap. 18, pp. 492–3), 4.2.

[41] Below, appendix 6.1 (from 'Livre des Assises de la Cour des Bourgeois', *RHC Lois*, 2, cap. 2, p. 20).

[42] Below, appendices 5.2 (from Philip of Novara, caps 32–5, pp. 508–12), 5.4 (from Novara, cap. 92, pp. 564–7).

[43] Below, appendix 5.3.3 (from Geoffrey Le Tor, 'Livre', *RHC Lois*, 1, MS B cap. 16, p. 449; James of Ibelin, cap. 68, p. 467).

[44] Below, appendix 5.5 (from *Li Livres dou Tresor de Brunetto Latini*, ed. Francis J. Carmody (Berkeley and Los Angeles, 1948), caps 74–5, pp. 392–5).

[45] Below, appendices 5.1, 5.3.1, 5.3.2, 6.2, 6.3.

the view that it was indeed composed as the concluding chapter. In B, however, it is given a different rubric and re-positioned earlier in the treatise.[46]

Like MS A, MS B contains a number of other legal texts from the Latin East, including the earlier recension of the *Lignages d'Outremer*. But whereas in A John's treatise and the *Lignages* are separated by other material and no connection is made between them, in B the *Lignages* follows John's treatise and is treated as if it were an integral part of it. The chapter numbers follow in an unbroken sequence (285–301) with the opening chapter bearing the rubric:

> Puis que vos avez oi et entendu les assises et les usages dou reaume de Jerusalem et qui les commença premierement, droit est que nos vos dions et devisons les hoirs qui descendirent d'eaus de quoi le pais est aangé.[47]

In MS B the *Lignages* is followed by James of Ibelin's treatise, and here the opening rubric reads:

> Puis que nos avons parlé ci desus des assises et des usages de la haute court les quex fist le bon Jahan d'Ybelyn, conte de Japhe et d'Escalone et seignor de Rames, nos vos dirons aucunes assises les quex messire Jaque d'Ibelyn, a qui Diex pardoint, fist ou lit de la mort.[48]

Anyone using this manuscript would therefore be left with the impression that John was the author of that version of the *Lignages d'Outremer* and that the seventeen chapters into which the text is divided were actually part of his treatise. In fact, as Marie-Adélaïde Nielen-Vandevoorde has pointed out, this was not the case and its composition dates to the period after John's death.[49] However, as will be seen, the association of the *Lignages* with John's treatise is also a feature of MS V.

MS V appears to date from the early fifteenth century and contains the text as preserved as an official work of reference in the High Court of Cyprus. In January 1369 the king of Cyprus, Peter I,

---

[46] Below, appendix 3.13. (cf. Philip of Novara cap. 94, pp. 569–70).

[47] BN MS fr. 19026, fols 28^{v} (table of rubrics), 214^{v}. Cf. *Lignages d'Outremer*, *RHC Lois*, 2, p. 439 n. 1. The wording in MS A is virtually identical, but there it refers back to the writings of Geoffrey Le Tor and James of Ibelin as well as to John of Jaffa.

[48] BN MS fr. 19026, fols 28^{v} (table of rubrics), 221^{r}. Fol. 221^{r} lacks 'et seignor de Rames'. Cf. James of Ibelin, p. 453 n. 2.

[49] Nielen-Vandevoorde, 'Un livre méconnu', pp. 109–11.

was murdered in a palace *coup*, and immediately afterwards the Cypriot vassals decided that a version of John's treatise should be prepared for use as a work of reference in the High Court. This decision is described at some length in a preface to this text which also recounts the accession of the young Peter II and the regency arrangements agreed directly after the murder.[50] The members of the High Court

> ordained that all the ancient books of *assises* that the old count of Jaffa had written should be brought and checked in the presence of the court; that the most accurate of them all should be found and should be written out; that other chapters of ordinances that had been made should be added to this book, together with the recognition made by the liege men concerning King Hugh [IV] and the other *assises* and ordinances made by the lord kings and liege men of the court in times past . . .

It would appear, however, that no action was taken until the following November when it was agreed that a commission of sixteen leading vassals should be set up to prepare this version of John's treatise. The regent, the prince of Antioch, then

> had the greater part of the most accurate books of *assises* by the count collected, and in the presence of those mentioned above (the sixteen vassals) they were checked. They chose the most accurate book of the *assises* and this was copied out and the above mentioned ordinances made by the liege men were added, together with the recognition made in respect of King Hugh and the rest of the *assises* and others made in time past.

The regent swore to uphold the law as enshrined in the book and the book itself was placed in a locked chest in the treasury of Nicosia cathedral.

An examination of the text as preserved in MS V shows that the commission established in 1369 followed its instructions carefully. The new material comprises a block of twenty-one chapters inserted into John's text between chapters 224 and 225. It consists of a detailed account of the disputes over the regency of Jerusalem in the 1260s, the text of an ordinance issued by King Henry II of Cyprus in January 1311 dealing with legal problems resulting from his brother's usurpation which had ended the previous year, an

[50] Below, appendix 7.1.

account of the arguments put forward at the time of King Hugh IV's accession in 1324 (this is the 'recognition' referred to in the 1369 prologue), an *assise* issued by the king in 1355 which from other evidence may in fact have been the reissue of an enactment dating to the 1310s, and the text of the *remède* drawn up in January 1369 in the aftermath of Peter I's death which, like the 1369 prologue, records among other things the decision to find the best version of John's treatise, 'correct' it and place it in a chest in the cathedral treasury.[51] This material is of great interest and for the most part owes its preservation to its inclusion in this version of the text.

It is clear that the members of the 1369 commission went to a good deal of trouble to establish what they considered to be the best readings. How many manuscripts they consulted is not known, but they evidently had at least two and may well have had several. There is no particular reason to assume that they used any of the extant manuscripts, but they certainly had at their disposal at least one that belonged to the CO family and one other that belonged to the AB family. So far as the detailed readings are concerned, it would seem that they had gone through the whole text to produce a pastiche, sometimes following one recension and sometimes the other. MS V contains none of the material found in C or O but not in A and B, but it does have almost all the additional chapters common to A and B,[52] and most, but not all, of the chapters found in B but not A.[53] So although V contains one chapter drawn from Philip of Novara's treatise found in A but not B,[54] it is generally closer in content to B. Thus, for example, it follows B in repositioning A's concluding chapter earlier in the treatise. On the other hand, the commissioners evidently decided to follow C and O in putting the two chapters describing the coronation towards the end where John had originally intended, although the text of these chapters in V follows the distinctive recension found in MSS A and B. There is of course no way of knowing whether the commissioners suppressed any of the chapters they found in only some of the manuscripts that were available to them or whether they included everything they

[51] Below, appendix 7.11.

[52] But not appendices 3.6.1, 3.10.1.

[53] Of the eleven chapters in B but not A (above notes 38–42), V lacks only appendices 6.1, 6.2, 6.3.

[54] Below, appendix 4.1.

could find. Perhaps the clearest indication that they were working from a text that is no longer extant is provided by the version of the *Lignages d'Outremer* that V preserves. Whereas A and B contain a version datable to c. 1270, V has a totally different text which from internal evidence had been composed around 1309.[55] The 1369 commissioners had made no attempt to bring it up to date, and it has to be assumed that they had found it in one or more of the manuscripts they had used. There was thus yet another recension of the text, and one that dated from the end of the first decade of the fourteenth century. Scattered through MS V are eleven more chapters not found in any of the other extant John of Jaffa manuscripts, and it is likely that these chapters, which unlike the material added in 1369 have no specific historical content, were present in some of the manuscripts the commissioners consulted. Two of these chapters are loosely adapted from James of Ibelin,[56] and there are one each from the *Livre au Roi*, and Philip of Novara.[57] The others are not identified as coming from any known source.[58]

Because the commissioners evidently used versions of John's treatise that have not survived, it is difficult to know how far the variant readings unique to MS V indicate that they themselves were introducing deliberate alterations into the texts at their disposal. One likely example, however, should be noted. King Peter I of Cyprus had treated his vassals high-handedly and, in their view at least, with scant regard for their legal rights. One of Peter's victims was a knight named John Viscount who had alerted the king to the queen's adultery with one of the leading Cypriot aristocrats. In reporting the queen's behaviour, John had acted as a faithful vassal should, but Peter had hounded him to death for his temerity. Chapter 175 of John of Jaffa's treatise includes a discussion of the obligations of the vassal who has done homage to a lord to do everything in his power

[55] P.W. Edbury, 'The Ibelin Counts of Jaffa: a Previously Unknown Passage from the "Lignages d'Outremer"', *English Historical Review*, 89 (1974), pp. 604–5 (dating it to 1305 x 1315); Nielen-Vandevoorde, 'Un livre méconnu', pp. 111, 112 (dating it to 1309).

[56] Below, appendices 7.8.1 (from James of Ibelin cap. 62, p. 467), 7.10 (from James of Ibelin cap. 1, pp. 453–4).

[57] Below, appendices 7.8.2 (from Philip of Novara, cap. 30, p. 507); 7.9 (from *Livre au Roi*, ed. M. Greilsammer, Documents relatifs à l'histoire des croisades 17 (Paris, 1995), cap. 21, pp. 195–9).

[58] Below, appendices 7.2, 7.3, 7.4, 7.5, 7.6, 7.7.

to protect his lord and his lord's interests, and among other things the vassal should not engage in illicit sexual relations with his lord's wife or daughter. The passage in MS V seems to make the point much more explicitly, extending it to require the vassal to take action to prevent anyone else from transgressing so far as he is able:

> . . . ne ne doit a la feme de son seignor ne a la fille requerre vilainie de son cors ne *soffrir ne consentir a son escient ne a son pooir que autre li face, ce est asavoir de* gesir o lui charnelment coment que se soit, se se n'est par mariage, ne a sa seur tant con ele est damoisele en son hostel, ne soufrir ne concentir a son *escient ne a son* pooir que autre li face.

The phrases unique to V are in italics. Although it cannot be proved beyond doubt, it could well be that it was the 1369 commission that made these emendations in the aftermath of the injustice committed against John Viscount.

What this analysis of the variants in the manuscripts shows is that in the century following John's death, people were deliberately altering his text to include additional material and to make minor changes. The fact that all five extant medieval manuscripts preserve unique recensions suggests that there were once in existence many more manuscripts and, in all likelihood, several more versions. None of the surviving manuscripts, however, has any appreciable marginalia which might indicate that any of them was used as a 'working copy' either by people seeking to amplify or 'improve' the text, or by lawyers who were actively consulting it when preparing a case. Even so, the fact that there was so much revision, not to mention the standing the book had evidently acquired in the eyes of the Cypriot vassals in 1369, is a clear indication of the attention and interest that the work continued to generate in the East long after it was written.

5. The stemma

The foregoing discussion mentions various recensions that are not represented by any of the extant manuscripts. The distinctive features of MS A and MS B would indicate that both represent further developments from their common ancestor, the '*z*' recension. The similarities between MS B and MS V would suggest that they shared a common ancestor which itself was derived from '*z*'. On the diagram below this version is designated 'z_1'. Precisely what the 1369 commissions used in preparing their recension is complex. They seem to have based their version on a text that was more closely related to MS B than to any of the other extant manuscripts, but one that was itself a development from 'z_1'. Hence 'z_2'. It might be suggested here that 'z_2' already included the 1309 version of the *Lignages* and much of the material edited below as appendices 7.2–7.7. On the other hand, as mentioned above, in preparing the text of MS V, the 1369 commissioners also utilised a manuscript from the CO family. It is with these points in mind that I offer this diagram showing the relationship between the extant manuscripts:

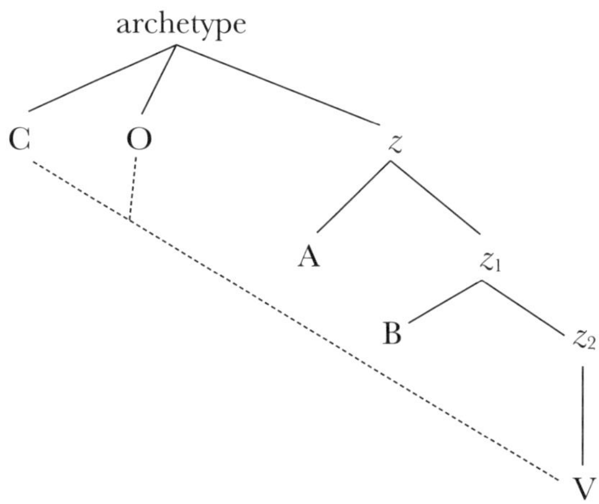

This edition of John's treatise uses MS C as its base. In deciding what editorial policy to adopt, it has been important to recognise a tension between two seemingly conflicting considerations. On the one hand the editor will want to produce—and the reader will want to have—an edition that as nearly as possible presents the text as it left the pen of the author; on the other, the editor has a duty to respect the integrity and authority of each of those texts that exist, preserved in the extant manuscripts. To an extent we are fortunate: in the case of John of Ibelin, the manuscript which appears to come closest to the author's original is also the oldest and so will be the most likely to preserve his syntax and orthography. But even MS C contains instances of what are self-evidently copyists' blunders, and, where the other four manuscripts agree on a reading that differs from C's, it has often been thought advisable to accept the majority verdict. The danger in this approach is obvious: we might easily end up with a version that is not John's original, nor that of any one manuscript, but is simply a pastiche based on the editor's subjective judgement. Here again, however, we are fortunate in that instances of MS O sharing readings with MSS ABV—the '*z*' recension—against the reading found in MS C are comparatively scarce. The policy has therefore been adopted of listing in the apparatus all instances in which the readings given by MS C have been rejected.

So if this edition essentially follows the text given by MS C, how are the texts given by the other four manuscripts to be displayed? Variant readings of closely parallel passages have been listed in the apparatus. More significant differences, such as the start of a new chapter or a significant omission, are signalled in footnotes. Only rarely has it been found necessary to set out passages in parallel. For the benefit of anyone wishing to consult the manuscripts, at the end of each chapter the foliation for each manuscript is noted. As has been described, all the manuscripts, even MS C, contain additional material, and these additions have been published in a series of appendices which, in the light of the stemma, follow in a logical sequence:

- Appendix 1 Additional material unique to MS C
- Appendix 2 Additional material unique to MS O
- Appendix 3 Additional material common to MSS ABV—i.e. the '*z*' recension.
- Appendix 4 Additional material unique to MS A
- Appendix 5 Additional material common to MSS BV—i.e. the 'z_1' recension.
- Appendix 6 Additional material unique to MS B
- Appendix 7 Additional material unique to MS V—i.e. the 'z_2' recension plus the 1369 additions.

The table that follows is designed to show how all this material fits together, and also how the chapter numbering in this edition differs from that adopted by Beugnot in his nineteenth-century version in *Recueil des Historiens des Croisades*.

LEGEND

app.	appendix
x	un-numbered chapter (The numbers added subsequently in MS O have been disregarded.)
pt	part
ct	continued

Chapter numbers in **bold** type denote large decorated capitals in the manuscript (or, in the case of MS B cap. 194, a large space for an unexecuted capital).

This edn	RHC	A	B	C	O	V	
app.7.1	x					**x**	(1369 prologue)
Prologue	1/5	**1**/5	1/5	**x**	**x**	**x**/1/2/3/4	
app.3.1.1	4(pt)	4(pt)	4(pt)			3(pt)	
app.3.1.2	5(pt)	5(pt)	5(pt)			4(pt)	
1	8/10	8/10	8/10/11	x	**x**	5/7	
app.6.1			9				(cf. *RHC Lois*, 2, p. 20)
2	11	11	12	1	**x**	**8**	
3	12	12	13	2	x	9	
4	13	13	14	3	x	10	
5	14	14	15	4	x	11	
6	15	15	16	5	x	12	
7	16	16	17	6	x	13	
8	17	17	18	7	x	14	
9	18	18	19	8	x	15	
10	19	19	20	9	x	16	
11	20	20	21	10	x	17	
12	21	21	22	11	x	18	
13	22	**22**	23	12	**x**	**19**	
14	23	23	24	13	x	20	
15	24	24	25	14	x	21	
16	25	25	26	15	x	22	
17	26	26	27	16	**x**	23	
18	27	27	28	17	x	24	
19	28	28	29	18	x	25	
20	29	29	30	19	x	26	
21	30	30	31	20	x	27	
22	31	31	32	21	x	28	
23	32	32	33	22	x	29	
24	33	33	34	23	**x**	**30**	
25	34	34	35	24	x	31	
26	35	35	36	25	x	32	
27	36	36	37	26	x	33	
28	37	37	38	27	x	34	
app.3.2.1	38	38	39			35	
app.3.2.2	39	39	40			36	
app.3.2.3	40	40	41			37	
29	41	41	42	28	x	38	
30	42	42	43	29	x	39	
31	43	43	44	30	x	40	

This edn	**RHC**	**A**	**B**	**C**	**O**	**V**	
32	44	44	45	31	x	41	
app.2.1					x		(cf. *RHC Lois*, 1, pp. 523–4)
33	45	45	46	32	**x**	42	
34	46	46	47	33	x	43	
35	47	47	48	34	x	44	
36	48	48	49	35	x	45	
37	49	49	50	36	x	46	
38	50	50	51	37	**x**	**47**	
39	51	51	52	38	x	48	
40	52	52	53	39	x	49	
41	53	53	54	40	x	50	
42	54	54	55	41	x	51	
43	55	55	56	42	x	52	
44	56	56	57	43	x	53	
45	57	57	58	44	x	54	
46	58	58	59	45	x	55	
47	59	59	60	46	x	56	
48	60	60	61	47	x	57	
49	61	61	62	48	x	58	
50	62	62	63	49	x	59	
51	63	63	64	50	x	60	
app.7.2	63bis					61	
52	64	64	65	51	**x**	**62**	
53	65	65	66	52	x	63	
app.1.1				x			(insertion into C 52)
54	66	66	67	53	**x**	64	
55	67	67	68	54	x	65	
56	68	68	69	55	x	66	
app.4.1	69	69				67	
57	70	70	70	56	x	68	
58	71	71	71	57	x	**69**	
59	72	72	72	58	x	70	
60	73	73	73	59	x	71	
61	74	74	74	60	x	72	
62	75	75	75	61	x	73	
63	76	76	76	62	x	74	
64	77	77	77	63	x	75	
65	78	78	78	64	x	76	
66	79	79	79	65	x	77	

This edn	RHC	A	B	C	O	V
app.7.3	p. 128n					78
67	80	80	80	66	x	79
68	81	81	81	67	x	80
69	82	82	82	68	x	**81**
70	83	83	83	69	**x**	82
71	84	84	84	70	x	83
72	85	85	85	71	x	84
73	86	86	86	72	x	85
74	87	87	87	73	x	86
75	88	88	88	74	x	87
76	89	89	89	75	x	88
77	90	90	90	76	x	89
78	91	91	91	77	x	90
79	92	92	92	78	x	91
80	93	93	93	79	x	92
81	94	94	94	80	x	93
82	95	95	95	81	x	**94**
83	96	96	96	82	x	95
84	97	97	97	83	x	96
85	98	98	98	84	x	97
86	99	99	99	85	x	98
87	100	100	100	86	x	99
88	101	101	101	87	x	**100**
89	102	102	102	88	x	101
90	103	103	103	89	x	102/103
91	104	104	104	90	x	104
92	105	105	105	91	x	105
93	106	106	106	92	x	106
94	107	107	107	93	x	107
95	108	108	108	94	x	108
96	109	109	109	95	x	109
97	110	110	110	96	x	110/111
98	111	111	111	97	x	**112**
99	112	112	112	98	x	113
100	113	113	113	99	x	114
101	114	114	114	100	x	115/116
102	115	115	115	101	x	117
103	116	116	116	102	x	118
104	117	117	117	103	x	119

This edn	RHC	A	B	C	O	V
105	118	118	118	104	x	120
106	119	119	119	105	x	121
107	120	120	120	106	x	122
108	121	121	121	107	x	123/124
109	122	122	122	108	x	125
110	123	123	123	109	x	126
111	124	124	124	110	x	127
112	125	125	125	111	x	128
113	126	126	126	112	x	129
114	127	127	127	113	x	130
app.7.4	127bis					131
115	128	128	128	114	x	132
app.4.2	129	129				
116	130	130	129/30	115	x	133
117	131	131	131	116	x	134
118	132	132	132	117	x	135
119	133	133	133	118	x	136
120	134	134	134	119	x	137
121	135	135	135	120	x	138
122	136	136	136	121	x	139
123	137	137	137	122	x	140
124	138	138	138	123	x	141
125	139	139	139	124	x	142
126	140	**140**	140	125	x	**143**
127	141	141	141	126	x	144
128	142	142	142	127	x	145
129	143	143	143	128	x	146
app.1.2				129		(cf. *RHC Lois*, 1, pp. 543–4)
130	144	144	144	130	x	147
131	145	145	145	131	x	148/149
132	146	146	146	132	x	150
133	147	147	147	133	x	151
134	148	148	148	134	x	152
135	149	149	149	135	x	153
136	150	150	150	136	x	154
137	151	151	151	137	x	155
138	152	152	152	138	x	156/157
139	153	153	153	139	x	158
140	154	154	154	140	x	159

This edn	RHC	A	B	C	O	V
141	155	155	155	141	x	160
142	156	156	156	142	x	161
143	157	157	157	143	x	163
app.3.3	158	158	158			162
144	159	159	159	144	x	164
145	160	160	160	145	x	165
146	161	161	161	146	x	166
147	162	162	162	147	x	167
148	163	163	163	148	x	168
149	164	164	164	149	x	169
app.3.4	165	165	165			170
150	166	166	166	150	x	171
151	167	167	167	151	x	172
152	168	168	168	152	x	173
153	169	169	169	153	x	174
app.3.5	170	170	170			175/176/177
app.7.5	170bis					178
154	171	171	171	154	x	179
155	172	172	172	155	x	180
app.7.6	172bis					181
156	173	173	173	156	x	182
157	174	174	174	157	x	183
158	175	175	175	158	x	184
159	176	176	176	159	x	185
app.6.2	176bis					177
160	177	177	178	160	x	186
161	178	178	179	161	x	187
162	179	179	180	162	x	188
163	180	180	181	163	x	189
164	181	181	182	164	x	190
165	182	182	183	165	x	191
166	183	183	184	166	x	192
167	184	184	185	167	x	**193**
168	185/6	185/6	186/7	168	x	194/195/196
169	187	187	188	169	x	197
170	188	188	189	170	x	198
171	189	189	190	171	x	199
172	190	190	191	172	x	**200**
173	191	191	192	173	x	201

This edn	**RHC**	**A**	**B**	**C**	**O**	**V**	
174	192	192	193	174	x	202/203	
app.3.6.1	193	**193**	**194**				
app.3.6.2	194	194	195			285	
175	195/6	195/6	196/7	175	x	**204**/205	
176	197/8	197/8	198/9	176	x	206/207/208	
app.3.7	199	199	200			209	
177	200	200	201	177	x	210	
178	201/4	201/4	202/5	178	x	211/212/213/214	
179	205	205	206	179	x	215	
180	206/7	206/7	207/8	180	x	216/217	
181	208	208	209	181	x	218	
app.3.8.1	209	209	210			219	
app.3.8.2	210	210	211			220	
182	211	211	212	182	x	221	
183	212	212	213	183	x	222	
184	213	213	214	184	x	223	
213	214	214	215	213	x	224/225/226	
185	215	215	216	185	x	227	
186	216	216	217	186	x	228	
187	217	217	218	187	x	**229**	
188	218	218	219	188	x	230	
189	219	219	220	189	x	231	
190	220	220	221	190	x	232	
191	221	221	222	191	x	233	
192	222	222	223	192	x	234	
193	223	223	224	193	x	235	
194	224	224	225	194	x	236	
195	225	225	226	195	x	237	
app.7.7						238	(not in *RHC Lois*)
196	226	226	227	196	x	239	
app.5.1	226bis		228			**240**	
197	233	233	235	197	x	**248**	
198	234	234	236	198	x	249	
199	227	227	229	199	x	241/242	
app.3.9	228	228	230			243	
200	229	229	231	200	x	244	
201	230	230	232	201	x	245	
202	231	231	233	202	x	246	
203	232	232	234	203	x	247	

This edn	RHC	A	B	C	O	V	
app.6.3	234bis		237				
204	235	235	238	204	x	250	
205	236	236	239	205	x	251/252	
206	237	237	241	206	x	253	
app.5.2			240			254 + 255 (pt)	(cf. *RHC Lois*, 1, pp. 508–12)
app.3.10.1	238	238	242			255 (ct)	
app.3.10.2	239	239	243			257	
207	240	240	244	207	x	256	
208	241	241	245	208	x	258	
209	242	242	246	209	x	259	
210	243	243	247	210	x	260	
211	244	244	248	211	x	261	
212	245	245	249	212	x	262	
213	214	214	215	213	x	224/225/226	
214	246	246	250	214	x	263	
app.3.11	247	247	251			264	
app.7.8.1						265	(cf. *RHC Lois*, 1, p. 467)
app.7.8.2						266	(cf. *RHC Lois*, 1, pp. 277–9)
215	248	248	252	215	x	267	
216	249	249	253	216	x	272	
217	250	250	254	217	x	271	
app.5.3.1	250bis		255			268	
app.5.3.2	250ter		256			269	
app.5.3.3			257			270	(cf. *RHC Lois*, 1, pp. 449, 467)
app.7.9						273	(cf. *Livre au Roi*, cap. 21)
app.5.4			258			**274**	(cf. *RHC Lois*, 1, pp. 564–7)
app.3.12.1	251	251	259			275	
app.3.12.2	252	252	260			277	
app.3.12.3	253	253	261			276	
app.3.12.4	254	254	262			278	
app.3.12.5	255	255	263			279	
app.3.13	273	273	264			280	
app.5.5.1			265			281	(from Brunetto Latini)

This edn	RHC	A	B	C	O	V	
app.5.5.2			266			282	(from Brunetto Latini)
app.7.10.1						283	(= *RHC Lois*, 2, p. 397)
app.7.10.2						284	(cf. *RHC Lois*, 1, p. 454)
218			218		x		(not in *RHC Lois*)
219	6	6	6	219	**x**	286	
220	7	**7**	7	220	**x**	**287**	
221	256	256	267	221	x	288	
222	257	257	268	222	**x**	289	
223	258	258	269	223	x	290	
224	259	259	270	224	x	291	
app.7.11.1						292	(= *RHC Lois*, 2, pp. 401–2)
app.7.11.2						293	(= *RHC Lois*, 2, pp. 403–4)
app.7.11.3						294	(= *RHC Lois*, 2, pp. 405–7)
app.7.11.4						295	(= *RHC Lois*, 2, pp. 407–9)
app.7.11.5						296	(= *RHC Lois*, 2, pp. 409–10)
app.7.11.6						297	(= *RHC Lois*, 2, pp. 410–12)
app.7.11.7						298	(= *RHC Lois*, 2, pp. 412–13)
app.7.11.8						299	(= *RHC Lois*, 2, pp. 413–14)
app.7.11.9						300	(= *RHC Lois*, 2, pp. 414–15)
app.7.11.10						301	(= *RHC Lois*, 2, p. 415)
app.7.11.11						302	(= *RHC Lois*, 2, pp. 415–16)
app.7.11.12						303	(= *RHC Lois*, 2, pp. 416–17)
app.7.11.13						304	(= *RHC Lois*, 2, pp. 417–18)
app.7.11.14						305	(= *RHC Lois*, 2, p. 418)
app.7.11.15						306	(= *RHC Lois*, 2, pp. 418–19)
app.7.11.16						307	(= *RHC Lois*, 2, pp. 368–70)
app.7.11.17						308	(= *RHC Lois*, 2, pp. 419–22)
app.7.11.18.1						309	(= *RHC Lois*, 2, pp. 373–4)
app.7.11.18.2						310	(= *RHC Lois*, 2, pp. 374–5)
app.7.11.18.3						311	(= *RHC Lois*, 2, p. 375)
app.7.11.18.4						312	(= *RHC Lois*, 2, pp. 376–7)
app.7.11.19						313	(= *RHC Lois*, 2, pp. 378–9)
225	260	260	271	225	x	314	
226	261	261	272	x	x	315	
227	262	262	273	x	x	316	
228	263	263	274	x	x	317	
229	264	264	275	x	x	318	
230	265	265	276	x	x	319	
231	266	266	277	x	x	320	

This edn	RHC	A	B	C	O	V	
232	267	267	278	x	x	321	
233	268	268	279	x	x	322	
234	269(pt)	269(pt)	280(pt)	x	x	**323**(pt)	
235	269(ct)	269(ct)	280/1	x	x	323(ct)	
236	270	270	282	x	x	324	
237	271(pt)	271(pt)	283(pt)	x	**x**	325	
238	271(ct)	271(ct)	283(ct)	x	x	326/329	
239	272	272	284	x	x	330	
app.3.13	273	273	264			280	
app.8.1	x						(*RHC Lois*, 2, pp. 397–401)
app.4.3	x	x					(*RHC Lois*, 1, pp. 431–2)

6. Structure and Content

Now that the extent of the later additions and alterations to the text have been identified, it is possible to return to the most primitive form of the text—that preserved in MSS C and O—to analyse its structure and content. Briefly stated, the work can be divided into four: two main sections preceded by a prologue and followed by appendices:

1. The Prologue
2. Court procedures and how to plead (caps 1–126)
3. The laws of fiefs and vassalage (caps 127–217)
4. Appendices: the constitution of the kingdom (caps 218–239)

Chapters 126 and 218 each form a 'hinge' between the sections.

The Prologue begins with the myth of Godfrey of Bouillon as the kingdom's law-giver. It is an attribute shared by other founding fathers of their respective realms including men as diverse as Moses and Chinggis Khan. John then explains that Godfrey instituted a division between the High Court, where matters concerning fiefs and vassals would be heard, and the burgess court for the affairs of people of lesser rank, before mentioning that he and later kings gave away baronies and lordships with the juridical franchises covered by the expression *cour, coins et justise*. The laws themselves were later revised in the light of advice from visitors from the West. At the request of the *Suriens*, the indigenous Christian inhabitants of the kingdom, Godfrey further agreed that they could have their own tribunals for regulating their own disputes. The High Court, the lords' seigneurial courts, and the burgess courts thus constituted the principal Latin tribunals, while the Syrians had a measure of judicial autonomy. As a historical explanation of how the system had come into being, John's account is seriously flawed, but he has provided his readers with a brief explanation of the legal system. He now comes to the nub:

> Because it seems to me right and proper that the chief lord of the kingdom of Jerusalem and the barons and the other rich men who have *cour et coins et justise* know the *assises* and the usages of the said kingdom . . . I have begun this book, even though I well recognise that I lack the sense and knowledge by which I ought to undertake to do it.

At the time John was writing, a generation had passed since a king had presided at the High Court of Jerusalem. Instead, the kingdom had been governed by regents, a position John himself had held briefly in the mid-1250s, and it is for this reason that John uses 'chief lord' as a portmanteau expression to denote 'the king or the regent'. He makes the point that when a king is crowned or a regent takes office he swears an oath to uphold the *assises* and usages, as do the vassals and rear vassals, all of whom share in the obligation of participating in the judicial processes of the court, and he also makes it clear that the same law and procedures should be applied in the seigneurial courts. So John's purpose is to educate all who preside or participate in the business of the courts. He then concludes his prologue with a prayer for himself and his readers, adding that he is anxious that no one should use his book to find ways of depriving others of their rights or perverting the course of justice.

Coming now to the section on court procedures and how to plead, John starts in his opening chapter by listing the qualities he would expect of those who preside in the courts, those who sit in judgement and those who plead. He ends his discussion with an explanation of his plan for what follows: he first will describe pleading and only later turn to the *assises* and usages. Taking the first part of the book (caps 1–126) as a whole, he broadly adheres to this programme, concentrating on procedures in chapters 2–97, and then giving a comparatively brief account of particular *assises* in chapters 98–126.

The first thing a litigant needs is the services of an experienced counsel to speak on his behalf, and so John begins (caps 2–12) with a description of how to request counsel and highlights various problems that might be encountered, including the objections of the other party and the need for the lord to retain an experienced member of the court to advise him on his conduct of the case. He then (caps 13–17) returns to the characteristics of a good counsel, and addresses specific issues such as the classes of people for whom one can plead without having been appointed by the High Court, the categories of business for which one cannot plead because they fall outside the jurisdiction of the High Court, and the circumstances under which one may plead against one's own lord or one's own vassal before coming back to the attributes of a successful counsel. John goes on to list things that a counsel should know (cap. 18), and in so doing sets out his own agenda for much that follows: he should know that a litigant cannot start pleading without counsel and then get one later; that a litigant cannot unsay what he has said in person or what he has confirmed after his counsel has said it (although he can contradict his counsel if his counsel errs); the correct procedural sequence; when the hearing will take place unless it is a plea which demands that the defendant denies the claim immediately;[59] how a litigant can assert that he had indeed appeared on the prescribed day and so avoid losing his case by default;[60] how to register an *essoin*;[61] how to prove by guarantors;[62] how to challenge the right of your opponent's guarantors to bear witness, and how to challenge their testimony by wager of battle;[63] what sort of people cannot bear witness in the High Court;[64] for what sorts of thing one cannot bear testimony; what types of thing one can claim by *assise*; for which categories of claim an *assise* prescribes that the defendant must answer immediately;[65] what penalties are laid down by *assise* for particular wrongs;[66] what is murder, and how to plead in cases of murder;[67] how to plead if the defendant is held in irons and will have to defend himself by battle;[68] rules about the use of champions and their non-attendance;[69] the nature of homicide and how to defend against the charge of homicide,[70] and so on. John then (caps 20–2) describes how to initiate a plea and the correct procedure if the other party accepts the claimant's case and wishes to make an out-of-court settlement. There follows a brief statement (cap. 23) noting that in all those cases for which an *assise* does not require the defendant to answer immediately there shall be a delay of fifteen days before the case is heard, and the announcement that before listing those cases

---

[59] Cf. caps 23, 38–40.
[60] Cf. caps 40–6.
[61] Cf. caps 47–8.
[62] Cf. caps 56–7.
[63] Cf. cap. 61–2.
[64] Cf. cap. 58.
[65] Cf. cap. 67.
[66] A subject not dealt with in the text.
[67] Cf. caps 68–79.
[68] Cf. cap. 76.
[69] Cf. cap. 93.
[70] Cf. caps 80–2.

in which the defendant must reply immediately John will describe various ploys that can be used in pleading.

At the end of the prologue John had expressed the desire that no one should use his book to deprive anyone of his rights, and so it comes as something of a surprise to find that he now (caps 24–37) begins a lengthy section describing procedural devices that a clever counsel can use to obfuscate the issues, delay judgement and ultimately secure a verdict that is unjust, although he also indicates how these devices can be countered. There then (caps 38–48) follows a description of the procedure to secure a day for the hearing, emphasising the need to ensure that there is no change to the plea when the case is presented, and at the same time explaining what is to be done if the lord or whoever is to preside at the court fails to appear or indeed what is to be done if the other party fails to appear. These considerations lead naturally to the means of notifying the court of an *essoin*. Behind much of this discussion lies the idea that failure to appear at the appointed time will lead to the case being lost by default, but, as John goes on to state (caps 49–51), the defendant who leaves the court without replying to the claim or without requesting an adjournment will automatically lose his case unless the claimant does not offer to prove what he alleges. This remark prepares the reader for the next main section which describes the modes of establishing proof, but, before John comes to this subject, there are two chapters which seem to be misplaced: one deals with *Novel Disseisin*, the other, discussed earlier, with the principle 'Fors de Turs ne tolt seisin' (caps 52–3). Both would seem to belong more properly in the description of fiefs and property law in the second half of the work. The question of establishing proof, whether by privilege, record of court or witnesses, then follows (caps 54–65). Here again John describes in some detail the legal chicanery that can be used to prevent a witness being permitted to bear testimony (cap. 61).

It is only at this point that John's subject-matter allows him, almost imperceptibly, to begin to touch on the substance of the law rather than describe procedure. He lists those categories of pleas to which the defendant must reply immediately and not simply ask for an adjournment (in the legal jargon of the time, those things for which 'assise tot le jor'), and then those categories, most of which feature in the previous list, which can only end in a judicial duel if the defendant persists in denying the charge (caps 67–8). (Many cases no doubt ended in an out-of-court composition, but this is a topic to which John rarely alludes.)[71] Top of this second list come murder, homicide, treason, and disputes over property worth more than a mark of silver, and John now embarks on a lengthy discussion of murder (secret killing, to which, by definition, there can be no witness) and homicide (witnessed killing). An appeal of murder will end in a judicial duel between the accuser and the accused, while an appeal for homicide will end in a judicial duel between the accused and the witness in which the outcome of the contest will establish whether or not the witness had perjured himself. In each case the defeated party will be hanged, unless already killed on the field (caps 69–81). John next comes to appeals of treason and the related charge of making a false claim against one's lord under oath (caps 82–7), before describing in detail the procedures for the conduct of judicial duels (caps 88–96). (As will be seen, disputes over property in excess of a silver mark are only considered very much later.) This section is rounded off by a chapter (cap. 97) describing the procedure in the event of someone impugning the integrity of the court by declaring its verdict false: that person will have to fight a judicial duel with every member of the court in turn until he is defeated, whereupon he will be hanged.

John at long last comes to the procedures in particular types of case which are governed by an *assise*. He begins (cap. 98) with a chapter explaining what is meant by *assise* in which he makes it clear that it is really only what custom and long usage regard as an *assise*. Even so, because the lord and his men all swear to maintain the *assises* and the good customs and usages, they ought to enforce them even more assiduously than the Courts Christian enforce the *decreta* and the *decretales*.[72] There then follows discussion of the procedure in disputes over the buying and selling of restive mounts (cap. 99), assault (caps 100–1), debt and pledge (caps 102–16, 119 cf. 66), restitution of lost property (cap. 117), leprous slaves (cap. 118), payments to mercenaries (caps 120–3), and the public auction and private sale of horses (caps 124–5). This section dealing with *assises* ends with 'the *assise* that lords and men should take the most trouble to know' (cap. 126). This is the *Assise sur la ligece*, and John gives a brief account

[71] But see cap. 22.

[72] Cf. Philip of Novara, pp. 521–4.

of its origin in the conflict between Gerard of Sidon and King Amaury over Gerard's treatment of one of his vassals and describes what the *assise* entailed. This is the first time since the prologue that John has referred to any historical event, but, in contrast to his treatment of the other *assises*, he does not discuss procedure. Instead the whole chapter is conceived as a curtain-raiser for the second half of his treatise—his description of the law of fiefs and vassalage—and at its end John set out his programme for what will follow:

> But (before returning to the *Assise sur la ligece*) I shall speak first of many aspects of fiefs and of the faith that is between lord and man, and afterwards I shall explain the services men owe their lords, and how lords should summon their men to do their services, and how men can and should distrain their lords to pay them what they owe them for their fiefs, and how to withdraw their services.

The chapter thus forms a hinge, linking the two principal parts of the work.

Beugnot claimed that this second part of John's work forms 'le traité le plus complet sur les fiefs qui ait été écrit au moyen âge'.[73] It is certainly comprehensive. It begins with grants of fiefs by the chief lord and lords with *cour et coins et justise*, and then describes the penalty for other fief-holders who alienate feudal property without permission and contrary to legal custom (caps 127–9). The question of alienation leads directly to the special rights of the first holder or 'conquereor' of a fief to determine the succession (caps 130–3), and that in turn leads to a lengthy section on inheritance. John here (caps 134–47) discusses the question of the man who inherits more than one fief, the requirement for co-heiresses to divide the inheritance, the right of the son or daughter of a deceased fief-holder to take possession, and the obligation of the lord to ensure that no one other than the rightful heir gains seisin. Clearly lords did not always fulfil this obligation, and so John (caps 148–52) broaches the issue of how a man can prove that his lord is withholding all or part of his fief, and then, by extension, how to prove one's right to a fief against someone other than one's lord. He then (caps 153–5) returns to the question of inheritance to consider how a minor heir enters his fief on his majority and the rights of a minor heiress on marrying, as well as the position of an unmarried woman who holds a

[73] *RHC Lois*, 1, p. 215 note b.

wardship. Up to this point John's discussion of feudal law has followed a reasonably logical sequence, but the organisation of his material now breaks down and it is less easy to see a pattern in his argument. The next two chapters (caps 156–7) deal with what may well have been a major source of friction at the time of writing: what to do if the source of a fief-rent is insufficient to cover all the payments assigned against it—a topic to which John will return much later.[74] We then come back to the basic principles of inheritance law (caps 158–9), before turning to two questions that might more properly belong in the later section on service and to which John does indeed return later: *servise de mariage*[75] and commendation of fiefs instead of performing military service.[76]

The next block of material has rather more coherence, dealing with the circumstances in which a man might alienate or forfeit his fief. John discusses the legal limitations concerning the division or alienation of fief, the question of fief-holders who wish to exchange all or part of their fiefs, and he then begins his treatment of forfeitures (caps 165–7). But before enlarging on this subject (caps 172–4), he has a lengthy account of the right of a fief-holder to sell his fief as a last resort to pay his debts, and a digression on validity of privileges as evidence in disputes over feudal property (caps 168–71).

John now comes to homage, fealty and *ligece* and their implications for the relationship between a lord and his vassals. He stresses mutual obligation, the right of a vassal to due judicial process before dispossession, imprisonment or exile, and the duty of his peers to take up his cause. It is here that the *Assise sur la ligece*—the *assise* 'that lords and men should take the most trouble to know'—and its implications are considered, although John avoids using this title, preferring instead to speak of those who make 'ligece par l'assise' (caps 175–82). There then follows a section on summons to perform service and *essoins*, and it is in this context that John describes (caps 183–96) the various forms that feudal service can take. Along the way he explains the rights of a man summoned when the lord is withholding part of his fief or his fief-rent is in arrears, the rule that the lord cannot summon his man without some reason, what the summoners should do if they cannot find the man, and the prob-

---

[74] Cap. 204.
[75] Caps 160–2, cf. 199–203.
[76] Caps 163–4, cf. 212, 214.

lems caused by the last-minute indisposition of the vassal's feudal companion (when the service of a companion is owed) or the indisposition of the vassal's horse. This discussion would naturally lead on to an account of the lord's rights to summon an heiress to perform *servise de mariage* (caps 199–203), but once again the arrangement of the material seems poor, for in MSS C and O, though not in A, B or V which here arranges the chapters in a more logical sequence, John interrupts himself to include two chapters (caps 197–8) which introduce the subject of the rights of a vassal to bring pressure to bear on his lord or to distrain his lord to fulfil his obligations.

Aspects of the right of redress a vassal has against his lord form the last major element in John's treatment of feudal law. John discusses the problem of how the vassal can act in concert with his peers to distrain his lord without breaking his oath of fealty, and considers various scenarios: what to do if the lord withholds all or part a of fief-rent; what to do if the source for the fief-rent proves insufficient; what to do if a lord holds part of a fief without judgement of the court; what to do if a third party takes a fief or part of a fief by force; what to do if the lord fails to implement the *esgart* or *conoissance* of the court; what a vassal should do if he is summoned to perform service when the lord is holding all or part of his fief (caps 197–8, 204–11, 213). (It might be noted that the chapter dealing with this last topic is placed earlier in ABV with the material on summonses.) John then returns to the subject of commendation of fiefs as a means of avoiding service (caps 212, 214, cf 163–4), and goes on to describe the things a lord should do for his vassal without a formal hearing, the circumstances under which a vassal should sell his wife's fief to pay his lord's ransom, and the procedure for the mutual renunciation of homage (caps 215–17). It is on that note that the discussion of feudal law in earliest recension of the treatise ends.

We come now to the material which provides a survey of the constitution of the kingdom of Jerusalem and that can be thought of as an appendix to the work. In MSS C and O this section is prefaced by a chapter (cap. 218) omitted from the other manuscripts and not published by Beugnot. It concerns a subject which should have been dealt with in the first half of the treatise: trial by battle in a dispute over property worth more than a mark of silver. It ought logically to have come after John's discussion of treason (cap. 68), and its appearance here suggests that these two manuscripts have preserved a relic of an earlier draft of the treatise in which the material was arranged very differently. The point about this chapter is that its concluding sentences announce what is to follow:

> Well ought there to be other things in this book, but because it would be too much trouble I do not want to include them . . . Next I shall speak of the manner of the coronation of the king of the kingdom of Jerusalem and role of his officers of the said kingdom and what by [virtue of] their office they are bound to do on the day of the coronation and afterwards. Then I shall describe for you in order all the other things as I have undertaken to do: . . . the baronies, the lordships which have *cour et coins et justise*, and where the king of the kingdom of Jerusalem ought to be crowned, and who crowns him, and the suffragans, and the services that there are and that are owed in the said kingdom, and the aids that each owes when there is need in the land, and the knights and sergeantries by name and then in total.

So what was presumably originally intended as the conclusion of one section of the work also, as in the case of the chapter on the *Assise sur la liegece*, acts as curtain-raiser for the next. John now describes the royal coronation:

> The king of the kingdom of Jerusalem does not hold his kingdom except from God, and he ought to be crowned in Jerusalem, if it is in Christian hands. When it is not, he ought to be crowned at Tyre. The patriarch ought to crown the king, if there is a patriarch in the kingdom when the king is to be crowned. If there is no patriarch in the kingdom, the archbishop of Tyre ought to crown him, because he is the primate of the archbishops of the kingdom. If there is no archbishop at Tyre, [the archbishop] of Caesarea ought to crown him, and if there is no archbishop of Caesarea, [the archbishop] of Nazareth ought to crown him (cap. 219).

In the next chapter (cap. 220) John describes the coronation ceremony, mentioning the ceremonial role of the seneschal, constable, marshal and chamberlain on that occasion. This leads naturally into a series of chapters detailing the duties of these four officers both at the coronation and more generally (caps 221–4). He then turns to the structure of the ecclesiastical hierarchy as touched on in the chapter just quoted, giving an account of the provincial structures in the patriarchate of Jerusalem and listing the suffragan bishops together with the major abbeys that lay under episcopal jurisdiction (caps 225–33). Having dealt with ecclesiastical structures, he now turns to the secular hierarchy and examines the four baronies of the kingdom of Jerusalem (caps 234–5)—a subject which has puzzled historians who have looked, largely in vain, for evidence to support the ideas John advances here. He then lists the lords who hold *cour et coins et justise* and control burgess courts, before enumerating the number of knights owed by the major lords and by the vassals in the cities of the royal domain. A final chapter lists the sergeants that were to be mustered when the king called on the *arrière ban* (caps 236–9). It is here that the book, in its earliest recension, ends. The lists of prelates, lords with *cour et coins et justise*, and military service of knights and sergeants appear to be taken from much older materials, some of it evidently dating from shortly before the collapse of the kingdom in 1187.[77]

John's treatise is a major source for the legal, social and constitutional ideas and assumptions of the Latin Syrian aristocracy in the mid-thirteenth century. It spoke to those who presided in the High Court and the seigneurial courts, to the legal experts and the others who sat in the courts, and to the litigants. All vassals were members of the court by virtue of their homage and fealty, and those who represented the parties in any dispute were drawn from their number. The work was evidently held in high esteem, although it is less clear which parts retained their value and which parts came to acquire little more than an antiquarian interest.[78] As the works of Philip of Novara, Geoffrey Le Tor and James of Ibelin show, the writing of treatises on the customary law of the Latin East enjoyed something of a vogue in the middle years of the thirteenth century, but John's work is far longer and fuller than any of the others. Why John and his contemporaries wrote is a question that deserves more attention than it has generally received. Clearly they had a didactic purpose, but the suspicion must remain that there was more to it than simply the desire to instruct their fellows. It may well be that the practitioners in the courts were finding it hard to justify their customary procedures and practices against the challenge of lawyers trained in Roman law and that the treatises by John and the others were designed to bolster the traditional system against an alternative that was more streamlined and more rational in its application.

---

[77] See Edbury, *John of Ibelin*, chapters 5–8 passim.

[78] An indication of which chapters were deemed most significant may perhaps be gained from those chapters which warranted a large decorated capital in the manuscripts (in bold on the table at pp. 25–33) or from the summary table of contents added to MS A later in the middle ages (below appendix 4.3).

It has to be said that some of the procedures—in particular the insistence on trial by battle as the ultimate means of establishing proof—seem antiquated by the standards of the time, even if cases rarely ended in that way. (Writing of the year 1314, the Cypriot chronicler took the trouble to record an appeal of murder that ended in a duel—evidence perhaps that such procedures were by then a rarity.)[79] Again John's insistence on hanging as the penalty for both the defeated party and the defeated party's champion seems harsh by the standards of the time. According to John, the greatest mercy the lord could show to a defeated witness in a dispute over property valued at more than a mark of silver was to substitute both the cutting out of his tongue and the cutting off of his right hand for hanging. That measure of clemency was allowable only to knights: base-born men were to be hanged as a matter of course.[80] (It might be noted that a silver mark was only worth the equivalent of around 225 grammes of pure silver or 25 Cypriot white bezants.)[81] There are other aspects of John's treatise that do not ring true: for example, the description of what a vassal who has two lords is to do if they come into armed conflict shows a naivety that defies belief, while much of the treatment of how a man might conjure his peers to distrain his lord sounds impracticable and relies too heavily on the unanimity of the vassals to be effective.[82] But before we conclude that the whole treatise and the legal system it described were anachronistic even when John was writing, we must remember that the work was copied and expanded after John's death and was still being added to and modified a century later. The manuscript copies that survive would have been expensive to produce and were evidently treasured. Though flawed, over long, and, in places, unrealistic, it is nonetheless impressive, and it is hoped that this new edition will reveal its full potential as a source for the legal, social and cultural history of the Latin East.

---

[79] 'Chronique d'Amadi', ed. R. de Mas Latrie in *Chroniques d'Amadi et de Strambaldi* (Paris, 1891–93), 1, p. 396.

[80] Cap. 218.

[81] 'Abrégé du Livre des Assises de la Cour des Bourgeois', *RHC Lois*, 2, p. 258. The white bezant was a debased gold coin weighing around 3.8 grammes and containing about 16.7% gold and 64.4% silver. I thank Professor D.M. Metcalf for his advice on these values.

[82] Caps 182, 205.

7. Editorial Considerations

The primary purpose in preparing this edition has been to provide a text that is dependable and clear. Beugnot's edition had serious defects. It failed to distinguish John's original text from later accretions, and was based on a version that came mid-way through the development of the manuscript tradition. Although he provided variant readings in his apparatus, it is often difficult to work out precisely what the individual manuscripts actually say, and in any case the manuscripts he used for the 1369 version were corrupt. The textual development as revealed by the five manuscripts used in this edition is complex, but it is hoped that the additions are set out in the appendices in a way that can be readily understood. These additions are often of considerable intrinsic interest as they show what sort of extra information people wanted and so shed light on the ways in which later legal experts considered John's original defective.

But besides the accretions to John's texts, the manuscripts contain countless minor variants. Some are plainly copyists' mistakes. Some could be instances of a scribe trying to correct what appeared to be a blunder in his exemplar. But in very many cases the variants would appear to have been simply a matter of someone polishing the style or modernising the orthography. Professional copyists commonly showed less respect for texts in vernacular languages than for those in Latin. Most of the variant readings are trivial in themselves, but from time to time we find examples that seem to indicate a definite change in meaning. Sometimes a later re-working does seem to be an improvement, but inevitably scribes also introduced mistakes of their own. They might try to correct the content of the treatise or bring it up to date—thereby perhaps signifying a change in procedure or legal practice since the time John was writing. Thus for example, the fourteenth-century MS B substituted 'Hermenie' (Armenia) for 'Romanie' (Romania) in the account of the delays allowed to bring witnesses to court from overseas, although it is unclear whether in this instance the change should be regarded as a deliberate attempt at an improvement or an error.[83]

Categorising the variants can easily turn into a question of the editor's subjective judgement, and so in preparing the apparatus I

[83] Cap. 63.

have not attempted to distinguish blunders from possible improvements to content or style. Rather, I have made the apparatus as full as practicable, omitting for the most part only minor orthographical variants or tiny changes in word order. There are, for example, at least eight spellings of the word 'royaume'—often two of three different spellings on a single page of just one of the manuscripts—and it is difficult to see what purpose listing these could serve. Similarly a change in the wording, for example from 'qu'il dit et fait' to 'qu'il fait et dit', can scarcely be of interest, and including such examples in the apparatus will only serve to make more significant variants less easily noticed. On the other hand, instances where the words differ or, in the case of verbs, where the tense or mode varies, have to be recorded.

The apparatus will show the numerous examples of the readings in MSS C and O at variance with those in MSS A and B or MSS A, B and V (the '*z*' recension). In the light of the stemma that will come as no surprise. The apparatus will also record all instances where the reading of MS C has been rejected in the face of the unanimity of all those other manuscripts, instances where MSS B and V share common readings distinct from those in the other manuscripts (the 'z_1' recension), and also those rare instances of the variant readings cutting across the lines of filiation, as for example where MSS CB agree against MSS AOV.

Although punctuation and capitalisation have been modernised and contractions restored, no attempt has been made to standardise orthography. The spellings and syntax of MS C are thus retained in this edition, while examples of those of the other manuscripts are to be found in the appendices as well as in the apparatus. Thus MS A has been used as the base manuscript in appendix 3 and MS B as the base for appendix 5, while appendices 2, 4, 6, and 7 comprise chapters unique to MSS O, A, B and V respectively.

In an article published in 1947 Edith Brayer identified some distinctive linguistic and orthographical characteristics in an Old French manuscript thought to come from the Latin East, and some at least of these features are also to be found in the John of Ibelin manuscripts.[84] For example, she noted instances of sentence-construction in which

[84] E. Brayer, 'Un manuel de confession en ancien français conservé dans un manuscrit de Catane (Bibl. Ventimilians, 42)', *Mélanges d'archéologie et d'histoire*, 59 (1947), pp. 155–98, at pp. 161–6.

an accusative pronoun is placed after an infinitive, and this feature appears fairly frequently in John's text. Thus we find 'il est prest de prover li' (cap. 77); 'ou rebuter les' (cap. 80); 'et mostrer les' (cap. 89). Other distinctive traits seem to have been the province of only certain manuscripts. Doubling a medial *s* is commonly found in MS A: *raisson, pluissors, faissoient, essient, dissant, maisson.* The other manuscripts much prefer a single *s*, although MS O occasionally has doublings of its own: *consseil, vissconte, averssaire, esscrit.* Brayer also noted the mutation of a medial *s* to *h*, but this phenomenon is largely restricted to MS V: *ehmolue, ehliront, dehloiaument, ehloignera* etc. MS V is also more prone than the others to add an initial *h* as in *huser, husages, horent, heuffre.* In the parallel passages none of the other manuscripts have these spellings, although C does have *henemis* and B *hoste* (from *oste*). Similarly V frequently has *gu* for *g* in, for example, *guarder* and *esguart.* A and B normally have *garder* and *esgart*; C sometimes has *guarder*, and O goes its own way with *guoverner* and *guarnisse.* In a few instances MS B has a *c* cedilla. Some examples come where we would expect to find them in modern French: *reçoive* (fol. 182^{v}), *reçoit* (fol. 187^{r}), *façon* (fol. 190^{r})—but others do not: *reçevoir, reçeoit* (both fol. 187^{r}). Consistency is not a feature. Take for example the *oi* and *ei* diphthongs. A almost always has *deit* whereas B and V regularly have *doit*, and C and O usually have *doit.* But while A almost always has *quei* and B and V normally have *quoi*, C and O usually have *quei.* All the manuscripts occasionally have *cui* for *qui*, but only A regularly has *carelles* for *quereles.* But note that C sometimes has *cantité* for *quantité.* AB and V almost always have *car* while C and O more usually have *quar.* B and the second scribal hand in C (fols 101^{v}–114^{r}) prefer *puet* where the others have *peut.* All the manuscripts sometimes have *y* where in modern French we would expect *i*, and this trait is especially noticeable in O and V: *roy, foy, moy, quoy*, (where A consistently has *roi, fei, moi, quei*) are not particularly remarkable, but V sometimes has the first person singular in *-ay* or *-oy*, e.g. *parleray, demanday, doy, croy*, as well as *droytement, playdoiant, doyt, rayson, estoyent, avoyent.* C too occasionally has the first person in *-ay*, for example *diray*. It is difficult to know what significance to attach to these variants. Many of them may represent no more than the foibles of the particular scribe, perhaps following the contemporary trends. The real question is whether any of them reflect the pronunciation or syntax characteristic of the French spoken in the Latin East, but that remains a subject for further research.

A NOTE ON *SIGLA*

Five manuscripts giving the text of John's treatise have been used in the preparation of this edition. They are:

- A: Venice Marciana: Ms fr. App. 20 (= 265)
- B: Paris Bibliothèque Nationale: MS fr. 19026
- C: Paris Bibliothèque Nationale: MS fr. 19025
- O: Oxford Bodleian: MS Selden 3457 (otherwise MS Selden Supra 69)
- V: Rome Vatican: Codex Vaticanus latinus 4789

As described earlier, both MS A and MS B contain a number of other legal texts from the Latin East including the treatise by Philip of Novara. A number of chapters edited here in the appendices are derived from Philip or from other authors. References are made to these manuscripts where appropriate, and it has occasionally been thought useful to indicate some of the variant readings they give. To avoid confusion where Philip or other authors are indicated, MSS A and B are designated A' and B'. A third manuscript containing Philip's text is the Munich Bayerische Staatsbibliothek: Codex Gallus 771 and this is designated 'M' in the apparatus.[85]

[85] See Grandclaude, 'Classement sommaire', pp. 467–71.

LE LIVRE DES ASSISES ET DES USAGES ET DES PLAIS DE LA HAUTE CORT DOU REIAUME DE JERUSALEM

JOHN OF IBELIN

*[Prologue] C'est le prologue de cest livre qui est des assises et des usages et des plais de la haute cort dou reiaume de Jerusalem, el quel prelogue est devisé coment les assises dou[1] reiaume furent faites et les cours et les usages establis.[2] [a]

Quant la sainte cité de Jerusalem fu conquise sur les henemis de la crois[3] [b] et remise en la main et[4] el pooir des feaus Jhesu Crist[5] par les pelerins, qui se murent[6] a venir conquerre la[7] par le preeschement de[8] la crois, qui fu preeschee par l'enortement Pierre l'Ermite,[9] et que les princes et les barons, qui l'orent conquise, orent esleu a roy et a seignor dou reiaume de Jerusalem le duc Godefroi de Buillon, et il en ot receue la seignorie et ne vost estre sacré ne en oint a roy[10] el dit royaume, por ce qu'il ne vost porter corone d'or la ou le roy des roys[11] Jesu Crist, le fis Dieu, porta corone d'espines le jor de la passion, il, qui fu moult ententif et mout curious a metre le dit roiaume[12] en bon point et en bon estat et que ses homes et son peuple et toutes manieres de gens alans et venans et demorans el dit roiaume fucent governés, gardés, tenus et maintenus, menés et justisés a droit et a raison, eslut par le conseill dou patriarche de la sainte[13] yglise de Jerusalem et par le conceill des princes et des barons

---

A: fols i^{r}–iii^{v} caps 1–5; **B:** fols 33^{r}–35^{v} caps 1–5; **C:** fols 2^{r}–5^{r}; **O:** fols 1^{r}–4^{r}; **V:** fols i^{r}–iv^{v} un-numbered chapter followed by caps 1–4; Beugnot, pp. 21–8, caps 1–5.

---

[a] B lacks rubric. Rubric in AB (from table of rubrics at fol. 17^{r}) V: Ci comence le (V rubrics fol. 3^{r}: Ci comencent les rebrices dou) livre des assises et des bons usages dou roiaume de Iherusalem qui furent establis et mis en escrit par le duc Godefroi de Buillon, qui lor (A: lor par comun acort; V: lequel) fu esleu a roi et a seignor dou dit roiaume, et par l'ordenement dou patriarche de Jherusalem, (A: qui lors primes fu esleu et sacré) et par le conseill des autres rois, princes (B et princes) et barons qui aprés le duc Godefroi furent.

[b] ABV specify 1099 as the date. See notes 3 and 5.

---

[1] O adds: dit [2] C: qui sont establis [3] BV add: en l'an de l'incarnacion nostre seignor Ihesu Crist .M. et .lxxxxix. (V: .M.xcix.) par .i. vendredi [4] en la main et] ABV lack [5] A adds: en l'incarnacion de .M. et .lxxxxviiii. par en vendredi [6] se murent] B: esmurent [7] conquerre la] B lacks [8] de] C lacks [9] l'Ermite] A: li Ermites; B: le Hermite [10] a roy] A lacks [11] C adds: de [12] fu moult ententif . . . roiaume] ABV: fu ententif (BV: ententis) a metre le roiaume (B: reaume) [13] V adds: cité et

et des plus sages homes, que il lors[14] pot avoir, sages homes[15] a enquerre et savoir des gens des diverces terres, qui la estoient, les usages de lor terres. Et tout quanque ceaus, que il orent[16] esleu a ce faire, en porent savoir ne aprendre, il[17] firent metre en escrit et aporterent cel escrit au[18] duc Godefroi. Et il assenbla le patriarche et les avant dis et lor mostra et fist lire devant eaus cel escrit, et aprés par lor conseill et par lor acort il concuilli de ceaus escris ce que bon lor senbla et en fist assises et usages que l'on deust tenir et maintenir et user el roiaume de Jerusalem, par lesqués lui et ses homes[19] et son peuple et les[20] alans et les venans et les estagans en son reiaume[21] fucent governés, gardés, tenus, maintenus et menés et justisés[22] a droit et a raison el[23] dit roiaume.[c]

Et y[24] establi .ii. cours secuilliers:[25] l'une la haute court, de quei il fu governeor et justisier; l'autre la court de la borgesie, de laquel il establi .i. home en son leuc a estre en governeor et justisier, lequel est apelé 'visconte'. Et establi a estre juges de la haute court ses homes chevaliers, qui li estoient tenus de foi par l'omage[26] que il li avoient fait, et de la cort de la borgesie, borgeis de la dite cité des plus loiaus et des plus sages, qui en la dite cité fucent. Et lor fist jurer le sairement que les jurés de la cort de la borgesie jurent, lequel est devisé el livre des assises[27] de la court de la borgesie.[28] [d] Et establi que lui et ses homes et lor fiés et tos chevaliers fucent menés par la haute court, et que les autres gens,[29] que il ne vodreit qu'il fucent[30] menés par la haute court, fucent menés par la cort de la borgesie,[31]

[c] ABV begin a new chapter: Ci dit coment (A: Coment) le duc Godefroi establi .ii. cours seculiers: l'une (V: l'une ci est) la haute court, de quei (B rubrics fol. 17[r]: dont) il fu gouverneor et justisier, et l'autre (V: ci est) la court de la borgesie, (de la borgesie] V: des borges) laquel est apelee la court dou visconte.

[d] See 'Livre des Assises de la Cour des Bourgeois', *RHC Lois*, 2, pp. 23–6. This source does not supply the text of the oath, for which see the fourteenth-century Cypriot treatise: 'Abrégé du livre des assises de la cour des bourgeois', *RHC Lois*, 2, pp. 237–8.

[14] lors] ABV lack [15] que il lors . . . homes] O lacks [16] orent] A: ot; BV: out [17] V adds: mirent et [18] au] A: devant le [19] lui et ses homes] ABV: il et ses genz [20] les] ABV: et totes autre manieres (V: manires) de genz [21] les venans et . . . reiaume] ABV: venans et demorans [22] gardés, tenus, maintenus . . . justisés] AV: et menés; B: et maintenuz [23] el] B: ou devant [24] et y] A: Le duc Godefroi; B: Le dit Goudefroi; V: Le duc Godeffroy de Buillon [25] secuilliers] V lacks [26] l'omage] C: homage [27] des assises] A lacks [28] de la borgesie] V: des borges [29] gens] ABV lack [30] que il ne vodreit qu'il fucent] AB: qu'il ne vodreit qui ne fucent; C: que il ne vodra qu'il fucent; V: qui ne vodroyent estre [31] de la borgesie] V: des borges

et que les[32] borgesies fucent menees et determinees[33] par la cort de la borgesie, que les plais des borgesies[34] ne pevent ne ne doivent estre plaidiés ne jugiés qu'en la court de la borgesie. Que[35] enssi fu lors establi par comun acort dou seignor et de ses homes et des borgeis, et enssi a esté ades puis tenu et maintenu el dit roiaume. Et il ne fist mie ne establi les[36] usages des .ii. dites cors senblans en toutes choses, por ce que haus homes et ceaus qui sont tenus au seignor de foy, et le seignor a iaus, et lor fiés et chevaliers ne doivent pas estre ensi menés come borgeis ne borgesies ne gens de bace main ne peuple.[37] Et establi qu'en toutes les cités et en tos les autres[38] leus dou reiaume, ou[39] il avroit justise, eust visconte et[40] jurés et court de borgeis[41] por le peuple governer, maintenir[42] et justiser par les assises et les usages qui lors et puis[43] furent establis a tenir et user en la court de la borgesie.[44]

Et il et les autres seignors et roys[45] dou dit reiaume, qui aprés lui furent, donerent a aucuns haus homes el roiaume baronies, seignories, court,[46] coins et justise, des ques il lor devoient[47] servise[48] de lor cors et de quantité de chevaliers. Et le servise que il en devoient ains que la terre fust perdue sera devisé en la fin de cest livre.[e]

Et aprés ce que les avant dites assises furent faites et les usages establis, le duc Godefroy et les rois et les seignors, qui aprés lui furent el dit roiaume, les amenderent par pluisors feis. Quar les choses que il veoient et conoissoient et qu'il[49] lor senbloient bones a joindre ou a croistre ou a amermer es assises et es usages do dit reiaume, il le faisoient par le conceill dou patriarche et des barons et des haus homes dou dit reiaume et des plus sages gens[50] que il pooient avoir,[51] clers et leis. Et a[52] chascun passage le roi do reiaume, se il avoit leisir, asenbloit a Acre le patriarche et les avant dis, et

---

[e] See below chaps 237–8. ABV begin a new chapter: Ci dit coment les assises et les usages (A: Coment les assises) dou (V: dit) roiaume de Jerusalem furent par (B rubrics fol. 17r: qui furent) pluissors fois amendees par le duc Godefroi et par les autres rois et seignors qui aprés lui (B: le duc) furent.

---

[32] les] ABV: totes [33] et determinees] A lacks [34] des borgesies] B: de la borgesie [35] Que] ABV: Et [36] ne establi les] ABV: establir les assises et les [37] ne borgesies ne . . . peuple] V: Ne pourgois (*sic*) ne gens de basse main ne peuple com chevaliers [38] autres] ABV lack [39] ou] C: d'ou [40] visconte et] A lacks [41] borgeis] AB: borgesie; V: bourgosie [42] AV add: mener et juger; B: mener juger [43] et puis] ABV lack [44] de la borgesie] V: des bourgois [45] et roys] AB lack [46] ABV add: et [47] devoient] C: devoit [48] servise] C: servises [49] et qu'il] AB: qui; V: et qui [50] gens] AV lack; B: homes [51] A adds: chevaliers et [52] a] C lacks

faisoit[53] enquerre a pluisors sages gens qui i venoient[54] des diverces parties dou monde les usages de lor terres. Et ceaus[55] les faisoient tous escrire[56] et puis li portoient ceaus escris,[57] et il les mostroit[58] au patriarche et as avant dis, et par lor acors et lor conceill[59] croissoit ou amermoit ou ajuignoit[60] es assises et es usages dou roiaume, amender ce que bon lor senbloit a amender les par les dis escris ou autrement.[61] Et pluisors[62] des rois dou dit[63] reiaume envoierent[64] pluisors feis mesages[65] es diverces parties do monde[66] por enquerre et savoir les usages de celes terres por amender a lor poeir et a lor essient les assises et les usages dou dit reiaume. Et les amendoient par le conseill des avant dis en ce que[67] il lor senbloit que bon fust. Et enssi le firent pluisors fois par pluisors ans tant que il orent faites les assises et les usages les meillors et les plus covenables que il[68] porent ne sorent a lor esient au seignor et a ses[69] homes et as chevaliers et as pelerins et as marchans et au peuple et as[70] alans et as venans et as demorans el dit roiaume governer, garder, tenir et maintenir, mener et justisier, bien et loiaument et droiturierement selonc ce que chascun[71] est.[72] [f]

Et aprés que le duc Godefrei et les autres, qui aprés lui furent seignors et roys dou dit reiaume, orent establi les assises et les usages dou dit reiaume[73] et les .ii. cours secuilliers[74] si con est avant dit,[75] [g] le peuple de Suriens[76] vindrent devant .i. des rois[77] dou dit reiaume,

---

[f] ABV begin a new chapter: Ci dit coment (A: Coment) le peuple des Suriens vint (B: des serjanz Suriens vindrent; V: des sergens vint) devant le roi dou roiaume de Jerusalem et li proierent et requistrent que il fucent menés par l'usage des Suriens.

[g] ABV insert a passage adapted from Philip of Novara at this point. See appendix 3.1.1

---

[53] faisoit] AV: faissoient; B: fesoient [54] qui i venoient] A: qu'il ve<n>oient; B: qui venoient; V: que il y venoient [55] ABV add: qu'il establissoit a ce faire [56] escrire] ABV: metre en escrit [57] li portoient ceaus escris] ABV: portoient ciaus escris (B: ces escrit) au roi [58] BV add: touz [59] O adds: le roi [60] ou ajuignoit] A lacks; B: ou joingnoit; V: ou junoit [61] V adds: non [62] pluisors] AV: aucuns; B: aucun [63] dit] C lacks [64] envoierent] AV: enveoit; B: envoioit [65] mesages] ABV lack [66] C adds: et [67] avant dis en ce que] V: devans dis ensi come [68] V adds: onques [69] a ses] C: as [70] as marchans et . . . as] ABV: a totes autres manieres de genz [71] B adds: et chascune [72] V adds before the rubric the words then repeated as the opening of the next chapter: Et aprés ce que le duc Godeffroy et les autres que aprés lui furent seignors et roys dou dit royaume orent establi less assises et les husages dou dit royaume [73] dou dit reiaume] AB lack [74] cours secuilliers] ABV: dites cours [75] dit] BV: devisé [76] Suriens] B: serjans; V: sergens [77] .i. des rois] ABV: le roi

et li prierent et requistrent que il vosist que il fucent menés par l'usage des Suriens, et qu'il[78] eust d'eaus chevetaine et jurés de court, et que par cele court il fucent menés selonc lor usages[79] des quereles qui venroient des uns d'eaus as autres. Et cel roi lor[80] otroia la dite court sauf[81] querele de sanc et querele de coi l'on pert[82] vie ou menbre et querele de borgesie, lesquels il vost qu'il fucent plaidees et determinees devant lui ou devant son visconte. Et enssi fu establi par[83] toutes les seignories dou reiaume.[84] Et le chevetaine de cele cort est apelé 'reys' en leur lenguage arabic et les autre 'jurés'. En aucun leuc dou reiaume a jurés de la cort de Suriens et n'i a point de reys, mais le bailli de la fonde de cel leuc est come reys. Et les plais des Suriens des quereles avant[85] dites vienent devant[86] lui et sont determinés par les jurés de cele cort ausi con devant le reis, qui vaut autant a dire en cest cas come visconte[87] a mener les Suriens ou dit reiaume.[88] [h]

Et por ce que il me semble droit et raison que le chief seignor dou reiaume de Jerusalem et les barons et les autres riches homes, qui[89] ont court et coins et justise, sachent les assises et les usages dou dit reiaume que le chief seignor jure, ains qu'il soit receu a seignor ne en oint ne sacré a roy, de tenir les a son pooir et faire les tenir en son reiaume, et que tos[90] ses homes et les homes de ses homes le doivent aussi[91] jurer, por governer, garder, maintenir, juger, justisier leur homes et leur peuple, si con il doivent, chascun en droit soi par les dites assises et usages,[92] et por ce que lor homes, qui doivent estre juges[93] de lor cors, sachent bien et droitement[94] juger les jugemens que il devront faire, selonc celes assises et ceaus usages, ai je comencié[95] cest livre, tout soit ce que je conoisse bien qu'en moi n'a sen ne conoissance[96] par quei je le deusse enprendre a faire.

---

[h] ABV begin a new chapter: Ci dit coment (A: Coment) le chief seignor (V: le seignor) dou roiaume de Jerusalem et les barons et les autres homes, (et les autres homes V lacks) qui ont court et coins et justise, doivent savoir les assises et les usages dou (B: dou devant) dit roiaume.

---

[78] AV add: y; B: i [79] selonc lor usages] A lacks [80] cel roi lor] ABV: il [81] sauf] AV: sanz [82] pert] V: perdist [83] par] C: que [84] Et enssi fu . . . reiaume] ABV lack [85] avant] V: devant [86] devant] B: avant [87] ABV add: et des (B: de) lors en sa ont (B: a) esté usé [88] ABV add: si come il est devant dit [89] C adds: i [90] tos] A: totes ces choses [91] aussi] AV: ensi [92] por governer, garder . . . usages] ABV lack [93] et por ce . . . juges] C lacks [94] droitement] ABV: droiturierement [95] AB add: a faire [96] qu'en moi . . . conoissance] C lacks

Mais par[97] la fiance et esperance[98] que je ai en la puissance de Dieu le pere et en la sapience[99] de Dieu le fis et en la bininité[100] dou saint Esprit, qui me[101] doignent sen et grace de bien faire[102] le, selonc ce que je ai oy et[103] apris et retenu de ceaus[104] qui ont esté les plus sages homes de mon tens a qui je ai oi parler des assises et des usages dou dit reiaume[105] et des plais de la dite court, et par ce que je lor ai veu faire et user l'ai je enpris a faire. Si pri la sainte Trinité qu'ele m'envoit la grace do saint Esperit, si que je puisse mener cest livre a tel perfeccion qu'il soit a l'enor de Deu et au profit de m'arme et au droit[106] governement dou peuple dou reiaume de Jerusalem, selonc les droites[107] assises et les drois usages dou dit reiaume et au profit des armes et des cors de tos ceaus[108] qui le liront ne lire l'oront.[109] Lesqués je pri et requier et conjur[110] de par Deu, que il de chose que il y ait n'en usent[111] malement[112] a tolir ne esloigner le droit d'autrui,[113] mais que il en usent a lor droit ou a celui d'autrui aprochier ou defendre, selonc ce que mestier lor sera. Car m'entencion n'a esté ne n'est[114] de cest livre faire que por enseignier a ceaus qui mestier en avront et avront droit et le requerront[115] de savoir le aprocher et desraigner, et a ceaus a qui l'on le requerra ce qui est lor droit de savoir[116] le esloigner et defendre. Et por ce que il me senble[117] que ains que je parole en cest livre des assises et des usages ne des plais de la haute court dou dit roiaume, que je doie[i] deviser ques il me senble que il seroit mestier que les chiés seignors do dit roiaume fucent por bien et droitement[118] le dit roiaume et lor homes et lor peuple tenir et garder, maintenir et justisier si con il doivent, et ques il seroit mestier que les barons et les riches homes qui ont court et justise el dit roiaume fucent por lor baronies[119] et leur seignories et leur homes et leur peuple tenir et maintenir et justisier selon les assises et les usages dou dit reiaume, et ques les juges et les plaideors de la haute court dou dit roiaume

[i] For the rest of the prologue, ABV diverge from CO. See appendix 3.1.2

[97] par] ABV lack [98] esperance] ABV: l'esperance [99] sapience] A science [100] bininité] ABV: beneurté; O: begninité [101] me] C: n'en [102] faire] A: parfaire [103] oy et] ABV lack [104] V adds: a cui je ais oy parler et [105] dit reiaume] B: reaume devant dit [106] droit] A lacks [107] droites] A: droitures [108] C adds: que [109] ne lire l'oront] ABV lack [110] et conjur] C lacks [111] il de chose... usent] B: de chose que i soit mise [112] malement] A: faucement [113] B adds: que il n'en doient user [114] ne n'est] A lacks [115] et le requerront] A lacks [116] aprocher et desraigner... savoir] A lack [117] A adds: avis [118] O adds: governer [119] baronies] O: barons

doivent estre por les plais bien plaideier et leiaument juger. Car sans ces avant dis, haute court en aucune seignorie dou dit royaume ne peut estre ne plait plaideé ne jugé ne determiné ne assise tenue ne usage maintenu en la haute court de cele seignorie. Por ce que chascun seignor est chief de sa court, et que tous ses homes ou partie d'eaus ou lui, ou celui que il establi en son leuc, sont court, deviserai je au comencement de mon livre ques il seront mestier que les avant dis fucent ou reiaume por bien et droiturierement governer.[j]

[j] AB insert here the chapters on the coronation which form chapters 219 and 220 of this edition.

***[1]** Ci fine le prologue dou livre des assises et des usages et des plais de la haute court dou reiaume de Jerusalem et comence le livre.[a]

Le chief seignor dou reiaume de Jerusalem[1] et tos les barons et[2] seignors dou dit reiaume, qui ont cours et coins et justise,[3] doivent[4] estre sages, loiaus, droituriers et bons justisiers. Sages, por eaus et leur homes[5] et leur peuple et leur terres governer sagement, et qu'il sachent[6] leur honors[7] et lor seignories et leur raisons bien[8] garder, si con il doivent, et lor droit requerre et desraigner. Loiaus, que il loiaument tieignent, mainent[9] et mantieignent et governent eaus et leur homes et leur peuple, que il ne facent a leur ecient ne ne seufrent a faire a lor pooir en lor seignories desleiauté ne fauceté. Droituriers, que il facent,[10] tieignent et maintieignent droiture droitement a chascun en leur cours et en leur seignories, selonc ce que chascun est en droit soi.[11] Bons justisiers, que il n'espargnent[12] aucun de justise quant il ne doit estre espargnés, cruex justisers la ou il s'afiert, et pitous et misericors en justise[13] la ou il s'afiert. Et ces choses conoistront et feront ceaus qui avront en eaus les .iiii. avant dites choses.[14]

Et[b] les homes qui sont juges de[15] la haute court doivent estre loiaus et ententis d'oir et de bien retenir les paroles et les poins, que les plaideors dient en la court el plait, et juger le plus droit et le plus loiaument, que il poront ne savront, selonc les paroles que il avront

A: fol. v[r–v] caps 8–10; **B:** fols 37[r], 37[v]–38[r] caps 8, 10–11; **C:** fols 5[r]–6[v]; **O:** fols 4[v]–5[v]; **V:** fols iv[v]–vi[r] caps 5–7; Beugnot, pp. 31–4, caps 8–10.

[a] Rubric in ABV: Si dit quel (V: Ci dit coument ne lequel) doit estre le chief seignor dou roiaume de Jerusalem, soit roi ou autre, et toz les (B: autres) barons et seignors dou dit roiaume qui ont court et coins et justise.

[b] ABV begin new chapter here with the rubric: Si dit quels doivent estre les homes qui sont juges en la haute court.

[1] ABV add: seit rei ou autre [2] barons et] B: autres barons ou; C: homes et [3] C adds: et [4] C adds in margin in different hand: avoir .iiii. chozes, ce est [5] homes] B: henor; V: cors, honour [6] leur homes et . . . sachent] A lacks [7] honors] CO: homes [8] V adds: gouverner et [9] mainent] C lacks [10] facent] ABV lack [11] droit soi] V: son droit [12] n'espargnent] B: n'esparaigne; O: n'en espargnet [13] B adds: et en droiture [14] Et ces choses . . . choses] ABV lack [15] de] ABV: en

oies et entendues. Que autrement il ne doivent juger ne por amor,[16] ne por haine, ne por poor, ne por loer,[17] ne por autre chose. Il ne doivent[18] laisser ajuger a lor escient ce que plus lor senblera raison, selonc les paroles qu'il avront oies et entendues el plait.[19] Que chascun doit plus amer et douter Deu et s'arme et s'enor que home,[20] ne gré ne maugré d'ome ne de feme, ne perte ne guaain d'avoir. Et il me senble que tos les juges qui sont[21] en la court sont mout chargés de honte et de pechie, se aucun pert sa querele par defaute[22] de non estre entendu de ce que il a dit el plait. Por quei il me senble que tos les homes de la[23] court, quant il sëent en court,[24] devroient laisser toutes autres ententes por entendre et retenir bien les paroles que les avantparliers[25] dient en la court, por bien et droitement recorder[26] les en jugemens et juger les leiaument.[27] Car grant honte est a tos ceaus qui sëent en la court, quant parole i est dite et ele n'est bien retenue et droit recordee au jugement faire et droitement jugee.[28]

Et[c] le plaideor doit estre loial et celable,[29] que il doit bien et loiaument conceiller tos ceaus et toutes celes a[30] qui conceill il est doné et plaideer por eaus leiaument au meaus que il savra contre toutes gens, ne mais que contre lui.[31] Ne ne le doit laisser, por amor que il ait a celui contre qui il plaidoie, ne por haine qu'il ait a celui a qui conceill il est doné, ne por dote,[32] ne por poor que il ait d'avoir honte ne damage ne maugré, ne por don,[33] ne por promesse que l'on li fase, que il bien et loiaument ne conceille celui ou cele a qui conceill le seignor l'a doné, que se il le faisoit autrement, il feroit que desloial. Et doit celer toutes[34] les privautés[35] que celui ou cele a qui conceill il est, li dira des choses de quei il est a son conceill, ne ne doit dire en court ne dehors court chose de ce dont il est a son conceill[36] que il cuide qui[37] li griege. Et se il dit sa parole en la

[c] ABV begin new chapter here with the rubric: Ci dit de (A: De) quel maniere doit estre le plaideor.

[16] Ne por amor] A: Ne por amor aveir; V lacks [17] A adds: ne por gré [18] B adds: juger ne [19] plait] V: plaint [20] B adds: ne feme [21] sont] A: seent; BV: soient [22] par defaute] A lacks [23] ABV add: haute [24] quant il sëent en court] ABV lack [25] paroles que les avantplariers] B: les avantplariers de ce que il [26] recorder] A: retorner [27] et juger les leiaument] A lacks [28] Car grant honte . . . jugee] ABV lack [29] celable] A: estable; V: feable [30] a] C lacks [31] lui] ABV: soi [32] ne por dote] V lacks [33] ne por don] V lacks [34] toutes] ABV lack [35] privautés] B: privances [36] ne ne doit . . . conceill] ABV lack [37] qui] C: que

court, il la doit dire au meaus et au plus loiaument que il porra, sans aucune chose taire[38] ne laisser que il entende que mestier li soit a dire, et se autre l'a dit et il li senble qu'il i puisse amender, il le doit faire ou dire le priveement a celui a qui conseill il est, et a celui qui a dite la parole, et avant que sele faute de quey celui qui avra dite la parole avra failli, grege ou puisse gregier a celui a qui conceill il est,[39] si qu'il la puisse amender a hore et a tens sans son damage.

Et por ce que il me senble qu'en plaidoiant sont les assises et les usages dou dit reiaume requis, debatus[40] et determinés par les homes de la haute court et des autres cours dou dit reiaume, parlerai je avant en cest livre des plais que des assises ne des usages.[d] Et por ce que il me senble que celui qui viaut[41] plaideer en la haute court doit, avant que il comence le plait, demander conceill au seignor, diray je coment et de coy et por qui on doit demander au seignor conceill de cort avant que l'on comence[42] a plaidoier.[e] Et aprés dirai en ordene[43] les autres choses de quei je ay enpris a parler en cest livre, selonc ce que Dex m'en donra[44] sen et grace.[45]

[d] The discussion of how to plead occupies caps 2–97.
[e] Below caps 2–12.

[38] taire] ABV: traire [39] et a celui . . . est] ABV lack [40] AB add: jugiés; V: jugés [41] viaut] C: vait [42] comence] V: face coumenser [43] ordene] AB: ordre [44] donra] C: dora [45] B adds: lequel il me veulle otroier par sa sainte merci

***[2]** Ci devise coment et por qui[1] et de quey l'on doit demander conceill de court.

Qui viaut plaidoier en la haute cort dou reiaume de Jerusalem, il doit demander au seignor conceill[2] le meillor plaideor de la cort a son escient, se il est plaideor ou se il ne l'est, por ce que se il n'est plaideor,[3] que son conceill li sache sa raison garder et sa querele desraigner de ce dont il est requereor et defendre de ce dont il est defendeor, et se il est plaideor por ce que il ait plus de conceill. Que il n'est nul si sage plaideor qu'il ne puisse bien et sovent estre averti el plait de ce que bon li est par .i. autre plaideor o lui. Que .ii. plaideors sevent plus que .i. et voient plus cler el plait et faillent mains. Que se l'un faut, l'autre l'amende. Et por ce qu'a enuis plaideera l'on ja si bien por soi come por autre, que[4] courous ou male volenté tot et amerme sovent conoissance d'ome et l'esmeut en ire qui desvoie sen d'ome plus tost et plus sovent por sa querele que por cele d'autre. Et por ce doit encor le plaideor ou celui qui n'est plaideor demander conseill a droit.[5] Que[6] qui dit sa parole en court, se il faut ou mesprent, il n'i peut amender, et qui la fait dire a autre et celui a qui il la fait dire mesprent ou i faut, il et son conceill i pevent amender ains jugement,[7] se il n'otroie ce que celui qui est a son conceill a dit por lui. Et por[8] ces raisons et por pluisors autres, qui trop seroient longues a dire, doit chascun de ceaus qui veut[9] plaidoier en la haute court demander au seignor conceill avant qu'il comence a plaidoier.

A: fols v^{v}–vi^{r} cap. 11; **B:** fol. 38^{r-v} cap. 12; **C:** fols 6^{v}–7^{r} cap. 1; **O:** fol. 6^{r-v}; **V:** fol. vi^{r-v} cap. 8; Beugnot, pp. 34–5, cap. 11.

---

[1] qui] ABV: quoi [2] ABV add: de court [3] n'est plaideor] B: ne l'est [4] que] C: qui [5] encor le plaideor. . . droit] B: en court le plaideor demander conseill a droit a celui qui n'est plaideor [6] Que] BV: Car [7] jugement] V: que jugement soit fait [8] V adds: toutes [9] veut] B: veulent

*[3] Qui demande conceill,[1] cui il doit demander a son conceill.[2]

Qui demande[3] conceill de court au seignor, il peut demander a son chois lequel que il vodra de tos ceaus qui lors sont en cor, soit[4] home dou seignor ou autre. Et doit demander celui que il cuide qu'il soit le meillor plaideor de la court. Et quant il en avra eu .i. a son conceil a son chois, si doit demander .i. autre, et le seignor li doit le segont doner tel con il vodra. Et se le seignor li done celui que il a requis a son chois et l'autre tel con le seignor vodra, si comence son plait le plus tost[5] et le meaus que il savra. Et se le seignor retient a son conceill ou a sa parole garder celui que il avra premier requis, et il veuille plaideer contre le seignor, si demande .i. autre a son conceill, celui que il cuidera que meillor plaideor soit aprés le premier. Que se il se met en plait de requerre et avoir par esgart celui que il a premier requis et que le seignor a retenu a son conceill, il esloignera son plait et ne le porra avoir. Que le seignor a pooir de retenir a son conceill[6] ou sa parole garder[7] lequel que il viaut[8] de ces homes. Et se le plait est contre autre que contre le seignor, et il retient a sa parole garder celui que l'on li a demandé a conceill, celui qui li a demandé li[9] doit dire: 'Sire, je ne vueill pas plaidoier contre vos, ains veuill plaidoier contre .i. autre. Si vos pri et requier que vos me donés a conceill celui que je vos ai requis'. Et ce le seignor ne li done, se il est requerant, si li demande .i. autre, et se il est defendant et il veaut le plait fuïr, si requiere au seignor pluisors esgars de court, disant pluisors raisons le meaus qu'il savra,[10] por quei il viaut celui avoir a son conceill, puis que il l'a trové en court et premier requis et que le plait n'est contre le seignor, et metre[11] soi de chascune chose par soi en esgart et en chascun esgart[12] metre son retenaill.

A: fol. vi^{r-v} cap. 12; **B:** fols 38^{v}–39^{r} cap. 13; **C:** fol. 7^{r-v} cap. 2; **O:** fols 6^{v}–7^{r}; **V:** fols vi^{v}–vii^{r} cap. 9; Beugnot, pp. 35–6, cap. 12.

---

[1] V adds: de court [2] a son conceill] B lacks [3] demande] A: viaut demander [4] lors sont en cor, soit] B: la sont, encor soit il [5] V adds: que il pora [6] il esloignera son. . . conseill] A lacks [7] A adds: le seignor peut retenir [8] viaut] B: voudra [9] li] V: a conseill [10] savra] B: porra [11] metre] B: mette [12] et en chascun esgart metre] A: de court et metre; B: et en chascune chose mete

***[4]** Coment l'on doit demander conceill, si que celui que on demandera a conceill ne puisse de cele querele conceillier son aversaire.

Qui viaut demander conceill de cort au seignor, si que se[1] le seignor le retient a sa parole garder, que il ne[2] le puisse de cele querele doner au conceill de son aversaire, ne celui que le seignor[3] retient a sa parole garder n'i puisse aler, se il viaut aler[4] de sa volenté, si die enssi quant il demandera[5] conceill: 'Sire, donés moi tel a mon conceill', et le nome, 'contre tel de tel chose', et nome[6] celui contre cui il viaut plaidoier et die de quei il viaut plaidoier.[7] Et se le seignor[8] le retient a sa parole garder, si li die: 'Sire, ce[9] plait de quei je veuill plaideer n'est pas contre vos, por quei je n'entens que vos a vostre parole garder puissiés ne deés tel retenir', et le nome, 'puis que il est present en la court, et que je qui sui vostre home le vos ay demandé a mon conceill contre tel et de tel chose', et die de quei, 'et que ce[10] n'est de riens contre vos, si[11] ne veuill que il demore por chose que vos aiés dite,[12] que vos ne me le donés a mon conceill, ains le veuill avoir a mon conceill[13] par les raisons que je ai[14] dites, se la court[15] l'esgarde, et de ce me met je en l'esgart de la court', et mete son[16] retenaill. Et a ce peut le seignor dire: 'Je ne veuill que il demore por chose que vos aiés dite, que je ne le reteigne[17] a ma parole garder et di por coi: por ce que je entent que le seignor a pooir par l'assise ou l'usage de cest[18] roiaume de retenir a son chois a son conceill et a sa parole garder lequel que il viaut de ses homes. Por quei je le veuill avoir a ma parole garder, puis que je l'ai retenu, se la court l'esgarde. Et de ce me met je en l'esgart de la court, sauf mon retenaill.' Et[19] la court doit esgarder que le seignor le peut[20] retenir a sa parole garder.

Et se il le retient aprés le dit esgart et il aprés le done au conceill de l'aversaire de celui qui premier[21] le requist, ou se celui i vait de

---

A: fols vi^{v}–vii^{v} cap. 13; **B:** fols 39^{r}–40^{r} cap. 14; **C:** fols 7^{v}–9^{v} cap. 3; **O:** fols 7^{r}–9^{r}; **V:** fols vii^{r}–viii^{v} cap. 10; Beugnot, pp. 36–8, cap. 13.

---

[1] se] BCV lack [2] ne] C lacks [3] le seignor] A: l'on [4] se il viaut aler] V lacks [5] demandera] A: viaut demander [6] A adds: la chose et [7] et die de . . . plaidoier] AV lack [8] le seignor] B: li sires [9] Sire, ce] V: sur cest [10] ce] C lacks [11] si] A: por quei je [12] dite] AV: faite dire [13] ains le veuill. . . conceill] ABV lack [14] ABV add: devant [15] V adds: ne [16] et mete son] A: sauf mon; BV: et metre son [17] reteigne] V: teigne [18] de cest] ABV: dou [19] Et] C lacks [20] peut] A: doit [21] premier] C: premierement

sa volenté, die celui qui premier[22] le demanda a son conseill, 'Sire, je n'entent que vos tel', et le nome, 'puissés ne deiés doner a conceill de mon aversaire de ceste querele, ne qu'il de sa volenté l'en puisse conceillier contre moy, puis que je avant le vos demandai a mon conceill de ceste querele contre lui, et que vos le retenistes a vostre parole garder,[23] et que je le vos contrebati par esgart de court. Et que vos par esgart de court l'avés desraigné vers moi a vostre parole garder de ceste querele, si ne veuill que vos, aprés les erremens devant dis, le doignés a conceill de mon aversaire de ceste querele,[24] ne que il l'en[25] conseille contre moi, et di por coi: por ce que trop seroit forte chose et contre[26] droit et raison et tort apert,[27] se me senble, que vos, qui estes seignor et justisier,[28] qui devés faire droit et maintenir ygaument a chascun sa raison, peusiés doner a conseill de mon aversaire celui que je vos ai demandé devant[29] a mon conceill contre lui de ceste querele, ne que il[30] de sa volenté, por chose que vos en aiés faite, l'en peut conceillier contre moy. Que s'ensi estoit, que vos ne le li peussiés faire, donc[31] poriés vos tolir a cui que vos vodriés[32] le conceill que l'on vos avroit premier requis, et[33] son aversaire l'avroit a son conceill contre lui de cele querele, se vos le poés doner[34] a son conceill et vos le voliés faire, et se vos ne le poés faire ou ne voliés faire,[35] et il de sa volenté peust mon aversaire conceillier contre moi de ceste querele aprés les dis erremens, ce ne seroit que por ce que vos l'avriés retenu et eu par esgart de court a vostre parole garder, quant je le vos demandai a mon conseill, laquel chose seroit contre[36] l'assise et l'usage de cest roiaume. Que par l'assise ne l'usage de cest roiaume[37] ne par raison vos ne le poés doner a conceill de mon aversaire contre moi de ceste querele, ne faire chose par coi il puisse mon aversaire conceillier contre moi de ceste querele, puis que je avant le vos demandai a mon conceill contre lui de ceste querele, et que vos l'avés retenu a vostre parole garder, et que je le vos ai contrebatu, et que vos l'avés par esgart de court. Por quey je ne veuill que vos le facés, ne[38] que il mon aversaire conceille[39] contre moi de ceste querele aprés les erremens devant dis, se la court

[22] premier] C: premierement [23] B adds: de ceste querele [24] si ne veuill . . . querele] ABV lack [25] l'en] ABV: le [26] et contre] C: encontre [27] apert] ABV: aparant [28] justisier] ABO: justise [29] devant] AB lack [30] que il] V lacks [31] donc] C: dont [32] ne le li . . . vodriés] A: vodreiés retenir; B: vousissiés retenir [33] et] C: a [34] poés doner] V: voliés doner et poiciés [35] faire] C lacks [36] V adds: droit et contre [37] Que par l'assise . . . roiaume] B lacks [38] ne] A lacks [39] conceille] A: dee conseillier

ne l'esgarde, et por tant plus di ge que vos ne le poés doner au conceill de mon aversaire contre moi de ceste querele, ne que il l'en puisse[40] conceillier. Que se vos le faisiés, ou se il l'en[41] conceilloit[42] de sa volenté, j'entens que ce seroit contre l'esgart de la court, laquel chose vos ne devés faire ne sofrir que autre le[43] fase. Que la court a esgardé que vos le poés retenir a vostre parole garder de ceste querele. Si est clere chose que il autre ne peut ne doit faire par raison de ceste querele[44] que vostre parole garder aprés les dis eremens. Et se il autre en faisoient,[45] j'entent que ce seroit tort apert[46] contre l'esgart de la court. Et por toutes les raisons que je ai dites ou por aucunes d'eles, je ne veuill que il conceille mon aversaire contre moy de ceste querele, se la cort ne conoist[47] que il faire le doie, et de ce me met[48] je en la conoissance de la court[49] sauf[50] mon retenaill.'

Et se le seignor comande a faire la dite conoissance, il ne[51] me senble que il, ne celui qu'il a retenu a sa parole garder, puissent[52] chose dire par quei la court conoisse que il doive conceillier de cele querele l'aversaire de celui qui premier le requist a son conceill en la maniere avant dite. Que s'autrement estoit, les seignors poroient tolir a lor homes le conceill que il avroient premier requis et doner le a leur aversaire, ou ce selui i voloit aler de sa volenté, il le poroit faire,[53] par ce que le seignor l'avroit retenu a sa parole garder laquel chose me senble qu'il[54] seroit tort apert.[55] Et se le seignor ne li viaut la conoissance faire faire, si le destraigne[56] si com il devise[57] aprés en cest livre, c'on peut et doit seignor destraindre de faire li faire conoissance de court.

---

[40] que il l'en puisse] AV: qu'il ne le peut (V: poet); B: que je ne le puet [41] l'en] ABV: le [42] conceilloit] B: conseille; V: conseillet [43] le] ABV lack [44] Si est clere . . . querele] AB: Ne qu'il autre chose ne deit faire [45] faisoient] A: faisseit; B: faisoit [46] apert] AB: apert et; V: aparant et [47] conoist] A: conut; V: l'esguarde ou counoist [48] met] C lacks [49] la conoissance de la court] V: l'esguart de la court et en la counissance [50] sauf] BV: sans [51] ne] OV lack [52] puissent] ABV: puisse [53] faire] C lacks [54] qu'il] AV: que ce; B: que [55] apert] V: aparant [56] destraigne] A: destreignent [57] il devise] AV: est devisé; B: il est devisé

***[5]** Por qui l'on peut[1] demander conceill[2] par esgart.

L'on peut por soi ou por sa feme ou por son fiz ou por sa fille merme d'aage demander conseill au seignor par esgart de court, et por celui ou sele a qui le seignor l'a doné a conseill, se il n'a motié la querele en la court de quei il viaut plaideer, quant il le demanda a son conseill. Quar[3] qui ne la motit au demander conseill[4] il peut par son conseill demander autre a son conceill,[5] et defendre celui qui avant[6] est a son conceill, se l'on li viaut tolir, ou desraignier celui qui a esté a son conceill se il n'i[7] viaut plus estre ou se le seignor ou son aversaire li defent[8] que il n'i aille par esgart ou autrement, tout soit ce que il[9] le demanda a son[10] conceill ne dist que il le demandoit por[11] conseill[12] requere[13] ou defendre.[14] Que puis que on demande conseill sans motir de coi, et le seignor le[15] li done, il peut celui a qui conceill il est donés conceiller de toutes quereles de quei celui qui l'a demandé a son conceill li dira lors de quei il l'a demandé a son conceill.[16] Mais d'autre[17] ne le doit il pas conceillier se le seignor ne le done a son conceill autres fois de[18] celes autres quereles, ne de querele de quei il ait esté donés avant a autre conceill ne le peut il conceillier. Mais qui a motié au demander conceill contre qui[19] il le demande ou por coi il le demande a son conceill, il ne le doit d'autre chose conceillier[20] se il ne viaut, et, se il le viaut conceiller, il le peut faire contre chascun qui ne soit son seignor ou son home a qui il soit tenus de foi ou contre autre a qui conceill il ait esté de cele querele de quei il avra[21] esté a son conseill.

A: fols vii^{v}–viii^{r} cap. 14; **B:** fol. 40^{r} cap. 15; **C:** fols 9^{v}–10^{r} cap. 4; **O:** fol. 9^{r-v}; **V:** fols viii^{v}–ix^{r} cap. 11; Beugnot, pp. 38–9, cap. 14.

---

[1] l'on peut] A: on deit [2] ABV add: de court [3] quar] O lacks [4] Quar qui ne . . . conseill] AB lack [5] A adds: c'il n'a motié la carelle au demander conseill si come est dessuz dit; B adds: si come est desus dit [6] avant] A lacks [7] n'i] AV: ne [8] defent] V: defendoit [9] ABV add: quant il [10] son] ABO lack [11] C adds: son [12] conseill] AB lack [13] requere] V: querre [14] ou defendre] B lacks [15] le] C lacks [16] li dira lors . . . conceill] BC lack [17] d'autre] ABV: des autres [18] de] C: que [19] qui] C lacks [20] a son conceill . . . conceillier] B lacks [21] A adds: avant

*[6] Por quei l'on peut demander conceill de court[1] sans esgart.

L'on peut por qui que l'on viaut demander au seignor conceill de court, mais que l'on[2] au seignor ne requiere[3] de ce esgart ne conoissance de court, ne s'i mete, se le seignor ou[4] autre ne[5] s'i viaut metre. Quar[6] qui le fera,[7] se il n'est a son conceill par court ou que ce soit l'un de ceaus de quei il est devant dit por qui[8] l'on peut demander conceill par esgart de court, il mesprent[9] vers le seignor,[10] et le seignor le porra achaisoner et gregier se il viaut. Et coment et de quei il mesprent vers le seignor,[11] et coment et de coi[12] le seignor le peut ataindre et droit avoir, et quel droit il en doit avoir, sera devisé aprés en cest livre.

A: fol. viii^{r} cap. 15; **B:** fol. 40$^{r\ v}$ cap. 16; **C:** fol. 10^{r} cap. 5; **O:** fols 9^{r}–10^{r}; **V:** fol. ix^{r-v} cap. 12; Beugnot, p. 40, cap. 15.

[1] de court] A lacks [2] que l'on] V lacks [3] requiere] B: quiere [4] ou] C: ne [5] ne] BCOV lack [6] A adds: por [7] B adds: ensi [8] qui] ABV: quoi [9] mesprent] C: me senble [10] V adds: de sa foi [11] et le seignor . . . seignor] V lacks [12] et de coi] ABV lack

***[7]** A qui le seignor[1] ne peut doner[2] conceill de cort se son aversaire le contrebat.[3]

Le seignor ne peut ne ne doit doner conceill de court a home qui sans conceill de court plaidoie, ne comence plait, ne fait clain d'autre, ne requiert chose a autre en court en forme de plait, ne qui ait respondu a clain ni a requeste que l'on li a faite en court de cele querele, se son aversaire le contredit ou defent, si com il doit, por ce qu'il est assise ou usage el roiaume de Jerusalem, que qui plaidoie en la haute cort sans avoir[4] conceill de cort, que il ne le peut ne ne[5] doit d'aprés[6] avoir se son aversaire ne li contredit.[7] Et qui viaut tolir a celui que a fait l'une des chozes devant dites conceill de court, si die au seignor quant celui demande conceill:[8] 'Sire, je vos pri et requier com a seignor et justise,[9] et defent enci come je puis et doi que vos a tel', et le nome, 'ne donés conceill de ceste querele, de quei il a comencé[10] a plaidoier contre moi sans conseill. Ne je n'entent que vos faire le puissiés ne deés, ne je ne veuill que vos le facés se vostre court ne l'esgarde, et di por coy: por ce que il n'est costume ne usage ne assise el roiaume de Jerusalem, que qui plaidoie ou comence a plaidoier[11] en court sans conseill, que il aprés de[12] cele querele[13] puisse ne dee aver conceill de court. Et tel a bien comencé a plaideer, quant il a ce dit et fait en la court', et die laquel des choses desus dites[14] il a dites et faites. 'Et por toutes les[15] raisons que je ai dites ou por aucunes d'eles, ne veuill je que il ait conceill,[16] se la court ne l'esgarde, et de ce me met je en l'esgart de la court', et mete son[17] retenaill. Et je ne croi[18] que celui[19] qui a comencié a plaidoier sans conceill puisse chose dire par coy la court esgarde[20] que celui qui a plait comencié sans conceill[21] doit aprés[22] avoir conceill[23] de court de cele querele.

A: fol. viii[r–v] cap. 16; **B:** fol. 40[v] cap. 17; **C:** fols 10[r]–11[r] cap. 6; **O:** fol. 10[r–v]; **V:** fols ix[v]–x[r] cap. 13; Beugnot, pp. 40–1, cap. 16.

[1] le seignor] AV: l'on [2] doner] V: demander [3] contrebat] AV: contredit [4] avoir] C lacks [5] peut ne ne] A lacks [6] d'aprés] A: plus; B: puis; OV: aprés [7] ne li contredit] A: li viaut defendre; V: li contredit [8] AV add: de court [9] justise] V: a justizier [10] a comencé] C: comence; O: comensié [11] a plaidoier] V: plait [12] de] C lacks [13] de cele querele] A lacks [14] laquel des choses desus dites] A: lesquels choses [15] les] AV: ces [16] ABV add: de court [17] et mete son] A: sauf mon; V: save mon [18] croi] B: cuit [19] celui] B: cil; O: ce l'on [20] esgarde] V: esgardera [21] A adds: de court [22] aprés] A: puis [23] doit aprés avoir conceill] V lacks

***[8]** A ques gens le seignor ne peut ne ne doit veer conceill de court.

Le seignor ne peut ne ne doit veer conceill de court[1] a aucune persone qui li requiert conceill[2] qui soit present en la court, se le seignor ne le retient a son conceill ou a sa parole garder et se il n'a[3] home a son conceill que le seignor li ait doné de cele querele[4] qui[5] soit present en la court, ou se il n'a plaidoie sans conceill, si com est avant dit, ou se il ne l'a doné avant a autre contre lui de cele querele. Et se le seignor li a doné conceill de cele querele,[6] et il ne soit present en la court,[7] et il li demande[8] autre[9] en eschange de celui, tant qu'il soit en la court, le seignor ne li peut veer se il n'a dit ou fait aucune des choses avant dites par quei le seignor li puisse veer conseill.[10] Et se le seignor vee conseill a aucune persone que[11] par l'une des dites choses, celui a qui il le vee[12] li doit dire: 'Sire, vos estes seignor et justisier[13] et droiturier, se Deu plaist,[14] et avés juré de tenir et maintenir les us et les costumes et les assises dou reiaume de Jerusalem, et il est us ou costume ou assise el dit roiaume que seignor ne peut ne ne doit veer conceill a qui qui[15] li requiert[16] en sa court, se il n'a chose faite ou dite par quei il a perdu a aveir conseill de court. Ne je n'ai chose faite ne dite par quei je l'aie perdu a avoir. Si le veuill avoir[17] por tant con je ai dit, se vostre court l'esgarde, et de ce[18] vos requier je l'esgart de la court', et mete son retenaill. Et se le seignor se met de ce en esgart, je cuit que la court esgardera que le seignor li doit doner conceill de court, se le seignor ou autre ne dit que il ait chose faite ou dite par quey il ne doit avoir conceill de court et die por coi et l'eufre a prover et le preuve,[19] si con il doit, et tel preuve ne peut[20] estre faite que par recort de court.

A: fols viii^{v}–ix^{r} cap. 17; **B:** fols 40^{v}–41^{r} cap. 18; **C:** fol. 11$^{r\ v}$ cap. 7; **O:** fols 10^{v}–11^{r}; **V:** fol. x^{r-v} cap. 14; Beugnot, pp. 41–2, cap. 17.

---

[1] de court] V lacks [2] C adds: de court [3] n'a] V: n'en a demandé (demandé in the margin in cursive hand) [4] V adds interlined in cursive hand: a autre [5] qui] C: qu'il [6] Et se le . . . querele] V lacks [7] V adds interlined in cursive hand: et se il demande home qui'l n'est present en la curt [8] li demande] A: ait demandé; B: a demandé; V: demande [9] autre] A: autre au seignor; V: conseill au seignor [10] conseill] C lacks [11] aucune persone que] A: aucune persone sanz ce que; B: aucun [12] le vee] V: nee conseill [13] justisier] ABO: justise [14] se Deu plaist] A lacks [15] qui qui] AV: qui; B: qui que [16] requiert] B: demande [17] avoir] C lacks [18] ce] C lacks [19] et le preuve] A lacks [20] peut] V: doit

***[9]** A qui le seignor doit doner conceill de cort quant on li requiert.

Le seignor doit doner conceill[1] a qui li[2] requiert en sa court et celui que l'on li requiert,[3] se il est present en la court quant l'on li requiert,[4] se il ne le retient a son conceill ou a sa parole garder, ou se celui qui li requiert le conceill[5] n'a fait l'une des dites choses si con il est dit[6] en l'autre chapitle por coi l'on pert a aver conceill de court, ou se le seignor ne l'a doné a autre a conceill de cele querele contre lui.

Et se celui que l'on li requiert a conceill n'est present en la court quant on li requiert a conceill,[7] il[8] doit dire: 'Celui que vos me requerés a conceill n'est pas en la court'. Et se celui li dit: 'Sire, celui que je vos demant a conceill est en ceste vile. Enveés le querre, et le me donés a conceill', se il doit servise de son cors au seignor, le seignor doit respondre: 'Je l'enveerai querre, et quant il sera en la court je vos en ferai ce que je devrai'. Et lors le doit mander[9] semondre par le banier que il veigne a court, et le banier[10] le doit querre la ou il le cuidera meaus trover es[11] leus covenables ou il le cuidera[12] trover. Et se le banier le treuve, il le doit semondre de venir a court, et se il le semont et il i vient, le seignor le peut retenir a son conceill ou[13] a sa parole guarder, ou doner le au conceill de celui qui li a[14] demandé, lequel qu'il meaus vodra. Mais se le seignor dit 'volentiers', quant celui vendra que il a demandé a conceill et requis qu'il li envoe querre, si con est devant dit, le seignor ne le pora[15] puis retenir[16] a sa parole garder, se il vient en la court, por ce que il li avra otroie en la court de doner le li a son conceill. Quar bien li otree, quant celui[17] li dit, 'Sire, envoiés le querre', et le seignor li dist: 'Volentiers',[18] ou[19] 'de par Deu', ou aucun tel mot por quei il li otree sa requeste.

A: fols ix^r–x^r cap. 18; **B:** fols 41^r–42^v cap. 19; **C:** fols 11^v–13^v cap. 8; **O:** fols 11^r–13^r; **V:** fols x^v–xii^v cap. 15; Beugnot, pp. 42–4, cap. 18.

---

[1] A adds: de court [2] qui li] B: qui que le [3] en sa court . . . requiert] A lacks [4] li requiert] B: li requiert, ou; V: le requerra [5] qui li requiert le conceill] A: qui li requiert; V: que l'on requiert a son conseill [6] si con il est dit] ABV: qui sont escrites [7] n'est present . . . conceill] C lacks [8] il] A: le seignor [9] mander] A: faire [10] que il veigne . . . banier] O lacks [11] es] BV: et en touz les; O: les [12] la ou il . . . cuidera] A: en toz les leus covenables ou il le cuidera miaus [13] ou] C: et [14] a] B: avoit [15] pora] B: puet [16] ABV add: a son conseill ne (A: ni) [17] celui] C: il [18] quant celui vendra . . . Volentiers] BV repeat
[19] ou] C lacks [20] au] C: o [21] le seignor] O lacks [22] ne] C: n'en [23] hors de] A:

Et se celui que l'on a demandé a conceill n'est en la vile ou ne doit servise de son cors au[20] seignor, le seignor[21] n'est pas tenus d'enveer le quere se il ne[22] viaut. Et se celui li requiert par esgart, il s'en peut bien defendre se il dit: 'Je n'entent que je le doie mander querre hors de[23] la vile por doner le vos a conceill, et di por quei'. Por ce que s'ensi estoit que le seignor fust tenus de mander[24] querre hors[25] de la vile, celui que l'on li requiert[26] a conceill, dont ne seroient ceaus qui fuïent les plais atains en lonc tens, que il demanderoient a conceill[27] quant il vodroient le plait fuïr, celui des homes dou seignor qui seroit plus loing de la vile[28] et avroient respit de lor plais[29] tant que celui seroit venus en la court ou avroit fait respons au seignor que il n'i[30] porroit venir. Et se il n'i venoit par essoigne que il eust ou autrement, celui qui vodroit le plait esloigner et demander[31] .i. autre de plus lontains, et le poroit tel demander vers qui il porchaceroit bien que il se feroit[32] esoigne quant le seignor le manderoit semondre de venir a court. Et enssi le porroit faire de pluisors de quei le requerant seroit lonc tens esloigné de sa raison, de quei[33] il poroit avoir grant damage por[34] sa raison perdre par moult[35] de choses qui el tens de cel delay poroient avenir. 'Por quei je n'entent que je hors de[36] la vile le doie enveer[37] querre por doner le vos a conceill, ne faire ne le veuill, se la court ne l'esgarde.' Et de ce metre soi[38] en l'esgart de la court et metre son[39] retenaill.

Et ceste defence doit le seignor faire contre[40] le defendeor. Et contre[41] le requereor die, 'Je ne le veuill mander querre hors[42] de la ville, se court ne l'esgarde, et di por quei: por ce que il n'est assise ne usage en cest roiaume que je faire le doie, por coy je n'entent[43] que je[44] soie tenus dou faire, ne faire ne le veuill, se court ne l'esgarde', et mete[45] s'en[46] en l'esgart de la court sauf son retenaill.

Et qui requiert au seignor a[47] conceill home qui n'est en la court[48] et ne li doit servise de son cors, le seignor n'est pas tenuz d'enveer

defors; V: dehors de [24] de mander] B: d'envoier [25] hors] A: fors [26] requiert] A: requereit; B: requerroit [27] a conceill] AB lack [28] B adds: a conseill [29] de lor plais] A: et delaiz [30] n'i] ABV: ne [31] et demander] A: demandereit; BV: demanderoit [32] se feroit] B: avroit [33] de quei] B: dont [34] por] A: de; O: ou [35] B adds: de raisons et [36] hors de] A: defors [37] enveer] B: mander [38] metre soi] V: me met je [39] et metre son] A: sauve son; B: et mete son; V: sauf mon [40] contre] BOV: encontre [41] contre] ABV: encontre [42] hors] A: fors [43] je faire le . . . n'entent] B: l'on le doie faire por quoi je m'entens [44] AV add: en [45] mete] AV: metre [46] s'en] A: sei; B: soi; V: se [47] AV add: son [48] A adds: present le querre. Si s'en peut le seignor[a] defendre, se il viaut, et enssi que il die: 'Je n'entent que je soie tenus d'enveer querre celui que vos me requerés que je vos done a vostre conceill, et di por coi: por ce qu'il ne me doit servise de son cors ne home qui[49] ne me doit servise de son cors, je n'entent que je soie tenus de faire[50] le semondre de venir a court, ne de servise faire que il ne me doit. Que se il fust en la court present et vos le me demandés[51] a vostre conceill, ne le poroie[52] je destraindre[53] d'aler y autrement que de comander li[54] que il i alast, et se il n'i voloit aler, et se partoit[55] de la court, ne le poroie je retenir[56] en la court ne destraindre le de demorer[57] y, n'achaisoner l'en, n'avoir[58] en droit par la court[59] n'amende de ce que il ne feroit mon comandement et qu'il se partiroit de court sans mon congié,[60] por ce qu'il ne m'avroit[61] mesfait. Que puis que il ne me[62] doit servise de son cors, je ne le puis destraindre[63] que il le me fase. Et por toutes les raisons que je ai dites, ou por aucunes d'eles, ne le veuill je mander querre, se la court ne l'esgarde', et mete[64] se en l'esgart[65] de la court sauf[66] son retenaill. Et se l'autre se met en l'esgart[67] vers le seignor d'aucune des dites choses, je cuit[68] que la cort esgardera que le seignor n'est pas tenus d'enveer querre hors[69] de la vile[70] celui que l'on demande a conceill, ne d'enveer quere de[71] la vile celui que l'on li demande a conceill qui[72] ne li doit servise de son cors.

Et quant le seignor a doné a conceill celui que l'on li demande,[73] et l'on li en demande .i. autre, il li doit doner et tel que il cuide qu'il sache[74] covenablement plaideer selonc les autres homes[75] de la court. Quar il ne li doit doner le meillor plaideor de la court aprés

---

[a] Following the reading of A. The readings of COV are corrupt: '. . . de son cors, et (et] V lacks) aprés ce le seignor d'esgart (V: esguart) d'enveer le quere, le seignor s'en peut . . .' B, perhaps trying to remedy the corruption, reads: '. . . de son cors aprés ce le seignor demande esgart d'envoier le querre, le seignor se puet . . .'

---

[49] ne home qui] A: et puis qu'il; V: et home qui [50] de faire] A: d'enveer [51] demandés] B: demandissiés; V: demandisiés [52] poroie] B: peusse [53] destraindre] A: semondre [54] comander li] AB: semondre le [55] partoit] C: paroit [56] retenir] A: tenir [57] demorer] B: venir [58] l'en, n'avoir] V: le avoir [59] par la court] ABV lack [60] congie] V: gré [61] B adds: riens [62] me] V: m'avroit mesfait ne ne [63] destraindre] B: constraindre [64] mete] AV: metre [65] l'esgart] C: esgart [66] sauf] V: sans [67] l'esgart] C: esgart; V: l'esguart de la court [68] cuit] B: entens [69] hors] A: fors [70] A adds: ne dedenz la ville [71] d'enveer quere de] B: de mander querre en [72] ne d'enveer . . . qui] A: puis qu'il [73] demande] AV: a demandé [74] cuide qu'il sache] V: li puisse [75] homes] B: persones

celui que il a demandé a son chois, por ce que son aversaire ne soit gregé, ne des mains sachans de la court, por ce que il ne soit gregé,[76] que le seignor doit estre en la court con[77] droite balance. Que il ne doit plait esloigner quant il entent que le requerant ait[78] droit, ne aprochier quant il entent[79] que le fuïant ait[80] droit, que le seignor ne doit maintenir partie en la court, ains doit estre dreiturier[81] et juste a chascun. Et il doit estre plus favorable as veves et as orfenins en lor droit et en lor raisons que as autres gens, por ce que il sont en sa garde plus especiaument que les autres gens, et que il ont sovent plus grant mestier de conceill et d'aie que les autres gens,[82] mais que il le fase enssi que il ne mespreigne[83] vers Dieu ne vers home ne vers feme.

[76] ne des mains . . . gregé] AB lack [77] con] B: ausi come [78] entent que le requerant ait] B: verra que le requereor avra [79] entent] AV: cuide; B: verra [80] ait] B: avra [81] V adds: et justizier [82] et que il . . . gens] AV lack [83] mespreigne] C: mesparaigne

***[10]** Quel diference il i a entre ce que le seignor retient[1] home a son conceill ou[2] a sa parole garder.[3]

La diference qui est[4] entre ce que seignor retient home a son conceill aucune fois[5] et aucune fois le retient[6] a sa parole garder est tel: que quant le seignor viaut plaideer a[7] aucun ou aucun a lui, il peut et doit retenir home a son conceill, et quant gent plaidoient l'un a l'autre il peut et doit retenir home a sa parole garder por les raisons aprés dites.

A: fol. x[r] cap. 19; **B:** fol. 42[v] cap. 20; **C:** fol. 13[v] cap. 9; **O:** fol. 13[r]; **V:** fol. xii[v] cap. 16; Beugnot, p. 44, cap. 19.

---

[1] retient] V: tient [2] ou] ABV: et [3] son conseill ou . . . garder] C: sa parole garder ou a son conceill [4] qui est] V: que il y a [5] aucune fois] B: ou a sa parole garder et aucune fois le retient a son conseill [6] et aucune fois le retient] V lacks [7] a] C lacks

***[11]** Coment le seignor doit retenir home a son conceill, et coment a sa parole garder.[a]

Le seignor doit retenir home a son conceill, quant il viaut plaideer a aucun de ses homes ou a autre,[1] ou quant l'on viaut plaideer a lui. Et quant il plaidoie a aucun de ces homes ou aucun de ses homes a lui, il ne peut avoir que .ii. de ces homes a son conceill. Et quant il plaidoie a autre qu'a son home ou autre que son home[2] a lui, il peut avoir tant de ces homes a son conceill con il veaut,[3] ne l'autre ne peut aveir de ceaus de la court que .ii. a son conceill. Et quant le seignor viaut retenir home a son conceill, il peut l'un de ces homes lequel qu'il veaut[4] a son chois retenir a son conceill, et doner a celui contre qui il plaidoie l'autre lequel qu'il[5] li[6] demandera. Et aprés peut le seignor a son chois prendre a son conceill[7] lequel que il vodra de ses autres[8] homes, et aprés[9] doner a son aversaire .i. autre a son conceill tel come il vodra. Et quant le seignor retient home a son conceill, il doit dire: 'Je retiens tel', et le nome, 'a mon conceill contre tel', et le nome, 'de tel querele', et la motisse. Et se il viaut, il peut dire en sa court au comencement des plais ains que il ait doné a aucun conceill: 'Je retiens tel home', et le nome, 'a mon conceill contre tos[10] ceaus qui vodront hui plaideer a moy et contre tos ceaus a qui je vodrai hui plaideer'. Et se il enssi le fait et aucun le demande aprés ce cel jor a[11] conceill et le seignor li done et il viaut plaideer au seignor, celui ne le[12] porra[13] conceillier, por ce que le seignor l'avra avant[14] retenu a son conceill, et que, quant il le dona au conceill de celui qui li[15] demanda, il ne savoit pas que ce fust contre lui, quar il ne dist[16] quant il li[17] demanda

---

A: fol. x^{r-v} cap. 20; **B:** fols 42^{v}–43^{r} cap. 21; **C:** fols 13^{v}–14^{r} cap. 10; **O:** fols 13^{r}–14^{r}; **V:** fols xii^{v}–xiii^{r} cap. 17; Beugnot, pp. 44–5 cap. 20.

---

[a] The second part of the rubric more properly relates to chapter 12.

---

[1] ou a autre] A lacks [2] son home ou . . . home] A: ces homes ou autre que ces homes [3] veaut] V: vodra [4] veaut] A: vodra [5] qu'il] C: qu [6] li] AV lack [7] a son conceill] V lacks [8] autres] BV lac [9] aprés] B lacks [10] tos] C lacks [11] AB add: son; V: cel [12] le] CV: li [13] porra] A: poreit; B: puet; V: poroit [14] V adds: heu et [15] dona au conceill . . . li] V lacks [16] dist] A: li dist pas; B: li dist mie [17] li] ABV: le

a son conceill, ne le seignor ne sot[18] quant il li dona, contre qui il voleit plaideer, et que[19] il avoit avant retenu a son conceill contre tos ceaus qui a lui plaidieroient.[20] Et por ce ne peut il autre en cel jor conceillier[21] contre le seignor.

---

[18] ne sot] A: ne saveit pas; BV lack [19] que] ABV lack [20] contre tos ceaus . . . plaidieroient] A: contre toz ciaus qui a lui plaidieroient ou a qui il plaideeroit; V: que a lui plaideeroit [21] autre en cel jor conseillier] B: avoir en cel jour a son conseill

***[12]** Coment et por quey le seignor doit retenir home a sa parole garder.

Le seignor peut retenir lequel que il viaut de ses homes a sa parole garder contre tous ceaus qui plaidoient[1] en la court les uns as autres, et il le doit faire por ce que sovent avient que, quant l'on plaidoie l'un a l'autre,[2] que il font sovent requestes[3] ou defences au seignor et a qui[4] il covient qu'il responde; et sovent li requierent[5] esgars ou conoissances de court de quei[6] il covient que il s'i[7] mete vers les .ii. parties ou vers l'une; ou l'un requiert a l'autre vilains ou terre ou aucune autre chose en quei[8] il covient que le seignor i mete contredit ou defence por droit que il y entent a avoir; et por plusors autres choses[9] qui sovent avienent et pevent avenir en la court doit le seignor ades retenir a sa parole garder le meillor plaideor de la court a son escient. Et quant le seignor retient aucun de ces homes a sa parole guarder quant on[10] li demande a conceill ou avant,[11] il doit dire a sa court, 'Je retiens tel a ma parole guarder contre tos ceaus qui hui plaideeront devant moy l'un contre l'autre ou de tel querele' et la motisse. Aprés ce il ne le doit doner a conceill de nul qui le demande se il ne veaut; mais aprés il le peut doner a conceill s'il ne li est defendu ou contredit par esgart si come est devant[12] dit.

A: fols x^{v}–xi^{r} cap. 21; **B:** fol. 43^{r-v} cap. 22; **C:** fol. 14^{r-v} cap. 11; **O:** fol. 14^{r}; **V:** fol. xiii^{r-v} cap. 18; Beugnot, p. 45 cap. 21.

---

[1] plaidoient] A: plaideeront; B: plaidoieront [2] quant l'on plaidoie . . . l'autre] B: quant les uns pladoient as autres [3] requestes] B: enquestes [4] a qui] B: as queles; O: a quei [5] requierent] V: requiert [6] quei] C: qui [7] s'i] BV: se [8] quei] C: qui [9] autres choses] A: raissons [10] quant on] B: et l'on [11] avant] B: avant ce [12] devant] V: avant

*[13] Coment l'on doit plaideer en la haute cort.[1]

Qui plaidoie en la haute court do reiaume de Jerusalem ou en cele de Chipre, il doit plaideer sagement, leiaument et cortoisement. Sagement, que il se garnisse quant il viaut plaidoier ains que il comence a plaidoier dou plus sage conceill que il porra avoir, et qu'il fase dire sa parole par son conceill ou par autre ce que miaus li senblera, et que il ne die chose en court qui li griege ne n'otroie[2] chose[3] de quei son aversaire[4] li demande otroi,[5] s'il ne le fait par le conceill de[6] son conceill, et que il n'eufre[7] en court chose a prover qu'il ne puisse prover se son aversaire li noie, et que il n'esloigne plait que il doie ataindre, ne aproche[8] plait que[9] il doie fuïr.[a] Leiaument, que il ne plaidoie de tort a son escient contre droit, et que il ne plaidoie faucement ne face fauce preuve en plait par faus garans ne autrement, ne que il ne toille a son escient le droit de celui contre[10] qui il plaidoie par point de plait ne autrement. Cortoisement, que il[11] el plait ne die ne fase dire[12] vilaines paroles ne outragoses ne ranponoses au seignor ne a la cort ne a celui[13] contre qui il plaidoie n'a son conceill, mais fase dire ces paroles le plus bel et le[14] plus cortoisement que il porra, disant a son escient ce que mestier li est el plait, et non laissant[15] a son escient[16] a dire ce que mestier li sera el plait.[17]

A: fol. xi[r] cap. 22; **B:** fol. 43[v] cap. 23; **C:** fols 14[v]–15[r] cap. 12; **O:** fol. 14[r–v]; **V:** fols xiii[v]–xiv[r] cap. 19; Beugnot, p. 46 cap. 22.

---

[a] A adds: et ce il est requerant qu'il die le plus brief qu'il pora. Car en brieve clamor a .ii. proufiz. L'un est que la court retient et recorde miaus le court que le lonc. L'autre si est, se l'aversaire nee, l'on peut miaus prover le court que le lonc.

---

[1] V adds: dou royaume de Ihersualem ou en cele de Chipre. In the table of rubrics (fol. 3[v]) V merely adds: dou royame de Jerusalem. [2] ne n'otroie] A: ne otreie; B ne otroie [3] qui li griege ne n'otroie chose] V lacks [4] chose de quei son aversaire] B: chose a son adversaire de quoi il [5] otroi] V: otroi en court [6] le conceill de] ABV lack [7] n'eufre] A: n'en euffre; V: n'en heuffre [8] aproche] A: aprocher; V: aprochier [9] que] C: que que [10] contre] V: encontre [11] il] V: il a [12] ne fase dire] B lacks [13] ne a celui] A: ni; B: ne a cel; V: ne [14] le plus bel et le] B: au plus bel et au [15] non laissant] V: ne laisse [16] disant a son . . . escient] A: dissant a son essient sanz rienz laissier [17] escient a dire . . . plait] B: escient ce que mestier li fera ou plait

*[14] Por qui[1] l'on peut plaideer en la haute court.

L'on peut plaideer[2] contre chascun sans estre doné a conceill par court por son droit desraigner ou[3] defendre et por celui de sa feme et de ses enfans mermes d'aage; c'est assaver des choses qui soues sont ou deivent estre de par sa feme par la raison do mariage ou de ces enfans par baillage. Et por son seignor peut l'on plaideer contre chascun autre que contre soi ou un autre sien seignor a qui il ait fait avant homage save la foi de celui qu'il doit[4] saver.[5] Et por son home peut l'on plaideer contre qui que l'on viaut, mais que contre[6] son seignor et celui a qui l'on est doné a conceill par court ou .i. autre sien home. Que l'on ne peut pas[7] plaideer por l'un de ces homes contre l'autre, se il n'est[8] a son conceill par court. Et por son ami peut l'on plaideer contre qui que l'on viaut mais que contre[9] son seignor ou contre son home, a qui l'on est tenus de foy, et contre celui, a qui conceill l'on est[10] par court de cele querele.[11]

A: fol. xi^{r-v} cap. 23; **B:** fols 43^{v}–44^{r} cap. 24; **C:** fol. 15^{r-v} cap. 13; **O:** fols 14^{v}–15^{r}; **V:** fol. xiv^{r} cap. 20; Beugnot, pp. 46–7 cap. 23.

---

[1] qui] BV: quoi [2] A adds: en la haute court [3] ou] A: et [4] qu'il doit] BV lack [5] avant homage save . . . saver] A: avant lige homage ou ne li eust fait homage avant de lui et ne l'eust sauvé [6] contre] BV: encontre [7] pas] B: mie [8] n'est] C: est [9] contre] ABV: encontre [10] est] A: est doné [11] de cele querele] A: de celle carelle a conseill; V lacks

***[15]** Des ques chozes l'on ne[1] doit plaideer en la haute cort.

L'on peut plaideer en la haute cort de toutes choses que[2] de sa foy, ce est de sa creance, et de mariage et de testament et des autres choses de quei l'on est[3] tenus[4] de respondre ne[5] faire droit qu'en la court de l'iglise, et de borgesie de quei l'on ne doit plaideer qu'en la cort de la borgesie.[6] Que[7] ceste franchise ont ancienement les seignors dou reiaume de Jerusalem donee as borgeis par la volenté et l'otroi et le conceill de lor homes, et ades puis l'ont enssi les seignors dou dit reiaume tenu et maintenu et les borgeis usé.[8]

A: fol. xi^{v} cap. 24; **B:** fol. 44^{r} cap. 25; **C:** fol. 15^{v} cap. 14; **O:** fol. 15^{r}; **V:** fol. xiv^{r-v} cap. 21; Beugnot, p. 47 cap. 24.

---

[1] ne] BV lack [2] choses que] A: carelles mes que [3] est] AB: n'est; V: n'en est [4] tenus] A lacks [5] ne] B: ne de [6] de la borgesie] B: des borgois [7] Que] AB: Car [8] usé] B: aussi

***[16]** Por qui[1] l'on peut plaideer contre son seignor et encontre son home.

L'on ne peut por aucune[2] persone plaideer en la haute court contre son seignor ne contre son home, se le seignor ne le done a conceill, se ce n'est por soi[3] ou por sa feme ou por ces enfans mermes d'aage et por les choses qui devant sont devisees en cest livre, por quei on peut plaideer contre les avant dis. Mais se le seignor le done au conceill d'aucun, il peut, tant con il sera a son conceill, plaideer contre son seignor et contre son home sans mesprendre; mais que ce soit de cele querele dont il est a son conceill par le comandement dou seignor. Et qui plaidoie contre son seignor ou contre son home a qui il est tenus de foi sans ce que le seignor l'ait doné au[4] conceill de celui por qui il plaidoie, se ce n'est por aucunes des avant dites choses por quei il le peut faire ou qu'il plaidoie d'autre chose que de ce de quei[5] le seignor l'a doné a conceill contre son seignor ou son home, le seignor et l'ome contre qui il le fera le pevent[6] moult gregier.[7] Et coment et de quoi il le pevent[8] gregier sera devisé aprés en cest livre.

Et se le seignor done aucun de ces homes au conceill d'aucune persone ou celui ou cele a qui conceill il est doné veaut plaideer contre home ou feme a qui il soit tenus de foi, il doit maintenant,[9] que[10] celui a qui conceill il est demoré[11] li[12] a dit contre qui il veaut plaideer, venir devant le seignor en la court[13] et dire li: 'Sire, vos m'avés doné au conceill de tel qui viaut plaidoier contre tel a qui je suis tenus de foi. Ne[14] je n'entent que je[15] deie[16] conceiller ne plaideer por lui contre celui a qui je suis tenus de foi, ne faire ne le veuill se vostre court ne conoit[17] que je faire le puisse sans mesprendre vers lui de ma[18] foy.' Et le seignor deit comander a la court

A: fols xi^{v}–xii^{v} cap. 25; **B:** fols 44^{r}–45^{r} cap. 26; **C:** fols 15^{v}–17^{r} cap. 15; **O:** fols 15^{r}–17^{r}; **V:** fols xiv^{v}–xvi^{r} cap. 22; Beugnot, pp. 48–9 cap. 25.

[1] qui] BV: quoi [2] aucune] ABV: autre [3] por soi] C lacks [4] au] A: a son; V: au son [5] de quei] B: dont [6] le pevent] B: le puet; V: peut [7] le seignor et . . . gregier] A: la le peut moult gregier le seignor ou l'ome contre qui il le fera [8] pevent] A: peut [9] B adds: demander [10] que] BV: a [11] demoré] A: doné [12] li] V: et il li [13] venir devant le . . . court] B: en la court par devant le seignor et come il li a dit il doit venir au seignor [14] Ne] V: Pour que [15] je] AV: je le; O: jel [16] V adds: faire ne [17] conoit] V: esgarde ou counoisse [18] ma] C: la

qu'ele fase cele conoissance,[19] et la court doit conoistre, se me senble, que il peut conceiller de cele querele celui a qui le seignor l'a doné a conceill contre son seignor ou contre son home sans mesprendre vers lui de sa foi. Et aprés la dite conoissance celui que le seignor a doné a conceill peut conceiller de cele querele celui a qui conceill il est doné contre son seignor et contre son home sans mesprendre vers iaus de sa foi.

Et celui que le seignor a doné enssi a conceill doit celui a qui conceill il est doné conceiller a son escient le meaus et le plus leiaument que il porra et savra de cele querele de quei[20] il li a esté doné a conceill; et doit estre curious et ententif de son droit desraigner ou defendre selonc ce que il est requereor ou defendeor par sotilance de plait ou par point de plait ou autrement, se il entent que celui a qui conceill il est[21] ait droit, et, se il n'entent que il ait droit, si li die: 'Il ne me senble pas que vos aiés droit en ce que vos requerés' ou 'defendés'[22] selonc ce que la querele sera. Et se celui a qui conceill il est[23] dit qu'il a droit en cele querele, die li: 'Dites me vos en vostre loiauté que vos entendés avoir droit en ce que vos volés requerre' ou 'defendre,[24] de quei vos m'avés demandé a vostre conceill'. Se il dit: 'Je vos di en ma[25] leauté que je i entent[26] a avoir droit', si plaidoie d'enqui en avant por lui le meaus que il savra. Quar se celui a qui conceill il est a tort et il li a[27] ce dit qu'il y a droit,[28] le peche et la colpe est soue, non pas[29] de celui qui est a son conceill. Et se il a droit et celuy qui est a son conceill li conquiert[30] et defent sa querele,[31] il a[32] henor et amosne et fait ce que il doit. Et por ce le doit chascun plaideor faire enssi qui aime[33] s'arme et s'enor et dote peche et honte, que nul ne doit plaideer de tort a son escient de la querele de celui ou de cele a qui conceill il est. Et se celui, a qui conceill l'on[34] est[35] et a qui l'on fait la demande en la maniere devant[36] dite, ne dit[37] a celui qui est a son conceill qui la demande li[38] fait ce qui est devant[39] devisé,[40] celui qui est a

[19] A adds: c'il faire le deit [20] de quei] B: dont [21] est] ABV: est doné [22] defendés] A: que voz defendés; B: defendés de quoi vos m'avés demandé a vostre conseill [23] est] A: est doné [24] vos volés requerre' ou 'deffendre] BV: vos requerés' ou 'deffendés [25] ma] C: la [26] je i entent] ABV: je entens [27] il li a] O: il y a; V: il ait [28] et il li . . . droit] A lacks [29] pas] B: mie [30] conquiert] V: requiert [31] querele] A: raisson [32] il a] AB: il y a [33] qui aime] A: come il aint [34] l'on] C: il [35] Et se celui . . . est] V lacks [36] devant] A: avant [37] ne dit] B: dit la verité; V: n'en ait renoie [38] qui la demande li] V: que il a demandé [39] devant] A: avant [40] ce qui est devant devisé] B: se il n'a bone raison

son conceill se doit partir de son conceill le plus tost que il porra et non conceiller le plus de cele querele, se il s'en peut bien[41] defendre, et, se il ne s'en peut defendre[42] enssi, il ne doit pas[43] son aversaire prendre a point[44] a la querele desraigner, se il y faut, se il bien le peut prendre a point. Et tant con il sera a son conceill de cele querele, il doit plaideer por lui et dire sa parole sinplement et selonc le[45] cours des plais et metre s'en[46] en esgart ou en conoissance de court le plus tost que il porra, mais que il ne le fase en tel maniere a son escient que celui a qui conceill il est perde[47] sa querele par lui, ne que il par point de plait ne la desraigne[48] contre son aversaire por ce que il n'ait honte en perdre[49] ne pechié en desraigner la.

[41] bien] A: biau; B: loiaument; V: beau [42] et se il . . . defendre] BV lack [43] il ne doit pas] B: qu'il ne doit mie [44] a point] B: par poins [45] le] AB: les [46] metre s'en] A: metre sei; B: motir ce en [47] perde] C: perdre [48] desraigne] C: destraigne [49] ABV add: la

*[17] Quel le bon plaideor doit estre, et qu'il li covient faire, et de quey il li covient a garder el plait.

Il covient a celui qui est bon plaideor et soutil que il soit sage de sen naturel, et que il ait prest sen et soutil engin, et qu'il ne soit doutif, ne esbay, ne hontous, ne hastif, ne nonchalant el plait, et que il n'ait s'entente ne sa pencee aillors tant con[1] il plaidoie, et qu'il se garde de soi trop courocier ne ayrer ne esmovoir en plaideant, que ces choses font tost home tresaillir de raison[2] et li tolent sen et conoissance. Et le bon plaideor doit dire ces paroles baudement et entendaument, et doit estre gaitant de dire ses paroles si que son aversaire ne le puisse prendre a point por quoy il perde sa querele, ne par quei le plait soit esloigné, se il est requereor, et ne l'aproche,[3] se il est defendeor. Et doit estre bien et soutilment notant tos les dis de son aversaire, et bien pointeant chascun par soi,[4] que il sache respondre ce que mestier li est et trover raisons a[5] desfaire ceaus des[6] dis que son aversaire avra dis, que il verra[7] qui facent a desfaire, et les desfase, se il[8] porra, par les raisons[9] que il dira, et que il le preigne a point, se il peut, se il dit chose por quei il a point le puisse prendre. Et se il entent que son aversaire die mal, si n'en face senblant que son aversaire[10] ne s'en parceive[11] de sa faute et l'amende, mais court[12] sinplement et sans faire senblant que il les veuille prendre a point sans otroy demander.[13] Et se il enssi ne le peut faire, si demande otroy a celui de qui la querele est, et a sa feme, se il plaidoient ensenble, et le fase a mains de contenances que il porra de voloir le prendre a point, por ce que il de cele faute ne se gardent et l'amendent. Et[14] maintenant que[15] celui de qui la querele est avra otroie ce que l'on avra dit por lui, le bon plaideor doit dire a ceaus de la court: 'Vos avés oi que tel a dit tel chose',

---

A: fols xii^{v}–xiii^{v} cap. 26; **B:** fols 45^{r}–46^{r} cap. 27; **C:** fols 17^{r}–18^{v} cap. 16; **O:** fols 17^{r}–18^{v}; **V:** fols xvi^{r}–xvii^{r} cap. 23; Beugnot, pp. 50–51 cap. 26.

---

[1] tant con] B: fors qu'en ce dont [2] de raison] A: en desraisson; BV: en desraison [3] ne l'aproche] A: ne apreuchié; B: ne aprocchier; V: n'en aproche [4] par soi] ABV: por ce [5] a] BO: et [6] ceaus des] AB: tos les [7] verra] A: cuidera; B: crera [8] se il] A: ce qu'il; B: en ce que il [9] a desfaire ceaus . . . raisons] V lacks [10] que son averaire] B: qu'il [11] perceive] A: aparceive; B: aparçoive; V: aparsoive [12] court] A: tot; B: tout; V: que tout [13] BOV add: se il peut [14] et] A lacks; V: le [15] que] AV: Et quant; B: com

et di quei, 'et que tel a otree ce que il a dit por lui', et les nome et di, por la court[16] meaus avertir, ce que il a dit[17] de quei il le veuille prendre a point, et aprés face celui qui les a[18] pris a point bien et entendaument entendre a la court coment et de coy il les a pris a point.

Et quant le bon plaideor voit que son aversaire dit bien se que mestier[19] li est, se il[20] cuide[21] par cel dit le plait perdre ou que sa raison soit enpiree, il doit metre point[22] de geter le de cele voie en toutes les manieres qu'il porra par lui traverser d'aucunes paroles, ou par eschanpes querre, ou par mostrer diverces[23] raisons a son dit desfaire ou faire changer, ou par atainer le en plaidoiant en cortoise maniere, ou par faire senblant qu'il le veuille prendre a point de ce que il avra meaus dit et[24] demander otroy de celui ou de cele de qui est la querele en[25] grant cenblant de voloir avoir otroi de la parole que son avantparlier avra meaus dite, por ce que il le veaut prendre a point de cele parole, por veir se il peut faire laissier a son conceill cele parole[26] que il avra bien dite, et que il entendra qui li[27] doive plus gregier por le senblant que il fera de voloir avoir l'otroi de celui de qui est la querele, por prendre le a point, que espoir por ce li fera il laisser la parole que il avra bien dite et qui greignor force li avra, et dire autre tel conceill porra il avoir.

Et bon[28] plaideor doit savoir bien ataindre plait et bien fuïr selonc ce que mestier li est,[29] et doit savoir atraire la preuve a soy quant mestier li est, et quant mestier li est[30] doner la a son aversaire, et doit savoir prover la negative quant il voit que mestier li est. Et moult d'autres senblances de plait covient il que[31] le bon plaideor sache, lesqués seroient trop longues et[32] riotouses a escrire en cest livre ce que l'on en poroit escrire, ne nul ne les y poroit[33] toutes metre. Mais tant con le[34] plaideor est plus soutil et meillor plaideor de l'autre,[35] en treuve[36] il plus, que je ne cuit que hom mortel les seust onques toutes ne que nul ja[37] les sache. Car aussi con l'on ne

---

[16] court] A: chose [17] por lui', et . . . dit] B lacks [18] les a] ABV: l'a [19] mestier] A: besoin; B: besoing; V: besoign [20] se il] ABV: si que il [21] A adds: bien [22] point] A: peine; O: poine [23] V adds: paroles et [24] meaus dit et] A: mau dit a [25] en] AV: o; B: a [26] por veir se . . . parole] V lacks [27] qui li] C: qu'il y [28] bon] ABV: le bon [29] li est] A lacks [30] li est] A: ne li est; C lacks [31] covient il que] C: coment que il [32] AB add: trop [33] ne nul ne les y poroit] B: ne je ne les i porroie [34] tant con le] AB: tant come le bon; V: que tant com bon [35] V adds: Et meillour plaideoir [36] treuve] AB: contrueve; V: contreuve [37] ja] C: y a; V: jamais

peut savoir toute clergie,[38] ne me senble il que l'on puisse savoir tout le plait[39] ne toutes les forces et[40] les soutilances qui sont en plait, mais qui[41] plus en set meillor plaideor est. Et quei que nul die je tiens a peor[42] plaideor qui seit ne qui puisse estre celui qui[43] pert s'arme por plaideer. Si pri et requier et conceill a tos les plaideors que il se guardent sur toutes choses de perdre lor armes por plaideer que trop avroit mau plaidee et le plait[44] cher acheté celui qui s'arme en perdra.

[38] toute clergie] ABV: toutes clergies [39] tout le plait] A: toz les plais; B: touz les plaiz; V: tout les plais [40] forces et] B: fuites ne [41] qui] C: que [42] peor] V: meillor [43] V adds: ne [44] plait] AV: plaideer

***[18]** Ques chozes[1] doivent savoir ceaus qui s'entremetent de plaideer en la haute court dou reiaume de Jerusalem et en cele de Chypre.

Tos ceaus qui s'entremetent de plaideer en la haute court dou reiaume de Jerusalem et[2] de Chipre doivent savoir por eaus et por ceaus qu'il vodront conceillier et avertir,[3] que qui plaidoie en la dite[4] cort sans avoir conceill de court qu'il ne peut puis avoir conceill de cele querele, se son aversaire le viaut et set defendre. Et qui dit parole por soi en court, ou qui[5] otroie ce que son conceill a dit, qu'il ne le peut puis desdire ne neer. Et que la premiere clamor doit avant aler, et que l'eufre premier oferte doit avant aler,[6] et que l'esgart premier[7] requis doit avant aler, et que l'on a jor a tos noviaus clains se assise ne le tot.[a] Et qui demande jor a clain que on fait de lui, et il l'a par cort, et il ne garde son jor a hore ne a tens, si con il doit la ou il est ajorné, ou[8] ne contremande c'essoine, si con il doit, qu'il[9] pert sa querele. Et coment l'on doit jour garder,[10] et coment l'on doit jor contremander, et par ques et par quans home on doit jor contremander,[11] et que ceaus par qui l'on contremande son jor doivent dire et faire quant il vienent la ou celui qui les i[12] a envoiés est ajorné,[b] et coment l'on doit prover par garans et qui die[13] por les garans en la haute court que les garans doivent dire et faire a lor guarentie porter, et coment l'on doit contredire et rebuter garans qui les conoit et le[14] viaut faire, et coment l'on doit torner garans par gage de bataille, et quel maniere de gens ne pevent porter garantie en la haute court, et por ques gens l'on ne peut porter garantie,[15] [c] et de quel choze l'on se peut clamer par l'assise, et de

---

A: fols xiii^{v}–xiv^{r} cap. 27; **B:** fol. 46^{r-v} cap. 28; **C:** fols 18^{v}–19^{v} cap. 17; **O:** fols 18^{v}–19^{v}; **V:** fols xvii^{r}–xviii^{r} cap. 24; Beugnot, pp. 51–2 cap. 27.

---

[a] Below caps 23, 38–40.
[b] Below caps 40–8.
[c] Below caps 56–8, 61–2.

---

[1] Ques chozes] ABV: quel chose [2] AV add: de celle [3] ceaus qu'il vodront . . . avertir] V: tous ceaus qui conseill vodront avoir [4] dite] AB: haute [5] qui] BV: que il [6] l'eufre premier . . . aler] B lacks [7] premier] AV: avant [8] A adds: c'il est essoigné [9] qu'il] B: si qu'il; V: il [10] Et coment l'on doit jour garder] Added in margin in C [11] et par ques . . . contremander] V lacks [12] i] ABV lack [13] qui die] A: qu'il deit dire; V: qu'il die [14] le] C: les [15] en la haute . . . garantie] ABV lack

ques choses l'assise tot le jor au noviau clain,[d] et de ques choses on fait amende par l'assise, et a qui l'on fait amende par l'assise, et quel amende l'on fait par l'assise selonc le mesfait, et quei est murtre, et coment l'on doit faire apeau de murtre,[e] et coment l'on se doit defendre[16] de murtre[17] ou d'autre malefaite,[18] de quey il covient que il s'en defende de son cors par bataille et il est en fers ou en liens et il noie le murtre ou l'autre malefaite ou il respont au clain ains[19] qu'il soit geté des fers ou des liens ou il est que il li covendra a conbatre se enssi con il sera en fers ou en liens,[f] et que se il est tel qu'il se puisse defendre par chanpion, et on se clame de lui des choses[20] de quei[21] il li estuise[22] a defendre, et il s'eufre a defendre par .i. home, et il ne l'a aprestè au jor que la court li donra que il est ataint de la malefaite que l'on li mete[23] sus,[g] et que[24] est homecide, et coment l'on doit faire apiau d'omecide, et coment[25] l'on se doit defendre d'omecide,[h] et pluisors autres choses doivent savoir ceaus qui s'entremetent d'estre plaideors[26] en la haute court. Que se il ne sevent[27] les choses devant[28] dites et pluisors autres, il porront sovent meschever[29] en plaidoiant et perdre le droit de celui a qui conceill il est celui qui ne le savra se aucun des dis cas avienent[30] qui li soit besoing de plaideer. Si se doit chascun de[31] ceaus qui veuillent plaideours estre[32] travaillier[33] de savoir les[34] dites choses.

---

[d] Below cap. 67.
[e] Below caps 68–79.
[f] Below cap. 76.
[g] Below cap. 93.
[h] Below caps 80–81.

---

[16] coment l'on se doit defendre] AB: qui est apelé [17] et coment l'on . . . murtre] V lacks [18] d'autre malefaite] B: d'autres mesfais [19] ains] B: avant [20] des choses] ABV: de chose [21] de quei] B: dont [22] li estuise] A: l'estuet; B: le couvient; V: esteut [23] mete] A: metra [24] que] C: qui; O: quei [25] l'on doit faire . . . coment] A lacks [26] d'estre plaideors] A: de plaideer [27] sevent] C: seguent [28] devant] B: desus [29] meschever] B: meschiver; C: mescheyer; V: mescheir [30] aviennent] B: avera; C: aviegnent [31] qui li soit . . . chascun de] ABV: et [32] AB add: se deivent [33] ceaus qui veuillent . . . travaillier] V: qui viaut estre plaideoir travaille soi [34] V adds: avant

***[19]** Que doit faire celui[1] qui est a conceill d'autre et veaut dire la force de sa parole et seir a l'esgart.

Qui est a conceil d'autre et il viaut dire la force de la parole et seir a l'esgart, face la parole comencier a autre qui die enssi: 'Sire, faites entendre a la parole de tel', et le nome. 'Je la dirai par amendement de li et de son conceill, que se je y mespernoie que lui et son conceill y peust[2] amender', et a tant se taise. Et l'autre die le remanant de sa parole en[3] jusques au poser sur cort.[4] Die celui qui la parole avra comencee: 'Selonc ce[5] que nos avons dit, et vos dit sur la cort, soit au retenaill que nos y avons mis'. Et qui enssi le fera, il dira[6] la force[7] de la parole, et sera a l'esgart se il viaut. Que le seignor ne la cort ne l'aversaire ne li porront[8] defendre, se il est tel que il puisse[9] seir a esgart et juger o les autres homes de la cort.

A: fol. xiv^{r-v} cap. 28; **B:** fol. 46^{v} cap. 29; **C:** fol. 19^{v} cap. 18; **O:** fol. 19^{v}; **V:** fols xvi–xvii^{r-v} cap. 25; Beugnot, p. 53 cap. 28.

[1] celui] BOV lack [2] peust] ABV: peussent [3] de sa parole en] B lacks; AV: de sa parole [4] ABV add: Et au poser sur court [5] ce] C lacks [6] dira] A: dit [7] la force] C: de la force de la force; O: la force de la force [8] porront] A: poreit; V: poroit [9] V adds: estre et

***[20]** Qui se viaut clamer d'ome ou de feme qui est present en court, coment il le doit faire.

Qui a conceill de court, et il se viaut clamer d'ome ou de feme qui est present en la court, il doit faire dire par son conceill au seignor si que celui de qui il se[1] viaut clamer l'oie: 'Sire, tel se clame a vos et de tel de tel[2] chose, et en viaut avoir droit par vos et par la court', et les[3] nome et die de quei il se clame et as plus briés paroles que il porra face son clain, mais que il ne laisse[4] a dire chose que mestier li est[5] a dire, et le plus[6] entendaument[7] que il porra die ses paroles. Que[8] les paroles brieves et entendaument[9] dites sont meaus entendues, retenues, recordees et jugees quant mestier est que les autres. Et face le clamant son clain enssi que, se[10] celui de qui il se claime noie ce que il li met sus el clain, que il li puisse prover si com il a dit en la cort. Et enssi le face que ce que il li covendra a prover soit le plus brief que il pora, mais que tot quanque mestier li est[11] a prover y soit, que l'on peut les preves qui sont[12] brieves meaus faire que les longues, et mains si[13] peut son aversaire acrocher[14] et dire encontre.

A: fol. xiv^{v} cap. 29; **B:** fols 46^{v}–47^{r} cap. 30; **C:** fols 19^{v}–20^{r} cap. 19; **O:** fols 19^{v}–20^{r}; **V:** fol. xviii^{v} cap. 26; Beugnot, pp. 53–4 cap. 29.

---

[1] V adds: claime ou [2] de tel de tel] BV: de tel; O: de tel del [3] les] ABV: le [4] ne laisse] A: ne laist; B: n'a lessé [5] est] A: seit; B: ait [6] plus] A: miaus [7] entendaument] B: entendablement [8] Que] ABV: Car [9] entendaument] B: entendablement [10] se] BV lack [11] li est] A: i soit [12] qui sont] ABV lack [13] si] AB: se; V: s'em [14] acrocher] A: apreuchier

***[21]** Quant home ou feme de qui l'on se viaut clamer[1] n'est en la cort, coment l'on se doit clamer de luy.

Qui se viaut clamer d'ome qui n'est present en la cort, celui qui viaut le clain faire doit faire dire par son conseill au seignor: 'Sire, tel', et le nome, 'se claime a vos de tel', et le nome, 'de tel chose', et la[2] motisse, 'et vos prie et requier[3] que vos le faites venir en la court, et, quant il i sera,[4] vos et la cort orrés lors coment et de coi il porportera[5] son clain contre[6] lui'. Et adonc le seignor le doit mander semondre par le banier ou par .iii. de ces homes come cort, que il veigne maintenant en la cort qui est assenblee por faire droit a celui qui de lui c'est clamés. Et se le seignor ne le veaut ensi faire semondre, si le face semondre[7] a jor moti que il soit a cel[8] jor devant lui en la court, et qui le semondra[9] li nome le jor et li motisse le leuc ou il le semont d'estre por faire droit a celui qui de lui c'est clamés. Et li face nomer le clamant[10] et dire de quei il c'est de lui clamés.[11] Et que le jor a quey il le fera semondre soit raisonable et tel que il y puisse estre. Et se il est ensi semons de venir maintenant a court faire droit a celui qui de lui c'est clamés, et il ne vient[12] ou ne dit qu'il est essoinés par quei il n'i peut aler, ou se il est[13] semons si com est avant dit a jor moti, et il n'i vient au jor[14] que le seignor l'avra fait semondre en la maniere avant dite, ou il dedens celui jor ou en cel jor ne fait assaveir au seignor que il est essoiné si que il ne peut estre[15] en la court a celui jor por faire droit a celuy qui de lui c'est clamés, et le clain est de chose de quei le clamant die que celui de qui il c'est clamés l'a desaisi ou de chose que il die que il a et tient dou sien, le seignor l'en doit faire metre en saisine, et il en doit avoir la saisine[16] tant que celui de qui il se clama[17] vieigne en court et requiere la saisine de cele chose de quei le clamant avra esté saisi. Et se il le fait,[18] il en avra la saisine, que le clamant ne

---

A: fols xiv^{v}–xv^{r} cap. 30; **B:** fol. 47^{r-v} cap. 31; **C:** fols 20^{r}–21^{r} cap. 20; **O:** fols 20^{r}–21^{r}; **V:** fols xviii^{v}–xix^{v} cap. 27; Beugnot, pp. 54–5, cap. 30.

---

[1] se viaut clamer] V: s'en claime [2] la] C lacks [3] requier] ABV: requiert [4] il i sera] A: il sera venus et [5] porportera] AB: portera [6] contre] A: envers [7] si le face semondre] V lacks [8] cel] AB: tel [9] qui le semondra] AB: que le semoneor; V: que le semouneoir [10] face nomer le clamant] A: nome le requerant [11] Et li face . . . clamés] V lacks [12] ne vient] AB: n'i vient; C: ne veaut [13] est] B: n'est [14] et il n'i vient au jor] V lacks [15] estre] AV: venir [16] et il en . . . saisine] A lacks [17] clama] AB: claime; V: clame [18] AB add: enssi

le porra defendre. Et quant il avra la saisine, il est tenus de faire droit au clamant en la court de ce qu'il[19] se clama[20] de lui. Et se[21] est terre ou rente[22] ou aucune autre chose et le clamant en ait[23] aucun profit, il n'est pas tenus de rendre cel[24] profit[25] a celui de qui il se clama, quant il recovra la saisine de la chose de quei[26] le seignor l'avra[27] mis ou fait[28] metre en sa saisine, por ce qu'il en ot la saisine par le seignor[29] et par la court. Et ce qui est desus devisé fu fait et establi por destraindre les gens a venir faire droit en la cort a ceaus qui d'eaus se claiment,[30] que se il n'estoient par ce destrains a venir[31] faire droit, a enuis en vendroient[32] ceaus de qui l'on se clameroit[33] qui vodroient[34] le plait fuïr.

[19] qu'il] B: dont il [20] clama] ABV: clamera [21] se] AV: ce ce; O: se ce [22] terre ou rente] C: rente ou terre [23] en ait] B: en a ja eu [24] cel] AB: le dit; V: le [25] il n'est pas . . . profit] O lacks [26] de quei] B: dont [27] l'avra] C: l'avera [28] fait] B: le doit [29] le seignor] A: lui [30] claiment] B: clameroient; V: clameront [31] venir] ABV lack [32] en vendroient] B: vendroient a court [33] de qui l'on se clameroit] A lacks [34] vodroient] C: vodroit

***[22]** Que doit faire celui qui est droiturier et loial, quant l'on li requiert aucune chose en court[1] ou quant l'on se claime de lui.

Celui de qui l'on se claime en cort ou a qui l'on requiert aucune chose en la cort,[2] se il est droiturier et doute Deu et aime tant que il ne veuille mentir, il doit conoistre le voir de ce que l'on li requiert ou de quei l'on se claime de lui. Et se le clain[3] est tel qu'il en doie soufrir mort ou desheritement ou honte ou aucune autre chose tel qu'il[4] aime meaus mentir[5] que conoistre en le voir,[6] il le doit neer se c'est chose[7] que[8] l'on[9] deie neer sans demander jor, et se c'est chose de quei l'on doit jor demander, il doit demander jor[10] au clain que on fait de lui. Que meaus li vaut il ces[11] choses neer que conoistre les en court, tout soit ce que l'on les li puisse prover. Que se il est sage, dedens le jor ou dedens le terme[12] de la preuve, que l'on vodra faire contre lui, il finera a son aversaire si que il ne fera plus parole en court.[13] Que se il le fait,[14] il eschevira la honte et le perill qu'il avroit en la conoissance que il feroit en la cort, ou de ce que on avroit prové contre lui en cort ce que il avroit neé en la court.[15] Et por eschiver le peche qu'il avroit, se il faucement rebutoit ou tornoit par gage[16] de bataille aucun des garans qui[17] cele garentie vodront[18] porter contre lui, le doit il enssi faire con je ai devant dit. Et qui viaut jor demander a clain que on fait de lui, si le demande enssi con il est devisé aprés en cest livre que[19] l'on doit jor demander.[a]

A: fol. xv^{r-v} cap. 31; **B:** fols 47^{v}–48^{r} cap. 32; **C:** fol. 21^{r-v} cap. 21; **O:** fol. 21^{r-v}; **V:** fols xix^{v}–xx^{r} cap. 28; Beugnot, pp. 55–6, cap. 31.

---

[a] Below caps 23, 38–40.

---

[1] en court] V: encontre [2] ou a qui . . . court] V lacks [3] ABV add: ou la requeste [4] en doie soufrir . . . qu'il] AB lack [5] mentir] CO: morir [6] conoistre en le voir] B: dire voir ne conoistre [7] tel qu'il aime . . . chose] V lacks [8] que] AO: de quei [9] A adds: en deit soufrir mort ou honte ou deseritement ou aucune chose qu'on [10] et se c'est . . . jor] V lacks [11] A adds: devant dites [12] terme] A: termine [13] V adds: contre lui [14] AB add: ensi [15] en la court] A: avant [16] gage] C: esgart [17] qui] OV: que [18] vodront] AV: vodroient; B: voudroit [19] que] B: coment

***[23]** Quans jors l'on a de respondre a noviau clain quant l'assise ne tot le jor.

Il est assise ou usage el[1] royaume de Jerusalem et en celui de Chipre, que l'on a jor de quinzaine a respondre a tos noviaus clains, se il n'est assise qui le jor toille. Et quels les assises sont[2] qui tolent le jor seront devisees aprés en cest livre.[a] Mais je dirai avant quantes fuites principaus il a[3] en plait et coment l'on doit plait fuïr et coment ataindre[4] selonc ce qu'a moy senble.

A: fol. xv[v] cap. 32; **B:** fol. 48[r] cap. 33; **C:** fol. 21[v] cap. 22; **O:** fol. 21[v]; **V:** fol. xx[r] cap. 29; Beugnot, p. 56, cap. 32.

---

[a] Below cap. 67.

---

[1] el] AB: ou; V: au [2] toille. Et quels . . . sont] V: tout lequesles assises [3] V adds: en la haute court [4] ataindre] B: atendre

***[24]** Quantes fuites principaus il a en plait, et qués eles sont.[1]

Il i[2] a .iii. fuites principaus en plait, et[3] chascune de .iii.[4] dites fuites a pluisors manieres de fuites que trop seroient longues et riotouses[5] a metre en escrit, ce que l'on en porroit en escrit metre,[6] ne[7] nul ne les y porroit toutes metre. Quar enssi con chascun est plus sage et plus soutill et meillor plaideor, l'un que l'autre, en contreuve il plus.[8] Et por ce que je veuill que l'on sache ques[9] sont les .iii. principaus fuites de plait dont les autres meuvent, les veuill je esclarsir et faire entendre a ceaus qui les oront.[10] L'une est de respondre au dit de son aversaire en paroles, et au pozer son esgart[11] non aerdre se a lui d'esgart, mais pozer s'en en vuid,[12] metant se en esgart d'autre chose que ce de quei le requerant s'i met, si que il n'i ait point d'esgart. L'autre est de dire: 'Je ne vos veuill respondre a ce que vos me requerés, se la cort ne l'esgarde, por tel[13] et por tel raison', et dire les raisons qui meillors li senblent[14] por coi il ne li doit respondre et metre se en esgart de cort sauf[15] son retenaill. La tierce est de dire: 'Je ne veuill ce faire que vos me requerés, se la court ne l'esgarde', et dit por coi, 'por tel[16] et por tel raison', et dire toutes les raisons que il cuidera que bones li soient, et les die l'une aprés l'autre enssi con eles se sivent[17] meaus, et se mete en esgart[18] de chascune chose par soi, sauf son retenaill.

A: fols xv^{v}–xvi^{r} cap. 33; **B:** fol. 48^{r} cap. 34; **C:** fols 21^{v}–22^{r} cap. 23; **O:** fols 21^{v}–22^{r}; **V:** fol. xx^{r-v} cap. 30; Beugnot, pp. 56–7, cap. 33.

---

[1] V adds: a royame de Jerusalem et de Chipre [2] i] ABO lack [3] ABV add: en [4] .iii.] AV lack [5] riotouses] A: riotes a reconter et [6] ce que l'on . . . metre] A lacks [7] ne] C lacks [8] C adds: et plus [9] ques] B: que; V: qui [10] oront] V: voront oir [11] au pozer son esgart] B: au poser sur esgart; V: oposer son esgart et [12] pozer s'en en vuid] A: passer ce en voit; B: passer soi en vuit; V: paser s'en huit [13] B adds: chose [14] senblent] AV: sembleront [15] sauf] V: sans [16] B adds: chose [17] eles se sivent] A: souficent; B: eles soufisent [18] A adds: de court

*[25] Coment l'on doit plait fuïr par la premiere fuite principal de plait.

Qui viaut[1] fuïr par la premiere[2] fuite principal de plait, qui n'est pas[3] bele, si responde[4] au dit dou requereor en paroles, sivant son dit le plus pres que il porra, et au poser sur cort ne s'aerde pas a lui d'esgart, tant con il le porra eschiver sans la querele perdre ou estre ataint de ce que l'on li met sus. Mais die au poser sur cort autre chose que cele que son aversaire avra dite et mete soi en esgart dou sien dit sans plus et requiere en esgars[5] et conoissances et recors[6] de court tant con il porra, et contreuve sur ce toutes les eschanpes qu'il porra,[7] metant soy en esgars et en conoissances[8] et en recors de cort, et de chascune choze par soi por le plait esloigner. Et que il en chascun esgart et en chascune conoissance[9] de cort en quei il se metra, mete son retenaill. Et que il de nul esgart ne s'aerde au dit de son aversaire tant con il s'en porra defendre, ains se defende et eschanpisse, si con est devant devisé.

A: fol. xvi^{r} cap. 34; **B:** fol. 48^{r-v} cap. 35; **C:** fol. 22^{r-v} cap. 24; **O:** fol. 22^{r-v}; **V:** fols xx^{v}–xxi^{r} cap. 31; Beugnot, pp. 57–8, cap. 34.

---

[1] Qui viaut] B: Quant l'on doit plait [2] premiere] A: segonde [3] pas] B: mie [4] responde] C: respondre [5] dou sien dit . . . esgars] AO lack [6] conoissances et recors] A: en conoissance et en recort dou sien dit sanz plus et requiere esgart [7] et contreuve sur . . . porra] C lacks [8] et recors de . . . conoissances] V lacks [9] B adds: et en chascune recort

***[26]** Coment l'on doit fuïr par la seconde fuite principal de plait.

Qui par la premiere fuite principal de plait ne viaut fuïr ou il ne puisse plus, si fuie par la seconde fuite[1] qui est mains laide. Et dit se la querele n'est de murtre ou tel chose de quei l'on est ataint et pert sa querele qui ne respont au clain que l'on fait de lui et le noie ou[2] a ce que l'on[3] li requiert ou met sus en la court par clain ou par requeste ou autrement: 'Je ne veuill respondre a[4] vostre clain ou a ce que vos me requerés, se cort ne l'esgarde, por tel[5] et por tel raison', et die toutes les raisons et les eschanpes que il porra trover[6] a ce que il ne li doit[7] respondre, et chascune chose par soi. Et a chascune fois die une sole raison por coi il ne viaut respondre, et de chascune chose par soi se mete en esgart ou en conoissance[8] de court sauf son retenaill. Quar le[9] fuïant ne se doit nule fois metre de pluisors choses ensenble en esgart que il cuide perdre, por ce que il porra plus le plait esloigner, se il requiert esgart ou conoissance[10] de cort de chascune chose par soi que de pluisors ensenble, et metre son retenaill totes les fois que il se metra[11] en esgart ou en conoissance de court. Et se le clain est de murtre ou d'aucune des autres choses de quei l'on est ataint qui ne respont au clain et le noie, si die et fase ensi com il est aprés devisé en cest livre que l'on le doit dire et faire la ou il parole de murtre et des autres dites[12] choses.

A: fol. xvi^{r-v} cap. 35; **B:** fols 48^{v}–49^{r} cap. 36; **C:** fols 22^{v}–23^{r} cap. 25; **O:** fols 22^{v}–23^{r}; **V:** fol. xxi^{r-v} cap. 32; Beugnot, p. 58, cap. 35.

---

[1] fuite] B: maniere; V lacks [2] ou] AB lack [3] fait de lui . . . l'on] V lacks [4] a] C: au [5] B adds: chose [6] trover] B: traïant [7] doit] V: pora [8] B adds: ou en recort [9] le] C lacks [10] AB add: ou recort [11] metra] C: metre [12] dites] A lacks

***[27]** Coment l'on doit fuïr plait par la tierce dite fuite.[1]

Qui ne viaut ou ne peut plus fuïr par la premiere ne par la seconde fuite principal de plait, si se preigne a la tierce fuite, qui est la droite fuite principal[2] de plait qui cortoisement veaut fuïr plait, et[3] die: 'Je ne veuil ce faire que vos me requerés, se court ne l'esgarde, por tel[4] et por tel raison', et die toutes[5] les raisons et les eschanpes[6] que il porra ne savra trover au[7] plait esloigner, descendant d'un en autre si con meaus li senblera, et con les paroles se porsivent[8] meaus et plus bel,[9] et metre soi en esgart de chascune chose par soi et tousjors[10] sauver[11] son retenaill.

A: fol. xvi^{v} cap. 36; **B:** fol. 49^{r} cap. 37; **C:** fol. 23^{r} cap. 26; **O:** fol. 23^{r}; **V:** fol. xxi^{v} cap. 33; Beugnot, p. 59, cap. 36.

---

[1] dite fuite] A: fuite devant dite; BV: fuite [2] principal] ABV lack. [3] fuïr plait, et] A: fuyr, si; B: plait fuïr, si; V: fuïr, si [4] B adds: chose [5] toutes] C lacks [6] et les eschanpes] AV lack [7] porra ne savra trover au] A: savra ne porra miaus trover en [8] porsivent] C: porsivrent [9] et plus bel] A: plus bel est; V: est plus beau [10] metre soi en . . . tousjors] B: meaus valent en mete son esgart de chascune chose par soi et de toutes [11] sauver] ABV: sauf

***[28]** Coment l'on doit et peut[1] longuement plait fuïr.

Qui viaut plait de chose en quei il n'a[2] droit longuement fuïr, si teigne les .iii. dite voies, l'une avant l'autre, et de chascune d'eles treuve tant de manieres de fuites con il porra plus trover. Et s'il ne viaut par la premiere fuite fuïr, par laquel l'on peut moult plait[3] fuïr et esloigner qui faire le viaut et set, si fuie par la seconde fuite,[4] par laquel l'on peut moult esloigner plait qui le set et viaut faire. Que[5] esgart que il perde, qui par cele voie fuit, ne li griege a ce que il perde la[6] querele. Et se il ne viaut ou ne set ou ne peut plus par les premieres .ii. dites fuites[7] fuïr, si fuie par la tierce, par laquel l'on peut longuement plait fuïr qui faire le set.

Et qui par ceste fuite[8] viaut fuïr, se le plait est de monoie, si die que il viaut qu'il li esclarsise coment il dit qu'il li doit cele monoie par prest ou autrement. Et se il ne li viaut esclarsir, die[9] qu'il ne li viaut respondre a sa requeste tant que il li ait[10] ce[11] esclarzi, se la cort ne l'esgarde, et mete son retenaill. Et se il dit que il li presta, die que il viaut que il li esclarsise[12] ou ce fu qu'il dit qu'il[13] li presta cele monoie. Et se il ne li viaut esclarsir, die que il ne li viaut respondre a ce que il li requiert, se la cort ne l'esgarde, tant que il li ait esclarzi ce que il li requiert, que il li esclarsise,[14] et mete son retenaill. Et aprés die que il li die[15] quant ce fu[16] que il li presta, et aprés die et[17] qui fu la quant il[18] li presta, et aprés die[19] se cele monoie que il dit qu'il li doit fu contee, et aprés die s'ele fu pesee, et aprés die qui la[20] conta,[21] et aprés die qui la[22] pesa, et aprés[23] quel maniere de monoie se fu, et plusors autres chozes peut l'on dire a tel plait fuïr que[24] trop seroient longues a metre en escrit.

Mais au senblant des avant dites paroles peut l'on mout trover eschanpes[25] et de fuites, qui bien set plait fuïr au plait longuement

---

A: fols xvi^{v}–xviii^{v} cap. 37; **B:** fols 49^{r}–51^{r} cap. 38; **C:** fols 23^{r}–26^{r} cap. 27; **O:** fols 23^{v}–26^{r}; **V:** fols xxi^{v}–xxiv^{r} cap. 34; Beugnot, pp. 59–63, cap. 37.

---

[1] doit et peut] A: deit; B: puet; A rubrics (fol. 1^{v}) V: peut [2] n'a] BV: n'ait; CO: a [3] plait] V: plus [4] fuite] ABV lack [5] Que] A: Et si que [6] la] AV: sa [7] fuites] C: voies [8] fuite] A: vee [9] se il ne . . . die] A lacks [10] ait] B: avra [11] ce] AB lack [12] esclarsise] B: die [13] qu'il] C: qui [14] que il li esclarsise] V lacks [15] que il li die] A lacks [16] V adds: et que ce fu [17] et] ABV lack [18] ABV add: dit qu'il [19] die] AB lack [20] die qui la] V: que il li [21] et aprés die . . . conta] B lacks [22] die qui la] V: que il li [23] ABV add: die [24] que] AB: qui [25] eschanpes] BV: d'eschampes

fuïr,[26] a celui acrocher de preuve,[27] que il ne[28] le puisse prover, par quei il perde sa querele, se il faut a prover ce que il avra[29] ofert a prover en court. Et de chascune chose par soi que le fuïant dira, die que il viaut[30] que il li esclarsise ce que il li requiert, se la cort l'esgarde, ne que il ne li viaut respondre,[31] se la court ne l'esgarde, tant que il li ait esclarsi ce que il li requiert, et de ce requiere esgart de court et de chascune chose par soi, et metre son retenaill en chascun esgart. Et se son aversaire dit[32] aucune chose el plait qu'il entende que il ne le[33] puisse prover, si[34] la nee, por ce que se il faut a sa preuve que il perde sa querele.

Et quant toutes ces[35] manieres d'eschanpes li seront faillies ou il ne vodra plus par tels eschanpes fuïr et il viaut la paie de la dete esloigner en maniere qui n'est[36] bele ne couvenable, mais faire se peut, se me senble, si die: 'Sire, tel', et le nome, 'a tant dit et de tant de choses m'a fait menbrant que je sui bien menbrant que[37] je li doi cele dete que il dit, mais je l'en ai paié bien et enterinement. Si me merveill con[38] il cele dete me requiert aprés ce que je l'en ai paié bien et enterinement.[39] Et se il par obli ou autrement[40] noie que je de cele dete que je li dui et que il dit que je encore li doy ne l'en ai paié bien et enterinement, je suis prest que je li preuve, si con la court esgardera ou conoistra que je prover le doie, que je l'ai[41] paié bien et enterinement.' Et se le requerant noie la paie, la cort doit esgarder ou conoistre que celui li doit prover par .ii. loiaus garans de la loy de Rome que il l'a paié si com il dit,[42] et que celui contre qui il preuve se par guarans en peut l'un torner par gage de bataille, se la querele est d'un marc d'argent ou de plus. Et quant la cort avra ce esgardé, celui qui le plait veaut fuïr, se il le veaut esloigner peut dire:[43] 'Et je suis prest que je li preuve par .ii. loiaus garans si con la cort l'a esgardé ou coneu, mais mes garans sont outre mer. Si requier a la cort qu'ele me doint jor avoir mes garans amenés en la court garantir moy ce que je ai dit et faire que loyaus garans.' Et a moi senble que la court li donra .i. an et .i. jor de

[26] ABV add: ou [27] acrocher de preuve] A: apreuchier qui le viaut apreuchier et garder de ce offrir preuve en court; B: aprochier de preuve; V: aprochier de preuve en court [28] ne] C lacks [29] avra] A: a; V: li avra [30] que il viaut] B lacks [31] A adds: a sa requeste [32] dit] A: deist [33] le] ABV lack [34] si] BV: se il [35] V adds: choses et [36] n'est] A: n'est pas; O: est; V: n'en est [37] je sui bien menbrant que] V lacks [38] con] A: coment; V: coument [39] aprés ce que . . . enterinement] AV lack. Si me merveill . . . enterinement] B lacks [40] autrement] A: par autre chose [41] l'ai] AB: l'en ai; O: l'en ay [42] dit] C: doit [43] peut dire] V: si die ensi

respit de[44] ces garans amener, se il les voche[45] outre mer. Et enssi avra delee la paie de la dete l'an et le jor. Et adonc dire que il ne peut avoir ses garans au jor que la court li a doné,[46] si est prest de la dete paier. Et tout nel die il[47] conoistra la cort que, puis que il n'a ses garans amenés au jor que la cort li a doné,[48] que il a sa querele perdue. Si li doit[49] paier ce de coi il se claime[50] de lui qu'il li devoit, ou que il li requist en la cort, et que il dist que il li dut,[51] mais que il l'en avoit paié.

Que de toutes quereles de quei l'on vouche garans en court, et court[52] li done jor de ses garans amener, et il ne les amoine au jor que la cort li a doné que il ait ses garans amenés en la court[53] a prover par iaus ce que il a ofert a prover,[54] il pert sa querele. Et garde se bien que qui noie chose en cort[55] que il aprés ne[56] la conoisse[57] en cort, sans ce que ele ait esté provee contre lui par recort de cort ou par garans ou autrement. Que, qui la conoistra puis que il l'avra noiee, s'ele n'est avant[58] provee, il sera ataint de faucetė faite en cort et perdra vois et respons en cort con home ataint en cort de faucetė. Por quei a moi senble qu'il vaut meaus de totes choses de quei l'on est araisné en cort, que l'on ne viaut otroier ou conoistre, dire: 'Je n'entent pas qu'enssi soit con vos dites', que neer les tout outre, sauf celes choses qu'il covient a neer si con est[59] murtre, traïson et plusors autres choses que il covient a neer sans[60] demander jor, et aucunes[61] aprés le jor que on a eu selonc ce que eles sont.

Et se la clamor est de terre ou de leuc moti, requiere le fuïant jor, si con il est devisé en cest livre que on doit demander jor, qui viaut plait longuement fuïr. Et aprés le jor requiere mostre de ce que celui li requiert. Et le requerant li doit faire la mostre, mais non mie de toutes choses quant[62] d'un casal nomé et coneu, ne d'un leuc qui a[63] non et apartenances, et que en cele terre n'a autre que[64]

---

[44] de respit de] A: d'aveir [45] voche] A: voe (here and elsewhere in this chapter) [46] a doné] AB: dona [47] nel die il] A: fust ce qu'il nel deist mie si; B: ne le deist il; V: ne le doit il si [48] a doné] ABV: dona. C repeats: si est prest de la dete paier [49] B adds: faire [50] claime] BV: clama [51] dut] B: devoit; OV: doit [52] et court] CO lack [53] que il ait . . . court] B lacks [54] par iaus ce . . . prover] O lacks [55] que qui noie . . . court] A: qu'il ne nee chose; B: que se il nee chose en court; V: que se il ne noie en court aucune chose [56] ne] A lacks [57] conoisse] B: reconoisse [58] avant] ABV: ainz [59] C adds: de [60] sans] V: puis [61] AV add: eschampes [62] quant] AV: Car [63] a] AV: ait [64] n'a autre que] A: n'a autre leuc qui; B: n'est autre leuc qui; V: ne en autre leu que

enssi ait non,[65] ne deit on avoir point de mostre. Mais se c'est cazal ou prestrie ou abaie ou autre leu qui ait non et apartenances, et il a[66] en cele seignorie autre leuc qui enssi ait a[67] non, de celui doit on avoir mostre. Et de chose qui est dedens autre apartenances si con est jardin et vigne[68] et[69] molin, champ, piece de terre, maison ou autre chose, doit l'on avoir mostre. Et de toutes choses que l'on requiert dedens vile doit l'on avoir mostre.[70] Et quant le requerant fait la mostre au fuïant, si l'enpeesche et enconbre le fuïant tant con il plus porra por le plait esloigner. Et de chascune des avant dites[71] choses par sei peut l'on requerre esgart et avoir le, ou dire que l'on le viaut avoir, se la cort l'esgarde, et metre se[72] en esgart de cort sauf[73] son retenaill. Et sur[74] chascune chose peut l'on trover asés esloignes[75] que l'on ne peut pas totes metre en escrit, et de chascun par soy metre se en esgart ou en conoissance de cort, et sauver ades son retenaill. Que enssi con les cas vienent[76] et les paroles sont dites, covient il au plaideor controver[77] ses fuites et ses eschanpes et ses esloignes. Et s'aucune[78] des choses devant[79] dites a preuve que il coveigne a prover par garans, et le requerant les eufre et amene en[80] cort, si enpeeche le fuïant[81] ou enconbre ou rebute ou torne par gage de bataille aucun des[82] garans, si con il est devisé en cest livre que l'on le doit faire, et le fuïant doit demorer longuement a soi conceiller par laquel des .iii. dites voies qu'il[83] veuille fuïr, ou par celes qui d'eles meuvent. Et doit querre[84] totes les esloignes et les eschanpes que il pora[85] et prendre respit toutes les fois qu'il le pora avoir, se son plait n'est en tel point que il cuide avoir damage par le respit. Et toutes les fois que il[86] fera dire sa parole, si la face dire o longes paroles, provant o senblance de raison son dit a bon, et defaisant le dit de son aversaire ce que il porra[87] por le plait esloigner, et doner a entendre as juges que il a droit et[88] dit raison, et mete souvent sus a son aversaire, recordant son dit que il a dit autrement la parole,[89] que il n'a cele que il plus doutera qui[90] li griege. Et enssi

[65] A adds: n'a n'i [66] a] AB: ait; V: y a [67] a] ABV lack [68] et vigne] B lacks [69] et] AB: aigüe [70] Et de toutes . . . mostre] V lacks [71] avant dites] B: autres [72] se] C: s'en [73] sauf] V: sans [74] sur] AV: de; B: a [75] esloignes] B: eschampes [76] les cas vienent] AV: le cas vient [77] controver] AB: trover; V lacks [78] s'aucune] A: se en aucune; B: de ce est avenu; V: se en aucunes [79] devant] AV: avant [80] en] ABO: a [81] fuiant] B: fait [82] aucun des] AV: aucun de ces; B: a un de ses [83] qu'il] A: devant dites il; BV: il [84] querre] A: aquerre; C: requerre [85] C adds: avoir [86] le pora avoir . . . il] V lacks [87] ce que il porra] A lacks [88] a droit et] A: y ait dreit et qu'il [89] la parole] B: son dit [90] qui] B: que; V: qu'il

la change[91] en aucun mot le plus pres et le plus senblant que il porra de ce que son aversaire avra dit, que ce que gregier[92] li deust li aide, se son aversaire ne li contredit. Et se il li[93] contredit,[94] si s'en[95] mete sur le recort de la cort que il enssi a dite la parole con il l'a retraite, et enssi le face sovent. Si porra par ce moult esloigner son plait. Mais s'il entent que son aversaire die si mal que il cuide sa querele desraigner por le mal dit de son aversaire,[96] laisse toutes les[97] fuites et les eschanpes, et au mal dit de son aversaire se preigne si qu'il puisse tost sa querele desraigner et metre soi maintenant sur l'esgart de la cort, et mete ades son retenaill en[98] tos les dis de quei[99] il se posera sur cort, soit d'esgart[100] ou de conoissance.

---

[91] change] C: griege [92] que ce que gregier] B: que ce grignor; V: que ce se gregier [93] li] C: le [94] Et se il li contredit] V lacks [95] s'en] ABV: se [96] die si mal . . . aversaire] V lacks [97] V adds: voyes de [98] en] A: sur; B: de [99] de quei] B: dont; V: en quoy [100] d'esgart] B: de recort

***[29]** Coment l'on doit demander jor quant l'on viaut plait fuïr.

Se le fuïant demande jor au clain que l'on fait de lui et il viaut cel plait fuïr, il le doit premier[1] demander o si feble raison se il peut, que, quant il se metra en l'esgart de la cort sauf son retenaill, que la cort esgarde que il n'a chose dite par coi il doie jor avoir. Et quant il avra cel esgart perdu, si redie[2] .i. autre feible[3] raison et se mete en esgart sauf son retenaill, et tel que il perde se il peut cel autre esgart. Et enssi se mete tant de[4] fois con il[5] porra en esgart que il perde, mais que il sauve tosjors son retenaill. Et enssi porra il mout le plait fuïr[6] et aprés avoir le jor,[7] se le requerant ne s'en[8] seit garder. Et quant totes les foibles[9] raisons faudront au fuïant par quei il perdra les esgars d'avoir le jor, die lor que il viaut le jor avoir se la cort l'esgarde, por ce que il est assise ou usage en la haute cort dou reiaume de Jerusalem que l'on a a tos[10] noviaus clains[11] jor se l'asise ne le tot ne il n'a[12] assise que le jor toille de cel clain, et mete se en l'esgart[13] de la cort sauf son retenaill. Et enssi avra le jor se ce n'est de clain[14] de quey assise tot le jor, et que[15] son aversaire li sache le jor defendre a avoir.

A: fol. xix^{r-v} cap. 41; **B:** fols 51^{v}–52^{r} cap. 42; **C:** fol. 26^{r-v} cap. 28; **O:** fol. 26^{r-v}; **V:** fol. xxv^{v} cap. 38; Beugnot, p. 66, cap. 41.

---

[1] premier] V: premierement [2] redie] A: die [3] feible] B: fausse [4] tant de] AB: tantes [5] A adds: onques [6] Et enssi porra . . . fuïr] A lacks [7] avoir le jor] A: le jor aveir autre jor [8] ne s'en] C: n'en se [9] foibles] B: fausses [10] a tos] V: tousjours [11] V adds: et [12] il n'a] A: n'i a; B: il n'i a; V: il n'en a [13] l'esgart] C: esgart [14] clain] B: chose [15] et que] V: de quoi

***[30]** Coment le requerant se doit garder que le fuïant n'ait plusors esgars et aprés ait[1] le jor.

Se le requerant se viaut garder que le fuïant ne delaie le plait par perdre[2] plusors esgars d'avoir jor,[3] quant il voit que le fuïant ne demande jor si come il doit por non avoir le tost a clain de quei assise ne tot le jor, die le requerant si feible raison par quei il perde cel esgart et que le fuïant ait jor par esgart de cort[4] le plus tost que il porra. Que meaus li vaut il le jor tost laissier[5] avoir de clain de quei[6] assise ne tot le jor, mais que il soit par esgart de court, que metre soy en plusors esgars qui aloignent[7] son plait, et que le fuïant ait[8] aprés jor.

A: fol. xix^{v} cap. 42; **B:** fol. 52^{r} cap. 43; **C:** fol. 26^{v} cap. 29; **O:** fols 26^{v}–27^{r}; **V:** fols xxv^{v}–xxvi^{r} cap. 39; Beugnot, pp. 66–7, cap. 42.

[1] ait] AV lack; B: avra [2] perdre] A: prendre [3] jor] ABV lack [4] de cort] A lacks [5] il le jor tost laissier] A: il tost le jor a aveir que laissier le a; B: le jor tost que laissier a; V: il le jour tost avoir que laisser [6] de clain de quei] A: de claim de claim que de [7] aloignent] V: ehloigent [8] ait] B: avra

*[31] Qui viaut plait fuïr, coment il doit demander jor a clain[1] de quei assise tot le jor.

Qui viaut plait fuïr a clain de quei l'on dit[2] que assise tot le jor, et le clain n'est[3] de murtre ou d'omecide ou de chose qu'il couveigne a neer ains que on demande jor[4] ou l'on est ataint, si demande jor au clain, et die enssi: 'Je voill avoir jor[5] a cest[6] clain, se la cort l'esgarde', et mete[7] son retenaill sans plus dire a cele fois. Et quant il avra perdu cel esgart, die: 'Je veuill avoir jor, se la cort l'esgarde, por ce que l'on onques de se[8] clain ne se clama de moy a[9] cort', et metre[10] son retenaill. Et quant il avra cel esgart perdu, die ce meimes et tant plus, que l'on onques ne se clama de lui de ce en court 'ou je fuse[11] present', et mete[12] soy en esgart sauf son retenaill.

Et aprés die: 'Je voill avoir jor, se la cort l'esgarde, por ce que j'entens que l'on a de tos noviaus clains jor', et mete son retenaill. Et aprés die: 'Je veuill avoir jor, se la cort l'esgarde, por ce que j'entens que l'on doit avoir de tous noviaus clains jor se usage ne le tot', et mete son retenaill. Et aprés die: 'Je veuill avoir jor, se la cort l'esgarde, por ce que j'entens que l'on doit avoir jor a noviaus clains[13] se costume ne le tot', et mete son retenaill. Et aprés die: 'Je veull avoir jor a ce[14] clain, por ce que j'entent que l'on doit avoir a tos noviaus clains jor se assise ne le tot', et mete son retenaill. Et aprés[15] die: 'Je veuill avoir jor, se la cort l'esgarde, por ce que de tos noviaus clains a l'on jor se assise ou usage ou costume ne le tot, ne je n'entens qu'il y ait costume qui cel[16] jor toille', et mete son retenaill.

Et aprés die: 'Je voill avoir jor, se la cort l'esgarde, por ce que je n'entens qu'il soit usage qui ce[17] jor toille', et mete son[18] retenaill. Et aprés die: 'Jel voill avoir,[19] se la cort l'esgarde, por ce que je n'entens qu'il y ait[20] assise qui ce[21] jor toille', et mete son retenaill.

A: fols xix^{v}–xxi^{r} cap. 43; **B:** fols 52^{r}–53^{v} cap. 44; **C:** fols 26^{v}–29^{r} cap. 30; **O:** fols 27^{r}–29^{r}; **V:** fols xxvi^{r}–xxviii^{r} cap. 40; Beugnot, pp. 67–9, cap. 43.

---

[1] clain] B: plait [2] l'on deit] A: on dit; CO: l'on deit [3] n'est] V: est [4] AB add: au claim; V: a cest clain [5] au clain, et . . . jor] V lacks [6] a cest] A: au [7] mete] V: metre (and elsewhere in this chapter) [8] se] AB: cest; O: celui [9] a] AV: en [10] metre] ABO: mete [11] je fuse] A: il fust [12] mete] AV: metre [13] a noviaus clains] A: a toz noviaus claims; B: a touz noviaus claims; V: au noviau clain [14] a ce] AV: en cest; B: a cest [15] B adds: ce [16] cel] ABV: cest [17] ce] AB: cest; V: ceste [18] mete son] V: se mete en esgart et en [19] Jel voill avoir] A: Je viaus aveir jor; BV: Je veull avoir jour [20] qu'il y ait] A: qu'il seit; B: quel soit; V: que il ait [21] ce] AB: cest; V: ceste

Et aprés die: 'Je voill avoir jor, se la cort l'esgarde, por ce que il n'i a[22] costume qui[23] cel[24] jor toille', et mete son retenaill.[25]

Et aprés die: 'Jel voill avoir,[26] se la cort l'esgarde, por ce qu'il n'a usage en cest roiaume qui le jor toille', et mete son retenaill. Et aprés die: 'Je voill avoir jor, se la cort l'esgarde, por ce qu'il n'i a costume en cest roiaume qui le jor toille', et mete son retenaill.[a] Et aprés die: 'Je vueil aver jor[27] a cest clain, por ce qu'il n'i a assise en cest roiaume qui le jor toille', et mete son retenaill.

Et se le requerant[28] dit qu'il n'i a point de creissance en ces .iii.[29] derrains dis ou en aucun d'eaus, die le fuïant que si a, et die coment il i a creissance. Que il dist en son autre[30] dit qu'il n'entendoit qu'ensi fust, et ore dit sans entendement que si n'est mie por quei il entent[31] que ce soit creissance, et de ce se met il en la conoissance de la cort se c'est creissance ou non.

Et aprés die: 'Je voill avoir jor, se la cort l'esgarde, por ce que se l'on ne[32] seit que ce soit usage que on a[33] jor de tel clain, ce n'est que por ce que il n'i a[34] nul de ceaus qui ores sont ci en la cort, qui ait veu ceste chose faire ne user, et tout soit ce que nul de ceaus qui ores sont si en la cort n'ait veu ce faire ne user,[35] n'est il pas si come j'entens qu'il ne soit usage el roiaume de Jerusalem, que l'on[36] doit avoir jor de tel clain? Quar il ne sera ja trové qu'en la haute cort dou royaume[37] de Jerusalem, s'il plaidoie en Chipre, n'en cest ait esté trové, qu'il soit usage que ce[38] jor toille, et se il estoit[39] usage qui ce jor tosist, donc avroit esté coneu et usé l'usage[40] en

---

[a] ABV lack this last sentence. Beugnot (p. 65 n. 5) believed it repeated the idea in a previous sentence (two sentences above). But he was mistaken, since the addition of the phrase 'en cest roiaume' is crucial, as the argument goes on to discuss specifying custom of this kingdom as opposed to that of Cyprus or Jerusalem. CO speak of usage, custom and *assise* 'en cest roiaume' while ABV only have usage and *assise* which presumably explains why AB (though not V) change .iii. to .ii. (see note 29). The omission of the last but one sentence above in B (see note 25) appears, however, to be the result of homeoleteusis.

---

[22] il n'i a] A: je n'entens qu'il seit [23] qui] C: qu'il [24] cel] AV: cest [25] Et aprés die . . . retenaill] B lacks [26] Jel voill avoir] A: Je viaus aveir jor; BV: Je veull avoir jour [27] V adds: se la court l'esgarde [28] requerant] A: requereor [29] .iii.] A: .ii.; B: deus [30] autre] A: dereain [31] il entent] V: je entens [32] se l'on ne] B: semblant me [33] on a] AV: l'on ait; B: l'on a [34] B adds: ores [35] B adds: et [36] B adds: ne [37] dou royaume] B lacks [38] s'il plaidoie . . . ce] A: ni en ceste de Chipre, c'il plaidee en Chipre, n'en ait esté coneu qui cest; B: ne de Chipre, qui i plaide qu'il ait esté coneu qu'il soit usage qui cest; V: si plaidoie en Chipre n'en ceste ait couneu que il soit husage qui cest [39] estoit] B: est [40] l'usage] B lacks

cele cort et en ceste. Mais por ce que il n'est[41] ne fu il onques coneu, por quei je ne voil que il demore por chose que vos aiés dite, que je n'aie le jor, se la cort l'esgarde', et mete son retenaill.

Et aprés die: 'Je veuill avoir le jor, se la court l'esgarde, por ce que je n'entens que il ait esté coneu en la haute cort dou dit reiaume', se il plaidoie en[42] Chipre, 'n'en ceste[43] qu'il soit costume qui ce jor toille, et[44] se il fust costume qui ce jor tosist, donc eust il esté coneu et acostumé[45] en ceste cort et en cele dou roiaume de Jerusalem.[46] Et puis qu'il n'a esté coneu ne[47] acostumé en ceste cort ne en cele, voill je avoir le jor, se la cort l'esgarde', et mete son retenaill.

Et aprés die: 'Je veuill avoir le jor, se la cort l'esgarde, por ce que je n'entens[48] que il[49] ait esté coneu en la haute cort dou dit reiaume', s'il plaideoie en Chipre, 'n'en[50] cest, qu'il[51] soit assise qui ce jor toille, et se il fust assise qui ce jor tosist, dont[52] eust il esté coneu et fait en ceste cort et en cele dou reiaume de Jerusalem.[53] Et puis que il n'a esté coneu[54] en ceste cort n'en cele,[55] ne qu'il y a[56] assise qui ce jor toille, je[57] voill avoir le jor, se la cort l'esgarde', et mete son retenaill.

Et aprés redie[58] si com est[59] devant dit, mais qu'il met[60] en chascun dit en leuc de 'la conoissance', 'esgart'. Et se le requerant dit[61] que il n'i a pas[62] creissance, si die qu'il y a changement ou creissance,[63] et tel par quei il entent que il doive jor avoir. Et de ce se met il en la conoissance[64] de la cort sauf son retenaill, et die que le changement ou la creissance[65] est en ce que il dist avant 'conoissance' et[66] ore dit 'esgart', et que esgart ne conoissance n'est mie une meime chose. Car l'on fait d'une parole conoissance de[67] court, ne esgart ne peut l'on faire d'une parole por coi il est clere chose que esgart ne conoissance n'est mie une meismes chose. Por quei il dit qu'en son dit a changement ou creissance, si viaut avoir de ce jor, se la cort l'esgarde, et mete son retenaill.

---

[41] n'est] AB: ne l'est; V: ne l'est ne [42] V adds: celle de [43] se il plaidoie . . . ceste] B: ne en cele de Chipre [44] AB add: que [45] et acostumé] B: a costume [46] dou roiaume de Jerusalem] B: de Chipre [47] puis qu'il . . . ne] B: por ce qu'il n'a esté [48] n'entens] V: entens [49] C adds: y [50] n'en] C: ne [51] s'il plaideoie . . . qu'il] A: qu'il; B: qui i plaidoie, ne en cele de Chipre qui [52] dont] AOV: donc [53] dou reiaume de Jerusalem] A lacks; B: de Chipre [54] A adds: ne fait [55] B adds: de Chipre; V lacks: dou reiaume . . . Chipre [56] ne qu'il y a] A: qu'il seit; B: qu'il i ait; V: qu'il ait [57] je] C lacks [58] redie] AB: die [59] est] B: il a [60] met] C: n'i ot [61] mais qu'il . . . dit] V lacks [62] pas] B: point de [63] si die qu'il . . . creissance] O lacks [64] la conoissance] V: l'esgart [65] creissance] O: conoissance [66] et] ABV lack [67] de] B: en

Et se il pert tos les devant[68] dis esgars ou conoissances, si die: 'Je veuill avoir jor, se la cort l'esgarde. Et por ce que j'entens qu'il n'i[69] ait costume el royaume de Jerusalem n'en cestui',[70] s'il plaidoie en Chipre,[71] 'qui cel jor toille, por quei je ne veuill que il demore, por chose que vos aiés dite, que je le jor n'aie, se il n'est[72] avant prové par la cort dou reyaume de Jerusalem qu'il y ait[73] costume qui le jor toille de tel[74] clain', et mete se en esgart[75] sauf son retenaill. Et enssi le fase aprés[76] de l'usage et aprés de l'assise. Et se le requerant dit aucune fois en sa parole qu'il est us ou costume ou assise el roiaume de Jerusalem qui ce jor tot, neé le maintenant le defendeor. Que se le requereor[77] ne l'eufre a prover, il[78] avra le jor, et s'il l'eufre a prover si die le defendeor: 'Je ne vos veuill[79] respondre au clain que vos faites[80] de moy, se cort ne l'esgarde, tant que vos aiés prové si con vos devés ce que vos avés dit et ofert a prover, et que je ai neé', et mete se de ce en esgart sauf son[81] retenaill. Et se le requerant se garde de la preuve[82] acuillir a soy, si que le defendeor[86] ne la[84] puisse faire acuillir, die le defendeor quant il avra perdu tos les dis esgars et totes les dites conoissances, que il viaut le jor avoir, se la cort l'esgarde, por ce que il est usage el roiaume de Jerusalem que l'on a de tel clain jor ou dou senblant,[85] et ce est il prest dou prover tot enssi con la cort esgardera ou conoistra que il prover le doie. Et aprés le face enssi de la costume et aprés[86] de l'assise, l'un avant l'autre. Et[87] enssi avra jor le fuïant au clain de quei assise tot le jor, ou il esloignera plus le plait que dou jor avoir se le requerant ne s'en[88] seit garder.

---

[68] devant] ABV: avant [69] j'entens qu'il n'i] AB: je n'entens qu'il; V: je entens que il [70] cestui] A: cestui de Chipre; B: celui de Chipre [71] s'il plaidoie en Chipre] B lacks [72] n'est] V: est [73] y ait] A: ait esté; O: n'ait [74] tel] BV: cest [75] esgart] AB: l'esgart de la court [76] aprés] B lacks [77] requereor] B: requerant [78] il] AV: qu'il [79] Je ne vos veuill] V: que il ne veut [80] faites] B: facies [81] mete se de . . . son] A: me met de ce en l'esgart de la court sauf mon [82] preuve] B: premiere [83] defendeor] B: deffendant [84] ABV add: li [85] dou semblant] B: de semblable [86] le face enssi . . . aprés] B lacks [87] Et] C lacks [88] ne s'en] C: n'en se

*[32] Coment le requerant se doit garder que le fuïant n'esloigne le plait par demander jor.

Se le requereor[1] se viaut garder que le fuïant n'esloigne le plait par demander jor en la maniere avant dite a clain de quei assise tot le jor, il doit dire maintenant que le fuïant demande jor au clain de quei assise tot le jor, que il ne viaut que il ait le jor por tel[2] et por tel raison, et die toutes les raisons ensenble par quei il li cuide le jor tolir. Et aprés die et por tant plus que il est us ou costume[3] ou assise el roiaume de Jerusalem qui tot le jor a tel[4] clain, et ce est il prest de prover tot ensi con la cort esgardera ou conoistra que il prover le doie, por quei il ne viaut que il ait jor, se la cort ne l'esgarde, et sauve[5] son retenaill. Et je croi[6] que la cort esgardera que, se il peut prover par recort de cort que il soit us[7] ou costume ou assise qui le jor toille de tel clain, que le fuïant n'avra point de jor. Et se il y a .ii. homes de la cort ou plus qui recordent qu'il aient veu esgarder ou conoistre a la cort que il i a[8] assise ou usage qui cel[9] jor tot, que le requerant a prové son dit si con il doit. Ou se pluisors de ceaus de la cort dient qu'il[10] ont veu ades[11] user que l'on de tel clain n'a pas jor, ne que il ne virent onques avoir jor de cel[12] clain, et que il aient plusors autres fois veu tel cas avenir[13] en la cort, de quei le fuïant demanda[14] jor au clain et ne l'ot[15] mie, a mei senble que le requerant a prové soufisaument que le fuïant ne doit pas avoir jor de tel clain, et por ce le me senble il enssi que a paines me senble il[16] assise prover que l'on a oy dire, et par ce que l'on voit[17] user com assise ou que l'on a tosjors acostumeement usé a faire en la cort de tel[18] cas ou dou senblant.[19] Et se le requerant ne peut ce prover, il n'i pert que tant[20] que le fuïant a jor, et meaus li vaut il que son aversaire ait tost jor, se il n'i[21] peut prover que il

A: fol. xxi^{r-v} cap. 44; **B:** fol. 53^{v} cap. 45; **C:** fol. 29^{r-v} cap. 31; **O:** fols 29^{r}–30^{r}; **V:** fol. xxviii^{r-v} cap. 41; Beugnot, pp. 70–1, cap. 44.

[1] requereor] ABV: requerant [2] B adds: chose [3] ou costume] AB lack [4] tel] BV: cel [5] et sauve] B: sauf [6] croi] A: cuit [7] us] B lacks [8] a] ABV: ait [9] cel] AV: tel [10] dient qu'il] CO: dont il [11] ades] B lacks [12] cel] AOV: tel [13] tel cas avenir] AV: avenir de tel cas; B: de tex cas [14] demanda] A: demandeit; B: demandoit; V: demande [15] l'ot] B: l'avoit; V: l'eut [16] me senble il] A: que l'on puisse; B: me semble il que l'on puisse; V: puisse l'en [17] voit] AB: l'a veu; V: veaut [18] tel] C: cel [19] B adds: me semble il et est raison por les choses desus ditez qu'il ne doit avoir point de jour [20] B adds: fors [21] n'i] A: ne le; BV: ne; C lacks

y a[22] assise ou us ou costume qui le jor toille, que deleer le plait par tant d'esgars com est avant dit, et perdre aprés[23] le jor. Et ce fasse se il ne[24] senble qu'il puisse prover, si con il doit, qu'il soit assise ou usage qui le jor toille. Et que il ait ce prové en plus brief terme[25] que n'est le jor qui n'est que de .xv. jors.[26] et se il ne le cuide prover en plus brief terme que les[27] .xv. jors,[28] si li laise[29] le jor avoir le plus tost que il porra, mais que ce soit par esgart de court.

[22] y a] AV: ait; B: i ait [23] aprés] B lacks [24] ne] ABV: li [25] terme] A: termine [26] qui n'est . . . jors] A: de quinzaine [27] que les] A: qu'en [28] et se il . . . jors] V lacks [29] si li laise] C: si li plaise; O: si si laisse

***[33]** Coment le clamant[1] doit le plait abregier.

Se le clamant viaut son plait abregier, otroie ce que le fuïant dira el plait qu'il cuidera perdre[2] par esgart ou par conoissance de cort, se ce n'est[3] de quei il perde la[4] querele ou[5] de quei il receive mort ou honte ou desheritement ou autre damage. Que tes choses[6] ne doit nul otroier ne conoistre en cort por .ii. raisons: l'une por ce qu'espoir[7] la cort ne l'esgardera pas[8] si come il entent; l'autre que tout le deust la cort enssi esgarder ne le doit il[9] faire. Qu'il li est mains mal et mains lait que ce soit fait par esgart ou par conoissance de cort que par son otroi ou par sa conoissance en la cort, que nul ne doit aucunes[10] des dites choses otroier ne conoistre en[11] cort tant con il s'en puisse garder ne defendre.

A: fol. xxi^v cap. 45; **B:** fols 53^v–54^r cap. 46; **C:** fols 29^v–30^r cap. 32; **O:** fol. 31^r; **V:** fols xxviii^v–xxix^r cap. 42; Beugnot, p. 71, cap. 45.

[1] clamant] A: requerant [2] perdre] C lacks [3] n'est] V: n'en est chose [4] la] BV: sa [5] A adds: de chose [6] Que tes choses] B: Car tel chose [7] por ce qu'espoir] B: por ce espoir que; V: ci est que il espoir [8] ne l'esgardera pas] A: ne l'esgardereit pas; B: n'esgardera mie [9] O adds: mie [10] aucunes] B: nules [11] C adds: la

*[34] Que doit faire celui qui viaut tost son plait ataindre.[a]

Qui viaut tost son plait ataindre, il doit faire estre en la cort tant de ses amis con il plus[1] porra, et prier les que il soient ententis[2] as paroles qui seront dites el plait et bien entendre et retenir, si que il les sachent recorder as esgars et as conoissances se mestier li est, et que se il[3] voient ou conoissent, quant il seront as esgars ou as conoissances[4] de son plait, que[5] cel esgart ou cele conoissance est por lui, qu'il n'en preignent nul respit ains dient lor avis sans respit[6] prendre, se il en sont[7] apencés.

Et se les autres veulent respit prendre,[8] ne le seufrent ains les[9] fasent destraindre, si con il doivent, au conestable, ou a celui qui sera en son leuc en la cort, a demander as homes de dire leur avis, et enssi les porront il destraindre. Que quant il avront dit lor avis, se[10] les autres ne veulent dire le leur,[11] por ce[12] que il veulent[13] prendre respit d'eaus apencer ou conceiller ou le plait esloigner et dient que il[14] ne sont mie bien apencés do dire,[15] ceaus qui ont dit leur avis requierent au conestable, se il est en la cort,[16] ou a celui qui sera par le seignor estably en la cort, a demander[17] que il les destraigne, si con il doit, de dire lor avis puis[18] que il ont dit le leur. Et[19] le conestable, ou celui qui sera establi par le seignor a demander en la cort,[20] lor doit dire: 'Je vos comant de[21] par mon seignor tel', et le nome, 'que vos[22] dites vostre avis, et[23] que vos vos[24] aquités si con vos devés'. Et[25] ceaus qui dient qu'il ne sont pas apencés doivent dire lor avis, ou dire par la foy que il doivent au seignor qu'il ne

---

A: fols xxi^{v}–xxii^{v} cap. 46; **B:** fols 54^{r}–55^{r} cap. 47; **C:** fols 30^{r}–31^{v} cap. 33; **O:** fols 31^{r}–32^{v}; **V:** fols xxix^{r}–xxx^{r} cap. 43; Beugnot, pp. 71–3, cap. 46.

---

[a] Rubric in B: Qui veut tost son plait ateindre que doit il faire.

---

[1] plus] BV lack [2] ententis] C: entendis [3] se il] A: ciaus; B: ceaus [4] V adds: se mestier li est [5] A adds: ce; B: se [6] C adds: de [7] sont] C: soit [8] se il en . . . prendre] V: et que il [9] les] CV: le [10] enssi les porront . . . se] V lacks [11] le leur] B: lor avis [12] por ce] V lacks [13] veulent] A: vodront [14] A adds: entendent qu'il [15] A adds: Se [16] se il est en la court] ABV lack [17] qui sera par . . . demander] AB: qui sera (B: est) en son leuc; V: que en son leu est [18] puis] A lacks; B: et puis [19] le leur. Et] A: le leur; B: leur avis [20] sera establi par . . . cort] AB: sera en son leuc; V: en son leuc sera [21] de] OV lack [22] tel', et le . . . vos] B: que vos tel', et le nome [23] et] ABV: ou [24] C adds: en [25] A adds: ce

sont pas apencés si que il le puissent dire a nete concience.[26] Et[27] lors ceaus qui ont dit lor avis pevent[28] l'esgart que il avront fait retraire devant le seignor, se il sont .ii. ou plus. Quar puis que partie de la cort a son avis dit, l'autre partie tout soit ele le plus ne peut l'esgart respiter, se se n'est par la volenté de ceaus qui ont dit lor avis, qu'il les pevent faire destraindre, si con il est desus dit par le conestable ou par celui que[29] le seignor avra establi en son leuc en la cort a demander.[30]

Et se le conestable n'i est ne n'a[31] esté estably por le seignor a ce demander,[32] ceaus qui ont dit leur avis doivent venir au[33] seignor ou mander[34] requerre li que il comande a aucun de ses homes qui est en la cort que il destraigne, si con il doit, ses homes qui n'ont dit[35] lor avis qu'il le dient,[36] ou que il s'en aquitent si com il doivent. Et le seignor le doit comander a aucun[37] de ces homes, et celui le peut faire ausi con le conestable. Et quant ceaus qui ont dit[38] lor avis s'en seront aquités,[39] si con il[40] est devant dit, ceaus qui ont l'esgart fait le pevent retraire,[41] se il veulent,[42] se il sont .ii. ou plus, que puis que .ii. l'ont fait, la cort la fait. Quar les .ii. sont cort en cest cas. Quar ceaus qui dient qu'il ne sont apencés et se sont aquités, si com il doivent, n'ont en cel esgart ou en cele conoissance vois de cort.[43] Et celui qui ne dira son avis ou ne s'en aquitera ains que la court retraie l'esgart, s'il en est destraint si con il est desus dit,[44] le conestable, ou celui qui sera establi par le seignor a demander en la cort,[45] le doit dire au seignor maintenant que l'esgart sera retrait.

Et se celui qui ne se[46] sera aquité de dire son avis ou ne l'avra dit[47] doit servise de son cors au seignor, il en porra avoir tel droit de luy con[48] defailli de servise. Quar tos ceaus qui doivent servise[49]

---

[26] doivent dire lor . . . concience] A: de dire lor avis, deivent dire que par la fei qu'il deivent au seignor qu'il ne sont pas si apencés qu'il le puissent dire o nete conscience sont quittez; B: si qu'il le puissent dire a nete consience, par la foi que il doivent au seignor, ou il doivent dire autrement leur avis, si ne veulent jurer la foy que il doivent au seignor; V: si que il puissent dire a nete consience [27] concience. Et] O: conoissance. Et [28] pevent] A: poront faire; O: peusent; V: poront [29] que] BV: qui [30] a demander] A: por demander; B: a comander [31] n'a] A: nul n'a; BV: nul n'i a [32] demander] B: comander [33] au] AV: devant le [34] mander] CV: demander [35] n'ont dit] B: ont a dire [36] dient] O: doient [37] aucun] A: un; BV: l'un [38] ont dit] A: n'ont dit; B: doivent dire [39] aquités] V: quités [40] il] OV lack [41] retraire] B: recorder [42] se il veulent] ABV lack [43] n'ont en cel . . . cort] AV: en cel esgart ou (V: et) en celle conoissance (V: counoisance) ont vois de court perdue [44] ains que la . . . dit] A: si come il devra, c'il en est destraint, si come il est dessuz dit, ainz que la court retraie l'esgart [45] establi par le . . . cort] ABV: en son leuc [46] se] AV lack [47] ou ne l'avra dit] A lacks [48] AO adds: de [49] B adds: au seignor

de lor cors et seent[50] en la cort, quant ele fait esgart ou conoissance, doivent dire lor avis ou aquiter s'en enssi[51] con il doivent, se il en la maniere desus dite en sont destraint. Que cestui servise doivent il au seignor. Quar s'ensi n'estoit, le seignor ne porroit[52] cort tenir tel con il doit[53] ne les gens[54] avoir lor raisons, se le seignor ne peut ses homes destraindre, si con il est desus[55] dit, a faire les esgars et les conoissances qui sont mises sur eaus a faire. Et celui qui est quite dou servise de son cors se doit partir de la cort ou dire son avis ou aquiter s'en[56] si con les autres.

Et se les amis dou requerant conoissent que l'esgart ou la conoissance[57] doit estre contre lui si que il perde sa querele,[58] si[59] facent a lor pooir coment l'esgart soit respité, se il le poient faire sans mesprendre et sans peche, por ce que espoir il y avra tel gent en la cort au jor qu'ele respitera l'esgart[60] par quei lor ami[61] ne perdra mie sa querele ains la gaaignera. Et le fuïant doit ausi faire estre[62] en la cort tant de ses amis con il[63] porra por aidier li a[64] garder sa raison en la maniere desus dite, mais que tant qu'ensi con[65] les amis dou requerant veulent le plait aprocher que ceaus dou defendant[66] l'esloignent,[67] se que il poront par raison et sans peche.

[50] et seent] B: sont [51] aquiter s'en enssi] A: eaus aquiter si; V: quiter soi si [52] porroit] A: peust [53] doit] B: devroit [54] gens] A: requeranz [55] desus] B: devant [56] s'en] A lacks; BV: soi [57] ou la conoissance] B lacks [58] AV add: par lui [59] si] C: il [60] qu'ele respitera l'esgart] AB: que l'esgart sera respité; C: que l'en respitera l'esgart [61] ami] ABO: amis [62] estre] B: et avoir [63] A adds; plus [64] aidier li a] O lacks [65] qu'ensi con] B: que; O: qu'ensi que [66] defendant] B: deffendeor [67] l'esloignent] A: le aloignent; B: aloignier; V: ehloigner

***[35]** Qui viaut plait ataindre, coment il doit plaideer se le fuïant fuit[1] par la premiere fuite principal de plait.

Celui qui viaut son plait ataindre doit dire ce que besoing li est a brieves paroles et le plus entendaument[2] que il porra, et requerre maintenant esgart de son dit[3] por le plait aprocher. Et se le fuïant fuit par la premiere des .iii. dites voies principaus[4] de plait, non aerdant[5] soy a l'esgart dou requerant, mais qu'il se mete d'autre choze en esgart que de ce que le requerant li requiert, et s'i mete por faire passer l'esgart en vuit[6] et le plait esloigner, die le requerant: 'Je ne veuill qu'il demore por chose que vos diés[7] de ceste[8] non aerdre[9] vos a mon esgart, que vos ne me faciés ce que je voz[10] ai requis en la court, ou que vos ne vos aerdés[11] a mon esgart que je ai premier requis, se la cort ne l'esgarde, ains veuill que vos me fasiés ce que je vos ai[12] requis en la cort ou que vos ne[13] vos aerdés a mon esgart que j'ai premier requis, et qu'il aille devant le vostre, et di por coi:[14] por ce que il est us ou[15] costume ou assise en cest roiaume ou raison,[16] que l'esgart premier requis doit avant[17] aler, et, puis qu'il doit avant[18] aler, donc est il clere chose que l'on[19] s'i doit aerdre. Que se l'un ne[20] se[21] aerdeit, il ne porroit avant aler, por ce qu'il n'i avroit point d'esgart, que la cort ne deit faire esgart[22] se l'un des querelous[23] ne s'aert a l'autre d'esgart,[24] et por ce est il certaine chose que l'on s'i[25] doit aerdre d'esgart a celui qui[26] premier li requiert. Que s'ensi[27] n'estoit que le defendant[28] fust destraint d'aerdre soi a l'esgart dou requerant par ce que l'esgart premier requis doit avant aler, il ne s'i prendreit se il ne voloit, et se il ne s'i pernoit il ne porroit estre jamais ataint, et s'il ne poeit estre[29] ataint, donc ne vau-

A: fols xxii^{v}–xxiii^{v} cap. 47; **B:** fols 55^{r}–56^{r} cap. 48; **C:** fols 31^{v}–33^{r} cap. 34; **O:** fols 32^{v}–34^{v}; **V:** fols xxx^{r}–xxxi^{v} cap. 44; Beugnot, pp. 74–6, cap. 47.

[1] fuit] B: plaidoie [2] entendaument] O: tendaument [3] son dit] B: court [4] des .iii. dites voies principaus] A: de ces treis dites voies principaus; V: fuit principau [5] aerdant] B: atandant [6] vuit] B: vain [7] diés] A: aiés dire; B: aiez dite; V: ayés dit [8] ceste] AV: coste; C reads 'ceste' with the final 'e' deleted. [9] aerdre] AV: aerdant; B: aherdant [10] voz] C lacks [11] aerdés] B: acordés [12] A adds: premier [13] ne] ABV lack [14] et di por coi] ABV lack [15] ou] OV: et [16] ou raison] B lacks [17] avant] B: premier [18] avant] B: devant [19] l'on] B: bien [20] ne] C added in margin; O lacks [21] se] AO: s'i; V: s'i ne [22] que la court . . . esgart] B lacks [23] l'un des querelous] A: l'un des carellanz; B: l'une des raisons; V: l'un des requerans [24] d'esgart] A lacks [25] s'i] ABV: se [26] qui] C: que [27] s'ensi] B: ce se [28] ABV add: ne [29] A adds: jamés; B: jamais

droit riens[30] la haute cort de cest roiaume puis que l'on n'i[31] porroit plait ataindre ne avoir droit que par la[32] volenté do fuïant, laquel choze seroit tort apert et contre droit et[33] raison et l'usage et l'assise de cest roiaume. Et por toutes les raisons que je ai[34] dites ou por aucunes d'eles, veuill je que vos me fasiés ce que je vos ai requis, ou que vos a mon esgart, que je ai premier requis, vos aerdés, et qu'il aille devant le vostre, se la cort l'esgarde, et de ce me met je en l'esgart de la cort sauf mon retenaill.'

Et il me senble qu'il[35] ne se peut[36] defendre que il ne se preigne a cest[37] esgart, et, se il s'i[38] prent, il me senble qu'il a en cest dit .ii. esgars: l'un est de ce que le requerant dit qu'il ne viaut por choze que le fuïant ait dite qu'il demore que il ne li fase ce que il li a requis en la cort, ou qu'il ne s'aerde[39] a son esgart que il a premier requis, se la cort ne[40] l'esgarde; l'autre esgart[41] est de ce qu'il dit que il viaut que il li face ce que il li requiert, ou que il s'aerde a son esgart que il a premier requis, et que il aille[42] devant le sien, se la cort l'esgarde, et dit raison por quey, et de ce c'est mis[43] en l'esgart de la cort sauf son retenaill. Et je cuit[44] que la cort doit faire ces .ii. esgars ensenble et doit esgarder, se croy, qu'il ne doit demorer por chose[45] que le fuïant ait dite, que il ne face au requerant ce que il li a requis en la cort ou qu'il ne[46] s'aerde a son esgart. Et maintenant aprés doit la cort faire l'autre esgart, et deit, se me senble, esgarder que le fuïant doit faire au requerant ce que il li a requis[47] en la cort ou aerdre[48] soi[49] a son esgart qu'il a premier requis, et que l'esgart premier requis[50] doit avant aler, et doit sauver les retenaus[51] des .ii. s'il y sont.[52] Et aprés ces .ii. dis[53] esgars ne vaut, se me senble, le retenaill[54] dou fuïant, qu'il covient que il fase au requerant sa requeste[55] ou qu'il s'aerde[56] a son esgart.[57] Si[58] me senble que le fuïant ne peut plus fuïr par la premiere fuite principal de plait se le requerant le fait si com est avant[59] dit. Et quant[60] les .ii. dis esgars

[30] riens] A: neent [31] n'i] ABO: ne [32] la] V: droite [33] droit et] B lacks [34] V adds: devant [35] qu'il] ABV: que le fuïant [36] se peut] A: s'en puisse; B: se puisse; O: s'en peut [37] cest] ABV: cel [38] s'i] AV: se [39] s'aerde] A: s'i aerde; B: s'acorde [40] ne] V lacks [41] AB add: si [42] aille] O lacks [43] c'est mis] A: est il mis; B: se met il [44] je cuit] B: me semble [45] chose] B: ce [46] ne] B lacks [47] a requis] A: requiert [48] aerdre] B: aherde [49] soi] A: ce [50] que l'esgart premier requis] V lacks [51] sauver les retenaus] B: savoir la raison; V: savoir les retenaills [52] s'il y sont] B lacks [53] .ii. dis] B: deus; V: dis [54] le retenaill] V: les retenaills [55] sa requeste] B: ce qu'il li requiert [56] s'aerde] B: s'aherdre [57] son esgart] V: lui d'esgart [58] Si] BV: Ce [59] avant] AV: devant [60] quant] B: aprés

avront esté fais et retrais,[61] face le requerant maintenant sa requeste tot aussi con il l'avoit avant faite.

Et se le fuïant ne fait la requeste dou requerant[62] ou ne se prent a son esgart et que por son retenaill qui li a esté sauvé dit aucune[63] chose por le plait fuïr et[64] non aerdant soy a l'esgart dou requerant, die le requerant au seignor: 'Sire, vos et vostre cort avés oy et[65] entendu les esgars[66] que la[67] cort a fais et retrais', et die ques il sont[68] esté, 'et tel', et le nome, 'ne m'a[69] fait ne ne fait ce que la cort a esgardé,[70] que il ne[71] me fait[72] ce que je li requis en la cort, ne ne se prent a mon esgart.[73] Si vos pri et requier com a seignor et justise,[74] que vos me faites faire et tenir[75] ce que la cort a esgardé.' Et le seignor doit lors dire au fuïant: 'Aerdés vos a son esgart, ou vos li faites sa requeste. Et se vos ne li faites,[76] je ne puis faillir au requerant que je ne li face ce que ma cort a esgardé.' Et se il aprés ce ne s'aert a son esgart ou ne li fait sa requeste, le seignor li doit faire faire sans delay ce qu'il li a requis. Que les seignors doivent faire tenir les esgars et les conoissances et les recors que lor[77] cors font.

---

[61] avront esté fais et retrais] AV: seront fais (V: fait); B lacks [62] requerant] A: requereor [63] que por son . . . aucune] A: que por son retenaill qu'il a sauvé vueille dire aucune; B: qu'il por son retenaill a sauver veulle dire; V: que pour son retenaill il a esté doné sauve die aucune [64] et] ABV lack [65] oy et] ABV lack [66] les esgars] ABV: l'esgart [67] la] B: vostre [68] il sont] AV: il ont; B: y ont [69] ne m'a] A: ne m'a pas; B: n'a [70] a esgardé] O: esgarde [71] ne] A lacks [72] que il ne me fait] V lacks [73] que il ne . . . esgart] B lacks [74] justise] AB: a justise; O: juste; V: a justizier [75] et tenir] V lacks [76] C adds: ne [77] lor] AV: les

***[36]** Coment l'on doit plait ataindre quant le fuïant fuit par la seconde fuite principal de plait.

Qui viaut plait ataindre quant le fuïant[1] veaut fuïr par la seconde fuite principal de plait, se le plait est de requeste sans clain ou a[2] clain, que le requerant face au fuïant,[3] die le requerant a[4] sa premiere parole maintenant qu'il avra faite sa requeste, que il viaut que le fuïant li face ce que il li requiert por tel et por tel raison,[5] se la cort l'esgarde, et die totes les raisons que il cuidera[6] qui li doivent valoir et mete[7] son retenaill. Et se le fuïant dit que il ne li viaut respondre a sa requeste ou a son clain por tel[8] et por tel raison, disant les raisons que il cuidera qui li doivent valoir et que[9] bones li seront[10] a ce qu'il ne li doive[11] respondre, die le requerant: 'Je ne veuill que il demore por chose que vos diés que vos ne me respondés, se la cort l'esgarde, por tel[12] et por tel raison', et die les raisons que il avra[13] dites, se il li senble que il ne[14] puisse meaus dire, et se il li senble que autres raisons[15] vaillent meaus que seles que il a dites, si les die. Et quant il les avra dites, si die: 'Ains veuill[16] por les raisons que je ai dites que vos me respondés,[17] et por tant plus qu'il est us et costume ou assise en cest roiaume ou raison que l'esgart premier requis doit avant aler',[18] donc est il clere chose que le fuïant doit respondre au requerant. Que se[19] il ne respondoit il n'i poroit[20] avoir esgart, por ce que cort ne peut ne ne doit faire esgart dou clain ne[21] de la requeste dou requereor, se le defendeor[22] ne li respont a sa requeste ou a son clain, et se preigne a lui d'esgart. Que cort ne peut faire esgart d'une parole, et puis que court ne peut faire esgart d'une parole[23] et que l'esgart premier requis doit avant aler,

---

A: fols xxiii^{v}–xxv^{r} cap. 48; **B:** fols 56^{r}–57^{r} cap. 49; **C:** fols 33^{r}–35^{r} cap. 35; **O:** fols 34^{v}–36^{r}; **V:** fols xxxi^{v}–xxxiii^{v} cap. 45; Beugnot, pp. 76–8, cap. 48.

---

[1] A adds: fuit et [2] a] C lacks; O: o [3] que le requerant . . . fuïant] A lacks [4] a] ABV: en [5] por tel et por tel raison] AV lack; B: a lui [6] cuidera] A: cuide [7] mete] V: metre [8] B adds: chose [9] qui li doivent valoir et que] A: qui; BV: que [10] seront] A: seent; BV: soient [11] doive] B: doient; V: doivent [12] B adds: chose [13] ABV add: avant [14] li senble que il ne] A: ne li semble qu'il [15] AB add: li [16] Ains veuill] A: Je viaus; V: Je veull [17] die. Et quant . . . respondés] B: responde [18] ABV add: et puis qu'il doit (A: deit) avant aler [19] se] C lacks [20] ne respondoit il n'i poroit] B: ne li respont donc n'i porroit il; C: n'i respondoit; V: n'i respondoit il ne poroit [21] ne] ABV: ou [22] requereor, se le defendeor] B: requerant, se le deffendant [23] et puis que . . . parole] C lacks

il est sertaine[24] chose que le fuïant doit respondre a la requeste et au clain[25] dou requerant et prendre s'en a lui d'esgart. Que se il ne le faisoit il ne porroit avoir esgart sans la volenté dou fuïant ne l'esgart premier[26] requis ne porroit avant aler, laquel choze seroit contre l'assise ou l'usage de cest roiaume et tort apert. Qu'il n'est assise ne usage en cest roiaume,[27] ne droit ne raison,[28] que le fuïant ne[29] doive respondre, se il ne viaut, au requerant de[30] ce que il li requiert en la cort ou[31] de quei il se clama[32] de lui. Et por toutes les raisons que je ai dites ou por aucunes d'eles, veuill je que vos me faites ce que je vos requier[33] que[34] vos me respondés a mon clain ou a ma requeste, se la cort[35] l'esgarde. Et de ce me met je en l'esgart de la cort sauf mon retenaill.'

Et se le requerant le fait enssi, il ne me senble que le fuïant s'en puisse[36] defendre de prendre se a lui d'esgart. Et se il s'i prent il y avra[37] .ii. esgars, se cuit,[38] et la cort doit faire, ce m'est avis, ces .ii. esgars ensenble. Enssi se croi que le fuïant n'a dite chose por quei il doive demorer qu'il ne responde au clain ou a la requeste dou requerant, se il n'a dite chose par qu'il senble a la cort qu'il ne li doit respondre et qu'il ont[39] leisir de dire.[40] Et maintenant aprés doit la cort faire l'autre esgart. Et enssi se me senble que le fuïant doit[41] respondre a la requeste dou requerant[42] ou faire li ce que il li requiert, et que l'esgart premier requis doit avant aler, et qu'il ont lisir de dire.[43] Et aprés ces esgars covient, se me senble, que le fuïant responde[44] au requerant, se il n'a tel raison[45] dite[46] que il senble a la cort qu'il ne li doit respondre. Que son retenaill ne li vaudra riens, se cuit, aprés les[47] dis esgars a fuïr plus par cele voie, puis que la cort avra esgardé que l'esgart premier requis doit avant aler, et que il s'i doie prendre[48] par les raisons avant dites. Que se il s'i

---

[24] et que l'esgart premier . . . sertaine] A: deit l'esgart premier requis avant aler, et puis qu'il deit avant aler, donc est il certaine; B: et que le regart avant requis doit avant aler, il est certaine; O: et que l'esgart premier requis doit avant aler, donc est il clere [25] et au clain] A lacks [26] premier] B: avant [27] et tort apert . . . roiaume] B lacks [28] B adds: n'est [29] ne] O lacks [30] se il ne . . . requerant de] B: au requerant se il ne veut doner au requerant [31] A adds: de ce; B: ce [32] clama] ABV: claime [33] requier] V: ais requis [34] que] A: ou que; B: et que [35] B adds: ne [36] ne me senble . . . puisse] BV: me semble que le fuïant ne se puisse (V: ne s'em pora) [37] il y avra] A: a lui il y avreit; B: il avra [38] se cuit] AB lack [39] ont] A: a [40] et qu'il ont . . . dire] B lacks [41] A adds: dire et [42] B adds: ou au claim [43] et qu'il ont . . . dire] B lacks [44] covient, se me . . . responde] V: doit, se me semble, le fuïant respondre [45] raison] V: chose [46] B adds: par quoi [47] A adds: .ii. [48] prendre] A: prendre a son esgart; O: respondre

prent, donc covient il que il responde a la requeste dou requerant, que autrement il ne s'en prendroit[49] a son esgart ne l'esgart premier requis n'iroit[50] avant. Et se il li respont[51] donc ne peut il[52] plus fuïr par la seconde fuite principal de plait.

Et se le requerant se claime, et le defendant[53] dit que il ne[54] viaut respondre a cel clain, se la cort ne l'esgarde, et dit raison por coi, le requerant ne li peut le jor defendre a respondre par la voie avant dite:[55] 'Je ne veuill que il demore por chose que vos diés, que vos ne me respondés a mon clain, se la court ne[56] l'esgarde, por tel[57] et por tel raison', et die totes les raison ensenble a une fois qu'il cuidera qui[58] li doivent valoir a ce que il responde a son clain. Et de ce se mete en l'esgart de la cort, sauf son retenaill. Et enssi le face toutes les fois que le fuïant dira que il ne li viaut respondre a son clain, se la cort ne l'esgarde, disant raison por quey. Que se le fuïant ne li respont[59] a son clain ains[60] que la cort se parte, ou ne dit tel raison que[61] la cort esgarde ou conoisse que il ne li doit respondre, le requerant avra desrainee sa querele. Qu'il est assise ou usage en cest roiaume que qui ne respont a clain que l'on fait de lui[62] en cort en sa presence ains que la cort se parte, ou ne dit chose par quei la cort esgarde ou conoisse qu'il n'i[63] doit respondre ou[64] l'eufre a respondre, se le seignor ou[65] la cort[66] le viaut oir, et qu'il ne demore qu'il ne[67] responde au clain que on fait de lui, que par ce que le seignor ou la cort ne le veulent oir,[68] il pert sa querele, et meaus ne peut l'on plait ataindre que gaaigner sa[69] querele.

---

[49] s'en prendroit] A: respondreit c'il ne s'i perneit] BO: se prendroit [50] V adds: jamais [51] Et se il li respont] A: c'il ne li respondeit; V: se il ne li respondoit [52] peut il] B: li puet [53] defendant] BV: fuïant [54] ABV adds: li [55] B adds: mais die [56] ne] ABV lack [57] B adds: chose [58] qui] B: qu'eles; O: qu'il [59] se le fuïant ne li respont] V: le fuïant ne li respondre [60] ains] O lacks [61] que] B: par quoi [62] lui] O lacks [63] n'i] ABV: ne li [64] A adds: ne [65] ou] O: en [66] ABV add: ne [67] demore qu'il ne] AB: demorre (B: demore) en lui qu'il ne; V lacks [68] oir] B lacks [69] sa] B: la

*[37] Se le fuïant fuit par la tierce fuite principal de plait, coment l'on le doit ataindre.

Se le fuïant fuit par la tierce fuite principal de plait disant que il ne viaut faire au requerant ce que il li requiert, se la cort ne l'esgarde, por tel[1] et por tel raison, die le requerant: 'Je ne voill que il demore por choze que vos aiés dite, que vos ne me[2] faciés ce que je vos requier por tel[3] et por tel raison', et die toutes les raisons ensenble a une fois[4] qu'il cuidera que bones li soient[5] a desfaire[6] le[7] dit de son aversaire et a aveir[8] ce que il li requiert. Et ce die tousjors le plus brief et le plus entendaument que il porra, tant que il l'ait ataint, mais ne laisse a dire chose que mestier li est[9] au plait ataindre por brief dire, et garde soi bien le requerant qu'il ne se mete en esgart qui[10] pase en vuit,[11] que son plait en seroit esloigné et il tenu a simple. Et il me senble que le requerant se peut bien garder de ce, et enssi qu'il ne se mete d'autre choze en esgart que de ce que son aversaire s'i met. Et se son aversaire ne se prent[12] a lui d'esgart, destraigne[13] le ensi con est dit en l'autre[14] chapitle devant que il a lui se preigne d'esgart. Et quant il se poze en esgart que il[15] die tousjors que il ne viaut que il demore por chose que son aversaire ait dite,[16] que il ne li face[17] ce que il li requiert, se la court ne l'esgarde, et de ce se mete[18] en l'esgart[19] de la cort sauf son retenaill. Et mete son retenaill[20] en chascun esgart et en chascune conoissance de court en quey il se metra.

A: fol. xxv^{r} cap. 49; **B:** fol. 57^{r} cap. 50; **C:** fol. 35^{r-v} cap. 36; **O:** fol. 36^{r-v}; **V:** fols xxxii^{v}–xxxiv^{r} cap. 46; Beugnot, pp. 78–9, cap. 49.

---

[1] B adds: chose [2] me] ABV lack [3] B adds: chose [4] fois] A: vois [5] qu'il cuidera que . . . soient] V: que bones li semblent [6] desfaire] BC: defendre [7] le] B: se dou [8] a aveir] B: avra [9] est] B: soit [10] qui] C: que [11] pase en vuit] B: passer en veut [12] ne se prent] C: mesprent [13] destraigne] V: destraindre [14] C adds: devant [15] que il] A lacks [16] quant il se . . . dite] B: die [17] face] B: fera [18] se mete] V: me met je [19] l'esgart] C: esgart [20] Et metre son retenaill] B lacks

***[38]** Coment l'on doit demander jor a tos les clains que l'on fait de lui en court, mais que a ceaus de quei l'on est ataint qui n'i[1] respont sans jor demander.

Qui se claime d'autre, celui de qui l'on c'est clamés doit demander jor au clain que on fait de lui ains que il[2] responde, se le clain est novel,[3] se il n'est de l'une des choses de quei l'on est ataint se il[4] ne respont au clain que on fait de lui sans jor demander. Et celes chozes sont devisees aprés en cest livre.[5] Et se il demande jor, il le doit faire en la maniere qui est devant devisee en cest livre que on le[6] doit faire,[7] et le clamant doit contrebatre le jor, si con il est devant[8] devisé en cest livre que on[9] doit jor contrebatre, soit[10] au clain de quey assise ne tot le jor ou au clain de quei assise tot le jor.[11] [a]

A: fol. xxv^{r-v} cap. 50; **B:** fol. 57^{r-v} cap. 51; **C:** fol. 35^{v} cap. 37; **O:** fols 36^{v}–37^{r}; **V:** fol. xxxiv^{r} cap. 47; Beugnot, p. 79, cap. 50.

---

[a] Above caps 23, 29–31. Below caps 39–46.

---

[1] n'i] ABV: ne [2] il] ABV: l'on [3] A adds: et [4] il] AV: l'on [5] ABV add: come (B: coment) l'on doit (A: deit) faire [6] on le] AB: l'on [7] Et se il . . . faire] V lacks [8] devant] B: avant [9] que on] B: coment l'on [10] soit] A: fors [11] ou au clain . . . jor] A lacks

***[39]** Quant aucun se claime d'autre, et il demande jor et l'a par court, por coy l'un et l'autre doit metre en escrit[1] le clain tel come il a esté.

Qui se claime, et l'autre demande jor et l'a par court, le clamant et le defendant doivent[2] metre en escrit coment et de quey le clain a esté fait, et a quel jor et a quans jors dou quel mois sera le jor de la quinzaine a qu'il[3] sont ajornés[4] par court, et ou il sont ajornés a lor jor garder, et le non de ceaus qui estoient en la cort quant il furent ajornés par court, si que, quans les parties guardent[5] le[6] jor, que le clamant soit bien menbrant coment il se clama, por ce que, se il li covient a clamer au jor que il est ajorné par court, que il ne croisse[7] en son clain ne le change,[8] por ce que le defendant n'ait jor noviau de la croissance ou do changement dou clain. Car se la croissance ou le changement dou clain i est, le fuïant[9] en avra noviau jor, se il le requiert par esgart. Et por ce le doit le clamant faire escrire que il dedens le jor devant plusors homes de la cort, ceaus qu'il[10] tendra plus a amis, lize l'escrit[11] et recorde coment il fist le clain, si que il en soient recordans, et en quel leuc il fu[12] ajornés par court, et a quel jor et[13] le jor,[14] et leur prie que il soient bien[15] recordans se mestier[16] li est, por ce que ce il covient que la cort recorde le clain ou aucune des choses desus dites ou toutes ensenble, qu'ele le sache faire sans riens croistre ne amermer. Et si[17] le recorde ou face tant recorder[18] a ses amis que il le sachent bien, et se il y faillent, si les en avoie.[19] Et tantes fois[20] le fase qu'il soit certain que il savront bien recorder en la cort, quant[21] mestier sera, quel le clain fu. Et le defendant le doit faire[22] enssi escrire, por ce que se le clamant au jor ou aprés fait changement ou croissance au clain que il fera de lui, que il demande noviau jor, et por ce que,

A: fols xxv^{v}–xxvi^{r} cap. 51; **B:** fol. 57^{v} cap. 52; **C:** fols 35^{v}–36^{v} cap. 38; **O:** fol. 37^{r-v}; **V:** fol. xxxiv^{r-v} cap. 48; Beugnot, pp. 79–80, cap. 51.

[1] metre en escrit] B: avoir en recort [2] ABV add: faire [3] qu'il] A: quei il; C: qui; V: quoi il [4] sont ajornés] B: soit nomez [5] guardent] B: garderont [6] le] A: leur; O: lor [7] croisse] A: truisse [8] le change] A: creissance ne changement [9] Car se la . . . fuïant] V: le deffendant [10] qu'il] C: qui [11] l'escrit] A: cel escrit [12] fu] A: furent [13] et] C: est [14] et a quel jor et le jor] A lacks [15] soient bien] C: en soient [16] recordans se mestier] B: remembrant et recordant se besoing [17] si] C: s'il; V: se il [18] ou face tant recorder] C lacks [19] en avoie] V: a envoié [20] tantes fois] A: tant de feis; B: tant; V: a tant de fois [21] quant] C: se [22] faire] V lacks

s'il li covient a respondre au clain que le clamant fera de lui enssi[23] com il autre fois c'est clamés, que il y[24] sache respondre, et por ce que il sache varier le clain que on[25] fait de lui, se le clamant le refait ensi con il autre fois le fist, et s'il[26] le viaut varier, enssi le varie el clain[27] por le plait esloigner, et se l'autre le desdit, si s'en mete el recort de la court qu'il le dist, enssi con il l'a retrait, et enssi porra le plait asés[28] esloigner.

---

[23] enssi] B: autressi [24] y] ABV: li [25] ABV add: a [26] B adds: ne [27] el clain] B lacks [28] asés] V lacks

***[40]** Quant les parties sont ajornees par cort, coment et por coi chascun doit demander au seignor ou il comande que il garde son[1] jor.

Quant l'on c'est clamés d'autre, et celui de qui l'on c'est clamé a jor demandé et l'autre l'a contrebatu et court a esgardé[2] qu'il doit avoir jor et il sont ajorné par cort, l'un et l'autre doivent demander[3] au seignor ou il comande[4] que il gardent lor jor, et se le seignor lor dit: 'Gardés le la ou je serai', chascune des parties doit dire, ou celui a qui le seignor le dira: 'Sire, només moi leuc certain ou je puisse estre au jor que la court m'a doné por mon jor garder si con je doy'. Et se il ne li viaut nomer leuc certain, ou il li nome leuc ou il ne li senble que il[5] puisse estre au jor, si die:[6] 'Sauve vostre grace, je n'entent que je tel ajornement doie acuillir con vos me faites, ne acuillir ne le vueill, se la court ne l'esgarde, et di por coi. Por ce que vos ne me motissés leuc certain ou je soie[7] a mon jor garder, et por ce, sire, que vos serés ou porés estre en tel leuc a cel jor ou je ne porrai aler, ou je ne savrai quel[8] part vos serés, et enssi poree je perdre ma querele par jor gardant, par defaute de ce que je ne[9] savroie ou vos seriés a cel[10] jor, ou que je ne poroie aler la ou vos seriés', et mete son[11] retenaill. Et il ne me senble que le seignor puisse contre ce dire[12] chose par coi la court ne doit esgarder que le seignor li doit nomer[13] leuc certain et tel ou les parties puissent le[14] jor garder.

Et se le seignor lor nome leuc certain ou il gardent lor jor, et tel qu'il y puissent[15] estre, il doivent venir a cel leuc au jor que la court lor avra doné avant que le soulaill soit couché ou au mains ains[16] que les estoiles soient aparans[17] au ciel, et amener chascun d'eaus[18]

A: fol. xxvi^{r-v} cap. 52; **B:** fol. 58^{r-v} cap. 53; **C:** fols 36^{v}–37^{v} cap. 39; **O:** fols 37^{v}–38^{v}; **V:** fols xxxiv^{v}–xxxv^{v} cap. 49; Beugnot, pp. 81–2, cap. 52.

---

[1] garde son] B rubrics (fol. 18^{v}): doient garder leur [2] a esgardé] B: esgarde [3] V adds: jour [4] comande] V: a coumandé [5] ou il ne . . . il] A: qui li semble qu'il n'i; B: ou il li semble qu'il ne [6] AB add: Sire [7] ou je soie] A lacks [8] quel] B: ou en quel; C: que [9] ne] C: n'en [10] cel] A: tel [11] mete son A: de ce me met je en l'esgart de la court sauf mon [12] ne me senble . . . dire] B: me semble que le seignor ne puet contrebatre ne dire contre ceste [13] nomer] B: motir [14] le] B: lor [15] puissent] O: puise [16] ains] V: avant [17] aparans] A: paranz [18] A adds: au meins .ii.; B: au mains deus

de ses amis qu'il[19] soient homes de cort tant con il plus pora.[20] Et le clamant y doit avoir tant con il plus[21] porra[22] de ceaus qui furent la quant la court les ajorna, et, s'il treuve le seignor, il doit faire dire en la presence de .ii. homes de la court et de tant plus con il pora,[23] 'Sire, la court m'ajorna au jor de hui contre tel', et le nome, 'de tel querele', et die la querele,[24] 'de quei je me clamai[25] de lui. Et vos, sire, me coumandastes que je gardasse[26] ci mon jor. Sire, et je i sui venus a hore et a tens garder mon jor et le garde si con je doi et en trai[27] vos et vostre cort a[28] garans.' Et ce face dire .ii. ou .iii. fois ains que les estoilles aperent[29] ou ciel. Et celui de qui l'on c'est clamé doit aussi faire et dire com il est devisé dou clamant, mais que tant qu'il doit dire: 'Sire, je garde mon jor contre tel[30] de tel choze de quei[31] il se clama de moi', et nome le clamant et die de quei il se clama. Et se l'un et l'autre gardent lor jor si con il doivent, si tost con le clamant a dit ce qui est dit desus et le defendant[32] aussi, le clamant doit renoveler son clain en tel maniere com il est aprés dit.[33] [a]

---

[a] Below caps 41–2.

---

[19] qu'il] AB: qui [20] chascun d'eaus de . . . pora] V: au meaus que il poront chascun de yaus de lor amis au plus que il porent mais que il soient homes de cort [21] tant con il plus] V: au mains tant que il [22] Et le clamant . . . porra] C lacks [23] V adds: et dire [24] die la querele] A: la moutisse; V: die laquele [25] je me clamai] B: il se clama [26] gardasse] O: gaitasse [27] en trai] V: entre [28] a] A: qui si estes; B: de; V: en cestes [29] aperent] V: perent [30] V adds: et le nome [31] de quei] B: dont [32] defendant] A: defendeor [33] dit] B: devisé

***[41]** Quant les parties sont ajornees par court et il gardent bien lor jor si con il doivent, coment le clamant doit renoveler son clain.[1]

Quant les parties ont lor jor gardé si com eles[2] doivent, et il sont present en la court au jor que la cort lor a doné, et[3] le clamant viaut renoveler son clain, si die: 'Sire, vos et la court oistes et entendistes .i. jor qui[4] pasés est coment et de coy je me clamai a vos en la cort[5] de tel en sa presence', et le nome, 'et il demanda jor a respondre au clain que je lors fis de lui, et le jor est a hui. Sire, et tout enssi[6] con je me clamai lors de lui, je me clain encore,[7] et en voill avoir droit par vos et par la court.' Et por ce le doit enssi faire le clamant, que se il refait[8] son[9] clain de novel, et il i fait aucune croissance ou il change le[10] clain en aucune chose, l'autre avra noviau jor de la croissance ou dou changement dou clain. Et se il riens[11] n'i croist ne ne change el clain, si pora le defendor[12] dire que il a changé ou creu en son clain et demandera jor de la croissance ou dou change[13] que il li metra sus qu'il avra fait el clain. Et se le clamant dit qu'il n'a creu ne changé el clain, le defendant dira que[14] si a, et motira aucune[15] creissance ou aucun changement qu'il dira que il avra fait en son clain, et se metra el[16] recort de la court. Et sera deleé tant le plait que le recort soit[17] fait. Et enssi porra de plusors chozes dire et plusors fois que il i a creissance ou changement[18] el clain et en avra plusors[19] recors. Mais qui se clamera[20] tout enssi con il autre fois c'est clamés, il n'a ne ne[21] peut aver creissance ne changement[22] en cel clain, por quei on ne peut jor demander ne aveir de creissance ne de changement[23] de[24] clain, ne le fuïant ne le pora dire ne deleer[25] le plait plus que d'un esgart et d'un recort.[26]

A: fol. xxvi^{v} cap. 53; **B:** fol. 58^{v} cap. 54; **C:** fols 37^{v}–38^{r} cap. 40; **O:** fols 38^{v}–39^{r}; **V:** fols xxxv^{v}–xxxvi^{r} cap. 50; Beugnot, pp. 82–3, cap. 53.

---

[1] clain] B: jour [2] eles] ABV: il [3] et] A: se; V: et se [4] qui] C: que [5] en la cort] AV lack; B: et [6] enssi] B: aussi [7] V adds: de lui [8] refait] ABV: fait [9] son] A: autre [10] il change le] AB: il change son; V: changement en [11] riens] V: vient [12] defendor] B: deffendant [13] dou clain. Et . . . change] A lacks [14] il a changé . . . que] B lacks [15] et motira aucune] AV: aucune; B: et metra avant [16] metra el] B: mete ou; V: metra en [17] soit] V: sera [18] creissance ou changement] B: croissement ou change [19] A adds: feis [20] qui se clamera] B: se il se clame; O: qui clamera; V: que il se clamera [21] n'a ne ne] A: n'i a ne; C: n'a ne [22] changement] O: change [23] en cel clain . . . changement] V lacks [24] de] C: del [25] deleer] B: declairier [26] A adds: de court

***[42]** Quant l'on garde le jor que l'on a par court, et le clamant se claime si[1] con il autre fois c'est clamé, coment le fuïant doit respondre.

Se le clamant se claime au jor qu'il est ajorné par court si con il autre fois c'est clamé, le defendeor[2] doit respondre le meaus que il savra au clain qui[3] avra esté de lui[4] autres fois[5] de quei il avra esté ajorné par court a respondre a cel clain a cel jor, se il viaut le plait abregier. Mais se il viaut le plait esloigner, si[6] die: 'Sire, je a son clain ne veuill respondre, se la court ne l'esgarde, se il le clain ne fait ore en ma presence, si que je li sache respondre a son clain, et di por coy: por ce que trop seroit grief chose a faire et estrange[7] de respondre au clain que l'on ne feist maintenant de lui en sa presence, car on poroit faillir a respondre isi con l'on devroit, par ce que l'on ne seroit pas menbrant quel le clain fu que on avroit[8] autre fois[9] fait de lui, que[10] mermoire d'ome est moult escoloriant. Si en poroit l'on perdre sa querele par ce que on ne seroit mie bien menbrant quel le clain fu que on avroit[11] fait autre fois de lui. Et por ce ne veuill je respondre, se la cort ne l'esgarde, au clain que il ore fait[12] de moi, si con il le[13] fist lors, se il ore ne se claime de moi en ma presence, et de ce me[14] met je en l'esgart de la court sauf mon retenaill.'

Et contre ce peut le clamant respondre et dire: 'Sire, il est voir que[15] .i. jor qui passés est je me clamai a vos et a la cort de lui et en sa presence, et la court entendi de coi et coment. Et il demanda jor a respondre a celui clain et l'ot par esgart de court, et le jor est a hui, et je ai hui[16] bien mon jor gardé, si con je doi. Et je me suis de lui clamés[17] en sa presence au jor que la cort me dona tout enssi con je lors m'en[18] clamai, et encor me clain, por quei je entent que il a mon clain doit respondre que je fais de lui, si con je le fis en

A: fols xxvii^{r}–xxviii^{r} cap. 54; **B:** fols 58^{v}–59^{v} cap. 55; **C:** fols 38^{r}–40^{r} cap. 41; **O:** fols 39^{r}–41^{r}; **V:** fols xxxvi^{r}–xxxvii^{v} cap. 51; Beugnot, pp. 83–5, cap. 54.

1 se claime si] A: seit clamés; B: se clama si 2 autre fois . . . defendeor] B: s'est autre foiz le deffendant 3 au clain qui] C: el clain que 4 de lui] A: de lui fait; BV: fait de lui 5 autres fois] V lacks 6 abregier. Mais il . . . si] B: esloignier 7 B adds: response 8 avroit] O: l'avroit 9 autre fois] A lacks 10 l'on ne seroit . . . que] B: la 11 avroit] B: avoit 12 ore fait] A: a fait orres; V: a orés fait 13 si con il le] A: qu'il 14 me] C lacks 15 A adds: par 16 hui] AV lack 17 clamés] C lacks 18 m'en] ABV: me

la court[19] en sa presence quant il ot jor a respondre a cel clain. Ne je ne vueill que il demore por choze que il ait fait dire[20] que il n'i[21] responde, se la cort ne l'esgarde, et di por coi: por ce que je lors me clamai de lui a vos en la court et en sa presence, et que il demanda jor a respondre a cel clain, et que il l'ot par esgart de cort, et que le jor que il ot par esgart de court[22] a respondre a mon clain est hui, et que[23] je hui me sui clamé et encore me clain de lui, si con je lors me[24] clamai, si ne vueill por chose que il die que il demore que il ne me responde a mon clain, se la court ne l'esgarde, et de ce me met je en l'esgart de la court sauf[25] mon retenaill.' Et je ne cuit que le defendant puisse chose dire por quei la court doit esgarder qu'il ne li doit respondre a cel clain que il lors fist de lui, por ce que il demanda jor a respondre au clain que le clamant fist de lui lors et l'ot par court, et que ce est celui que il ot par court a[26] respondre a cel clain. Et puis que le clamant se claime tout enssi com il lors se clama et que ce est celui jor que il ot par court a quei il[27] devoit respondre a celui clain, est il tenus, se me senble, de respondre a celui clain.[28]

Et se la cort fait l'esgart desus dit, le defendeor doit requerre au seignor que il li fase recorder a la court[29] quel le clain fu, por ce que il li[30] sache respondre si con il[31] devra, et le seignor[32] li doit faire faire cel recort. Et quant il avra enssi respondu[33] au clain que la court avra recordé, si con il devra, que contre cel clain ne peut il trover[34] eschanpes ne fuites que il ne responde ou die raison por quei il n'i doit respondre.[35] Et se il fuit disant raison por quei il ne viaut respondre a celui clain, si l'ateigne[36] le requerant en la maniere que il[37] est devant devisé que l'on doit home ataindre qui fuit par la seconde fuite principal de plait. Et se le clamant n'est bien certain que ceaus de la court[38] recorderont[39] son clain si con il le fist,

---

[19] le fis en la court] B: fiz de lui [20] fait dire] C: dite [21] n'i] ABV: ne [22] et que le . . . court] A: et que le jor que il ot; B lacks [23] que] ABV lack [24] me clain de . . . lors me] B: m'en claim si com je lors m'en [25] sauf] V: sans [26] et que ce . . . court a] A: et que ce est celui jor a quoi il deveit; B: a; O: et que ce est de lui qu'il l'ot par court a; V: et que ce est celui jour que il ot par court a qui il li devoit [27] a quei il] AB: et qu'il [28] Et puis que . . . clain] V lacks [29] a la court] A lacks [30] li] ABV lack [31] si con il] A: ce qu'il [32] A adds: qui ne deit faillir [33] avra enssi respondu] A: l'avra eu si respont; O: l'avra fait enssy responde; V: avra heu si responde [34] V adds: nulles [35] n'i doit respondre] AB: ne viaut (B: veut) respondre; V: ne responde [36] l'ateigne] C: l'atarge [37] que il] ABV: qui [38] B ads: ne [39] recorderont] AV: recordent

si le reface[40] de rechief le plus tost que il porra, et se garde de croistre[41] ne de changer aucune[42] choze el clain que son aversaire n'ait noviau jor. Que, se il ne renovele son clain, il i porra[43] avoir damage se la cort n'estoit[44] bien recordant de son clain.

Et qui renovele son clain, se il n'i croist ou[45] change aucune chose, et l'autre die que il a creu el clain,[46] die que non a. Et se il demande jor por dire qu'il i a el clain changement ou croissance sans dire quel le changement ou la croissance est,[47] disant que il viaut que la court, qui oi la premiere clamor et a oie ceste, recorde se il[48] a croissance ou changement en son clain ou c'ele n'i est, et que il de ce requiert le recort de la cort et le viaut avoir, se la court l'esgarde, et mete son retenaill, die le clamant,[49] 'Vos requerés recort de chose descovenable et de[50] tel que vos ne devés avoir recort, quant vos requeres[51] recort de cort[52] de ce que vos dites que je ay creu ou changé[53] mon clain et ne dites de coi. Et[54] trop avroit[55] la court a faire, se il li covenoit retenir et recorder a la requeste dou fuïant toutes les paroles que les avantparliers avroient[56] dites en la court por esclarsir li se il a creissance ou non el clain sans la creissance motir. Ne enssi ne peut l'on ne ne doit jor avoir, ne la cort ne doit faire recort se il a creissance el clain ou non, se celui qui dit qu'ele[57] y est ne dit quel la creissance est. Et por les raisons que je ai dites ou por aucunes d'eles ne vueill je que vos aiés jor, ne que la cort face cest recort, c'ele ne l'esgarde, et de ce me met je en l'esgart de la court sauf mon retenaill.' Et il ne me senble que le fuïant puisse chose dire[58] par quei la court doit faire cel recort que il requiert, se il ne dit quel creissance il a el clain, ne qu'il doie avoir jor por tant con il a dit, mais il a lisir de dire.[59]

---

[40] reface] AV: face [41] croistre] O: conoistre [42] C adds: autre [43] i porra] A: poreit; O: porra; V: poroit [44] n'estoit] A: n'est [45] n'i croist ou] A: n'i creist ou ne; B: i croist ou; V: ne croise ou ne [46] el clain] A: ou changié; V: ou changié au clain [47] i a el . . . est] AB: a creissance (B: croissance) ou changement [48] AV add: y [49] clamant] ABV: requerant [50] de] A: di [51] A adds: a aveir; B: avoir; V: a avoir [52] de court] V lacks [53] ABV add: a [54] Et] ABV: Que [55] avroit] O: avoit [56] avroient] C: avoient [57] qu'ele] A: qu'il [58] chose dire] B: faire chose; C: choses dire [59] mais il a lisir de dire] B lacks

***[43]** Se l'un[1] de ceaus qui est ajorné[2] par court garde[3] son jor si con il doit, et l'autre ne le garde ne contremande si con il doit, que[4] celui qui l'a gardé doit dire et faire.

Quant l'on est ajorné par court et l'on viaut[5] a hore et a tens garder son jor et le garde si con il doit, et l'autre n'i vient[6] ne ne le garde si con il doit ne ne contremande si con il doit, celui qui l'a gardé si con il doit,[7] quant il verra les estoiles aparans au ciel, il les doit mostrer as .ii. ou a[8] plus des homes de la court, et tels que il cuide que il[9] soient ses amis, et aprés venir devant le seignor et dire li: 'Sire, je ai bien mon jor gardé si con je doi jusques as estoiles aparans el ciel. Mandés les veir.' Et le seignor les doit mander veir a sa requeste par .ii. de ces homes ou plus. Et quant il les avront[10] veues, il le doivent dire au seignor et en la court. Et lors celui qui a son jor gardé doit dire au seignor: 'Sire, je me clamai a vos et[11] en la cort .i. jor qui pasés est de tel et de tel[12] chose', et die de qui et de quel.[13] 'Sire,[14] il demanda jor a mon clain, et je le contrebati, et il l'ot par esgart de court. Sire, et je vins a hore et a tens[15] mon jor garder, et l'ai gardé si con je doi jusques[16] as estoiles aparans el ciel.[17] Et ceaus que vos envoiastes veir les estoiles les ont veues et le vos ont dit en la court. Si vos pri et requier que vos me faites conoistre a vostre court se je ai bien mon jor gardé si con je doi.' Et le seignor doit comander a la court qu'ele face[18] cele conoissance, et la court la doit faire et doit conoistre, se croy,[19] que il a bien son jor gardé si con il doit. Et maintenant il doit dire au seignor: 'Sire,[20] vostre court a coneu que je ai mon jor gardé si con je doi, et mon aversaire n'a[21] le sien jor gardé ne contremandé si con il doit. Si vos pri et requier que vos me faites conoistre a vostre court se j'ai vers lui desraigneé par jor gardant ma querele de quei je me cla-

A: fols xxviii^{r}–xxix^{v} cap. 55; **B:** fols 59^{v}–61^{v} cap. 56; **C:** fols 40^{r}–42^{v} cap. 42; **O:** fols 41^{r}–43^{v}; **V:** fols xxxvii^{v}–xl^{r} cap. 52; Beugnot, pp. 85–9, cap. 55.

[1] Se l'un] A: Celui; V: Quant celui [2] est ajorné] B (fol. 18^{v}): sont ajornés; V: sont ajournés [3] B adds: bien [4] que] C: quey [5] viaut] ABV: vient [6] vient] O: viaut [7] celui qui l'a gardé si con il doit] A lacks [8] a] C lacks [9] que il] ABV: qui [10] avront] B: avroit [11] et] ABV lack [12] de tel et de tel] A: de tel de tel; B: de tel et le nomme de tel; V: de cel [13] qui et de quel] AV: quoi et de qui; B: quoi; O: quei et de quoi [14] Sire] A: Sire, et; B: dont; V: et [15] A adds: por; B: a [16] jusques] A: trusque; V: treusques [17] el ciel] BV lack [18] qu'ele face] A: qu'il facent [19] et doit conoistre se croy] B: ce quit [20] Sire] BV lack [21] B adds: mie

mai de lui, de quei[22] nos fumes ajornés par court au jor de hui, puis que je ai mon jor gardé si con je doi et il n'a le sien gardé ne contremandé si con il doit.' Et le seignor doit comander a la cort qu'ele face cele conoissance, et la cort la doit faire et doit, se cuit, conoistre[23] que il a la querele desraignee,[24] se son aversaire n'a son jor gardé ne contremandé[25] si con il doit. Et coment l'on doit jor garder et coment[26] contremander est devisé[27] en cest livre.

Et a mei senble que se celui, qui est ajorné par court, peut mostrer si con il doit que il mut[28] a hore et a tens por venir[29] son jor garder, et que il ot el chemin[30] essoigne tel qu'il ne pot venir a hore et a tens[31] son jor garder,[32] et qu'il de la[33] ou il fu esoigné contremanda son jor a hore et a tens[34] si con il dut, et que ceaus par qui il contremandoit son jor orent essoigné por quei il n'i[35] porent venir a hore et a tens en la court[36] dire c'esoigne et faire ce que il lor avoit enchargé[37] de dire et faire a son jor contremander, que[38] celui qui n'a son jor gardé ne contremandé a hore et a tens por essoigne que il ou ceaus par qui il le contremandoit ont eu, que il n'a pas sa querele perdue par jor gardant. Et doit venir le plus tost que il porra en la court et doit ces choses faire assaveir[39] au seignor et a la court et ofrir a mostrer, si con la court esgardera ou conoistra que il les doive mostrer. Et la court doit esgarder ou mostrer, se me senble, que il les doit mostrer[40] si con il est devisé[41] en cest livre que l'on doit tel chose mostrer.

Et maintenant que l'avant[42] dite conoissance est faite et retraite, se c'est celui qui se clama, il[43] doit requere au seignor que il[44] fase avoir et delivrer ce de quei[45] il se clama et que il a[46] gaaigné par jor gardant. Et le seignor le li doit faire delivrer le plus tost que il porra et sans delay. Et se le seignor met ou fait metre le clamant

---

[22] de quei] B: dont [23] doit, se cuit, conoistre] B: dire, ce cuit; V: doit, je cuit, counoistre [24] desraignee] V: guaaignee [25] n'a son jor . . . contremandé] O: ne son son jor garde ne contremande [26] coment] ABV lack [27] devisé] B: escrit [28] mut] B: vint [29] por venir] A: por; BV lack [30] ot el chemin] V: a heu au chemin aucune [31] A adds: venir; C: por venir [32] que il ot . . . garder] C repeats (but lacking 'por venir' as previous note) [33] ot el chemin . . . de la] B: dou leuc [34] a hore et a tens] A lacks [35] n'i] ABV: ne [36] en la court] B lacks [37] enchargé] V: chargié [38] Que] C: Et que [39] venir le plus . . . assaveir] A: ces choses faire assaveir le plus tost qu'il peut; B: venir le plus tost qu'il puet au seignor en la court et dire ces choses [40] les doive mostrer . . . mostrer] AV: mostrer le dee (V: doie); B: le doit mostrer [41] devisé] A: escrit [42] l'avant] B: la devant [43] se c'est celui . . . il] AV: celui qui se clama [44] ABV add: li [45] de quei] B: dont [46] a] ABV: l'a

en la[47] saisine de ce dont il se sera clamé, et le defendant peut mostrer c'essoigne ou cele de ceaus par qui il contremandoit son jor, si con la court esgardera ou conoistra que il mostrer la doive, le seignor le redoit metre[48] ou faire metre en tel saisine et en tel teneure con il estoit devant de ce de quei il avra[49] mis ou fait metre le clamant en saisine et en teneure con de ce que il l'a desraigneé par jor gardant, por ce que il ne l'avra pas desraigneé par jor gardant, puis que l'autre avra s'esoigne mostree si con il[50] est avant[51] dit.

Et se[52] le seignor ne viaut faire faire les dites conoissances a celui qui les[53] requiert ou aucunes d'eles, celui a qui il ne les[54] vodra faire faire li die, 'Sire, je[55] vos ai requis que vos comandisiés a la cort qu'ele feist la conoissance que je vos avoie requise que vos me feisiés faire, et vos ne l'avés faite. Et j'entent que vos ne devés faillir d'esgart ne de conoissance de court a qui qui le[56] vos requiert en court. Si me devés faire faire la conoissance que je vos requier puis que je la vos ai requis[57] en la court con celui qui en estes tenus par les us ou les costumes ou les[58] assises dou reiaume de Jerusalem que vos avés juré a tenir et a faire tenir[59] en cest roiaume. Si vos requier que vos me faites faire la dite conoissance que je vos ai requise. Que vos qui estes seignor et justise[60] et droiturier, se Deu plaist, ne devés voloir[61] que je ne autre perdiens[62] nostre raison en vostre cort ne ne seons deleé d'avoir la par defaut d'avoir esgart ou conoissance de court. Et por toutes les raisons que je ai dites ou por aucunes d'eles, veuill je que vos la dite conoissance me faites[63] faire, se la court l'esgarde, et de ce me met je en l'esgart de la court sauf mon retenaill.' Et le seignor li doit faire faire[64] la dite conoissance, ou se doit metre vers lui en esgart de court de ce qu'il li requiert esgart, disant raison por quei il ne le doit faire et tel que court esgarde[65] ou conoisse qu'il ne li doit faire. Que[66] autrement seignor ne doit faillir d'esgart ne de conoissance de cort a home ne a feme qui la requiert en la cort. Et se le seignor se met de ce en esgart[67] de la cort, il ne me senble qu'il puisse chose dire par coi la cort doit

[47] la] ABV lack [48] redoit metre] B: doit metre; V: doit remetre [49] avra] V: avroit [50] il] ABV lack [51] avant] AO: devant [52] se] B lacks [53] les] ABV: li [54] les] BV: la [55] je] O lacks [56] qui qui le] B: qui que la [57] ai requis] C: requier [58] les] ABV lack [59] et a faire tenir] B: et a faire toz jors; C lacks [60] justise] B: justisier; O: juste [61] se Deu plaist, ne devés voloir] ABV: et qui ne devés voloir (A: voleir) se (V: si) Dieu (B: Deu) plaist [62] perdiens] B: perdons; V: perdisiens [63] faites] A: fassiés; B faciés [64] faire faire] AOV: faire [65] esgarde] O: l'esgarde [66] Que] C lacks [67] esgart] ABO: l'esgart

esgarder que le seignor ne doit comander a la cort qu'ele face[68] la dite conoissance. Mais la court doit esgarder que le seignor doit comander a la court qu'ele face la dite conoissance.[69] La cort doit conoistre, se cuit, que celui qui a son jor gardé si con il doit a sa querele desraigneé, se son aversaire n'a son jor gardé[70] ne contremandé si con il doit, et por ce doit la court en ce[71] cas metre le 'si' si[72] con est devant devisé. Que s'ele faisoit la conoissance tout outre sans metre y[73] le 'sy' devant,[74] celui qui avroit esté essoigné el chemin et qui avroit s'esoigne contremandee a hore et a tens, si con il devroit, dou chemin ou de son hostel, et que[75] ceaus par qui[76] il la contremandoit[77] orent tel essoigne el chemin par quei il[78] ne porent venir a court[79] a hore ne a tens s'esoigne dire et faire ce que il devroit,[80] et que il eust tout ce prové, si con cort esgarderoit ou conoistroit que il le deust faire, avroit il encore a tot ce[81] perdue sa querele. Que essoigne ne autre ne li vaudroit se la cort faisoit[82] la conoissance sans le 'sy', et ce seroit desraison et tort apert, se me senble. Que par esoigne ne doit l'on mie perdre sa querele par jor gardant, se il l'a contremandé si con est avant[83] dit ou en[84] fait son leau pooir en la maniere devant[85] devisee. Si doit bien faire la court[86] la dite conoissance en la maniere devant[87] dite[88] selon droit et raison, se me senble. Que autrement ne seroit la dite essoine[89] valable.

Et maintenant que ceste conoissance sera faite, se celui qui a son jor gardé est requerant, il doit requerre au seignor que il cele querele que il a desraignee[90] li face delivrer, et le seignor li doit faire sans delai. Et se celui qui a son jor gardé est defendant, il doit les conoissances[91] requerre en la maniere desus[92] devisee, et aprés ce qu'il les avra eues[93] le plus tost que il trovera la cort bien esforcee, il doit faire[94] recorder les dites conoissances en la cort pleniere a ceaus qui furent la ou eles furent retraites[95] devant le seignor, por ce que se

---

[68] qu'ele face] AB: de faire [69] Mais la court . . . conoissance] ABV lack [70] A adds: si come il deit [71] ce] ABV: cest [72] 'si' si] C: si; V: ensi [73] tout outre sans metre y] A: sanz metre [74] ABV add: dit [75] que] C: ques [76] qui] O: quei [77] contremandoit] B: comanderoit [78] par quei il] B: qu'il [79] a court] A lacks [80] devroit] A: deveent; B: devoient; V: dovroient [81] encore a tot ce] AB: a tort; V: a tout ce [82] essoigne ne autre . . . faisoit] AB: le seignor ne autre ne li vodreit fausser (B: voudroit fauser); V: s'essoigne ne autre ne li vaudroit faissant [83] avant] BV: devant [84] en] C: eust [85] devant] A: avant [86] la court] AV lack [87] devant] A: avant [88] dite] V: devisé [89] essoine] V: counoissance [90] AB add: par jor gardant [91] les conoissances] ABV: la conoissance [92] desus] AB: devant [93] les avra eues] AB: l'avra eue [94] ce qu'il les . . . faire] V lacks [95] retraites] AB: recordees

celui contre qui il avra sa querele desraignee par jor gardant ou aucun autre requiert a lui ou a son heir ou a autre por lui cele meisme querele,[96] que il puisse bien prover[97] par recort de court quant mestier li sera que cele querele a esté desrainee par jor gardant, por quei il en[98] est quite et delivre, et n'en est tenus aprés de respondre a aucune persone quel qu'ele soit. Mais se le clamant ot essoine el chemin et a[99] ceaus par qui il contremandoit s'esoigne et il le peut mostrer si con il est avant[100] dit, le defendant[101] n'avra pas[102] sa querele desraineé[103] vers lui por les raisons avant dites, ains seront en tel point l'un vers l'autre[104] de cele querele com il estoient[105] ains[106] que le clamant se clamast de lui.

[96] requiert a . . . querele] A: por lui requist celle carelle a lui ou a son heir [97] prover] A: mostrer [98] en] ABV lack [99] et a] ABV: ou [100] avant] AV: devant [101] deffendant] A: defendeor [102] pas] B: mie [103] desraineé] A: desrainieé ne gaaignieé; B: gaaignié ne desraisnié [104] l'un vers l'autre] AB lacks [105] estoient] C: estoit [106] ains] AB: avant

***[44]** Quant l'on viaut[1] garder son jor el leuc ou[2] l'on est[3] ajorné par court, et l'on ne[4] treve le seignor ne home que il ait establi en son leuc, quey[5] l'on doit dire et faire.

Quant celui qui est ajorné par court venra[6] el leuc ou il est ajorné a son jor garder, se il ne treuve le seignor ou home que il ait establi en son leuc devant qui il doie son jor garder, si face et die en la presence de tant des homes dou seignor con il porra, et qu'il en[7] ait .ii. au mains,[8] ce qui est devant[9] devisé que il die et face au seignor en la court quant il vient[10] son jor garder et le garde, mais que de requere[11] esgart ne conoissance de cort. Et puis lor mostre les esteles, et lor prie et requier que il[12] soient recordant de ce que il ont[13] veu et oy si que il le recordent en la court[14] quant mestier li sera. Et aprés ce, au plus tost que il porra trover le seignor en court, si li die que il a son jor gardé si con il doit[15] vers tel de tel querele et le nome et motisse la querele. Et se son aversaire ne l'a gardé ne s'esoigne contremandee[16] si con il doit, si die au seignor que il a sa querele desrainee par jor gardant, si li prie et requiert que il la[17] li face delivrer se de quei il se clama de son aversaire. Et quant il a ce dit, se le seignor[18] viaut estre sertefié[19] que il ait son jor gardé si com il dit,[20] il l'en doit faire sertain par le recort des homes de la court[21] qui furent la ou[22] il garda son jor. Et se son aversaire est en la cort et dit que il n'a pas son jor gardé si con il doit, il le doit prover vers lui[23] par le recort des avant[24] dis homes de la court. Et qui viaut de ce qui est avant dit faire sertain le seignor ou prover le vers son aversaire, il le doit ensi faire: que il doit dire au seignor, quant il viaut estre sertefié de son dit ou quant son aversaire desdit[25] que il n'a son jor gardé,[26] si die: 'Sire, tel et

A: fols xxix^{v}–xxxi^{v} cap. 56; **B:** fols 61^{v}–63^{r} cap. 57; **C:** fols 42^{v}–45^{r} cap. 43; **O:** fols 43^{v}–46^{r}; **V:** fols xl^{r}–xlii^{v} cap. 53; Beugnot, pp. 89–93, cap. 56.

[1] viaut] A rubric (fol. 2^{r}) V: vient [2] el leuc ou] B: en leu que [3] est] C: c'est [4] ne] B: n'i [5] quey] ABV: que [6] venra] AB: vient; O: vera [7] BO add: i [8] et qu'il en . . . mains] V: avoir ou qu'il en y ait .ii. au mains et face [9] devant] AB: avant [10] vient] C: viaut; V: vient en la court [11] de requere] A: qu'il requiert; B: de ce requerre [12] V adds: en [13] ont] B: a [14] en la court] V lacks [15] si con il doit] A lacks [16] l'a gardé ne s'esoigne contremandee] A: l'a gardé ne contremandé; B: le garde ou contremande [17] la] ABV lack [18] V adds: en [19] sertefié] B: certain [20] dit] A: deit; BV: doit [21] de la court] B lacks [22] ou] A: quant [23] vers lui] B lacks [24] le recort des avant] A: les avanz; B: les avant [25] desdit] B: dit [26] B adds: ne contremandé

tel de vos homes', et les nome,[27] 'furent la ou je gardai mon jor, et aucuns autres de quei il ore ne me sovient. Si vos pri et requier com a mon seignor que vos comandés a ceaus que je ai només et a vos autres homes que il recordent ce que il virent et oirent[28] que je dis et fis a mon jor garder.' Et se il sont present en la cort, le seignor lor doit comander[29] que il recordent ce que il[30] virent et oirent. Et se ceaus qui ont esté[31] només ne sont en la cort, le seignor les[32] doit faire venir, et quant il i seront,[33] il doit comander a iaus[34] et a tos ses autres homes que il recordent ce que il sevent de cel fait. Et lors tos les homes de la court doivent estre[35] ensenble et seoir et recorder se que il sevent de cel fait.[36] Et se il i a en la cort .ii. homes ou plus qui soient recordans que celui qui a son jor gardé venist la ou il fu[37] ajorné a son jor garder, ains que les estoiles furent[38] aparans el ciel, et dist en leur presence que il estoit venus garder son jor contre tel de tel querele, et le noma et dist la querele,[39] et que aprés ce il demora la tant que les estoiles furent aparans au ciel, et que il lor mostra et puis lor dist: 'Je vos tray a garans coment[40] je ai mon jor gardé, et vos pri et requier que vos en soiés recordans si que vos le puissiés recorder en la cort[41] quant mestier me sera', il me senble qu'il a bien fait le seignor certain et prové vers son aversaire que il a bien[42] son jor gardé si con il doit.[43] Et que se[44] son aversaire n'a le jor enssi[45] gardé ou contremandé s'esoigne a hore et a tens si con il doit, que[46] celui qui a son jor gardé, si con est avant[47] devisé, a sa querele desrainee par jor gardant vers celui qui n'a son jor gardé ne s'esoigne contremandee si con il doit.

Qu'en cest cas est le recort des homes de la cort ausi valable et doit estre ausi tenu et maintenu ferm et estable, con le recort des homes de la cort fait ou dit en la presence dou seignor et de ces homes. Qu'en cest cas et en aucuns autres, qui sont aprés devisés[48] en cest livre, font les homes de la cort a croire[49] tout n'i soit le

[27] et les nome] A lacks [28] que il virent et oirent A: qu'il oyrent et qu'il virent [29] comander] C: mander [30] C adds: en [31] qui ont esté] V: que il a [32] OV add: y [33] i seront] A: seront venus; B: seront venu [34] iaus] A: ciaus; BV: ceaus [35] estre] C: entrer [36] Et lors tos . . . fait] B lacks [37] fu] C: fust [38] furent] A: fucent; BV: fussent [39] et le noma . . . querele] B lacks [40] coment] B: come; V que [41] en la cort] A lacks [42] fait le seignor . . . bien] V lacks [43] a bien son . . . doit] A: aveit bien son jor gardé si come il deveit; B: avoit son jor bien gardé si com il devoit [44] que se] BV: que; C: se [45] le jor enssi] AB: ensi son jor; V: le sien jour [46] V adds: se [47] avant] V: devant [48] devisés] V lacks [49] font les homes . . . croire] A: sont et deit l'on les homes de la court creire; B: doivent les homes de la court estre creus; V: et doit l'en les homes de la court croire

seignor. Et les choses que les homes de cort font sans le seignor sont tenues et maintenues con chose faite[50] en court en quey le seignor et ces homes[51] sont[52] ensenble. Quar s'ensi n'estoit, a enuis porroit l'on plait ataindre ne querele desraigner par jor gardant. Que sovent avient et est avenu que les seignors ne sont[53] mie es leus ou les gens sont ajornés a lor jor garder a celui jor a quei il sont ajornés,[54] et que por ce ne doit demorer que les parties ne gardent lor jor[55] ou eles sont ajornees et si con eles doivent[56] garder, et que se l'un le garde, si con il doit, et l'autre ne le garde ne contremande,[57] si con il doit, que celui qui l'a gardé,[58] si con est avant[59] dit, a sa querele desrainee par jor gardant vers celui qui ne le garde ne contremande[60] si con il doit. Et s'aucun dit que recort de court ne peut ne ne doit estre en cel[61] cas, por ce que court n'est ne estre ne peut[62] se le seignor et .iii.[63] de ces homes ne sont[64] o lui, je dis que si doit, et que en cest cas et en aucuns[65] autres qui aprés seront[66] devisees en cest livre doit le seignor[67] comander a ses homes que il recordent se que il sevent[68] de cel fait, et que les homes de court pevent[69] et doivent recorder come court se que il en[70] ont veu et oy,[71] et que ce que il en[72] recorderont doit estre tenu et maintenu ferm et estable aussi con ce que la court recorde qui a esté fait[73] devant le seignor et plusors de ces homes, et qu'en cel cas doit estre ce que les homes[74] de la court[75] en[76] ont veu et oi et[77] mené con recort de cort.

Que con garantie ne doit il mie estre mené,[78] por ce que le seignor ne peut ne ne[79] doit par nos usages[80] destraindre garans de porter

[50] con chose faite] B: come les choses faites; C: en chose faire [51] et ces homes] C lacks [52] sont] A: seient; B: soient [53] les seignors ne sont] AB: le seignor n'est [54] a celui jor . . . ajornés] B lacks [55] ABV add: la [56] doivent] B: devront [57] le garde ne contremande] V: l'a gardé ne contremandé [58] l'a gardé] AB: le gardera [59] avant] AB: devant [60] le garde ne contremande] ABV: l'a gardé ne contremandé [61] cel] AV: tel; B: cest [62] n'est ne estre ne peut] A: n'en est ni ne peut ni ne deit estre [63] .iii.] AV: .ii. [64] ne sont] A: ou plus ne sont; B: ou plus; V: et plus ne sont [65] et que en . . . aucuns] A: et ce cest cas avient ou aucuns; B: et quant cest case ou aucuns; V: quant a cest cas et a [66] seront] B: sont [67] doit le seignor] B: avienent, le seignor doit; V: Et doit le seignor [68] sevent] B: savront [69] de court pevent] B: s'en doivent pener [70] en] ABV lack [71] ont veu et oy] AB: oyrent (B: oirent) et virent [72] en] ABV lack [73] ce que la . . . fait] A: la cort recordereit ce qui avreit esté fait; B: ce que la cort regarderoit; V: ce que la court recorde quant il a esté fait [74] Et qu'en cel cas doit estre ce que les homes (= O)] A: Et quant en cest cas deit estre ce que les homes; B: et que cest cas que les homes; C lacks; V: Et quant tel cas doit estre, se les homes [75] de la court] B lacks [76] en] BO lack [77] et] A lacks; B: doit estre [78] Que con garantie . . . mené] B: et non pas que il doit estre mené come garantie de court [79] ne ne] A: ni ne; C: ne [80] par nos usages] A: par usage; B lacks

garantie. Et puis que il ne les en[81] peut destraindre, il ne lor[82] doit comander. Que le seignor ne doit comander a sa cort n'a son home chose que il ne li soit[83] tenus de faire ou qu'il li puisse refuser sans mesfaire,[84] et que se il la li refuse[85] que il ne l'en puisse destraindre ne a autre chose mener par raison, et por tant plus ne[86] doit ce mie estre mené con garantie. Qu'en[87] garantie a sairement, et que on peut le garant rebuter et torner[88] par gage de bataille, se la querele est dou vaillant[89] d'un marc d'argent ou de plus. Et garantie d'omes de court d'un home a autre n'est neent plus valable que d'autres gens qui ne sont de cort, por ce que on les[90] peut ausi bien geter et torner de garantie con autres gens, ce que on ne peut mie[91] de ce que il recordent en la court par le comandement dou seignor. Que par la foi de quei il sont tenus au seignor qui lor comande[92] ce que il ont veu et oy de ce de quei l'on se met en lor recort; par la leiauté dont il sont tenus de jugier,[93] conoistre et recorder[94] leiaument en la court ce que il ont veu et oy selonc ce que les cas escheent,[95] lor est doné foi tel que[96] nul ne peut faucer esgart ne conoissance ne recort[97] que homes de court facent aprés ce que le seignor lor a comandé a faire l'esgart ou la conoissance ou le recort qui ne viaut toute la cort faucer. Mais il i a bien maniere[98] coment l'on poroit aucun des homes de la cort[99] faucer d'esgart ou de conoissance de court que il avroit fait se il ne s'en[100] savroit garder. Et coment l'on le porroit faire a qui ne s'en set[101] garder ou ne viaut garder sera aprés devisé en cest livre, et coment l'on se peut et doit garder qui garder s'en viaut. Et por les raisons avant[102] dites et por plusors[103] autres, que l'on porroit dire que trop seroient longues a metre en escrit[104] en cest livre, me senble il que tel[105] cas doit estre mené[106] con recort de court et non pas con garantie.

Et quant[107] le recort[108] des homes de la court sera fait et retrait, si con est avant dit, se[109] l'aversaire de celui qui a son jor gardé, si

---

[81] en] ABV lack [82] lor] V: les peut ne ne [83] soit] V: sont [84] mesfaire] AB: mesfait [85] la li refuse] B: li a refusé; V: li refuse [86] C adds: le [87] Qu'en] ABV: Car en [88] on peut le . . . torner] B: l'on ne puet le garant rebuster et retorner [89] dou vaillant] ABV lack [90] que on les] B: com le; V: hom le [91] B adds: faire [92] qui lor comande] AB: il lor comande a recorder; V: qui lor coumande de recorder [93] ABV add: et [94] recorder] B: retreire [95] les cas escheent] V: le cas eschiet. Et [96] tel que] B: Ne [97] AB add: de court [98] Mais il i a bien maniere] B: se l'on n'a bien oi [99] de la court] V lacks [100] se il ne s'en] A: qui ne se; B: qui ne s'en; V: qu'il ne [101] set] B: seust; C: savroit [102] avant] V: devant (and elsewhere in this section) [103] plusors] B lacks [104] en escrit] BV lack [105] tel] AB: cest [106] mené] B lacks [107] quant] C: que [108] A adds: de court [109] se] C: sire

con est avant dit, n'a le sien jor gardé si con il doit, si requiere au seignor la conoissance ou l'esgart en la maniere desus[110] devisee. Et se le seignor ou son aversaire defent par esgart de court que il ne li doit cel esgart ou cele conoissance faire avoir, ou dit que il n'a pas son jor gardé ne la querele desrainee par jor gardant, et die tel raison que court l'esgarde ou conoisse, si recomence son clain de rechief le requerant[111] en la maniere desus devisee.[112]

[110] desus] B: devant [111] le requerant] A lacks [112] le requerant en . . . devisee] B lacks

***[45]** Quans gens sont ajornés par court et il gardent lor jor si com il doivent, et il n'i treuvent[1] home devant qui le defendant soit tenus de respondre, et le clamant se clame a .i. autre jor[2] aprés tout ensi con il autre fois c'est clamé, quey[3] le fuïant[4] doit respondre.[5] [a]

Se .ii. homes ou femes sont ajornés par court en leuc moti, et chascun d'eaus i vient a hore et a tens garder son jor et le garde bien si con il doit[6] en dit et en fait, et il n'i treuvent la ou il sont ajornés a lor jor garder le seignor ne home qui soit en son leuc devant qui[7] le fuïant soit tenus de respondre de cele querele, et il enssi se partent[8] sans plus[9] faire, et aprés aucun jor le clamant treuve le fuïant en la cort devant le seignor, et il se claime de lui enssi con il autre fois c'est clamé sans creissance faire el clain ne changement aucun, celui de qui il se clama doit demander jor au clain. Et se il le demande si con il doit, il l'avra,[10] se croi, de quinzaine par esgart de court. Et qui de tel cas viaut demander jor et avoir,[11] il le doit demander enssi que il doit dire quant le clamant se claime de lui:[12] 'Je voill avoir jor a cest clain et di por coi: por ce que je a cest jor de hui de cestui clain, ne sui je[13] ajorné par court, por quei le jor je vueill avoir, se la cort l'esgarde', et mete son retenaill. Et a ce[14] peut le clamant dire que il ne viaut qu'il ait jor, por ce que il autre fois c'est de lui clamés et en court de cest clain, et que l'on n'en a ne[15] ne doit avoir jor que a noviau clain se il n'a[16] creissance ou changement el clain ou que se soit[17] clain de quei assise tot le jor, et que cestui n'est pas noviau clain ne creissance ne changement n'i

---

A: fols xxxi^{v}–xxxii^{r} cap. 57; **B:** fol. 63^{r-v} cap. 58; **C:** fols 45^{r}–46^{r} cap. 44; **O:** fols 46^{v}–47^{r}; **V:** fols xlii^{v}–xliii^{v} cap. 54; Beugnot, pp. 93–4, cap. 57.

---

[a] From here until cap. 92 B lacks the rubrics in the text, although they are present in the table of rubrics (fols 18^{v}–20^{v}).

---

[1] treuvent] C: treuve [2] jor] C lacks [3] autre fois c'est clamé, quey] B (fol. 18^{v}): s'est clamés a autre, quel chose [4] quey le fuïant] V: que le clamant [5] doit respondre] A: peut respondre et deit [6] garde bien si con il doit] A: gardent bien si come il deivent [7] qui] C: que [8] se partent] V: s'em partoit [9] A adds: dire et [10] l'avra] AV: avra [11] V adds: le [12] de lui] B lacks [13] je a cest jor . . . je] A: je ai cest jor de hui de cestui claim ne fu; B: a cest jor de hui de cestui claim ne sui je mie; V: a cestui jour d'uy de cestui clain ne fu [14] V adds: ne [15] n'en a ne] B lacks [16] n'a] AB: n'i a [17] que se soit] A: ce ce n'est; B: se ce est; V: se soit

a, n'i n'est tel[18] de quei assise toille le jor, et que[19] autre fois c'est de lui clamé en court et encor s'en claime tout enssi[20] con il lors se clama, por quei il ne viaut que il le jor ait, se cort ne l'esgarde, et mete[21] son retenaill. Die[22] le respondant: 'Se vos autre fois vos clamastes de moi en court, je demanday jor et l'os par court et gardai mon jor si com je dui et fis quanque je dui a mon jor garder, et me delivrai de vostre[23] clain quant a celui jor. Ne[24] vos a celui jor ne vos clamastes de moi, ne la court ne m'ajorna de celui clain[25] a aucun[26] jor moti. Por quei j'entens[27] que je de celui[28] clain sui quite et delivre, quant a ce qui a celui jor fu fait, et que se vos or vos clamés de moi, si con vos lor vos clamastes, por tant ne doit demorer que je n'aie jor a cest clain, que[29] cestui clain est novel, por ce que ce[30] qui lors fu fait ne vaut ne ne doit valoir a ce que je soie tenus de[31] respondre a vostre clain sans jor avoir. Si voill le jor avoir por toutes les raisons que je ai dites ou por aucunes d'eles, se la court l'esgarde', et mete[32] s'en[33] en l'esgart de la cort sauf[34] son retenaill. Et a moi senble que le requerant ne porra chose dire par quei la cort ne doit[35] esgarder[36] que le fuïant[37] doit avoir[38] jor a cel clain de quinzaine con de noviau clain[39] por les raisons avant[40] dites.

[18] tel] A: clain [19] cestui n'est pas . . . que] B lacks [20] tout enssi] AB lack; V: si [21] mete] V: metre [22] Die] A: Die lors; B: Lors die [23] vostre] B: mon [24] a celui jor, ne] V lacks [25] clain] A: jor [26] aucun] AB: autre [27] j'entens] C: je n'entens [28] celui] O: lui [29] que] ABV: car [30] ce] ABV: celui [31] soie tenus de] A: dee; BV: doie [32] mete] V: metre [33] s'en] A: sei; C: se [34] s'en en l'esgart de la cort sauf] B lacks [35] ne doit] A: deie; B: doie; V: doive [36] A adds: que por chose qu'il ait ditte [37] V adds (interlined): ne [38] doit avoir] AB: n'ait [39] de quinzaine con de noviau clain] B lacks [40] avant] V: devant

***[46]** Quant gens sont ajornés par court et il gardent[1] lor jor si con il doivent et le seignor[2] ne peut ou[3] ne viaut cel jor entendre a oir[4] le[5] plait, quei il[6] lor doit dire, et quei il li[7] doivent respondre.

Quant gens sont ajornés par court et il gardent bien lor jor si con il doivent, et le seignor n'a leisir d'entendre a oir cel jor le[8] plait qui est entre iaus,[9] il lor doit dire et comander que il soient a tel jor devant lui en la court en tel leuc et en tel point con il sont lors,[10] et lor doit dire le jor et motir[11] lor le[12] leuc et dire a chascun que il l'otroie. Et se il l'otroient, il sont tenus d'estre y, et qui n'i sera[13] il perdra sa querele. Et s'il i vienent, il seront en tel point con il sont a[14] celui jor. Et qui ne l'otroiera se il n'i vient il n'i perdra pas sa querele. Et se le clamant n'i[15] vient a celui jor, et il aprés .i. autre jor treuve en la court celui de qui il se clama, et il se claime de lui de cel clain, le fuïant avra jor[16] se il le requiert si con[17] est devisé en cest[18] livre que on doit jor requerre a clain que on fait de lui de quei assise ne tot le jor des qu'il[19] n'a respondu en cort, ne que[20] il n'est ajorné par court de respondre a cel clain. Que comandement que seignor face[21] a son home ne a autre que il soit a jor moti devant lui faire[22] droit a celui qui de lui se claime[23] ne tot[24] querele. Mais se il le comande es parties en la maniere desus[25] dite,[26] et celui de qui l'on c'est clamé n'otroie[27] de venir en tel[28] point[29] con il est et il n'i vient, il se[30] sera ataint et puni[31] com home qui[32] defaut de venir faire droit a home qui se claime de lui. Et quel paine il en

A: fol. xxxii^{r-v} cap. 58; **B:** fols 63^{v}–64^{r} cap. 59; **C:** fol. 46^{r-v} cap. 45; **O:** fols 47^{r}–48^{r}; **V:** fols xliii^{v}–xliv^{r} cap. 55; Beugnot, pp. 94–5, cap. 58.

[1] B (fol. 18^{v}) adds: bien [2] V adds: ou celui qui est en son leuc [3] ne peut ou] AV lack [4] a oir] O: avoir [5] cel jor entendre a oir le] B: faire entendre leur [6] quei il] A: qu'il; B: que il; V: qui [7] quei il li] A: que il; B: qu'il li; V: qui li [8] d'entendre a . . . le] AB: d'entendre celui (B: a ce) jor le; V: celui jour d'entendre y au [9] B adds: en cel jor [10] lors] B: ores [11] motir] B: nomer [12] le] C lacks [13] n'i sera] AV: ne sera; B: ne sera la [14] sont a] V: seroient en [15] n'i] B lacks [16] A adds: de cel claim [17] ABO add: il [18] cest] C: ce [19] des qu'il] A: de quei il; B: et de quoi il; V: de que il [20] que] A: de quei; B: de quoi [21] AV add: en court [22] faire] A: fornir [23] a celui qui . . . claime] A lacks [24] ne tot] B: li toille [25] desus] A: avant [26] dite] B: devisee [27] l'on c'est clamé n'otroie] A: il est clamés otree [28] tel] C: cel [29] en tel point] AB: faire dreit (B: droit) a celui qui se clama de lui en tel maniere (B: point) [30] se] ABV lack [31] puni] ABV: prové [32] C adds: de

doit soufrir est devisé autre part en cest livre, por quei il n'est[33] mestier que je ci le redie.[34]

Mais se la court ajorne les parties a jor nomé qu'eles soient en tel point com eles sont lors, il ne pevent contredire ne refuser l'ajornement[35] que la cort lor fait, ains covient que il soient en la cort au jor qu'eles les ajornent,[36] et que il se gardent ou contremandent[37] cel jor a quei la court les avra ajornés enssi, aussi con le jor que il avront[38] eu par court au noviau clain. Et qui ne le fera,[39] il perdra sa querele ausi[40] con par jor gardant.

---

[33] n'est] C: n'en est [34] redie] ABV: die [35] l'ajornement] B: le jor nomé [36] qu'eles les ajornent] A: que la court les a ajornés; B: que la court lor a doné; O: qu'ele les ajorne; V: que elle les ajourne [37] contremandent] C: contremande [38] avront] B: ont; O: avroit [39] AB add: ensi [40] ausi] AB lack

***[47]** Qui est ajorné par court et il viaut son jor contremander, coment il le doit contremander et par quans et par ques homes.

Qui viaut jor qui li est doné par court contremander si con il doit, si le doit contremander par .ii. homes de la loi de Rome qui ne soient de ceaus qui n'ont vois ne respons en court, et que il soient a tens et a hore au jor que la court li avra doné au leuc ou celui qui les envoie est ajorné por son jor garder. Et ceaus doivent[1] dire ou faire dire au seignor ou a celui qui sera en son leuc en la presence[2] de partie de sa cort ains que les estoiles soient aparans el ciel,[3] 'Sire, tel home qui fu ajorné par vostre court au jor de hui contre tel et[4] de tel querele', et nomer[5] les .ii., le clamant et le defendant, et motissent[6] la querele, 'vos fait par nos assaveir que il est essoiné[7] si que il ne peut hui venir a cort por son jor garder contre tel et de tel querele', et noment qui[8] et de coy, 'et por ce a il son jor contremandé[9] par nos, et nos por lui, sire,[10] faisons assaveir a vos[11] et a la court s'esoine. Et se vos, sire, ou la court qui ajorné l'a,[12] mescreés qu'il ne soit essoinés si con nos disons,[13] nos somes prest de faire en ce que la court esgardera que[14] faire doions.'[15] Et lors le seignor doit comander a la court qu'ele conoisse que ceaus qui sont venus[16] dire l'essoine de celui qui a son jor contremandé en doivent faire, et la court doit conoistre,[17] se me senble, qu'il doivent jurer sur sains que tel, et le noment,[18] qui les a enveés la est essoinés si que il ne puet venir garder son jor, et qu'il[19] les a enveés la son jor contremander et s'esoine faire assaveir au seignor et a la court. Et lors le seignor doit comander[20] que l'on aporte une evangile, et

---

A: fols xxxii^{v}–xxxiii^{r} cap. 59; **B:** fol. 64^{r-v} cap. 60; **C:** fols 46^{v}–48^{r} cap. 46; **O:** fols 48^{r}–49^{v}; **V:** fols xliv^{r}–xlv^{r} cap. 56; Beugnot, pp. 96–7, cap. 59.

---

[1] au leuc ou . . . doivent] A: por; BV lack [2] AB add: de la court ou [3] V adds: et die [4] contre tel et] AV: encontre tel [5] nomer] B: nome [6] motissent] C: motissant [7] que il est essoiné] O: essoine [8] noment qui] B: nomer quoi [9] contremandé] O: gardé; V: contremander [10] sire] A: si; B: le vos; V: le [11] a vos] B lacks [12] ajorné l'a] V: ajorne le [13] essoinés si con nos disons] V: ensi com nous vous disons s'essoigné [14] que] A: ou conoistra que noz [15] doions] A: en deons; B: en doions; O: le deons; V: en devons [16] O adds: a la court [17] conoistre] B: esgarder [18] noment] BO: nome [19] les a enveés . . . qu'il] ABV lack [20] comander] O contremander

quant on la li avra[21] aportee, il doit comander a ceaus .ii. que il facent le sairement si con la court l'a comandé,[22] et il le doivent faire. Et se il le font, celui qui avra son jor contremandé par yaus l'avra bien contremandé si con il doit, ne il n'a pas[23] sa querele perdue par jor gardant.[24] Mais se il ne font le dit sairement, il n'a pas[25] bien son jor contremandé ne si con il doit et perdra cele querele par jor gardant se son aversaire garde ou contremande son jor si con il doit. Et l'aversaire de celui qui contremande son jor[26] ne peut nul de ceaus .ii.[27] torner de garantie par gage de bataille, por ce qu'il eufre[28] a certefier le seignor et[29] la court qui ajorna les parties et les fait certain par le sairement de[30] .ii. homes, si en doit[31] bien estre creu.

Et se ceaus qui vienent faire le contremant dou jor ne treuvent le seignor el leuc ou celui qui les avra enveés por son jor contremander fu ajornés, ne home que il ait establi en son leuc, il doivent venir en cel leuc ou celui qui les envoie est ajorné et ofrir a faire devant .ii. ou .iii. homes de cele court ou plus ce qui est devant devisé que l'on doit faire de tel chose, et dire que se il trovasent la[32] le seignor ou home en son leuc en cort ou sans court que il diroient et[33] feroient devant[34] lui ce qui est devant[35] devisé en cest livre que on[36] doit faire de tel chose. Et puis lor[37] prient que il soient bien recordans de ce qu'il ont dit et ofert, si que quant besoin sera a[38] celui qui les a la[39] envoiés son jor contremander[40] que il recordent[41] coment il sont venus[42] a hore et a tens faire assaveir au seignor et a la court, se il les eusent trovés ou home qui fust en leuc dou seignor,[43] coment celui qui envoiés les a la est essoinés si que il n'a peu[44] venir garder son jor, et por ce qu'il n'ont trové[45] le seignor ne la court la ou celui qui les a envoiés fu ajornés, ont il dit a hore

---

[21] on la li avra] AB: l'on l'avra; V: l'on li avra [22] comandé] ABV coneu [23] ne il n'a pas] B: ne n'avra mie; OV: ne il n'avra pas [24] ne il n'a . . . gardant] A lacks [25] n'a pas] ABO: n'avra pas (B: mie) [26] contremande son jor] AB: a son jor contremandé [27] ABV add: homes [28] eufre] A: euffrent [29] le seignor et] A: son essoine au seignor et a; B: son essoine a [30] de] ABV: des [31] doit] A: deivent; B: doivent [32] la] ABV lack [33] et] C: ou [34] devant] ABV: de [35] devant] C lacks [36] C adds: en [37] lor] AV: les; O: li [38] si que quant besoin sera a] A: si que quant le seignor vendra el leuc ou; B: ce que est besoing a; V: si que quant le seignor dira rien a [39] la] B lacks [40] contremander] C: comander [41] que il recordent] B lacks [42] venus] C lacks [43] fust en leuc dou seignor] BV: fussent (V: fust) en son leuc [44] n'a peu] B: n'i puet [45] trové] V: peu trover

et a tens[46] ofert en lor presence ce que il ont oy. Et se celui de qui la querele est a[47] aprés mestier de cel recort, il le doit faire si com il est[48] devisé el chapitle devant la ou il dit que[49] l'on doit dire et faire quant l'on a son jor gardé si con il doit la ou l'on fu ajorné[50] a son jor garder[51] et le seignor ne fu la a cel jor.

---

[46] AB add: et [47] a] C lacks [48] V adds: devant [49] dit que] C: dit quei; O: doit que [50] fu ajorné] C: ajorne; V: fu [51] a son jor garder] AB lack

***[48]** Qui est ajorné par cort, et il meut[1] a hore et a tens por venir a[2] son jor garder, et il a tel essoigne el chemin que il ne peut aler[3] son jor garder, coment et par qui il le[4] peut contremander.

Se celui qui est ajorné par court est hors[5] de la vile ou il est ajorné, et il meut[6] a hore et a tens por venir garder son jor, et essoine li avient el chemin por quei il n'i puisse aler a hore et a tens garder son jor[7] la ou il est ajorné, et il n'a o lui home que .i.[8] de la loi de Rome en tel[9] point, peut il bien[10] son jor contremander par .i. home de la loy de Rome, et, se il n'a o lui aucun home de la loy de Rome et il contremande son jor par[11] autre crestien, il vaut.[12] Et se il n'a crestien et il treuve juif[13] ou sarazin par qui il le contremande, il vaut[14] quant il est en tel point. Quar en tel[15] cas doit un home estre creu de l'esoine de celui qui par lui l'a contremandé de quelque nacion que il soit, mais que il jure selonc sa loy que celui qui son jor contremande par lui et fait savoir[16] s'esoine au seignor et a la court est ensi essoinés el chemin venant[17] garder son jor que il n'a peu venir garder son jor.[18]

Et se il ne treuve[19] home par qui il puisse[20] son jor contremander[21] et il treuve aucune gent a qui il puisse s'essoine mostrer, il le doit faire, et en cest cas sera .i. home creu de quelque nacion que il soit, se il ne peut plus trover a mostrer s'esoine, mais que il face le dit sairement. Et qui ensi contremande son jor il n'a pas failli, se me senble,[22] a son jor garder, ains l'a bien gardé puis que en lui n'est remés[23] a venir garder son jor la ou la court l'avoit ajorné et[24] garder le. Et aussi doit estre de ceaus par qui il contremande son

---

A: fols xxxiii^{r}–xxxiv^{r} cap. 60; **B:** fol. 65^{r-v} cap. 61; **C:** fols 48^{r}–49^{v} cap. 47; **O:** fols 49^{v}–51^{r}; **V:** fols xlv^{r}–xlvi^{v} cap. 57; Beugnot, pp. 98–100, cap. 60.

---

[1] meut] B (fol. 19^{r}) V rubric (fol. 5^{r}): vient [2] a] ABV lack [3] aler] B: venir; V lacks [4] par qui il le] B: por quoi il [5] hors] A: fors [6] meut] B: n'en vient [7] et essoine li . . . jor] ABV lack [8] o lui home que .i.] B: ou lui homes deus [9] tel] ABO: cel [10] bien] ABV lack [11] home de la loy de Rome, et se . . . par] ABV lack [12] crestien, il vaut] A: crestien, ce il viaut; B: se il veut; O: crestien il viaut [13] juif] AB: jude [14] il vaut] A: il vaut que; B: se il veaut; O: il viaut [15] point. Quar en tel] ABV lack [16] savoir] A: assaveir; V: assavoir [17] est ensi essoinés el chemin venant] A: qu'il a eu a la court venant; B: est ensi essoinez qu'il l'a envoié; V: que il est ensi essoignés au chemin venant [18] n'a peu venir . . . jor] B: ne puet venir garder [19] ne treuve] C: n'i treut [20] puisse] V: ne peut [21] son jor contremander] A lacks [22] se me senble] A lacks [23] n'est remés] A: ne remest [24] et] ABV: a

jor. Ou se il ou[25] aucun de ceaus sont enpeeschés[26] par prison ou par lor henemis, qui les asaillent ou gaitent el chemin par quei il ne[27] puissent paser a aler la ou il doivent lor[28] jor garder,[29] ou par aigue qu'il ne[30] puissent paser sans perill de mort ou par aucunes autres choses tes que court conoisse qu'il lor est avenu d'enpeeschement,[31] il doit valoir se il le pevent mostrer si com il doivent.[32] Et qui enssi[33] mostre que aucun des enpeeschement li soit avenu el chemin par[34] quei il ne peut[35] venir a hore ne a tens garder son jor, il ne doit pas sa querele perdre[36] par jor gardant, se me senble. Et il doit venir a[37] la court faire asseveir[38] s'esoine au plus tost que il porra,[39] et que il die[40] au seignor et a la court coment il a esté essoiné et l'eufre a prover si con court esgardera ou conoistra que il le doie prover. Et la court doit conoistre, se me senble, que se il jure sur sains que il mut a hore et a tens por venir garder son jor, et que il fu si[41] essoinés el chemin par quei[42] il ne pot venir garder son jor au jor que la court li dona, et que il ait .ii. homes de la loi de Rome que il jurent sur sains que il le virent enssi[43] esoinés el chemin par quei il ne pot venir garder son jor la ou il estoit ajorné,[44] se il fu essoiné en leuc ou il eust [45] gens[46] de la loy de Rome,[a] et se il fu essoignié en leuc ou il n'i eust genz de la lei de Rome,[a] et il a[47] .ii. crestiens de quelque nacion que il soient,[48] que il[49] facent le dit sairement, et se il fu essoinés en leuc ou il n'avoit[50] crestien et il a[51] juis ou sarazins qui jurent si com il doivent selonc lor loi, il me senble que il a asés fait ce que il doit[52] de son jor garder, ne

[a–a] Following the unique reading of A. CO is undoubtedly defective here, probably as the result of a homeoteleuton, and BV (see note 45) provide what appears to be an attempt at correcting CO.

[25] Ou se il ou] A: Que se; B: Ou se; V: Ou se il avient que [26] sont enpeeschés] A: seit enpeeschié; B: soit empeeschié; V: soit empachiés [27] ne] OV: n'i [28] lor] OV: le [29] par quei il . . . garder] A lacks [30] ne] OV: n'i [31] qu'il lor est avenu d'enpeeschement] A: qu'il lor seit avenu aucun enpeeschement; B: qui lor sont avenues aucuns empeschement; V: que lor soit a avenir d'empeescheement [32] pevent mostrer si com il doivent] ABV: peut (B: puet) mostrer si com il deit (B: doit; V: doivent) [33] qui enssi] V: que ensi le [34] par] C: por [35] quei il ne peut] V: qui il n'ont peu [36] sa querele perdre] V: avoir perdu sa quarele [37] a] C: en [38] faire asseveir] AB: mostrer [39] porra] O: pot venir a court [40] que il die] A: deit dire; V: die [41] si] BV lack [42] quei] C: que [43] enssi] ABV lack; O: si [44] estoit ajorné] B: fu essoiné [45] se il fu . . . eust] BV: Et se il fu essoiné (V: essoignés) en leuc ou il n'eust (V: n'i eust) [46] gens] A lacks [47] et il a] A: qu'il ait; B: et il i a; V: et il y avoit [48] il soient] V: ce fust [49] que il] ABV: qui [50] n'avoit] A: n'i avoit; B: n'eust; V: n'i eust [51] a] A: y a; BV: y avoit [52] ce que il doit] AB lack

qu'il n'a pas sa querele perdue par jor gardant, por ce qu'en lui ne remest que il son jor ne gardast a hore et a tens si com il[53] dut, et que il avra juré et .ii. autres homes o lui puis que par[54] essoine avra esté enpeesché si que il ne pot[55] son jor garder ne contremander.

Et il est bien raison, se me senble, qu'ensi doie estre. Que chascun qui meut a venir son jor garder n'a pas .ii. homes de la loy de Rome[56] o soi, que ce[57] il est esoigné el chemin ou enpeesché par[58] qui il puisse son jor contremander, ne chascun qui meut a venir garder son jor ne cuide pas estre essoinés ne enpeeschés el chemin, por quei il n'est merveille s'il ne meine apencement gens o lui[59] par quei il puisse s'esoine contremander se besoing li est, tout soit il tel que il ait[60] pooir de mener les. Que maintes fois est avenu ou porroit[61] avenir que celui qui est ajorné par court est sain[62] et en tel leuc que il cuide venir seurement et sauvement a hore et a tens garder son jor la ou il est ajorné, si meut soul ou aveuc .i.[63] home en sa conpaignie, et que il a[64] essoigne ou[65] enpeeschement el chemin tel par quei il ne peut[66] aler son jor garder ne contremander. Et s'ensi estoit que se il estoit[67] essoigné ou enpeesché en l'une des manieres avant dites[68] que il perdist sa querele, ce seroit tort apert, que nul ne doit par raison perdre[69] querele par jor gardant se il ne demore par lui et[70] en sa defaute qu'il ne garde ou[71] contremande son jor[72] si con il doit.

---

[53] C adds: i [54] par] O: passer [55] V adds: venir [56] AB add: apareilliez (B: appareilliés) por mener; OV: aprestés d'amener (V: de mener) [57] C adds: soit [58] par] C: por [59] apencement gens o lui] A: genz a son plait apenseement; B: genz a son plait o lui [60] ait] A: n'ait; V: n'a [61] porroit] A: peut; B: puet [62] sain] B: asseur [63] soul ou aveuc .i.] A: celui tot soul ou aveuc un autre; B: celui tout soul ou aucun; V: soul ou auchun autre [64] et que il a] A: Car il ne cuide pas aveir; B: Car il ne cuide mie qu'il ait; V: et que il ait [65] ou] B: ne; C: et que ot [66] ne peut] B: ne puisse; C: n'i peut [67] que se il estoit] ABV: qu'il fust [68] en l'une des . . . dites] B: par les manieres devant dites et [69] BV add: sa [70] par lui et] A lacks [71] et en sa . . . ou] B: qu'il defaille ou ne [72] ne garde ou contremande] AV: n'a gardé son jor ne contremandé

***[49]** Por quei home de quei[1] on se claime en court ou il est present ne se doit partir de la cort sans respondre au clain ou demander jor.

Selui[2] de qui l'on c'est clamé en court[3] en sa presence garde soi qu'il ne se parte de la cort qu'il n'ait ains respondu au clain que l'on[4] fait de lui, ou qu'il n'ait demandé jor, ou qu'il n'ait ofert au mains[5] a respondre se le seignor et la court le veulent entendre[6] et que il de ce traïe la cort a garant. Quar s'il l'une des dites chozes ne faisoit[7] ains que la cort se parte ou ne disoit[8] raison por quei il ne devroit[9] respondre au clain et tel que cort l'esgardast ou coneust,[10] il perdra sa querele, por ce que il est assise et usage el roiaume de Jerusalem que qui ne respont au clain que l'on fait[11] de lui en cort ou il est present ou ne fait[12] l'une des avant dites chozes, qu'il pert sa querele, se la cort se parte et il n'a aucune des avant dites choses[13] faite[14] avant[15] que la court s'en[16] parte.

A: fol. xxxiv^{r-v} cap. 61; **B:** fols 65^{v}–66^{r} cap. 62; **C:** fol. 49^{v} cap. 48; **O:** fol. 51^{r-v}; **V:** fols xlvi^{v}–xlvii^{r} cap. 58; Beugnot, pp. 100–1, cap. 61.

[1] quei] AB (fol. 19^{r}): qui [2] Selui] A: Ce celui; O: A celui [3] V adds: de lui [4] AB add: a [5] ofert au mains] B: avant offert [6] entendre] B: ataindre [7] l'une des dites . . . faisoit] AB: ne fait l'une des dittes choses [8] disoit] AB: dit [9] devroit] A: dee; B: doie [10] l'esgardast ou coneust] AB: l'esgarde ou conoisse [11] fait] A: face [12] fait] C: fert [13] qu'il pert sa . . . choses] BV lacks [14] faite] AB lack; V: faire [15] avant] A: ainz [16] s'en] C: se

[50]* Por quei celui a qui l'on met sus aucune malefaite[a] en cort[1] ou a qui l'on requiert aucune choze, il det respondre et neer la se l'on l'eufre a prover.

Qui requiert a autre chose en la[2] cort[3] ou li met sus aucune malefaite et l'eufre a prover ce que il li requiert ou la malefaite qu'il li met sus, et celui a qui l'on fait la requeste ou sur qui l'on met sus la malefaite ne noie ce que l'on eufre contre lui a prover en la cort,[4] et la cort[5] se parte ains qu'il l'ait neé ou ofert a respondre,[6] se le seignor ou[7] la court le veulent escouter, ou n'a dit[8] raison por quei il ne le doit faire[9] et tel que cort l'esgarde ou conoisse, il est ataint de ce que l'on li a requis ou[10] mis sus en la maniere avant[11] dite, se il n'a[12] fait l'une des dites[13] choses ains que la court s'en parte.[14]

A: fol. xxxiv^{v} cap. 62; **B:** fol. 66^{r} cap. 63; **C:** fols 49^{v}–50^{r} cap. 49; **O:** fol. 51^{v}; **V:** fol. xlvii^{r} cap. 59; Beugnot, p. 101, cap. 62.

[a] B throughout this chapter and the one that follows consistently uses the form 'mesfait' for 'malefaite' as a masculine noun.

[1] aucune malefaite en cort] B (fol. 19^{r}): aucun mesfait [2] requiert a autre chose en la] B: demande aucune chose en [3] V adds: aucune chose [4] en la cort] V lacks [5] et la cort] B lacks [6] respondre] B: deffendre [7] ou] ABV: et [8] n'a dit] A: ne die; B: ne dit [9] le doit faire] AB: dee (B: doie) respondre [10] requis ou] A lacks [11] avant] A: devant [12] n'a] AB: ne [13] dites] B: deus [14] s'en parte] B: se departe; C: se parte

***[51]** Coment et por coi celui a qui l'on met sus malefaite en court et il la[1] noie et l'on ne li eufre a prover ains que la court s'en parte, celui[2] qui li a mis sus[3] ne li peut aprés[4] riens demander.

Quant l'on se claime[5] en court d'autre ou[6] li[7] met sus aucune malefaite, et celui de qui l'on c'est clamé ou[8] sur qui l'on a mis[9] la malefaite noie ce que l'on li met sus el clain ou autrement, et le clamant ou celui qui la malefaite li a mis sus ne l'eufre a prover ains que la court s'en parte, je cuit[10] qu'il est quite et delivre de cele querele et n'en est plus tenus de respondre a celui qui de lui c'est clamé ou qui li a la malefaite mise sus. Que aussi con[11] celui de qui l'on se claime en court en sa presence ou a qui l'on met sus malefaite,[12] se[13] il ne respont au clain ou ne noie la malefaite ou[14] n'eufre a respondre,[15] se le seignor et la court le veulent escouter, ou il ne demande jor au clain[16] ains que la court s'en parte ou ne dit raison por coi il ne li[17] doit respondre a cel clain ou a ce[18] que l'on li met sus, et tel que court l'esgarde ou conoisse, est ataint de ce[19] que l'on li met sus el clain ou autrement[20] est quite, se me senble, celui de qui l'on se claime[21] ou a qui l'on met sus malefaite de ce que l'on li met sus el clain[22] ou autrement, se il le noie, et le clamant ne l'eufre a prover ains que la cort se parte. Car droit doit estre comun et ygal, et il ne le seroit mie en cest cas[23] s'ensi n'estoit.[24]

A: fols xxxiv^{v}–xxxv^{r} cap. 63; **B:** fol. 66^{r} cap. 64; **C:** fol. 50^{r} cap. 50; **O:** fols 51^{v}–52^{r}; **V:** fol. xlvii^{r-v} cap. 60; Beugnot, p. 102, cap. 63.

---

[1] malefaite en court et il la] B (fol. 19r): aucun mesfait en cort et il le [2] celui] B: et que cel [3] celui qui li a mis sus] A: l'on [4] aprés] AB lack [5] se claime] B: plaidoie [6] d'autre ou] B: a autre et [7] li] AB: l'on li [8] B adds: celui [9] C adds: sus [10] cuit] A: crei; B: croi [11] aussi con] B: quant [12] malefaite] B: aucun mesfait [13] se] ABV: et [14] il ne respont . . . ou] V lacks [15] B adds: deffendre [16] au clain] A lacks [17] li] ABV lack [18] ce] C: cel; V: celui [19] ce] V: celle quarele [20] A adds: tot aussi; V: ains [21] se claime] A: c'est clamés; B: s'est clamez; C: se claime de lui [22] el clain] B lacks [23] en cest cas] A lacks [24] V adds: mais aprés vous dirai em poi de conseill esclarzi

***[52]** Quei[1] l'on doit dire et faire qui viaut recovrer saisine de ce de quey l'on l'a desaisi.

Quant aucun desaisist[2] autre d'aucune choze et celui qui a esté desaisi en veaut recovrer sa saisine, il doit venir devant le seignor et dire li: 'Sire, tel', et le nome, 'm'a de noviau desaisi de tel choze', et die de coy. 'Si vos pri et requier que vos me faites remetre[3] en ma saisine de ce de coi il m'a desaisi, et quant je serai en[4] saisine, s'il me set que demander, je li en feray droit par vostre cort.[5] Sire, et se vos ce[6] mescreés qu'ensi ne soit[7] con je vos ai dit, faites le enquerre et me faites, si con vos devés, par l'assise ou l'usage de cest roiaume con[8] de novele desaisine.' Et lors le seignor doit mander .ii. ou .iii. de ses homes ce enquerre et les[9] doit conjurer par la foi que il li doivent qu'il enquierent[10] par leal enqueste se celui, qui[11] dit que l'on l'a de novel desaisi, estoit saisi[12] de cele chose de quei il dit que l'on l'a[13] desaisi. Et quant il avront enquis, il doivent dire au seignor en sa cort ce qu'il en avront[14] trové. Et se il treuvent qu'il ait .xl. jors ou mains qu'il en ait esté desaisi, le seignor ou celui qui sera en son leuc a qui celui qui avra esté desaisi l'avra requis si con est devant dit,[15] le doit maintenant faire resaisir[16] et defendre a l'autre devant .ii. ou plus de ses homes qu'il ne s'en saisise[17] et dire li que, se il le fait, il l'en menra[18] a ce qu'il pora et devra. Mais s'il cuide avoir droit, qu'il le requiert si con il doit, et il li en fera droit par sa court, et se celui a qui la defence avra esté ensi faite s'en saisist[19] sans esgart ou[20] sans conoissance de court ou sans le congé de son[21] seignor, il fera force, et s'il en est ataint ou prové, il en sera encheu en la mersi do seignor con ataint de force.

Et qui de ce viaut faire leal enqueste,[22] il doit venir el leuc ou ce est de quei l'on a dit au seignor que l'on a esté de novel desaisi, et

---

A: fols xxxv^r–xxxvi^v cap. 64; **B:** fols 66^r–67^v cap. 65; **C:** fols 50^r–52^r cap. 51; **O:** fols 52^r–54^v; **V:** fols xlviii^r–l^r cap. 62; Beugnot, pp. 103–7, cap. 64.

---

[1] Quei] AB (fol. 19r) V: Que; O: Quant [2] V adds: aucun [3] remetre] V: metre [4] ABV add: ma [5] s'il me set . . . cort] A: je li fornirai dreit par vostre court se il me set riens que demander; B: je li en ferai droit se il m'en set que demander par vostre court [6] ce] A: me; BV lack [7] ne soit] V: n'estoit [8] vos devés par . . . con] C lacks [9] les] O: leur [10] enquierent] B: enquerront [11] qui] C: con [12] C lacks: estoit saisi [13] l'on l'a] A: on l'a de noviau [14] B adds: enquis et [15] ou celui qui . . . dit] ABV lack [16] resaisir] C: desaisir [17] qu'il ne s'en saisise] V: et dire li que il ne les desaisise [18] l'en menra] ABV: le (B: l'en) metra [19] saisist] A: ressaissist [20] ou] V: et [21] de son] ABV: dou [22] leal enqueste] AB: l'enqueste; V: enqueste

enquerre par sairement as plusors des voisins de cel leuc,[23] a ceaus qu'il tendront[24] a plus loiaus et qu'il entendront[25] qui miaus sachent cel fait, conbien il[26] a de tens que celui qui au jor en est saisi en fu premier[27] saisi aprés la saisine d'autre et qui en estoit saisi derainement ains que celui[28] en fust saisi ou qu'il s'en saisist. Et selonc ce qu'il oront dire a seaus a qui il[29] feront l'enqueste, si leur demandent et enquierent au miaus qu'il savront ce qu'il cuideront par quei il puissent estre et soient plus certains de cel fait. Et quant il avront enquis au meaus qu'il savront, si dient[30] au seignor en sa court[31] ce qu'il avront trové. Et se .ii. ou plus de ceaus a[32] qu'il avront enquis par lor sairement et[33] dient que celui que l'on a de noviau desaisi fu[34] saisi et tenant de cele chose, ou autre por lui, quant celui qui au jor la tient l'en[35] desaisi, le seignor le doit remetre[36] en sa saisine se il[37] a .xl. jors ou mains qu'il en fu desaisi.[38] Car se il[39] a plus de .xl. jors qu'il en ait esté desaisi et il n'a requis au seignor que il le remete ou face remetre[40] en la saisine de cele chose ou[41] qu'il[42] face enqueste con de novele desaisine, il ne peut ne ne doit cele desaisine apeler novele,[43] ne le seignor ne li est[44] pas tenus de faire li ce que il li requiert con de novele desaisine, por ce qu'il me senble[45] qu'il ait desprisé[46] et despité le seignor quant il a tant demoré a[47] mostrer li que l'on l'a desaisi et requerre li[48] la saisine ou que il[49] face l'enqueste desus dite ou qu'il ait esté negligant de son droit requerre tant que le terme qui est establi que l'on peut apeler[50] la desaisine novele est pasé.

Si ne doit plus la desaisine estre tenue a novele, se il n'a esté en celui terme hors[51] do pais ou si[52] essoinés de son cors par maladie ou par prison ou par ce que son seignor le semonst de son servise ou por aucune autre essoigne qu'il a eu, par quei il dedens les .xl. jors ne peut venir a cort devant le seignor ce requerre qui est devant dit. Et se il le dit, et[53] le seignor ou celui qui dit qu'il de novel l'a

[23] AB add: et [24] tendront] AB: cuident; O: tendroit [25] entendront] AB: entendent [26] il] A: qu'il y; O lacks; V: il y [27] premier] B: premierement [28] A adds: qui orrés est saissi [29] ABV adds: en [30] dient] A: deivent dire [31] en sa court] A lacks [32] a] C lacks [33] et] AB lack; V: ci [34] fu] A: esteit [35] l'en] C: la [36] doit remetre] A: redeit metre [37] AV add: y [38] desaisi] C: saisi [39] AV add: y [40] remete ou face remetre] BV: mete ou face metre [41] ou] C lacks [42] BO add: en (O with dots under to denote deletion) [43] A adds: dessaissine [44] ne li est] A: n'est [45] me senble] V: resemble [46] desprisé] B: mesprisé [47] B adds: requerre le qu'il le saisisse et ce [48] li] A: li ent; B lacks [49] AB add: li [50] apeler] B: requerre; C: apeler a [51] hors] A: fors [52] si] A: c'il n'a esté; B: se il n'est; V: ensi [53] il le dit, et] A lacks

desaisi dit qu'il ne l'en croit[54] qu'il ait esté si esoinés con il dit, il doit dire: 'Je suis prest que je de ce[55] en face se que la court[56] conoistra que je en doie faire que si ay'. Et la cort doit conoistre, se cuit, qu'il doit dire en la presence dou seignor et de la court que par la foy qu'il doit au seignor qu'il a esté si esoinés con il[57] dit,[58] et s'il n'est home dou seignor qu'il[59] doit jurer sur sains, et autres .ii. homes de la loy de Rome o lui. Et qui enssi le fera il porra bien la desaisine apeler novele par raison dedens autres[60] .xl. jors puis que[61] par lui ne sera demoré,[62] mais par l'essoine qu'il avra en qu'il n'ait[63] fait ce qu'il doit de ce si con il est avant[64] devisé. Et s'il est hors[65] dou pais quant on le desaisist,[66] dedens les .xl. jors qu'il sera revenus el pais peut il venir devant le seignor et dire[67] que l'on l'a desaisi de novel et requerre li qu'il le face resaisir de ce que l'on[68] l'a de novel desaisi ou enquerre le et li en face ce qu'il doit con de novele desaisine. Et le seignor li est tenus de faire faire l'enqueste[69] si con est avant[70] dit, et se il le[71] treuve par l'enqueste que il soit si con il dit, il est tenus de faire le metre[72] en la saisine et de faire la defence[73] devant[74] dite a celui qui l'avra[75] desaisi.

Mais se les .xl. jors pasent, il ne peut dire que sele[76] desaisine[77] soit novele, ne le seignor ne li est pas tenus de faire li en par l'assise ne l'usage ce qu'il doit con de novele desaisine. Et se celui qui a esté desaisi laisse les .xl. jors paser, si con est desus[78] dit, sans faire requeste au seignor qu'il li face faire l'enqueste de la novele desaisine, il ne peut puis[79] avoir[80] par raison la saisine de ce de quei il dit que l'on l'a[81] desaisi que par clain et par respons et par preuves de garans en quei il i[82] avra tornes de bataille se la querele est de plus d'un marc d'argent. Et s'ele est de mains d'un marc d'argent[83] et il li[84] met sus force au clain de la saisine[85] et l'eufre a prover, il i[86] avra bataille[87] se l'autre noie[88] la force, et s'il ne[89] la noie il sera

[54] B adds: mie [55] de ce] BV lack [56] AB add: en; V: esguardera ou [57] BV add: a [58] AV adds: ce il (V: s'il) est home dou seignor [59] qu'il] A: il le; BV: il [60] autres] B lacks [61] puis que] A lacks [62] sera demoré] A: demora [63] n'ait] C: n'a [64] V adds: dit et [65] hors] A: fors [66] desaisist] C: saisist [67] ABV add: li [68] que l'on] A: de quei l'on; B: dont on [69] l'enqueste] V: novelle enqueste [70] avant] V: devant [71] le] ABV lack [72] metre] A: remetre [73] V adds: si com est [74] devant] AB: avant [75] A adds: de noviau [76] sele] AB: la; O: tele [77] il ne peut . . . desaisine] V: si ne peut dire de celle dessaisine que [78] desus] V: devant [79] puis] C: pas [80] avoir] V: faire ne avoir [81] A adds: de novel; B: de nouveau [82] i] ABV lack [83] Et s'ele est . . . d'argent] B: Et se ele est de mains; V lacks [84] li] OV lacks [85] de la saisine] B: de la dessaisine; O: dessaisine [86] i] BV lacks [87] bataille] V: tournes de batailles. Et [88] noie] A: l'a neé [89] ne] B lacks

ataint de force et encheu en la merci dou seignor con[90] ataint de force. Et se il l'une des dites chozes ne fait et il requiert par court a celui qui l'avra desaisi ce dont il l'a[91] desaisi, celui en plaideera come saisi,[92] et il porra trover et faire[93] moult d'eschanpes et de fuites et tant que celui qui en avra esté desaisi en sera moult travaillés ains que il l'ataigne[94] se le fuïant le viaut et set faire et enssi[95] porra avoir grant damage le requerant. Si n'est pas sage celui que l'on desaisist d'aucune chose se ce n'est par assise ou usage ou esgart ou[96] conoissance de cort qu'il ne vient au plus tost qu'il peut[97] devant le seignor en sa cort et ne li mostre que l'on l'a de novel desaisi au plus tost qu'il peut au mains dedens les .xl. jors et ne li requiert qu'il li face recevoir[98] sa saisine ou faire l'enqueste con de novele desaisine et li en face ce qu'il doit par l'assise ou l'usage con de novele desaisine.[99] Que ce est la plus prochaine et la meillor[100] et la plus seure voie a revenir[101] tost en sa saisine de ce de quei l'on l'a desaisi, et por ce n'est pas sage qui laisse cest voie et se prent a nule des autres.

---

[90] V adds: home [91] l'a] AB: l'avra [92] saisi] V: desaisi [93] trover et faire] A: dire; BV: dire et faire [94] ains que il l'ataigne] A lacks [95] enssi] ABV: en ce [96] esgart ou] AB lack [97] peut] V: onques pora [98] recevoir] A: raveir; B: ravoir [99] et li en . . . desaisine] ABV lack [100] et la meillor] B: et la plus bone; V lacks [101] revenir] ABV: venir

*[53] En quel cas force de turs tot saisine[1] et en quel quas ele ne la tot.[2]

Moult de[3] gens dient que force de turs ne tot saisine. Ce est voirs en plusors cas, mais non[4] en tos, et il me senble que par tel senblance le peut on trover.[5] [a] Il avint chose[6] que .i. home qui a[7] non Pierre[8] tint le Daron come sien en tens de trive en[9] pais et sans chalonge, et sil Pierre ot .ii. fis: l'un ot non Fouque et l'autre Ote,[10] et ceaus siens fis orent femes et anfans. Et avint que el vivant de Pierre[11] guerre fu[12] et le Daron fu perdu et sarazins le tindrent. Et en tant com il le tenoient[13] cil Pierre morut, et demorerent ses .ii. fis sans saisine avoir do Daron ne de rien qui de la seignorie fust. Et puis morut Fouques, l'aisné des fis Pierre, sans aucune[14] saisine avoir des choses devant[15] dites par la force que les sarazins li faisoient, et .i. fis de Fouques demora qui ot a non Tibaut[16] et vint en aage. Et puis trive fu,[17] et le Daron fu rendu as crestiens, et Ote vint avant, qui fu[18] fis Pierre, et requist[19] la saisine dou Daron con le plus dreit heir aparant de Pierre qui fu seignor do Daron et[20] derainement en fu saisi et tenant con de son fié.[21] Et puis sa mort nul autre crestien n'en ot saisine ne teneure.[22] [b] 'Et se nus mescroit que Pierre ne me tenist a son fis leal, je suis prest de prover le tout enssi con[23] court conoistra[24] que je prover le doie. Et por ce que fis est plus droit

A: fols xxxvi^{v}–xxxvii^{r} cap. 65; **B:** fols 67^{v}–68^{v} cap. 66; **C:** fols 52^{r}–53^{v} cap. 52; **O:** fols 54^{v}–56^{r}; **V:** fols l^{r}–li^{r} cap. 63; Beugnot, pp. 107–9, cap. 65.

[a] None of the individuals named in the dispute described here are known from other sources, and, indeed, it is unclear whether Daron was ever granted as a fief. The use here of the word 'senblance' may indicate that this example is fictive.

[b] Beugnot (p. 107 n. 61) considered there to be a lacuna in the text at this point as Ote's speech evidently begins part way through. However, despite the abrupt switch to direct speech, the line of argument seems to be complete.

[1] saisine] B (fol. 19^{r}): assise [2] B adds: mie [3] Moult de] A: Totes [4] non] A: ne mie; BV: non mie [5] trover] AV: torner; B: ravoir [6] chose] ABV lack [7] a] A: ot a; B: avoit; V: ot [8] V adds: Celui Piere [9] en] V: et de [10] Ote] A: Otte; B: Othes; V: Othe (and elsewhere in this chapter) [11] de Pierre; V: dou pere [12] el vivant de Pierre guerre fu] B: celui Pierre out guerre [13] tenoient] CO: tenoient et; V: tindrent [14] aucune] A lacks [15] devant] ABV: avant [16] Tibaut] ABO: Thibaut (and elsewhere in this chapter) [17] trive fu] B: treves furent [18] fu] V: estoit [19] requist] B: quist [20] qui fu seignor do Daron et] A: et qui [21] et tenant con de son fié] A: come dou sien [22] teneure] B: tenement [23] ABV add: la [24] conoistra] BO: esgardera

heir de pere[25] que[26] autre, et que le fié dou pere dont nul crestien n'a esté[27] entre .ii. saisi[28] et tenant con de son droit, doit meaus venir[29] au fis que a nul autre. Et por ce que mon pere fu plus[30] derainement saisi de cest fié que nul autre crestien et por les autres raisons que je ai dites, le veuill je avoir, se la cort l'esgarde.' Et Tibaut vient avant et dit: 'Sire, je requier la saisine dou Daron con le plus droit heir aparant, et di coment. Fouques, qui fu mon pere, fu fis ainsné et dreit heir de Pierre[31] qui fu seignor[32] dou Daron. Et quant Pierre morut, tos ses drois escheirent a Fouques mon pere, con a droit heir, et a son fis ainsné et son droit heir,[33] et il ot et tint tos les biens de Pierre son pere de quei sarazins ne[34] li faisoient force. Et se sarazins firent[35] force a mon pere dou Daron, je ne doi[36] pas[37] por ce perdre mon droit ne ma saisine, quar je n'entens que force de turs toille saisine. Et se nus mescroit que Pierres ne tenist Fouques a son fis leal[38] et que il ne fust ainsné d'Ote et que Fouque ne me tenist a son fis leal[39] et qu'il n'eristast[40] as biens de Pierre come son ainsné fis et son droit heir, je le[41] suis prest de prover tout ensi con[42] court conoistra[43] que je prover le doie. Et por toutes les raisons devant[44] dites veuill je avoir la saisine dou Daron, se court l'esgarde'.

Et a moi[45] senble que Ote, qui fu fis[46] Pierre qui derainement fu[47] saisi et tenant do Daron[48] con de son fié, soit plus dreit heir a avoir le Daron, et que le fié de son pere dont autre crestien n'a eu[49] saisine entre .ii. doit meaus venir a lui que a[50] Tibaut son nevou, fis de l'ainsné fis de Pierre. Quar se le nevou[51] en estoit son plus droit heir, par ceste meimes raison seroient tos ceaus qui de Fouques seroient descendus ses plus drois heirs jusques en[52] la fin do siecle[53] au fié[54] avoir devant Ote le fis Pierre, laquel chose seroit descovenable et dou tot contre raison. Que par l'assise ou l'usage dou reiaume de Jerusalem on ne peut requere et avoir[55] le fié, que on dit[56] qui

[25] pere] C: Pierre [26] A adds: nul [27] esté] CO: est [28] entre .ii. saisi] B: saisi entr'eaus deus [29] meaus venir] B: meauir [30] plus] AB lack [31] Pierre] V: pere [32] seignor] O lacks [33] et son droit heir] BV lack [34] ne] deleted in C [35] firent] V: faisoient [36] doi] C: doit [37] pas] AB: mie; V lacks [38] leal] AV lack [39] A adds: et a son dreit heir [40] n'eristast] B: n'entrast [41] le] ABV lack [42] ABV add: la [43] conoistra] B: esgardera; V: esguardera ou conoistra [44] devant] AB: avant [45] a moi] B: ensi me [46] BV add: de [47] fu] A: en morut; V: en fu [48] do Daron] A lacks [49] n'a eu] B: n'ont; V: n'en a heu [50] a] C lacks [51] nevou] B: menour; V: nevou fis [52] en] AV: a [53] siecle] B: monde [54] au fié] A: dou fié a; B: le fié; V: dou fié [55] et avoir] B lacks [56] que on dit] A lacks

li soit escheu, que par celui qui derainement en ait[57] esté saisi et tenant con dou sien,[58] et le fis[59] est plus droit heir[60] dou pere a heriter en ce dont il a eu derainement la saisine et la teneure que ne soit[61] le fis[62] de son ainsné fis.[c]

Et par ces raisons et par plusors autres peut on bien conoistre que force de turs[63] tot saisine en aucun cas.

[c] C inserts a unique passage here. See below, appendix 1.1.

[57] en ait] B: en a; V: a [58] dou sien] B: de son fié [59] C adds: et la fille [60] AV add: aparant [61] soit] V: soroit [62] C adds: ou la fille [63] C adds: ne

*[54] Quant le plaideor doit acuillir la preuve a soy et quant doner a son aversaire, et coment l'on doit prover la negative.

Qui viaut estre bon plaideor, il li covient a gaitier sur toutes riens es plais en quei[1] il[2] covient a faire preuve coment il puisse acuillir la preuve a soi quant besoin li est se il la peut faire, et, se il ne la peut faire,[3] que il la doigne a son aversaire. Quar par bien prover ce que l'on eufre a prover en la cort se gaaignent[4] les plus des plais, et par faillir a prover[5] se perdent. Et la preuve premier oferte doit avant aler par l'assise ou l'usage dou reiaume de Jerusalem. Ne nul ne peut faire preuve de non, qu'en tel maniere ou par le senblant: 'Je di que tel home n'est pas nés de leal mariage et di coment qu'il[6] estoit nés avant que son pere tel', et le nome, 'espousa[7] sa mere tele', et la nome. 'Et ce suis je prest de prover tot enssi con la court esgardera ou conoistra[8] que je prover le doie.' Et en ceste maniere ou par le senblant peut l'on prover le non, ne autrement ne[9] peut l'on prover se me senble. Quar enssi preuve l'on le non par ce que[10] la preuve chet sur la parole afirmative et non pas sur la[11] negative.

A: fol. xxxvii^{r-v} cap. 66; **B:** fol. 68^{v} cap. 67; **C:** fol. 53^{v} cap. 53; **O:** fol. 56^{r-v}; **V:** fol. li^{r-v} cap. 64; Beugnot, p. 109, cap. 66.

---

[1] en quei] A: es quels; B: ou; V: es ques [2] BV add: li [3] se il ne la peut faire] A: quant besoin ne li est [4] gaaignent] B: gaaigne [5] a prover] A lacks [6] qu'il] A: il; B: et que il [7] espousa] AB: espousast [8] ou conoistra] B lacks [9] AB add: le [10] par ce que] A: quant [11] pas sur la] B: mie

***[55]** Coment l'on doit defendre d'acuillir la preuve a soy quant son aversaire viaut que il preuve a sien ce que il a et tient come sien.

Se home ou feme est saisi et tenant d'aucune choze et en[1] use con la soue chose, et autre li requiert disant qu'ele n'est mie soue et li viaut geter la preuve sus par aucune maniere de soutillance[2] de plait, celui qui est saisi et tenant de la[3] chose se peut bien defendre de la preuve acuillir a soi, se me senble, et enssi: que quant celui qui li requiert cele chose dit qu'ele n'est mie soue, que il a ce li[4] responde que, sauve sa pais, il est asés clere chose qu'ele est soue[5] qu'il l'a et tient come soue et en[6] use come de la soue, et que sa saisine et sa[7] teneure[8] et son usage preuvent assés[9] qu'ele est soue. Ne quant a ce il n'entent qu'il autre preuve en doie faire ore que de la saisine et de la teneure qu'il en a et a eu.[10] Que[11] s'ensi estoit qu'il[12] covenist a prover a soue[13] chascune chose que l'on a et tient come soue et de quey l'on a usé et use[14] con de la soue autrement que par sa saisine et sa teneure et[15] son usage, les saisines[16] et les teneures vaudroient poi, et moult de gens perdroient par ce lor raison, por quei il ne viaut[17] ore autre preuve faire, se la court ne l'esgarde, et de ce se met il en l'esgart de la court sauf son retenaill. Et as autres choses que son aversaire avra dites responde le meaus que il savra, sans[18] qu'il s'acroche[19] a prover autrement[20] que par sa saisine et sa teneure que ce qu'il a et tient soit[21] sien. Et qui enssi le fera, il ne me senble que son aversaire li puisse la preuve geter[22] sus de[23] ce qu'il a et tient come sien,[24] ne que il puisse dire chose par coi la cort doie esgarder que il doie prover a sien ce qu'il a et tient come le sien[25] et de quei il use come dou sien[26] par sa saisine et sa teneure

A: fols xxxvii^{v}–xxxviii^{r} cap. 67; **B:** fol. 69^{r-v} cap. 68; **C:** fols 53^{v}–54^{v} cap. 54; **O:** fols 56^{r}–57^{v}; **V:** fols li^{v}–lii^{r} cap. 65; Beugnot, pp. 110–11, cap. 67.

[1] en] ABV lack [2] soutillance] C: cenblance [3] A adds: soe; V: soue [4] li] ABV lack [5] AV add: et [6] l'a et tient . . . en] V: la tient et [7] sa] C: la [8] et la teneure] A lacks [9] assés] ABV lack [10] et a eu] B: ore [11] Que] C: Qu'en [12] estoit qu'il] A: n'estoit et il [13] a soue] BV lack [14] et use] V lacks [15] sa saisine et sa teneure et] B: teneure ou saisine ou [16] V adds: et les usages [17] viaut O: vaut [18] ABV add: ce [19] s'acroche] C: s'acroiche; V: ne s'acroche [20] autrement] A: autre [21] soit] A: est; O: soy [22] geter] C: getre [23] sus de] AV: dessus de; B: que il doie prover [24] sien] A: le sien; B: la soue chose; V: le sien et de quoi il use com dou sien [25] come le sien] AB: come sien; V lacks [26] AV add: que

et son usage, se son aversaire ne preuve avant qu'il ait droit en cele chose.

Mais se il preuve que il y a[27] droit, il covient aprés que il preuve que sele chose soit[28] soue, si que le droit que son aversaire avra prové qu'il[29] ne li vaille. Et se il ne peut prover aprés la preuve de son aversaire, il perdra cele chose et son aversaire l'avra par raison gaaignee.

Et qui viaut prover a[30] soue chose, se[31] que autre que son seignor ait et tieigne, il le doit prover par prevelige ou par recort de court ou par garans, et se l'on preuve par garans et la chose vaut[32] .i. marc d'argent ou plus, il i a[33] tornes de bataille, se celui contre qui l'on preuve viaut l'un des garans torner[34] par guage de bataille.

[27] a] AB: ait [28] que sele chose soit] A: coment elle fu; BV: que cele (V: celle) chose fu [29] qu'il] A: qu'il a; B lacks; O: que il y a [30] a] V: la [31] se] AB lack [32] vaut] B: monte a [33] a] B: avra [34] l'on preuve viaut . . . torner] A: il le preuve le viaut faire et il en viaut lever l'un des garenz; B: il le preuve le veut faire et il lieve l'un des garanz; V: l'om preuve en veaut l'un des guarens tourner

***[56]** Coment et por quei et par qui[1] l'on doit prover en la haute court.

Qui viaut prover en la haute court aucune chose, il la doit prover par prevelige ou par recort de court ou par garans. Ne l'on ne peut prover contre son seignor chose que l'on vouche[2] a son fié que par prevelige ou par recort de court.[3] Mais chose que l'on vouche[4] a partie de son fié et[5] de quey l'on est saisi et tenant peut l'on prover contre son seignor par son sairement. Et contre tos autres[6] peut l'on prover par prevelige et par recort de court et par garans toutes choses, soit fié ou autre chose.[7] Et qui viaut prover par garans fié ou chose de fié ou autre chose,[8] il covient qu'il soient .ii. loiaus[9] garans ou plus de la loy de Rome, se ce n'est de prover aage ou lignage.[10] Que[11] l'on peut prover ses .ii. dites choses par chascun home ou feme, mais que il soit crestien batié[12] et qu'il soient .ii. ou plus et que il s'acordent bien ensenble a une parole. Ne il n'a[13] point de tornes de[14] bataille contre garans qui preuvent aage ne contre ceaus qui preuvent lignage que en .i. cas, et cel cas sera devisé aprés en cest livre. Et en la haute cort dit l'avantparlier por les garans, et en cele dou visconte dit chascun guarant[15] par soy sa garantie.

A: fol. xxxviii^{r} cap. 68; **B:** fol. 69^{v} cap. 69; **C:** fols 54^{v}–55^{r} cap. 55; **O:** fols 57^{v}–58^{r}; **V:** fol. lii^{r-v} cap. 66; Beugnot, pp. 111–12, cap. 68.

---

[1] et par qui] B (fol. 19^{r}) lacks [2] vouche] A: voe [3] que par prevelige . . . court] B lacks [4] vouche] A: voe [5] et] ABV lack [6] tos autres] V: toutes autres manieres de gens [7] ou autre chose] A: seit autre [8] qui viaut prover . . . chose] A lacks [9] loiaus] A lacks [10] lignage] C: lingnage; V: linguage [11] Que] B: Car [12] soit crestien batié] A: seient crestiens batisiés; B: soit crestien bautiçé [13] n'a] AV: n'i a [14] tornes de] A lacks [15] guarant] V lacks

***[57]** Qui viaut prover par garans,[1] ques et quans ses guarans doivent estre.

Qui viaut prover par garans,[2] il doit querre tes garans que l'on ne puisse dire contre yaus chose par quei il ne puissent[3] la garantie porter, et qu'il por Deu et por leauté et por lui portent cele garantie et facent tout quantque[4] garans doivent faire de sairement et de bataille et d'autres choses.[5] Que le seignor et la court ne autre ne peut garant constraindre[6] a garantie porter en la haute court. Et celui qui[7] viaut prover par garans se doit garder que son aversaire ne le[8] sache qui sont ses garans qui doivent cele garantie porter, por ce qu'il ne les coronpe par loier ou par poour ou par aucune autre maniere, ou qu'il ne porchase chose par quei il les[9] mete en tel point ains qu'il portent la garantie, qu'il ne puissent cele garantie porter[10] au jor que celui avra[11] par court d'avoir ses garans amenés et[12] de prover par iaus ce qu'il avra ofert a prover.

A: fols xxxviii^{v}–xxxix^{r} cap. 70; **B:** fols 69^{v}–70^{r} cap. 70; **C:** fol. 55^{r} cap. 56; **O:** fol. 58^{r-v}; **V:** fol. liii^{r} cap. 68; Beugnot, pp. 113–14, cap. 70.

[1] B (fol. 19^{r}) adds: en la haute cort [2] par garans] C lacks [3] ne puissent] C: puissent; O: ne puisse [4] quantque] B: ce que [5] AB add: qui (A: i) besoignent [6] Que le seignor . . . constraindre] A: Ne le seignor ne la court ne peut garant defendre; B: Ne la court ne puet deffendre garant; V: Que le seignor ne la court ne peut deffendre [7] qui] C lacks [8] le] ABV lack [9] les] B: le [10] portent la garantie . . . porter] A: portent celle garentie, qu'il ne la puissent porter; B: porte la garantie qu'il ne puisse cele garantie [11] avra] B lacks [12] et] AV lack

***[58]** Ques gens ne pevent porter[1] garantie en la haute cort.[2]

Ces sont ceaus qui ne pevent porter garantie en la haute court et qui n'ont vois ne respons en court: parjurs,[3] foy menties, traytors, bastars,[4] avoutres, ceaus de qui le chanpion a[5] esté vencu en chanp, ceaus qui ont esté reneés ou qui ont servi an et jor sarrasins contre crestiens ou gres,[6] [a] ou gens de tel nacion qui ne sont obeissans a Rome: gres ne suriens ne ermins ne jacopins. Ne gens de[7] nassion qui ne sont[8] obeissans a Rome[9] ne pevent[10] porter garantie en la haute cort, se ce n'est contre celui ou[11] ceaus qui sont de sa nacion que des .ii. dites choses. Que nul ne peut porter garantie en la haute court[12] contre[13] persones qui ne sont[14] de sa nacion,[15] se il[16] n'est de prover aage ou[17] lignage. Ne feme ne home[18] de religion ne prestre ne clerc,[19] tout soit[20] il de la loy de Rome, ne pevent porter garantie en la haute court[21] que de prover aage ou lignage. Ne enfans de mains de .xv. ans ne pevent [22] porter garantie en la haute court. Ne nul ne peut porter garantie en la haute court[23] de ce dont il est parsonier. Ne serf ne peut porter garantie en la haute court.[24]

A: fol. xxxix^r cap. 71; **B:** fol. 70^r cap. 71; **C:** fol. 55^r–v cap. 57; **O:** fols 58^v–59^r; **V:** fol. liii^r–v cap. 69; Beugnot, p. 114, cap. 71.

---

[a] There is a significant difference here in the MSS. I understand the phrase as found in CO to mean '... who have served Saracens or Greeks for a year and a day against the Christians' and this reading receives qualified support from the parallel passage in Philip of Novara (p. 502). The alternative is to punctuate it so that 'gres' is linked to 'gens de tel nacion' in a new sentence, but that is unlikely in view of the repetition of 'gres' that follows. B omits the words 'ou gres'. A and V re-write the passage so that 'grex' now becomes part of the subject of the main verb in the sentence that follows: 'Greeks or people of those nations ...' and suppress the list of eastern Christian groups. In V 'ou gres' or 'ou grex' is heavily scored out, perhaps a reflection of opinion in Cyprus in the fifteenth century.

---

[1] porter] V: prover [2] V adds: dou royaume de Jerusalem et de Chipre [3] parjurs] A: esparjurés; V: sparjurés [4] bastars] A lacks [5] de qui le chanpion a] B: qui ont [6] ou gres] A: Grex (beginnings new sentence); B lacks; V heavily scored out [7] B adds: nule [8] sont] B soit [9] gres ne suriens ... a Rome] AV lack [10] pevent] B: puet [11] ce n'est contre celui ou] A: ne sont contre [12] se ce n'est contre ... court] B lacks [13] V adds: toutes [14] persones qui ne sont] B: persone qui ne soit [15] sa nacion que ... nacion] A: leur nassion [16] se il] A: ou ce ce; B: se ce [17] ou] C: et [18] feme ne home] AB: home ne feme [19] de religion ne prestre ne clerc] V: ne prestre ne clerc ne home de religion [20] soit] AB: soient [21] en la haute court] BV lack [22] enfans de mains ... pevent] ABV: enfant de meins (V: mains) de .xv. anz ne peut [23] Ne nul ne ... court] A: Ne nul; OV lack [24] en la haute court] ABV lack

***[59]** Que doit faire celui encontre qui l'on viaut prover par prevelige.[1]

Se vostre aversaire viaut prover contre vos par preveliges, soies guaitans soutilment de noter[2] les poins dou prevelige savoir se vos par aucun point poés[3] vostre aversaire acrocher a faire[4] faillir a sa preuve. Et s'il y a aucun point a coi vos le puissés acrocher, si le faites desfaisant sa[5] preuve, mostrant raisons que sa preuve ne vaut, et si clerement le faites que la cort l'entende.[6]

A: fol. xxxix^{r} cap. 72; **B:** fol. 70^{r} cap. 72; **C:** fol. 55^{v} cap. 58; **O:** fol. 59^{r}; **V:** fol. liii^{v} cap. 70; Beugnot, p. 115, cap. 72.

[1] prevelige] A rubrics (fol. 2^{v}): garentie; V: guarentie [2] noter] C: noier [3] poés] B: porriez [4] faire] B lacks [5] sa] C: la [6] et si clerement . . . l'entende] B: riens

***[60]** Quant l'on viaut prover aucune choze par recort de court, que celui doit dire et faire contre qui l'on viaut prover.

Se vostre aversaire viaut prover contre vos par recort de court et il a[1] en la court aucun home qui ne soit vostre per ou qui n'ait vois en court que vos doutés qu'il ne porte cel recort contre vos, si le getés de la cort. Et qui viaut geter de cort home qui n'est[2] son per ou qui n'a[3] vois en court,[4] il doit dire au seignor et a la cort quant la court s'asiet[5] por jugier et celui ou ceaus qui n'ont[6] vois en court[7] aveuc yaus: 'Sire, je pri et requier[8] a vos et a la court que vos ne soufrés que tel ou tes', et les nome,[9] 'qui ne sont mes[10] pers ou qui ont perdu[11] vois de[12] court soient[13] a cest esgart ou a ceste conoissance ou a cest recort. Que[14] je n'entent qu'il puisse de[15] chose qui soit de mon cors ne de m'enor ne de mon fié faire[16] esgart ne[17] conoissance ne recort,[18] por ce qu'il est tel por quei il ne le peut ne ne doit faire', et die ques il[19] est, 'por quei je ne vueill que il le face, se la court ne l'esgarde, et de ce me met je en l'esgart de la court sauf mon retenaill.' Et se il n'est son per si qu'il le puisse juger, ou il n'est tel qu'il ait[20] vois de cort, il ne peut[21] chose dire par quei la court esgarde que il doie seir en la court faire esgart ne conoissance ne recort de[22] chose qui soit de son cors ne de son fié ne de s'enor. Et se ceaus de la cort sont tes qu'il n'en puisse nul[23] geter de recort, si note bien ce que la court[24] retraira qu'ele avra recordé.[25] Et se il y ait[26] choze a quei il se puisse prendre a faire faillir a son aversaire a sa preuve, si le face le meaus et le plus soutilment et le plus entendaument qu'il porra.[27]

A: fol. xxxix^{r-v} cap. 73; **B:** fol. 70^{r-v} cap. 73; **C:** fols 55^{v}–56^{r} cap. 59; **O:** fol. 59^{r-v}; **V:** fols liii^{v}–liv^{r} cap. 71; Beugnot, pp. 115–16, cap. 73.

---

[1] a] A: n'ait [2] n'est] A: ne seit [3] n'a] B: n'ait [4] ou qui n'a vois en court] A lacks [5] s'asiet] AB: se siet [6] n'ont] O: ont [7] A adds: ou qui ne sont ces pers [8] et requier] AB lack [9] quant la court . . . nome] V: 'Je vous pri que vous ne souffrés que tel home', et le nome, 'ou tel [10] mes] B: mie [11] ont perdu] AB: n'ont [12] de] ABV: en [13] soient] C: seent; V: soient a cest recort ou [14] Que] B: Car [15] puisse de] A: puissent jugier; B: puissent de [16] cors ne de . . . faire] B: cors fyé ne de mon henor [17] ne] C: ou [18] faire esgart ne . . . recort] A: ni esgart ni conoissance ni recort faire; B: esgart ne conoissance ne recort faire [19] por quei il . . . il] B: qu'il ne le puet faire ne doit faire', et die ce qu'il [20] ait] BV: n'ait [21] peut] A: pora; V: porra [22] de] CO: ne [23] puisse nul] B: puissent nul hoster ne [24] la court] A: la court recordera et; B: l'on recordera et [25] recordé] C: recort [26] Et se il y ait] A: Et se il y a; B: si il y a [27] B adds: ne savra

***[61]** Coment l'on doit garans enpeescher et coment rebuter et coment torner.[1]

Se vostre aversaire viaut contre vos prover par garans, se il sont tes que il puissent garantie porter,[2] et vos les conoissés et vos ne volés que cele garantie soit portee contre vos, se vos avés droit en cele querele et que vos cuidiés que lor[3] garantie vos toille[4] vostre droit, metés les avant que il portent cele garantie en tel point par quei il ne la puissent porter contre vos. Et se vos ce volés faire, si le faites enssi:[5] quant vostre aversaire avra jor par cort de ses garans amener,[6] venés en la court avant celui jor[7] et vos clamés ou faites aucun autre clamer d'aucun de ceaus que vos savrés[8] qui la garantie devront[9] porter contre vos, et el clain lor metés sus ou faites metre aucune malefaite[10] et tel qu'il coveigne a prover par garans en quei il i ait[11] tornes de bataille, et ofrés[12] a prover ce que vos li metés sus, si con la court esgardera ou conoistra que vos prover le doiés. Et la court esgardera, se croy, que vos le devés prover par .ii.[13] loiaus garans.[14] Et quant la court avra ce esgardé, vouchés[15] vos garans si loins que vos aiés si lonc jor a vos garans amener,[16] que le jor que la court avra doné a vostre aversaire de ses garans amener soit ains pacé que le jor veigne que la court vos avra doné a[17] vos garans amener a prover contre celui qui la garantie devra[18] porter contre vos. Et puis que vos avrés ce fait, se vostre aversaire ameine a son jor le garant[19] a qui vos ou autre avrés[20] mis sus la malefaite et ofert a prover le par garans, et celui vueille[21] porter[22] garantie contre vos, quant vostre aversaire l'amenra[23] en la court et l'oferra a garant por

A: fols xxxix^{v}–xli^{v} cap. 74; **B:** fols 70^{v}–72^{v} cap. 74; **C:** fols 56^{r}–58^{v} cap. 60; **O:** fols 59^{v}–63^{r}; **V:** fols liv^{r}–lvi^{v} cap. 72; Beugnot, pp. 116–20, cap. 74.

[1] coment rebuter et coment torner] B (fol. 19^{v}): rebuter et torner; O: coment rebuter et coment torter [2] que il puissent garantie porter] A: qu'il puissent celle garentie porter par court; B: c'on les puisse geter par court; V: que il puissent guarentie porter par tout [3] lor] A: celle leur; B: cele [4] toille] C: faille [5] AB add: que [6] AB add: et vos [7] jor] V lacks [8] savrés] A: savés; B: savez [9] devront] A: deivent; B: doivent [10] aucune malefaite] B: d'aucun mesfait. Throughout this chapter B has 'mesfait' (m) for 'malefaite' (f) with consequent changes of gender for pronouns and adjectives. [11] en quei il i ait] A: et en quei il y a; BV: et en qui il ait [12] ofrés] C: ofert [13] .ii.] B: .iii. [14] A adds: de la lei de Rome [15] vouchés] A: voés; B: devochiez [16] amener] A: amenés [17] a] AB: de [18] devra] A: deit; B: devoit [19] le garant] V: les guarens [20] avrés] B: avez; O: avés [21] O adds: prover par garans [22] ABO add: la [23] l'amenra] B: le metra

la garantie porter, dites au garant[24] maintenant ains qu'il[25] porte la garantie ne qu'il s'agenoille por faire le sairement que guarant doit faire:[26] 'Tien toi', et le només[27] par son non et dites [28] au seignor: 'Sire, je ne vueill que cestui garant soit reseu[29] a garant contre moi, ne qu'il garantie porte contre moi tant que il s'en soit[30] aleiauté de la malefaite que l'on li met sus. Qu'il ne[31] peut garantie porter ne faire ce que garant peut et doit faire contre celui qui vodroit[32] sa garantie faucer, se il n'est avant aleiautés de la malefaite[33] que l'on li a mise sus en vostre court et qu'on a ofert a prover contre lui, si con vostre[34] cort l'a esgardé,[35] et de quei l'on a jor par cort a ses garans amener a prover li ce que l'on li met sus. Quar home, a qui l'on a mis sus en court[36] tel malefaite, con l'on a mis sus a cestui, et que on li[37] a ofert a prover si con court esgardera ou conoistra et que court a esgardé ou coneu coment l'on li doit[38] prover, ne peut ne ne doit garantie porter par l'assise ou l'usage dou reiaume de Jerusalem tant qu'il s'en[39] soit aleiauté, si com il doit, de la malefaite qu'on li a mise sus, si qu'il puisse la garantie porter et faire ce que[40] loiaus garans doit faire. Et por totes les raisons que je ai dites ou por aucunes d'eles ne vueill je que sa garantie soit receue[41] contre moi ne qu'ele vaille a mon aversaire n'a moi griege, se la court ne l'esgarde, et de ce me met je en l'esgart de la court sauf mon retenaill.' Et le garant ne celui qui l'a amené [42] en la court por la garantie porter ne poront[43] chose dire, se me senble, par quei la court doit esgarder que celui doie estre receu[44] en garantie tant qu'il se[45] soit aleauté en la cort,[46] si com il doit, de la malefaite que l'on li a sus mise en court avant[47] que il ait esté[48] moti ne ofert en cort[49] a garant.

Et se vos ne volés le garant enpeescher en la maniere desus dite, si notés le dit que l'avantparlier des garans[50] dira por eaus au plus

[24] garant] A: garant tot; B: seignor tout [25] ains qu'il] V: que il n'em [26] B adds: Frere [27] només] O: nome [28] et le només . . . dites] AB: et le nome par nom et puis dittes (B: ditez); V: par non et puis doit dire [29] cestui garant soit reseu] A: cestui seit receu; B: cestui garant soit retenuz; O: vos cestui garant recevés [30] s'en soit] ABV: se soit (A: seit); C lacks [31] ne] A lacks [32] vodroit] AV: vodra; B: voudra [33] la malefaite] V: de querele faite [34] vostre] C lacks [35] l'a esgardé] B: esgardera [36] en court] B lacks [37] li] AB lack [38] li doit] V: le doit faire [39] s'en] AB: se [40] ce que] A: que; B: com [41] receue] A: portee; B: retenue [42] le garant ne . . . amené] V: les guarens ne celui qui les a amenés [43] poront] A: peut; B: puet [44] A adds: en court [45] se] BV lack [46] en la cort] A lacks [47] avant] A: anseis [48] esté] O lacks [49] en cort] AB lack [50] des garans] A lacks

soutilment que vos porrés et savrés et l'enpeeschés et desfaites tant con vos porrés,[51] mostrant raisons et senblances[52] de droit por cel dit caser[53] et varier. Et se vos ne le poés[54] faire ou ne savés ou ne volés, quant l'avantparlier aura dit por yaus, et il se traïent[55] avant por le sairement faire, ains que il s'agenoillent por faire le sairement dites a[56] celui que vos vodrés geter de garantie:[57] 'Tien toy. Je[58] dis que tu n'es pas tel que tu puisses ceste garantie porter contre moy, et di por coy: por ce que tu es tel',[59] et dites ce que vos savrés de lui, c'est assaveir[60] une des choses qui devant sont devisees en cest livre por quei on ne peut garantie porter en la haute court, et ofrés a prover ce que vos li metés sus, si con la court esgardera ou conoistra que vos le doiés prover. Quar autrement vostre dit ne vaudroit riens. Et ce faites ains qu'il aient fait le sairement, que se celui que vos volés ensi geter de la garantie porter avoit fait le sairement, vos ne li poriés puis[61] metre sus nule des[62] choses devant[63] dites qui vos vausist[64] a geter le de[65] garantie. Car se il font[66] ce que leiaus garans doivent[67] faire, et vos ne l'aiés contredit ou enpeesché[68] avant en l'une des manieres desus dites, vostre aversaire avra celui plait desrainé contre[69] vos et sa querele gaaignee,[70] se ce n'est de querele de quei vos volés torner con faus garant l'un des garans par gage de bataille et lever le con parjor.

Et se ce est[71] de querele en[72] quei il i a tornes de bataille et vos volés l'un des garans torner de garantie come faus garant et lever l'en con parjuir et aerdre vos en a lui,[73] se lor dit[74] est tel que vos ne le poés[75] contredire et les persones sont tes que vos ne les puissés coronpre n'enpeescher ne contredire par les raisons desus dites, quant[76] il avront juré ce qu'il vos metront sus, si en poés[77] l'un d'eaus lever, le quel que vos vodrés, et conbatre vos en a lui de vostre cors ou metre[78] chanpion en vostre leuc, se vos estes tel que vos faire le

---

[51] tant con vos porrés] A: au miaus que voz savrés; B: au meaus que vos savrez [52] raisons et senblances] B: raison et semblance; V: raisons semblables [53] caser] B: tenser [54] ne le poés] A: ce ne volés; B: ce ne poez [55] traïent] AB: traïront [56] a] O lacks [57] de garantie] B: dou garant [58] A adds: te [59] que tu puissés . . . tel] V lacks [60] c'est assaveir] ABV lack [61] puis] B lacks [62] nule des] B: nulles; V: nulle chose de [63] devant] AB: avant [64] vausist] B: vausissent [65] ABV adds: la [66] font] V: fait [67] doivent] V: doit [68] vos ne l'aiés . . . enpeesché] AB: il ne seent contredis ou (B: soient contredit ne) empeeschiez [69] desrainé contre] AB: gaaignié contre; O: desarmé couverte [70] gaaignee] A: desrainiee; B: desraisnee [71] est] C: n'est [72] en] ABV: de [73] aerdre vos en a lui] B lacks [74] dit] C lacks [75] poés] B: puissés [76] quant] B: si com [77] poés] AV: porés [78] metre] B: metre un; O: metre y; V: mete y

puissés et deés par raison. Et se vos ce volés faire, si le faites enssi que si tost con celui que vos vodrés torner avra le sairement fait, pernés le maintenant par le poin, ains qu'il se lieve, et dites li: 'Tu mens come faus garant, et je t'en[79] lief come parjur'.[80] Et l'en levés et dites maintenant: 'Et je suis prest que je le te preuve de mon cors contre le tien, et que je te rendrais[81] mort ou recreant en une hore de jor, et vez ci mon gage.' Et tende son[82] gage au seignor a genous.

Et por ce que l'assise[83] ou l'usage dou reiaume de Jerusalem est tel que de querele d'un marc d'argent ou de plus que il a tornes de bataille quant l'on l'eufre a prover si con court esgardera ou conoistra que prover le doie, et que la court esgarde ou conoisse[84] que l'on le doit prover par .ii. loiaus garans de la loy de Rome, et que l'on peut l'un des garans torner con faus garant et lever con parjur et conbatre s'en a lui,[85] di je que l'on le face en cest cas aprés le sairement, quar l'on[86] ne porroit lever le garant con parjur devant le sairement.[87] Car nul n'est esparjuré de sairement qu'il ait a faire[88] tant qu'il ait fait le sairement. Ne il n'est faus garant tant que il ait[89] la garantie portee faucement. Ne il ne l'a[90] faucement portee[91] tant qu'il s'en[92] soit parjuré. Et qui l'en[93] leveroit devant[94] ce qu'il eust le sairement fait, il ne le levroit mie come parjur ne ne torneroit come faus garant, et se il se conbatoit a lui il se metroit en faus gages se il disoit qu'il se[95] fust parjuré et il ne le fust. Que nul ne le[96] peut a droit dire que nul [97] soit parjuré tant qu'il ait le sairement fait, ne bataille ne peut[98] estre[99] par assise ne par usage ne par raison de choze que on veulle faire tant qu'ele soit faite. Que[100] qui vodroit .i. home murtrir ou seignor traïr et eust juré sur sains de faire[101] ne le porroit on pas[102] apeler dou murtre ne de la traïson tant qu'il eust le murtre ou la traïson faite.[103] Que moult de choses enprent on a faire et dit on que l'on les fera qu'on ne fait pas.[104]

---

[79] t'en] ABV: te [80] parjur] V: faus esparjur [81] te rendrais] A: te rende; B: t'en rendrai; OV: t'en rende [82] tende son] B: rende son; OV: tendés le [83] O adds: est [84] que la court . . . conoisse] B: la cort esgardera [85] et conbatre s'en a lui] A lacks [86] l'on] B: il; V: nul [87] quar l'on ne . . . sairement] A lacks [88] n'est esparjuré de . . . faire] B: est parjuré de chose que il face ne die [89] V adds: le serement fait et [90] ne l'a] O: aie la [91] Ne il ne l'a faucement portee] C lacks [92] s'en] ABV: se [93] l'en] OV: le [94] devant] B: avant [95] se] AB lacks [96] le] ABV lack [97] ne le peut . . . nul] C lacks [98] peut] A: poreit; B: porroit [99] V adds: faite [100] Que] ABV: Et [101] ABV adds: le [102] on pas] B: l'on mie; V: l'em plus [103] la traïson faite] V: le larrecin faite ou la trayson [104] les fera qu'on . . . pas] AB: fera que l'on ne fait pas (B: mie); V: les fera que ne les fait pas

Et por ces raisons et por pluisors autres que l'on[105] i porroit[106] dire est il cler[107] a conoistre que l'on doit au[108] garant[109] laissier faire le sairement ains que l'on le torne come faus garant ne leve con parjur[110] ne s'aerde a lui par gage de bataille ne se mete en droite loy de[111] bataille vers lui.

Et le garant que l'on lieve, si con est desus dit, con parjur doit respondre maintenant a celui qui enssi l'a levé:[112] 'Tu mens, et je suis prest que je m'en aleaute contre toi et m'en defende[113] mon cors contre le tien et t'en rende[114] mort ou recreant[115] en une hore de jor, et vés ci mon gage.' Et tende au seignor a genos son gage.[116] Et le seignor doit ces gages[117] recevoir et acener[118] lor le[119] jor de la bataille au quaranteime jor,[120] se ce n'est d'omecide en quei il n'a que .iii.[121] jors de respit,[122] ausi con de murtre.[123] Et il doivent a celui jor que le seignor lor avra asené a[124] venir devant le seignor[125] yaus[126] porofrir de la bataille faire, apareillés et adreciés de lor armes,[127] si con est dit aprés en ce livre que chanpion le doivent[128] faire de tel querele con il avront les gages donés. Et le garant qui est ensi torné et levé com est avant dit, se il[129] ne s'en aleiaute si con est desus[130] devisé, il a perdu a tos jors[131] vois et respons en court et sera tenus a faus et a desloiaus toute sa vie, et celui[132] por qui il devoit[133] la garantie porter perdra sa querele[134] que la garantie ne sera mie fornie. Que garantie n'est mie[135] fornie,[136] puis qu'on maintenant le torne[137] con faus garant et lieve con parjur et l'eufre l'on a prover, tant que le garant se soit aleiauté si com il doit.[138]

[105] que l'on] C: qu'on [106] i porroit] A: i peut; B: puet; V: porroit [107] cler] AB: clere chose [108] au] AV lack [109] que l'on doit au garant] B: qu'il covient [110] torne come faus . . . parjur] A: lieve come esparjuré ne torne come faus garent; B: lieve come parjuré ne come faus garant ne [111] loy de] B: de la [112] l'a levé] V: le lieve [113] AO add: de [114] rende] BV: rendrai [115] recreant] B: vencu [116] au seignor a . . . gage] B: le au seignor a genous [117] ces gages] AB: le gage; O: les gages; V: les guages [118] acener] AB: asseir [119] lor le] ABV: le; C: lor [120] au quaranteime jor] B: a quarante jors [121] en quei il n'a que .iii.] B: qu'ele n'a que .xv. [122] ABV adds: de la bataille [123] ausi con de murtre] B lacks [124] a] ABV lack [125] lor avra asené . . . seignor] O lacks [126] yaus] A: et eaus; B: et soi; V: et yaus [127] armes] A: armeures [128] doivent] B: doit venir [129] se il] V lacks [130] desus] B lacks [131] il a perdu a tos jors] B: a perdu toutes; V: il y a tout jours perdue [132] B adds: aussi [133] devoit] V: devroit [134] A adds: por ce [135] porter perdra sa . . . mie] B: faire [136] fornie] BC lack [137] qu'on maintenant le torne] A: que l'on torne maintenant le garant; B: qu'on la torne maintenant; V: que home maintenant la torne [138] le garant se . . . doit] V: les garens se sont aleautés si com il doivent

*[62] Quant chevalier porte garantie contre home qui n'est chevalier, coment il le peut rebuter et coment torner.

Se .i. chevalier porte garantie contre .i. home qui n'est[1] chevalier de choze de quei[2] il i a tornes de bataillle, et celui qui n'est chevalier le viaut torner par gage de bataille et[3] conbatre s'en a lui, il le doit faire en la maniere qu'il est devant dit[4] qu'on doit torner garant. Et se il le fait enssi, il ne me senble que le chevalier en cest[5] cas se puisse defendre d'aerdre s'en a lui de bataille par ce qu'il est chevalier et l'autre n'en est mie, tout soit ce que chevalier n'est pas tenus d'aerdre[6] se de bataille a home qui n'est[7] chevalier qui l'apele de murtre ou de traïson ou de pluisors[8] choses, se il ne viaut, tant qu'il soit chevalier. Car puis que le chevalier de sa volenté se mete a porter garantie contre home qui n'est[9] chevalier de chose qu'il y[10] a tornes de bataille, il est bien[11] aparant qu'il de sa volenté se mete a la[12] bataille, se celui contre qui il porte[13] la garantie le viaut lever[14] come parjur et torner[15] con faus garant, que nul seignor ne autre[16] ne le peut esforcier ne destraindre[17] de porter garantie en la haute court, se il ne le fait de sa volenté. Et l'assise ou l'usage[18] est tel que[19] qui porte garantie en la haute court de chose en quei[20] il i a[21] querele d'un marc d'argent ou de plus ou[22] de quei l'on perde vie ou[23] menbre ou s'enor qui en est ataint, qu'il le peut torner con faus garant et lever con parjur et aerdre s'en[24] a lui par gage de bataille. Ne chevalier ne autre n'en est excepté[25] en l'assise ne en l'usage.

Et est bien droit, se me senble, qu'enssi doive[26] estre, que s'enssi estoit que chevaliers peucent[27] porter garantie sur autres gens et que l'on ne les peut torner par gage de bataille, chevaliers avroient trop

A: fols xli^{v}–xlii^{v} cap. 75; **B:** fols 72^{v}–73^{v} cap. 75; **C:** fols 58^{v}–60^{r} cap. 61; **O:** fols 63^{r}–65^{v}; **V:** fols lvi^{v}–lviii^{v} cap. 73; Beugnot, pp. 120–3, cap. 75.

[1] n'est] A: n'est pas; B: n'est mie; O: ne soit [2] de quei] A en quei; B: dont [3] celui qui n'est . . . bataille et] CV lack [4] qu'il est devant dit] A: avant dite; B: qui est avant dite; V: qui est devant devisé [5] cest] C: ce [6] s'en a lui . . . d'aerdre] V lacks [7] A adds: pas; B: mie [8] AV adds: autres [9] AB add: mie [10] de chose qu'il y] A: de chose de quei il y; B: des choses de quoi il i; V: de chose de que il n'i [11] bien] O lacks [12] a la] AB: en la; V: em [13] porte] V: a porté [14] lever] AB: faire et lever le (B: l'en) [15] torner] ABV lack [16] autre] O: avra [17] destraindre] B: deffendre [18] A adds: dou reiaume [19] que] AO lack [20] en quei] AV: de quoi; B: dont [21] a] C: ait [22] A adds: de chose [23] vie ou] B lacks [24] s'en] A: sei; B: soi [25] excepté] A: en epté; C: expeté [26] doive] A: dee; BOV: doit [27] chevaliers peucent] V: chevalier peust

grans avantages sur toutes autres[28] gens, et autres gens que chevaliers seroient trop[29] malbaillis qu'il poroient[30] estre tos[31] mors et detruis quant les chevaliers vodroient ce, qui ne peut ne ne doit estre par raison ne par l'assise ne[32] l'usage dou reiaume de Jerusalem. Que[33] l'assise est tel que qui porte garantie contre autre de chose de quei la querele est d'un marc d'argent ou de plus[34] ou de chose de quei l'on doit perdre[35] vie ou[36] menbre ou de[37] s'enor, qu'il peut torner le garant par guage de bataille. Ne en cest cas ne doit pas estre ce que l'on dit que chevalier ne se doie aerdre par guage de bataille a home qui n'est[38] chevalier por ce que celui n'est[39] son per. Que celui contre qui l'on doit porter[40] la garantie ne savra pas espoir que chevalier doive la garantie porter contre lui por quei il ne se sera[41] mie fait faire chevalier, et se il ne le peut torner ou rebuter se il n'estoit[42] chevalier, il avroit sa querele perdue. Que l'on[43] doit le garant[44] rebuter ains qu'il face le sairement et torner maintenant qu'il l'a fait,[45] si nel porroit celui qui n'est chevalier faire ce, se il n'est[46] chevalier. Por quei il[47] me senble que il le peut bien torner, tout ne[48] soit il chevalier, et conbatre s'en a lui. Mais que il soit chevalier quant il se vodra[49] porofrir. Que se il n'estoit chevalier au porofrir et a la bataille faire, il ne me senble que le chevalier fust tenus de conbatre s'en[50] a lui, que[51] chevalier n'est tenus par l'assise ou l'usage dou reiaume de Jerusalem[52] de conbatre se a home qui l'apele se il n'est[53] chevalier. Que par l'asise ou l'usage dou dit reiaume[54] l'apeleor doit sivre le defendeor en sa loy, ne home qui n'est chevalier ne se peut conbatre en[55] loi de chevalier. Si est clere chose, se me senble, que quant home qui n'est[56] chevalier apele chevalier, qu'il covient qu'il se face faire chevalier ains qu'il se conbate a lui, et ce est[57] en ce cas. Mais en autre[58] cas covient il que il soit chevalier ains qu'il l'apele, ou le chevalier ne s'aerdra[59] mie a lui. Mais le cas en quei home qui n'est chevalier n'est[60] per dou chevalier ne ne peut dire chose ne faire contre chevalier qui[61] li

[28] V adds: manieres de [29] trop] OV lack [30] poroient] B: em porroient; C: porront [31] tos] V: tos jours [32] AOV add: par [33] Que] B: Car; O: Quar [34] ou de plus] B: en amont [35] doit perdre] V: pert [36] B lacks: vie ou [37] de] AB lack [38] AB add: mie [39] AB add: mie [40] doit porter] V: porte [41] sera] A: savra [42] n'estoit] AB: n'est [43] V adds: ne [44] O adds: torner ou [45] l'a fait] A: a fait le seirement [46] n'est] V: n'estoit [47] V adds: ne [48] ne] C: ni [49] se vodra] AO: se vendra; V: s'en vera [50] s'en] A: sei; B: soi [51] que] BV: car [52] de Jerusalem] C lacks [53] l'apele se il n'est] B: n'est mie [54] par l'asise ou . . . reiaume] B lacks; V adds: de Jerusalem [55] en] ABV: a [56] n'est] O: est [57] et ce est] A: et ce est ensi; B: enssi est [58] autre] ABV: l'autre [59] s'aerdra] B: s'aherdroit [60] n'est] AB: ne [61] qui] V: et ce que

vaille est devisé en ce livre la ou il parole de la franchise que les chevaliers ont sur les autres gens. Et se .i. chevalier[62] viaut porter garantie contre[63] home qui n'est chevalier, et celui le veuille geter de la garantie,[64] metant li sus l'une des choses desus[65] devisees par quei l'on ne peut porter garantie, et l'eufre a prover, si con la cort esgardera ou conoistra qu'il prover le doie, faire le peut. Et se il le fait, il me senble que la court doit esgarder ou conoistre qu'il le doit prover par .ii. loiaus garans de la loy de Rome qui facent que loiaus garans et qu'il soient chevaliers. Et il me senble qu'enssi doive estre con je ai dit en ce chapitle por .ii. raisons. L'une, que le chevalier porte la garantie de sa[66] volenté sans ce que nul l'en[67] puisse esforcier, et qu'il set ou doit savoir que qui porte garantie contre autre qu'il l'en peut torner et[68] rebuter par l'assise ou l'usage dou dit reiaume[69] si con est avant[70] dit. L'autre raison[71] est que le chevalier s'aleaute contre celui qui li met desleauté sus,[72] que[73] qu'il dit qu'il ne peut porter garantie contre lui. Que chevalier nés de leal mariage[74] qui n'a esté ataint ou prové en court de l'une des choses par quei l'on pert vois et respons en court se peut et doit aleauter contre chascun, soit chevalier ou[75] autre, qui desloiauté li met sus ou aucune des avant dites choses par quei l'on ne peut garantie porter en la haute court.

Et se home qui n'est chevalier porte garantie contre chevalier et[76] chevalier le veut torner de la garantie et lever con[77] parjur et conbatre s'en a lui, il se conbatra a pié come sergent por ce que l'apelor doit sivre[78] le defendeour en sa lei. Car[79] le chevalier en cest cas est apeleor et le sergent defendeor.[80] Et se chevalier viaut rebuter de garantie home qui n'est[81] chevalier et li met sus l'une des choses par quei l'on ne peut porter garantie et il l'eufre a prover si con la court esgardera ou conoistra qu'il prover le doive, la court doit esgarder ou conoistre, se cuit,[82] qu'il le doit prover par .ii. loiaus garans de la loi de Rome, et qu'a ceste preuve faire soufist bien autre que chevalier, se me senble, por ce que la preuve est contre autre que chevalier.

---

[62] chevalier] O: home [63] ABV add: un [64] la garantie] B: garant; O: gartie [65] desus] AV: devant [66] le chevalier porte . . . sa] ABV: les chevaliers portent garentie (B: garantie; V: la guarentie) de lor (A: leur) [67] l'en] AV: les; BO: le [68] et] ABV: ou [69] dit reiaume] V: roiame de Jerusalem [70] avant] A: devant [71] A adds: si; V: ci [72] li met deleauté sus] B: le veut desleauter [73] que] AB: de ce; V lacks [74] nés de leal mariage] B: n'est desloiau garant [75] ou] A: ou seit; B: soit [76] ABV add: le [77] lever con] O: levet [78] sivre] B: ensivre [79] Car] V: en quoi [80] en sa lei . . . defendeor] CO lack [81] AB add: mie [82] cuit] B: me semble

***[63]** Quel terme l'on a d'amener[1] ses garans selon le leuc ou il les vouche.[2]

Qui eufre a prover par garans et il vouche ses garans el[3] roiaume ou il est, il a .xv. jors de respit d'avoir les amenés en la court a prover par iaus ce qu'il a ofert.[4] Et qui les vouche deça mer[5] hors[6] dou reiaume, il en a .xl. jors de respit. Et se il est yver et il les a vouchés[7] en leuc ou il les coveigne mer a paser, il a .iii.[8] mois de respit. Et qui les vouche en Romanie[9] et il est eysté, il a .iii. mois de respit, et se il est yver, il en a .vi. mois.[10] Et qui les vouche outre mer, il en a .i. an et .i. jor de respit.[11]

A: fol. xlii^{v} cap. 76; **B:** fol. 73^{v} cap. 76; **C:** fol. 60^{r} cap. 62; **O:** fol. 65^{v}; **V:** fol. lviii^{v} cap. 74; Beugnot, p. 123, cap. 76.

---

[1] d'amener] V: de mener [2] vouche] A: a voés; V: a vochés [3] et il vouche ses garans el] A: et il les voe ou; B: que il vouche ou; V: et il les a avochés a [4] AB add: a prover [5] deça mer] B: d'eaus [6] hors] A: fors [7] a vouchés] A: voe; B: vouche [8] .iii.] B: quatre [9] Romanie] B: Hermenie [10] BV add: de respit [11] de respit] AB lack

***[64]** Quant l'on a amenés ses guarans a court, quei l'on doit dire et faire et quei les guarans doivent dire et faire en la garantie porter.[1]

Quant celui qui a ses garans vouchés les a[2] amenés en la court, il doit par son conseill faire dire[3] au seignor: 'Vés ci les garans de tel', et le nome, 'qu'il a amenés por garantir ce qu'il a ofert a prover par yaus, et il sont prest de porter l'en[4] garantie et de faire que loiaus garans. Donés lor conseill por lor parole dire[5] de la garantie porter ensi con il la li enchargeront.' Et le seignor doit lors demander a celui qui les garans a vouchés, 'Sont ce vos garans?' Et s'il dit 'oyl', il lor doit doner conceill tel com il le demanderont,[6] se il ne le retient a sa parole garder ou se il ne l'a doné a conceill de l'autre partie de cele querele. Et quant il avront conceill, le conceill doit dire por iaus[7] ce que il li enchargeront. Et se il ne viaut dire lor[8] parole, yaus ou celui por qui il portent la garantie doivent .i. home aveir aponsté qui dit por iaus lor parole,[9] por ce que le seignor ne peut destraindre celui de ses homes qu'il done a conceill de dire la parole se il ne viaut, tout soit ce que il le puisse destraindre de doner le au conceill de celui qui le requiert, puis qu'il li doit servise de son cors, et por ce doivent les garans avoir home qui die lor parole. Que lor guarantie doit estre portee ensenble par[10] une vois, qu'en la haute court les .ii. garans[11] font dire ensenble la parole de lor garantie et aprés jurent[12] que il est enssi con celui l'a dit por yaus quant l'on lor seufre[13] le sairement a faire.

Et celui por qui il la[14] portent la garantie, se il est sage,[15] sera bien certain, ains qu'il les amoine[16] a court, qu'il porteront[17] por lui la garantie enssi com il l'a oferte et qu'il feront[18] dou jurer et de la bataille, s'ele i eschet, tot quantque garans doivent faire. Et quant il sont paiés de conceill, il lor doit dire devant lor conceill: 'Je vos

---

A: fols xlii^{v}–xliii^{v} cap. 77; **B:** fols 73^{v}–74^{v} cap. 77; **C:** fols 60^{r}–61^{r} cap. 63; **O:** fols 65^{v}–67^{r}; **V:** fols lviii^{v}–lix^{v} cap. 75; Beugnot, pp. 124–5, cap. 77.

---

[1] en la garantie porter] AB (fol. 19^{v}) lack [2] vouchés les a] V: avochiés et [3] faire] V lacks [4] l'en] ABV: la [5] dire] V: mostrer [6] demanderont] C: demanderoit [7] AV add: leur (V: lor) parole [8] ne viaut dire lor] B: veulent dire la [9] V adds: ce que il lor enchargeront [10] par] ABV: a [11] les .ii. garans] ABV lack [12] jurent] AV jurent ensemble; B: jurer ensemble [13] seufre] A: euffre [14] la] ABV lack [15] est sage] ABV: fait que sage, il [16] amoine] B: amerme; O: a nomé [17] porteront] O: portent [18] et qu'il feront] V: a faire

ai ci amenés por porter garantie de tel choze que je ai ofert a prover par vos con par garans', et die lor la chose qu'il a oferte a prover et coment il l'a oferte a prover.[19] Si lor prie et requiert qu'il portent cele garantie por lui si con il doivent. Et se il sont menbrans qu'enssi soit et qu'il en[20] puissent faire come leaus garans, si[21] li doivent dire: 'Nos somes bien menbrans qu'enssi fu con vos dites, et de ce vos porterons nos[22] bien[23] garantie et ferons come leaus garans.' Et aprés doivent encharger a leur avantparlier que il die[24] por yaus qu'il furent el leuc et en la place ou il virent et oirent tel chose faire et dire, et dient coi[25] selonc ce que la garantie est qu'il veulent porter et qu'il[26] eufrent a faire ce que leaus garans doivent faire. Et lors l'avantparlier doit dire por iaus: 'Sire, tel et tel', et les nome, 'vos dient, et je por yaus, qu'il furent el leuc et en la place ou il virent[27] tel chose faire et oirent tel chose[28] dire', et die[29] a qui et coy, 'et de ce eufrent il a faire que[30] loiaus garans.' Et lors le seignor doit faire aporter une evangile et dire as garans: 'Venés avant et jurés qu'il est enssi con vostre avantparlier l'a dit por vos'. Et il si[31] doivent traïre avant por[32] le sairement faire. Et adonc[33] celui contre qui il veulent porter[34] la garantie, se il viaut aucun d'eaus contredire et geter de garantie, il le doit faire enssi com il est devant[35] dit qu'on le doit faire[36] ains qu'il portent la garantie ne[37] qu'il facent le sairement. Et se il en[38] viaut l'un[39] torner par[40] bataille, il doit[41] a[42] celui qu'il viaut torner par bataille[43] laisser faire le sairement et lever le maintenant con parjur et torner con faus guarant et aerdre[44] s'en a lui en la maniere devant devisee.

[19] a prover] O lacks; et coment il . . . prover] V lacks [20] en] ABV lack [21] si] A: et ciaus; B: Et cil; O: cil [22] porterons nos] V: proumetons que nous vous porterons [23] bien] V lacks [24] die] B: dient [25] coi] B: ensi [26] C adds: en [27] virent] O: viaut [28] tel chose] O: chose; V lacks [29] die] ABV: dient [30] que] B: come; V: ce que [31] si] ABV: se [32] C adds: ofrir [33] Et adonc] B: et lors die; O: a droit [34] veulent porter] A: portent [35] devant] V: avant [36] enssi com il . . . faire] A lacks [37] ne] C lacks [38] en] AV lack; O: ne [39] A adds: lever ou [40] torner par] O: lever et torner par gage de [41] doit] V: li doit dire [42] a] C lacks [43] torner par bataille] A: lever par bataille; B: torner; C: torner de bataille [44] aerdre] C: aerde

*[65] Por quei[1] le guarant vif peut porter guarantie por le mort, et coment il la doit porter.

En la haute court peut porter guarantie le vif por le mort. Et quant on viaut prover par garans vif et mort, il doit dire au seignor quant son guarant vif est en la cort au jor qu'il a[2] de prover ce qu'il a ofert:[3] 'Sire, vostre cort m'ajorna a hui de prover par .ii. loiaus garans ce que je ofris[4] a prover, et vés ci tel qui est[5] mon guarant qui portera guarantie por lui et por tel qui est mort que au jor que ce que j'ai ofert a prover[6] fu fait[7] estoit vif et fu o cestui present la ou ce fu.[8] Et se il vesquist encor,[9] il me portast garantie aussi[10] con cestui fera.'[11] Et lors le seignor doit dire a celui: 'Porterés[12] vos guarantie a tel por vos et por tel qui est mort de ce dont il vos a vouchés[13] a garans?' Et il doit dire: 'Oil, Sire', et aprés faire en[14] ce qu'il doit. Ce est qu'il doit faire dire par son conceill: 'Sire, je et tel qui mort est qui au jor que[15] tel chose fu faite estoit vif fumes el leuc et en la place ou nos veimes et oimes tel chose', et die coy,[16] 'et se il vesquist il portast[17] ceste garantie aussi con je fais, et de ce sui je prest de faire quanque[18] loiaus garans doit faire.' Et le seignor doit faire aporter l'evangile et dire a celui: 'Venés avant. Jurés ce que vos devés[19] por vos et por le mort.' Et il se doit traïre avant por faire le sairement. Et adonc, se celui contre qui il viaut la garantie porter en[20] viaut torner ou geter de guarantie le vif, il le doit faire en la maniere desus dite. Et se il viaut aucune des choses devant[21] dites par quei l'on ne peut garantie porter metre sus au mort, il le peut faire. Et se il l'eufre a prover si con court esgardera ou conoistra qu'il le doit faire, se celui por qui la garantie doit estre portee veaut que la garantie vaille, il le doit aleauter et defendre de ce que l'on li avra mis sus ou faire aleiauter et defendre[22] par tel qu'il le

A: fols xliii[v]–xliv[r] cap. 78; **B:** fols 74[v]–75[r] cap. 78; **C:** fols 61[r]–62[r] cap. 64; **O:** fols 67[r]–68[v]; **V:** fols lix[v]–lx[v] cap. 76; Beugnot, pp. 125–6, cap. 78.

[1] Por quei] A: Coment [2] a] O lacks [3] a de prover . . . ofert] A: a de prover ce qu'il a offert de prover; B: offeri a prover [4] offris] V: ai offert [5] est] O: n'est [6] a prover] C lacks [7] ce que j'ai ofert a prover fu fait] B: je offri ce a prover [8] ce fu] O: ce fu fait; V: je fus [9] vesquist encor] B: fust vif [10] aussi] A lacks [11] fera] ABV: fait [12] a celui: 'Porterés] B: 'Portés [13] a vouchés] V: a avoué [14] faire en] B: face [15] que] C: qui [16] et die coy] B: dire ou faire; V: et dient quoi [17] portast] A: portereit [18] quanque] A: ent ce que [19] ce que vos devés] A: ce que voz dites; B: si com vos devez; O: ce que vos dites et que vos devez [20] en] ABV lack [21] devant] A: dessus [22] de ce que . . . defendre] ABV lac

puisse et doive faire. Et se il ne le fait, il avra failli a sa preuve et sa querele perdue. Et se celui contre qui la garantie doit estre portee[23] veaut torner le garant vif et aerdre s'en[24] a lui par bataille, il le doit faire en la maniere desus dite. Mais le garant mort ne peut on pas torner de garantie ne lever con parjur por ce qu'il ne fait nul sairement por quoi l'on ne l'en porroit lever con parjur,[25] ne l'on ne se poroit aerdre a lui par[26] bataille, n'apeler le, quar home mort ne se peut defendre ne conbatre soy. Et se l'on l'eufre[27] a faire le sairement a celui qui porte la garantie por lui et por le mort, il doit jurer qu'il est enssi con son avantparlier a dit por lui, et quant il a fait le dit[28] sairement, se celui contre qui il porte la garantie l'en[29] viaut torner par gage de bataille, il le peut faire en la maniere avant[30] dite.

[23] la garantie doit estre portee] V: il veaut la guarentie porter doit estre [24] s'en] A: sei; B: soi [25] por ce qu'il . . . parjur] AV lack [26] B adds: gage de [27] l'on l'eufre] ABV: l'on (B: l'en) seuffre (A sueffre) [28] dit] C lacks [29] l'en] AB: le; C: l'en li; V: l'on [30] avant] V: devant

***[66]** Qui conoit[1] devant gent que il doit a aucune persone dete ou qu'il est son plege ou qu'il i[2] ait aucuns[3] autres covenans, et celui a qui il dit que il est d'une[4] des dites chozes tenus n'est la present, se la dite conoissance[5] li doit valoir.

Se home ou feme conoist devant gens qu'il doit a aucun aucune dete et die conbien, ou qu'il est son plege d'aucune chose et die de coi, ou aucuns[6] covenans que il ait[7] a aucun, et celui a qui il dit[8] qu'il doit la dete ou vers qui il dit qu'il est[9] plege ou qu'il dit[10] qu'il a eu covenans est la present, cele conoissance li vaut, si[11] qu'il porra prover par la garantie de ceaus devant qui il avra ce coneu, la dete ou la plegerie[12] ou les covenans, et vaudra, se cuit,[13] la preuve de ceste conoissance autant con se il eussent esté present la ou celui li fist le prest, ou[14] la ou il entra vers lui en plege,[15] ou la ou il li ot les covenans. Mais se aucun dit devant gens: 'Je doi a tel tant',[16] et le nome et die conbien, ou die: 'Je suis plege vers tel de tel chose', et le nome et die de coi, ou: 'Je ai a tel tes covenans',[17] et les motisse, et celui a qui il dit qu'il[18] doit la dete ou vers qu'il[19] est plege ou a qui il a les covenans n'est la present, ceaus qui li avront ce oi dire ne pevent[20] porter garantie de cel dit que il[21] vaille a celui qu'il dist a qui il devoit la dete ou de qu'il dist qu'il estoit plege n'a celui a qui il dist qu'il avoit les covenans, por ce qu'il covient par la dite[22] assise ou le dit usage que[23] les guarans dient a la garantie porter qu'il furent[24] el leuc et en la place ou il oyrent a tel conoistre a tel[25] qui estoit present qu'il li[26] devoit tel chose ou qu'il estoit son plege de tel chose[27] ou que il li avoit tes[28] covenans et les noment et motissent[29] la dete[30] ou la plegerie[31] ou les covenans,[32] que autrement la garantie ne vaudra[33] par l'assise ou l'usage dou dit reiaume.[34]

A: fol. xliv^{r-v} cap. 79; **B:** fol. 75^{r-v} cap. 79; **C:** fol. 62^{r-v} cap. 65; **O:** fols 68^{v}–69^{r}; **V:** fols lx^{v}–lxi^{r} cap. 77; Beugnot, p. 127, cap. 79.

[1] conoit] A: conut [2] i] AB (fol. 19^{v}) V lack [3] aucuns] AV lack [4] d'une] A: de l'une; B: tenu de l'une; V: d'aucune [5] se la dite conoissance] B lacks [6] V adds: autres [7] ait] A: ont [8] dit] A: a dit [9] dit qu'il est] O: doit que il n'est [10] qu'il dit] AV: que il a dit; B lacks [11] Si] C: se [12] plegerie] B: plege [13] cuit] B: me semble [14] prest, ou] O: present en [15] plege] V: plegerie [16] tant] AB lack [17] V adds: et le nome [18] dit qu'il] O lacks [19] V adds: dit que il [20] pevent] B: porront; V: li peut [21] que il] B: qui; O: qui li [22] dite] B: droite [23] que] C: ou [24] furent] O: fucent [25] a tel conoistre a tel] B: a tel conoistre; V: tel et le nome a tel counoistre [26] li] BV lack [27] de tel chose] A lacks [28] li avoit tes] A: y aveit entr'iaus; B: li avoit; V: avoit [29] noment et motissent] B: motisse et; O: nome et motisse [30] B adds: motisse [31] ou la plegerie] V lacks [32] ou les covenans] B lacks [33] vaudra] B: vaudroit [34] dit reiaume] BV: reaume (V: royaume) de Jerusalem

***[67]** Des ques chozes[1] l'on[2] se peut clamer par l'assise de quei assise tot le jor.

Ce sont les choses de quei il me sovient[3] ore[4] de quei l'on se peut clamer par l'assise, et de quei l'on n'a point de jor au clain qu'on fait des dites choses por[5] ce qu'assise en[6] tot le jor:

De murtre aparant mostré a[7] court.[a]

D'omecide aparant mostré a[7] court.[8] [b]

De cop aparant mostré a[9] court.[10]

De rap,[11] ce est[12] de feme esforcee.[13] [c]

De force palaise[14] qu'on mostre au seignor et a[15] la court aparant,[16] si con est de chose dont l'on ait[17] esté saisi, et autre l'en a[18] dessaisi sans esgart ou sans conoissance de court.[19]

De defaut de servise.[20]

De defaut de homage.

De chose de quei il y a amende, con de foi mentie entre[21] seignor et home.

De dete[22] quant[23] l'on se claime par l'assise.[d]

De dete que sodeer requiert au[24] seignor de sa deserte.[e]

De plegerie de terre.[25]

De chose mal adiree.[26]

A: fol. xliv^{v} cap. 80; **B:** fol. 75^{v} cap. 80; **C:** fols 62^{v}–63^{r} cap. 66; **O:** fol. 69^{r-v}; **V:** fols lxi^{v}–lxii^{r} cap. 79; Beugnot, pp. 128–9, cap. 80.

---

[a] Below caps 69–79.
[b] Below caps 80–81.
[c] Below cap. 91.
[d] Below caps 102–16.
[e] Below caps 120–3.

---

[1] Des ques chozes] B (fol. 19v): De quele chose; V: Des choses [2] C adds: ne [3] sovient] C: senble [4] AV add: et [5] por] C: par [6] qu'assise en] V: que l'assise [7] a] AV: en [8] D'omecide aparant . . . court] B lacks [9] a] V: en [10] De cop aparant . . . court] A lacks [11] rap] C: rapt [12] De rap, ce est] B lacks [13] esforcee] A: esforsier [14] De force palaise] V: palesement [15] et a] AB: en [16] aparant] A lacks [17] dont l'on ait] A: de quei on a; B: dont l'on a [18] l'en a] B: l'en ait; V: l'a [19] A adds: De cop aparant (cf note 10) [20] servise] B: saisine [21] entre] A: contre son [22] entre seignor et home. De dete] B: come seignor et home doit doner [23] quant] AV: que [24] au] ABV: a (V: au) son [25] De plegerie de terre] A: De plegerie. De plegerie de dette; B: De plegerie; V: De plegerie de dete. De plegerie de terre [26] adiree] A: atiriee; BV: atiree

De chose prestee.

De guage perdu.

De chose vendue qui est[27] aparant de quei l'on n'en[28] a paie[29] receue.

De chose vendue a l'enchantement.[f]

De beste restive.[g]

De beste[30] vendue[31] sans enchantement[32] qui n'est restive.[h]

D'esclaf ou d'esclave[33] mezel ou mesele ou qui chiet dou mauvais mau.[i]

---

[f] Below cap. 124.
[g] Below cap. 99.
[h] Below cap. 125.
[i] Below cap. 118.

---

[27] qui est] B lacks [28] n'en] ABV lack [29] paie] O: point [30] De beste] O lacks [31] vendue] B: vendre [32] sans enchantement] V: a l'enchantement [33] A adds: qui est

***[68]** Des ques chozes l'on ne se[1] peut defendre par l'assise ne par l'usage d'aerdre se de bataille quant l'on en est apelé.[2]

Ce sont les choses de quey il i a bataille par l'assise ou l'usage dou reiaume de Jerusalem de quei l'on ne se peut defendre par esgart ne par conoissance de court sans bataille:

De murtre aparant mostré a[3] court.[a]

D'omecide aparant mostré a[3] court.[b]

De traïson aparant.[c]

De querele d'un marc d'argent ou de plus.[d]

D'atraire contre[4] son seignor chose a son fié qui n'en[5] soit.[e]

Et de toutes autres choses de quei on[6] perdroit vie ou menbre ou s'enor qui en seroit ataint ou prové[7] en cort.[8]

A: fol. xliv[v] cap. 81; **B:** fol. 75[v] cap. 81; **C:** fol. 63[r] cap. 67; **O:** fols 69[v]–70[r]; **V:** fol. lxii[r] cap. 80; Beugnot, p. 129, cap. 81.

---

[a] Below caps 69–79.
[b] Below caps 80–81.
[c] Below caps 82–5.
[d] Below cap. 218.
[e] Below caps 86–7.

---

[1] se] C lacks [2] quant l'on en est apelé] AB (fol. 19[v]) V lack [3] a] AV: en [4] D'atraire contre] AB: De traïre contre; O: D'atrane court [5] n'en] ABV: ne [6] de quei on] A: que on; B: dont l'on; V: c'om [7] prové] C: povré [8] en cort] A lacks; V: en la haute court

***[69]** Ques gens pevent faire apeau de murtre a qui l'on est tenus de respondre.

Por ce que le murtre est avant devisé en ce[1] livre que les autres choses de quei[2] on[3] se peut clamer par l'assise et avoir en droit,[4] et auquel clain il n'a point de jor et il[5] y a torne de bataille par l'assise ou l'usage dou reiaume de Jerusalem, en parlerai je premier. Si veuill avant deviser quel maniere de gens pevent faire apeau de murtre, vers qui on ne se peut defendre de respondre del[6] murtre par l'assise ou l'usage dou reiaume[7] de Jerusalem:

Feme espouse dou murtri.

Home espous de la murtrie.

Tos parens et parentes de sanguinité.

Tos parens et parentes d'afinité.[8]

Tous parains.

Toutes maraines.

Tos fileuls.

Toutes filleules.

Tos conperes.

Toutes comeres.

Tos ceaus et totes celes qui sont dou pais do murtri se il est pelerin estrange.

Tos ceaus et totes celes qui vindrent[9] au pasage a quei[10] il vint se il est d'outre mer.

Tos ceaus et toutes celes qui avront esté asos[11] aveuc le murtri ou aveuc la murtrie[12] an et jor.[13]

Le seignor ou la dame ou[14] qui le murtri ou la murtrie[15] avra[16] esté an et jor,[17] si con est devant[18] dit.

Tos ceaus et toutes celes qui sont tenus de foy au murtri ou a la murtrie, soit seignor ou dame, home ou feme.

A: fols xliv^{v}–xlv^{r} cap. 82; **B:** fol. 76^{r} cap. 82; **C:** fol. 63^{r-v} cap. 68; **O:** fols 70^{r}–71^{r}; **V:** fol. lxii^{r-v} cap. 81; Beugnot, pp. 130–1, cap. 82.

---

[1] ce] ABV: cest [2] quei] C: qui [3] B adds: ne [4] B adds: par l'assise [5] il] ABV lack [6] de respondre del] A: dou; BV: de respondre dou [7] dou reiaume] V lacks [8] d'afinité] A: de finité; B: de feauté; V: de fauté [9] vindrent] B: furent [10] a quei] B: ou; V: que [11] avront esté asos] AV: ont esté [12] murtrie] O: murtriere [13] qui avront esté . . . jor] B: avec qui le murtri ou la murtrie a esté an et jor [14] ou] AB: a [15] ou la murtrie] O: en la m<u>rtriere [16] avra] A: ait; B: a [17] Le seignor ou . . . jor] V lacks [18] devant] C: avant

Tos ceaus et toutes celes qui ont esté en la conpaignie dou murtri ou de la murtrie an et jor ou plus.[19]

Tos ceaus et toutes celes qui sont dou comun dou murtri ou de la murtrie, s'il est de[20] comune.

Tos ceaus et toutes celes qui sont de la frairie do murtri ou de la murtrie, s'il est de frairie.[21]

Feme s'ele a esté soignant[22] dou murtri.

Home se il[23] a tenue la murtrie[24] en soignantage.[25]

Mais feme qui a baron ne peut faire apeau[26] que par l'otroi de son baron.

Et por ce le pevent ces manieres de gens faire,[27] et autres non. Que il est bien senblant que amors les moine a ce, que il font[28] l'apel por l'amor qui a esté entre iaus et le murtri ou la murtrie, et non por haine ne por loer ne por malice.

---

[19] In C this sentence comes before the preceding sentence; in V it follows the next sentence. [20] C adds: la [21] la frairie do . . . frairie] B: sa frairie et [22] soignant] C: essoignant [23] se il] A: qui [24] murtrie] A: feme [25] en soignantage (following O)] A: en soignante; B: assoignante; C: essoignantage; V: asoignante [26] AV adds: de (V: dou) murtre [27] pevent ces manieres de gens faire] V: peut tel maniere de gens apeler [28] font] B: facent

***[70]** Quant[1] l'on doit plaideer de murtre soutilment[2] et quant selonc[3] le cours[4] usé.

Plait de murtre est moult soutil, et moult le peut l'on soutilment plaideer qui faire le set, mais que l'on soit bien entendu. Et[5] quant on est bien entendu,[6] il peut moult valoir a celui por qui[7] on plaidoie soutilment. Et quant l'on n'en est bien entendu,[6] le plaideor dou murtre soutilment est[8] perillous, por ce que l'on porroit metre en perill celui a qui conceill l'on est par non estre bien[9] entendu, se il est defendeor, d'estre ataint et[10] pendu, et, se il est apeleor, de perdre sa bataille[11] si[12] que celui que il apele s'en ira quite et delivre sans bataille. Que maintes fois avient que plaideor[13] dit bien et soutilment ce qu'il doit, et que la cort l'entent mal et recorde[14] et juge les paroles autrement que il ne les a dites, par ce que la court n'a les paroles bien[15] entendues. Et por ce doit celui qui de murtre viaut plaideer[16] soutilment, se il faire le set,[17] esgarder et veir, quant il viaut de murtre plaideer soutilment, ques sont les homes de la cort qui lors y sont por juger ce que il dira, et se il cuide[18] qu'il soient sages et bien entendans et qu'il entendent[19] et retienent[20] bien et sotilment les paroles[21] qu'il dira, si plaidoie do murtre le plus soutilment qu'il porra ne[22] savra. Et se il ne[23] li senble que ceaus qui lors sont en la cort[24] soient tes que il entendent[25] bien et soutilment[26] ce qu'il dira, si ne s'entremete[27] mie de plaideer soutilment[28] en maniere que celui a qui conceill il est se il est[29] apelé soit ataint dou murtre s'il n'est bien entendu, et se il est apeleor que le defendeor s'en delivre sans aerdre s'en a lui de bataille.

A: fol. xlv^{r-v} cap. 83; **B:** fol. 76^{r-v} cap. 83; **C:** fols 63^{v}–64^{r} cap. 69; **O:** fol. 71$^{r\ v}$; **V:** fols lxii^{v}–lxiii^{r} cap. 82; Beugnot, p. 132, cap. 83.

---

[1] Quant] A: Coment [2] soutilment] A lacks [3] selonc] V: se [4] cours] B (fol. 19^{v}): cas [5] entendu. Et] B: entendant. Car [6] entendu] B: entendant [7] qui] C: que [8] B adds: mout [9] bien] A lacks [10] et] C: ou [11] bataille] A: carelle; B: querele [12] si] A: ensi; B: enssi; V: enci [13] plaideor] A: le parleor; B: le plaideour; V: le plaideoir [14] B adds: mal [15] bien] A lacks [16] de murtre viaut plaideer] V: plaidoie de murtre [17] set] A: seit [18] cuide] V: cuident [19] entendent] A: entent [20] retienent] B: recordent [21] les paroles] B: ce [22] porra ne] AV lack; B: porra et [23] ne] B lacks [24] sont en la court] AV: sont; B: i sont [25] entendent] B: n'entendent [26] bien et soutilment] AV lack [27] s'entremete] V: s'entremetent [28] soutilment] O lacks [29] se il est] CO lack

***[71]** Quel soutilance il[1] a en plait de murtre.

La soutilance dou plait dou murtre est en ce, se me senble, que qui plaidoie de murtre et il est au conceill de l'apeleor, qu'il le garde sur toutes choses[2] que il, a l'apel faire et a son gage doner, ne le face enssi que il s'i[3] mete en faus guages, ne que celui que il apele s'eschanpisse[4] de cel apel sans bataille, et que celui qui est au conceill de celui qui est apelé[5] de murtre se garde qu'il ne die chose por quei celui qui est apelé de murtre en[6] soit ataint, ne que .ii. homes ou plus le puissent apeler de cel murtre a qui il li covient a respondre et aerdre s'en a yaus[7] de bataille, et qu'il s'en[8] paine se qu'il porra de faire celui a qui conceill il est partir s'en quite de[9] bataille se il faire le peut sans metre le en perill d'estre ataint dou murtre, et se il faire ne le peut, de metre son aversaire en faus guages et lui en loiaus guages,[10] gardant soy des choses devant[11] dites.

A: fol. xlv^{v} cap. 84; **B:** fol. 76^{v} cap. 84; **C:** fol. 64^{r-v} cap. 70; **O:** fols 71^{v}–72^{r}; **V:** fol. lxiii^{r-v} cap. 83; Beugnot, p. 133, cap. 84.

---

[1] V adds: y [2] choses] A: riens [3] s'i] ABV: se [4] s'eschanpisse] A: s'en eschampisse; V: n'eschampisse [5] qui est apelé] A: qu'on a apelé; B: que on apele; V: c'om apelle [6] de murtre en] B lacks; V: de murtre ne [7] yaus] C: lui [8] s'en] ABV: se [9] AB add: la [10] guages] AV lack [11] guages et lui en . . . devant] B: gage et lui en leal et gardoit se bien des choses avant

***[72]** Quel chose est murtre, et por quei l'on le doit savoir, et que doit faire et dire[1] qui viaut faire apeau de murtre.

Qui viaut faire apeau de murtre, il doit savoir que est murtre por garder soi quant il fera l'apel dou murtre[2] qu'il ne se mete en faus guages. Murtre est quant home est tué de nuit ou en[3] repost dehors[4] ou dedens vile.

Et qui viaut faire apeau de murtre, il doit faire aporter le cors murtri devant l'ostel dou[5] seignor ou el leuc ou il[6] est establi que l'on porte les murtris, et[7] aprés doit venir devant le[8] seignor et demander conceill. Et quant il avra conceill, si die:[9] 'Sire, mandés faire[10] veir cel cors qui la aval[11] gist, qui a esté murtri'. Et le seignor i doit mander[12] maintenant .iii. de ces homes, l'un en son leuc et les .ii. en leuc de[13] cort, et les .iii. homes que le seignor y envoie doivent aler veir sel cors et quere se il a cos et, se il a cos, veir ques les cos sont que cel cors a,[14] et puis revenir devant le seignor et dire li en la presence de la court: 'Sire, nos avons veu cel cors que vos nos mandastes veir et avons veu[15] les cos que il a'. Et doivent dire quans cos il y[16] a et en quel leuc il les a et de quel chose il lor senble qu'il aient esté fais. Et se il n'a cos et il ait aucune autre[17] entreseigne par quey il[18] senble que il ait esté murtri, il le doivent dire au seignor. Et s'il n'i voient aucune entreseigne en celui cors,[19] il doivent dire au seignor:[20] 'Sire, nos avons veu cel cors, mais nos n'i avons veu nul cop ne bleceure nule ne chose par quei il nos senble que il ait esté murtri.'

Et se il a en cel cors aucune chose par quei il senble qu'il ait esté murtri, maintenant aprés ce que les .iii. devant dis l'avront dit au seignor en la cort,[21] celui qui veaut faire l'apeau doit faire dire par son conceill au seignor: 'Sire, tel se clame a vos de tel qui tel a

A: fols xlv^{v}–xlvi^{v} cap. 85; **B:** fol. 77^{r-v} cap. 85; **C:** fols 64^{v}–65^{v} cap. 71; **O:** fols 72^{r}–74^{r}; **V:** fols lxiii^{v}–lxiv^{v} cap. 84; Beugnot, pp. 133–5, cap. 85.

[1] A adds: celui [2] quant il fera . . . murtre] AV lack [3] B adds: leuc [4] A adds: ville [5] l'ostel dou] B: le [6] ou il] A: qui [7] et] ABV lack [8] devant le] B: au [9] die] A: face dire par son conseill; V: die son conseill [10] mandés faire] A: faites [11] aval] B: hors [12] mander] AV: envoier [13] en leuc de] V: coume [14] cos sont que cel cors a] A: sont et quanz [15] V adds: le cors et [16] y] ABV lack [17] et il ait aucune autre] A: ou il n'a aucune; BV: et il a (V: aucune) autre [18] BV add: lor [19] V adds: par quoi il lor semble que il ait esté murtri [20] Et s'il n'i . . . seignor] A lacks [21] devant dis l'avront . . . court] B: avant diz homes l'avront dit au seignor

murtri. Faites le venir[22] en vostre presence. Si orrés coment il portera[23] son clain contre lui.' Et l'avantparlier doit nomer tos les .iii. par lor nons et dire lor surnons, se il les set,[24] c'est assaveir celuy a qui conceill il est et celui sur qui il met le murtre et le murtri.[25] Et maintentant le seignor doit faire quere celui a qui l'on met sus le murtre, se il n'est[26] son home, et prendre le[27] et metre le en sa prison. Et maintenant que il l'avra en son pooir, il le doit faire assavoir[28] au clamant.

Et il me senble que se le seignor veaut bien faire, il li[29] doit mander a celui qui est aresté por le murtre[30] .iii. de ces homes, l'un en son leuc et les .ii. come court, et que celui qui est el leuc dou seignor li die: 'L'on te met sus tel murtre. Coment ne[31] por quei le feis tu, et qui fu o toi a faire le?' Et se il le conoist et nome aucuns qui fucent en sa conpaignie, le seignor doit faire celui pendre come murtrier[32] et les autres prendre et metre en[33] prison, et enquerre le meaus que il porra se il est voir si con il a dit[34] que il fucent o lui au murtre faire. Et se il en peut estre certain par autre que par celuy,[35] il en doit faire de s'autorité justise.[36] Que chascun bon seignor doit estre bon justisier et droiturier. Et celui qui dist qu'il avoit[37] le murtre fait et que ceaus avoient esté o lui[38] ne doit mie estre creu de ce que il dira d'eaus, si que par son dit il soient justisiés, mais il doivent bien estre arestés por son dit tant que la verité en soit seue. Et por ce ai je devant dit que le seignor doit faire justise de ceaus qui furent o le murtrier au[39] murtre faire, se il est certain que il donerent force ne[40] aie au murtre faire, que autant vaut qui tient come[41] qui escorche.[42] [a] Que espoir celui qui fist ce murtre ne l'eust mie fait, se ce[43] ne fust par l'aie et la force de ceaus qui o lui furent.

Et se il noie le murtre, il le doit faire garder an et jor en sa prison se celui qui se claime[44] de lui do murtre ou autre ne le viaut apeler

[a] A saying or proverb denoting common purpose.

[22] de tel qui . . . venir] B: por tel qui a esté murtri. Faites le venir devant vos [23] portera] A: porportera; V: pourportera [24] et dire lor . . . set] A: se il seit et leur surnoms [25] et le murtri] crossed out in O [26] n'est] AB: est. A has 'n'en' in the margin in a later hand. [27] et prendre le] V lacks [28] assavoir] B: savoir [29] li] ABV lack [30] B adds: par [31] ne] ABV: et [32] murtrier] C: murtriere [33] AV add: sa [34] il a dit] A: li a dit celui; B: il li a dit [35] A adds: qui le murtre avra fait [36] de s'autorité justise] B: la justise de s'auctorité [37] avoit] B: a; C: l'avoit [38] A adds: qui sont arestés [39] au] C: o le [40] ne] AB: et [41] se il est . . . come] V: que a tant vaut cil qui tient come celui [42] escorche] C: escorge [43] ce] ABO lack [44] claime] ABV: clama

de cel murtre, et se l'an et le jor pase que celui qui se claime[45] de lui do murtre ou autre[46] qui apeler l'en puisse par raison ne l'apele,[47] le seignor le doit[48] laisser aler, et il est quite de cel[49] murtre si que il n'est plus[50] tenus[51] de respondre a nul qui l'en apelast.[52] Et por ce li doit le seignor faire demander en la maniere desus dite se il a fait le murtre, que se il le conoisse[53] qu'il en face justise sans apel et sans bataille. Que chascun seignor doit estre curious et ententif de faire justise de murtriers[54] por chastier les autres qu'il ne le soient.

---

[45] claime] B: clama [46] ne le viaut . . . autre] AV lack [47] A adds: et se le dit terme passe [48] V adds: faire [49] de cel] C: do [50] n'est plus] B: n'en est puis [51] tenus] C lacks [52] apelast] A: apelle; B: apele [53] que se il le conoisse] B lacks [54] murtriers] A: murtrier; O: murtre

***[73]** Que doit faire celui ou cele qui le murtre a presenté a court, et[1] se il set que le murtre[2] est[3] aresté.

Quant celui qui a le murtre presenté set par le seignor ou par autre que celui sur qui il a mis le murtre est[4] aresté, il doit venir[5] devant le seignor en la court, et, se il viaut maintenant faire[6] l'apel, il le doit faire si con est aprés devisé en cest livre.[7] Et se il maintenant ne le viaut faire et il est tel qu'il le puisse faire par chanpion, il doit dire au seignor: 'Sire, vos avés[8] tel home aresté de qui[9] je me clamai de tel murtre. Je vos pri et requier que vos le faites[10] garder en vostre prison tant que je soi aisé[11] de mon clain por sivre contre lui, si con je doi.' Et le seignor li doit respondre: 'Je en[12] ferai se que je devrai'. Et il le doit faire garder si com il est dit desus.

Et se celui de qui l'on se claime de[13] murtre se met en yglise ou en maison de relegion tel que le seignor[14] ne le puisse[15] faire prendre,[16] si tost con le seignor le set, il doit[17] faire garder cel leuc qu'il ne s'enfuïe et le doit faire semondre a jor nomé et en leuc moti par .iii. de ces homes, et qu'il establisse l'un en son leuc et les autres .ii. en leuc de[18] court. Et les .iii. semoneors doivent querre celui de qui l'on c'est clamé de murtre tant qu'il le treussent,[19] et quant il l'avront trové, celui qui est en leuc de[20] seignor li doit dire: 'Mon seignor',[21] et le nome, 'vos semont, et je por lui, que vos soiés a tel jor devant lui en tel leuc[22] por respondre a tel qui de vos c'est clamé que vos avés tel murtri', et le nome. Et ce die[23] par .iii. fois et li mete[24] le jor que le seignor li avra comandé et nome le[25] leuc ou il le semondront[26] de venir faire droit dou murtre. Et puis die a ceaus qui sont venus o lui: 'Je vos comant de par mon seignor que vos seés guarans de la semonce que je ai faite en vos presences[27] por

A: fols xlvi^{v}–xlviii^{r} cap. 86; **B:** fols 77^{v}–79^{r} cap. 86; **C:** fols 65^{v}–67^{v} cap. 72; **O:** fols 74^{r}–77^{r}; **V:** fols lxiv^{v}–lxvi^{v} cap. 85; Beugnot, pp. 136–9, cap. 86.

[1] presenté a court et] B (fol. 19^{v}): present en cort [2] murtre ABV: murtrier; C: murtrer [3] est] B: soit; V: ai (rubrics fol. 6^{r}: aie) esté [4] est] B: soit [5] A adds: avant [6] viaut maintenant faire] ABV: maintenant fait [7] en cest livre] ABV lack [8] vos avés] V: nous avons [9] qui] C: quey [10] faites] B: faciés [11] aisé] B: aaisiez [12] en] ABV lack [13] de] B: dou; V: de tel [14] tel que le seignor] B: de quoi la seignorie [15] puisse] A: peut [16] V adds: ne arester [17] ABV add: bien [18] en leuc de] V: coume [19] qu'il le treussent] V: que home le treusse [20] de ABV: dou [21] AV add: tel [22] que vos soiés . . . leuc] V lacks [23] die] A: deit dire [24] mete] B: motisse [25] le] V: celui [26] semondront] ABV: semont [27] vos presences] BV: vostre presence

lui, si que vos le puissés recorder come court quant besoin[28] sera.' Et se celui que il semont[29] se part de la et ne vueille la semonce oir, ne laisse pas por ce le semoneor a faire la semonce. Que por sa partie[30] ne demore que la semonce ne soit valable puis qu'il la comença[31] en sa presence.

Et se celui que l'on viaut semondre de murtre est home dou seignor, le seignor ne peut metre main en lui ne en son fié ne as soues[32] choses que par l'esgart ou la conoissance de la court. Et se il defuit[33] par la seignorie dou seignor por ce que l'on ne le truisse a semondre de venir faire droit au clain dou murtre ou por autre chose, le seignor le doit faire querre par .iii. de ces homes tant que il le treussent et faire le semondre en la maniere desus dite. Et se il c'est mis en yglise ou en[34] religion, il le doit[35] faire semondre en la maniere desus dite.[36]

Et se[37] le seignor a fait aucun de ces homes semondre ou autre de murtre, si con il est desus[38] dit, il doit faire les semoneours venir en la court et retraire la semonce qu'il ont faite. Aprés ce doit le seignor dire: 'J'ai fait tel semondre par court,[39] si com ele[40] l'a recordé, de venir faire droit de tel murtre dou quel[41] tel s'estoit clamé de lui.[42] Soiés en[43] recordans quant mestier sera.' Et aprés ce il doit faire assaveir[44] a celui qui c'est clamé dou murtre[45] le jor de la semonce por ce[46] qu'il veigne a cel jor en la cort por sivre son[47] clain, se celui de qui il c'est clamé i vient. Et se celui qui est enssi semons ne vient au jor que les semoneors li ont mis por soi defendre dou murtre ou ne contremande s'esoigne si com il doit, il est ataint dou murtre. Et quant le jor sera passé de la semonce,[48] se il n'i est venus ou n'a contremandé s'esoigne si com il doit,[49] le seignor doit retraire a sa court le clain dou murtre et la semonce[50] et dire que celui n'est[51] venus au jor a quei[52] il fu semons a venir respondre dou murtre que l'on li a mis sus, ne contremandé n'a le jor si com il doit, ne fait assaveir qu'il eust essoigne por quei il n'i peut venir au

[28] besoin] V: l'en [29] semont] B: a semons [30] sa partie] V: son partir [31] la comença] A: l'a comensiee [32] soues] AV: ces; O lacks [33] defuit] AV: fuit; B: ne s'enfuit [34] A adds: maisson de [35] doit] A: deivent; V: doivent [36] dite] A: devizee [37] il c'est mis . . . Et se] B lacks [38] desus] V: devant [39] court] C: recort [40] si come ele] B: enssi com l'on [41] dou quel] V: dont [42] AB add: en la court [43] en] O lacks [44] assaveir] B: savoir [45] dou murtre] V: de lui [46] por ce] ABV lack [47] son] ABV: le [48] il est ataint . . . semonce] B lacks [49] se il n'i . . . doit] AB lack; V adds: il est ataint dou murtre [50] et la semonce] A lacks [51] B adds: mie [52] a quei] ABV: que

jor de la semonce faire droit au clamant. Si requiert et comande a sa court qu'ele li conoisse se il est ataint do murtre. Et se les semoneors ont retrait[53] en la court que il aient fait la semonce si con est desus devisé,[54] la cort doit conoistre, se croi,[55] que il est ataint dou murtre puis[56] qu'il en fu semons et que il au jor[57] n'est venus ne n'a fait assaveir au seignor ne a la court s'esoigne ne contremandé son jor si con il doit. Et aprés la dite conoissance le seignor peut metre main en lui et es soues[58] choses, soit[59] fié ou autre chose, com en home qui est ataint de murtre, et faire con de murtrier se il le peut avoir en son pooir, soit son home ou autre. Et se il est[60] home dou seignor et il en fait justise ou il[61] meurt[62] sans ce que justise en soit faite el pooir dou seignor ou aillors, le fié doit revenir[63] a ses heirs, mais des muebles[64] croi je que le seignor peut faire sa volenté con des soues choses, puis que cil a esté semons et il est[65] en la maniere devant dite defailli[66] de venir faire droit do murtre et que la cort a coneu qu'il est ataint del murtre.

Et se il est alé hors de la seignorie dou seignor sans son congé, le seignor, se il viaut, le peut bien[67] faire semondre de son servise en son ostel ou en son fié si com il est devisé en cest livre. Aprés ce le seignor[68] doit faire son home semondre[69] dou servise qu'il li doit, et quant il sera venus devant le seignor, le seignor[70] le doit semondre[71] en sa court ou faire le semondre par .iii. de ces homes[72] come court qu'il soit a jor nomé devant lui faire droit a tel[73] de tel murtre que il li met sus et de coi il c'est clamé de lui, et li doit nomer le clamant et le murtri et motir le jor a quei il le semont et le leuc ou il l'a ajorné. Et se il n'i vient[74] a la semonce dou[75] servise, le[76] seignor se peut faire servir de son fié en la maniere qu'il est[77] devisé en cest livre que le seignor le doit faire d'ome qui defaut de venir au[78] jor que il a esté semons de son servise.

Et se celui de qui l'on c'est clamé[79] de murtre est home dou seignor, se il defuit par la seignorie do seignor si que il ne le puisse

---

[53] ont retrait] AB: retraient; V: ont recordé [54] devisé] V: dite [55] croi] A: cuit [56] puis] C lacks [57] et que il au jor] V: au jour et il [58] es soues] B: en ses; V: en ces [59] soit] O lacks [60] C adds: autre [61] ou il] V: et il en [62] meurt] B: muire [63] revenir] B: torner [64] des muebles] C: des meillors; V: dou meuble [65] est] B: a [66] defailli] ABV: failli [67] bien] AV lack [68] le seignor] AB: que seignor; V: que le seignor en [69] A adds: en sa court [70] le seignor] A: il [71] dou servise qu'il . . . semondre] B lacks [72] V adds: l'un en son leuc et les .ii. [73] a tel] O lacks [74] vient] O: viaut [75] dou] ABV: de son [76] le] AB: son [77] qu'il est] BV: qui est (V: devant) [78] venir au] V: servise et de venir faire droit a [79] c'est clamé] A: se claime

trover a faire semondre, il doit establir .iii. de ses homes come cort qu'il le quierent[80] tant que il le treussent et le semonent. Que il ne le doit faire[81] semondre de son servise[82] tant con il est en sa seignorie, se il n'a[83] besoin de son servise, et se il[84] le fait a moi senble que il mesprent[85] vers lui. Si se doit chascun seignor[86] garder de faire le.

Et se[87] celui de qui l'on c'est clamé de murtre n'est home dou seignor et il se destorne si que le seignor ne le puisse trover[88] a prendre ou a faire semondre, il peut prendre toutes les soues choses et user en come des soues[89] tant que celui veigne en la presence dou seignor et[90] de la court et eufre a faire droit de ce que l'on li savra que demander, et ce faisant le seignor[91] li doit toutes[92] les soes choses faire rendre sans delai. Quar il n'est pas[93] ataint de murtre por defuite[94] qu'il ait faite se il n'a esté semons si come est desus dit et defailli[95] de venir au jor ou de contremander c'esoigne.

---

[80] quierent] C: requierent [81] ne le doit faire] B: aille droit faire ou [82] de son servise] A lacks [83] n'a] B: a; V: n'en a [84] B adds: ne [85] mesprent] A: mesfait [86] seignor] V lacks [87] V adds: il le fait [88] trover] C: torner [89] V adds: choses [90] dou seignor et] ABV lack [91] ce faisant le seignor] B: par faisant ce la seignorie [92] toutes] V lacks [93] pas] B: mie [94] defuite] ABV: defaute; O: defuïre [95] defailli] B: defaille

***[74]** Qui viaut faire apeau de murtre et le murtre[1] est present en[2] la court, que il doit faire et dire quant il apele.[3]

Qui fait maintentant[4] apeau de murtre d'ome ou de feme ou d'enfant qui ait esté murtri et mostre a[5] court si con est avant[6] dit, et[7] celui ou cele que il[8] viaut apeler est present en la cort, il doit en la court faire dire au seignor[9] par son coneill ensi: 'Sire, tel se claime a vos de tel qui la est qui a tel murtri, et se il le noie il est prest que il le li[10] preuve de son cors contre le sien, et qu'il l'en rende mort ou recreant[11] en une hore de jor. Et veés enssi son guage.' Et nome tos les[12] .iii.: l'apelor,[13] l'apelé et le murtri. Lors l'apelor s'agenoille devant le seignor et li tende son guage.

A: fol. xlviii^{r} cap. 87; **B:** fol. 79^{r} cap. 87; **C:** fol. 67^{v} cap. 73; **O:** fol. 77^{r-v}; **V:** fols lxvi^{v}–lxvii^{r} cap. 86; Beugnot, p. 139, cap. 87.

---

[1] murtre] A rubrics (fol. 3^{r}) B (fol. 19^{v}) V: murtrier [2] en] C lacks [3] apele] A rubrics: l'apelle; B: l'apele; V: l'a apelé [4] fait maintentant] A: viaut faire; BV: veut (V: veaut) maintenant faire [5] et mostre a] B: si le mostre a la [6] avant] V: devant [7] B adds: se [8] que il] A: qui [9] en la court . . . seignor] ABV: faire dire en (A: a) la court [10] li] ABV lack [11] recreant] B: vencu [12] les] AV lack [13] ABV add: et

***[75]** Quant on[1] viaut faire apeau de murtre par chanpion, coment on[2] le doit faire.

Qui viaut faire apeau de murtre par chanpion et il est tel que il le puisse et doie faire, si doit en la court faire dire au seignor en la presence de celui que il[3] viaut[4] apeler: 'Sire, tel se claime a vos de tel qui a tel murtri', et nomer les[5] .iii., l'apeleor et le murtri et le murtrier,[6] 'et s'il le noie, il est prest que il li face[7] prover par .i. home contre son cors au jor que la court li donra, et qu'il l'en[8] rendra mort ou recreant en une hore de jor, ou qu'il de son cors le li preuve,[9] se il a cel jor n'avoit son chanpion aploresté,[10] et que il l'en[11] rende mort ou recreant en une hore de jor. Et[12] veés enssi son guage.' Et s'agenoille l'apeleor devant le seignor et li tende son gage. Et garde se bien celui qui fait apeau[13] par chanpion que il l'ait apresté au jor que la court li donra d'avoir le amené, que se il ne l'a apresté de la bataille faire au jor que la court li donra, il sera ataint de murtre se il ne peut parfaire[14] ce qu'il avra ofert a faire en court par chanpion ou par son cors et[15] de quei il avra doné son guage et le seignor receu.

A: fol. xlviii^{r-v} cap. 88; **B:** fol. 79^{r-v} cap. 88; **C:** fols 67^{v}–68^{r} cap. 74; **O:** fols 77^{v}–78^{r}; **V:** fol. lxvii^{r} cap. 87; Beugnot, pp. 139–40, cap. 88.

---

[1] on] AB (fol. 19^{v}) V: l'on [2] on] AB: l'on [3] que il] B: qui [4] A adds: faire [5] nomer les] A: nomer toz les; B: nome [6] murtrier] V: deffendeor [7] face] B: fera [8] qu'il l'en] A: qu'il le; BV: qui le [9] le li preuve] A lacks [10] A adds: contre le sien [11] l'en] AV: le [12] ou qu'il de . . . Et] B lacks [13] V adds: de murtre [14] parfaire] V: faire [15] et] ABV lack

***[76]** Qui est en fers ou en liens amené en la court et on se claime de lui de murtre ou d'aucune autre malefaite,[1] qu'il doit dire au seignor ains que il responde.

Celui de qui l'on se claime de murtre en sa presence doit demander conceill, et aprés faire dire par son conceill[2] au seignor se il est en fers ou en liens: 'Sire, faites geter tel', et le nome, 'des fers ou[3] des liens ou il est et metre[4] le en sa delivre poesté,[5] et aprés il respondra et fera ce que il[6] devra'. Et se le seignor ne le fait ou celui qui l'apele le contredit, si die celui qui est a son conceil: 'Sire, il ne viaut respondre a riens que l'on li met sus tant que il soit[7] en sa delivre poesté, se la court ne l'esgarde'. Et de ce se met il en l'esgart de la court sauf son retenaill. Et la cort doit esgarder, se cuit, qu'il doit estre geté des fers ou[8] des liens, se il i est,[9] et mis en sa delivre poesté.[10] Et maintenant le seignor le doit faire, et faire le si bien garder qu'il ne s'en puisse foïr ne destorner. Et por ce le doit celui qui est au conceill de celui qui est en fers ou en liens[11] enssi faire,[12] que se il noie le murtre tant con il est en fers ou en liens[13] ou respont au clain, il li covendroit[14] enssi a conbatre a celui qui l'apele con il seroit quant il avroit[15] le murtre noie ou respondu au clain, fust en fers ou en liens ou en autre destresce.

Et quant il sera[16] en sa delivre poesté, se l'on se claime de lui de murtre en la maniere avant[17] dite, celui qui est a son conceill doit dire au seignor: 'Sire, tel', et le nome, 'noie et defent le murtre[18] que tel li met sus', et le nome, 'et est prest qu'il s'en defende de son cors contre le sien. Mais il n'entent que il a lui s'en doie aerdre ne faire ne[19] viaut, se la court ne l'esgarde, et dit por coi: por ce[20] que il n'entent que celui[21] soit parent de celui que il dit qui

---

A: fols xlviii^{v}–l^{v} cap. 89; **B:** fols 79^{v}–81^{r} cap. 89; **C:** fols 68^{r}–70^{v} cap. 75; **O:** fols 78^{r}–82^{r}; **V:** fols lxvii^{r}–lxx^{r} cap. 88; Beugnot, pp. 140–3, cap. 89.

---

[1] d'aucune autre malefaite] B (fol. 19^{v}): d'aucun mesfait [2] et aprés faire . . . conceill] V lacks [3] ou] AB: et [4] metre] A: metés [5] sa delivre poesté] B: son delivre pooir [6] ce que il] B: que [7] soit] B: sera [8] qu'il doit estre . . . ou] V: que hom le doit geter [9] se il i est] A lacks [10] se la court . . . poesté] B lacks [11] au conceill de . . . liens] A: a son conseill [12] doit celui qui . . . faire] B: dit celui qui est au conseill de celui qui est en fers ou en liens [13] enssi faire, que . . . liens] V lacks [14] li covendroit] B: li covient; V: couveroit [15] seroit quant il avroit] B: estoit quant il avoit [16] sera] B: seroit [17] avant] AV: devant [18] et defent le murtre] V: le murtre et se deffent [19] ABV add: le [20] Por ce] ABV lack [21] celui] ABV: cestui

est[22] murtri ne tel qui de tel murtre le puisse ne[23] doie apeler, et se il est parent de celui qu'il dit qui est[24] murtri, si a il plus prochain parent de lui[25] por quei il a cestui ne s'en viaut aerdre, se la court ne l'esgarde.' Et mete[26] son retenaill.[27] Et l'apeleor doit lors faire dire par son avantparlier: 'Sire, il ne viaut que il demore[28] por chose qu'il ait faite dire que il a lui ne s'en aerde, et di[29] por coi: por ce que il est de ceaus qui pevent et doivent faire apeau de murtre, et ce est il prest de prover tot enssi con la court[30] conoistra qu'il prover le doie. Que trop seroit fort chose et grief, se il covenoit[31] mostrer a chascun qui viaut faire apeau de murtre qu'il fust le plus prochain parent do murtri ou le plus prochain[32] de tos[33] ceaus qui pevent et doivent[34] faire apeau de tel murtre et que on a autre que au plus prochain ne se[35] deust l'on aerdre. Quar s'ensi estoit poy i[36] poroit on faire apel de murtre, et enssi avroient trop grans avantages les murtriers et les maufaitors. Que il porroient les povres pelerins et les estranges et autres[37] murtrir sans ce qu'il les covenist a conbatre, qu'a[38] envis seroit trové le plus prochain parent dou murtri ou celui ou cele qui seroit[39] plus droit a l'apel faire dou murtre qui l'apel en feist.[40] Si porroient ensi[41] le plus des murtriers[42] sans bataille, laquel chose seroit tort[43] et peché et contre droit et[44] raison et moult de maus en avendroient. Et por toutes les raisons que je ai dites ou por aucunes d'eles ne viaut il[45] qu'il demore por chose que il ait dite qu'il a lui ne s'en aedre,[46] se la court l'esgarde.' Et de ce se met il en l'esgart de la court[47] sauf son[48] retenaill. Et le defendeor doit faire[49] dire par son conceill: 'Sire, le murtre il noie et defent, mais a lui ne s'en viaut il aerdre por les raisons que je ai dites por lui si com[50] la court les a entendues, et por tant plus. Que trop

---

[22] parent de celui . . . est] A: parent dou; BV: parent de celui qui est; C: que il dit qui est [23] qui de tel . . . ne] ABV: que (B: qui) de tel (V: cel) murtre le (V: l'en) [24] de celui qu'il dit qui est] A: a celui qui est; B: dou; V: a celui que il dit qui est [25] lui] B: cestui [26] mete] V: metre [27] se la court . . . retenaill] C lacks [28] que il demore] BV lack [29] V adds: raison [30] V adds: l'esguardera ou [31] covenoit] C: covient [32] V adds: parent [33] tos] ABV lack [34] et doivent] V lacks [35] se] AB: s'en [36] i] ABV lack [37] estranges et autres] A: estranges et autres genz; B: autres estranges; C: estrangiers et autres [38] qu'a] AV: car a; B: car [39] seroit] V: seroient [40] dou murtre qui l'apel en feist] AB: ne poreit (B: porroit) ou ne vodreit (B: voudroit) faire l'apel (B: l'apeau); V: que l'apeau feist [41] Si porroient ensi] A: ensi poreient; V: et ensi se porroient [42] le plus des murtriers] AB: le plus des murtriers partir (B: aler); O: les plus des murtres; V: eschampir le plus des murtriers [43] BV add: apert [44] et contre droit et] B: contre Dieu et contre [45] viaut il] V: veut je [46] s'en aedre] AO: s'aerde [47] la court] B lacks [48] se met il . . . son] V: me mete en l'esguart de la court sauf mon [49] faire] V lacks [50] si come] A: se

seroit fort chose et estrange, se il a cestui s'en aerdoit et en venoit au desus ou[51] pais en estoit faite et .i. autre qui parent fust dou murtri plus prochain que cestui n'est, se il est son parent, venist avant et l'en apelast, qu'il a celui respondist de cel murtre ne a cestui[52] s'en aersist, s'il n'en estoit quite vers[53] tous autres. Et por toutes les raisons que je ai dites por lui ore et autresfois ou por aucunes d'eles, il n'entent[54] qu'il a lui s'en doie aerdre ne faire[55] ne le viaut, se la cort ne l'esgarde.' Et de ce se met en l'esgart de la court sauf son retenaill. Et la cort doit esgarder, se me senble, que por chose que le defendeor ait dite ne doit demorer[56] qu'il ne s'aerde[57] a lui de son cors contre le sien, et que s'il s'i aert, qu'il n'est tenus de respondre a autre de cel murtre. Et por ce le doit le defendeor faire enssi con est devant dit. Que se il enssi s'en[58] defent d'aerdre s'en a lui[59] et il par esgart s'aert,[60] il n'est aprés ce tenus de respondre a nul autre de cel murtre. Et se il enssi[61] ne s'aert par esgart ou par conoissance de court et l'apeleor n'est parent do mutri et pais en est faite et .i. parent dou murtri[62] vient avant en la court et l'apele de cel murtre, il covendra que il li responde et s'en defende et s'en aerde[63] a lui de bataille. Et se il est son parent et plus prochain l'en apele, covendra il que il a lui s'en aerde, se il a l'autre ne c'est aers[64] par esgart de court ou se bataille n'en a esté faite que il ait otreie, que .i. murtre ne peut avoir qu'une bataille, se me senble. Mais d'un home ocis sans murtre qui ait eu[65] plusors cos peut bien[66] avoir pluisors batailles, se m'est avis, et coment et par quel raison ce[67] peut estre sera aprés devisé en cest livre. Et aucuns dient[68] que se le defendeor s'aert a l'apeleor de bataille autrement que par esgart ou par conoissance de court et bataille en est ferue[69] et il vaint[70] son aversaire, qu'il li covendroit[71] aprés a conbatre a son plus prochain parent se il l'en[72] apeloit. Mais a moi ne me senble il pas[73] raison,

---

[51] ou] V: et [52] celui respondist de . . . cestui] B: cestui respons feist de cel murtre ne a celui [53] vers] A: por [54] n'entent] A: n'en entent [55] faire] V lacks [56] doit demorer] V: demore [57] s'aerde] B: s'en aherde; V: s'en aerdre [58] s'en] A: se; BV: ne se [59] s'en a lui] A: se; B soi [60] et il par esgart s'aert] A: et il par esgart de court s'i aert; B lacks; V: et il par esguart aprés s'en aert [61] enssi] V lacks [62] et pais en . . . murtri] O lacks [63] .i. parent dou . . . aerde] V: aprés .i. autre venist qui en fust plus prochain parent dou murtri en la court et l'apelast de cel murtre, il couvendroit que il respondist et s'en deffendist et s'en aerdeist [64] c'est aers] AB: s'en est aers (B: ahers); V: s'en aerde [65] eu] ABV lack [66] bien] A lacks [67] par quel raison ce] B: quel raison i [68] aucuns dient] B: se aucun dit [69] ferue] B: faite; C: ferme [70] vaint] B: venque; O: viaut; V: vainc [71] covendroit] A: covendra [72] l'en] C: le [73] a moi ne . . . pas] A: a mei ne semble il pas; B: en ce ne me senble il mie; V: a moi semble il que ce n'est pas

que puis que bataille est fornie et outree d'un murtre que bataille en doive avoir plus,[74] mais se pais en estoit faite et il[75] ne s'en estoit aers par esgart ou par conoissance de court et .i. plus prochain parent[76] dou murtri l'en apelast,[77] il l'en covendroit a respondre et aerdre s'en a lui de bataille por ce que, s'ensi n'estoit, moult de malices se poroient faire a estordre le murtrier de la bataille.

Et quant le devant dit[78] esgart sera fait, celui qui est au conceill de l'apelor doit dire por lui: 'Sire, tel se claime a vos de tel[79] qui a tel murtri, et se il le noie il est prest qu'il li[80] preuve de son cors contre le sien et qu'il l'en rende[81] mort ou recreant en une hore de jor, et veés ci son guage', et nomer[82] l'apeleor et l'apelé et le murtri. Et lors l'apeleor s'agenoille et tende son guage au seignor. Et celui qui est au conceill dou defendeor doit por lui dire:[83] 'Sire, tel', et le nome, 'noie et defent le murtre que tel li met sus', et le nome, 'et est prest qu'il s'en defende de son cors contre le sien, et veés enssi son gage.' Et lors le defendeor s'agenoille devant le seignor et li[84] tende son guage, et le seignor doit les guages recevoir et lor doit comander que il soient atirés au tiers jor et[85] aprestés de la bataille faire[86] armés de tes armes con il covient a chanpions qui se conbatent de murtre. Et lors il doivent dire au seignor:[87] 'Sire, faites nos conoistre[88] a la court ques armes nos devons avoir[89] a nos conbatre.' Et le seignor[90] doit faire conoistre a la court[91] de ques armes il doivent[92] estre armés, et la court le doit conoistre selonc ce que il sont chevaliers ou sergens. Et coment les chevaliers doivent estre armés qui se conbatent de murtre, et coment[93] les sergens, sera devisé aprés[94] en cest livre.

Et aprés ce que les guages sont[95] donés et receus, le seignor les doit faire garder andeus les .iii. jors sans fers et sans liens et[96] en large leuc ou il n'aient nule destrece, et que chascun d'eaus[97] soit par soi, et qu'il lor face bien et largement avoir ceaus .iii. jors[98] ce

[74] doive avoir plus] A: dee puis estre; B: doie estre puis; V: doit estre plus [75] et il] B: qu'il [76] parent] A lacks [77] apelast] A: apeleit; B: appeloit [78] V adds: counoissance ou [79] se claime a vos de tel] A: clame a vos [80] li] ABV: le [81] l'en rende] A: le rende; BV: le rendra [82] nomer] ABV: nome [83] doit por lui dire] AB: si die; V: doit dire [84] li] AB lack [85] atirés au tiers jor et] ABV: au tiers jor [86] faire] B lacks [87] lors il doivent dire au seignor] A: il deivent dire lors; BV: lors doivent dire [88] conoistre] ABV: dire [89] nos devons avoir] A: il nos covendra aveir; B: il nos covendra; V: nous couvient avoir [90] ABV adds: lor [91] a la court] A lacks [92] doivent] C: doit [93] coment] B lacks [94] aprés] C lacks; V: ci aprés [95] sont] ABV: seront [96] et] ABV lack [97] d'eaus] B lacks [98] ceaus .iii. jors] ABV lack

que mestier lor sera[99] de manger et de boivre et de lis a dormir,[100] se il ne l'ont dou leur ou se il le requierent. Et por ce doit le seignor faire garder l'apeleor del murtre, que se il ne le faisoit, plusors malices en[101] porroit on[102] faire au murtrier eschanper[103] sans bataille, et se seroit legiere[104] chose a faire qui faire le vodroit et en avroit .i. poi d'espase, et enssi me senble que on le porroit faire. Que[105] quant l'apeleor feroit l'apel que le defendeor s'en aersist[106] a lui par esgart de court et que l'apeleor se destornast et ne venist mie au jor de la bataille et ensi seroit quite et delivre le murtrier. Et por ce que malice ne s'en face, les doit le seignor faire[107] garder andeus,[108] si con est devant[109] dit, qu'en la garde n'a damage ne[110] perill, et en la non garde[111] y porroit estre.

Et se la feme ou le fis ou la fille[112] font l'apel, et il sont[113] tes que il puissent faire apel de murtre, ou le pere ou la mere, se il n'a feme n'enfant qui puisse l'apeau faire ou se[114] le frere ou la seur do murtri font l'apel,[115] se il n'a feme ni enfant ne pere ne mere qu'il puisse[116] faire l'apel do murtre,[117] il le doivent faire en la maniere devant dite,[118] et au plus brief que il porra[119] le doit[120] faire celui ou cele qui fera l'apel,[121] et le defendeor s'i doit aerdre le plus tost que il pora sans riote.[122] Et por ce di ge que a tes manieres de gens le doit le defendeor enssi faire, que il ne me senble que plus prochains d'eaus[123] soient dou murtri. Car l'on doit respondre au murtre[124] le plus brief[125] que on porra la ou l'on ne se[126] peut eschanper de respondre y, se l'apeleor est tel qu'autre ne le puisse apeler de cel murtre a qui il en soit tenus de respondre par les raisons avant dites.

---

[99] sera] A: est; B: soit [100] lis a dormir] AB: bien gesir; V: lis a gesir [101] en] AB lack [102] porroit on] V: poroient evenir et [103] eschanper] B: et eschampes [104] legiere] O: la grief [105] Que] C: Quar [106] s'en aersist] A: se aersist; B: se hardist; V: s'aersit [107] les doit le seignor faire] AB: les fait le seignor; V: le seignor les doit [108] andeus] A lacks [109] devant B: avant [110] qu'en la garde . . . ne] A: que on les garde que au garder n'a damage ne; B: que l'on les garde qu'il n'i ait damage ne; V: que hom les doit guarder ne o damage ne a [111] et en la non garde] AB: ou (A: et ou) non garder [112] la fille] AB: le frere; V: la seur [113] sont] A: seient; B: soient [114] se] AB lack [115] se il n'a . . . l'apel] V: Et [116] qu'il puisse] AB: qui puissent; V: qui puisse [117] l'apel do murtre] A: le dit apel [118] devant dite] A: avant devizee; V: devant devisee [119] porra] B: porront [120] doit] V: doivent [121] fera l'apel] V: l'apeau vodra faire [122] A adds: faire [123] Et por ce . . . d'eaus] B: qu'il me semble que le deffendeor ne doit querre fuites contre tex manieres de gens, qu'il ne m'est pas avis que plus prochainz parenz de ceaus desus diz [124] murtre] B: murtri [125] brief] ABV: tost [126] on porra la . . . se] A: l'on porra la ou l'on ne s'en; B: l'on puet quant on ne s'en; V: l'om peut la ou l'on ne se

***[77]** Qui viaut faire apeau de persone qui ait esté tuee autrement qu'en murtre,[1] qu'il doit faire por metre se en drois guages.

Qui viaut faire apel de murtre[2] d'ome ou de feme ou d'enfant[3] qui ait esté tué autrement qu'en murtre et metre s'en[4] en drois guages se son aversaire ne s'en set guaitier,[5] si face[6] dire au seignor en la presence de celui ou de cele que il viaut de ce apeler aprés ce que le cors et les cos avront esté mostrés a[7] court si con est avant[8] dit: 'Sire, tel', et le nome, 'se claime a vos de tel qui la est', et le nome, 'qui a tel murtri', et le nome,[9] 'et donés les cos[10] dont il a mort receue. Et se il le noie, il est prest de prover li[11] de son cors contre le sien et de rendre l'en[12] mort ou recreant[13] en une hore de jor. Et veés en si son[14] guage.' Et s'agenoille devant le seignor et li tende son guage.[15]

Et se celui de qui l'on se claime enssi[16] noie et defent ce que le clamant li met sus et s'en eufre a defendre et[17] en[18] tent son guage, die celui qui est au conceill dou clamant la parole en la maniere desus[19] devisee, mais que tant[20] que il mete 'ou' por 'et'[21] la ou il dit qu'il l'a murtri *et* doné le cop dont il a mort receue die qu'il l'a murtri *ou* doné le cop dont il a mort receue, et mete a la premiere parole le 'et'. Por ce que son aversaire ne conoisse[22] la desjointive a la premiere[23] parole, que se il dit au premier[24] le 'et' et il dit au doner des gages le 'ou', son aversaire ne s'en prendra pas si tost gardé[25] se il le dit tost en ce que il[26] sont[27] eschaufés as guages doner com il fera au comencement de la parole.[28] Por ce que il seront[29] esmeus et eschaufés plus as guages doner[30] et mains guaitans que il

A: fols l^{v}–lii^{v} cap. 90; **B:** fols 81^{r}–83^{r} cap. 90; **C:** fols 70^{v}–73^{v} cap. 76; **O:** fols 82^{r}–86^{v}; **V:** fols lxx^{r}–lxxii^{v} cap. 89; Beugnot, pp. 143–7, cap. 90.

[1] qu'en murtre] B (fol. 20^{r}): que murtrie; V: que murtre [2] de murtre] V lacks [3] V adds: ou d'autre [4] s'en] A: se; OV: soi [5] guaitier] A: garder; V: guarder [6] V adds: ensi [7] a] AB: en la; V: en [8] avant] AV: devant [9] tel murtri', et le nome] V: murtri [10] donés les cos] A: doné le cop ou les cos; B: doné le cop [11] li] C lacks [12] l'en] ABV: le; C lacks [13] recreant] B: vencu [14] en si son] B: ci mon [15] Et s'agenoille devant . . . guage] B lacks [16] enssi] V lacks [17] et] B: ou [18] ce que le . . . en] V: et [19] desus] V: devant [20] que tant] B lacks [21] por 'et'] B: par [22] A adds: pas; B: mie [23] a la premiere] C lacks [24] que se il dit au premier] V: et c'il dit a sa premiere parole [25] prendra pas si tost gardé] V: dora gardé si tost [26] en ce que il] B: enssi qu'il; V: ensi com il [27] sont] A: seit; B: soit [28] de la parole] AB lack [29] seront] A: seit plus; B: soit plus [30] com il fera . . . doner] V lacks

ne sont[31] au comencer[32] de la parole, que espoir il cuidera qu'il dist[33] la parole si com il fist[34] au comencement. Et se il se garde lors de la desjointive et dit qu'il n'en[35] s'en viaut enssi[36] aerdre a luy, se court ne l'esgarde, et que cort esgardera[37] que il ne le doit faire, si y[38] mete le 'et'. Que meaus li vaut faire son[39] clain aveuc le 'et', se il ne le peut faire aveuc[40] le 'ou', que faire le sans 'et', et sans[41] 'ou' se son aversaire ne s'en set de ce[42] garder.[43] Mais se il voit et conoit[44] que il s'en sache garder, si n'i[45] mete le 'et' ne[46] le 'ou', se il s'en[47] viaut conbatre por cel[48] home ou feme ou enfant qui avra esté tué,[49] ne se viaut garder de metre[50] se en faus gages. Quar se le clamant met le 'et' el clain et l'autre ne s'en garde et il se parjure[51] do murtre, l'autre se parjure[52] des cos. Si seront les .ii. esparjurés el champ. Et por ce doit l'on l'apel faire aveuc le 'ou' en cest cas qui faire le peut. Que se celui qui se defent noie et defent ce qu'il li a mis sus et s'en aert a lui, l'apeleor c'est mis[53] en drois guages de ce qu'il dist que il li dona les cos ou le cop dont[54] il a mort receue. Car s'il n'eust dit en son clain autre mais qu'il l'a murtri, il n'eust pas voir dit si se[55] fust mis en faus guages. Se il eust[56] dit qu'il l'a murtri et doné les cos ou le cop dont il a mort receue,[57] ne diroit il pas voir,[58] qu'il ne l'a pas murtri por quei il seroit[59] en faus guages[60] por ce qu'il avroit[61] ajoint le cop o le murtre. Mais quant il dit qu'il l'a murtri ou donés les cos ou le cop dont il l'a mort,[62] il dit voir dou quelque ce soit dou murtre ou des cos. Si s'en[63] met en drois[64] guages,[65] se son aversaire ne s'en set garder.

Et se l'apeleor[66] fait l'apel en la maniere devant dite[67] et celui qui est au conceill dou defendeor[68] noie le murtre sans plus et as cos[69]

---

[31] plus as guages . . . sont] B: et mains gaitans [32] comencer] A: comensement; B: comencement; V coumencement [33] dist] AV: die [34] dist la parole si come il fist] B: la dist [35] n'en] AB: ne [36] enssi] V lacks [37] esgardera] AB: esgarde; V: esguarde [38] y] O lacks [39] Que meaus li vaut faire son] A: et que moult miaus li vaut a faire le; B: que mout de caus li voient faire son; V: Et qui mout meaus li vaut que il face le [40] aveuc le 'et' . . . aveuc] A: aveuc le 'e', et; B: ou le 'et', et se il ne le puet avec; V: aveuc le 'e', ou que faire [41] 'et' et sans] A: le 'e' et sans le; B: le 'ou' et sanz [42] de ce] A lacks [43] garder] V: esguarder [44] et conoit] A lacks [45] n'i] AB: i; V: ne [46] ne] A: et non; B: non [47] s'en] BO: se [48] cel] ABV lack [49] avra esté tué] AB: ait esté tué, se il [50] se viaut garder de metre] V: si veaut metre ou guarder soi de metre [51] se parjure] AV: s'en esparjure [52] se parjure] A: s'en esparjure [53] c'est mis] AB: se met [54] dont] A: de quoi [55] si se] V: s'il s'en [56] eust] B: n'eust [57]dont il a mort receue] A lacks [58] A adds: en ce qu'il dit qu'il l'a murtri [59] A adds: mis [60] Se il eust . . . guages] V lacks [61] avroit] B: n'avroit [62] l'a mort] AV: a mort receue [63] Si s'en] A: Si se; V: c'il se [64] drois] A: leaus; V: loyaus [65] dont il l'a . . . guages] B lacks [66] l'apeleor] A: son aversaire [67] devant dite] A: dessus dite; V: dessus devisee [68] defendeor] B: deffendant [69] et as cos] AB: ne au cop

ne fait respons ne ne[70] dit aucune chose contre cel dit, demande celui qui est au conceill de l'apeleor otroi a celui qu'on apele, et, s'il l'otroie, si die que il le viaut avoir ataint de la malefaite que il li a mise[71] sus en la court que il n'a noie. Ce est[72] de ce que il dist a son clain qu'il avoit tel murtri et doné ou doné[73] les cos de quei[74] il avoit mort.[75] Et die lequel que il dist en son clain: le 'et' ou le 'ou', et il les cos ne noia[76] por quei il de ce le viaut avoir ataint, se la court l'esgarde, et avoir en tel droit con d'ome ataint[77] en court[78] de cos fais a home de quey[79] il a mort receue et mete son retenaill. Et il ne me senble que aprés les dis erremens que[80] celui qui ne nea[81] les cos[82] puisse chose dire que la court n'esgarde que il est[83] ataint de ce que celui li mist sus en la court et se clama[84] de lui[85] qu'il avoit a celui doné le cop ou les cos de quei il avoit mort receue, et[86] il ne le nea ne ne dist por quei il a ce ne devoit respondre ne autre raison por quei il soit de ce delivre si con il doit, et en pora le seignor faire[87] justise con d'ome qui a fait homecide.

Et se celui qui est au conceill de celui que l'on apele ensi set,[88] il le defendra[89] sans bataille se celui qui est au conceill de l'apeleor ne s'en set garder. Il l'en porra estordre sans bataille,[90] se son aversaire ne s'en set garder.[91] Et coment son aversaire s'en peut[92] garder[93] sera devisé aprés en ce[94] livre.

Et qui ne le savra defendre sans bataille et le viaut metre en drois guages, il doit dire quant il oit[95] que l'on fait l'apel si con est avant[96] dit: 'Sire, tel vos dit, et je por lui, qu'il noie le murtre et defent, ne as cos il ne viaut respondre tant con il enssi porportera[97] son clain des[98] cos et dou murtre ensenble. Mais se il laisse le clain[99] dou murtre et se tient a celui des cos, il y[100] respondra si com il devra. Car nul n'est tenus a[101] respondre a .ii. clains ensemble qui ne soient[102]

[70] ne ne] V: n'en a [71] de la malefaite . . . mise] B: dou mesfait qu'il li a mis [72] Ce est] A lacks [73] a son clain . . . doné] A: a son claim tel murtri ou dona; B: tel murtre ou doné; V: a son clain tel murtri et doné [74] les cos de quei] B: tex cos dont [75] avoit mort] AV: avoit mort receue; B: a mort receue; C: l'avoit mort [76] les cos ne noia] V: a les cos couneu [77] se la court . . . ataint] V lacks [78] en court] B lacks [79] a home de quey] A: de que [80] aprés les dis erremens que] B lacks [81] ne nea] V: noya [82] A adds: ne [83] est] A: en seit; V: soit [84] clama] V: claime [85] de lui] O: que celui [86] et] AB: ne [87] faire] A: aveir [88] set] B: set respondre a ce; V: soit [89] defendra] AB: destornera [90] se celui qui . . . bataille] V lacks [91] Il l'en porra . . . garder] AB lack [92] peut] AV: pora; B: porra [93] garder] V: deffendre [94] en ce] A: en cest; B: dedenz cest; V: en cestui [95] oit] V: veaut [96] avant] ABV: devant [97] porportera] B: portera [98] des] V: ensi de [99] le clain] A: celui [100] y] ABV lack [101] a] ABV: de [102] qui ne soient] A: et qui ne sont mie; B: qui ne sont; V: et ne sont pas

une meisme chose. Et en cest clain que tel a fait de lui a .ii. clamors ensenble et ne sont[103] pas une meime chose,[104] qu'eles soient sevrees[105] l'une de l'autre[106] par le 'et' ou[107] par le 'ou' qui les despart. Si ne doivent aler ensi[108] ensemble con il les viaut faire aler. Que le murtre peut l'on autrement prover que les cos, et que au murtre covient autre respons que as cos. Por quei il, por[109] les raisons que je ai dites[110] ou por aucunes d'eles, ne viaut[111] respondre as cos se il avant[112] ne se relaisse dou clain do murtre, se la court ne l'esgarde.' Et de ce se met il en l'esgart de la court sauf son retenaill. Et l'autre[113] ne porra chose dire contre ce,[114] se me senble, por quei la cort ne doit[115] esgarder que celui de qui l'on c'est enssi clamés n'est pas[116] tenus de respondre[117] as cos, se l'apeleor ne se relaisse avant[118] dou clain do[119] murtre. Que la ou il dit que il l'a murtri et doné[120] ou doné le cop ou les cos dont il a mort receue, depart il les cos dou murtre por ce que il[121] dit 'murtri' *et* 'doné' *ou* 'doné[122] les cos dont il a mort receue'. Qu'en ce peut l'on entendre et doit estre entendu l'un ou l'autre, et por ce ne doit il pas respondre as cos puis que il a le murtre neé.

Mais se il disoit el clain qu'il fait que il l'a murtri et donés les cos ou le cop dont[123] il a mort receue, tout soit ce q'il ajoigne par le 'et' et le murtre et les cos ensenble,[124] n'est pas tenus celui de qui l'on se clameroit enssi de respondre au murtre et au clain ensenble, por ce qu'il ne dit 'les cos dont il l'a murtri', mais dit 'les cos dont il a mort receue'. Et home murtri et home tué autrement qu'en[125] murtre n'est pas[126] une chose. Quar le tué sans murtre est homecide, et por ce qu'il ajont le clain dou murtre et de[127] l'omecide ensemble[128] par le 'et', et[129] quant il dit qu'il l'a murtri et doné les cos[130] de quei il a mort receue, et que l'on n'est pas tenus de respondre

---

[103] ne sont] AB: non [104] Et en cest . . . chose] V lacks [105] qu'eles soient sevrees] A: car elles sont decevrees; B: que eles sont dessevreez; O: quei les sont sevrees; V: que elles son desevrees [106] l'une de l'autre] A lacks [107] ou] B lacks [108] ensi] O lacks; V: si [109] Por quei il, por] AB: Et por; V: Pour quoi pour [110] dites] A: dites por lui; V: devant dites [111] AB add: il [112] avant] AB: ains [113] A adds: ce me semble [114] chose dire contre ce] A: chose dire; B: dire encontre [115] ne doit] A: deie; B: doie; OV: ne doive [116] n'est pas] A: seit; B: soit [117] de respondre] V lacks [118] avant] A: quant [119] clain do] V lacks [120] et doné] V lacks [121] V adds: l'a [122] AB adds: le cop ou [123] que il l'a . . . dont] A: de lui quu'il l'a murtri et doné ou doné les cos ou le cop de quoi [124] ensemble] ABV lack [125] qu'en] ABV: que [126] pas] A: pas tot; B: mie tout [127] de] AB lack [128] ensemble] B lacks [129] et] AO lack [130] les cos] AB: le cop

a .ii. clains ensemble de murtre et d'omecide,[131] s'en peut bien garder le defendeor de respondre as cos, se il set. Et se il s'en viaut defendre, il doit le murtre neer et defendre, et aprés dire[132] qu'il ne viaut respondre,[133] se la court ne l'esgarde, se il ne relaisse le[134] clain dou murtre et dit raison por quei; por ce qu'il se claime de .ii. clains ensenble, de murtre et d'omecide, la ou il fait en son clain mension de murtre, et aprés die[135] qu'il li a doné les cos 'dont il a mort receue' et ne dit 'dont il l'a murtri', fait il .ii. clains ensemble, l'un dou murtre[136] l'autre des cos. Por quei[137] il as cos ne viaut respondre, se la court ne l'esgarde, se il[138] ne se relaisse dou[139] clain dou murtre, et se il dou clain[140] dou murtre se relaisse, il respondra a celui[141] des cos si con il devra. 'Et por toutes les raisons que je ai dites por lui[142] ou por aucunes d'eles ne viaut il respondre au clain do murtre et des cos ensenble si con il a fait[143] de lui, se la court ne l'esgarde.' Et de ce se met il en l'esgart de la court sauf son retenaill. Et a moi ne senble que aprés ce dit le clamant puisse chose dire par coi la court doie esgarder[144] que celuy de qui il se claime[145] doive respondre au clain do murtre et des cos ensenble, se le clamant ne dit quant il a[146] fait mention des cos 'et doné[147] les cos de quei il l'a murtri'. Que se il dit 'de quei[148] il l'a tué' ou 'de quei il[149] a mort receue', il ajont o le clain do murtre clain[150] d'omecide, laquel chose l'on ne doit faire ne nul ne le peut faire[151] se son aversaire s'en set garder. Et il sera aprés devisé coment l'on s'en[152] peut et doit garder qui faire le viaut.

Et quant la court avra fait le dit esgart, il covendra que[153] l'apeleor se relaisse do clain[154] dou murtre et se claime des cos, ou qu'il se relaisse dou clain des cos et se teigne a celui[155] dou murtre. Et se il se tient au clain dou murtre et laisse celui des cos, il se[156] metra[157] en faus guages. Si il[158] devra mescheir de la bataille. Qu'il se parjura[159]

[131] de murtre et d'omecide] AB: del (B: dou) murtre et de l'homecide (B: l'omicide) [132] dire] AB: die [133] A adds: as cos [134] relaisse le] A: se relaisse dou; B: laisse le [135] aprés die] A: puis dit aprés; B: puis dit [136] AB add: et [137] por quei] B lacks [138] AB add: premier [139] dou] C: d'un [140] dou clain] C lacks [141] a celui] AB: au claim [142] por lui] B lacks [143] a fait] B: fait; C: a faire [144] par coi la . . . esgarder] A: que la court esgarde [145] claime] ABV: clama [146] a] AB lack [147] AB add: le cop ou [148] de quei] AB: dont [149] l'a murtri'. Que . . . quei il] V lacks [150] clain] A: cop [151] faire] B lacks [152] s'en] AOV: se [153] que] C lacks [154] do clain] ABV lack [155] teigne a celui] AB: teigne (B: tiegne) au claim; V: claime [156] il se] O lacks [157] metra] AB: sera mis [158] Si il] AOV: Si li; B: Se li [159] se parjura] AV: s'esparjurera; B: se parjurera

el champ quant il jura[160] que il l'a murtri, quar il ne l'avra[161] pas murtri. Et se il relaisse le clain dou murtre et se prent a celui des cos, il li covendra faire l'apel si con l'on[162] doit faire d'omecide. Et coment que l'apeleor face l'apel de murtre ou d'omecide defende s'en[163] celui qui est apelé si con il est devisé en ce[164] livre que il se doit defendre selonc la maniere que le clain sera que on fera de lui dou tué. Et se l'apeleor ajont les cos[165] ou le murtre disant qu'il li a doné les cos[166] de quei[167] il a mort receue, et le defendeor[168] s'aert enssi a lui, quant il feront le sairement ou chanp andeus[169] seront parjurs:[170] l'apeleor de ce qu'il jurra et[171] dit que l'autre l'a[172] murtri, et le defendeor de ce qu'il jurra[173] qu'il ne li dona le cop ou les cos de quei[174] il a esté mort.[175]

[160] jura] ABV: jurera [161] l'avra] ABV: l'a [162] l'on] AB: il le [163] s'en] A: sei; B: soi [164] ce] ABV: cest [165] les cos] A: le cop [166] C adds: ou le cop [167] de quei] BV: dont [168] defendeor] A: defendant; B: deffendant [169] V adds: ensemble [170] parjurs] AV: esparjurés; B: parjurés [171] jurra et] ABV: avra; O: jura [172] l'autre l'a] V: il a [173] jurra] AB: jure; V: li jura [174] de quei] ABV: dont [175] esté mort] AB: mort receue

***[78]** Quant home se claime de murtre et il ajont el clain[1] homecide o le murtre, coment l'apelé[2] s'en peut partir sans bataille.

S'aucun se claime d'autre de murtre et son conceill dit por lui en son clain:[3] 'Sire, tel se claime a vos de tel qui a tel murtri et doné le cop ou les cos de quei[4] il a mort receue', se celui qui est au conceill de celui que l'on apele enssi dou[5] murtre est bon plaideor, il me senble que il l'en[6] peut faire partir sans bataille se le clamant maintient son clain en la maniere avant dite. Et qui faire le vodra, si demande au clamant quant son avantparlier avra[7] fait le dit[8] clain, se il otroie ce que il a dit por lui, et se il l'otroie[9] si die: 'Sire, tel', et le nome, 'noie et defent mot a mot le murtre et les cos que tel li met sus, et est prest qu'il s'en defende de son cors contre le sien, se la court l'esgarde qu'il[10] a lui s'en doie aerdre. Mais il n'entent que il a[11] lui s'en doie aerdre[12] ne faire ne le viaut, se la court ne l'esgarde, et dit por quei: por ce que il c'est clamés de lui de .ii. choses ensenble, lesqués ne pevent[13] ne doivent estre conduites ne menees[14] ensemble,[15] que l'une est contraire a l'autre. Quar murtre et homecide ne peut[16] estre en .i. cors. Por quei la clamor est fauce, et di coment: que quant il dist que il l'avoit murtri et doné les cos[17] dont il avoit mort receue, il ajonst murtre et omecide ensemble, laquel chose ne peut estre faite en .i. cors ensenble.[18] Quar murtre est chose[19] faite en repost, et por ce est l'assise[20] tel que l'on peut prover murtre[21] par son cors. Car en ce[22] cas le cors murtri porte partie de la garantie et l'apeleor l'autre. Et celui a qui l'on done cos de quei il receit mort[23] est homecide, ne homecide ne peut l'on prover par l'assise ou l'usage dou reiaume de Jerusalem que par .ii. loiaus garans de la loy de Rome qui facent que loiaus garans,[24] que

---

A: fols lii^{v}–liii^{v} cap. 91; **B:** fols 83^{r}–84^{r} cap. 91; **C:** fols 73^{v}–74^{v} cap. 77; **O:** fols 86^{v}–88^{r}; **V:** fols lxxii^{v}–lxxiv^{r} cap. 90; Beugnot, pp. 147–9, cap. 91.

---

[1] el clain] AV lack [2] l'apelé] A rubrics (fol. 3^{r}): l'apeleor; V: l'apelleoir [3] en son clain] V lacks [4] de quei] BV: dont [5] dou] AB: de [6] l'en] AB: le; V lacks [7] V adds: dit et [8] fait le dit] B: dit son [9] et se il l'otroie] V lacks [10] qu'il] BV: que [11] que il a] C: qu'a [12] Mais il n'entent . . . aerdre] V: s'en [13] A adds: ni; B: ne [14] conduites ne menees] A: conjointes ne vouees; B: conjontes ne nomeez [15] lesqués ne pevent . . . ensemble] V lacks [16] peut] A: pevent; B: pueent [17] murtri et doné les cos] B: murtre et doné le cop [18] laquel chose ne . . . ensenble] V lacks [19] chose] V lacks [20] V adds: faite [21] murtre] V lacks [22] ce] ABV: cest [23] de quei il receit mort] A: dont il a mort receue; B: dont il recoit la mort [24] A adds: deivent faire ce est qu'il jurent; B: doivent faire

il li[25] virent[26] les cos doner de quei il a[27] mort receue. Si est clere chose que sa clamor est fauce. Et puis que sa clamor est fauce, par l'assise ou l'usage dou dit reiaume[28] celui de qu'il c'est clamé[29] doit estre quite et delivre vers lui de cele querele. Por quei tel vos dit, et je por lui, qu'il a luy ne se viaut aerdre[30] de ce qu'il li a mis sus[31] par fauce clamor, se la court ne l'esgarde,[32] ains en viaut demorer vers lui quite et delivre por tant con je ai dit por lui, se la court l'esgarde.' Et de ce se met[33] en l'esgart de la cort sauf son retenaill.

Et a mei senble que la clamor faite en la maniere avant dite est fauce. Et puis qu'ele est fauce, et[34] le clamant otroie ce que son avantparlier a dit,[35] il ne me semble qu'il puisse dire aprés chose por quei la court ne[36] doive esgarder que celui de qui[37] il c'est clamé est[38] quite et delivre[39] vers lui de cele querele. Et se celui qui est au conceill dou clamant[40] qui fait le clain en la maniere avant dite por metre le en drois guages, si com il est avant[41] dit, se son aversaire ne s'en set garder, se viaut garder[42] que celui qu'on apele en la maniere avant[43] dite[44] ne[45] s'en[46] parte quite et delivre sans bataille, si s'en garde enssi[47] que, quant l'autre demande[48] otroi a celui a qui conceill il est,[49] ne seufre que il l'otroie mais change son clain enssi qu'il face l'apeau dou murtre sans ajondre y les cos de quei il a mort receue ou faire[50] le clain de l'omecide sans ajondre y le murtre. Et se il le fait ensi, celui qui sera[51] apelé ne se[52] porra defendre que il ne responde au clain dou murtre ou de l'omecide.

Et quant il covendra a[53] celui qui est apelé a respondre au murtre ou a l'omecide, si le face si com il est devisé devant en ce livre que on le doit faire selonc le clain qu'on fait de lui. Que se il ne le fait, il en sera ataint, et se il est ataint dou murtre ou de l'omecide, il avra deservi a estre[54] pendu et le doit estre par l'assise ou l'usage

---

[25] li] ABV lack [26] AB add: le cop ou [27] il a] A: celui aveit [28] dit reiaume] B: reaume de Jerusalem [29] qu'il c'est clamé] V: qui il se claime [30] se viaut aerdre] B: s'en veut prendre [31] sus] A lacks [32] l'esgarde] C: conoisse [33] BV add: il [34] et] CO lack [35] A adds: por lui [36] ne] ABV lack [37] qui] O: quei [38] est] A: ne seit; B: ne soit [39] et delivre] ABV lack [40] dou clamant] A: de celui [41] il est avant] V: est devant [42] se viaut garder] A: et il ne viaut; B: se il veut; V: s'il ne veaut [43] avant] V: devant [44] la maniere avant dite] B: tel maniere [45] ne] A lacks; V: n'en [46] s'en] C: se [47] s'en garde enssi] AB: se garde; V: se guarde [48] demande] AB: demandera [49] B adds: qu'il [50] faire] A: face; B: il face [51] V adds: ensi [52] se] O: s'en; V: s'em [53] a] ABV lack [54] il en sera . . . estre] A: il est ataint dou murtre ou de l'homecide et c'il en est ataint, il a decervi d'estre; B: et il est ataint dou murtre ou de l'omicide, il a deservi d'estre; V: et il est ataint del murtre ou de l'omecide, il avra deservi estre

dou dit[55] reiaume. Et se le clamant y veaut ajoindre el clain dou murtre les cos o[56] le murtre, faire le peut sans perill, mais que il die qu'il l'a murtri et doné le cop ou les cos dont[57] il l'a murtri. Et se il fait enssi son clain, le defendant doit mot a mot neer[58] le murtre et les cos que celui li met sus et ofrir s'en[59] a defendre de son cors contre le sien et tendre[60] son guage au seignor a genos. Qu'en tel clain n'a[61] mestier de maistroier[62] que de guarder se[63] qu'autre ne le puisse apeler de cel murtre, se il s'en estoit aers a lui par guage de bataille et pais en estoit faite. Et en[64] la maniere con[65] l'on doit ce[66] faire est devisé en ce livre.

[55] dit] C lacks [56] o] ABV: et [57] dont] AB: de quoi [58] AB add: maintenant [59] s'en] ABV lack [60] tendre] C: tende [61] Qu'en tel clain n'a] A: Que en tel claim n'i a; B: Que or n'i a [62] maistroier] A: maistreer ce; B: mestrance [63] se] ABV lack [64] en] A lacks [65] con] AB: que [66] Et en la . . . ce] V: en la maniere com la doit

***[79]** Quant home[1] apele autre de murtre et il n'est[2] de ceaus vers qui l'on ne se peut defendre de respondre, coment l'on se doit[3] defendre.

Se aucun apele autre de murtre et il n'est de ceaus de qui il[4] est devant[5] dit qui pevent[6] apeau faire de murtre, l'apelé s'en doit[7] enssi defendre: qu'il doit faire dire que il nee et defent le murtre mot a mot, si con il le[8] li met sus, et qu'il est prest qu'il s'en defende de son cors contre le sien, se la court esgarde[9] que il a lui s'en doive aerdre, mais il n'entent que il a lui s'en doive aerdre[10] ne faire ne le viaut, se la court ne l'esgarde, et di por quei: por ce que il n'est pas parent dou mort[11] ne ataignant a luy d'aucune chose tel por quei il puisse faire apeau[12] de murtre de cel cors. Por quei il a lui ne s'en viaut aerdre, se la court ne l'esgarde. Et de ce se met en l'esgart de la court sauf son retenaill. Et je cuit que la court doit esgarder qu'il ne s'i doit pas aerdre, se il ne preuve si con il doit qu'il est[13] parent dou murtri ou ataignant a lui en l'une[14] des manieres devant devisee.[15] Que s'ensi n'estoit, chascun et chascune porroit faire apeau de murtre, laquel chose seroit moult descovenable et moult de maus en porroit l'on faire. Que chascun home, qui seroit grant et fort ou qui seroit chanpion afaitié, porroit par ce raembre[16] moult de gens se il voloit faire[17] aporter .i. cors en court qui eust[18] cos et le mostrast a la court et[19] se clamast d'aucun riche home ou d'aucun qui eust parens et[20] amis riches.[21] Et s'ensi estoit que chascun peust apeler de murtre, ceaus et[22] celes qui font apel de murtre et[23] guagent bataille par chanpion feroient moult que fos de faire l'apel et d'estre en perill d'estre justisié se lor chanpion estoit vencu,

---

A: fols liii^{v}–liv^{r} cap. 92; **B:** fol. 84^{r-v} cap. 92; **C:** fols 74^{v}–75^{v} cap. 78; **O:** fols 88^{r}–90^{r}; **V:** fols lxxiv^{r}–lxxv^{r} cap. 91; Beugnot, pp. 149–51, cap. 92.

---

[1] Quant home] A: Se aucun [2] n'est] B (fol. 20^{r}): est [3] coment l'on se doit] B: et coment s'en puet home [4] il] ABV lack [5] devant] V: avant [6] pevent] A: peut [7] s'en doit] A: se deit; O: son dit; V: se peut [8] le] ABV lack [9] esgarde] C: l'esgarde [10] mais il n'entent . . . aerdre] BV lack [11] mort] ABV: murtri [12] apeau] C: apeaus [13] est] B: soit son [14] en l'une] AV: d'aucune; B: d'aucunes [15] devant devisee] A: avant dites; B: devant ditez [16] raembre] C: raenbler [17] voloit faire] A: le voleit faire et ensi qu'il poreit; B: le voloit faire et porroit [18] A adds: pluissors [19] le mostrast a la court et] ABV lack [20] et] ABV: ou [21] A adds: et les poreit apeler [22] et] AB: ou [23] apel de murtre et] A: apeler et qui; B: apeler et

puis que le chanpion le porroit faire ou autre que le parent ou la[24] parente ou aucun des avant dis qui pevent faire apeau[25] de murtre,[26] puis que il porroient avoir por monoie home qui feist l'apel et les[27] getast dou perill d'estre justisiés se lor[28] chanpion estoit vencus. Et il me senble que, se il covient a aucun a[29] prover qu'il est[30] tel qu'il puisse faire apeau de murtre, qu'il le doie[31] prover si con l'on preuve parenté, et que tos ceaus qui pevent porter garantie de parenté la[32] pevent porter en cest cas aussi des autres con des[33] parens, et qu'il n'i a point de tornes de bataille en ce[34] cas contre les garans. Quar s'ensi n'estoit, jamais apeau de murtre ne seroit fait de quei l'on venist a bataille. Que l'apelé porroit dire a celui qui l'apeleroit qu'il n'est mie de ceaus qui pevent et doivent faire apeau de murtre. Et se l'apeleor[35] l'ofroit[36] a prover si con[37] court esgarderoit ou conoistroit q'il prover le deust, court esgarderoit ou conoistroit, se croi,[38] qu'il li[39] deust prover par .ii.[40] garans. L'apelé porroit dire contre les garans et contredire ou torner[41] si con il est devisé en ce[42] livre que on le peut faire de garans, laquel chose seroit tort apert et contre tos drois et tos usages et toutes assises. Si soufist asés quant home ou feme fait apel de murtre et se met en perill[43] de mort hontoze, se il[44] a .ii. homes ou femes qui jurent sur sains qu'il est ataignant[45] au murtri en la maniere qu'il avra dit, se l'apelé[46] contredit[47] qu'il ne soit ataignant au murtri. Et asés doivent[48] ceaus qui le jurent estre creu en cest cas, mais qu'il soient crestiens batiés de quelque nacion que il soient, mais que il ne soient de ceaus qui n'ont vois ne[49] respons en court. Et aprés cest esgart il covient que celui[50] qui fait l'apel preuve si con il doit qu'il soit parent dou mort[51] ou qu'il soit en tel cas vers lui con il est avant devisé[52] que ceaus sont qui pevent et doivent faire apeau de murtre.

---

[24] le parent ou la] AB: parent ou [25] avant dis qui . . . apeau] B: devant diz qui pueent apeler [26] ou aucun des . . . murtre] V: dou murtri [27] les] A: le [28] lor] ABV: le [29] a] ABV lack [30] est] A: seit [31] doie] V: peut faire [32] la] AV: le [33] des autres con des] A: come des autres [34] ce] ABV: cest [35] l'apeleor] A: il [36] l'ofroit] B: l'offre [37] AB adds: la [38] croi] AB: cuit [39] li] ABV: le [40] C adds: loiaus [41] contredire ou torner] A: rebuter ent aucuns et torner; B: rebuter en aucun; V: contredire et tourner [42] ce] AB: cest; V: cestui [43] AB add: dou (B: de) cors et [44] AV add: y [45] ataignant] O: ataint [46] l'apelé] B: le deffendeor [47] contredit] AV: le contredit [48] doivent] A: devront; B: devroient [49] n'ont vois ne] V: ont perdu vois et [50] celui] C: cestui [51] mort] AV: murtri [52] lui con il . . . devisé] B: le mort com il est devisé devant

Et quant la preuve sera faite et l'apel sera fait et[53] les guages donés et receus, le seignor doit faire bien[54] garder l'apeleor et le defendeor jusques au jor de la bataille en la maniere devant[55] devisee en ce livre, et au jor de la bataille il se doivent venir porofrir ensi armés et atirés com il est aprés devisé[56] et ce dire et faire qui est aprés dit.[57]

---

[53] la preuve sera . . . et] A: il l'avra prové et; B: il l'avra prové et l'apeau sera fait et; C: la preuve sera faite et; V: la preuve et l'apeau sera fait et [54] bien] AB lack [55] devant] A: qui devant est [56] en la maniere . . . devisé] V: que il doivent estre armés et atirés com il est aprés devisé en cestui livre [57] il se doivent . . . dit] B: coment il doivent estre arméz est aprés devisé

***[80]** Coment et por quey l'apeau d'omecide est grief a amener[1] a bataille se le defendant[2] s'en[3] set garder, et coment l'on le doit faire et coment l'on s'en[4] doit guarder.

Apeau d'omecide est moult grief a faire si que celui qu'on apele s'en[5] conbate se il s'en set et viaut garder. Et qui veut apeau faire d'omecide, il doit faire le cors aporter en la court et doit dire et faire[6] dou cors et des cos mostrer a la court si con il est devant[7] devisé en ce[8] livre que l'on le[9] doit faire de murtre. Et quant celui qui viaut faire l'apeau de l'omecide en veaut faire l'apeau,[10] il doit faire dire ensi au seignor par son conceill: 'Sire, tel se claime a vos de tel', et le[11] nome, 'qui a a tel', et le nome, 'doné le cop ou les cos par quei il a mort receue, et se il le noie il est prest de prover le[12] li tot enssi con la court esgardera ou conoistra qu'il[13] prover le doie. Et veés en si son guage.' Et lors celui qui fait[14] l'apel s'agenoille devant le seignor et li tende son guage. Et se celui qui est enssi apelé est present en la court, il doit demander conceill au seignor,[15] et aprés faire dire[16] au seignor, s'il est en fers ou en liens, qu'il le face desferer ou deslier. Et quant se sera fait, l'apeleor doit refaire son clain[17] si com il[18] est desus dit. Et adonques celui qui est au conceill do defendeor doit dire:[19] 'Sire, tel', et le nome, 'noie et defent les cos et la malefaite que tel li met sus', et le nome, 'et est prest[20] qu'il s'en defende tout ensi con la court esgardera qu'il s'en doie defendre. Et veés en si son guage.' Et lors celui qui est apelé se doit agenoiller devant le seignor[21] et tendre[22] son guage. Et la court doit esgarder que celui ou cele qui fait enssi l'apel doit prover se qu'il a dit par .ii. loiaus garans de la loy de Rome, et que l'apelé en doit[23] l'un torner par guage de bataille et conbatre s'en a lui, se il viaut.

A: fols liv^{r}–lv^{v} cap. 93; **B:** fols 84^{v}–86^{r} cap. 93; **C:** fols 75^{v}–77^{v} cap. 79; **O:** fols 90^{r}–93^{r}; **V:** fols lxxv^{r}–lxxvii^{r} cap. 92; Beugnot, pp. 151–3, cap. 93.

---

[1] amener] AB (fol. 20^{r}): mener [2] defendant] B: deffendeor [3] s'en] AB: se [4] s'en] A rubrics (fol. 3^{r}) BOV: se [5] s'en] ABV: se [6] A adds: dire [7] devant] AB: avant; V: devant dit et [8] ce] AB: cest; V: cestui [9] le] AB lack [10] de l'omecide en . . . l'apeau] V lacks [11] le] AO: les [12] le] ABV lack [13] qu'il] V: que je [14] fait] V: a fait [15] au seignor] C: a la court; V: a la court et au seignor [16] A adds: par son conseill [17] refaire son clain] A: faire son reclain; B: faire son claim [18] il] ABV lack [19] B adds: au seignor [20] prest] C lacks [21] devant le seignor] B lacks [22] AO adds: li [23] doit] AV: peut; B: puet bien

Et quant la court a ce esgardé,[24] se celui qui fait[25] le dit[26] apel n'a ses garans aprestés, il doit faire dire[27] au seignor: 'Sire, soiés seur de tel', et le nome, 'tant que je aie mes garans amenés en la[28] court[29] porter me la dite[30] garantie au jor que la court me[31] donra'. Et le seignor li doit demander ou ses guarans sont, et il doit dire ou il sont[32] ou reiaume ou[33] hors[34] la ou il cuide que il soient.[35] Et la court li doit doner jor d'avoir[36] ses garans amenés [37] en la court por la garantie porter. Et le jor doit estre selonc ce qu'il est[38] devant dit en ce[39] livre que l'on a jor de guarans amener selonc le leuc que[40] l'on dit[41] que[42] il sont quant on les vouche.[43] Et le seignor doit celui de qui l'on c'est ensi clamé faire bien[44] garder en prison et en fers jusques[45] au jor que la court avra doné a son aversaire d'avoir ses garans amenés.

Et se celui qui a tel apel fait con[46] est devant[47] devisé a ses garans aprestés et il viaut maintenant faire l'apel, il doit faire dire[48] aprés l'esgart de la court: 'Sire, et je suis prest que je le li preuve tout enssi[49] con la court esgardera,[50] et veés ci mes garans par coi[51] je li proverai', et dire[52] as garans: 'Venés avant. Dites et[53] faites de cest fait ce que loiaus guarans doivent faire.'[54] Et lors ceaus doivent ensenble demander conceill au seignor, et le seignor lor doit doner. Et quant il avront[55] lor conceill doit dire por eaus: 'Sire, vés ci tel et tel[56] qui vos dient, et je por eaus, que il furent el leuc et en la place ou il[57] virent que tel', et le nome,[58] 'fist a tel', et le nome, 'le cop ou les cos de quei il a mort receue, et de ce sont il prest de faire que loiaus garans'.[59] Et[60] le seignor doit maintenant faire aporter une evangile et doit dire: 'Venés avant. Jurés que il est enssi com vostre avantparlier a dit por vos'. Et il se doivent agenoiller por le sairement faire. Et se l'apelé[61] les viaut contredire ou rebuter ou torner[62] par guage de bataille en aucune des manieres devant[63] dites, il le

[24] esgardé] O: esgardera [25] fait] B: a fait [26] dit] O lacks [27] dire] C lacks [28] en la] AB: a [29] B adds: a; C: por [30] me la dite] AB: ceste; V: la dite [31] me] OV: m'en [32] AB adds: se il sont [33] ou] C lacks [34] hors] A: defors; BV: dehors [35] soient] A: sont [36] d'avoir] AB: a; V: que il ait [37] amenés] AB: amener [38] qu'il est] V: que je ai [39] ce] AB: cest; V: cestui [40] que] ABV: ou [41] l'on dit] V: il dist [42] que] AOV: ou [43] vouche] A: a voués; V: a voé [44] bien] B lacks [45] jusques] A: trusques [46] C adds: il [47] devant] ABV: avant [48] A adds: par son conseill [49] tout enssi] ABV: si [50] esgardera] A: a esgardé [51] quoi] ABV: qui [52] dire] AB: die [53] Dites et] AB lack [54] faire] B lacks [55] A adds: conseill [56] A adds: et les nome [57] ou il] AB: qu'il [58] nome] V: noument [59] que loiaus garans] AB: ce que leaus garenz deivent (B: garanz doivent) faire [60] B adds: lors [61] l'apelé] A: l'apeleor [62] ou torner] ABV lack [63] devant] AB: avant

peut faire si con est[64] devisé en cest livre que on le doit faire qui viaut torner garant par guage de bataille ou rebuter les.[65] Et se l'apelé[66] torne l'un de garans[67] par guage de bataille, le seignor doit recevoir les gages. Et quant il les a[68] receus, il doit dire a sa court qu'ele li conoisse coment cele bataille doit estre faite et a quel jor. Et la court doit conoistre, se cuit, qu'ele deit estre au tiers jor et ensi armés et apareillés com il est dit devant que les chanpions de murtre le doivent estre, et que l'apeleor en[69] doit rendre le defendeor mort ou recreant en une hore de jor. Quar il ne[70] me senble qu'il ait[71] diference entre murtre et homecide autre que de ce que l'on peut l'apel dou murtre[72] faire et prover de son cors, et celui de l'omecide covient a[73] prover par guarans, et por ce doit l'on estre mené come l'autre en toutes choses, mais que de la preuve qui est diverce con de cors a garans. Et quant les dis chanpions ont doné lor guages au seignor et il les a receus, il les[74] doit lors andeus faire[75] bien garder, et[76] celui qui a fait l'apel doit il ensi bien faire[77] garder et tenir le o son chanpion jusques au tiers jor.[78]

Et au tiers jor il[79] se doivent venir porofrir ensi con ceaus do murtre et ce faire et dire con[80] est devisé en ce livre,[81] que les chanpions de murtre doivent faire et dire jusques au sairement. Et le sairement[82] que il feront doit estre tel: que celui qui est apelé de l'omecide[83] doit jurer enmi le chanp sur les saintes evangiles[84] que il n'a a tel, et le nome, doné le cop ou les cos de quei il a mort receue, et celui qui l'apele[85] le doit maintenant prendre par le poing et dire li:[86] 'Tu mens, et je t'en lief come parjur. Et jur sur ses[87] saintes evangiles que tu li as[88] doné le cop ou les cos de quei il a mort receue.' Et aprés les gardes dou chanp les doivent mener chascun a l'une des parties[89] dou chanp et partir lor le souleill et faire toutes[90] les autres choses qui sont devant[91] devisees que l'on doit

---

[64] AB: add: avant; O: devant [65] les] AB lack [66] l'apelé] AB: il [67] de garans] A lacks [68] il les a] V: le seignor a les guages [69] en] AB lack [70] ne] B lacks [71] qu'il ait] ABV lack [72] et homecide autre . . . murtre] V lacks [73] a] ABV lack [74] les] O: lor [75] lors andeaus faire] V: an .ii. [76] A adds: aussi [77] il ensi bien faire] B: il autresi bien; V: auci bien [78] et tenir le . . . jor] B: come l'autre et son champion avec lui. [79] Et au tiers jor il] V: qu'il [80] con] B: que; OV: qui [81] C adds: et [82] Et le sairement] C lacks [83] de l'omecide] B: dou murtre [84] les saintes evangiles] A: l'evangille; B: l'evangile; V: les evangiles [85] qui l'alepe] A: qui l'a apelé] V: qu'il l'a apelé [86] li] AV lack [87] ses] AV lack [88] dire li: Tu . . . as] B: lever le come parjuré et jurer sur saint evangile qu'il li a [89] chascun a l'une des parties] AV: a une part; B: en une part [90] toutes] B: jurer [91] devant] AB: avant

faire[92] des[93] champions qui se conbatent por murtre. Et de celui qui est vencu ou recreant doit le seignor faire faire justise, si com[94] est avant dit, et ausi de celui ou de cele qui fait l'apel se son chanpion est vencu.

Et se l'apelé de l'omecide rebute l'un des garans et dit que il n'est pas[95] tel que il puisse garantie porter contre lui et l'eufre a prover si con la court esgardera ou conoistra qu'il le doive prover, et[96] la court esgarde ou conoisse[97] qu'il le doit prover par .ii. loiaus garans de la loi de Rome,[98] le garant[99] que l'on enssi rebute s'en[100] doit aleauter et peut torner[101] lequel qu'il vodra des garans qui portent[102] cele garantie contre lui[103] et conbatre s'en a lui. Et se il ne le viaut torner par guage de bataille et il le viaut geter de cele garantie porter contre lui, faire le porra[104] si con est avant dit qu'il[105] doit tel chose faire. Et enssi porra la chose longuement estre deleeye des[106] garans contre garans tant que aucun des guarans que on viaut geter de la[107] garantie torne aucuns des garans[108] qui doivent garantie[109] par quei il doive estre geté de garantie et s'aerde[110] a lui de bataille. Et por ce ai ge devant[111] dit qu'il est grief chose[112] a faire de conbatre se a home d'omecide[113] qui s'en set garder. Quar[114] il fera cheir la[115] bataille sur .i. des[116] guarans se il viaut rebuter .i. des guarans qui la[117] garantie veullent[118] porter contre lui de l'omecide que l'on li met sus.

---

[92] B adds: jurer [93] des] AB: a; V: de [94] C adds: il [95] rebute l'un des . . . pas] AB: viaut (B: veut) rebuter les garenz (B: garanz) et dit a l'un que il n'est mie [96] et] AV lack [97] esgarde ou conoisse] AB: deit (B: doit) esgarder; V: doit counoistre [98] A adds: et aprés le dit esgart [99] le garant] B: et les garanz [100] s'en] ABV: se [101] torner] V: aloyauter [102] portent] O: porteront [103] A adds: par gage de bataille [104] porra] A: peut; B: puet [105] dit qu'il] A: devisié qu'on; B: devisé c'on; O: dit qui; V: devisé c'om [106] des] AV: de [107] la] C lacks [108] de la garantie . . . garans] B: trove autres deus [109] doivent garantie] A: veulent garentir; B: veulent garantie porter; V: veullent guarentir [110] s'aerde] A: s'en aert; B: s'en aherdre; V: se aerdre [111] devant] AB: avant [112] chose] ABV lack [113] d'omecide] C: de [114] qui s'en set garder. Quar] A: quant il s'en set garder. Que se il s'en set garder; B: Que se il se set garder; V: quant il s'en set garder. Que [115] la] C lacks [116] .i. des] A: l'un des; B: l'un de ses; O: .i. de ces [117] la] A: celle; B: cele [118] veullent] V: veulle

***[81]** Coment il[1] peut avoir plusors batailles d'un[2] home ocis[3] qui a plusors cos.

Je ai dit en cest livre que d'un home tué[4] autrement que en[5] murtre, se il a plusors cos, peut avoir pluisors batailles. Et por ce que je ai devisé ore[6] coment l'on peut faire apeau d'omecide,[7] veuill je deviser coment il peut avoir plusors batailles d'un home qui ait esté tué, si con est[8] devant dit, ou il a plusors cos. Et[9] la maniere est tel. Quant il est aporté[10] a court et la court avra veu les cos et dire[11] les au seignor,[12] si con[13] est dit devant, cil[14] qui viaut faire l'apel d'omecide[15] si se clamera[16] au seignor de celui de qui[17] il se vodra[18] clamer, et ne se clamera que de l'un des cos de celui de qui il est verais[19] qu'il[20] ait[21] mort receue et[22] dire: 'Sire, je me clain a vos de tel qui a tel a doné cel[23] cop de quei[24] il a mort receue.' Et die lequel,[25] et aprés die et face ce qui est devant[26] devisé que on doit dire et faire a loy de l'apel de l'omecide.[27]

Et aprés ce[28] se .i. home ou feme qui veuille aucun autre home[29] mener a guage de bataille veigne devant le seignor et li demande conceill et[30] li die: 'Sire, je me clain a vos de tel qui a tel fist cel[31] cop d'arme esmolue[32] et de tel armeure.' Et die se qu'il li senblera meaus de coi le cop ait[33] esté, d'espee ou de coteau ou d'autre armeure, et die:[34] 'Et se il le noie, je suis prest que je li preuve[35] si con la court esgardera[36] que je prover le[37] doie.' Et se celui le conoist, il est en la merci dou seignor par l'assise ou l'usage de faire li coper

---

A: fols lv^{v}–lvi^{v} cap. 94; **B:** fol. 86^{r-v} cap. 94; **C:** fols 77^{v}–78^{v} cap. 80; **O:** fols 93^{r}–94^{v}; **V:** fol. lxxvii^{r-v} cap. 93; Beugnot, pp. 154–5, cap. 94.

---

[1] il] V: l'on doit et [2] d'un] B (fol. 20^{r}): en [3] ocis] A lacks [4] d'un home tué] V: .i. houme tué .i. autre [5] autrement que en] AB: sans [6] ore] AB lack [7] C adds: coment [8] est] A: j'ais; B: je ai [9] Et] BOV lack [10] aporté] V: porté [11] dire] A: retrais; B: dit; V: retraire [12] au seignor] B: enseignes [13] ABV adds: il [14] cil] A: celui; B lacks; V: et celui [15] d'omecide] A: de l'homecide; O: de l'omeside; V: de l'omecide [16] clamera] AB: deit (B: doit) clamer [17] qui] O: quei [18] vodra] A: viaut; B: veut; V: veaut [19] qui il est verais] O: quei il est vrais [20] de qui il est verais qu'il] A: qu'il cuide miaus que il; B: que il meaus cuide de qui il [21] clamer, et ne . . . ait] V: de quoi ill a [22] A adds: deit; B: doit [23] a tel a doné cel] AV: a tel dona tel; B: a a tel doné le [24] quei] OV: qui [25] Et die lequel] AB lack; OV: Et die lequel cop [26] devant] AB: avant [27] de l'apel de l'omecide] A: d'apel d'omecide; B: d'apel d'omicide [28] ce] ABV lack [29] home] B: claim; V lacks [30] A adds: puis [31] cel] ABV: tel [32] esmolue] BV: molue [33] se qu'il li . . . ait] AB: de quoi il li semble miaus que le cop ait (B: a); V: ce que li semblera meaus de que le cop avra [34] A adds: quel elle est [35] que je li preuve] B: de prover li [36] A adds: ou conoistra [37] le] AV: li

le poing destre. Et se il le noie, celui qui de lui c'est clamés le doit prover par .ii.[38] loiaus garans,[39] et il en peut l'un lever[40] et conbatre s'en a lui ou geter de guarantie porter, si con est avant[41] dit. Et s'il ne le fait et les guarans fornisent la guarantie, il en sera ataint et avra le poing copé, si com je ai[42] dit. Et ensi le peut on faire de chascun des cos[43] que l'ome ocis a. Et por ce ai je dit que d'un home ocis qui a plusors cos poroit[44] on avoir pluisors batailles, que je ne cuit qu'il[45] soit home[46] qui[47] avant ne se[48] defendist[49] contre .i. autre par lui ou par chanpion, se il estoit tel que par chanpion s'en[50] deust[51] defendre, qu'il soferroit[52] le poing destre a coper. Et il est[53] droit et raison et bien le[54] senble, que l'on peut et doit l'un de[55] ses menbres defendre par gage de bataille avant que soufrir le a[56] perdre quant l'on de querele d'un marc d'argent se peut l'on et doit defendre par bataille, que moult est plus grant et[57] grief la querele d'un menbre[58] perdre que d'un marc d'argent.

Et qui fait apel d'omecide, il doit savoir ques[59] est homecide, si qu'il se mete en drois guages quant on[60] fait l'apel. Homecide est quant home[61] est tué en apert devant la gent en meslee ou sans meslee.[62] Et l'omecide ne peut l'on pas prover de son cors, si le covient a prover[63] par garans, et la preuve des guarans est moult grieve a faire venir a bataille qui s'en set defendre[64] et le viaut faire. Et il est asés devisé en cest livre coment on le[65] porroit faire,[66] si ne[67] veuill orés plus[68] esclarzir.[a]

[a] For proof by 'garans', above caps 57–8, 61–5.

[38] .ii.] B: trois [39] A adds: de la lei de Rome [40] lever] A: lever par gage de bataille; B: torner [41] avant] V: devant [42] AV add: devant [43] chascun des cos] AB: chascune des plaies [44] poroit] A: peut: B: puet [45] V adds: ne [46] home] ABV: nul [47] qui] C: que [48] se] OV: s'en [49] defendist] A: combatist; B: conbatist [50] s'en] ABV: se [51] deust] B: peust [52] sofferroit] A: se soufrist; B: s'en souffrist; V: se soffriroit [53] est] O: dist [54] ABV add: me [55] l'un des] B: bien [56] le a] B: les [57] et] AB: chose et plus [58] d'un menbre] B: de ses membres [59] ques] ABV: que; C: queus [60] on] AB: il [61] home] C: on [62] en meslee ou sans meslee] A: en meslee ou sans meslee ou en ville ou fors ville; B: en vile ou sanz vile; V: en mehlee [63] de son cors . . . prover] A: par son cors, ains le covient prover; B: par son cors solement que; C lacks [64] defendre] B: aparcevoir [65] on le] AB: l'on le; O: il [66] on le porroit faire] V: et pour quoi [67] ne] AB: ne le; C: n'en [68] plus] B: mie

***[82]** Quant on apele home de traïson qui[1] n'est[2] aparant et[3] s'en eufre a defendre de son cors[4] et tent son guage, coment et quant le seignor peut la bataille desfaire.

Qui viaut apeler home de traïson qui n'est[5] aparant, savoir se il s'en aerdra[6] a lui sans esgart de cort por haine[7] ou por atine ou par despit ou par volenté que il ait de conbatre se[8] a lui, il doit motir la traïson[9] de coi il l'a apelé,[10] et dire enssi en la presence[11] de celui qu'il viaut apeler: 'Sire, tel', et le nome, 'come faus et desloiaus fist[12] tel traïson contre tel', se c'est contre[13] le seignor ou autre et nome les .ii. et la traïson. Et die aprés:[14] 'Et se il le noie, je suis prest que je li preuve de mon cors contre le sien, et que je[15] l'en rende mort ou recreant[16] en une hore de jor. Et veés enssi mon[17] guage.' Et s'agenoille devant le seignor et li tent son gage.[18] Et se celui que l'on apele ensi s'en viaut aerdre a celui qui l'a apelé[19] de son cors au sien,[20] il le doit desmentir mot a mot[21] et ofrir se a defendre de son cors contre le sien et en tende[22] son guage au seignor a genous. Et se il le fait, le seignor en peut recevoir les guages se il viaut.

Et se il ne les viaut recevoir, il lor doit dire que il s'en seufrent de cele haitine, que il ne viaut ore que bataille en soit[23] guagee en sa cort, se ce n'est par esgart ou par conoissance de court ou par assise. Et se le seignor dit ce, il n'i avra[24] point de bataille, que[25] se il requiert esgart ou conoissance de court de la bataille aveir dont l'apel et la defence[26] est[27] faite si con il est devant dit,[28] la court n'esgardera ne conoistra[29] que bataille en doive estre par assise.[30] Que

A: fols lvi^{v}–lvii^{v} cap. 95; **B:** fols 86^{v}–87^{v} cap. 95; **C:** fols 78^{v}–79^{v} cap. 81; **O:** fols 94^{v}–96^{r}; **V:** fols lxxvii^{v}–lxxix^{r} cap. 94; Beugnot, pp. 155–7, cap. 95.

[1] qui] AV: et elle [2] n'est] B (fol. 20^{r}): est [3] ABV add: il [4] A adds: contre le sien [5] n'est] C: est [6] aerdra] O: aerde [7] haine] ABV: honte [8] se] A: s'ent; V: s'en [9] traïson] O: raison [10] de coi il l'a apelé] AB: dont il l'apelle (B: l'apele) [11] AB add: de la court et [12] come faus et desloiaus fist] ABV: a come faus et desleau (B: desloiaus; V: dehloyaus) faite [13] se c'est contre] A: seit; BV: soit [14] nome les .ii. . . . aprés] A: le nome et die aprés la traysson [15] je] O: il [16] rende mort ou recreant] B: rendrai mort ou vaincu [17] mon] C: son [18] et li tent son gage] C lacks [19] l'a apelé] BOV: l'apele [20] au sien] AB: contre le sien; C: ausi [21] desmentir mot a mot] A: maintenant desmentir; B: desmentir maintenant [22] en tende] ABV: tendre [23] AB add: faite ne [24] ce, il n'i avra] B: qu'il ne veut [25] que] AV: car; B: ore [26] la defence] B: l'affense [27] est] C: a esté [28] dit] V: devisé [29] ne conoistra] A: ja [30] en doive estre par assise] A: en deit estre ne seit par assise ne par usage; B: ne doie estre ne ne soit pas assise; V: en doit estre ne ne peut par assise em peut estre

bataille ne doit[31] estre[32] de traïson par esgart ne par conoissance de court ne par assise, se la traïson n'est aparant.[33]

Mais se le seignor en receit les guages, la bataille ne peut demorer[34] que par l'asent des .iii. parties, dou seignor et de l'apeleor[35] et dou defendeor, que le seignor de soi[36] ne la peut desfaire se aucun des chanpions l'en viaut et set mener a ce qu'il porra[37] par l'esgart de la cort.[38] Que se l'apeleor s'en vosist[39] relaisser de son rapel[40] et desdire s'ent en court et l'apelé s'en tenist apaié et font[41] pais ensenble, ne peut la bataille demorer sans la volenté do seignor, puis que il en a les gages receus. Que la ou la volenté de l'apeleor et de[42] l'apelé[43] s'acordent[44] ensemble au doner des[45] guages et les eufrent au seignor,[46] il metent[47] lor volenté el pooïr de cele dou seignor, et se cele[48] dou seignor s'acorde ave la leur au recevoir des guages[49] et il les receit,[50] les .iii. volentés se joignent[51] ensenble et sont une[52] volenté et un meimes[53] otrei. Quar bien otreie[54] l'apelé la volenté[55] de l'apeleor quant il s'aert a lui de[56] bataille sans esgart et sans conoissance de court et sans assise[57] et sans destresce de raison.[58] Et le seignor otroie bien et s'asent[59] a la volenté des .ii. quant il receit les guages sans esgart et[60] sans conoissance de court et sans force d'assise ne d'usage. Que[61] dreit ne le destraint ne raison ne li fait ce[62] faire, dont otroie il bien en court[63] la bataille, et ajont sa volenté o les leur quant il de sa propre volenté receit les guages. Et chose otroiee et faite en court ne peut estre desdite[64] ne desfaite par rai-

---

[31] doit] A: peut [32] Que bataille ne doit estre] B: Car; O: Que bataille en doit estre; V lacks [33] B adds: n'i a point de bataille [34] demorer V: estre demoree [35] de l'apeleor] V: dou requereoir [36] le seignor de soi] A: le seignor; B: nesun des trois [37] a ce qu'il porra] A lacks; B: a ce que il l'en puet mener [38] de la court] ABO lack [39] s'en vosist] A: se voleit; B: se voloit [40] rapel] AB: apel; V: apeau [41] font] AB: feissent [42] la ou la . . . de] A: puis que l'apeleor et; B: l'apeleor et [43] de l'apelé] V: dou deffendeor [44] s'acordent] B: s'acorderent [45] au doner des] AB: par leur (B: lor) volenté a doner les [46] et les eufrent au seignor] A: au seignor et li euffrent; B: et les offrirent au seignor [47] metent] B: mirent; C: mentent [48] il metent lor . . . cele] V: et il metent lor pooïr et lor volenté el pooïr dou seignor et la volenté [49] au recevoir des guages] O: aversaire des gages; V: as guages douner [50] V adds: et [51] joignent] V: conjoignent [52] sont une] ABV: font (V: sont) une meismes (A: meismes) [53] un meimes] V lacks [54] Quar bien otreie] O lacks [55] la volenté] A: le assent; B: l'assent [56] C adds: la [57] et sans assise] V lacks [58] et sans destresce de raison] A: et sans destrece de la traysson que l'on li met sus; B lacks [59] otroie bien et s'asent] A: se otreie bien et assent; B: otroie bien et assent [60] et] A: ou [61] A adds: puis que [62] force d'assise ne . . . ce] B: assise ne usage. Ne droit ne raison ne le fait [63] en court] A: de estre; B: d'estre [64] desdite] A: deslaissiee; B: delaissie; V: des o otroie

son, se ce n'est par la volenté de toutes les parties qui sont parsonieres de cel fait. Et a moi senble par les raisons devant dites que toutes les .iii. parties sont parsonieres en cel fait,[65] et lor volenté de la[66] bataille est conjointe[67] ensenble com chose otroiee et faite en court puis que le seignor et[68] l'apeleor et l'apelé[69] ont fait en la[70] court les choses avant[71] dites, por coi il ne me senble que la bataille puisse demorer puis que les guages en sont donés et receus si con il est avant dit que par l'asent[72] et la volenté des .iii. parties.[73] Et se aucun dit que les seignors ont desfait bataille ensi guagee et que il le pevent faire,[74] je di que se il l'ont fait, ce n'a esté par esgart ne[75] par conoissance de court aprés ce qu'il a[76] esté defendu et contrasté[77] en cort[78] par aucun des chanpions si con il doit.[79] Que ce que seignor fait sans[80] esgart de court n'est[81] pas assise[82] ne ne doit estre maintenu come assise si l'en[83] peut mostrer raison a l'encontre[84] tel que court l'esgarde ou conoisse,[85] que ce qui a esté fait autrefois ne doit lor estre fait[86] por les raisons que l'on a dit encontre, que la court ne doit faire esgart ne conoissance que des paroles que l'on[87] dit[88] quant l'on se pose sur court.

[65] devant dites que ... fait] V: avant dites que les parties sont persouniers en cel cas [66] la] OV lack [67] AB add: et otreiee (B: otroiee) [68] et] BOV lack [69] et l'apelé] O lacks [70] la] OV lack [71] avant] B: devant [72] l'asent] A: l'acort [73] que par l'asent ... parties] B lacks [74] les seignors ont ... faire] AB: le seignor peut (B: les seignors pueent) desfaire bataille ensi gagiee [75] l'ont fait ... ne] AB: le (B: l'ont) fait, se a par esgart ou [76] ce qu'il a] A: ce qu'il avra; V: qu'il l'a [77] contrasté] C: constratés [78] en cort] A lacks [79] doit] A: est devant dit; B: est dit [80] sans] OV: ne [81] n'est] O: n'i est [82] fait sans esgart ... assise] A: ne esgart de court n'est pas tenu [83] si l'en] A: se l'un; B: se l'on ne; V: se l'on [84] l'encontre] AB: l'autre [85] l'esgarde ou conoisse] A: esgarde [86] ne doit lor estre fait] C lacks [87] A adds: a [88] que des paroles que l'on dit] V: des paroles que l'on a dites

***[83]** Qui apele home de traïson qui[1] n'est aparant et il ne s'en viaut a lui aerdre, coment il le doit faire.

Se celui[2] que l'on apele de traïson, et la traïson n'est aparant, et il ne s'en viaut aerdre par[3] bataille a celui qui l'a apelé,[4] il l'en doit desmentir mot a mot[5] ce que il li a mis sus et li peut dire et metre sus moult de lait et[6] de vilainie[7] et aprés dire qu'il est prest que il s'en defende de la traïson que il li met sus, tout aussi con la cort esgardera ou conoistra qu'il defendre s'en doie, et metre[8] se en l'esgart de la cort sauf son retenaill. Que[9] la cort n'esgardera[10] ja,[11] se cuit, qu'il i ait bataille de traïson, se ele n'est aparant.

A: fol. lvii^{v} cap. 96; **B:** fol. 87^{v} cap. 96; **C:** fol. 79^{v} cap. 82; **O:** fol. 96^{r-v}; **V:** fol. lxxix^{r} cap. 95; Beugnot, pp. 157–8, cap. 96.

---

[1] Qui apele home de traïson qui] A (rubrics fol. 3^{r}): Quant l'on apelle home de traysson et elle [2] celui] V: aucun [3] par] C: por [4] l'a apelé] B: l'apele [5] mot a mot] A: mout a mout de; B: maintenant de [6] de lait et] A lacks [7] et li peut . . . vilainie] B lacks [8] metre] AB: mete [9] Que] A: Et; B lacks [10] n'esgardera] B: esgardera [11] ja] ABV lack

***[84]** Coment et de quey la traïson est aparant.

Qui viaut faire apeau de traïson aparant, il doit savoir[1] de quei la traïson est aparant. Et ce sont les choses de quei il me senble[2] orés que la traïson est aparant et de quei l'on peut faire apeau de traïson aparant de quei l'on ne se peut defendre de non aerdre se[3] de[4] bataille par esgart ou par conoissance de court.

Se le seignor a aucun[5] chastel ou forteresce qui li ait esté enblee ou traïe ou que aucuns l'aient[6] traïe[7] ou vendue a autre[8] sans son congé ou que par aucune autre maniere ait esté traïe la forteresce, la traïson est aparant dou chastel ou de la forteresce que le seignor avra perdue. Si peut l'on[9] apeler de cele traïson qui que l'on viaut et metre li sus, ce il estoit en la forterese, qu'il l'ait traïe et que par lui a esté perdue, et se il n'estoit[10] dedens que par son porchas a esté cele traïson faite, et que puis que il la porparla[11] et la porchaça qu'il la fist[12] et que se par lui ne fust ele ne fust[13] pas esté faite[14] et que puis[15] que par lui a esté faite, il l'a bien faite. Et de ce me senble il qu'il y avroit[16] bataille de la forterece qui a esté perdue, et que l'on met sus a celui que l'en a apelé[17] que par lui a esté[18] porchacee et faite cele traïson. Si ne me senble que il s'en peust[19] defendre par esgart ne par conoissance de court que il de cele traïson ne l'en covenist a[20] defendre et par bataille.

Et se le seignor a esté nafré ou asailli ou aguaité[21] de gens armees[22] par le chemin ou il est pasé ou qui[23] devoit paser,[24] ou gens armees qui ne sont amis[25] dou seignor sont[26] venus en l'ostel dou seignor soudainement ou autre part ou le seignor soit, ou d'ou[27] il se soit[28]

A: fols lvii^{v}–lviii^{v} cap. 97; **B:** fols 87^{v}–88^{v} cap. 97; **C:** fols 79^{v}–80^{v} cap. 83; **O:** fols 96^{v}–98^{r}; **V:** fols lxxix^{r}–lxxx^{r} cap. 96; Beugnot, pp. 158–60, cap. 97.

[1] doit savoir] V: la doit savoir et [2] senble] A: souvient [3] de non aerdre se] A: d'aerdre se; B: d'aherdre le [4] C adds: la [5] a aucun] ABV: ait [6] aucuns l'aient] A: aucun l'ait; V: aucunes l'aie [7] V adds: a vendre [8] vendue a autre] A: rendue [9] AB add: bien [10] et se il n'estoit] B: se il estoit [11] et que puis . . . porparla] C: que puis que il la parla [12] la porchaça qu'il la fist] AB: porchassa (B: porchaça) qu'il l'a faite [13] ne fust] AB: n'eust [14] faite] C lacks [15] que puis] B: depuis [16] avroit] AB: a tornes de [17] que l'en a apelé] A: qui est apelé; B: que l'on apele [18] faite, il l'a . . . esté] V lacks [19] peust] AV: puisse [20] l'en covenist a] A: li coveigne; B: le coviegne a [21] ou aguaité] A: en agait; B: en aguait [22] de gens armees] B: d'aucunes genz [23] qui] A: qu'il; OV: il [24] ou qui devoit paser] B lacks [25] sont amis] A: seient coneus; B: soient coneuz [26] sont] A: seient; B: soient [27] d'ou] ABV: dont [28] soit] C: sont

briement[29] parti, soit de jor ou de nuit, se il ne sont venus par son comandement ou par besoin[30] aparant qui[31] les i covenist[32] venir armés, et l'on met sus a home[33] dou seignor que les gens avant dites vindrent par son porchas la c'il[34] ont esté por le seignor murtrir ou prendre, la traïson est aparant des gens armees[35] qui la vindrent. Si ne se porra[36] mie defendre par esgart de court celui a qui l'on mete[37] sus cele traïson, se il en est apelé,[38] ains li covendra, se me senble, a defendre et a conbatre se.

Et se la feme ou la fille ou la mere ou la seur dou seignor ont esté enblees ou prizes a force et menees[39] hors de l'ostel ou[40] de la forterece dou seignor ou[40] de la ou il les avra[41] mises ou laissees en garde, ou se le fis ou le pere ou le frere do seignor fust pris et[42] osis en traïson, la traïson[43] est aparant dou fait qui a esté et est fait contre le seignor. Quar tos sont si prochains dou seignor qui[44] sont ausi[45] come sa char et lui meimes.

Et de cest cas et de plusors autres senblans a ces, me senble il que il i a bataille de traïson, se aucun en apele autre sans ce que l'on se[46] puisse defendre par esgart de cort, mais que celui qui fait le dit apel[47] ne soit de ceaus qui n'ont vois ne[48] respons en court, por ce que les choses ont esté et sont aparans de quei on li met sus la traïson, quar s'il n'i avoit bataille de traïson qui[49] s'en vodroit defendre par esgart de court. Quar la traïson ne porroit[50] estre aparant en court qu'il eust[51] fait[52] se il ne la faisoit[53] en court ou se il ne la conoissoit en court ou se il[54] n'estoit ataint ou prové[55] par esgart ou par conoissance de court. Et se il n'estoit ausi[56] ataint ou prové ou il[57] eust la traïson faite[58] ou coneue en court, il n'i covient[59]

[29] briement] B: maintenant [30] besoin] AB: essoine [31] qui] AB: que il [32] i covenist] B: coviegne [33] home] A: aucun des homes [34] c'il] ABV ou il [35] armees] CV: armés [36] porra] A: peut; B: puet [37] mete] V: metra [38] en est apelé] V: n'est apellés [39] A adds: a force [40] ou] C lacks [41] avra] A: avreit; B: avroit; V: avoit [42] et] A: ou [43] la traïson] O lacks [44] qui] ABV: qu'il [45] ausi] C lacks [46] se] BV: s'en [47] le dit apel] A: l'apel; B: l'apeau [48] vois ne] V: point de vois ne de [49] qui] A: a qui; B: on [50] ne porroit] B: ne puet; V: doit [51] eust] B: l'ait [52] Quar la traïson . . . fait] A: la traïsson que il ait faite ne peut estre aparant en court [53] V adds: ou counoisoit [54] ne la conoissoit . . . il] CV lack [55] A adds: qu'il eust la traïsson faite [56] n'estoit ausi] A: en esteit ensi; B: est aussi; V: n'estoit ensi [57] ou il] V: qu'il [58] ou prové ou . . . faite] B: come il voust la trayson faire [59] covient] V: couvendroit

point de bataille, que celui qui de l'une des dites choses est ataint qu'il[60] doit estre pendu come traïtor, se le seignor le peut avoir, et ses heir desherités a tos jors come heirs de traïtor[61] par esgart ou par conoissance de court, se le seignor viaut aprés les erremens devant dis[62] comander a sa court que ele li en face esgart ou conoissance.

---

[60] qu'il] AB: il [61] A adds: ataint ou prové [62] devant dis] A lacks

***[85]** Qui viaut faire apeau de traïson aparant,[1] coment il le doit faire.

Qui d'une des avant dites choses ou d'aucunes senblans[2] a eles de quei la traïson est aparant viaut faire apel,[3] il doit venir devant[4] le seignor en la court et demander conceill. Et quant il avra[5] conceill, se celui que il viaut apeler de la traïson n'est present en la court, il doit faire dire[6] au seignor: 'Sire, je vos fais assaveir en[7] vostre court[8] que tel', et le nome, 'est vostre traïtor con celui qui tel traïson a faite contre vos', et dire quel.[9] 'Et[10] mandés le[11] querre, et quant il sera venus en vostre court, se il viaut neer ce que je li met sus, je li proverais de mon cors contre le sien.' Et le seignor le doit mander querre, et, se il se destorne et il est son home, il le doit faire querre et semondre[12] par .iii. de ces homes, l'un en leuc de lui[13] et les .ii. come court. Et ceaus .iii. le doivent[14] querre tant que il le treussent.[15] Et quant il l'avront trové, celui qui est en leuc dou seignor li doit dire enssi: 'Tel', et le nome, 'je vos semons de par mon seignor tel que vos soiés a tel jor[16] devant lui en tel leuc', et nomer[17] le jor et le leuc, 'por aleauter vos vers tel de tel traïson[18] qu'il vos met sus', et die la traïson que celui li avra mise sus en la cort. Et puis redie ce meimes autres .ii. fois, et quant il l'avra[19] ensi semons par .iii. fois die as autres .ii. qui sont venus aveuc lui come cort: 'Je vos tray a garant coment et de quei je ai tel', et le nome, 'semons.' Et puis doivent venir devant le seignor en sa[20] court, et celui qui a la semonce faite la doit retraire au seignor en sa[20] court, et les autres .ii. qui ont esté aveuc lui a la semonce faire li doivent garantir.

Et quant ce sera fait, le seignor doit faire[21] assaveir a celui qui la traïson a mis[22] sus a l'autre le jor a quei ceaus qui ont celui sur qui il met la traïson semons, et il doit[23] estre en la court celui jor. Et

---

A: fols lviii^{v}–lix^{v} cap. 98; **B:** fols 88^{v}–89^{v} cap. 98; **C:** fols 80^{v}–82^{r} cap. 84; **O:** fols 98^{r}–100^{v}; **V:** fols lxxx^{v}–lxxxii^{r} cap. 97; Beugnot, pp. 160–2, cap. 98.

---

[1] aparant] A rubrics (fol. 3^{v}) V rubrics (fol. 6^{v}) lack [2] d'aucunes senblans] AB: de aucune semblable; V: d'aucunes semblables [3] V adds: de traïson [4] devant] B: avant [5] V adds: son [6] V adds: en la court [7] en] V: et a [8] en vostre court] A lacks [9] A adds: la traysson est [10] Et] AOV lack [11] le] C: les; O lacks [12] et semondre] B: et faire semondre; C lacks [13] leuc de lui] V: son leu [14] V adds: semondre ou [15] treussent] V: treuvent [16] que vos soiés a tel jor] V: et le nome, 'que vos seés [17] nomer] AV: nome [18] traïson] O: raison [19] l'avra] V: l'a [20] sa] ABV: la [21] B adds: ce; OV: se [22] a mis] B: met [23] V adds: dire a

se celui qui a esté ensi semons n'i[24] vient a celui jor[25] en la court ou ne contremande s'esoigne si con il doit, il me senble qu'il est ataint de la traïson que celui li met[26] sus, et que le seignor peut d'enqui[27] en avant faire de son cors et de son fié et de toutes ses autres choses ensi con d'ome ataint de traïson.[28] Mais il doit dire a sa court avant coment on li mist[29] traïson sus, et quel et qui et coment il le fist semondre de venir s'en[30] aleauter a jor nomé et il n'i est venus ne contremande[31] s'esoigne, si lor requiert[32] que il li conoissent[33] que il en peut[34] faire de lui et des soues choses. Et la court li doit conoistre, se me senble, que puis que il l'a fait ensi semondre com il a dit et il ne c'est venus aleauter[35] de la traïson que l'on li met sus ne n'a contremandé c'essoine si con il doit, qu'il peut de lui et des soes choses faire con d'ome ataint de traïson.

Et se il[36] vient a celui jor en la court, celui qui li met sus la traïson i doit estre et doit faire dire par son conceill au seignor en la presence de celui sur qui il met sus[37] la traïson: 'Sire, tel vos dit, et je por lui, que tel est vostre traïtor', et le nome, 'de tel traïson que il fist contre vos', et die quel, 'et se il le noie il est prest que il li preuve de son cors contre le sien, et que il l'en rende mort ou recreant en une hore de jor. Et veés ensi son guage.' Et lors celui qui[38] fait l'apel aille avant et s'agenoille devant le seignor et li tende son guage. Et il covient que la traïson ait esté ou soit aparant si con il est devant[39] devisé. Et celui que l'on apele enssi de traïson doit demander conceill, et quant il l'avra[40] celui qui est a son conceill doit dire, 'Sire, tel a conseill.[41] S'il est aucun qui veuille dire aucune chose contre lui, il l'ora et respondra et fera ce que il devra.' Et lors[42] l'apeleor doit dire: 'Sire, tel', et le nome,[43] 'vos fait assaveir, et je por lui, que tel', et le nome, 'est vostre traïtre de tel traïson que il a faite contre vos, et se il le noie il est prest que il li preuve de son cors contre le sien, et qu'il l'en rende mort ou recreant en une hore de jor. Et veés enssi son guage.' Et die quel la[44] traïson[45]

---

[24] n'i] ABV: ne [25] V adds: qui l'a esté ensi semons [26] celui li met] A: il li a mus [27] d'enqui] A: de iqui; V: de qui [28] traïson] V: traytour [29] mist] AB: a mis [30] venir s'en] A: sei venir [31] ne contremande] A: ni n'a contremandé [32] requiert] O: requierent [33] il li conoissent] B: li conoissent; C: lor conoisse; V: il counoissent [34] en peut] A: deit; B: doit [35] ne c'est venus aleauter] V: n'en estoit venus aloyauter ce [36] il] V: celui y [37] sus] B lacks [38] A adds: a [39] devant] AB: avant [40] l'avra] A: l'avra eu; CV: avra [41] doit dire: 'Sire, tel a conseill] C lacks [42] A adds: celui qui est au conseill de [43] et le nome] B lacks [44] quel la] A: que la; BO: quel; V: quelle [45] B adds: ce

est qu'il li met sus. Et lors celui qui fait l'apel s'agenoille devant le seignor et li tent son guage. Et adonc celui qui est au conceill do defendeor[46] doit dire se le fait a esté[47] aparant de quei il li met sus la traïson: 'Sire, la traïson il defent et noie mot a mot si con il la[48] li met sus et l'en desment tout[49] mot a mot[50] et est prest qu'il s'en defende de son cors contre le sien. Et veés ensi son guage.' Et lors celui qui se defent aille avant et s'agenoille devant le seignor et li tent son guage. Et adonc l'apeleor die: 'Et je suis prest que je li preuve de mon cors contre le sien, et que je l'en rende mort ou recreant en une hore de jor. Et veés ensi mon gage.' Et le defendeor die:[51] 'Et je suis prest que je li preuve[52] de mon cors contre le sien,[53] et que je l'en rende mort ou recreant[54] en une hore de jor. Et veés ensi mon guage.'[55]

Et lors le seignor doit recevoir les gages et[56] comander a sa cort qu'ele li conoisse coment cele bataille doit estre faite[57] et a quel jor et de quei et coment il doivent estre armés[58] el chanp. Et la cort doit conoistre que la bataille doit estre a cheval au carantime jor et que les chanpions doivent estre armés come chevaliers chanpions de[59] bataille faire doivent estre de tel querele. Et la maniere coment il le doivent estre est aprés devisé en cest livre et coment il se doivent[60] porofrir. Et quant la court avra ceste conoissance faite, le seignor doit comander as chanpions qu'il soient au carantime jor devant lui[61] apareillés de cheval[62] et d'armes,[63] si con la cort l'a coneu, aprestés de[64] faire ce que chascun a ofert a faire, et lor doit nomer le leuc ou il viaut qu'il soient devant lui a celui jor, et il i doivent[65] estre por iaus porofrir,[66] et por totes les autres choses faire qu'il covient a faire a chanpion. Et les[67] doivent faire si com est[68] devisé en cest livre que l'on le[69] doit faire la ou l'on parole de ces choses.[70] [a]

---

[a] Below, cap. 90.

---

[46] defendeor] A: l'apeleor [47] a esté] AB: est [48] la] ABV lack [49] tout] B lacks [50] si con il . . . mot] C lacks [51] die] A: deit dire; B: doit dire [52] li preuve] A: me defende; B: m'en defende. O has 'li preuve' corrected to 'me deffende' in a later hand. [53] de mon cors contre le sien] B lacks [54] recreant] B: veincu [55] Et le defendeor . . . guage] V lacks [56] A adds: deit [57] faite] C lacks [58] armés] V lacks [59] A adds: tel; B: tele [60] doivent] V: doive [61] devant lui] A lacks [62] de cheval] A: de chevaus; B: des chevaus [63] d'armes] A: d'armeures [64] de] AV: a; B: por [65] doivent] C: veut [66] porofrir] V: offrir [67] les] ABV: le [68] V adds: devant [69] l'on le] A: l'en; BV: l'on; O: l'on l'en [70] ces choses] AB: tel chose

*[86] Coment il peut avoir bataille d'atraire contre son seignor choze a son fié qui ne[1] soit.

La maniere coment il peut avoir bataille d'atraire aucune[2] chose a son fié contre son seignor est tel: que se il[3] a aucun des homes dou seignor qui[4] atraie a[5] son fié contre son seignor aucune chose qu'il ait et tiegne qui[6] ne soit de son fié, et le seignor li[7] requiert, et il dit que cele chose est de son fié et qu'il l'atrait a son fié[8] et est prest de faire en ce qu'il doit qu'ele est de son fié si con il dit, le seignor li doit[9] dire: 'Faites ent donc ce que vos devés par l'assise'. Et lors il doit jurer sur sains que ce qu'il a[10] atrait a son fié est de son fié, et le seignor ne li[11] peut plus demander.

Mais se il i a aucun des homes dou seignor qui sache qu'il ait fait[12] faus sairement de ce, il l'en doit lever con parjur et foi mentie vers son seignor et ofrir li a prover de son cors contre le sien et qu'il l'en rendra mort ou recreant[13] en une hore de jor et tendre son guage au seignor a genous. Et celui qui a fait le dit sairement et qui on a enssi apelé doit respondre a celui qui l'a[14] apelé[15] et dire: 'Tu mens,[16] et je suis prest que je m'en defende de mon cors contre le tien, et veés en si mon guage', et tendre[17] son guage au seignor.[18] Et celui des homes dou seignor qui ne fait l'apel desus dit, se il set que l'autre a[19] fait faus sairement de ce, il ment sa foi vers son seignor. Et se il i a aucun des homes dou seignor qui ne fust present au sairement faire desus dit[20] et il sache[21] que .i. autre s'en soit parjuré atraiant contre son seignor aucune chose a[22] son fié qui n'en soit, il l'en doit apeler quant il le savra en la maniere avant[23] dite. Et se celui qui avra atrait contre son seignor[24] chose a son fié qui n'en soit en est ataint ou prové par bataille ou autrement, le seignor recovera[25] ce qu'il avra atrait a son fié et peut faire de lui justise con de foi mentie.

A: fols lix^{v}–lx^{r} cap. 99; **B:** fols 89^{v}–90^{r} cap. 99; **C:** fol. 82^{r-v} cap. 85; **O:** fols 100^{v}–101^{v}; **V:** fol. lxxxii^{r-v} cap. 98; Beugnot, p. 163, cap. 99.

[1] A adds: le [2] aucune] C: d'aucune [3] A adds: y; B: i [4] qui] CO: qu'il [5] atraie a] O: atraire; V: atraire a [6] tiegne qui] B: regehist que [7] li] ABV: la [8] a son fié] B lacks [9] A adds: lor [10] qu'il a] B: que; V: que il [11] li] B: l'en; O: li en [12] V adds: faire [13] recreant] B: vaincu [14] qui on a . . . l'a] V: que hom ensi apelle doit respondre a celui qu'il y a ensi [15] l'a apelé] B: l'apele [16] 'Tu mens] A lacks [17] tendre] AB: tende [18] A adds: a genoills [19] a] AV: ait [20] sairement faire desus dit] B: dit sairement faire [21] sache] A: seit; V: set [22] a] V: contre [23] avant] B: devant [24] AB add: aucune [25] recovera] B: recovre; V: doit recouvrer

*[87] Qui viaut apeler home de choze que il ait atraite a son fié contre son seignor, coment il le doit faire.

Qui viaut apeler home de chose qu'il ait atraite contre son seignor a son fié et qu'ele ne[1] soit, il doit venir en la court devant le seignor et demander li[2] conceill, et aprés faire li dire par son conseill, 'Sire,[3] tel', et le nome, 'vos dit, et je por lui, que tel', et le nome, 'a qui vos requeistes tel chose', et die de coi, 'et il[4] vos respondi que ce estoit partie de son fié, et l'atraist a son fié contre vos qui estes son[5] seignor et a qui il doit foi et le jura menti de cel sairement come faus et desloiaus et foi mentie vers vos. Et se il le noie, il est prest qu'il le li[6] preuve de son cors contre le sien et qu'il l'en rende[7] mort ou recreant[8] en une hore de jor. Et veés ensi son guage.' Et lors celui qui fait l'apel s'agenoille devant le seignor et li tent son guage. Et[9] celui qui est enssi apelé doit demander conceill et aprés son conceill faire le desmentir[10] mot a mot et ofrir s'en a defendre de son cors contre le sien et aprés s'agenoille et tende son guage au seignor.[11] Et le seignor doit recevoir les guages et comander a la cort qu'ele li conoisse coment et a quel jor cele bataille doit estre. Et la cort doit conoistre qu'ele doit[12] estre au carantime jor et qu'il doivent estre ensi armés et apareillés et ensi se doivent porofrir[13] com il est devisé[14] aprés que chanpions d'autre querele que de murtre ou d'omecide le doivent faire.[15] [a]

A: fol. lx^{r-v} cap. 100; **B:** fol. 90^r cap. 100; **C:** fols 82^v–83^r cap. 86; **O:** fols 101^v–102^r; **V:** fols lxxxii^v–lxxxiii^r cap. 99; Beugnot, p. 164, cap. 100.

---

[a] Below, cap. 90.

---

[1] et qu'ele ne] A: por quoi elle ne le; B: por quoi ele n'en [2] li] ABV lack [3] par son conseill, 'Sire] C lacks [4] C adds: si [5] son] AB lack [6] li] AB lack [7] rende] BV: rendra [8] recreant] B: veincu [9] A adds: lors [10] son conceill faire le desmentir] A: faire dire par son conseill et desmentir le [11] et tende son guage au seignor] B: devant le seignor et li tende son gage [12] qu'ele doit] V lacks [13] porofrir] AB: paroffrir (B: poroffrir) por combatre; V: combatre et pouroffrir [14] il est devisé] V: est devisé ci [15] d'autre querele . . . faire] AB: deivent (B: doivent) faire que l'on apelle de murtre ou d'omicide

***[88]** Coment toutes manieres de chanpions doivent estre armés quant il se vienent[1] porofrir a cort por[2] la bataille.[3]

C'est la maniere coment toutes manieres de[4] chanpions chevaliers et autres se doivent conbatre, et coment il se doivent avant[5] porofrir au seignor,[6] et coment et de ques armeures[7] il doivent venir armés[8] a court porofrir eaus de bataille, et coment et de ques armeures il doivent[9] estre armés el chanp, et, se la bataille est[10] a cheval, coment et de quei les chevaus doivent estre covers.

A: fol. lx^v cap. 101; **B:** fol. 90^r cap. 101; **C:** fol. 83^r cap. 87; **O:** fol. 102^r–v; **V:** fol. lxxxiii^r cap. 100; Beugnot, p. 165, cap. 101.

---

[1] vienent] AB (fol. 20^r) V: vont [2] por] A: au jor de; V: a [3] BOV add: faire. A rubrics (fol. 3v) reads: 'a bataille faire quant il se vont poroffrir' for 'quant il se . . . bataille' [4] V adds: gens [5] avant] A: avant venir; B: armer quant il se doivent venir [6] AV adds: et ou [7] armeures] O: armes [8] venir armés] ABV: estre armés por (V: et) venir [9] C adds: venir [10] V adds: el champ

***[89]** Coment chevaliers doivent estre armés qui se conbatent por murtre, et coment por autre querele, et coment il se doivent venir[1] porofrir, et ou et a quel hore.

Les chevaliers qui se conbatent por murtre ou por homecide se doivent conbatre a pié et sans coife et estre[2] roignés a la reonde, et[3] vestus de cotes vermeilles[4] ou de doubles ou de chemises de sendel vermeill, cortes jusques au genoill[5] et les manches copees desus[6] le coude,[7] et avoir chauces vermeilles de drap ou de sendel a estrier[8] sans plus,[9] et une targe, que l'on apele harace, qui soit plus grant de lui demi pié ou plaine paume,[10] en laquel ait .ii. pertuis de comunal grant[11] en tel endroit qu'il puisse veir son aversaire par ceaus pertuis, et doit avoir une lance et .ii. espees, l'une sainte qui ait le feure trenché jusques as renges, et l'autre atachee a sa harace,[12] si qu'il la puisse avoir quant il en avra mestier.[13] Et il n'a[14] que .iii. jors de respit de tel bataille puis que les guages sont donés et receus.

Et quant les chanpions qui ont guagé tel bataille se veulent porofrir au jor de la bataille, il doivent venir a pié entre prime et tierce en[15] l'ostel dou seignor, et l'apeleor avant, ensi vestus et chaucés[16] com il est desus devisé, et faire porter devant yaus[17] plusors haraces et pluisors lances et espees si qu'il puisse prendre a l'entree dou chanp lesqués[18] qu'il vodra.[a] Car se chascun ne presentoit qu'une[19] et ele estoit brisee ou perdue ou enpiree en aucune maniere ains qu'il fust el chanp, il n'en poroit nule autre avoir puis fors cele qu'il avroit presentee au seignor et a la cort. Et l'apeleor se doit avant[20] porofrir et dire ce[21] quant il sera venus enssi a[22] la court[23] dou seignor, ou

A: fols lx[v]–lxii[r] cap. 102; **B:** fols 90[r]–91[v] cap. 102; **C:** fols 83[r]–84[v] cap. 88; **O:** fols 102[v]–104[r]; **V:** fols lxxxiii[r]–lxxxv[r] cap. 101; Beugnot, pp. 165–9, cap. 102.

[a] O has a substantial *lacuna* beginning here.

[1] venir] B (fol. 20[r]) lacks [2] coife et estre] A: coifes les testes [3] V adds: estre [4] vermeilles] B lacks [5] genoill] C: genous [6] desus V: jusques desous [7] le coude] A: les coudes [8] estrier] A: estriers; B: estrivieres [9] plus] A: soliers [10] que l'on apele . . . paume] A: plus grant de lui de mi pié ou plain paume que l'on apelle harace [11] de comunal grant] B: granz [12] sa harace] ABV: son escu; O: son arson [13] il en avra mestier] V: mestier li sera [14] n'a] ABV: n'i a [15] en] AB: devant [16] B adds: ensi [17] yaus] A: sei; B: lui; V: soi [18] lesqués] AV: lequel; B: laquele [19] B adds: espee [20] avant] B lacks [21] ce] AB lack [22] a] BV: en [23] enssi a la court] A: en l'ostel

de celui qui sera en son leuc, et de la cort:[24] 'Sire, je present moi et mes armeures[25] a vos et a la cort, et veés les ci',[26] et mostrer les, 'et me poreufre a fornir ce que je ai ofert a faire et a fornir de la bataille que je ai guagee contre tel', et le nome. Et lors le seignor doit faire totes les armeures veir a sa cort[27] s'eles sont tels con eles doivent estre, et puis livrer les[28] a ses homes et comander au chanpion qu'il aille[29] el chanp et ceaus qui portent les armeures o luy. Et le defendeor doit aprés venir porofrir soi, si con il est desus dit[30] de l'apeleor, et le seignor doit enssi faire et dire a lui com[31] a l'apeleor. Et se l'une des lances est plus longe que[32] l'autre, le seignor les doit roigner d'un grant.[33] Et doit les .ii. chanpions bien faire garder, alant[34] el chanp, que aucun d'eaus ne s'enfuie ou destorne ne que l'on ne lor face mal ne ennui de cors ne die ne face honte ne vilainie.[35] Car le seignor les doit de tot ce faire garder, qu'il sont en sa garde.

Et quant il seront andeus el chanp, le seignor i doit[36] metre de ses homes por le chanp garder, et l'un de ceaus doit dire devant les autres a chascun des chanpions: 'Choisisés de vos armeures[37] lesqués[38] que vos vodrés avoir a la bataille faire'. Et il le doivent faire, et il[39] doivent celes[40] retenir el chanp et les autres oster[41] del chanp. Et aprés doivent faire jurer a chascun des chanpions qu'il ne porte[42] brief ne charei[43] ne sorcerie, ne qu'il por cele bataille ne l'a fait ne[44] fait faire, ne autre por lui qu'il sache, ne n'a doné ne promis a autre[45] persone quelqu'ele soit aucune maniere de chose[46] por faire brief ou esperiment[47] ou charei[48] ne sorcerie que a cele bataille li puisse aider, ne a son aversaire nuire, ne qu'il n'a autres armeures sur[49] soi que celes que la cort a veues. Et puis doivent estre[50] les chanpions ensenble en mi le[51] chanp a[52] avoir la une evangile. Et le

[24] et de la cort] V lacks [25] armeures] BV: armes [26] les ci] V: en ci mes armes [27] totes les armeures . . . cort] B: venir toutes les armeures en sa cort savoir [28] les] AV: les armeures; B lacks [29] au chanpion qu'il aille] V: as champions que il aillent [30] dit] A: devisié [31] il est desus . . . com] B lacks [32] longe que] A: grant de; B: granz de [33] roigner d'un grant] AB: faire reoignier a un (B: reoingner d'un) point [34] alant] AB: a l'aler [35] ennui de cors . . . vilainie] V: vilainie dou cors ne die ne face honte ne ennuy [36] A adds: faire [37] armeures] AB: armes [38] lesqués] B: celes [39] il] ABV lack [40] doivent celes] B: les doivent [41] oster] C: ostel [42] port] V: portent [43] charei] B: charme [44] la fait ne] A: les a [45] autre] ABV: aucune [46] aucune maniere de chose] B: nule chose en nulle maniere; V: en aucune maniere de chose [47] esperiment] ABV: espirement [48] charei] B: charme [49] sur] B: sus [50] estre] AB: metre; V mener [51] en mi le] AB: ou [52] a] AV: et

defendeor doit premier jurer[53] sur sains a genous, la main destre sur l'evangile, et dire ensi[54] li ait Des et les saintes evangiles qu'il n'a celui[55] murtri, et le nome. Et l'apeleor doit dire qu'il ment et qu'il l'en lieve[56] come parjur et prendre le par le poing et lever et jurer maintenant qu'ensi li ait Dex et les saintes evangiles[57] qu'il a cel[58] murtri, et le nome. Et aprés ce les guardes doivent chascun des chanpions mener[59] a une part dou chanp, et le ban doit estre crié tel as[60] .iiii. cantons dou chanp, qu'il n'i ait nul si hardi, de quelque lenguage[61] qu'il soit, qui oze faire ne dire chose par quei l'un des chanpions, ne les .ii., soient[62] en aucune chose aidés ne aveés, ne estre ne le puissent,[63] et se aucun le faisoit que son cors et son avoir seroit encheu en la merci dou seignor.[b] Et se le murtré est en presence, il doit estre a une part dou chanp tout descovert. Et se il i a home ou feme qui ait fait l'apel par chanpion, il doit estre delés le cors en tel maniere que il ne nuise nen[64] aide a nule des .ii. parties,[65] ne en dit ne en fait ne en contenance que[66] de Des prier en tel maniere que les chanpions ne le puissent oïr.

Et les armeures dou vencu et celes qui cheent au venqueor, brisees ou entieres, doivent estre dou seignor, et, s'il i a conestable, do conestable. Et se pais[67] est faite puis qu'il sont laissés aler ensenble et aucunes des armeures dou quelque ce soit est brisee ou chet el chanp, ele est[68] dou seignor ou do conestable se il i est.

Et aprés les gardes dou chanp doivent partir le souleill si qu'il ne soit contre la chiere[69] de l'un plus que de l'autre. Puis doit dire l'une des guardes au seignor: 'Sire, que comandés vos? Nos avons fait quanque nos devons faire.' Et le seignor lor doit lors dire: 'Laissés les aler ensenble.' Et il les doivent laisser aler ensenble[70] et traire soi[71] a une part dou chanp et laisser les covenir. Et se le chanpion porte arme reposte[72] autre que cele que la cort a veue, et il s'en

---

[b] End of *lacuna* in O.

---

[53] doit premier jurer] B: premier jure [54] dire ensi] AV: dire que ensi; B: die si [55] celui] ABV: tel [56] qu'il l'en lieve] V: l'en doit lever et lieve [57] maintenant qu'ensi li . . . evangiles] B lacks [58] cel] ABV: tel [59] mener] B: metre [60] tel as] A: en; B: es; V: et tel a [61] lenguage] B: lengue [62] l'un des chanpions . . . soient] A: nul des .ii. champions seit; B: l'un des champions foloit; V: l'un ne le .ii. champions soient [63] aidés ne aveés . . . puissent] A: ne aidiés ne aveés ne estre ne le puisse; B: ne ne soit aidiez ne auciez [64] nen] ABV: ne [65] parties] B: persones [66] que] V: fors [67] ABV adds: en [68] est] A: deit estre [69] chiere] C: chere [70] Et il les . . . ensenble] V lacks [71] soi] A: se arieres; B: eaus arriere [72] arme reposte] A: resposte armeure

veut aider por son aversaire gregier, et les gardes dou chanp s'aparçoivent, eles[73] le doivent maintenant prendre, et le seignor en doit faire justise[74] com de murtrier.[75] Et se l'un prent l'autre et il s'entr'abatent,[76] les guardes do chanp se doivent traire cele part et estre au plus pres qu'il poront d'eaus si que, se l'un[77] dit le mot dou recreant, qu'il le puissent oïr. Et se il le dit et il l'oïent, il doivent maintenant dire a l'autre: 'Asés en[78] avés fait', et maintenant celui prendre et livrer au comandement dou seignor. Et le seignor le doit maintenant de la[79] faire trainer jusques as forches et pendre[80] par la goule, et celui ausi[81] qui avra esté ocis, tot n'ait il dit le mot recreant.

Et qui viaut faire apeau de murtre et il n'est chevalier,[82] il doit faire et dire[83] si con est devant[84] dit toutes les[85] choses fors tant que les chanpions doivent estre armés autrement que les chevaliers. Et il doivent estre ensi armés et avoir tels armeures[86] com il est devant[87] devisé que[88] chanpions autres que chevaliers doivent avoir. Car sergens a pié se conbatent de toutes quereles d'unes armeures.[c]

[c] O has drawings (perhaps of the fifteenth or sixteenth century) in the bottoms of fol. 103v and fol. 104r of men atired as described in this chapter.

[73] s'aparçoivent, eles] B: se parçoivent, il; V: s'en aparsoivent, si [74] justise] ABV lack [75] murtrier] O: murtre [76] s'entr'abatent] A: s'entreluitent et abatent; B: s'entreluitent [77] l'un] A: aucun d'iaus [78] Asés en] V: Laissés, assés [79] de la] B lacks [80] OV adds: le [81] ausi] ABV lack [82] chevalier] C: chevaliers [83] et dire] BO dire; V lacks [84] devant] BV: avant [85] toutes les] A: de totes; B: toutes; V: de toutes [86] armeures] B: armes [87] devant] A: aprés [88] ensi armés et . . . que] V: autrement armés et ensi et de telz armeures com est devisé en cestui livre ci aprés que les

***[90]** Quans jors l'on a de respit a la[1] bataille faire[2] aprés ce que les guages sont donés et receus.

De toutes manieres de bataille[3] que de murtre et d'omecide a l'on .xl. jors de respit puis que les guages sont donés, et au[4] caranteime jor, entre prime et tierce, se doivent les chanpions venir porofrir en l'ostel dou seignor, et l'apeleor avant et le defendeor aprés. Et se il sont chevaliers, il doivent venir a cheval en l'ostel dou seignor por iaus porofrir. Et doivent avoir les chauces de fer chaucees et lor espalieres vestues. Et doivent faire amener lor[5] chevaus covers de fer et de toutes autres[6] choses apareillés si com por entrer el chanp, et[7] faire aporter lor autres armeures de coi il doivent estre armés el chanp. Et doivent estre armés el champ[8] de haubers[9] et de chauces[10] et de heiaumes a visiere, et que[11] chascun ait[12] cote a armer et guanbeison se il viaut. Et se il ne viaut ganbeison, il peut metre devant son pis et devant[13] son ventre[14] .i. contrecuer[15] de tele ou de coton[16] ou de boure de see, tel et si fort con il vodra. Et doit avoir .i. escu et une lance et .ii. espees, et que les lances soient d'un lonc et que les fers des lances et des espees soient tes come fers de lances et d'espees de[17] chevaliers qui se conbatent en chanp guagé de bataille doivent estre. Et il doivent estre[18] de tel façon con il vodront et de tel grant, mais qu'il ne soient pas[19] tes qu'il puissent paser par[20] les mailles dou hauberc[21] sans tailler ou rompre maille. Et doit avoir en l'orle[22] dou heiaume tot entor orlés[23] de broches[24] de fer tel con il vodra[25] ou razors, et en l'escu doit avoir .ii. broches,[26] l'une en mi l'escu et l'autre au pié desout, et doivent estre de tel groisse[27] con il vodront et de tel longor jusques a .i. pié[28] mais neent plus. Et

---

A: fols lxii^{r}–lxiv^{r} cap. 103; **B:** fols 91^{v}–93^{v} cap. 103; **C:** fols 84^{v}–87^{r} cap. 89; **O:** fols 104^{r}–105^{v}; **V:** fols lxxxv^{r}–lxxxviii^{r} caps 102–3; Beugnot, pp. 170–4, cap. 103.

---

[1] a de respit a la] A: a de; O: a la; V: a a la [2] l'on a de . . . faire] B (fol. 20^{r}): a la bataille faire a l'on [3] bataille] A: carelles autre [4] au] C: a [5] lor] BOV: les [6] autres] A lacks [7] A adds: deivent [8] Et doivent estre armés el champ] C lacks [9] haubers] AB: hauberc [10] A adds: de fer [11] heiaumes a visieres, et que] AB: heaume a visiere, et [12] ait] A: deit aveir [13] son pis et devant] OV lacks [14] A repeats: et devant son pis [15] contrecuer] V: contrecuree [16] tele ou de coton] AB: teille (B: toile) et de coton ou de laine [17] de] OV: des [18] Et il doivent estre] V lacks [19] pas] B: mie [20] par] B: par mi [21] dou hauberc] A: des haubers [22] l'orle] O: l'ourle; V: l'oreille [23] orlés] A: orlé; O: ourlés [24] de broches] ABV lack [25] tel con il vodra] A: trenchant [26] AV adds: de fer [27] groisse] A: groissece; B: grossece [28] pié] A: paume

entor l'escu, tant con il vodra, si ait[29] broches de fer[30] agües ou[31] razors.[a] Et le cheval doit estre covers de covertures de fer et avoir une testiere de fer,[32] et en mi la testiere une broche[33] tel con cele de l'escu. Et peut metre chascun entor ses covertures de fer[34] chenevé[35] si lonc[36] con il vodra por les jarés[37] et les chanpes[38] de son cheval covrir et garder. Et chascun doit avoir l'une de ses .ii. espees atachee a l'arçon devant la sele,[39] et l'autre doit avoir sainte et le feurre taillé jusques as renges. Et peut avoir, se il viaut, lié a sa sele[40] .i. ou .ii. foriaus plains de ce qu'il vodra,[41] mais que de chose de quei[42] il[43] puisse son aversaire[44] gregier. Et peut covrir son cheval d'autres covertures[45] sur celes de fer tel con il vodra.[46]

Et ains que la carantaine[47] soit, le seignor doit avoir fait faire le chanp hors de la vile et pres.[48] Et doit estre le chanp[49] de .xl. canes de careure et bien yguale[50] et clos de foce et de palus[51] qui soit entor lacé de cordes si que par mi les pels ait cordes trelees, si[52] que se aucun des chevaus est tirans qu'il ne surporte son seignor hors do chanp. Car le chanpion est vencu qui ist[53] hors dou chanp ou qui en est geté[54] par quelque maniere que ce soit, tant que la bataille soit fornie ou que pais en soit faite.[b]

Et au carantime jor les chanpions se doivent venir porofrir en l'ostel dou seignor, entre prime et tierce, l'apeleor avant et le defendeor aprés, et doit chascun d'eaus pluisors chevaus avoir covers si con est devant[55] devisé, et faire porter[56] des armeures devant[57] dites

[a] O has a substantial *lacuna* beginning here.
[b] V begins a new chapter here with the rubric: Coument au jour de la bataille se doivent venir pouroffrir les champions.

[29] si ait] AB: d'autres [30] con il vodra . . . fer] V: de broches de fer com il vodront [31] ou] B: et [32] de fer] B lacks [33] V adds: de fer [34] entor ses covertures de fer] V: en ces couvertures de fer d'entour [35] de fer chenevé] A: chaeenes de fer; B: de fer chainvré [36] si lonc] A: tels [37] jarés] B: garrez; V: jarrés [38] chanpes] ABV: jambes [39] devant la sele] AB: devant de la scelle (B: sele); V: de sa celle devant [40] lié a sa sele] A: lié a sa scelle; B lacks; V: bien [41] vodra] V: vodront [42] de quei] B: dont [43] A adds: ne [44] de quei il puisse son aversaire] V: que il puisse nuire son aversaire ne [45] son cheval d'autres covertures] C lacks [46] vodra] V: vodront [47] la carantaine] A: le quarantisme jor [48] et pres] C: et aprés [49] hors de la . . . chanp] V lacks [50] et bien yguale] A: lacks; B: bien ygueles [51] palus] A: paleys; B: paliz [52] entor lacé de . . . si] A: si entrelassié de cordes treilliees; B: entrelacié de cordes si que par mi les paus ait cordes entrelacieez, si; V: entour passé et lassé de cordes si que par mi les pies ait cordes treiletés, si [53] ist] AB: est [54] ou qui en est geté] C lacks [55] devant] AB: avant [56] porter] V: aporter [57] devant] AV: avant

de chascune plusors, por ce que, se il n'i portoit qu'une et il n'i faisoit mener que .i. cheval et celui cheval fust mort ou essoignés ou aucune des armeures[58] maumise[59] ou enpiree,[60] il n'i porroit autre recovrer[61] puis qu'il l'avroit presenté[62] a court. Et quant l'apeleor vient devant le seignor, il doit dire ou faire dire:[63] 'Sire, je sui venus au jor que vos et la cort m'avés doné, garni et apareillé de ce que mestier m'est a[64] [c] ma bataille fornir, et me poreufre de faire de ma bataille en fait ce que je[65] ai ofert de[66] faire en dit. Et vos pri et requier que vos comandés que je aille el chanp por ma bataille faire.' Et le seignor li doit dire: 'Soufrés vos ent tant que je le vos comande.' Et adonc il se doit tenir[67] a une part en l'ostel dou seignor. Et quant le defendeor vient devant le seignor, il[68] doit ensi faire dire[69] com il est devisé[70] desus de l'apeleor. Et quant il ensi se sont porofers, le seignor doit comander avant a l'apeleor qu'il voise el chanp et aprés[71] au defendeor, et doit a chascun bailler de ses homes qui les aconpaignent[72] jusques[73] el chanp et qu'il[74] les gardent que nul d'eaus ne s'en destorne,[75] ne que l'on ne lor dit ne face mal ou outrage ne vilainie. Et quant il vendront pres dou chanp, chascun doit avoir tentes tendues[76] ou loges faites hors dou chanp la ou il s'armeront.[77] Et le seignor doit la venir[d] et les[78] homes et establir de ses plus prodes homes au chanp garder, et doit avoir asés[79] de ces gens armees[80] entor le chanp por[81] garder que tort ne force ne outrage ne soit faite a sa seignorie ne a aucun des chanpions.

Et quant il sont la venus, le seignor doit faire venir les chanpions devant lui et dire a chascun: 'Lequel est le cheval sur quei vos vos volés[82] conbatre, et ou sont vos armeures de[83] quei vos vos volés[84]

---

[c] End of *lacuna* in O.
[d] O has a substantial *lacuna* beginning here.

---

[58] V adds: fust [59] maumise] B: mauvaise [60] maumise ou enpiree] A: maumises ou empiriees [61] autre recovrer] V: avoir ne recovrer autre [62] l'avroit presenté] AB: les avreit (B: avroit) presentees [63] V adds: au seignor [64] O adds: por faire [65] AB add: en [66] de] ABV: a [67] tenir] AV: traire; B: trayre [68] quant le defendeor . . . il] A: aprés le defendeor deit venir devant le seignor et; B: adonc le deffendeor doit venir avant devant le seignor et [69] dire] AB: et dire; V lacks [70] est devisé] C: devise [71] aprés] A: puis [72] aconpaignent] O: aconpaigne [73] jusques] A lacks [74] qu'il] ABV: qui [75] s'en destorne] AB: se destorne et (B: ne) ne s'en aille [76] tentes tendues] B: contretendues [77] s'armeront] BV: s'arment [78] et les] ABV: o ses (A: ces) [79] avoir asés] A: aussi aveir assés; B: enssi avoir [80] gens armees] V: homes armés [81] entor le chanp por] A: au champ [82] volés] B: devez [83] de] C: sur [84] volés] A: devés

conbatre?' Et il les doivent mostrer, et le seignor les doit faire[85] veir a sa cort s'eles sont tes com eles doivent estre a tel fait faire. Et lor la cort doit les lances mezurer et, se l'une est plus grante de l'autre, roigner la si qu'eles soient igaus.[86] Et se nule[87] des espees ou le fer de la lance[88] est tel qu'il puisse passer[89] la maille del hauberc[90] sans ronpre ou tailler[91] maille, l'on les[92] doit faire changer, et qu'il lors[93] aient tes com est devant dit qu'eles doivent estre. Et quant ce sera fait, le seignor doit dire as chanpions qu'il se voisent armer de toutes lor armeures[94] fors que dou heiaume et de l'escu et de la lance.[95] Et le seignor doit comander a ses homes qu'il les mainent[96] el chanp, et l'on meine[97] devant eaus lor chevaus et porte[98] lor escus et lor lances et lor heiaumes, et entrent a pié el chanp et mener les chascun a une part del chanp.[99] Et quant ce sera fait, ceaus homes qui[100] le seignor a establis[101] a garder le chanp[102] doivent[103] porter une evangile et faire jurer a chascun des chanpions por soi qu'il ne porte sur lui ne sur son cheval[104] armeures aucunes par quei il puisse son enemi gregier[105] autres que celes que la cort a veues, ne qu'il ne porte sur soi ne sur son cheval qu'il sache[106] brief ne chartre[107] ne sorcerie ne autre que[108] lui qu'il sache.[109]

Et aprés ce sairement il doivent faire venir en mi le chanp les .ii. chanpions, et avoir une evangile que .i. des gardes dou chanp tieigne.[110] Et doit dire au defendeor: 'Venés avant.[111] Jurés ce que vos devés.' Et il se doit agenoiller et metre la main sur l'evangile et dire enssi: 'M'ait Des et ses saintes evangiles[112] que je n'ai pas[113] faite la traïson que tel me met sus', et le nome. Et l'apeleor le doit maintenant

---

[85] ABV add: prendre et faire [86] qu'eles soient igaus] A: que l'une seit igual de l'autre; B: que l'une soit ygal a l'autre; V: que elles soient d'un grant [87] nule] V: l'une [88] le fer de la lance] AV: le fer des lances; B: des fers des lances [89] AV add: par; B: par mi [90] la maille del hauberc] B: les mailles des haubers [91] tailler] A: trenchier; B: trencher [92] les] AB: la [93] lors] ABV: les [94] armeures] V: armes [95] dou heiaume et . . . lance] B: de lors heaumes et de lor escuz et de lor lances [96] mainent] V: metent [97] l'on meine] A: que il meinent; B: qu'il meignent [98] porte] AB: portent [99] del chanp] V: par soi [100] ceaus homes qui] AB: l'un de ceaus a qui; V: ceaus des homes que [101] a establis] A: avra comandé; B: a comandé [102] A adds: et establi [103] doivent] A: deit; B: doit [104] porte sur lui . . . cheval] V: portent sur eaus ne sur lor chevaus [105] gregier] A: grever [106] armeures aucunes par . . . sache] B lacks; V: armeures par quoi il puissent l'un l'autre gregier autres que celles que la cort a veus, ne qu'il ne portent que il sachent sur eaus ne sur lor chevaus [107] chartre] A: charai; B: caraut [108] que] AB: por [109] que lui qu'il sache] V: pour eaus que il sachent [110] tieigne] V: doit tenir [111] venés avant] B: premierement [112] ses saintes evangiles] B: ceste sainte evangile [113] pas] AB: mie

prendre par le poing et dire: 'Tu t'es esparjuré,[114] et je t'en lief come parjur[115] et jure[116] qu'enssi m'ait Des et ces saintes evangiles que tu as la traïson faite que je t'ai mise[117] sus.' Et adonc les gardes doivent mener chascun des chanpions a une part dou chanp et comander que le ban soit crié en .iiii. parties do chanp,[118] si con il est avant[119] dit que l'on doit ban[120] crier en chanp. Et doivent[121] chascun des chanpions metre[122] sur son cheval et adonc lacer son heiaume et prendre son escu et sa lance, et les gardes[123] doivent tenir chascun des chanpions par le frain do cheval et les autres lor doivent le soulaill partir. Et quant le soulaill sera parti et le ban crié, il doivent dire au seignor qui doit estre dehors le[124] chanp a cheval: 'Sire, nos avons fait tot[125] quanque nos devons. Que comandés vos?' Et le seignor lor doit dire: 'Laissés les aler ensenble'. Et lors ceaus qui les tienent les doivent laisser aler,[126] et[127] l'un doit venir[128] contre l'autre et faire le[129] meaus qu'il savra.[130] Et se aucun des chanpions porte[131] armeure reposte et il la trait hors por son aversaire gregier, il en doit estre fait[132] si con il est dit la ou il parle dou murtre et de l'omecide, qu'on en doit faire. Et celui des .ii.[133] qui[134] sera mort ou recreant el chanp, le seignor le doit faire trainer et pendre.

Et le cheval et les armeures dou vencu[135] doivent estre dou conestable et[136] celes dou venqueor qui sont brisees ou qui cheent[137] el chanp. Et se pais est faite de la bataille puis que les chanpions sont[138] laissés aler ensenble, totes les lances[139] qui sont cheues el chanp, brisees et entieres, doivent estre do conestable. Et s'il n'i a conestable, eles doivent estre dou seignor.

Et se celui qui est apelé de[140] traïson est veincu, il est ataint de la traïson, car l'on li a prové si con l'on doit. Si doivent estre ses heirs desherités com heirs de traïtor ataint et prové de traïson. Et se le seignor viaut avoir le fié de celui qui est ataint et prové de la traïson,[141] si con il est avant[142] dit, con[143] il avra esté outré[144] et la

[114] t'es esparjuré] A: es parjur; B: t'esparjures; V: es esparjuré [115] parjur] V: esparjurés [116] jure] C: jur [117] t'ai mise] V: te met [118] do chanp] B lacks [119] avant] A: devant [120] ban] AB: faire [121] AB add: faire [122] metre] ABV: monter [123] gardes] C lacks [124] dehors le] A: fors dou; BV: hors dou [125] tot] BV lack [126] A adds: ensemble [127] lors ceaus qui . . . et] B lacks [128] venir] A: moveir; B: manoir; V: movoir [129] le] AB: dou [130] savra] V: savront [131] A adds: aucune [132] A adds: de lui [133] des .ii.] V lacks [134] celui des .ii. qui] B: se l'un des deus [135] dou vencu] A lacks [136] A adds: aussi [137] qui cheent] B: cheues [138] sont] AB: seront; V: s'en sont [139] lances] ABV: armeures [140] AB adds: la [141] B adds: et prové [142] avant] V: devant [143] con] AB: quant [144] outré] V: otreé

justise[145] en sera faite, il doit faire assenbler[146] sa court et[147] dire coment tel, et le nome, fu apelé de traïson et qu'il en[148] a esté ataint con celui a qui l'on l'a provê par bataille et qui en a esté veincu.[149] Si requiert a sa cort qu'ele li conoisse se ses heirs[150] sont desherités del fié qui fu[151] de celui qui a esté ataint de la traïson par ce que l'on li a provê en chanp par bataille. Et la cort doit conoistre, ce m'est avis, que ses heirs sont desherités[e] del fié qu'il tenoit[152] et de tot quanque de par lui lor est escheu, si con heirs de traïtor[153] ataint et provê de traïson. Et lors le seignor peut faire[154] saisir son fié et avoir le et[155] tenir et faire ent totes ses volentés[156] con del sien, puis qu'il ensi l'a eu par esgart ou par conoissance de cort.

[e] End of *lacuna* in O.

[145] justise] A: bataille [146] C adds: en [147] V adds: doit [148] qu'il en] AB: coment il [149] V adds: par bataille [150] heirs] B lacks [151] qui fu] V lacks [152] V adds: de lui [153] V adds: aparant et [154] peut faire] B: doit faire et puet [155] V adds: faire [156] totes ses volentés] A: tote sa volenté; B: tot a sa volunté

***[91]** Coment l'on doit apeler home de rap.[1]

Qui viaut apeler home de rap,[2] ou de briseure de chemin, ou de force quelqu'ele soit, ou[3] d'un marc d'argent ou de plus, ou d'aucune[4] chose de quei l'on pert vie ou menbre qui en[5] est ataint ou prové, il doit faire dire au seignor en la presence de celui qu'il viaut apeler: 'Sire, je me clain[6] a vos de tel', et le nome, 'qui tel chose a faite', et die quel, 'et se il le noie je suis prest que je li preuve tout[7] ensi con la cort esgardera ou conoistra que je prover li doie, et que je l'en rende ou face rendre[8] mort ou recreant en une hore de jor. Et veés ensi mon guage.' Et l'autre doit demander conceill et faire dire au seignor: 'Sire, je noie et defent mot a mot se qu'il me[9] met sus', et l'en desment mot a mot, 'et suis prest que je m'en defende tout ensi con la court esgardera[10] que je defendre m'en doie. Et veés ensi mon guage.' Et s'agenoille devant le[11] seignor et li tent son guage. Et la court doit esgarder[12] que celui qui l'eufre a prover[13] le[14] doit prover par .ii. loiaus garans de la loy de Rome, et que celui contre qui l'on viaut[15] prover aucune des choses desus[16] dites par guarans[17] peut torner ou rebuter lequel qu'il viaut[18] des garans. Et qui viaut torner[19] ou rebuter ou geter garant de garantie, si face ensi con[20] est devant[21] devisé en cest livre qu'on le[22] doit faire contre garant que on[23] viaut lever de chose en quei il y[24] a tornes de bataille ou rebuter et[25] geter[26] de garantie.[a] Et se[27] la querele[28] est de chose que l'on[29] a mort deservie qui en est ataint ou prové, et le garant

A: fol. lxiv^{r-v} 104; **B:** fol. 93^{v} cap. 104; **C:** fol. 87^{r-v} cap. 90; **O:** fols 105^{v}–106^{v}; **V:** fol. lxxxviii^{r-v} cap. 104; Beugnot, pp. 174–5, cap. 104.

[a] Above cap. 61.

[1] de rap] B (fol. 20^{v}): rapine ou de brisure de chemin; C: rapt; V: d'arap [2] de rap] B: de rapine; C: de rapt; V: d'arap [3] quelqu'ele soit ou] A: quelqu'elle seit ou de carelle; C: que querele soit ou ('ou' crossed out) [4] d'aucune V: d'autre [5] en] AB lack [6] clain] V: plains [7] tout] A lacks [8] l'en rende ou face rendre] A: le rendrai; B: l'en rendrai ou ferai rendre; V: le rende [9] qu'il me] A: que tel me; B: que tel [10] A adds: ou conoistra [11] le] B: son [12] V adds: ou counoistre [13] qui l'eufre a prover] A lacks [14] le] AB: li [15] viaut] V: doit [16] desus] V lacks [17] par guarans] A lacks [18] viaut] A: vodra; B: voudra [19] torner] V: lever [20] AB add: il [21] devant] B: avant [22] qu'on le] ABV: que l'on [23] le doit faire contre garant que on] C lacks [24] en quei il y] B: ou il [25] rebuter et] A: lacks [26] geter] B: torner [27] se] A lacks [28] la querele] AV: la bataille; B: bataille [29] que l'on] AB: de quei (B: quoi) l'on; V: c'om

est veincu, il et celui por qui il fait la bataille seront[30] pendus. Et se le garant est tel qu'il puisse[31] metre chanpion por soy, si con il est devant dit,[b] et il li[32] met,[33] et son chanpion est veincu, il seront[34] tos .iii. pendus. Et se feme fait l'apel et son garant et[35] son chanpion est veincu, ele sera arce, et le garant, se il se conbat,[36] pendu. Et se il met chanpion por soi et il est veincu, il seront andeus[37] pendus et la feme arce. Et se la bataille est por querele et tel[38] que l'on ne doit[39] mort recevoir qui en sera[40] ataint,[41] celui ou cele por qui il se conbat de qui le chanpion est veincu pert la querele et vois et respons en court, et le chanpion doit estre pendu.

[b] Below cap. 93.

[30] seront] A: deivent estre; B: sont [31] puisse] V: puissent [32] li] A: le; B: i; O: y [33] V adds: sus si come est devant dit [34] seront] B: sont [35] et] AB: ou [36] il se conbat] A: il se conbate sera; V: combat et est vencu sera [37] andeus] V: tous .ii. [38] querele et tel] A: tel carelle; B: querele tele; V: la quarele est tel [39] doit] C: doute [40] sera] B: est [41] qui en sera ataint] A lacks

***[92]** Coment qui apele feme des choses[1] en quei il i a bataille et ele a baron, son baron la peut defendre, et coment se il ne l'en viaut defendre, ele se peut defendre par .i. autre.[2]

Se l'on apele d'aucune chose feme qui avra baron et il la veaut defendre, il la peut defendre de son cors. Et se il ne la veaut defendre, ele s'en peut defendre par .i. autre chanpion, enssi com feme qui n'a baron. Ne son baron ne peut ce defendre ne[3] contredire, por ce que se[4] l'on apeloit feme de murtre ou d'autre chose dont ele se deust defendre et son baron ne la vosist defendre de son cors et il la peust defendre qu'ele n'i[5] feist defendre[6] par .i. autre home, ele en seroit atainte, ou l'on ne porroit feme apeler por mesfait qu'ele feist se son baron ne voloit, lesqués choses seroient contre droit et[7] raison. Et por ce doit il estre et est ensi con je ai dit devant par l'assise ou l'usage dou reiaume de Jerusalem. Et se son chanpion est veincu, ele doit estre[8] arce, et il doit estre pendu.[9] De quelque querele que ce soit le chanpion veincu doit estre pendu[10] par l'assise ou l'usage dou dit reiaume.

Et se[11] feme qui a baron veut faire apeau de murtre ou d'omecide ou de rapt[12] ou de briseure de chemin ou de chose qu'il i[13] ait bataille qui ne soit de querele d'un marc d'argent,[14] [a] et[15] son baron viaut por li entrer el chanp,[16] il le peut faire. Et se il n'i[17] viaut entrer[18] et il seufre qu'ele face l'apel, ele peut metre chanpion, mais que ce soit par l'otroi de son baron, que feme ne peut faire apel sans l'otroi de son baron[19] por les raisons que je ai avant[20] dites. Et[21] se son chanpion est veincu, il sera fait de li et de son chanpion

A: fols lxiv^v^–lxv^v^ cap. 105; **B:** fol. 94^r^ cap. 105; **C:** fols 87^v^–88^r^ cap. 91; **O:** fols 106^v^–107^v^; **V:** fols lxxxviii^v^–lxxxix^r^ cap. 105; Beugnot, pp. 175–6, cap. 105.

[a] The text as emended in A (note 14) seems to make better sense.

[1] des choses] ABO: de chose [2] l'en viaut defendre . . . autre] V: veaut deffendre la, elle s'em peut deffendre par champion [3] V adds: dehdire ne [4] se] C lacks [5] n'i] AB: ne se [6] qu'ele n'i feist defendre] V lacks [7] B adds: contre [8] doit estre] A: sera [9] A adds: Que [10] de quelque querele . . . pendu] O lacks [11] se] A lacks [12] de rapt] AO: de rap; B: de rapine; V: d'arap [13] qu'il i] V: ou il [14] qui ne soit . . . d'argent] A: ou de carelle qui seit d'un marc d'argent ou de plus, elle le peut faire par l'otrei de son baron [15] AB add: se [16] el chanp] V: em bataille [17] n'i] AV: ne [18] el chanp, il . . . entrer] O lacks [19] que feme ne . . . baron] A lacks [20] avant] AV: devant [21] Et] A: Que

si[22] com il[23] est avant[24] dit. Mais se le baron ne viaut soufrir que sa feme[25] face l'apel, ele ne le porra faire por ce que l'on ne respondra pas a li sans son baron ou sans l'otroi de son baron. Que s'ensi[26] li respondoit sans l'otroi de son baron et[27] la bataille estoit gagee et le baron ne vosist que la[28] bataille fust, il en peut[29] partir sa feme sans bataille qui en fust[30] se il disoit qu'ele n'a pooïr de rien faire sans son congé puis qu'ele est sa feme. Et por ce ne doit l'en respondre a feme qui a baron d'apel qu'ele face, se son baron n'otroie[31] avant en cort que ce est par sa volenté qu'ele fait cel apel. Et se il l'otroie, il ne peut puis defendre a sa feme qu'ele ne face l'apel ne desfaire[32] la bataille de[33] l'apel qu'ele avra fait par son otroi, que chose faite et otroiee[34] en cort ne doit aprés estre desfaite ne desdite.[35]

---

[22] si] AV: ensi; B: enssi [23] il] C lacks [24] avant] AV: devant [25] sa feme] A: elle [26] s'ensi] AB: se l'on [27] Que s'ensi li . . . baron et] V: et se [28] la] C lacks [29] peut] A: poreit; B: porroit; V: poroit [30] A adds: et ensi [31] n'otroie] A: n'en otreit; V: n'en otroi [32] desfaire] A: desfaire ne desdire; C: defaire [33] la bataille de] A: ce de; B lacks [34] et otroiee] A lacks [35] desdite] B: desdire

***[93]** Ques gens se pevent defendre par chanpion.

Ce sont les gens qui se pevent defendre par chanpion: feme, home mahaigné, ou home qui a pasé aage de[1] .lx.[2] ans. Et se leur chanpion est veincu, il sera d'andeus[3] fait si com est desus devizé.[a]

A: fol. lxv^{v} cap. 106; **B:** fol. 94^{v} cap. 106; **C:** fol. 88^{r} cap. 92; **O:** fol. 107^{v}; **V:** fol. lxxxix^{r} cap. 106; Beugnot, p. 176, cap. 106.

[a] Above caps 91–2.

[1] aage de] AB lack [2] .lx.] B: quarante [3] d'andeus] C: des .ii

***[94]** Qui se claime de force et ne l'eufre a prover, par quei celui de qui l'on se claime n'est tenus de non neer la.[a]

Qui se claime de force, il doit dire de quel chose[1] l'on li fait force et ofrir la[2] a prover si con court esgardera ou conoistra qu'il prover la[3] deie, ou autrement n'est tenus celui de qui l'on se clame de force de neer la. Car se il ne la nee, il ne sera pas[b] ataint se l'on la motit et eufre[4 c] a prover si con la cort esgardera ou conoistra qu'il[5] prover la deie. Ce est selon l'assise ou l'usage dou reiaume[6] de Jerusalem. Et celui de qui l'on se claime de force, tout soit ce que l'on l'eufre a prover si con est avant dit, il doit demander jor au premier clain sans la force neer, car s'il la nee sans demander jor, il ne peut puis avoir[7] jor, car il a respondu au clain quant il a la force neee. Car le clain est de la force, et qui nee la force[8] dont respont il au clain. Mais se il au jor que la cort li donra ne la nee, se l'on l'eufre a prover et a[9] dit de quei il li fait force et se il en est[10] ataint ou prové, il est encheu en la merci do seignor dou cors et de canqu'il a. Et qui la noie, la cort doit esgarder ou conoistre que l'on la[11] li doit prover par .ii. loiaus garans[d] de la loy de Rome, et que celui sur qui l'on la met peut lever l'un lequel qu'il vodra et conbatre se a lui ou contredire et rebuter, si con est devant[12] devizé que l'on[13] le doit faire.[e]

A: fol. lxv^{v} cap. 107; **B:** fol. 94^{v} cap. 107; **C:** fol. 88^{r-v} cap. 93; **O:** fol. 107^{v}; **V:** fol. lxxxix^{r-v} cap. 107; Beugnot, p. 177, cap. 107.

---

[a] From here until chapter 102 B lacks the rubrics in the text, although they are present in the table of rubrics (fol. 20^{v}).
[b] O begins *lacuna* here.
[c] The text as emended in A (note 4) seem to make better sense.
[d] End of *lacuna* in O.
[e] Above caps 90–91.

---

[1] quel chose] A: quei [2] la] ABO: le [3] la] AB: le; V: li [4] se l'on la motit et eufre] A: se l'on ne l'a moutie et offerte; B: selonc la motie et offre; V: se lon l'a motie et offert [5] qu'il] A: que [6] dou reiaume] B lacks [7] avoir] V: demander [8] et qui nee la force] B lacks [9] a] V lacks [10] li fait force . . . est] A: a fait force il est; B: li fait force se en n'est; V: y a fait force et il en est [11] la] ABV lack [12] devant] B: avant [13] que l'on] BV: c'om

***[95]** Coment toutes manieres de gens autre que chevaliers qui gagent[1] bataille doivent estre armés a la bataille faire.

Toutes manieres de gens mais[2] que chevaliers[3] por quelque querele que ce soit se doivent conbatre a pié en bliaut a cortes robes[4] et chauces a estrier[5] et braies et braiers, tel com il est usé que chanpion a pié les ont, et estre roignés a la reonde et avoir tanevas[6] et bastons de chanpions, et qui avoir ne les peut[7] autres bastons[8] qui soient[9] d'un lonc.[10] Et des armeures dou vencu et do venqueor sera fait[11] en la maniere avant devisee.[12] Et apel qui est fait de murtre ou d'omecide n'a de respit dou jor que les guages sont[13] donés[14] jusques[15] au jor de la bataille que .iii. jors, et de totes autres[16] quereles[17] jusques au jor de la bataille a[18] .xl. jors. Et au jor qu'il[19] lor est doné de la bataille par le seignor et par la court,[20] il dovient venir iaus[21] porofrir en l'ostel dou seignor apareillés ensi con il[22] est devant[23] dit, fors tant que chascun doit porter .i. de ses bastons et puis en la maniere qu'il est desus devisé se doit representer et ofrir a faire ce qu'il doit, et le seignor en doit dire et faire se con est avant[24] dit en cest livre que le seignor le doit faire.[25] Et quant il seront au chanp, les sairemens et le ban[26] et les autres choses devant devisees[27] doivent faire faire les gardes do chanp, si con il est devant devizé[28] en cest livre.[29] [a]

A: fols lxv^{v}–lxvi^{r} cap. 108; **B:** fols 94^{v}–95^{r} cap. 108; **C:** fol. 88^{v} cap. 94; **O:** fols 107^{v}–108^{v}; **V:** fols lxxxix^{v}–xc^{r} cap. 108; Beugnot, p. 178, cap. 108.

[a] Above cap. 90.

[1] gagent] C: ont guagé [2] mais] ABV: autres; O lacks [3] chevaliers] A: chevaliers qui bataille gagent; B: cavaliers [4] a cortes robes] ABV: ou en cotes rouges (B: roges) [5] a estrier] A: rouges a estrivieres sanz soliers [6] A adds: reont dessuz [7] V adds: si ait [8] B adds: avoir [9] qui soient] C lacks [10] et qui avoir . . . lonc. A: qui seient de cor nervés o une boce dessuz et une broche de oz dessouz [11] sera fait] A: deit estre; V: seront faites [12] avant devisee] B: avant dite ou devissee; V: devant dite [13] sont] V: seront [14] AB adds: et receus; V: et resseus [15] jusques] A lacks [16] autres] B: batailles et [17] A adds: dou jor que les garenz sont donés [18] a] ABV: lack [19] qu'il] AB: qui [20] par le seignor . . . court] A: faire de par le seignor [21] iaus] A lacks; B: a eaus; V: et eaus [22] il] ABV lack [23] devant] B lacks [24] dit, fors tant . . . avant] BV lack [25] fors tant que . . . faire] A lacks [26] le ban] V: les bans [27] devisees] ABV: dites [28] B adds: et declaré [29] en cest livre] C lacks

***[96]** Que le seignor doit[1] faire quant pere et fis ou[2] .ii. freres qui donent[3] lor guages l'un contre l'autre.

Il est assise el roiaume de Jerusalem que[4] seignor ne doit recevoir les gages de pere a fis ne de fis a pere ne de .ii. freres l'un contre l'autre.

A: fol. lxvi^{r} cap. 109; **B:** fol. 95^{r} cap. 109; **C:** fol. 88^{v} cap. 95; **O:** fol. 108^{v}; **V:** fol. xc^{r} cap. 109; Beugnot, p. 179, cap. 109.

---

[1] le seignor doit] AB (fol. 20^{v}) V: les seignors doivent (A: deivent) [2] ou] C: et [3] qui donent] ABV: tendent; C: qui doivent [4] ABV add: le

***[97]** Qui viaut la cort faucer qu'il doit faire et dire, et qui la fauce en dit, coment et por quei tos les homes de la haute cort[1] la doivent aleauter.

Se .i. home viaut la cort faucer et dit que le jugement ou l'esgart ou la conoissance et[2] le recort que la court a fait[3] est faus ou desleiaument fait ne[4] qu'il n'est mie de droit fait ou en aucune autre maniere la veulle faucer disant encontre[5] aucune des choses avant dites que la court avra faites ou retraites,[6] tos ceaus de la court le doivent maintenant desmentir et ofrir[7] aleauter en la cort[8] de lors cors contre le sien. Et s'il la veaut faucer, il covient qu'il se conbat a tos les homes de cele court l'un aprés l'autre,[9] ausi[10] ceaus qui n'avront[11] esté a[12] la conoissance ou[13] a l'esgart ou au recort[14] faire come[15] ceaus qui l'avront fait. Car se il fauce la cort, il ne fauce pas tant solement ceaus qui l'esgart ou la conoissance ou le recort avront fait, mais tos ceaus qui sont homes de cele court. Et por ce que l'ennor et la honte de la[16] court est comun a tos ceaus[17] de cele court, le doit chascun des homes de cele court defendre et aleiauter la[18] de son cors contre celui qui la veaut faucer. Car cort qui est faucee ne peut puis faire esgart ne conoissance[19] ne recort qui soit valable se aucun veaut dire a l'encontre.[20] Car ensi com home ataint et vencu[21] de fauceté ne peut[22] puis garantie porter, ne ne peut home de la court faucee garantie porter[23] qui soit valable qui a l'encontre viaut dire, ne[24] la court faucee ne peut puis faire esgart ne conoissance ne recort de court[25] qui soit valable qui viaut dire a l'encontre, et tos ceaus de cele court ont perdu a tos jors[26] vois et respons en

A: fols lxvi^{r}–lxvii^{v} cap. 110; **B:** fols 95^{r}–96^{r} cap. 110; **C:** fols 88^{v}–90^{r} cap. 96; **O:** fols 108^{v}–111^{v}; **V:** fols xc^{r}–xcii^{r} caps 110–11; Beugnot, pp. 179–82, cap. 110.

[1] haute cort] C: cort haut [2] et] ABV: ou [3] fait] C: faite [4] ne] ABV: ou [5] encontre] ABV: contre [6] faites ou retraites] C: faites; V: fait ou retrait [7] AB add: a [8] aleauter en la cort] V: maintenant a la court aleauter [9] V adds: et [10] ausi] A: aussi a; B: autresi a [11] B adds: mie [12] A adds: cel recort ou a [13] ou] C: et [14] recort] A: jugement [15] AB adds: a [16] la] A: celle [17] de la court . . . ceaus] V: est au tous coumune ceaus qui sont [18] de cele court, le doit . . . la] B: qui sont de cele court, por ce doit chascun de cele cort faire et deffendre a aleauter la corte [19] ne conoissance] C lacks [20] se aucun veaut . . . l'encontre] A: qui a l'encontre viaut dire [21] ataint et vencu] C: est vencu; V: ataint vencu et prové [22] peut] A lacks [23] porter, ne ne . . . porter] AB: porter; V: ne peut porter home qui soit de la court faucee guarentie [24] ne] AB lack [25] de court] AB lack [26] a tos jors] AV: a tot (V: tout) tens; B lacks

cort[27] et ne peut[28] puis nul d'eaus leal[29] garantie porter.[30] Por ce doit chascun prendre le fais sur lui de[31] la maniere avant[32] dite.

Et celui qui a dites aucune[33] des avant dites choses contre la cort[34] faucer,[35] si con est desus dit, et il[36] tent son guage contre tos ceaus de la court, et le seignor[37] le receit,[38] quant il sont el chanp por la bataille faire, il doit estre d'une part et tos les[39] homes de la court[40] de l'autre.[41] Et .i. des homes, lequel qu'il esliront, se doit premier conbatre[42] a lui soul a soul, et se[43] celui qui s'est parti est vencu maintenant doit venir[44] .i. des autres[45] en quelque point que celui qui vodra[46] la cort faucer soit.[47] Et se il vaint l'autre,[48] .i. autre doit maintenant venir,[49] et ensi se conbatront[50] .i. a .i., et qu'il les venque tos[51] en .i. jor. Et se il ne les vaint tos en .i. jor, il doit estre pendu.

Et se aucuns dit a ceaus de la court[52] aprés ce qu'il avront fait une des dites choses et retrait: 'Qui a ce fait?' et aucuns die: 'Je l'ai fait', et il n'en face[53] mencion de la court, l'autre peut bien dire a tos ceaus qui ce diront: 'Je di que se vos dites que vos avés ce[54] fait',[55] et die quei, 'vos[56] l'avés fait faucement et desloiaument. Et se vos le volés neer, je suis prest de prover le vos[57] de mon cors contre le vostre ou les vos',[58] se il sont plusors, 'et rendre vos mors ou recreans en une hore de jor. Et veés ensi mon guage', et le tende[59] au seignor. Et a tos ceaus qui avront ce dit, se peut il[60] conbatre sans la court faucer. Et se[61] celui ou ceaus que l'on ensi faucera ne s'en defendent et aleiautent de lor cors, il sont atains d'estre faus et[62] desloiaus et ont perdu vois et respons en cort a tot tens. Et se il sont plusors, il se doit conbatre a tos .i. a .i., si con est dit desus.[63]

---

[27] en cort] B lacks; O: en tous [28] peut] C: pevent [29] leal] B: lacks [30] A adds: et; B: en cort [31] chascun prendre . . . de] V: chascuns d'eaus prendre le fait sur soi en [32] avant] OV: devant [33] aucune] C: aucunes [34] ABV adds: por (V: pour) la court [35] faucer] B: desleauter [36] C adds: en [37] le seignor] V lacks [38] A adds: il se deit combatre a toz et en tel maniere que [39] et tos les] A: dou champ et toz les autres [40] ABV lacks: de la court [41] de l'autre] B: d'autre; O lacks; V: d'un autre [42] conbatre] A: partir et combatre sei [43] se] C lacks [44] venir] A: moveir; BV: movoir [45] des autres] B: autre [46] vodra] B: veut [47] soit] V: cera [48] l'autre] B: cel autre; V: maintenant cel autre [49] venir] BV: movoir [50] conbatront] B: combatent; V: combatent tous [51] en quelque point . . . tos] A: et combatre sei a celui qui vodra la court fausser en quelque point que il seit. Et ce il venque celui, un autre deit maintenant moveir et combatre sei a lui, et ensi se deit combatre a toz un a un tant qu'il les ait toz vencuz [52] aucuns dit a . . . court] BV: aucun (V: aucuns) de ceaus de la court dit [53] n'en face] A: ne fait; B: ne face [54] se vos dites . . . ce] A: ce que vos avés; B: vos avez ce; V: vous dites que vous avés ce [55] fait] O: peut [56] vos] OV lack [57] de prover le vos] B: que je le vos preuve [58] vos] B: vostres; C lacks [59] tende] C: tent [60] il] BV lack [61] se] BOV lack [62] faus et] C lacks [63] est dit desus] A: il est devant dit

Et se il les vaint tos, por ce n'est pas[64] la court faucee, ne ne pert riens de s'enor et le jugement qu'ele a[65] fait[66] est estable. Et tos ceaus qu'il vaincra seront pendus, et il sera pendu se il est vencu. Et se plusors dient: 'Nos feimes ce', et il ne s'en viaut prendre qu'a .i., il le peut faire au quel qu'il vodra qui li avront[67] ensi dit, car il ne dit riens contre la court. Et se il s'en[68] prent a plusors et il ne vaint[69] en .i. jor tos ceaus contre qui il se doit conbatre,[70] il doit est pendu et tos ceaus qu'il vaincra le doivent estre ausi. Ne por nul de ceaus qu'il vainque,[71] tot les venquist il tos, ne doit demorer que l'esgart ou la conoissance[72] que la court avra fait ne doit estre tenus, car il n'a pas la cort faucee.[a]

Et por les raisons desus dites et por autres assés doivent tos ceaus qui veulent[73] esgart ou conoissance faire ou recort de court estre ensenble o tos les autres qu'il poront avoir de la court. Et quant il vodront retraire ce qu'il avront fait, .i. doit dire au seignor en la presence des .ii. parties, se eles i sont: 'Sire, vostre court a ce esgardé ou coneu ou ele est de tel chose recordant', et dire[74] ce qu'ele avra fait, et enssi ne se pora nul[75] aerdre a nul de[76] ceaus de la court, se il ne s'aert a tous[77] si con[78] est desus dit. Et se aucun de[79] ceaus de la cort, quant ce qu'il avront fait sera retrait une des dites choses, die,[80] 'Lequel de vos a ce fait?' il doivent respondre, 'La court l'a fait'. Et se il demande a .i. par non ou a plusors d'eaus: 'Avés vos ce fait?' il doivent respondre: 'La court l'a fait[81] et nos aveuc, car nos i avons esté.[82] Et se vos volés rien dire contre[83] la cort, nos l'orons.' Et ensi covendra qu'il fauce la court ou il demorera desjuglé,[84] puis que tant en avra fait. Por quei a moi senble que nul ne doit dire contre esgart ou recort ou conoissance.[85] Car se il le fait, il viaut

[a] V begins a new chapter here with the rubric: Ci dit coument l'on se doit guarder que nul ne le puisse faucer se il ne fauce toute la court.

[64] pas] AB: mie [65] a] C lacks [66] A adds: si [67] qui li avront] A: de ciaus qui l'avront; C: qui li avroit [68] s'en] ABV: se [69] ne vaint] A: nes vainc toz; B: ne les vainc; V: ne les veinc tous [70] tos ceaus contre . . . conbatre] A: ciaus contre qui il se prendra; B lacks [71] vainque] A: veincra; B: a vanqui [72] A adds: ou le recort [73] veulent] V: doivent [74] dire] A: die [75] nul] B: il mie [76] nul de] ABV lack [77] V adds: ensemble [78] AB adds: il [79] de] ABV: dit a [80] die] ABV lack [81] Et se il . . . fait] B lacks [82] avons esté] A: fumes [83] contre] V: a l'encontre de [84] demorera desjuglé] C: demora dejuglé [85] esgart ou recort ou conoissance] A: esgart ne conoissance ne recort de court; V: l'esgart ou la conoissance ou le recort de la court

la court faucer, et covient qu'ele s'en[86] defende[87] et qu'il se conbate[88] a tos ceaus de la court, si con est devant[89] dit, ou qu'il ait la teste copee, se il ne se[90] viaut a tos conbatre, l'un aprés l'autre. Et se il si[91] conbat et il ne les[92] vaint tous,[93] il sera pendu par la goule. Si[94] me senble que nul home, se Des ne faisoit apertes miracles por lui, qui la fausast en son[95] dit la peust faucer[96] en fait, et, se il s'en asaiast, qu'il peut eschaper d'avoir le chief copé ou d'estre pendu par la goule. Si ne le doit nul home qui aime s'ennor et s'arme[97] enprendre a faire, que qui s'esaiera[98] a faire, il en morra[99] de vil mort et de hontouze.[100]

[86] s'en] AV: se [87] C adds: et qu'il s'en defende [88] qu'ele s'en . . . conbate] B: qu'il s'en conbate et s'en deffendre [89] devant] B: avant [90] se] BV: s'en [91] si] AB: se; V: s'en [92] il ne les] B: ne [93] A adds: en un jor [94] A adds: ne [95] son] BV lacks [96] peust faucer] V: fausast [97] s'arme] ABV: sa vie [98] s'esairera] A: si assaiera; B: s'en essaiera; V: s'en assaiera [99] en morra] C: covendra qu'il muire; V: mora [100] B adds: et vergougneuse

*[98] Coment les assises doivent estre tenues et maintenues fermement en totes choses, et coment les usages.[1]

Les assises doivent estre tenues[2] fermement en toutes chozes, et de ce de quei on ne sera certain que soit assise doit on[3] tenir selonc usage que[4] la longue acostumance.[5] Et de ce que court avra fait esgart ou conoissance ou recort qui soit assise doit estre tenu et maintenu come assise, car les assises ne pevent en plusors choses estre provees que par le lonc usage ou por ce que l'on l'a veu faire et user come assise. Et ce[6] est maniere de la preuve[7] et doit estre et est[8] tenue ou reiaume de Jerusalem et[9] de Chipre meaus que loys ne decres ne decretales, que le sire[10] dou reiaume doit jurer et jure, ains que il soit receu a seignor, de garder et maintenir les assises et les bons us[11] et les bones costumes do reiaume de Jerusalem[12] et de mener chascun selonc les dites assises ou us ou costumes. Et tos les homes dou roiaume doivent jurer ausi[13] de garder les bons us et les bones costumes et les assises dou roiaume[14] de Jerusalem et[15] tenir et maintenir.[16] Et por ce les doit l'en ensi[17] tenir et maintenir et garder[18] en ces .ii. roiaumes en la court laie fermement sur toutes choses, et ausi le doit l'on faire[19] en cele de l'yglise quant cas de ce y escheet.

Et se aucun home a[20] aucun covenant contre l'assise[21] qu'on a juree a tenir doit estre premierement tenue et aprés se l'autre peut les covenans[22] prover si con il doit,[23] les .ii. doivent[24] estre tenues,

A: fols lxvii^{v}–lxviii^{r} cap. 111; **B:** fol. 96^{r-v} cap. 111; **C:** fol. 90^{r-v} cap. 97; **O:** fols 111^{v}–112^{r}; **V:** fol. xcii^{r-v} cap. 112; Beugnot, pp. 182–3, cap. 111.

[1] et coment les usages] V lacks [2] A adds: et maintenues; V: et maintenues et [3] on] AB: l'on; V lacks [4] usage que] ABV: l'usage et. In O 'que' is struck through and 'et' interlined in a later hand. [5] acostumance] V: coustumance [6] In O the words 'et ce' interlined in a later hand over an erasure. [7] la preuve] A: lei; B: loy; V: loi. In O 'del preuve' is struck through and 'de lei' written in the margin in a later hand. [8] et est] AB lack. In O 'et est' is struck through. [9] A adds: en celui [10] sire] V: seignour [11] us] V: husages [12] et de Chipre . . . Jerusalem] O lacks, but written in the margin in a later hand: et de Cypre miaus des leis ne decreis ne decrets Et de le [13] ausi] B lacks [14] doivent jurer ausi . . . roiaume] A lacks [15] et] B: aussi [16] et maintenir] O lacks [17] ensi] ABV lack [18] et garder] AB lack [19] le doit l'on faire] A lacks [20] a] ABV: fait [21] A adds: et l'on se claime par l'assise, l'assise; BV: l'assise [22] covenans] C: covens [23] se l'autre peut . . . doit] A: l'assise les covenans, se il les peut prover si come il deit, et [24] doivent] C: devent

por ce que[25] chascun peut le sien doner et aliener par sa volenté par assise et sans assise, et que les covenans fais et provés, si con il doivent, doivent[26] estre tenus et maintenus.[27] Car l'on dit:[28] 'Covenant veint ley'.

[25] por ce que] B: car [26] doivent] OV lack [27] et maintenus] A lacks [28] V adds: tous jours que

***[99]** Ques est l'assise des bestes restives,[1] et coment l'on se doit clamer.

Par l'assise dou dit reiaume,[2] se .i. home a acheté[3] une beste restive, et que le vendeor li dit: 'Ceste beste[4] est restive, et je por restive la vos vens', et l'achetor dit:[5] 'Et je por restive l'achate, et bien m'en tiens apaié, tout soit ele restive',[6] aprés qu'il a achetés, et la beste[7] restive[8] dedens l'an et le jor qu'il l'a achetee, et il la veut rendre, il doit faire si que .ii. homes la voient restiver qui jurent sur sains, se mestier li est, qu'il l'ont veue restiver, et aprés ce, le plus tost qu'il porra, il doit[9] venir en la court dedens l'an et le jor et dire: 'Sire, je achetai de tel home', et dire de qui,[10] 'une beste que est restive, et di[11] por quei je vueil[12] recovrier[13] mes deniers par l'assise et qu'il preigne[14] sa beste. Et je suis prest de fornir l'assise[a] se il est qui[15] me mescroie[16].' Et le seignor li doit faire rendre sa monoie[17] et reprendre a l'autre sa beste, se il fornist l'assise, se il n'a la beste faite faire[18] mareschacer de cuitures ou de traire dens ou descoler, qu'il[19] i a une propre assise[20] de ce. Et ele[21] est tel que qui achate beste et il la fait mareschaucer de cuitures ou de dens traire ou descoiller[22] la et il aprés la treve restive, qu'il[23] ne la peut rendre par l'assise, et se il n'a la beste[24] faite mareschaucer de l'une[25] des .iii.[26] dites choses et ele[27] restive et il la veut rendre,[28] faire le peut

A: fol. lxviii^{r-v} cap. 112; **B:** fols 96^{v}–97^{r} cap. 112; **C:** fols 90^{v}–91^{r} cap. 98; **O:** fol. 112^{r-v}; **V:** fols xcii^{v}–xciii^{r} cap. 113; Beugnot, pp. 183–4, cap. 112.

[a] O begins *lacuna* here.

[1] des bestes restives] A: de la beste restive [2] dit reiaume] A: reiaume de Jerusalem; V: royaume [3] a acheté] A: achate; B: achete [4] beste] C lacks [5] l'achetor dit] B lacks [6] ABV add: et [7] beste] B lacks [8] aprés qu'il a . . . restive] C lacks [9] il doit] B lacks [10] et dire de qui] A lacks; B: et die de qui; V: et le nome [11] et di] A: et die quel beste; B lacks; O: et die li [12] veull] C: vire il(?) [13] recovrier] B: recevoir; O: resivre; V: ressevoir [14] preigne] A: recuevre [15] qui] A: que il [16] mescroie] A: mescreit; C: moscroir [17] sa monoie] V: ses deniers [18] faire] BV lack [19] traire dens ou descoler, qu'il] B: faire traire denz ou descoullier, quar il [20] se il n'a . . . assise] A lacks [21] ele] A: l'assise; V lacks [22] qui achate beste . . . descoiller] A: celui qui achate la beste deit jurer sur sainz que il n'a la beste faite mareschaussier de cuitures ou de traire denz ou descoiller ne faite chose par quei elle ait celle restiveté, que il y a une preupre assise de ce, et elle est tel: que qui achate beste et il la fait mareschaussier de cutures ou de denz traire ou descoillier [23] qu'il] BV: il [24] V adds: restive [25] l'une] B: nulles [26] V adds: devant [27] B adds: est [28] et il la veut rendre] A lacks

par la dite assise. Et l'assise de ce est tel que se il dedens l'an et le jor qu'il a achetee la beste peut prover par .ii. loiaus garans qui jurent qu'il ont[29] veu cele beste restiver et qu'il aprés jure sur sains que cele beste n'a la restiveté par lui, il doit rendre la beste et recevoir tant con[30] ele li costa de celui qui li vendi la beste,[31] se il ne la fait mareschaucer d'aucune des avant[32] dites chozes.

Et se le vendor peut puis prover si con il doit par garans les covenans desus dis, il recovera les deniers de l'achetor[33] de la beste, et il ravra[34] la beste tout ait il bien[35] fornie l'assise. Car ensi sera l'assise[b] premier[36] tenue, et aprés les covenans. Ne celui contre qui l'on porte la garantie de la beste restive ne peut par l'assise torner nul des guarans, mais celui contre qui l'on viaut prover les covenans peut l'un des garans torner qui portent[37] la garantie desus dite contre lui, por ce que de ce n'a point d'assise qui toille les tornes ne la[38] bataille.

[b] End of *lacuna* in O.

[29] ont] ABV: aient [30] aprés jure sur . . . con] A: facent le seirement dessuz dit, il deit rendre la beste et receveir ce que [31] li vendi la beste] B: la li vendi [32] avant] V: .iii. devant [33] de l'achetor] V lacks [34] ravra] ABV: avra [35] bien] V lacks [36] premier] A: premierement [37] portent] AV: portera; B: porteront [38] ne la] AV: de; B: ne ne la

*[100] Ques est l'assise de cop aparant et coment l'on se doit clamer.

Qui se viaut clamer de cop aparant par l'assise dou roy Bauduin,[1 a] il doit venir devant le seignor en sa cort et mostrer a lui et a sa cort les cos aparans[2] qu'il a et[3] dire: 'Sire, faites veir[4] a vostre court le cop ou[5] les cos que tel m'a fait', et le nome, et le seignor doit maintenant comander a .iii. de ces homes,[6] l'un en son leuc et les .ii. come cort, qu'il aillent veir le cop ou les cos que celui lor mostera. Et il dovient maintenant aler et veir[7] ce que celui lor mostera,[8] et quant il l'avront[9] veu il doivent venir devant le seignor en sa cort et dire li: 'Sire, tel', et le noment,[10] 'a bien cop ou[11] cos aparans', se il sont plusors,[b] 'et nos les avons veus', et dire quels[12] les cos aparans sont, por ce que celui qui a les cos[13] eus[14] se viaut clamer de plusors homes se les cos[15] sont plusors qu'il le puissent[16] faire. Que[17] l'on se peut de chascun cop clamer d'un home et avoir en droit par la dite assise. Et quant la cort avra les cos veus et retrais les[18] au seignor, celui qui en viaut faire son[19] clain par la dite assise[20] doit dire au seignor en sa cort enssi se il ne s'en viaut clamer que[21] d'un sol home: 'Sire, je me clains a vos par l'assise do roi Bauduin de tel', et le nome,[22] 'qui m'a le cop ou les cos fais', se il sont plusors, 'que vostre cort a veus. Et[23] vos pri et requier que vos me faites[24] droit de lui par la dite assise.' Et lors le seignor le doit mander querre,[25] et quant il sera[26] devant lui le seignor li doit dire: 'Tel',

---

A: fols lxviii^{v}–lxix^{r} cap. 113; **B:** fol. 97^{r-v} cap. 113; **C:** fols 91^{r}–92^{r} cap. 99; **O:** fols 112^{v}–113^{r}; **V:** fols xciii^{r}–xciv^{r} cap. 114; Beugnot, pp. 185–6, cap. 113.

---

[a] Which King Baldwin issued this *assise* is not known. It is discussed at length by Philip of Novara (pp. 546–8) and mentioned by both Geoffrey Le Tor (p. 441) and James of Ibelin (p. 465).
[b] O begins *lacuna* here.

---

[1] Bauduin] AB: Baudoyn (and similarly throughout this chapter) [2] aparans] AB lack [3] et] AV: ou; B: ou fait [4] veir] O: venir [5] le cop ou] A lacks [6] de ces homes] V: homes de la court [7] veir] O: venir [8] Et il dovient . . . mostera] B lacks [9] l'avront BOV: avront [10] noment] C: nome [11] cop ou] V: mostre le cop ou le [12] quels] ABV: quans [13] V adds: aparans [14] celui qui a les cos eus] AB: se celui qui a les cos (B: cous) [15] se viaut clamer . . . cos] B: se il [16] puissent] AV: puisse [17] le puissent faire. Que] B: se puisse clamer de tant de gens com il a cous se il veut. Car [18] les AB lack [19] son] A lacks [20] la dite assise] B: l'assise [21] ne s'en viaut clamer que] A: se viaut clamer [22] et le nome] A lacks [23] Et] A: Si [24] faites] B: faciez [25] le doit mander querre] A: deit mander querre celui de qui l'on sera clamés [26] AV add: venus

et le nome, 'c'est a moi clamés de vos par l'assise dou roy Bauduin de cop aparant que vos li avés fait, et m'a requis que je li en face droit par la dite assise.[27] Et je ai le cop fait veir a ma court, et il est aparant. Si vos comant de fornir l'assise.'[28] Et celui maintenant sans avoir jor au clain doit fornir l'assise ensi qu'il doit conoistre ou neer ce que celui qui c'est de lui clamés li a mis[29] sus. Et se il le conoist,[30] il[31] doit paier l'assise au seignor et a celui qui avra fait le clain l'amende establie qui est[32] aprés devisee. Et se il le noie, il doit jurer sur sains de son poing destre en la presence dou seignor et de la cort et dou clamant, se il i est, qu'il ne li a cel cop fait ou ceaus[33] cos[34] de quei il c'est de lui[35] clamés par la dite assise.

Et se il fait le dit sairement, il fornit[36] l'assise et en est quites a tos jors de cel clain,[37] si que aucun ne li en[38] peut aucune[39] chose demander, non[40] se celui moroit[41] dou cop ou des cos dont il se seroit clamé par la dite assise, puis que celui de qui il se clama par l'assise[42] en a l'assise fornie en l'une des .ii.[43] dites manieres. Et bien est raison,[44] car[45] l'on[46] ne doit d'un mesfait soufrir .ii. paines, ne estre .ii. fois justisié.[47]

Et se il a plusors cos, et se[48] viaut clamer de plusors[c] homes, de chascun de ceaus de qui il se viaut clamer[49] il doit dire lequel des cos[50] aparans est celui que cil[51] li a fait de qui il se viaut clamer,[52] et aprés claime ce[53] en la maniere desus dite. Et l'autre li doit conoistre ou neer, et se il le conoist si paiera[54] l'amende aprés devisee,[d] et se il le neie[55] faire le sairement avant dit.[56]

---

[c] End of *lacuna* in O.
[d] Below cap. 101.

---

[27] la dite assise] ABV: l'assise [28] V adds: enci [29] a mis] V: met [30] conoist] A: conut [31] il] V: si [32] V adds: ci [33] cel cop fait ou ceaus] BV: le coup (V: cop) fait ou les [34] A adds: se il sont pluisors [35] de lui] AV lack [36] fornit] A: a forni [37] en est quite . . . clain] ABV: est quite de cel claim tous (A: tot) tens [38] en] AV lack [39] aucun ne li en peut aucune] B: nul ne li en puet nulle [40] non] A: neis [41] demander, non se celui moroit] V: que demander ou celui morir [42] l'assise] V: la dite assise [43] .ii.] A lacks; V: .ii. devant [44] A adds: que ensi deit estre [45] car] V: ce. Que [46] l'on] ABV: nul [47] paines, ne estre . . . justisié] V: justizes ne pennes [48] se] A: il se; BV: il s'en [49] homes, de chascun . . . clamer] A lacks [50] des cos] C: de ces [51] cil] A: tel; V: celui [52] de plusors homes . . . clamer] B lacks [53] et aprés claime ce] A: et aprés se claime des autres; B: si s'en claime; O: aprés claime se; V: et aprés clamer se [54] conoist si paiera] A: conut il deit paier; B: conoist ou nee a faire le sairement devant dit, il doit paier; V: counoist paier [55] le neie] A: ne viaut si deit [56] et se il le neie . . . dit] B lacks

***[101]** Quel amende doit faire celui par l'assise de qui[1] l'on se claime de lui[2] de cop aparant.[3]

L'amende de[4] celui de qui l'on se claime de cop aparant par l'assise[5] doit faire[6] est tel, que se chevalier bat ou fiert chevalier et il[7] fait cop aparant et il se claime de lui par l'assise et il ne le nee en la cort et en fornit l'assise[8] faisant l'avant[9] dit sairement,[a] il li covendra a fornir l'assise[10] ensi[11] que il paiera au seignor de l'amende de celui mesfait .m. besanz de la monoie de celui pais et au clamant harnes de chevalier si covenable et tel qu'il ne puisse estre refusé par raison d'estre en restor,[12] se celui a qui il le done[13] veut demorer au[14] seignor ou a autre. Et se il a plusors cos et il de chascun cop[15] se claime d'un chevalier, il avra l'amende desus dite et le seignor ausi, se celui de qui il se claime ne[16] nee qu'il ne li a fait cel cop de quei il c'est de lui clamés et en fornit l'assise faisant le dit sairement. Et c'il se claime d'aucun des cos de chevalier et d'aucun des cos[17] d'autre que de chevalier, il en avra de celui qui n'est pas[18] chevalier l'amende qui est aprés devisee de celui qui n'est chevalier et fait au[19] chevalier cop aparant, se celui en est ataint ou prové si con est aprés dit. Que qui a plusors cos aparans il peut par la dite assise de chascun des cos[20] clamer par soi[21] d'un home ou d'une feme et avoir ent droit si con est avant[22] dit.

Et se autre home[23] que chevalier bate ou fiert ou fait cop aparant a chevalier, et il en est ataint, si con est devant dit, il doit par l'assise[24] perdre le poing destre[25] por l'ennor et la hautece[26] que

---

A: fols lxix^{r}–lxx^{r} cap. 114; **B:** fols 97^{v}–98^{r} cap. 114; **C:** fol. 92^{r-v} cap. 100; **O:** fols 113^{r}–114^{r}; **V:** fol. xciv^{r-v} caps 115–16; Beugnot, pp. 186–7, cap. 114.

---

[a] Above cap. 100.

---

[1] qui] C: quei [2] de lui] AB (fol. 20^{v}) lacks [3] A adds: se il ne le nee et a qui; BV: se il le nee (V: noie) et a qui [4] de] A: que deit faire [5] B adds: et que il [6] doit faire] A lacks; V: si [7] il] AV: li; B: il li [8] et il ne . . . l'assise] B lacks [9] l'avant] B: le devant [10] faisant l'avant dit . . . l'assise] A lacks [11] ensi] A: est ce; BV: en ce [12] en restor] A: a soz [13] done] ABV: paie [14] au] C: a [15] cop] B lacks [16] il se claime ne] B: il s'est clamé le; V: c'est clamés ne [17] de chevalier et d'aucun des cos] BC lack; V: et d'aucun des cos [18] pas] ABV lack [19] au] A: a celui qui est; BV: a [20] des cos] B: coup [21] par soi] AB lack; V: ce par soi [22] avant] A: devant [23] home] V lacks [24] est devant dit . . . l'assise] AB: il deit (B: doit) par l'assise, il deit (B: doit); V: il doit, il doit [25] poing destre] B lacks [26] et la hautece] B lacks

chevalier et chevalerie[27] a et doit avoir sur toutes autres manieres de gens.[b]

Et se chevalier ou autre persone[28] que chevalier bat ou fiert autre persone[29] que chevalier et li fait cop aparant, se celui se claime par la dite assise[30] dou roi Bauduin, se l'autre ne le noie et ne[31] fait le sairement desus devisé,[32] il doit paier au seignor por l'amende dou mesfait .c. besanz et au clamant .c. sos. Et se le clamant est d'autre nacion que de la loy de Rome et l'autre ne[33] noie qu'il ne li a cel cop fait et ne fait le dit sairement, le seignor en avra de lui en amende .l. besanz et le clamant .l. sos.

Et se home bat ou fiert sa feme ou sa feme a lui et[34] se aucun d'eaus l'a[35] fait a son fis ou a sa fille tant con il sont familians,[36] ce est ains qu'il les ait mancipés,[37] ce est partis de lui, ou a son serf ou a sa serve ou a sa chanbriere, et il se claime par la dite assise, il ne ele n'est pas tenus de paier la paine desus devizee, por ce que tes manieres de gens ne se pevent clamer par la dite assise,[38] car il[39] sont exceptés.

---

[b] V begins a new chapter here with the rubric: L'amende dou cop aparant par l'assise dou roy Bauduin d'autre personne que de chevalier.

---

[27] chevalier et chevalerie] V: le chevalier [28] persone] BV lack [29] persone] V lacks [30] la dite assise] V: l'assise [31] ne] C lacks [32] sairement desus devisé] A: dit sairement [33] ne] V lacks [34] et] ABV: ou [35] l'a] ABV: le [36] sont familians] A: est *in familias*; V: soit famillans [37] les ait mancipés] A: mansipe; B: soient mancipez [38] la dite assise] A: l'assise [39] B adds: en

***[102]** Quel est[1] l'assise do chevalier qui doit dete et la conoist, ou[2] l'on la li preuve, et il n'a de quei paier la.[3]

Por ce qu'il est devant dit que chevalier doit paier paine motie par la dite assise,[a] veuill je esclarsir[4] une assise propre[5] qui est faite de chevalier: ce est assaveir que chevalier ne peut ne ne doit par l'assise dou reiaume de Jerusalem estre aresté por dete.[6] Mais l'on peut bien toutes les soues chozes arester et faire vendre por la dete paier qu'il doit[7] aussi por cele qu'il doit[8] por l'amende de l'assise, con por l'autre soue dete, quant ele a esté coneue ou provee en cort si con ele doit, et le fié, se il l'a, si[9] doit estre vendu ausi, mais qu'il soit vendu par l'assise.

A: fol. lxx[r] cap. 115; **B:** fol. 98[r–v] cap. 115; **C:** fol. 92[v] cap. 101; **O:** fol. 114[r–v]; **V:** fols xciv[v]–xcv[r] cap. 117; Beugnot, p. 188, cap. 115.

---

[a] Above cap. 101.

---

[1] Quel est] C: Quel qu'est [2] conoist ou] A rubric (fol. 3[v]): conut et [3] la] BV rubric (fol. 7[r]) lack [4] esclarsir] C: o sele issir; O: o oele issir [5] assise propre A: ditte assise [6] peut ne ne . . . dete] A: deit estre aresté por dette que il deit [7] A adds: et [8] aussi por cele qu'il doit] B lacks [9] si] AB: en

***[103]** Ques est l'assise d'autre home[1] que de chevalier, quant il conoist[2] dete en cort ou[3] vers qui l'on la preuve.[a]

Se aucun autre[4] que chevalier doit dete qu'il ait coneue en court ou qui li ait esté provee, si con la court l'a esgardé ou coneu,[5] et le seignor li comande[6] qu'il l'ait paiee dedens .vii. jors, et il ne la paie[7] et[8] il a choze de quei il la puisse paier, et le seignor la peut[9] trover[10] ou faire trover, il la doit faire prendre et[11] vendre guage abandon tant que celui a qui il doit la dite[12] dete en[13] soit paié. Et se il n'a de quei paier la que de son fié[14] et il est home dou seignor, le fié doit estre vendu[15] si com est avant dit[16] por la[17] dete paier.[b] Et se il n'est home dou[18] seignor, le peut et doit faire arester por la dete[19] et faire le metre en prison tant qu'il ait cele dete paiee ou faite[20] en le gré de celui a qui il la deit, se il ne fornit l'assise. Mais se il eufre a fornir l'assise,[21] le seignor le doit faire mener et tenir selonc l'assise de ce. Et l'assise en[22] est tel: qu'il doit jurer sur sains qu'il n'a dou sien a covert ne a descovert[23] que la robe de son vestir[24] et les dras de son lit, ne autre por lui, et aprés ce sairement il doit estre livré a celui a qui il doit la dite dete, et il le peut tenir con son esclaf tant qu'il ou autre por lui[25] l'aient paié[26] ou fait son gré de la dite dete. Et il le doit[27] tenir sans fers mais que[28] .i. aneau de fer au bras por reconoissance qu'il est au poeir d'autrui por dete qu'il li doit,[29] et li doit doner a mangier et a boivre soufisaument,[30]

A: fol. lxx[r–v] cap. 116; **B:** fols 98[v]–99[r] cap. 116; **C:** fols 92[v]–93[r] cap. 102; **O:** fols 114[v]–115[v]; **V:** fol. xcv[r–v] cap. 118; Beugnot, pp. 188–9, cap. 116.

---

[a] B lacks the rubric in the text, although it is present in the table of rubrics (fol. 20[v]).
[b] Below caps 168–70.

---

[1] home] B (fol. 20[v]) lacks [2] conoist] A: conut; V: counut [3] ou] C: et [4] aucun autre] A: autre home [5] V adds: ou recordé [6] comande] B: ait comandé [7] dedens .vii. jors . . . paie] B lacks [8] la paie et] A: l'a paiee et [9] peut] V: puisse [10] trover] B: prover [11] V adds: faire [12] dite] AB lack [13] la dite dete en] V lacks [14] la que de son fié] B lacks [15] vendu] O: dou seignor; V: aresté [16] est home dou . . . dit] A: livre son fié au seignor, le seignor le peut et deit faire vendre par l'assise [17] AV add: dite [18] vendu si come . . . dou] B: doit seignor le [19] Et se il . . . dete] A lacks; C adds: paier [20] cele dete paiee ou faite] C: celui paié ou faire [21] Mais se il . . . l'assise] B lacks [22] en] A: de ce; V lacks [23] n'a dou sien . . . descouvert] A: a descovert ne a covert n'en a; B: n'a a covert ne a descouvert [24] vestir] C: vestiment [25] et aprés ce . . . lui] B lacks [26] l'aient paié] C: l'ait paiee [27] B adds: faire [28] B adds: il ait [29] li doit] B: doit a autrui [30] soufisaument] B lacks

au mains pain et aigue, et a vestir[31] une robe l'iver et une cote l'isté et .ii. chemises, et la mesion que il[32] fera doit estre contee a la dete. Et se l'aresté por dete fait servise a celui[33] en cui pooir il est, le servise qu'il li fera doit il conter resnablement et abatre[34] de la dete, tant[35] con le servise qu'il li avra fait vaudra. Et se il le sert tant qu'il s'aquite vers lui en servant le, il doit estre[36] maintenant qu'il est aquité delivrer le[37] et li doit oster l'aneau[38] dou bras, et peut aler et venir quite et delivre,[39] come home qui est en sa delivre[40] poesté.

[31] O adds: et [32] que il] C: qui [33] a celui] V lacks [34] il conter resnablement et abatre] AB: estre conté raisnablement (B: resonablement) et abatu; O: il contre regnablemant et abatu; V: estre conté raisounablement abatant [35] de la dete, tant] V lacks [36] estre] C lacks [37] qu'il est aquité delivrer le] AV: quitte (V: quite) et delivre; BO: que il est quite delivre [38] l'aneau] V: le fer [39] quite et delivre] V quitement [40] delivre] B lacks

***[104]** Coment l'on se doit clamer de plegerie.

Qui se viaut clamer de plegerie, il se doit clamer par l'assise, et[1] l'on n'a pas jor, car l'assise tot le jor. Et aucuns des bons plaideors que je ai veus et oi parler ont dit que l'on ne peut par l'assise les garans qui portent guarantie de plegerie rebuter ne torner par guage de bataille, et aucuns des autres bons plaideors que je ai veus et oy parler ont dit[2] que si peut, se la querele est do vaillant[3] d'un marc d'argent ou de plus, mais je n'en oy[4] onques dire as uns ne as autres que il fust esgardé ni[5] coneu que ce fust assise, ne qu'il eussent[6] esté en leuc[7] ou l'un ou[8] l'autre eust esté[9] esgardé ou coneu. Et a moi senble que ceaus qui ont dit et qui diront que l'on peut les garans rebuter et torner[10] par gage de bataille ont dit et dient meaus et plus grant raison que ceaus qui dient que l'on ne les peut rebuter ne torner. Et les raisons por quei il le me senble sont[11] tes: qu'il[12] est assise et usage[13] que de querele d'un marc d'argent ou de plus qu'il a tornes de bataille, et que l'on peut le garant rebuter ou torner[14] par guage de bataille, et qu'ausi est querele le fait de plegerie con d'autre,[15] se celui qui se claime la[16] viaut faire.[17] Qu'ausi peut il dire en ce[18] clain qu'il est son plege de .iii. mars d'argent ou d'or ou de plus come de .v. sos ou de .x. ou de plus[19] ou de mains, et por ce le[20] me senble il ensi con je ai dit.[21]

Que se ensi n'estoit que l'on ne peust rebuter ne torner[22] aucun des garans qui portent[23] garantie de plegerie, moult de maus en porroit[24] l'on faire qui vodroit[25] maligner et avoir de l'autrui[26] a tort. Que se .i. home se claime[27] d'un autre par l'assise et deist qu'il fust son plege d'une quantité[28] d'avoir et deist de conbien et celui neast la plegerie ou deist qu'il n'en fust menbrant et l'autre le[29] provast

---

A: fols lxx^{v}–lxxi^{v} cap. 117; **B:** fol. 99^{r-v} cap. 117; **C:** fols 93^{r}–94^{r} cap. 103; **O:** fols 115^{v}–117^{v}; **V:** fols xcv^{v}–xcvi^{v} cap. 119; Beugnot, pp. 190–2, cap. 117.

---

[1] ABV add: par l'assise [2] que je ai . . . dit] V: dient [3] do vaillant] A lacks; C: do vaillanc [4] n'en oy] C: n'en n'oy; V: n'oy [5] ni] AV: ne; B: ou [6] eussent] V: eust [7] leuc] ABV: court [8] ou] A: ne; C lacks [9] eust esté] B: est; V lacks [10] torner] B: retorner [11] A adds: et deivent estre [12] tes: qu'il] B: ces: quar il [13] et usage] A: ou usage; B lacks [14] Et les raisons . . . torner] V lacks [15] ABV add: chose [16] la] ABV: le [17] faire] A lacks [18] ce] ABV: son [19] ou de plus] ABO lack [20] por ce le] B: paier li; V: paier li ce [21] V adds: devant [22] torner] B: retorne [23] portent] O: porteront [24] porroit] O: porront [25] vodroit] V: vodront [26] l'autrui] O: l'autre [27] claime] V: clamast [28] par l'assise et . . . quantité] B lacks [29] le] AB: la; V: li

par le sairement de .ii. homes et que l'on ne peust aucuns d'eaus rebuter ne torner par guage de bataille, celui que l'on diroit qui seroit[30] son plege perdroit quanque[31] l'on diroit el clain de coi il seroit son plege, se il neoit la plegerie. Que puis que l'on nee plegerie[32] en court, se ele li est aprés provee, celui por qui il fu plege n'est pas tenus d'amender li le damage que celui qui est[33] plege en avra[34] receu. Et se il neoit la plegerie et disoit qu'il n'en fust menbrant et l'autre l'en peust faire[35] menbrant[36] par .ii. homes qui juracent qu'il fu[37] son plege, se la plegerie estoit por tant provee et que celui por qui l'on dit que l'on est plege qui le damage recevroit[38] ne peust aucuns des guarans rebuter ou torner par gage de bataille, ensi poroit chascun estre destruit de si grant cantité d'avoir, con celui qui le vodroit avoir a tort[39] vodroit[40] dire en son clain que l'autre li fust plege. Et asés de legier troveroit l'on .ii. homes qui se parjureroient[41] por monoie ou por[42] amor ou por poor ou por heine ou[43] por aucune autre choze et porteroient garantie de tel cantité d'avoir con l'on vodroit dire que l'on fust plege de l'autre qui de lui c'est clamé, puis qu'il seroit seur[44] qu'il ne poroient estre rebutés ne tornés de cele garantie.[45] Si[46] avroient les faus[47] et les desloiaus trop[48] grant avantages sur les prodes homes, laquel chose ne peut ne ne doit estre par droit ne par raison ne par assise ne par usage. Si ne me senble[49] que l'assise soit tel con ceaus ont dit qu'ele est qui ont dit[50] que on[51] ne peut torner ne rebuter garans de plegerie, ains est tel con les autres ont dit.[52]

Et por ce que celui qui preste le sien n'est mie destraint de prester le[53] se il ne viaut, si ne le doit prester qu'a tel[54] qu'il conoist a[55] leau ou qu'il cuide fermement qu'il le soit ou qu'il[56] l'ait tel plege qui ne li faille[57] de la plegerie ou qui[58] ne le moine[59] a tornes de bataille por damage qui li en dee avenir ou qu'il en reçoive la plegerie en

---

[30] qui seroit] A: qui fu; B lacks [31] l'on diroit . . . quanque] C lacks [32] l'on nee plegerie] V: plegerie se nee [33] est] ABV: l'avra [34] V adds: eu et [35] faire] V: faire faire [36] et l'autre l'en . . . menbrant] A: et l'on li provast; B lacks [37] fu] ABV: fust [38] qui le damage recevroit] A lacks [39] tort] O: court [40] avoir a tort vodroit] C lacks [41] se parjureroient] A: s'esparjurereient [42] por] C: par [43] por amor ou . . . ou] A lacks [44] seroit seur] ABV: seroient (A: sereient) seurs [45] de cele garantie] A: par gage de bataille de celle garentie porter [46] Si] A: Et ensi; B: enssi [47] faus] BV: fors [48] trop] A: moult; B: mout [49] semble] B: sembla [50] ont dit qu'ele . . . dit] A: qui ont dit que elle est tel [51] que on] C: qu'ele [52] ont dit] B lacks [53] V adds: sien [54] tel] C: cel [55] conoist a] B: condisse [56] cuide fermement qu'il . . . qu'il] V lacks [57] qui ne li faille] A: doné qui ne li faut [58] qui] AB: que il; V: que [59] moine] AB: meine; OV: mene

la cort ou se face reconoistre la dete en cort, et ensi pora estre gardé de damage. Et que se il autrement le fait et il i a damage, se[60] soit[61] en sa coupe. Que[62] puis qu'il le peut faire en maniere qu'il n'i avra[63] damage et il le fait autrement et damage[64] et ennui li avient,[65] nul n'est tant a reprendre[66] con il est. Et por les raisons avant dites et por[67] plusors autres[68] que l'on en[69] porroit encores[70] dire, me senble il qu'il doit estre en cest cas ensi[71] con je ai devant[72] dit.

[60] se] C: si [61] soit] AB: sera; V: cera [62] Que] ABV: Et [63] n'i avra] AB: n'i ait; V: n'ait [64] et il le . . . damage] O lacks [65] avient] BV: en vient; O: avoient [66] reprendre] B: respondre [67] por] ABV lack [68] autres] C: avant [69] en] ABV lack [70] encores] V lacks [71] ensi] AV lack; B: si [72] devant] A lacks

***[105]** Que doit faire celui qui est plege vers .i.[1] autre et il en est menbrant.[a]

Qui est plege vers aucun[2] d'aucune choze et il en[3] est menbrant qu'il doit faire,[4] se il est prodome et leal, il doit faire que[5] plege et fornir le des guages[6] tant con il a[7] de coi,[8] et quant il n'a de coi[9] il le doit dire vers[10] celui de qui il est plege, et se il l'en mescroit, il li en doit fornir l'assise en la cort. Et l'assise de ce est tel: que qui est plege por[11] autre, et celui a qui il est plege li demande guage, et il dit qu'il n'a de quei il li puisse faire que plege, l'autre li doit dire: 'Fornissiés ent donc[12] l'assise', et il la doit fornir ensi qu'il doit jurer sur sains qu'il n'a, ne autre por lui, dou sien a covert ne a descovert de quei il li puisse faire que plege que la robe de son vestir et les dras[13] de son lit. Et se le[14] plege fait le dit sairement, il fornit l'assise que[15] l'autre ne le peut ne[16] deit guagier par[17] l'assise de la robe de son vestir ne des dras de[18] son lit, si covient qu'il s'en[19] seufre tant qu'il treusse[20] aucune chose dou sien qu'il[21] le puisse guager.[22] Et se il set qu'il a dou sien autre que les avant dites choses, il le peut guager, et il le peut bien faire[23] par l'assise et ausi bien le peut[24] guagier de ce qu'on li avra presté come dou sien, mais il ne peut ne ne[25] doit guager de ce qu'il[26] avra loué. Et la raison por quei[27] est tel qu'il est tenus d'amender ce qui li est presté, mais[28] ce qu'il a loué n'est il pas[29] tenus dou rendre et que la chose prestee

A: fols lxxi^{v}–lxxii^{r} cap. 118; **B:** fol. 100^{r} cap. 118; **C:** fol. 94^{r-v} cap. 104; **O:** fols 117^{v}–118^{v}; **V:** fols xcvi^{v}–xcvii^{r} cap. 120; Beugnot, pp. 192–3, cap. 118.

[a] From here until chapter 132 B lacks the rubrics in the text, although they are present in the table of rubrics (fols 20^{v}–21^{v}).

[1] .i.] AB (fol. 20^{v}) V lack [2] vers aucun] A: vers aucun autre; B: vers autre; V lacks [3] en] ABV lack [4] qu'il doit faire] B: que doit il faire [5] que] ABV: come [6] de guages] A: plegerie et garder le de damage [7] a] B: avra [8] C adds: et dire [9] et quant il n'a de coi] B lacks [10] vers] AB: a [11] est plege por] A: plege; BV: est plege (V: pleges) a [12] donc] V lacks [13] les dras] B lacks [14] le] A: celui qui est [15] que] A: si que; B: quar [16] le peut ne] B: puet ne ne; V: peut ne ne [17] par] C lacks [18] de la robe . . . de] V: la robe de son vestir ne de son lit [19] s'en] ABV: se [20] treusse] AO: truisse; B: triuise; V: trove [21] qu'il] B: dont il [22] guager] C: garder [23] guager et il . . . faire] A: bien faire gagier [24] le peut] B lacks; C: le peut il [25] peut ne ne] A: le peut ni ne le [26] qu'il] A: que l'on li; V: que il li [27] por quei] V lacks [28] C adds: de [29] est tenus d'amender . . . pas] ABV: n'est (V: est) tenus (B: tenu) de rendre ce qui li est presté, mais ce que il a luie (B: loué; V: loé) est il

par le prest faire est[30] soue tant con il l'a qu'il li[31] doit amender se ele est perdue ou enpiree en quelque maniere que ce soit ou enconbree ou enpeeschee si que celui qui la li[32] presta ne l'ait. Si est clere chose, se me senble, que l'on peut son plege guager de ce qui li est presté si con dou sien et que l'on ne le peut par raison guager de ce que l'on li a loé.[33]

[30] le prest faire est] A: le prester est faite; B: le preste est faite; V: l'emprest est faite [31] l'a qu'il li] A: l'a que il la; B: l'a que il; V: la [32] la li] BV: li; C: la [33] a loé] V: loe

***[106]** Ques est l'assise de la choze prestee que l'on pert.

L'assise de la chose prestee quant ele est perdue par mort ou autrement ou ele est enpiree est tel: que celui a qui l'on a la chose prestee, se il[1] la pert por mort ou autrement,[2] doit jurer conbien il croit qu'ele valoit et rendre[3] au seignor de la chose tant con il jura[4] qu'ele valoit.[5] Et se ele n'est perdue et ele est enpiree en la faute[6] de celui a qui ele a[7] esté prestee, il doit amender a celui qui li presta tant con vaut ce qu'ele[8] est enpiree. Et ce doit jurer celui a qui ele a esté prestee.[9] Et por ce est[10] doné par l'assise[11] le sairement a celui a qui l'on a la chose prestee, que se[12] celui de qui la chose est et a qui l'on la requiert en prest[13] ne la prestera,[14] se il ne viaut, et il ne la doit prester a home se il n'entent[15] ou ne cuide qu'il soit tel que se il la pert ou enpire, qu'il la li amende ou qu'il face leal sairement dou pris de la chose. Et se il n'est tel et celui qui la chose li presta i a damage, c'est en[16] sa coupe quant il presta[17] le sien a home que il ne conoissoit[18] a prodome et a leal. Et por ce est doné[19] le sairement a celui a qui la chose a esté prestee, que se il s'en viaut parjurer qu'il ne peut[20] faire damage a l'autre que de tant con la chose qu'il[21] li presta valoit,[22] et que se[23] le sairement fust[24] doné premier a celui qui li[25] presta, et il se[26] voloit parjurer, il porroit l'autre destruire,[27] tant porroit il[28] jurer que ce que il li presta valoit.[29] Mais se celui a qui l'on a la chose prestee[30] qui est perdue, coment que ce soit, ou enpiree ne viaut faire le[31] sairement dessus[32] dit, celui qui la chose li presta doit le sairement faire.[33] Et tant con il jurera que sa[34] chose valoit, celui a qui il la presta li est tenus dou[35] rendre, et

---

A: fol. lxxii^{r-v} cap. 119; **B:** fol. 100^{r-v} cap. 119; **C:** fols 94^{v}–95^{r} cap. 105; **O:** fols 118^{v}–119^{r}; **V:** fols xcvii^{r}–xcviii^{r} cap. 121; Beugnot, pp. 193–4, cap. 119.

---

[1] il] C lacks [2] ou ele est . . . autrement] A: celui a qui elle a esté prestee [3] rendre] V: rende [4] jura] BV: avra juré [5] et rendre au . . . valoit] A lacks [6] faute] B: defaute [7] a] B: avra [8] vaut ce qu'ele] B: ele [9] Et ce doit . . . prestee] A lacks [10] est] V: a esté [11] par l'assise] A lacks [12] se] AB lack [13] en prest] AV: a emprest [14] A adds: ja; B: mie [15] a home se il n'entent] V: se ne seit a houme que entent [16] en] C: a; V lacks [17] presta] A: preste [18] conoissoit] C: conoisse [19] est doné] A: encores a esté doné; V: done [20] peut] B: puisse [21] qu'il] C: qui [22] A adds: ou de tant come elle est empiriee [23] et que se] A: Que se; C: et que [24] fust] B lacks [25] li] A: la chose [26] il se] A: il s'en; C: se il [27] V adds: et destraindre [28] B adds: dire et [29] B adds: tant [30] l'on a la chose prestee] A: a esté prestee la chose; BV: la chose a esté prestee [31] V adds: dit [32] dessus] B: devant [33] V adds: dessus dite [34] sa] AV: la [35] dou] ABV: de

le seignor li doit faire rendre[36] come dete coneue en cort. Et par les raisons avant dites est doné par l'assise[37] premier[38] le[39] sairement de la chose prestee et perdue[40] ou enpiree a celui a qui ele a esté prestee,[41] et se celui[42] de qui le sairement est[43] premier ne le viaut faire et le laisse faire a l'autre et il i a damage tel[44] soit de lui que nul ne le doit par raison[45] plaindre.[46]

[36] doit faire rendre] B: est tenuz de faire a l'autre tendre [37] par l'assise] A lacks [38] premier] B lacks [39] le] C: au [40] et perdue] A: qui a esté perdue coment que ce seit; B: perdue; V: ou perdue [41] prestee] V: emprestee [42] a qui ele . . . celui] B lacks [43] est] A: a esté [44] tel] B: tout [45] par raison] A lacks [46] plaindre] B: preindre

***[107]** Quant l'on dit a home qu'il est son plege et il le noie, que celui vers qui l'on est plege doit faire.[1]

Se celui qu'on dit qui est son plege nee en cort la plegerie, il covient que celui qui la li met sus li preuve par .ii. loiaus garans de la loy de Rome qui jurent[2] sur sains que celui est son plege si con il dit, et qu'il oirent a[3] tel reconoistre a tel, et les[4] noment, qui estoit present qu'il[5] estoit son plege de tel chose, et dient de quei. Et se il dient que la plegerie est de plus d'un marc d'argent[6] et celui qu'il[7] dient qu'il[8] est plege si con est avant dit et il[9] en viaut l'un lever et torner par guage de bataillle, il le[10] peut faire, et i avra bataille. Et[11] il[12] est bien droit, se me senble, qu'il i ait bataille en cest cas par les raisons avant dites[13] en cest livre. Et c'il en[14] est ataint par bataille ou sans bataille, il covient qu'il face que[15] plege, et celui de qui il est plege ne li est pas tenus de rendre ne amender le damage[16] qu'il en recevra[17] puis qu'il a la plegerie neee. Et qui[18] par bataille en est ataint, il doit soufrir la poine qui est desus devisee[19] que ceaus qui perdent[20] querele de plus d'un marc d'argent[21] par bataille doivent soufrir.[a] Et se celui qui nee la plegerie contre qui l'on la viaut prover par garans torne l'un des garans et se conbat a lui et il est vencus, l'on fera de lui justise con de chanpion vencu, et des soues chozes seront[22] tant donees a vendre[23] come gage a celui qui li avra prové qu'il estoit son plege qu'il ait en ce de quei il fu son[24] plege, se tant des soues choses pevent estre trovees. Que s'ensi n'estoit, celui qui avroit la plegerie provee contre lui avroit damage en ce que son

A: fols lxxii^{v}–lxxiii^{r} cap. 120; **B:** fols 100^{v}–101^{r} cap. 120; **C:** fol. 95^{r-v} cap. 106; **O:** fols 119^{r}–120^{r}; **V:** fol. xcviii^{r-v} cap. 122; Beugnot, pp. 194–5, cap. 120.

[a] Below cap. 218.

[1] plege doit faire] V: som plege doit faire et dire [2] jurent] C: jure [3] a] AB lack [4] les] C: le [5] qu'il] V: qui [6] de plus d'un marc d'argent] A: d'un marc d'argent ou de plus [7] qu'il] C: qui [8] qu'il] ABV: qui [9] et il] AB lack [10] il le] O lacks [11] le peut faire . . . Et] B lacks [12] il] ABV lack [13] A adds: qui sont [14] c'il en] A: qui en; B: il; C: c'il; V: il en [15] que AB: come; V: coume [16] le damage] A: les damages [17] recevra] A: avreit receus; BV: a receu [18] qui] B: que il; C: que [19] qui est desus devisee] V: dessus dite [20] perdent] B: pardesus [21] de plus d'un marc d'argent] A: d'un marc d'argent ou de plus [22] seront] A: seient; BV: soient [23] tant donees a vendre] B: vendues [24] il fu son] AB il li fu; V: il li avra prové qui li fu

chanpion avroit la bataille vencue qu'il perdroit ce qu'il avroit[25] de quei celui li seroit plege. Que l'on ne peut de plegerie[26] riens demander a home[27] de plege en autre cas qu'en cestui.[28] Et par .i. autre raison me senble il que ce soit droit, qu'il est assise ou usage[29] que qui se conbat por[30] querele et il ou son chanpion venquent[31] la bataille, qu'il a cele querele guaaignee. Si me senble bien raison qu'il doive enssi estre con je ai devant dit, quant tel cas avient.[32]

[25] qu'il perdroit ce qu'il avroit] A: et il perdreit ce que il avreit prové [26] plegerie] O: plege [27] home] AV: heir; B: hoir [28] qu'en cestui] V: que cestui cas [29] A adds: ou reiaume de Jerusalem [30] A adds: aucune [31] venquent] AV: venque; B: vainc [32] avient] V: vient

***[108]** Quant .i. home[1] dit a[2] autre que il est son plege, et celui dit que il n'est mie menbrant.

Se .i. home dit a .i. autre: 'Vos estes mon plege por tel', et le nome, 'de tel chose', et die de quei, et celui li dit:[3] 'Je ne suis pas[4] menbrant que je soie vostre plege. Faites m'en[5] menbrant si con vos devés, et je ferai vers vos ce que je devrai', celui li doit dire ou ce fu et[6] devant qui ce fu et de tant[7] d'autres raisons com[8] il porra a faire le menbrant.[9] Et se il por tant con il li dira dit qu'il n'est[10] menbrant, il se doit clamer au seignor, et le seignor le doit mander querre et comander li qu'il li face que plege de ce de quei il li est plege.[11] Et s'il dit: 'Je ne suis mie menbrant que je soie son plege, mais se il me viaut faire[12] menbrant si con il doit, je li ferai[13] ce que je devrai', celui qui dit qu'il est son plege[14] doit dire lors: 'Et je suis prest que je le[15] face menbrant, si con la cort[16] conoistra, que je faire le doie.' Et la court doit conoistre[17] qu'il le[18] doit faire[19] menbrant[20] par recort de court, se il l'a, et se il n'a recort de cort par .ii. loiaus garans de la loi de Rome. Et se il le fait menbrant par recort de court, la plegerie est bien provee. Et se il le fait menbrant par .ii. loiaus garans[21] et la querele est d'un marc d'argent ou de plus, celui qui[22] dit qui li doit la dete de quei il[23] dit que l'autre li est plege peut l'un des garans[24] torner par guage de bataille. Et por ce le doit celui faire en cest cas, et non le plege, que le damage seroit sien, se la garantie estoit portee[25] tout outre contre celui que l'on dit qui l'a plegé, et il covendroit qu'il amendast le damage[26] dou plege qui seroit vendu por lui, que aprés ce que la plegerie

---

A: fols lxxiii^{r}–lxxiv^{v} cap. 121; **B:** fols 101^{r}–102^{v} cap. 121; **C:** fols 95^{v}–97^{r} cap. 107; **O:** fols 120^{r}–122^{v}; **V:** fols xcviii^{v}–c^{r} caps 123–4; Beugnot, pp. 195–7, cap. 121.

---

[1] .i. home] A: on; B (fol. 21^{r}): home; V: houme [2] C adds: .i. [3] celui li dit] AB: celui respont; V: se il respont [4] ne suis pas] A: ne sui mie; B: n'en sui mie; V: n'en sui pas [5] m'en] OV: me [6] et] BV: ou [7] de tant] A: tant; B: ce; V: acés [8] raisons com] A: enseignes come; BV: enseignes que [9] le menbrant] V: loyaument remembrant [10] dit qu'il n'est] A: ne dit que il est [11] de ce de . . . plege] A lacks [12] viaut faire] AV: fait [13] li ferai] A: ferais vers lui [14] Et s'il dit . . . plege] B: il [15] le] AV: l'en; BO: li [16] A adds: esgardera ou [17] conoistre] A: esgarder ou conoistre se cuit [18] menbrant, si con . . . le] B: ce que je devrai, se il me fait menbrant.' Celui que il dit qui est son plege doit dire lors: 'Et je sui prest que je l'en [19] doit faire] AB: face [20] si con la . . . menbrant] V lacks [21] A adds: de la lei de Rome [22] qui] B: qui il; V: qu'il [23] dit qui li . . . il] A: deit la dette a celui qui [24] V adds: lever et [25] portee] ABV: provee [26] damage] B: gage; V: guage

seroit[27] provee, si con est avant dit, il ne poroit metre contens ne debat en la plegerie puis qu'il seroit prové si con est avant dit[28] qu'il fust son plege. Et il senble bien[29] raison qu'ensi doie estre, que se ensi n'estoit, que celui qu'on dit qui est detour[30] ne[31] peust torner le garant en cestui cas,[32] trop de maus se poroient faire, et en poroit l'on maliner en moult de manieres, mais qu'il eust .ii. homes de la loy de Rome qui se voreent[33] parjurer[34] de quei moult de maus poroient venir,[35] que l'on poroit qui que[36] l'on vodroit[37] legierement destruire. Que se .i. home eust[38] .ii. faus garans de la loy de Rome, de quei l'on troveroit assés por monoie, et deist a aucun autre: 'Vos estes mon plege de tel home', et le nomast, 'de tant de monoie', et deist de si grant cantité con il vodroit, et l'autre respondist: 'Je ne suis pas[39] menbrant. Faites me[40] menbrant.[41] Je ferai[42] vers vos ce que je devrai', et l'autre se clamast de lui, et il deist ce meimes en la court, et l'autre l'ofrist a prover si con la court esgarderoit ou conoistroit,[43] et la cort esgardast ou coneust qu'il le deust prover par recort de cort ou par .ii.[44] loiaus garans de la loi de Rome, et celui qu'il diroit[45] qui li doit[46] la dete ne[47] peust torner l'un des garans[48] par guage de bataille ne dire[49] contre aucun des garans por ce qu'il le rebutast de cele guarantie,[50] l'on poroit destruire qui que l'on vodroit, et avoir dou sien tant con l'on[51] diroit que celui sur qui l'on metroit la plegerie seroit son plege, de quei moult de maus vendroient[52] et seroit[53] tort[54] apert et grant[55] pechié. Por quei[56] il est droit et raison,[57] se me senble, qu'ensi doit estre con je ai dit[58] en cest chapitle[59] quant plegerie vient en tel cas.[a]

---

[a] V begins a new chapter here with the rubric: Coument le plege doit faire venir celui de qui l'on dit pour qui il est plege pour savoir se il vodra riens dire contre les guarens.

---

[27] vendu por lui . . . seroit] AB lack [28] il ne poroit . . . dit] ABV lack [29] il senble bien] A: ce me semble [30] detour] B: dette [31] ne] V lacks [32] A adds: ne dire a l'encontre par quei il le rebutast de la garantie porter [33] voreent] A: vosicent; BV: vosissent [34] parjurer] A: esparjurer [35] venir] ABV: avenir [36] qui que] B: que qui [37] vodroit] A: vodreit par ce; C: voroit [38] eust] B: avoit [39] ne suis pas] B: n'en suis mie [40] me] A: m'ent; B: m'en; O lacks [41] AV add: et [42] C adds: volentiers [43] A adds: qu'il prover le deust [44] .ii.] V lacks [45] diroit] C: diront [46] C adds: la monoie ou [47] ne] B: en [48] des garans] BV lack [49] dire] B: die [50] por ce qu'il . . . guarantie] A: chose par quei il le rebutast de celle garentie porter [51] l'on] B: l'on voudroit et; O: il en; V: il [52] vendroient] C: avendroient; V: verroient [53] seroit] OV: seroient [54] tort] B: trop [55] grant] A lacks [56] quei] O lacks [57] et raison] V lacks [58] con je ai dit] A lacks [59] cest chapitle] B: ceste capistre; V: ce chapitre

Et quant l'on oferra[60] a faire menbrant le plege en la maniere avant dite, il doit dire au seignor:[61] 'Sire, faites venir devant vos celui de qui cestui dit que je sui son plege. Si orra[62] parler les garans par quei[63] cestui me viaut faire menbrant que je suis son plege saver se il vodra[64] riens dire a l'encontre, por ce que le damage en[65] seroit sien, se je damage i avoie.'[66] Et le seignor li doit mander dire[67] qu'il veigne a cort oir cele garantie, et faire li dire le jor et l'ore que les guarans li doivent porter cele guarantie, et dire li coment celui qui[68] dit que l'autre est son plege[69] a ofert a faire l'avant dit[70] menbrant qu'il est son plege por lui, et dire[71] de quei et de conbien il dit que celui est son plege por lui[72] por ce que se il viaut estre a cel jor en la cort, qu'il i puisse estre et dire contre les[73] garans se il viaut. Et se il i[74] vient et il aportent la garantie,[75] il en peut[76] l'un[77] torner par les raisons avant dites.[78] Et se il ne vient en[79] la court au jor oir ce[80] que le seignor li avra fait savoir[81] que cele garantie doit estre portee[82] ou il ne contremande s'esoigne si con il doit,[83] les guarans doivent porter la garantie, et s'il la portent si[84] con il doivent la plegerie est provee, et covendra que le plege face que plege[85] et que[86] l'autre li amende le damage qu'il avroit[87] eu por lui.

Et garde se bien que qui entre en plegerie[88] qu'il sache[89] coment et por quei il i entre. Que se il viaut faire que[90] leal et il est menbrant qu'il est[91] plege si con celui qui li requiert le guage,[92] il li doit faire que plege quelque damage qu'il en doit avenir.[93] Que se il ne le faisoit, il feroit autre que loiauté. Que sovent avient que le prestor[94] ne preste le sien que por la fiance qu'il a en la leiauté dou plege qui li doit faire que plege sans plait et sans riote, que miaus vaut

---

[60] oferra] AV: euffre; B: offre [61] au seignor] C lacks [62] orra] V: oyrai [63] quei] AB: qui; V: que [64] vodra] C: vora [65] en] ABV lack [66] se je damage i avoie] ABV: se damage y aveit (B: avoit; V: avroit) [67] dire] A lacks [68] qui] A: a; BV lack [69] ABV add: et [70] l'avant dit] V: le [71] AO adds: li; V: le [72] et dire de . . . lui] B lacks [73] contre les] V: a l'encontre des [74] i] ABO lack [75] aportent la garantie] AV: portent la garentie (V: guarentie); B: la portent [76] peut] ABV: peut (B: puet) bien; C: pora [77] V adds: des guarens [78] par les raisons avant dites] A: par gage de bataille par les raissons avant dittes et combatre sei a lui [79] vient en] B: venoit a [80] oir ce] AB lack; V: oyr la garentie [81] savoir] V: assavoir [82] A adds: oyr ce que ciaus qui vodront la garentie porter diront et por dire encontre eaus ce il viaut [83] A adds: ce il est essoigniés [84] si] A: tot outre; B: la [85] face que plege] A: face come plege a celui a qui il avra esté plege; C: lacks [86] que] BV lack [87] avroit] ABV: avra [88] garde se bien . . . plegerie V: qui entre en plegerie si se guarde [89] qu'il sache] ABV lack [90] C adds: plege [91] A adds: son [92] A adds: dit [93] qu'il en doit avenir] V: il en doit avoir [94] prestor] B: porteour

au plege sa loiauté et sa verité[95] garder, quelque damage qu'il en doive avoir, que faire chose par quei il soit tenus a autre qu'a[96] leal. Si se doit chascun garder d'entrer en plegerie hors de court, s'il n'i entre por tel home qu'il conoisse a tel qu'il[97] le gardera[98] de damage[99] de la plegerie en quei il est entré[100] por lui. Et qui plege home qu'il ne conoisse[101] a[102] tel com est avant[103] dit, et il y a damage, il est en sa colpe, si ne l'en doit nul plaindre qu'il s'en peut bien garder se il viaut.[104] Et qui preste le sien et il ne viaut avoir autre seurté que plegerie, se il est sage, il recevra la plegerie en la court, por ce qu'on ne li puisse la plegerie neer[105] ne maliner par tornes de bataille ne autrement. Que de chose faite en cort et qui est prové[106] par recort de court ne peut nul dire encontre qui ne viaut la court faucer, et qui la fauce[107] le perill en est si grant, con il est devisé en ce[108] livre, por quei il ne me senble que nul l'osast enprendre a faire.[b] Et qui autrement preste le sien par plegerie et il y a damage, nul ne l'en doit plaindre, car il ne le feroit s'il ne voloit.

---

[b] Above cap. 97.

---

[95] et sa verité] B lacks [96] qu'a] B: que [97] qu'il] AV: qui [98] gardera] B: garde [99] de damage] A lacks [100] est entré] B: entre [101] home qu'il ne conoisse] A: qu'il ne conut a leau [102] a] ABV: ou [103] avant] V: devant [104] viaut] B: vousist [105] neer] B: veer [106] qui est prové] ABV: que on (V: hom) preuve [107] et qui la fauce] O lacks [108] ce] AB: cest; V: cestui

***[109]** Coment l'on doit faire que plege par l'assise ou l'usage dou reiaume de Jerusalem.

Se .i. home est plege d'aucun vers .i. autre et il li veuille faire que plege par l'assise ou l'usage dou reiaume de Jerusalem, et celui a qui il est plege li demande guage, il li doit doner guage[1] par quinzaine, et celui le doit recevoir, et puis recroire[2] li tant que la quinsaine soit pasee. Et quant la quinzaine sera pasee, si[3] li demande gage, et il li doit doner dou[4] tiers jor, et il le doit prendre et faire le[5] .iii. jors[6] crier come gage au[7] crior establi par seignor ou par visconte, et aprés faire le livrer par lendemain toute jor. Et se celui qui le gage fait vendre le veut recevoir par lendemain tote jor[8] por rendre le a celui de qui il est,[9] il le peut[10] avoir por le pris qu'il avra esté vendu, et ausi le peut faire[11] celui por qui le guage avra[12] esté vendu ou celui de qui le gage est provant[13] ce qu'il avra esté vendu.[14] Mais se lendemain que le gage avra esté livré pase, nul ne le peut puis recovrer, se par la volenté de celui qui l'avra acheté.

Et aprés ce que le premier guage et le segont[15] avra esté crié[16] et vendu et livré, et[17] le terme pase, si con[18] est dit desus, il doit demander gage a celui qui est son[19] plege, et celui[20] li en doit tant doner qu'il soit parpaié de ce de quei il li est[21] plege, et celui les peut[22] tos faire vendre maintenant, l'un aprés l'autre, au criage au[23] dit crior et dire les .iii. mos et livrer puis que le premier gage et le segont[24] est vendu et encoru si con est desus[25] dit.

Et se[26] celui a qui l'on est plege ne veut[27] guage que son plege li doint[28] de[29] .i. besanz ou de plus,[30] que se il[31] le refuse et son plege

---

A: fols lxxiv^{v}–lxxv^{r} cap. 122; **B:** fols 102^{v}–103^{r} cap. 122; **C:** fols 97^{v}–98^{r} cap. 108; **O:** fols 122^{v}–123^{v}; **V:** fols c^{r}–ci^{r} cap. 125; Beugnot, pp. 198–9, cap. 122.

---

[1] il li doit doner guage] O: par quinzaine il li doit doner [2] recroire] AB: racreire; O: racroire; V: racrere [3] si] A: celui [4] dou] ABV: au; O: de [5] le] AB lack; O: le crier [6] le .iii. jors] V: au tiers jour [7] au] A: aveuc le; O: a; V: a .i. [8] Et se celui . . . jor] AB lack [9] de qui il est] A: qui l'a doné a vendre c'il le viaut recovrer et [10] il le peut] B: et il le porra [11] faire] A: aveir; BV lack [12] avra] ABV: a [13] provant] A: receveir le, paiant; BV: recevoir, paiant; O: recovrer, prouvant [14] vendu] V: paié [15] avra esté livré . . . segont] B lacks [16] Mais se lendemain . . . crié] V lacks [17] livré pase, nul . . . et] A: crié et vendu et livré passe, il ne le deit plus recouvrer que il est encoru. Et aprés [18] BO add: il [19] son] V: en son leu [20] qui est son plege, et celui] B lacks [21] O adds: son [22] peut] B: doit [23] l'un aprés l'autre au criage au] A: au criage par le [24] et le segont] ABV lack [25] desus] B: devant [26] se] ABV lack [27] veut] ABV: doit (A: deit) refuser [28] li doint] AV: li done; B: li doinst; C: doit [29] A adds: la value de [30] ou de plus] B: en amont [31] que se il] B: car se il; C: qu'il

li peut prover si con il doit, il ne li est plus[32] tenus de doner li[33] guage, ains li peut des lors en avant refuser par l'assise a doner[34] autre guage, por ce qu'il refusa a prendre le guage qu'il li vost doner par l'assise ou l'usage dou dit reiaume.[35]

Et se aucun crior establi par le seignor ou par visconte vent .i. guage[36] au criage, et il a le gage livré, et aprés en cel jor il vait en l'ostel de celui qui acheta le guage [37]por respiter le et il le treuve et il li[38] dit que le guage est respité et[39] qu'il li[40] rende, il le doit faire. Et se il ne le treuve en son ostel, il le doit dire a sa mainsnee. Et se celui qui a acheté[41] le gage nel viaut rendre, por ce qu'il le jor ne li dist, por ce ne doit[42] demorer que le crior ne recuevre[43] le gage[44] par l'assise ou l'usage dou reiaume de Jerusalem[45] par[46] .i. tel sairement qu'il ala en son ostel et qu'il ne le trova pas,[47] et qu'il le dist a sa maisnee et[48] qu'il estoit la venus por respiter le guage por[49] celui qui le gage faisoit vendre par son comandement.[50]

[32] plus] ABV: puis [33] li] AB lack [34] doner] C: doné [35] par l'assise a . . . reiaume] A: a doner li autre gage par l'assise ou l'usage dou reiaume de Jerusalem por ce que il refusa a prendre le gage que il li vost doner [36] vent .i. guage] B: veut gager [37] acheta le guage] A: avra le gage acheté [38] il li] AV: li; O: il [39] que le guage est respité et] B lacks [40] et qu'il li] A: a vendre et qu'il le [41] a acheté] B: acheta; V: achete [42] por ce ne doit] A: il ne deit mie por ce [43] recuevre] C: requevre [44] nel viaut rendre . . . gage] V lacks [45] dou reiaume de Jerusalem] B: de cest reaume [46] A adds: ensi qu'il deit faire [47] pas] A: mie; BV lack [48] et] BOV lack [49] por] B: de part [50] por celui qui . . . comandement] A: par le comandement de celui qui le faisseit vendre

***[110]** Quant home[1] demande guage a son plege, et il li[2] dit: 'Faites m'en[3] menbrant que je suis vostre plege',[4] que l'on doit dire et faire.

Qui demande gage a son plege, et le plege li dit: 'Je ne suis pas[5] menbrant que je soie vostre plege.[6] Faites me menbrant que je soie vostre plege, et[7] je lors[8] vos ferai que plege',[9] celui qui[10] requiert le guage li peut dire:[11] 'Donés moi vostre guage, et se je le vent a tort, je le vos rendrai[12] a dreit.' Et celui li doit lors doner le gage. Et se il ne li done, il le peut prendre et dire li: 'Je vos guage come mon plege, et se je vens vostre guage a tort, je le vos amenderai[13] a dreit.' Et lors le plege li doit laisser le guage. Car se il ne[14] le fait et il li[15] rescout son guage, se il[16] peut mostrer si con il doit qu'il est son plege et qu'il li[17] ait son guage rescous a force, il la ataint de force, et qui est ataint de force[18] il est encheu en la merci dou seignor dou cors et de quanqu'il a. Et se aucun prent guage d'autre[19] qu'il[20] die qu'il soit[21] son plege et il le vent et celui de qui est le guage vendu se claime de lui par l'assise de ce qu'il a pris son gage et vendu autrement qu'il ne doit et il n'a prové[22] si con il doit qu'il soit son plege, il li doit rendre le[23] guage cel jor sans enpirement. Et se il ne li rent, celui de qui le guage fu doit jurer[24] que[25] le guage valoit, et le seignor li doit faire rendre a celui qui le gage avra[26] fait vendre tant con[27] celui de qui il[28] fu vodra jurer qu'il valoit sans contredit qu'il i puisse metre ausi con de dete provee ou[29] coneue en court. Et se[30] il ne veut le sairement faire, l'autre doit jurer que[31]

A: fol. lxxv^{r-v} cap. 123; **B:** fol. 103^{r-v} cap. 123; **C:** fol. 98^{r-v} cap. 109; **O:** fols 123^{v}–124^{v}; **V:** fol. ci^{r-v} cap. 126; Beugnot, pp. 199–200, cap. 123.

---

[1] Quant home] V: Qui [2] li] AB (fol. 21r)V lack [3] m'en] C lacks; V: me [4] ABV add: et je (B: ge) le voz (V: vous) donrai [5] li dite: 'Je ne suis pas] B: dit: 'Je n'en sui mie [6] le plege li . . . plege] A: il deu [7] que je soie vostre plege, et] B lacks [8] lors] AB lack [9] que je soie . . . plege] V lacks [10] celui qui] B: et celui qui li [11] A adds: ce il viaut, et mener le par l'autre veie devant devisiee, et se il ne se viaut tenir a l'autre veie dessuz dite, si li die; B: se il veut, et se il ne veut il se puet tenir a l'autre voie desus dit; V: se il veaut et se il ne veaut tenir se a l'autre voie dessus dite [12] rendrai] V: ferai [13] amenderai] A: renderais [14] ne] V lacks [15] fait et il li] C: faisoit et il [16] se il] A: a force et l'autre; B: et il le; V: se il le [17] li] ABV lack [18] et qui est ataint de force] OV lack [19] d'autre] V: d'aucun autre [20] qu'il] BOV: qui [21] soit] B: est; C: soie [22] il n'a prové] A: celui qui le gage a pris ne preuve; BV: il ne preuve [23] le] ABV: son [24] A adds: sur sains [25] que] B: combien [26] avra] A: aveit; BV: avoit [27] con] C: que [28] il] A: le gage [29] ausi con de dete provee ou] B: autressi come de chose provee et [30] se] C lacks [31] que] B: combien; C: quei

le guage valoit qu'il fist vendre et tant paier a celui de qui le guage fu, et atant en est quite. Et se il li rent le guage, et celui de qui il le prist,[32] si con est avant dit, dit[33] qu'il est enpiré, tant con il jurera qu'il a de damage[34] a l'enpirement de son[35] guage, celui qui prist le guage en la dite maniere[36] li rendra[37] si con dete[38] provee.[39] Et se celui de qui le guage fu pris ne viaut faire le dit[40] sairement, celui qui le prist doit jurer que vaut le damage de l'enpirement dou guage et rendre au seignor dou guage[41] en la maniere avant[42] dite. Et celui qui prent guage d'autre qu'il dit qu'il est son plege et le fait vendre fait moult que fos, qu'il en peut[43] estre destruit se l'autre s'en[44] viaut parjurer,[45] por ce qu'en cest cas est doné le sairement a celui de qui le guage[46] a esté vendu, et tant con il jurera que son guage vaudra[47] covendra[48] que l'autre li rende con dete[49] provee en court. Et por ce se doit chascun guarder de ce faire, se il ne[50] peut prover si con il doit que l'autre soit son plege.

[32] Et se il . . . prist] A: ou que il li rent le gage. Et ce celui de qui il prist le gage [33] dit] A: deist; BC lack; V: si dit [34] a de damage] A: y a d'amende [35] a l'enpirement de son] B: en l'enpirement dou [36] dite maniere] V: maniere devant dite [37] li rendra] B lacks [38] A adds: coneue ou [39] AV add: en court [40] dit] V lacks [41] dou guage] V: de la chose [42] avant] BV: devant [43] peut] A: poreit [44] s'en] C: se [45] parjurer] A: esparjurer [46] A adds: esteit qui [47] vaudra] A: valeit; BV: valoit [48] covendra] O lacks [49] dete] A: de dette coneue ou [50] C adds: li en

***[111]** Se[1] gage dou plege[2] est vendu por plegerie, quant il se peut clamer de celui por qu'il[3] est vendu.

Se aucun est plege d'autre, si tost con le premier de ses[4] guages[5] est[6] vendu, il se peut clamer au seignor par l'assise de celui por qui son guage est vendu. Et se il se[7] claime et l'autre le nee, il le doit ofrir a prover si con court esgardera ou conoistra qu'il prover le doie. Et la cort doit esgarder,[8] se croi, que la preuve doit estre tel, que se celui de qui le guage a esté vendu peut prover par recort de court ou par .ii. loiaus guarans de la loy de Rome qu'il le mist en plege[9] de cele[10] plegerie ou qu'il le reconut[11] qu'il l'avoit mis en plege,[12] la plegerie est provee si con ele doit. Mais il peut torner l'un des garans[13] se la querele est d'un marc d'argent ou de plus. Et celui por qui le guage a esté vendu le doit amender. Mais se il li en done[14] gage de sa volenté sans se que il l'en a fait menbrant en la maniere avant devisee, et[15] celui por qui le guage a esté vendu dit au plege: 'Je ne suis pas menbrant que vos fusiés mon plege', l'autre le doit faire menbrant en la maniere desus[16] devisee.[17] Et[18] se il dou tot nee qu'il ne fust[19] son plege, l'autre le doit prover par .ii. loiaus garans de la loy de Rome qui facent[20] que loiaus garans, et se la querele est d'un marc d'argent ou de plus, il[21] en[22] peut l'un torner et y[23] avra bataille. Et se il en est ataint par bataille, il en[24] soufrira la poine qui est devisee la ou il parole des[25] batailles, et y[26]

A: fols lxxv^{v}–lxxvi^{r} cap. 124; **B:** fols 103^{v}–104^{r} cap. 124; **C:** fols 98^{v}–99^{r} cap. 110; **O:** fols 124^{v}–125^{r}; **V:** fols ci^{v}–cii^{r} cap. 127; Beugnot, pp. 200–1, cap. 124.

---

[1] Se] A: Quant [2] plege] B (fol. 21^{r}) V: plegerie [3] qu'il] AB: qui le gage [4] de ses] AB: des [5] A adds: qu'il avra doné [6] est] V: sera [7] se] AB: s'en [8] doit esgarder] A: deit esgarder ou conoistre; B: esgardera [9] qu'il le mist en plege] A: qui facent que leaus garenz que il l'eust plegié [10] plege de cele] V lacks [11] le reconut] A: reconeust; B: recounut; V: l'a couneu [12] plege] V: plegerie [13] Mais il peut . . . garans] A: et celui por qui le gage est vendu le deit amender, mais il peut bien torner l'un des garenz par gage de bataille [14] en done] B: a doné le; V: a doné [15] C adds: se [16] Et celui por qui le guage a esté vendu le doit amender . . . desus] A: ce celui qui dona le gage n'ait dit a l'autre: 'Faites m'ent membrant', et l'autre l'ait fait membrant si come est devant dit. Mais se il li a le gage doné de sa volenté, sanz ce qu'il li ait dit: 'Faites m'ent membrant', ne que l'autre l'en ait fait membrant en la maniere devant [17] et celui por . . . devisee] B lacks [18] devisee. Et] V: dite. Et [19] se il dou . . . fust] A: celui por qui le gage fu vendu nee dou tot que il ne fu [20] facent] B: feissent; V: jurent et facent ce [21] il] C lacks [22] en] O: ne [23] l'un torner et y] A: torner l'un des garenz par gage de bataille et il [24] en] O: ne [25] des] CV: de [26] y] ABV lack

amendera le guage[27] en la maniere desus dite. Et il est bien[28] raison, ce me senble, qu'ensi doit estre, que se ensi ne fust[29] l'on en poroit trop[30] maligner et faire d'engins et de maus[31] a la gent. Et se il torne le garant et se conbate a lui et est vencu, il sera de lui fait[32] come d'ome vencu en chanp, et le senblant de la raison por quei il doit estre ensi est[33] devant escrit.

[27] le guage] O: les gages [28] bien] B lacks [29] ne fust] A: n'esteit [30] trop] B lacks [31] d'engins et de maus] AB: de granz damages; V: de grant damage [32] est vencu, il . . . fait] A: le garent est vencu il sera ataint de fauceté et fait de lui [33] A adds: si come est

***[112]** De qui est le sairement de la valor[1] do guage qui est[2] vendu por plegerie.

Quant aucun[3] est plege d'un autre[4] et il done guage a celui vers qui il est plege[5] et celui[6] gage est vendu, celui de qui il est plege et[7] por qui son guage est vendu li doit rendre tant con son gage valoit. Et en cest cas cuit je[8] que le sairement est[9] premier de celui por qui le guage a esté vendu, ne il ne peut mains jurer que tant con le gage a esté[10] vendu. Et se il jure qu'il valoit plus, il doit dire conbien et rendre le a celui de qui le guage a esté vendu. Et se il ne viaut le sairement faire, tant con l'autre jurera que son guage valoit, il li doit rendre si com est devant[11] dit.

A: fol. lxxvi^{r} cap. 125; **B:** fol. 104^{r} cap. 125; **C:** fol. 99^{r} cap. 111; **O:** fol. 125^{r-v}; **V:** fol. cii^{r-v} cap. 128; Beugnot, p. 201, cap. 125.

---

[1] valor] AB (fol. 21^{r}) V: value [2] est] A: a esté [3] aucun] C lacks [4] d'un autre] ABV: d'autre [5] a celui vers . . . plege] V lacks [6] celui] A: le [7] gage est vendu . . . et] B lacks [8] cuit je] A: covient; B: covient il; V: couvient il [9] est] BV: soit [10] a esté] A: est [11] devant] B: avant

***[113]** Por quei l'ome[1] qui est semons dou servise qu'il doit n'est tenus de faire que plege tant con il est en sa[2] semonce.

Se .i. home est plege por .i. autre et il est semons de par le seignor dou servise qu'il li doit, il n'est pas tenus par l'assise[3] de faire que plege tant con il est en la semonce, por ce que, se il faisoit que plege et il donoit a vendre[4] tout ou partie de son harnois de quei il fait[5] le servise au seignor, il ne porroit faire le servise sans harnois au seignor qu'il li doit, et ensi porroit le seignor perdre son servise ou le plege[6] son fié an et jor,[7] se il defailloit[8] do servise de quei[9] il avroit esté semons. Que laquel de ces .ii. choses avenist, ele seroit trop[10] grevable au seignor et au plege. Si est meaus raison que celui vers qui l'on est plege s'en seufre[11] tant qu'il soit revenus de la semonce, que le seignor ne le plege i[12] eucent tel damage[13] con il est devant[14] devizé[15] que il poroient avoir s'ensi estoit.[16]

A: fol. lxxvi^{r-v} cap. 126; **B:** fol. 104^{r-v} cap. 126; **C:** fol. 99^{r-v} cap. 112; **O:** fols 125^{v}–126^{r}; **V:** fol. cii^{v} cap. 129; Beugnot, p. 202, cap. 126.

[1] l'ome] AB (fol. 21^{r}): home; V: houme [2] sa] ABV: la [3] A adds: ou l'usage dou reiaume de Jerusalem [4] donoit a vendre] ABV: devoit (A: deveit) amender [5] fait] C: faisoit [6] plege] A: chevalier [7] C adds: que; V: et [8] defailloit] C: faisoit [9] de quei] ABV: dont [10] trop] B lacks [11] s'en seufre] ABV: se sueffre (B: suffre; V: soffre) de la plegerie [12] i] V: fors tant que il soit revenus de la semonce que le seignor ne le plege [13] tel damage] A: damage si [14] devant] BOV: avant [15] devizé] AV: dit [16] que il poroient avoir s'ensi estoit] B: qu'il porroient avoir se enssi estoit que le pleige feist que plege; C lacks

***[114]** Qui est semons dou servise que il doit, por quei il ne doit amender guage qui ait esté vendu por lui de plegerie tant con il est en la semonce.

Se .i. home qui doit servise au seignor doit amender[1] guage qui ait esté vendu por lui de plegerie et il est semons de son servise, il n'est pas tenus,[2] s'il ne viaut, par l'assise ou l'usage dou dit reiaume[3] d'amender cel[4] guage tant con il est en la semonce, por ce que se[5] il li covendroit[6] son harnois a vendre por le guage amender ou enguager le de quei il deit le servise au seignor[7] ou[8] autre meschief faire par quei il ne peust aler a la semonce por le servise qu'il doit au seignor faire, le seignor perdroit son servise et[9] il seroit deserité de son fié an et jor[10] con de defailli de servize,[11] puis que il ne seroit alé[12] a la semonce de son seignor si con il devroit. Laquel chose ne doit estre par la raison avant dite.[13]

A: fol. lxxvi^{v} cap. 127; **B:** fol. 104^{v} cap. 127; **C:** fol. 99^{v} cap. 113; **O:** fol. 126^{r}; **V:** fols cii^{v}–ciii^{r} cap. 130; Beugnot, pp. 202–3, cap. 127.

---

[1] amender] B: mander [2] C adds: de son servise; V: d'amender [3] dit reiaume] A: reiaume de Jerusalem [4] d'amender cel] V: et amender celui [5] se] ABV lack [6] covendroit] C: covenoit [7] le servise au seignor] BV: au seignor servir [8] por le guage . . . ou] A: ou a engagier de quei il deit au seignor le servise por le gage amender ou aucun [9] et] ABV: ou [10] an et jor] AB: un an et un jor [11] C adds: et [12] alé] BV lack [13] la raison avant dite] B: les raisons devant nommees

***[115]** Quant home est semons de son[1] servise, por quei celui qui est por lui plege ne doit mie faire que plege tant con il est en la semonce.

Se aucun[2] qui doit servise au seignor est semons do servize qu'il li doit et aucun est plege por lui, le plege[3] de celui qui est semons ne doit par l'assise[4] faire[5] que plege tant con celui por qui il est plege est[6] en semonce, por ce que tant con celui qu'il a plege est en[7] semonce[8] il ne li est[9] tenus d'amender guage qui por lui ait esté vendu tant con il sera en la semonce ni rendre[10] damage[11] qu'il ait de cele plegerie eu[12] por lui. Car se il le faisoit, son seignor en porroit son servise perdre et[13] il son fié an et jor.

A: fol. lxxvi^v cap. 128; **B:** fol. 104^v cap. 128; **C:** fols 99^v–100^r cap. 114; **O:** fol. 126^r–v; **V:** fol. ciii^r cap. 132; Beugnot, p. 203, cap. 128.

---

[1] son] V: d'aucun [2] Se aucun] V: Quant home [3] por lui, le plege] C lacks [4] A adds: ou l'usage dou reiaume de Jerusalem [5] V adds: riens [6] por qui il est plege est] B: qui est plege soit [7] celui qu'il a plege est en] ABV: il sera (A: est) en la [8] semonce] C: servise [9] il ne li est] A: il n'est pas; B: il n'est; V: n'est [10] guage qui por . . . rendre] A: a son plege; V lacks [11] ni rendre damage] B: ne de mander damage [12] eu] ABV lack [13] et] AV: ou

***[116]** Coment celui vers qui l'on est plege et dete peut celui qui li est ensi tenus mener[1] par laquel des .ii. voies qu'il viaut.[2][a]

Il[3] avient aucune fois que l'on est plege et dete, et[4] selui a qui l'on est plege et dete[5] peut celui qui ensi li[6] est tenus mener par laquel des .ii. voies[7] qu'il viaut.[8] Se il le viaut mener[9] par cele de la plegerie, il doit faire et dire si com est avant dit de la plegerie. Et se il le viaut[10] mener par la deterie[11] et il li demande guage et celui li done, il le peut faire crier et livrer au tiers jor, qu'il n'a en ce point de quinzaine ne plus de terme[12] que le tiers jor, et aprés ce qu'il a celui guage vendu il doit[13] tos les autres guages que cil[14] li donra ou qu'il meimes prendra vendre[15] si con est avant[16] dit de plegerie. Et se il dit qu'il n'est mie menbrant de la plegerie et deterie, il le doit faire menbrant[17] en la maniere desus devizee. Et se il la noie, il la doit prover si con est avant dit de la[18] plegerie.[19] Et se celui qui est plege et dete[20] moroit,[21] celui vers qui il est tenus peut par la raison[22] de la deterie demander et requerre[23] a celui de ces heirs qui herite en ces biens ce qui li[24] defaut de ce que l'ancestre de lui[25] li estoit tenus

---

A: fol. lxxvii^{r-v} cap. 130; **B:** fols 104^{v}–105^{v} caps 129–30; **C:** fol. 100^{r} cap. 115; **O:** fols 126^{v}–127^{r}; **V:** fol. ciii^{r-v} cap. 133; Beugnot, pp. 204–5, caps 129–30 (and see note a).

---

[a] B gives this chapter twice (numbered 129 and 130 in the MS) with minor variations. In the apparatus the second version is designated B'. A has both a shortened version of this chapter as cap. 129 (see appendix 4.2) and then the version (cap. 130) collated here. Beugnot edited A cap. 129 with variants from B cap. 129, C and the MSS derived from V as his cap. 129 and then edited his chapter 130 from A and B caps 130.

---

[1] li est ensi tenus mener] V: est enci tenus [2] laquel des .ii. voies qu'il viaut] AV: laquel des deus voies que il vodra tenir; B (fol. 21^{r}): l'une des .ii. voies; B': laquele des .ii. voies que il voudra [3] Il] AB': Se il [4] aucune fois que . . . et] A: que aucun seit a autre plege et dette [5] et selui a . . . dete] O lacks [6] li] C lacks [7] voies] A: manieres de voie; B: manieres; V: choses [8] viaut] A: vodra. Et; B: veaut. Et [9] viaut mener] B moine [10] Se il le viaut . . . viaut] V lacks [11] deterie] BB': dette (here and elsewhere throughout this chapter) [12] plus de terme] V: de plus termine [13] il doit] A: vendera il; BB'V: vendra il [14] cil] AB: celui [15] vendre] ABB': vendra (A: vendera) il; V: vendra [16] avant] A: devant [17] menbrant] B': remenbrant [18] de la] A: que on deit faire preuve de [19] Et se il dit . . . plegerie] BV lack [20] et dete] BB'OV: de ce [21] moroit] AB': muert; BV: meurt [22] par la raison] A lacks [23] requerre] C: requerir [24] ce qui li] B: de celui qui est plege et dette ce qui li en [25] lui] A: l'heir; BB': l'oir; V: l'eir

por la raison de la deterie. Car les heirs qui abitent[26] as biens de celui qui estoit[27] plege et dete sont[28] tenus par la rayson de la deterie[29] de respondre li et[30] paier come l'autre[31] dete.[32] Car[33] il ne sont[34] tenus de respondre li ent ne faire que[35] plege por lor ancestre de plegerie. Et por ces raisons fait meillor[36] recevoir plege et[37] dete[38] que plege sans plus.

---

[26] les heirs qui abitent] A: l'eir qui irrite [27] estoit] ABB'V: est [28] sont] A: est [29] Car les heirs . . . deterie] C lacks [30] li et] AV: li ent et; B: l'en; B': et [31] l'autre] B lacks [32] A adds: Et ce celui qui est plege sans plus muert, ces heirs ne responderont neent a celui de qui leur ancestre esteit plege. [33] Car] B: Et; B': Mais [34] AV adds: pas; BB': mie [35] ent ne faire que] B: ne faire que; B': ne faire li come; V: ent ne faire li ent que [36] meillor] V: il meaus [37] et] CO lack [38] recevoir plege et dete] A: prendre plege et dette et plus fort est

***[117]** Quel est l'assise de la choze maladiree,[1] et coment l'on se doit clamer.[2]

Qui se viaut clamer par l'assise de chose qui a esté maladiree,[3] ce est qu'il ait[4] perdue, se il treuve cele chose el pooir d'autrui, il la doit[5] arester et faire la aporter[6] ou amener au[7] seignor et dire li: 'Sire, tel choze que je ai perdu[8] je l'ai trovee o tel. Faites la garder tant que droit en soit coneu entre moi et lui.' Et s'il ne la peut arester, il doit dire a celui qui la choze a devant guarans[9] qui li puissent la[10] guarantie porter se mestier li est: 'Tel choze que vos avés est moie, et je la perdi. Si vos pri que vos la me rendés.'[11] Et se il ne li rent, il li doit dire: 'Donc vos defent[12] je de par le seignor que vos ceste choze qui moie est', et die quei, 'ne partés de vostre[13] pooir tant que droit en soit coneu entre moy et vos. Et de ceste defence que je vos fais, trais je a guarant ces prodes homes qui sont ci.' Et aprés doit venir devant le seignor et dire li: 'Sire, tel', et le nome, 'a tel chose qui est moie que je perdi. Et je l'ai[14] requise, et il ne[15] la me viaut rendre. Si me clain a vos de lui[16] par l'assise, et en[17] eufre a fornir l'assise,[18] et vos pri et requier que vos me faites droit par l'assise.' Et lors[19] le seignor le doit mander querre et dire li: 'Tel', et le nome, 'm'a dit que vos avés[20] tel chose qui est soue qu'il perdi. Rendés la et faites la me[21] venir en mon pooir tant que droit en soit coneu[22] entre vos .ii.'[23] Et se il conoist[24] qu'il l'a, il la doit faire venir el pooir del[25] seignor, et le seignor la doit faire garder tant que droit en soit coneu des[26] .ii. dou quel ele doit[27] estre. Et quant il[28] sera coneu, il la doit rendre a celui de qui ele sera. Et le

---

A: fols lxxvii^{v}–lxxviii^{r} cap. 131; **B:** fols 105^{v}–106^{r} cap. 131; **C:** fols 100^{r}–101^{r} cap. 116; **O:** fols 127^{r}–128^{r}; **V:** fols ciii^{v}–civ^{v} cap. 134; Beugnot, pp. 205–6, cap. 131.

---

[1] maladiree] A: malatiree; B (fol. 21^{r}): qui est perdue; V: malatiree et est de prest perdu [2] V adds: par l'assise [3] qui a esté maladiree] V: que il a presté et li a esté malatiree [4] qui a esté . . . ait] A: qui li ait esté malatiree, ce est qu'il l'ait; B: que il a [5] d'autrui, il la doit] ABV: d'autre, et il la peut (B: puet) [6] faire la aporter] A: il la fait aporter; V: il la fait porter [7] au] A: devant le; BV: maintenant devant le [8] ai perdu] A: perdis; BV: perdi; O: perdue [9] guarans] A: genz [10] la] AB lack [11] vos la me rendés] B: le me gardez [12] defent] OV: deffens [13] vostre] C: nostre [14] l'ai] AV: li ais [15] ne] A lacks [16] de lui] AB lack [17] en] BV lack [18] et en eufre a fornir l'assise] A lacks [19] lors] ABV lack [20] avés] C lacks [21] la et faites la me] ABV: li ou faites la; C: la me et faites la me [22] droit en soit coneu] A: raisson en seit coneue [23] .ii.] A: et lui; B: et deus [24] conoist] A: conut [25] del] ABV: dou [26] des] V: entre eaus [27] doit] A: devra [28] il] A: dreit en; V: elle

droit en doit estre coneu[29] et l'assise fornie[30] ensi: que celui qui requiert ce qu'il dit que il a perdu[31] doit prover par .ii. loiaus garans de la loi de Rome qui jurent sur les saintes evangiles[32] qu'il li[33] virent de cele choze qu'il requiert saisi et tenant con dou sien. Et il[34] doit aprés jurer qu'il ne l'a donee ne vendue ne prestee ne enguagee ne en aucune maniere alienee par quei il ne la puisse et doive[35] reçoivre[36] par l'assise. Et se il le preuve en la maniere avant[37] dite et il fait le dit sairement, il a l'assise fornie, et cele choze qu'il requiert[38] li doit estre[39] rendue.

Et se celui a qui il a la choze trovee l'a eue d'aucune par[40] d'achat ou autrement, il[41] doit dire de qui il l'ot et coment il l'ot et s'il l'ot en eschange d'aucune autre choze. Et quant celui qui dit qu'il la perdi l'a recovré par l'assise, celui de qui il l'a recovré doit recovrer par l'assise ce que cele choze li costa de celui de qui il l'ot ou ce que il dona en eschange ou le vaillant. Que[42] se autrement estoit, ce seroit tort apert. Et se celui de qui il ot cele choze le noie, l'autre le doit prover par .ii. loiaus garans de la loi de Rome,[43] et celui en peut l'un torner[44] par gage de bataille se la chose vaut .i. marc d'argent ou plus. Que se autrement estoit, ce seroit contre droit et raison por ce qu'on[45] porroit faire mot de maus. Et[46] se il preuve par guarans ou autrement, si con il doit, qu'il ot cele choze de lui en achat ou por aucune autre choze,[47] celui de qui il l'avra eue li doit rendre ce qu'il avra eu de lui por cele choze ou le vaillant.

---

[29] il la doit . . . coneu] B lacks [30] fornie] C: fornir [31] ce qu'il dit . . . perdu] A: la chose deit mostrer si come il deit que il a perdue celle chose et; B lacks [32] les saintes evangiles] AB: sains [33] li] ABV: le [34] C adds: li [35] doive] V: doie avoir et [36] reçoivre] A: recouvrer; BV: recevoir; O: recovrer [37] avant] B: devant [38] requiert] O: requerroit [39] B adds: livree et [40] d'aucune par] A lacks; BV: d'autre part; C: d'aucune part [41] C adds: le [42] le vaillant Que] B: la value. Et [43] A adds: qui facent que leaus garenz [44] celui en peut l'un torner] A: l'un en peut torner l'autre; B: il en puet lever l'un; V: l'un em peut lever l'autre et tourner [45] ce qu'on] A: quei on; B: quoi l'en; V: quoi hom [46] Et] C: Que [47] por aucune autre choze] A: autrement; BV: par aucune autre maniere

***[118]** Quel est l'assise[1] qui achete esclaf ou esclave mezel ou mezele ou qui chiet do mauvais mal.

Qui se viaut clamer par l'assise d'esclaf ou d'esclave qu'il ait acheté[2] qui soit mezel[3] ou qu'il[4] chet dou[5] mauvais mal, il doit venir devant le seignor en sa court dedens l'an et le jor que il l'avra acheté ou achetee[6] et dire au seignor:[7] 'Sire, je achetai de tel', et le nome, '.i. esclaf ou une esclave', et die lequel, 'et il[8] est malade de tel maladie',[9] et die de laquel des dites maladies il est malade, 'si veuill[10] recovrer par l'assise ma monoie et rendre li son esclaf ou s'esclave. Et je en[11] eufre a fornir l'assise.' Et lors le seignor doit mander querre celui de quei[12] il dit que il l'acheta[13] et dire li: 'Tel', et le nome,[14] 'm'a dit que il acheta de vos .i. esclaf ou une esclave', et die lequel, 'et dit que il est malade de tel maladie', et die de quel.[15] 'Si[16] en[17] eufre a fornir l'assise. Et se vos volés receivre l'esclaf ou l'esclave et rendre li sa monoie, il est prest de faire le. Et se vos recevre ne le volés, je li comant de fornir l'assise,[18] et a vos comant je[19] quant il l'avra fornie[20] que vos li rendés sa monoie et reprenés[21] vostre esclaf ou vostre esclave.' Et l'assise doit estre ensi fornie que celui qui l'eufre[22] a fornir doit amener[23] .ii. loiaus garans de la nacion de quei celui est[24] contre qui il viaut ce qui est avant dit prover qui jurent sur sains que l'esclaf ou l'esclave que celui eufre a rendre est mezel[25] ou qu'il l'ait veu chair[26] dou mauvais mal. Et aprés ce[27] que[28] celui

---

A: fol. lxxviii^{r-v} cap. 132; **B:** fol. 106^{r-v} cap. 132; **C:** fol. 101^{r-v} cap. 117; **O:** fols 128^{r}–129^{r}; **V:** fols civ^{v}–cv^{r} cap. 135; Beugnot, p. 207, cap. 132.

---

[1] C adds: de [2] ait acheté] B: achete; C: ait [3] A adds: ou meselle; B: ou mesele; V: ou mezele [4] qu'il] ABO: qui [5] chet de] B: a chasie de [6] ou achetee] O lacks [7] A adds: ou faire dire [8] et il] A: qui; V: et il ou elle [9] et die lequel . . . maladie] B lacks [10] des dites maladies . . . veuill] V: maladie il est malade, 'si veull je avoir et [11] en] A: de ce en; C lacks [12] quei] AB: qui; V: que [13] l'acheta] A: acheta l'esclaf ou l'esclave; O: l'achate [14] et le nome] A lacks [15] et dit que . . . quel] B lacks [16] de quel, 'si] A: laquel, 'si; V: laquelle, 'si [17] en] C lacks [18] de fornir l'assise] AV: que il fornisse (V: fornist) l'assise; B: qu'il offre l'assise et fornisse [19] a vos comant je] A: si voz comans que [20] l'avra fornie] A: avra l'assise fornie; B: avra fornie; V: avra fornie l'assise [21] reprenés] C: repernés [22] ensi fornie que celui qui l'eufre] V: tel et enci fornie que celui qui l'euffre a prover et [23] amener] C lacks [24] quei celui est] B: belui [25] A adds: ou meselle; B: ou mesele; V: ou mezele [26] l'ait veu chair] A: l'aient veu cheir; B: l'ont cheoir [27] ce] C lacks [28] que] A: que ces avront fait le dit seirement; B lacks

qui requiert sa monoie doit jurer qu'il n'a chose faite a cel esclaf ou a cele esclave par quei il ou ele ait acuilli cele maladie.[29] Et a tant est l'assise fornie, si doit celui recovrer sa monoie, et l'autre l'esclaf ou l'esclave.

[29] ait acuilli cele maladie] A: tel maladie deie acuillir; V: ont celle maladie doie acuillir

***[119]** Ques est l'assise de dete de quei l'on n'a[1] guage ne plege ne garans.

Se aucun se viaut clamer par l'assise en la haute court[2] de dete de monoie qu'il dit qu'il[3] li doit de quei il dit qu'il n'a ne plege ne guage[4] ne guarans, il doit dire au seignor en sa court: 'Sire, je me clains a vos par l'assise de tel qui me doit tant de monoie', et die conbien il li doit et de quel monoie, 'et vos pri et requier, sire, que vos me faites[5] droit[6] par l'assise.'[7] Et lors le seignor deit mander querre celui de qui l'on ensi se claime et dire li[8] en la presence de la court et do clamant: 'Tel se claime de vos par l'assise[9] que vos li devés tant de tel monoie', et die[10] la quantité et motisse la monoie. 'Si vos comant que vos la li paiés, se vos li devés, et, se vos ne li devés, que vos en fornisés l'assise.' Et celui doit la dete conoistre ou neer, et se il la conoist il la doit paier dedens .vii.[11] jors. Et se il la noie, il doit lors jurer[12] sur sains que il cele dete de quei celui c'est clamés de lui ne li doit. Et se il le jure, il en est quite, que il a l'assise fornie. Et se il le sairement ne[13] viaut faire et il le viaut doner au clamant, le clamant doit jurer sur sains que il li doit cele dete de quei il c'est de lui clamé, et ce faisant le seignor la li[14] doit faire paier come dete coneue[15] en court.

A: fol. lxxviii[v] cap. 133; **B:** fol. 106[v] cap. 133; **C:** fol. 101[v] cap. 118; **O:** fol. 129[r–v]; **V:** fol. cv[r–v] cap. 136; Beugnot, p. 208, cap. 133.

---

[1] n'a] AB (fol. 21[r]): n'a ne; V: n'en a [2] A adds: d'aucun autre [3] dit qu'il] B: die que aucun [4] ne plege ne guage] A: gage ne plege; B: gages ne pleges; O: ne pleges ne gages; V: pleges [5] faites] C: facés [6] droit] O: doner [7] qui me doit . . . l'assise] B: et le nomme [8] A adds: quant il sera venus [9] A adds: et m'a dit [10] die] C: dit [11] .vii.] O: .viii. [12] doit la dete . . . jurer] A: maintenant sanz aveir jor au claim deit fornir l'assise ou paier le. Et l'assise deit estre ensi fornie qu'il deit jurer; BV: doit jurer [13] ne] A lacks [14] la li] ABV: le [15] A adds: ou provee

***[120]** A qui[1] sodeer se doit clamer de son seignor de ce que il li doit de ses sodees, et quel assise est[2] de ce.

Se chevalier ou sergent d'armes ou autre qui ait esté sodeer se viaut clamer de son seignor ou de sa dame de ce que l'on li doit de sa deserte de ses sodees, il s'en[3] doit clamer au conestable et[4] par l'assise, et dire conbien celui li doit de qui il se claime et nomer le. Et quant il c'est enssi clamé, le conestable doit[a] mander querre celui ou cele de qui l'on c'est[5] clamé et dire li: 'Tel', et le nome, 's'est a moi clamé de vos et par l'assise, et m'a dit que vos li devés tant de sa desserte', et dire[6] conbien, 'et[7] si vos comans que vos li paiés ce que vos li devés[8] sans delai.' Et se il dit que il ne li cuide riens dever, le conestable li doit maintenant dire: 'Paiés li la dette[9] que vos li devés, ou vos fornissiés l'assise.'[10] Et se il ne fait l'une des .ii.[11] choses, le conestable doit faire[12] prendre tant do sien[13] et[14] vendre que celui qui requiert la dette de sa desserte soit paié de ce que il requiert. Et se il noie la dette, die le conestable: 'Fornissiés ent l'assise.'[15] Et qui l'assise[16] viaut de ce[17] fornir, il doit jurer que il a celui qui la dette li requiert ne doit riens de sa desserte. Et se il li doit aucune chose[18] de sa deserte de quoi il s'est clamé, die: 'Je ne li doi que tant', et die conbien et le jure. Si a l'assise fornie quant[19] en ce cas. Et de ce que il a neé par son sairement, est il quite. Et se il aucune chose en conoist, l'on ne li puet riens demander que[20] tant com il conoist[21] par son seirement que il li doit. Et se il ne viaut l'assise fornir faisant le dit sairement et il done le sairement au sodoier, le sodoier[22] doit fornir l'assise ensi qu'il jure conbien son seignor li doit de sa desserte, et tant come il jurera que il li doit le

---

A: fols lxxviii[v]–lxxix[r] cap. 134; **B:** fols 106[v]–107[r] cap. 134; **C:** fols 101[v]–102[r] cap. 119; **O:** fols 129[v]–130[r]; **V:** fols cv[v]–cvi[r] cap. 137; Beugnot, pp. 209–10, cap. 134.

---

[a] Change of hand in C.

---

[1] AB (fol. 21[r]) V add: le [2] quel assise est] A: quels est l'assise; B: quele l'assise en est; V: quelle est l'assise [3] s'en] ABV: se [4] et] BV lack [5] A adds: ensi [6] dire] A: die [7] et] ABV lack [8] AB adds: et [9] li la dette] AV: la dette; B: le de ce [10] A adds: Et il le deit paier ou fornir l'assise. [11] ABV add: dites [12] faire] ABV lack [13] do sien] B: de ses choses [14] A adds: faire [15] A adds: Et il deit fornir l'assise [16] C adds: en [17] de ce] ABV lack [18] aucune chose] V: riens [19] quant] C: et [20] riens demander que] V: que demander fors [21] Et de ce . . . conoist] A: si le deit paier de ce qu'il a juré; B: de ce que il l'a nee [22] ABV add: en

conestable li doit maintentant faire paier se celui est parti de lui ou faire tant prendre dou sien et vendre que celui en soit paiés. Et se il est encore[23] a[24] lui et le terme de la paie est passé,[25] le conestable li doit comander[26] que il l'ait paié ou fait paier dedens .vii. jors de ce que il[27] sera coneu ou prové devant lui[28] que il li doit, aussi come de dette coneue ou provee en cort. Et se il ne le paie[29] ou fait paier ou fait[30] son gré et le clamant dit au conestable que le terme des .vii. jors est passé[31] et que il ne l'a paié[32] ne fait paier, le conestable le doit faire paier si com est devant[33] dit.

[23] encore] O: en cort [24] a] ABV: o [25] est passé] V: passe [26] comander] C: mander [27] que il] AV: qui; B: que [28] V adds: et devant court [29] le paie] B: l'a paié [30] paier ou fait] C lacks [31] est passé] O: pase [32] il ne l'a paié] V: se il ne le paie ne [33] devant] ABV: avant

***[121]** Quel est l'assise quant l'on done congié a son sodoier et l'on ne le paie de ce que l'on li deit de ses sodees.

Qui done congié a son sodoier et il ne le paie, et celui dit:[1] 'Je n'acueill pas[2] le congié sans la paie',[3] de tant de tens com il sera sans sos,[4] celui qui li donra[5] congié sans paier li[6] doit paier par l'assise ou l'usage[7] de Jerusalem. Que nul ne doit doner congié a son sodoier que il ne le paie ou fasse paier.[8] Et le conestable le puet de ce destraindre. Mais se le sodoier demande[9] congié et le seignor li done, il n'est pas tenus de paier le que[10] de tant de tens com il l'a servi. Et se le sodoier li requiert[11] de ce sa paie et il ne le paie,[12] il s'en puet clamer au conestable et avoir en droit si com est avant dit.[a]

A: fol. lxxix^{r-v} cap. 135; **B:** fol. 107^{r} cap. 135; **C:** fol. 102^{r-v} cap. 120; **O:** fol. 130^{r-v}; **V:** fol. cvi^{r} cap. 138; Beugnot, pp. 210–11, cap. 135.

[a] Above cap. 120.

[1] et celui dit] A: de ce qu'il li deit de ces sodees, et il li die; O: et celui li dit [2] pas] ABV lack [3] la paie] A: la paie de ce que voz me devés; B: la paga; C: bataille [4] sos] A: sodees [5] donra] ABV: dona [6] paier li] A: paier le de ce qu'il li deveit le; V: la paie li [7] A adds: dou reiaume; B: dou reaume; V: dou royaume [8] que il ne . . . paier] A: se il ne le paie ou face paier de ce qu'il li deit [9] demande] V: prent [10] que] A: fors; B lacks [11] le sodoier li requiert] B: le seignor ne le paie aprés ce que le sodoier li avra requis [12] et il ne le paie] AB lack

***[122]** Quans jors a l'entree[1] dou mois le seignor puet doner congié a son sodoier sans ce qu'il soit tenus de paier le de cel mois.[2] Et quant jors a l'issue le sodoier puet prendre congé sans perdre[3] les sos[4] de cel mois.[5]

Qui done congé a son sodoier dedens le mois .iii. jors, il le doit paier de tout le mois par l'assise ou l'usage dou roiaume de Jerusalem. Et le sodoier qui prent congié de son seignor et il demore dou mois[6] .iii. jors ou plus, il pert sa desserte de cel mois, ne n'en[7] doit estre paiés par l'assise ou l'usage dou dit reiaume.[8]

A: fol. lxxix^{v} cap. 136; **B:** fol. 107^{v} cap. 136; **C:** fol. 102^{v} cap. 121; **O:** fol. 130^{v}; **V:** fol. cvi^{r-v} cap. 139; Beugnot, p. 211, cap. 136.

---

[1] l'entree] C: l'entrant [2] sans ce qu'il . . . mois] A rubric (fol. 4^{r}) lacks [3] perdre] C: prendre [4] sos] B (fol. 21^{v}): soudees [5] perdre les sos de cel mois] A rubric: ce que l'un ne l'autre y ait damage [6] V adds: a parfaire [7] n'en] AOV: ne [8] dit reiaume] B: reaume de Jerusalem

***[123]** Por quex choses le sodoier qui est a foi et a fiance a son seignor et a terme nomé s'en[1] puet partir de lui dedens le[2] terme sans sa foi mentir.[3]

Quant aucun home, chevalier ou autre, demore a seignor a foi ou[4] a fiance a terme moti, il ne s'en[5] puet devant[6] le terme[7] partir dou servise de son[8] seignor, se ce n'est por les choses dessous devisees.[9] Ce est: s'il est pelerin et il s'en viaut aler en son pays, il le puet faire sans mesprendre; ou se il a voé d'aler en pelerinage es parties d'outremer et il y vait; ou se fié li est escheu que il aille requerre hors dou pays; ou se fié li est escheu[10] ou pays[11] qui doive[12] servise de son cors; ou se fié li est doné por le servise de son cors;[13] ou se il se marie;[14] ou se il entre en religion; ou se il prent la crois a estre au servise de Nostre Seignor;[15] ou[16] se il vait au[17] servise de la crois en cel pays que[18] son seignor ne vait ne ne veaut que il aille.[19]

Et se il autrement s'en[20] part, il ment sa foi. Et se il en est ataint ou prové, le chevalier ou le sergent d'armes doivent perdre lor hernois de cheval et d'armes et estre bani[21] dou pays, et les autres gens doivent avoir les paumes percees d'un fer chaut. Et les hernois de ceaus qui les perdent por tel mesfait doivent[22] estre dou seignor de cele seignorie en quei ce avra esté.[23] Et des avant dis fois menties qui sont a sos doit[24] estre le plait devant le conestable, et il en doit faire la justise, mais[25] que des escuiers des ques[26] le plait doit estre devant le mareschal, et il en doit faire la justise.

A: fols lxxix^{v}–lxxx^{r} cap. 137; **B:** fol. 107^{v} cap. 137; **C:** fols 102^{v}–103^{r} cap. 122; **O:** fols 130^{v}–131^{r}; **V:** fol. cvi^{v}–cvii^{r} cap. 140; Beugnot, pp. 211–12, cap. 137.

---

[1] s'en] AB (fol. 21^{v}): se [2] A rubric (fol. 4^{r})BV add: dit [3] sans sa foi mentir] AB lack; A rubric: sanz menti sa fei [4] ou] BV: et [5] s'en] ABV: se [6] devant] A: dedens [7] B adds: moti [8] dou servise de son] B: de son; C: dou [9] dessous devisees] A: aprés dittes; BV: aprés devisees [10] que il aille . . . escheu] B lacks [11] requerre hors dou . . . pays] A: hors dou pays [12] qui doive] ABV: de quoi il deit (B: doie; V: doive) [13] ou se fié . . . cors] AO lack [14] ou se il se marie] C lacks [15] A adds: ou sien; V: et au sien [16] ou] C: et [17] servise de Nostre . . . au] B lacks [18] en cel pays que] AB: fors (B: hors) dou pays ou quel [19] que il aille] AB: aler [20] s'en] AO: se [21] le chevalier ou . . . bani] A: c'il est chevalier ou sergent d'armes, il deit perdre son harneis de chevau et d'armeures et deit estre bani fors [22] les hernois de . . . doivent] A: le harneis de ciaus qui le perdent por tel mesfait deit [23] V adds: fait [24] doit] V: doivent [25] mais] V: fors [26] des ques] AB lack

***[124]** Qui fait chose vendre a l'enchantement par autre que par crior establi,[1] por quoi le seignor la puet prendre come[2] soue.

Qui veaut faire vendre aucune chose a l'enchantement, il la doit faire crier par le crior qui est establi par le seignor ou par le visconte, que nul autre ne doit crier chose au criage. Et qui la fait crier par autre,[3] le seignor par l'assise ou l'usage la puet faire prendre come soue, et celui qui la crie est en la merci dou seignor.

Et qui[4] la fait crier par le dit crior establi autrement qu'ele ne doit estre criee, et le seignor, ou celui qui est en son luec, le set, il la puet faire prendre come soue. Et se le crior le sot, il est ataint de faucetė[5] et est en la merci dou seignor de perdre quantque il a et la lengue.[6] Et s'il ne le sot, il ne portera nule poine, et quant il en est achoisonés, il en doit estre creus par son sairement.

A: fol. lxxx^{r} cap. 138; **B:** fol. 108^{r} cap. 138; **C:** fol. 103^{r} cap. 123; **O:** fol. 131^{r-v}; **V:** fol. cvii^{r} cap. 141; Beugnot, pp. 212–13, cap. 138.

[1] establi] B (fol. 21^{v}) lacks [2] C adds: la [3] par autre] B lacks [4] A adds: ne [5] de faucetė] O lacks [6] A adds: aussi

***[125]** Quex est l'assise de beste vendre[1] sans enchantement.

Qui veaut une beste vendre sans enchantement et le vendeor dit au vendre qu'il la vent par l'usage dou pays, et l'acheteor dit: 'Et je l'achat par l'usage dou pays', ou n'i soit ja moti l'usage, celui qui l'achate la puet tenir celui jor qui[2] l'avra achetee et[3] la nuit et lendemain jusques a tierce mais[4] que il ne l'abevre[5] ne face abevrer la matinee, et aprés rendre[6] la[7] se ele ne li siet.[8] Mes se il l'abevre ou[9] tierce est sonee[10] ou chantee a la mere[11] yglise ains que il la rende, il ne la puet plus[12] rendre par l'assise ou l'usage dou dit roiaume,[13] se celui qui la li vendi ne la veaut recevoir,[14] ains covient qu'ele li demore et qu'il paie a celui de qui il[15] l'acheta[16] tant come il l'acheta. Et s'il[17] a contens entreaus dou marche, le coretier ou celui qui fist le marche[18] de la beste en doit estre creu par son sairement. Et se il n'i ot corretier ou[19] home qui fist le marche entreaus[20] et il[21] a guarans, le vendor doit prover a l'acheteor par[22] leiaus guarans de la loi de Rome ce qu'il dit qu'il li vendi, et l'acheteor puet l'un[23] torner par guage de bataille, se le contens est d'un marc d'argent ou de plus. Et se il n'i ot que le vendeor et l'acheteor, l'acheteor doit estre creu par son sairement, por ce que se le vendeor estoit creu par son sairement et il se voloit parjurer, il li porroit metre sus[24] si grant quantité par quei l'acheteor seroit destruit. Car il ne le porroit contredire, et covendroit que le seignor l'en[25] feist paier. Et l'acheteor, se il se[26] voloit parjurer, ne porroit le pris amermer[27] que de la valor de la beste, que mains de .i. besanz ou de .ii. besanz[28]

A: fol. lxxx^{r-v} cap. 139; **B:** fol. 108^{r-v} cap. 139; **C:** fol. 103^{r-v} cap. 124; **O:** fols 131^{v}–132^{v}; **V:** fol. cvii^{r-v} cap. 142; Beugnot, pp. 213–14, cap. 139.

[1] vendre] A rubric (fol. 4^{v}) OV: vendue [2] qui] BO: que il [3] celui jor qui . . . et] A lacks [4] jusques a tierce mais] C lacks [5] C adds: mie [6] rendre] B: rende [7] la] C lacks [8] V adds: mais que il ne l'aboivre [9] ou] AV: et [10] est sonee] A: seit sonnee; V: soune [11] mere] C: maire [12] plus] V: puis [13] dit roiaume] V: royaume de Jerusalem [14] recevoir] AV: recouvrer; B: recovrer; O: resevre [15] paie a celui de qui il] O lacks [16] qui il l'acheta] A: qui l'a achetee; V: qu'il l'a achetee [17] AV add: y [18] AV add: entre eaus; B: entreaus [19] ou] A: ne [20] entreaus] AB lack [21] AV add: y [22] A adds: .ii. [23] A adds: des garenz [24] sus] ABV lack [25] l'en] A: le; BV: li [26] se] B: s'en; V: ne s'en [27] amermer] B: amener [28] de .ii. besanz] A: de .ii.; BV: d'un denier; O: du denier

ne porroit il dire qu'il eust[29] la beste acheté. Et se l'acheteor ne viaut faire le[30] sairement, le vendeor le doit faire, et tant com il jurera que il li vendi[31] la[32] beste ou quelque autre chose que ce soit, l'acheteor le doit paier con dette provee[33] en court.

[29] O adds: perdu [30] viaut faire le] V: voloit faire le dit [31] li vendi] O: lendi [32] la] AOV: sa [33] A adds: ou coneue

***[126]** C'est l'assise de quei les seignors et les homes se doivent plus pener[1] de savoir la.[2]

Entre les autres[3] assises qui furent faites et establies el roiaume de Jerusalem en y ot une faite au tens dou roi Amauri qui est propre des seignors as homes et des homes as seignors. Et cele assise[4] fu faite a la pais faire de la guerre et del[5] contens qui fu entre le roi Amauri et messire Girart qui fu seignor de Seete et de Beaufort. Et cele guerre mut entreaus por ce que le dit Girart desherita .i. sien home sans esgart et sans conoissance de cort dou fié qu'il tenoit de lui en la seignorie de Seete que il tenoit[6] dou roi et de quei il estoit[7] son home. Et la pais de cele guerre fu ensi faite que le dit Gerart rendi a cel sien home qu'il avoit desherité sans esgart et sans conoissance de court son fié et li amenda tout le domage qu'il li avoit fait, et fu par[8] la court dou dit roi et dou dit Gerart et de toz les autres[9] barons et[10] haus homes dou reiaume et de tous ceaus qui avoient homes qui tenoient[11] fié[12] d'eaus el[13] dit roiaume. Et fu cele assise ensi faite et establie: que tous[14] les homes des homes dou chief seignor[15] dou roiaume feissent ligesse par l'assise au chief seignor dou reiaume des fiés qu'il tenoient de ses homes, et que tous ceaus qui avroient[16] fait homage au chief seignor ou ligesse[17] fust par l'assise ou autrement fussent[18] tous[19] tenus les uns as autres, et aussi les homes de ces homes[20] les uns as autres[21] de chascune court par soi, et que, se le roi voloit avoir la feiauté[22] des gens qui estoient manans es cités et es chasteaus et es bors que ses homes tenoient de lui, que il li jurassent[23] feauté, et que il[24] li[25] fussent tenus[26] par cele feauté de ce que les homes de ses homes li sont tenus par la ligesse faite par l'assise. Et fu devisé et acordé lors coment il feroient la

---

A: fols lxxx[v]–lxxxi[r] cap. 140; **B:** fols 108[v]–109[r] cap. 140; **C:** fols 103[v]–104[r] cap. 125; **O:** fols 132[v]–133[r]; **V:** fols cvii[v]–cviii[v] cap. 143; Beugnot, pp. 214–15, cap. 140.

---

[1] plus pener] B (fol. 21[v]): travaillier [2] et les homes . . . la] V: se doivent plus pener de savoir et toutes manieres de gens [3] autres] AB lack [4] ABV add: si [5] del] ABV: dou [6] V adds: de lui [7] estoit] B: est [8] par] BV lack [9] autres] ABV lack [10] A adds: les; V: de tous les [11] homes qui tenoient] O lacks [12] fié] AO: fiés [13] d'eaus el] B: ou [14] tous] A lacks [15] chief seignor] C: seignor chief [16] avroient] A: avoient [17] ou ligesse] A lacks [18] fussent] C: furent [19] tous] ABV lack [20] de ces homes] O lacks [21] les uns as autres] ABV lack [22] feiauté] O: fiance; V: feance [23] A adds: toz; B: touz; V: tous [24] li jurassent feauté, et que il] O lacks [25] li] BV lack [26] V adds: par l'assise et

ligece par l'assise[27] au chief seignor, et de quoi il seroient[28] tenus a lui[29] par la dite ligesse, et de quei le seignor seroit tenus a ceaus qui la dite ligesse li feroient,[30] et de quei les homes seroient tenus[31] les uns as autres et tous ensemble, lesqués choses le chief seignor et chascun des homes dou dit roiaume doivent metre poine dou savoir. Et je les deviserai aprés en cest livre.[a]

Mais je parlerai avant de pluisors cas des fiés et de la foi qui est[32] entre seignor et home, et aprés deviserai les servises que les homes doivent as seignors, et coment les seignors doivent leur homes semondre de lor servises, et coment les homes pueent et doivent destraindre leur seignors[33] d'avoir leur paies que il lor doivent[34] de lor fiés et coment guager de lor servises.[b]

---

[a] The conflict between King Amaury (1163–74) and Gerard lord of Sidon (fl. 1147 × 1170) which resulted in the promulgation of the so-called *Assise sur la ligece* has received much scholarly attention. It should be noted that neither here nor later, when he discusses the significance of this assise, does John refer to it by this name, although he does uses phrases such as 'faire la ligece par l'assise' (below caps 175–7). For a recent discussion, see R. Hiestand, 'Die Herren von Sidon und die Thronfolgekrise des Jahres 1163 im Königreich Jerusalem', in *Montjoie. Studies in Crusade History in Honour of Hans Eberhard Mayer*, ed. B.Z. Kedar, J. Riley-Smith and R. Hiestand (Aldershot, 1997), pp. 88–90. Hiestand rejects the view that the king involved in the dispute was Baldwin III, and not Amaury, and draws attention to Gerard's role in obliging Amaury to divorce his wife at the outset of his reign.

[b] It is with this statement that John of Ibelin signals that he is moving on to consider the laws and customs governing fiefs and vassalage, topics which occupy him as far cap. 217.

---

[27] Et fu devisé . . . l'assise] ABV lack [28] seroient] V: seront [29] a lui] C lacks [30] dite ligesse li feroient] V: ligesse li feront [31] ceaus qui la . . . tenus] B: eaus et [32] est] B: estre doit [33] destraindre leur seignors] A: semondre lor seignors destraindre [34] doivent] A: deit

***[127]** Coment le chief seignor dou reiaume[1] puet fié doner.

Le chief seignor dou roiaume de Jerusalem puet fié doner dou demaine de sa seignorie, fié et fiés tel com il viaut, a servise et[2] sans servise. Et ceaus que il done a servise, il les puet doner por tel servise com il viaut.[3] Et ceaus que il done sans servise, il les puet doner si franchement com il viaut. Et puet de son demaine doner ce que il viaut et a qui que il viaut et[4] si franchement com il viaut, a yglise, a religion,[5] a comune, et[6] a gent laye. Et puet quiter tout le servise que l'on li doit dou fié que l'on tient de lui ou partie. Et ce que le chief seignor fait des choses devant[7] dites doivent estre et sont fermes et[8] estables. Quar il est de sa seignorie soul[9] seignor et chief, ne ne la tient d'autre[10] seignor que de[11] Dieu, ne il n'en[12] doit a home ne a feme homage ne servise ne aucune autre redevance, por quei il ne puisse faire toutes les choses avant dites et chascune d'eles. Et chose que il[13] fasse ses heirs ne pueent ne ne doivent rapeler ne desfaire[14] par raison ne par l'assise ne l'usage[15] do dit roiaume.

A: fol. lxxxi^{r-v} cap. 141; **B:** fol. 109^{r} cap. 141; **C:** fol. 104^{r-v} cap. 126; **O:** fol. 133^{r-v}; **V:** fols cviii^{v}–cix^{r} cap. 144; Beugnot, pp. 215–16, cap. 141.

[1] V adds: de Jerusalem [2] et] V: ou [3] por tel servise com il viaut] B lacks [4] ce que il . . . et] V: si come il veaut a qui que il veaut [5] a religion] AO: et a religion (O: relegion) et; V: ou a relygion ou [6] et] C lacks; V: ou [7] devant] A: avant [8] et sont fermes et] B: et fermes et; V: fermes et sont [9] soul] C lacks [10] d'autre] AO: d'aucun; B: de nul; V: d'aucun autre [11] que de] V: fors que [12] n'en] ABV: ne [13] ABV add: en [14] desfaire] C: defaire [15] ne par l'assise ne l'usage] B: ou usage

***[128]** Coment ceaus qui sont homes dou chief seignor, qui ont court et coins et justise, poent fiés[1] doner.

Les homes qui tiennent fié dou chief[2] seignor, soit baronie ou seignorie, qui ont cort et coins et justise, ou[3] autre fié, et ceaus qui tienent fié[4] d'aucun des homes dou chief seignor pueent tous lor fiés[5] vendre par l'assise et partie de lor fié doner et desmenbrer por partie dou servise, mais que ce soit par l'assise ou l'usage dou dit roiaume. Et qui autrement le fait, chose que il[6] face n'est valable ne estable, soit fait[7] en court ou dehors[8] court, par otroi ou sans otroi dou seignor de qui il tient le fié, se ce n'est a aucun de ses homes,[9] et par l'otroi dou seignor, si come est aprés devisé en cest livre.[a] Et qui autrement le fera, son heir le puet[10] rapeler, se il viaut, et se il le rapele, chose[11] que il fait[12] ne vaudra ne ne sera tenue. Et se le fié vient en la main dou seignor par escheete ou par defaut de servise ou autrement, le seignor puet rapeler et avoir ce qui[13] sera fait sans assise et sans usage, se le seignor ne la otroie en cort, ou se il ne li a doné adonc[14] pooir en cort de faire le.

A: fol. lxxxi^{v} cap. 142; **B:** fol. 109^{r-v} cap. 142; **C:** fol. 104^{v} cap. 127; **O:** fols 133^{v}–134^{r}; **V:** fol. cix^{r} cap. 145; Beugnot, pp. 216–17, cap. 142.

---

[a] Below caps 129, 165.

---

[1] fiés] AB (fol. 21^{v}) V: fié [2] chief] B lacks [3] ou] C: et [4] et ceaus qui tienent fié] BO lack [5] pueent tous lor fiés] B: puet tout leur fye; O: pevent tout lor fié [6] ABV add: en [7] fait] A lacks [8] dehors] A: fors; BV: hors de [9] homes] AV: heirs; B: hoirs; O: heirs (corrected over erasure) [10] puet] B lacks [11] chose] ABV: la chose [12] fait] B: a faite [13] qui] A: qui en [14] adonc] ABV lack

***[129]** Quele assise est[1] quant l'on aliene tout son fié ou partie de son fié[2] autrement que par l'assise ou l'usage do reiaume de Jerusalem.[3]

Qui aliene tout son fié ou partie de son fié sans l'otroi dou seignor et[4] autrement que par l'assise ou l'usage dou dit roiaume et le met en main d'yglise[5] ou de relegion ou de comune ou d'autre, le seignor de qui il tient cel fié puet prendre ce que il[6] a aliené[7] et tenir et user con la soue chose. Quar le seignor dou fié qui l'a tout ou partie aliené sans assise et sans usage et sans otroi dou seignor de qui il tient le fié est par le fait qu'il en a fait encheu vers son seignor[8] de perdre a toz jors, lui et ses heirs, ce que il a dou dit fié aliené sans assise[9] et sans usage et sans otroi dou seignor, et le puet et doit avoir le seignor de qui il le tenoit en fié a lui et a ses heirs com la soue chose propre et faire en toutes ses volentés com dou sien.[a]

A: fols lxxxi^{v}–lxxxii^{r} cap. 143; **B:** fol. 109^{v} cap. 143; **C:** fols 104^{v}–105^{r} cap. 128; **O:** fol. 134^{r-v}; **V:** fol. cix^{r-v} cap. 146; Beugnot, p. 217, cap. 143.

---

[a] C inserts here a chapter from Philip of Novara. See appendix 1.2.

---

[1] assise est] AB (fol. 21^{v}) V: est l'assise [2] ou partie de son fié] A: ou partie de son fié sanz otrei dou seignor; A rubric (fol. 4^{v}) BV add: ou; O lacks [3] de Jerusalem] ABO lack [4] et] AV: ou [5] l'assise ou l'usage . . . d'yglise] V: l'usage dou royaume de Jerusalem et l'assise et le met en la main de l'yglise [6] O adds: en [7] a aliené] B: aliene [8] V adds: de qui il tenoit le fié [9] sans assise] V lacks

***[130]** Quel chose le conquereor dou fié puet faire dou fié qu'il a[1] conquis.

Celui qui a conquis fié a lui et a ses heirs, soit a toz heirs et as heirs[2] de feme espouse, le puet[3] bien[4] par l'assise ou l'usage dou roiaume de Jerusalem rendre et aquiter[5] au seignor de qui il le tient. Et se il le fait, ses heirs n'i[6] poent puis recovrer. Mais se le fié que le conquereor a conquis eschiet et vient a ses heirs, lequel que ce soit d'eaus, por saisine ne por teneure que il en[7] ait, ne le puet rendre ne quiter au seignor de qui il le tient, si que les heirs dou conquereor en soient desherités ne les siens, por ce que l'escheete est escheue a tous heirs dou conquereor,[8] tout soit ce que le plus prochain en ait la saisine et la tenure, s'il[9] la veaut requerre. Que quant aucun la requiert et l'a, il ne l'a[10] que por l'escheete qui lor est escheue dou conquereor, et tous les autres heirs dou conquereor sont ygaus a lui quant a ce que le fié lor est escheu,[11] tout soit ce que le plus droit heir et le plus prochain de ceaus qui le fié requierent en ait la saisine et la teneure devant[12] les autres. Par quei aucuns d'eaus ne puet les autres desheriter por rendre le[13] ne quiter au seignor de qui il le tient. Mais le conquereor qui n'a nul[14] per ne compaignon[15] el fié que il a conquis, et que nul de ses heirs n'est en tel degré del fié come il est et qui n'ont riens el fié qui lor soit[16] escheu, le puet rendre et quiter[17] au seignor de qui il le tient, que nul de ses heirs ne[18] puet[19] faire. Que tout soit ce que il dit el previlege que le seignor face le don a lui et a ses heirs, n'est le don parvenu[20] a ses heirs tant que il lor soit escheu, por ce que il n'ont riens el fié tant que il lor eschee. Que se .i. seignor done a un home un fié et li en fait

---

A: fol. lxxxii^{r-v} cap. 144; **B:** fols 109^{v}–110^{v} cap. 144; **C:** fols 106^{r}–107^{r} cap. 130; **O:** fols 134^{v}–136^{r}; **V:** fols cix^{v}–cx^{v} cap. 147; Beugnot, pp. 217–19, cap. 144.

---

[1] a] B (fol. 21^{v}): avra [2] soit a toz . . . heirs] A: seit a tos heirs ou as heirs; B: ou a hoir; V lacks [3] puet] C: poent [4] bien] AB lack [5] aquiter] AB: quiter; C: 'aquiter' altered to 'quiter' [6] n'i] AB: ne le; V: ne [7] en] ABV lack [8] en soient desherités . . . conquereor] A: ne le puissent recouvrer; B: en soient deseritez ne les siens, por ce que l'escheet est escheue a touz hoirs; V lacks [9] s'il] C: si [10] B adds: mie fors [11] tout soit ce . . . est escheu] V repeats [12] la teneure devant] ABV: l'a avant [13] le] ABV lack [14] nul] A: ne; BV lack [15] compaignon] C: compaignons [16] soit] A: est [17] quiter] AV: aquiter [18] AV add: le; B: 'ne' corrected to 'le'; O: 'le' interlined in later hand [19] puet] A: pevent [20] parvenu] B: mie venu

prevelige et dit el prevelige: 'Je tel doing a toi[21] et a tes heirs tel et tel casaus', et les nome,[22] 'ou tant de besanz asenés en tel leuc', et les motisse, et que ceaus casaus ou cel leuc ou les besanz sont assenés soient en la seignorie dou[23] seignor qui[24] cel don a fait de[25] son demaine, et sarazins ou autres gens tienent ceaus casaus[26] ou cel luec,[27] si que cil a qui le don en est[28] fait, ou autre[29] por lui, n'en ait[30] la saisine ne la teneure de tout ou de partie, ou tout soient[31] il en la main dou seignor et celui a qui il en a le don fait et saisi l'en d'une[32] verge et son homage receu n'en a aucune[33] teneure ou aucun usage, ou autre por lui en son nom, et se le fié est en besanz que un terme ou pluisors[34] de l'assenement soient passés que il ou autre por lui en son nom n'en aient paie receue, et le seignor qui l'avra ensi fait meurt ou est par aucune chose que il mesface[35] desherité en sa vie de son fié, ou lui ou ses heirs,[36] le don que il[37] avra fait en dit ne sera valable ne estable,[38] ne celui a qui la seignorie[39] en quei ceaus casaus seront ou le luec en quei le dit assenement des besanz avra[40] esté asené, si come[41] est avant dit, vendra par escheete ou par esguart ou par conoissance de cort, ne tendra cel don[42] se il ne viaut,[43] soit l'eir ou le[44] seignor, por ce que ce n'avra esté que promesse. Car le don n'avra esté fait qu'en dit et non en fait. Car[45] le don n'est pas parfait qui n'est fait[46] qu'en dit sans fait, que la saisine et la teneure de la chose donee en dit parfait le don en fait.[47] Et se un seignor dit a .i. home ou feme:[48] 'Je te doing le fié de tel home ou de tel feme aprés son decés', et que celui n'ait[49] nul heir si que le fié doit escheir au seignor par raison, et que celui qui tendra[50] le fié au jor que il l'avra doné[51] survive le seignor qui[52] le don avra fait et que il avra doné soit tel chose[53] que il[54] mesavient de celui ou de cele qui le fié tient[55] que le fié[56] vieigne au seignor, et

[21] toi] C: tel tel [22] nome] V: noment [23] seignorie dou] A lacks [24] qui] OV: que [25] cel don a fait de] A: fait le don en; BV: cel don fait en [26] casaus] C lacks [27] cel luec] B: ceaus leus [28] est] A: a esté [29] autre] C: autrement [30] n'en ait] A: n'en a; B: n'a; V lacks [31] soient] A: seit; BV: soit [32] d'une] CO: done [33] aucune] C: autre [34] pluisors] ABV: plus [35] mesface] B: mesfait [36] lui ou ses heirs] A: ou ces heirs ne veulent le don tenir [37] ABV add: en [38] ne estable] O lacks [39] la seignorie] ABV: le seignor [40] avra] B: avront [41] C adds: il [42] don] C: fié [43] A adds: encor [44] l'eir ou le] A: il heir dou; B: l'oir dou; V: l'eir dou [45] Car] AOV: Que [46] fait] A: en fait; B lacks; V: pas en fait [47] que la saisine . . . fait] AB lack [48] ou feme] A lacks [49] n'ait] A: n'a; C: n'en ait [50] tendra] C: rendra [51] que il l'avra doné] B lacks [52] que il l'avra . . . qui] V: survivant le seignor que il li avra doné que [53] que il avra doné soit tel chose] A: puis soit chose tel; B: ou soit chose tele [54] que il] C: que s'il [55] AB adds: et [56] tient que le fié] C lacks

qu'il soit sien quite et delivre a faire sa volenté, celui a qui il avra fait le don[57] de cel fié aprés le decet de l'autre n'avra, par l'assise ne par l'usage ne par raison, point dou fié quant l'autre mora, por ce que le seignor n'avoit ne tenoit cel fié quant il le dona ne autre por lui, ni n'ot en la vie dou seignor qui le fié li dona[58] en dit saisine ne teneure, ne il ne autre por lui,[59] n'en usa con dou sien en la vie dou doneor. Et por ces raisons et por pluisors autres que l'on porroit[60] dire que[61] trop seroient longues a metre en escrit en cest livre, qui en y metroit ce que on y[62] porroit metre, est il bien aparant que don que seignor fait[63] a home et a ses heirs dou fié n'est parvenu as[64] heirs tant que il lor soit escheu, ains est jusques lors[65] tout propre de celui a qui le don a esté fait,[66] que[67] celui a qui nul de ses heirs[68] n'est ygual en ce[69] fié ne rien n'a en la proprieté dou fié tant qu'il lor soit escheu. Por ce est il bien raison que le conquereor dou fié le puet rendre et quiter[70] au seignor de qui il le tient, et s'il le fait que ses heirs n'i poent plus[71] recouvrer.

---

[57] il avra fait le don] A: le don avra esté fait [58] dona] O: donra [59] ni n'ot en . . . lui] ABV lack [60] porroit] A: poroit encores; O: y porroit; V: y poroit [61] que] AB: qui [62] ce que on y] A: ce que l'on; B: ce que on y en; O: se que on en y; V: si com il [63] fait] ABV: face [64] heirs dou fié n'est parvenu as] A: heirs n'est pas venus a ces; B lacks; V: heirs n'est parvenu as [65] jusques lors] B lacks [66] C adds: et [67] que] AB: come; V: com [68] nul de ses heirs] B lacks [69] ce] ABV: son [70] quiter] A: aquiter [71] plus] AV: puis; B: pouis

***[131]** En quel maniere celui qui a fié conquis le puet doner auquel que il viaut de ses heirs.

Selui qui a fié conquis le puet doner par l'assise ou l'usage[1] de cest roiaume[2] auquel qu'il viaut de ses heirs, mais que ce soit par l'otroi dou seignor[3] de qui il tient le fié. Et ce me distrent le sire[4] de Seete,[5] mesire[6] Balean,[7] et sire Nicole Antiaume,[8] desqués Deux ait les armes.[9] [a] Et je lor enquis ce por ce que le baill d'Ermenie me manda priant que je lor enqueisse se il porroit,[10] par l'assise ou l'usage dou dit[11] roiaume de Jerusalem, doner le fié que il avoit[12] de son conquest auquel que il vodroit de ses enfans par l'otroi dou seignor de qui il tenoit le fié. Et ce que il me manda que je lor enqueisse fu por le Courc[13] que il disoit que il avoit conquis,[14] que il[15] voloit doner a baron Oysin[16] son fis, et que baron Senbat,[17] le conestable d'Ermenie, qui estoit[18] son ainsné fis, contredisoit cel don et disoit qu'il ne le porroit faire.[b] Et por ce[19] me manda il que je lor enqueise se il le porroit faire, et il me distrent que oil bien. Car ausi[20] con le conquereor dou fié le puet rendre[21] au seignor[22] de qui il le tient, et que, se il le fait, ses heirs ne pevent[23] puis recovrer le fié par l'assise ne[24] l'usage de cest roiaume,[25] le puet il par la dite assise ou[26] usage[27] doner auquel que il viaut de ses heirs[28] par l'otroi dou seignor,[29] a l'un de ses heirs,[30] soit a son dreit heir ou a autre. Et

---

A: fols lxxxii^{v}–lxxxiii^{v} cap. 145; **B:** fol. 111^{r-v} cap. 145; **C:** fols 107^{r}–108^{r} cap. 131; **O:** fols 136^{r}–137^{v}; **V:** fols cx^{v}–cxii^{r} caps 148–9; Beugnot, pp. 220–1, cap. 145.

---

[a] Balian lord of Sidon (d. 1240); Nicholas Antiaume (fl. 1225 × 1245).
[b] Constantine, the regent (*baill*) of Cilician Armenia (d. 1263), was the father of King Hethum I (1226–69, d. 1270). John of Ibelin had married his daughter Maria.

---

[1] ou l'usage] C lacks [2] par l'assise de cest roiaume] B lacks [3] dou seignor] A: de celui [4] le sire] AB: le seignor; V: les seignors [5] Seete] B: Saete; V: Sayete [6] mesire] C lacks [7] Balean] A: Bellian; B: Balyan; O: Baillian; V: Belian [8] Antiaume] B: Anteaume [9] ait les armes V: en ait l'arme [10] porroit] C: parreit [11] dit] ABV lack [12] B adds: conquis et qui estoit [13] Courc] AB: Corc; V: Courq [14] AV add: et [15] avoit conquis que il] B lacks [16] Oysin] A: Oissin; OV: Oyssin [17] Senbat] A: Sembat; OV: Semblat [18] qui estoit] ABV lack [19] porroit faire. Et por ce] ABV: pooit (A: poeit) faire [20] ausi] C: ensi [21] A adds: et aquiter [22] au seignor] B: a celui [23] pevent] C: porront [24] ne] AB: ou; V: et [25] de cest roiaume] V: dou royaume de Jerusalem [26] A adds: par le dit [27] la dite assise ou usage] V: l'assise et l'usage [28] C adds: mes que ce soit [29] dou seignor] A: de celui de qui il tient le fié ou [30] a l'un de ses heirs] B: qui (added in margin)

se[31] celui a qui il ensi le doneit[32] muert[33] sans heirs de sa[34] feme espouse, que le fié eschiet as heirs dou conquereor qui[35] le fié[36] li[37] dona. Et se le don dou fié[38] ne fu qu'a heirs de feme espouse, autre[39] heirs que ceaus[40] n'i poent riens avoir, que celui des heirs dou conquereor a qui il done[41] son fié par l'otroi dou seignor,[42] ensi com il est avant dit en cest livre el point[43] dou conquereor, sauf ce qu'il ne le puet[44] rendre ne quiter au seignor de qui il le tient.[c] Et je, ensi com il le me distrent, le mandai au[45] dit baill, et il dona a baron Oyssin[46] le Courc[47] qu'il ot et tint tant com il vesqui[d] l'oiant et le veant dou dit[48] conestable, son ainsné fis[49] qui eust, se cuit,[50] mis contredit[51] et chalonge el dit don[52] se il faire le peust.[53 e]

Et il[54] semble bien[55] raison que ensi doie estre,[56] que[57] l'on[58] a veu pluisors preveliges en quei le seignor fait don d'un fié a un home et a ses heirs, et aprés ce que il li a fait le don generaument a lui et a ses heirs, li done il plain pooir en celui prevelige de doner cel fié a qui[59] que il viaut de ses heirs ou a aucun de ses heirs par nom et as heirs[60] de celui a qui il le done. Et l'on dit comunaument que quant le prevelige est ensi fait, que celui a qui le seignor a doné le fié et le pooir de doner le auquel que il viaut de ses heirs, et il le done a autre de ces heirs[61] que a son dreit heir, que cel don vaut et est estable a celui de ses heirs a qui il l'a doné[62] et a ses heirs. Ne que le dreit heir dou conquereor[63] ne puet faire ne dire chose par quei cel don ne soit valable a celui de ses heirs a qui il l'a doné

[c] Above cap. 130.

[d] Oshin of Gorhigos died in Dec. 1264. *Chronique attribueé au Connétable Smbat*, trans G. Dédeyan (Paris, 1980), p. 116. Evidently John composed this passage after that date.

[e] V begins a new chapter here with the rubric: Ci devise l'esclerissement coument l'om peut fié douner de son conquest auquel que il veaut de ces heirs.

[31] se] BV lack [32] ensi le doneit] AV: le done; B: done [33] muert] BV lack [34] sa] ABV lack [35] qui] C: que [36] fié] A: don [37] li] AB lack [38] dou fié] B lacks [39] autre] BOV: autres [40] que ceaus] A lacks [41] done] B: a doné [42] A adds: de qui il le tient [43] cest livre el point] A: cest livre en est ou point; B: cest livre en est il ou pooir; O: est el point; V: cestui livre en est el pooir [44] puet] O: pevent [45] V adds: devant [46] Oyssin] A: Oissin; B: Oysin [47] Courq] AB: Corc; V: Corq [48] dit] C lacks [49] fis] ABV: frere [50] se cuit] ABV lack [51] contredit] C: contens [52] el dit don] A lacks; B: ou dit don; V: dou dit don [53] B adds: par raison; V: par raison mais il ne post. Si demoura a baron Oyssin le devant dit Courq. [54] BV add: me [55] il semble bien] A: por ce me semble il encores [56] V adds: com l'on a dit au devant dit chapistle [57] que] BV: car [58] l'on] C: l'en [59] a qui] ABV: auquel [60] ou a aucun . . . heirs] ABV lack [61] et il le . . . heirs] C lacks; V: et il le doune a autre [62] l'a doné] A: le done [63] C repeats: ne que le dreit heir

et a ses heirs.[64] Et se le seignor done a celui a qui il a[65] fait le don dou fié, si com est avant dit, pooir en son privilege de doner le auquel qu'il viaut[66] de ses heirs, aprés ce que il li[67] a fait le don[68] general a lui et a ses heirs, donc, di ge, que il le puet faire toutes les fois que il viaut, soit en cel prevelige devisé ou en autre. Que autel pooir en a le seignor de faire le quant il viaut com il a aprés ce que il a[69] fait le don generaument a lui et a ses heirs. Car ausi come il le puet faire[70] .i. hore[71] aprés le don, le puet il faire .i. jor ou un mois ou[72] .i. an ou tant plus come il viaut.[73]

---

[64] Ne que le dreit . . . heirs] AB lack [65] a] O lacks [66] viaut] V: vodra [67] li] AV lack [68] dou fié, si . . . don] B lacks [69] com il a . . . a] A: avant come aprés ce qu'il; B: com il a aprés ce que il en a; V: come il l'a aprés ce que il li a [70] le puet faire] B: puet [71] .i. hore] ABV: en un horre (B: une houre; V: une oure) ou en un moment [72] ou un mois ou] C: et un mois et [73] ABV add: Car la longour (A: longuor) de la demorre (B: demoure; V: demoree) dou terme ne tolt (V: tot) au seignor, se me semble, en cest cas son poeir, ne faire ne le doit par raison (A: deit par

***[132]** Qui a fié de[1] conquest ou d'escheete,[2] coment il le[3] puet doner a son dreit heir.

Selui qui a fié de[4] conquest ou d'escheete le puet doner par l'assise ou l'usage de cest roiaume a son dreit heir par l'otrei dou seignor de qui il tient le fié. Et qui ensi le fait, l'eir a qui il le done deit faire au seignor de qui il tient le fié[5] quantque le fié doit d'omage et de servise et toutes les autres[6] redevances que le fié doit. Et[7] celui qui a ensi doné[8] son fié a son dreit heir est quite vers le seignor de qui il tenoit[9] le fié de tout quantqu'il li[10] devoit por cel fié, que .ii. homes ne doivent par l'assise ne l'usage de cest roiaume por un fié estre tenus au seignor de ce que le fié doit. Et puis que le seignor otroie au seignor dou fié que il le doigne[11] a son dreit heir[12] et il reseit de celui a qui le fié se done[13] l'omage et le servise[14] et les autre redevances que le fié doit, bien est clere chose que il en quite[15] l'autre. Et se il ne le[16] fait en dit, si est il fait[17] en fait par l'assise ou l'usage de cest roiaume. Et quant le fié est doné ensi come il est dessus[18] devisé,[19] et celui a qui l'on l'a doné[20] meurt sans heirs que il ait de sa feme espouse, le fié eschiet par l'assise ou l'usage de cest roiaume a son[21] plus droit heir de cele part dont le fié meut, ce est assaveir a ceaus heirs a qui cel fié puet escheir de par celui qui le fié li dona.[22]

A: fols lxxxiii^{v}–lxxxiv^{r} cap. 146; **B:** fol. 111^{v} cap. 146; **C:** fol. 108^{r-v} cap. 132; **O:** fols 137^{v}–138^{r}; **V:** fol. cxii^{r} cap. 150; Beugnot, p. 222, cap. 146.

---

[1] ABV add: son [2] ou d'escheete] A: et de s'escheete [3] V adds: doit et [4] de] ABV: de son; C: dou [5] Et qui ensi . . . fié] B lacks [6] O adds: choses et [7] B adds: se; V: ce [8] a ensi doné] V: enci done [9] tenoit] BOV: tient [10] li] ABV lack [11] doigne] A: doint [12] a son dreit heir] AB au dreit heir (B: droit hoyr) qu'il a [13] se done] ABV: est doné [14] le servise V: les servises [15] quite] B: a quité [16] le] C: la [17] est il fait] A: est il; B: le fait il bien [18] dessus] A: devant [19] devisé] BV: dit [20] l'on l'a doné] A: il le done; V: il l'a douné [21] a son] ABV: au [22] dona] B: done

***[133]** Qui a fié de son conquest et il le rent et quite au seignor de qui il le tient, et le seignor le done au dreit heir de celui qui li a rendu et quité et[1] a ses heirs, a qui cel[2] fié puet escheir se il muert sans heir de sa[3] feme espose.[4 a]

Se aucun a fié conquis, et[5] viaut que son dreit heir ait son fié, ensi que il le rende et quite au seignor de qui il le tient[6] par condicion que le seignor le doigne[7] a son dreit heir et a ses heirs de sa feme espouse ou a tous heirs selonc ce que le fié est, et le seignor en receit la quitance et la rendue que le conquereor dou fié li fait,[8] et il aprés le done au dreit heir dou[9] conquereor dou fié, et le fié est a tous heirs, et celui qui a le don dou dit fié receu[10] meurt sans heirs que il ait[11] de sa feme espouse, cel fié escharra au plus prochain de ses heirs aussi bien a ceaus qui ne[12] li apartienent de par le premier conquereor dou fié com a ceaus qui li apartienent de par lui. Et se le fié est as heirs de feme espouse, et celui a qui il a esté[13] doné si con est avant[14] dit[15] muert sans heirs que il ait de sa feme espouse, le fié revient au seignor. Ne nul des heirs dou premier conquereor[16] dou fié, qui le rendi et quita au seignor et qui[17] le tenoit, ne puet ne ne doit heriter[18] par l'assise ne[19] l'usage de cest roiaume, por ce que il est assise ou usage en cest[20] roiaume que le conquereor dou fié le puet rendre et quiter au seignor de qui il le tient, et que, se il le fait, ses heirs n'i[21] pueent aprés ce heriter en cel fié par les raisons qui sont devisees en l'autre chapistle qui parole de cest cas. Et se le seignor le done a aucun des heirs de celui qui li a rendu et quité,[22] celui a qui il le done n'i a riens de par le conquereor

---

A: fol. lxxxiv^{r-v} cap. 147; **B:** fols 111^{v}–112^{r} cap. 147; **C:** fols 108^{v}–109^{r} cap. 133; **O:** fol. 138^{r-v}; **V:** fols cxii^{r}–cxiii^{r} cap. 151; Beugnot, pp. 222–3, cap. 147.

---

[a] B lacks the rubrics to chapter 133 and 134 in the text, although they are present in the table of rubrics (fol. 21^{v})

---

[1] et] CV lack [2] cel] AB (fol. 21^{v}): celui [3] sa] AV lack [4] se il muert . . . espose] B: de par celui qui le fié li dona [5] ABV add: il [6] et quite au . . . tient] C lacks [7] doigne] AV: done [8] li fait] A: fait a lui [9] dreit heir dou] A lacks [10] ABV add: dou seignor [11] V adds: eu [12] ne] AB lack [13] a esté] AB: est [14] avant] B lacks [15] si con est avant dit] C lacks [16] C adds: au seignor. Ne nul [17] et qui] AB: de qui il [18] A adds: el fié [19] ne] C: ou [20] en cest] A: ou dit; V: dou dit [21] n'i] ABV: ne [22] a rendu et quité] V: rendi et quite

dou fié ne de[23] par nul autre[24] que de par le seignor[25] qui li done.[26] Si ne se doit en cel don a[27] plus estendre que tant come il est devisé el don que le seignor en fait. Et por les raisons devant dites et por[28] pluisors autres est il si cler a conoistre, ce me semble, que les heirs do conquereor dou fié n'ont droit de par lui el fié qu'il a[29] conquis et que il a aprés rendu et quité au seignor, tout soit ce que le seignor l'ait doné a aucun des heirs dou conquereor.

[23] de] C lacks [24] autre] ABV lack [25] AV add: dou fié [26] done] B: a doné [27] en cel don a] A: cel fié; B: en cel don; V: a cel don [28] devant dites et por] AV: avant dites et [29] a] A: aveit; O lacks

***[134]** Quant fie eschiet qui doit servise de cors a home ou a feme qui a fié el roiaume[1] de quei il a fait homage, et autre fié li eschiet qui doit tel servise et tel homage com est avant dit, coment il le puet avoir et deservir.

Se aucun home ou feme a fié en cest royaume de quei il doive homage en chief et servise de son cors, et il en a fait l'omage a celui ou a cele a qui il le doit, et fié li eschiet el dit roiaume qui doive homage en chief et servise de cors, il le puet[2] requerre et avoir par l'assise ou l'usage de cest roiaume, faisant l'omage de cel fié qui li est escheu sauve[3] la feauté de celui ou de ceaus de qui il tient[4] el dit reiaume fié[5] a qui il a fait[6] homage avant que cel fié li estoit[7] escheu, et deservir le par chevaliers ou par chevalier[8] selonc ce que le fié doit servise. Et se[9] pluisors fiés li escheent[10] en un jor ou en pluisors,[11] il les avra par l'assise ou l'usage de cest roiaume, l'un avant l'autre, si come il escheent,[12] et il les requera, l'un avant l'autre,[13] faisant l'omage et le servise en la maniere avant[14] devisee.

Et se il muert et il n'a que un soul[15] heir, il avra et tenra tous les fiés qui li seront escheus si com celui de par qui il[16] li escheirent les teneit quant il li escheirent, faisant en homage[17] et de servise ce[18] que celui en faisoit de par qui il li escheirent.[19] Et s'il y[20] a pluisors[21] qui li teignent[22] en un degré de cele part dont les fiés muevent, chascun avra l'un[23] des fiés par l'assise ou l'usage de cest[24] roiaume, se il li requierent.[25] Et se il sont plus heirs que fiés, chascun des heirs mahles qui li seront[26] en .i. degré avra .i. des fiés qui doivent[27] homage en chief[28] et servise de cors et fera chascun d'eaus ce que le fié doit d'omage et de servise,[29] et les ainsnés choisiront des dis

A: fols lxxxiv^{v}–lxxxv^{r} cap. 148; **B:** fol. 112$^{r–v}$ cap. 148; **C:** fol. 109$^{r–v}$ cap. 134; **O:** fol. 139$^{r–v}$; **V:** fol. cxiii$^{r–v}$ cap. 152; Beugnot, pp. 223–4, cap. 148.

[1] B (fol. 21^{v}) adds: de Jerusalem [2] puet] A: viaut [3] sauve] A: et sauver [4] tient] V: tienent [5] fié] A: fié et; B: lacks [6] B adds: ou dit reaume [7] estoit] A: seit; B: fust; V: soit [8] chevaliers ou par chevalier] A: un chevalier ou par pluisors [9] se] C lacks [10] escheent] C: escheoient [11] fiés li escheent . . . pluisors] B lacks [12] escheent] A: li escharont [13] si come il . . . l'autre] BV lack [14] et le servise . . . avant] B: en la maniere devant [15] soul] V lacks [16] de par qui il] C: qui [17] homage] A: de homage; O: d'omage [18] ce] C lacks [19] faisant en homage . . . escheirent] V lacks [20] y] ABO lack [21] A adds: heirs [22] teignent] O: teigne; V: atiegnent [23] avra l'un] A: deit aver l'un; B: d'eaus avra un [24] ou l'usage de cest] V: et l'usage dou dit [25] requierent] B: requiert [26] A adds: apartenans [27] doivent] B: doit [28] en chief] O lacks; V: au chief [29] A adds: et le mainzné partira les fiés

fiés l'un avant l'autre si come il sont ainsnés. Et s'il y a plus[30] fiés qui doivent homage ou[31] servise de cors que heirs masles, et il[32] y ait heirs femeles ataignans el dit degré a celui de par qui les fiés escheirent,[33] et il y a tant[34] com il y a fiés remés, chascune d'eles en avra .i. si com est avant dit des heirs masles, et se il y a .ii. fiés et il y ait .iii. ou .iiii. filles,[35] seurs ou parentes en .i. degré, l'ainsnee avra l'un des fiés a son chois et les autres partiront l'autre, se il est de pluisors chevaleries,[36] si com est aprés[37] devisé en l'autre chapistle qui parole[38] coment seurs doivent partir fiés.[39][a] Et s'il n'est que d'une chevalerie, cele qui sera l'ainsnee de celes[40] qui deust[41] le fié partir se il fust de[42] plus[43] d'une chevalerie, l'avra tout puis que il n'est que d'une chevalerie.[44] Que par l'assise ou l'usage de cest roiaume, fié qui ne doit servise que d'une chevalerie ne se part mie entre seurs.

[a] Below chapter 136. Note that all the MSS except C speak of this topic coming earlier ('avant').

[30] plus] V: plusours [31] ou] AB: et [32] il] C lacks [33] escheirent] ABV: escheent [34] tant] AB: tantes filles; V: tantes [35] ait .iii. ou .iiii. filles] AB: a .ii. ou .iii.; O: ait .iii.; V: a .ii. ou plus ou .iii. [36] chevaleries] ABV: chevaliers [37] aprés] A: sa avant; BOV: avant [38] parole] A: devise [39] fiés] A: fiés quant il lor escheit; BV lack [40] celes] C: cele [41] deust] ABV: deussent [42] de] ABV lack [43] B adds: que [44] tout puis que . . . chevalerie] B lacks

***[135]** Quans[1] pluisors fiés escheent en .i. jor ou en pluisors, por quei[2] l'ainsné de ceaus a qui il escheent, qui est plus[3] dreit heir de celui ou de ceaus de par qui il escheent,[4] les puet avoir toz, s'il les requiert.

Se pluisors fiés escheent a home ou a feme ensenble ou par parties[5] et que il ne doivent homage en chief ne servise de cors, il seront tous dou plus droit heir de celui a qui il seront[6] escheus aprés son decet, se il les viaut requerre. Et il puet[7] faire l'omage que les fiés doivent, sans ce que nus des autres y puisse ne doive[8] avoir droit ne requerre[9] par l'assise ou l'usage de cest roiaume. L'ainsné des freres ou des seurs ou des autres parens ou parentes qui apartienent[10] en .i. degré a celui de par qui le fié lor eschiet de cele part dont le fié muet a[11] devant[12] les autres parens[13] qui li escheent[14] qui ne doivent servise de cors ne homage, se il les requiert[15] en la cort si come il doit. Et s'il doivent homage et il les puet faire si com les fiés les doivent, il les doit tous avoir.

A: fol. lxxxv^{r} cap. 149; **B:** fols 112^{v}–113^{r} cap. 149; **C:** fol. 109^{v} cap. 135; **O:** fols 139^{v}–140^{r}; **V:** fols cxiii^{v}–cxiv^{r} cap. 153; Beugnot, pp. 224–5, cap. 149.

[1] Quans] AB: Se [2] por quei] C lacks [3] escheent, qui est plus] B: eschiet qui eschiet; B rubric (fol. 22^{r}): escheent qui est; V: eschet qui est plus [4] escheent] B: eschiet (B rubric: escheent); V: eschet [5] a home ou . . . parties] B: en .i. jor ensemble ou par parties a home ou a feme [6] C adds: tous [7] puet] A: puisse [8] puisse ne doive] V: puissent ne doivent [9] A adds: que [10] apartienent] V: apartient [11] muet a] V: vient et meut l'a [12] A adds: toz [13] ABV add: touz (A: toz) les fiés (B: fiez) [14] escheent] C: escheirent [15] requiert] O: requierent

***[136]** Coment[1] fié ou fiés doivent[2] estre parti entre seurs.[3]

Quant fié eschiet a pluisors seurs qui doit[4] servise de pluisors chevaleries,[5] le fié doit par l'assise ou l'usage[6] de cest roiaume estre parti entre eles en tel maniere que se eles sont. ii. seurs[7] et il y a .ii.[8] chevaleries[9] chascune doit avoir l'une des chevaleries,[a] [10] et la mainsnee le doit partir et l'ainsnee doit choisir et prendre laquel partie qu'ele vodra, et la mainsnee tenra sa partie de l'ainsnee et li en devra[11] tot quantque le fié doit[12] d'omage et de servise de mariage et d'estage[13] et de toutes les autres redevances que le fié doit. Et se le fié est de .iii.[14] chevaleries ou de plus et il y a[15] tant de seurs con de chevaleries,[16] chascune des seurs doit avoir une chevalerie,[17] et toutes doivent tenir ce que eles avront de cel fié de l'ainsnee et faire li en quantque le fié doit, et la mainsnee[18] doit faire la partison des fiés, et l'ainsnee doit premier choisir et aprés chascune des autres, ausi[19] com ele est ainsnee, doit avant choisir. Et s'il a el fié plus de[20] chevaleries[21] que de[22] seurs, chascune des seurs avra une chevalerie,[23] et tant come il y avra plus de chevaleries que de seurs[24] sera parti entre eles[25] a chascune son avenant, tant a l'une come a l'autre dou surplus des chevaleries. Et s'il y a plus de seurs qu'il n'a[26] de chevaleries el fié, tant com il y avra de chevaleries[27] l'ainsnee en avra l'une et la mainsnee[28] aprés li l'autre, et des autres chevaleries chascune des autres seurs[29] tant com eles se porront estendre, que une chevalerie ne se part mie entre seurs par l'assise ne l'usage de cest[30] roiaume.

Se le fié n'est de plus de chevaleries qu'il n'a[31] de seurs et la mainsnee[a] des seurs qui ont part[32] el fié fait la partie[33] et les ainsnees

A: fols lxxxv[r]–lxxxvi[r] cap. 150; **B:** fols 113[r]–114[r] cap. 150; **C:** fols 109[v]–111[r] cap. 136; **O:** fols 140[r]–141[v]; **V:** fol. cxiv[r–v] cap. 154; Beugnot, pp. 225–7, cap. 150.

a–a This passage is missing from V.

[1] Coment] V: Ci orrés coument [2] doivent] O: doit [3] doivent estre parti entre seurs] B: doit ou doivent estre parti ou partiz entre serours [4] doit] V: doivent [5] chevaleries] BV: chevaliers [6] ou l'usage] B lacks [7] seurs] BV lack [8] .ii.] C: .iii. [9] chevaleries] BV: chevaliers [10] chevaleries] BV: chevaliers [11] B adds: faire [12] doit] B: devra [13] d'estage] B: d'ostage [14] .iii.] B: .ii. [15] y a] A lacks [16] chevaleries] B: chevaliers [17] une chevalerie] A: l'une des chevaleries; B: l'un des chevaliers [18] C adds: des seurs [19] ausi] AB: si [20] de] C lacks [21] de chevaleries] B: des chevaliers [22] de] C lacks [23] chevalerie] B: des chevaliers [24] que de seurs] AB lack [25] C adds: et [26] qu'il n'a] AB: que [27] el fié, tant . . . chevaleries] B lacks [28] la mainsnee] O: l'ainsnee [29] A adds: en avra une [30] de cest] A: dou dit [31] chevaleries qu'il n'a] B: chevaliers que il n'i a [32] part] O: parti [33] partie] V: partison

choisissent, et prenent[34] chascune sa part l'une avant l'autre si come eles sont ainsnees, les unes[35] devant les autres, et cele qui part le fié, soit en .ii. pars[36] ou en plus, si[37] a .xl. jors de respit par l'assise ou l'usage dou[38] reiaume de faire la partie aprés ce que ele li[39] ait esté requise en cort ou que le seignor li a comandé en cort que ele le[40] face ou li mande[41] comandant[42] par court. Et court est .iii. homes ou plus que[43] le seignor a establi, l'un d'eaus en son luec et les autres[44] come court, mes que il ait ce fait en[45] la[46] presence d'autres[47] de ces homes qui li en puissent porter recors de court se mestier li est. Et quant la partie dou fié est faite,[48] celui ou cele qui l'a faite doit chascune des parties faire escrire[49] en une chartre, et dedens .xl.[50] jors ou au quarantime jor il doit venir en la court devant le seignor ou devant celui[51] qui sera en son luec, et se il treuve celui ou cele ou ceaus ou celes qui doivent choisir, il doit offrir les chartres des parties[52] devant le seignor et la court et baillier[53] li. Et se il ne les treuve, il les doit offrir[54] a[55] baillier[56] au seignor et a la cort et baillier[57] leur, se il les vorront[58] recevoir, et traire la court a garant de ce de quei il[59] est venus a hore et a tens[60] ofrir les parties[61] qu'il a faites do fié que il devoit partir, et doit retenir et avoir le transcrit[62] des parties qu'il offrira et baillera. Et[63] celui ou cele qui doit choisir et prendre lequel que il viaut a[64] .xv. jors de respit de choisir et de[65] prendre[66] laquel que il vodra des parties, et a celui jor ou avant il doit venir[67] devant le seignor en sa cort[68] et dire li en la presence de celui ou de cele qui a la partie faite, se il y est, laquel des parties il prent, et retenir cel escrit en quei cele partie qu'il a prise est escrite, et rendre l'autre a celui qui la fist,[69] se il est en la cort, et se il n'i est[70] baillier la au seignor et a la court. Et celui qui baille les chartres de la partie dou fié les doit faire lire en la court

---

[34] prenent] C: prent [35] unes] C: uns [36] pars] AB: parties [37] si] ABV lack [38] dou] AB: de cest [39] li] ABV lack [40] le] AV: la [41] C adds: en court [42] comandant] BO: comandement [43] que] ABV: quant [44] autres] B: deus; V: autres .ii. [45] en] C lacks [46] la] AV lack [47] d'autres] B lacks [48] BV add: ou [49] escrire] B: escrivre [50] .xl.] B: .x. [51] celui] B lacks [52] parties] V: partizons [53] baillier] A: doner; O: batailler [54] offrir] O: soffrir [55] a] B: et [56] baillier] C: prover; O: bataille [57] au seignor et . . . baillier] B lacks [58] vorront] A: viaut; B: veulent [59] de quei il] AB: que il [60] B adds: pour [61] parties] V: partizons [62] transcrit] AV: contre escrit; B: contrescrit [63] Et] C lacks [64] lequel que il viaut a] B: laquele que il veut des parties a; V: doit avoir [65] et prendre lequel . . . parties] A: ou prendre laquel qu'il vodra des parties le deit aveir fait dedenz .xx. jors [66] et de prendre] V lacks [67] venir] O lacks [68] en sa cort] AV: en la court; B lacks [69] fist] B: fit; V: fait [70] n'i est] AV: n'est

au jor[71] que il les baille au seignor ou a celui qui doit choisir. Et celui qui a pris[72] sa partie[73] doit faire lire en la court la chartre en quei sa partie est escrite, et chascun le doit faire[74] por ce que la court en soit[75] recordant,[76] se mestier lor est. Et guarde[77] soi[78] celui ou cele qui fait la partie qu'il ne[79] laisse riens a partir[80] do fié; ce qu'il en laissera sera do seignor dou fié[81] qui avra a choisir.

Et se eles sont pluisors seurs,[82] il sera parti entre les autres,[83] s'il en y a plus d'une qui doivent avoir part el fié, et se il n'i[84] a que une, tout quanque il n'en[85] sera mis en la[86] partie dou fié sera sien. Et quant les parties sont[87] faites et les chartres baillees et receues en la court, chascun de ceaus ou de celes qui ont chartres des parties doivent prier et requerre[88] le seignor que il face escrire[89] en la secrete les parties si come eles sont escrites en lor chartres, et le seignor le doit faire a lor requeste por avoir ent plus grant memoire et greignor[90] seurté, ce aucune des parties en a[91] mestier a aucun de lor heirs.[92]

[71] au jor] ABV: avant [72] pris] C: prise [73] Et celui qui . . . partie] B lacks [74] A adds: ensi [75] en soit] C: estoit [76] recordant] ABV: membrant [77] guarde] B: garder [78] soi] C: se [79] qu'il ne] BO: que se il; V: que si [80] A adds: que c'il en laisse riens a partir [81] ce qu'il en . . . fié] O lacks [82] C adds: se [83] autres] A: autres suers; B: seurs; V: autres seurs [84] n'i] A: n'en y; B: n'en i [85] quanque il n'en] A: quan qui ne; B: ce qui ne; O: quanque; V: quanque ne [86] C adds: par [87] sont] ABV: seront [88] et requerre] A lacks [89] escrire] B: escrivre [90] grant memoire et greignor] V: memoire et plus grant [91] a] B: avoit [92] a aucun de lor heirs] ABV lack

***[137]** Coment et por quey le fiz ou la fille se peut metre de s'autorité el fié qui li est escheu de son pere ou de sa mere.[a]

Quant fié eschiet, le fis ou la fille qui est droit heir de celui ou de cele de par qui il[1] eschiet se puet metre par sei, se il est d'aage, au[2] fié avoir en la saisine de cel fié quant le pere ou la mere meurt saisi et tenant con dou sien, sans ce que il mesprent vers le seignor d'aucune[3] chose, por ce que il est assise ou usage en cest reiaume que le fis ou la fille demore en la saisine et[4] en la teneure de ce de quei leur pere ou leur mere meurt[5] saisi et tenant come do sien, mais que de baillage. Que de baillage[6] ne demore mie le fis ne la fille en la saisine dou pere ne de la mere.

A: fol. lxxxvi^{r-v} cap. 151; **B:** fol. 114^{r} cap. 151; **C:** fol. 111^{r} cap. 137; **O:** fols 141^{v}–142^{r}; **V:** fols cxiv^{v}–cxv^{r} cap. 155; Beugnot, p. 227, cap. 151.

---

[a] From here until chapter 148 B lacks the rubrics in the text, although they are present in the table of rublics (fol. 22^{r-v}).

---

[1] il] B: le fié [2] au] AV: a; B: et [3] mesprent ver le seignor d'aucune] B: mespreigne vers le seignor de nulle [4] en la saisine et] O lacks [5] meurt] C: morut [6] Que de baillage] A: Que dou baill; B: que dou baillier; C lacks; V: Car dou baliage

***[138]** Por quey le seignor ne doit soufrir[1] que autre que l'ainsné des fiz ou des filles de celuy ou de celle de par qui le fié leur eschiet se met[2] de[3] s'autorité en saisine ne en teneure de cel fié.[4]

Se home ou[5] feme qui a fié muert et il a pluisors enfans, et aucuns de ces enfans autre que son dreit heir se met de s'auctorité en saisine dou fié de son pere ou de sa mere sans requerre[6] au seignor la saisine dou fié com le plus dreit heir aparant et requerant de cel fié en la court, le seignor de qui l'on tient cel fié ne le doit soufrir, ce me semble. Car se il le soufroit, le droit heir[7] a cui il est tenus de garder sa raison, com a droit heir de son home, lui et ses heirs en porroient estre travailliés au recovrer dou fié ou[8] estre en desherités de tout le fié[9] ou de partie. Et por guarder le droit heir de travaill et de perill et de desheritement, et por maintenir l'assise ou l'usage qui est tel, que quant fié eschiet a pluisors enfans ou a pluisors[10] heirs[11] qui sont en un degré apartenans[12] a celui de par qui le fié est escheu, et le droit heir ne s'i met ou[13] le requiert, selonc ce que le cas eschiet et que il le puet faire, selonc l'assise ou l'usage dou reiaume de Jerusalem,[14] et[15] l'un des autres heirs le requiert, com le plus dreit heir aparant[16] en la court tant que plus dreit heir y vieigne,[17] et se l'assise ou l'usage est tel, il est clere chose que celui des enfans qui n'est dreit heir des enfans[18] ne s'i puet ne[19] doit metre de s'autorité ne[20] autrement que par requerre au seignor de qui l'on tient cel[21] fié la saisine de cel fié[22] com le plus droit heir aparant et requerant le en la court.

Et par raison[23] me semble il bien que il ensi le doie[24] estre, que

---

A: fols lxxxvi^{v}–lxxxviii^{r} cap. 152; **B:** fols 114^{r}–116^{r} cap. 152; **C:** fols 111^{r}–113^{v} cap. 138; **O:** fols 142^{r}–145^{v}; **V:** fols cxv^{r}–cxvii^{v} caps 156–7; Beugnot, pp. 228–31, cap. 152.

---

[1] soufrir] O: offrir [2] met] B (fol. 22^{r}): metre [3] de] C: en [4] saisine ne en . . . fié] ABV: la saisine (A: saissine) ne en la teneure (B: teneure dou fié) [5] home ou] V: .i. home ou une [6] sans requerre] C lacks [7] le droit heir] B: l'oir [8] ou] AV: a; B: et; O lacks [9] le fié] B lacks [10] enfans ou a pluisors] C lacks [11] heirs] A: parens [12] apartenans] A lacks [13] ABV add: ne; O has 'ne' in margin in later hand [14] dou reiaume de Jerusalem] V: de cestui royaume [15] et] A: ce [16] O adds: et requerant [17] en la court . . . vieigne] A: qu'il ait et y aveigne; BV: et y viegne [18] des enfans] ABV lack [19] puet ne] A: peut ni ni; B: puet ne ne; V lacks [20] A adds: non [21] cel] A: le; V: son [22] la saisine de cel fié] A lacks [23] C adds: le [24] il bien que . . . doie] A: qu'ensi deit; B: il bien qu'il doit enssi; O: il bien que il en doye ensi; V: il que il doie enci

raison done que por soufrance que le droit heir face a aucun de ses freres ou[25] de ses seurs ou de ses parens d'avoir[26] le fié qui li est[27] escheus, il ne ses heirs ne doivent estre desherités ne travailliés de ravoir[28] le quant il le vodront[29] avoir. Que se il estoit ensi que autre des[30] enfans que le droit heir se peust metre en la saisine et[31] en la teneure dou fié de son pere ou de sa mere de s'auctorité ne autrement que par la condicion avant[32] dite, ce est com le plus dreit heir aparant et requerant en la court tant que[33] plus dreit heir y viegne, et le droit heir vosist aprés avoir le fié et celui qui de s'auctorité se seroit mis[34] le vosist deffendre, il le porroit longuement faire[35] par eschampes et par fuites et par delais, por ce que il covendroit que il se clamast de lui. Que puis que il en[36] avroit eu la saisine par le seignor, le seignor ne seroit tenus de respondre ent au[37] requerant, se il li en[38] requeroit la saisine, ne autre[39] chose ne li en[40] avroit a faire que d'avoir li a droit celui qui en avroit la saisine et la teneure,[41] puis que il par le seignor ne l'avroit[42] eue. Que le seignor n'est tenus de respondre, se cuit, de chose que autre ait[43] et teigne,[44] se celui qui en a[45] la saisine et la teneure ou[46] son ancestre ne l'a eue par le seignor ou par son ancestre. Et ensi porroit le droit heir estre moult[47] travaillié et esloignié de son droit, se il ne[48] pooit venir que par la[49] clamor que il feist de son frere ou de sa seur ou de[50] cel sien parent a qui il avroit le fié escheu,[51] com a droit heir, soufert a tenir, se il li voloit defendre et le plait fuïr. Que plait en quei il y a[52] clain puet l'on moult fuyr par les jors et[53] les fuites qui sont en plait,[54] et por tant plus que les dreis heirs et lor heirs[55] en porroient estre desherités de tout le[56] fié qui lor seroit escheu ou de partie se autre que eaus[57] se poent[58] metre en saisine et en teneure dou dit fié autrement que con[59] le plus droit heir[60] aparant et requerant en la court. Car celui qui el[61] dit fié se seroit mis autrement que

---

[25] ou] C: et [26] ses parens d'avoir] A: autre siens parenz a aveir [27] est] V: estoit [28] de ravoir] C: d'avoir [29] vodront] V: vodroit [30] des] C: de ses [31] et] A: ne [32] avant] AB: devant [33] que] V: com le [34] A adds: en la saissine dou fié [35] faire] V lacks [36] en] A: n'en [37] ent au] BV: en autre [38] en] ABV lack [39] requeroit la saisine, ne autre] V: requiert la saisine ne autrement [40] en] AOV lack [41] la saisine et la teneure] B: eu la saisine [42] l'avroit] C: l'averoit [43] de chose que autre ait] V: que autre l'ait [44] teigne] C: teignent [45] en a] A: est a; O: en ot [46] ou] ABV: de [47] moult] V lacks [48] ne] AB: n'i [49] la] AB lack [50] de] C lacks [51] avroit le fié escheu] V: avoit le fié [52] y a] BV: a; C: y ait [53] ABV add: par [54] en plait] V lacks [55] et lor heirs] O lacks [56] de tout le] C: del [57] que eaus] ABV lack [58] se poent] A: se poeit; B: s'en pevent; O: se pevent; V: s'i peut [59] que con] O lacks [60] heir] C lacks [61] el] B: est ou

par la maniere[62] devant[63] dite le porroit vendre par l'assise, et se il le vendoit,[64] le droit heir et ses heirs en seroient desherités de tout le fié. Et se le fié estoit de pluisors chevaleries, il porroit partie dou fié doner por partie dou servise. Si seroit[65] ensi le droit heir et ses heirs desherités de partie dou[66] fié.[67] Et se celui qui seroit[68] saisi et tenant autrement que con le plus dreit heir aparant et requerant en la court moroit saissi et tenant dou fié, le droit[69] heir n'i poroit recovrer ne ses heirs, se cuit, devant les enfans de celui qui derrainement en seroit[70] mort saisi et tenant se il avoit enfans, por ce que ses enfans[71] seroient plus droit heirs[72] de celui qui derrainement morut saissi et tenant dou fié sans condicion et con de son droit heir,[73] que[74] ne seroit son frere ainsné. Qu'il est assise ou usage[75] que l'on ne puet requerre et avoir[76] fié que l'on die qui li soit escheus qui ne le requiert de par celui qui derrainement en[77] morut saisi et tenant com de son droit, et est assise ou usage que le fis ou la fille dou mort se puet metre[78] en la saisine et en la teneure dou fié de quoi son pere ou sa mere morut saissi et tenant con de son droit. Et par ces raisons et por pluisors autres se ensi estoit[79] avroient les enfans dou derrain saissi et tenant le fié devant[80] lor oncle qui seroit droit heir dou fié,[81] et il et[82] ses heirs en seroient desherités a tort et a pechié et sans mesfait.[a]

Et se aucun dit que puis que[83] l'assise ou l'usage est tel que le fis ou la fille demore en la saisine dou fié que son pere ou sa mere morut saisi et tenant con son droit,[84] et puis que ensi est, donc ne covient il mie que fis ne fille autre que le droit heir[85] requiere au seignor con le plus droit heir[86] aparant et requerant en la court escheete[87] qui li soit[88] escheue de pere ou de mere de fié de quei il

---

[a] V begins a new chapter here with the rubric: Coument fis ou fille ne demeure en saisine dou fié de quoy som pere morut saissi et tenant se il n'est le droit heir.

---

[62] maniere] BV: teneure [63] devant] ABV: avant [64] vendoit] B: vendroit [65] seroit] B: seroient [66] servise. Si seroit . . . dou] O lacks [67] Et se le fié . . . fié] A lacks [68] seroit] A: en sereit ensi; BV: enssi (V: enci) seroit; O: en seroit [69] le droit] V lacks [70] seroit] ABV: sera [71] por ce que ses enfans] V lacks [72] droit heirs] A: dreis; O: dreis heirs [73] et con de son droit heir] A: de son dreit [74] que] BV: qui [75] A adds: en cest reiaume [76] et avoir] B lacks [77] en] CV lack [78] dou mort se puet metre] A: demorre; BV: en demoure (V: demore) [79] estoit] V: estoient [80] devant] ABV: de [81] dou fié] B lacks [82] il et] C lacks [83] puis que] B lacks [84] son droit] B: dou sien [85] autre que le droit heir] A lacks; C adds: le [86] requiere au seignor . . . heir] B lacks [87] la court escheete] ABV: l'echeete [88] soit] A: est

ou ele morut saisi et tenant com de son droit,[89] por quoi il ne doit[90] mie estre si com je ai devant dit, mais que chascun fis ou fille se puet metre en la saisine et en la teneure de s'autorité sans aucune[91] requeste faire ent au seignor, je di que non doit, por ce que se il est en l'assise ou en l'usage que fis ou fille demore en la saisine et en la teneure[92] dou fié de quei son pere ou sa mere morut[93] saisi et tenant con de son dreit,[94] que ce est le dreit heir et non[95] autre, qu'en l'assise n'en l'usage[96] n'est mie que les fis et les filles demorent en la dite saisine, ains est que le fis et[97] la fille y demorent.[98] Et puis qu'il n'i a que le fis ou la fille,[99] donc n'est ce que l'un. Et puis que ce n'est que l'un, donc est ce l'ainsné des fis, et quant il n'i a fis, l'ainsnee des filles. Que par l'assise ou l'usage dou[100] reiaume, l'ainsé de ceaus qui sont en un degré est le droit heir.

Et se tous[101] les anfans ou chascun d'eaus ou autre que l'ainsné se pooit[102] metre de s'autorité en saisine et en teneure dou fié, donc en porroit l'un l'autre geter toutes les fois que il vodroit et metre se en[103] saisine, de quei guerre et contens poroit movoir et movreit[104] entre les freres[105] et les autres parens por le fié qui seroit escheu au dreit heir, et por neent seroit l'assise faite[106] ou l'usage establi que l'on a veu ades user qui est tel: que quant autre heir[107] que[108] le droit heir veaut avoir la saisine et la teneure dou[109] fié qui lor est escheu de pere ou de mere ou d'autre parent, et l'ainsné ne[110] le requiert par ce que il n'est present ou autrement, que celui qui le veaut avoir le doit requerre con le plus droit heir[111] de celui[112] de par qui le fié est escheu qui soit aparant et requerant en la court de cel fié. Et quant il ensi le requiert, que le seignor le doit metre en saisine tant que plus droit heir de lui[113] a avoir cel fié vieigne[114] en la court et le requiert. Et puis que l'assise ou l'usage est tel, il est cler a conoistre que nul des anfans autre que le dreit heir ne

[89] V adds: heir [90] il ne doit] B lacks [91] aucune] B lacks [92] de s'autorité sans . . . teneure] V lacks [93] morut] A: muert [94] dreit] B lacks [95] le dreit heir et non] A: a son dreit heir et non a [96] qu'en l'assise n'en l'usage] A: que en l'assise; V: que l'assise ou l'usage [97] et] ABV: ou [98] demorent] A: demore; B: demoure [99] ou la fille] C lacks [100] dou] A: de cest; B: de ceste; V: de cestui [101] se tous] AB: certes se; V: sertes [102] pooit] AV: peust [103] se en] A: s'ent en; B lacks; V: s'en en [104] movoir et movroit] AB: avenir et movreit (B: movroit); C: movoir; V: avenir et movoir [105] C adds: et les seurs [106] faite] A lacks [107] autre heir] AB: aucun heir (B: hoir) autre; V: aucun heir ou autre [108] que] C: qui [109] dou] C: de [110] ne] V lacks [111] heir] B lacks [112] celui] C: lui [113] plus droit heir de lui] A: le plus dreit heir; B: le plus droit hoir; V: le plus droit heir de lui [114] B adds: avant

demore en la saisine ne[115] en la teneure dou fié que[116] lor pere ne[117] lor mere morut[118] saissi et tenant con de son droit, ne que il ne s'i puet metre de s'autorité ne autrement avoir ent la saisine que con le plus droit heir aparant[119] requerant en la court et[120] tant que plus droit heir y vieigne. Car quant il a ensi toutes les avant dites assises et toz les dis[121] usages sont bien gardés et[122] tenus et maintenus et le droit heir gardé de travaill de ravoir le fié, quant il le veaut avoir,[123] et lui[124] et ses heirs[125] guardé de desheritement. Que quant aucun est saisi de[126] fié con le plus dreit heir aparant et requerant en la court tant que[127] plus droit heir de lui a avoir cel fié y vieigne en la court[128] et le requiere, il ne puet cel fié vendre par l'assise ne doner partie dou fié por partie dou servise. Et se il le done, quant le dreit heir requerra le fié et l'avra, il n'est pas tenus de tenir cel don, et que le droit heir n'a a requerre le fié qui li est escheu que au seignor de qui il le doit tenir, et s'il le[129] requiert, que le seignor ne se[130] pora deffendre por chose que il[131] ne celui qui a et tient le fié dient que il au dreit heir ne responde et que il en saisine ne le mete. Si est clere chose, ce me semble, que il doie ensi estre com je ai dit en cest chapitle par les raisons que je ai dites, se tel cas avient en la court.

[115] ne] AV: et [116] que] B: dou quel; V: qui lor est escheu dont [117] ne] AB: ou; V: et [118] morut] AB: muert; V: meurt [119] BV adds: et [120] et] C lacks [121] toutes les avant . . . dis] B: fait toutes les dites assises et toutes les [122] et] OV lack [123] avoir] BV: ravoir [124] lui] C: celui [125] et lui et ses heirs] B: lui et ses hoirs sont [126] de] V: et tenant dou [127] que] V: com le [128] tant que plus . . . court] AB lack [129] le] OV: li [130] se] AB: s'en; V: s'em [131] V adds: die que il

***[139]** Por quey fis ou fille ne se doit metre de s'autorité en saisine ne en teneure de fié de quey son pere ou sa mere ne soient mors saisis et tenans con de lor droit, ou[1] que il en aient esté les derains crestiens[2] saisis et tenans con de lor droit.[3]

Se aucun fis ou fille se met de s'autorité en saisine sans le seignor de qui cel fié muet[4] d'aucune choze dont son pere ne sa mere ne morurent saisis et[5] tenans, et qu'il dit que ce est le fié qui fu de son pere ou de sa mere et qu'il en[6] furent saisi[7] et tenant en aucun tens, il ne le peut ne[8] doit faire par l'assise ne l'usage de cest[9] royaume se[10] son pere ou sa mere n'en[11] fu le derain crestien[12] saisi et tenant et que il puisse ce prover si come il[13] est[14] devisé en cest livre que on doit tel chose prover.[a] Et se il ensi ne le puet[15] prover, il est ataint de force faite[16] au seignor et[17] encheu en la merci dou[18] seignor en qui seignorie cel fié est[19] con home ataint de force. Por quoi il est plus seure chose de metre soi en saisine et en teneure[20] par[21] le seignor que autrement de ce de quei son pere ou sa mere ne[22] muert[23] saisi et tenant con dou sien, se la chose n'est si clere que il puisse prover si con il doit[24] que son pere[25] en ot eu la derraine saisine des crestiens.

A: fol. lxxxviii^{r-v} cap. 153; **B:** fol. 116^{r-v} cap. 153; **C:** fol. 113^{v} cap. 139; **O:** fols 145^{v}–146^{r}; **V:** fols cxvii^{v}–cxviii^{r} cap. 158; Beugnot, p. 231, cap. 153.

---

[a] Above cap. 53; below caps 158–9.

---

[1] ou] C lacks [2] crestiens] AV lack [3] droit, ou que . . . droit] B (fol. 22^{r}): fiez; CO lack the final 'droit' [4] muet] C: vient [5] morurent saisis et] B: mourure saisi ne [6] en] AV lack [7] en furent saisi] O: fu saisis [8] ne] A: ni ne; B: ne ne le; V: ne ne [9] ne l'usage de cest] C: do [10] se] A: de puis que [11] n'en] ABV: ne [12] crestien] A: qui en morut [13] il] ABV lack [14] V adds: devant [15] puet] B lacks [16] faite] A: faire [17] AV add: est [18] dou] C: au [19] est] B lacks [20] et en tenure] ABV lack [21] par] AB: de par [22] ne] V lacks [23] muert] AV: morut; B: mourut [24] doit] A: dit [25] ABV add: ou sa mere

***[140]** Por quei nul ne se doit[1] metre[2] en saisine de fié qui li[3] soit escheu d'autre que de pere ou de[4] mere, se il ne le fait par le seignor de qui il doit tenir celuy[5] fié.[6]

Nul ne se puet ne[7] doit par l'assise ne[8] l'usage de cest roiaume saisir de chose qu'il die[9] qui[10] li soit escheue de ses ancestres ne d'aucun ne d'aucune de son lignage autre que[11] pere ou mere que[12] par le seignor de qui le fié muet, qui ne soit encheu en la merci dou seignor com[13] ataint de force, se ce de quei il[14] sera saisi[15] doit venir en la main dou seignor par quel que maniere que ce soit. Et se le seignor en viaut avoir droit,[16] il le pora avoir par sa cort. Et coment il le pora avoir[17] sera devisé aprés[18] en cest livre.

A: fol. lxxxviii^v cap. 154; **B:** fol. 116^v cap. 154; **C:** fol. 113^v cap. 140; **O:** fol. 146^r; **V:** fol. cxviii^r cap. 159; Beugnot, pp. 231–2, cap. 154.

---

[1] B (fol. 22^r) adds: saisir ne [2] A adds: de sa auctorité [3] qui li] B: que il; V: que il li [4] pere ou de] A (rubrics fol. 4^v) B: son pere ou de sa [5] celuy] A (rubrics) V: le [6] de qui il . . . fié] A lacks [7] ne] A: ni ne; BV: ne ne [8] ne] AB: ou [9] die] C: dit [10] qui] AV: que [11] A adds: de par [12] pere ou mere que] B: de pere ou de mere que de [13] V adds: home [14] BO add: se [15] V adds: et tenant [16] droit] C lacks [17] A adds: et quel dreit [18] aprés] C lacks

***[141]** Coment l'on doit[1] requerre la saissine dou fié qui li est escheu de par autre que de par son pere ou sa[2] mere, et quey le seignor en[3] doit faire, et coment il la peut[4] esloigner, et coment on[5] le peut ataindre.[a]

Se fié eschiet a home ou a feme de par autre que son pere ou sa mere, et celui ou cele de par qui il li est escheu en morut[6] saisi et tenant con dou sien, et il le viaut requerre, il doit venir devant le seignor et demander li conseill, et aprés faire li dire par son conseill: 'Sire, tel', et le nome, 'vient devant vos com devant son seignor et vos fait assavoir que Deu a fait son comandement de tel[7] qui li apartenoit en tel degré de cele part dont le fié muet. Sire, et celui fié li est escheu com a celui qui estoit[8] apartenant a[9] tel', et le nome, 'de par qui le fié li est escheu et qui dou dit fié morut saisi et tenant con dou sien. Sire, et se vos mescreés qu'il ne[10] li atainsist[11] en tel degré con je ai dit por lui[12] et de cele part dont le fié muet, il est prest de prover tout ensi con la cort esgardera ou connoistra que il prover le doie. Si vos requiert la saisine et la teneure de cel fié qui li est escheu[13] si com je ai dit, et la viaut avoir por tant come je ai dit por lui, se la cort l'esgarde.' Et se la court ne l'esgardoit[14] que por tant la[15] deust avoir, il iroit a son conseill et diroit tant que il sa raison avroit.[16] Et se le seignor set que[17] ensi soit come il dit, il le doit metre en saisine et en teneure debonairement[18] sans plait et sans contens.

Et se le seignor veaut maliner en cele chose et tenir le fié, moult y puet avoir d'eschampes et de fuites, laquel chose bon seignor ne doit faire. Et se le seignor n'est certain que il soit ensi,[19] il li puet

---

A: fols lxxxviii^{v}–xc^{v} cap. 155; **B:** fols 116^{v}–118^{v} cap. 155; **C:** fols 113^{v}–116^{v} cap. 141; **O:** fols 146^{v}–150^{r}; **V:** fols cxviii^{r}–cxxi^{r} cap. 160; Beugnot, pp. 232–5, cap. 155.

---

[a] This chapter is adapted from Philip of Novara, pp. 503–6 cap. 29.

---

[1] doit] V: peut [2] son pere ou sa] A: pere ou; B (fol. 22^{r}) son pere ou de par sa; V: pere ou de par [3] en] C: li [4] il la peut] A: il le peut; B lacks; V: hom le peut [5] on] B: celui ou ceaus a qui il est escheu [6] morut] C: muert [7] A adds: et le nome [8] estoit] B: est [9] a] A: en tel deg<r>é de [10] mescreés qu'il ne] V: me mescreés qu'il ne soit ensi que il ne [11] atainsist] A: apartenist [12] por lui] A lacks [13] qui li est escheu] A lacks [14] se la court ne l'esgardoit] B: la court se ele n'esgardoit; V: se la court ne l'esguarde [15] la] BV: ne le [16] avroit] A: gardereit [17] ABV add: il [18] C adds: et [19] A adds: come il a dit

respondre lui[20] deleant en[21] semblant de raison que il n'entent que celui fié fust onques de celui que le requerant[22] a voué a son ancestre, et se il avint en aucune maniere que il ot et tint cel fié, il ne l'ot de don de[23] seignor ne en autre maniere qu'il peust ne deust venir ne escheir a lui[24] qui le[b] requiert, et a ce qu'il euffre a prover le parenté, il n'a mie ore[25] grant talent de savoir son lignage. Mais se il fust prové que le fié eust esté doné a celui qu'il a voé a son ancestre en maniere que il deust ne peust escheir a lui, se il fust dessendu de lui si come il[26] dit,[27] adonc[28] quant leuc et tens seroit,[29] le seignor respondroit au parenté si con il devroit. Et de toutes les choses dessus dites et de chascune par sei l'une aprés l'autre puet le seignor, qui veaut tenir le fié et la saisine que on li requiert, esloignier et[30] metre s'en[31] en esguart[32] et dire que por tant en veaut il demorer en pais, se la cort l'esguarde, et tous jors metre retenaill de court as esgars et as conoissances[33] en quei il se metra.[34]

Et se le requereor a prevelige ou recort de court dou[35] don qui fu fait a[36] son ancestre saisi et tenant[37] de cel fié con dou sien fié,[38] si li doit soufire, se me semble, a la saisine et a la teneure avoir del dit fié,[39] se il par le[40] prevelige ou par le recort de la cort le prouve,[41] si con il doit, et puis prover[42] le parenté que il a dit qui[43] est entriaus, si con la court esgardera[44] que il prover le doie. Et se il avient que le requereor n'ait prevelige qui ait esté fait a[45] son ancestre de cel fié, die celui qui est a son conseill: 'Sire, celui ou celle qui avoit et tenoit cestui fié, de qui Des a fait son comandement, aparteneit a tel[46] en tel degré de celle part dont le fié meut, et se est il prest de prover si[47] con vostre court esgardera ou conoistra[48] que il prover

[b] Change of hand in C.

[20] li puet respondre lui] A: li respondra lui; B: li respondra; V: respondera lui [21] en] AV: o; B: ou [22] requerant] V: requiert [23] don de] BV: son [24] lui] O: autre [25] ore] BV lack [26] V adds: a [27] dit] B: doit [28] C adds: et [29] seroit] B: sera [30] et] AO lack [31] s'en] C: sei [32] A adds: de court [33] de court as . . . conoissances] A: es esgars et es conoissances de court [34] en quei il se metra] B: ou il se met [35] dou] V: que de [36] dou don qui fu fait a] C: qui ait veu [37] saisi et tenant] ABV lack [38] con dou sien fié] A: ou garent qui ait veu son ancestre saissi et tenant come dou sien; B: qui ait veu son ancestre saisi et tenant de cel fié come dou sien; V: ou recort de court qui ait veu son ancestre saisi et tenant de cel fié com dou sien [39] del dit fié] A: dou dit fié ou; B: dou fié devant dit ou; V: dou dit fié et [40] le] ABV lack [41] prouve] A: peut prover [42] prover] ABV: preuve [43] que il a dit qui] V: si que il a dit que il [44] AV add: ou conoistra [45] fait a] A: de [46] a tel] BV lack [47] si] A: tot ensi [48] ou conoistra] V lacks

le doie. Sire,[49] et[50] il est us ou costume ou assisse en cest royaume ou raison que quant fié eschet qui est a touz heirs que il eschet as parens de celui de par qui il eschet et que le plus prochain qui en[51] requiert la saissine et la teneure la[52] doit avoir devant[53] les autres et l'a,[54] s'il[55] la requiert, et c'il n'est que as heirs de feme espouse, que il eschiet a ceaus heirs, et que le plus prochain de ceaus heirs l'a devant les autres, s'il la requiert. Sire, tel et tel[56] aparteneit[57] a tel en tel degré de celle part dont le fié meut qui[58] en mourut saisi et tenant.[59] Si est clere chose que il doit avoir cele meimes saisine selon l'assise ou l'usage dou reaume de Jerusalem ou raison. Et il est choze certaine que les[60] fiés de Chypre[61] sont useement fais as heirs de feme espouse de celui a qui l'on done le fié, et que ce[62] est le cours des dons des fiés de Chypre[63] dont il, provant[64] le parenté[65] dou derain[66] qui[67] morut saisi et tenant de cestui fié, et ensi que il soit des heirs qui de celui[68] sont decendus de sa feme espouse, veaut il[69] avoir la saisine,[70] se la court l'esgarde.' Et se la court n'esgarde[71] que il[72] por tant con je ai dit por lui[73] la deust[74] avoir, il[75] diroit et[76] feroit tant[77] dire que il garderoit sa raison. Et contre ce peut le seignor[78] trover mout d'eschanpes et[79] delais et de fuites, mais il ne[80] me semble que il a la fin puisse defendre au requerant a avoir la saisine. Et se[81] il dit que le don[82] ne fu doné en maniere que il, a celui qui le requiert, peust ne deust escheir, por quei il[83] ne le veaut metre en saisine, se court ne l'esgarde, ains en veaut demorer vers lui quite et en pais, se la cort l'esgarde, tant que il ait prové si con il doit que le fié fu doné a celui qui le conquist[84] en maniere que il a lui qui le requiert peust escheir, et de ce se met en l'esgart de la court sauf son retenaill, a ce peut respondre le requerant, et dire: 'Sire, certaine choze est que le cours et l'usage des dons que les

[49] Sire] C lacks [50] et] BV lack [51] et que le . . . en] O: a ceaus heirs et que le plus prochein de ceaus [52] la] C lacks [53] la doit avoir devant] A: l'a devant toz [54] et l'a] A lacks; B: et [55] s'il] C: si [56] V adds: et le nome [57] aparteneit] C: apartenant [58] qui] A: et qui; BV: et [59] A adds: come dou sien [60] B adds: dons des [61] de Chypre] A: que l'on done orres [62] ce] ABV: tel [63] dons des fiés de Chypre] A: fiés des dons de orres [64] provant] B: provent [65] le parenté] C: les parentés [66] dou derain] V lacks [67] ABV adds: en [68] celui] C: lui [69] il] BV lack [70] A adds: dou fié [71] n'esgarde] AB: n'esgardast; O: n'esgardoit [72] que il] V lacks [73] por lui] B: ne; V: pour lui ne [74] deust] V: poist [75] A adds: ireit a son conseill et [76] et] AB: ou [77] tant] V lacks [78] V adds: dire et [79] AOV add: de [80] ne] B lacks [81] Et se] A: Que ce; BV: Que [82] le don] A: cel fié; BV: son don [83] por quei il] A: et que por ce il; B: por ce; V: pour ce que il [84] qui le conquist] A: et que il le conoist

seignors ont adés fais[85] en cest royaume de Chypre[86] ont esté a ceaus a qui il ont[87] doné les fiez[88] et a lor heirs de feme espouse, et je qui[89] suis prest de prover, si con court esgardera ou conoistra que je prover le doie, que je suis des heirs descendus de tel et de tel', et le[90] nome, 'doy[91] avoir s'escheete et la saisine et la teneure del[92] fié qui fu sien qui de par lui m'est escheu. Quar par le cours qui est usé corsablement en Chypre[93] des dons des fiés qui sont adés fais acostumeement a heirs de feme espouse est il asés[94] prové et coneu que le fié fu doné a mon[95] ancestre, a lui et a ses heirs de sa feme espouse. Et se vos volés dire que ce[96] don fu doné autrement que selon le cours des dons des fiés de Chypre,[97] je di, sauve soit vostre henor, que non, place Deu, ne ne veull[98] que il demore por chose que vos aiés fait dire que je n'aie la saisine dou fié que je vos ay requis et requier come mon droit, ains le veull[99] avoir por toutes les raisons que je ais dites ou por aucunes d'elles se la court l'esgarde. Et de ce me met je en l'esgart de la court sauf mon retenail.' Et a moy semble, que par le cours et l'usage des dons des fiés de Chypre,[100] que le seignor ne peut defendre au requereor[101] la saisine, se il ne preuve par recort de court si con il est desus[102] dit,[103] ou par prevelige qui[104] soit el pooir et en la garde de l'ome et que il en use ou en ait usé en court[105] a son besoing, que le don de cel fié[106] fu[107] fait a l'ancestre dou requereor[108] si que l'escheete[109] ne peut ne ne doit venir a lui par assise ne par usage ne par raison, tout soit ce que le prevelige que le seignor[110] fait a l'ome porte guarentie encontre le seignor por[111] son seel qui y pent, mais encontre l'ome ne porte il nule[112] garentie de chose qui soit encontre luy, mais que tant que se le seignor fait aucun prevelige de dons ou de covenans, et le prevelige est[113] el pooir et en la guarde[114] de l'ome, et il en a usé et use[115] a son besoing, se il y a aucune chose qui soit au profit dou

---

[85] adés fais] A: fait des fiés; V: adés fais des fiés [86] de Chypre] A lacks [87] qui il ont] C: qu'il ot [88] A adds: au meins a eaus [89] qui] ABV lack [90] le] AB: les [91] doy] A: et par ce deis; B: et doi; V: et doit [92] del] AB: dou [93] en Chypre] A lacks [94] asés] B: bien [95] mon] V: son [96] ce] A: cest; B: le; V: son [97] dons des fiés de Chypre] A: fiés de cest reiaume [98] ne ne veull] A: si ne viaus [99] le veull] A: la viaus [100] dons des fiés de Chypre] A: fiés d'orres [101] requereor] AB: requerant [102] desus] C: devant [103] dit] V: devisé [104] qui] C: qu'il [105] use ou en . . . court] A: use; B: usoit en cort; V: huse en court [106] de cel fié] B lacks [107] fu] A: ne fu [108] requereor] AV: requerant [109] l'escheete] V: celle escheete [110] B adds: a [111] le seignor por] V lacks [112] nule] A: mie; V: point nulle [113] est] A: seit [114] et en la guarde] B lacks [115] et use] A lacks

seignor et au damage de l'ome, ausi[116] bien doit estre cel prevelige grevable a l'ome come au seignor. Quar aussi con le don et le profit de l'ome doit estre contre[117] le seignor des choses qui sont[118] el prevelige qui est en la guarde de l'ome et de quei il a usé et use,[119] redoit estre contre l'ome et gregier le, se il y a chose qui li griege, por ce que il est en la garde de l'ome et que il en a usé[120] a son profit en la court, si en repeut le seignor bien user au sien[121] profit, puis que court est[122] recordant de ce que il a el prevelige, ou ce celui qui derainement ot la saisine dou[123] dit fié ne fist choze par quey lui et ses heirs fussent[124] desherités de cel fié par esgart ou par conoissance de court ou par assisse ou par usage.

Et se l'avant dite requeste est faite el royaume de Jerusalem ou le[125] cors des anciens fiés est a touz heirs et des noviaus as[126] heirs de feme espouse, le seignor peut molt mains esloigner et defendre la saisine et la teneure dou dit fié au requereor que el royaume de Chypre, por ce que c'il est des anciens dons qui sont a toz heirs la preuve est plus legiere a faire au requereor dou parenté en general que de prover que il soit des heirs[127] de par qui il requiert l'escheete decendus de lui[128] de sa feme espouse. Quar prover le parenté en general soufist en tant, se me semble, que ce celui qui prover le veaut preuve[129] par .ii. homes ou femes crestiens[130] que il oirent que[131] celui de par qui le requerant[132] requiert l'escheete le teneit a parent et il lui, il a bien prové le parenté si com il doit.[133] Et se le fié est des noviaus dons qui sont as heirs[134] de feme espouse, la preuve dou parenté[135] est[136] autel con cele de Cypre. Et se le seignor noie que le don ne fu[137] fait a l'ancestre dou requereor[138] en maniere que l'escheete puisse a lui venir por doner li la prouve de ce, si que c'il n'en a prevelige ne recort de court dou don qui en a[139] esté fait a son ancestre si que a lui puisse escheir[140] que il faille a la preuve et que por ce perde sa querelle. Tout soit ce que le requereor n'ait

[116] ausi] B: autressi [117] contre] C: encontre [118] V adds: contre le seignor [119] a usé et use] A: en a usé et use a son besoin [120] B adds: et use [121] au sien] AB: a son [122] court est] A: la court en est bien [123] dou] V: de celui [124] fussent] B: fussent estre; C: furent [125] le] C: les [126] as] C lacks [127] AB add: de celui [128] AV add: et [129] preuve] C: peut prover; V: le preuve [130] homes ou femes crestiens] V: loyaus homes ou femes crestiens de la loi de Rome [131] oirent que] O: l'oirent que se [132] requerant] C: requereor [133] si com il doit] B lacks [134] as heirs] B lacks [135] dou parenté] B lacks [136] dou parenté est] C: est dou parenté [137] fu] A: fust [138] requereor] A: requerant [139] qui en a] C: que n'a; V: qui ait [140] A adds: et

prevelige ne recort de court de ce qui est avant dit se porra[141] il defendre d'acuillir la preuve a soi en cest cas et doner la au seignor par les raisons qui devant[142] sont dites et devisees[143] del don corsable des fiés, ce est assaveir des anciens[144] a touz heirs et des noviaus[145] as heirs de feme espouse, et a ce[146] li devroit[147] bien valoir les dites raisons, se me semble, que se autrement estoit, mout de gens en[148] porroient[149] perdre lor raisons et estre desherité a tort et sans raison.

---

[141] porra] A: peut [142] devant] ABV: avant [143] dites et devisees] AV: dites; BO: devisees [144] anciens] A: ancestres [145] V adds: c'est assavoir [146] a ce] A: assés [147] devroit] BO: devront [148] en] C lacks [149] porroient] V: poroit

***[142]** Por quey le seignor n'est tenus de respondre dou[1] fié que[2] autre ait et teigne, de quey il ait esté saisi[3] con de son droit par esgart ou par conoissance de court ou par assise ou par usage.[4]

Se aucun requiert au seignor saisine de fié qui li soit escheu, et le seignor dit aucune chose a l'encontre por quei le requerant ne doie cele saisine avoir, et le requerant dit raison et tel que court esgarde[5] ou conoisse que il en doit avoir la saisine, et il l'a par esgart ou par conoissance de court, et .i. autre vient[6] aprés[7] devant celui seignor ou autre ou el[8] tens de celui qui en avra eu la saisine par esgart ou par conoissance de court ou de son heir et requiert au seignor cel fié disant que il est dreit heir a cel fié avoir devant tous les autres et[9] ofrant[10] le a prover si con la court esgardera ou conoistra que il prover le doye, le seignor li doit respondre que il n'a ne tient cel fié por quey il n'entent que il li en ait a respondre, mais ce il se claime de celui qui l'a et[11] tient, il l'avra[12] a droit en sa court, ne il n'entent que il autre li en ait a faire, puis que il ou son ancestre par esgart ou par conoissance de court ont eue la saisine dou dit fié, ne faire ne le viaut, se la court ne l'esgarde,[13] et de ce se met il en l'esgart de la court sauf son retenaill. Et aprés cest dit, ce le requerant viaut son plait abregier,[14] il se clamera de celuy qui tient le fié et requerra au seignor que il le face venir en la cort faire li droit de ce que il li requerra. Que il ne me semble que il puisse chose dire par quei la court esgarde ne[15] conoisse que le seignor li soit tenus de respondre de cel fié ne de faire autre que ce que il li a ofert, que il est assise ou usage el royaume de Jerusalem que de fié de quei home ou feme ait esté saisi et tenant par conoissance de court et que il ou son heir teigne, que le seignor ne doit respondre ne entrer en plait ne autre chose faire que aver a droit[16] celui qui le tient se l'on se claime de luy.

A: fols xc^{v}–xci^{r} cap. 156; **B:** fols 118^{v}–119^{r} cap. 156; **C:** fols 116^{v}–117^{r} cap. 142; **O:** fols 150^{r}–151^{r}; **V:** fol. cxxi^{r-v}–cap. 161; Beugnot, p. 236, cap. 156.

---

[1] dou] AB (fol. 22^{r}) V: de [2] que] B adds: nul [3] ait esté saisi] A: l'a saissi; A rubric (fol. 5^{r}): l'ait saissi; B: l'ait mis en saisine et en teneure; C: ait esté saisi et tenant; V: l'ait [4] de court ou . . . usage] B: ou par assise de cort [5] esgarde] C: l'esgarde [6] vient] BOV: revient [7] aprés] B lacks [8] ou el] AV: el; B: ou [9] et] C lacks [10] ofrant] ABV: offrir [11] l'a et] A: le [12] l'avra] A: l'avera; O: le li avra [13] l'esgarde] V: le veaut esgarder [14] abregier] C: abergier [15] ne] C: ou [16] a droit] B: droit de; V: droit

***[143]** Quant fié eschiet a plusors gens et aucun autre que le droit heir[1] en requiert la saisine au seignor come droit heir, por quey le seignor ne le doit metre en saisine,[2] se il ne l'en requiert con le plus dreit heir aparant et requerant en la court.

Se aucun requiert fié qui dit qui[3] li soit escheu de par aucun sien[4] ancestre, et il li requiert[5] con dreit heir de celui de par qui[6] il dit que le fié li est[7] escheu a avoir cel fié, et le seignor cret ou set[8] que il y a[9] plus droit heir de lui[10] a cel[11] fié avoir, il li doit respondre: 'Vos me requerés cel fié con le plus droit heir de tel', et le nome, 'et je entens que il y a plus droit heir de vos[12] a avoir le dit fié,[13] por quey je a vos con a plus dreit heir[14] ne veull respondre, se la court ne l'esgarde, et di por quey: por ce que je entens que il y a plus dreit heir[15] de vos, et que je doi garder la raison de chascun que j'entent que raison ait en ma seignorie,[16] et que se je vos metoie en saisine dou dit[17] fié si con vos le me requerés, il porroit torner a perjudice d'autre se il estoit[18] plus dreit heir de vos a avoir le fié. Mais se vos le me requerés[19] come le plus droit heir aparant et requerant en la court au dit fié avoir, je vos[20] eufre a faire ce que je doi par ma court, ne je n'entens que je autre[21] vos en doie faire ne faire ne le veull por les raisons que je ais[22] dites ou por aucunes d'elles, se la court ne l'esgarde que je faire le doye, se vos avant ne le[23] provés si[24] con court esgardera ou conoistra que vos faire le doiés que vos[25] soiés le plus dreit heir de celui de par qui vos requerés cel fié a avoir le,[26] et de ce me met je en l'esgart de la court sauf mon retenaill.' Et aprés ce[27] il ne[28] me semble que le requereor

---

A: fol. xci^{r-v} cap. 157; **B:** fol. 119^{r-v} cap. 157; **C:** fol. 117^{r-v} cap. 143; **O:** fols 151^{r}–152^{r}; **V:** fols cxxi^{v}–cxxii^{v} cap. 163; Beugnot, p. 237, cap. 157.

---

[1] B (fol. 22^{r}) adds: vient en cort et [2] saisine] B: la saisine dou fié [3] dit qui] B: die qu'il; O lacks [4] sien] O lacks [5] requiert] B: quiert [6] qui] C: quey [7] est] O: soit [8] cret ou set] A: set; BV: croit; O: set ou creit [9] a] BV: ait [10] lui] C: celui [11] cel] A: le dit [12] de vos] AV lack [13] dit fié] A: fié de voz [14] por quey je . . . heir] V: si [15] heir] A lacks [16] ait en ma seignorie] A: y ait si come je le truis escrit en ma secrete; B: ait en ma secrete; V: ait [17] dit] A lacks [18] perudice d'autre se il estoit] B: prendre d'autre se il est [19] il porroit torner . . . requerés] A: je ne voz metre autrement que [20] en la court . . . vos] A: au dit fié aveir et je voz en [21] B adds: chose [22] que je ais] O: dessus [23] le] ABV lack [24] si] C lacks [25] faire le doiés que vos] C lacks [26] le] BO lack [27] aprés ce] C: ce (deleted) [28] ne] BO lack; V interlined in later hand

puisse[29] chose dire par quei[30] le seignor le mete en saisine de cel fié si con il la requis, ce il ne preuve si con il doit que il est le plus droit heir de celui de par qui il le requiert le dit fié a avoir.[31] Si me semble que se il viaut son plait[32] abergier que[33] il le doit requerre con le plus droit heir aparant et requerant en la court a avoir cel fié, se il ne peut[34] la prove avant dite faire, et que[35] se il ensi le requiert que le seignor ne li porra defendre la saisine dou fié[36] se son ancestre de par qui il le requiert en morut saisi et tenant con dou sien, et il preuve le parenté si con il doit, se son ancestre[37] n'a chose faite par quei il et ses heirs soient desherités[38] de cel fié par assisse ou par usage ou par esgart ou par[39] conoissance de court.

---

[29] puisse] B: ne puet [30] A adds: la court dee esgarder que [31] si con il la requis . . . avoir] ABV: a avoir (A: aveir) le [32] plait] B lacks [33] que] C: se [34] V adds: prover ou a [35] que] C lacks [36] la saisine dou fié] B lacks; V: le fié [37] de par qui . . . ancestre] A lacks [38] desherités] O lacks [39] esgart ou par] B lacks

***[144]** En quel cas le seignor est tenus de respondre a[1] qui li requiert saisine de fié que autre ait et teigne et de quey il soit[2] son home.

Se home ou feme requiert au seignor come le plus dreit heir aparant et requerant en la court fié qu'il dit qui[3] li soit escheu[4] de par aucun de ses ancestres, et le seignor le met en saisine sans esgars ou[5] sans conoissance de court, et home ou feme veigne[6] aprés devant le seignor et li requiert la saisine de cel fié que celui a,[7] et dit coment que celui qui le fié a et tient estoit apartenant a celui de par qui le fié lor eschey[8] en tel degré et il en tel, et die en[9] quans degrés[10] il li apartenoit,[11] et s'il li apartenoient[12] en .i. degré et il est l'ainsné, ou s'il est home et l'autre[13] feme, si le die et die[14] que il est prest de prover tout ensi con la court esgardera[15] qu'il prover le doye, que il estoit[16] ataignant[17] a celui de par qui le fié lor est escheu en tel degré con il a dit,[18] ou que il est ainsné de celui qui tient le fié, se il sont en .i. degré a celui de par qui il dit que le fié lor[19] est escheu, et que ce provant viaut il que le seignor le mete en saisine del[20] dit fié por tant come il a dit, se la court l'esgarde, et de ce se met il[21] en l'esgart de la court sauf son[22] retenaill, et se le seignor li respont que il n'a le fié ne[23] tient, por quei il n'entent qu'il soit tenus de respondre[24] ne faire ne le veaut, se la court ne l'esgarde, mais se il viaut aucune chose requiere a celui qui l'a et[25] tient, il le li avra a droit en sa court, ne autre chose il n'i entent[26] qu'il[27] en ait a faire ne faire ne le[28] viaut, se la court ne l'esgarde, et de ce se met il en l'esgart de la court sauf son retenaill, a ce peut respondre le requerant et[29] dire: 'Sire, je ne veull que il demore por chose que vos

---

A: fols xcii[r]–xciii[r] cap. 159; **B:** fols 119[v]–120[v] cap. 159; **C:** fols 117[v]–119[r] cap. 144; **O:** fols 152[r]–154[v]; **V:** fols cxxii[v]–cxxiv[r] cap. 164; Beugnot, pp. 238–40, cap. 159.

---

[1] B (fol. 22[v]) adds: celui [2] soit] A: est [3] dit qui] O: die qu'il [4] escheu] C: escheue [5] ou] ABV: et [6] veigne] V: meut [7] de cel fié que celui a] A: come le plus dreit heir que celui qui l'a; B: de cel fié come plus droit hoir de celui qui l'a et tient; V: de cel fié come plus droit heir que celui qui l'a [8] eschey] ABV: est escheu [9] en] ABV: de [10] quans degrés] A: quel degré [11] apartenoit] O: apartenoient [12] apartenoient] C: apartient; V: apartenoit [13] et l'autre] AV: et l'autre est; C: ou [14] C adds: coment [15] A adds: ou conoistra [16] estoit] AB: est [17] A adds: en tel degré [18] en tel degré . . . dit] O: et que se prouvant [19] lor] ABV: li [20] del] ABV: dou [21] il] AB lack [22] son] A: mon [23] ne] A: ni nel; V: ne ne le [24] A adds: li ent [25] l'a et] C: la [26] n'i entent] ABV: n'entent [27] AB add: li [28] le] C: li [29] respondre le requerant et] B: le requerant

aiés dite que vos ne me[30] respondés a ma requeste et me metés a la[31] saisine dou fié que je vos requier, et di por coy: que vos, sire, tel', et le nome, 'avés mis en saisine dou dit fié con le plus dreit heir aparant et requerant en la court,[32] et ce que vos en feistes ne fu par esgart ne par conoissance de cort, et que je[33] suis plus dreit heir et plus aparant[34] de lui au dit fié avoir, et que[35] ce suis je prest de[36] prover tout enssi con la court esgardera ou conoistra que je prover le doye, et que je entent que vos, qui estes seignor et a qui je doi mon fié et m'escheete requerre con de celui de qui je la doy tenir et a qui j'en doy faire l'omage et le servise que le dit fié doit, ne vos[37] poés par l'assise ne l'usage dou reaume de Jeruslem ne par droit ne par[38] raison defendre en cest cas de respondre a ma requeste, ne de metre moy[39] en saisine dou dit fié, se provant que je ai ofert,[40] et[41] s'enssi fust que vos en cest cas vos peuciés vers moi defendre de non respondre me[42] a ma requeste, por ce que tel', et le nome, 'en est[43] saisi si con je ai devant dit, trop porroient estre les drois heirs des fiez gregés[44] et travaillés ains que il en[45] eussent la saisine, se il les covenist[46] a clamer de ceaus qui la saisine des fiés avront[47] con le[48] plus droit heir aparant et requerant[49] en la court, se ceaus qui avroient tels saisines[50] voloient maligner et le plait fuïr et esloigner a ceaus qui plus drois heirs seroient d'eaus. Que molt peut plait fuïr et esloigner[51] qui est saisis[52] d'aucune chose et autre se claime de lui se il faire[53] le viaut et set. Et por toutes les raisons que je ai dites ou por aucunes d'eles veull je que vos me[54] respondés a ma requeste et me metés en saisine[55] dou fié que je vos[56] requier ce provant que je ai ofert, se la[57] court l'esgarde, et de ce me met je en l'esgart de la court sauf mon retenaill.' Aprés ce dit ne me senble que le seignor puisse chose dire par quey il se puisse defendre de respondre[58] au requerant, et que[59] la court n'esgarde que il li doit respondre a sa requeste et que il a leisir de[60] dire.

---

[30] me] AB lack [31] a la] A: en la; BV: en [32] la court] A: l'escheete [33] C adds: y [34] et plus aparant] V: aparant et requerant [35] que] AB lack [36] ce suis je prest de] V: je suis prest dou [37] BOV add: ne [38] droit ne par] A lacks [39] ne de metre moy] B: et que vos ne mettés [40] A adds: a prover [41] O adds: que [42] me] ABV lack [43] en est] AV: c'est; B: s'est [44] gregés] B: grevez [45] en] ABV lack [46] covenist] B: covenoit [47] avront] ABV: avroient [48] le] C: les [49] le plus droit . . . requerant] A: les plus dreis heirs aparanz et requeranz [50] tels saisines] A: tel saissine [51] a ceaus qui . . . esloigner] B lacks [52] C adds: et tenant [53] faire] A: foyr; BV: fuïr [54] me] BV lack [55] ABV add: et en teneure [56] vos] BV lack [57] se la] V: en la court se [58] V adds: a sa requeste [59] que] C: se [60] de] AV: dou

Et aprés le dit esgart le seignor doit dire que puis que celui qui[61] a et tient le dit fié en est son home et que il le tient de lui, il entent qu'il en[62] doit avoir .i. respit resnable a faire assavoir a celui qui a et tient le[63] fié la requeste[64] et le response qu'il li a fait et l'esgart que la court a fait[65] savoir se il voudra venir en la court[66] dire aucune chose contre le dit et la requeste dou requerant, si viaut avoir le respit se la court l'esgarde, et tel con court esgardera ou[67] conoistra qu'il avoir le doie. Et a moi ne me[68] senble que le requereor[69] puisse chose dire contre[70] ce par quei la court n'esgarde que le seignor doit avoir le respit et tel con la court conoistra que il avoir le doie.[71] Et a moy senble que le respit seroit covenable ce celui qui tient le fié est en la vile de .iii. jors, et ce il est au reaume de .xv. jors, et se il est hors dou reaume .xl. jors, et[72] se il est yver et il li coveigne mer a[73] passer .iii. mois, et se il est[74] en Roumanie .iii. mois se il est ysté et se il est yver[75] .vi. mois,[76] et se il est[77] outre mer .i. an. et .i. jor. Et quant la court avra coneu quel respit le seignor en[78] doit avoir, le seignor[79] doit faire assavoir le plus tost que il pora a celui qui tient le fié la requeste dou requerant et son respons et l'esgart de la court et mander que, se il viaut venir en la court dire aucune chose contre le requerant, que il y soit au jor que il a de respit par la conoissance de la court et dire au requerant que il y soit a celui jor.[80] Et ce selui qui tient le fié y vient a cel jor et die raison por quoy le seignor ne doit de cel fié respondre au requereor,[81] et tel que la[82] court l'esgarde ou conoisse, si oie le plait de l'un et de l'autre, et ce il ce[83] ne fait ou ne vient a celui jor en la court, si responde le seignor et face au requerant[84] ce que il entendra que[85] il respondre et[86] faire l'en doive[87] par raison et selon l'usage dou reaume de Jerusalem. Et se celui qui tient le fié vient en la court

[61] qui] C lacks [62] en] BV lack [63] AV add: dit [64] A adds: dou requerant [65] V adds: pour [66] en la court] C lacks; V: en la court pour [67] esgardera ou] AOV lack [68] me] AOV lack [69] requereor] A: requerant [70] contre] O lacks [71] Et a moi . . . doie] B lacks [72] et] C lacks [73] a] BV lack [74] hors dou reaume . . . est] A lacks [75] .iii. mois se . . . yver] C lacks [76] .vi. mois] B: demi an [77] A adds: desa mer fors dou reiaume .xl. jors, ce il est esté, et se il est yver qu'il coveigne mer a passer .iii. meis, et se il est [78] en] ABV lack [79] en doit avoir, le seignor] C lacks [80] a celui jor] B: au jour que il a de respit par la conoissance de la court [81] au requereor] A lacks; B: au requerant [82] la] ABV lack [83] ce] O lacks [84] et face au requerant] A: au requerant et li face [85] que] C: et [86] respondre et] B lacks [87] l'en doive] A: li en deie; B: li doie; V: le doie

et il ne[88] dit raison por quei le seignor n'est tenus de respondre au requerant et il dit aucune chose contre le requerant ou contre ses preuves, si les teigne et maintiegne[89] le seignor a droit par sa court si con il devra par l'assise ou l'usage dou dit royaume.[90]

[88] il ne] AB lack; V: il [89] et maintiegne] C lacks [90] dit royaume] BV: reaume (V: royaume) de Jerusalem

***[145]** En quel cas le seignor ne se peut defendre de respondre a[1] qui li requiert saisine de fié que autre ait et teigne, et de quey il[2] est en l'omage et[3] servise dou seignor.[4] [a]

Se .i.[5] home ou feme meurt qui a[6] fié, et le fié[7] vient en la main dou seignor, et il le tient .i. espace de tens quelqu'ele soit, et aprés se aucun veigne en la cort devant le seignor[8] et li requiert cel fié, disant que il li est[9] escheu de par celui ou cele qui derainement[10] morut saisi et tenant con dou sien,[11] con celui qui li aperteneit de cele part dont le fié moveit en tel degré, et die quel, et l'eufre a prover si con cort esgardera ou conoistra que il prover le doie, et le preuve si con il devra,[12] et que[13] le seignor li contrebate[14] la saisine[15] disant raison contre son dit tel con il li semblera[16] que faire le doie, et que aprés il s'en[17] saisi[18] par esgart ou par conoissance de court, et[19] aucun autre vient aprés devant le seignor et li requiert cel fié disant que il est droit heir a avoir cel fié,[20] et que ce est il prest de prover tout ensi con la[21] court esgardera ou conoistra que il prover le doye, et que celui qui l'a et tient n'i a droit con celui qui n'est de riens apartenant a celui de qui le fié estoit et qui derainement[22] morut saisi et tenant con dou sien, et que ce que il ot le dit fié fu par la[23] preuve que il prova par faus garans qui se parjurerent[24] et cele guarentie porterent faucement par seurté de[25] ce qu'il ne cuiderent qu'il n'eust mie[26] tornes de bataille en preuve de parenté, de laquel chose il furent et sont deceus, que ele y est bien d'un home a .i.[27] autre en aucun cas, tout soit ce que de preuve de parenté

A: fols xciii^{r}–xcvi^{r} cap. 160; **B:** fols 121^{r}–123^{v} cap. 160; **C:** fols 119^{r}–123^{r} cap. 145; **O:** fols 154^{v}–160^{v}; **V:** fols cxxiv^{r}–cxxviii^{r} cap. 165; Beugnot, pp. 240–5, cap. 160.

---

[a] This rubric does not accurately describe the content of this chapter.

---

[1] B (fol. 22^{v}) adds: celui [2] de quey il] A: qu'il [3] A adds: ou; BV: en; O: au [4] dou seignor] B lacks [5] .i.] ABV lack [6] a] AOV: ait [7] le fié] B: il [8] le seignor] C lacks [9] est] A: seit [10] AB add: en [11] ABV add: et [12] devra] B: doit [13] que] AB lack; V: se [14] contrebate] V: contredit [15] la saisine] ABV lack [16] semblera] C: semblara; V: resemblera [17] s'en] O: l'en [18] et que aprés il s'en saisi] A: et que por chose que le seignor die ne demorre que court n'esgarde ou conoist qu'il le dee metre en saissine, et qu'il le met en saissine; BV lack [19] B adds: se; V: ce [20] cel fié] A: le [21] tout ensi con la] A: si come la; BV: si come [22] AB add: en [23] la] BV lack [24] se parjurerent] AV: s'esparjurerent [25] par seurté de] A: por; B: et de; V: de [26] ne cuiderent qu'il n'eust mie] A: ne cuidierent mie qu'il eust; BV: cuiderent que il n'i eust (B: eust mie) [27] .i.] ABV lack

d'ome a seignor n'ait point de tornes de bataille,[28] et que s'il eust la esté quant les faus garans se parjurerent[29] et la fauce guarentie porterent dou parenté, il en eust l'un levé come parjur[30] et torné come faus guarant par guage de bataille, et que ce il estoient tel que il vousissent lor faus dis maintenir, que il est prest de torner ent[31] l'un par guage de bataille, et que ce provant, faisant ce[32] que il a ofert, veaut que le seignor le mete en saisine dou dit[33] fié, se la court l'esgarde, et de ce se met il en l'esgart de la court sauf son retenaill, contre ce peut le seignor dire[34] qu'il cel fié que il li[35] requiert n'a[36] ne tient, et que celui, qui l'a et tient et qui son home en est[37] et servise li en doit,[38] l'ot par esgart de court, ne que por chose que il deyst contre son dit qui disoit le meaus que il savoit a defendre li par raison la saisine dou dit fié, ne demora que il par esgart de court[39] n'eust la saisine: 'et puis que il par esgart de court l'ot, je n'entent que je vos soie tenus de respondre ne d'autre chose faire vos ent que d'avoir le vos a droit, se vos vos clamés de lui, ne faire ne le veull, se la court ne l'esgarde. Et de ce me met je en l'esgart de la court sauf mon[40] retenaill.' Et aprés ces dis[41] je cuit que la court doit esgarder que le seignor ne li[42] a pas a[43] respondre ne autre chose faire, que[44] ce que il li a ofert, ce est d'avoir le li a droit en sa court.

Et aprés cest esgart, c'il[45] se claime de celui qui a et tient le dit fié, le seignor le doit faire venir en sa[46] court le plus tost que il porra et avoir le a droit au requerant. Et quant il sera en la court, se le requerant se claime de lui, si cora[47] le plait entr'yaus si con il devra par l'usage de la court. Et se le requerant dit el plait que la preuve que celui fist dou parenté quant il ot la saisine dou fié[48] fu fauce,[49] et que les guarans s'en parjurerent[50] desleiaument et porterent fauce guarentie en seurté de ce que il cuidoient[51] que on ne peust torner guarans par guage de bataille qui portent guarentie de parenté, et

[28] bataille] C: batailles [29] se parjurerent] A: se esparjurerent; V: c'esparjurerent [30] parjur] V: esparjuré [31] de torner ent] B: qu'il en torne [32] que ce provant faisant ce] B: qu'il ce provent et faisant [33] dit] B lacks [34] dire] B: respondre [35] li] BO lack [36] n'a] A: n'a ni; B: ne n'a [37] et qui son home en est] B: en est son home [38] BV add: et [39] de court] V lacks [40] me met je . . . mon] V: se met en l'esgart de la court sauf son [41] ces dis] AB: cest dit; V: ce dit [42] C adds: en [43] a pas a] B: est mie tenuz de [44] B adds: faire [45] c'il] A: se le requerant; BV lack [46] sa] ABV: la [47] cora] AV: corera; B: courra; O: corra [48] quant il ot . . . fié] A lacks [49] fu fauce] V: fausement [50] s'en parjurerent] AV: s'esparjurerent; B: se parjurerent [51] cuidoient] A: cuidierent; V: cuiderent

que se il eust esté la quant yaus[52] celle fauce guarentie porterent, il en eust l'un levé come parjur[53] et torné par guage de bataille con faus guarans, et que se il encores voloient[54] lor faus dis maintenir, que il seroit prest de torner ent l'un par gage de bataille et conbatre s'en a lui et rendre le[55] mort ou[56] recreant en une hore dou[57] jor, por quei il ne viaut que cele fauce guarentie li vaille ne a lui grege,[58] que il dit bien et voirs est que il ne fu[59] onques apartenant a celui de qui le fié li eschey, mais que[60] il est son parent et[61] de cele part dont le fié meut et ensi que il a lui est escheu, et[62] que ce est il prest de prover tout ensi con la court esgardera ou conoistra que il prover le doie,[63] et que ce[64] la cort esgarde ou conoit[65] qu'il le doit prover par guarens, que il le[66] provera par bons et leaus guarens non pas par faus guarens si come celui fist, et que[67] por les raisons que il a[68] dites ou por aucunes d'eles viaut il le dit fié avoir ce faisant et provant qu'il a ofert, se la court l'esgarde, et de ce se met il en l'esgart de la court[69] sauf son retenaill. A ce peut celui qui tient le fié respondre et dire que il ment[70] de ce que il a dit que il par faus guarans prova[71] le parenté.[72] Quar il le[73] prova bien et leaument si con il doit[74] et[75] con la court l'esgarda[76] et conut[77] et par bons et loyaus[78] guarans qui bien firent ce que il durent come loyaus guarans[79] et prodes homes que il sont, ne que por chose que il ait dite il ne viaut qu'il ait le fié qui li[80] requiert qui est sien et que il ot come s'escheete[81] par esgart de court, et que il l'a et tient con se qui est son droit, ne[82] chose que il ait dite contre ses guarens ne li vaut ne valoir ne li doit,[83] que puis que ses guarans ont dit ou fait[84] dire lor guarentie et il ont le[85] sairement fait de la guarantie et il se sont levés sans se que nul ne[86] les ait rebutés de celle guarantie ne levés con parjur[87] ne tornés con faus guarans, lor guarentie est bien

---

[52] yaus] A: ciaus; B: il; V: ceaus [53] parjur] V: esparjur [54] V adds: celle fauce garentie et [55] le] A lacks; B: l'en [56] ou] C: au [57] dou] A: de; C: del [58] grege] V: gregier [59] fu] C: fust [60] que] ABV lack [61] et] ABV lack [62] et] C lacks [63] prover le doie] C: le doit prover [64] que ce] B lacks [65] esgarde ou conoit] AOV: esgarde (V: esguarde) ou conoist (A: conoisse); B: doit esgarder [66] que il le] B: et il [67] que] BV lack [68] il a] V: je ais [69] de la court] C lacks [70] il ment] A lacks; BV: il [71] par faus guarans prova] V: l'a par faus guarens prové [72] parenté] A: parenté que non, place Dieu; C: parenteis [73] Quar il le] B: Que il le; V: Que il [74] doit] ABV: dut [75] et] C: si [76] l'esgarda] BV: esgarda [77] et con la . . . conut] A lacks [78] et loyaus] A lacks; C: loyaus [79] qui bien firent . . . guarans] B lacks [80] qui li] A: que il; V: que il li [81] ot come s'escheete] B: l'out come escheete; V: ot par escheete et [82] A adds: que [83] doit] C: 'veut' corrected to 'peut' [84] dit ou fait] C: dite ou faite [85] ont le] V: l'ont leur [86] ne] ABV lack [87] parjur] B: parjurés; O: parjurs; V: esparjurés

fornie si con ele doit,[88] ni ne peut nul aler a l'encontre par l'assisse ne[89] l'usage dou reaume de Jerusalem[90] par raison, 'por quey chose que vos ayés dite contre mes guarens ne vos vaut n'a moy griege,[91] ne por chose que vos aiés dite le fié que vos[92] requerés qui est mien vos ne[93] devés avoir, ne je ne[94] veull que vos l'aiés[95] por toutes les raisons que je ai dites ou por aucunes d'eles, se la court ne l'esgarde, et de ce me met je en l'esgart de la court sauf mon retenaill.'

Et aprés ces dis la court doit esgarder, se me senble, que le requerant n'a chose dite par coy il doive avoir le dit fié et que il a leisir de dire. Et la raison por quey il le me senble est que je entent qu'il est assisse ou usage[96] au reaume de Jerusalem que puis que guarentie[97] est bien fornie si con ele doit, que nul ne peut aler a l'encontre, et que il me senble que la guarentie avant dite fu bien fornie si come ele dut par les raisons avant dites, et que bien est raison et droit que ensi doit[98] estre, que se autrement estoit les guarans ne vaudroient riens se l'on pooit[99] guarans rebuter et torner par guage de bataille .i. espace de tens aprés ce que la guarentie seroit bien[100] fornie si con ele devroit.[101] Si me semble que aprés les erremens[102] avant dis le requerant ne poroit[103] dire chose qui li vaille[104] au dit fié avoir,[105] que[106] celui qui l'a et tient fust ataignant a celui de par qui il eschei, et que il fust plus prochain de lui et[107] plus dreit[108] a avoir le dit fié, por ce que il avroit dit en la court que celui qui le fié tient[109] n'estoit de riens apartenant[110] a celui de par qui le fié eschey, que chose dite en court ne peut on desdire.[111]

Si me semble que s'il avenoit que fié fust escheu et[112] venu en la main dou seignor, et aucun en eust la saisine requise et eue, si con est avant dit, fust parent ou autre de celui de par qui[113] le fié est[114] escheu,[115] mais qu'il en eust le parenté prové si con est avant[116] devisé, et aucun qui[117] fust plus dreit heir de celui qui avreit eue la

---

[88] AB add: et de garentie fornie si come elle deit (B: com ele doit) [89] ne] AB: ou; V: et [90] A adds: ne [91] griege] B: grieve; V: gregier [92] ABV add: me [93] V adds: le [94] ne devés avoir ne je ne] B: nel devez ne je nel [95] l'aiés] C: aiés [96] est que je . . . usage] A: qu'il est assise ou usage si come je entens [97] puis que guarentie] V: garentie puis que elle [98] doit] BO: doie; V: doive [99] pooit] O: porroit; V: ne pooient [100] bien] C lacks [101] devroit] B: devra [102] erremens] B: sairement; V: saremens [103] poroit] A: peut [104] vaille] B: valust [105] avoir] B: ravoir [106] ABV add: se [107] plus prochain de lui et] B: au plus prouchain de lui et au [108] AV add: heir; B: hoir [109] celui qui le fié tient] A: cestui qui le tient; B: cestui; V: cestui qui tient le dit fié [110] apartenant] C: apertenant [111] on desdire] A: estre desdite [112] escheu et] B lacks [113] qui] C: quey [114] est] AB: fust [115] et venu en . . . escheu] V lacks [116] V adds: dit et [117] qui] ABV lack

saisine dou dit fié en la maniere avant dite[118] voloit cel fié requerre et avoir, que il ne devroit pas dire que celui qui la dite saisine dou fié[119] avroit n'estoit[120] pas ataignant a celui de par qui le fié eschei,[121] que son dit ne vaudroit riens, se cuit, par les raisons avant[122] dites, puis que il avroit le parenté prouvé en l'avant dite maniere. Mais l'autre qui le fié[123] requiert devroit dire, se m'est avis, s'il voloit le fié avoir, que il estoit[124] plus prochain parent de celui de qui le fié eschey et qui derrainement en morut saisi et tenant con dou sien de cele part dont le fié movoit[125] que celui qui l'a et tient,[126] et que ce est il prest dou[127] prover tout ensi con la court esgardera ou conoistra que il[128] prover le doie, por quei il est plus dreit heir a avoir le dit fié que celui qui l'a, si[129] le veaut avoir ce provant qu'il a ofert, se la court l'esgarde, et de ce se met il en l'esgart de la court sauf son retenaill. Et tout soit ce que le saisi dou fié puisse plusors esloignes et eschanpes faire[130] au plait[131] esloigner, se il viaut et set, si ne[132] me semble il[133] que il a la parfin puisse le fié defendre que l'autre ne l'ait, ce provant que il a ofert si con la court esgardera ou conoistra que il faire le doive,[134] se il ne demore par faute[135] de plaideor que le requerant face. Et quant le plait sera a ce venus[136] que le requerant amenra ses guarans a prover le parenté si con il a[137] ofert, aucuns[138] de ceaus que je ai oy tenir a bons plaideors ont dit que il en peut l'un des guarens torner ou rebuter.[139] Et les raisons que je ai oi dire en cel[140] cas dient[141] que s'ensi n'estoit que l'en ne deust[142] torner,[143] mout de maus en poroient avenir et mout de gens perdre[144] lor droit et[145] estre desherités de ce qui seroit lor clere raison.[146] Que se aucun parent qui fust dreit heir a avoir l'escheete dou fié qui li seroit escheue et seroit en la main dou seignor la li requeroit et[147] ofroit a prover le parenté si con court esgarderoit ou conoistroit

---

[118] dite] B: dite et il] O: motie [119] dou fié] A lacks [120] n'estoit] V: n'est [121] le fié eschei] B: muet le fié [122] avant] B: devant [123] le fié] V lacks [124] estoit] A: est [125] movoit] C: meut [126] B adds: n'estoit [127] dou] ABV: de [128] il] A lacks; V: je [129] qui l'a, si] AB: qui l'a et tient, si; C: qu'il l'a, s'il; V: qui [130] faire] ABV: trover [131] C adds: faire [132] ne] BV lack [133] il] C lacks [134] il faire le doive] AV: faire le dee (V: doie); B: il prover le doie [135] faute] AB: defaute [136] venus] C lacks [137] a] OV: l'a [138] A adds: dient que l'autre en peut rebuter ou torner l'un des garenz par gage de bataille, mais aucuns [139] il en peut . . . rebuter] ABV: non peut (B: puet) [140] cel] AB: cest; V: tel [141] dient] A: a aucuns ont dit [142] l'en ne deust] A: l'on peust rebuter ou; B: l'on ne peust; O: l'on le peust; V: l'on peust [143] A adds: le garent par gage de bataille [144] perdre] A: poroient perdre; O: perdroient; V: em perdroient [145] lor droit et] A: leur dreis et poreient [146] clere raison] A: Si est clere chose; B: Clere raison est [147] et] C lacks

que il prover[148] le deust et le provast[149] et[150] eust la saisine par esgart ou par conoissance de court, et un[151] autre qui n'apartenist mie a celui de par qui le fié eschey venist aprés devant le seignor et se clamast de celui[152] qui le fié avroit[153] et tendroit et deist en son clain qu'il est plus prochain parent[154] de celui de qui le fié[155] lor estoit escheu[156] qui derainement[157] morut saisi et tenant con de son droit[158] de celle part dont le fié moveit[159] que celui qui le fié[160] aveit et teneit,[161] et ofrist a prover si con la court esgarderoit ou conoistroit[162] que prover le deust, et que[163] ce provant qu'il[164] estoit plus dreit heir a aveir le dit fié que celui qui l'avoit por quey il le voloit avoir se la court l'esgardast,[165] et de ce[166] se meist[167] en l'esgart de la court sauf son retenaill, je cuit que[168] la court esgaderoit que il devroit[169] ce prover par .ii. loyaus guarans de la loy de Rome et que se l'on ne peut[170] en cest cas l'un des guarens[171] torner, que dont[172] poroit[173] chascun qui vodroit maligner et troveroit[174] .ii. homes de la loi de Rome qui por lui se vodroient[175] parjurer, desques l'on troveroit plusors por monoie puis que il seroient[176] seur que il n'avroient[177] en celle guarentie tornes de bataille[178] ne autre peril que de sei[179] parjurer, poroit[180] desheriter quelque il[181] voudroit[182] de son droit et de c'escheete, laquel chose[183] seroit tort apert et contre droit[184] et raison et justise, por quei il lor senbleit qu'en tel cas eust[185] tornes de bataille[186] contre le guarant dou parenté, ne[187] que l'asisse ne l'usage ne toloit en cest cas la torne de bataille.

---

[148] que il prover] B lacks [149] A adds: si come la court l'avreit esgardé ou coneu [150] le provast et] BV lack [151] un] C lacks [152] celui] C: lui [153] le fié avroit] C: avroit le fié [154] de celui qui . . . parent] B lacks [155] de qui le fié] AB: qui le fié avreit (B: avroit) et tendreit (B: tendroit) et deist encores (B: encore) en son claim qu'il est dessendu (B: descendu) de celui de (A adds: par) qui le fié; V: qui le fié avroit et tendroit et deist en son clain que il est de celui qui le fié [156] estoit escheu] A: est escheu et; B: escheut; V: est escheu [157] AB add: en [158] de son droit] B: dou sien [159] B adds: estoit plus son prochain parent [160] le fié moveit . . . fié] A: il le fié [161] aveit et teneit] V: a et tient [162] esgarderoit ou conoistroit] C: esgardera ou conoistra [163] que] ABV lack [164] qu'il] A: il en; BV: il [165] voloit avoir se la court l'esgardast] B: veut avoir se la cort l'esgarde [166] de ce] A lacks [167] meist] B: met il [168] je cuit que] A: et; V: Se cuit que [169] esgarderoit que il devroit] A: esgardast ou coneust qu'il deust [170] peut] AB: peust [171] A adds: rebuter ne; C: lever et [172] dont] OV: donc [173] que dont poroit] A: par gage de bataille donques [174] troveroit] A: qui troveroient [175] vodroient] A: vosicent [176] seroient] O: seroit [177] n'avroient] B: n'avroit [178] bataille] C: batailles [179] de sei] B: Diex [180] poroit] A: poroient [181] quelque il] ABV: qui que il [182] voudroit] A: vodroient [183] laquel chose] C lacks [184] droit] BV: Dieu; O: Deu [185] tel cas eust] A: cest cas avoit [186] bataille] C: batailles [187] ne] ABV lack

Et les autres disoient que il n'avroit point de tornes[188] de bataille contre guarant qui[189] porteroit[190] guarentie de parenté en nul cas et disoient por quey: por ce que l'assisse ou l'usage le toloit,[191] et[192] que il estoit[193] assise ou usage que[194] toutes manieres de gens crestiens[195] pevent porter[196] guarentie en la haute court de prover[197] parenté[198] et aage, et que prestres et clers et gens de relegion et femes[199] pevent par l'assisse ou l'usage[200] dou reaume de Jerusalem porter guarentie en la haute cort des .ii. dites choses, et que il est certaine chose que prestres ne clers ne gens de religion ne feme ne se pevent[201] conbatre de lor cors, ne prestre ne clerc ne gens de religion[202] metre chanpions por eaus aleiauter, que bataille de champions ne peut[203] estre fornie ne otree[204] que l'un des chanpions ne muire el champ ou ne die le mot[205] recreant, par quey il doit estre pendu, se il le[206] dit. Sy est[207] clere chose que les avant dis ne pevent guager[208] ne faire guager[209] bataille, por ce que lor condition le[210] defent, que le prestre par qui ce avroit esté[211] ne poroit messe chanter ne le clerc venir a ordre de prestre, et puis que il ne la pevent guager ne faire gager l'on ne les peut torner[212] par gage de bataille, et se l'on ne[213] les pooit torner par gage de bataille et l'on peust[214] autrement lor garentie contredire ou faucer, lor garentie ne vaudroit riens, et s'ele ne valoit, por neent fust il en l'assise ou[215] en l'usage que il peucent porter guarentie des .ii. dites choses. Mais por ce que par l'assisse ou l'usage[216] dou dit reiaume pevent les avant[217] dis porter guarentie de .ii.[218] dites choses et que lor guarentie vaut et est receue, est il legier[219] a conoistre que il n'i a[220] tornes de bataille contre les guarans par qui l'on preuve parenté ou aage,[221] et que se l'asisse ou l'usage[222] ne[223] tosist la bataille, que aucune fois fust avenu el reyaume

[188] n'avroit point de tornes] A: n'i avoit torne; BV: n'avoit tornes (V: tournes) [189] qui] C: que [190] porteroit] AV: portoit; B: porte [191] B adds: ou reaume de Jerusalem [192] et] ABV lack [193] estoit] AV: est [194] il estoit assise ou usage que] B lacks [195] crestiens] B lacks; C: crestiens ne [196] porter] C: torner [197] prover] B: preuve de [198] parenté] A: lignage [199] femes] O: feaus [200] ou l'usage] A lacks [201] pevent] B: puet [202] A adds: ne pevent [203] peut] C: pevent [204] ne prestre ne . . . otree] B: ne de prestre ne de clerc ne de genz de religion ne puet estre fornie ne outree bataille por ce [205] AB add: dou [206] le] B: ne [207] A adds: donc [208] C adds: la [209] guager] ABV lack [210] le] C: les; V: lor [211] V adds: fait [212] les peut torner] B: se puet deffendre; V: ce peut [213] ne] C lacks [214] et l'on peust] C: ou [215] por neent fust . . . ou] C: n'en por neent seroit il en l'assise ne [216] que il peucent . . . l'usage] V lacks [217] avant] B: devant [218] V adds: devant [219] legier] V: legiere chose [220] AOV add: pas [221] parenté ou aage] ABV: le parenté ou l'aage [222] B adds: est tel que [223] ne] BV lack; O: n'en

de Jerusalem ou de Chypre que il eust eu[224] tornes de bataille en preuve[225] de parenté ou d'aage, mais por ce que l'assise ou l'usage[226] le tot, ne le vit on[227] onques[228] avenir, ne n'oy l'on[229] dire que il avenist[230] en aucun cas,[231] et se il ne fust assise ou usage qui la torne en tousist et que il y eust torne de bataille contre[232] les guarans par qui l'on[233] prove le parenté ou l'aage, a enuis poroit[234] on trover guarans de ce qui en portacent guarentie, et se l'on les trovoit, que l'on les torneroit ou rebuteroit sovent, et que il n'est chose, se cuit, de quey l'on puisse guarant torner que l'on ne puisse[235] rebuter, et que par ce perdroient ou seroient esloignees lonc[236] tens plusors gens de leur drois et de lor raisons,[237] laquel chose seroit[238] mal et peché et contre droit et raison.

Et selonc les raisons que je lor[239] ai oy dire, que a moi semble, se il[240] n'est assise propre qui tolle[241] torne de bataille en cel cas ou en tous cas, je di que en tel cas doit avoir tornes de batailles par raison, que s'ele[242] n'i estoit, trop en poroit l'on de mal faire[243] sans perill de mort ne de honte que[244] le guarant ne celui de qui la querele est[245] y eucent, que asés plus de gens se guarderoient de maligner[246] en cel[247] cas en quey il y avroit peril a celui de qui la querele seroit de perdre[248] vois et respons[249] en court se son chanpion estoit[250] vencu, et au chanpion d'estre mort ou vencu et justisié ou[251] avilaini con guarant rebuté, que se la torne de bataille n'i estoit. Mais se il est assise que il en tel cas n'ait torne de bataille ou en nul autre de preuve de parenté, je ne di riens contre l'asisse, ains di qu'ele soit bien tenue et guardee tel con ele est por ce que le seignor et ses homes jurent les assises a tenir.[252]

---

224 eu] BV lack 225 en preuve] A lacks 226 ou l'usage] AV: ne (V: et) l'usage ne 227 on] ABV lack 228 A adds: nul 229 ne n'oy l'on] A: ne ne l'oy; B: ne oi; V: ne ne l'oi onques 230 V adds: onques 231 cas] C: tens 232 contre] C: entre 233 l'on] C: la 234 poroit] V: poroient 235 que l'on ne puisse] A: que l'on ne le puisse; B: ne; V: ou 236 lonc] C: leur 237 A adds: aveir 238 de leur drois . . . seroit] O: Et selonc les raisons que je lor ai oy dire, que a moi 239 lor] ABV lack 240 se il] B: qu'il 241 tolle] A: tolle la; B lacks 242 s'ele] B: elle 243 de mal faire] AB: faire de maus 244 que] C lacks 245 est] A: sereit 246 de maligner] ABV lack 247 cel] ABO: tel 248 A adds: a toz jors 249 et respons] BV lack 250 estoit] V: seroit 251 ou] C: et 252 B adds: et maintenir

***[146]** En quel cas il n'i a[1] tornes de bataille contre le[2] guarant qui a porté[3] la guarentie de[4] parenté, et en quel cas la torne y doit estre par raison, se il n'i a[5] propre assise qui en tel cas[6] toille[7] la torne de la bataille ou qui en touz cas[8] la toille[9] de[10] preuve de parenté, quar s'ele n'i estoit, mout de maus en poroient avenir et[11] de gens estre desherités a tort et sans raison.[12]

Se fié eschet et vient en la main dou seignor par ce que[13] celui ou cele de qui il est escheu n'avoit[14] fiz ne fille qui fust[15] demoré a avoir de[16] cel fié en tel saisine et en tel teneure con le pere et la mere en[17] avoient quant il alerent de vie a mort, et celui qui seroit plus dreit heir a avoir cel fié venist en la court por requerre le, et .i. autre qui ne fust son parent requerroit[18] au seignor cel fié, disant qu'il li est[19] escheu com a[20] celui qui est le[21] plus prochein parent de celui de par qui le fié est escheu et le plus dreit heir[22] a avoir cel fié et dit coment que il estoit[23] ataignant de parenté a celui de par qui le fié eschey et de cele part dont le fié movoit[24] et en tel degré que autre qui ne li fust fiz ne[25] fille ne li peust de[26] plus pres ataindre et ofrir a prover le parenté si con la court esgarderoit ou conoistroit que il prover le deust, et celui qui seroit le droit heir a avoir le dit fié et venus[27] la por requerre le,[28] quant il avroit ce oy, deist au seignor: 'Sire, cestui qui requiert[29] cest fié n'i a[30] droit, quar il n'est de riens ataignant a celui de qui le fié est escheu, mais je, sire,[31] sui ataignant a celui de qui le fié est escheu[32] et son dreit heir a aveir le[33] devant tos[34] autres con celui qui li ataignoie[35] en tel degré, et ce suis je prest de prover par bons et leiaus garans tot ensi con la court esgardera ou conoistra que je[36] prover le doie. Mais les

---

A: fols xcvi^{r}–xcix^{r} cap. 161; **B:** fols 123^{v}–126^{r} cap. 161; **C:** fols 123^{r}–126^{r} cap. 46; **O:** fols 160^{v}–165^{v}; **V:** fols cxxviii^{r}–cxxxi^{v} cap. 166; Beugnot, pp. 246–50, cap. 161.

---

[1] n'i a] B (fol. 22^{v}): n'a point de [2] le] B: celui [3] a porté] ABV: porte [4] de] ABV: dou [5] n'i a] C: n'a [6] en tel cas] A lacks [7] toille] V lacks [8] cas] C lacks [9] toille] V: bataille [10] de] B: la [11] B adds: mout [12] sans raison] B: a pechié [13] par ce que] B: et [14] n'avoit] C: n'ait [15] fust] C: fu [16] a avoir de] ABV: en [17] en] ABV lack [18] requerroit] B: requeist [19] li est] A: est a lui; B: li [20] a] AV lack [21] le] C lacks [22] et le plus dreit heir] B lacks [23] que il estoit] A: qu'il est; BV: il est [24] movoit] A: muet [25] ne] AB: ou [26] de] ABV lack [27] le dit fié et venus] B: cel fié fust venu [28] le] BV lack [29] requiert] B: quiert [30] A adds: point de [31] sire] V lacks [32] mais je, sire . . . escheu] O lacks [33] A adds: fié [34] ABV add: les [35] ataignoie] C: ataignoit; O: teignoye [36] je] C: il

guarans par qui tel', et le nome, 'viaut prover ce que il dit[37] sont faus, ce il tel guarentie li veullent porter, quar de chose qui n'est ne onques ne fu ne poroit nul porter leal guarentie disant que ele eust esté ou fust, que tel', et le nome, 'ne fu onques apartenant a celui[38] de qui le fié m'est escheu[39] con a son droit heir. Por quey je vos pri et[40] requier con a seignor et[41] justise que vos sa preuve ne recevés de ce de quey il la vos eufre,[42] et que vos la moye recevés con de celui qui suis drois heir a cest fié avoir, et veull que ce que je vos ais requis faciés par les raisons que je ai dites se la court l'esgarde, et de ce me met je en l'esgart de la court sauf mon retenaill.'

Contre ce peut respondre le premier requerant et dire: 'Sire, vos et la court avés oy et entendu coment je vos ais[43] requis le fié qui m'est escheu de par tel', et le nome, 'et coment j'ay ofert a prover le parenté qui estoit[44] entre moy et lui, et avant que celui',[45] et le nome, 'que ce fié en quey il n'a[46] droit vos requiert le vos eust requis ne ofert preuve de parenté ne d'autre, si ne veull que il demore por chose que il ait dite que vos, sire,[47] ne recevés ma preuve que je vos ai premier oferte, ains[48] veull que vos la recevés avant de la soue,[49] se la court l'esgarde, et di por quei: por ce que il est asisse ou usage en cest[50] roiaume que la premiere requeste doit avant aler, si veulle que ma requeste aille devant[51] la soue et que ma preuve que je ai premier oferte soit avant receue,[52] se la court l'esgarde, et de ce me met je[53] en l'esgart de la court sauf mon retenaill.' Et aprés ces dis[54] le seignor doit dire: 'Je comant a la court qu'ele l'esgarde[55] que j'en ay a faire selonc le dit et la requeste de l'une partie[56] et de l'autre.' Et la court doit esgarder, se cuit, qu'il ne doit demorer por chose que le derain requerant ait dite que la premiere requeste et l'eufre premier oferte n'aille[57] avant. Et aprés cest esgars il ne me senble que le derain requerant[58] puisse chose dire por quei

[37] ce que il dit] B lacks [38] celui] ABV: tel [39] ne fu onques . . . escheu] O lacks but repeats: veaut prouver se que il dit sont faus, se il tel garantie [40] pri et] C lacks [41] ABV add: a [42] la vos eufre] V: vous a offert [43] ais] B lacks [44] qui estoit] B lacks [45] celui] ABV: tel [46] n'a] AV: n'i a [47] sire] A: sire, ne faites ma requeste que je voz ais premier requise et que voz; B lacks [48] premier oferte, ains] B: a prover offerte et [49] recevés avant de la soue] B: recevois avant de la siene [50] ou usage en cest] V: et usage au [51] devant] A: avant [52] A adds: que la soe [53] je] C lacks [54] ces dis] B: cel dit [55] l'esgarde] A: esgarde ce; B: l'esgarde en ce; V: esguarde [56] l'une partie] A: l'un [57] n'aille] A: ne voisse; V: voise [58] derain requerant] C: requerant derain

la premiere requeste et l'eufre premier oferte[59] n'aille[60] avant. Et quant l'esgart[61] avra esté fait, et la court avra esgardé ou coneu coment le premier requerant doit[62] prover ce que il a ofert, je cuit que la court esgardera ou conoistra que il doit ce[63] prover par .ii.[64] guarans crestiens,[65] homes o femes.[66] Et quant il les amenra en la court a[67] prover ce que il a ofert, et il vodront[68] la guarentie porter, si se traie avant le derain requerant et torne l'un des guarans si con[69] est avant[70] devisé en cest livre que on[71] doit guarent[72] torner.[73 a] Et se il le torne, le guarant qui est torné doit respondre a celui qui le torne et dire li que il ment de ce qu'il li met sus, ne[74] que il a lui ne s'en viaut aerdre, se la court ne l'esgarde, et dit por quey: por ce il entent que[75] par l'assisse ou[76] l'usage dou reyaume de Jerusalem n'a tornes[77] de bataille en preuve de parenté ne[78] d'aage, por quey il a lui ne s'en viaut aerdre se la court ne l'esgarde, et de ce se met il en l'esgart de la court sauf son retenaill. Et le premier requerant de la querelle doit dire: 'Sire, tel', et le nome, 'ment de ce que il a mis sus a mon guarant tel qui s'est parjuré[79] et que il a fauce guarentie portee, quar il a fait sairement bon et leal et garentie portee.[80] Ne je n'entent que il mon[81] guarant puisse de ceste guarentie torner[82] ne mon droit ne ma raison encombrier ne que mon garant s'en[83] doive a lui aerdre, et di[84] por quey: por ce que il n'est assise ne usage en cest reaume que l'on[85] puisse par gage de bataille guarant torner qui portent[86] guarentie de parenté ne d'aage.'

Et que bien est[87] clere chose que il n'a[88] pas tornes de bataille en ces .ii. cas[89] par les raisons qui sont devant dites[90] en l'autre chapitle la ou il dit que prestres et clers et gens de religion et femes

[a] Above caps 60–62.

[59] oferte] V lacks [60] n'aille] A: ne voisse; B: ne voise; V: voise [61] l'esgart] C: il [62] A adds: premier [63] doit ce] ABV: le doit (A: deit) [64] A adds: leaus; BV: loiaus [65] crestiens] V lacks [66] C adds: de la loy de Rome [67] a] BOV lack [68] et il vodront] B: je cuit que la cort esgardera qu'il voudront; C: et il voudroient [69] AB add: il [70] avant] AV lack; O: devant [71] que on] V: coment l'on [72] guarent] C: guarentie [73] C repeats: en cest livre [74] ne] AV: et [75] il entent que] A: qu'il n'i a; B: que; V: que il [76] ou] A: ne [77] n'a tornes] A: torne; O: il n'a tornes; V: que il n'i a [78] B adds: en preuve [79] tel qui s'est parjuré] A: tel', et le nome, 'qu'il est parjuré; B: qu'il s'est parjurez; C: tel qui est parjur; V: tel que il c'est esparjuré [80] quar il a . . . portee] AV lack; B: car il a fait bon sairement et loyau et bone garantie et loial apportee [81] mon] B lacks [82] torner] A: porter faire tenir [83] s'en] C: se [84] di] AO: dis [85] l'on] C: l'un [86] portent] A: porte [87] C adds: il [88] n'a] AV: n'i a [89] A adds: et die [90] dites] C: devisees

pevent porter guarentie de prover aage et[91] parenté, et les die si con eles sont devisees en l'autre[92] chapitle.[b] Et que por toutes les raisons que il a dites ou por aucunes d'elles, il n'entent que il de ceste guarentie puisse son guarant torner ne que son guarent a lui s'en doie[93] aerdre, ne ne viaut que il[94] le face, se la court ne l'esgarde, et de ce se met il en l'esgart de la court sauf son retenaill. Contre ce peut le derain requerant[95] dire: 'Je ne veul que il demore por chose que vos aiés dite que le guarant que je ai levé[96] come parjur[97] et torné come faus guarant ne s'aerde a moy ou que sa guarantie soit nule et il est[98] tenus a faus[99] et a[100] desloiaus tel con il est, et di por quei: por ce que c'il est assise ou[101] usage[102] qui toille la preuve de la[103] bataille[104] contre le guarant par qui l'on preuve aage ou[105] lignage,[106] ce n'est[107] que de querele qui est dou seignor a home ou dou[108] merme d'aage contre le baill qui tient son baillage, mais d'un home a .i.[109] autre n'est il assise ne usage que[110] en tel cas tosist les tornes[111] de bataille,[112] que se il en tel cas n'avoit tornes de batailles,[113] chascun droit heir poroit estre desherité de s'escheete qui li seroit escheue,[114] fust grant ou petite, se aucun fust qui avoir la[115] vosist a tort, mais que il trovast .ii.[116] crestiens, homes ou femes, qui por[117] lui se vosissent parjurer.[118] Et le siecle est ores tel que molt y a de ceaus qui feroient volentiers coment il fucent riches, tout fust ce a tort, que poi de force feroient el peché d'avoir .i. bon fié a tort, mais que il le peucent[119] avoir sans perill de cors et legierement. Et par noz pechiez de legier troveroit l'on qui faire le vodroit[120] .ii. homes ou femes crestiens[121] de la loy de Rome ou d'autre nacion

[b] Above cap. 145.

[91] prover aage et] B: preuve d'aage et de [92] l'autre] O: cel autre [93] guarent a lui s'en doie] O: gage se doive a lui [94] il] V: son guarent [95] requerant] V: requerreour [96] que je ai levé] C lacks [97] parjur] V: esparjuré [98] est] AOV lack [99] A adds: garent; B: garanz; V: garens [100] a] C lacks [101] que c'il est assise ou] AB: qu'il n'est assise ne; V: que il est assise ou [102] A adds: en cest reiaume [103] preuve de la] ABV: torne de [104] A adds: en cest cas [105] par qui l'on preuve aage ou] B: qui porte garantie d'aage ou de [106] lignage] C: lingnage [107] n'est] B: c'est [108] que de querele . . . dou] ABV de querele (A: carelle; V: quarele) qui est de seignor a home ou de [109] .i.] AV lack [110] que] ABV: qui [111] les tornes] A: la torne [112] bataille] C: batailles [113] que se il . . . batailles] A: que ce ensi n'esteit qu'il n'eust torne de bataille en cest cas; B: car [114] de s'escheete qui li seroit escheue] V: des escheetes qui li seroient escheus [115] la] BV: le [116] A adds: garenz [117] por] C: par [118] parjurer] V: esparjurer [119] peucent] V: puissent [120] l'on qui faire le vodroit] A: on [121] crestiens] ABV lack

qui se parjureroient[122] por monoie puis que il seroient seurs[123] que il n'avroient autre perill que d'eaus parjurer, que plus de gens que mestier ne seroit font mains de force en yaus parjurer que[124] il ne devroient. Si entent que[125] por toutes les raisons que je ai dites ou por aucunes d'eles que je puis par raison[126] le guarent torner en cest cas, et que il[127] a mey s'en doit aerdre ou que sa guarentie est[128] nule. Si veull que[129] puis que je l'ai torné con faus guarant et levé con parjur,[130] que il s'en aerde[131] a moy ou que sa guarentie soit nulle, se[132] la court l'esgarde, et de ce me met je[133] en l'esgart de la court sauf mon retenaill.' Et[134] a moy semble que se la court set que il soit assise ou usage el royaume de Jerusalem qui en tel cas toille les tornes[135] de bataille ou en touz cas de parenté, qu'ele por[136] l'assise[137] ou le dit[138] usage maintenir doit esgarder que le derain requerant ne peut le guarant[139] torner[140] ne que le guarent a lui ne s'en doit[141] aerdre. Et que se la court ne set qu'il[142] soit assise ou[143] usage qui toille la torne[144] de[145] bataille en cel[146] cas de parenté, qu'ele doit esgarder selon[147] raison que le derain requerant peut le guarant torner en cest cas et que le guarant se doit a lui aerdre ou que sa guarentie est[148] nule.

Et por les raisons qui devant sont dites en cest chapitle et en l'autre le[149] me senble il et por tant plus, que se aucun[150] viaut dire que se il n'i eust assise ne usage qui la torne de bataille en[151] tosist, si en poroient estre mout de maus fais, et de[152] gens qui avroient droit en l'escheete et[153] qui seroient[154] drois heirs a avoir la[155] estre en[156] desherités[157] et ahontés et vilainement[158] travaillés en tel maniere que, quant .i.[159] dreit heir requeroit s'escheete au seignor et amenroit ses guarans a prover le parenté, que .i. home estrange ou champion afaitié venist[160] et deist que celui qui le fié requiert n'a[161] droit

---

[122] se parjureroient] V: s'en parjuroient [123] seurs] C: seur [124] plus de gens . . . que] V lacks [125] que] BV lack [126] par raison] ABV lack [127] il] C lacks [128] est] A: seit [129] que] ABV lack [130] parjur] V: esparjuré [131] aerde] C: aerdre [132] se] C: que [133] je] C lacks [134] Et] V: Car [135] les tornes] A: la torne [136] por] C: par [137] l'assise] ABV: la dite assise [138] le dit] B lacks [139] le guarant] V: les guarens [140] A adds: par gage de bataille [141] ne s'en doit] A: s'en dee [142] qu'il] A: que ce [143] ou] C: ne [144] torne] O: court [145] C adds: la [146] cel] AV: tel; B: cest [147] C adds: la [148] est] A: seit; V: soit [149] le] ABV lack [150] B adds: dit ou [151] en] ABV lack [152] de] C: des [153] et] ABV lack [154] seroient] V: seroit [155] B adds: en porroient; V: et [156] en] ABV lack [157] C adds: a avoir la [158] et vilainement] AB: vilainement et; V: vilainement [159] .i.] A lacks [160] .i. home estrange . . . venist] A: .ii. homes estranges ou champion afaitiés venist avant [161] n'a] ABV: n'i a

el fié[162] con celui qui de riens n'estoit ataignant a celui de par qui le fié est escheu, mais qu'il est le[163] droit heir a cel fié avoir con celui qui ataignoit de parenté[164] celui de par qui il li[165] est escheu[166] de cele part dont le fié muet[167] en tel degré, et deyst si prochain degré que le requerant ne autre n'eust[168] le dit[169] fié devant lui, et l'ofrist a prover si con la court esgarderoit ou conoistroit qu'il[170] prover le deust,[171] et que por ce que l'eufre premier oferte doit avant aler,[172] que il l'un des guarans tornast et que il y eust torne de[173] bataille, molt en poroit de maus avenir, que chascun n'a pas guarans aprestés a tel preuve faire, qui se peust defendre contre .i. chanpion afaitié ou contre[174] .i. grant et fort home qui par tel malice voudroit ce[175] fié avoir, si en seroit le droit heir deserité[176] dou fié se son chanpion estoit vencu et il ahonti a tous jors[177] con celui qui avreit[178] perdu vois et respons en court,[179] puis que son chanpion avroit esté outré en chanp, et que le chanpion en seroit pendu, et que se ensi n'estoit[180] l'on troveroit trop a enuis home ne feme[181] qui portast guarentie de parenté, por quei mout de gens perdroient lor droit et lor raisons. Contre ce di je que tout soit ce que les dis perils[182] y sont, a il plus de perill en l'autre. Et por ce que l'on deit eschiver les choses en quey il y a plus de perills et faire celes en quey il en[183] a mains[184] quant l'on ne les peut faire sans perill, me semble il que se[185] il n'i a propre assise ou propre usage qui toille la torne de la[186] bataille de la preuve de[187] parenté en cest cas ou[188] en tous cas, que ele y doit estre par raison.

Que s'ele n'i estoit qui onques[189] vodroit fié avoir qui fust escheu et venu en la main dou seignor le poroit avoir se il le requeroit premier[190] et ofroit a prover le parenté en la maniere avant[191] dite, qui[192] eust .ii. homes ou femes qui por lui se vosissent parjurer,[193] et[194] que ensi l'avroit[195] il sans perill de mort ne de honte ne de damage que a

[162] el fié] B lacks [163] le] AB lack [164] de parenté] AO: de parenté a; B: a [165] il li] A: le fié li; B: le fié [166] mais qu'il est . . . escheu] V lacks [167] muet] A: vient; C: mueut [168] n'eust] AV: n'en eust [169] dit] B lacks [170] qu'il] AB: que [171] le deust] A lacks; O: le doie [172] aler] C: aleir [173] torne de] A lacks; BO: tornes de [174] contre] C lacks [175] ce] ABV: cel [176] deserité] C: descheeté [177] a tous jors] A lacks [178] avreit] V: a [179] A adds: a toz jors; V: a tous jours [180] n'estoit] A: esteit; C: estoit [181] home ne feme] C: homes ou femes [182] C adds: en l'autre [183] en] AV: y; B: en y [184] V adds: de perills [185] se] C lacks [186] la] ABV lack [187] de] AV: dou [188] ou] C: et [189] qui onques] AB: quiconques [190] V adds: requis [191] avant] B: com il est devant [192] qui] A: mais qu'il [193] parjurer] V: esparjurer [194] et] ABV lack [195] l'avroit] O: l'avra

lui ne a[196] ses guarans en peust avenir mais que dou pechié que il l'avroit a tort, et dou sairement que il avroit fait faire faus, et le guarant dou peché de ce que il se seroit parjuré[197] et tolu le dreit d'autrui, et que l'on troveroit trop plus de gent qui s'entremeteroient[198] de[199] fié requerre et avoir par ceste voie que par l'autre, puis que il le porroient[200] avoir sans bataille et si de ligier.[201] Que chascun grant home et fort et chascun chanpion afaitié qui guage bataille n'est mie seur de vaintre[202] son aversaire, que mainte fois a l'on veu avenir que .i. petit home et foible vaintra[203] .i. grant et fort, et que aucun qui n'estoit[204] mie chanpion afaitié vencoit le[205] chanpion afaitié. Et Dex est droiturier, si[206] ne devroit soufrir que celui qui si[207] desleyaument com est avant dit tornast le guarant et en[208] venist au desus[209] par bataille, et chascun home doute la mort ou la doit doter et doit[210] douter d'entrer en champ a tort et en faus guages que il li couvendroit[211] conbatre a tort et[212] parjur,[213] et mout de fois a l'on veu mesavenir a ceaus qui le faisoient. Et par les raisons avant[214] dites et par plusors autres que l'on poroit[215] dire que trop seroient longes a metre[216] en cest livre ce que l'on en[217] porroit metre, est il[218] cler,[219] se m'est avis, que il doit ensi estre con je ai dit[220] en cest chapitle se .i. tel cas avenoit[221] en la court.

[196] a] C lacks [197] parjuré] V: esparjuré [198] s'entremetroient] B: s'entremetoient; C: se tremetroient [199] de] AV: dou [200] porroient] B: porroit; V poroit [201] C adds: et [202] vaintre] AV: vencre; B: vaincre [203] vaintra] AV: vencre; B: vaincre; C: abatra [204] n'estoit] A: n'est [205] vencoit le] A: vencre un autre qui est [206] droiturier, si] V: si droiturier que il [207] si] B lacks; V: ensi [208] et en] AO: en; C: et [209] au desus] B lacks [210] doter et doit] V lacks [211] couvendroit] C: couveroit [212] C adds: estre [213] parjur] B: parjurés [214] avant] V: devant [215] que l'on poroit] A: qui se poroient; V: que il poroient [216] BV adds: en escrit [217] en] C lacks [218] est il] B: qu'il est; V: qui est [219] AB add: chose [220] V adds: devant [221] avenoit] V: avenist

***[147]** En quel cas le seignor ne se peut defendre a celui qui li requiert saisine de[1] fié qu'il die[2] qui li est escheu par dire[3] que il n'a ne tient cel fié et que autre l'a et tient,[4] et qu'il[5] li avra a droit[6] se il se viaut clamer de lui.[7]

Se il avient que home ou feme qui ait fié muire,[8] et le seignor se saisist de cel fié et aprés le done ou vent ou eschange ou en[9] aucune autre maniere l'aliene et met hors[10] de sa main, et aprés le dreit heir[11] a cel fié avoir ou aucun des heirs qui cel fié pevent avoir[12] par raison se il le requierent[13] con le plus dreit heir aparant et requerant en la court venist devant le seignor en la court et li requeist la saisine de cel fié si com il deust et ofrist[14] a prover le parenté qui estoit entre lui et celui de par[15] qui le fié li[16] seroit escheu si con la court esgarderoit ou conoistroit que il prover le deust, et le seignor li respondist que il n'a ne tient cel fié mais que tel l'a et tient et en est[17] son home, et ce il se claime de lui que il le[18] li avra a droit en sa court, ne que il de[19] fié que il n'a[20] ne tient et que autre a et tient et dont il est son home n'entent il que il autre li en ait a faire, ne faire ne li viaut, se la court ne l'esgarde, et de ce se met il en l'esgart de la court sauf son retenaill.

Contre ce peut respondre le requerant et dire:[21] 'Sire, je ne veull que il demore por chose que vos dites[22] que vos ne me respondés a ma requeste, et di por quei: por ce que vos estes seignor et con seignor vos saisistes dou fié qui fu de mon ancestre tel', et le nome, 'et que vos, sire, aprés l'avés enconbré et parti de vostre main sans ce que il le vos covenist a faire par destrece d'esgart ne de conoissance de court. Sire, et il est assise ou usage en cest royaume ou raison que l'on doit requere son fié et s'escheete au seignor de qui l'on le doit tenir et a qui l'on en doit l'omage et le servise, ce se

A: fol. xcix[r–v] cap. 162; **B:** fols 126[r]–127[r] cap. 162; **C:** fols 126[r]–127[r] cap. 147; **O:** fols 165[v]–166[v]; **V:** fols cxxxi[v]–cxxxii[v] cap. 167; Beugnot, pp. 250–1, cap. 162.

[1] de] B (fol. 22[v]) V rubric (fol. 9[v]): dou [2] qu'il die] OV lack [3] dire] V: droit [4] cel fié et . . . tient] C lacks [5] qu'il] C: qui [6] A adds: en sa court [7] de lui] C lacks [8] muire] A: muert; V: meurt [9] en] C lacks [10] hors] A: fors; B: de hors [11] V adds: vient [12] ou aucun des . . . avoir] O lacks [13] requierent] AV: requiert [14] ofrist] O: offrir [15] par] A lacks [16] li] B lacks; V: lor [17] est] C: c'est [18] le] AB lacks [19] de] AV: dou [20] n'a] C: n'en a [21] peut respondre le requerant et dire] B: porroit dire le requerant [22] dites] AO: diés; B: die

n'est fiz ou fille qui demore en la saisine et[23] en la teneure,[24] de quey son pere[25] ou sa mere[26] morut saisi et tenant con dou sien, por quey je a vos le doy requerre et le vos requier, ne de[27] vos ne me[28] veull[29] partir de qui[30] je doy cest fié tenir et a qui je doy[31] l'omage et le servise, et je entens que vos me devés respondre puis que vos come seignor[32] par[33] raison de vostre seignorie en eustes la saisine et que vos de vostre main le partistes[34] sans destrece d'esgart ne de conoissance de court, et que puis que vos l'avés enconbré sans esgart ne[35] sans conoissance de court[36] que vos le devés desenconbrer. Si veull por toutes les raisons que je[37] ai dites ou por aucunes d'eles que vos m'en[38] respondés et le dit fié me desenconbrés et en saisine me metés, ce provant que je ai ofert se la court l'esgarde, et de ce me met je en l'esgart de la court sauf mon retenaill.'

Et il me semble que aprés ces dis[39] la court doit esgarder que il ne doit demorer por chose que le seignor ait dite que il ne responde dou dit[40] fié au requerant et que il ne li desenconbre, puis que il l'a enconbré[41] sans destrece d'esgart ne de conoissance de court, et que il l'en[42] doit metre en saisine ce provant que il a ofert, se le seignor ne dit chose por quey il en saisine ne le doie metre et tel que court l'esgarde ou conoisse.

---

[23] en la saisine et] B lacks [24] BV add: dou fié [25] C adds: en la saisine et en la teneure de quoy son pere [26] ou sa mere] A: et sa mere en [27] ne de] V: pour ce [28] me] AV lack [29] C adds: je [30] qui] C: quoy [31] cest fié tenir . . . doy] B lacks [32] come seignor] A lacks [33] BV add: la [34] le partistes] B: la preistez [35] ne] BV: et [36] que puis que . . . court] A lacks [37] C adds: vos [38] m'en] ABV: me [39] ces dis] V: ce dit [40] dit] C lacks [41] enconbré] C: enconbrés [42] l'en] AB: le; V lacks

***[148]** Quant le seignor a et tient chose que autre[1] dit qui est[2] son fié ou partie de son fié[3] et il li en[4] requiert la saisine, coment il doit ce prover a son fié ou a partie de son fié,[5] et coment l'on use[6] con de son fié que on a et tient.

Se[7] aucun requiert au seignor chose que il die qui est de son fié ou partie de son fié et[8] que il die[9] que lui ou son ancestre[10] ont esté saisis et tenant et usant con de lor fié, il le doit ofrir a prover si con la court esgardera ou conoistra que il prover le doie. Et la court doit[11] esgarder ou conoistre, se croy, que il le doit prover[12] par le recort de la court ou de partie des homes de la court. Et aprés ce il doit dire au seignor: 'Sire, je entens que tel et tel de vos homes', et les nome, 'en sont recordans et plusors autres. Si vos pri et requier, sire,[13] que vos[14] ceaus que je ai només[15] faites venir en la court[16] et tant de vos autres homes con vos porrés[17] avoir, et que vos[18] lor comandés que il facent le recort[19] que je vos requier.'

Et se le seignor ou autre dit que le recort de partie des homes de la court n'est ne ne peut estre porté come recort de court ne tenu a recort de cort[20] d'autre chose que[21] de ce qui a esté fait en court, et que court n'est se le seignor ou home que il ait establi en son leuc et .ii. de ses[22] homes ou plus ne sont ensemble la ou les choses ont esté faites et que court et homes[23] de court les[24] recordent, mais quant le seignor ou home[25] que il ait establi en son leuc et .ii. ou plus des homes dou seignor sont ensemble ce est court, et ce qui[26] est fait devant yaus peut on[27] recorder come recort de court et autres choses[28] non, por quei il ne li viaut faire ce que il li requiert, se la court ne l'esgarde, et se court esgarde[29] que il faire le doie, et

A: fols xcix^{v}–c^{v} cap. 163; **B:** fols 127^{r}–128^{r} cap. 163; **C:** fols 127^{r}–128^{r} cap. 148; **O:** fols 166^{v}–168^{v}; **V:** fols cxxxii^{v}–cxxxiv^{r} cap. 168; Beugnot, pp. 252–3, cap. 163.

[1] autre] B: aucun autre home; V: l'autre [2] ABV add: de [3] ou partie de son fié] V lacks [4] en] C lacks [5] de son fié] B lacks [6] use] B: en a usé; V: a usé [7] Se] C: Quant [8] et] C lacks [9] qui est de . . . die] A lacks [10] lui ou son ancestre] B: la ou son ancestre en [11] V adds: maintenant [12] prover] O: conoistre [13] sire] B lacks [14] O repeats: sire [15] ai només] V: vous ais nomé les [16] en la court] B lacks [17] porrés] B: porrois [18] A adds: sire [19] C adds: de la cort [20] ne tenu a recort de cort] A lacks [21] que] C lacks [22] .ii. de ses] B: se .ii. [23] et homes] A: ou home; B: ou .ii. homes; V: ou homes [24] les] ABV: le [25] que il ait . . . home] O lacks [26] qui] C: que [27] B adds: bien [28] autres choses] ABV: autre chose [29] et se court esgarde] C lacks

ceaus des homes[30] de la court que il a només et[31] autres le recordent, si con il dit,[32] n'entent[33] que il li doive[34] recort de court par les raisons que il a avant dites ne ne viaut que il li vaille a avoir ce que il li requiert, se la court ne l'esgarde, et de ce se met il en l'esgart de la court sauf son retenaill.[35] Die le requerant que en cest cas est il bien recort de court qui preuve par plusors homes de la court dou seignor qui recordent que il aient veu lui ou son ancestre saisi et tenant et usant de ce que il li[36] requiert con de son fié.[37] Quar se il ensi le preuve, il a bien prové par recort de court, que bien est recort de court a prover et[38] a avoir la saisine de ce que il[39] dit qui[40] est de son fié. Por quey il ne viaut que il demore por chose que il ait dite que il ne li face avoir le recort que il[41] requiert en la maniere que il l'a requis, et que cel recort li vaille ausi[42] con recort de court a avoir ce que il requiert, ains viaut que il li face si con il l'a requis et que il li vaille a avoir ce que il li requiert[43] se la court l'esgarde, por les raisons que il a dites, et de ce se met il en l'esgart de la court sauf son retenaill.

Et je cuit que la court doit esgarder que le seignor li doit faire le recort si com il li requiert[44] et que il li doit valoir ausi con recort de cort[45] a avoir sa requeste se les[46] homes de la court le recordent si con il l'a[47] dit, se il[48] ou aucun de ces ancestres n'ont[49] fait chose par quei il aient cel fié perdu par assise ou par usage ou par conoissance de court. Et ce il est ensi con il a dit, ceaus qui doivent faire cel recort doivent dire quant il sont[50] asis en la court por le dit recort faire, qu'il ont veu saisi et tenant et usant celui qui fait la requeste ou son ancestre de ce que il requiert[51] con de son fié, et doivent dire la maniere coment il l'ont[52] veu user con de son fié.[53]

Et les manieres que l'on use de fié,[54] selonc se que il[55] me senble, sont tes: que l'on en[56] use ausi[57] con les autres homes dou seignor de faire de cel fié homage au seignor, ou seir en cort et juger o[58]

---

[30] V adds: dou seignor et [31] et] BV: ou [32] que il a . . . dit] A: le recordent [33] AOV add: il [34] ABV add: faire le [35] sauf son retenaill] O: ne l'esgarde [36] li] BV lack [37] de son fié] A: dou sien [38] que bien est . . . et] V: a prover [39] AB add: a; V: l'a [40] qui] V: que il [41] ABV add: li [42] ausi] B: autressi [43] ains viaut que . . . requiert] ABO lack; V: ains veaut que il face ce que il li a requis et que il li vaille a avoir ce que il requiert [44] si com il li requiert] C lacks [45] ausi con recort de cort] B: autressi come recort [46] se les] C: et ses [47] l'a] AV: a; C lacks [48] C adds: le dit [49] n'ont] C: n'ait [50] sont] C: soit [51] requiert] V: requierent [52] l'ont] AO: l'en ont; B: ont [53] et doivent dire . . . fié] V lacks [54] fié] B: faire [55] A adds: orres; B: ore; V: hores [56] en] AV lack [57] ausi] B lacks [58] o] C: ou

les autres homes dou seignor tenant cel fié, ou estre a faire recort de court[59] par comandement dou seignor, ou faire aucun servise par comandement dou seignor[60] ou par semonce de banier ou de .iii. homes dou seignor[61] come cort, ou user dou fié en aucune autre[62] maniere si con l'on peut et doit user de fié, ce est de requerre[63] en court aucune chose de cel[64] fié, terre, vilains ou autre chose, ou respondre en court a chose que l'on li requeist[65] de cel fié, soit terre,[66] vilains ou autre chose qui soient de cel fié ou[67] que il ou ses ancestres les aient contredites et[68] defendues en la court come chose de lor fié.[69] Et qui en l'une des dites manieres le preuve, il me senble que il l'a[70] bien prouvé que il et[71] son ancestre l'ot et tint et[72] usa come de son fié. Que plusors choses qui[73] sont faites devant les[74] homes de court sans ce que le seignor soit aveuc yaus[75] pevent et doivent les homes de court recorder come recort de cort et doivent[76] par raison estre apelés recort de court,[77] se les homes de court devant qui[78] il est fait en sont menbrant et le recordent. Et ce[79] est aparant, quar[80] il avient plusors feis en plusors cas que les homes de court font recort de chose a[81] quey le seignor n'avra ja esté, et cel recort vaut et est tenus con recort de court.

---

[59] de court] B lacks [60] ou faire aucun . . . seignor] AOV lack [61] C adds: ou par semonce do seignor (over an erasure) [62] autre] V lacks [63] de requerre] O: d'enquerre [64] cel] A: son [65] chose que l'on li requeist] B: ce que l'on li requiert [66] soit terre] A: contre genz ou; B: soit terre ou; V: terre ou [67] ou] AV lack [68] et] ABO: ou [69] fié] C: fiés [70] l'a] A: ait; BV: a [71] et] ABV: ou [72] O adds: en [73] qui] BV lack; C: qui y [74] C adds: autres [75] B adds: Quar [76] recorder come recort . . . doivent] V lacks [77] et doivent par . . . court] AB lack [78] se les homes . . . qui] C: avant que [79] ce] C lacks [80] quar] C: quart [81] font recort de chose a] A: de chose en

***[149]** Coment l'on doit prover contre[1] son seignor tout son fié ou partie de son fié.[2]

Qui viaut prover contre son seignor tot son fié ou partie,[3] il le doit prover par prevelige que le seignor ou son ancestre ont fait[4] a celui[5] ou a son ancestre[6] dou don dou[7] fié ou[8] dou confermement de cel fié, ou le doit prover[9] par le recort de la court de cele seignorie dont cel[10] fié meut. Que homes d'autre cort ne[11] pevent porter recort de court des choses[12] de celle seignorie, ne seir en court, ne faire esgart ne conoissance de court, se le chief seignor ne les a donés en esforcement de celle court[13] a la requeste dou seignor de celle court,[14] se ce n'est en la haute cort et que ce soit de ceaus homes qui ont fait au seignor la[15] ligece par l'assise. Mais[16] en la haute cort pevent tous les homes des autres cours dou reyaume qui ont fait la ligece par l'assise au chief seignor seir[17] as esgars et as conoissances[18] et recorder et avoir vois de court[19] en toutes choses ausi con les propres homes de celle court, por ce que il sont tenus au chief seignor de foy par la ligece qu'il li ont faite[20] par l'assise. Et les haus[21] homes de la court ne pevent seir ne esgarder ne faire les autres choses que les homes de court pevent et doivent faire es cours des homes dou seignor, se le chief seignor ne les a donés en esforcement de celle court par la requeste dou seignor[22] de la court, por ce que il ne li sont tenus de foy, ne sont il mie[23] pers des homes de cele court[24] quant as choses devant[25] dites faire.[26] Et qui viaut prover contre son seignor saisine de fié que il dit que lui ou son ancestre aient eue, il la doit prover par le recort des homes de cele court dont le fié meut, que nul ne peut prover par[27] recort de court aucune chose se les

A: fols c^{v}–ci^{r} cap. 164; **B:** fol. 128^{r-v} cap. 164; **C:** fol. 128^{r-v} cap. 149; **O:** fols 168^{v}–169^{v}; **V:** fol. cxxxiv^{r-v} cap. 169; Beugnot, p. 254, cap. 164.

[1] contre] B: encontre [2] B adds: coment il le peut prover [3] AOV add: de son fié [4] ont fait] A: ait doné [5] celui] ABV: lui [6] ont fait a . . . ancestre] O lacks [7] don dou] ABV: dit; O: don de [8] ou] C lacks [9] prover] C lacks [10] cel] ABO: le [11] ne] C lacks [12] des choses] V: de chose [13] esforcement de celle court] B: l'esforcement de cele court et [14] a la requeste . . . court] C lacks [15] la] ABV lack [16] Mais] B: mise [17] seir] A: estre [18] A adds: que la court fait [19] de court] AV lack; B: et recort [20] par la ligece . . . faite] V lacks [21] haus] V autres [22] se le chief . . . seignor] O lacks [23] ne sont il mie] B: ne ne sont [24] par la requeste . . . court] AV lack [25] devant] AOV: avant [26] as choses devant dites faire] B: a faire les choses devant ditez [27] le recort des . . . par] O lacks

homes qui portent cel recort ne sont des[28] homes de la court dont cel fié meut et l'estoient[29] au jor que ce fu[30] de quey il doivent[31] porter le recort, ou s'il n'ont esté donés en esforcement[32] de cele court par le chief seignor a la requeste de son home qui est seignor de cele cort.

[28] des] AB lack [29] l'estoient] A: l'esteit; V: l'estoit [30] que ce fu] A: de quoi ce fu fait [31] doivent] A: deveit; O: devroit [32] en esforcement] C: enforcement

***[150]** Qui viaut requerre au[1] seignor cazal ou terre ou autre chose que rente de besanz disant que ce est[2] son fié ou partie de son fié, coment il le doit requerre et par quei[3] et par qui il le doit[4] ofrir a prover, et coment et por quoy et de coy[5] le recort des homes de la court de chose ou le seignor n'est present est portee con recort de court[6] et est tenu ausi con recort[7] de court[8] la ou le seignor est[9] present.[10]

Qui viaut[11] requerre et avoir del[12] seignor saisine de fié qui est en casaus ou en terre ou en[13] autre leu qu'en besanz que il die que lui ou son ancestre aient[14] eue, et prover la vers lui si com il doit, il doit venir[15] et demander[16] conseill et[17] faire dire:[18] 'Sire, l'ancestre de tel', et le nome, 'ou lui', et selon ce qui[19] avra esté, 'die[20] con[21] de tel chose con de son fié, et se vos, sire, ce mescreés, il est prest dou[22] prover le par[23] le recort de partie des homes de vostre cort. Si vos pri et requier[24] con a son seignor que vos en saisine de tel chose',[25] et die de quoy, 'le metés. Et il[26] entent que vos le devés faire, ce provant qu'il a ofert a prover se vos de ce que je ai dit por lui le[27] mescreés. Si viaut que vos le facés[28] por tant con je ai dit por lui,[29] se la court l'esgarde.' Et de ce se met il en l'esgart de la court sauf son retenaill.

Et se le seignor viaut[30] esloigner cele requeste, il li peut respondre: 'Je n'entens que je en saisine vos en doie metre de ce que vos me requerés, se vos ne provés avant par le[31] prevelige[32] ou par recort de court la saisine que vos[33] dites que[34] vos ou vostre ancestre en eustes, por ce que je n'entent[35] que preuve de fié d'ome a seignor

---

A: fols ci^{r}–cii^{v} cap. 166; **B:** fols 128^{v}–129^{v} cap. 166; **C:** fols 128^{v}–130^{v} cap. 150; **O:** fols. 169^{v}–172^{r}; **V:** fols cxxxv^{r}–cxxxvi^{v} cap. 171; Beugnot, pp. 255–7, cap. 166.

---

1 au] C: a son 2 B rubric (fol. 22^{v})V add: de 3 et par quei] ABV lack 4 requerre et par . . . doit] C lacks 5 coy] V: qui 6 V adds: et des houmes de court 7 O adds: d'omes 8 V adds: des homes de court 9 est] AV: n'est 10 et est tenu . . . present] B lacks 11 AV add: fié 12 del] ABV: dou 13 en] C lacks 14 aient] A: aveit 15 A adds: devant le seignor en la court; B: devant le seignor 16 BOV add: li 17 A adds: puis 18 ABV add: par son conseill 19 qui] AV: qu'il; B: que 20 die] AV: si die; B: le dit; O: le die 21 con] A: a esté saissi 22 dou] ABO: de 23 le par] O lacks 24 requier] AB: requiert 25 tel chose] A: cel fié 26 Et il] A: Qu'il 27 por lui le] C: l'en 28 facés] OV: faites 29 por lui] V lacks 30 B adds: dire riens ou 31 le] ABV lack 32 prevelige] V: preveliges 33 B adds: me requerez et por ce que vos; V: me requerés et 34 vos dites que] C lacks 35 n'entent] AB: entens

puisse ne doie[36] estre faite si que ele vaille se ele n'est faite par[37] prevelige ou par recort de court. Et que ce que vos ofrés a prover la saisine de vos ou de vostre ancestre de ce que vos[38] requerés par le recort[39] de partie[40] des homes de ma[41] court, je n'entent que je[42] tel recort vos en[43] doie faire faire,[44] ne que il vos vaille ne doie valoir a avoir la saisine que vos[45] requerés, tout l'eusiés vos ensi provee[46] con vos dites se je[47] ou mon ancestre ne fumes o les homes de nostre cort par qui vos volés prover en dit la[48] ou ce fu fait[49] que vos ofrés a prover. Que je n'entent que court soit, ce le seignor et .ii. de ces homes ou plus ne sont ensemble ou se le seignor n'establit[50] en leuc de lui[51] .i. home et .ii. autres homes[52] o lui come court a oir ou a veir ou a dire ce qu'il[53] comande que il en facent come court, et que court n'est ne ne peut estre sans seignor,[54] si n'entent que[55] por chose que vos aiés dite ne oferte a prover que je vos en doie faire le recort que vos me requerés, ne que il vos vaille ne doive valoir a la saisine avoir que vos me[56] requerés,[57] si ne veull faire recort ne metre vos en saisine de ce que vos me requerés[58] por chose que vos aiés dite se la court ne l'esgarde, et de ce me met je en l'esgart de la court sauf mon[59] retenaill.'

Contre ce peut le requerant dire: 'Sire, a ce que vos dites que court n'est que la ou le seignor et .ii. de[60] ses homes ou plus[61] sont, vos dites vostre volenté, mais je entent que si est. Que se[62] ensi[63] fust[64] con vos dites, il n'avroit jamais[65] esgart de court ne conoissance ne recort, quar seignor ne peut ne ne doit estre ne seir a[66] la court ou les homes de la court as esgars ne as conoissances ne as recors que il font, ains le font il[67] sans le seignor, et quant il les ont fais, il les font retraire[68] devant le seignor ce que la court a fait,[69]

[36] puisse ne doie] A: ne puisse ni ne deit [37] par] C: por [38] ABV add: me [39] C adds: de la court [40] de partie] V lacks [41] ma] A: la [42] je] C: il [43] en] ABV lack [44] faire faire] A: faire; B: faire a faire [45] ABV add: me [46] provee] A: a prover [47] je] A: mei; C: vos [48] en dit la] A lacks; B: la; V: dites la [49] B adds: et [50] n'establit] A: n'en establist; O: n'estoit; V: n'establi [51] leuc de lui] B: son leuc [52] homes] A lacks [53] AV add: lor; O: luer [54] que court n'est . . . seignor] A: puis que court n'en est ni ne peut estre sanz seignor ou sans home qu'il ait establi en son leuc [55] que] B: mie; V lacks [56] me] C lacks [57] ne que il . . . requerés] B lacks [58] si ne veull . . . requerés] ABOV lack [59] mon] V: son [60] de] C: des [61] A adds: ne [62] se] A lacks [63] BV add: ne [64] B adds: mais fust enssi [65] n'avroit jamais] B: ne seroit jamais fait; V: n'i avroit jamais [66] a] BV: en [67] le font il] B: les font [68] il les font retraire] A: et il les ont retrais [69] ce que la court a fait] B lacks

soit esgart ou conoissance de court,[70] et[71] celui qui le retrait en la court[72] dit: "Sire, la court a ce fait". Por ce que la court l'a[73] fait, si est clere chose que les homes sont court en aucun cas sans le seignor, et puis qu'il le sont en aucun cas sans le seignor,[74] ne il n'est assise ne usage qui toille[75] que[76] en tel cas les homes de la court dont le fié meut ne puissent et doivent recorder en la court se il ont veu, celui qui requiert la saisine dou fié ou son ancestre saisi et tenant ou usant de ce que il requiert con de son fié ne autrement que par le recort des homes de cele court ne peut l'on prover la saisine de lui ou de son ancestre dou fié que il requiert que[77] le recort d'autre[78] gens ne seroit mie recort de court. Et que se l'on doit prover sa[79] saisine ou celle de son ancestre par recort de court[80] et l'on ne peut ce prover[81] que ce soit recort de court que par le recort[82] des homes dou seignor[83] de celle court, dont il est clere chose que je qui eufre a prover la saisine de moi ou de mon ancestre par le recort des homes[84] de vostre court de la dont le fié meut dont je vos requier la saisine, que je l'eufre bien a prover si con je doi, et que[85] en cest cas est bien recort de court[86] ce que les homes de la court[87] en recordent. Por quey je ne veul que il demore por chose que vos aiés dite que vos[88] ne me faciés aveir le recort que je vos ai requis, et que il y a des homes de vostre court qui recordent qu'il aient veu moy ou mon ancestre saisi ou[89] tenant[90] de ce que je vos requier con de son fié que lor recort ne[91] vaille a la saisine avoir que je vos requier,[92] si la voill avoir, ce provant que je ai ofert a prover, por toutes les raisons que je ai dites ou por aucunes d'eles se la court l'esgarde, et de ce me met je en l'esgart de la court sauf mon retenaill.'

Et selonc ce qui est avant[93] dit, il me senble que la court devroit[94] esgarder que le seignor n'a[95] chose dite par quei il doive demorer que il ne face avoir au requerant le recort que il[96] requiert, et que[97]

---

[70] de court] A: ou recort; B: ou recort de court [71] et] ABV lack [72] en la court] A lacks [73] l'a] AV: le [74] et puis qu'il . . . seignor] ABOV lack [75] toille] AV: vaille [76] que] C: qui; V: que que [77] que] C lacks [78] d'autre] C: d'autres [79] sa] C lacks [80] Et que se . . . court] AV lack [81] BV add: si [82] que par le recort] C lacks [83] dou seignor] B lacks [84] dou seignor de . . . homes] AV lack [85] que] C: qui [86] de court] V lacks [87] de la court] B lacks [88] C adds: dites que vos [89] ou] ABV: et [90] BV add: et usant (V: husant); O: ou usant [91] ne] C: n'a [92] que je vos requier . . . requier] A: come de son fié et que leur recort que je voz requier a la saissine aveir me vaille; B: que je vos requier [93] avant] AV: devant [94] devroit] B: doie; V: doit [95] n'a] V: n'ait [96] AO add: li [97] que] AV lack

se il y a des homes de la court qui soient recordans qu'il veicent le requerant ou son ancestre saisi et tenant ou usant[98] con de son fié et il le recordent en la court, que cel recort[99] li vaut[100] et doive valoir a la saisine avoir que il requiert, et que le seignor le doit en saisine metre se provant que il a ofert.[101] Que se autrement estoit, mout a enuis porroit nul prover[102] saisine de fié[103] de lui ou de son ancestre, por quey molt de gens perdroient lor droit et lor raison par defaute de recort de court, laquel chose seroit contre droit et raison et tort apert.

Et se le fié de qui l'on veaut prover la saisine de lui ou de son ancestre est assené en besanz et le requerant peut prover par la secrete dou seignor que lui ou son ancestre aient receu paie de cel fié, il me senble que il a prové[104] sofisaument la saisine et la teneure dou fié, ou se il peut prover par le recort de partie des homes[105] de la court[106] que il aient veu lui ou son ancestre receveir paie de cel fié,[107] il a bien prové la saisine et la teneure de cel fié si con il doit, mais l'usage dou fié covient il que l'on preuve par les homes de la court si con est devisé[108] el chapitle qui vient aprés cestui.

---

[98] ABV add: de ce qu'il (AB: li) requiert [99] le recordent en . . . recort] V: recordent en la court, que ce [100] vaut] C: vaille [101] A adds: a prover [102] nul prover] A: l'on prover nulle [103] de fié] B lacks [104] a prové] ABV: preuve [105] V adds: dou seignor et [106] de la court] B lacks [107] C adds: si con il doit [108] devisé] B lacks

***[151]** Que il covient a dire as homes de court qui recordent[1] saisine et teneure et usage de fié si que le recort vaille[2] a avoir la saisine dou fié[3] a celui ou a celle qui l'a oferte a prover par leur recort.[4]

Qui viaut prover saisine de fié de lui ou de son ancestre par le recort des homes de la court, il covient que ceaus qui cel[5] recort feront soient recordans[6] qu'il aient veu celui qui requiert la saisine dou fié ou son ancestre saisi et tenant de ce que il requiert,[7] et que il l'en ont veu user con de son fié, et ensi que il li[8] aient veu de cel fié faire homage au seignor ou servise en tel maniere que il tenant cel fié l'aient oy semondre au banier dou[9] servise ou[10] aler en aucune semonce dou servise[11] o[12] les autres homes dou seignor, ou seir[13] en court et jugier ou conoistre ou recorder[14] o[15] les autres homes dou seignor, ou faire ou les autres homes dou seignor[16] aucunes des autres choses que les homes de la court[17] pevent et doivent faire, ou requerre en la court[18] vilains ou vilaines[19] de cel fié ou aucune autre[20] chose de cel fié come soue, ou que autre li requeist[21] en la court et qu'il le defendist con chose de son fié. Que a moy senble[22] que qui a et tient aucune chose et il en use en aucune des[23] manieres devant dites, que il est clere chose que il en use[24] con de son fié.[25]

A: fol. cii[v] cap. 167; **B:** fols 129[v]–130[r] cap. 167; **C:** fols 130[v]–131[r] cap. 151; **O:** fol. 172[r–v]; **V:** fols cxxxvi[v]–cxxxvii[r] cap. 172; Beugnot, p. 258, cap. 167.

---

[1] recordent] V rubric (fol. 9[v]): requirent [2] vaille] AV lack [3] le recort vaille . . . fié] B: la cort a avoir la saisine dou fié soit vaillable [4] recort] A: recort li vaille; B: esgart [5] cel] AV: tel [6] feront soient recordans] B: font ou feront soient [7] A adds: come dou sien [8] li] BV lack [9] dou] ABV: de [10] ou] C: o [11] ou aler en . . . servise] A lacks [12] o] B: avec [13] seir] B: soit [14] A adds: ou esgarder [15] o] B: avec [16] ou faire ou . . . seignor] B lacks; V: ou faire [17] de la court] C: dou seignor [18] en la court] AB lack [19] ou vilaines] C lacks [20] autre] BV lack [21] requeist] B: requerist [22] Que a moy senble] A lacks; B: A moi semble [23] en aucune des] O: come de son fié [24] use] AB: a usé; V: a husé [25] de son fié] V: dou sien

***[152]** Coment l'on peut[1] prover son fié ou partie de son fié contre autre que contre son seignor.

L'on peut contre autre que contre son seignor prover son fié ou[2] partie de son fié par prevelige ou par recort de cort ou par guarans. Et peut l'on prover la saisine de son fié[3] de lui ou de son ancestre en la maniere que il est devisé en l'autre chapitle devant que l'on la peut prover contre son seignor.[a] Et par guarans la peut l'on prover contre autre que contre son seignor.[4] Mais[5] l'usage dou fié ne peut l'on contre l'autre prover qu'en la maniere avant[6] dite. Et qui viaut prover par previlige ou par recort de court contre autre que contre son seignor tout[7] ou[8] partie ou la saisine ou la teneure de lui ou de son ancestre de cel fié et l'usage, il le doit faire en la maniere avant dite.[9] [b] Et qui le viaut prover par guarans, il le[10] doit prover par[11] .ii. loyaus guarans de la loy de Rome et qu'il soient tes que il puissent guarentie porter sans estre rebutés ne contredis. Et quant il vodra se prover que il a[12] dit par guarans, se son aversaire ne torne l'un des guarans ou contredie ou[13] rebute a hore et a tens si con il est devisé en cest livre que l'on le doit faire,[c] celui qui l'a ensi prové l'a bien prové si con il doit, et[14] il doit venir devant le seignor et dire li: 'Sire, je ai tel chose provee si con je doy a mon fié ou a partie de mon fié ou a la saisine de moy ou de mon ancestre de cest fié et l'usage dou dit fié.[15] Faites le moy delivrer.' Et le seignor le doit faire sans delai.[16] Et se son aversaire torne l'un des guarans, si en doit estre la bataille con de querelle de plus d'un marc d'argent,

A: fols cii^{v}–ciii^{r} cap. 168; **B:** fol. 130^{r-v} cap. 168; **C:** fol. 131^{r-v} cap. 152; **O:** fols 172^{v}–173^{v}; **V:** fol. cxxxvii^{r-v} cap. 173; Beugnot, pp. 258–9, cap. 168.

[a] Above cap. 150.
[b] Above cap. 151.
[c] Above caps 55–8.

[1] l'on peut] A: on deit [2] ou] AB: et [3] de son fié] A: dou fié; B: lacks [4] Et par guarans . . . seignor] A: Et par garenz ne la peut l'on prover contre son seignor; B: Et par garanz la puet on prover contre autre; O lacks; V: et par guarens [5] A adds: la saissine de [6] avant] V: devant [7] A adds: son fié [8] BO add: en [9] de lui ou . . . dite] A: avant dite faire le peut; BV: avant dite [10] le] A: la [11] guarans, il le doit prover par] V lacks [12] a] B lacks [13] contredie ou] AB: contredit ou; V: ne contredit ou ne [14] A adds: quant il l'a prové [15] A adds: et die ce qu'il avra prové [16] delai] B: nul deleement

et la maniere de la torne de bataille[17] et de la bataille[18] en tel cas est devisé en cest livre la ou il parle des batailles.[d] Et se il le contredit ou rebute, si s'en defent le guarant et aleaute si con est avant dit[19] en cest livre des guarenties et des guarans.[e]

[d] Above cap. 90.
[e] Above caps 61–2.

[17] con de querelle . . . bataille] ABV lack [18] et de la bataille] CV lack [19] avant dit] V: devant devisé

***[153]** Coment enfant a qui fié eschey tant[1] con il fu[2] merme d'aage peut avoir cel[3] fié quant il est d'aage.

Se[4] fié eschiet a enfant[5] merme d'aage et le seignor ou autre tiegne son baillage, quant il a .xv. ans complis, se il viaut entrer en son fié,[6] il doit venir devant le seignor en sa[7] court et dire li: 'Sire, je ai .xv. ans d'aage ou plus, et se vos[8] ou autre le mescreés, je le suis prest de[9] prover tout ensi con la cort esgardera ou conoistra que je prover le doie.' Et aprés cest[10] dit, se le seignor tient le baillage et il seit que il a .xv. ans conplis,[11] il li doit dire: 'Je vos en croy bien, et metés vos en vostre fié quant vous vodrés.' Et se[12] autre tient le baillage de cel fié, et[13] se le seignor ne set que il ait .xv. ans[14] ou plus, il doit dire:[15] 'Je veull bien que la court conoisse coment vos devés vestre aage prover.' Et celui li doit dire: 'Sire, comandés a la court qu'ele face ceste conoissance.' Et le seignor le doit comander[16] a la court,[17] et la court le[18] doit faire ensi, se cuit, que elle[19] doit conoistre que il doit prover par .ii. leiaus guarans crestiens, homes ou femes, que il a .xv. ans d'aage ou plus et que il le jurent.[20] Et se il ensi le preuve,[21] il avra bien[22] prouvé son aage si con il doit. Et quant il l'avra prové, il se peut metre en son fié toutes les fois[23] que il voudra[24] sans ce que nul qui le baillage tiegne de cel fié[25] li en doive ne puisse contredit metre por achaison dou bailliage. Que nul baill ne peut nule chose dire qui li[26] vaille contre la preuve de l'aage[27] de l'eir.

Et se il n'est chevalier quant il preuve[28] son aage, se il fait que sage il dira au seignor quant il avra son aage prové: 'Sire, donés

---

A: fol. ciii^{r-v} cap. 169; **B:** fols 130^{v}–131^{r} cap. 169; **C:** fols 131^{v}–132^{r} cap. 153; **O:** fols 173^{v}–174^{v}; **V:** fols cxxxvii^{v}–cxxxviii^{v} cap. 174; Beugnot, pp. 259–60, cap. 169.

---

[1] tant] B: entretant [2] fu] A: est [3] cel] C: cest [4] Se] C: Le [5] O adds: quant il est [6] son fié] A: saissine de son fié; BV: saisine [7] sa] BV: la [8] A adds: sire [9] le mescreés, je . . . de] B: m'en mescreez, je sui prest dou; V: me mescreés je suis prest dou [10] cest] B: cel; V: ce [11] a .xv. ans conplis] B: ait quinze anz acompliz [12] C adds: vostre [13] et] B: ou [14] conplis, il li . . . ans] AO lack [15] Je vos en . . . dire] V lacks [16] comandés a la . . . comander] V: dons coumandes [17] a la court] A lacks [18] le] A: la; V lacks [19] que elle] B: qu'il; C: que elle ne [20] doit prover par . . . jurent] A: le deit prover par .ii. leaus crestiens, homes ou femes, qui jurent qu'il a .xv. anz ou plus d'aage [21] preuve] V: preuvent [22] bien] ABV lack [23] fois] C: fiés [24] voudra] A: viaut; B: veut; V: veaut [25] de cel fié] B lacks [26] li] OV lack [27] de l'aage] B lacks [28] preuve] A: a prové; V: fait la preuve de

moy .i.[29] respit resnable de moi faire chevalier por faire vous le servise que je vos doy de mon fié.' Et le seignor li doit doner, se cuit, le respit. Et le respit[30] me senble resnable de .xl. jors, se le seignor n'a besoing hastif de chevaliers[31] por afaire[32] d'armes, et se il l'a selonc le besoing le respit. Et je cuit que celui qui eufre son aage a prover si con est avant dit feroit que sage se il se faisoit faire[33] chevalier puis que il avroit .xv. ans conplis[34] ains que il ofrist son aage a prover, et que maintenant que il l'avroit prouvé[35] que il ofrist au seignor son homage de cel fié tel con le fié le doit ou ensi con il le peut et doit faire par l'assise ou l'usage de cest roiaume, et se le seignor le voloit recevoir que il le feist, et se il[36] ne le voloit recevoir ou le deleast de recevoir le, qu'il[37] traisist la court a guarant de ce que il a son homage ofert a ore et a tens si con il doit, et[38] que se le seignor disoit raison por quoy il n'entendist[39] que il deust son homage recevoir, si con il a[40] ofert, qu'il deist contre le seignor raison por coy il[41] entent que il ensi le doit recevoir, et se meist en esgart ou en conoissance de court.

[29] Sire, donés moy .i.] B: Donez moy [30] le respit] ABV: il [31] de chevaliers] A lacks [32] afaire] B: fait; OV: faire [33] faire] A lacks [34] conplis] A: complis et; B: acompliz [35] l'avroit prouvé] A: seroit chevalier et qu'il avroit prové son aage [36] Et se il] V: en nom de Dieu fust receu. Et se le seignor [37] le qu'il] C: lequel il [38] et] C lacks [39] n'entendist] C: n'en rendist; V: n'entent [40] a] BV: l'a [41] si con il . . . il] O: et se meist en esgart ou en conoissance de court

***[154]** Por quey celui ou cele qui tient baillage de damoisele[1] le doit tenir tant que ele soit mariee tout ait ele .xii. ans ou plus, et coment ele peut avoir le fié qui li estoit[2] escheu quant ele a pasé .xii. ans.[3]

Se fié eschet a damoisele qui ait .xii. ans ou plus, celui ou celle qui devoit tenir son baillage s'elle eust[4] mains de .xii. ans le devra tenir par l'assise ou l'usage de cest reiaume tant que ele soit mariee, tout soit ce que ele ait .xii. ans conplis.[5] [6] Et le seignor, puis que elle avra .xii. ans[7] passés, la peut semondre de prendre baron. Et s'il l'en veaut semondre,[8] il le doit faire ensi[9] con il est devisé[10] en cest livre que l'on doit faire[11] feme semondre de tel chose. Et se il ensi[12] la semont et ele ne prent[13] baron a la semonce dou seignor, il en peut avoir droit, et coment et quel sera aprés[14] devisé en cest livre.[a]

Et se aucun tient le fié qu'il[15] soit tel que le seignor aime meaus qu'il le teigne que marier la damoiselle, et les parens et les amis de la damoiselle[16] veulent qu'ele soit mariee et que ele entre en son fié, il doivent venir devant le seignor et dire li: 'Sire, nostre parente est[17] tel qui fu[18] fille de tel', et nomer la[19] et son pere,[20] 'a pasé .xii. ans, et ele provera[21] son aage se aucun l'en mescroit. Si vos prions et requerons que il uos plaise que noz la puissons marier si qu'ele entre[22] en son fié et que vos en aiés le servise.' Et se le seignor ne fait lor priere, laquele je ne cuit pas qu'il face[23] volentiers s'il n'est mout tenus a iaus, por ce que le fait des mariages[24] est une des choses[25] de quei le seignor peut avoir plus de profist et l'a[26] sovent,

---

A: fols civ[r]–cv[v] cap. 171; **B:** fols 131[v]–132[v] cap. 171; **C:** fols 132[r]–133[v] cap. 154; **O:** fols 174[v]–176[v]; **V:** fols cxxxix[v]–cxli[r] cap. 179; Beugnot, pp. 263–6, cap. 171.

---

[a] Below cap. 199.

---

[1] de damoisele] B lacks [2] estoit] ABV: est; O: soit [3] B adds: et est mariee [4] eust] V: fust [5] ait .xii. ans conplis] A: a .xii. anz passés; B: ot passé .xii. anz [6] tant que ele . . . conplis] V: et pour ce que il a esté usé longuement et se use encores que puis que damoysele a compli .xii. ans peut requerre son fié au seignor et aver le se la dite damoisele le veut requerre le doit avoir [7] conplis. Et le . . . ans] O lacks [8] C adds: de prendre baron [9] ensi] BV: si [10] devisé] V lacks [11] faire] O lacks [12] ensi] V: est ensi que il [13] prent] C: prist [14] aprés] V lacks [15] qu'il] ABV: qui [16] de la damoiselle] B lacks [17] est] AB lack [18] V adds: telle et [19] nomer la] AV: noment li; B: le nomment, 'lui [20] pere] C: aage; V: pere, si [21] AV add: bien [22] entre] V: puisse entrer [23] pas qu'il face] B: mie qu'il feist [24] des mariages] V: de mariage [25] des choses] AV: chose [26] l'a] B: les a

si li dient: 'Sire, nos vos donrons tant se il vos plaist et soufrés que nos la marions', et dient tel quantité de monoie que il puissent soufrir et que il entendent que le seignor le doit faire, et se faisant se il entendent que il la puissent bien marier a tel de[27] qui soit le profist et l'ennor de la damoisele.[28] Et se le seignor ne viaut finer a iaus de cel mariage, si li dient: 'Sire, dont vos prions nos[29] et requerons que vos la[30] mariés si con vos devez par l'usage.'[31] Et se le seignor ne le fait por ce que il tieigne le fié et que il aime miaus avoir le profit des rentes dou fié que se qu'il avroit por le mariage, ne que la damoisele eust baron, laquel chose bon seignor ne fera ja, se Dieu plaist, ou por aucune chose deleast le mariage, se les parens de la damoisele ou la damoisele[32] veulent tout outre qu'ele soit mariee, la damoisele doit venir devant le seignor en la court et demander conceil et faire dire par son conseill: 'Sire, tel', et la nome, 'qui fu fille de tel', et le nome, 'est venue devant vos come devant[33] son seignor et vos fait assaveir que ele a .xii. ans pasés. Et se vos, sire,[34] ou autre se ne creés,[35] ele est prest de prover le tout ensi con la court esgardera ou conoistra qu'ele[36] prover le doie.' Et se le seignor dit que il viaut bien que la court li conoisse,[37] si[38] die: 'Sire,[39] comandés a la cort qu'ele le face.' Et le seignor le doit comander a la court[40] et la[41] doit faire ensi, se cuit, con il est devisé en l'autre chapitle[42] que on[43] doit prover aage.[b] Et se le seignor li eschanpist[44] ou deleye la conoissance, si le destraigne[45] si con est devisé en cest livre que on[46] doit seignor[47] destraindre d'avoir conoissance de court.[48] [c] Et quant la dite conoissance sera faite et ele[49] avra prouvé son aage si con la court l'a[50] coneu, si die celui qui est a son conseill: 'Sire, tel', et la nome, 'a[51] son aage provè si con ele doit. Si vos pri et requier et semont[52] con a son seignor que vos de hui en .xv. jors ou de demain en .xv.

[b] Above cap. 153.
[c] Below cap. 210.

[27] de] BV lack [28] A adds: si le facent [29] dont vos prions nos] B: nos vos prions [30] la] C: le [31] A adds: de cest reiaume [32] ou la damoisele] AB lack [33] vos come devant] C lacks [34] sire] B lacks [35] ne creés] ABV: mescreés [36] qu'ele] CV: que [37] li conoisse] V: conoist [38] AB add: li [39] V adds: dons [40] a la court] A lacks [41] la] ABV: la court le [42] l'autre chapitle] B: cest livre [43] on] AV: l'on [44] eschanpist] V: champist [45] AV adds: d'avoir (A: la) conoissance de court [46] on] AV: l'on [47] prover aage. Et . . . seignor] B lacks [48] d'avoir conoissance de court] AV lack [49] ele] B: cele; V: celle [50] l'a] AB: l'avra; V: avra [51] A adds: bien [52] et semont] B lacks

jors ou depuis demain en .xv. jors[53] li aiés oferte par l'usage[54] de cest reiaume .iii. barons soufisans a lui par le dit usage,[55] et ele entent que vos faire le devés par le dit usage,[56] et que[57] se vous ne le faites, qu'ele[58] se peut marier a son gré sans mesprendre[59] vers vos. Si vos requier que vos le faciés conoistre a vostre court, se vous dedens le dit terme ne li avés[60] fait se qu'ele vos a requis et semons, et[61] ele aprés se marie se ele le puet faire sans se que vous d'aucune chose[62] la puissés achaisoner de son mariage.' Et le seignor qui ne doit faillir d'esgart ne de conoissance de court doit comander a la court qu'ele cele conoissance de court[63] face, et[64] ofrir li maintenant baron par le dit usage. Et se le seignor comande a la court que ele[65] face[66] cele dite conoissance, je cuit que la court doit conoistre que se le seignor ne li eufre baron si com il doit dedens le dit terme, qu'ele aprés se peut marier a sa volenté[67] sans ce que ele de riens mespreigne vers le seignor. Que se autrement estoit, les[68] seignors qui[69] vodroient maliner en poroient[70] tout tens mais[71] tenir le baillage des fiés[72] des damoiseles quant il[73] seroient en leur mains, ou se il le[74] voloient faire tenir a celui ou a cele qui le[75] tenroient[76] en baillage, que se la damoisele se marie sans le congé de celui ou de cele de qui ele doit le fié[77] tenir, ele perdra son fié si con il est devisé en cest livre que l'on doit perdre son fié[78] por tel[79] mesfait.[d] Et quant la court avra la dite conoissance faite, se le seignor ne li a ofert baron dedens le dit terme selonc le dit usage, elle se peut marier a sa volenté, que le seignor ne l'en pora de riens achaisoner. Et tout soit ce que il me senble que se la damoisele semont le seignor si con est avant[80] dit[81] et le seignor ne li eufre[82] dedens le dit terme baron[83] par le dit

[d] Below cap. 201.

[53] ou depuis demain en .xv. jors] BC lack [54] l'usage] A: l'assise [55] par le dit usage] B lacks [56] par le dit usage] V lacks [57] que] AV lack [58] qu'ele] B: ele [59] a son gré sans mesprendre] A: sanz congé prendre [60] avés] A: ais; B: aiez; V: aiés [61] a requis et semons, et] AV: requiert et semont et; B: requiert que vos li faciés conoistre que [62] vous d'aucune chose] B: elle d'aucune chose vos mesface ne que vos [63] de court] AV: li [64] et] ABV: ou [65] a la court que ele] B: que la cort [66] face] A: li face [67] dit terme qu'ele . . . volenté] A: terme devant dit et le dit terme passe qu'elle se peut marier [68] les] C: le [69] A adds: ce; O: li [70] les seignors qui . . . poroient] BV: le seignor qui voudroit (V: vodroit) maligner porroit (V: poroit) [71] mais] V lacks [72] des fiés] BV lack [73] il] B: eles; V: elles [74] il le] V: elle [75] le] C: l'en [76] tenroient] B: tenroit [77] doit le fié] B: le doit [78] si con il . . . fié] O lacks [79] por tel] C lacks [80] est avant] A: il est devant [81] dit] C lacks [82] V adds: si come est devant dit [83] baron] O lacks

usage, qu'ele se peut aprés marier a sa volenté[84] sans ce que le seignor l'en puisse gregier,[85] por ce que il me senble que il est plus seure chose de[86] la dite conoissance requiere avant le mariage que aprés[87] l'ai je[88] dit en cest chapitle.

---

[84] que le seignor . . . volenté] B lacks [85] gregier] A: de riens gregier et; B: grever [86] de] C: que [87] B adds: tot [88] l'ai je] V: l'aage

***[155]** Coment damoisele qui a[1] pasé .xii.[2] ans peut avoir bailliage[3] qui li eschiet.

Se baillage eschiet a damoisele qui ait[4] .xii. ans ou plus d'aage[5] et ele le veulle avoir et tenir et user ent, li et[6] ces amis doivent faire et dire de[7] son aage prover et le[8] seignor prier et requerre[9] que il lor doint poier de marier la et[10] de finer a lui de son mariage, et ele[11] requere et semondre[12] le seignor[13] qui[14] la marit[15] et de conoissance de court requerre et des autres choses requerre[16] si con il est devisé el chapitle[17] devant que la damoisele qui a .xii. ans ou plus et fié[18] li escheyt et ces amis le doivent faire.[a] Que[19] il me senble que en cest cas doit estre mené[20] le fait dou baillage a celui[21] con celui dou fié.

A: fol. cv^{v} cap. 172; **B:** fol. 132^{v} cap. 172; **C:** fol. 133^{v} cap. 155; **O:** fols 176^{v}–177^{r}; **V:** fol. cxli^{r-v} cap. 180; Beugnot, p. 267, cap. 172.

---

[a] Above cap. 154.

---

[1] a] V: ait [2] .xii.] C: .xv. [3] bailliage] A rubric (fol. 5^{v}): fié [4] V adds: passé [5] d'aage] B lacks [6] ent li et] A: c'est ce que li et; B: por lui; V: li et [7] de] A: et de; B lacks [8] le] AV: dou [9] et requerre] A lacks; C: et querre [10] et] A: ou [11] B adds: doit [12] ele requere et semondre] V: se elle requiert et semone [13] le seignor] B lacks [14] qui] BOV: que il [15] marit] AV: marie [16] de conoissance de . . . requerre] B: doit requerre connoissance de court [17] el chapitle] A lacks [18] fié] B: baillage [19] et ces amis . . . Que] B lacks [20] doit estre mené] A lacks [21] a celui] A: a celui a qui il escheit; B: aussi

***[156]** Se aucun seignor done fié en besanz a home ou a feme et l'asene en aucun leuc moti, et se de la defaut[1] sur toutes ses[2] autres rentes que il a et avra, et aprés done a un autre home fié et l'en asene en aucun[3] autre[4] leu moti, et il defaille[5] dou leuc ou le premier[6] est asené par non, et il veulle estre paié avant de l'autre dou leuc ou il est asené,[7] lequel des .ii. doit estre avant payé de cel[8] leu.

Se .i. home ou plusors sont[9] asenés de leur fié[10] en .i. leu moti,[11] et se de la defaut sur toutes les autres rentes que il a ou[12] avra en cele seignorie, et que[13] le seignor, qui lor dona les fiés en la maniere avant dite, die es preveliges[14] que il lor a fais[15] des fiés, que il les asene[16] des lors de ce que il[17] leur defaudroit de lor dis[18] fiés, fust de tout ou de partie, sur toutes ces autres rentes de sa seignorie que il a et avra,[19] et aprés une espace de tens il done[20] a aucun autre fié et l'assene[21] sur aucun leuc[22] moti autre[23] que celui que il a[24] les autres asenés motiement, et celui qui avra le derain don a[25] receu aucune paie de son fié dou leu ou il est asené, et il defaut dou leu ou les premiers[26] sont asenés par non, et celui ou ceaus a qui sa paie sera defaillie requiert[27] que il le face paier de ce[28] que il est failli[29] de son asenement des rentes dou leu ou le derain asené[30] est asené[31] par non, por ce que il contient en son prevelige que se il defaut de la ou[32] il est assené par non,[33] par quel[34] maniere que se soit, que il est assené des que le seignor fist le don dou fié a son ancestre ou a celui[35] sur toutes les rentes que le seignor[36] avoit au

A: fols cv^v–cvii^r cap. 173; **B:** fols 132^v–134^r cap. 173; **C:** fols 133^v–135^v cap. 156; **O:** fols 177^r–179^v; **V:** fols cxli^v–cxliii^v cap. 182; Beugnot, pp. 270–2, cap. 173.

[1] defaut] A: faut [2] ses] C lacks [3] en aucun] V: a .i. [4] autre] AB lack [5] il defaille] A: ce il li defaille; A rubric (fol. 5^v): si defaut; O: il defailli; V: il deffailist [6] leuc ou le premier] B: premier leuc ou il [7] AB add: avant [8] cel] AB rubric (fol. 23^r) V: celui [9] V adds: en .i. leuc [10] fié] AV: fiés [11] A adds: par le seignor [12] ou] O: et [13] que] C: se [14] es preveliges] A: el prevelige [15] a fais] A: fait; V: a fait [16] asene] V: a assenés [17] ce que il] A: qui; B: ce qui [18] dis] AV lack [19] ces autres rentes . . . avra] B: les autres rentes que il a et avra en sa seignorie [20] done] C: doit [21] et l'assene] A lacks [22] leuc] B: autre [23] fié et l'assene . . . autre] C lacks [24] que il a] B: sur quoi il a [25] a] B: avra [26] premiers] B autres [27] A adds: au seignor [28] requiert que il . . . ce] B lacks [29] que il est failli] A: qu'il est defaillant; B lacks; V: qui li defailli [30] asené] AB lack [31] asené] C lacks [32] ou] V: dont [33] por ce que . . . non] A lacks [34] quel] ABV: quelque [35] celui] ABV: lui [36] fist le don . . . seignor] O lacks

jor et avroit en cele seignorie, et que il avoit[37] cele rente au jor que il le fié dona a lui[38] ou a son ancestre, por coi il dit que il est asené sur cel leu qui estoit dou seignor au jor que il dona son[39] fié a lui ou a son ancestre,[40] si[41] viaut estre[42] paiés des rentes de cel leu devant celui qui aprés est asené[43] par non, por ce que son don et son asenement fu fait avant dou sien, se la court conoist que il estre[44] le doie, et de ce se met il en la conoissance[45] de la court sauf son retenaill.

Celui qui est asené par non en sel leu[46] ou l'autre demande a estre paié le peut bien contredire et defendre par raison, se me senble, qu'il ne sera pas paié de ce que il[47] defaut de son fié des rentes de cel leu ou il est asené par non, tant que il soit avant paié de son fié,[48] se le requerant ou son ancestre ne furent[49] onques paié del defaut de l'asenement[50] en cel leu, et se[51] il le veaut defendre, je cuit que il le peut ensi faire. Quant celui requiert au seignor[52] en la maniere avant dite que il le face paier sur l'asenement de l'autre, die au seignor celui qui le viaut defendre: 'Sire, je n'entent que vos tel', et le nome, 'puissés ne deés faire paier dou defaut de son fié des rentes de mon asenement tant que je soye avant paié de mon fié et[53] enterinement por chose que il die, et dis[54] raison por coy: por ce que je suis asené en cel[55] leu motiement, et il ne l'est mie, et que se[56] le seignor qui[57] dona son fié l'asena de ce qui en[58] defaudroit de son asenement sur ces autres rentes, il ne l'asena pas[59] sur mon[60] fié. Et je veull bien, sire,[61] que de ce que vos avez el leu[62] que vos l'en paiés se il[63] vos plaist, mais de ce qui est de mon fié ne veull je mie que vos le paiés, ainz[64] vos pri et requier et defent con a mon seignor que vos de ce qui est de mon fié ne le paiés ne le[65] faites paier. Car je n'entent qu'il[66] ait[67] riens en mon fié ne en mon asenement se se n'est aprés ma paie. Que asenement que il ait eu en general sans avoir paie ne li vaut ne valoir ne li doit quant a ce que il resoive devant moy paie, que son don ne li fu fait en

---

[37] avoit] V: avroit en [38] dona a lui] B: li dona [39] son] B: cel [40] por coi il . . . ancestre] A lacks [41] si] B: por quoi il dit qu'il [42] estre] C lacks [43] est asené] V: fu assenés [44] conoist que il estre] V: ne conoist que il [45] la conoissance] C: l'esgart [46] en sel leu] B lacks [47] A adds: li [48] des rentes de . . . fié] O lacks [49] furent] O: recurent [50] l'asenement] A: leur assenement; V: son assenement [51] se] C: que [52] requiert au seignor] A: le requiert; V: ne requiert [53] et] ABV lack [54] dis] AB: di; V: dirai [55] cel] AB: tel; V: celui [56] se] ABV lack [57] AB add: li [58] en] BV lack [59] pas] ABV: mie [60] B adds: assenement ne sur mon [61] sire] A lacks [62] el leu] A: celui assené; C: et; O: el [63] se il] B: si com [64] ainz] B lacks [65] le] AB lack [66] C adds: y [67] n'entent qu'il ait] A: entens qu'il n'a

maniere que il eust asenement en[68] leu ou je sui asené que il[69] li vaille a estre[70] paié devant moy. Que il ne li[71] fu mie asené par non, ne il n'ot de l'asenement que il dit qui[72] li fu fait el leu ou je sui asené que promese. Que tant con il fu vostre sans ce que vos y eussiés[73] riens doné ne asené et qu'il estoit en vostre main tout delivre, il ne resut aucune paie ne son ancestre ne autre por aucun d'eaus, por quoy il aprés se que vos ou vostre ancestre avez doné a moi ou a mon ancestre et asené motiement sur celui leu, et que moy ou mon ancestre[74] avons reseu paie de cel[75] leu et en avons usé con de nostre fié, il ne peut[76] ne[77] doit paie recevoir devant moy. Ne raison n'est ne asisse ne usage qu'il faire le doie. Car trop seroit descovenable[78] chose et contre raison se .i.[79] seignor donoit[80] a aucun .i.[81] fié et l'en asenast si con il dit que il est assené, que il aprés ce[82] ne peust[83] aucune chose doner de sa seignorie de quey celui ne fust la[84] paié se il vosist se aucune chose li defailloit[85] de[86] paie dou leu ou il seroit asené par non. Et s'ensi estoit, les seignors qui avroient aucun tel don fait avroient acervi trop malement toute lor seignorie,[87] laquel chose ne peut ne ne doit estre par assise ne par usage ne par raison. Et por tant plus di je qu'il ne doit estre paié[88] devant moy de mon asenement,[89] qu'il ne fu asené que sur les rentes dou seignor, ne il ne doit faire[90] requerre ne avoir paie d'aillors que dou leu ou il est asené par non tant que il li defaille de la, ne[91] il ne doit resoivre paie dou defaut de son asenement que[92] des rentes que le seignor a au jor[93] que il li defaut de sa paie. Ne mon fié ne[94] mon asenement n'est mie des rentes dou seignor, dont est il clere chose que il ne doit mie estre paié dou defaut de[95] son asenement sur mon fié. Si ne veull, sire,[96] por toutes les raisons que je ai dites ou por aucunes d'eles que vos le faciés paier de[97] mon asenement se vostre court ne conoist[98] que vos faire le deés, et de ce me met je en[99] la conoissance de vostre[100] court sauf mon retenaill.'

---

[68] il eust asenement en] B: l'assentement ou [69] que il] B lacks; V: qui [70] devant moy paie . . . estre] A lacks [71] li] ABV lack [72] qui] C: qu'il [73] eussiés] AV: eustes; C: eciés [74] et que moy ou mon ancestre] A: moi ou mon ancestre et [75] cel] BV: celui [76] il ne peut] B lacks [77] ne] A: ni ne; BV: ne ne [78] descovenable] AB: desrainable; V: desrenable [79] .i.] A: le [80] donoit] V: done [81] a aucun .i.] A: aucun; BV: a aucun [82] ce] ABV lack [83] peust] AV: peut [84] la] B: ja [85] defailloit] B: defaillist; V: defailist [86] AC (interlined) add: sa [87] toute lor seignorie] B: leurs seignories [88] A adds: par raisson [89] B adds: ne [90] faire] ABV lack; C: faire ne [91] ne] B lacks [92] que] C: ne [93] que le seignor a au jor] V: dou seignor a jour [94] mon fié ne] C lacks [95] B adds: sa paie et de [96] sire] B lacks [97] de] ABV: sur [98] conoist] A: conut; C: conoisse [99] V adds: l'esguart et en [100] vostre] A: la

Et le seignor lor[101] deit lors[102] respondre: 'Et je veull et comant a ma court que ele conoisse[103] se je por la requeste de tel', et le nome, 'le doie faire paier de tel leu', et le motisse, 'si con il me[104] requiert par les raisons que il a dites,[105] ou se je por la defence que[106] tel', et le nome, 'm'a fait[107] ne le dey faire paier[108] de son fié ne de son asenement por les raisons que il a[109] dites.' Et la court doit faire la dite conoissance puis que le seignor le comande.

Et a moi senble que la court doit conoistre que le seignor ne doit mie faire paier le requerant dou defaut de l'asenement ou il est assené par non sur le fié de l'asenement[110] de l'autre, se il ou son ancestre n'ont receu paie del defaut de[111] leur[112] assenement de celui leu ou le derain est assené par non, et dont il ou son ancestre ont receu paie ains que le don fust doné au derain ou aprés.

---

[101] lor] AV lack [102] lors] B: maintenant [103] conoisse] AV: conoist [104] me] V: le [105] il a dites] V: je ais dit [106] que] ABV: de [107] m'a fait] B lacks [108] O adds: ne [109] il a] C: je ai [110] C adds: ou il est assené [111] l'asenement ou il . . . de] V lacks [112] leur] O: 'son' crossed through

***[157]** Qui est asené de son fié en .i. leu moti, et il defaut de cel leu une anee ou plusors, si que celui qui est asené n'ait[1] pou estre payé de son fié, et il rent[2] .i. autre anee aprés el tens d'autre[3] seignor ou baill tant[4] que il puisse estre payé de quanque l'on li doit de son fié de vieill et de noviau, coment et en quel cas il en doit estre paié sans ce que le seignor ne le baill ne s'en puisse defendre por dire: 'que[5] ce que[6] l'on vos doit n'est[7] mie de mon tens, por quey je ne vos veull payer que ce que l'on vos doit de mon tens'.

Se .i. home est asené de son fié que il a[8] en besanz sur .i. leu moti, soit casal ou terre ou rente, et cel leu ne rent tant de quey[9] il puisse estre paié, et il demore a estre paié[10] .i. an. ou plus ou mains por ce que le leuc ou il est assené n'a[11] tant rendu[12] qu'il ait peu[13] estre paié, et il en cest[14] tens que la[15] paie li defaut, si con est avant dit, ne guage[16] son seignor dou servise que il li doit ains tient et fait le servise adés si con il doit atendant sa paie, et aprés une espace de tens cel leu vaut tant de quei[17] il puisse[18] estre bien paiés de ce que[19] il est la asené de son fié de cele anee, et il y a autres gens que luy asenés en cel leu[20] aprés lui de lor fiés, et il ait[21] tant en cel leu de rente par quey il soient paiés de ce que l'on lor deit de cele anee se c'est casal et il[22] a plus de rentes el casal[23] de cele annee que la paie des asenés ne monte de cele annee, celui qui premier[24] est asené de[25] ceaus a qui il est[26] premier defailli de la[27] paie peut requerre a celui qui a cel jor tendra cel leu,[28] soit droit seignor ou baill, se qui[29] li sera defailli de sa paie en[30] son tens ou el tens d'autre et la doit, se me senble, avoir par[31] raison selonc[32] l'assise ou l'usage dou reaume de Jerusalem.[33] Que le seignor ne s'en[34] peut defendre par dire: 'Ce

A: fols cvii^{r}–cviii^{r} cap. 174; **B:** fols 134^{r}–135^{r} cap. 174; **C:** fols 135^{v}–137^{r} cap. 157; **O:** fols 179^{v}–181^{v}; **V:** fols cxliii^{v}–cxlv^{r} cap. 183; Beugnot, pp. 273–4, cap. 174.

[1] n'ait] A: n'en a [2] rent] B: rent tant; V: tent [3] d'autre] B rubric (fol. 23^{r}) C: d'un autre [4] tant] B lacks [5] que] C lacks [6] que] ABV lack [7] n'est] A: ce n'est; B: aucune chose ce n'est; V: se n'en est [8] a] B: l'ait; V: l'a [9] tant de quey] V: pas tant coment [10] et il demore a estre paié] B lacks [11] n'a] A: n'en a [12] tant rendu] B: mie tant valu [13] ait peu] B: puisse; V: peust [14] cest] AO: cel; B: tel; V: celui [15] la] ABV: sa [16] ne guage] B: n'a gaigié [17] quei] C: quex [18] puisse] B: puet [19] que] B: dont [20] en cel leu] B lacks [21] ait] ABV: a [22] AV add: y [23] et il a . . . casal] C lacks [24] premier] V lacks [25] de] C lacks [26] est] A: a; V: l'a [27] premier defailli de la] B: failli premier de sa [28] leu] A: fié [29] qui] BV: que [30] en] ABV: de [31] par] C: per [32] selonc] B: par [33] C adds: et [34] s'en] ABV: se

que l'on vous doit de vostre fié n'est pas de mon tens ainz est dou tens de tel qui lors estoit[35] seignor[36] ou de tel[37] qui adonc estoit baill. Ne je ne suis tenus de paier vos[38] se qu'il vos devoient[39] de vostre fié.' Ne le baill ne se peut defendre par dire: 'Ce que l'on vos devoit de vostre fié[40] et de quey[41] vos me requerrés[42] paie n'est pas dou tens de mon bailliage ainz est dou tens de tel seignor ou de tel baill qui fu baill[43] devant moy. Ne je ne sui[44] tenus de paier ce que il devoient, por quei je[45] ne vos en veull paier, se la court ne l'esgarde, et de ce me met je en l'esgart de la court sauf mon retenaill.'

Et a se porra respondre au seignor ou au baill celui qui requera sa paie: 'Sire, vos dites[46] ou ferés dire vostre volenté, mais por chose que vos diés[47] je ne veull que il demore que vous ne me facieés[48] paier de ce que l'on me doit de mon fié de quey je suis asené en tel leu et de coy je ai esté merme de ma paye, par ce que le leu ne rendeit tant que[49] je peuce estre paiés[50] de ce qui m'est defailli de ma paie. Et puis que il adonc ne rendi[51] et il ore l'a[52] rendu, et que il a el leu ou je sui asené de quey je puisse[53] estre payé[54] de mon fié, et que je ai adés tenu et bien fait si con je doi le servise que je devoye et doy de cel[55] fié, car je onques ne fu[56] defaillant[57] dou servise faire que je devoie et doy de cel fié, por quey je entens que je doy estre paiés de mon fié de ce[58] que le leu ou je sui asené n'a[59] rendu[60] puis que il a hore tant rendu de quey je puis estre payé, et le veull estre[61] por toutes les raisons que je ai dites ou por aucunes d'eles se la court l'esgarde, et de ce me met je en l'esgart de la court sauf mon retenaill.'

Et a moy ne[62] semble que le seignor ne le baill qui se mete en esgart de ce[63] puisse chose dire contre ce par quey la court ne doive esguarder que le requerant ne doive[64] estre payé de ce qu'il y a esté defailli de sa paye de son fié, puis que le leu a tant rendu de quey

[35] lors estoit] B: adons fu [36] seignor] C: seignors [37] de tel] B: del tens [38] AB add: de [39] devoient] V: devoit [40] Ne le baill . . . fié] ABV lack [41] de quey] B: ce dont [42] de quey vos me requerre] V: de que vous requerés a me [43] A adds: ou seignor [44] sui] C: sus [45] de paier ce . . . je] A: ni [46] dites] BV: dirés [47] diés] AB: aiés dite; V: ayés dit [48] facieés] V: faites [49] que] AB: de quoi; V: de qui [50] peuce estre paiés] B: me peusse paier [51] B adds: tant [52] ore l'a] A: a orres; B: a ores; V: a ores bien [53] puisse] V: puis [54] payé] A: assené [55] de cel] B: dou; V: de celui [56] car je onques ne fu] A: ne je ne fui onques; BV: Car je ne fui; O: car je onques ne sui [57] defaillant] V: faillant [58] de ce] B: ce qui m'est defialli por ce [59] B adds: tant valu ne [60] AV adds: puis et; B: et [61] C adds: payé [62] ne] ABV lack [63] de ce] C: ne [64] ne doive] A: deit

il peut estre paié de[65] tout ou de partie. Que fort chose seroit, se me senble, et contre droit et raison, que por changement de seignor ou de baillage[66] celui qui est asené el leu moti de son fié et a adés fait le[67] servise si con il doit et[68] .i. espace de tens a esté par guerre ou autrement, que le leu ou il est asené n'a rendu tant de quey il peust[69] estre payé de ce que l'on li doit de son fié et aprés le rende, que celui qui est asené ne deust estre payé de ce que on li doit de son fié[70] de quei il est asené en cel leu puis que le leu le rent et que il n'a son servise guagé ne defaillant n'a esté de son servise.[71] Et qui est[72] assené sur rente de besanz, si con est fonde ou cheene ou loge ou boucherie[73] ou molins ou monoie[74] ou aucune[75] autre rente, a estre payés de .iii. meis en .iii. meis ou[76] de demi[77] an en demi an, et les rentes de cel leu ou il est asené sont apautees ou le seignor l'a[78] en sa main, et il li[79] est defailli .i. espace de tens d'estre payé de ce que l'on li doit de son fié, et il ait fait[80] le servise que il doit de sel fié si con est avant dit, et cele rente[81] vaille aprés[82] tant que tous ceaus qui y sont[83] acenés soient paiés dou[84] terme enterinement de ce de quey[85] il sont assenés sur cele rente[86] de leur[87] fié et il[88] y a remanant,[89] le premier asené de ceaus a qui l'on devra de son fié en la maniere avant dite le doit, se cuit, avoir par raison s'il le requiert si con est avant dit, por ce que on li doit de son fié[90] de quey il est asené en cel leu, et c'il ne le requiert, celui des autres qui le requerra et sera premiers asené le devra avoir, que ausi con il est avant dit de l'annee dou cazal por ce que les rentes dou casal se revont[91] et se parfont en l'annee doit estre, se me senble, de la rente des besanz de[92] .iii. mois en .iii. mois ou de[93] demi an en demi an, selonc se que les assis[94] sont assenés[95] en cel leu d'estre payés. Et ensi croi je que l'on l'a usé et use el[96] reyaume de Jerusalem.

---

[65] ce qu'il y . . . de] ABV lack [66] baillage] ABV: baill [67] le] B: son [68] V adds: aprés [69] peust] A: puisse [70] et aprés le . . . fié] ABV lack [71] et que il . . . servise] A: et qu'il n'a son seignor de son servise gagié ne defaillant n'a esté de servise; B: ne qu'il n'a esté gagié de son servise ne defaillant [72] est] V: a esté [73] A adds: ou pescherie [74] ou monoie] O lacks [75] aucune] C lacks [76] ou] C: et [77] demi] C: demin [78] l'a] AB: les a [79] li] AV lack [80] ait fait] AV: fait; B: a fait [81] rente] V: terre [82] C adds: y [83] sont] C: son [84] dou] C: d'un [85] de quey] B dont [86] cele rente] C: rentes [87] leur] A: cel; V: ce lor [88] il] C lacks [89] remanant] C: remant [90] V adds: si come est avant dit [91] revont] A: refont [92] de] C: des [93] de] C lacks [94] assis] C: assenés [95] assenés] BV: assis [96] l'a usé et use el] A: a usé ou; B: l'a usé ou; V: a husé au

***[158]** Quant home ou feme qui a et tient[1] seignorie[2] meurt et il a plusors parens[3] a qui son[4] fié puisse[5] escheir, a qui il escheent,[6] et lequel doit avoir cele escheete devant[7] les autres.[8]

Se[9] home ou feme qui ait et tiegne seignorie ou fié meurt et a plusors parens et parentes d'aage qui li apartienent[10] de cele part dont la seignorie ou le fié meut ou[11] escheu[12] si que il y[13] puissent heriter par l'assise ou l'usage de cest reaume,[14] la seignorie ou le fié[15] eschiet a tous ces parens et parentes qui[16] de cele part dont le fié meut[17] li apartienent, mais l'ainsné de ceaus qui sont en vie et li sont[18] pres ataignans en .i. degré le[19] doit avoir devant[20] les autres par l'assise ou l'usage de cest royaume et l'a, se il le[21] requiert, mais que tant que l'eir femele ne le[22] doit avoir par ainsneese[23] devant l'eir mahle quant il sont en .i. degré apartenans a celui ou a cele de par qui l'escheete lor est escheue, que l'ainsné[24] de l'eir femele ne li vaut[25] a avoir l'escheete de l'eritage devant le[26] mahle quant il sont apartenans[27] en .i. degré a celui ou a cele de par qui l'eritage lor est escheu. Car l'eir mahle erite en tous heritages devant l'eir femele par l'assise ou l'usage de cest reyaume, se la femele n'apartient de plus pres que l'eir mahle a celui de par qui le fié ou la seignorie ou l'eritage lor eschiet et[28] de cele part dont le fié meut.[29]

A: fol. cviii^{r} cap. 175; **B:** fol. 135^{r-v} cap. 175; **C:** fol. 137^{r-v} cap. 158; **O:** fol. 182^{r-v}; **V:** fol. cxlv^{r-v} cap. 184; Beugnot, p. 275, cap. 175.

---

[1] a et tient] B: ait et tiegne [2] seignorie] C: seignor [3] B adds: et parentes d'aage qui li apartienent [4] son] A: se; B: celui; V: ce [5] puisse] B: puet; V: peut [6] escheent] A: escheit; B: eschiet; V: eschet [7] AB adds: toz [8] B adds: parenz [9] OV add: .i. [10] apartienent] C: apertienent; V: aparteignent [11] ou le fié meut ou] A: muet qui lor est; V: meut ou [12] escheu] B: eschiet; V: eschee [13] y] ABV lack [14] de cest reaume] V: dou royaume de Jerusalem [15] ou le fié] ABV lack [16] qui] C lacks [17] C adds: et [18] sont] AV: sont plus; B: est plus [19] le] A: la [20] BV add: tous [21] le] AV: la [22] le] A: la [23] ainsneese] V: ancieneté [24] l'ainsné] A: l'ainzneece; B: l'ainsneeté; V: l'ainsnee [25] B adds: noient [26] le] A: l'eir [27] apartenans] A lacks [28] eschiet et] A: escheit; V: est escheu [29] ou l'eritage lor . . . meut] B: muet ou l'eritage leur eschiet

***[159]** Quant aucun[1] home ou feme qui a et tient seignorie ou fié meurt, et il a plusors fis ou filles ou autres parens a qui se[2] fié puisse[3] escheir, et l'ainsné des fiz en a aprés lui[4] la saissine et la teneure, et ces freres ou ses seurs[5] ont enfans et[6] meurent avant de celui qui a et tient la seignorie ou l'eritage, et il meurt aprés sans heir qui de lui soit descendu,[7] lequel des heirs qui seroient[8] descendu de ces freres ou de ses seurs ou de ces autres parens doit avoir c'escheete[9] d'eritage ou de bailliage.

Se[10] home ou feme qui a et tient seignorie ou[11] fié a plusors enfans ou freres ou seurs ou nevous ou nieces ou autres parens[12] apartenans en .i. degré, et ces enfans ou les autres[13] enfans devant dis[14] ont enfans nés en[15] leal mariage, et les enfans de celui qui a et tient la seignorie ou le fié ou ces autres dis parens meurent avant[16] de lui, et il aprés .i. espace de tens meurt, et les fiz ou les filles de ces fiz ou de ses filles ou de ses freres[17] ou de ces seurs[18] ou de ses nevous ou de ces nieces[19] ou d'aucun de ces[20] autres parens requiert[21] c'escheete, et que l'un des requerans[22] soit le fiz ou la fille de l'ainsné des devant[23] dis enfant ou parens de celui de par qui le fié est escheu et soit[24] mainsné de l'autre requerant,[25] soit fis ou fille des autres devant[26] dis enfans ou[27] parens de celui de par qui le fié est escheu et soit ainsné de l'autre requerant, et les .ii. apartenisent en .i. degré de celui de qui le fié est escheu,[28] et que lor peres ou leur meres aient survescu lor ancestre[29] ou[30] n'aient eu saisine ne[31] teneure de ce que il requierent, et que le fis de l'ainsné ou de l'ainsnee[32] dit

---

A: fols cviii^{r}–cix^{r} cap. 176; **B:** fols 135^{v}–136^{r} cap. 176; **C:** fols 137^{v}–138^{v} cap. 159; **O:** fols 182^{v}–184^{r}; **V:** fols cxlv^{v}–clxvi^{v} cap. 185; Beugnot, pp. 276–7, cap. 176.

---

[1] aucun] A rubric (fol. 5^{v}) B lack [2] se] A: cest; B: celui; V: le [3] puisse] B: puet [4] a aprés lui] V: aprés lui la seignorie et [5] ou ses seurs] C lacks [6] ont enfans et] B: ou lor enfanz [7] heir que de lui soit descendu] AB: heirs (B: hoirs) qui de lui soient dessenduz (B: descendant) [8] seroient] BV: seront [9] c'escheete] AV: l'escheete [10] Se] O: Se .i.; V: Quant aucun [11] ou] C: de [12] C adds: ou; V: ou parentes [13] autres] C lacks [14] enfans devant dis] A: enfanz; B: enfanz desus ditez; V: dis enfans [15] en] A: de [16] avant] AB: ainz; V: ains [17] ou de ses freres] O lacks [18] ou de ces seurs] A lacks [19] A repeats: ou de ces filles [20] de ces] AB: des [21] requiert] AV: qui requierent; B: qui requiert [22] des requerans] B: requerant [23] devant] V: avant [24] soit] A: set; B: sont [25] OV add: et que l'autre requerant [26] devant] A lacks [27] ou] C lacks [28] et soit ainsné . . . escheu] ABV lack [29] que lor peres . . . ancestre] A: que leur ancestre ait survescu leur peres ou leur meres [30] lor ancestre ou] B: l'ancestre et [31] C adds: en [32] ou de l'ainsnee] A: ne

que il viaut avoir cele escheete devant son parent qui est ainzné de lui par l'ainsneece[33] de son pere ou de sa mere, disant raison por coy il por ce[34] le doit[35] avoir, et l'autre viaut avoir l'escheete par la soue ainsnece[36] et dit por quei,[37] je di que, se chascun[38] dit en sa requeste se que l'on peut meaus dire a avoir la dite escheete, que l'ainsné des .ii. requerans qui sont en .i. degré apartenans a celui ou a cele de par qui ele[39] est escheue la doit avoir par l'assise ou l'usage dou reyaume de Jerusalem devant celui qui est mainsné de lui, tout ait esté son pere ou sa mere ainsné dou pere ou de la mere de l'autre requerant, por ce que a mort ne a morte ne[40] peut aucune chose escheir. Que par l'usage dou dit[41] reiaume le fiz ne[42] la fille ne demore en la teneure[43] des dreis[44] de[45] son pere ne de sa mere que de ce que[46] il meurt saisi et tenant con de son droit ou de ce de quey il ou[47] ele ont esté le derrain crestien[48] saisi et tenant con de lor droit,[49] por[50] ce que par l'assise ou l'usage dou dit royaume ne peut l'on[51] requerre ne avoir escheete, que on die qui li soit escheue, qui ne la requiert de par le derain saisi et tenant con dou sien, et que l'ainsné des .ii. avant dis requerans est plus prochein de celui qui derainement en morut saisi et tenant que le mainsné et[52] meaus doit avoir s'escheete puis que il li ataignent[53] en .i. degré, que leur pere[54] ne leur mere ne autre por yaus[55] n'en orent[56] saisine ne teneure en lor vie,[57] et que l'on par assise ou par usage[58] dou dit reyaume ne peut escheete requerre et[59] avoir que de par celui[60] qui derainement en morut saisi et tenant come dou sien ou qui a esté saisi et tenant come dou sien[61] derainement[62] d'autre crestien, car qui de par autre la requiert le seignor ou autre a qui il la requiert[63] ne li est tenus de respondre par l'usage dou dit reyaume. Et en cest cas doit estre ausi dou baillage con il est avant[64] dit que il doit estre de seignorie ou de fié.

---

[33] l'ainsneece] BV: l'ainsneeté [34] por ce] ABV lack [35] doit] A: viaut [36] ainsnece] B: ainzneeté; V: ainsneeté [37] V adds: pour ce que il est ainsné [38] chascun] V: aucun [39] ele] A: l'escheete; B: la seignorie [40] ne] B lacks [41] dit] A lacks [42] ne] BV: ou [43] en la teneure] ABV lack [44] dreis] C: dreit [45] de] AB lack [46] que] A: de quoi; B: dont [47] ou] C: et [48] le derrain crestien] A: les dereains crestiens [49] ou de ce . . . droit] B lacks [50] por] ABV: et por [51] l'on] C: on; V: hom [52] A adds: qui [53] ataignent] A: ataignoient [54] leur pere] V: l'eir [55] que leur pere . . . yaus] A: puis que les heirs ne leur peres ne leur meres [56] n'en orent] B: ne ourent onques [57] lor vie] A: leur vies [58] assise ou par usage] B: l'assise ou l'usaje [59] et] AB: ne [60] de par celui] ABV: par celui ou celle [61] ou qui a . . . sien] V lacks [62] saisi et tenant . . . derainement] A: derainement saissi et tenant [63] requiert] V: requis [64] con il est avant] A: si come il est; B: com est avant; V: si come est avant

***[160]** De quel maniere dou[1] fié feme doit au seignor de qui ele le tient le[2] mariage[3] de marier soy par semonce, et de quel[4] maniere de fié[5] ele ne se peut marier sans l'otroy dou seignor ne il ne la peut esforcier de marier la par sa[6] semonce ne autrement.[7]

Quant feme a et tient fié qui doit servise de cors et ele le tient en heritage ou en baillage,[8] ele en doit le mariage par l'assise ou l'usage dou reaume de Jerusalem au seignor de qui ele le tient, se il la semont ou fait semondre si con il doit de prendre baron. Et feme qui a et tient doaire de fié qui doit[9] servise de cors ne doit pas[10] mariage au seignor de qui ele tient le doaire de cel fié, ni[11] ele ne se peut marier sans[12] le congé de celui ou de cele de qui ele tient cel doaire,[13] et se ele le fait, ele doit perdre[14] le fié qu'ele tient en doaire. Et[15] le seignor ne peut destraindre de marier feme[16] qui tient fié qui ne doit servise de cors, ne ele ne se peut marier sans son congé, et se ele le fait ele perdra[17] son fié. Et il sera aprés devisé[18] en cest livre coment le seignor de qui feme[19] tient son fié la peut semondre ou faire semondre[20] de prendre baron, et se il l'en[21] semont ou fait semondre si con il doit et[22] ele ne le prent ou ne dit raison por coy ele ne le doit prendre et tel que court l'esgarde ou conoisse, quel amende le seignor en doit avoir, et quel de cele qui se marie sans le congé de celui ou de cele[23] de qui elle tient son fié, soit d'eritage[24] ou de baillage ou de doaire.[a] Et par l'assise ou l'usage dou

---

A: fol. cix^{r-v} cap. 177; **B:** fol. 137^{v} cap. 178; **C:** fol. 138^{v} cap. 160; **O:** fol. 184^{r-v}; **V:** fols clxvi^{v}–cxlvii^{r} cap. 186; Beugnot, pp. 279–80, cap. 177.

---

[a] Below cap. 199.

---

[1] dou] ABV: de [2] le tient le] OV: tient [3] de qui ele . . . mariage] B: mariage de qui ele tient [4] quel] C: quelque [5] de fié] A: de fei; V lacks [6] esforcier de marier la par sa] A: marier ne esforsier par; A rubric (fol. 6^{r}): marier ne esforsier de marier la par [7] l'otroy dou seignor . . . autrement] B: la volunté et l'otroi dou seignor ne il ne l'en puet esforcier de marier soi par la semonsse ne autrement se ele ne veut [8] ou en baillage] C lacks [9] doit] A: ne det [10] ABV add: le [11] ni] ABV: ne [12] sans] V: soi sans la volenté et [13] cel doaire] ABV: le (V: celui) doaire de cel fié [14] doit perdre] ABV: perdra [15] B adds: se [16] de marier feme] A: feme; V: feme de marier soi [17] perdra] ABV: doit (A: deit) perdre [18] aprés devisé] V: devisé si aprés [19] feme] V: elle [20] ou faire semondre] C lacks [21] l'en] AV: la [22] il l'en semont . . . et] B lacks [23] ou de cele] C lacks [24] d'eritage] CO: de mariage

reaume de Jerusalem chascune franche feme[25] a en doaire la meyté de tout quanque son baron a a l'ore qu'il[26] vait de vie a mort, mais[27] que la raine et les femes des .iiii. barons[28] dou reiaume, qu'il[29] est propre assise et usage, usé et acostumé[30] el dit reiaume, que le reiaume[31] ne aucune des .iiii. baronies ne peut ne ne doit[32] estre parti par douaire ne[33] entre seurs.

---

[25] feme] A: dame [26] qu'il] V: que son baron [27] mais] V: fors [28] barons] A: baronies [29] qu'il] ABV: qui [30] usé et acostumé] A: et costume [31] que le reiaume] C lacks; A: que reiaume; V: que royaume [32] peut ne ne doit] B: pevent ne ne doivent [33] ne] A: ni; B lacks

*[161] De qui[1] les femes qui ont doaire le doivent tenir, et a qui le baillage peut et doit escheyr par rayson.

Les femes qui ont doaire en fié le doivent tenir par l'assise ou l'usage[2] dou reaume de Jerusalem de celui ou de celle qui a et tient con sien[3] le fié de quei[4] le doaire est[5] heritage ou en baillage.[6] Et quant home qui a fié meurt et il a feme et enfans[7] mermes d'aage, la mere doit avoir le baillage de ses enfans de tout quanqu'il lor[8] est escheu de par lor pere. Car il est assise ou usage el royaume de Jerusalem que le pere ou la mere doit avoir le baillage de l'escheete de ses enfans, et que nul autre que pere ou mere ne doit avoir ne tenir baillage de fié se le fié ne li peut escheir se il mesavient de l'enfant merme d'aage a qui le fié est escheu et por qui l'on requiert le baillage. Et est assise ou usage el dit reaume que le plus dreit heir a avoir le fié, se il escheoit,[9] doit avoir le baillage de cel fié devant tous les autres heirs,[10] se il le[11] requiert.[12]

A: fol. cix^{v} cap. 178; **B:** fols 137^{v}–138^{r} cap. 179; **C:** fol. 139^{r} cap. 161; **O:** fols 184^{v}–185^{r}; **V:** fol. cxlvii^{r-v} cap. 187; Beugnot, pp. 280–1, cap. 178.

[1] qui] B rubric (fol. 23^{v}) V: quoi [2] l'assise ou l'usage] V: assise et husage [3] con sien] A: come son fié; B: come fié; V: son fié [4] quei] C: quex [5] le doaire est] A: elle a en doaire la moitié ou en; B: ele a en douaire la moitié en [6] en baillage] C has dots above and below to indicate deletion [7] B adds: qui sont [8] quanqu'il lor] A: quan qui; B: ce qui lor [9] a avoir le . . . escheoit] V lacks [10] de cel fié . . . heirs] B: devant touz les autres [11] le] C lacks [12] A adds: si come il est devant devisié en cest livre

***[162]** Quant baillage eschiet a feme, coment ele se peut garder que le seignor de qui ele le doit tenir ne la puisse[1] marier por le[2] baillage.

Se feme a qui[3] baillage et doaire de fié[4] eschiet ensemble par la mort de son baron[5] ne veaut que le seignor de qui ele doit tenir[6] son doaire ait poeir en li marier, ou quant baillage de fié[7] eschiet a feme qui a[8] doaire d'autre fié et ele ne veaut que le seignor la[9] marie, ele le[10] peut faire ensi: que quant son baron est trespassé qu'ele veigne devant le seignor avant qu'ele requiere le[11] baillage de ces enfans, et li die ou face dire: 'Sire, Des a fait son comandement de mon baron, et je doy avoir la moitié de son fié en doaire et l'autre meytié por le baillage de[12] mes enfans. Sire, et le baillage de mes enfans de cest fié[13] je ne veull avoir ore ne tenir ne[14] deservir, ne ne vos requier ore de cest fié que mon doaire. Si vos porrés[15] ore faire servir come seignor de ce qui est le[16] baillage de mes enfans, et je tendrai ore mon doaire sans plus, et de mon doaire vos eufre je l'omage et le servise que je en doy.' Et aprés cest dit il ne me senble que le seignor puisse la dame[17] destraindre dou baillage tenir ne de li marier, por ce qu'ele n'avra ne tendra le baillage qui doit le mariage. Mais se la dame requiert[18] le baillage ou s'i met[19] et[20] en use, et ele le viaut puis laisser et tenir se au doaire sans plus, ele ne le peut laisser[21] sans la volenté dou seignor de qui ele le tendra, tout soit ce que ele die les raisons avant dites ou autres. Que puis que ele l'a requis[22] en court et eu par court ou autrement et que ele l'a tenu, ele l'a assés otroyé clerement de tenir le par le fait que ele en a fait, por[23] coy ele ne le peut puis[24] laissier par sa volenté

A: fols cix^{v}–cx^{r} cap. 179; **B:** fol. 138^{r-v} cap. 180; **C:** fol. 139^{r-v} cap. 162; **O:** fols 185^{r}–186^{r}; **V:** fols cxlvii^{v}–cxlviii^{r} cap. 188; Beugnot, pp. 281–2, cap. 179.

[1] B adds: constraindre de [2] por le] A rubric (fol. 8^{r}) BV: par [3] a qui] A: qui a [4] de fié] V lacks [5] A adds: et elle [6] doit tenir] B: tient [7] de fié] V lacks [8] a] B: ait [9] la] C: le [10] le] B: ne [11] le] A: son [12] por le baillage de] B: en baillage por; C: por le baillage des; V: em bailliage pour [13] de cest fié] A lacks [14] veull avoir ore ne tenir ne] A: viaus ores tenir ni; V: veull ores tenir ne [15] porrés] B: poez [16] le] A: dou; BV: de [17] dame] ABV: feme [18] dame requiert] ABV: feme tient [19] ou s'i met] A lacks [20] et] A: et elle; BV: ou [21] laisser] ABV: faire [22] V adds: devant le seignor [23] clerement de tenir . . . por] A: el tenement que elle a fait par le tenir por; B: ou tenement de tenir le par fait que ele en a fait par; V: autrement de tenir le par fait que elle en fait par [24] puis] A: mais

sans cele dou seignor en maniere que ele soit[25] quite dou mariage qu'ele doit au seignor, et que[26] ele a et tient le baillage[27] et aprés le lasse, et le seignor la semont ou fait semondre si con il doit de prendre baron et ele ne le prent ou[28] ne dit raison por coy ele ne le doit prendre[29] et tel que la[30] court l'esgarde ou conoisse, le seignor en avra l'amende[31] de li[32] con de defaut de servise et ausi dou doaire con dou[33] baillage.

[25] C adds: au seignor [26] et que] A: jusque [27] qu'ele doit . . . baillage] B lacks [28] ou] B: ne; O: et [29] prendre] O: prent [30] la] ABV lack [31] l'amende] ABO: amende [32] de li] A: de li si; B: ausi [33] dou doaire con dou] ABV: de douaire come de

***[163]** Por quey celui qui ne viaut deservir son fié le doit comander au seignor de qui il le tient avant que estreer le.[1]

Qui s'en[2] viaut partir dou pais ou en aucune autre maniere laissier son fié, il le doit comander au seignor. Quar la comande est plus seure chose et mains y a de perill qu'en l'estraier por tel raison que se .i. home[3] comande son fié par l'asisse ou l'usage dou reyaume de Jerusalem,[4] il le puet aveir[5] aprés .i. an et .i. jor toutes les foys que il le requerra sans autre amende que le seignor en puisse[6] avoir, se il ne le comandoit[7] el point que il fust semons d'aucune des semonces qui aprés sont dites[8] por quey on pert son fié sa vie[9] qui en defaut.[a] Et se[10] le seignor l'a en sa main par la comande et aucun autre s'i[11] viaut metre, le seignor le li doit garentir que autre ne s'i met. Et qui comande son fié a son[12] seignor ou a son baill par l'assise ou l'usage dou dit reyaume, le seignor ou le baill a qui l'on veaut comander le fié[13] doit[14] recevoir ou dire que il ne viaut le fié recevoir se court n'esgarde que recevoir le doye et dire aucune raison por coy. Car il est plus seure chose au seignor de receveir le par esgart ou par conoissance de court que autrement. Et se il l'esgart ou la conoissance ne veaut avoir, si le doit recevoir[15] par l'assise, et se le seignor ou le baill ensi ne le fait, il vait[16] contre l'assisse ou l'usage dou dit reyaume. Et se le seignor ou le baill dit raison por coy il ne le veaut recevoir et s'en[17] mete en esgart de court, die celui qui li comande raison por coy il entent que il le doive resevoir et por coy il viaut que il le resoive et s'en mete en esgart[18] ou en conoissance[19] de court. Que se il[20] ensi ne le fait, sa comande ne vaudra ainz sera

---

A: fol. cx^{r-v} cap. 180; **B:** fols 138^{v}–139^{r} cap. 181; **C:** fols 139^{v}–140^{v} cap. 163; **O:** fols 186^{r}–187^{r}; **V:** fols cxlviii^{r}–cxlix^{r} cap. 189; Beugnot, pp. 282–3, cap. 180.

---

[a] Below caps 212, 214.

---

[1] le] A rubric (fol. 8^{r}) B: lack [2] s'en] ABV: se [3] .i. home] AV: home; B: il [4] reyaume de Jerusalem] B: dit reaume [5] aveir] V: ravoir [6] en puisse] ABV: i peust [7] comandoit] A: comande [8] dites] A: devisiees [9] sa vie] A lacks; B: a sa vie; V: toute sa vie [10] se] B lacks [11] s'i] AV: se [12] a son] A: a; V: au [13] veaut comander le fié] ABV: le comande le [14] doit] C: doir [15] recevoir] A: aveir; BV: avoir [16] ensi ne le fait, il vait] A: qui ensi ne le fait vait; B: qui autrement le fait va [17] s'en] AB: se; V: ce [18] de court, die . . . esgart] AV lack [19] de court, die . . . conoissance] B lacks [20] il] A: l'autre

nule. Et quant home comande[21] a[22] seignor,[23] il le doit comander par l'assise ou l'usage dou dit reaume, car ce[24] est la plus seure chose[25] a faire. Mais guart se bien en quel point il l'estraiera ou comandera,[26] car en tel point le porroit il faire que il en porroit le fié perdre[27] sa vie par les raisons qui aprés seront[28] dites en cest livre.[b] Ne il ne le peut comander par raison puis que il est semons dou servise, ne le seignor n'est tenus de recevoir[29] le, se il ne viaut, puis que il l'a semons dou servise[30] tant con cele semonce dure. Et qui comande son fié par l'assise ou l'usage de cest reyaume, il ne le peut avoir[31] sans la volenté de celui a qui il l'a comandé[32] tant que l'an et le jor soit passé,[33] et maintenant que il est passé toutes les foys que il requerra[34] son fié, celui qui l'a receu en comande li[35] doit rendre sans eschanpe et sans delay. Et ce celui a qui l'on a[36] le fié comandé meurt dedens l'an et le jor, son[37] heir doit le fié tenir[38] jusques au perfait de l'an et dou jor, que celui qui l'a comandé ne le peut recovrer[39] devant lors.[40] Et ce celui qui l'a comandé meurt dedens l'an et le jor, son heir le peut raveir[41] toutes les foys que il le requerra aprés la mort de son ancestre, tout ne soit l'an et le jor de[42] la comande dou fié acompli,[43] [44] car il est asisse ou usage en cest reyaume que la comande dou fié[45] ne s'estent a plus[46] que a la vie de celui qui le comande.[47]

---

[b] Below caps 164, 167, 173.

---

[21] comande] C: comanda [22] a] ABV: au [23] AB add: son fié [24] ce] A: elle; B: ele; V: celle [25] chose] V: voie [26] l'estraiera ou comandera] A: comandera ou estreera son fié; BV estraera (V: estrayera) ou comandera son fié [27] porroit le fié perdre] C: porroit le fié perdre et; V: perderoit son fié toute [28] seront] ABV: sont [29] recevoir] C: servir [30] ne le seignor . . . servise] V lacks [31] avoir] A: recouvrer; B: recevoir; V: faire [32] l'a comandé] V: le comande [33] soit passé] AV: passe [34] requerra] ABV: requiert [35] li] ABV: le [36] a] V: n'a [37] son] B: sanz [38] doit le fié tenir] O: le puet ravoir [39] recovrer] B: recevoir [40] que celui qui . . . lors] C lacks [41] raveir] A: aveir; V: avoir [42] de] A: passe ne; V: passe [43] son heir le . . . acompli] B: la comande dou fié a compli passé [44] acompli] V: acomplir [45] dou fié] C lacks [46] a plus] AB lack [47] le comande] A: l'a comandé

***[164]** Coment le seignor[1] se peut et doit metre el fié estreé,[2] et quel[3] perill et quel damage a et peut avoir celui qui estree son fié plus que celui qui le comande.

Qui estree son fié et le seignor le viaut avoir, il le doit faire semondre de son servise si con il est devisé en cest livre que l'on doit home semondre de son servise,[4][a] et s'il ne vient a la semonce, le seignor doit faire venir en la presence de sa court ceaus qui la semonce ont faite et dire la semonce que il ont[5] faite,[6] et puis que le jor de la semonce est pasé, le seignor peut dire a sa court quant il[7] viaut qu'ele li[8] conoisse quel droit il en doit avoir de celui qui li[9] est defailli[10] dou[11] servise, si con il ont oy que la court l'a recordé.[12] Et la court doit conoistre, se cuit, que le seignor se peut faire servir dou fié tant que le semons soit venus en la presence de lui et de sa court et que il li[13] ait le fié requis, et que si tost con il le requerra que il l'en[14] mete en saisine sans delay, et puis se il li[15] set[16] que demander qu'il li requiert droit par sa court et que celui li face. Et se[17] le seignor s'en[18] claine[19] a sa court si con il doit de celui qui a son fié estraié[20] et que il en a la saisine recovree, il avra aprés[21] le fié par conoissance de court .i. an et .i. jor en amende de ce que il li defailli dou servise de quey[22] il le fist semondre[23] si con est avant dit. Et[24] encore y a greignor perill a celui qui estree son fié, que se le seignor ne[25] veaut metre main et[26] aucune autre persone s'i mete et le seignor le seufre et celui qui s'i[27] est mis l'a et tient quant celui de qui le fié est revendra ou aucun de ces heirs aprés son deces, il covendra que il requiert[28] a celui le fié qui saisi s'en sera, et il en

---

A: fols cx^{v}–cxi^{r} cap. 181; **B:** fol. 139^{r-v} cap. 182; **C:** fols 140^{v}–141^{r} cap. 164; **O:** fols 187^{r}–188^{r}; **V:** fol. cxlix^{r-v} cap. 190; Beugnot, pp. 283–4, cap. 181.

---

[a] Below caps 188, 190.

---

[1] le seignor] A: l'on [2] estreé] B: qui est estrae [3] quel] C: que [4] si con il . . . servise] ABV lack [5] ont] V: a [6] ont faite et dire . . . faite] A: ont faite et il la deivent dire; B: firent et dire la semonse que il ont faite; C: de sa court que il ont faite [7] quant il] ABV: qu'il [8] li] ABV lack [9] li] ABV lack [10] defailli] B: defaillant [11] dou] ABV: de [12] l'a recordé] A: l'a retrait; B: le recorde [13] li] ABV lack [14] l'en] ABV: le [15] li] C lacks [16] A adds: riens [17] se] B: que; V lacks [18] s'en] AB: se [19] A adds: lors [20] estraié] C: destraié [21] aprés] A: puis; C lacks [22] quey] V: ce que [23] li defailli dou . . . semondre] B: le semons ou fist semondre de servise et il li defailli [24] Et] ABV lack [25] ne] AB: n'i [26] et] C lacks [27] s'i] AV lack [28] requiert] V: le requiere

respondra et plaidera come saisi[29] et porra metre mout[30] d'eschanpes et avoir mout de fuites a cel fié defendre por coy celui qui l'avra estree[31] sera lonc tens esloigné de ravoir son fié et[32] ces heirs aprés lui. Et par les raisons avant dites me senble il plus seure chose et meylor le comander[33] del fié[34] que l'estreer.

---

[29] C adds: et tenant [30] mout] O: plus [31] C adds: por quei [32] et] ABV: ou [33] le comander] V: la comande [34] del fié] OV lack

***[165]** Coment l'on peut et doit fié desmenbrer par l'assise ou l'usage dou reaume de Jerusalem.[1]

Nus ne peut desmenbrer fié par l'assise ne[2] l'usage dou reyaume de Jerusalem[3] se le fié ne doit servise de plus d'une chevalerie. Et qui viaut desmenbler fié qui doit servise de plusors chevaleries,[4] il doit doner partie dou[5] fié por partie dou servise[6] que le fié doit, et enssi que le plus dou fié[7] demore au seignor qui le[8] desmenbre en la maniere avant dite, et en tel maniere ou par le semblant de ce. Que qui a .ii. .m. besanz et il[9] doive servise de son cors et[10] d'un autre chevalier ou de .ii. chevaliers[11] sans son cors, il en peut doner les .ix.[12] .c. besanz[13] por le servise d'un chevalier et que les .m. et .c.[14] besanz[15] li demorent. Et s'il y a .iii. .m. besanz de fié por le servise de soy tiers, il[16] peut bien[17] doner les .m. besanz por le servise d'un chevalier et tenir les .ii. .m. besanz por lui[18] et por .i.[19] sodeer.

Et aucuns de ceaus que l'on tient a bons plaideors dient que celui qui a les .iii. .m. besanz de soy tiers de servise[20] peut bien doner de cel fié a[21] .ii. chevaliers a chascun .viiii.[22] .c.[23] besanz por le servise de son cors ou d'un chevalier,[24] et que les .m. et .ii. .c. besanz[25] des .iii. .m. li demorent, et que, se il le fait ensi, il a le fié desmenbré si con il doit[26] par l'assise ou l'usage dou dit reaume,[27] et que ceaus dons sont valables.

Et aucuns des autres que on tient a[28] bons plaideors dient que qui a fié de .iii. .m. besanz por le servise de soi tiers et il viaut doner les .ii. chevaliers[29] en fié, que il ne peut doner as .ii. fiés que[30] mains de .m. et .vc. besanz, et les partisse[31] si con il voudra, por ce dient ceaus qui a se s'acordent que il covient que le seignor dou fié

A: fols cxi^r^–cxii^r^ cap. 182; **B:** fols 139^v^–140^r^ cap. 183; **C:** fols 141^r^–142^r^ cap. 165; **O:** fols 188^r^–189^v^; **V:** fols cxlix^v^–cl^v^ cap. 191; Beugnot, pp. 284–5, cap. 182.

---

[1] de Jerusalem] BV lack [2] ne] A: ou; V: et [3] dou reyaume de Jerusalem] V: de cestui royaume [4] chevaleries] V: chevaliers [5] dou] ABV: de son [6] dou servise] AB: de son servise; V: de son servise dou servise [7] C adds: en [8] le] C: les [9] O adds: en [10] et] C lacks [11] chevaliers] AB lack [12] .ix.] O: .viii. [13] besanz] C lacks [14] .m. et .c.] B: .xi^c^. [15] besanz] AB lack [16] O adds: en [17] bien] B lacks [18] lui] C: l'un [19] V adds: autre chevalier [20] de soy tiers de servise] B: por le servise de soi tierz [21] a] C lacks [22] .viiii.] C: .viii. [23] .c.] B lacks [24] ou d'un chevalier] B lacks [25] besanz] B lacks [26] si con il doit] A lacks [27] dit reaume] A: reiaume de Jerusalem; O: reaume devant dit [28] que on tient a] ABV: qui sont [29] chevaliers] ABO: chevaleries [30] que] B lacks; V: de [31] partisee] C: partisent

reteigne plus por son cors dou dit fié qui[32] n'est quanque il done en fiés[33] por le servise que le[34] fié doit et que autrement ne demore mie le plus dou fié au seignor dou fié, et qui autrement le fait que[35] les dons ne sont mie valables, por ce que le fié n'est mie desmenbré si con l'on peut et doit desmenbrer fié[36] par l'assise ou l'usage dou dit reaume.

Et les autres dient que puis que il done toutes les chevaleries[37] que il doit de[38] servise en fié[39] et il[40] retient plus a son cors[41] que il ne[42] done[43] a celui a qui il done plus de son fié,[44] que il desmenbre son fié bien selonc l'assise ou l'usage[45] dou dit reiaume, et que ceaus dons sont valables por ce que le fié est desmenbré si con il doit par la dite assise ou[46] usage.

Et[47] en la maniere avant dite a esté le descort dou fié desmenbré entre ceaus[48] que je ai oi tenir as plus sages plaideors de mon tens, et ausi bien[49] les uns come les autres dou grant fié con dou fié,[50] que il n'i a autre tache en l'un qu'en l'autre conbien l'on peut doner de son fié que le seignor en reteigne le plus dou fié, ne le descort qui a esté entriaus de ce qui a esté[51] que je aie oy[52] qu'en[53] se qui est desus devisé. Car tous[54] s'acordent a se que le seignor done[55] tant de son fié por le servise que le fié doit qu'il li en[56] remaigne plus que n'est tout[57] quanque il en a doné qu'il a son fié[58] desmenbré par l'assise si[59] con il doit, et que les dons sont valables et estables, ne l'eir ne le chief seignor ne pevent rapeler ceaus[60] dons par l'assise[61] ne[62] l'usage dou reiaume de Jerusalem. Por coy il me senble que l'on peut mout de bones raisons et de vives dire et mostrer por l'une et por l'autre partie, ne je ne veull[63] ore dire[64] a laquel des parties je m'acort,[65] mais espeir je le dirai aprés en cest livre.

[32] qui] ABO: que [33] fiés] AV: fié [34] le] C: son [35] que] BV lacks [36] fié] V lacks [37] chevaleries] V: chevaliers [38] de] ABV: dou [39] fié] C: vie [40] ABV add: en [41] cors] AB: eus; V: heus [42] ne] BO: n'en [43] C adds: plus [44] son fié] ABV: cel (V: celui) fié et [45] ou l'usage] B lacks [46] A adds: le dit [47] Et] BV lack [48] desmenbré entre ceaus] A: desmembrer entriaus et sont esté ciaus [49] bien] ABV lack [50] fié] ABV: petit [51] entriaus de ce qui a esté] A lacks; B: entre eaus de ce [52] A adds: n'est [53] qu'en] C: quan [54] tous] B: trop [55] done] C lacks [56] V adds: retiegne et en [57] que n'est tout] V: qui n'est [58] AB add: doné et [59] si] C: osi [60] pevent rapeler ceaus] V: le peut rapeler ces avans dis [61] si con il . . . l'assise] AB lack [62] ne] AB: ou; V: et [63] ne je ne veull] A: et por ce ne viaus je; BV: ne veull je [64] dire] C lacks [65] m'acort] V: m'en acort

***[166]** En quantes manieres l'on peut son fié eschanger, et coment l'on peut[1] eschanger si que l'eschange soit valable.[2]

L'on peut son fié eschanger en plusors manieres. Que l'on peut son fié eschanger[3] a tout le fié d'autre ou partie de son fié a partie dou fié[4] d'autre ou tout son fié[5] a partie dou fié d'autre,[6] mais que l'on le face[7] par l'usage dou reiaume de Jerusalem.[8] Et qui le viaut faire par le dit usage,[9] ceaus qui font l'eschange le doivent faire a[10] la court et par l'otroy dou seignor de qui il les fiés tienent. Et quant il veulent faire l'eschange de lor fiés, il doivent venir devant le seignor et[11] en la court et dire li: 'Sire, nos somes acordés[12] de faire de noz fiez tel eschange', et dire quel, 'si vous prions et requerons con a nostre[13] seignor que il vos plaise que nos faciens[14] cest eschange et que vos l'otroyés.' Et le seignor le doit otroier se il ne set que il facent cel eschange por le deseritement de[15] lui ou de[16] ces heirs de cel[17] servise ou d'escheete[18] qui peust venir d'aucun[19] des fié de ceaus qui font[20] l'eschange ou qui les face[21] por le desheritement d'aucun a qui aucun[22, 23] des fiés doit[24] escheir. Et se[25] le seignor otroie l'eschange, et l'eschange est de tout le fié de[26] l'un a tout le fié de l'autre, chascun doit dire au seignor quant il ont fait l'eschange: 'Sire, je vos sui tenus de cel[27] fié que je ay en eschange dou mien de ce que je vos estoie tenus por le mien d'omage et de servise et de toutes autres choses que je vos[28] devoye por le dit fié que je ai eschangé a cestui[29] que je ai,[30] et se vos otroye je si[31] en la court.' Et se l'eschange est de partie de l'un fié a partie de l'autre, chascun de ceaus qui font l'eschange doivent dire a l'eschange faire:

A: fol. cxii^{r-v} cap. 183; **B:** fols 140^{r}–141^{r} cap. 184; **C:** fol. 142^{r-v} cap. 166; **O:** fols 189^{v}–191^{r}; **V:** fols cl^{v}–cli^{v} cap. 192; Beugnot, pp. 286–7, cap. 183.

---

[1] ABV adds: fié [2] soit valable] ABV: soit (A: seit) estable; A rubric (fol. 8^{r}): vaille [3] en plusors manieres . . . eschanger] C lacks [4] a partie dou fié] C lacks; V: a partie [5] partie de son . . . fié] B lacks [6] ou tout son . . . d'autre] AV lack [7] que l'on le face] V: le face hom [8] l'usage dou reiaume de Jerusalem] AB: le seignor [9] le dit usage] C: l'usage [10] a] ABV: en [11] et] ABV lack [12] acordés] AB: concordés [13] V adds: chier [14] faciens] B: façons; V: faisons [15] le deseritement de] CV lack. In O these words are interlined in a later hand. [16] de] CV lack. In O this word is interlined in a later hand. [17] de cel] V: pour celui [18] d'escheete] C: de c'escheete [19] d'aucun] C: d'aucuns [20] font] A: ont fait; C: fait [21] qui les face] AB: qu'il le facent [22] a qui aucun] C: por qui aucuns [23] des fiés de . . . aucun] V lacks [24] doit] B: deust [25] se] BV lack [26] de] B: que [27] cel] ABV: tel [28] je vos] C: vos je [29] B adds: autre [30] V adds: ores [31] si] ABV lack

'Sire, je atray tel chose a mon fié que je ai eu de tel[32] en eschange de tel chose qui estoit de mon fié.' Et doit chascun[33] d'eaus dire que la chose[34] est que il atrait a son fié et quel[35] cele est que il a donee en eschange por cele qu'il a traite[36] a son fié.[37]

Et se le seignor n'otroye l'eschange a la requeste de ceaus[38] a qui l'eschange plaist plus et que[39] plus y cuide faire son profit, li doit dire: 'Sire, je entent que par l'usage dou reyaume de Jerusalem[40] les homes qui ont fiés pevent lor fiés eschanger les uns as autres tous[41] ou partie, mais que le servise dou seignor y soit[42] sauf et que l'eschange ne[43] soit trop descovenable ensi que se que l'un done a l'autre ne vaille au jor que l'eschange est fait[44] plus de l'autre. Sire, et cest eschange[45] que nos volons faire est asés comunau,[46] que poy vaut plus se que l'un de nos done a l'autre que ce que[47] il en a d'eschange.[48] Et se il vaut ore plus en autres choses,[49] l'autre[50] cuide bien tant esvancier[51] en se change[52] con se vaut et plus. Si entent chascun de nos a aveir profit en cest eschange,[53] ne vos, sire, n'estes mermé de vostre servise por[54] cest eschange.[55] Et puis, sire, que vos n'estes mermé de vostre servise, et que chascun de nos cuide faire son profit en l'eschange, vos ne le devés desvoloir,[56] ains vous doit plaire et le devez otroyer. Si veull que vos l'otroyés, et qu'il soit estable por toutes les raisons que je ai dites ou por aucunes d'eles se la court[57] le conoist, et de ce me met je en la conoissance de la court sauf mon retenaill.' Et a moy semble que se le seignor ne dit raison por coy il ne[58] doit cel eschange otroyer et tel que la court le conoisse que il ne la doit otroyer[59] ne que l'eschange ne doit estre estable, que la court doit conoistre que il doit l'eschange[60] otroier et qu'il doit estre estable. Et aprés la dite conoissance le doit le seignor otroier,[61] et est l'eschange estable.

[32] de tel] V: a tel chose [33] chascun] C: chascuns [34] que la chose] A: quel la chose; B: quele la chose; V: la chose quelle elle [35] quel] BV: que [36] traite] AB: atraite [37] et quel cele . . . fié] O lacks [38] de ceaus] A: d'iaus celui [39] que] AB: qui [40] AB add: que [41] tous] A lacks [42] y soit] V: doit estre [43] ne] C: n'i [44] ABV add: trop [45] eschange] C: change [46] comunau] V: couvenau [47] l'un de nos . . . que] C lacks; V: l'on done a l'autre que ce que [48] en a d'eschange] V: a eschangié. [49] autres choses] A: aucune chose; BV: aucunes choses [50] que ce que . . . l'autre] O lacks [51] esvancier] B: avancier [52] se change] AB: cest (B: ceste) eschange; V: cestui change [53] cest eschange] ABV: l'eschange; O: cest change [54] por] ABV: en [55] cest eschange] B: ces eschanges [56] desvoloir] B: contredire [57] O adds: ne [58] ne] C: en [59] et tel que . . . otroyer] AB lack [60] l'eschange] B: cel eschange [61] et qu'il doit . . . otroier] ABV lack

***[167]** Por quel choze l'on peut perdre son fié an et[1] jor et por quel[2] sa vie et por quel[3] ces heirs.

L'on peut par l'assise ou l'usage[4] dou reyaume de Jerusalem perdre son fié en .iii. manieres: l'une[5] an et jor; l'autre toute sa vie; la tierce lui et ses heirs. An et jor[6] le peut on perdre[7] par defaut[8] de servise. Toute sa vie le[9] peut on perdre[10] par defaut de homage[11] et par autres choses qui seront aprés devisees en cest livre. Et l'on le peut perdre et pert[12] par Deu renoyer et par estre traïtor vers son seignor de coy[13] on tient le fié et a[14] qui on[15] a[16] fait homage de cel fié, et par vendre le par l'assise.[17] Et coment l'on[18] le pert a lui et a ces heirs par vendre le par l'assise[19] et[20] par Deu renoyer et par estre traïtor vers son seignor sera aprés devisé en cest[21] livre.[a]

A: fol. cxii[v] cap. 184; **B:** fol. 141[r] cap. 185; **C:** fols 142[v]–143[r] cap. 167; **O:** fol. 191[r]; **V:** fol. cli[v] cap. 193; Beugnot, p. 287, cap. 184.

[a] Below caps 168–74.

[1] an et] B: .i. and et .i. [2] quel] A: quei tote; B: quoi toute; V: quoi tout [3] quel] AV: quei (V: quoi) lui et; B: quel raison lui et; C lacks [4] l'assise ou l'usage] V: assise et husage [5] V adds: est [6] An et jor] V: L'an et le jour [7] ABV add: et pert [8] defaut] B: defaillement [9] le] C: l'en [10] V adds: et pert [11] Toute sa vie . . . homage] A: Et par defaut d'omage a sa vie [12] A adds: lui et ces heirs [13] coy] AB: qui [14] a] C lacks [15] on] OV: l'on [16] a] AB lack [17] l'assise] OV: assise [18] l'on] A: on [19] Et coment l'on . . . l'assise] BV lack [20] a lui et . . . et] A lacks [21] cest] BV: cestui

***[168]** Coment et por quey l'on ne[1] peut vendre par l'assise partie de son fié, et coment et por quey on le peut tout[2] vendre par l'assise,[3] et coment il doit estre vendu, et coment l'on[4] doit fornir l'assise, et coment[5] quant le fié est vendu coment[6] et dedens quel terme doit le seignor[7] faire paier les detes[8] de celui[9] de qui le fié a esté vendu et lesqués detes. Et que celui a qui l'on a[10] dete coneue en court ou qui l'a provee[11] doit dire et faire quant il en viaut estre paié.[12] Et quant home ou feme de qui le fié a esté[13] crié a vendre par l'assise ne veaut fornir l'asise, quey le seignor en doit faire.[14]

Home ou feme qui a fié ne peut par l'assise ou l'usage dou reyaume de Jerusalem vendre partie de son fié, mais tout son fié peut l'on bien[15] vendre par la dite assise. Et l'assise de la vente[16] des fiés[17] est tel que l'on peut et doit fié vendre por dete coneue ou provee en cort, se celui de qui le fié est n'en a autre chose de ce qu'il[18] puisse la dete paier que[19] de[20] la vente dou fié. Et quant aucun doit dete a .i. home ou a plusors, et celui ou ceaus a qui il doit la dete[21] la li requiert[22] en la court ou il se claiment[23] de la dite dete, et il la conoist,[24] le fié doit estre vendu por paier cele dete se il n'a autre chose de quey paier la,[25] se[26] celui ou ceaus a qui il la doit et[27] a qui il l'a[28] coneue[29] ne se veulent soufrir ou deporter l'en. Et se il noie la[30] dete en la court a la requeste que on li fait ou au clain que on[31] fait de lui et l'on la preuve vers lui si con l'on doit, le fié doit estre vendu[32] por la dete paier. Et quant la dete est coneue ou

A: fols cxii^{v}–cxvii^{v} caps 185–6; **B:** fols 141^{r}–146^{v} caps 186–7; **C:** fols 143^{r}–149^{v} cap. 168; **O:** fols 191^{r}–201^{v}; **V:** fols cli^{v}–clix^{r} caps 194–6; Beugnot, pp. 288–97, caps 185–6.

[1] l'on ne] A rubric (fol. 8^{r}): on [2] tout] B lacks [3] l'assise] ABV: la dite assise [4] l'on] C: l'en [5] coment] B lacks [6] coment] A lacks [7] le seignor] V lacks [8] les detes] A: la dette [9] de celui] V lacks [10] Et que celui . . . a] V: que l'on doit a celui a qui l'on a la [11] l'a provee] B: l'a provee par garanz ou autrement; V: la preuve [12] Et que celui . . . paié] A lacks [13] C adds: vendu [14] Et quant home . . . faire] AB lack [15] l'on bien] B: on [16] de la vente] B: des ventes [17] des fiés] A: dou fié [18] chose de ce qu'il] A: de quei il; B: chose dont il; V: chose que ce que il [19] que] C lacks; O added in margin in later hand [20] que de] B: fors que [21] a .i. home . . . dete] A: et on [22] requiert] B: requierent [23] claiment] C: claime [24] A adds: ou l'on la li preuve [25] n'a autre chose . . . la] V: n'en a autre chose de que il puisse celle dete paier [26] se] A: ou se [27] a qui il la doit et] ABV lack [28] l'a] B: a la dette [29] A adds: ou qui li ont provee [30] BV add: dite [31] on] AB: l'on [32] vendu] A: paié

provee en court, celui ou ceaus[33] a qui il la doit, quant il en veulent estre paiés,[34] doivent requerre au seignor que il les en[35] face payer come de[36] dete coneue ou provee en court, et le seignor doit comander a celui qui la[37] doit que il l'ait payee[38] dedens .vii. jors. Et ce il dedens cel terme ne l'a paiee[39] et[40] celui ou ceaus a qui il la[41] doit dient[42] au seignor que les .vii. jors sont pasés et qu'il ne sont paiés, le seignor[43] le doit faire semondre de venir en sa court, et quant il y sera,[44] il li doit[45] dire: 'Vos coneustes[46] en ma court tel dete a tel et[47] tel', ou, 'Tel et tel proverent en ma court si con il durent que vos lor devés tant', et les nome et die conbien la dete est,[48] 'et aprés il me requistrent que je les feise paier con de dete coneue ou provee en court.[49] Je vos comandai que vos les eusiés paiés dedenz .vii. jors, et il me dient que[50] vos ne l'avés pas[51] fait.[52] Si veull savoir por coy se a esté.' Se celui dit que il n'a de quey payer cele dete[53] que de son fié et que il[54] livre son fié a vendre[55] por la dite dete paier, le seignor li doit respondre: 'Je suis prest de reseveir le, se ma court conoit[56] que je faire le doye, et faire quanque ele me conoistra', et aprés dire a la court[57] que il en a a faire selonc[58] les erremens qui ont esté. Et la court li doit conoisstre, se cuit, que il doit le fié recevoir et faire le crier et vendre par l'assise. Et aprés le seignor doit le fié recevoir et faire le crier et vendre par l'assise.[59]

Et l'asise[60] est tele: que il le doit faire comencer a[61] crier[62] par .iii. quaranteines, et les criors qui le crient par les .iii. cités le doivent ensi crier le premier jor: 'Qui veaut acheter et metre[63] au fié de tel', et le nome, 'que je cri par le comandement de mon seignor tel', et le nome, 'a vendre par l'assise o toutes ces apartenances et ces raisons[64] et ces droitures ou qu'eles soient et ques qu'eles soient,[65] lequel[66] fié est a tous heirs', ou 'as heirs[67] de feme espouse', selonc se qu'il sera, 'et doit tel servise a tel', et die quel servise il doit[68] et

---

[33] A adds: a qui on la deit [34] ABV add: si [35] en] ABV lack [36] de] AV lack [37] A adds: dette [38] l'ait payee] A: les ait paiés [39] ne l'a paiee] A: n'a paié; V: ne l'ait paié [40] et] AB lack [41] la] ABV lack [42] dient] A: dit; V: di [43] O adds: sy [44] y sera] A: sera venus [45] C adds: lors [46] coneustes] B: reconeustes [47] ABV add: a [48] la dete est] C: est la dete [49] ABV add: Et [50] V adds: encor [51] que vos ne l'avés pas] B: ne l'avez mie [52] V adds: paier [53] B adds: que dette [54] AV adds: li [55] et que il . . . vendre] B: il doit livrer son fié au seignor [56] conoit] A: conut [57] A adds: qu'elle li conoist [58] selonc] AB: aprés [59] Et aprés le . . . l'assise] BV lack [60] AB add: en [61] comencer a] ABV lack [62] A adds: par .iii. cités dou reiaume et [63] B adds: ou faire metre [64] et ces raisons] V lacks [65] et ques qu'eles soient] V lacks [66] lequel] C: et lequel [67] ou as heirs] C lacks [68] il doit] C lacks

a qui il le doit,[69] 'si soit de hui en .xl. jors, de demain en .xl. jors, ou depuis demain en .xl. jors[70] en tel leuc ou le fié[71] sera crié et livré par l'asise, et qui plus i metra si l'avra', et motise le leu ou il sera livré. Et le segont jor le[72] crie en la maniere avant[73] dite jusques au quaranteine,[74] et lors die: 'De yer en .xl. jors, et de hui en .xl. jors et de demain en .xl. jors.' Et au tiers jor die:[75] 'Devant[76] yer en .xl. jors, et de yer en .xl. jors et de[77] hui en .xl. jors.'

Et au jor qu'il doit estre livré, le seignor doit estre el leu ou il doit estre crié a livrer, et le doit faire[78] crier par cele ville .ii. ou .iii. fois le jor. Et le crior qui lors le crie le doit ensi[79] crier par la ville ou il sera livré ains que il soit livré:[80] 'Qui voudra metre a tel fié viegne devant mon seignor tel', et le nome, 'en tel leu et a tel hore', et dira[81] l'ore[82] quant il sera livré et le leu.[83] Et a la dite hore le seignor et la court doivent estre ensemble[84] la ou le fié doit estre livré, et le fié doit estre la[85] crié une piece en la court tant que il soit monté a ce que il pora selonc les acheteors qui y metront, et puis doit dire le crior par le comandement dou seignor les .iii. mos selonc[86] l'usage de[87] la court. Et au livrer dou fié doit dire le seignor a celui qui a livré son fié a vendre, se il est present, que il fornise l'asise si con il doit, et celui ou cele qui vent son fié doit fornir l'assise ensi que il doit jurer sur les[88] saintes evangiles[89] que il doit cele dete que il conut en la court que il devoit[90] por quey il livra son fié a vendre, et que il cele dete ne fist por achaison de son fié vendre, et qu'il ne autre por lui n'a[91] dou sien a covert ne a descovert la ne aillors dont il puisse cele dete paier[92] que[93] la vente de son[94] fié.

Et se il ou autre por lui a dedens les dites quaranteines aucune chose payé de cele dete que il conut en la court ou que l'on li prova en court, il doit dire ou[95] faire le sairement: 'Je' ou 'autre por moy avons tant[96] payé de cele dete',[97] et die la quantité de ce qui en a esté payé et qui le paia.[98]

---

[69] il doit et . . . doit] B: et a qui [70] de demain en . . . jors] AB lack [71] fié] B lacks [72] le] ABV lack [73] avant] B: devant [74] A adds: jor; BV: jour [75] die] AB lack [76] Devant] A: De avant; V: Desavant [77] yer en .xl. jors et de] C lacks [78] le doit faire] B: doit faire le fier [79] C adds: faire [80] ains que il soit livré] AV lacks [81] dira] A: dirre; BV: die [82] l'ore] C: lors [83] et le leu] AB: et le leuc meismes; C lacks; OV et le leu (V: leuc) ou il sera livré [84] ensemble] B: asemblé [85] la] AB lack [86] selonc] AB: par [87] de] A: en [88] les] ABV lack [89] A adds: de Dieu [90] V repeats: en la court [91] qu'il ne autre por lui n'a] V: que lui ne autre por lui n'en a [92] V adds: fors [93] ABV add: de [94] son] V: celui [95] ou] ABO: au [96] tant] AB lack [97] A adds: tel quantité', et nome celui qui l'a paiee; B: tele quantité [98] de ce qui . . . paia] A lacks; B: et a qui il l'a paiee; V: de ce qui en a esté paié et qui l'a paié

Et aprés le seignor doit comander a livrer le fié. Et lors le crior doit livrer au seignor le baston que il tient en sa main, et le seignor doit livrer le[99] fié[100] par cel baston a celui qui plus y avra[101] mis s'il est tel persone que fié puisse[102] et doye acheter par l'assise selonc ce qui[103] est aprés[104] dit. Et quant le seignor a le baston receu dou crior, il doit comander[105] a la court que ele li conoisse se l'asisse est bien fornie si con ele doit,[106] et lors le seignor doit le fié[107] livrer par le baston a celui qui plus y a mis,[108] se il a la[109] tant de monee aprestee de payer[110] con il[111] a le fié[112] acheté.[113] Et se il ne l'a[114] toute aprestee, et il en a partie, et il en face[115] le seignor seur a son gré[116] de ce qui en defaut ou fait vers les[117] detours tant que il s'en[118] teignent a paiés de leur detes s'eles montent[119] tant con le parfait[120] des besanz est, le seignor li doit livrer le fié et recevoir la monoie et le peut faire sans[121] perill aprés la dite conoissance. Et por ce ay je dit devant[122] que le seignor doit requerre la conoissance[123] a[124] la court se l'assise est bien[125] fornie si con ele doit de la vente dou fié.[126] Que le seignor est tenus par son sairement de tenir et faire tenir les assises et les usages dou reyaume de Jerusalem, et fié ne doit ne peut estre vendu que[127] par l'assise, si doit a son pooir le seignor des fiés qui li sont livrés a[128] vendre par l'assise faire ent fornir l'assise, et il le fait bien si con il doit quant il le fait par[129] conoissance de court. Et toutes les cas qui vienent en sa court doit il mener et faire mener[130] selonc les assises et les usages dou dit reaume. Et se le seignor par obli ou autrement ne requiert a la court la dite conoissance, celui qui plus y a mis ou[131] fié la doit requere ainz que il resoive[132] le fié ne que il paie la monoye. Que, se la court conoist a sa requeste ou a cele dou seignor[133] que l'assise de la vente[134] dou fié est bien fornie si con ele doit, il est hors[135] dou perill de l'achat dou fié, por ce que aprés la conoissance de la court nul ne peut dire chose qui li griege,[136]

---

[99] le] AB: cel [100] Et lors le . . . fié] O lacks [101] avra] ABV: a [102] fié] V: le fié puisse acheter [103] qui] B: que il [104] est aprés] V: aprés sera [105] comander] AB: demander [106] AB add: et la court li deit (B: doit) conoistre [107] le fié] A: faire [108] AB add: et celui [109] la] ABV lack [110] de payer] AB lack [111] C adds: li [112] il a le fié] V: le fié que il a [113] A adds: il la deit livrer au seignor; B: la doit paier; V: li a cousté [114] BO add: la [115] face] AB: fait [116] a son gré] A lacks [117] les] C: le [118] s'en] BV: se [119] detes s'eles montent] ABV: dette se elle monte [120] parfait] B: fait [121] A adds: delai et sanz [122] devant] AV: avant [123] Et por ce . . . conoissance] B lacks [124] a] BV: de [125] bien] AB lack; V: bien faite et [126] dou fié] B lacks [127] que] V lacks [128] a] C: au [129] C adds: la [130] et faire mener] C lacks [131] ou] OV: au [132] resoive] V: resoit [133] ou a cele dou seignor] B lacks [134] de la vente] AB lack [135] hors] A: fors [136] griege] C: greige

que le fié n'ait esté vendu si con il doit par l'assise, por ce que les esgars et les conoissances et les recors que la court fait doivent estre et sont tenus et maintenus fermes et estables.

Et le seignor doit faire garder la monoie que le fié a esté vendu .vii. jors por faire paier ceaus a qui celui de qui le fié a esté vendu devoit.[137] Et quant le fié est[138] vendu,[139] le seignor doit faire crier par la ville ou le fié a esté vendu que ceaus a qui celui de qui le fié a esté vendu[140] devoit aucune chose qu'il[141] soient[142] a tel jor devant lui por estre paiés si con il devront de ce que tel, et le nome,[143] lor devoit et nomer le seteime jor que le fié a esté vendu. Et a cel jor tous ceaus a qui il avra dete coneue en court avant que le fié ait esté vendu et tous ceaus qui dedens les .vii. jors[144] avant dis avront prouvé si con il devront[145] que il lor deust aucune chose[146] doivent estre paiés en[147] la monoie que le seignor a fait garder de la vente dou fié se la monoie[148] est tant ou plus con la dete.[149] Et se aucune chose en demore aprés ce que les .vii. jors seront pasés, le seignor la[150] doit faire rendre a celui de qui le fié fu qui a esté vendu[151] s'il a l'assise fornie. Et se la dete est plus que la monoie, le seignor la doit faire[152] paier par quarobles a chascun son avenant.[153] [a]

Et ce il avient que celui qui a livré son fié a vendre par l'assise por dete coneue[154] ou provee en cort se destorne de venir en la court fornir l'assise, ou s'il est en la court et il ne viaut le sairement avant dit faire a[155] l'assise fornir,[156] por tant ne me senble il mie que il doit demorer d'estre[157] vendu puis que la dete a esté coneue ou provee en cort si con ele doit, se il n'a autre[158] de quey la dite dete soit paiee.[159] Car il y a propre assise que fié se peut vendre por dete coneue ou provee en court,[160] se celui qui la conoist ou vers qui l'on

---

[a] V begins a new chapter here with the rubric: Ci dit coment celui qui a son fié livré a vendre, quant il ce destorne de fornir l'assise, coment l'on le doit conduire

---

[137] .vii. jors por . . . devoit] B lacks [138] est] V: a esté [139] vendu] B lacks [140] que ceaus a . . . vendu] A: que ce celui qui le fié a vendu; CO lack; V: que tout ceaus a qui devoit celui de qui le fié a esté vendu [141] qu'il] B lacks [142] soient] A: soit [143] nome] V: noment [144] que le fié a esté vendu. Et . . . jors] ABV: et quant les [145] devront] BV: doivent [146] AB add: il [147] en] ABV: de [148] monoie] AB: vente [149] tant ou plus con la dete] V: autant come la dette est ou plus [150] la] AV lack; B: le [151] A adds: ce qui sera demoré [152] faire] BV lack [153] son avenant] V: soi ravenant [154] V adds: en court [155] a] O: en; V: et [156] fornir] C: fornie [157] A adds: le fié [158] autre] AV: autre chose; B: chose [159] la dite dete soit paiee] V: il puisse la dite dette paier [160] si con ele . . . court] O lacks

l'a provee[161] n'a[162] autre chose de quey payer la que de la vente de son fié. Et si a un autre assise que dete coneue ou provee en court doit estre paiee dedens .vii. jors et que le seignor doit comander a celui qui la doit que il l'ait paiee dedens .vii. jors, et se il dedens le terme ne l'a paiee et celui a qui il doit la dete le li fait assaveir et li requiert que il l'en face paier si con il doit par l'assisse, que le seignor doit faire prendre de celui qui doit la dete tant des soes choses et faire les[163] vendre tant que la dete soit paiee.[164] Et puis que les dites assises sont tez, donc est il clere chose que le seignor peut[165] le fié[166] de celui qui a dete coneue en court ou vers qui ele est[167] provee faire[168] vendre par l'assise, se il ne peut tant recovrer de ces choses autre que le fié de coy la dete soit paiee,[169] tout soit ce que celui qui doit la dete se destorne por non fornir l'assise ou por autre chose ou que il soit present en la court et ne veulle le sairement faire de l'assise fornir. Que se[170] ensi n'estoit, les .ii. assises ne seroient pas tenues, ains seroient faites de droit a l'encontre puis que fié ne seroit vendu por dete. Que se fié ne poeit estre vendu par l'assise por dete[171] coneue ou provee en cort ou celui qui l'a coneue ou vers qui l'on la preuve[172] ne livroit son fié a vendre et il ne faisoit l'avant dit sairement[173] a la vente dou fié, fié ne seroit jamais vendu por dete se celui de qui le fié est ne voloit. Que nus ne li porroit faire livrer son fié a vendre se il ne voloit, et, s'il[174] [b] l'avoit livré, ne le porroit autruy esforcier de faire le dit sairement, por coy fié ne seroit jamais vendu por dete se celui de qui le fié est ne voloit,[175] laquel chose seroit contre les avans dittes assises. Mais por ce que les avant dites assises doivent estre tenues[176] fermement et[177] que il ne me semble qu'eles le puissent estre se le seignor ne peut faire vendre le fié selon assise[178] por dete coneue ou provee en court,[179] fust livré ou non livré a vendre par l'assise, puis que il autre chose que le fié ne troveroit a faire vendre de celui de qui le fié

---

[b] O lacks a folio beginning at this point.

---

[161] l'a provee] AO: la preuve [162] n'a] V: en court n'en a [163] tant des soes ... les] AV: son fié et faire le [164] et celui a ... paiee] B: on doit faire vendre son fié pour la dette paier [165] B adds: faire [166] le fié] O lacks [167] vers qui ele est] A: qu'elle soit; B: que ele li est [168] faire] B lacks [169] Et puis que ... paiee] V lacks [170] se] C lacks [171] Que se fié ... dete] A lacks [172] la preuve] AV: l'a provee; B: l'a prové [173] sairement] C: seirament [174] V adds: le voloit ne [175] se celui de ... voloit] B lacks [176] AB add: et maintenues; V: et maintenus [177] et] AB lack [178] assise] ABV: l'assise [179] en court] B lacks

seroit a[180] la dete payer,[181] me semble il que se le seignor fait le fié[182] crier et livrer por la dite dete paier si con est usé que on le fait dou[183] fié que on vent par l'assise, que la vente est estable, ne que celui de qui le fié est ensi vendu con est avant dit ne ses heirs ne[184] pevent puis recovrer au dit fié. Que par l'assise ou l'usage dou dit[185] reyaume, se .i. home qui a fié meurt, celui de ses heirs qui a son fié est tenus de paier sa dete, et se la dete dou mort a esté coneue ou provee[186] en cort a sa vie ou aprés sa mort prové[187] si con ele doit et son heir ne l'a[188] payé et celui ou ceaus a qui il la devoit requiert son heir[189] au seignor que il les face paier de cele dete si con il doit par l'assise et le seignor comande a l'eir de celui qui[190] devoit la dite conoissance et dete[191] et qui tient le fié qui fu sien que il l'ait payé[192] dedens .vii. jors et s'il[193] ne le fait, le fié qui fu[194] de celui qui doit[195] la dite[196] dete doit estre, se me semble, vendu selonc l'assise por la dite[197] dete paier ausi bien aprés sa mort con a sa vie,[198] puis que il conut la dete[199] a sa vie ou qu'ele li fu provee si con ele dut.[200] Si est clere chose que fié peut et doit estre vendu selonc l'asisse ou l'usage dou dit reyaume por dete provee ou coneue en cort tout soit ce que celui qui la dete devoit n'a[201] fait l'avant dit sairement de fornir l'assise. Qui est sertaine chose que le mort ne peut fornir l'assise par le sairement avant dit, ne por ce ne demore que le fié qui a esté sien ne soit vendu en la maniere avant dite por sa dite[202] dete paier. Si ne peut demorer par raison selonc l'assise ou l'usage dou dit[203] reaume que fié ne soit vendu si con est avant dit, tout soit ce que celui de qui le fié est ne[204] fait l'avant dit sairement de fornir l'assise.

Et s'aucun home ou feme qui ait fié a[205] dete coneue en cort ou il l'a[c] nee et ele li est[206] provee si con l'on doit par l'asise et l'on

[c] End of *lacuna* in O.

[180] de qui le fié seroit a] A: qui la dette devroit por [181] B adds: ne [182] que se le . . . fié] A: se il fait le seignor le fié vendre; BV: que (B: que se) le seignor fait le fié vendre (V: et) [183] dou] ABV: de [184] ne] AV: n'i [185] dou dit] A: de cest; B: dou [186] ou provee] B lacks [187] prové] ABV lack [188] ne l'a] C: n'a la [189] requiert son heir] ABV: requierent [190] qui] B: a qui il [191] la dite conoissance et dete] A: la ditte dette; B: la dite dete; V: celle dette paier [192] l'ait payé] A: ait paiee la dette [193] s'il] ABV: il [194] qui fu] A lacks [195] doit] BV: devoit [196] dite] AB lack [197] dite] B lacks [198] a sa vie] B: devant [199] la dete] V lacks [200] dut] V: doit [201] n'a] V: ne [202] dite] BV lack [203] dou dit] V: de cestui [204] ne] B: n'ait; V: n'a [205] a] AV: ait la; B: a la [206] est] A: ait esté; V: a esté

li[207] a livré son fié a vendre por la dite dete paier,[208] ou se il est destorné aprés la[209] dete coneue en court, et le seignor a fait saisir[210] son fié par conoissance ou avoiement de court[211] et faire le crier a vendre en la maniere avant dite de[212] dete paier, et[213] celui de qui le fié est meurt ains que le fié soit vendu[214] et il n'a nul autre heir a qui le fié puisse escheir mais que au[215] seignor, a moy senble que cel fié doit estre vendu por la dite dete paier se le seignor a qui il devroit[216] revenir[217] ne paie celle dete.[218] Car puis que celui de qui le fié estoit le livra en court por la dite[219] dete paier, ou que le seignor l'ot saisi par conoissance ou par avoiement de court et fait crier si con est avant dit por la dite dete paier, il me senble que il ne doit demorer por la mort de celui de qui le fié fu, ne[220] por ce que il soit escheu a aucun de ces heirs ou que il soit revenus au seignor que il ne soit vendus[221] por la dite[222] dete paier, se celui a qui le fié est escheu ou le seignor a qui il[223] est revenus ne paie la dite[224] dete[225] d'autre part, ou se celui de qui le fié fu n'avoit autre chose que le fié de coy la dete soit[226] paiee, puis que il[227] fu obligé en aucune des manieres avant[228] dites a la dite[229] dete paier avant[230] que celui de qui il fu mort.[231]

Et ce celui ou celle[232] qui a fié a dete coneue en court, ou ele li a esté provee en court morut[233] sans heir a qui son fié puisse et doive escheir et il n'a livré en sa vie son fié a vendre[234] par l'assise por la dite[235] dete paier ou le seignor ne l'a saisi par esgart ou par conoissance ou par avoiement de cort por faire vendre por la dite dete paier,[236] le dit fié ne doit mie estre vendu, se me senble, por cele dete paier por ce qu'il[237] est revenus au seignor dont il mut sans ce que il soit en aucune des .ii.[238] dites manieres obligé a la dete

---

[207] par l'asise et l'on li] ABV: et l'on [208] paier] BV lack [209] A adds: ditte [210] saisir] A: vendre [211] ou avoiement de court] AV: de court ou autrement; B: ou autrement [212] en la maniere . . . de] A: par la maniere avant ditte por la ditte [213] et] A: ou ce; V: et ce [214] meurt ains que . . . vendu] A: morust [215] escheir mais que au] A: ni dee escheyr que le [216] devroit] BV: devoit [217] V adds: ne fust en la maniere avant dite [218] a qui il . . . dete] A: ne la paie a qui il devreit revenir ou se il ne fust en la maniere avant ditte qu'il trovast tant des choses de celui de qui le fié fu que celle dette fust paiee [219] dite] B lacks [220] ne] C lacks [221] vendus] C: venus [222] dite] B lacks [223] il] A: le fié [224] dite] B lacks [225] paier, se celui . . . dete] O lacks [226] soit] AB: fust [227] il] A: le fié [228] avant] V: devant [229] dite] ABV lack [230] avant] B lacks [231] mort] A: moreust; B: morust; V: morut [232] ou celle] ABV lack [233] morut] AB: morust [234] fié a vendre] A: avant dit fié a vendre; B: fié devant dit; V: fié avant dit [235] dite] B lacks [236] ou le seignor . . . paier] B lacks [237] por ce qu'il] B: quar il [238] .ii.] AB lack

paier, car le seignor n'est pas tenus par l'assise ne[239] l'usage dou dit reyaume[240] de paier la dete que son home conut en court ou que l'on li prova,[241] tout soit ce que le fié que celui avoit qui la dete conut et[242] vers qui ele fu provee en court li soit revenus por ce que il soit[243] mort sans heir. Mais par l'assise ou l'usage dou dit[244] reyaume son heir qui a ses biens en[245] est tenus de la dite[246] dete paier, et por ce ay je devant dit que le fié qui eschiet a l'eir doit estre vendu par l'assisse por paier la dete que celui de qui le fié fu[247] conut en court ou que l'on li prova en court que il devoit.[d]

Et quans gens a qui l'on a la[248] dete coneue en court ou qui l'ont provee si con il doivent veullent estre paiés de cele dete, celui qui en veaut estre paiés doit[249] venir devant le seignor en la court et requerre li[250] que il le face paier si con il doit par l'assise,[251] con de[252] dete coneue ou provee[253] en court, de tel dete[254] que tel li conut en la[255] court ou de cele dete que il li prova[256] en la court,[257] et le nome et die la dete. Et le seignor li doit respondre que il[258] en fera volentiers se que il[259] devra par[260] l'avoiement de sa court et aprés doit dire a la court que ele l'avoie[261] qu'il en a a faire.[262] Et la court doit, se me senble, avoier[263] de ce ensi le seignor que il doit mander[264] semondre[265] par .iii. de ces homes come court celui ou cele qui la dete conut en la court que il veigne devant lui en la court a hore motie ou au jor nomé faire a[266] celui a qui il doit la dite[267] dete se qu'il doit,[268] et ce les semoneors[269] ne le treuvent, que il le[270] dient as gens de son hostel. Et se il i vient,[271] quant il i sera,[272] le seignor li doit comander qu'il ait la dite dete[273] paiee dedens .vii.

---

[d] ABV begin a new chapter here with the rubric: Coment celui a qui l'on a dette coneue en court (A: cort) ou qui l'a prouvé (B: provê en court) doit (A: deit) dire et faire quant il en veut (A: viaut; V: veaut) estre paié par le seignor.

---

[239] ne] BV: ou [240] dit reyaume] ABV: reiaume (B: reaume; V: royaume) de Jerusalem [241] prova] V: a provê en court [242] et] AB: ou [243] soit] B: est [244] dou dit] AB: dou; V: de cestui [245] en] ABV lack [246] dite] B lacks [247] de qui le fié fu] B: qui le fié fu qui [248] la] AB lack [249] doit] C: doivent [250] la court et requerre li] A: sa court et dire li et requerre; V: court et requerre au seignor [251] BV add: si [252] de] CV lack [253] ou provee] V lacks [254] C adds: coneue ou provee en court [255] la] C lacks [256] que il li prova] A: que il prova vers tel; V: provee [257] ou de cele . . . court] B lacks [258] C adds: li [259] A adds: en [260] par] C: por [261] l'avoie] A: li conoisse ou avee; V: avoie ce [262] faire] V: fera [263] avoier] C: avoir [264] doit mander] ABV: mande [265] semondre] O lacks [266] a] C lacks [267] dite] B lacks [268] doit] A: devera [269] ce les semoneors] B: que les semoneors doivent faire enssi et se il [270] le] BV lack [271] vient] O: vienent [272] i sera] B: sera venuz; V: sera [273] la dite dete] B: de ce

jors a celui ou a cele a qui il la doit ou a son comandement[274] quant[275] il counut la dete en la court.[276] Et ce il ne le fait dedens cel terme aprés le comandement dou seignor et celui a qui il doit la dete vient devant le seignor aprés les .vii. jors que le seignor li avra fait[277] le dit comandement et il dit que celui ne l'a mie paié si con il comanda dedens le terme des .vii. jors et les[278] jors sont pasés, si le[279] prie et requiert que il le face paier de cele dete si con il faire le doit par l'assise. Et le seignor doit faire semondre en la maniere avant[280] dite celui qui doit la dete qu'il soit devant lui a .i.[281] jor moti et brief. Et se il n'i vient et il a en la seignorie de celui seignor autre chose a vendre que son fié que le seignor puisse avoir, il la[282] doit faire prendre et vendre guage abandon et paier ent la dete coneue ou provee en court. Et se il de ce ne peut faire paier la dite[283] dete et celui ou cele qui la dete doit n'a autre chose dou sien que son fié de coy la dite[284] dete puisse estre paiee et il ne vient a court livrer au seignor son fié a vendre[285] par l'assise por la dite[286] dete paier, ou il se destorne si que le seignor ne le puisse faire trover a faire semondre[287] en la court faire se que il doit de la dite[288] dete paier, ou[289] se le seignor le fait semondre et il n'i vient en[290] la semonce et[291] celui a qui il doit la dete requiert au seignor qu'il le face paier si con il doit de la dete qui a esté coneue ou provee devant lui en la[292] court ou que il li en face ce que il doit[293] par l'assise ou l'usage de cest reyaume, le seignor li doit dire en la presence de la court que il ensi fait, et que[294] por ce que il ne veaut mesprendre[295] envers aucune des[296] parties ne faire chose qu'il ne[297] doive est il prest de faire ent ce que la court[298] conoistra que il faire en doie, si comande a sa court que[299] li conoisse qu'il en a a faire. Et quant le seignor avra comandé a sa court[300] qu'ele li face la dite conoissance, la court li[301] doit faire et doit[302] conoistre, se me semble, que le seignor doit faire saisir le[303] fié de celui ou de cele qui

[274] O adds: se il ne li fist cest comandement; V: se il ne fist son coumandement [275] quant] V: et [276] quant il counut . . . court] AB lack [277] V adds: doner [278] A adds: .vii. [279] le] ABV: li [280] avant] B: devant [281] .i.] ABV lack [282] la] ABV: le [283] dite] B lacks [284] dite] B lacks [285] vendre] C: vendr [286] dite] B lacks [287] B adds: de venir [288] dite] B lacks [289] il se destorne . . . ou] A lacks [290] n'i vient en] ABV: ne vient a [291] et] BV lack [292] la] ABV lack [293] doit] A: li en deit; B: l'en doit faire [294] il ensi fait, et que] ABV lack [295] mesprendre] B: respondre [296] envers aucune des] C: enver aucune de [297] ne] B lacks [298] court] A lacks; B: court en [299] que] V: qu'elle [300] que li conoisse . . . court] ABO lack [301] li] AV: la; B lacks [302] doit] B: dire et [303] le] B: son

a la dete coneue en court et livrer le au crior a crier[304] a vendre si con l'on crie fié que l'on vent par l'assise. Et aprés la dite conoissance le seignor doit comander[305] le fié a crier en la maniere avant devisee.[306] Et se le seignor ou la dame dou fié[307] ne vient[308] dedens le terme des .iii. quaranteines que le fié sera crié[309] a livrer[310] paier ou faire[311] paier celui a qui la dete est coneue en court ou que il l'a prové[312] de ce que il li a provee[313] en court[314] ou faire li en[315] son gré si que le fié soit par lui respité a vendre ou dire chose por coi le fié ne doit estre vendu, que le seignor peut et doit faire le[316] vendre par les .iii. quaranteines que il avra esté crié en .iii. cités si con fié que l'on vent par l'assise doit estre crié.

Et a cel jor que le fié[317] avra esté crié[318] a livrer le[319] seignor doit estre el leu ou il l'a[320] fait crier que le fié doit estre[321] livré, et doit cel[322] jor faire crier le fié par cele vile ou il est .ii. ou .iii. fois et dire le leu ou cel fié sera livré et a quel hore, et a cele hore[323] il doit estre la et avoir ce que il pora de ces homes et y doit avoir le crior de la ville et faire crier .ii. fois ou .iii. le dit fié en sa presence et[324] de la court. Et quant le fié sera monté a ce que il porra, il doit faire dire les .iii. mos, et quant les .iii. mos seront dis,[325] le crior doit livrer le baston que il tient[326] au crier dou fié au seignor, et[327] lors le seignor doit dire a celui qui plus y a mis: 'Venez avant. Recevez ce fié qui a esté crié selonc l'assise en quex vos avez plus mis que nul des autres, et paiés ce que vos y avés mis et aprés faites ce que vos devez por le dit fié.' Et celui qui plus y a[328] mis doit respondre au seignor: 'Sire, il[329] est veir que je ais plus mis a cel[330] fié que nus autre, et je suis prest de paier tant con je y[331] ay mis et de faire les autres choses que le fié doit se la court conoit[332] que l'achat que je en fai[333] soit ferme et estable et valable a moy et a mes heirs a tous tens,[334] car je n'i voy[335] pas ci en[336] present[337] celui

[304] ABV add: et [305] comander] C: mander [306] devisee] B: dite [307] dou fié] V: qui le fié est [308] vient] B: vienent [309] crié] B: cité [310] A adds: et a; B: a; O (in margin in later hand): pour [311] faire] A: face [312] l'a prové] AB: a provee; O: la preuve; V: l'a provee [313] de ce que . . . provee] B lacks [314] en court] V lacks [315] li en] ABV lack [316] le] A: le fié; BV lack; C le fié ('fié' interlined) [317] avra esté crié . . . fié] V lacks [318] Et a cel . . . crié] B lacks [319] a livrer le] C: et livré le [320] l'a] C: a; V: le [321] B adds: crié et [322] cel] AV: celui [323] et a cele hore] C lacks [324] et a quel . . . et] B: en la presence [325] dis] V: crié [326] tient] C: tien [327] et] BV lack [328] plus y a] V: a plus [329] il] B: bien [330] a cel] AB: en cest; V: en ce [331] y] AV lack [332] conoit] AV: l'esgarde (V: l'esguarde) ou conoisse; B: esgarde ou conoist [333] en fai] AO: en fas; B: ai fait; V: ais fait [334] a tous tens] C lacks [335] n'i voy] V: ne vois [336] en] ABV lack [337] present] C: presence

ou cele de qui le fié est que l'assise en fornise. Si vos pri et requier que vos me faites faire a vostre cort la dite conoissance.' Et le seignor deit comander a la court qu'ele li face. Et il me senble par les raisons avant dites que la court doit conoistre que la vente est estable et que[338] l'achat doit estre estable a celui qui achate[339] le fié et a ces heirs a tous tens. Et ensi sera la vente parfaite[340] si con ele doit et les .ii. avant dites assises maintenues et tenues fermes et estables, se m'est avis.

Et ce celui qui achate le fié en aucune des avant dites manieres fait que sage, maintenant que il avra receu[341] la saisine dou dit fié, il en offrira son homage au seignor et li[342] fera se il le viaut recevoir, por ce que le seignor li soit tenus de foy et il a lui, et que se aucun le vosist metre en plait de cel fié par aucune maniere, que le seignor li fust plus tenus d'aidier li et[343] defendre[344] par raison. Et le seignor doit recevoir l'omage de celui qui a le fié acheté en aucune[345] des avant dites manieres se il l'eufre a faire tel[346] con le fié doit. Que quant le fié a esté vendu en aucune des avant dites manieres,[347] le seignor est quite de sa foy vers celui de qui le fié fu, et celui est ausi quite de sa foy[348] que il doit[349] au seignor[350] par l'omage que il li avoit fait de cel fié, que puis que home pert son fié toute sa vie, ou lui ou[351] ces heirs, par assise ou par usage[352] ou par esgart ou par conoissance de court il n'en est[353] plus tenus de foy au seignor de ce[354] que il tenoit et a qui il en[355] avoit fait homage, ne le seignor a lui.

Et[356] se aucun home ou feme a livré son fié a vendre por dete coneue ou provee en court et le fié a esté crié si con est avant dit que on doit fié crier que on[357] vent par l'assise, et celui qui le livra se destorne de non[358] venir a cort quant le fié doit estre vendu por ce que il ne fornise l'assise ou por autre chose et le fié est vendu por plus que la dete n'est et il aprés vient devant le seignor et li requiert se qui[359] est demoré en sa guarde outre la paye des detors

[338] que] C lacks [339] l'achat doit estre . . . achate] A: la vente deit estre valable a celui qui a acheté [340] parfaite] B lacks [341] receu] C: eu [342] li] C: le [343] d'aidier li et] A: a aider le et a; B: a aidier li et; V: de ayder le et [344] C adds: li [345] aucune] C: aucunes [346] tel] V: celui servise si [347] avant dite manieres] C: manieres avant dites [348] vers celui de . . . foy] ABV lack [349] doit] V: devoit [350] A adds: de cel fié; BV: dou fié [351] lui ou] B lacks [352] assise ou par usage] C: l'assise ou par l'usage [353] n'en est] ABV: n'est [354] de ce] A: por cel fié; BV: pour ce [355] tenoit et a qui il en] AV: teneit (V: tenoit) et qu'il en; B: ne tient mie ce dont il li [356] Et] A: Car [357] on] BOV: l'on [358] non] A lacks [359] qui] B: que li

de ce que le fié a esté vendu, le seignor li doit respondre que il en fera volentiers se que il[360] devra par sa court. Et quant il li requerra en la[361] court, si die[362] le seignor: 'Je n'entent que je[363] ceste monoie que vos me requerés vos doie rendre se vos avant ne[364] fornisés l'assise de la vente de vostre fié[365] que vos livrastes a vendre por dete coneue ou provee en court et qui a esté vendu selon l'assise par conoissance de court. Ne faire ne le veull se la court ne conoist[366] que je faire le doie. Et de ce me met je en l'esgart et en[367] la conoissance de la court.' Et a moy ne semble que celui qui requiert la monoie puisse chose dire par coy la court ne doit conoistre que il doit fornir l'asisse, faisant le sairement que l'on fait au fornir de l'assise quant les fiés sont vendus si con est avant dit ains que il ait la monoie que il requiert. Et quant la court avra se coneu, le seignor li doit dire et requerre que il fornise l'asisse. Et se il la veaut fornir, il doit faire l'avant dit sairement. Et se[368] il le[369] fait, le seignor li doit faire rendre sans delay ce qui en demora[370] de la vente de son fié aprés la paie de ceaus a qui il devoit et qui en furent paiés si con il durent. Et ce il aprés ceste conoissance ne fornit[371] l'assise, ou se il est present en la court au vendre dou fié et le seignor li dit que il fornise l'assise et il ne le fait ou ne[372] dit raison por coy il ne la doit fornir et tel que la court l'esgarde ou conoisse, la dite monoie, se me senble,[373] remaint au seignor quite et delivré. Et le siegnor peut[374] celui qui l'a[375] refusé a[376] fornir l'asisse[377] prendre et laidir a sa[378] volenté, puis que son fié a esté par esgart ou par conoissance de court crié et vendu en aucune des avant dites manieres, por ce que il ne li est plus tenus de foy, et que il a son fié livré a vendre par barat et malesiousement et est alé a son pooir contre l'assise laquel le seignor est tenus par son sairement de tenir et[379] faire tenir en son royaume. Si n'est[380] merveille se le seignor aprés le punit, puis que il est quite de sa foy vers lui, et qu'il a[381] fait si lait barat et en court et encontre[382] l'assise que le seignor doit tenir et faire tenir en sa seignorie.

[360] BV adds: en [361] la] A: sa [362] die] B: responde [363] je] A: vos [364] B adds: faites et [365] de vostre fié] B: dou fié qui vostre fu [366] conoist] A: conut [367] l'esgart et en] AB lack [368] se] B lacks [369] le] C lacks [370] demora] V: demorera [371] fornit] AV: fornist; C: fornise [372] le fait ou ne] B lacks [373] se me senble] AB lack [374] V adds: de [375] l'a] AB: a [376] a] ABV: de [377] A adds: faire [378] a sa] C: assa [379] AB add: de [380] n'est] AB: n'est mie; C: n'i est [381] a] BV: ait [382] encontre] BV: contre

***[169]** Ques gens ne pevent fié acheter par l'assise, et la raison por coi il ne le pevent[1] acheter,[2] et que[3] feme peut fié acheter,[4] et par quel raison cele le peut acheter le fié ou non.[5]

Par l'assise ou l'usage dou reaume de Jerusalem, qui a fié ne peut fié acheter qui ne peut faire ce que le fié doit[6] qu'il viaut acheter d'omage et de servise. Mais qui le peut[7] faire le peut bien acheter, qui n'a en lui autre chose par coy on[8] ne puisse ne doive fié acheter par l'assise ou l'usage devant dit.[9] Ne fiz de chevalier et[10] de dame né en leal mariage ne peut fié acheter tant que il ait .xv. ans complis, ne damoisele fille de chevalier et[11] de dame nee[12] en leal mariage por aage que ele ait ne peut fié acheter, car le fiz merme d'aage n'a vois ne respons en court, ne chose qu'il face n'est valable ne estable[13] tant que il ait .xv. anz complis, ne chose que la fille face de quelque aage qu'ele soit n'est mie estable en la haute cort tant que ele soit mariee.

Mais a moy semble que la dame veve fille de chevalier et[14] de dame nee en leal mariage[15] peut bien acheter fié par l'asise ou l'usage dou dit reyaume.[16] Et la raison por coy si est tel, que je croi qu'en l'assise de coy home[17] ne peut fié de chevalier acheter qui n'est chevalier,[18] fis de chevalier et[19] de dame, né en leal mariage, et se ensi est donc[20] n'est mie la feme degetee par l'assise de[21] fié acheter, et puis que ele ne l'est ele le peut bien acheter par l'asise.[22, 23] Et se aucun dit que il est en l'assise[24] que nul ne peut fié acheter par l'assise c'il n'est chevalier, fiz de chevalier et de dame, nés en leal mariage,[25] et puis que il y[26] a que nul autre ne le peut acheter[27] que feme ne le peut acheter[28] par l'assise, je di contre[29] ceaus qui se

A: fols cxvii^{v}–cxix^{r} cap. 187; **B:** fols 146^{v}–148^{r} cap. 188; **C:** fols 149^{v}–151^{r} cap. 169; **O:** fols 201^{v}–204^{r}; **V:** fols clix^{r}–clx^{v} cap. 197; Beugnot, pp. 297–9, cap. 187.

[1] pevent] V: peut [2] par l'assise et . . . acheter] C lacks [3] que] AV: quel [4] acheter et que . . . acheter] B: et que feme puet fié acheter et quel non [5] cele le peut . . . non] ABV: elle le peut (B: puet) acheter [6] doit] A lacks [7] le peut] B: puet ce [8] on] B: il [9] devant dit] B: dou dit reaume [10] et] V: ou [11] et] V: ou [12] nee] B lacks [13] estable] B lacks [14] et] V: ou [15] nee en leal mariage] B lacks [16] V adds: de Jerusalem [17] de coy home] A: est que nul; V: pour quoi hom [18] qui n'est chevalier] B lacks [19] fis de chevalier et] V: ou fis de chevalier ou [20] donc] C: dont [21] de] AV: dou [22] et, puis que . . . l'asise] A lacks [23] par l'asise] V lacks [24] en l'assise] AV: assise [25] et se ensi . . . mariage] B lacks [26] y] A: n'i; V: n'en [27] peut acheter] A: puisse acheter que chevalier [28] que feme ne le peut acheter] CV lack [29] di contre] B: contredi

dient que si peut:[30] que tot soit il ensi con il dient que en l'assise est que nul ne peut fié acheter qui n'est chevalier, fiz de chevalier et de dame,[31] néz en leal mariage, ne se rapose[32] le 'nul' que a[33] home soulement, que par le 'nul' ne doit estre entendu n'en est[34] que a home, que ce ceaus qui firent l'assise vosissent et eussent establi que les femes ne peucent[35] fié acheter par l'assise il eussent clerement dit en l'assise que feme ne peut fié acheter,[36] si con il ont dit de plusors autres qui ne pevent fié acheter par l'assise, ou au mains dit[37] 'nul ne nule' ne peut fié de chevalier acheter que chevalier, fiz de chevalier et de dame,[38] nés en leal mariage. Mais[39] en nul endroit de l'assise[40] ne me senble qu'il[41] soit que feme ne puisse fié acheter par l'assise[42] por les raisons avant dites, por coy il me semble par les dites raisons que ele le peut bien acheter. Et por tant plus le me semble il qu'ele le peut bien acheter[43] par la dite assise, que[44] selonc se que je ay entendu et que il me semble raison que quant l'assise fu faite il y ot .iii. choses gardees especiaument: l'une le servise dou seignor; l'autre que les detes deussent estre[45] paiees de la vente dou fié se la vente s'estendoit[46] a tant ou a plus con la dete montoit[47] et s'ele[48] ne s'estendoit a[49] tant que les detours fucent paiés[50] par caroble; la tierce que celui de qui le fié estoit peust[51] avoir le plus qu'il porroit de la vente de son[52] fié por la chevance de lui et de ces heirs. Et se la dame veve, fille de chevalier et de dame, nee en leal mariage, met el fié qui se crie par l'assise plus que home qui puisse fié acheter, je di que toutes les .iii. avant dites choses y sont bien guardees et maintenues, que le servise dou seignor y[53] est premierement bien guardé et y a l'avantage et le[54] proufit dou seignor quar il la peut maintenant marier que ele avra[55] le fié acheté mais que il ne la desparage et peut metre a son servise qui qu'il[56] viaut selon la valor[57]

---

[30] peut] V: pevent [31] et de dame] BV lack [32] rapose] ABV: raporte [33] a] A: en; BV lack [34] n'en est] A: ni n'en est; V: ne il n'est [35] peucent] V: puissent [36] fié acheter par . . . acheter] A: fié acheter il l'eussent dit; B: acheter; V: fié acheter [37] dit] A: dit que; B: dire que [38] dame] C: dames [39] dit 'nul ne . . . Mais] V lacks [40] ABV adds: il [41] qu'il] C: qui [42] l'assise] B: les assises et [43] Et por tant . . . acheter] ABV lack [44] que] AB lack [45] deussent estre] A: fucent [46] s'estendoit] B lacks [47] montoit] B: monte; V: monteroit [48] s'ele] B: se la vente [49] ne s'estendoit a] V: n'estendoit [50] ou a plus . . . paiés] A: que les dettors peussent estre paiés ou se non [51] peust] V: peut [52] plus qu'il porroit . . . son] A: surplus de ce qui seriet de la vente dou [53] y] C lacks [54] et le] A: au; BV: et au [55] avra] B: a [56] qui qu'il] A: qui que; V: quaque il [57] la valor] B: l'avoir

dou fié ou avoir en deniers et[58] home asés covenable.[59] Et se .i. home met a[60] fié qui soit coneu a vil recreant coart, ou qu'il soit bosu, ou que il soit mahaigné d'aucun des menbres, ou yvroigne ou enteché d'aucun mauvaiz vice et vilain, mais que il soit fiz de chevalier et de dame nés en leal mariage, l'on ne le[61] peut pas contredire que il n'achate le fié de quey le seignor peut estre enpiré et amermé[62] de son servise. Si est[63] clere chose que le servise dou seignor y est bien sauvé et amendé se la dame[64] achete le fié par les raisons avant dites, et de tant con ele metra plus el fié que nul autre est le proufit de ceaus a qui le seignor dou fié doit por qui de ce[65] paier est le fié vendu ou dou seignor dou fié. Si me semble que toutes les .iii. avant dites choses[66] y sont bien guardees et maintenues.

Et se aucun dit que feme ne peut fié deservir por coy ele ne le peut acheter,[67] je di que si peut. Que sovent est avenu et avient que fié qui doit servise de cors et[68] eschiet[69] a feme et que ele le desert par .i. chevalier tant que il plaise au seignor de marier la, et lors ele le desert par[70] le mariage[71] que ele doit au seignor, et quant ele est mariee par le seignor son baron le[72] desert le fié por li[73] et en fait au seignor[74] tout[75] quanque le fié doit. Si est[76] chose certaine que feme peut bien deservir fié, et puis que ele le peut deservir[77] donc ne doit mie por ce remanoir[78] que la dame veve fille de chevalier et de dame nee en leal mariage ne puisse fié acheter par l'asisse que ausi le peut ele deservir con cele a qui il eschiet. Et puis[79] que a la feme n'est en nul endroit[80] de l'assise contredit que ele n'i[81] puisse fié acheter, et que feme peut fié deservir, et que les .iii. avant dites choses[82] sont bien gardees et sauvees se la dite dame achate le fié, je di que la dame veve fille de chevalier et de dame nee en leal mariage peut bien fié de chevalier acheter par l'assise ou l'usage dou dit reiaume.[83]

---

[58] et] B: ou [59] home asés covenable] A: homes assés covenables [60] met a] A: achate le; B: a; V: qui a [61] le] ABO: li [62] amermé] B: amermer [63] A adds: donc [64] se la dame] A: de la dame se elle [65] de ce] AV: dette; B: dete [66] choses] V: raisons [67] C adds: et [68] et] ABV lack [69] eschiet] C: eschiest [70] .i. chevalier tant . . . par] ABV lack [71] A adds: se elle est a marier [72] le] A: qui; V lacks [73] li] C: lui [74] son baron le . . . seignor] B lacks [75] tout] ABV lack [76] C adds: clere [77] fié, et puis . . . deservir] C lacks; V: et puis que elle le peut servir [78] por ce remanoir] C: remanoir por ce [79] puis] A: puisse [80] endroit] A: leuc [81] ni] ABV: ne [82] AV adds: y; B: i [83] dit reiaume] AB: reiaume (B: reaume) de Jerusalem

Et toutes manieres de gens pevent bien fié de sergent acheter par l'assise ou l'usage dou royaume de Jerusalem,[84] mais q'il soient tes[85] que il aient vois et respons en court et qu'il puisse[86] faire ce que le fié doit d'omage et de servise, mais que ceaus qui ne pevent fié acheter et chevaliers et dames veves.[87]

[84] Et toutes manieres . . . Jerusalem] A: Et toz homes fiz de chevalier et de dame né en leau mariage peut bien fié de chevalier acheter; B lacks [85] tes] C: ces [86] qu'il puisse] B: que eles puissent [87] mais que ceaus . . . veves] A: mais a ciaus qui ne pevent fié acheter n'est mie la dame veve; B lacks; V: mais que ceaus qui ne pevent fié acheter de chevalier et de dame veve

***[170]** Que on doit faire de celui ou de cele de qui le[1] fié a[2] esté vendu, se la dete que il ou ele[3] a coneue[4] ou qu'on[5] li a[6] provee[7] en court est[8] plus que la vente dou fié.

Se chevalier ou dame qui a fié[9] doit dete et il la conoist[10] en court, ou se il[11] la noie et on la[12] li preuve en court si con l'on doit, et son fié est vendu por la dite[13] dete paier en aucune des manieres avant[14] dites el chapitle qui[15] parle de la vente des fiés,[16] [a] et[17] la vente de son[18] fié[19] ne peut parpaier[20] la dite dete, et que ceaus a qui il doit soient paiés par carobles as chascun son avenant, por tant n'est[21] il ou ele[22] quite de ce qu'il[23] remaint a payer de cele dete. Et[24] por ce que il[25] a une propre assise que chevalier ne dame ne doit estre aresté por[26] dete quelqu'ele soit, ne doit[27] mie le seignor faire arester[28] chevalier ne dame[29] por leur dete qui demore a paier de la vente de[30] son[31] fié ne por autre dete que il ne ele doive.[32]

Mais se home ou feme autre que chevalier ou dame ait fié et il ou ele doit[33] dete et la conoisse[34] en[35] court ou ele li est provee[36] en court[37] se il la noie et son fié en[38] est vendu en aucune des dites manieres avant dites,[39] et[40] la vente de son fié n'est tant con la dete, et les gens a qui celui ou cele de qui le fié est vendu[41] sont paiés de la vente[42] dou fié de lor detes[43] par carobles, et ce[44] celui ou cele qui doit la dete ne fait le gré de ceaus a qui il doit de ce qui[45] leur

---

A: fols cxix^{r}–cxx^{r} cap. 188; **B:** fols 148^{r}–149^{r} cap. 189; **C:** fols 151^{r}–152^{r} cap. 170; **O:** fols 204^{r}–206^{r}; **V:** fols clx^{v}–clxi^{v} cap. 198; Beugnot, pp. 300–1, cap. 188.

---

[a] Above cap. 168.

---

[1] le] B: son [2] a] BV: avra [3] ou ele] B lacks [4] coneue] AC: coneu [5] qu'on] A rubric (fol. 8^{r}) BV: que l'on [6] a] B rubric (fol. 24^{r}) V: avra [7] provee] C: prové [8] est] B: monte [9] C adds: et [10] conoist] A: conut [11] se il] B lacks [12] on la] A: l'on la; B: on; V: l'on [13] dite] B lacks [14] avant] A: qui sont; O: devant; V lacks [15] qui] AV: lequel [16] des fiés] B: dou fié [17] A adds: que; B: se [18] de son] ABV: dou [19] C adds: .i. [20] parpaier] ABV: parfaire [21] A adds: mie [22] il ou ele] B: celui ou cele [23] qu'il] BV: qui [24] Et] BV lack [25] ABV add: y [26] V adds: nulle [27] estre aresté por . . . doit] A lacks [28] C adds: ne [29] chevalier ne dame] A lacks [30] la vente de] B lacks [31] son] A: leur [32] ne ele doive] A: deivent; B: ou ele doient; V: ou elle doivent [33] doit] B: ait [34] conoisse] ABV: conoist [35] BV add: la [36] ele li est provee] B: l'en la li prouve [37] en court] A lacks [38] en] CV lack [39] dites manieres avant dites] AB: avant dittes (B: ditez) manieres [40] et] A: si que; V: de [41] vendu] O lacks [42] de la vente] B lacks [43] sont paiés de . . . detes] A: ne sont paiés de la vente dou fié de leur dettes que [44] ce] AB lack [45] qui] OV: que il

demore a paier, et celui ou ceaus a qui il doit cele dete requiert[46] au seignor[47] que il les en face paier ou[48] faire leur gré ou que il lor face ce qu'il doit par l'assise ou l'usage dou reiaume de Jerusalem, le seignor lor[49] doit respondre que il lor[50] fera ce que la court conoistra que il faire lor[51] doie, et lors il[52] doit comander a sa court que ele li conoisse que il lor en a a faire. Et quant le seignor comande[53] a la court de faire la dite conoissance, ele la doit faire. Et[54] ensi se m'est avis que la court doit conoistre que le seignor doit comander a celui ou a cele de qui le fié a esté vendu que il paie cele dete ou que il face le gré de ceaus a qui il doit ou que il les face seurs covenablement de paier lor cele dete dedens .i. terme resnable,[55] et que se il lors[56] les dites choses ne fait que le seignor le doit faire garder en prisone[57] tant que lui ou autre por lui l'ait fait ou que il le livre a ceaus a qui il doit[58] si con l'on doit[59] par l'assise prisoner qui doit dete que il ne peut paier ne faire le gré de ceaus a qui il[60] doit. Et a moy senble que en tel cas seroit la seurté de la[61] dete payer covenablement[62] et le terme resnable,[63] se il lor donoit pleges de cele dete as us et as costumes[64] ou gagiere[65] que aucun de ces amis li prestast d'avoir les paiés dedens .i. an. et .i. jor. Et la raison por coy il[66] me senble que la[67] court doit faire la dite[68] conoissance en la maniere avant devisee[69] si est tel, que il y a une propre assise que le seignor peut arester por dete home ou feme qui n'est chevalier ou[70] dame ou a[71] qui il n'est tenus de foy, et que il y a une[72] autre assise que quant home est aresté por dete que il ne puisse paier et[73] celui ou ceaus a qui il doit et que il ne paie[74] requierent au seignor que il lor livre par l'assise celui qui lor[75] doit la dete, que[76] le seignor lor doit livrer et que il le peuvent tenir en fers se

[46] requiert] B: requierent [47] de ce qui . . . seignor] A: la dette et il requierent au seignor celui ou ciaus a qui il deit la dette [48] A adds: face [49] par l'assise ou . . . lor] B: il [50] lor] AV: lor en; B lacks [51] que il faire lor] AB: qu'il faire lor (B: leur) en; V: que faire en [52] il] ABV lack [53] comande] A: a comandé [54] la doit faire. Et] BV: li doit faire [55] resnable] B: couvenable; V: covenable [56] lors] C: lor [57] prisone] O: persone [58] A adds: la dette [59] AB add: livrer [60] AB add: la [61] V adds: dite [62] payer covenablement] BV: couvenable [63] de la dete . . . resnable] A: raisnable de la ditte dette et le terme covenable [64] et as costumes] A: ou a costumes dou reiaume [65] gagiere] B: plegerie; C: guagier; V: a gagere [66] AB add: le [67] la] C: le fié [68] dite] A lacks [69] devisee] A: ditte; V: dite [70] ou] O: ne [71] ou a] AV: a; B: et [72] une] C: un [73] puisse paier et] B: puet paier et que [74] et que il ne paie] A: la dette qu'il ne peut paier; B lacks; V: et ne peut paier [75] livre par l'assise celui qui lor] C lacks [76] que] A lacks; V: et

il ne les paie ou en prison toute sa vie et doner[77] li a manger et a boivre[78] soufisaument a sa vie sostenir[79] pain et aigue et robe a vestir si que il ne muire de froit par defaute de[80] robe, et se il le fait[81] laborer que son labor soit conté au feur corsable des laborans[82] qui laborent[83] de tel labor con l'on le fera[84] labourer et abatre de sa dete se que il deservira de son labor. Et que[85] puis que les dites assisses sont teles con est avant dit et celui ou cele qui doit la dete qui n'est chevalier ne dame ne[86] le seignor n'est tenus a lui[87] de foy par les raisons qui sont devisees el chapitle ou il devise coment et par quel raison le seignor est quite de sa foy vers ceaus et vers celes de qui les fiés sont vendus en aucune des avant dites[88] manieres qui devant sont devisees coment et por coy l'on[89] doit fié vendre, me semble il que il doive[90] enssi estre con je ay devant dit.[b]

[b] Above cap. 168.

[77] et doner] ABV: donant [78] C adds: toutse sa vie [79] A adds: au meins [80] par defaute de] B: pour defaute et [81] fait] ABV: font [82] laborans] A: laborors [83] laborent] C: laborant [84] con l'on le fera] A: come il le feront; B: come l'en li fera; V: que li fera [85] que] ABV lack [86] et celui ou . . . ne] A: ce celui ou celle qui deit la dette n'est chevalier ou dame ne; B: a celui ou a cele qui doit la dete se il n'est chevalier ou dame; V: se celui ou celle qui doit la dette n'est chevalier ne dame a qui [87] n'est tenus a lui] AB: ne lor (B: li) est tenus; V: li est tenus [88] avant dites] V lacks [89] l'on] ABV: l'on peut (B: puet) et; C lacks [90] doive] A: deit

***[171]** Sur lesqués des fiés des homes dou seignor son prevelige ne peut[1] ne[2] doit porter guarentie qui soit valable, et sur lesqués des fiés des homes le prevelige de lor seignor[3] leur[4] peut porter garentie con vos avez oy.[5]

Prevelige dou chief seignor ne peut ne ne doit valoir a porter guarentie sur le fié de ces[6] homes, c'est assavoir de ceaus qui ont court et coins[7] et qui pevent faire prevelige donatif, se le donatif do seignor en cui seignorie ce est de quey le prevelige dou[8] seignor parole n'est aveué,[9] ou que celui qui[10] requiert puisse prover qu'il eust la saisine et la teneure en pays en[11] tens de quey le previlige parole. Et c'il cele saisine ne peut prover, por ce que toute[12] la gent de cel tens soient mors, et il puisse prover la saisine et la teneure[13] longue en pais et sans chalonge en tens des seignors[14] de cel leu, ensi li porroit valoir le prevelige dou[15] chief seignor sans le donatif dou seignor de qui on tendroit cel[16] fié, et autrement non. Que se le prevelige dou chief seignor[17] peut de tout en tout guarentie porter[18] et avoir force sur les fiés des seignors de ces homes qui ont dou don dou seignor les seignories qui ont[19] court et coins,[20] et enssi ne lor avroit il riens doné ne nule seignorie n'en avroit,[21] se les seignors par les seignories[22] par leur provelige[23] pevent[24] sur les seignories[25] de lor homes sans le[26] leur proveliges doner fiés ou guarentir que il les eussent[27] donés.[28] Et s'ensi n'estoit,[29] por neent lor avroient[30] il donés ne court ne coins, et[31] se les homes qui ont court et coins doivent[32] a[33] aucune persone aucune[34] chose ou fié, bien[35] devroient[36] requerre

---

A: fol. cxx^{r-v} cap. 189; **B:** fol. 149^{r-v} cap. 190; **C:** fols 152^{r}–153^{r} cap. 171; **O:** fols 206^{r}–207^{v}; **V:** fols clxi^{v}–clxii^{v} cap. 199; Beugnot, pp. 302–3, cap. 189.

---

[1] A adds: ni; BV: ne [2] peut ne] O lacks [3] le prevelige de lor seignor] B rubrics (fol. 24^{r}): dou seignor son privilege [4] leur] ABV lack [5] con vos avez oy] AV lack; B: qui soit vaillage (B rubrics: vaillable) [6] ces] C: lor [7] et coins] ABV lack [8] ABV add: chief [9] aveué] A: ausé; B: aucé [10] AV adds: li; B: le [11] en] AB: ou [12] toute] C: toutes [13] en pays en . . . teneure] V lacks [14] des seignors] ABV: dou seignor [15] dou] C: del [16] cel] A: le [17] sans le donatif . . . seignor] O lacks [18] guarentie porter] B: garantir; V: guarentir [19] dou don dou . . . ont] AV lack [20] A adds: et justise [21] n'en avroit] AB: ne vaudroit; V: n'en avroient [22] par les seignories] AB lack [23] provelige] AOV: preveliges [24] pevent] V: puissent [25] seignories] A: seignors [26] le] ABV lack; O: les [27] eussent] A: peussent [28] donés] A: doner [29] n'estoit] A: esteit; B: estoit [30] avroient] ABV: avroit [31] et] ABV lack [32] doivent] AV: donoient; BO: devoient [33] a] C lacks [34] aucune] O lacks [35] bien] C: li en [36] devroient] O: devoient

et avoir celui a qui le fié est doné de celui qui le don li avroit fait prevelige, que sans son[37] prevelige ou le recort de sa court ne devroit estre ne est[38] estable vers ces heirs que il deist que il li eust donee.[39]

Mais les preveliges des seignor portent[40] et doivent porter force de guarentie des[41] dons des fiés et des[42] autres covenances que les homes font de lor fiés, ce est assavoir de ceaus qui n'ont court ne coins. Car bien senble[43] raison que toutes manieres de dons des[44] fiés et d'autres choses que l'on viaut faire estable,[45] que l'on les doit faire en court por avoir le recort de la court. Et por ce que la memoire des[46] gens est[47] escoloriant, et que chascun n'est pas bien menbrant des lointaines choses, et que les gens sont mortels et durent petit et[48] en cest tens,[49] fait on des dons et[50] des autres covenances des[51] fiés preveliges por estre en leuc de recort de court, et ceaus qui n'ont court ne coins et doivent[52] aucune chose de lor fiés, soit en fié ou en[53] aucune autre maniere, il les[54] doivent[55] faire en la court dou seignor de qui il tienent[56] cel fié, et le prevelige qui en sera fait doit estre coignés des coins[57] dou seignor de qui celui tient le[58] fié de quey il done partie[59] por partie dou[60] servise si con il doit par l'assise. Et ce celui de qui il tient cel[61] fié n'a court ne coins et que il le teigne d'autre, le prevelige doit estre coingné des coins dou chief seignor del fié qui a court et coins en quey[62] il guarantise le don que son home a fait en sa court et l'otroye et conferme por ce[63] que celui qui[64] fait le don ou le covenant n'a court ne coins,[65] et puis que il ne les a ne son seignor meaus est estable se qui sera fait par la court ou par prevelige dou chief seignor de cel fié que par autre chose, por ce que il tient cel fié dou seignor et que le seignor est tenus a lui de foy con a son home et les homes de cele court li sont tenus con a lor[66] per.

---

[37] son] AB lack [38] ne est] AB lacks; V: ne n'en est [39] donee] ABV: doné [40] portent] AV: pevent; B: pueent [41] des] A: le; V: les [42] fiés et des] ABV lack [43] senble] V: resemble [44] des] A: de; B: et [45] C adds: que l'on viaut et doit faire estable [46] des] C: de [47] est] O lacks [48] et] AB lack [49] en cest tens] V: pour ce [50] et] V: ou [51] des] C: de [52] doivent] AO: donent; V: donent autre [53] fié ou en] C: fiés ou; O lacks [54] les] ABV: le [55] doivent] C: doit [56] tienent] V: tient [57] coignés des coins] A: coignié dou coin [58] le] O: cel [59] partie] AV: partie de son fié; B: partiere son fié [60] dou] ABV: de son [61] cel] BV: le [62] en quey] ABV: ou que [63] por ce] A: puis; BV lack [64] V adds: a [65] A adds: ne son seignor [66] a lor] B: deu

***[172]** Por quantes choses et por ques l'on peut et doit[1] estre desherités, lui et ces heirs.

Se sont les choses de quey il me sovient ore par coy on peut et doit par l'assise ou l'usage dou reiaume de Jerusalem estre desherités lui et ses heirs: qui est herege; qui se renoye; qui met main sur le cors de son seignor; qui vient a armes contre son seignor en champ; qui rent sans le congé de son seignor sa cité ou son chastiau[2] [a] ou sa forterece a son henemi tant con il ait a boivre et[3] a manger tant ne quant; qui trait son seignor et livre[4] a ces henemis; qui porchace la mort et le desheritement de son seignor et est de ce ataint et[5] provó; qui ne[6] vent son fié par l'assise; qui est apelé de trayson et vencu en chanp[7] ou defaillant de venir soy defendre en la court de son seignor de la traïson que l'on li met sus, se il[8] est semons si con il doit.

A: fol. cxx^v^ cap. 190; **B:** fols 149^v^–150^r^ cap. 191; **C:** fol. 153^r^ cap. 172; **O:** fols 207^v^–208^r^; **V:** fols clxii^v^–clxiii^r^ cap. 200; Beugnot, pp. 303–5, cap. 190.

[a] A clear instance where the reading of ABV is to be preferred to CO.

[1] et doit] AB lack [2] chastiau] CO: cheval [3] ait a boivre et] V: a a boire ne [4] livre] C: livrer; V: le livre [5] et] A: ou [6] ne] ABV lack [7] chanp] B: court [8] AB add: en

***[173]** Par quantes choses[1] l'on peut et doit estre desherités de son fié[2] sa vie, et por quel chose[3] on le pert an et jor.

Se sont les choses que[4] il me semble por coy l'on peut et doit[5] estre desherités sa vie. Se .i. home tient .i. fié dou[6] seignor de coy[7] il li doive[8] homage et il ne le fait ou[9] ne l'eufre a faire si com il doit dedens .i. an. et .i. jor. Mais ceaus qui doivent homage a baill et il[10] ne le font dedens l'an et le jor ou ne li eufrent a faire si con il doivent, il perdront leur fiés[11] tant con[12] celui baill tendra le[13] baillage se il en veaut avoir droit par sa court.[14] Et se .i. home fait murtre ou homecide et il est semons par court de venir faire droit et il ne[15] vient au jor de la semonce, se il n'a[16] esoigne tel por coy il ne peust[17] venir et ne la contremande si con il doit, il est encheu en la merci dou seignor con ataint de cel clain[18] et pert le fié[19] sa vie, se le seignor viaut. Et qui est ataint de force, il est en la merci dou seignor et pert le fié sa vie, se le seignor veut.[20] Et qui est ataint de foy mentie vers son seignor, il pert son fié[21] sa vie, se le seignor viaut con celui qui est encheu en la merci dou seignor[22] dou cors et dou[23] fié et de tout[24] quanqu'il a, mais ces heirs ne doivent mie estre desherités por estre ataint de foy mentie, se il n'est en la foy mentie[25] ataint de trayson. Et se le seignor semont ou fait semondre aucun de ces homes dou servise que il li doit que il[26] aille o lui por conbatre soy a ces henemis qui sont entrés en sa terre ou por defendre que il n'i entrent ou por entrer o lui[27] en une forterece qui est assegee[28] ou doit estre asegee de ces henemis ou por desasager la contre yaus[29] et il n'i vait,[30] se il n'a esoigne aparrant et qu'il la[31]

A: fols cxx^{v}–cxxi^{r} cap. 191; **B:** fol. 150^{r-v} cap. 192; **C:** fols 153^{r}–154^{r} cap. 173; **O:** fols 208^{r}–209^{r}; **V:** fol. clxiii^{r-v} cap. 201; Beugnot, pp. 305–6, cap. 191.

---

[1] choses] V: raisons [2] V adds: toute [3] quel chose] A: quelles choses [4] que] B: dont; V: pour quoi [5] et doit] B lacks [6] .i. fié dou] B: fié de [7] de coy] A: dou quel; V: de qui [8] doive] A: deit [9] ou] C lacks [10] il] ABV lack [11] leur fiés] B: lor fié [12] con] O lacks [13] le] V: celui [14] sa court] A: l'assise; BV: la court; C: 'l'assise' altered to read 'sa court' [15] ne] AB: n'i [16] n'a] A: eu [17] tel por coy il ne peust] B: pour quoi il ne puisse [18] con ataint de cel clain] ABV lack [19] V adds: toute [20] Et qui est . . . veut] ABV lack [21] son fié] V: le fié toute [22] la merci dou seignor] B: sa merci [23] dou cors et dou] ABV: de cors et de [24] tout] BV lacks [25] en la foy mentie] B: o la mentie [26] A adds: y [27] o lui] ABV lack [28] assegee] C: assagee [29] desasager contre yaus] A: desassigier la contre ciaus; B: desaangier la contree de ceaus; V: desaseger la contre ceaus [30] vait] B: va [31] la] V: l'ait

contremande a hore et a tens si que[32] court conoisse que il peut por ce[33] demorer, ou se il meut ou[34] son seignor et il le laissa[35] alant ou[36] demorant en .i. des fais devant[37] dis, se ce n'est par esoigne qui li aveigne el chemin[38] tel qu'il puisse et doive demorer par esgart ou par conoissance de la court de son seignor, il pert le fié sa vie, se le seignor en viaut avoir droit par sa court, se il n'est demoré de la semonce ou parti par[39] le seignor. Et de toutes autres manieres de choses de quey l'on est ataint de foy mentie pert l'on son fié sa vie, se le seignor vers qui l'on a sa foy mentie[40] en viaut avoir droit par sa court.[41]

Et de toutes autres dou[42] defaut dou servise pert l'on[43] son fié an et jor[44] sans plus par esgart ou par conoissance de court aprés ce que le seignor c'est de lui clamés et l'en a[45] ataint si com il[46] doit.

---

[32] que] A: come [33] peut por ce] V: pour ce puisse [34] meut ou] B: vient avec [35] laissa] A: laist; BV: laisse [36] ou] C: et [37] devant] C: avant [38] el chemin] V: au chemin et [39] par] C lacks [40] pert l'on son . . . mentie] V: se le seignor [41] pert l'on son . . . court] A: et le seignor en viaut aveir dreit par sa court celui qui a sa fei mentie pert son fié a sa vie [42] dou] A lacks; B: faiz. De [43] l'on] AB: l'ome [44] an et jor] ABV: un an et un jour (A: jor) [45] l'en a] A: l'on l'a; B: l'en; V: l'on a [46] il] A: l'on

***[174]** Quant .i.[1] home est forsjugé[2] par court con traytor por traïson[3] que il a[4] faite vers son seignor, coment et por quey ces heirs doivent estre desherités dou[5] fié et[6] des fiés dou traytor.

Se .i. home ou plusors ont fait trayson vers le[7] seignor et il sont forsjugés par esgart ou par conoissance de court come traytors, a moy senble que ceaus[8] et tous les[9] heirs de celui ou de ceaus qui sont ensi forjugés sont desheritez dou fié et de l'eritage qui estoit do forsjugé,[10] ains que il feyst la[11] trayson, et ausi des heirs qui estoient[12] nés ains qu'il feist[13] cele traïson[14] con ceaus qui puis furent[15] nés, et ausi tos ses[16] heirs costiers con ces heirs descendus[17] de lui. Et la raison por quoi il le me senble[18] est[19] que l'on dit[20] par l'assise ou l'usage dou reyaume de Jeruzalem peut l'on son[21] fié perdre en trois manieres: l'un,[22] an et jor; et[23] l'autre, toute sa vie;[24] la tierce, lui et ces heirs. Por le defaut dou[25] servise le pert on an et jor. Por defaut d'omage et por les[26] choses qui sont devant[27] devisees[28] en l'autre chapitle[29] le pert on toute sa vie. Et[30] por estre traïtre[31] vers son seignor et por aucunes des autres[32] choses qui sont avant[33] dites en l'autre chapitle le pert l'on[34] et ces heirs a tous jors.[a]

Ne il n'est mie en l'assise ne en l'usage quant il dit que le traïtor et ces heirs doivent estre desherités que ceaus heirs[35] qui sont engendrés et[36] naistront puis la trayson soyent[37] deserités sans plus ou ceaus qui de lui descendirent[38] ou sont descendus sans plus[39] et que les

---

A: fols cxxi^r^–cxxiii^r^ cap. 192; **B:** fols 150^v^–152^v^ cap. 193; **C:** fols 154^r^–156^v^ cap. 174; **O:** fols 209^r^–213^r^; **V:** fols clxiii^v^–clxvi^v^ caps 202–3; Beugnot, pp. 307–10, cap. 192.

---

[a] Above caps 172–3.

---

[1] .i.] C: aucun [2] forsjugé] C: jugé [3] por traïson] B: par raison [4] a] BV: ait [5] dou] V: de son [6] et] A: ou [7] le] A: leur [8] ceaus] AV: eaus; B: il [9] les] B: leur [10] do forsjugé] V: des forjugiés [11] la] C: cele [12] estoient] AV: ont esté; B: furent [13] feist] V: feissent [14] traïson] B: raison [15] puis furent] B: furent; V: y furent puis [16] ses] BV: les [17] descendus] A: dessendans; B: descendanz; V: desendans [18] le me senble] V: me semble que il [19] B adds: tele [20] A adds: que [21] son] ABV lack [22] l'un] AB: l'une; V: l'une ci est [23] et] ABV lack [24] toute sa vie] C: sa vie toute [25] dou] AV: de [26] B adds: autres [27] devant] BV lack [28] devisees] A: dittes; O: dites seés [29] B adds: desus escrit [30] Et] ABV lack [31] traïtre] A: traïtor; BV: traïtour [32] autres] AB lack [33] avant] B lacks [34] ABV add: lui [35] heirs] ABV lack [36] et] B: qui [37] soyent] ABV: sont [38] descendirent] A: dessenderont; V: desendront [39] ou ceaus qui . . . plus] B lacks

heirs qui devant se que il fist[40] la trayson[41] furent nés ne furent mie desherités ne les heirs costiers; ne par l'assise ou[42] l'usage dou dit reyaume[43] nul des heirs dou traïtor forjugés n'est excepté d'estre desherités. Ains en est l'assise ou l'usage tel que le traïtor et ces heirs doivent estre a touz jors desherités dou fié et de l'eritage que il tenoit dou seignor avant que il feist la trayson contre lui. Por quey il est clere chose, se me senble, que touz les heirs dou traytor[44] doyvent estre[45] desherités de tout quanque il tient[46] dou seignor vers qui il a faite la trayson et de quey il est forsjugié con traïtor par esgart ou par conoissance de la[47] court dou seignor.[48]

Et por tant plus me senble il que les heirs dou traytor forsjugié doivent estre desherités si con je ay devant dit, que il est assise[49] ou usage el royaume de Jerusalem et de Cypre que nul ne peut requerre ne avoir escheete que il dit[50] qui li soit escheue que de par celui ou cele qui derainement en ot la saisine et la teneure con de son droit heritage, se le seignor ou celui qui la tient la[51] viaut defendre. Et bien est rayson que ensi doive[52] estre, car s'ensi n'estoit[53] que on[54] peust avoir et eust escheete que on[55] requeroit[56] de par autre que de par le derrain[57] saisi et tenant con de son droit, les ventes des fiés[58] ne vaudroient riens que les heirs dou conquereor le[59] requeroient[60] le fié de par le conquereor dou fié ou de par aucun des autres qui l'avroient eu et tenu ains que de celui qui l'avroit vendu par l'assise,[61] puis que l'on porroit requerre et avoir escheete de par autre que de par le derain saisi,[62] ne les enfans de l'ainsné fiz dou conquereor n'entreroient[63] pas el fié dou conquereor devant les autres enfans dou conquereor[64] aprés son decés[65] saisi et tenant con de c'escheete[66] qui li seroit escheu con a droit heir dou conquereor et l'avroit tenu tant con il avroit vescu et en seroit mort saisi et tenant con de son droit, car son frere ou sa seur seroit plus dreit heir et plus prochein

[40] fist] AB: feist [41] fist la trayson] C: la trayson fist [42] ne par l'assise ou] A: ainz est en l'assise ou en [43] A adds: que [44] dou traytor] V: de traytours [45] B adds: esté [46] tient] AV: tienent; B: tenoit [47] C adds: haute [48] la court dou seignor] B: court [49] est assise] C: assise est [50] que il dit] V lacks [51] la tient la] B: le tient le; V: la tient le [52] doive] A: deit; V: doit [53] n'estoit] B: estoit [54] on] AB: l'on; V: l'om [55] on] AB: l'on [56] requeroit] AV: requiert [57] le derrain] B: celui qui daesrainement en morut [58] des fiés] B lacks; V: dou fié [59] le] AV: li; B lacks [60] requeroient] V: requeroie [61] par aucun des . . . l'assise] ABV lack [62] ABV add: et tenant [63] n'entreroient] C: n'en tenroient V: ne terroient [64] B adds: tout eust est l'ainsné fiz dou conquereour; OV: tout (O: tout en) eust il esté l'aisné fiz dou conquereor [65] A adds: qui seroient [66] de c'escheete] ABV: d'escheete

dou conquereor qui en avroit esté[67] premier[68] saisi et tenant con de son droit que le fiz de son ainsné fis ne seroit[69] que nevou dou conquereor dou fié qui avroit esté premier saisi et tenant con de son droit[70] et ensi perdroit le fiz de l'ainsné fiz dou conquereor le droit que il avroit aquis dou conquereor de par son pere a qui le fié eschey[71] con a droit heir dou conquereor qui en morut saisi et tenant derainement con de son droit, laquel chose seroit tort apert et contre l'assise de cest reyaume. Car il est assise ou usage en cest roiaume que quant .i. home ou une feme qui a fié[72] meurt et il y a plusors heirs[73] qui requierent c'escheete[74] de cel fié, que[75] le plus prochain de ces heirs requerant de cele part dont cel fié li est venu[76] l'a devant tous ces[77] autres[78] heirs. Et s'ensi n'estoit que[79] la requeste que on feroit[80] vausist[81] a requerre la de par le premier saisi et tenant con de son droit, donc[82] avroit le frere ou la seur de l'ainsné fiz[83] dou conquereor[84] le fié devant les[85] fiz de l'ainsné fiz dou conquereor,[86] tout fust le fié dou conquereor escheu[87] a son pere con a l'ainsné fiz dou conquereor et son droit heir, et il[88] en eust esté en saisine et en teneure toute sa vie jusques a sa mort. Car le fiz ou la fille dou conquereor dou fié seroient[89] plus prochain de celui qui premier en avroient[90] esté saisi et tenant dou fié que le fiz de son ainsné[91] fiz,[92] et ensi perdroit le fiz de l'ainsné fiz dou conquereor dou fié[93] son droit et c'escheete, laquel chose seroit tort apert et contre l'assise ou l'usage,[94] qui est tel que, quant home ou feme meurt saisi et tenant d'un fié ou d'un heritage come[95] son droit, que son fiz ou sa fille demore en tel saisine et en tel teneure con son pere ou sa mere avoit quant il[96] morut. Et por les raisons avant dites et por ce que l'on ne peut par l'assise ou l'usage de cest reyaume requerre et[97] avoir escheete qui ne la requiert de par celui ou cele qui derainement en morut saisi et tenant con de son droit,[98] a l'on veu et voit[99]

[67] en avroit esté] C: esté en avroit [68] premier] AB lack [69] V adds: qui ne seroit [70] que le fiz . . . droit] ABO lack [71] eschey] A: escheit [72] C adds: et [73] heirs] B: requeranz [74] c'escheete] ABV: l'escheete [75] que] BV: come [76] cel fié li est venu] A: le fié muet; B: cel fié muet; V: le fié meut et [77] ces] ABV: les [78] autres] C lacks [79] que] ABV lack [80] AB adds: de s'escheete; V: d'escheete [81] vausist] A: vaudreit; B: vaudroit [82] donc] A: dont si; BV: dont [83] fiz] C: ne fiz de l'ainsné [84] conquereor] B: requereour [85] les] BV: le [86] devant les fiz . . . conquereor] A lacks [87] escheu] A lacks [88] heir, et il] B lacks [89] seroient] ABV: seroit [90] avroient] ABV: avroit [91] ainsné] B: premier [92] de son ainsné fiz] V: de l'ainsné fis dou conquereor dou fié [93] dou fié] B lacks [94] A adds: de cest reiaume [95] AB adds: de [96] C adds: en [97] et] A: ne [98] V adds: et souvent [99] B adds: on; V: l'on

toz jors avenir que, quant le conquereor dou fié meurt saisi et tenant dou fié que il a conquis, que son ainsné fiz a son fié[100] devant touz les autres heirs con celui qui en demore en la saisine et en la teneure de son pere, et que se il y entre et[101] use con de[102] c'escheete et[103] il ne fait chose par coy lui et ses heirs en puissent estre desheritez par assise ou par usage ou par raison, que ces enfans eritent en cel fié devant toutes autres manieres de gens con ceaus qui[104] demorent en tel saisine et en tel teneure con lor[105] pere estoit. Et par les raisons avant[106] dites et par plusors autres que on y poroit dire, est il clere[107] a conoistre que l'on doit requerre l'escheete de son fié que l'on dit[108] qui li est escheu de par le derain[109] saisi et tenant et usant con de son droit et non de par autre, et qui de par autre[110] le requiert que[111] le seignor ne autre qui le fié teigne ne li est tenu de respondre. Et par les[112] avant dites raisons est il cler a conoistre que l'eir d'un[113] traïtor ne peut par raison requerre le fié do traïtor forsjugé que de par celuy qui derainement en fu[114] saisi et tenant et usant con dou sien. Et puis que il de par autre ne le peut requerre, donc est il clere chose que il ne le peut avoir, puis que il[115] et ces heirs en sont desherités par esgart ou par conoissance de court.

Et[116] se .i. comun a en la seignorie dou seignor faite franchise ou court ou rente ou casal ou heritages[117] ou quelque posesion que se soit et il l'ait[118] eue de don ou autrement, et cel comun est traïtor vers le[119] seignor de cele seignorie, ou il li guerroient[120] aparaument et par comun[121] prenent ou assaillent le cors dou seignor ou[122] aucune soue forterece ou sont contre lui a armes[123] par comun, il perdent[124] a touz jors perpetuelment par l'usage ou l'assise dou reiaume de Jerusalem et par droit escrit[125] tout quanqu'il ont des choses devant dites en la seignorie de celui seignor en une des manieres avant[126] dites. Et puis que le comun qui n'est tenu de foy au seignor le pert par les dites choses[127] a touz jors si que aucun de cel comun n'i peut[128] jamais recovrer par droit et par raison, meaus doivent tous

---

[100] son fié] V lacks [101] AB add: en [102] V adds: son droit et [103] et] A: ce; B lacks [104] ABV adds: en [105] lor] ABV: le [106] avant] B: devant [107] B adds: chose [108] dit] C: doit [109] derain] C: derains [110] et qui de par autre] BC lack [111] que] A lacks [112] V adds: autres [113] d'un] ABV: dou [114] fu] AB: morut [115] il de par . . . il] A: lui [116] Et] A: Car [117] heritages] A: irritage; B: heritage [118] l'ait] B: l'a; V: ait [119] le] B: son [120] guerroient] C: requeroient; O: querroient; V: requierrent [121] et par comun] A: par comun ou [122] ou] B: en [123] V adds: contre lui [124] perdent] A: perderont; BV: perdront [125] escrit] B: estroit [126] avant] V: devant [127] par les dites choses] B lacks [128] peut] A: pevent

les heirs de l'ome dou seignor qui li est tenus de foy[129] et que lui ou ces ancestres orent le fié que il tient de don dou[130] seignor estre desherités[131] quant il est traytor vers celui[132] et forsjugié par esgart[133] de court,[134] que le comun n'en est qui n'est[135] mie tenu de foy au seignor.[b]

Et el coude de l'enperere Justignien,[136] qui est .i. des meillors livres de lais des enpereors qu'il firent ancienement et establisement[137] que il vostrent qu'il[138] fucent tenus par le monde, et que cel livre fu des autres livres des leys concuillis et amendés et fait par grant sen et par grant estuide, estuidit[139] et devise[140] que les heirs des traytors[141] doivent molt plus grief[142] peine soufrir que estre desherités del fié del traytor et[143] forjugé. Et se que l'enperere Achades[144] en dist[145] trova[146] l'on qui quere le voudroit[147] el noveime[148] livre dou code en la loy qui[149] est apelee la loy Julie.[150] Et je cuit qu'il dist en celle loy que le traytor devroit[151] morir de mort hontouse et que tous les biens doivent venir a l'enpereor.[c]

Et plusors autres raysons y a[152] por coy l'on doit entendre que les heirs dou traytor[153] sont et doivent estre desherités de tous ces biens. Et por les raisons qui devant sont dites et par plusors autres que on[154] porroit encores dire et mostrer,[155] me senble il que tous les heirs de celui qui est forsjugiés con traytor doyvent estre desherités a tous jors de tout[156] quanque le traytor avoit en la seignorie dou seignor vers qui il fist la trayson au jor que il la fist, ausi ceaus qui estoient néz et engendrés ains que il feist[157] la trayson[158] con ceaus

[b] V begins a new chapter here with the rubric: Ci dit coment as livres des empereors dient coument les traytours doivent estre deserités.
[c] *Cod.* 9.8.5 cf. *Dig.* 48.4. As Beugnot (p. 309 note c) remarked, the phrase 'je cuit' implies that John had no first-hand knowledge of the *Codex Iustinianus.*

[129] heirs de l'ome . . . foy] V: autres heirs des homes dou siengor qui est tenus de foi au seignor [130] dou] AB: de [131] estre desherités] V: bien doit il estre deserité [132] celui] A: celui seignor; B: lui [133] A adds: ou par conoissance [134] de court] V lacks [135] qui n'est] V lacks [136] Justignien] ABV: Justinien [137] et establisement] A: establirent il; BV: et establirent [138] qu'il] B: qu'eles [139] estuidit] AB lack [140] estuidit et devise] V: estudie et devisee [141] des traytors] AB: dou traytor (B: traytour) [142] molt plus grief] A: plus grant [143] et] ABV lack [144] Achades] B lacks; V: Acades [145] B adds: as occles *(sic)* [146] trova] AB: trovera [147] voudroit] A: vodra; B: voudra; O: vorra; V: vora [148] noveime] A: noviau [149] C adds: i [150] Julie] AV: Julien [151] devroit] A: deveit; BO: devoit [152] y a] BV lack [153] dou traytor] V: des traïtors [154] on] AB: l'on [155] et mostrer] C lacks [156] tout] AB lacks [157] feist] AV: fist [158] trayson] B: raison; V: traïson auci

qui puis nasquirent[159] qu'il ot la trayson[160] faite, et ausi ces heirs costiers[161] con les decendus[162] de lui. Que[163] forjugié a[164] traytor par conoissance ou par esgart de cort n'a[165] ne peut avoir heir qui erite aprés lui en son fié de quey[166] il est desherité par ce que il a esté forsjugié par esgart ou par conoissance de court, car il pert a lui et a ces heirs par la trayson[167] que il a faite de quey il a esté forsjugié come traïtor, et[168] le fié qu'il tenoit dou seignor vers qui il fu traytor[169] cel fié revient au seignor de qui il le tenoit[170] et a ses heirs, et en pevent[171] le seignor et ces heirs faire toutes[172] lor volenté con de leur propre chose.

---

[159] nasquirent] B: vesquirent [160] trayson] B: raison [161] costiers] B: coustoiens [162] decendus A: dessendans; B: descendanz; C: decendu; V: desendans [163] de lui. Que] A: Que celui qui est; B: de lui. Quar [164] a] A: come; BV: ne [165] A adds: ni; B: ne [166] en son fié de quey] A: en ce dont; B: en ce de quoi; V: de ce en quoi [167] trayson] B: raison [168] et] ABV lack [169] ABV add: et [170] revient au seignor . . . tenoit] A: qu'il teneit revient au seignor; V: revient au seignor de qui il le tient [171] pevent] AV: peut; B: puet [172] toutes] ABV lack

***[175]** Coment l'on doit faire homage au chief seignor dou reyaume[1] et coment a celui qui n'est chief[2] seignor, et de coy l'ome[3] est tenus a son seignor par l'omage que il li a fait, et de quoy le seignor[4] a son home.[5]

Quant home ou feme[6] fait homage au chief seignor dou reyaume,[7] il doit estre a genous devant lui et metre ses mains jointes entre[8] les soues et dire li: 'Sire, je deviens[9] vostre home[10] lige de tel fié', et dire quel fié ce[11] est por quey il li fait homage,[12] 'et vos promet[13] a garder et sauver contre[14] toutes riens qui vivre et morir puissent'. Et le seignor li doit lors[15] respondre: 'Et je vos en resoy[16] en Dieu foy et en la moie',[17] et le doit baiser en[18] bouche en fey.[19]

Mais se celui qui fait homage si con est desus dit[20] au chief seignor a fait avant ligece ou homage a home ou a feme qui ne soit home dou chief seignor ou a home[21] qui soit home dou chief seignor,[22] il le doit saver a l'omage faire, por ce que nul qui est home d'autre[23] ne peut aprés faire homage a autre, se il ne sauve son premier seignor,[24] s'il ne le fait par son congé[25] que il ne mente sa foy vers celuy de qui il est[26] avant home. Et qui fait homage de chose qui soit ou reyaume a autre que au chief seignor[27] dou reyaume,[28] il le doit faire en la maniere devant[29] devisee, mais que tant que il ne[30] li doit[31] faire[32] ligece, por ce que nul home ne peut faire plus d'une[33] ligece, et que tous les homes des homes dou chief seignor dou reyaume[34] li doivent faire la[35] ligece par l'assise, et puis que l'on li doit la ligece,[36] l'on ne la peut a autre faire sans mesprendre devant luy.[37]

A: fols cxxiv^{r}–cxxv^{r} caps 195–6; **B:** fols 153^{v}–155^{r} caps 196–7; **C:** fols 156^{v}–158^{r} cap. 175; **O:** fols 213^{r}–215^{v}; **V:** fols clxvi^{v}–clxviii^{v} caps 204–5; Beugnot, pp. 313–16, caps 195–6.

---

[1] C adds: de Jerusalem [2] chief] B: mie [3] l'ome] C: l'on [4] V adds: est tenus [5] et de quoy . . . home] AB lack [6] ou feme] A lacks [7] V adds: de Jerusalem [8] jointes entre] B: en [9] deviens] C: deveins [10] home] A lacks [11] quel fié ce] A: quel fié il; B: que le fié; V: li quel le fié [12] homage] AB: l'omage [13] V adds: je [14] V adds: tous ceaus et [15] lors] ABV lack [16] resoy] O: resoif [17] A adds: sauve mes dreis; V: de vos drois sauve les miens [18] ABV add: la [19] en fey] C lacks [20] si con est desus dit] B lacks [21] a home] B lacks; V: a home ou feme [22] ou a home . . . seignor] C lacks [23] d'autre] AV: d'autrui [24] AV add: ou [25] s'il ne le . . . congé] B lacks [26] est] V: fu [27] a autre que au chief seignor] B lacks [28] dou reyaume] ABV lack [29] devant] A: dessus; B: avant; V: desus [30] ne] C lacks [31] AV add: pas; B: mie [32] faire] C: parfaire [33] plus d'une] V: que une [34] dou reyaume] C lacks [35] la] AV lack [36] par l'assise, et . . . ligece] B lacks [37] devant luy] AV: vers lui; B lacks

Et home ou feme qui fait homage a autre est tenus a son seignor par la foy que il li[38] doit et par l'omage que[39] il li a fait de luy guarder et sauver contre toutes riens[40] qui vivre et morir puissent, et se li promet il a l'omage faire.[41] Et por ce me senble il que il li est tenus de non metre[42] ne faire metre main[43] en[44] son cors ne concentir ne soufrir a son poeir que autre li mete; ne ne[45] doit prendre ne faire prendre ne[46] retenir[47] aucune chose de son seignor sans son congé,[48] se[49] il ne le fait par l'esgart[50] ou par la conoissance de la court de son seignor[51] de cele seignorie ou son fié est por coy il li a fait l'omage; ne ne doit home ne feme conceller contre son seignor, se il ne li a doné[52] a son conceill; ne ne doit por home ne por feme parole mostrer en court, se il n'est a son conceill[53] de quey il se mete en esgart ou en conoissance de court de chose qui contre son seignor soit;[54] ne ne[55] doit porter armes contre son seignor, se ce n'est aveuc .i. autre sien seignor a qui il soit tenus de foy ains que a lui; ne ne doit faire a son escient ne faire faire[56] ne porchacer la honte ne le damage de son seignor ne soufrir ne concentir a son ecient[57] a son poier que autre li face; ne[58] ne doit a la feme de son seignor ne a la[59] fille requerre vilainie de son cors ne[60] gesir o lui[61] charnelment coment que se soit, se se n'est par mariage, ne a sa seur tant con ele est damoisele en son hostel, ne soufrir ne concentir a son[62] pooir que autre li face; et doit conceiller loyaument a son ecient son seignor de ce que[63] il li demandera conceill.[64] [a]

[a] ABV begin a new chapter here with the rubrics: A: Si dit coment le seignor est tenu a son home et de quoi por l'omage qu'il en a receu; B: Ci dit coment le seignor est tenu a son home et de quel chose par l'omage et la ligece que il li a fait; V: Ci dit coment le seignour est tenus a son home et de quoi par l'omage que il li a fait.

[38] li] C lacks [39] et par l'omage que] B: par l'omage [40] C adds: et [41] faire] B lacks [42] B adds: autre [43] metre main] C: main metre [44] en] A: a; V: sur [45] ne ne] A: ni ne (a similarly throughout this paragraph) [46] faire prendre ne] C lacks [47] retenir] V: tenir [48] A adds: ne outre son gré; B: contre; V: outre son gré [49] se] C lacks [50] l'esgart] C: esgart [51] sans son congé . . . seignor] O lacks [52] il ne li a doné] A: son seignor ne l'a doné; B: le seignor ne li a doné; V: le seignor ne le done [53] ne ne doit . . . conceill] A lacks [54] qui contre son seignor soit] A lacks; BO: qui (B: que) soit contre son seignor [55] ne ne] C: ne [56] ne faire faire] AV lack; B: ne querre [57] ABV add: ne [58] face; ne] B lacks [59] la] A: sa [60] V adds: soffrir ne consentir a son escient ne a son pooir que autre li face, ce est asavoir de [61] o lui] AV: a li [62] V adds: escient ne a son [63] que] B: dont [64] conceill] A lacks

Et le seignor ne[65] doit metre main ne faire metre main el cors ne el[66] fié de son home, se ce n'est[67] par l'esgart ou par la conoissance de sa court, et est tenus[68] a son home, se me senble, par la foy qui est entr'iaus de toutes les choses avant dites de quey home est tenus a son seignor. Car entre l'ome et le seignor a[69] fey, et la fey doit estre coneue[70] entr'iaus des[71] choses avant dites, mais que tant que l'ome doit au[72] seignor reverence[73] en toutes choses. Et chascun doit garder sa foy,[74] l'un vers l'autre, fermement et enterinement[75] en droit soy por sa foy et sa leiauté et s'enor garder et sa bone renomee.

Et l'ome doit tant plus au seignor por la fey que il li est tenus que le seignor a lui,[76] que[77] l'ome doit entrer en ostage por son seignor[78] geter de prison s'il[79] l'en requiert ou fait requerre par certains mesages.[80] Et chascun home qui a[81] fait homage a autre est tenu par[82] foy se il treuve son seignor en besoing d'armes a pié[83] entre ces henemis ou en leuc qu'il[84] soit en perill de mort ou de prison de faire son leal poeir de remetre[85] le et geter[86] le de cel perill, et se il autrement ne le peut faire, il li doit doner son cheval ou sa beste sur coy il chevauche, s'il la requiert, et aider le a metre[87] sus[88] et aider le a son poeir a son cors sauver. Et qui[89] faut vers[90] son seignor d'aucune des avant[91] dites choses, il ment sa fei vers lui,[92] et se le seignor l'en poeit[93] prover par recort de court, il porra faire de luy et des soues choses con d'ome ataint de foy mentie. Et qui fait aucune des dites choses por son seignor, le seignor est tenus par sa foy de delivrer le[94] a son leal pooir celui ou ceaus de ces homes que[95] il a mis en ostage por sa delivrance. Et[96] celui ou ceaus de ces homes[97] qui le remonteront, si con est avant dit, se il ou ceaus[98] sont por achaison de ce pris et enprisonés, est il tenus d'eaus delivrer[99] a son[100] poeir.

---

[65] le seignor ne] C: ce le seignor ne li [66] main el cors ne el] B: ou cors ne ou; V: au cors ne au [67] se ce n'est] C: se n'en est [68] tenus] BOV: tenu [69] l'ome et le seignor a] AV: seignor et home n'a (V: n'en a) que la [70] coneue] A: coneue et gardee; C: coneu [71] des] AB: es; C: de; V: as [72] doit au] B: a a son; V: doit a son [73] reverence] C: reverances [74] C adds: vers le seignor [75] A adds: chascun [76] lui] A: l'home [77] que] B: quar [78] C adds: et [79] s'il] C: si [80] certains mesages] ABV: certain mesage (A: message) [81] home qui a] A: qui [82] ABV add: sa [83] pié] C: paié [84] qu'il] B: ou il [85] remetre] ABV: remonter [86] geter] V: regeter [87] C adds: le [88] sus] A: sur; B: desus [89] qui] C: qu'il [90] vers] V: a [91] avant] B: devant [92] lui] V: son seignor [93] poeit] AV: peut; B: puet [94] le] AB lack [95] que] A: qui le remontent ou ciaus a qui [96] AV add: ce [97] de ces homes] O lacks [98] remonteront, si con . . . ceaus] AV: remontent si come est dessuz dit (V: dit desus) [99] d'eaus delivrer] AV: de delivrer les; B: dou delivrer [100] V adds: loyal

Et chascun qui tient fié d'autre de quey il est son home est tenus a son seignor d'entrer por lui en hostage por dete et[101] en plegerie de tant vaillant con le fié qu'il tient de luy[102] et de quey il est son home vaudroit resnablement au vendre par l'assise. Et qui de ce faut[103] a son seignor je croi qu'il doit perdre[104] le fié que il tient de luy toute[105] sa vie. Et se le seignor laisse encorre son home de tel maniere d'ostage ou de plegerie et il y a damage, il est tenus de restorer lui tout le damage qu'il avroit eu par se. Et[106] celuy de ces homes qu'il a laissé[107] encorre[108] d'ostage por dete ou de[109] plegerie quelque la quantité soit, petite ou grant, n'est tenus d'entrer por lui en ostage por dete ne plegerie[110] tant que il li ait amendé tout le damage que il avra por lui reseu, et le seignor doit croire son home dou damage que il dira[111] por la foy que il li doit que il en a reseu et restorer[112] li ou[113] amender tant con il avra dit en la maniere avant[114] dite[115] que il en a eu de damage.

[101] hostage por dete et] A: tel point por dette ou [102] V adds: vaut [103] de ce faut] A: defaut; V: ce defaut [104] doit perdre] A: perdreit [105] toute] AV: a; B lacks [106] V adds: ce [107] a laissé] AB: laisse [108] encorre] C: core [109] de] AV: por [110] por dete ne plegerie] A: ni en dette ni en plegerie; B: ne en plegerie de dete; O: por dette n'en plegerie] V: de dette ne de plegerie [111] dira] C: dit [112] restorer] C: retorner [113] ou] O: et [114] avant] A: dessuz [115] en la maniere avant dite] V lacks

***[176]** Coment les homes des homes[1] dou chief seignor dou reiaume[2] li deivent faire la ligece par l'assise, et de quey il li sont tenus par la dite[3] ligece,[4] et coment[5] les autres gens dou[6] reyaume doivent jurer au chief seignor[7] feiauté.[8]

Quant les homes des homes dou chief seignor dou reiaume font au chief seignor la ligece par l'asise, celui qui le[9] fait[10] doit estre a genous devant luy et metre ces mains jointes[11] entre les soues et dire li: 'Sire, je vos fais la ligese par l'assise de tel fié que je tiens de tel', et nomer celuy de qui il tient le fié et dire quel le[12] fié est, 'et vos promet[13] a garder et a[14] sauver contre toutes riens qui vivre et morir puissent, si con je faire le doie de ligece faite[15] par l'assise'. Et le seignor li doit respondre: 'Et je ensi vos resoif en Dieu foy et en la moye con je faire le doie de ligece faite par l'assise',[16] et baiser le en fey en la bouche. Et quant la ligece est ensi faite les homes qui l'ont faite sont tenus au chief[17] seignor de garder le et sauver le[18] contre toutes riens qui vivre et morir puissent, mais que contre[19] lor seignor de qui il tienent[20] le fié por quey il[21] ont faite la ligece par l'assise, et[22] en tel maniere que[23] [a] se[24] il avient que le chief seignor ait contens ou guerre au seignor[25] de ses homes qui ait homes qui li aient[26] faite la dite ligece, ceaus[27] homes doivent venir a lor seignor et dire leur:[28] 'Sire, vos savés que nos somes homes[29] liges dou chief seignor dou reyaume devant vos, por quey nos ne devons estre contre luy, se en luy ne remaint. Si vos prions et requerons que vos vos

A: fols cxxv[r]–cxxvi[v] caps 197–8; **B:** fols 155[r]–156[r] caps 198–9; **C:** fols 158[r]–159[r] cap. 176; **O:** fols 215[v]–217[v]; **V:** fols clxviii[v]–clxx[r] caps 206–8; Beugnot, pp. 317–19, caps 197–8.

[a] V begins a new chapter here with the rubric: Ci orrés quez est l'assise pour quoi l'on fait la ligesse par l'assise.

[1] des homes] C lacks [2] B adds: de Jerusalem [3] dite] V lacks [4] B rubrics (fol. 24[v]) adds: au seignor [5] et coment] C: comment [6] B adds: dit [7] au chief seignor] AB lack [8] feiauté] A: feaument [9] le] ABV: la [10] B adds: au seignor [11] jointes] ABV lack [12] le fié et dire quel le] B: cel [13] vos promet] C: promet vos [14] a] C lacks [15] faite] B: faire [16] Et le seignor . . . l'assise] B lacks [17] chief] A lacks [18] le] AB lack [19] contre] AV: encontre [20] tienent] V: tient [21] tienent le fié por quey il] B lacks [22] et] B lacks [23] et en tel maniere que] V: en telle maniere come vous troverés si aprés en escrit. [24] se V: Et se [25] au seignor] A: a aucun des seignor; B: as seignors; V: a aucun [26] qui ait homes qui li aient] A: qui li ont; V: qui ait houme qui li ait [27] ceaus] B: ses [28] leur] ABV: li [29] homes] O lacks

adreciés[30] vers luy, et que vos li mandés que il vos maint[31] par l'esgart de sa court. Et se vos ce ne faites dedens .xl. jors, nos vos guerpirons et irons a lui aider[32] et conseiller[33] contre vos, ce en lui ne remaint. Et se vos[34] faites ce que nos vos requerons et il vos faut de faire droit par sa court, nos ne vos guerpirons[35] pas. Mais se vos dedens ces[36] .xl. jors feysiés chose qui fust encontre[37] lui, nos ne le vos[38] soufrirons pas, se nos le poons[39] amender, et se nos ne le poons[40] amender[41] ne destorber son mal,[42] nos vos guerpiriens[43] lors et yriens a luy et feriens vers luy ce que nos devriens.'[b]

Et se le chief seignor fait semondre son home si con il doit[44] de venir faire li droit[45] par sa court et il n'i vient ne[46] contremande s'esoigne si con il doit ou mande[47] par ces homes en la court dou chief segnor dire raison por coy il n'i doit aler et tel que court l'esgarde ou conoisse, et se[48] le chief seignor requiert ou fait requerre les homes de celuy qui defaut de venir li[49] faire droit par[50] sa court que il en[51] facent vers luy ce que il doivent, il doivent tous venir devant le seignor et dire:[52] 'Sire, tel', et le noment, 'a qui nos[53] avons fait la ligece par l'assise des fiés que nos tenons de vos, nos a tel choze[54] requise ou fait[55] requerre', et dient li coy, 'si vos prions et requerons que vos ne faillés a vostre seignor et a nostre[56] droit faire si con vos devés par sa court. Et vos requerons que vos dedens .xl. jors[57] aillés en la court de vostre seignor et dou nostre[58] faire li droit si con vos devés. Et se vous y volés aler, nos yrons o vos se il vos plaist et vos ayderons et maintendrons et vos[59] conceillerons si con

---

[b] ABV begin a new chapter here with the rubric: Si dit (B adds: et devise) coment (B adds: et en quel maniere) les homes des homes dou chief seignor se deivent contenir vers le chief seignor quant il li ont faite la ligece (A: lige) par l'assise (B: quant ont faite la ligece).

---

[30] adreciés] C: adriciés [31] maint] V: mene [32] BO add: le [33] C adds: le [34] B adds: ne [35] guerpirons] C: grepirons [36] ces] AV lack; B: ceaus [37] encontre] AV: contre [38] vos] AV lack [39] poons] A: poriens; B: porons; V: poissens [40] poons] B: porons [41] et se nos . . . amender] AOV lack [42] A adds: et se noz ne le porieens destorber [43] guerpiriens] C: grepiriens et yre [44] si con il doit] V lacks [45] V adds: si come il doit [46] ne] AB: ne ne; V: ou ne [47] mande] A: mander [48] se] AB lack [49] defaut de venir li] A: defailli li est de venir [50] B adds: l'esgart de [51] en] ABV lack [52] le seignor et dire] AV: leur seignor et dire li [53] O adds: vos [54] tel choze] B lacks [55] fait] V: faire [56] a vostre seignor et a nostre] ABV: a (A: au; B: mie a) nostre seignor et au vostre de [57] jors] C: jor [58] de vostre seignor et dou nostre] ABV: de (A: dou) nostre seignor et dou vostre [59] vos] ABV lack

nos porons[60] con[61] nostre seignor.' Et ce il y vait[62] et il viaut que il aillent[63] o lui, il y doivent aler et aider le et conseiller le[64] et maintenir contre le chief seignor tant con il voudra faire droit par sa court. Et se il li[65] dit quant le chief seignor le[66] fait semondre de venir li faire droit en sa court ou quant ces homes li requierent que il y[67] aille, si con est avant[68] dit, qu'il n'est mie aseur de son cors por quey il n'i ose aler, mais se le[69] seignor le[70] veaut aseurer et faire aseurer[71] de tel, et le nome,[72] de coy il est en regart de son cors il yra et[73] le seignor le doit lors faire aseurer,[74] et se il ne le fait ces homes ne le doivent mie laiser et aler au[75] chief seignor. Mais se il ne dit se et les .xl. jors pasent et lor seignor n'a[76] fait ce que il li ont requis ou ne dit rayson por coi il ne le[77] doit faire et tel que court l'esgarde[78] ou conoisse qu'ensi doit estre, il se doivent tuit[79] partir de lui et aler au chief seignor a cheval ou[80] a armes ou a tel servise con il doivent de lor fiés et dire li: 'Sire, nos vos somes venus servir[81] et aider et conseiller con nostre seignor lige,[82] se par vos ne remaint, puis que nos veons et conoissons que nostre seignor vos defaut de droit faire par vostre court. Si vos requerons que vos nos maintenés ou restorés nos fiés au vaillant et nos amendés les damages[83] que nos avons eu de noz choses por achaison de ce que nos somes venus a vos. Et se vos se nos[84] faites dedens .xl. jors, nos serons a vos encontre[85] nostre seignor. Et se vos se ne[86] nos[87] faites,[88] nos retornerons[89] a noz fiéz et aidrons et maintendrons nostre[90] seignor contre vos, et se ne sera pas par nos defautes, ains sera par[91] vos, se vos ne faites vers nos se que vos devés faire de nos fiés[92] et de noz damages amender et restorer.' Et[93] se le chief seignor lor fait ce que il li requierent, il ne le doivent pas[94] guerpir[95] tant con le

[60] porons] A: devons; BV: devrons [61] A adds: au; V: a [62] vait] B: va [63] aillent] B: i aillent; C: aylle [64] le] AB lack [65] li] AV lack [66] le] C: li [67] y] C lacks [68] avant] A: devant [69] aler, mais se le] B: mie aler, mais [70] le] V: l'en [71] aseurer et faire aseurer] A: asseur; OV: aseurer et faire aseur (V: seur) [72] le nome] V: nome celui [73] yra et] B: i ira; V: yra [74] faire aseurer] A: asseur; O: aseurer [75] mie laiser et aler au] V: laisser aler devant le [76] n'a] BV: ne [77] ne le] B lacks [78] l'esgarde] AB: esgarde; V: esguarde [79] tuit] A: toz; B: touz; V: tous [80] ou] ABV: et [81] A adds: a cheval et as armes [82] lige] B lacks [83] les damages] AB: le damage [84] nos] OV: ne [85] encontre] A: contre [86] ne] C lacks [87] vos se ne nos] O: ne [88] nos serons a . . . faites] V lacks [89] B adds: arries [90] V adds: premier [91] A adds: les [92] V adds: faire [93] Et] C lacks [94] pas] ABV lack [95] guerpir] C: grepir

contens durera, et se il ne lor fait lor requeste, ceaus a qui il ne le fera doivent retorner a lor[96] seignor[97] et aider le et maintenir le[98] et conceiller le[99] contre le chief seignor tant con celui contens durera. Et le chief seignor[100] les doit croire de la valour[101] de lor fiés[102] par leur dit[103] sur[104] la fey que il li doivent et dou damage qu'il[105] ont[106] eu de lor choze[107] par lor sairement sur l'evangile.[108]

[96] ceaus a qui . . . lor] B: il doivent retorner a son [97] seignor] V: premier seignor [98] et maintenir le] C lacks [99] le] AB lack [100] A adds: ce il fait lor requeste [101] valour] A: value [102] fiés] BO: fié [103] par leur dit] A lacks [104] sur] B: par [105] C adds: li [106] ont] A: avront [107] choze] ABV: choses [108] l'evangile] B: saintes evaingiles

***[177]** De coy le chief seignor est tenus a ceaus des[1] homes de ces homes qui li ont faite la ligece par l'assise, et[2] coment et de quey tous les homes[3] sont tenus les uns as autres par la dite assise.[4]

Le chief seignor[5] est tenus as homes de ces homes[6] qui li ont fait la ligece par l'assise[7] que il ne[8] doit metre main ne faire metre[9] en leur cors ne en leur fiés de coy il li ont faite la ligece, ce se n'est par esgart ou par conoissance de sa[10] cort, ne ne doit soufrir a son pooir que autre li mete.

Et se aucun de lor seignor[11] met main en leur cors ne en leur fiés, se il ne le[12] fait par l'esgart ou par la[13] conoissance de sa court, le chief seignor ne le doit pas[14] soufrir, ains le doit faire delivrer le plus tost que il pora, ce il est pris et aresté,[15] et doit celui[16] de ces homes qui se avra fait mener a quanque[17] il porra et devra par sa cort. Et se aucun de lor seignor[18] faut a aucun d'eaus de faire li droit par sa court, ou ne li tient et[19] fait tenir ce que sa court a esgardé ou coneu ou recordé,[20] ou le desaisist de son fié sans esgart ou sans conoissance de court,[21] et celui a qui l'on a fait aucune des dites choses le mostre au chief seignor et li requiert que il li face a son seignor faire droit par sa court ou que il li face a son seignor[22] tenir ou faire tenir ce que sa court a esgardé ou coneu ou recordé ou le face metre en la saisine de son fié de quey il l'a desaisi sans esgart ou sans conoissance de court,[23] le chief seignor le doit faire[24] venir devant luy en sa court, et quant il i[25] sera il li doit dire:[26] 'Tel vostre home', et le nome, 'm'a dit tel chose', et die ly ce que celui

---

A: fols cxxvii^{r}–cxxviii^{r} cap. 200; **B:** fols 156^{v}–157^{v} cap. 201; **C:** fols 159^{r}–160^{v} cap. 177; **O:** fols 218^{r}–219^{v}; **V:** fols clxxi^{r}–clxxii^{r} cap. 210; Beugnot, pp. 321–2, cap. 200.

---

[1] a ceaus des] V: as [2] et] C lacks [3] B adds: dou reaume de Jerusalem [4] par la dite assise] A: par l'assise; A rubrics (fol. 6^{v}) B lack; V: par l'assise dou royaume de Jerusalem [5] V adds: dou royaume [6] de ces homes] A lacks; B: des homes [7] par l'assise] A lacks [8] ne] B lacks [9] B adds: main [10] sa] A lacks [11] seignor] AB: seignors [12] ne le] B lacks [13] l'esgart ou par la] V: esguart ou par [14] pas] ABV lack [15] ce il est pris et aresté] AB lack [16] et doit celui] V lacks [17] a quanque] V: en quant que [18] seignor] B: seignors [19] et] AB: ou [20] coneu ou recordé] C: recordé ou coneu [21] ou le desaisist . . . court] B lacks [22] faire droit par . . . seignor] C lacks [23] ou le face . . . court] B lacks [24] le doit faire] A: deit faire celui [25] i] AC: li; BV lack [26] il li doit dire] B: venuz dire li

li a dit. 'Si vos comant si destretement[27] con je puis et doy que vos li faciés droit par vostre court si con vos devés dedens .xl. jors'.[28] Et ce c'est d'esgart ou de conoissance ou de recort de cort[29] qu'il ne li a fait[30] faire si con la court l'a esgardé ou coneu ou recordé, si li die: 'Tel vostre home', et le nome, 'm'a dit que vostre court a esgardé ou coneu ou recordé tel chose.[31] Si[32] vos[33] comant con a mon home si destretement con je puis et doy, que vos li faciés[34] et faites faire se que vostre court a esgardé ou coneu ou recordé dedens .xl. jors, et de ce vos semons je en la presence de mes homes et de ma court qui si est et les en tray a garant.' Et ce celui a qui le seignor avra le dit comandement fait et qu'il avra ensi semons con est avant dit ne le fait dedens le dit[35] terme ou ne dit raison por coy il ne le doit faire et tel que la[36] court l'esgarde ou conoisse,[37] et ce celui a qui il a[38] fait aucune des[39] dites choses revient devant le chief seignor et li mostre que son seignor ne li a fait ce que il li comanda et de quey il le semonst et n'en a[40] dit chose par coy court n'ait esgardé ne[41] coneu que il ne li doive faire, si li prie et requiert, con a celui qui est le chief seignor dou reyaume,[42] que il li en face ce qu'il doit par l'assise ou l'usage dou reyaume de Jerusalem, le seignor doit mander querre son home[43] et dire li en sa court ce que le sien home[44] li a dit. Et se il le conoist ou[45] ne mostre par les homes de la soue court qu'il est[46] autrement que celui ne li a fait assaver et ensi qu'il li a[47] fait se que le seignor li comanda,[48] le chief seignor le doit[49] des lors en avant faire remetre en sa[50] saisine de ce de[51] son fié de coy son seignor l'avoit desaisi sans esgart et[52] sans conoissance de court et maintenir le tant con il[53] voudra que il doit[54] faire a son seignor par sa court. Et se il li failli de ce que court a esgardé ou coneu[55] et il dedens xl. jors n'a[56] fait a son home[57] ce que la[58] court a esgardé ou coneu et que le seignor li a comandé et de coy

---

[27] destretement] V: estroitement [28] B adds: se il li defaut de droit faire par sa court [29] de cort] A lacks [30] a fait] AV: fait; B: faut [31] tel chose] BV lack [32] li die: 'Tel . . . Si] A lacks [33] C adds: pri et [34] faciés] V: faites [35] dit] A lacks [36] la] AB lack [37] l'esgarde ou conoisse] A: l'esgardera ou conoistra [38] a] V lacks [39] B adds: devant [40] et n'en a] ABV: ne n'a [41] n'ait esgardé ne] AB: ait esgardé (B: esgarder) ou; V: n'a esguardé ou [42] C adds: de Jerusalem [43] querre son home] C: son home querre; V: querre celui son home [44] le sien home] B: son home de lui [45] ou] A: et; B: et il [46] est] A: seit [47] a] A lacks] C: en a [48] comanda] A: comande [49] O adds: faire [50] sa] A lacks; V: la [51] de] C: que [52] et] V: ou [53] V adds: vodroit ou [54] que il doit] A: dreit; V lacks [55] failli de ce . . . coneu] AV: a defailli (V: failli) de faire ce que sa cort (V: court) a esgardé ou coneu ou recordé [56] n'a] V: ne [57] n'a fait a son home] A lacks [58] la] AV: sa

il l'a semons si com est avant dit, il doit perdre[59] sa court,[60] se le seignor l'en[61] veaut mener a se que il pora[62] par sa court, por ce que il me[63] senble que il est assise ou usage que le seignor doit tenir et faire tenir les esgars et les conoissances et les recors que sa court dit et fait.[64] Et por ce que le chief seignor est tenus par son sairement de tenir et faire tenir en sa seignorie les assises et les usages de son reyaume, me senble il que puis que son home, qui a[65] la court del don de lui[66] ou de son ancestre, n'en[67] euvre si com il doit par l'assise ou l'usage dou dit[68] reiaume, que il la doit perdre,[69] et que le seignor le[70] peut tolir,[71] se il viaut par la[72] conoissance de sa court, se il requiert a sa court qu'ele li conoisse quel droit il en doit avoir[73] aprés ce[74] que il avra les avant[75] dis erremens retrais ou fait retraire en la court. Que il ne me senble que celui qui sera defaillant de l'avant[76] dite semonce puisse choze dire par coy la court ne conoisse que il ne doit plus avoir[77] court en sa seignorie[78] aprés le comandement et la semonce dou chief seignor, puis que il a defailli a son home de faire li droit par sa court ou de faire li se que la court[79] a esgardé ou coneu ou recordé.

---

[59] remetre en sa . . . perdre] B: et celui qui ne fait son dit comandamant ne sa dite semonse perdra [60] A adds: a sa vie [61] l'en] A: le; CV lack [62] pora] B: porroit [63] ce que il me] A: ce se me; B: ce ce me; V: ce [64] dit et fait] AV: fera; B: fait [65] a] B lacks [66] lui] C: celui [67] n'en] B: ne; C: non [68] dit] ABV lack [69] perdre] B: prendre [70] le] ABV: li [71] A adds: a sa vie [72] la] C: l'assise [73] il en doit avoir] A: en deit aveir. Et [74] de sa court . . . ce] O lacks [75] avant] B: devanz; V lacks [76] l'avant] V: la dessus [77] plus avoir] V: pas avoir plus [78] A adds: a sa vie et [79] ou de faire . . . court] B: de ce que ele

***[178]** Coment et de quoy tous les homes dou dit reyaume sont tenus les uns as autres par la dite assise.[a]

Tous les homes dou dit reyaume sont par la dite assise tenus les uns as autres si con est avant[1] dit,[2] [b] et en tel maniere que se leur seignor met main[3] el cors ou el fié d'aucun d'eaus sans esgart ou sans conoissance de sa court, que tous les homes[4] doivent venir devant lor seignor, se il a son home aresté ou fait arester[5] sans esgart ou sans conoissance de court et le tient ou fait tenir en prison, se[6] aucun des parens ou des autres amis de celuy qui est pris[7] le requierent[8] de par luy que yaus le facent delivrer et que il en[9] eufre a faire droit par yaus con[10] par ces pers, il doivent tous venir devant le seignor et dire li: 'Sire, nos avons entendu que vos avés tel nostre per aresté.[11] Si vos prions et requerons si[12] destretement con nos poons et devons que se il est aresté en vostre pooir, que vos le faciés[13] delivrer sans delay, et que vos le menés par[14] vostre court.' Et se le seignor le fait,[15] tant con celuy qui avra esté arestés vodra faire droit par ces pers, il le doivent maintenir a droit con leur per. Et se le seignor ne le fait delivrer a lor requeste ou ne dit choze[16] por quoy il ne le doit faire et tel que cort l'esgarde ou conoisse, tos les homes ensenble doivent aler la ou il sevent qu'il[17] est aresté et delivrer le a force ou autrement, se le cors de lor seignor ne lor defent a[18] armes, contre lequel il ne pevent ne ne doivent porter

---

A: fols cxxviii[r]–cxxx[v] caps 201–4; **B:** fols 157[v]–160[v] caps 202–5; **C:** fols 160[v]–164[r] cap. 178; **O:** fols 219[v]–225[r]; **V:** fols clxxii[v]–clxxvi[r] caps 211–14; Beugnot, pp. 323–8, caps 201–4.

---

[a] Rubric in A: Si esclarsisse coment toz les homes des homes sont par la ditte assise tenus les uns as autres si come est avant dit et coment il se deivent aider et conseillier; B: Ci esclarcit coment et en quel maniere touz les homes (B rubrics (fol. 24[v]) adds: dou reaume) par la devant dite assise sont tenuz les uns as autres; V: Ci esclersisse coment tous les homes des homes dou chief seignor sont par la dite assise tenus les uns as autres et coment il se doivent entreayder et conseillier.

[b] Above cap. 177.

---

[1] avant] V: dessus [2] C adds: et devisé [3] AB add: ou fait metre main; V: ou face metre [4] homes] A: autres homes; BV: autres [5] ou fait arester] V lacks [6] se] A: et [7] pris] A: aresté [8] le requierent] A: les requiert; BV: le requiert [9] en] BV lack [10] yaus con] B: ceaus ou; V: eaus ou [11] aresté] B: fait arrester [12] si] B: tant [13] faciés] AV: faites [14] A adds: l'esgart de [15] AV add: delivrer [16] choze] B: raison [17] sevent qu'il] B lacks [18] a] C lacks

armes ne faire choze a[19] force, et dire li que tant con il voudra faire droit par ces pers que il le maintendront con[20] leur per. Et se le seignor le defent contre yaus[21] a armes ou autrement a force, yaus[22] li doivent dire: 'Sire, vos estes nostre seignor. N'encontre[23] vostre cors nos ne porterons mie armes ne ne ferons choze[24] a force. Et puis que vos nos defendés[25] a force a delivrer[26] nostre per qui est pris et enprisonés sans esgart ou[27] sans conoissance de cort, nos vos gagons tos ensenble et chascun par soi dou servise que nos vos devons tant que vos ayés nostre per tel[28] delivré[29] ou fait delivrer ou dites[30] raison por quei vos ne le devés faire et tel que cort l'esgarde ou conoisse.'[c]

Et se le seignor a le fié d'aucun d'iaus[31] aresté ou fait arester sans esgart ou[32] sans conoissance de court, celuy de qui le fié est ensi aresté sans esgart ou sans conoissance de cort[33] doit assenbler tant de ces pers con il pora et dire leur et mostrer coment leur seignor son fié a aresté sans esgart et sans[34] conoissance de court.[35] Si lor prie et requiert et conjure con a ces pers[36] que il li facent son fié rendre ou que il se portent vers luy si con il doivent con vers lor per, et bien eufre a faire[37] droit par yaus con par ces pers quant il ravra[38] son fié. Et lors tous ensenble[39] doivent venir devant le seignor et dire li: 'Sire nostre per tel', et le noment,[40] 'nos a tel chose dite, et nos a ensi requis et conjurés', et dire li coment. 'Si vos prions et requerons que vos a nostre per tel rendés sans delay son fié, et le[41] remetés ou faites remetre en sa[42] saisine. Et se vos aprés[43] li savés que demander, que vos li demandés en[44] vostre court et que vos le

[c] ABV begin a new chapter here with the rubric: Se le fié d'aucun des homes (B: homes liges) est aresté par le seignor sanz esgart ou (B: et) sanz conoissance de court, (B: la court), coment (coment V lacks) celui (B: celui qui est arresté; B rubrics (fol. 24[v]): celui de qui le fié est arresté) le peut (V: doit) destraindre par le conjurement (A: l'esconjurement) de ces pers.

[19] a] B: par [20] con] B: contre [21] contre yaus] V lacks [22] yaus] AB: il [23] N'encontre] AB: ne contre [24] porterons mie armes . . . choze] A: porteremes armes ni ne feriens chose; B: porterions mie armes ne ferions choses; V: porteriens mie armes ne ne ferons chose [25] defendés] B: feffendez [26] a delivrer] A lacks [27] ou] A: ne; B: et [28] tel] V lacks [29] delivré] A: delivrer [30] dites] A: dite; B: dire; V: dire la [31] d'iaus] V: des homes [32] ou] B: et [33] celuy de qui . . . cort] O lacks [34] sans esgart ou sans conoissance . . . sans] A: deit assembler tant de ces pers come il porra et dire lor coment leur seignor et le sien a son fié aresté sans [35] doit assenbler tant . . . court] BV lack [36] con il pora . . . pers] O lacks [37] a faire] B lacks [38] ravra] AB: avra [39] A adds: et chascun par sei [40] noment] O: nome [41] le] O: l'en [42] sa] ABV lack [43] V adds: ce [44] en] A: par

menés par vostre court. Et[45] se vos ne le faites, nos ne porrons muer que nos ne faisons vers luy se que nos devons.'[46] Et se le seignor ne le fait, et il[47] requiert ces pers que il li doignent force et poier de remetre se en sa[48] saisine et que il le maintienent si con il doivent, il doivent tous aler o luy et remetre[49] le en sa[50] saisine[51] et maintenir le contre tous homes, ne[52] mais que contre[53] le cors dou[54] seignor ou de autre home a qui il soient tenus de foy. Et se le seignor lor defent a armes ou autrement que en dit, et il est la present, il[55] doivent dire: 'Sire, vos estes nostre seignor, et contre vos nos ne porterons mie armes ne forceerons[56] contre vos[57] tant con vos serés present, mais[58] contre tous autres que vos ferons[59] nos nostre leal poier[60] de remetre nostre per en la saisine de son fié et maintenir le en sa[61] saisine tant con il voudra faire droit. Et puis que ensi est que vos qui[62] estes nostre seignor[63] et contre qui nos ne poons porter armes ne faire choze a force la ou vostre cors est, et nos defendés a force que nos ne remetons[64] nostre per[65] en saisine de ce de que[66] il a esté desaissi sans esgart et sans conoissance de court, nos tous ensenble et chascun par soy vos guagons de servises[67] que nos vos devons tant que vos aiés rendu a nostre per tel', et le noment,[68] 'son fié ou dite[69] raison por quoy vos ne le devés faire et tel que court l'esgarde ou conoisse.' Et aprés ce il ne li doivent faire servise ne faire[70] choze qu'il leur comande tant qu'il ait fait se que il li ont requis.[d]

Et[71] se le seignor faut[72] a aucun de ces homes de faire li faire[73] esgart, si con il doit, ou conoissance ou recort[74] de court, ou[75] se

[d] AV begin a new chapter here with a rubric which consists of the following paragraph.

[45] que vos le . . . Et] A lacks [46] devons] B: devrirons [47] A adds: en [48] sa] BV lack [49] remetre] V: metre [50] sa] BV lack [51] et que il . . . saisine] A: il le deivent faire et metre le en sa saissine par force ou autrement; O lacks [52] ne] A lacks [53] tous homes, ne mais que contre] B lacks [54] cors dou] V: chief [55] A adds: li [56] porterons mie armes ne forceerons] V: porriens mie armes porter ne nous esforcerons [57] contre vos] A lacks [58] vos serés present, mais] V: nous seroiens en present, mais que [59] ferons] AV: feriens; B: ferions [60] poier] A lacks [61] sa] B: la; V lacks [62] qui] V lacks [63] nostre seignor] C: seignor nostre [64] remetons] AO: metons [65] V adds: tel [66] de que] AO: de quei; B: dont; C: que [67] de servises] AV: dou servise; B: des servises [68] noment] C: nome [69] dite] BO: dites; V: ne dites [70] faire] A lacks [71] Et] AB lack [72] faut] V: defaut [73] faire] V lacks [74] ou recort] B lacks [75] ou] A rubrics (fol. 6v) V: a

que[76] court a esgardé ou coneu ou recordé en[77] aucune choze, et[78] le seignor ne le tient et[79] fait tenir, et[80] celui a qui le seignor[81] faudra d'aucune des devant[82] dites chozes requiert[83] ces pers que il[84] facent vers lui ce qu'il doivent,[85] il doivent lor seignor requerre que il les[86] face ou[87] guager le[88] de leur servise[89] en la maniere avant devisee tant[90] qu'il ait[91] fait.[e]

Et[92] se le seignor faut[93] a aucun de ses homes de son fié, et celui li requiert sa paye et aprés l'en[94] semont si con il doit par les termes qui sont establis a se, et il ne le paye par les dis[95] termes, se[96] selui qui avra son seignor ensi semons, si con il doit, d'avoir sa paye et ne l'avra eue et requiert[97] et conjure[98] ces pers, si con il[99] doit, que il destraignent le seignor si con il pevent et doivent que il le face[100] payer si con il doit de ce que il[101] li doit de son fié, les homes en doivent faire se qui est aprés devisé en cest livre[102] que il doivent faire quant tel cas avient.[f] Et je[103] qui ay fait ce[104] livre ay veu plusors des avant dites chozes faire[105] en la haute cort dou reyaume de Jerusalem et aucunes en celles de Cypre et les autres[106] oi dire a plusors sages homes[107] de mon tens. Car au tens que l'enpereor Fedric[108] tenoit le baillage dou reiaume de Jerusalem fu fait a mon seignor mon oncle le veil seignor de Barut,[109] et au seignor de Cesaire mon cozin, et a moi, et au seignor de Caifas[110] mesire Rohart,[111] et

---

[e] B begins a new chapter here with the rubric: Se le seignor faut de paier aucun sien home (sien home] B rubrics (fol. 24^v): de ses homes) de son fié puis que il l'avra requis, coment il doit conjurer ses pers.

[f] Below caps 197–8.

---

[76] que] B: se [77] en] AOV: ou; B lacks [78] choze, et] A: autre chose [79] le tient et] A: li tient ou ne li; B: le tient ne ne; V: li tient ou [80] et] B: a; C lacks [81] ne le tient . . . seignor] C repeats [82] devant] AV: avant; B lacks [83] requiert] AV: requerra; B: requiere [84] B adds: en [85] doivent] C: doivent et; V: devront [86] les] AV: le; B: li [87] ou] A rubrics (fol. 7^r) BOV: et [88] le] O lacks [89] servise] A rubrics (fol. 7^r) BO: servises [90] avant devisee tant] A: avant dite tant; B: lacks; V: devant devisee tant [91] ait] AV: l'ait [92] Et] AV lack [93] B adds: de paier si com il doit [94] l'en] AV: le; B: li [95] dis] C lacks [96] il ne le . . . se] V: ce il ne les paie et les dis termes passent [97] eue et requiert] B: ne requiere [98] et requiert et conjure] V: doit requerre et conjurer [99] O adds: pevent et doivent qu'il le face paier si com il [100] face] BV: facent [101] destraignent le seignor . . . il] A: le facent paier de ce que son seignor [102] en cest livre] C lacks [103] je] V lacks [104] ce] A: cest; B: ceste; V: cestui [105] faire] V lacks [106] les autres] A: aucunes ais; V: les autres ais [107] sages homes] V: autres sages [108] Fedric] A: Federit; B: Frederic [109] Barut] BOV: Baruth [110] Caifas] A: Kayphas; B: Caiphas; O: Cayphas [111] Rohart] B: Richart

a sire Felipe l'Ahne et a sire[112] Johan Moriau, que nos pers[113] a nostre requeste nos donerent force de nos resaisir de[114] noz fiés de quey le seignor de Sayete[115] mesire Balean,[116] qui estoit baill de l'enperere Fedric,[117] nos avoit desaisi[118] sans esgart et[119] sans conoissance de court par le[120] comandement[121] que le dit enpereor li fist. Et vis[122] et oy[123] as homes dou dit reyaume le dit seignor de Seete,[124] qui estoit baill dou dit enpereor, guager dou servise que il devoient a l'enpereor,[125] por ce que il ne tenoit[126] ne faisoit tenir a parfaire[127] a la princece Aalis, qui fu[128] mere dou prince Rupin, se que la haute cort dou dit reyaume avoit esgardé dou plait qui estoit entre li et les freres de l'ospitau des Alamans de la seignorie[129] dou Thoron,[130] laquel ele desraina vers yaus par l'esgart de la haute cort dou dit reyaume. Ne por ce que le dit seignor de Seyete[131] disoit que il ne se pooit de cel fait entremetre, car[132] l'enpereor li avoit mandé defendant que il ne s'entremeist de cel fait[133] et mostreit[134] le comandement qu'il en avoit eu par[135] letres de l'enpereor, ne por ce ne remest[136] que les homes dou dit reyaume a la requeste de la dite princese[137] ne le gaiasent[138] dou servize q'il devoient au dit enpereor tant que il eust fait a la dite princesse se que la court avoit esgardé. Et aprés, par le gré et l'otroy de la dite princesse et des dis homes, il se laisserent[139] de cel guagement et retornerent[140] au dit servize que il devoient[141] au dit enpereor.[g, h] Et[142] en Chypre au tens le roy Henri ay je veu[143] a la requeste de mesire Phelippe[144] de Gibelet,[145]

[g] These two disputes both appear to date to 1229. For a discussion of their historical context, see J. Riley-Smith, *The Feudal Nobility and the Kingdom of Jerusalem, 1174–1277* (London and Basingstoke, 1973), pp. 170–2.

[h] V begins a new chapter here with the rubric: Coment ce guagement desus dit fu fait meismes en Chipre a tens de roi Henri.

[112] Felipe l'Ahne et a sire] AO: Phelippe l'Asne (O: l'Ahne) et a sire; B lacks; V: Phelipe l'Ahne et a mesire [113] V adds: estoient [114] nos resaisir de] B lacks [115] Sayete] A: Seete; B: Sete [116] Balean] A: Beleem; BO: Balian; V: Ballian [117] Fedric] A: Federic; B: Frederic; V: Fredric [118] A adds: de nos fiés [119] et] V: ou [120] V adds: dit [121] comandement] BO: mandement [122] vis] BV: vi [123] oy] A: oys [124] Seete] B: Saete; V: Sayete [125] devoient a l'enpereor] V: li doivent au dit empereor [126] A adds: ni; V: ne [127] a parfaire] A lacks; B: et parfaire [128] fu] V: estoit [129] V adds: qui estoit [130] Thoron] C: Thouron [131] Seyete] AO: Seete; B: Saete; V: Saiete desus dit [132] car] A: que [133] cel fait] B: cel plait; V: celui plait [134] et mostreit] B: et monstroit; O: entremetre [135] eu par] B: par les [136] por ce ne remest] A: remest mie; B: pour ce ne demoura [137] princesse] A: prince [138] gaiacent] C: jaiacent [139] laisserent] A: relaissierent [140] de cel guagement et retornerent] B lacks [141] devoient] CV: devoit [142] Et] ABV lack [143] ay je veu] A: vi ge [144] Phelippe] C: Phelipe [145] Gibelet] B: Gibellet; V: Giblet

a qui le roy devoit de son fié, que[146] le terme de sa paye estoit pasé et que il avoit sa paye requise au roy[147] plusors foys en court et hors[148] court et aprés semons par les .iii. quinzaines et les .iii. quaranteines qui sont establiés a son seignor semondre de faire le paier de son fié et qu'eles estoient pasees[149] et tous les termes qui sont[150] establis par l'assise qu'on[151] doit son[152] seignor atendre de sa paye,[153] que tous les homes qui la furent vindrent devant[154] le roy et li prierent et requistrent que il paiast ou[155] feyst payer le dit Phelippe de ce qui il li devoit de son fié ou[156] feyst faire son gré, et que[157] le roy le fist, ne[158] ne vost atendre que l'on le guagast si con l'on doit faire[159] par l'asise, ains li fist maintentant son gré[160] de ce que il li devoit.[161] Et lors le dit Phelippe[162] mercia tous[163] les homes[164] de ce que il[165] avoient fait[166] et lor dist que le roy li[167] avoit tant fait[168] de sa paye que il se[169] tenoit apayé, et par ce demora que les homes ne guagerent le roy de lor servise.[i, j]

Et je ay[170] oy dire a mon seignor mon oncle le viell seignor de Barut,[171] que, quant le roy Heimeri[172] congea mesire Raoul[173] de Thabarie[174] dou reyaume de Jerusalem, que mesire Raoul requist et conjura ces pers que il le maintenissent[175] a droit[176] con a[177] lor per, et que il[178] ofroit a faire droit par eaus con par ces[179] pers se il estoit aucun qui[180] rien li demandast en la court, et ofroit a[181] aleiauter

[i] This dispute may relate to the financial problems King Henry experience at the end of the civil war of 1229–33 in Cyprus. See below appendix 1.2; Philip of Novara, pp. 543–4.

[j] AB begin a new chapter here with the rubric: A: Si devise (Si devise] A rubrics (fol. 7r) omit) coment toz les homes gagierent le roi quant il congea dou reaume mesire Raou de Thabarie; B: Ci devise coment les homes gagierent le roi Aymeri quant il congea messire Raoul de Thabarie dou reaume de Jerusalem, et coment il les conjura.

[146] que] A: et que; V: dont [147] roy] A: seignor [148] hors] A: fors; B: hors de; C: sans [149] pasees] B: paiés [150] establiés a son . . . sont] V lacks [151] par l'assise qu'on] A: que l'on [152] son] B lacks [153] A adds: par l'assise [154] devant] O lacks [155] paiast ou] AV lack [156] A adds: paiast ou [157] faire son gré et que] V: son gré, et [158] ne] AV: et [159] doit faire] B: devoit [160] C adds: par l'assise [161] de ce que il li devoit] B lacks [162] Phelippe] C: Phelipe [163] tous] ABV lack [164] A adds: liges [165] BO add: li [166] de ce que il avoient fait] A lacks [167] li] AB lack [168] et lor dist . . . fait] V lacks [169] se] AOV: s'en [170] ay] ABV lack [171] Barut] AOV: Baruth; B: Baruch [172] Heimeri] A: Henri [173] Raoul A: Raou (and similarly throughout this paragraph) [174] Thabarie] BV: Tabarie [175] maintenissent] V: menassent [176] a droit] B lacks [177] a] ABV lack [178] A adds: li; V: en [179] ces] B lacks [180] estoit aucun qui] V: y avoit nul que [181] a] C lacks

s'en[182] en la court le roy de ce que l'on[183] li metoit sus, si les requeroit[184] semonoit et conjuroit que il alassent o luy devant le roy, et[185] que il li voloit se ofrir devant yaus,[186] et que il y alasent,[187] et que mon seignor[188] mon oncle fu l'un d'eaus[189] que mesire Raoul semonst et conjura si con est avant dit, et que il et les autres homes le roy alerent en la court o luy, et que,[190] quant il furent devant le roi,[191] mesire Raoul li dist: 'Sire, vos m'avés congeé de vostre reyaume sans esgart et sans conoissance de court, laquel choze vos ne poés ne devés faire par l'assise ne l'usage de cest reyaume tant con je vodray faire droit par vostre court. Sire, et je eufre si en vostre court de faire droit si con je dois par mes pers, se il est[192] aucun qui aucune choze me requiert[193] en vostre court, et me offre a aleiauter en vostre court[194] de ce que vos m'avés mis sus, que je ai fait contre vos, se il est home[195] qui le veulle metre avant et maintenir dou[196] plus bas home de vostre reyaume jusques au plus haut. Et tant con je eufre se a[197] faire en vostre court, vos ne me devés congeer de vostre reyaume sans esgart ou sans conossance de court. Si vos requier et conjur come mon seignor que vos aprés se que je ay ofert en vostre court ne me congeés de vostre reyaume, et que vos me tenés a droit en vostre cort con vostre home[198] et me menés par l'esgart de mes pers.' Et que[199] por chose qu'il deist que le roy Heimeri[200] ne s'en vost soufrir et que[201] il requist[202] et conjura[203] ces pers qu'il[204] le maintenisent a droit si con il doivent[205] con lor per, puis que il avoit ofert et eufre[206] en la court se que il avoient oy, et que[207] lors[208] tous les homes dou rey li respondirent que ce[209] feroient il volentiers, et il les[210] mercia et s'en parti de la court. Et que[211] tous les homes dou rey requistrent au roy que il s'en soufrist de ce que il avoit[212] lor per congeé, et que, se il ne[213] s'en soufroit

[182] et ofroit a aleiauter s'en] A: et offreit a aleauter sei; B: a aleauter s'en; V: que il estoit prest d'aloyauter soi [183] l'on] AB: il [184] AV adds: et [185] et] ABV lack [186] A adds: en la court [187] et que il y alasent] A lacks; B: et que il alassent; V: et que eaus y alassent [188] seignor] A lacks [189] l'un d'eaus] A: un de ciaus; BV: l'un de ceaus [190] le roy alerent . . . que] B: alarent devant le roy o lui, et [191] ABO add: que [192] est] A: y a; V: li est [193] requiert] B: requiere; C: requeroit [194] et me offre a aleiauter en vostre court] AC lack [195] home] B lacks [196] le veulle metre . . . dou] A: metre en avant le vueille des le; B: le veull maintentir des le; V: metre le veulle avant et maintenir de le [197] B adds: prover et a [198] home] C: homes [199] que] V lacks [200] Heimeri] A lacks [201] que] V lacks [202] requist] B: requiert [203] AV adds: la; B: a [204] qu'il] A: qui [205] doivent] A: deveient; BV: devoient [206] eufre] A: offreit; BV: offroit [207] que] V lacks [208] lors] A lacks [209] ce] BO: si; V: ci [210] AV add: en [211] que] V lacks [212] A adds: ensi; B: enssi; V: enci [213] ne] C: n'en

et ne[214] menoit mesire Raoul par l'esgart de sa court, que il le guageroient tous ensenble et chascun par soy dou servize que il li[215] devoient tant que il eust faite lor requeste, et que[216] bien seust il que il[217] maintendroient contre lui mesire Raoul si con il devroient[218] con leur per, et que plusors[219] grans paroles y ot dite au roy. Et a tant s'en partirent devant[220] le roy et alerent a mesire Raoul et li distrent[221] coment il avoient le roy guagé de leur servize et que il[222] ofroient tous ensenble et chascun par soy de luy aidier et maintenir en cel fait si con il devroient[223] con leur per. Et que[224] il les en mercia mout[225] et lors[226] dist que il s'en soufriroit[227] lors de sa requeste et del conjurement[228] que il lor avoit fait que, puis que le roy estoit de tel portement vers luy, que il ne le serviroit ne[229] demoreroit en son reiaume por chose que il li feyst, ne que il li donast,[230] et que il s'en parti dou reyaume dedens le terme que le roy li avoit mis, et que[231] le guagement de quoy il avoient[232] le roy guagé demora[233] par se que mesire Raoul s'en[234] soufri de la requeste que il lor avoit faite[235] et del conjurement que[236] il les avoit conjurés. Et oy dire a mon dit[237] oncle, que[238] Dieus ait l'arme, que se aucun tel[239] cas avenoit[240] con il est avant dit[241] de mesire Raoul de Thabarie[242] et dou roy Heymeri,[243] que les homes de la court comunalment le doivent ensi faire con il est[244] devisé que il et les autres le firent quant le roy Heimeri[245] congea mesire Raoul de Thabarie[246] dou reyaume de Jerusalem sans esgart et sans conoissance de court.[k]

---

[k] The conflict between King Aimery of Lusignan and Ralph of Tiberias dates to 1198. For discussion, see Riley-Smith, *Feudal Nobility*, pp. 151–2, 156–9.

---

[214] ne] V lacks [215] li] CV lack [216] que] V lacks [217] il] V: eaus [218] devroient] A: deveent; B: doivent; V: devoient [219] C adds: autres [220] s'en partirent devant] A: laissierent; B: se partierent de devant [221] distrent] C: requistrent [222] AB adds: li [223] devroient] A: deveent; BV: devoient [224] que] ABV lack [225] mout] V lacks [226] lors] A: lor; BV: leur [227] soufriroit] B: soufroit [228] del conjurement] V: des esconjuremens [229] ne] A: ni ne; BV: ne ne; O: ni [230] feyst, ne que il li donast] A: seust doner ne qu'il li feist; B: dounast; V: feist ne li donast [231] avoit mis, et que] V: dona et [232] avoient] C: avroit [233] demora] C lacks [234] s'en] BV: se [235] faite] A: dit et fait [236] que] B: dont [237] dit] A: seignor mon; B: devant dit [238] que] A: de cui; BV: de qui [239] aucun tel] A: un tel; B: un autel [240] avenoit] A: avenist; C: avient [241] con il est avant dit] A: come est devant dit come celui; V: come celui [242] Thabarie] V: Tabarie [243] Heymeri] A: Henri [244] B adds: avant; V: dessus [245] Heimeri] A: Henri [246] de Thabarie] A lacks; BV: de Tabarie

***[179]** Se le seignor congee son home de sa seignorie sans esgart ou[1] sans conoissance de[2] court de la ou celui[3] est son home, que[4] l'ome qui est ensi congeé doit dire et requerre a son seignor et quey a ces pers, et que ces pers[5] doivent dire et faire.

Se il avient que .i. seignor de sa volenté congee .i. de ces[6] homes de sa seignorie sans ce qu'il l'a[7] ataint des choses par[8] quey il le puisse[9] congeer par esgart ou par conoissance de court, il me senble que il doit dire[10] en la presence de partie de ces homes:[11] 'Sire, je sui vostre home et aprestés sui[12] de droit faire en vostre court, se vous ou autre me savés[13] que demander. Et tant con je sui droit ofrant par vostre court, vos pri[14] et requier et conjur come[15] mon seignor que vos ne me congeés de vostre terre, ne ne veull que vos le facés, se vostre court n'esgarde[16] que vos faire le doyés. Et de ce vos[17] requier je l'esgart[18] de vostre court', et metre[19] son retenaill.

Et se le seignor ne s'en[20] seufre por tant de lui congeer, et cel esgart et[21] celle conoissance ne fait faire, il doit venir a ces pers et lor doit[22] dire: 'Seignors, mon seignor[23] m'a congeé de sa seignorie sur ce que je[24] li ay[25] droit ofert a faire par sa court et esgart[26] li en ay requis, et il[27] ne me le[28] viaut faire ne de moy congeer ne s'en[29] seufre. Por quey je vos pri et requier et conjur come mes pers que vos alés a mon seignor et le[30] priés et requerés que il ne me congee de sa seignorie tant con je[31] voudrays faire drois par sa court con celui qui eufre a faire droit par vos qui mes pers estes a lui ou a autre qui rien me savra que demander, et se li ofrés de par moy.

A: fols cxxx^{v}–cxxxi^{r} cap. 205; **B:** fols 160^{v}–161^{r} cap. 206; **C:** fol. 164^{r-v} cap. 179; **O:** fols 225^{r}–226^{v}; **V:** fols clxxvi^{r}–clxxvii^{r} cap. 215; Beugnot, pp. 328–9, cap. 205.

---

[1] ou] CV: et [2] AB rubrics (fol. 24^{v}) add: la [3] celui] A: il [4] que] V: car [5] ABV add: en [6] de ces] C: des [7] l'a] AB: l'ait; V: ait [8] des choses par] B: de chose par; V: de chose de [9] puisse] ABV: face [10] V adds: au seignor [11] de ces homes] V: des homes de sa court [12] sui] A lacks [13] V adds: riens [14] AB add: je [15] A adds: a [16] n'esgarde] A: ne conut; V: ne l'esguarde ou conoist [17] C adds: en [18] A adds: ou la conoissance [19] metre] AO: mete [20] s'en] A: se; B: le [21] et cel esgart et] A: ne cel esgart ne; B: et cel esgart ou; V: ou celui esgart ou [22] doit] B lacks [23] A adds: et le vostre; V: ci [24] je] C lacks [25] V adds: dit et [26] et esgart] A: et esgart ou conoissance; B: esgart; C: et esgard; V: et [27] il] A: dire li coment il li a requis ne il l'esgart ne la conoissance; B: dire coment il li a l'esgart requis et [28] ne me le] A: ne me; V: li ne me [29] s'en] AB: se [30] le] BOV: li [31] V adds: devrais et

Et tant con je eufre droit a faire par mes pers, je n'entent que il me doye ne puisse par raison[32] congeer de sa seignorie. Por quey je vos pri et requier et conjur come mes pers que vos ne me soufrés ensi a surmener[33] tant con je eufre[34] droit a faire par vos, ains me maintenés si con vos devez con vostre per.' Et a moy senble que aprés ce tous les homes[35] doivent venir devant le seignor et dire li: 'Sire, tel',[36] et le noment, 'est venus a nos et nos a dit que vos l'avés[37] congeé de vostre seignorie sur droit ofrant, et dit que il vos a ofert a faire droit en vostre court par ces pers, et a nos meymes l'a il[38] a ofert et prié et requis nos a[39] que nos le vos ofrons de par luy. Et il[40] nos a conjurés que nos le faisons tenir a droit par l'esgart de vostre[41] court ou que nos[42] le maintenons si con nos devons con nostre per. Por quei nos vos prions et requerons con nostre seignor que vos nostre per tel teignés a droit et menés par[43] vostre court et li faites faire l'esgart que il vos a requis ou que vos vos soufrés de lui congeer de vostre seignorie. Et[44] tant que vos li aiés fait faire l'esgart que il vos a requis ou dites[45] raison por coy vos ne li devés faire et tel que vostre court l'esgarde ou conoisse,[46] nos tous ensenble et chascun par soi[47] vos guagons dou servise[48] que nos vos devons. Et bien sachés que tant con il vodra faire droit[49] en vostre court par ces pers nos ne soufrerons que vos le surmenés,[50] ains le maintendrons[51] a droit si con nos devons.'[52] Et se le seignor li viaut aprés ce[53] mal faire, il le doivent aider et[54] defendre contre tous homes sauf le cors dou seignor tant con il voudra droit faire par ces pers.

---

[32] par raison] C lacks [33] surmener] B: formener [34] eufre] B: offrerai [35] tous les homes] V: que tous les homes de la court [36] V adds: vostre home [37] l'avés] V: l'en avés [38] l'a il] C: la ou il a; V: a il [39] nos a] AB lack [40] il] AB lack [41] vostre] A: la [42] ou que nos] C: onques nos ne [43] A adds: l'esgart de [44] Et] AB lack [45] dites] A: ditte [46] A adds: et se voz ce ne faites [47] soi] C: son [48] dou servise] B: des servises [49] droit] C lacks [50] surmenés] B: formenez [51] maintendrons] A: maindrons [52] B adds: come nostre per [53] ce] C lacks [54] et] V: a

***[180]** Coment et de coy l'ome ment sa foy vers son seignor, et coment et de coy le seignor ment sa foy vers son home, et coment l'un en[1] peut ataindre l'autre, et quel amende l'un en doit avoir de l'autre.[2]

L'ome[3] ment sa foy vers son seignor et[4] le seignor vers son home, se[5] il l'ocit ou fait ocire ou porchace[6] sa mort ou la consent[7] ou la seufre,[8] se il la set et il l'en[9] peut garder ou defendre se il ne le fait[10] a son poeir, et se il faire ne le peut que il[11] au mains l'en guarnise le plus tost qu'il porra por garder soy;[12] ou se il le prent ou fait prendre ou porchace[13] ou consent ou seufre[14] que il soit pris par ces enemis se il l'en[15] peut defendre ou guarder c'il ne le fait[16] a son poeir, et se il faire ne le peut que il l'en guarnise[17] par soy ou par autre le[18] plus tost que il pora; et[19] se il le tient ou fait tenir[20] en prison ou seufre que autre li[21] teigne se il l'en peut geter et il ne le[22] gete a son pooir a bone foy;[23] ou s'il le fiert par ire ou fait ferir ou consent ou seufre a son pooir[24] qu'il soit[25] ferus ou laydis et il le peut defendre et il ne le fait a son pooir; ou[26] s'il li court sus ou fait coure por metre[27] main a[28] son cors ou en ces choses de sa seignorie de cele dont il est son home; ou se le seignor met main[29] el cors ou el fié de son home ou[30] por luy desheriter, tout ne le face il, ou se il le fait ou fait faire, ou se il li met sus que il[31] a esté ou est ou a volu estre ou veaut estre mesprenant[32] vers lui de sa foy; ou que il fist trayson vers luy ou porchasa[33] ou soufri ou concenti ou sot et ne le[34] guarda ou au mains ne l'en guarnist,[35] ou aucune autre maniere de trayson ou de foy mentie li mete sus[36] et il ne l'en

---

A: fols cxxxi^{r}–cxxxii^{v} caps 206–7; **B:** fols 161^{r}–162^{v} caps 207–8; **C:** fols 164^{v}–166^{r} cap. 180; **O:** fols 226^{v}–228^{v}; **V:** fols clxxvii^{r}–clxxviii^{v} caps 216–17; Beugnot, pp. 330–2, caps 206–7.

---

[1] en] AV lack [2] doit avoir de l'autre] B: puet avoir de l'autre par l'assise [3] L'ome] AV: Se home; BO: Home [4] et] A: ou [5] se] AV: et [6] porchace] A: porchassier [7] la consent] A: la counoissent; O: consent [8] seufre] A: sueffrent; B: soufret [9] l'en] AB: le; V: la [10] se il ne le fait] A lacks; V: se il ne la fait [11] fait a son . . . il] B: puet [12] soy] BV: s'en [13] porchace] C: porchacer [14] B adds: ce [15] l'en] AV: le [16] c'il ne le fait] B: si le faca [17] guarnise] V: garnit [18] par soy ou par autre le] B: por lui ou por autre au [19] et] AOV: ou [20] A adds: come [21] li] ABV: le [22] le] BO: l'en [23] a bone foy] A lacks [24] a son pooir] A lacks [25] soit] B lacks [26] ou] C: et [27] por metre] A: ou mete [28] a] ABV: en [29] met main] B lacks [30] se le seignor . . . ou] V lacks [31] A adds: y [32] mesprenant] A: mesprent [33] porchasa] V: pourchasse [34] le] ABO: l'en [35] guarnist] AB: garni [36] ou de foy . . . sus] A: vers lui ou de fei mentie

ataint si con est devisé en l'autre chapitle que le seignor peut son home ataindre de sa foy ou l'ome son seignor;[a] ou se il gist charnelment o sa fille, ou la requiert de folie, ou le[37] porchace par autre a faire, ou ce il quiert[38] ou fait ou[39] porchace l'une des choses desus[40] dites a la fille[41] son seignor ou a la seur, tant con ele est damoiselle en son hostel,[42] ou seufre ou concent que autre le face c'il le peut destorner et il ne le fait ou au mains n'en[43] face son pooir. Et de laquel des choses desus[44] dites que l'un mesprent vers l'autre, il ment sa foy l'un vers l'autre.

Et se le seignor en ataint son home, il est[45] encheu en sa merci dou cors et dou[46] fié et de[47] quanque il a, et se il en viaut avoir droit[48] et il le requiert a sa court qu'ele li conoisse quel droit il en doit avoir, je cuit que la court esgardera que il[49] peut de son cors faire justize selonc ce que le mesfait sera de traïson ou de foy mentie et qu'il peut son fié et toutes ses autres chozes prendre et faire ent con de choze de traïtor et[50] de foy mentie. Et se l'ome ataint son seignor en court qu'il a[51] mespris vers luy de sa foy et il en requiert a[52] avoir droit par esgart ou par conoissance de court, je cuit que la court esgardera ou conoistra que l'ome est quite vers luy de sa foy et a son fié[53] toute[54] sa vie sans servise. Et se l'ome met sus a son seignor en court que il a mespris vers luy de sa foy et il ne l'en ataint si con il doit, il avra sa fey[55] mentie vers luy et sera encheu en la merci dou seignor con de foy mentie. Et bien se guart le seignor[56] que il ne mete sus a son home en court que il ait[57] sa fey mentie vers lui, que c'il le fait[58] et il ne[59] l'en ataint si con est avant[60] dit, il mentira sa foy vers luy, et l'ome avra l'amende de luy desus[61] dite, se il viaut. Ne l'un ne peut de ce ataindre l'autre, se ce[62] n'est par reconissance[63] que il[64] ait faite en court ou par quey[65] l'un mespreigne vers l'autre en court[66] d'aucune des avant[67] dites

[a] Above cap. 174.

[37] le] B: la; V: li [38] quiert] C: requiert [39] fait ou] B lacks [40] desus] B: devant [41] V adds: de [42] son hostel] A: l'ostel de son frere [43] n'en] AB: en [44] desus] B: devant [45] est] A lacks [46] dou cors et dou] AV de cors et de [47] de] C: que [48] et se il . . . droit] B: se il l'en veut avoir [49] esgardera que il] A: conoistra qu'il en [50] de choze de traïtor et] A: de traïtor ou [51] a] BV: ait [52] en requiert a] B: l'en requiert [53] et a son fié] A lacks [54] toute] B lacks [55] et il ne . . . fey] B lacks [56] con de foy . . . seignor] B lacks [57] ait] A: a [58] le fait] B: ne faut [59] ne] C: n'en; V lacks [60] avant] A: devant; V: dessus [61] desus] B: devant [62] ce] AB lack [63] reconissance] V: conoissance [64] ABV add: en [65] par quey] B: por ce que [66] en court] A lacks [67] avant] AO: devant; V: dessus

choses, car seignor ne peut prover vers son home aucune chose qui monte a sa foy ne l'ome vers son seignor autrement que par le recort des homes de la court dou seignor. Mais .i. home peut bien metre sur[68] .i. autre[69] qu'il est traytre vers son seignor ou qu'il a mespris vers luy d'aucunes des avant[70] dites choses, et se la trayson est aparant en tel maniere le peut il[b] apeler qu'il y avra bataille, et s'il en est ataint ou prové par bataille ou autrement il en sera fait de lui[71] con de traïtor ou de foy mentie selonc ce que le cas sera et la maniere coment se ce peut faire est devant[72] devisee la ou il parla[73] coment l'on deit bataille guager de fei mentie ou de traïson aparant.[c, d]

Et qui est home d'autre[74] et fait justise d'ome ou de feme[75] en la seignorie de son[76] seignor, s'il[77] ne le fait par son comandement ou ce le seignor ou son ancestre ne dona[78] a lui ou a son ancestre la justize do leuc ou[79] celuy l'a fait,[80] il mesprent de sa foy vers son seignor, et le seignor en pora avoir droit de lui et amende par sa court come de foy mentie, s'il en[81] est ataint ou prové.[82] Et se autre

[b] Change of hand in C.
[c] Above caps 84–5, 90.
[d] ABV begin a new chapter here with these rubrics:

A

Si dit qui fait justise en sa terre c'il ne le fait par comandement dou seignor de qui la seignorie est, ou se le chief seignor ou son ancestre n'en ait doné a lui ou a son ancestre la justise il se mesfait vers son seignor, et quel amende le seignor en deit aveir et a quei le seignor le peut mene<r> par sa court (et a quei . . . court] rubrics (fol. 7[r]) lack) sera devisié si dessout en cest chapitle.

B

Ci dit qui fait justise en sa terre se il ne le fait par comandement dou seignor de qui la seignorie est ou se le chief seignor ou son ancestre (ou son ancestre] rubrics (fol. 25[r]) lack) n'ait doné a celui ou a son ancestre, il mesfait vers son seignor, et en doit aveir amende tele con il voudra.

V

Ci dit que nus ne doit faire justize d'autrui en sa terre et c'il qui le fait si mesfait vers son seignor et quel amende le seignor en doit avoir.

[68] sur] BOV: sus a [69] A adds: home [70] avant] O: devant [71] de lui] BV lack [72] devant] B: avant [73] parla] AV: parle; B: parole [74] d'autre] V: d'autrui [75] B adds: ou d'enfant [76] de son] V: dou [77] s'il] C: si [78] ne dona] A: n'ont doné; B: ne done; V: ont doné [79] B adds: quel [80] V adds: il me semble que [81] en] C lacks [82] prové] C: povré

que home do seignor fait justize d'ome ou de feme ou d'anfant en la seignorie dou seignor, s'il ne le fait par son comandement,[83] le seignor de la seignorie[84] ou il fait la justise peut par raison faire de lui autel justise con il a fait de celui ou de cele qu'il a justisié sans[85] congé et plus grant se il viaut. Que par[86] le mesfait que il a fait[87] est il encheu en la mersi do seignor en qui seignorie[88] il a faite la justise de son cors et de[89] quanque il a. Si peut le seignor prendre et avoir tot[90] quanque il a en sa seignorie et son cors justisier[91] a sa volenté.

[83] en la seignorie . . . comandement] A lacks [84] dou seignor, s'il . . . seignorie] B lacks [85] V adds: son [86] Que par] B: Car pour [87] que il a fait] V lacks [88] seignorie] A lacks [89] A adds: tot [90] tot] A: ent [91] justisier] A: justisié; V: a justicier

***[181]** Se le seignor fait prendre son home et enprisoner sans esgart et[1] sans conoissance de sa[2] court, que[3] les pers de celui qui est ensi pris[4] doivent faire et dire a[5] lui delivrer.

Se aucun[6] seignor prent ou fait prendre aucun de ces homes, se ce n'est par l'esgart ou par la[7] conoissance de sa court de[8] la seignorie dont celui est son home, il mesprent de[9] sa foy vers lui, et ces autres homes ne le doivent soufrir, ains doivent tos ceaus qui le savront, maintenant qu'il avront seu qu'il l'a pris ou fait prendre un ou plusors de ces homes,[10] venir devant le seignor et dire li: 'Sire, l'on nos a dit que vos avés[11] nostre per tel', et le noment, 'ou nos pers tels',[12] se il sont pluisors, 'pris ou[13] fait prendre et arester sans esgart ou sans conoissance de court. Si vos prions et requerons que se vos l'avés pris ou fait prendre ou arester, ou s'il est en vostre poeir, que vos maintenant le faites delivrer et le faites venir en la cort. Si savrons se il eufre a faire[14] droit par vostre court a vos ou[15] a autre qui rien li savra que demander, et[16] nos le maintendrons si con nos[17] devons[18] con nostre per tant con il vodra droit faire par ces pers. Ne vos ne poés par l'assize ne l'usage de cest reiaume metre main ne faire metre[19] sur lui, se ce n'est par esgart ou par conoissance de court, ne tenir le pris[20] ne arester[21] tant con il eufre[22] droit a faire en vostre court par ces pers, que sa fey et son fié le plegent.'[23]

Et se[24] le seignor l'a pris ou fait prendre, il le doit maintenant[25] laisser aler, et garder soy que il ne die devant ces homes que il l'ait[26] pris ne[27] fait prendre ne que il le teigne en prison ne aresté, s'il ne peut mostrer par recort de court que il l'ait fait par esgart ou par conoissance de court. Que se il[28] le dit,[29] son home que il a[30] ensi aresté en avra, se il viaut, tel amende de lui que il sera quite vers

---

A: fols cxxxii^v–cxxxiii^v cap. 208; **B:** fols 162^v–163^v cap. 209; **C:** fols 166^r–167^v cap. 181; **O:** fols 228^v–231^r; **V:** fols clxxviii^v–clxxx^r cap. 218; Beugnot, pp. 332–4, cap. 208.

---

[1] et] ABO: ou [2] sa] AV lack [3] que] B lacks [4] pris] A: enprissoné; A rubrics (fol. 7^r)V: pris et enprissoné; B: enprisoné [5] a] B: quanqu'il porront por [6] aucun] V: le [7] par la] B lacks; C: la; V: par [8] sa court de] B lacks [9] de] C lacks [10] B repeats: doivent [11] avés] A lacks [12] B adds: et les noment [13] pris ou] B: en prison [14] a faire] C lacks [15] ou] BV: et [16] et] BV lack [17] nos] O lacks [18] devons] BO: devrons; V: porons [19] C adds: main [20] le pris] V lacks [21] ne arester] A: ni aresté; B: ne aresté [22] eufre] B: offrera [23] plegent] A: plege [24] se] B lacks [25] ABV add: faire [26] l'ait] B: l'a [27] ne] O: et [28] se il] A lacks [29] B adds: a [30] a] BV: l'a

son seignor toute sa vie de la foy et do servize que il li devoit et avra son fié,[31] et por ce ne sera pas quite le seignor de sa foy vers lui.[32] Et por ce est il ensi que l'ome n'a mie sa foy mentie vers son seignor et que le seignor l'a mentie vers son home, car quant l'un[33] ment sa foy l'un[34] a l'autre, celui a qui l'on la ment est quite[35] de la[36] foy que il doit a celui qui li a sa foi mentie, et celui qui la ment n'en est[37] mie quite por tant, ains en est aussi bien tenu con devant.

Et se il avient que le seignor die[38] qu'il le delivrera, si li dient: 'Quant?' et se il lor met jor ou terme et il a cel jor ou a cel[39] terme que il lor a[40] dit que il le delivrera[41] ne[42] le delivre et le tient plus[43] en prison, il li doivent dire: 'Sire, vos avés entendu coment nos vos avons requis que vos faites[44] tel qui est nostre per delivrer que vos tenés en[45] prison, et que[46] vos nos otroiastes[47] de delivrer le[48] et vos ne l'avés[49] fait encor que nos sachons. Si vos requerons et conjurons con nostre seignor que vos, par la fey que vos nos devés con a vos homes,[50] delivrés ou faites delivrer[51] sans delay nostre per tel', et le noment, 'que vos tenés et[52] faites tenir en prison. Et sachés, sire, que se vos ne le faites, nos ne porons laisser que nos ne fasons se que nos devons.'

Et se le seignor nee que il ne l'a pris ne fait prendre ne ne le tient ne fait tenir en prison, si li doivent dire: 'Sire,[53] donc nos abandonés que nos le puissons querre en tos les[54] leus que[55] nos cuiderons que il soit en prison,[56] et se nos le trovons[57] que nos le delivrons, se il veaut faire droit par vostre court a qui riens li savra que demander.' Et le seignor le doit faire. Et s'il l'abandone,[58] il le doivent querre en tos les leus ou il cuideront que il soit enprisoné. Et se il le treuvent, il[59] li doivent dire: 'O vos tel, vos estes nostre per. Se vos volés faire droit par la court de nostre seignor et do vostre de ce que l'on vos

---

[31] A adds: sanz servise [32] avra son fié . . . lui] B: le seignor ne sera mie quite vers lui de la foy que il li doit [33] l'ome n'a mie . . . l'un] ABV: le seignor a sa fei (B: foy; V: foi) mentie vers son home et que l'ome ne l'a pas (B: mie mentie; V: pas mentie) vers son seignor, quar (V: car) qui [34] l'un] deleted in C [35] vers son seignor toute sa vie . . . quite] O lacks [36] la] AV: sa [37] n'en est] A: n'est; B: ne est; V: ne [38] die] C: dit [39] a cel jor ou a cel] B: a cel jor ou; O: a cel jor et a cel; V: au jour ou a [40] a] B: avra [41] si li dient . . . delivrera] A lacks [42] ne] A: et ne; V: et il ne [43] le tient plus] B: tient [44] faites] B: facez; V: faciés [45] V adds: vostre [46] et que] B; et; C: que [47] otroiastes] O: otroiés [48] le] ABV lack [49] B adds: mie [50] ABV repeat: que voz (V: vous) [51] ou faites delivrer] B lacks [52] et] ABV: ou [53] Sire] V lacks [54] les] C lacks [55] que] ABV: ou [56] en prison] A: enprissoné; B: enprisoné [57] trovons] V: troverons [58] l'abandone] B: leur abandone; V: abandone [59] se il le treuvient, il] A: si

requerra ou que l'on vos[60] metra sus, nos vos delivrerons et maintendrons con nostre per.' Et se il l'eufre, il le doivent delivrer et maintenir con leur per[61] tant con il ofrira a faire droit par ces pers. Et s'il ne l'eufre, il le doivent laisser en prison,[62] ne plus ne se doivent de lui entremetre. Et se le seignor ne lor[63] viaut abandoner a querre, il ne doivent mie por ce laissier que il ne le quierent,[64] ains le doivent querre en tos les[65] leus ou il cuideront[66] qu'il soit,[67] et c'il le treuvent et il veulle ofrir a faire droit par ces pers, il le doivent delivrer a force ou autrement, se le cors do[68] seignor ne lor[69] defent a force,[70] a armes[71] ou autrement, car il ne pevent[72] porter armes contre le cors de[73] leur seignor ne faire li force. Et se le seignor le defent encontre yaus[74] a force ou autrement, il li[75] doivent dire: 'Sire, puis que vos[76] qui estes nostre seignor nos defendés a force nostre per a delivrer et maintenir a droit en vostre court tant con il vodra faire droit par ces pers, nos qui somes vos homes et qui[77] ne poons armes porter contre vos ne faire force,[78] vos guagons toz ensenble et chascun par soi do servize[79] que nos voz devons jusques a tant que vos aiés nostre per tel',[80] et le noment, 'delivré[81] et remis[82] en sa lige poesté.' Et de celui jor en avant iaus[83] ne li doivent obeir ne faire servise que il li doivent, ne faire[84] comandement que il leur fase tant que il[85] ait[86] leur per[87] delivré si con il li ont requis. Et se le seignor ne le delivre a lor requeste ou[88] ne lor defent si con est avant dit et il[89] le delivrent, il le doivent maintenir contre chascun tant con il vodra faire droit par ces pers, mais que contre[90] le cors do seignor contre qui nul de ces homes ne doit[91] autre maintenir, se ce n'est[92] aucun autre sien seignor a qui il ait avant fait homage.

---

[60] l'on vos requerra . . . vos] B: vos l'on; V: l'on vous requerra ou [61] Et se il l'eufre . . . per] V lacks [62] laisser en prison] C: en prison laisser [63] lor] C: le [64] quierent] V: quiert [65] les] C lacks [66] cuideront] B: tendront [67] ABV add: en (V: em) prison (A: prisson) [68] do] A: de leur [69] lor] ABV: le [70] a force] V lacks [71] a armes] A lacks [72] pevent] V: peut [73] le cors de] B lacks [74] encontre yaus] A: contre eaus; B: contra eaus; O entr'yaus; V lacks [75] li] BV lack [76] que vos] O lacks [77] qui] V: que nos [78] V adds: nos [79] do servize] B: de servises [80] tel] A lacks [81] delivré] C: delivrés [82] remis] BV: mis [83] iaus] AB: il; V lacks [84] faire] B lacks [85] V adds: lor [86] ait] A: aie [87] per] B lacks [88] ou] A: et [89] C adds: ne [90] contre] V: encontre [91] doit] C: doivent [92] ce n'est] A: n'est; C lacks

***[182]** Coment et por quei home qui a pluisors seignors peut porter armes contre son seignor sans mesprendre vers[1] lui de sa foy.

Se un home a pluisors seignors, il peut sans mesprendre de sa foy aider son premier seignor a qui il a fait homage devant les autres en totes choses et en toutes manieres contre tos ses autres seignors, por ce qu'il est devenus home des autres sauve sa feiauté. Et ausi peut il aidier a chascun des autres sauf le premier et sauf ceaus a qui il a fait homage avant que a celui que il vodra aidier. Car a moi senble que se .i. seignor eust un home ou plusors qui fust ou fucent home ou homes d'autre seignor[2] devant lui,[3] et il l'eust semons de venir le[4] aidier a defendre sa terre contre ces henemis mortels qui venissent por desheriter lui[5] et ces homes, et que se il ne[6] vient,[7] il est en perill d'estre desherité, si li covient sei a conbatre a iaus[8] sans delay, et quant il seroit[9] venus a sa semonce, et il fust armés el chanp aprestés de soy conbatre, et il seust sertainement que un de ces seignors de qui il seroit home devant celui o qui il seroit venus[10] el chanp par semonce[11] si con est desus dit,[12] et son premier seignor[13] fust armé d'autre part en la conpaignie de ceaus qui venroient[14] celui desheriter[15] a tort, cel home, por guarder soy de mesprendre vers son seignor[16] de sa fei, devroit venir devant son seignor, quant il seroit venus el chanp, et dire li en la presence[17] de ces homes: 'Sire, je sui vostre home sauve la feiauté[18] de tel', et nomer le,[19] 'et il vient a armes[20] contre vos, et moult me[21] peise de ce[22] que je ne vos puis aidier a cest besoing qui est vostre et mien, por ce

---

A: fols cxxxiv^{r}–cxxxv^{r} cap. 211; **B:** fols 164^{v}–165^{v} cap. 212; **C:** fols 167^{v}–169^{r} cap. 182; **O:** fols 231^{r}–232^{v}; **V:** fols clxxxi^{r}–clxxxii^{v} cap. 221; Beugnot, pp. 336–7, cap. 211.

---

[1] son seignor sans mesprendre vers] B: l'un des seignors sanz mesprendre envers [2] d'autre seignor] C: d'autres seignors [3] lui] A lacks [4] venir le] A: venir li; V: lui venir [5] venissent por desheriter lui] V: vienent pour lui deseriter et lui [6] ne] A: n'i [7] vient] V: vienent [8] si li convient . . . iaus] A: car il li covient sei combatre a eaus; B: se il li covient soi conbatre o ceaus; V: car conbatre se couvient a eaus [9] seroit] ABV: fust [10] venus] C lacks [11] et il fust . . . semonce] AB lack [12] si con est desus dit] A lacks [13] et son premier seignor] BV lack [14] venroient] B: voudroient; V: veroient [15] ABO add: et [16] vers son seignor] ABV lack [17] la presence] V: sa presence et [18] feiauté] V: foi [19] nomer le] A: le nome; B: le noment [20] a armes] V: armés [21] me] OV: m'en [22] de ce] A lacks

que celui qui est mon seignor devant vos est[23] de cele part, ne je ne doy[24] ne ne puis porter armes contre[25] lui en leuc ou son cors soit. Por laquel chose je m'en terai[26] a une part et n'aiderais[27] de mon cors[28] a cest besoing ne a vos ne a lui. Mais je veus bien que totes[29] mes gens vos aident contre celui[30] qui vos vient dezeriter et qui est[31] chief de la guerre contre vos.'

Et se son seignor li dit:[32] 'Vos savés que je vos semons que vos me venissiés aidier a defendre moy et ma terre contre mes mortels henemis qui a tort me veulent desheriter. Et vos mandai que se vos ne[33] me venés[34] aidier, que je[35] ne me conbatroie pas a iaus, et vos venistes a ma semonce, et sur[36] cest mandement et par fiance de vos me sui je venu conbatre a iaus, et vos me volés ore guerpir[37] en champ por dire que vostre seignor est venus o mes henemis, et si[38] est venus par son outrage sans ce que la guerre a monté de riens a lui,[39] je n'entent[40] pas que vos por ce me deiés guerpir en chanp, qui[41] por vostre fiance sui ci[42] venus conbatre a mes henemis. Et je vos pri et requier et conjur par la fei que vos me devés et semons sur[43] quanque vos[44] tenés de moy, que vos ne me guerpissiés[45] en chanp, ains vos venés conbatre o moy a[46] mes henemis. Et vos vos poés bien garder de metre main el[47] cors de vostre seignor, et ensi[48] li[49] porroit escheir que vos li avrés besoing.' L'ome peut a ce respondre: 'Sire, vos[50] dirés[51] quanque[52] vos vodrés,[53] mais sachiés[54] je ne porterai ja[55] armes por vos en chanp contre celui qui est mon seignor devant vos, puis que il est armés[56] de l'autre part. Car quant je devins[57] vostre home, si i fu[58] sauve sa feyauté,[59] por coy je ne puis porter armes contre lui por vos. Mais vés si que je vos lais tot le

---

[23] est] C lacks [24] C adds: de cele part [25] contre] B: encontre [26] m'en terai] A: me trais; B: me trai; O: me terrai; V: m'en trais [27] n'aiderais] O: m'ayderais [28] de mon cors] A lacks [29] totes] A lacks [30] celui] V: lui et contre tous ceaus [31] est] V: sont [32] se son seignor li dit] A: son seignor li peut dire [33] ne] V lacks [34] venés] A: venissiés; B: veniez; V: venisiés [35] V adds: me combatree. Et ce vous n'i veniciés je [36] sur] B lacks [37] guerpir] C: par grepir [38] si] A: c'il est venus il; B: se il i [39] a monté de riens a lui] V: n'a monté de rien a lui ne [40] je n'entent] A: por quei je n'entens [41] qui] V: car [42] sui ci] A: me sui si; V: suis je [43] sur] B lacks [44] V adds: me devés et [45] guerpissiés] C: grepissiés [46] venés conbatre a moy a] V: en venés combatre a moi contre [47] el] BV: au [48] ensi] B: ausi [49] li] ABV lack [50] A adds: entendés si come il vos plaira et [51] dirés] B: dites [52] quanque] AB: ce que [53] vodrés] B: volez [54] ABV add: que [55] ja] A lacks [56] contre celui qui . . . armés] ABV: ou celui qui est mon seignor devant vos seit armés (BV: soit a armes) [57] devins] B: deveig [58] fu] O: fui [59] feyauté] C: feyance

servise que je vos doi do fié[60] que je tiens de vos mais que mon cors. Ne plus vos ne me poés requerre[61] par raison, car je ne vos suis pas tenus d'aider contre lui, ne[62] n'entens que je faire le puisse sans ma fei mentir. Et por ce je n'acuill n'acuillir ne veuill[63] la semonce ne le conjurement que vos m'avés fait. Et[64] vos dis come vostre home sur la foi que je vos doi[65] con a mon seignor, que se que[66] je ne[67] vos aide a[68] se[69] besoing de mon cors et que je part[70] de cest chanp n'est que[71] por ma fey guarder vers tel', et le nome,[72] 'qui est mon seignor devant vos, et que on ne me puisse de traïson reter,[73] se je portoie armes en chanp contre lui.' Et a tant s'en part et se traie a une part.[74] Et se il ensi le fait, je cuit que il fera ce que il devra vers chascun de ces seignors. Car c'il ne le fait enssi, il mentira sa foy vers son premier seignor et l'en porroit l'on apeler de trayson et son seignor[75] avoir en droit par sa court, et[76] se il ensi le fait le segont[77] seignor, se me senble, ne le peut par raison ataindre de foy[78] mentie ne de defaut de servize.

---

[60] fié] A: servise [61] A adds: autre [62] ne] ABV: et [63] n'acuillir ne veuill] A: ni ne viaus acuillir [64] Et] B: Ainz [65] doi] B lacks [66] se que] BV lack [67] ne] C lacks [68] aide a] B: aiderai en; V: ayderais a [69] ce] A: cest; B: ceste; V: cestui [70] que je part] B: que je me part; V: ce pour qui je depart [71] n'est que] B: tant soulement; V: n'est pour autre que [72] nome] B: noment [73] reter] B: arrester; V: apeller [74] A adds: dou champ [75] V adds: em poroit [76] et] V: Car [77] le fait le segont] B: li fait le [78] foy] A: sa fei ni de fei; O: sa foy

***[183]** Coment seignor doit faire semondre home ou feme de faire droit en sa court quant l'on c'est clamé[1] de lui,[2] et quant l'on est enssi semons et l'on a essoine,[3] coment l'on[4] doit contremander c'essoine et par qui, et se il ne vient au jor que[5] il est[6] semons ou ne contremande c'essoigne si con il doit, quei[7] son aversaire doit requerre au seignor, et quei[8] le seignor li[9] en det faire.

Se aucun se claime au seignor d'aucun des[10] homes de quelque chose[11] que ce soit, le seignor ne le peut ne ne[12] doit[13] par l'assise ou l'usage do reiaume de Jerusalem faire le semondre qu'en sa propre persone de[14] venir faire droit. Et se le seignor mande semondre par .iii. de ces homes come court aucun home[15] de venir faire droit[16] maintenant d'aucune choze dont on[17] se claime de luy, et il dit[18] au message: 'Je suis essoignés.[19] Je ne[20] puis ore aler', et se il y[21] met jor ou hore et il mande au jor ou[22] a l'ore que le seignor li avra mis de venir a court qu'il est essoignés si qu'il n'i[23] peut aler a court, il doit estre creus la premiere feis par sa sinple[24] parole. Et se le seignor l'a[25] fait semondre par letres ou par banier et il est essoinés, il doit c'essoine faire assavoir au seignor par son message. Et quant les .iii. homes avant dis le semonent et li[26] metent jor de venir a court et il mande au jor que les semoneors l'avront semons[27] de venir a court[28] faire droit a celui qui de lui c'est clamés[29] par un home qu'il est essoignés si que il ne peut venir a court,[30] et celui qui ce dit au seignor eufre a faire ce que court esgardera ou conois-

---

A: fols cxxxv^r^–cxxxvi^v^ cap. 212; **B:** fols 165^v^–167^r^ cap. 213; **C:** fols 169^r^–171^r^ cap. 183; **O:** fols 232^v^–235^v^; **V:** fols clxxxii^v^–clxxxiv^v^ cap. 222; Beugnot, pp. 338–40, cap. 212.

---

[1] c'est clamé] A: se claime [2] V adds: ou d'elle [3] a essoine] B: est essoignié [4] l'on] A: on; A rubrics (fol. 7^r^) BV: il [5] et se il ne vient au jor que] B lacks [6] est] V: avra esté [7] quei] ABV: que [8] quei] ABV: que [9] li] B lacks [10] des] AV: de ces; B: de ses [11] quelque chose] V: qui [12] ne ne] C: ne le [13] ne le peut ne ne doit] B: ne ne doit mie ne ne puet [14] de] C lacks [15] par .iii. de . . . home] A: un de ces homes par .iii. de ces homes come court; B: aucun de ses homes [16] Et se le . . . droit] V lacks [17] dont on] B: dont l'on; V: que l'on [18] dit] ABV: die [19] V adds: pour qui [20] ne] B: n'i [21] se il y] A: cel li; B: se il li; V: ce il [22] ou] V: et [23] n'i] ABV: ne [24] sinple] B: plaine [25] l'a] AV; le [26] et li] A: c'il li; V: s'il y [27] V adds: li ont mis et semons [28] a court] AV lack [29] Et se le seignor . . . clamés] B: quant il a dit a ceaus qui le semonent, et se il au jor ou a l'ore que il avra esté semons mande au seignor [30] par un home . . . court] A: qu'il est essoigniés

tra que il faire en doie, que[31] il est mesage de celui qui a esté semons[32] a ce dire que il a dit por lui, s'il est nul qui le mescree, il doit estre creu de sa plaine[33] parole, ausi con celui seroit qui la l'a[34] envoié, se il estoit present,[35] puis que il eufre a faire se que la cort conoistra qu'il[36] doie faire, que[37] il est son message et qu'il li a enchargé se que il a dit por lui.[38] Mais se il ne l'eufre, il ne me semble que son dit doie estre acuilli con de mesage,[39] por ce que se enssi n'estoit que le message ne fust tenus en tel cas de ofrir se qui est avant[40] dit, a paines seroit jamais home ne feme ataint de defaut de venir faire droit par semonce do seignor. Car qui seroit semons de venir faire droit au[41] jor nomé ou a hore motie et il ne venoit ne ne mandoit[42] au seignor ne a la[43] court faire assaveir c'essoine, quiconques[44] vodroit porroit dire: 'Sire, tel vos mande qu'il est essoiné si que il ne peut venir a court faire droit a celui qui se claima[45] de luy', et ensi seroit quite celui de cele semonce[46] de qui l'on ce[47] seroit clamé et qui avroit esté semons de venir faire droit[48] sans ce que il fust essoinés, ne que il eust dit ne mandé[49] que il fust essoignés.[50] Et ce seroit, ce me senble, contre l'assise ou l'usage do roiaume de Jerusalem, que[51] en l'assise ou en l'usage est que qui est semons de venir faire droit de clain que on a[52] fait de lui, que il doit estre creus la premiere feiz de c'essoine par sa plaine[53] parole. Et se enssi estoit que celui qui dit qu'il est essoignés[54] n'en[55] deust sertefier le seignor en la court, chascun qui vodroit se porroit faire son message et seroit escusé de la semonce do seignor de venir a court faire droit sans ce que il fust essoinés que qui[56] il eust dit ne mande que il fust essoinés.[57] Si[58] ne seroit pas l'assise ou[59] l'usage devant[60] dit tenue ne maintentue.[61] Et por le maintenir,[62] me senble il, que celui

---

[31] que] B: quar [32] esté semons] V: ceste semonce [33] plaine] AV: simple [34] la l'a] C: l'a; V: l'a yleuques [35] B adds: et [36] V adds: en [37] que] B: quar [38] et qu'il li . . . lui] BV lack [39] V adds: et que il li a enchargié ce que il li a dit por lui et [40] avant] V: desus [41] par semonce do . . . droit] AV: a [42] ne venoit ne ne mandoit] B: ne vient ne ne mande; V: n'i vient ou ne contremande [43] ne a la] V: et a sa [44] quiconques] A: qui onques [45] clama] C: claime [46] quite celui de cele semonce] A: que celui; B: celui [47] ce] BV lack [48] faire droit] C lacks; V: faire droit de clain [49] que il fust . . . mandé] CV lack [50] A adds: sereit quitte de celle semonce [51] que] B: quar [52] a] AV lack [53] plaine] A: simple [54] qu'il est essoignés] V: que le mesage de l'essoigné [55] n'en] ABV: ne [56] que qui] B: ne que; C: quei; O: quei que [57] que qui il . . . essoinés] A lacks [58] V adds: me semble que ce [59] pas l'assise ou] V: l'assise ne [60] devant] A: avant; V: dessus [61] tenue ne maintentue] B: tenuz; V: tenue et maintenue [62] le maintenir] AV: maintenir l'assise ou (V: et) l'usage; B: mainteni

qui dit[63] de par le semons de venir faire droit qu'il est essoinés doit sertefier le seignor et la court, si con est avant[64] dit, que il est son mesage, et que se il ne le fait, que[65] son dit ne doit valoir[66] a celui de qui il dist qu'il est mesage,[67] si[68] que il soit creu de c'essoine[69] par le dit de celui qui a dit[70] qui[71] estoit[72] son mesage. Et se celui de qui l'on c'est clamés et que le seignor a fait semondre de venir faire droit au clamant dit la premiere feiz[73] que il est essoignés si que il ne peut aler,[74] ou le mande[75] faire assaveir au seignor et a la cort si con il doit, il en est creus.

Et se le clamant aprés aucun jor dit au seignor que il ne croit[76] que il lors[77] soit essoinés, si li prie et requiert que il li ait a droit, le seignor le doit mander[78] semondre de venir faire droit a celui qui de lui c'est clamés. Et s'il dit qu'il est essoinés et le clamant dit que il ne le croit pas,[79] le seignor i doit mander .iii. de ces homes, l'un en leuc de lui[80] et les .ii. come[81] court, et ceaus le doivent semondre que il aille[82] a court faire droit a tel de tel choze, et nomer la persone et dire de quei. Et s'il dit qu'il est essoinés si que il ne[83] peut aler, il li doivent dire que celui ne le croit mie, et qu'il sont venus de par le seignor come court[84] semondre le que il aille a court,[85] ou que il s'escondise[86] en leur presence si con il doit par l'assise ou l'usage dou[87] reiaume.[88] Et il doit faire l'un des .ii.[89] aler au mandement do seignor, ou faire le sairement qui est establi a faire de ce. Et s'il dit lors qu'il est essoinés si que il ne peut aler a court, il li doivent dire: 'Faites nos ent sertains si con vos devés', et il doit jurer sur sains que il est essoinés si que il ne peut aler[90] a court.[91] Et s'il fait ce, il en[92] est creus a cele foiz. Et s'il ne le fait ou il ne vait maintenant a court,[93] il est encheu con defailli[94] de

[63] qui dit] V: que [64] avant] V: desus [65] que] B lacks [66] doit valoir] B: vaut riens; V: doit valoir ne [67] et que se il . . . mesage] A lacks [68] si] V: et [69] c'essoine] A: ces essoines [70] a dit] B: disoit [71] qui] ABV: qu'il [72] estoit] B: ostoit; V: est [73] la premiere feiz] A: au premier [74] aler] V: venir a faire droit [75] mande] B: manda [76] ne croit] A: n'entent; O: n'en croit [77] lors] C lacks [78] B adds: querre et [79] pas] ABV lack [80] leuc de lui] V: son leuc [81] come] C: en leuc de [82] aille] V: y veigne [83] ne] BV: n'i [84] come court] B: come; V lacks [85] faire droit a . . . court] O lacks [86] s'escondise] C: s'econdise [87] B adds: dit [88] O adds: de Jerusalem [89] faire l'un des .ii.] V: lors faire l'une des ces .ii. choses ou [90] aler] V: venir [91] il li doivent . . . court] A lacks [92] en] C lacks [93] a court] V lacks [94] defailli] AV: de defailli; B: defaillant

droit[95] et pert[96] sa querele en tel maniere con il est devisé en cest livre que home qui defaut de venir faire droit la pert.

Et aprés aucun jor, se le clamant entent que il se fait essoine[97] et il ne le soit ou que il soit garis de cel essoigne[98] que il avoit quant il fist[99] le dit sairement, il doit venir devant le seignor et dire li: 'Sire, je me clamai de tel', et le nome, 'un jor qui pasés est, et il dist lors que il estoit essoinés, et ge vos diz que je ne le creoie pas et vos[100] envoiastes .iii. de vos homes et il lor dist qu'il estoit essoinés et[101] en fist lors se que il dut.[102] Mais je ne croi pas que il ore soit essoignés, por quei je vos pri et requier que vos le m'aiés[103] a droit enssi con vos devés, que[104] je me clain de lui tot ensi con ge autre foiz m'en[105] sui clamés.' Et[106] le seignor doit mander lors chés celui[107] .iii. de ces homes come court et un fisisien ou selorgien selonc le dehait que il dit que il a qui soit son home lige et esconjurer[108] le par la fei que il li doit que il li die voir de l'essoine de celui.[109] Et s'il nul n'en y a qui soit son home lige, si[110] envoit un qui soit tenus par son sairement de dire voir a son escient de cel dehait. Et les .iii.[111] homes le doivent semondre de[112] par le seignor que il aille[113] a court faire droit a tel de tel choze et nomer la persone et dire de quey. Et s'il dit qu'il est essoinés, celui des .iii. homes de court[114] qui est la en leuc dou seignor li doit dire: 'Mostrés vostre essoigne a cest miege',[115] et il le doit faire. Et le miege le doit veir et taster son pous et veir[116] s'orine. Et se ce est de[117] choze que le[118] selorgien doie conoistre, il li doit mostrer la bleseure en la presence des .iii.[119] homes que le seignor avra enveés. Et se le miege[120] dit par la fei ou[121] le sairement de quei[122] il est tenus que il est[123] essoinés, l'on ne le peut a plus mener tant con il demorera en son ostel et dira

[95] droit] A: semonce et de dreit faire [96] pert] B: a perdu [97] se fait essoine] A: se fait essoigniés; B: face essoigniez [98] et il ne . . . essoigne] C lacks [99] fist] C lacks [100] pas et vos] B: mie et vos y [101] ge vos diz . . . et] V lacks [102] .iii. de vos . . . dut] A: lors a lui si come voz deustes [103] m'aiés] V: menés [104] que] B: quar; V: car [105] m'en] ABV: me [106] Et] B lacks; V: de lui [107] chés celui] A lacks; O: celui [108] esconjurer] AV: conjurer [109] voir de l'essoine de celui] V: verité de celui se il est essoigné [110] si] BV lack [111] A adds: de ces [112] de] C lacks [113] aille] V: veigne [114] de court] B: de la cort; V lacks [115] miege] C: mege (and similarly throughout this section) [116] veir] B: resgarder [117] de] BV lack [118] que le] B: que O: de quei [119] V adds: de ces [120] le miege] B: il [121] la fei ou] V lacks [122] de quei] O: ou [123] est] A lacks; B: soit

qu'il est essoiné. Maiz se[124] le fisisien ou le selorgien[125] ne conoist[126] en lui aucun[127] dehait por quei[128] il doit demorer d'aler a court, yl i doit aler faire droit, ou il est ataint come home[129] defailli[130] de venir faire droit. Si pert celle querele, si con est avant[131] dit en cest livre que home qui defaut de venir faire droit la pert.[a]

[a] Above cap. 43.

[124] se] C lacks [125] selorgien] O: cyrorgien [126] conoist] A conut [127] aucun] C: autre; V: aucune chose ou aucun [128] quei] C: que [129] home] A lacks [130] defailli] B: defaillant [131] avant] V: dessus

***[184]** Se le seignor fait semondre aucun[1] de son servise, et il[2] est mermé d'aucune chose de son fié que le seignor ait et tieigne sans esgart ou[3] sans conoissance de cort, ou que le seignor li doive aucune chose parfaire de son fié que il li[4] ait requis en cort que il li parface[5] et[6] il ne li a[7] fait, coment il se peut defendre d'acuillir cele semonce tant que le[8] seignor li ait[9] son fié parfait ou rendu se qu'il[10] li en tient[11] en la maniere avant dite.[12]

Se aucun home[13] est mermé d'aucune choze de son fié que le seignor ait et tieigne sans esgart ou sans conoissance de court, et que se soit[14] chose que le seignor li doive parfaire[15] de son fié, et il a cele choze requise en cort au seignor, et le seignor le fait semondre d'auctions de ces servizes que il li doit et il ne viaut sele semonce acuillir ne faire cel servize de son seignor,[16] il doit dire a celui qui le semont: 'Je n'entent pas[17] que je doie ceste semonce acuillir tant que mon seignor m'ait rendu tel choze que il tient de mon fié sans esgart et[18] sans conoissance de court, laquel choze je li ai requisse en sa court', et dire[19] que se est,[20] 'ne acuillir ne la veuill, se la court ne l'esgarde.' Et se il li faut de chose que le[21] seignor li doit parfaire de son fié, si li die que il n'entent que il cele semonce doie acuillir tant que il li ait parfait se que il li faut de son fié, et die quel choze ce est: 'laquel chose je li ai requise en sa court. N'acuillir ne la veuill, se la court ne l'esgarde.' Et aprés il doit venir devant le seignor et dire li: 'Sire, vos m'avés fait semondre de tel servise', et die[22] quel, 'et vos tenés sans esgart et sans conoissance de court tel choze de mon fié', et die quei, 'et[23] je la vos ai requise[24] en vostre court, et

---

A: fols cxxxvi^{v}–cxxxvii^{r} cap. 213; **B:** fols 167^{r}–168^{r} cap. 214; **C:** fols 171^{r}–172^{r} cap. 184; **O:** fols 235^{v}–237^{r}; **V:** fols clxxxiv^{v}–clxxxv^{v} cap. 223; Beugnot, pp. 340–1, cap. 213.

---

[1] AV add: home; B: de ses homes [2] et il] AB: et l'ome; V: ou [3] ou] BV: et [4] li] C lacks [5] de son fié . . . parface] A lacks [6] parface et] B: deust parfaire et [7] li a] B: l'ait; V: li ait [8] le] B: son [9] que le seignor li ait] V: come le seignor ne li ait fait [10] se qu'il] A: de ce que il; C: se il [11] li en tient] A: tient; BV: entent [12] en la maniere avant dite] B: que il li tient de son fié [13] home] AV lack [14] et que se soit] A: ou ce seit de; B: ou que ce soit; V: et que il se soit de [15] parfaire] B: faire [16] de son seignor] V lacks [17] pas] ABV lack [18] et] OV: ou [19] dire] B: die [20] se est] V: ceste semonce [21] de chose que le] B: chose que son [22] die] B lacks [23] vos tenés sans . . . et] V lacks [24] la vos ai requise] B: le vos ai requis; V: vous ais requis tel chose que vous me tenés de mon fié et die quel

vos ne me l'avés encore rendue, ne dit raison por coi court ait esgardé ou coneu[25] que vos ne[26] me devés rendre. Si n'entent que je doie vostre semonce acuillir, tant que vos m'aiés ce rendu qui est de mon fié que vos tenés sanz esgart et[27] sans conoissance de court, ou que vos aiés dite raison[28] tel que cort esgarde ou conoisse[29] que vos faire ne[30] le deés. Ne acuillir ne la veuill se la court n'esgarde[31] que je acuillir la doie, et di por coi: por ce que je ne vos doi servize que de mon fié, et que tel chose que vos tenés[32] est de mon fié, laquel chose[33] je[34] vos ai requise en vostre court', et die quei, 'et que je[35] mermé de mon fié ne vos doi servise.[36] Si ne le veul faire por les raisons que je ai dites,[37] se la cort ne l'esgarde, et de ce me met je[38] en l'esgart de la court sauf mon retenaill.' Et ensi se covera il d'esgart de cort. Et puis qu'il ensi ce sera covert, il ne me senble que il soit tenus de la dite semonce acuillir ne faire le servize de quei il a[39] esté semons, tant que la cort ait le dit esgart fait. Et il ne me senble que le seignor puisse dire[40] chose par coy la court doie esgarder qu'il doie cele semonce acuillir, tant que le seignor li ait rendu se que il a[41] et tient de son fié si con est avant dit, puis que il autre foiz li a requis en court et[42] que le seignor n'a chose dite par quei court ait esgardé ou coneu que il ne le[43] doive rendre.

---

[25] ou coneu] B: ne coneu; V lacks [26] A adds: la; BV: le [27] et] AV: ou [28] aiés dite raison] V: m'aiés dit raison dite [29] esgarde ou conoisse] B: ait esgardee ou coneue [30] ne] CV lack [31] n'esgarde] AB: ne l'esgarde; V: ne l'esguarde [32] tenés] V: me devés [33] que tel chose . . . chose] A: je sui mermé de mon fié de tel chose laquel [34] chose je] O: je [35] C adds: suis [36] servise] BOV: servir [37] si ne le . . . dites] A lacks [38] met je] V: mes [39] a] A: ait [40] dire] C lacks [41] a] BV: l'a [42] B adds: qu'ele et [43] le] BOV: li

***[185]** Se .i.[1] home se viaut defendre d'acuillir semonce dou[2] servise que il doive quant le seignor a et tient aucune chose de son fié sans esgart et[3] sans conoissance de court, ou que il li doit parfaire aucune chose de son fié, ou se il li doit[4] dete de son fié,[5] et il n'a requis au seignor aucune des dites choses, que il doit dire et faire quant il est semons dou servise que il doit.

Se le seignor fait semondre aucun sien home d'aucun de ces[6] servises que il li doit, et il est mermé d'aucune choze de son fié en aucune des manieres avant[7] dites,[a] et il n'ait cele chose requise au seignor en sa court avant que il ait esté semons, et il ne veulle cele semonce acuillir ne faire le servise de quei il est semons[8] se il n'a se de quei[9] il est mermé de son fié, il doit dire a celui qui le semont: 'Mon seignor tient tel choze de mon fié', ou, 'il me doit[10] tel chose parfaire de mon fié',[11] ou, 'il me doit de mon fié d'un terme ou de plus',[12] et die quei. 'Se il la me rent', ou, 'il me[13] parfait mon fié, je ferai vers lui se que je devrai.' Et aprés doit venir devant son[14] seignor et dire li: 'Sire, vos m'avés fait semondre de tel servise', et dit quel, 'et vos tenés tel chose de mon fié sans esgart et sans conoissance de court', ou, 'vos me devés tel chose parfaire de mon fié', ou, 'vos me devés de mon fié[15] d'un terme ou de plus', et die li laquel de ces choses ce est.[16] 'Se vos la me rendés ou parfaites, je suis prest d'aler et de faire[17] vostre servise si con je doiz.[18] Et se vos ne la me rendés', ou, 'ne[19] parfaites', ou, 'ne me paiés,[20] ne dites raison por coi vos ne le devés faire et tel que court l'esgarde ou conoisse, je n'entent que je doie vostre semonce acuillir, ne faire vostre servise tant que vos l'aiés fait, ne faire ne le veull se la cort ne l'esgarde, et di por coi: por ce que je ne vos doi servise[21] que

---

A: fol. cxxxviii[r–v] cap. 215; **B:** fols 169[v]–170[r] cap. 216; **C:** fol. 172[r–v] cap. 185; **O:** fols 237[r]–238[r]; **V:** fol. clxxxvii[r–v] cap. 227; Beugnot, pp. 343–4, cap. 215.

---

[a] Above cap. 184.

---

[1] .i.] ABV lack [2] dou] ABV: de [3] et] A rubrics (fol. 7[v]) B: ou [4] doit] A lacks [5] ou se il . . . fié] CV lack [6] de ces] AV: des; B lacks [7] avant] B: devant [8] et il ne . . . semons] O lacks [9] de quei] B: dont [10] C adds: de mon fié [11] de mon fié] A lacks [12] A adds: de la paie [13] il me] B lacks [14] son] ABV: le [15] ou, 'vos me . . . fié] A: ou, 'vos me devés; BV lack [16] de ces choses ce est] V: chose se est et [17] faire] V: parfaire [18] Se vos la . . . doiz] O lacks [19] B adds: me; V: la me [20] ne me paiés] ABV lack [21] tant que vos . . . servise] O lacks

de mon fié, et[22] se que je vos requiers[23] est de mon fié,[24] et se[25] vos mescreés que se ne soit de mon fié je le[26] suis prest de prover le[27] si con court esgardera ou conoistra que je prover le doie, et de ce me met je en l'esgart de la court sauf mon retenail.' Et qui ensi le fera com est avant[28] dit, il ne me senble que le seignor puisse chose dire par coi la court doie esgarder que l'ome doie sa semonce acuillir ne faire son servise tant qu'il li ait rendu se que il tient de son fié ou parfait se qu'il li en defaut ou paie[29] ce que[30] il li en doit[31] dont le terme est passé de sa paie ou dit[32] raison por coi il ne le doit faire et tel que court l'esgarde ou conoisse.

[22] BO add: que [23] requiers] BV: requier; C: requis [24] fié] O lacks [25] que je vos . . . se] A lacks [26] le] AV lack [27] le] B lacks [28] avant] V: desus [29] paie] B: paier; V: parpaie [30] parfait se qu'il . . . que] C: partie se qui li en faut ou partie se [31] B adds: paier [32] dit] B: dire

***[186]** Quant le seignor fait semondre aucun par .iii. de ces homes come court, se[1] celui qui fist la semonce en leuc do seignor n'est present en la cort, se les .ii.[2] qui furent[3] come cort la ou il la fist la[4] recordent[5] sans lui en la cort, se sele[6] semonce vaut ou ne vaut,[7] ou[8] se celui qui estoit[9] en leu do seignor est en la cort et l'un de ceaus qui fu come cort quant il fist la semonce et il recordent en la court la semonce qu'il a faite, se cel recort doit valoir?[10]

Se le seignor fait semondre aucun de ses homes dou servise qu'il li doit ou d'autre chose ou il fait semondre aucun autre que son home par .iii. de ces homes come court, l'un en leuc de lui et les .ii.[11] por[12] court, et celui qui est en leuc[13] dou seignor meurt ou forspaise ains que la semonce soit retraite devant le seignor et devant la[14] court, ou se le seignor a[15] mestier dou recort[16] de ceaus qui furent a la semonce faire come court et celui qui fist la semonce n'est present en la court quant il en avra mestier, il doit les .ii. qui furent[17] come court la ou la semonce fu faite[18] venir devant lui et devant tant de ces autres[19] homes que ce soit court, et[20] dire leur: 'Je establis .i. jor[21] qui passés est tel en mon leuc et vos[22] .ii. come court a faire tel[23] semonce', et doit nomer celui et devizer[24] la semonce. 'Je vos comant que vos recordés come court si[25] en la presence de moi et de ma court qu'en[26] fu fait de cele semonce.' Et il doivent lors recorder se que il en virent et oirent, et se que il en diront[27] et[28] doit estre creu[29] et maintenu come recort de court,[30] et[31] se le seignor

A: fols cxxxviii^{v}–cxxxix^{v} cap. 216; **B:** fol. 170^{r-v} cap. 217; **C:** fol. 173^{r-v} cap. 186; **O:** fols 238^{r}–239^{v}; **V:** fols clxxxvii^{v}–clxxxviii^{v} cap. 228; Beugnot, pp. 344–5, cap. 216.

[1] se] A: et [2] B adds: homes [3] furent] C: sont [4] la] AB: le [5] recordent] C: rendent [6] sele] AV: la [7] ou ne vaut] C lacks [8] ou] ABV: et [9] estoit] ABV: est [10] fu come cort . . . valoir] A: furent court se elle vaut ou non; A rubrics (fol. 7^{v}): furent court n'i est se elle vaut ou non; B: furent court vaut ele ou non vaut; V: furent come court faut se le recort vaut ou ne vaut auci [11] .ii.] B: autres [12] por] ABV: come [13] C adds: de lui [14] la] ABV: les autres (A: autres de ces) homes tant que se soit (A: seit) [15] se le seignor a] A: le seignor ait [16] V adds: de court [17] qui furent] V lacks [18] ABV adds: faire [19] de ces autres] B: de ses autres de ses; V: des autres [20] et] A: a [21] jor] C: jors [22] vos] B: puis [23] en mon leuc . . . tel] C lacks [24] devizer] B: devise [25] si] V: yci [26] qu'en] A: ce qui; B: que; V: qui [27] diront] C: diroit [28] et] ABV lack [29] creu] A: tenu [30] O adds: que ce est recort de court [31] Et] ABV: que

peut prover par recort de court que[32] il establi a faire cele semonce celui que il[33] a dit[34] en son leuc et ceaus[35] .ii. come court. Que le seignor peut faire en la court se que celui qu'il establi en son leuc feist, se il y fust, ce est a[36] dire que il semonst tel de par le seignor en tel maniere et nomer celui qu'il semonst et dire la maniere.[37] Et se les .ii. qui sont[38] court le guarantisent, la semonce est[39] faite en court et vaut. Mais s'il ne le guarantisent,[40] ele ne[41] vaut,[42] ne ne[43] sera creu de choze que il en die come court ne con recort de court[44] en maniere que son dit ait force come court[45] ne con d'ome qui ait vois de[46] court, ne son dit ne vaut que de raconter[47] se que il a[48] fait[49] por le seignor. Et puis que son dit n'a force d'autre,[50] se le seignor le dit en quel leuc il[51] fu a sa semonce faire, mais que il dit: 'Tel que[52] je mis en mon leuc a tel semonce faire la fist enssi', et dire[53] la maniere, il vaut autant con se il estoit present et le deist, et[54] se les .ii. devant dis le recordent en la court, que la force de la guarantie n'est que as .ii. Mais se les .ii. avant diz le recordent[55] ensenble,[56] ou que l'un le recorde si con l'autre[57] le recorde[58] sans aucun amermement faire,[59] le seignor ne porra cele semonce prover par recort de court, s'il est qui la noie, tout fust ce que les .ii. de ceaus[60] qui furent a la semonce faire[61] le recordassent en la[62] court, et que l'un de ceaus[63] fust[64] celui qui estoit en leuc do seignor a la semonce faire, por ce que puis que il avroit esté en leuc do seignor il n'avroit pas vois de recort[65] a court puis[66] que le seignor ne l'a, ne il ne le poroit[67] avoir en cel cas puis que le seignor ne l'a.[68]

---

[32] se le seignor . . . que] BV lack [33] establi a faire . . . il] C lacks [34] a dit] A: mist; V: establi a esté [35] ceaus] B: ces; V: les [36] a] AV: de [37] et nomer celui . . . maniere] V lacks [38] B adds: en; V adds: come [39] est] B lacks [40] guarantisent] C: guarnissent [41] C adds: le [42] Mais s'il ne . . . vaut] B lacks [43] ne ne] AB ne il ne; V: ne il ne vaut ne il ne [44] ne con recort de court] V lacks [45] en maniere que . . . court] B lacks [46] vois de] C lacks [47] raconter] V: recorder [48] a] C: ait [49] fait] A: dit [50] n'a force d'autre] V: n'en a force plus que .i. autre [51] il] C: ce [52] le dit en . . . que] A: dit que celui que [53] dire] A: dit [54] et] ABV lack [55] que la force . . . recordent] B lacks [56] ensenble] V: en la court ensemble [57] l'autre] C: la court [58] le recorde] B: l'a recordé [59] faire] A: faire et se l'un des .ii. fu en leuc de semonce; C: faite [60] de ceaus] V lacks [61] B adds: cele semonse [62] en la] A: come [63] ABV add: .ii. [64] fust] V: fu [65] V adds: de court [66] puis] B: porter [67] le poroit] A: la poreit pas; B: la porroit [68] V adds: quant il fist la semonce et il recordent en la court la semonce que il a faite se celui recort doit valoir

***[187]** Ques manieres[1] de servise[2] doivent ceaus qui doivent servise de lor cors au seignor a qui il le doivent, et en quel leuc il li doivent le servise.[3]

Ce[4] sont les servises de coi je suis ore menbrant que les homes doivent a celuy de[5] lor seignors[6] a cui il doivent servise de lor cors por les fiés que il tienent de lui quant il les semont ou fait semondre si con il doit.

Il li[7] doivent servise d'aler a cheval et a armes a[8] sa semonce en tous les leus dou reiaume ou il les semondra ou fera semondre o tes servises[9] con il doivent[10] et de[11] demorer y tant com il les semondra ou fera semondre[12] jusques a un an. Que plus d'un[13] an de terme ne doit l'on pas[14] acuillir semonce par l'assise ou l'usage do reiaume[15] de Jerusalem. Et celui qui doit servise de son cors ou de chevalier[16] ou de sergens en doit faire par tout le roiaume le servise[17] o lui ou sans lui, se il en est semons si con il doit.[18]

Et quant il est a court d'aler au conceill de celui ou de cele[19] a qui le seignor l'a doné[20] a conseill,[21] se il n'est au conceill de son aversaire ou se la querele n'est contre lui meime, que nul ne doit plaideer contre lui[22] par[23] comandement de seignor ne d'autre. Et doivent faire esgars et conoissances et recors de court, se le seignor[24] comande a faire. Et doivent aler veir murtre ou homecide, se le seignor lor comande d'aler veir come court. Et doivent par le comandement dou seignor veir les cos de quei l'on se claime que l'on veaut mostrer a court. Et doivent aler[25] par tout le reiaume semondre come

A: fols cxxxix^{v}–cxl^{r} cap. 217; **B:** fols 170^{v}–171^{v} cap. 218; **C:** fols 173^{v}–175^{r} cap. 187; **O:** fols 239^{v}–241^{r}; **V:** fols clxxxviii^{v}–clxxxix^{v} cap. 229; Beugnot, pp. 345–8, cap. 217.

[1] Ques manieres] A: Quel maniere; A rubrics (fol. 7^{v}): Quantes manieres; B: Quele maniere [2] servise] AO: servises; V: services [3] li doivent le servise] B rubrics (fol. 25^{v}): le doivent [4] Ce] V: Ces [5] celuy de] B lacks [6] lor seignors] ABV: leur seignor [7] li] AV lack [8] a armes a] A: as armes en [9] tes servises] ABV: tel servise [10] AB add: aler (A: a aler) en besoigne d'armes se il sont (B: en sont) semons si come il deivent (B: doivent) [11] de] AV lack [12] y tant com . . . semondre] C lacks [13] d'un] A: qu'un [14] doit l'on pas] A: peut on; B: doit l'on mie [15] do reiaume] V lacks [16] ou de chevalier] B: et des chevaliers; V: et de chevaliers [17] le servise] B lacks [18] se il en . . . doit] A lacks [19] ou de cele] A lacks [20] l'a doné] AB: le done; V: le donra [21] a conseill] C: a consiller; V lacks [22] meime, que nul . . . lui] A lacks; V: meymes que nul ne doit plaideoir [23] par] C: por [24] A adds: le; B: leur; V: lor [25] aler] B lacks

court quanque[26] le seignor lor comandera et oir come court[27] se que l'on[28] dira devant eaus, se le seignor lor comande,[29] et faire la messagerie que le seignor leur eschargera[30] par tot le reiaume. Et li doivent servise d'aler veir[31] devises[32] de terres et d'aigües entre gens qui ont contens quant le seignor leur comande.[33] Et doivent faire enquestes quant l'on requiert au seignor qu'il les fase requerre[34] et il lor comande a faire.[35] Et doivent venir[36] mostres de terres ou d'autres choses quesqu'eles soient que le seignor lor comande[37] a veir come court. Et doivent servise de faire[38] toutes les autres choses que les homes de cort doivent faire come cort quant le seignor lor comande.[39] Et tout le dit servise[40] le[41] doivent il faire par tout le reiaume.

Et li doivent servise hors dou reiaume en tos les leus la ou le seignor ne le chief seignor ne vait por[42] .iii. choses:[43] l'une[44] por le mariage de lui ou d'aucun[45] de ces enfans; l'autre por sa foi ou por[46] s'enor garder ou[47] defendre; la tierce por le besoing aparant de sa seignorie ou le comun profit de sa terre. Et celui ou ceaus qui[48] le seignor semont ou fait semondre si con il doit de l'une de ces[49] .iii. dites[50] choses et il l'aquiaut[51] la semonce et vait el servise dou seignor, le seignor li doit doner ces estoviers soufisaument tant con il sera en cel sien[52] servise, tout soit ce que il n'ait mie en fié[53] estoveirs[54] ens et hors. Et celui ou ceaus que le seignor a semons ou fait semondre dou dit servise et il[55] n'aquiaut[56] la semonce ou[57] ne dit raison[58] por quoi il ne la doit acuillir et tel que court l'esgarde[59] ou conoisse, le seignor en peut avoir droit con[60] defailli de servise. Que chascun[61] des homes[62] dou reiaume qui doivent servise de lor cors doivent par

---

[26] quanque] V: quant [27] quanque le seignor . . . court] C lacks [28] l'on] A: on lor [29] C adds: et oir come court se que l'on dira devant eaus, se le seignor lor comande [30] escharera] V: comandera [31] veir] ABV: faire [32] devises] CV: devise [33] comande] A: comandera a faire [34] requerre] BV: enquerre [35] Et doivent faire . . . faire] A lacks [36] venir] A: veyr; OV: veir [37] comande] C: mande [38] faire] A lacks [39] comande] C: coumanda [40] tout le dit servise] AB: toz les dis servises [41] le] AV: li; B: si [42] seignor ne vait por] B: ne va de [43] Et li doivent . . . choses] A: en toz les leus la ou leur seignor ou le chief seignor vait ou ne vait quant il sont semont si come il deivent, et hors dou reiaume sont il tenus d'aler et de faire .iii. choses por le seignor [44] A adds: est [45] d'aucun] C: d'aucune [46] ou por] A: et; B: por; V: ou [47] ou] A: et [48] qui] ABV: que [49] de ces] AV: des [50] dites] V lacks [51] l'aquiaut] C: l'aquiant [52] sien] A lacks [53] n'ait mie en fié] A: n'a mie [54] C adds: et [55] dou dit servise et il] A lacks [56] n'aquiaut] C: n'aquiant [57] ou] C: dou dit servise et il [58] dit raison] A: die [59] l'esgarde] B: esgarde; V: esguarde [60] AOV adds: de [61] chascun] B: aucun [62] des homes] A: home

l'assise ou l'usage de cest reyaume[63] de ces .iii. dites[64] choses servise[65] hors dou reiaume a celui a qui il doivent servise de lor cors. Et au chief seignor doivent il[66] tos les avant diz servises si con[67] est avant[68] devisé.

Et feme qui a et[69] tient fié qui doit servise de cors doit au seignor tel servise: qu'ele se doit marier a la semonce do seignor quant il la semont si con il doit de marier sey,[70] et quant elle s'est[71] mariee son baron[72] doit au seignor[73] les servises avant devizés.

[63] qui doivent servise . . . reyaume] C lacks [64] dites] V lacks [65] .iii. dites choses servise] A: dittes choses [66] il] ABV lack [67] A adds: il [68] avant] V: dessus [69] feme qui a et] V: ce feme [70] a la semonce . . . sey] V lacks [71] s'est] V: sera [72] baron] B: mari [73] doit au seignor] V: devra au seignor tous

***[188]** Coment et ou les seignors pevent et doivent faire[1] semondre leur homes des[2] servises qu'il[3] leur doivent.[4]

Ce sont les manieres selonc ce que a moi[5] sovient ore coment les seignors pevent et doivent faire leur homes et leur femes[6] semondre do servise que il li doivent et qui[7] les en peut[8] semondre si que la semonce soit valable. Le seignor les peut semondre[9] mais qu'il ait[10] court la ou il les semont, cest assaveir .ii. de ces homes ou plus, et les peut[11] faire semondre par .iii. de ses homes lesqués[12] il establise[13] l'un en son leuc et les .ii.[14] come[15] court, et que ce soit establi devant autres de ces homes.[16] Et les puet faire semondre par son banier. Et si[17] est devizé en cest livre quel droit le seignor[18] en[19] doit avoir de celui ou de ceaus de ces homes qui li defaillent do servize, et coment il en peut avoir droit.[a]

A: fol. cxl^{r-v} cap. 218; **B:** fols 171^{v}–172^{r} cap. 219; **C:** fol. 175^{r} cap. 188; **O:** fol. 241^{r-v}; **V:** fols clxxxix^{v}–cxc^{r} cap. 230; Beugnot, p. 348, cap. 218.

---

[a] Below cap. 190.

---

[1] faire] B lacks [2] des] ABV: de leur (B: lor) [3] qu'il] A: que eaus [4] B adds: faire [5] V adds: semble et [6] et leur femes] BV lack [7] qui] AB: qu'il [8] peut] V: pevent [9] si que la . . . semondre] CV lack [10] ait] V: aient [11] les peut] V: le pevent [12] lesqués] A: desquels; B: desquex; V: desqués [13] establise] V: establissent [14] les .ii.] A: que les .ii. seent [15] come] B: en leuc de [16] autres de ces homes] A: .ii. de ces homes ou plus [17] si] ABV lack [18] le seignor] V: il [19] en] AB lack

***[189]** Por quei le seignor ne doit son home faire semondre[1] de son servise se il n'en a[2] mestier, et por quoi[3] l'ome[4] ne se doit faire essoigne[5] se il ne l'est quant il est semons dou servise que il doit au seignor.

Le seignor ne doit son home semondre ne faire semondre[6] de son servise[7] se il n'en a[8] besoing. Et l'ome ne se doit faire essoine[9] quant son seignor l'en[10] semont ou fait semondre de son servise[11] se il n'est essoiné.[12] Et lequel des .ii. qui le[13] fait autrement ne fait pas[14] se que il doit, ne ne guarde sa foy vers l'autre si con il doit.

A: fol. cxl[v] cap. 219; **B:** fol. 172[r] cap. 220; **C:** fol. 175[r] cap. 189; **O:** fol. 241[v]; **V:** fol. cxc[r] cap. 231; Beugnot, p. 349, cap. 219.

[1] faire] AB lack [2] n'en a] A: n'a [3] mestier et por quoi] O: besoing et [4] l'ome] C: l'on [5] essoigne] AB: essoigniez [6] ne faire semondre] V lacks [7] B adds: faire [8] n'en a] A: n'a [9] essoine] A: essoignié [10] l'en] ABV: le [11] de son servise] A lacks [12] n'est essoiné] ABV: ne l'est [13] le] C lacks [14] pas] B: mie

***[190]** Coment[1] le seignor peut et doit semondre et faire semondre ces homes dou servise que il li doivent et ou, et quant il les a semons ou fait semondre que il[2] doit faire et dire. Et[3] quant l'ome defaut[4] dou servise que il li[5] doit aprés se que il[6] a esté semons si con il doit,[7] quel droit le seignor en doit avoir, et coment il le peut avoir. Et se le seignor ne le[8] fait si con il doit, quel amende l'ome en doit avoir. Et qui est semons dou servise que il doit et il est essoigné, coment et par qui il doit contremander c'essoine.

Se le seignor a besoing de tos ses homes ou d'aucun d'eaus, il les peut, si con est avant[9] dit,[a] semondre,[10] et se il meimes fait la semonce, il la doit faire devant .ii. de ces homes ou plus, por ce qu'il ait recort de court se mestier li est. Et quant le seignor semont son home, il doit dire a celui que il semont: 'Je vos semons de tel chose en tel maniere', et die[11] de quoi et coment il le[12] semont[13] et ou il le[14] semont et[15] fase la semonce en la maniere[16] aprés devisee. Et quant il l'avra faite, traie[17] a guarans ceaus de ces homes[18] qui la seront ou il fera[19] la semonce.

Et s'il la fait[20] faire par .iii. de ces homes, l'un en leuc de lui et les .ii. en leuc de[21] court, die celuy qui est establi en leuc do seignor a celui que il viaut semondre: 'Je vos semons de par mon seignor tel', et le nome, 'que vos seés a tel jor en tel leuc',[22] et die le jor et nomer[23] le leuc,[24] 'aprestés de tel servise faire con vos devés a mon seignor, et aiés ce que besoing vos est a demorer la jusques a tel terme',[25] et die le terme, 'et soiés au comandement de tel', et le nome, 'que mon[26] seignor a establi a estre[27] en son leuc.' Et se le

A: fols cxl^{v}–cxlii^{v} cap. 220; **B:** fols 172^{r}–174^{v} cap. 221; **C:** fols 175^{r}–178^{r} cap. 190; **O:** fols 241^{v}–245^{v}; **V:** fols cxc^{r}–cxcii^{v} cap. 232; Beugnot, pp. 349–52, cap. 220.

[a] Above caps 186–8.

[1] Coment] A rubrics (fol. 7^{v}): Por quei [2] O adds: en [3] Et] ABV lack [4] defaut] AB: faut [5] li] AV lack [6] ABV add: en [7] A adds: et [8] le] C lacks [9] avant] A: devant; V: dessus [10] BOV add: ou faire semondre [11] die] A: dire [12] le] V: les [13] et die de . . . semont] O: aprés devisee et quant il l'avra faite [14] le] V les [15] et ou il le semont et] B: et; C: ou cil le semont ou [16] en la maniere] A lacks [17] traie] A: traire [18] de ces homes] V lacks [19] fera] A: fait [20] s'il la fait] B: il la [21] en leuc de] AV: come [22] que vos seés . . . leuc] A lacks [23] le jor et nomer] A lacks; B: le jor et nome [24] et die le . . . leuc] V lacks [25] tel terme] B: tant [26] mon] C: le [27] ABV add: la

besoin est hastif, le seignor peut bien son home[28] semondre a hore motie[29] ou[30] a movoir maintenant selonc ce qu'il en avra besoin. Et se il le viaut ensi semondre, le semoneor le doit semondre si con est avant[31] dit, mais que tant que il li die l'ore a quei il le semont et le leuc. Et se le seignor le fait semondre par le banier, le banier doit faire la semonce en la maniere avant[32] devisee.

Et s'aucun des homes dou seignor defaut do servize de quei il a esté semons en la maniere avant[33] dite par[34] seignor ou par home en son leuc ou par banier et le seignor en viaut[35] avoir droit, le banier en doit estre creu s'il dit qu'il l'a semons, se celui ne dit[36] par la foy que il doit au seignor que le banier ne le semonst de cele semonce si con il l'a[37] dit et a[38] tant en est quite, ou se non, il pert son fié tant con il devise[39] en cest[40] livre que l'on pert son fié por defaut de servise.[b] Et se le seignor le semont devant .ii. ou plus de ces homes ou le fait semondre par .iii. de ces homes, l'un en leuc de lui et les .ii. come[41] court, il pert son fié en la maniere aprés dite,[42] car escondit que le semons[43] face ne li vaut riens,[44] se il n'estoit si[45] essoinés si qu'il ne[46] peust aler a la semonce et qu'il a c'essoine faite assaver au seignor a hore et a tens si con il doit, ou que il l'a contremandee si con il doit[47] a hore et a tens.[48] Et quant le seignor a son home semons ou fait semondre par .iii. de ces homes si con est avant devisé[49] en sa persone ou en son[50] hostel ou en son fié de son servise que il doit, il doit[51] faire reter[52] en la court ceaus de ces homes qui ont esté la ou la semonce fu[53] faite, et celui qui l'a faite doit retraire en la court coment il a la semonce faite et les autres le doivent guarantir,[54] et quant il ont ce dit en la court, le seignor doit comander[55] a la court qu'ele seit bien menbrant de cele semonce que la court a recordee.

---

[b] Above cap. 183.

---

[28] ABV add: faire [29] son home semondre a hore motie] B: semondre mové [30] ou] C: et [31] avant] AB: devant; C lacks [32] avant] AB: devant; V: desus [33] avant] AB: devant [34] ABV add: le [35] viaut] A: vueille; BV: veulle [36] se celui ne dit] V: Et ce celui ne dit que [37] l'a] AV lack; B: a [38] a] C lack [39] il devise] A: il est devisié; V: est devisé [40] cest] C: cel [41] et les .ii. come] B: l'autre en leuc de [42] dite] C: devisee [43] semons] C: seignor [44] riens] A: neent; B: nens [45] si] ABV lack [46] qu'il ne] C: que nul n'i [47] C adds: ou que il [48] ou que il . . . tens] AB lack; V adds: si come est dessus dit [49] avant devisé] V: dessus dit [50] son] C lacks [51] il doit] C lacks [52] reter] A: retraire; B: rester; V: recorder [53] fu] V: a esté [54] guarantir] C: guarantie [55] comander] C: mander

Et aprés ce que le terme de la semonce est pasé, se celui qui a esté semons do servise que il doit au seignor n'est venus ou alé la ou il a esté[56] semons ou[57] dite ou mostree c'essoine au seignor ou a celui qui est en son leuc, ou ne l'a[58] contremandee[59] si con il doit a hore et a tens, le seignor en peut[60] avoir droit par sa court totes le feis que il vodra. Et se il veaut avoir droit,[61] si face dire enssi en la presence de sa court: 'Je fis semondre tel[62] en tel maniere', et die[63] coment, 'laquel semonce fu retraite en la presence de moy et de ma court par tes', et les nome, 'qui furent presens[64] la ou la semonce fu faite. Et celui qui fu semons n'a fait ce de quei il fu semons[65] ne contremandé[66] a hore ne a tens si con il doit c'essoine, s'il ot essoine.[67] Si vos requier[68] que vos me counoissés quel droit je[69] en doie avoir.' Et la court[70] li doit[71] conoistre, se cuit, que il se peut saisir de son[72] fié de coi il doit le servise et[73] de coi[74] il[75] l'a fait semondre et faire s'en servir an et[76] jor, se il a esté semons en persone. Mais se il a esté semons[77] en son hostel ou en son fié, la cort doit conoistre que le seignor peut le[78] fié saisir et faire s'en servir tant que celui[79] qui a esté semons[80] en son hostel ou en son fié[81] si con est desus[82] dit veigne[83] en la presence de lui et de la court et li requiere la saisine de son fié, et que le seignor li doit maintenant rendre la saisine dou[84] fié quant il la[85] requera.[86] Et quant le seignor l'avra saisi de ce dont il ot la saisine, si con il[87] est avant[88] dit, le seignor se peut, se il viaut, maintenant clamer de lui de ce qu'il[89] li est defailli dou servize de quei il li fist la semonce[90] en la maniere avant dite.[91] Et quant il se clamera, celui de qui il se claime n'avra pas jor a cel[92] clain. Et se il nee que il n'est pas[93] defailli dou[94] servise, le seignor le[95] doit prover par le recort de la court, et se il

---

[56] a esté] B: estoit [57] do servise que . . . ou] A: a [58] ne l'a] ABV lack [59] V adds: la [60] en peut] C lacks [61] par sa court . . . droit] O lacks [62] V adds: et tel [63] die] B: dire [64] presens] A lacks [65] n'a fait ce . . . semons] C lacks [66] A adds: n'a [67] s'il ot essoine] V lacks [68] A adds: si come je dei [69] je] C: il [70] la court] C: laquel [71] li doit] B lacks; V: doit [72] de son] ABV: dou [73] et] AB lack [74] de coi] B: dont [75] doit le servise . . . il] V lacks [76] an et] ABV: .i. (B: et un) an et .i. [77] en persone. Mais . . . semons] O lacks [78] le] A: son [79] V adds: y viegne [80] la cort doit . . . semons] O lacks [81] en son hostel . . . fié] ABOV lack [82] desus] B: devant [83] veigne] CV lack [84] dou] A: de son [85] B adds: li [86] quant il la requera] V lacks. B adds: dou defau<t> dou servise se celui est defalli dou servise si com est avant dit requerre la ssasine de son fié [87] il] BV lack [88] avant] V: dessus [89] qu'il] A: quei il; C: qui [90] la semonce] A: semondre [91] en la maniere avant dite] V: dessus dit [92] cel] BV: celui [93] pas] A lacks; BV: mie [94] dou] AB: de [95] le] OV: li

le preuve ensi, la cort doit[96] esgarder que il se peut resaisir de cel[97] fié et faire s'en servir[98] .i. an et un jor, et[99] por ce que il est plus seure chose au seignor quant il l'a semons devant .ii. de ces homes ou plus ou fait semondre par .iii. de ces homes come court aucun de ses homes,[100] et il[101] li[102] est defailli de servise, que il li[103] fase la semonce retraire en la court a ceaus de ces homes qui furent la ou il les[104] semonst ou as devant diz.[105] Que se il se claime et la semonce a esté retraite, ceaus de la court sont certains que la semonce a esté faite. Si pevent et doivent l'esgart[106] faire si con est avant[107] dit. Mais se le seignor ne fait la semonce retraire en la court as avant[108] dis et dit que il a fait semondre tel son home[109] et le nome si con il doit[110] et il li[111] est defailli de servise et[112] requiert a la court qu'ele li conoisse quel droit il en doit avoir, la court doit conoistre, ce me semble, que se il est ensi con il dit qu'il se peut saisir dou[113] fié et faire s'en servir an et[114] jor ou tant que celui que il dit qui[115] li est defailli de servise li requiert[116] la saisine de son fié selon ce que la semonce avra esté faite, a son cors ou a son fié ou en sa maison.

Et quant celui que le seignor a dit qui li[117] est defailli de servise et de qui le fié[118] est saisi en la dite maniere vient en la court et requiert la saisine de son fié et l'a,[119] et le seignor se claime de lui si con est avant[120] dit, et il nee que le seignor ne l'a pas[121] fait semondre si con il a dit ne que il ne li est defailli de[122] servise que il[123] doit, et le seignor ne le peut prover par recort de court, ce est assaveir de ceaus siens homes devant qui il fu semons, celui[124] ne sera pas ataint de[125] defaut de servize. Et que se il[126] se claime do seignor de ce que il avra mis main en[127] son fié autrement[128] qu'il ne doit et qu'il en viaut avoir tel amende[129] con la court[130] conoistra qu'il avoir en doie,[131] la court doit conoistre,[132] se cuit, qu'il en

[96] doit] V: peut [97] cel] A: son; V: celui [98] s'en servir] C: son servise [99] et] C lacks [100] come court aucun de ses homes] C lacks [101] aucun de ses homes et il] B: et aucun de ses homes [102] li] AV lack [103] li] ABV lack [104] les] AO: le [105] A adds: homes [106] l'esgart] A: les garenz [107] avant] A: devant; V: dessus [108] avant] O: devant; V: dessus [109] tel son home] C: son home tel [110] si con il doit] B: si com il dut; V lacks [111] li] AB lack [112] et] B: si [113] dou] A: de son [114] s'en servir an et] B: servir un an et un [115] qui] OV: que il [116] requiert] B: quiert [117] qui li] V: que il [118] qui le fié] ABV: qui (V: que) fié il [119] et l'a] B lacks [120] avant] V: dessus [121] pas] ABV lack [122] de] A: de son; BV: dou [123] ABV add: li [124] qui il fu semons, celui] V: que il fu semons celui qui [125] ne sera pas ataint de] B: n'est mie a tant [126] que se il] ABV: qui [127] avra mis main en] V: y avra mis main sur [128] autrement] C: autorment [129] amende] B: enmende [130] V adds: esguardra et [131] doie] C: doive [132] doit conoistre] ABV: conoistra

doit estre quite vers le seignor[133] toute sa vie de la fei et do servise qu'il li doit de cel[134] fié et que le seignor n'est mie quite vers lui de la soue fei. Et por ce ai ge dit devant que le seignor doit faire retraire a sa court la semonce as[135] .iii.[136] homes si con il l'ont faite,[137] ou a ceaus[138] qui furent la ou il le[139] semonst, que se il le fait ensi, il est hors de cel[140] desus[141] dit perill. Et se le seignor fait ces homes semondre par banier ou par .iii. de ces homes d'aler a court et il n'i[142] vienent,[143] il sont defaillis[144] de servise, s'il ne sont essoinés et qu'il[145] fasent assaveir lor essoigne as .iii. homes ou au banier.

Et se il[146] vont a[147] la court par la semonce desus[148] dite, celui qui se partira de la court dou seignor[149] sans son[150] congé tant con ele se[151] tenra a celle fois sera defaillant de servize. Car ce est un propre servise que tous ceaus qui doivent servise au seignor de lor cors li doivent. Et[152] se il sel[153] servise ne li deusent et les autres qui sont devant[154] devisé[155] en cest livre, il ne poroit tenir court ne faire droit ne justise a ceaus qui la li[156] requeroient. Et por ce sont les diz servises establis, que il puissent[157] ces homes destraindre de venir a court et de demorer y et des avant[158] dites choses faire por les plais et les quereles oir et jugier. Car court ne vaudreit[159] ne plais,[160] se le seignor ne poeit[161] ces homes destraindre d'estre y a[162] faire en la court les avant[163] dites choses, que le seignor ne peut jugement faire ne estre au jugement.[164]

Et se le seignor semont ou fait semondre aucun de ces homes dou servise que il li doit et il[165] le fait[166] en la maniere devant[167] dite et il en defaut et le seignor en viaut avoir droit, il le doit faire en la maniere avant[168] dite.[169] Et se le seignor fait semondre aucun de ces homes[170] qui soit essoinés, il li doit faire assaveir c'essoigne et dire

[133] vers le seignor] A lacks [134] cel] BV: celui [135] as] A: a ciaus [136] A adds: de ces; O: de ses [137] il l'ont faite] B: il ont faite; V: l'on fait [138] ceaus] C: ces [139] le] V: les [140] cel] ABV: celui [141] desus] A lacks; B: devant [142] n'i] C: ne [143] vienent] A: vont; V: vient [144] defaillis] B: failliz [145] qu'il] A: il ne [146] V adds: y [147] a] ABV: en [148] desus] B: devant [149] dou seignor] A lacks; B: son seignor [150] son] BO lack [151] se] C: s'en [152] Et] A: Que [153] sel] A: tel; V: celui [154] devant] B: avant; O lacks [155] C adds: doivent [156] li] CV lack [157] puissent] A: peust; B: puisse; V: pevent [158] avant] V: dessus [159] V adds: riens [160] A adds: ne seroient oyr [161] poeit] V: poroit [162] a] ABV: et [163] avant] V: dessus [164] ne estre au jugement] C lacks [165] AB add: ne [166] BV add: semondre [167] devant] AO: avant; V: dessus [168] avant] B: devant; V: dessus [169] il en defaut . . . dite] O lacks [170] homes] O lacks

ensi a ceaus qui le semonent:[171] 'Je ai tel essoine', et die quel, 'por quei je ne veull acuillir ceste semonce[172] se cort n'esgarde ou conoisse[173] que je acuillir[174] la doive.[175] Et de m'essoine et de mon respons vos en[176] trai je a garans.'

---

[171] ceaus qui le semonent] A: celui qui le semont; V: ceaus qui le semont [172] V adds: n'acuillir ne la veull [173] n'esgarde ou conoisse] B: n'esgardoit ou conoissoit; V: ne l'esguarde [174] je acuillir] C: il cuillir [175] que je acuillir la doive] B: je acuellir la deusse; V lacks [176] en] ABV lack

***[191]** Quant home a qui le seignor doit de son fié est semons dou servise que il[1] doit, et il ne[2] veaut acuillir la semonce, coment il le[3] doit faire si que il n'ait[4] damage, et coment l'ome qui est semons de son seignor[5] doit faire assaveir c'essoigne et a qui.[6]

Se le seignor deit[7] de son fié a aucun de ces homes[8] ou il est mermé d'aucune chose de son fié et il le[9] fait semondre de son service et il[10] n'entent qu'il doie la semonce acuillir tant que il soit paié,[11] il doit dire la raison por quei il ne veaut la semonce acuillir[12] et metre soi en esgart ou en conoissance de court s'il la doit acuillir ou non.

Et s'il est si[13] essoiné avant le jor de la semonce[14] que il ne puisse venir[15] faire assaver au seignor c'essoine, contremande la si[16] con il doit.[17] Et qui viaut contremander c'essoine si con il doit, si doit[18] faire assaveir au seignor en sa court[19] avant dou jor de la semonce c'essoine[20] par .ii. homes de la loy de Rome et[21] tes que il[22] aient vois en[23] court. Et ceaus doivent venir devant le seignor en sa court ou devant celui qui sera en son leuc et aveir aveuc eaus .ii. ou plus des homes dou seignor et dire ensi:[24] 'Vos avés tel de vos homes fait semondre do servize que il vos doit', et nomer le, 'et[25] il vos mande par nos que il est essoinés si que il ne peut[26] aler en vostre servise. Et se vos, sire,[27] se[28] mescreés, nos somes prest de faire en ce que la court conoistra que nos en doions faire.' Et se le seignor comande a la court qu'ele li[29] conoisse que yaus[30] en[31] doivent faire, la court doit conoistre, se cuit, que il doivent jurer sur sains que celui qui a fait assaveir par yaus c'essoine est essoinés si con il dient. Et se[32] le seignor lor dit que il le jurent, il le doivent faire si con la court l'a coneu.

A: fols cxlii^{v}–cxliii^{r} cap. 221; **B:** fols 174^{v}–175^{r} cap. 222; **C:** fol. 178^{r-v} cap. 191; **O:** fols 245^{v}–246^{v}; **V:** fols cxcii^{v}–cxciii^{v} cap. 233; Beugnot, pp. 352–3, cap. 221.

---

[1] BV adds: li [2] et il ne] V: en il en [3] le] V lacks [4] n'ait] AB: n'i ait [5] de son seignor] AB: dou servise; V: de son servise [6] assaveir c'essoigne et a qui] V lacks [7] V adds: aucune chose [8] de ces homes] A: home [9] V adds: doit ou [10] le fait semondre . . . il] C lacks [11] tant que il soit paié] BV lack [12] tant que il . . . acuillir] O lacks [13] si] AV lack [14] A adds: si [15] B adds: a cort [16] la si] B: la li si; C: ausi [17] contremande si con il doit] V: ne [18] doit] V: doivent [19] V adds: ou [20] au seignor en . . . c'essoine] A: sa essoine au seignor [21] et] ABV lack [22] que il] AB: qui [23] vois en] B lacks [24] A adds: Sire [25] et] ABV lack [26] V adds: venir devant vous ne [27] sire] BV lack [28] se] V: nos [29] li] AB lack [30] yaus] AB: il [31] en] C lacks [32] dient. Et se] B: a devant dit

Et se le seignor[33] fait semondre aucun de ces homes d'aler[34] hors[35] do reiaume d'autre servize que[36] des .iii. avant[37] dites choses de quei les homes doivent servise au seignor[38] hors do reiaume sans ce que son cors y aille, il ne li doivent[39] pas tel servise ne ne doivent sa semonce acuillir, ains doit dire celui qui est ensi semons que il n'entent que il doive au seignor[40] tel servise por coi il ne viaut cele semonce acuillir, se la court ne l'esgarde ou conoisse que il[41] acuillir la doie, et de ce se met il en l'esgart de la court sauf son retenaill. Et se il ensi le fait, je cuit que la court esgardera ou conoistra que il ne doit la[42] semonce acuillir, por ce que il ne li doit mie le servise de coi il l'a semons.[43]

[33] lor dit que . . . seignor] A lacks [34] d'aler] V lacks [35] hors] A: fors [36] AB add: de l'une; V: l'une [37] avant] V: dessus [38] servise au seignor] B: servises as seignors [39] aille, il ne li doivent] A: soit, il ne le deivent faire ne aler. Car il ne li deivent [40] au seignor] V lacks [41] il] BV lack [42] doit la] V: doive celle [43] mie le servise . . . semons] V: le servise de ce que il l'a semons par l'asssise ne l'usage dou royaume de Jerusalem

***[192]** Que doit perdre l'ome qui est en .i.[1] leu par semonce, et il s'en part sans le[2] congé dou seignor ou de celuy qui est en son leuc.

Se aucun des homes dou seignor est semons de son servize[3] de demorer en .i. leuc moti .i. espace de tens, et il s'en part avant[4] le terme de la semonce sans le congé do seignor ou de celui qui est en son leuc ou il est defaillant de servise, il[5] pert son fié selonc le leuc et le besoin[6] dont il s'en part si con est avant[7] dit.[a]

A: fol. cxliii[r] cap. 222; **B:** fol. 175[r] cap. 223; **C:** fols 178[v]–179[r] cap. 192; **O:** fol. 246[v]; **V:** fol. cxciii[v] cap. 234; Beugnot, p. 353, cap. 222.

[a] Above cap. 190.

[1] .i.] BV lack [2] le] AB lack [3] de son servize] A: dou servise qu'il deit [4] V adds: le tens et [5] ou il est . . . il] A: il est defaillant dou servise et [6] A adds: est [7] est avant] V: il est dessus

***[193]** Quant[1] le seignor peut faire son home semondre en son ostel, et por quel chose, et que ceaus qui le semonent[2] doivent faire et dire a la semonce.[3]

Quant le seignor a besoing de son home[4] por son servise[5] et il ne le[6] peut trover ou[7] il ne le[8] veuille faire querre[9] ou il[10] est alé hors de sa seignorie sans son congé, il le peut faire semondre par .iii. de ces homes en son ostel, et, s'il n'a ostel,[11] ou[12] il a usé de demorer, et, s'il n'a manoir estable en la vile ou il[13] doit son estage,[14] il[15] le doit semondre en l'ostel ou il fu derainement manant en cele ville ou en son fié.[16] Et les homes qui font la semonce[17] doivent venir a la porte ou qu'il soit[18] dou dit ostel et dire: 'A il arme[19] seens?'[20] Et se il n'a arme[21] en l'ostel ou[22] se il[23] ne viaut respondre, dient le[24] a la porte de cel[25] maneir ou la ou le fié est de quei il doit le servize de quoi il a esté semons.[26] Et die celui qui est establi en leuc do seignor: 'O vos tel', et[27] noment[28] celui que il doivent[29] semondre, 'mon seignor tel', et le noment,[30] 'vos semont, et je por lui, que vos de hui en .xv. jors ou de demain en .xv. jors[31] ou de puis[32] demain en .xv. jors soiés en tel leuc aprestés de tel servise con vos li devés et[33] aiés ce que besoing vos sera jusques a tel terme', et motir le terme et[34] conbien il le semont de demorer el leuc qu'il avront[35] nomé. Et se le seignor ne viaut que il aille autre part que devant

---

A: fol. cxliii^{r-v} cap. 223; **B:** fol. 175^{r-v} cap. 224; **C:** fol. 179^{r} cap. 193; **O:** fols 246^{v}–247^{v}; **V:** fols cxciii^{v}–cxciv^{r} cap. 235; Beugnot, p. 354, cap. 223.

---

[1] Quant] ABV: Coment [2] semonent] O: savront [3] AV add: et aprés [4] son home] A: ces homes [5] por son servise] V lacks [6] le] A: les [7] ou] V: et [8] le] A: les [9] querre] C: requerre [10] il] A: celui de qui il a besoin [11] A adds: en la ville en l'ostel; B: en l'ostel [12] ou] C: et [13] A adds: a usé de demorer ou se il n'a maneir en la ville ou il [14] V adds: tenir [15] il] B: on [16] B adds: ou que il soit [17] font la semonce] A: le semonent [18] ou qu'il soit] B lacks [19] arme] B: ame; C: armes [20] ABV add: Et se (A: ce) il treuvent (B: trouvent) aucune persone (B: persone eaus) en la presence de celui doivent (A: deivent) faire la semonce [21] arme] B: ame; C: armes [22] ou] C: et [23] se il] A: il; V lacks [24] le] BV lack [25] cel] BV: celui [26] de quoi il . . . semons] B: dont l'on le semont [27] C adds: le [28] noment] A: nomer; BV nome [29] doivent] B: doit [30] noment] ABV: nome [31] ou de demain en .xv. jors] B lacks [32] puis] A: plus [33] et] C lacks [34] et] AB: a; V lacks [35] qu'il avront] A: qu'il avra; B: que il li avra; V: ou il l'ont

lui, si le semonent[36] si con le seignor[37] lor enchargera. Et celui qui dira[38] la parole si la die .iii. fois et puis doit dire[39] as autre .ii.: 'Je vos trai a garans de ce que je ai tel semons, et coment et de coi je l'ai semons'.[40]

[36] semonent] V: semont [37] seignor] A: roi [38] dira] A: dit [39] doit dire] V: la die
[40] coment et de . . . semons] V: die de quoi il l'a semons et coment

***[194]** Qui est semons do servise que il doit a son[1] seignor, et son[2] seignor li doit de son fié de quei le terme de sa paie est[3] passé, qu'il doit faire et dire se il ne viaut cele semonce acuillir tant que il soit paié de ce que il[4] li doit de son fié.

Se le seignor semont ou[5] fait semondre aucun de ces homes dou servise que il li doit, et il li doive aucune chose de son fié de quei le terme de sa paie soit[6] pasé, et il ne veulle acuillir la semonce ne aler la ou il a esté semons d'aler se il n'est paiés, il doit dire a celui qui l'a semons:[7] 'Mon[8] seignor[9] me doit de mon fié de coy le terme de ma paie[10] est pasé. Face me paier, et je ferai vers lui se que je[11] devrai. Et tant qu'il m'en ait[12] fait paier, je n'entent que je doie sa[13] semonce acuillir, ne acuillir ne la veull, se la cort ne l'esgarde.' Et aprés[14] il doit venir le plus tost que il pora devant le seignor, ou devant celui[15] qui est[16] en son leuc, avant le jor de la semonce, et dire li: 'Sire, vos m'avés semons ou fait semondre', selonc ce que il avra esté semons.[17] 'Faites me paier de ce que vos me devés de mon fié, et je irai[18] volentiers a vostrre semonce. Et[19] jusques a tant que vos m'aiés paié ou[20] fait[21] paier ce que vos me devés de mon fié de quei le terme de ma paie[22] est pasé,[23] je ne veuil vostre semonce acuillir ne vos servir, se vostre[24] court ne l'esgarde, et di por coi: por ce que je ne vos doi servise que de mon fié, et sans ma[25] paie de ce que vos me devés de mon fié de quei le terme de ma paie est[26] pasé, ne vos veuil je servir,[27] se la court ne l'esgarde,[28] et de ce met je en l'esgart de la court sauf mon retenaill.' Et aprés se il

---

A: fols cxliii^{v}–cxliv^{r} cap. 224; **B:** fols 175^{v}–176^{r} cap. 225; **C:** fols 179^{r}–180^{r} cap. 194; **O:** fols 247^{v}–248^{v}; **V:** fol. cxciv^{r-v} cap. 236; Beugnot, pp. 354–5, cap. 224.

---

[1] a son] ABV: au [2] son] AB: le [3] B adds: ja [4] il] ABV: l'on [5] semont ou] V lacks [6] soit] AV: est [7] l'a semons] A: le semont [8] semons. Mon] B: se. mon (*sic*) [9] A adds: tel [10] de ma paie] V lacks [11] B adds: faire [12] m'en ait] V: ne m'ait [13] sa] C: nule [14] ABV adds: ce [15] celui] C lacks [16] est] V: sera [17] ou fait semondre . . . semons] O lacks. A adds: Et vos, sire, me devés de mon fié de quei le terme de ma paie est passé. [18] V adds: mout [19] Et V: Car [20] de ce que . . . ou] A: de mon fié et je ferais vers voz ce que je deverais. Que tant que voz ne m'en aiés [21] m'aiés paié ou fait] V: me n'avés fait [22] de ma paie] C lacks [23] de quei le . . . pasé] A lacks [24] ne veuil vostre . . . vostre] V: n'en yrais a a vostre semonce se la [25] et sans ma] A: ni ne voz dei servir sanz la [26] B adds: ja [27] ne vos veuil je servir] A: por quei je ne dei cest semonce acuillir; B: je n'entent que je vos doie servir si le veull faire, tant que je soie paiez de ce que vos me devez de mon fié de quoi le terme de ma paie est passez [28] et di por . . . l'esgarde] V lacks

ne me semble que le seignor puisse chose dire par coi la court doie[29] esgarder que il doie sa[30] semonce acuillir ne faire le servise tant que il soit paiés de ce que il li doit de son fié de quei le terme de sa paie est pasé. Si s'en peut l'en[31] enssi defendre de la semonce avant[32] dite[33] quant l'on ne la veaut faire et[34] le seignor li doit de son fié et[35] ne le paie ou fait paier avant[36] dou jor de la semonce de ce[37] que il li doit de son fié de quei le terme de sa paie est pasé. Mais se il le paie ou fait paier, il ne peut la semonce ne le servise refuser. Que se il est paié et il defaut de la semonce ou dou servise, le seignor en[38] peut avoir droit come defailli[39] de servise.

[29] doie] C: doit [30] doie sa] V: en doie celle [31] s'en peut l'en] ABV: se peut l'on [32] avant] V: dessus [33] A dds: acuillir [34] A adds: se [35] et] A: si come est avant dit il ne deit la semonce acuillir ne le servise faire se le seignor; BV: se le seignor [36] le paie ou fait paier avant] C: l'a paié ou fait paier [37] de ce] V lacks [38] en] B: ne [39] defailli] B: d'ome; O: d'ome defailli; V: d'ome qui defaut

*[195] Qui doit servise de conpaignon,[1] et il le fait semondre de tel servise con il li doit ou de cel[2] conpaignon, et le[3] conpaignon est essoiné si que il ne puisse cel[4] servise faire, quey[5] le semons doit dire et[6] faire a garder se, si[7] que le seignor ne puisse avoir de lui amende nule[8] con de[9] defaut de son[10] servise.

Se le seignor semont ou fait semondre aucun de ces homes qui li doive[11] servise de conpaignons, .i. ou plusors,[12] et que cele semonce soit a jor moti que il aille en aucun leu[13] ou[14] il li[15] doit le servise,[16] et aucun de ces conpaignons est essoignés, il le doit dire a celui qui[17] le semont et doit[18] venir devant le seignor et dire li: 'Sire, vos m'avés[19] fait semondre que je aille en tel leuc o tel servise con je vos doi. Sire, et tel de mes conpaignons que je tenoie por vostre servise est dehaitiés[20] si que il ne peut ore[21] aler. Se il vos plaist a deporter vos[22] de son servise tant que il soit guaris, il venra aprés moi quant il sera guariz et fera son servise. Et se il ne vos[23] plaist a soufrir, je en querais un autre, et se je le puis trover a retenir,[24] je le retendrai[25] a tes[26] sos con celui qui est dehaitiés[27] estoit a[28] moi ou a sos[29] comuns de cest reiaume, et le menrais o[30] moi en vostre servise. Et se je ne le puis trover, je le vos ferai assaver.' Et se le seignor ne se viaut soufrir dou servise[31] qui est dehaitiés, celui qui a esté ensi semons con est avant[32] dit doit querre un autre chevalier a retenir[33] as sos qui sont usés de doner comunaument el pais, se le dehaitié[34] n'avoit plus grans sos. Mais se il les avoit plus grans et il ne le peut trover a retenir[35] as sos comuns de la terre, il li doit tant doner con celui avoit qui est demoré[36] por son dehait.

A: fol. cxliv^{r-v} cap. 225; **B:** fol. 176^{r-v} cap. 226; **C:** fols 180^{r}–181^{r} cap. 195; **O:** fols 248^{v}–249^{v}; **V:** fols cxciv^{v}–cxcv^{v} cap. 237; Beugnot, pp. 356–7, cap. 225.

---

[1] A adds: au seignor [2] cel] A: servise dou; A rubrics (fol. 8^{r}) B: servise de; V: celui dou [3] V adds: dit [4] cel] AB: le; V: celui [5] quey] ABV: que [6] dire et] A lacks [7] a garder se, si] V: et guarder se [8] nule] ABV lack [9] V adds: home qui [10] son] ABV lack [11] doive] A: deivent [12] plusors] B: plus; V: de plus [13] leu] B lacks; V: leuc moti [14] ou] A: si come [15] li] AV lack [16] B adds: o le servise que il li doit [17] a celui qui] V: quant home [18] doit] A lacks [19] m'avés] V: ci m'en avés [20] dehaitiés] V: essoignés [21] ore] A: o mei [22] vos] A: vos ent; C: nos [23] AB adds: en [24] retenir] B: recevoir [25] retendrai] B: detendrai; V: reterrais [26] a tes] C: aiés [27] V adds: qui [28] a] AO: o [29] sos] C: ces [30] menrais o] V: metrais a [31] ABV add: de celui [32] avant] AV: devant [33] a retenir] B: et retenir le; V et retenir [34] dehaitié] C: dehait [35] retenir] V: tenir [36] est demoré] V: demore

Et se il ne peut trover chevalier a retenir[37] en la maniere avant[38] dite dedens[39] le terme de la semonce, il doit venir devant le seignor et dire li: 'Sire, j'ai[40] quis[41] chevalier a retenir por faire vostre servise, et je ne le truis qui demore[42] a mei a[43] tes sos[44] con celui qui est essoignés[45] avoit de moi, ne por les sos comuns de cest[46] roiaume. Sire, et ce vos di je par la fey que je vos doi con a mon seignor.[47] Et vés ci[48] la monoie des sos dou chevalier selonc le cors[49] des sodeers comuns[50] de cest roiaume de tant de terme con vos m'avés fait semondre dou servise que je vos dei. Faites la reseveir et retenir[51] .i. chevalier ou faites ent vostre volenté.' Et ait au dire[52] la moneie aprestee la[53] et la baille[54] au comandement dou seignor se il la veaut faire[55] resevoir. Et se qui est devant dit li die et eufre[56] devant .ii. ou plus de ces homes, por ce qu'il en ait recort de court se mestier li est.

Et se le seignor fait son[57] home semondre en la dite maniere a movoir maintenant, die l'essoigne de son conpaignon a celui qui le semont[58] et veigne maintenant devant le seignor et si[59] die et fase se qui est avant[60] dit. Et se il fait ce a[61] laquel que ce[62] soit des semonces, il ne me senble que le seignor le puisse[63] achaisoner de defaut de servise en maniere que il en ait amende con de defaut de servise, qu'il s'en aquite[64] bien si com il doit ce me senble.

---

[37] a retenir] A lacks [38] avant] V: dessus [39] dedens] B: avant [40] j'ai] B: je vos ai; C: je [41] quis] AB lack [42] demore] V: veulle demorer [43] a] AB: por; V: pour [44] sos] A: sodees [45] essoignés] V: dehaitié [46] de cest] B: dou [47] BV add: Sire [48] vés ci] C: vest; V: veés enci [49] le cors] A: les cors; B: le comun cors [50] sodeers comuns] AV: sodees comunes; B: sodees [51] retenir] A: tenir; B: retenir en [52] au dire] V: atiré [53] la] V: yleuc [54] la baille] A: baillier la [55] faire] A lacks [56] li die et eufre] A: si li die et euffre a faire [57] ABV add: dit [58] a celui qui le semont] A lacks [59] si] A: li; V: si li [60] avant] V: desus [61] fait ce a] V: le fait en [62] laquel que ce] A: laquel que; B: la que ce; O: laquel ce [63] O adds: de rien [64] qu'il s'en aquite] B: quar il s'en va quite

***[196]** Qui est semons dou servise[1] de son cors ou[2] aler[3] en .i. leu[4] a cheval et a armes et il n'a que .i. cheval et cel[5] cheval est essoinés, que il doit faire et dire a guarder soy[6] que son seignor n'ait de lui amende con de[7] defailli[8] de servise.

Se le seignor semont ou fait semondre aucun de ces homes qui li doive servise de son cors d'aler[9] a cheval et a armes en aucun leu moti, et la semonce seit a moveir maintenant ou a jor moti, et[10] celui qui est semons n'a[11] que un cheval et cel[12] cheval est essoinés, il le doit dire a celui qui le semont et doit[13] porchacer un autre cheval,[14] se il aveir le peut. Et se il aveir ne le peut dedens le terme de la semonce, il doit venir devant le seignor ou devant celui qui est[15] en son leuc et dire li: 'Sire, je ai esté semons d'aler a cheval et a armes en tel leu', et die[16] ou, 'a movoir a tel houre ou[17] a tel jor', selonc ce que la semonce sera. 'Sire, et mon cheval est essoiné si que je ne le puis mener en vostre servise, et je ai fait mon leial poeir de recovrer[18] ent[19] un autre.[20] Et se vos di ge par la foi que je vos doi com a mon seignor. Sire,[21] et[22] en moi ne demore que je n'aille en vostre servise si con vos m'avés semons ou fait semondre[23] que par defaut de cheval. Et se vos, sire, m'en volés un prester ou faire prester tant que le mien soit gari ou que je en aie[24] un recovré, je irai[25] en vostre servise si con je ai esté semons. Que sans cheval je n'entens que je vos en[26] doie servir de tel servise con vos m'avés[27] fait semondre ne acuillir vostre semonce[28] aprés ce que je vos ai dit et ofert en la court. Por quei je faire ne le veuill por les raisons que je ai dites,[29] se la court ne l'esgarde, et de ce me met je en l'esgart de la court sauf mon retenaill.' Et aprés les dis erremens il ne me

---

A: fols cxliv[v]–cxlv[r] cap. 226; **B:** fol. 177[r–v] cap. 227; **C:** fol. 181[r–v] cap. 196; **O:** fols 250[r]–251[r]; **V:** fols cxcvi[r]–cxcvii[r] cap. 239; Beugnot, pp. 357–8, cap. 226.

---

[1] A adds: que il deit [2] ou] ABV: a [3] de son cors ou aler] B rubrics (fol. 26[r]): que son cors pout [4] A adds: mouti; B: moti [5] cel] ABV: le [6] a guarder soy] B lacks [7] de] B lacks; V: home [8] defailli] B rubrics: defaut [9] d'aler] B lacks [10] la semonce seit . . . et] O lacks [11] n'a] A: n'ait [12] cel] BV: celui [13] doit] A lacks [14] autre cheval] A: cheval; BV: autre; O: autre a cheval [15] est] AV: sera [16] die] B: dire [17] ou] C: et [18] recovrer] C: retrover [19] ent] AB lack [20] B adds: et je ne l'ai peu recovrer [21] Sire] A lacks [22] et] BV lack [23] que je n'aille . . . semondre] AV lack [24] je en aie] C: il en ait [25] recovré, je irai] V: trové, je vais [26] en] ABV lack [27] B adds: semons ou [28] V adds: ne veull [29] A adds: devant

senble que le seignor[30] puisse chose dire par coi la court doie[31] conoistre ne[32] esgarder que il doie sa semonce[33] acuillir ne faire le dit[34] servise tant que son cheval soit gari ou que il en ait un autre, coment que ce soit, en prest ou d'achat ou[35] en autre maniere. Et[36] il est tenus par la foy que il doit au seignor de faire ent[37] en son leau poeir d'aver le[38] plus tost que il pora covenablement un cheval, et quant il l'avra d'aler faire le servise de son seignor le plus tost[39] que il porra,[40] se le terme de la semonce a quey il a esté semons dure encore. Et se le seignor li preste ou fait prester .i. cheval, il doit aler a sa[41] semonce sans delai et sans eschanpe querre. Et s'il ne le fait, le seignor l'en porra mener con hom defailli de servize.

Et s'il doit servise d'un chevalier ou de plus[42] et le seignor l'en[43] semont ou fait semondre dou servise que il li[44] doit de ces conpaignons d'envoier les a cheval et a armes en un[45] leu moti, et le cheval[46] d'aucun d'eaus est esoinés, le seignor de celui chevalier de qui le cheval est essoinés[47] doit faire et[48] dire si con est devant[49] devisé[50] dou sien[51] cheval. Mais s'il peut recovrer a[52] cheval, il le doit bailler a son conpaignon et enveer le au servise dou seignor sans eschanpe querre.

---

[30] B adds: ne celui qui est en son leuc [31] doie] V: puisse chose [32] ne] A: ni; C: et [33] semonce] B: cort [34] dit] A lacks [35] ou] C lacks [36] autre maniere. Et] A: aucune autre maniere, que [37] ent] B: en; C: ent en; V lacks [38] V adds: au [39] le plus tost . . . tost] B: le le plus tost qu'il porra covenablement et quant il avra il doit aler faire le service son segnor le plus [40] covenablement un cheval . . . porra] V lacks [41] sa] ABV: la [42] plus] V: plusors [43] l'en] ABV: le [44] li] C lacks [45] un] AV lack [46] et a armes . . . cheval] B lacks [47] le seignor de . . . essoinés] A: il [48] faire et] V lacks [49] devant] B: avant; V: dessus [50] ABV add: qu'il doit (A: deit; B: le doit) faire et dire [51] dou sien] A: de son [52] a] V lacks

***[197]** Ce sont ceaus qui pevent guager ou[1] semondre ou conjurer le seignor de sa foy, et coment, et lesqués non, par l'assise[2] dou reiaume de Jerusalem.

Ce sont ceaus qui pevent guager ou semondre ou conjurer le seignor de sa foy. Celui a qui il[3] doit aucune choze de son fié le peut semondre ou guager do servise que il li doit de celui fié ou conjurer le[4] de sa foi, c'est assaveir en la maniere aprés devisee, et son heir aussi.[a] Mais s'il mesavenoit de celui a qui l'on doit[5] de son fié, et son heir est merme d'aage et aucune persone tient le baillage, le baill[6] ne peut semondre ne guagier ne conjurer por la dete[7] que le seignor[8] deveit a l'ancestre de celui por qui il tient le baillage. Mais quant l'eir sera d'aage, il peut guager ou semondre ou conjurrer le seignor por la dete que il[9] devoit a son ancestre ou por chose que l'on li doive[10] de son fié ou por force que l'on li fase si con est avant[11] dit. Et se le seignor doit aucune chose au baill do fié que il tient en baillage, le baill peut guager ou semondre ou conjurer por la dete que le seignor li doit del fié[12] en baillage. Mais l'eir, quant il sera d'aage, ne peut guager ne semondre ne conjurer[13] por dete que l'on deust a son baill. Et se le seignor doit a aucun de ces homes aucune chose de son fié et le seignor[14] meurt, celui a qui il[15] devra la dete[16] ou son heir peut guager ou semondre ou conjurer l'eir dou seignor ou son baill, se l'eir est merme d'aage. Et se le baill dou seignor doit de son tens[17] a aucun de ces homes aucune chose de son fié, selui a qui la dete sera deue ou[18] son heir peut guager ou semondre ou conjurer celui baill tant con il tendra le baillage, mais[19] autre non.

A: fols cl^{v}–cli^{r} cap. 233; **B:** fol. 183^{v} cap. 235; **C:** fols 181^{v}–182^{r} cap. 197; **O:** fol. 251^{r-v}; **V:** fols cciv^{v}–ccv^{r} cap. 248; Beugnot, pp. 369–70, cap. 233.

---

[a] Below caps 204–6.

---

[1] ou] B: et [2] A adds: ou l'usage [3] il] ABV: le seignor [4] le] BO: l'en [5] mesavenoit de celui . . . doit] B: ne s'avenoit a celui a qui l'on dit [6] le baill] C lacks [7] dete] B: dite [8] por la dete que le seignor] A: le seignor por la dette qu'il [9] il] O: le seignor; V lacks [10] doive] A: deveit; V: devoit [11] avant] A: devant; V: dessus [12] del fié] ABV: dou fié qu'il tient [13] A adds: le seignor [14] le seignor] V: li sires [15] il] C lacks [16] il devra la dete] AB: la dette sera deue; V: la dete est deue [17] de son tens] A lacks [18] ou] C: en; V: a [19] mais] AV: et

***[198]** Coment l'on doit[1] son[2] seignor destraindre que il le fase paier se que[3] il li doit de son fié, ou de raveir se il tient aucune chose de son fié, ou de faire[4] abatre force que crestien li fait[5] de son fié ou de partie de son fié.

Qui veaut son seignor destraindre qu'il le fase paier de ce que il li doit de son fié de quey le terme de sa paie est pasé, ou de ravoir ce que il tient[6] de son fié[7] sans esgart ou[8] sans conoissance de court, ne[9] sans l'assise ne l'usage dou reiaume[10] ne sans ce que il l'ait[11] recoumandé ne estreé ne eschangé ne[12] par mesfait que il ou aucun de ses ancestres aient fait, ou de faire li abatre force que crestien li[13] fait de son fié ou de partie de son fié, si le fase si con il[14] est aprés devisé.[a]

Mais avant que je die coment on peut son seignor destraindre des avant dites choses, dirai je contre ce que aucuns[15] de nos grans maistres plaideors[16] a[17] aucune[18] feis dit: que qui veaut son seignor destraindre d'aucune des[19] dites choses, qu'il le doit ensemble conjurer de sa foy et semondre par les .iii. quinzaines et les .iii.[20] quarantaines[21] qui sont establies a son[22] seignor semondre. Et aprés ce que les quinsaines[23] et les quarantaines[24] sont pasees, que il le peut guager de son servise. Je di que enssi ne le peut l'on ne ne doit faire[25] par l'assise ne par[26] l'usage dou reiaume de Jerusalem ne par raison. Et qui le fera, il ne fera mie que sage. Et di por coi: por ce que qui conjure son seignor de sa foi autrement que il ne doit, ou dit ou fait chose par coi son seignor soit ou doit[27] estre villainement

---

A: fols cli^{r}–clii^{r} cap. 234; **B:** fols 184^{r}–185^{r} cap. 236; **C:** fols 182^{r}–184^{r} cap. 198; **O:** fols 251^{v}–254^{r}; **V:** fols ccv^{r}–ccvii^{r} cap. 249; Beugnot, pp. 370–2, cap. 234.

---

[a] Below caps 204–6.

---

[1] Coment l'on doit] B: Qui veut [2] son] A lacks [3] que] A rubrics (fol. 8^{v}) BV lack [4] faire] A: faire li; V rubrics (fol. 14^{v}): refaire li. V has 'refaire' corrected to 'faire'. [5] fait] B: face [6] ou de ravoir . . . tient] B lacks [7] de quey le . . . fié] V lacks [8] ou] BV: et [9] ne] B: et [10] A adds: de Jerusalem [11] l'ait] C: ait [12] eschangé ne] A: eschangié ne perdu; B lacks; V; ne changé [13] V adds: ait [14] il] ABV lack [15] aucuns] C: aucun [16] plaideors] C: plaideor [17] a] B: ont [18] aucune] A: pluisors; BV: plusors [19] d'aucune des] B: d'aucune des avant; O: des avant [20] .iii. quinzaines et les .iii.] ABV: quinsaines (B: quinzaines) et les [21] quarantaines] B: quartaines [22] a son] A: au [23] C adds: sont [24] quarantaines] A: quarantaines qui sont establiés au seignor semondre; B: quartaines [25] ne ne doit faire] B: ne doit [26] par] ABV lack [27] soit ou doit] B: soit ou die; V: en doie

difamé, il ne garde mie bien sa foi vers son seignor; ou qui ensemble le conjure de sa foi et semont par les .iii. quinzaines et[28] les .iii. quarantaines, il ne le conjure pas si con il doit par l'assise ou l'usage dou dit[29] reiaume; et qui aprés ce que il l'a semons et[30] conjuré de sa foy le gage de son servise, il ne fait pas ce que[31] il[32] doit, et le difame[33] de sa foi vilainement, ou en lui ne remaint mie[34] que il ne le difame[35] vilainement ou[36] que il ne soit vilainement par lui difamé.[37] Que quant il conjure son seignor de sa foi por[38] l'une des avant dites choses, et il aprés le guage de son servise, il done bien a entendre a chascun que[39] son seignor n'a pas bien gardee sa foy vers lui ou que il ne se fie mie[40] en la foi de son seignor,[41] ne que il ne l'a mie bien gardee vers lui,[42] quant il aprés ce que il l'en a conjuré en court[43] le guage de son servise, por[44] quei il le difame vilainement[45] de sa foy, ou il ne remaint mie[46] en lui que il[47] vilainement ne difame.[48] Si me senble que celui qui ensenble[49] conjure et semont son seignor de sa foi et aprés le guage de son servise mesprent vers lui de sa foi,[50] et[51] le seignor en peut avoir droit par sa court, se il viaut,[52] con de foi mentie.

Et se l'ome le peut faire enssi con celui maistre plaideor le dist sans mesprendre vers son seignor de sa foi, di je qu'il ne le peut ne[53] doit faire.[54] Car[55] nul home[56] dou seignor ne doit par l'assise ne[57] l'usage dou reiaume de Jerusalem par[58] .ii. destreces[59] ensemble destraindre le seignor[60] de faire l'une des[61] dites choses aussi con, par l'assise ou l'usage dou[62] reiaume,[63] le seignor ne peut faire d'un mesfait .ii. justises. Et ce est aparant que le seignor ne le[64] peut ne ne doit faire[65] par la dite assise[66] ne par le dit usage. Car se .i. home se claime d'un autre[67] par l'assise d'un[68] cop aparant que il li a[69]

[28] AB add: par [29] dou dit] AB: de cest; V: de cestui [30] que il l'a semons et] A: qui l'a semons ou [31] fait pas ce que] A: le fait si come; B: le fait mie si com; V: le fait pas si come [32] l'a semons et . . . il] C lacks [33] difame] C: difaine [34] B repeats: en lui [35] difame] C: difaine [36] en lui ne . . . ou] V lacks [37] difamé] C: difainé [38] por] A: de [39] ABV add: il entent que [40] A adds: bien [41] ou que il . . . seignor] V lacks [42] ne que il . . . lui] BV lack [43] en court] A: et encore; B: et ancores [44] por] ABV: par [45] vilainement] B: malement [46] mie] ABV lack [47] que il] V lacks [48] difaime] ABV: l'ait diffamé [49] ensenble] V lacks [50] ou il ne . . . foi] O lacks [51] A adds: que [52] se il viaut] A lacks [53] ne] A: ni ne; B: ne ne [54] ABV add: par raison [55] qu'il ne le . . . Car] O: par l'assise ou l'usage dou reaume. Car [56] home] ABV: des homes [57] ne] BO: ou [58] ABV add: ces [59] destreces] C: crestiens [60] le seignor] B: son seignor; V lacks [61] l'une des] V: de l'une des .ii. [62] A adds: dit [63] BV adds: de Jerusalem [64] le] B lacks [65] faire] B lacks [66] la dite assise] V: l'assise [67] V adds: home [68] d'un] B: de [69] a] AB: ait

fait d'armeure[70] esmolue ou d'autre chose,[b] et celui de qui il c'est clamés conoist[71] en la court que il li[72] a[73] cel cop fait et en fornit l'assise, et celui qui a le cop meurt puis de cel cop,[74] aucun[75] sien parent ne autre ne[76] peut riens demander a celui qui conut en la court, si con est avant dit, que il li[77] avoit le cop fait, ne le seignor ne deit[78] faire justise, por ce que d'un mesfait ne doit nul .ii. paines[79] soufrir. Et por ce que le clamant vost meaus avoir la justise par l'assise de celui qui le cop li[80] fist que autrement, et puis que sa volenté fu tel et l'on li acompli, il, ne autre por lui, ne peut rien demander a celui de qui il enssi se clama.[81] Et[82] aussi vos di je par le senblant de ce, que ce .i. home est mermé de son fié ou d'aucune chose de son fié,[83] que il en[84] peut son seignor destraindre de faire li[85] sa requeste par pluisors voies qui sont establiés de faire[86] par l'assise ou l'usage de cest[87] reiaume, lesqués sont[88] aprés devisees en cest livre, et il est au chois[89] de l'ome de destraindre son seignor des dites choses par laquel des[90] voies que il vodra, ausi[91] con il[92] est au chois dou clamant avant[93] dit de clamer sei par laquel des manieres que il vodra par l'assise ou autrement. Et aussi con le clamant qui[94] se[95] claime par l'assise[96] ne se peut plus[97] clamer autrement[98] de cel cop,[99] ou se il[100] autrement s'en clameit ne s'en[101] peut puis[102] clamer par l'assise,[103] ne peut l'ome destraindre son seignor[104] de l'une des avant dites choses que par l'une des[105] voies aprés devisees.[c]

Et il est cler a conoistre a chascun que enssi doie estre, por coi a moi senble, par les raisons que je ai dites et mostrees et par plusors[106] autres que on i poroit dire et mostrer que trop seroient longues

[b] Above caps 100–1.
[c] Below caps 204–6.

[70] d'armeure] AV: d'arme [71] c'est clamés conoist] A: se claime conut [72] li] BV lack [73] a] A: ait [74] meurt puis de cel cop] B lacks [75] aucun] C: a aucun [76] autre ne] B lacks [77] li] BV lack [78] ne deit] B: n'en puet; V: n'en doit [79] paines] V: justizes [80] li] AV lack [81] de qui il enssi se clama] B: de qui il se claime; V: qui de lui se clame [82] Et] V: Tout [83] ou d'aucune chose de son fié] A lacks [84] en] ABV lack [85] V adds: faire [86] de faire] V lacks [87] de cest] C: dou [88] sont] B lacks [89] au chois] V: ançois [90] A adds: .ii. [91] ausi] V lacks [92] il] C lacks [93] au chois dou clamant avant] V: ançois dou clamant dessus [94] par l'assise ou . . . qui] A: que se il [95] le clamant qui se] BV: se le clamant se [96] ABV add: il [97] plus] A: pas; B: mie; O: puis; V lacks [98] V adds: il ne se peut clamer par autre maniere [99] de cel cop] A lacks [100] C adds: se [101] autrement s'en clameit ne s'en] AB: autrement se claime il ne se; V: se claime autrement il ne se [102] puis] A lacks [103] V adds: tout auci [104] V adds: que [105] V adds: avant dites [106] plusors] C: plus

a metre en[107] cest livre qui y metroit toutes celes que on i porroit dire et mostrer,[108] dis je que celui ou ceaus qui dient que on doit ensemble son seignor semondre et conjurer de sa foy et aprés guager de son servise ne dient, sauve leur pais, se me senble bien, ne droit ne raison, ne l'on ne le deit mie faire si con il dient, mais l'on le doit faire si com[109] est devisé si aprés en[110] cest livre. Car qui enssi le fera con il est devisé,[111] il le[112] fera si con il doit par l'assise ou l'usage de cest roiaume et par raison[113] et en tel maniere que nul ne porra dire par dreit que il ait mespris de sa foi vers son seignor, par ce que il l'ait conjuré de sa foi[114] autrement que il ne doit ne par se que il l'ait difamé[115] de sa foy ne d'autre chose.

[107] V adds: escrit en [108] V adds: pour quoi [109] il dient, mais . . . com] C lacks [110] en] C lacks [111] V adds: en cestui livre [112] le] CV lack [113] et par raison] A lacks [114] de sa foi] V lacks [115] ABO add: ne volu diffamer (B: defamer)

***[199]** Coment et ou et[1] par qui le seignor doit[2] faire semondre feme qui tient fié qui li doive servise de cors de prendre baron, et quant la feme est semonce si come ele doit de prendre baron et[3] ele[4] ne le prent, quel amende le seignor en peut[5] avoir.

Quant le seignor viaut semondre ou faire semondre si con il doit feme[6] de prendre baron, quant elle a et tient fié qui[7] li doive servise de cors, ou a damoiselle, a qui fié est escheu qui[8] li doit servise de cors,[9] il li doit ofrir .iii.[10] barons, et tels[11] que il soient a li aferans de parage ou a son autre baron. Et la doit semondre en la presence[12] de .ii. de ces[13] homes ou de plus, ou faire la semondre par .iii. de ces homes, l'un en son[14] leuc[15] et les .ii. come court, et celui qu'il[16] a establi en son leuc[17] a ce faire[18] doit dire enssi: 'Dame, je vos eufre de par mon seignor tel', et le nome, '.iii. barons, tel et tel et tel',[19] et les nome, 'et vos semons de par mon seignor[20] que vos dedens tel jor', et li motisse le jor, 'en[21] aiés pris baron l'un des .iii. que je vos ai només. Et de ce trai[22] je a guarans ces homes de mon seignor qui sont si come court.' Et enssi le dit[23] en leur presence .iii. fois. Et se le seignor la semont, si li eufre les[24] .iii. barons et la semone en la maniere avant dite. Et se l'on ne la treuve a[25] semondre en sa persone,[26] l'on la doit semondre en son ostel ou en son fié ou en l'ostel ou elle fu derainement c'ele n'a ostel sien en quei ele maigne. Et qui la vodra semondre[27] en un des dis leus, si le fase[28] si con[29] est avant[30] devisé en cest livre que l'on semont l'ome

---

A: fols cxlv^r^–cxlvi^v^ cap. 227; **B:** fols 177^v^–179^r^ cap. 229; **C:** fols 184^r^–186^r^ cap. 199; **O:** fols 254^r^–257^r^; **V:** fols cxcvii^r^–cxcix^r^ caps 241–2; Beugnot, pp. 359–61, cap. 227.

---

[1] ou et] B lacks [2] par qui le seignor doit] V: pour quoi le seignor peut [3] quant la feme . . . et] BOV lack [4] ele] AB lack [5] peut] A: deit; BV: doit [6] feme] O lacks [7] qui] V: que il [8] est escheu qui] V: eschet ou est escheu que il [9] ou a damoiselle . . . cors] B lacks [10] .iii.] B lacks [11] tels] C: tios [12] en la presence] V lacks [13] de ces] AV: des [14] l'un en son] O: ou de plus [15] son leuc] V: leuc de lui [16] qu'il] C: qui [17] en son leuc] A lacks [18] ce faire] B: cel fait [19] et tel] B lacks [20] A adds: tel', et le nome [21] en] ABV lack [22] trai] C: ten [23] le dit] A: le die; BV: li die [24] les] AB lack [25] l'on ne la treuve a] AB: on ne la treuve ou [26] sa persone] C: la presone; V: la persone [27] maigne. Et qui la vodra semondre] B: puisse maindre [28] si le fase] B: et si le face; V lacks [29] si con] O: ensi com il [30] avant] AV: devant; O lacks

de son servise[31] en son ostel, disant les paroles avant devisees que l'on doit dire[32] au semondre de la feme.[a]

Et[b] quant feme est enssi semonce, et ele ne prent dedens le[33] dit terme l'un des .iii. barons que l'on li a ofert et de quei l'on la semonce d'espouser l'un d'eaus, ou[34] ne vient dedens le jor qui li est doné a baron prendre devant le seignor c'ele le treve et die[35] raison por coi ele ne veulle sa semonce acuillir et tel que cort l'esgarde ou conoisse, et[36] s'ele ne treuve[37] le seignor en la[38] court, qu'ele le[39] die[40] en la presence de .ii.[41] homes ou de plus de la court que ele estoit la venue ou ele cuidoit trover le seignor et que[42] s'ele l'eust trové ele eust dite raison por coi ele n'entent que ele doive sa[43] semonce acuillir de prendre baron si con il l'en a fait[44] semondre, et que de ce les trait ele[45] a guarans et leur prie et requiert que il soient recordans dou jor que ele est la venue et des paroles que ele a dites si qu'il les puissent recorder en la court se mestier li est.

Ou c'ele est[46] essoinee dedens le jor[47] de la semonce, que ele fase assaveir[48] au seignor c'essoine par tel qui li eufre en la presence de .ii.[49] homes ou de plus a sertefier le qu'il est son message et que ele li a enchargé se que il a dit por lui,[50] et que ce ele li mande[51] faire assaveir c'essoine par message,[52] le message doit dire: 'Sire, tel', et la nome, 'vos fait par moi assavoir que ele est essoingee[53] si que ele ne peut venir devant vos respondre vos de vostre semonce, et dire por coi ele ne la doit acuillir',[54] ou, 'dire que ele est si essoinee que ele ne peut faire ce de quei vos l'avés semonce ou faite semondre.[55] Sire, et se vos mescreés que je ne[56] soie son mesage et que ele ne m'ait enchargé se que je ai por lui[57] dit, je en eufre a faire ce que la court[58] conoistra que je en doie faire.' Et se le seignor le[59] mescreit,

---

[a] Above caps 188, 190.
[b] The sentence-structure of what follows appears to be defective.

---

[31] l'ome de son servise] A lacks; BV: de son servise [32] B adds: et faire [33] dedens le] A: el [34] ou] A: ou elle; B: et ele [35] c'ele le treve et die] B: por dire [36] et] AO: ou [37] s'ele ne treuve] B: que se ele ne treuva [38] la] AB: sa [39] le] BO: li [40] die] C: doie [41] .ii.] B: trois [42] que] ABV lack [43] doive sa] B: deust [44] l'en a fait] AV: l'a faite [45] les trait ele] A: trait elle la court [46] est] A lacks [47] le jor] A: les jors [48] assaveir] B: savoir [49] A adds: de ces [50] lui] V: elle [51] que ce ele li mande] A: qu'elle a mandé; B: que ele mande la; V: que elle li mande [52] A adds: et que [53] que ele est essoingee] V lacks [54] acuillir] V lacks [55] vos l'avés semonce ou faite semondre] A: il la semone et dire ce por quei elle ne le peut faire; BV: il l'a semonse (V: semonce) ou fait semondre [56] mescreés que je ne] B: ne creez que je [57] lui] V: elle [58] A: adds: esgardera ou [59] le] AV: l'en

il doit comander a la court qu'ele li conoisse qu'il en doie faire. Et la court doit conoistre, ce me senble, que il doit jurer sur sains que il est son message et qu'ele li encharja[60] a dire se que il a dit por lui.[61] Et s'il le fait, il en doit[62] estre creu, et ele a bien contremandé c'essoine si con ele doit. Et s'il ne fait ce que la court avra coneu, ele[63] sera defaillant au seignor dou servise qu'ele li doit de soy marier a sa semonce. Que ce[64] celui qui se fait message en court d'ome ou de feme qui a esté semons de servise ou de venir faire droit n'eufre[65] a faire se qui est[66] devant dit et ne le fait, ne[67] doit pas[68] estre[69] tenus a message.

Et c'ele[70] vient dedens le dit terme en la court,[71] et[72] ele ne dit ou[73] fait dire chose dedens tel[74] terme[75] par coi court esgarde ou conoisse que ele n'est tenue d'acuillir la semonce de quei le seignor l'avra fait semondre,[76] ele sera defaillant[77] dou servise que ele doit au seignor, si en porra le seignor avoir droit et amende de li,[78] se il viaut,[79] con de[80] defaut de servise de baron prendre. Et c'ele fait assaveir au seignor c'essoine si con est avant[81] dit, et le terme de la semonce passe, le seignor la doit faire semondre de rechief si con est avant[82] devisé.[83] [c]

Et se la feme qui est semonce de prendre baron si con est avant[84] dit[85] ne le prent dedens le jor de la semonce, ou ele ne fait l'une des choses avant[86] devisees par quei ele n'est defaillant do servise c'ele[87] le fait, et elle, aprés ce que le jor de la semonce sera passé,[88] ait le seignor saisi son fié par[89] conoissance de court, ou ne l'ait, vient devant le seignor et li dit: 'Sire, vos me feistes .i. jor qui passés est ofrir[90] .iii. barons et semondre que je en[91] preise l'un dedens tel

[c] V begins a new chapter here with the rubric: Encor dit ci coment feme qui est semonce de baron prendre, coment elle doit respondre.

[60] encharja] A: a enchargié [61] lui] AO: li; V: elle [62] en doit] A: deit bien [63] A adds: n'avra mie contremandé son essoine si come elle deit, si [64] ce] AV lack [65] n'eufre] A: n'en euffre; V: ou n'en euffre [66] qui est] C: qui a esté; O: que est [67] et ne le fait ne] B: ne ne le fait ne ne [68] pas] ABV lack [69] A adds: creus ne; B: creu ne [70] A adds: ne [71] ABV add: devant le seignor [72] et] C: ne [73] BV add: ne [74] tel] O: cel; V: celui [75] dedens tel terme] AB lack [76] OV add: et [77] ele sera defaillant] C lacks [78] de li] AV: d'elle; B: d'ele [79] AB adds: si [80] de] V: feme qui [81] avant] AV: devant [82] avant] AV: devant [83] devisé] B: dit [84] avant] V: devant [85] se la feme . . . dit] B: ele [86] avant] A: devant [87] c'ele] V: ou elle [88] sera passé] B: passe [89] A adds: esgart ou par [90] A adds: des [91] en] C lacks

jor', et le motise, 'et se[92] que je ne le fis fu par essoine que je oi[93] ou par mauvais conseill. Et je suis ore prest de faire vostre comandement et d'espouser l'un des .iii. barons que vos m'ofristes.'[94] Se le seignor s'en[95] tient a paié et il a le fié saisi, il li[96] doit rendre, et ele doit faire son comandement. Et s'il ne s'en tient a paié, ains veulle meaus avoir l'amende dou defaut dou[97] servise,[98] si li die: 'Dame, il est voir que vos me devés servise de vos marier, et je vos fis semondre si con je duis, et a jor nomé, et vos dedens celui jor ne me feistes le servise que vos me devés, ne ne deistes en court raison por coi vos ne le deussiés[99] faire[100] tel que court l'esgardast ou coneust, ne ne fustes esoinés par coi vos ne deussiés ma semonce[101] acuillir et mon servise faire.[102] Por coi je entens que vos me soiés defaillie de[103] servise que vos me devés de prendre baron. Si en veuil avoir tel droit et tel amende con je doi par la conoissance de ma court, ne ne veuill que il demore[104] por chose que vos aiés dite que je ne l'aie, se ma court l'esgarde[105] que je faire le[106] dee, et de ce me met je en[107] la conoissance de ma court,[108] sauf mon retenaill.' Et aprés il ne me senble que la feme puisse chose dire que[109] la court ne doit conoistre que le seignor en peut et doit avoir[110] tel amende[111] con de defaut de servise. Et aprés la dite conoissance, se[112] le seignor comande a sa[113] court qu'ele li[114] conoisse quel droit il en doit avoir et quel amende,[115] la court li doit conoistre, se cuit, qu'il se peut faire servir de ce fié[116] .i. an et .i. jor, et aprés l'an et le jor toutes les feis qu'ele li[117] requera son fié qu'ele l'ait. Et quant la feme avra recovré son fié,[118] le seignor la peut de rechief faire[119] semondre de prendre baron en la maniere avant dite et en sera si con est avant[120] devisé.

---

[92] A adds: sire [93] oi] AV: os; B: ois [94] AV add: Et [95] s'en] BO: se [96] li] BV: le [97] dou] AO: de [98] C adds: et [99] le deussiés] A: le deveés; B: devez; V: le deviés [100] AO add: et [101] semonce] C: semoncs [102] acuillir et mon servise faire] V: faire ne acuillir [103] de] ABV: dou [104] demore] B lacks [105] l'esgarde] A: ne conoisse; B: ne conoist; V: ne counoisse [106] faire le] A: aveir ne le; B: avoir ne la; V: avoir ne le [107] B adds: exgart; V: l'esguart et en [108] ne ne veuill . . . court] O lacks [109] que] AB: par quoi [110] A adds: ce il viaut; B: se il veut; V: se il veaut [111] amende] C lacks [112] se] B lacks; V: et [113] sa] ABV: la [114] li] AV lack [115] et quel amende] A lacks [116] de ce fié] A: dou fié; B lacks; V: de celui fié [117] li] AB lack; V: le [118] recovré son fié] C: le fié recours [119] faire] A lacks [120] avant] V: devant

***[200]** Quant feme[1] tient pluisors fiés de plusors seignors, de[2] quel fié[3] ele doit le mariage de qui ele tient le fié.[4]

Se feme a et tient fiés de pluisors gens[5] et aucun des fiés doit[6] servise de cors, ele doit le[7] mariage a celui ou a cele de qui ele tient le fié qui doit servise de cors. Et se tous les fiés que ele tient ou partie d'eaus[8] doivent servise[9] et ele en desert[10] l'un de son cors et les autres[11] con d'escheete, ele doit le mariage a celui sans[12] plus de qui ele tient le fié que ele en[13] desert de son cors. Et quant feme qui a et tient pluisors fiés de pluisors gens[14] ce[15] marie par la semonce de celui de qui ele tient le fié qui doit servise de cors, nul des autres ne peut ne ne doit avoir amende de li de ce que ele est[16] mariee sans leur congié, por ce qu'en[17] l'assise ou l'usage dou reiaume de Jerusalem[18] est que[19] feme qui tient fié qui[20] doit servise de cors doit de cel fié[21] le mariage au seignor de qui ele le tient. Que autre servise ne doit feme por[22] fié que ele tiegne que de soi marier. Et puis que ele a celui seignor[23] de qui ele tient le fié de[24] servise de cors doit le mariage, et as autres non, et ele[25] par semonce de celui ou de cele a cui ele doit le servise de soy marier[26] se marie, ele ne mesprent mie[27] vers les autres. Que feme ne peut deveir mariage que a[28] un seignor, quar ele ne peut aveir .ii. maris ne plus ensemble, et s'ele devoit son mariage a pluisours,[29] chascun de ceaus a qui ele les[30] devroit[31] la porroit semondre de baron[32] prendre, et de divers

A: fol. cxlviii^{r-v} cap. 229; **B:** fol. 181^{r} cap. 231; **C:** fol. 186^{r-v} cap. 200; **O:** fol. 257^{r-v}; **V:** fol. cci^{r-v} cap. 244; Beugnot, pp. 364–5, cap. 229.

[1] V adds: a et [2] de] AB: dou [3] fié] B: des fiéz [4] de qui ele tient le fié] A lacks; B: et au quel seignor; B rubrics (fol. 26^{r}): et au quel des seignors [5] fiés de pluisors gens] A: pluisors fiés de pluissors seignor; BV: plusors fiés de plusors seignors [6] doit] C: doivent [7] B adds: servise et le [8] d'eaus] B lacks [9] A adds: de cors [10] desert] B: sert [11] B adds: sanz plus [12] sans] C: san [13] en] ABV lack [14] gens] AB: seignors [15] pluisors fiés . . . ce] V: fié qui plusours fiés se [16] est] V: c'est [17] qu'en] A: que par; BV: que [18] de Jerusalem] B lacks [19] est que] A lacks; B: est tele que; V: ci est tel que [20] qui] C: que [21] de cel fié] A: deveir; B: devoir [22] por] ABV: de [23] a celui seignor] C: au seignor celui [24] de] V qui doit [25] ele] C: autres [26] soy marier] B: son mariage [27] mesprent mie] B: respont [28] B adds: celui c'est assavoir a [29] C adds: a [30] les] AV: le [31] les devroit] B: le devoit [32] baron] V: mari

barons, et ele ne peut espouser que un, et enssi perdroit[33] ces autres fiés, laquel chose seroit contre droit[34] et raison et[35] tort apert. Si est raison clere et aperte qu'enssi doie[36] estre con il[37] est devant[38] devisé en cest[39] chapitle.

---

[33] perdroit] V: poroit perdre [34] droit] V: Dieu [35] raison et] BV: contre raison et seroit [36] doie] V: doive [37] il] C lacks [38] devant] ABV lack [39] cest] AV: cestui

***[201]** Quant feme tient .i. fié ou plusors d'un seignor ou de pluisors,[1] et ele se marie sans le congé de celui a qui ele doit le mariage, quel amende il et les autres seignors en[2] devent aver.[3]

Quant feme, qui a et tient .i. fié ou pluisors d'un seignor ou d'une dame[4] en heritage ou en baillage ou en doaire, se marie sans[5] congé,[6] celui ou[7] cele[8] de qui ele tient le fié ou[9] les fiés en peut[10] avoir droit et amende, et tel, se me senble, que il avra, ce il viaut,[11] cel fié que ele tient en fié par la conoissance de sa court tant con ele sera en celui mariage. Et quant le seignor viaut avoir fié de feme por tel mesfait, il le doit, ce m'est avis, ensi faire que, quant il est sertain que ele c'est[12] enci mariee, si doit[13] assenbler sa court et dire ou faire dire a ceaus de la court: 'Tel feme', et nomer la, 'qui a et tient[14] cel[15] fié de moi enssi', et dire quel le fié[16] est, et coument ele le tient de lui, et[17] se que ele doit de cest[18] fié, 'c'est[19] mariee sans mon congé. Si[20] vos comant que vos me conoissiés quel[21] amende et quel droit je en doi avoir.' Et la court doit faire cele conoissance et[22] enssi, se cuit, que le seignor se peut saisir dou fié que ele tient de lui et faire s'ent servir tant con ele sera en cel[23] mariage, se la feme a conneu en la court que elle enssi c'est[24] mariee. Et se la court n'en est certaine que par le dit dou seignor, ele doit faire la conoissance enssi, se me senble, que s'elle c'est mariee sans le congé dou seignor[25] de qui elle tient le fié si con il le[26] dit, que il en[27] peut saisir son fié et faire s'en servir tant con ele sera en cel[28] mariage. Et se feme tient pluisors fiés de pluisors gens[29] et ele se marie en la maniere avant dite, je cuit que chascun de ceaus de qui ele tient

A: fols cxlviii^{v}–cxlix^{r} cap. 230; **B:** fol. 181^{r-v} cap. 232; **C:** fols 186^{v}–187^{r} cap. 201; **O:** fols 257^{v}–258^{v}; **V:** fols cci^{v}–ccii^{r} cap. 245; Beugnot, pp. 365–6, cap. 230.

[1] seignor ou de pluisors] ABV: ou de plusors (A: pluisors) seignors [2] en] C lacks [3] B adds: par l'assise [4] A adds: ou de pluisors [5] AV add: le; C: son [6] A adds: de celui a qui elle deit le mariage et [7] celui ou] V: de celui ou de [8] A adds: ou ciaus [9] le fié ou] V lacks [10] peut] A: pevent [11] ce il viaut] V lacks [12] c'est] AB: est [13] AB add: faire [14] V adds: de lui [15] cel] ABV: tel [16] le fié] B: fié ce [17] de moi enssi . . . et] V lacks [18] cest] AB: cel; V: celui [19] fié, 'c'est] V: si est [20] Si] AB: Dont je [21] quel] C: que [22] faire cele conoissance et] V: conoistre [23] cel] BV: celui [24] c'est] A: se seit; B: si soit; V: se soit [25] dou seignor] A: de celui [26] il le] A: il; B: le; V: elle [27] en] AB lack; V: se [28] cel] ABV: celui [29] gens] AB: seignors

fié[30] peut aveir se que ele tient de lui en fié en amende dou mesfait que ele li a fait de marier sei[31] de s'atorité. Et qui en vodra avoir l'amende, il la peut avoir par la court do seignor en la maniere avant devisee.[a]

[a] Above cap. 199.

[30] fié] C lacks; V: celui fié [31] sei] C: la

***[202]** Quant home dou seignor prent feme qui tient fié dou seignor, et il l'espouse sans son congé, que il doit faire si que le seignor ne autre ne le puisse reter[1] de sa foy.

Se home dou seignor espouse feme qui tient fié do seignor de quei ele li en doit le mariage ou ne se puisse marier sans le congé dou seignor, et il ne le fait par le comandement dou seignor, il ne deit saisir ne tenir le fié de la feme,[2] se il ne le fait par le seignor, ains le doit laisser estreé,[3] por ce que s'il tient le fié de la feme qu'il a espousee sans le congé dou seignor, il c'est mis autrement que il ne doit el[4] droit de son seignor, si a mespris vers lui de sa foi,[5] se me senble. Et me senble[6] que le seignor en porra avoir droit con de foi mentie. Mais se il espouse la feme sans le congé dou seignor et il ne[7] saisist ne ne prent[8] le fié de la feme, il m'est avis[9] que le seignor ne porra pas[10] avoir droit de lui ne amende par sa court, por ce que la feme ne doit au seignor le mariage qu'ele li[11] doit que por le fié que ele tient de lui. Et puis que ele por autre[12] ne li doit le mariage[13] que por le fié,[14] et[15] que son home qui a la feme[16] espousee sans son congé ne c'est[17] mis el fié de sa feme, donc ne c'est[18] il mie mis el[19] droit de son[20] seignor autrement que il ne doit ne mespris vers lui de sa foi. Et puis que il ne c'est[21] mis ne n'a mespris de sa foi vers lui, le seignor ne peut ne ne doit avoir[22] amende[23] par sa court, ce m'est avis, de la feme[24] autre que d'avoir le fié que ele tient de lui. Quar feme n'est mie serve[25] por son fié que ele ne se puisse[26] marier sans le congé dou seignor la ou ele vodra, et c'ele le fait et le seignor viaut avoir le fié, si le fase si con est devisé el chapitle qui est devant cestui.

A: fol. cxlix^{r-v} cap. 231; **B:** fols 181^{v}–182^{r} cap. 233; **C:** fol. 187^{r-v} cap. 202; **O:** fols 258^{v}–259^{v}; **V:** fols ccii^{r}–cciii^{r} cap. 246; Beugnot, pp. 366–7, cap. 231.

---

[1] puisse reter] B: doie rester; V: puisse geter [2] V adds: que il a espousee [3] estreé] V: ester [4] el] A: es; B: ou; V: au [5] de sa foi] A lacks [6] Et me senble] B lacks [7] A adds: s'en [8] ne ne prent] A: ne prent; V lacks [9] m'est avis] AB: me semble [10] pas] ABV lack [11] li] BV lack [12] ele por autre] A: por autre chose elle; O: autre autre [13] B adds: fors [14] que ele tient . . . fié] V lacks [15] et] C lacks [16] la feme] C lacks [17] C adds: mie [18] donc ne c'est] B: dont ne s'est; V: dont n'est [19] fié de sa feme . . . el] C lacks [20] de son] AV: dou [21] c'est] AB: si est [22] A adds: dreit ne [23] amende] V: droit ne amende de lui [24] de la feme] A lacks [25] serve] B: seure [26] puisse] C: peut

Et se autre que home dou seignor, a qui il ne[27] soit tenus de foi, espouse feme qui teigne fié dou seignor[28] de qui ele le doit[29] le mariage ou[30] que ele[31] ne se puisse marier sans son congé[32] mete soi ou ne[33] mete en saisine do fié, le seignor, se m'est avis, le peut prendre ou faire prendre,[34] se il viaut, et justiser le a sa volenté, puis que la feme, qui[35] devoit au seignor[36] le mariage ou qui ne se peut sans son congé marier, a espousee[37] sans son congé.[38] Que s'il se saisist do fié, il se mete el droit dou seignor, et c'il[39] ne s'en saisist[40] si a il desprisé le seignor et fait[41] contre sa seignorie, quant il a la feme[42] qui li devoit mariage ou qui sans son congé ne se pooit[43] marier a espousee, et por ce me senble il que le seignor en peut[44] faire sa volenté puis que il n'est tenus de foy a lui.

[27] ne] V lacks [28] a qui il . . . seignor] B lacks [29] le doit] A: li deive; B: tient et doit; O: li doive; V: doive [30] AV add: tel; B: tele [31] que ele] B: qui [32] A adds: et ce; B: et [33] A adds: se; V: le [34] ou faire prendre] B lacks [35] qui] AB lack [36] au seignor] B lacks [37] a espousee] V: est espouse [38] a espousee sans son congé] B lacks [39] c'il] C: il [40] s'en saisist] V: se mete en saisine [41] fait] C: faire [42] quant il a la feme] B: que il a la feme prise [43] pooit] V: peut [44] V adds: avoir droit et em peut

***[203]** Quant aucun home dou seignor prent[1] feme qui tient fié dou seignor sans son congé,[2] et il[3] s'en saisist dou fié de la feme,[4] coment il peut aver tornes de bataille.[5]

Se aucun des homes dou seignor espouse feme qui tient fié do seignor de qui[6] ele li doive[7] le mariage, et il l'espouse sans le congé dou seignor, et il se[8] saisist dou fié de la feme, se ce n'est par le seignor, et le seignor[9] se deporte[10] de mener lui et sa feme a se que[11] mener les en porroit[12] par sa court, et ne[13] li otroie ne[14] consent[15] le mariage ne le fié a[16] tenir, et aucuns[17] des homes dou seignor ou aucun autre viaut celui, qui ensi[18] c'est mariés et mis au droit de son seignor autrement qu'il ne doit,[19] apeler par gage de bataile, il le pora faire, se me senble. Et qui faire le vodra, il le doit faire ensi, qu'il doit venir devant le seignor en la court et demander li[20] conceill, et quant il sera paiés de conceill, se celui que il vodra apeler[21] n'est[22] en la court, si fase dire au seignor par son conceill: 'Sire, je vos[23] requier que vos facés tel venir en la court, si orés[24] coment je li veuill metre sus que il a sa foi mentie vers vos de ce que il c'est mis[25] en vostre droit autrement que il ne doit.' Et se le seignor viaut la bataille soufrir, il doit faire celui semondre de venir en la court a jor moti[26] respondre a ce que celui li metra sus. Et quant il sera en la court, si die ou fase dire par son conceill celui qui apeler le veaut en la presence de celui qu'il viaut apeler:[27] 'Sire, tel', et le nome,[28] 'qui est vostre home et tenus a vos de fey a sa foi mentie vers vos con

---

A: fols cxlix^{v}–cl^{v} cap. 232; **B:** fols 182^{r}–183^{v} cap. 234; **C:** fols 187^{v}–189^{r} cap. 203; **O:** fols 259^{v}–261^{v}; **V:** fols cciii^{r}–cciv^{v} cap. 247; Beugnot, pp. 367–9, cap. 232.

---

[1] Quant aucun home . . . prent] ABV: Se aucun des homes dou seignor espouse [2] sans son congé] A rubrics (fol. 8^{r}) BV lack [3] il] BV lack [4] de la feme] O lacks [5] de la feme . . . bataille] A: quel amende le seignor en deit aveir, et coment un de ces pers le peut apeler de fei mentie; B: quele amende le seignor en doit avoir, et coment un autre home dou seignor qui soit son per l'en puet apeler de foy mentie; V: quel amende le seignor en doit avoir, et coment .i. des homes dou seignor le peut apeller de foi mentie [6] qui] A: quei; BV: quoi [7] doive] A: deit; B: doit [8] se] AV: s'en; C: le [9] et le seignor] B lacks [10] se deporte] A: s'en deporte; C: se departe [11] a se que] B: a ce que il; V: et ce qui [12] porroit] V: pora [13] et ne] BV: ne ne [14] ne] B: ne ne; V: et ne [15] otroie ne consent] C: otroient coment [16] a] C lacks [17] aucuns] ABV: aucun [18] ensi] V lacks [19] A adds: le peut [20] demander li] A: et li deit demander [21] vodra apeler] C: apele [22] n'est] O lacks [23] ABV add: pri et [24] si orés] O: a jor moti (struck through in later (?) hand) [25] c'est mis] B: est marié [26] AV add: a [27] la presence de . . . apeler] AB: sa presence [28] et le nome] B lacks

celui qui faucement et deleaument s'est mis en vostre droit autrement qu'il ne doit. Que il tel feme', et la nome, 'a espousee sans vostre congé, laquel vos deit[29] mariage dou fié qu'ele tenoit de vos, et il en celui fié c'est mis autrement que il ne doit, lequel[30] fié la feme a mesfait vers vos, par se qu'ele c'est mariee sans vostre congé.[31] De quei je dis que il a sa foy mentie vers vos et c'est mis en vostre droit autrement que il ne doit. Et se il le[32] veaut noier, je suis prest que je li preuve de mon cors contre le sien et que je l'en[33] rende mort ou recreant en une hore de jor, et vés enssi mon guage.' Et s'agenoille devant le seignor et li tende son guage.

Et se celui que l'on apele enssi le desment[34] mot a mot et s'en eufre sans esgart et[35] sans conoissance de court de[36] defendre de son cors contre le sien et en tent son guage et[37] le seignor resoit les guages,[38] la bataille doit estre au quarantaime jor,[39] s'il sont chevaliers a cheval a armes[40] apareillés come chevaliers chanpions, et s'il sont sergens[41] enssi adoubés et apareilliés come sergens chanpions.[42] Et se celui que l'on apele enssi desment celui qui l'a apelé[43] mot a mot de ce que il li met sus et s'en eufre a prover[44] tout enssi con la court esgardera ou conoistra que il deffendre s'en doie, je cuit que la court doit esgarder ou conoistre que[45] il s'en doit deffendre de son cors contre le sien, puis que la chose que l'on[46] li met sus est aparant et manifeste de ce que il a la feme espousee sans le congé do seignor qui devoit mariage au seignor[47] dou[48] fié que ele tient[49] de lui, et c'est mis el fié. Que la feme[50] a mesfait au seignor por ce que ele c'est mariee sans son congé, lequel fié le seignor doit aveir, se cuit, par l'assise ou l'usage dou reiaume de Jerusalem tant con la feme est en celui mariage.

Et por ce meismes me senble il[51] que la court doit faire la dite conoissance ou le dit esgart, que je entens que par l'assise[52] ou l'usage de cest roiaume que il y a bataille de murtre aparant mostré a court

---

[29] deit] V: devoit [30] lequel] V: douquel [31] laquel vos deit . . . congé] ABO lack [32] le] ABV: ce [33] l'en] AV: le [34] se celui que . . . desment] B: celui que l'en apele enssi le doit desmentir [35] et] A: ou; B lacks [36] de] ABV: a [37] en tent son guage et] V: tent son guage et se [38] resoit les guages] B: les reçoive ambedus et [39] au quarantaime jor] A: a .xl. jors [40] a armes] A: armés et; B: amez et; V: et a armes [41] B adds: si doivent estre en [42] et s'il sont . . . chanpions] A lacks [43] l'a apelé] A: l'apelle [44] prover] ABV: defendre [45] O adds: se [46] l'on] AV: il; B: on [47] qui devoit mariage au seignor] A: a qui elle deveit le mariage [48] dou] C: qui devoit dou [49] tient] A: teneit; OV: tenoit [50] que la feme] A: et que la feme B: de la feme de quoi ele [51] me senble il] AB lack [52] l'assise] V: la dite assise

et de traïson aparant et de querele d'un marc d'argent ou de plus et de totes choses de quei l'on pert vie ou menbre[53] ou vois ou[54] respons en court[a] qui[55] est ataint ou prové, et a moy senble que celui qui avroit la feme espousee qui doit[56] mariage au seignor et se seroit mis el fié avroit fait vers son seignor .i. rain de traïson, et cele traïson seroit bien aparant et manifeste. Por coi il me senble que la bataille i devroit bien estre, et por tant plus, que moult meaus[57] doit il[58] avoir bataille de chose de quei[59] l'on pert vie ou menbre ou s'enor[60] qui en est ataint ou prové que de querele d'un marc d'argent ou de plus. Que se celui que l'on avroit apelé si con est avant dit ne s'en[61] pooit defendre par guage de bataille,[b] il seroit[62] ataint de[63] foy mentie, et s'il en estoit ataint, il seroit en la merci dou seignor, si le porroit le seignor[64] faire morir vilainement ou[65] si con il[66] li plairoit, ou tolir li tant des menbres con il vodroit, et s'il li soufroit la vie, il avroit henor perdue a tos jors et seroit desherité de quanqu'il tenroit de celui[67] seignor,[68] se le seignor le voloit[69] avoir, qu'il[70] monteroit a plus grant chose que n'est[71] querele d'un marc d'argent ou de plus. Car s'il n'eust bataille es dites choses, qui vodroit maliner ou vodroit metre sus a qui que l'on vodroit[72] aucune chose de quoi il perdroit vie ou menbre ou s'enor s'il en[73] estoit ataint, laquel chose ne seroit aparant ne manifeste, et l'ofriroit a prover par guarans, et il trovast .ii. homes tes qui peucent[74] guarentie porter, et il feissent ce que guarans doivent faire a guarantie porter,[75] et se celui contre qui il vodroient[76] guarantie porter[77] ne peust l'un torner par guage de bataille, il seroit ataint de ce que l'on li avroit mis[78] sus. Si en perdroit vie ou menbre ou s'enor, selon se que l'on li

---

[a] O has a *lacuna* starting here.
[b] End of *lacuna* in O.

---

[53] ou menbre] V et membres [54] ou vois ou] AV: et vois et; B: vois ou [55] ABV add: en [56] espousee qui doit] V: a espouse qui devroit [57] ABV add: i [58] il] BV lack [59] de quei] B: ou [60] ou s'enor] B lacks; V: et son honor [61] s'en] AV: se [62] seroit] C: ce soit [63] ataint de] B lacks [64] le seignor] AB lack [65] vilainement ou] ABV lack [66] il] AB lack [67] de celui] C: do [68] B adds: et [69] voloit] C: voroit [70] qu'il] ABV: qui [71] n'est] A lacks [72] metre sus a . . . vodroit] B lacks; V adds: maligner ou metre sus [73] en] C lacks [74] peucent] BOV: puissent [75] et il feissent . . . porter] AB lack [76] AB add: la [77] et il feissent . . . porter] V lacks [78] avroit mis] V: metroit

avroit mis sus,[79] lesqués choses chascun doit meaus defendre.[80] Et par les raisons avant dites et par pluisors autres[81] que on i porroit encore dire, me senble il que il i[82] peut et doit avoir bataille en cest cas si[83] con il est[84] avant dit.[85]

[79] Si en perdroit . . . sus] B lacks [80] A adds: par torne aveir de bataille; B: que tornes avoir de bataille; V: que tourne avoir [81] autres] C lacks [82] i] AOV lack [83] cest case si] ABV: tel cas [84] est] A lacks [85] dit] B: devisé

***[204]** Coment l'on doit son seignor semondre de faire le paier de ce que il li doit de son fié de quei le terme de sa paie est passé, et coment guager.[a]

Se[1] .i. home est asené de son fié en .i. leu[2] qui ne rende tant que il puisse estre paiés[3] enterinement[4] de son fié si con il est asené a estre paiés, de .iii. meis en .iii. meis[5] ou de[6] demi an en demi an ou autrement, et[7] que se[8] le seignor ne prent ou ne[9] fait prendre aucune chose de cel leu[10] ou celui est asené de son fié, mais que ce qui li[11] defaut de sa paie d'un terme ou de plus, il peut guager le seignor de son servise en tel maniere que il doit[12] venir devant luy et dire li: 'Sire, le terme de ma paie en tel leu est pasé, et je ne puis estre paiés. Si vos pri et requier con a mon seignor que vos me faites[13] paier de mon fié par les termes si con je sui asené.' Et enssi le fase .ii. ou iii. fois, ains[14] que il[15] requiere en court. Et se le seignor ne le fait por tant paier,[16] il doit aprés venir en sa court une fois ou .ii. et faire li la requeste desus dite.

Et se por tant le seignor ne le fait paier, il doit aprés[17] venir devant lui[18] en la presence de sa court et demander conceill et[19] faire dire par son conceill: 'Sire, tel qui est vostre home de tel fié qui est asené en tel leu de quei il vos doit tel servise', et nome le leu ou il est asené[20] et die quel le fié[21] est et quel[22] servise il doit, 'n'a pas[23] esté paié de son fié si con son asenement le devise, ains li doit on d'un terme et[24] de plus. Et il vos a pluisors feis prié et requis en court et hors court que vos le feissiés paier de son fié, et vos ne

A: fols clii^r^–cliii^v^ cap. 235; **B:** fols 185^r^–187^r^ cap. 238; **C:** fols 189^r^–191^v^ cap. 204; **O:** fols 261^v^–265^v^; **V:** fols ccvii^r^–ccix^r^ cap. 250; Beugnot, pp. 373–6, cap. 235.

[a] Rubric in ABV: Se un home est assené de son fié en .i. leuc moti (A: mouti) qui ne rende (V: rent) tant qu'il puisse (A: en puisse) estre paié (puisse estre paié] V: soit paiés) enterinement de son fié si come il est assené paié, il peut (B: puet) le seignor gagier (gagier V: guager) de son servise si come il est aprés devisié (B: devisé aprés).

[1] Se] C: Pe [2] BV add: moti [3] paiés] V lacks [4] enterinement] C: enteriment [5] en .iii. meis] B lacks [6] de] C: dei; V lacks [7] et] C lacks [8] se] ABV lack [9] ou ne] AV: ou; B: ne ne [10] cel leu] B: celui leuc; V: celui fié [11] que ce qui li] C: ce qui; O: que ce qui li en [12] doit] V: peut [13] faites] B: faciez [14] ains] V: avant [15] AB add: li; V: le [16] paier] ABV lack [17] aprés] V lacks [18] devant lui] AB lack [19] V adds: puis [20] en tel leu . . . asené] V lacks [21] le fié] B: fié ce [22] quel] C: que [23] n'a pas] B: n'a mie; V: n'en a [24] et] B: ou

l'avés encore fait. Si vos pri et requier encore com a son seignor que vos le faciés paier de[25] ce que l'on[26] li doit de son fié, si que il vos en[27] puisse faire le servise que il vos en[28] doit. Car sans[29] paie de son[30] fié ne vos peut il servir.'[31] Et lors celui de qui le fié est doit dire au seignor: 'Sire, je vos semons que vos m'aiés paié ou fait paier de ce que vos me devés de mon fié[32] de hui en .xv. jors, ou[33] demain en .xv. jors, ou de puis[34] demain en .xv. jors.[35] Et de cest semonce que je vos ai faite[36] trai je vostre court a guarant.' Et a tant se taise por tant[37] que les .iii. quinsaines soient[38] pasees, qui sont .xvii. jors.

Et quant eles seront pasees,[39] si reveigne[40] devant son[41] seignor en sa court et li fase dire par son conceill coment il li a sa paie requise pluisors feis amiablement en court et hors[42] court, et coment aprés ce por ce que il ne le paie ou feist[43] paier il le semonst par les .iii. quinsaines qui sont establiés de semondre son seignor,[44] et eles sont pasees et il ne l'a paié ne fait paier[45] encore; si le[46] prie et requier con a son seignor que il le fase paier[47] de ce que il li doit de son fié. Et lors celui qui requiert sa paie dit: 'Sire,[48] je vos semons que vos m'aiés paié ou fait paier de ce que vos me devés de mon fié de hui en .xl. jors ou de demain en .xl. jors ou de[49] puis[50] demain en .xl. jors. Et de ce trai je vostre[51] court a guarant'.

Et se les[52] quarantaines, qui sont .xlii. jors, pasent que il ne l'ait paié ou fait paier de ce que il li doit de son fié, il doit revenir[53] devant le seignor en sa court et dire li: 'Sire, je vos ai pluisors feis requise ma paie de ce que vos me devés de mon fié, et vos ne me feistes paier, et aprés je vos[54] ai[55] semons par les .iii. quinsaines[56] que vos me paisiés ou[57] feissiés paier de ce que vos me devés de mon fié, et vos ne[58] l'avés fait, et les dites quinzaines et quarantaines sont

[25] faciés paier de] V: faites paier [26] l'on] AB: on [27] en] C lacks [28] en] ABV lack [29] AV add: la [30] son] C lacks [31] servir] B: servise faire [32] de mon fié] V lacks [33] AO add: de [34] puis] A: plus [35] ou de puis . . . jors] B lacks [36] AB add: en [37] por tant] ABV: tant; O: por tant tant [38] soient] V: seront [39] qui sont .xvii. . . . pasees] B lacks [40] reveigne] B: viegne [41] son] ABV: le [42] hors] A: fors; B: hors de [43] le paie ou feist] A: l'en a paié ou fist; B: l'en paia ou ne fist; V: l'a paié ou fait [44] de semondre son seignor] A: dou seignor semondre; BV: a (V: por) semondre son seignor [45] l'a paié ne fait paier] A: l'en a paié ou fait paier et [46] si le] AB: li [47] encore; si le . . . paier] V lacks [48] ABV add: et [49] demain en .xl. jors ou de] B lacks [50] puis] A: plus [51] trai je vostre] V: en trais je la [52] AV add: .iii.; B: trois [53] revenir] ABV: venir [54] me feistes paier . . . vos] A: m'avés paié ne fait paier de ce que vos me devés de mon fié et [55] ai] ABV lack [56] ABV add: et (B: et par) les .iii. quarantaines [57] paisiés ou] A lacks [58] me feistes paier . . . ne] O lacks

pasees, ne je ne suis paiés. Si vos guage dou servise que je vos doi de cest fié tant que vos m'aiés[59] fait paier de ce que vos me devés de cest[60] mien fié si con je suis asené, et veuill que le guagement vaille, se vostre court l'esguarde, por tant con je ai dit et fait. Et de ce me met je en l'esgart de la court.' Et mete son[61] retenaill. Et le seignor peut[62] respondre a se, se il viaut le guagement contrebatre.[63] Et se le seignor respont a se:[64] 'Il est voir que vos estes asené de vostre fié en tel leu, ne je n'ai pris ne fait prendre nule chose de vostre asenement. Et se autre l'a pris, dites le moi, et je le vos ferai rendre, ou je vos avrai[65] celui qui pris l'a a droit. Et je ai comandé et comanderai[66] encor que vos seiés paié de vostre fié en vostre asenement, si con vos en[67] estes asené, et[68] s'il i a de coi. Et se il demoure[69] que vos n'avés esté paié, se n'est[70] demoré en la faute[71] de moy ne d'autre, ains est por ce que le leu ne l'a pas rendu. Et puis que il par la defaute de moi ne d'autre n'est remés[72] que vos ne soiés paiés, ne par autre chose que par[73] le leu ou vos estes asené n'a pas[74] tant[75] rendu que vos puissés estre paiés, je ne veuill que vostre guagement vaille, se la court ne l'esguarde.' Et mete[76] son retenaill. Et lors celui qui l'a guagé[77] doit dire se il viaut que son guagement vaille:[78] 'Sire, vos ferés dire[79] vostre volenté, mais je ne veuill que il demoure por chose que vos diés ou fasés[80] dire que mon guagement ne vaille, et di por coi: por ce que je suis asené de mon fié de .iii. mois en .iii. mois',[81] ou selon ce que l'asenement sera, 'et le terme de ma paie est pasé,[82] et je n'ai esté paiés, ne je ne vos puis ne dois servir[83] de mon fié se je ne suis paiés coment qu'il me[84] faile, soit par vos ou par autre ou par le leu qui ne vaille.[85] Que sans paie de mon fié ne vos puis je ne doi servir. Puis que le terme de ma paie est pasé et que je ne suis paiés, je[86] n'entent que je servise vos[87] doie faire

---

59 m'aiés] B: m'avez paié ou; V: m'en aiés paié ou 60 cest] BV: cestui 61 Et mete son] V: sauf mon 62 peut] A: deit; BV: doit 63 contrebatre] O: combatre 64 Et se le . . . se] ABV lack 65 avrai] A: aveerai 66 comanderai] A: comande 67 en] AV lack 68 et] BV lack 69 demoure] AB: est demorré (B: demoré); C: i demoure; V: n'en est demoré 70 A adds: pas 71 vos n'avés esté . . . faute] B: n'estes paié ce n'est mie en la defaute 72 que vos n'avés . . . remés] V: en vie ne ne la faute de moi ne d'autre n'est demoré 73 que par] A: que por ce que] B: fors que por; V: fors que 74 pas] A lacks 75 n'a pas tant] B : qui n'a tant valu ne 76 mete] AV: metre 77 l'a guagé] AO: le gage; B: l'a gagié; V: le guage 78 se il viaut . . . vaille] V lacks 79 ferés dire] A: dittes; B: dites 80 diés ou fasés] B: doiez ou faciez; V: dites ou faites 81 en .iii. mois] C lacks 82 pasé] B lacks 83 servir] V: servise que 84 me] C lacks 85 vaille] A: vaille tant; B: le veut; V: le vaille 86 je] C: ne 87 AV add: en

de cel[88] fié tant que je en soie paiés si con je suis asené. Por coi je entent que mon guagement vaut[89] et doit valoir, et veuill que il vaille aprés se que je ai dit[90] et fait par les raisons que je ai dit[91] ou par aucunes d'eles, se la court l'esgarde, et de ce me met je en l'esgart de la court.' Et mete son[92] retenaill. Et je entent que la court doit esgarder que cel guagement vaut, et quant l'esgart sera fait, celui peut son seignor ensi guager que il ne li fera[93] servise d'aler ne de venir a[94] semonce qu'il li fase.[95] Mais il covendra que il tiegne cheval et[96] armes, et se le fié doit servize de conpaignons, que il tiegne[97] [b] le servise en piés de tant de conpaignons con le fié doit, tant que le leu ou il est asené vaille tant de quei[98] il puisse estre paiés, et qu'il soit paiés, de la ou d'aillors, de tout quantque l'on li[99] devra de son fié devant la semonce et aprés de tant de terme con il i[100] avra de terme de[101] paie passé.[102]

Et se celui qui ensi avra guagé[103] voit et conoist[104] que le leu ou l'en l'a asené ne vaille ou ne doie[105] valoir d'un lonc tens tant de quei[106] il puisse estre paiés, se[107] il peut trover chevance covenable de sodees ou d'autre fié ou d'autres choses,[108] se il fait que sage, il comandera son fié au seignor et prendra la chevance tant con[109] le leuc ou il est asené vaille tant que il puisse estre paiés de tout quantque l'on li doit[110] de son fié ou de ce qu'il deservira. Que il porroit[111] tant demorer a estre paié de tout quanque l'on li doit[112] de[113] son fié[114] que il i[115] avroit grant[116] damage en tenir le seignor guagé de son servise et tenir les conpaignons et le cheval[117] et les armes que il doit tenir tant que il soit paiés. Et se celui qui a guagé[118] son servise si com est avant dit viaut comander son fié, il le doit enssi

[b] A clear example of the reading of ABV being preferable to CO.

[88] cel] BV: celui [89] vaut] V: vaille [90] dit] B: doit [91] C repeats: et fait par les raisons que je ai dites (with all but the first two words deleted). [92] Et mete son] BV: sauf mon [93] ensi guager que . . . fera] V: guager et ne li fera nient de [94] BV add: sa [95] qu'il li fase] A: qu'il face; V lacks [96] cheval et] A: chevaus et; B: le cheval et les [97] tiegne] CO: ne tieigne (O: tiegne) pas [98] de quei] V: que [99] quantque l'on li] B: ce que il [100] i] BV lack [101] terme de] B: termes de; V lacks [102] terme con il . . . passé] A: termes come il avra de termes de paie passés [103] ensi avra guagé] A: ensi gage son seignor; B: enssi a gagié son seignor; O: ensi a gagé; V: est si gagé [104] conoist] A: conut [105] doie] C: doit [106] de quei] C: que [107] se] A: et [108] d'autre fié ou d'autres choses] A: d'autre chose [109] con] ABV: que [110] doit] A: deveit [111] porroit] C: pora [112] de tout quantque l'on li doit de son fié . . . doit] B lacks [113] tout quanque l'on li doit de] A lacks [114] ce qu'il deservira . . . fié] V: qui en defaudra [115] i] AB lack [116] grant] V: de [117] et le cheval] B: les chevaus [118] ABV add: son (A: le) seignor de

faire que il doit venir devant le seignor et dire li: 'Sire, .i. jor qui passés est je vos gajai de mon servise,[119] et la court entendi[120] de coi et coment. Sire, et[121] dou guagement je m'en relais et m'en seufre ore et rentre[122] el[123] servise et en trai vostre court a guarant.' Et quant il avra ce dit, si li die aprés aucuns jors:[124] 'Sire, je vos comans mon fié par l'assise ou l'usage de cest roiaume'. Et li doit tendre aucune chose par quoi il li comande son fié. Et se le seignor le reçoit, si ne die plus. Et s'il ne le reçoit sans dire raison por quoi il ne le doit recevoir,[125] si[126] die: 'Sire, je vos ai comandé mon fié par l'assise ou l'usage de cest roiaume, et encore[127] le vos comant, et en trai vostre[128] court a guarant coment je le vos ai comandé.[129] Et encore le vos comant, et vaille ce que valoir[130] devra.' Et se parte a tant. Mais quant il comande[131] le fié au seignor, se le seignor[132] dit aucune raison par coi il ne le viaut recevoir et se met en l'esgart[133] ou en la conoissance de la court sauf son retenaill,[134] celui[135] qui fait la comande die raison por coi il viaut que sa comande vaille et se mete en l'esgart ou en la conoissance de la court sauf son retenaill. Que se il ne le fait, sa comande ne vaudra riens. Et quant il avra son fié comandé, il porra aler la ou il[136] cuidera faire son meaus, se la court esgarde ou conoist[137] que la comande dou fié soit valable[138] si com il l'a fait.

[119] B adds: si com est avant dit [120] entendi] A: l'entendi; B: l'entendi et [121] et] C lacks [122] rentre] A: entre; C: rendre [123] el] V: en vostre [124] aucuns jors] C lacks [125] sans dire raison . . . recevoir] C lacks [126] AB add: li [127] et encore] V: en [128] vostre] ABV: la [129] comandé] AB: recomandé [130] valoir] C: valer [131] comande] V: coumandra [132] V adds: ne [133] V adds: de la court [134] sauf son retenaill] ABV lack [135] celui] BV: se celui [136] B adds: voudra ou; V: vodra et ou il [137] conoist] A: conut [138] soit valable] V: vaille

***[205]** Coment l'on doit son seignor destraindre de ce que il li doit de son fié de quei le terme de sa paie est passé, et coment conjurer ses pers et coment guager.[a]

Se un home ou[1] feme est assené de son fié en .i. leuc qui ait[2] tant valu de quei il puisse estre paiés, et le seignor l'ait pris ou fait prendre, et que par ce sa paie li est defaillie, et que .i. terme ou plus li defaut de sa paie, et il veuille destraindre son seignor coment[3] il le paie,[4] il doit venir devant lui et requere li[5] entre lui et lui[6] sa paie, et dire li: 'Sire, vos me devés de mon fié, et le leuc ou je sui assené a tant valu que je peuse[7] estre bien paiés de ce que l'on me doit de mon fié. Si vos pri et requier, com a mon seignor, que vos me faisiés[8] paier[9] de mon fié, si que je vos en puisse servir si con je doi.'

Et se le seignor ne l'en paie ou fait paier, il doit puis venir devant lui en sa cort et requerre li sa paie en la maniere avant[10] dite une feis ou .ii. ou .iii.

Et se il por tant ne le[11] fait paier, il doit venir en la court et demander conceill, et quant il sera paié de conceill, son conceill doit dire por lui: 'Sire, tel', et le nome,[12] 'vos dit, et je por lui, que il est assené de son fié en tel leuc', et die ou, 'a estre paiés a[13] tel terme[14] de l'asenement, et[15] l'on li doit de son fié d'un terme[16] et[17] de plus, et il entent que le leuc[18] ou il est asené de son fié ait[19] bien tant valu et plus de quei il peust estre paiés de son fié.[20] Si vos pri et requier come a son seignor que vos le fasiés[21] paier de[22] ce que l'on li deit de son fié de quei le terme de sa paie est passé.' Et lors

A: fols cliii^v–clvi^v cap. 236; **B:** fols 187^r–190^r cap. 239; **C:** fols 191^v–195^v cap. 205; **O:** fols 265^v–271^r; **V:** fols ccix^r–ccxiii^r caps 251–2; Beugnot, pp. 376–80, cap. 236.

[a] Rubric in ABV: Se un home ou une feme est assené (A: essenee) de son fié en un leuc qui ait tant valu qu'il puisse estre paié, et le seignor l'ait pris et que par ce li est sa paie defaillie, il le doit (A: deit) requerre au seignor par la maniere ci aprés devisee (A: aprés devisiee; B: ampés devisee).

[1] ABV add: une [2] ait] V: a [3] coment] A: que [4] et il veuille . . . paie] O lacks [5] li] A lacks; B: il [6] entre lui et lui] V lacks [7] peuse] ABV: puis [8] faisiés] V: faites [9] paier] C: paer [10] avant] ABV: devant [11] le] B: li; C: l'en [12] et le nome] V: home [13] a estre paiés a] V: estre paié en [14] terme] A: termine [15] et] V: que [16] terme] A: termine [17] et] ABV: ou [18] le leuc] B lacks [19] ait] ABV: a [20] peust estre paiés de son fié] V: puisse estre paié [21] fasiés] V: faites [22] son fié. Si . . . de] AB lack

celui qui requiert sa paie li[23] doit dire: 'Sire, je vos ai requise pluisors fois ma paie dehors[24] cort et en court amiablement, si con mon conceill le vos a dit por moi, et vos ne m'avés paié ne fait paier. Si vos semons come mon seignor que vos m'aiés paié ou fait paier de ce que vos me devés de mon fié de hui en .xv. jors, ou de demain en .xv. jors, ou de puis[25] demain en .xv. jors[26] et je trai[27] vostre court a guarant coment[28] je vos ai semons si con je doi par les .iii. quinsaines qui sont establies que home doit son seignor semondre d'avoir le paie de ce que il li doit de son fié puis que le terme est passé et que[29] le leuc ou il est assené de son fié[30] a tant valu que il puisse[31] sa paie avoir.' Et a tant se taist.

Et se les .iii. quinsaines, qui sont .xvii. jors, passent que le seignor ne l'ait paié ou fait son gré de sa paie,[32] il doit revenir[33] devant le seignor en la presence de sa court, et faire[34] que il ait lors de ceaus homes qui furent la ou il le semonst par les .iii. quinsaines, et faire li dire par son conceill: 'Sire, tel', et le nome, 'vos a pluisors fois entre vos et lui et puis en court requise sa paie de son fié dont il est vostre home et de quei il est assené en tel leuc et[35] a bien tant valu que il peust[36] bien estre paié, et vos ne l'en[37] feistes paier. Et aprés, sire, il vos semonst par les .iii. quinzaines, qui sont establies que[38] home doit son seignor semondre que il le fase paier de son fié,[39] que vos le feissiés paier de son fié.[40] Et les .iii.[41] quinsaines sont passees, et vos ne l'avés[42] fait paier. Si vos prie et requiert con son seignor que vos le fasiés[43] paier de ce que vos li devés de son fié.' Et lors celui qui requiert sa paie doit dire: 'Sire,[44] je vos semons con[45] mon seignor que vos de hui en .xl. jors, ou de demain en .xl. jors, ou de puis[46] demain en .xl. jors[47] m'aiés paié ou fait paier se que vos me devés de mon fié de tant con le terme de ma paie[48] est passé. Et de ceste semonce trai je vostre court a guarant.' Et a tant se taise.

Et se les .iii. quarantaines passent,[49] qui sont .xlii. jors, que le seignor ne l'ait paié ou fait paier ou fait[50] son gré de sa paie, se il

---

[23] sa paie li] AB lack; V: sa paie [24] dehors] B: dehors de; V: hors [25] puis] A: plus [26] ou de demain . . . jors] B: ou demain en quinze jors; C lacks [27] je trais] A: de ce trais je; B: de ce en trai je; V: en trais [28] coment] BV: come [29] que] AB lack [30] de son fié] B lacks [31] puisse] B: puet [32] ou fait son . . . paie] C lacks [33] revenir] V: venir [34] V adds: tant [35] et] A: lequel [36] peust] V: deust [37] l'en] ABV: le [38] que] B: par lesquex [39] de son fié] B lacks [40] que vos le . . . fié] V lacks [41] .iii.] AB lack [42] B adds: paié ne [43] fasiés] AOV: faites [44] ABV add: et [45] AV add: a [46] puis] A: plus [47] ou de puis . . . jors] B lacks [48] de ma paie] O lacks [49] passent] V: sont passees [50] paier ou fait] C lacks

viaut le seignor guager de son servise, il le peut faire ensi, que il veigne en la presence dou seignor et de la court et faire li dire par son conceill: 'Sire, tel', et le nome, 'vint pluisors fois devant vos et vos requist[51] pluisors fois[52] devant vos[53] dehors court et en court sa paie[54] de ce que l'on li doit[55] de son fié, et vos ne le feistes paier, et[56] aprés il vos semonst par les .iii. quinsaines, qui sont establies que home doit semondre son seignor que il le fase paier de ce que il li doit de son fié,[57] que vos le deussiés faire paier de ce que vos li devés de son fié, et le terme passa, et vos ne le feistes.[58] Et[59] aprés il vos semonst par les[60] quarantaines,[61] qui sont establies que on[62] doit son seignor semondre que il le fase paier de son fié, et eles sont passees, et vos ne l'avés fait. Et encore[63] vos prie il[64] come son seignor que vos l'en[65] faites[66] paier.' Et lors celui qui l'a semons doit dire: 'Sire, je vos ai requise ma paie[67] de ce que vos me devés de mon fié et semons que vos me[68] feissiés paier si come mon conceill vos a dit por moi, et vos ne l'avés fait. Si vos guage dou servise que je vos doi de cel fié en tel[69] maniere que je ne vos en veuill servir ne tenir cheval ne armes ne conpaignons de servise que je vos doi de cest fié, tant que vos me paiés[70] de ce que vos me devés dou dit fié, se vostre court ne l'esgarde, ains veuill que le guagement vaille, si con je l'ai fait, se vostre court[71] l'esgarde. Et de ce me met je en l'esgart de la court sauf mon retenaill.' Et se le seignor dit aucune chose contre son dit[72] por quei il ne viaut[73] que celui[74] guagement vaille, si fase dire a son conseill se que il cuidera que mestier li est[75] contre le dit do seignor a ce que cel guagement vaille. Que se il respont se que mestier li sera, il ne me senble que le seignor puisse dire chose par quei la court ne deie esgarder que le guagement vaut en la maniere que il l'a fait. Et quant il l'avra ensi[76] guagé, il ne doit plus[77] faire[78] servise au seignor ne tenir cheval ne[79] armes ne

[51] requist] O: requiert [52] pluisors fois] V lacks [53] devant vos] AOV lack [54] requist pluisors fois . . . paie] B: a plusors requis sa paie dedenz cort et hors cort [55] doit] V: devoit [56] et] ABV lack [57] que il li . . . fié] B lacks [58] C adds: paier [59] Et] AV lack [60] AV adds: .iii.; B: trois [61] quarantaines] B: quinzaines [62] on] A: l'on; BV: home; C: en [63] Et encore] V: encores paier si [64] il] A: il et requiert; BV: et requiert [65] l'en AB: le; V: li [66] faites] B: faciez [67] V adds: par plusor fois [68] me] BO: m'en [69] cel fié en tel] V: tel fié en [70] me paiés] BV: m'aiez (V: m'en aiés) paié ou fait paier [71] court] B lacks [72] contre son dit] B: de contredit [73] ne viaut] ABV: n'entent [74] celui] B: cel; V: son [75] est] B: soit [76] l'avra ensi] B: avra enssi fait et enssi; V: avra ensi [77] plus] ABV: puis [78] A adds: le; O: de [79] cheval ne] A: le cheval et les

conpaignons, se le fié doit servise[80] de[81] chevalier, et doit atendre .i. an et .i. jor.[82]

Et aprés ce que il l'avra enssi guagé et que l'an et le jor sera enssi[83] passé, il peut faire lequel que il meaus cuidera:[84] ou conjurer son seignor de sa foi que il le paie ou fase paier de se que il li doit de son fié, ou[85] conjurer[86] ses pers que il destraingnent le seignor, si con il doivent,[87] que il le paie ou fase paier de ce que il li doit, ou prendre fié ou sodees el[88] roiaume ou aillours, la ou il li plaira,[89] ou il cuidera son meaus faire.[90] Et se il prent fié d'autre, il doit sauver la foi de son seignor a l'omage faire. Et se il le fait enssi, il covenra que son seignor le paie de tot quantque il li devra de son fié, se il viaut avoir son servise, ausi dou tens[91] que il avra[92] le fié d'autre ou les sodees aprés les dis erremens con dou tens devant ce qu'il l'eust semons ne guagé.

Et s'il aime meaus faire destraindre le seignor[93] par ses pers[94] coment il le paie ou fasse paier de ce qu'il li doit de son fié que prendre fié ou sodees d'autre en la maniere desus[95] devisee, il doit assenbler tant des homes dou seignor com il porra, et puis lor doit dire coment le terme de sa paie passa,[96] et que le leuc ou il estoit asené rendi bien[97] tant ou plus que il peust aver esté paié[98] en[99] son asenement, et que il requist a son seignor[100] pluisors fois sa paie amiablement dehors cort et en court et il ne le paia[101] ne fist[102] paier, et aprés ce il le semonst si com il dut[103] par les quinsaines et les quarantaines qui sont establies a son seignor semondre por la paie de son fié, et les quinzaines et les quarantaines[104] passerent et il ne le paia ne[105] fist paier de ce que il li devoit de son fié, et aprés ce il le guaga de son servise, ne por tant il ne le paia ne fist paier de ce que il li doit[106] de son fié[107] ne il ne[108] viaut ne ne[109] peut plus

[80] fié doit servise] B: servise doit fié [81] au seignor ne . . . de] V: dou [82] B adds: sera [83] enssi] A lacks [84] cuidera] B: cuidera que li doie valoir; V: vodra [85] ou] C: et [86] son seignor de . . . conjurer] V lacks [87] V adds: ou conjurer son seignor de sa foi [88] el] AB: ou; V: au [89] ABO add: et [90] faire] V: trover [91] A adds: passé [92] AB add: eu; V: heu [93] faire destraindre le seignor] AB: le seignor (B: a) destraindre [94] par ses pers] A lacks [95] desus] BO: devant [96] coment le terme . . . passa] V: le terme coment il est passé de sa paie [97] bien] A lacks; B: l'an [98] peust aver esté paié] A: peust aveir sa paie; B: puet avoir esté paié; V: em peust bien estre paié [99] en] C: a [100] V adds: par [101] le paia] A: l'en paia; C: le paie; V: l'a paié [102] fist] V: fait [103] dut] V: doit [104] a son seignor . . . quaratainesl V: coment hom doit semondre son seignor pour la paie. Et les quinsaines et les quarantaines qui sont establés au seignor semondre pour la paie [105] ne] BV: ne ne [106] doit] B: devoit [107] et aprés ce . . . fié] AV lack [108] ne il ne] B: se il [109] ne ne] A: ni ne; V: ne il

sofrir de sa paie. Si les prie et requiert et conjure tos ensenble et chascun par soi con ses pers que il destraignent lor seignor si com il pevent et doivent, que il les[110] paie ou fase paier de ce que il li doit de son fié. Et lors tos les homes dou seignor doivent venir devant lui et dire li: 'Sire, tel qui est nostre per', et le noment, 'nos a dit tel chose, et enssi conjurés', et dire li ce que il leur a dit et coment il[111] les a conjurés.[112] 'Si vos prions et requerons que vos le paiés ou faciés[113] paier de[114] ce que vos li devés de son fié. Et tos ensenble et chascun par soi vos guagons dou servise que nos vos devons tant que vos aiés nostre per tel', et le noment, 'paié ou fait paier de ce que vos li devés de son fié,[115] ou que vos aiés dite raison en court[116] tel[117] par quei vos ne le devés faire et[118] que court l'esgarde ou conoisse.' Et aprés ce aucuns[119] de ces homes ne li doivent[120] faire servise[121] tant que il ait[122] ce por quei il l'ont guagé fait.[123]

Et se il ne viaut ses pers conjurer de son seignor destraindre de faire le paier si com est devant[124] dit, et il aime meaus querre sa chevance,[125] si com est devant[126] devisé, il le doit enssi faire. Il[127] doit venir devant le seignor et dire li coment[128] aprés ce que le terme passa[129] de son fié coment[130] il li requist[131] pluisors fois amiablement dehors court et en court sa paie, et coment il aprés le semonst par les dites[132] quinzaines et quarantaines, et coment il aprés[133] le guaga de son servise, et coment[134] aprés[135] tout ce a atendu[136] .i. an et .i. jor, ne il encor por tot ce ne l'a paié[137] ne fait paier[138] ce que il li doit de son fié. Si ne se peut plus soufrir de querre sa chevance.[139] Si[140] li covient a querre la ou il cuidera son meaus faire. Et il entent que il le puisse faire aprés les erremens avant diz par l'assise ou l'usage de cest roiaume[141] ou par raison, jusques a tant que il l'ait paié ou fait paier de tot[142] quanqu'il[143] li doit de son fié. Si li prie et requiert com a son seignor que il[144] le fase conoistre a sa court

[110] les] ABV: le [111] il] C: qu'il [112] et coment qu'il les a conjurés] B lacks [113] faciés] V: faites [114] de] AV lack [115] Et tos ensenble . . . fié] O lacks [116] en court] A lacks [117] tel] AB lack [118] et] A: et tel; B: et tele; V lacks [119] aucuns] B: nul [120] doivent] A: deit; BV: doit [121] servise] V lacks [122] il ait] A: il ait paié; B: il ait fait; V: elle ait compli [123] guagé fait] AB: gagié; O: gagé [124] devant] BOV: avant [125] A adds: aillors [126] devant] B: avant dit ou; V: avant [127] Il] AB: qu'il [128] li coment] B lacks; V: coment [129] passa] B: est passé [130] son fié coment] A: sa paie de son fié [131] li requist] B: le requist; V: requist par [132] dites] V lacks [133] aprés] C lacks [134] ABV add: il [135] AV adds: de [136] a atendu] V: atendi [137] l'a paié] B: le paie [138] tot ce ne . . . paier] V: tant ne la paié [139] C adds: Et [140] B adds: la [141] de cest roiaume] A: dou reiaume de Jerusalem [142] de tot] A lacks [143] quanqu'il] AB: ce qu'il [144] ABV add: ensi

se il enssi le peut faire com il a dit[145] sans mesprendre vers lui[146] et sans aver damage de la paie[147] de son fié.[148] Et se[149] le seignor, qui ne doit faillir a son home d'esgart ne de conoissance de court, doit comander a sa court qu'ele fase la dite conoissance. Et s'il le comande, je croi[150] que la court doit conoistre que il le peut bien[151] faire si com il l'a dit. Et se le seignor le[152] refuse ou delaie de la dite conoissance faire,[153] il le doit destraindre si com il est devisé en cest livre que on peut son seignor destraindre[154] de faire li faire conoissance de court.[155] [b]

Et a moi senble que qui veaut son seignor[156] guager et faire[157] guager a ces pers dou servise que il li doivent por ce que il ne l'a paié[158] ne fait paier de ce que il li doit de son fié, qu'il le[159] peut faire en moult[160] plus brief terme qu'il n'est devant devisé. Et qui faire le veaut, si le fase enssi que, quant les dites quinsaines et quarantaines seront[161] pasees, si die au seignor: 'Sire, vos me devés de mon fié de tant de termes, et[162] les termes sont pasés de ma paie', et die quans, 'et je vos ai pluisors feis requise ma paie en court et hors[163] court, et aprés vos ai semons par les quinsaines et les quarantaines qui sont establies que l'on doit son seignor semondre de sa paie avoir, ne vos por tout ce ne m'avés paié ne fait paier. Et puis que les dites[164] quinzaines et quarantaines sont pasees, je entent que vos me devés paier ou[165] faire paier sans delai de ce que vos me devés de mon fié de quei[166] je suis vostre home et de quei je vos ai fait le servise et fis.[167] Si vueill, sire, que puis que la dite semonce de quei je vos[168] semons est passee des .iii. quinsaines et des .iii. quarantaines de quei je vos semons si con je dui, que vos sans delai

[b] V begins a new chapter here with the rubric: Ci devise coment l'om peut son seignor guagier et faire guaigier dou servise por la paie de son fié en plus brief terme.

[145] com il a dit] AB lack [146] B adds: come il a dit [147] de la paie] O lacks [148] la paie de son fié] V: sa paie [149] se] V lacks [150] doit comander a . . . croi] B: le comande a faire je cuit [151] bien] B lacks [152] le] C: li; V lacks [153] de la dite conoissance faire] V: la dite conoissance faite [154] si com il . . . destraindre] O lacks [155] la dite . . . court] A: faire la ditte conoissance de court si le destraigne si come devant dit [156] de faire li . . . seignor] B lacks [157] guager et faire] A: faire; B: ou gagier ou faire; V lacks [158] l'a paié] B: le paie [159] qu'il le] B: quar il ne [160] moult] V lacks [161] seront] A: sont [162] et] ABV: dont [163] hors] B: dehors de; V: dehors [164] dites] V lacks [165] paier ou] V lacks [166] quei] V: ce que [167] fis] A: fas; BV: fais [168] AB add: ai; V: ais

me paiés ou faites paier de tout quanque[169] vos me devés de mon fié de quei le terme de ma paie est passé. Et je entent, sire, que vos faire le me devés. Si vueill que vos le me[170] fasiés por toutes les raisons que je ai[171] dites ou por aucunes d'eles, se vostre court esgarde ou conut[172] que vos faire le me devés.[173] Et se ele n'esgarde ou conoit[174] que vos faire le me[175] devés,[176] je irai a mon conseill et dirai et[177] ferai dire[178] tant que je garderai ma raison. Et de ce que je ai dit me met[179] je en l'esgart de la court, sauf mon retenaill.' Et se le seignor se met de ce en l'esgart,[180] il ne me senble que il puisse chose dire que[181] la court n'esgarde aprés les erremens avant[182] dis que il le doit faire paier. Et quant la court avra ce esgardé, se il ne le fait paier si con ele l'avra[183] esgardé,[184] si die a ses pers: 'Seignors, vos avés oi et entendu l'esgart que la court a fait. Ne je ne suis encore paiés si con la court l'a esgardé. Si vos pri et requier et conjur come a mes pers que vos destraignés mon seignor si con vos poés et devés, que il tieigne et face tenir et faire[185] ce que sa[186] court a esgardé.' Et lors tos les homes dou seignor doivent venir devant lui et dire li: 'Sire, nostre per tel', et le noment, 'nos a priés et requis et conjurés con ces pers que nos fasiens vers vos tant que vos faites[187] se que vostre court a esgardé. Si vos prions et requerons que vos enssi le faites[188] paier con vostre court l'esgarda.[189] Et[190] vos guagons tos ensemble et chascun par soi dou servise que nos vos devons[191] tant que vos l'aiés paié ou fait paier de se que vos li devés de son fié enssi con vostre court l'a esgardé.' Et il doit dire ausi:[192] 'Sire, et je ausi[193] vos guage dou servise que je vos doi tant que vos m'aiés paié ou[194] fait paier se que vos me devés de mon fié'. Et aprés se il ne nul des autres homes dou seignor ne li doit[195] faire servise tant que il l'ait[196] paié ou fait paier[197] se que il li doit de son

[169] tout quanque] AB: ce que [170] le me] C: me le [171] V adds: devant [172] ou conut] B lacks; O: ou conoit; V: ou conoist [173] devés] B: doiez [174] conoit] A: conut [175] le me] C: me le [176] Et se ele . . . devés] B: Et se ele n'esgarde; V lacks [177] et] ABV: ou [178] dire] A lacks [179] me met] O: m'en mes [180] l'esgart] ABO: esgart [181] que] ABV: par quoi (A: quei) [182] avant] B: devant [183] ele l'avra] B: il avra [184] se il ne . . . esgardé] V lacks [185] faire] ABV: parfaire [186] sa] C: la [187] faites] B: faciez [188] faites] A: fassiés; B: faciés [189] l'esgarda] A: l'a esgardé; B: a esgardé; V: l'a esguardé [190] A adds: nos [191] dou servise que nos vos devons] A lacks [192] ausi] C lacks [193] Sire, et je ausi] B lacks [194] paié ou] A lacks [195] doit] A: deivent [196] l'ait] B: l'a [197] ou fait paier] V lacks

fié, si con la court l'a esgardé.[198] Et se le seignor refuse l'esgart desus dit ou le[199] delaie, si le destraigne[200] d'aveir le, si con l'on doit seignor destraindre d'avoir l'esgart de sa court, et la maniere[201] est devisee en cest livre la ou il parle de tel[202] cas.[c]

[c] Below cap. 210.

[198] C adds: desus [199] le] ABV: l'en [200] destraigne] C: destraint [201] et la maniere] A: en la maniere come [202] tel] A: cest; B: cestui

***[206]** Qui veaut son seignor destraindre d'avoir sa paie de ce que il li doit de son fié par lui semondre et conjurer de sa foy, coment il le doit faire.[1]

Qui veaut son seignor destraindre d'avoir sa paie de ce que il li doit de son fié par lui semondre et conjurer le[2] de sa foi, il ne le doit pas faire ensenble, ains doit faire l'un avant[3] l'autre et ensi que il doit avant[4] pluisors fois prier et requerre son seignor en court et hors court[5] que il le fase paier de ce que il li doit de son fié. Et s'il ne le fait, il le deit semondre par les .iii.[6] quinzaines et[7] quarantaines devant dites en la maniere avant[8] devisee.[9] [a] Et quant les quinzaines et les quarantaines seront pasees, se il ne le fait paier ou fait[10] son gré de sa paie,[11] si li die: 'Sire, je vos ai pluisors fois requis en cort et hors court[12] que vos me feissiés paier de ce que vos me devés de mon fié, et vos ne le me[13] feistes.[14] Aprés je vos semons par les .iii.[15] quinsaines et[16] quarantaines qui sont establies a[17] son seignor semondre d'aveir se qu'il li doit de son fié, et eles sont passees, et vos ne[18] m'avés paié ne fait paier. Et je en suis vostre home de cest[19] fié et vos en doi servise, lequel servise[20] je vos en[21] ai fait et fais[22] si com je doi,[23] et vos sui tenus de foy dou dit fié et vos a moi com a vostre home. Sire, ne[24] je n'ai de quoi je vos puisse bien servir, se ce n'est de mon fié.[25] Si vos conjur com a mon seignor par la foi que vos me devés come a vostre home, que vos m'aiés paié ou fait paier[26] dedens tel jor', et li mete si resnable[27] jor que il entende que il

---

A: fols clvi^{v}–clvii^{r} cap. 237; **B:** fols 192^{r}–193^{r} cap. 241; **C:** fols 195^{v}–196^{v} cap. 206; **O:** fols 271^{r}–273^{r}; **V:** fols ccxiii^{r}–ccxiv^{v} cap. 253; Beugnot, pp. 381–2, cap. 237.

---

[a] Above cap. 205.

---

[1] coment il le doit faire] A: il ne le deit pas faire ensemble, ainz deit faire l'un avant l'autre; B: il ne le doit mie faire ne dire tot ensemble, mais le doit faire l'un amprés l'autre; V: il ne le doit mie faire ensemble mais l'un aprés l'autre [2] le] ABV lack [3] avant] AV: aprés; B: amprés [4] avant] V lacks [5] B adds: enssi; V: enci [6] .iii.] ABV lack [7] ABO add: les [8] avant] V: devant [9] devant dites en . . . devisee] AB: qui sont devisiees devant et en celle maniere [10] fait] V: face [11] de sa paie] AV: de la paie; B lacks [12] requis en cort et hors court] V: en court et hors court requise ma paie et [13] le me] AB: le; V: mei [14] AOV add: Et [15] .iii.] ABV lack [16] AB add: les [17] qui sont establies a] V: establies de [18] ne] B: le [19] cest] B: cestui; V: ce [20] servise] B: chose [21] en] ABV lack [22] B adds: encore; V: encor [23] si com je doi] V lacks [24] ne] A: et; BV lack [25] B adds: Sire [26] paié ou fait paier] C lacks [27] resnable] B: covenable

dedens cel[28] jor l'ait paié. Et avant que il fase ce,[29] il doit estre bien certain que le seignor li deit de son fié ce[30] que il li requiert, et garde[31] se bien que ce que il requiert soit si cler que il le puisse prover se le seignor nee la dete. Que nul ne doit[32] conjurer de sa foi de chose qui[33] ne soit tel com il dit et que il ne li[34] puisse prover si com il doit. Que qui le fait et il en est ataint ou prové, il en doit faire amende au seignor,[35] et quel amende en doit estre que[36] on fait au seignor de ce et de pluisors autres chozes est devisé en cest livre la ou il parle des amendes que les homes doivent au seignor faire[37] quant[38] tel cas avient.[b] Et qui conjure[39] son seignor si com il[40] est[41] dit, il ne le doit mie guager de son servise aprés ce de sa foi[42] par les raisons avant devisees.[43] Quar l'on ne peut ne ne doit par raison ces .ii. choses faire ensenble, et qui les fait le seignor[44] peut moult gregier[45] qui[46] viaut et seit.[47] Et qui conjure son[48] seignor de sa foi de nule des choses qui sont devisees en cest chapitle[49] par quoi on peut son seignor destraindre par conjurer le de sa foy, et le seignor ne[50] fait ce de coi son home l'a conjuré[51] ne dit raison por quei il ne le doit faire et tel que la court l'esgarde ou conoisse,[52] je ne sui mie[53] bien certain a quoi son home[54] le[55] peut mener par sa court ne quel amende il en doit avoir,[56] por ce ne le veuill je metre en cest[57] livre.[58] Mais a moi[59] senble que le seignor qui est loial et doute Deu et aime s'arme et son henor et sa bone renomee est moult[60] destraint de faire ce que l'on li requiert quant il en est conjuré de sa foy de chose que il doit faire que quant il est guagé dou servise que celui li doit, ne que[61] quant ses[62] homes le guagent de

---

[b] Above cap. 173.

---

[28] cel] B: tel; V: celui [29] que il fase ce] V: ce que il le face [30] ce] C: et [31] garde] B: garder [32] AB add: son seignor [33] qui] O: que il; B lacks [34] li] AB: le; C lacks [35] au seignor] A lacks [36] en doit estre que] AB lack; V: que [37] la ou il . . . faire] A: si aprés cest chapitle et [38] faire quant] B: quant [39] qui conjure] A: qu'il a conjuré; BV: qui a conjuré [40] il] AB lack [41] est] O lacks [42] ce de sa foi] B: ce; V: sa foi [43] devisees] C: dites [44] AV add: le; B: l'en [45] gregier] B: bien gagier [46] qui] A: ce il; B: se [47] A adds: Et de quei et coment le seignor le peut gregier sera devisié en cest livre; B: Et de quoi et coment le seignor l'en porra gagier est assez seu; V: de quoi et coment sera aprés devisé en cestui livre. [48] son] C: le [49] chapitle] B: livre [50] ne] B lacks [51] l'a conjuré] A: le conjure ne; B: le conjure et [52] et tel que . . . conoisse] B lacks. V adds: Et certes [53] B adds: mout [54] son home] B: l'ome [55] le] C: l'en [56] B adds: par sa cort et [57] cest] BV: cestui [58] B adds: mais quc tant come vos orrez amprés [59] C adds: s'en [60] moult] A: plus [61] que] V: pour [62] ses] A: toz ces; B: toz les; V: tout ces

lor servises. Que trop plus le doit[63] destraindre par raison le lien de sa foi que le guagement[64] dou[65] servise ne autre chose[66] par quei ses homes le puissent[67] destraindre. Et se le seignor n'est tel com il[68] est devant[69] dit, l'ome qui le viaut destraindre des choses avant dites par conjurer le n'est pas sage. Car tel seignor vaut meaus guager et faire guager[70] a ses pers ou querre[71] chevance que conjurer le, que[72] plus tost li fera sa[73] requeste par[74] le guager[75] ou[76] par ce que il querra[77] aillors sa chevance, et a la fin converra il[78] que il le paie de tout quantque[79] il li devra que par conjurer le de sa foy.[80] Que le seignor qui ne doute Deu ne honte ne pechié fera plus tost por estre destraint de l'une des .ii.[81] destresces que par cele d'estre conjuré[82] de sa foy.

[63] doit] V: doivent [64] doit destraindre par . . . guagement] B: doivent destraindre les liens de foy que les gagemenz [65] dou] AV: de [66] chose] B: choses [67] ses homes le puissent] ABV: son home le puisse [68] il] BV lack [69] devant] B: avant [70] et faire guager] B lacks [71] AB add: sa [72] que] B: quar il [73] plus tost li fera sa] AV: il plus tost le fera sanz (V: sans) [74] par] V: sans [75] guager] B: gagement [76] ou] A: et [77] querra] A: quiert [78] et a la fin converra il] A: que par concjurer le et a la fin covendra [79] converra il que . . . quantque] B: covendra il le paie de tot ce que [80] par conjurer le de sa foy] A lacks [81] .ii.] A: dittes; B: deus dites choses ou [82] conjuré] B: destrait par le conjurement

***[207]** Se le seignor tient aucune chose dou fié[1] de son home autrement que par assise[2] ou par usage ou par esgart ou par conoissance de[3] court,[4] coment[5] l'ome[6] le doit requerre.[7]

Se le seignor tient aucune choze dou fié de son home[8] autrement que par assise[9] ou par usage ou par esgart ou par conoissance de court ou par eschange[10] ou par ensens[11] ou par apaut ou par comande, enssi que celui de qui le fié est le viaut avoir, il li[12] doit requerre[13] .ii. ou .iii. fois entre lui et lui et aprés en la court autant[14] ou plus sans plait, et en tel maniere que il li doit dire: 'Sire, je vos[15] requier com a mon seignor que vos me rendés ou faites rendre tel choze que je entens qui est de mon fié', et die quel chose ce est[16] que il[17] requiert. Et se il ne la li rent aprés ce que il li avra requise si com est avant dit, il doit demander conseill et faire dire par son conseill: 'Sire, tel vos prie et requiert[18] que vos li rendés ou faites rendre tel choze que il vos a pluisors fois requise en court et hors[19] court que il entent qui est de son fié', et die quoi. Et se le seignor dit[20] que il n'entent que ce que il requiert soit[21] de son fié si com il dit, die[22] celui qui le requiert por son fié que il est prest dou prover que ce[23] qu'il requiert est de son fié, si con la court esgardera ou conoistra que il prover le doie. Et je cuit que la cort doit esgarder ou conoistre que il le doit prover enssi com il est devisé en cest livre que on doit prover fié ou partie de fié[24] vers son seignor quant le[25] seignor le tient.[a] Et s'il enssi le preuve, quant il[26] l'avra[27] prové, se le seignor

---

A: fol. clviii^{r-v} cap. 240; **B:** fols 193^{v}–194^{r} cap. 244; **C:** fols 196^{v}–197^{r} cap. 207; **O:** fol. 273^{r-v}; **V:** fol. ccxvi^{r-v} cap. 256; Beugnot, pp. 385–6, cap. 240.

---

[a] Above caps 148–51.

---

[1] dou fié] O: de sa foy [2] assise] BV: l'assise [3] ou par usage . . . de] B: ou par l'esgart ou par la conoissance de la [4] de court] V lacks [5] coment] A rubrics (fol. 8^{v}) BV lacks [6] l'ome] ABV: il [7] ABV add: au seignor par (AV: et par) court (AB sa cort) [8] de son home] B: d'aucun de ses homes [9] assise] B: l'assise; V: l'assie [10] eschange] B: eschampe; V: eschampes [11] ensens] V: contens [12] li] ABV: le [13] B adds: au seignor [14] au tant] B: autretant [15] ABV add: pri et [16] C adds: ce [17] AOV add: li [18] B adds: come a son seignor [19] hors] A: dehors; BO: hors de [20] dit] ABV: respont [21] soit] C: est [22] die] C: de [23] que il requiert . . . ce] V lacks [24] ou partie de fié] A: ou partie de son fié; B lacks [25] le] A: son [26] s'il enssi le preuve quant il] B: quant il enssi [27] l'avra] OV: avra

ne li rent ou ne dit raison por quoi il le tient et ne li[28] doit rendre et tel que court l'esgarde[29] ou conoisse que il ne le doit faire, si le destraigne celui qui li[30] requiert, si com est avant[31] dit que l'on doit son seignor destraindre d'avoir sa paie.[b]

[b] Above cap. 198.

[28] li] ABV: le [29] l'esgarde] AB: esgarde [30] li] AV: le [31] si come est avant] B: enssi come il est

***[208]** Quant[1] aucun crestien fait a aucun des homes dou seignor force de tot son fié ou de partie,[2] a qui il se doit clamer, et coment il se doit clamer.[3]

Se aucun crestien fait a aucun des homes do seignor force de tout son fié ou de chose qui soit de son fié,[4] il se doit clamer au seignor de qui il tient le fié, se il a court,[5] et, s'il n'a court, au chief seignor. Et qui de force se viaut clamer, il doit demander conseill, et aprés faire dire au seignor par son conseill: 'Sire, tel se claime a vos de tel qui li[6] fait force de tel choze[7] que il tient[8] et ne li viaut rendre, laquel chose est de son[9] fié'. Et die[10] quel chose ce est. Et[11] aprés die: 'Et se il le noie, il est prest que il le[12] li preuve[13] tout enssi con la court esgardera ou conoistra que il prover le doie. Si vos prie et requiert com a son seignor de qui il tient le fié de ce dont l'on li[14] fait force[15] et dou quel fié il est vostre home et a qui il doit et fait le servise de cel[16] fié, que vos li abatés ou[17] faites abatre la force que tel', et le nome, 'li[18] fait, et[19] que vos l'aiés a droit en vostre court. Et il entent que vos le devés faire et veaut que vos le fasiés,[20] por tant com je ai[21] dit por lui, se vostre court l'esgarde. Et de ce vos requiert il l'esgart de la[22] court, sauf son[23] retenaill'. Et se[24] le seignor, qui ne doit faillir a son home[25] d'esgart de court, li doit respondre que il[26] li[27] avra volentiers a droit en sa court celui de cui il se claime et a tel jor, et nomer[28] le jor. Et aprés le doit faire semondre de venir faire droit a cel[29] jor a celui qui de lui c'est clamés.[30] Et[31] se il i[32] vient, il doit faire droit au clamant par sa

A: fols clviii^{v}–clix^{r} cap. 241; **B:** fols 194^{r}–195^{r} cap. 245; **C:** fols 197^{r}–198^{v} cap. 208; **O:** fols 273^{v}–276^{r}; **V:** fols ccxvi^{v}–ccxviii^{v} cap. 258; Beugnot, pp. 386–8, cap. 241.

[1] Quant] ABV: Se [2] B adds: de son fié [3] a qui il . . . clamer] ABV: il se doit (A: deit) clamer au seignor de qui il tient cel (B: celui) fié (tient cel fié] V: le tient) qui (BV rubrics (fol. 15^{r}): que il) li abate la (li abate la] B: abbate cele) force, et, c'il ne le fait, il le doit (A: deit; B: puet et doit) destraindre par ces pers [4] ou de chose . . . fié] A: ou de partie; B lacks [5] A adds: qu'il li face abatre la force [6] qui li] V: que il li a [7] V adds: et [8] B adds: de son fié [9] son] V: mon [10] est de son . . . die] B: Et [11] die quel chose ce est. Et] V lacks [12] le] B lacks [13] que il le li preuve] A: de prover; O: de prouver li; V: dou prover le [14] A adds: a [15] force] C: faire [16] cel] BV: celui; C: tel [17] ou] C: et [18] li] V: me [19] et] A: ou [20] fasiés] V: faites [21] je ai] C: il a [22] la] A: vostre [23] son] V: mon [24] se] AO lack [25] ABV adds: de droit (A: dreit) ne [26] C adds: le [27] li] AV lack [28] nomer] AB: nome [29] cel] ABV: tel [30] qui de lui c'est clamés] V: de cui il se clame [31] a celui qui . . . Et] O: et nomer le jor et aprés le [32] i] C lacks

court. Et se il est semons et il ne[33] vient au jor de la semonce ou ne contremande c'essoine si con il doit,[34] le seignor doit le clamant metre en saisine de ce de quoi[35] celui[36] c'est clamés de lui tant que il[37] vieigne faire droit au clamant de ce de quei[38] il c'est[39] clamés de lui.

Et[40] se celui de cui l'on[41] c'est clamé[42] est tel que le seignor ne puisse ou ne veuille faire se qui est devant[43] dit, le clamant li doit dire[44] en la court: 'Sire, vos et la court oistes et entendistes .i. jor qui passés est[45] que je me clamai de tel, et coment et de quoi je m'en[46] clamai la court l'entendi. Sire, et vos me deistes[47] lors que vos le m'avroiés a droit en vostre court. Sire,[48] et je entens que vos le feistes semondre a jor nomé de venir faire me droit de ce de quei je me clamai de lui,[49] et il n'i vint ni[50] contremanda[51] c'essoigne si con il dut.[52] Si vos prie et requier que vos me metés ou faites metre en saisine et en teneure de ce de quei je me clamai de lui, si con droit[53] le done, puis qu'il a esté semons de venir[54] faire droit et il n'i est[55] venus ne n'a c'essoine contremandee si con il doit. Et vueill que vos[56] le faciés par les raisons que je ai dites,[57] se vostre court l'esgarde. Et de ce me met je en l'esgart de la court sauf mon retenaill.' Et se le seignor,[58] qui ne doit faillir d'esgart a son home, se met de ce en esgart de court,[59] il[60] me senble que la court doit conoistre ou esgarder que le seignor li doit faire abatre la force et metre le en saisine de ce de quei il se clama, tant que celui de qui il se clama li vieigne faire droit, puis que[61] il n'i vint ne[62] contremanda c'essoine si con il dut.[63] Et[64] quant la court a[65] fait le dit esgart ou la dite conoissance, si requiert le clamant au seignor qu'il li fase ce que la court a esgardé.[66] Et se le seignor ne le fait, et il le viaut destraindre de faire, il doit requerre et conjurer ses pers si con est avant[67] dit, que il destraignent le seignor si com il doivent, que il li fase ce que la court a esgardé ou[68] coneu. Et lors tos ses

---

[33] ne] A: n'i [34] A adds: se il est essoigniés [35] de quoi] V: dont [36] celui ABV: il [37] il ABV: celui [38] de quei] V: dont [39] c'est] BV: est [40] Et] BV lack [41] l'on] C: l'en [42] l'on c'est clamé] B: on se claime [43] devant] V: avant [44] li doit dire] B: doit dire au seignor [45] est] A lacks [46] m'en] AV: me [47] .i. jor qui . . . deistes] B lacks [48] Sire] A lacks [49] de lui] C lacks [50] ni] A: ni ne; BV: ne ne [51] contremanda] B: contremande [52] dut] V: doit [53] droit] A: raisson [54] AOV add: me [55] n'i est] AB: n'est [56] que vos] B lacks [57] A adds: ou fait dire [58] Et de ce . . . seignor] O lacks [59] sauf mon retenaill . . . court] A: sauf mon retenaill.' Et; BV lack [60] B adds: ne [61] puis que] V: et [62] ne] C: ni [63] puis que il . . . dut] AB lack [64] dut. Et] V: doit [65] a] B: avra [66] V adds: ou coneu [67] avant] V: devant [68] ou] C: et

pers[69] doivent venir devant le seignor et dire[70] coment et de coi celui les a requis et conjurés de prier li[71] et requerre que il tieigne et fase[72] tenir l'esgart ou la conoissance de sa court et guager de lor servises en la maniere devant[73] dite tant que il l'ait fait.[74] Et le clamant le doit en cest cas[75] ausi guager con ses pers. Ne nul d'eaus ne li[76] doit aprés[77] faire servise tant que il ait fait ce que la court a esgardé ou coneu, ou rendu a celui tant con vaut ce de quei il se clama de quei[78] l'on li faisoit[79] force de son fié. Que bien li abat la force quant il li rent tant con vaut ce de quei il li[80] fait[81] force, que[82] force[83] atainte ou provee en court n'a celui a qui l'on l'a[84] fait amende que ce de[85] que l'on li rent ce de quei l'on li fait[86] force. Mais l'amende do mesfait en est au seignor por l'outrage et le mesfait que l'on li[87] fait de faire force en sa seignorie. Et puis que celui a qui on a[88] fait[89] la force ne doit avoir autre amende,[90] le seignor li a bien la force abatue et l'esgart de la court tenu quant il[91] li a restoré ce[92] de quei il se clama de quei[93] l'on li avoit fait force ou le vaillant. Et le seignor doit faire cel[94] restor au gré dou clamant ou par la conoissance de .iii. de ses homes. Et aprés ce tos les homes qui ont le[95] seignor guagé de lor servise,[96] si com est avant[97] dit, doivent de cel jor en avant faire li[98] le servise que il li doivent, que il a bien tenu l'esgart de la court si com il doit, quant il li[99] a rendu ou fait rendre ce de quei il se clama ou[100] le vaillant au gré dou clamant ou par la conoissance de .iii.[101] de ces homes.

---

[69] destraignent le seignor . . . pers] AB lack [70] AOV add: li [71] et conjurés de prier li] A: et prier li; B: et prie li; V: prier le [72] et fase] O lacks [73] devant] A: avant [74] l'ait fait] A: ait fait ce de quei il l'ont requis; B: ait fait; V: ait fait ce que la court a esgardé ou coneu [75] en cest cas] B lacks [76] li] C: lor [77] ABV add: ce [78] ou rendu a . . . quei] B: rendu ce dont il se clama ou tant come il vaut de quoi [79] faisoit] V: fait [80] il li] A: on li a [81] fait] C: fase [82] ABV add: de [83] que force] C lacks [84] l'on l'a] A: on [85] que ce de] A: autre que ce; B: fors; C: que de [86] fait] A: a fait; B: faisoit [87] ABV adds: a [88] a] C lacks [89] de faire force . . . fait] A: de; BV lack [90] ne doit avoir autre amende] A: Et [91] tenu quant il] C: tot quantqu'il [92] restoré ce] B: abatue la force dont il se clama [93] il se clama de quei] C lacks [94] cel] AB: celui [95] qui ont le] O: dou [96] lor servise] BV: leur servises [97] avant] V: devant [98] li] ABV lack [99] li] AB lack [100] ou] C lacks [101] de .iii.] C lacks

***[209]** Quant un home ou une feme est assené de son fié de tout[1] ou de partie sur les rentes d'un casau ou d'un autre leuc moti que autre[2] que le seignor tieigne, et le terme de sa paie est passé, et il requiert ou fait requerre sa paie a celui qui tient le leuc, et il ne le paie ou fase paier, que il doit faire et dire si que il soit paié.[a]

Se un home ou une[3] feme est assené de son fié ou de partie de son fié sur les rentes d'un casau ou d'autre leu que[4] le seignor tieigne, et le terme de sa paie est passé, et il requiert[5] ou fait requerre sa paie a celui qu'il tient le leu, se il[6] ne le paie,[7] il doit venir devant le seignor en sa cort et dire li: 'Sire, je suis asené de mon fié ou de partie de son fié en tel leu', et le nome, 'et le terme de ma paie est passé, et je ai requise ma paie a tel', et le nome, 'qui le leu tient ou je sui asené, et il ne m'a paié ne[8] fait paier. Si vos pri et requier com a mon seignor que vos me faites paier de mon fié dou leu ou je suis asené.'[9] Et lors le seignor doit comander ou mander a celui, se il n'est prezent, qui le leuc tient que il dedens .xv. jors ait celui paié ou que il dedens tel[10] terme soit devant lui en la court por dire et[11] mostrer raison por coi il ne le doit[12] paier. Et se celui ne le paie dedens le dit terme ou ne vient devant le seignor et[13] dit raison por coi il ne le doit paier et tel que court l'esgarde ou conoisse, le seignor doit mander el leuc ou celui est assené[14] et[15] prendre tant des chozes de cel leu[16] qui bien vaillent[17] tant ou plus con l'on doit a celui qui a sa paie requise, et faire les vendre guage abandon, et[18] de ce que

A: fol. clix$^{\text{r-v}}$ cap. 242; **B:** fol. 195$^{\text{r-v}}$ cap. 246; **C:** fols 198^{v}–199^{r} cap. 209; **O:** fol. 276$^{\text{r-v}}$; **V:** fols ccxviii^{v}–ccxix^{r} cap. 259; Beugnot, pp. 388–9, cap. 242.

[a] Rubric in ABV: Se (V: Ci orrés coment se) .i. home ou une feme est assené de son fié (de son fié] AV lack) sur les rentes d'un casau que autre que le seignor teigne, et le terme de sa paie est passé et il n'a esté paié, il le doit (A: la deit) requerre au seignor, et le seignor le doit (A: deit) faire paier.

[1] de tout] O lacks [2] moti que autre] C lacks [3] un home ou une] V: home ou [4] ABV adds: autre que [5] requiert] C: requiet [6] a celui qu'il . . . il] A: et celui qui tient le leuc; B: a celui qui tient le leuc si; V: a celui qui tient le leuc et se il [7] paie] B lacks [8] m'a paié ne] V: me paie ou [9] et il ne . . . asené] AB lack [10] tel] A: cel; V: celui [11] dire et] B lacks [12] doit] A: deie [13] et] B: ou ne [14] ABV add: qui li a sa paie requise [15] V adds: faire [16] cel leu] C: celui; V: celui leuc [17] vaillent] V: vaille [18] tant des chozes . . . et] B: gages et faire les vendre abandon

ses chozes seront[19] vendues faire le paier de ce que l'on li doit de son fié. Et se le seignor ne le fait[20] a la requeste dou requerant, si li requiere l'esgart ou la conoissance de la court se il li doit ce faire ou non. Et je cuit que se il de ce li requiert esgart ou conoissance de court, et[21] le seignor si mete. Je cuit que[22] la court esgardera ou conoistra que le seignor le doit ensi faire, et aprés ce se le seignor ne le viaut faire si[23] l'en[24] destraigne par l'esgart ou par la conoissance que la court avra faite.

---

[19] seront] C: sereent [20] ne le fait] A: faut; B: fait [21] et] C lacks [22] je cuit que] A lacks [23] si] C: et [24] l'en] ABV: le

***[210]** Coment l'on doit destraindre le seignor de faire li tenir et faire esgart ou conoissance que la court avra faite.[a]

Se la court fait esgart ou conoissance et le seignor ne la tient et[1] fait parfaire, et se[2] celui por qui l'esgart ou la conoissance avra esté faite viaut le seignor destraindre a tenir le et[3] faire li parfaire ce que la court avra esgardé ou coneu, il le peut de ce destraindre[4] en l'une des .iii. manieres aprés devisees: l'une par conjurer le de sa foy et dou sairement que il a[5] fait de tenir les assises et les usages[6] do[7] reiaume, es ques[8] assises ou es ques[9] usages il est que chascun seignor qui a court et coins et justize el dit[10] reiaume doit tenir, et faire tenir[11] les esgars et[12] les conoissances que sa court fait; l'autre par semondre et conjurer ses pers, si com est avant dit,[b] que il li fasent au seignor tenir l'esgart ou la conoissance que sa court a fait;[13] la tierce par lui guager de son servise en la maniere avant[14] devisee o ses pers ou sans ses pers.[15] [c]

Et qui par l'une de ses voies[16] vodra destraindre son seignor, il li[17] doit avant requerre plusors fois en la presence de sa court qu'il li fase tenir et parfaire ce que la court avra esgardé ou coneu et die quoi. Et se le seignor ne le fait, et il le viaut gager do[18] servise, il le doit enssi faire con il est devant dit por la paie ou por les[19] choses[20] qui defaillent dou fié, fors tant que il doit dire: 'Je vos guage dou servise que je vos doi, jusques a tant que vos m'aiés tenu et fait parfaire ce que la court a[21] esgardé ou coneu', et die coi, 'se court

A: fols clix^{v}–clx^{v} cap. 243; **B:** fols 195^{v}–196^{v} cap. 247; **C:** fols 199^{r}–200^{r} cap. 210; **O:** fols 276^{v}–278^{v}; **V:** fols ccxix^{r}–ccxx^{r} cap. 260; Beugnot, pp. 389–90, cap. 243.

[a] Rubric in ABV: Se le seignor ne tient ou (A: ou ne) fait tenir l'esgart ou la conoissance que sa court a (B: la cort avra) fait, coment celui por qui l'esgart ou la conoissance avra esté fait peut le seignor destraindre par .iii. manieres (A: manieres qui sont) si desous devisiees (B: deviseez; V: devisés).

[b] Above caps 204–5.

[c] Above caps 178, 197.

[1] et] B: ne [2] se] ABV lack [3] B adds: a [4] a tenir le . . . destraindre] O lacks [5] a] A lacks [6] et les usages] O lacks [7] do] A: de cest; B: de cestui [8] es ques] A: lesquels [9] es ques] A: lesquels; B lacks [10] et justize el dit] A: ou [11] et faire tenir] A lacks [12] et] V: ou [13] l'esgart ou la . . . a fait] B: les esgart ou les conoissances que so cort avra faites [14] avant] ABV: devant [15] ou sans ses pers] C lacks [16] voies] C: forces [17] li] ABV: le [18] do] A: de son; V: de [19] V adds: autres [20] les choses] B: l'eschange [21] a] ABV: avra

esgarde[22] que je guager vos en puisse et doive, et de ce[23] vos requier je l'esgart de la court', et mete[24] son retenaill.

Et qui le viaut conjurer de sa foi, il li[25] doit requerre plusors fois hors de[26] court et en la[27] court que il li doie[28] faire tenir et parfaire se que la court a esgardé ou coneu, et die coy. Et se il ne li fait, si veigne devant lui en sa cort si[29] li die: 'Sire, je vos ai plusors fois prié et[30] requis en vostre court et dehors[31] que vos me feissiés tenir et parfaire ce que vostre court a esgardé ou coneu', et die quoi, 'et vos ne le m'avés[32] fait. Si vos conjur come mon seignor que par la fei que vos me devés con a vostre home et par le sairement que vos avés fait de tenir les bons us et les bones costumes et les assises dou reiaume de Jerusalem, que vos m'aiés tenu et[33] fait parfaire dedens tel jor ce que vostre cort a esgardé ou coneu.' Et die quoi, et i[34] mete .i. jor si resnable que il entende que le seignor[35] li puisse avoir fait ce que il li requiert. Et nul[36] ne doit son seignor conjurer de sa foi ne de son sairement de chose qu'il entende[37] que il ne li[38] puisse ou doie faire.

Et qui vodra son seignor destraindre par ses pers, si li requiere plusors fois en sa[39] court que il li fase tenir l'esgart ou la conoissance que sa court avra fait, et die quel, et s'il ne le fait, assenble[40] tant des homes dou seignor com il en porra avoir et lor die: 'Seignors, vos savés que la cort a fait tel esgart ou tel conoissance', et die quel et de quoi l'esgart ou la conoissance a[41] esté faite, 'et je ai mon[42] seignor plusors fois prié et[43] requis en sa cort que il l'esgart ou la conoissance que la court a faite me fase tenir et parfaire. Et[44] il ne le fait. Si vos prie et requiert et conjur come mes pers que vos destraignés mon seignor, si con vos poés et devés, que il l'esgart ou la conoissance[45] que sa court a faite me tieigne et fase parfaire.' Et lors tos les homes dou seignor sont tenus de venir devant lui et dire li: 'Sire, nostre per tel', et le noment,[46] 'est venus a nos, et nos a priés et requis et conjurés come ses pers, que nos vos destraignons,

[22] esgarde] C: a esgardé [23] ce] C lacks [24] mete] V: metre [25] li] BV: le [26] hors de] A: dehors; BV: hors [27] la] ABV lack [28] doie] C: doit [29] si] AB: et [30] prié et] A lacks [31] en vostre court et dehors] B: en cort et hors cort [32] le m'avés] AV: me l'avés; B: l'avez; O: le m'avés mie [33] m'aiés tenu et] B: m'avez tenu ou [34] i] ABV: li [35] ou coneu.' Et . . . seignor] O lacks [36] nul] A: il; B lacks [37] entende] A: n'entent; BV: n'entende [38] li] A: le; BV lack [39] sa] ABV: la [40] assenble] B: assembler [41] a] V: avra [42] mon] AB: le [43] prié et] A lacks [44] C adds: se (interlined in later (?) hand) [45] que la court . . . conoissance] B lacks [46] noment] CV: nome

si con nos poons et devons, et[47] que vos li teignés ou[48] faites parfaire l'esgart ou la conoissance que vostre court a faite. Et[49] vos guajons tos ensemble et chascun par soi dou servise que nos vos devons tant que vos[50] aiés tenu et fait parfaire a nostre per tel', et le noment, 'ce que vostre court a esgardé ou coneu.'[51] Et celui por qui il dient[52] ce si[53] doit dire: 'Et je, sire, vos guage aussi come mes[54] pers ont fait'. Ne nul des homes d'enqui[55] en avant ne doit aucune[56] chose de[57] servise faire au seignor jusques a tant que il ait l'esgart ou la conoissance que sa[58] cort a faite[59] tenu et fait parfaire.[60]

---

[47] et] ABV lack [48] ou] AV: et [49] A adds: nos [50] Et vos guajons . . . vos] V (in margin in cursive hand): et vous gagons tous ensemble du servize que nous vous devons tant que vous [51] (i) a nostre per . . . coneu] A: l'esgart ou la conoissance que vostre court a fait; (ii) Et vos guajons . . . coneu] B lacks; (iii) ce que vostre . . . coneu] V (in margin in cursive hand): ce que vostre court n'esgard [52] dient] V: doit [53] dient ce si] B: le dient; C: dient ce enssi [54] ABV add: autres [55] d'enqui] CV: de qui [56] aucune] B: nulle; C lacks; V: nul [57] de] ABV: dou [58] sa] AB: la [59] faite] V lacks [60] tenu et fait parfaire] B lacks

***[211]** Coment l'ome qui n'est home dou seignor qui viaut destrainde le seignor[1] de tenir ou faire tenir l'esgart ou la conoissance ou le recort que sa court a faite, coment il le doit faire.[a]

Se aucun qui ne soit home dou seignor le viaut destraindre de tenir ou faire tenir l'esgart ou la conoissance ou le recort[2] que sa court a[3] faite, il li doit requerre pluisors fois en sa cort que il li tieigne ou fase tenir et[4] parfaire l'esgart ou la conoissance ou le recort que sa court a faite, et die quel et de quel chose il a esté. Et s'il ne le[5] fait, si[6] die en sa court: 'Sire, il est us ou costume ou assise el roiaume de Jerusalem que seignor doit tenir et parfaire les esgars et les conoissances que sa court[7] fait. Si vos pri et requier qu'enssi con vos estes tenus de tenir et guarder les bons us et les bones costumes et les assises dou roiaume de Jerusalem, que vos me tenés et parfaites[8] tenir et parfaire sans delai l'esgart ou la conoissance ou le recort que vostre court a fait.' Et die quel.

Et se le seignor ne le fait, si assenble tant des homes dou seignor con il porra et lor die: 'Seignors, la court dont vos estes a fait tel esgart ou tel conoissance ou tel recort', et die quel, 'et je ai pluisors fois prié et requis le seignor[9] que il le dit esgart ou la dite conoissance ou le dit recort[10] me feist tenir et parfaire, et il ne l'a mie[11] fait. Et je aprés[12] li ai prié et requis qu'ensi[13] com il est tenus de tenir les bons us et les bones costumes et les assises[14] dou roiaume de Jerusalem, que il le me feist et[15] sans delay, et il ne me l'a pas[16] fait. Si vos pri et requier et conjur, si con je[17] puis et doi, com a

A: fols clx^v^–clxi^r^ cap. 244; **B:** fols 196^v^–197^v^ cap. 248; **C:** fols 200^v^–201^v^ cap. 211; **O:** fols 278^v^–280^r^; **V:** fols ccxx^r^–ccxxi^r^ cap. 261; Beugnot, pp. 391–2, cap. 244.

[a] Rubric in ABV: Coment celui qui n'est mie (mie] B rubrics (fol. 27^r^) V lack) home dou seignor le peut (B: puet) par ces homes (par ces homes] V lacks) constraindre (B rubrics V: destraindre) et faire (B adds: le) destraindre de faire (faire] B lacks) tenir l'esgart ou la conoissance que sa court avra (V: a) faite.

[1] qui viaut destrainde le seignor] O: le viaut destraindre [2] ou le recort] C lacks [3] a] B: avra [4] et] B: ou [5] le] C: l'a [6] BO add: li [7] AV add: a [8] ABV add: ou faites [9] le seignor] C lacks [10] ou le dit recort] ABV lack [11] mie] ABV lack [12] aprés] BV lack [13] qu'ensi] C: que si [14] les bones costumes et les assises] V: assises et costumes [15] et] ABV lack [16] me l'a pas] B: le m'a mie [17] si con je] V: tant come

ceaus qui estes homes[18] de cele court et estes tenus de garder l'ennor de vos et de la court dont vos estes et qui estes ou[19] devés estre tenus par sairement de tenir et maintenir les assises et les usages do roiaume de Jerusalem,[20] que vos destraignés, tant con vos poés et devés, vostre seignor qu'il me tieigne et parfase ou[21] face[22] tenir et[23] parfaire l'esgart ou la conoissance ou le recort que sa court,[24] dont vos estes, a fait.' Et die lequel, ce est[25] esgart ou conoissance ou recort. Et adonc tos les homes doivent venir devant le seignor et dire li: 'Sire, tel', et le noment,[26] 'nos a dit que vostre court a fait tel esgart ou tel conoissance ou tel recort', et dient lequel ce est, 'et que il vos a plusors fois requis que vos[27] li feissiés[28] tenir et parfaire ce que vostre[29] court a esgardé ou coneu ou recordé', et dient lequel ce est, 'et[30] que vos ne[31] li avés fait ne fait faire. Et nos a priés et requis et conjurés, si com il peut et doit, com homes de vostre[32] court, que nos vos prions et requerons et destraignons,[33] si con nos poons et devons, que vos li teignés et parfaites ou faites[34] tenir et parfaire ce que vostre cort a esgardé ou coneu ou recordé. Et por ce que nos somes homes de vostre court et[35] que nos somes tenus de garder et faire guarder[36] a nos poeirs l'ennor de la court dont nos somes et de maintenir les assises et les usages dou roiaume de Jerusalem, nos tos ensenble et chascun par soi vos guajons dou servise que nos vos devons, tant que vos aiés a tel', et le noment, 'tenu ou[37] parfait ou fait tenir et[38] parfaire ce que vostre court, dont nos somes,[39] a esgardé ou coneu ou recordé, ou dit en la court[40] raison tel que la court[41] esgarde ou conoisse que vos ne le devés faire.' Et aprés ce il ne doivent faire au seignor aucun[42] servise, tant que il ait tenu et parfait ou fait tenir et parfaire ce que la court a esgardé ou coneu ou recordé, ou dite choze en la court tel que court esgarde ou conoisse que il ne li doit[43] tenir ne parfaire ne faire tenir ne parfaire[44] ce que la court a esgardé ou coneu ou recordé.

[18] homes] C: home [19] ou] A: et [20] B adds: destreignez [21] ou] A: et [22] face] AO: faire [23] tenir et] B lacks [24] que sa court] B lacks [25] lequel, ce est] V: quel soit [26] V adds: est venus devant nos et [27] que vos] B: lacks [28] feissiés] V: faites [29] parfaire ce que vostre] B: faire ce que la [30] dient lequel ce est, 'et] B lacks [31] ne] O lacks [32] vostre] ABV lack [33] destraignons] B: deffragnons [34] ou faites] B lacks [35] court et] O: seignor [36] et faire guarder] OV lack [37] ou] AB: et [38] et] BV: ou [39] BV add: homes [40] ou coneu ou . . . court] B: coneu ou recordé ou vos dites [41] A adds: esgart [42] aucun] BV: nul [43] ou conoisse que . . . doit] B: que vos ne le devez [44] ne faire tenir ne parfaire] B lacks; V: ne faire tenir

***[212]** Se .i. home[1] est semons dou servise que il doit au seignor, et il lors viaut son fié comander au seignor ou livrer le a vendre par aucune des chozes qui sont avant[2] dites par quoy l'on peut son[3] fié vendre,[a] le seignor n'est pas tenus de recevoir le[4] fié et faire[5] vendre ne la comande dou fié, puis que il l'a avant semons de son servise, tant que celle semonce soit passee, ains le peut bien refuser par raison.

Se celui qui sera[6] semons comande son fié par l'assise au seignor tant com il est[7] en semonce, et le seignor ne[8] le reseit, disant li que il ne le viaut resevoir puis que il l'a semons et que il a besoing de son servize por quei il n'entent que il li puisse[9] ne doive comander son fié tant com il est en sa semonce, et se celui dit:[10] 'Sire, vostre court a bien oi[11] coment je vos ai mon fié comandé et bien entendu,[12] et vos ne le volés recevoir', vaille ce que valoir devra. Ou[13] se il se taist, et le seignor li respont: 'Et ma court a bien entendu coment et por coi je ai dit que je la[14] comande de vostre fié ne veul resevoir', et vaille ce que valoir devra. Et se[15] le seignor se taist[16] et l'ome se taist[17] aussi, et l'ome[18] ne vait a[19] la semonce de quei il avra esté semons, il sera defailli de servise et perdra son fié an et jor ou sa vie, selon ce que il sera[20] semons et selonc le besoing que son seignor avra de lui, si com est avant[21] devisé en cest livre que l'on[22] pert son fié qui defaut de servise, por ce que par l'assise ou l'usage dou dit roiaume nul ne peut son fié comander tant com il est en semonce se par la volenté dou seignor n'est.[b] Quar s'ensi n'estoit, trop seroit

---

A: fol. clxi^{r-v} cap. 245; **B:** fols 197^{v}–198^{r} cap. 249; **C:** fols 201^{v}–202^{r} cap. 212; **O:** fols 280^{r}–281^{r}; **V:** fols ccxxi^{r}–ccxxii^{r} cap. 262; Beugnot, pp. 392–3, cap. 245.

---

[a] Above cap. 168.
[b] Above cap. 163.

---

[1] .i. home] AV: home; B: l'ome [2] qui sont avant] ABV: devant [3] son] A lacks [4] le] C: son [5] ABV add: le [6] sera] A: est [7] est] V: sera [8] ne] C lacks [9] por quei il . . . puisse] C: que il li peusse [10] et se celui dit] A: et celui dit; BV: celui die [11] ABV add: et entendu [12] et bien entendu] ABV lack [13] Ou] ABV: Et [14] je ai dit que je la] B: que ai dit que je l'ai [15] se] V lacks [16] se taist] B lacks [17] se taist] V lacks [18] l'ome] A: il; B lacks [19] vait a] B: veut faire [20] sera] AB: avra esté; V: l'avra esté [21] V adds: dit et [22] l'on] AB: on; V: hom

contre[23] raison se .i. home qui avroit .i.[24] fié qui li seroit doné por servise moti ou qui li seroit escheu de par ses ancestres et[25] le tenoit et[26] usoit et enjoisoit un espasse de tens sans faire ent[27] servise au seignor por ce que il n'en avroit eu besoin, ou[28] por ce que le seignor l'avroit de la semonce et[29] dou servise esparaigné, et quant le seignor avroit besoin de son servise et il le semondroit, que il li peust son fié comander et non acuillir la semonce de son seignor ne aler a son besoing. Et se ensi n'estoit,[30] les seignors seroient trop gregiés et en porroient lor servise[31] perdre por coi il porroient estre desherités. Et por ce et por pluisors autres raisons est il bien aparant que l'assise est bone et[32] juste en cest quas.

---

[23] B adds: droit et contre [24] .i.] A lacks; B: un sien [25] et] A lacks [26] ABV add: en [27] ent] ABV lack [28] ou] C lacks [29] et] V: ou [30] n'estoit] A: esteit; O: estoit [31] servise] O: servises [32] bone et] B lacks

***[213]** Qui est semons de son servise, et l'on li doit de son fié ou il est mermé de son fié, et il ne viaut la semonce acuillir tant que il soit paié, que il doit dire et faire.[a, b]

Se le seignor doit de son fié a aucun de ces homes ou il est mermé[1] d'aucune chose de son fié, et il le fait semondre de son servise, et il ne viaut sa[2] semonce acuillir tant que il soit paié, il doit dire la raison[3] por coi et[4] venir le plus tost que il porra devant le seignor en la court et dire li: 'Sire, vos m'avés fait semondre de tel servise', et dire li[5] quel. 'Sire, et vos[6] me devés[7] de mon fié de quey je vos doy le servise de quei[8] le terme[9] de ma paie est pasé. Faites moi paier,[10] et je aquiaudrai[11] vostre semonce si con je devray. Car je n'entens que je deie vostre semonce acuillir, se vos ne me paiés ou faites[12] paier se que vos me devés de mon fié de quei le terme de ma paie est passé, ne acuillir ne la vueill se la court ne l'esgarde. Et de ce me met je en l'esgart de la court sauf mon retenaill.' Et aprés se il ne me senble que le seignor puisse choze dire par coy la court doie esgarder que le semons[13] doie la semonce acuillir tant que il soit paiés de ce que l'on li doit de son fié de quei le terme de sa

A: fols cxxxvii^r^–cxxxviii^r^ cap. 214; **B:** fols 168^r^–169^v^ cap. 215; **C:** fols 202^r^–203^v^ cap. 213; **O:** fols 281^r^–283^v^; **V:** fols clxxxv^v^–clxxxvii^r^ caps 224–6; Beugnot, pp. 341–3, cap. 214.

[a] Rubric in A: Si dit quant (A rubrics (fol. 7^v^): Ci dit coment se) le seignor semont son home dou servise qu'il li deit, et il li deit de son fié, coment l'ome se peut defendre de acuillir sa semonce, et coment il le deit faire se le seignor n'a essoine aparant, come de estre assegié de ces ennemis ou d'autre perill; B: Ci dit coment quant le seignor semont son home dou servise que il li doit de son fié, coment l'ome s'en puet deffendre d'acueillir sa semonse, et coment il le doit faire se le seignor n'a essogne apparant, come d'estre assigié de ses ennemis ou d'autre perill; V: Ci dit coment quant le seignor semont son home dou servise que il li doit. Et se le seignor li doit de son fié, coment home ce peut deffendre d'acuillir sa semonse, et coment il le doit faire se le seignor n'en a essoigne aparant, come de estre asegé de ce hennemis.
[b] A marginal note in O (fol. 281^v^) wrongly claims that this chapter is taken from Philip of Novara.

[1] ou il est mermé] B: mermez [2] sa] ABV: la [3] raison] B: traïson [4] A adds: puis [5] li] AB lack [6] et vos] V: vous ci [7] devés] O lacks [8] quei] B: qui; V: que [9] terme] B: termen [10] paier] A: ce que voz devés [11] aquiaudrai] C: irai a; V: acuillerais [12] faites] C: faces [13] le semons] A: l'ome

paie est passé, se ce n'est a defendre cité ou[14] borc,[15] vile ou chasteau qui soit dou seignor en quey cil[16] se treuve quant il est semons. Car a tel semonce ne me senble il mie que[17] defaut de la paie l'escuse selonc l'assise ou l'usage dou reiaume de Jerualem. Que selonc ce que je ai oy dire, cestui servise doit chascun a son seignor, et paié et non[18] paié.

Et s'il est essoiné avant[19] le jor de la semonce qu'il ne puisse venir en la court faire[20] assavoir au seignor c'esoine[21] ou ne la contremande[22] si con il doit, et qui[23] viaut faire au seignor assavoir[24] c'essoine, quant il est semons de son servise et il est essoiné,[25] il la deit faire assaveir[26] par .i.[27] crestien. Et celui par qui il la[28] fait assaveir[29] doit dire au seignor en la presence de .ii. de ces homes ou de plus:[30] 'Sire, tel vostre home', et le nome,[31] 'vos fait assaveir par moy que il est essoiné, si que il ne peut venir[32] faire le servise de quei vos l'avés semons ou[33] fait semondre.[34] Sire, et se vos mescreés que je ne soie son message et qu'il[35] ne m'ait enchargé a dire se que je vos ai dit por lui, je suis prest que je en face se que la court[36] conoistra que je faire en doie.' Et se le seignor[37] comande a la court que ele fase cele[38] conoissance, la cort doit conoistre, se cuit, que il doit jurer se le seignor viaut[39] qu'il est message de celui qu'il dit[40] qui la l'a envoié[41] et que il li a[42] enchargé a dire ce que il a dit por lui. Et se le seignor veaut que il le jure, il le doit faire.[43] Et se il[44] le jure,[45] ou[46] le seignor le[47] croit sans sairement, le semons[48] avra bien[49] contremandé c'essoine si com il devra.[c]

---

[c] V begins a new chapter with the rubric: Ci dit coment le banier doit semondre les homes dou seinor.

---

[14] ou] BV lack [15] AOV add: ou [16] cil] ABV: il [17] que] A: que le; C lacks [18] non] A: sanz; B: senz; V: sans [19] avant] V lacks [20] faire] AB: face; V: il doit faire [21] assavoir au seignor c'esoine] B: le au seignor assavoir [22] ne la contremande] A: le contremande; B: contremande la; V: contremander [23] qui] B: que il [24] assavoir] B: savoir [25] quant il est . . . essoiné] V lacks [26] assaveir] B: savoir [27] .i.] ABV lack [28] la] AB: le [29] fait assaveir] B: fera savoir [30] de ces homes ou de plus] A: homes ou plus, mais qu'il seent homes dou seignor [31] et le nome] B lacks [32] venir] AV lack [33] semons ou] AV lack [34] si que il . . . semondre] B lacks [35] et qu'il] B: que je [36] V adds: esgardera et [37] A adds: l'en mescreit et il [38] cele] A: la ditte [39] se le seignor viaut] A lacks [40] qu'il dit] ABV lack [41] qui la l'a envoié] C: qu'il l'a envoié; V: qui l'a yleuques mandé [42] li a] C: l'a [43] faire] BV: jurer [44] O adds: ne [45] jure] V: fait [46] ou] CO: et [47] le] AO: l'en [48] le semons] A: l'essoignié [49] bien] ABV lack

Et se[50] .iii. homes dou seignor ou le banier semont aucun home ou feme[51] de venir faire droit ou do[52] servise que il doit au seignor a faire le maintenant, et il lor dit que il est essoinés, il ne li covient mie aprés ce faire[53] assaveir[54] au seignor[55] c'essoine por ce que il l'a dit en court se il l'a[56] dit[57] au banier. Que[58] le banier est tenus en sa loiauté de dire au seignor le respons que l'ome fait a la semonce de quei il le semont, et que le seignor le doit croire par la foy de quei[59] il li est tenus. Mais s'il est semons[60] par letres a une choze faire maintenant et il est essoinés si qu'il ne la puisse faire, ou se les .iii. des homes[61] ou[62] le banier le semont a jor nomé et il dedens cel jor est esoinés, il doit au jor ou[63] .i. jor devant contremander[64] c'essoine en la maniere avant[65] devisee.[d]

Et se le banier[66] semont aucun d'aucune choze faire maintenant, et il li[67] dit que il est essoinés, et le banier ne le dit au seignor ou le seignor ne le veaut dire[68] et il[69] veuille avoir[70] droit ou[71] amende de celui qui ensi[72] avra esté semons, et[73] il[74] die[75] que il le[76] dist au banier quant il le semonst qu'il estoit essoinés, se le banier[77] li porte guarentie de ce, le seignor l'en doit croire par la foy que[78] il li est tenus, et se il noie que l'ome ne li dist et l'ome dist par la foi que il doit au seignor que il li dist, l'ome en[79] sera creu et le banier non contre l'ome, por ce que il n'est mie tenus a l'ome de foy et que l'ome est tenus[80] au seignor de foy.

Et se le seignor fait semondre aucun de ces homes d'aler hors[81] dou reiaume d'autre servise que de l'une des .iii. avant[82] [e] dites[83]

---

[d] V begins a new chapter with the rubric: Encor de ceste raison meimes, et se le seignor semont aucun d'aucune chose.

[e] In substituting 'aprés' for 'avant', MS A shows an awareness that the order of the chapters has been changed. (In ABV this chapter is placed earlier, directly after cap. 184.) The reference is to material in chapter 187.

---

[50] se] A lacks [51] .iii. homes dou . . . feme] B: le banier semont aucun home ou feme ou trois homes dou seignor le semonent [52] do] ABV: de [53] faire] C: faire faire [54] assaveir] B: savoir [55] au seignor] V lacks [56] l'a] O: le [57] ABV add: a (A: as) .iii. de ces homes (V: .iii. homes de sa court). Et se il le dit [58] Que] B lacks [59] de quei] C: que; V: de qui [60] est semons] A: semons; B: le semont [61] C adds: dou seignor [62] se les .iii. des homes ou] A: se les .iii. dis homes ou; B lacks; V: se les .iii. houmes devant dites ou [63] ou] BC lack [64] contremander] C: mander [65] avant] ABV: devant [66] banier] V: seignor [67] li] AV lack [68] dire] ABV: croire [69] il] C lacks [70] avoir] B lacks [71] ou] C: et [72] ensi] A lacks [73] et] C lacks [74] il] A: celui [75] die] ABV: dit [76] le] ABV lack [77] V adds: ne [78] par la foy que] B: de quoi [79] en] C: si [80] a l'ome de foy . . . tenus] BO lack [81] d'aler hors] A: d'aler fors; C lacks [82] avant] A: aprés; V: devant [83] B adds: trois

chozes de quey les homes doivent servise as seignors[84] dou reiaume de Jerusalem[85] sans ce que son cors y aille, il ne li doivent pas tel[86] servise ne ne doivent[87] sa semonce acuillir, ains doit dire celui qui enssi est semons que il n'entent que il doie[88] au seignor tel servise, por coi il ne viaut ceste semonce acuillir, se la court ne l'esgarde[89] ou conoisse que il acuillir la doie. Et de ce se[90] met il en l'esgart de la court sauf son[91] retenaill. Et se il enssi le fait, je cuit que la court esgardera ou conoistra[92] que il ne doit[93] cele semonce acuillir por ce qu'il ne li doit mie le servise de quey il l'a semons par l'assise ne[94] l'usage do reiaume de Jerusalem.

---

[84] as seignors] A: au seignor hors; C: a seignors; V: au seignor [85] de Jerusalem] ABV lack [86] tel] C: cel [87] doivent] A: deit [88] doie] A: deive; OV: doive [89] ne l'esgarde] AB: n'esgarde [90] se] BV lack [91] son] V: mon [92] ou conoistra] B lacks [93] doit] AV: doive; B: doit mie [94] ne] AB: ou; V: et

***[214]** Quant .i. home est semons et il veaut son fié comander, coment il le doit faire sans perill.[a]

Qui est semons et il veaut son fié comander, se[1] il le veaut faire sans perill quant il le comande au seignor, se le seignor ne le receit,[2] si li die: 'Sire, je entens que vos le devés faire por tel et por tel raison', et die quels,[3] 'por coi je veuill que vos le resevés, se vostre court l'esgarde. Et de ce me met je en l'esgart de vostre[4] court sauf mon retenaill.'[5] Et le seignor doit dire lors: 'Et je ne le veuill recevoir por tel et por tel raison', et die[6] les raisons que il cuidera qui li vaillent[7] a se que court esgarde ou conoisse que il ne doit la comande resevoir, et de ce se met en l'esgart ou en la conoissance de sa court sauf son retenaill. Et por ce que il ne me senble que celui qui le fié comande puis que il est semons puisse choze dire par quei le seignor le[8] receive par esgart ou par conoissance de court, se il se viaut et set defendre,[9] ne viaus je ci[10] aleguer ne dire ce que il me[11] semble que les .ii.[12] parties porroient[13] dire, ne ce que la court en devroit esgarder.[14] Car riote sans profit n'est pas bone.[15] Mais por ce di je que celui qui en tel point veaut comander son fié s'en[16] doit metre en esgart ou en conoissance de court. Car qui enssi le fait, il ne peut perill avoir de son fié perdre sa vie ne an ne[17] jor, se il ne fait contre ce que la cort avra esgardé ou coneu.[18]

A: fols clxi^{v}–clxii^{r} cap. 246; **B:** fol. 198^{r} cap. 250; **C:** fols 203^{v}–204^{r} cap. 214; **O:** fols 283^{v}–284^{r}; **V:** fol. ccxxii^{r-v} cap. 263; Beugnot, p. 393 cap. 246.

---

[a] Rubric in A: Qui viaut son fié comander et il le viaut faire sanz perill quant il le comande au seignor, se le seignor ne le receit si li die que il viaut que il le resseit par esgart; B: Qui veut son fié comander et il le veut faire sanz perill quant il le comande au seignor, se il ne le veut recevoir se li die qu'il veut qu'il le reçoive par esgart; V: Qui veaut son fié comander et il le veaut faire sans perill quant il le comande au seignor, se le seignor ne le resoit si li die que il veut que il le ressoive par esgart.

---

[1] se] A: et [2] receit] B: recevoit [3] quels] C: 'que' altered to 'quei' [4] vostre] BOV: la [5] sauf mon retenaill] AV lack [6] A adds: totes [7] qui li vaillent] C: qu'il li vaille [8] le] BV lack [9] set defendre] A: se defendre et set [10] ne viaus je ci] B: Et je ne veull ci; C: ne ne viaus [11] il me] C: a moi [12] .ii.] B lacks [13] porroient] C: povroient [14] en devroit esgarder] A: devereit esgarder de ce [15] n'est pas bone] V: ne vaut riens [16] s'en] A: se; C: si [17] ne] A: et [18] ou coneu] AB lack

***[215]** Ques[1] sont les choses que le seignor a la requeste de son home li[2] peut et[3] doit delivrer sans clamor.[4]

Il est costume, assise et usage par droite vive raison ou reiaume de Jerusalem et en celui de Chipre quant l'ome fait requeste au seignor d'aucune choze de fié que le seignor la li doit delivrer et faire avoir sans clamor, se le seignor conoist la raison de l'ome ou se l'ome la peut prover. Et les[5] chozes ce sont que le seignor est tenus par les desus dites raisons a delivrer sans clamor seront si desus devisees en cest chapitle.[a]

La premiere choze que l'on peut requerre au seignor et[6] que le seignor peut delivrer[7] est cele[8] que le seignor a et tient. Et aprés cele[9] que le seignor[10] a enpeeschee et enconbree. Et aussi cele que l'on requiert d'escheete come droit heir, se aucun[11] autre heir meindre de lui ou mains prochain de celui qui ot la deraine[12] saisine est[13] entré en la saisine de cele chose de[14] s'autorite ou par[15] seignor, requerant[16] come le plus droit heir aparant qui[17] en la court fust. Et ausi cele[18] de la novele desaisine dont le seignor fait enquestion[19] et met[20] le noviau desaisi en autel[21] saisine con il avoit devant ce qu'il fust desaisi par l'assise usee de la novele desaisine.[22] Et ces sont les choses que l'on peut requerre au seignor sans clamor. Et toutes autres

---

A: fol. clxiii^{v} cap. 248; **B:** fol. 199^{v} cap. 252; **C:** fol. 204^{r-v} cap. 215; **O:** fol. 284^{r-v}; **V:** fols ccxxv^{v}–ccxxvi^{r} cap. 267; Beugnot, p. 396, cap. 248.

---

[a] ABV lack this opening paragraph.

---

[1] Ques] ABV: Ce [2] li] A: le; V lacks [3] peut et] B lacks [4] clamor] B: delai [5] les] O: lesqueus [6] et] AV: par usage (V: husage) ou par raisson (V: raison) ou au plus pres de la raisson (V: raison); B: par usage ou par raison [7] delivrer] ABV: et doit (A: deit) delivrer sanz clamor [8] est cele] AV: ensi (V: enci) la chose [9] que le seignor . . . cele] B lacks [10] le seignor] ABV: il [11] aucun] V lacks [12] la deraine] B: desrainment la [13] est] V: ou que il soit [14] de] B: par [15] ABV add: le [16] requerant] B: la requeist [17] qui] BV: que [18] cele] ABV lack [19] fait enquestion] ABV: est esclarsi (B: esclarci; V: esclersi) par l'enquesicion (B: l'enquisicion; V: la question) [20] met] V: mist [21] autel] ABV: tel [22] par l'assise usee . . . desaisine] ABV lack

quereles se doivent conduire par forme de plait.[23] Car chascun sera plus curious de son avantage que le seignor qui dit tous[24] 'par droit sur la court' soit, et enssi le[25] doit il faire,[26] car il est balance[27] apareillé de faire ce que la court esgardera.[28]

[23] forme de plait] AV: point de plait et par forme (A: forme de raisson) [24] AB add: jors; V: jour [25] le] AV lack [26] et enssi le doit il faire] B lacks [27] balance] C: balanee [28] faire ce que la court esgardera] B: ce que sa cort esgardera ou conoistra

***[216]** Coment et por coi l'on doit[1] vendre le fié de sa feme sans son otroi ou[2] avant que le sien, laquel vente est contre[3] l'assise.[a]

Se il avenist[4] chose[5] que le rey chevauchast a host banie contre les henemis de la fey,[6] et il avenist par aucune[7] aventure que l'ost fust desconfite et le seignor fust pris en cele chevauchee ou[8] desconfiture ou en forteresce ou il ce[9] fust receté, et fust mené en prison, et aprés venist a fin de la[10] raançon, et l'on mandast[11] amacer la quantité de[12] la[13] raançon por la delivrance dou seignor, et il avenist que la raançon fust si grant que l'on ne la peust trover a amacer dou tresor ne dou meuble dou seignor ne a enprunter ce qui en defaudreit de la quantité de la dite[14] raançon, les homes dou seignor sont lors[15] tenus de foagier lor fiés par comun acort chascun[16] .i. besanz par centenar.[17] Et ce o[18] tout ce ne fust amacee l'avant dite cantité de[19] la raançon toute[20] enterinement, et il i eust[21] aucun des homes dou seignor[22] qui tenist fié[23] par sa feme franchement ou par servise de cors ou de conpaignon d'un ou de plusors,[24] celui doit venir en la presence des homes dou seignor,[25] ses pers, et faire les assembler tant con il porra, et se doit haster dou faire, et quant il seront

A: fols clxiii[v]–clxiv[r] cap. 249; **B:** fols 199[v]–200[v] cap. 253; **C:** fols 204[v]–206[r] cap. 216; **O:** fols 284[v]–287[v]; **V:** fols ccxxvii[v]–ccxxviii[v] cap. 272; Beugnot, pp. 397–9, cap. 249.

[a] As indicated in the apparatus, ABV supply a version of this chapter that is abridged.

[1] doit] AV: peut; B: puet [2] ou] ABV lack [3] contre] A: encontre [4] avenist] B: avenoit [5] chose] ABV lack [6] fey] V: crois [7] aucune] ABV lack [8] chevauchee ou] ABV lack [9] ce] ABV lack [10] la] ABV lack [11] B adds: a; V: pour [12] la quantité de] ABV lack [13] de la raançon . . . la] O lacks [14] dou tresor ne . . . dite] A: de son tresor et meuble et ne trovast l'on en enprunt la quantité de ce qui en defaudreit de la; B: de tresor ne de meuble et que l'on ne trovast en enrprunt ce qui faudroit de la; V: tresor meuble et ne trovast l'on emprunt de la quantité de ce qui en defaudroit de la [15] dou seignor sont lors] ABV: sont [16] par comun acort chascun] AV lack; B: a [17] par centenar] AB: por .c.; V: par cent [18] o] B lacks [19] l'avant dite cantité de] ABV lack [20] toute] ABV lack [21] eust] ABV: avoit [22] dou seignor] AB lack [23] A adds: de [24] plusors] ABV: plus [25] dou seignor] ABV: liges qui sont

assenblés, celui qui enssi a et tient .i. fié par sa feme, com est aprés[26] devisé,[27] doit dire l'oiant de ceaus qui la sont assenblés[28] en tel maniere:[29] 'Seignors, vos savés[30] coment le roy qui est[31] nostre seignor[32] de qui nos somes homes et de qui nos tenons nos fiés a finé de sa delivrance[33] a tel quantité de raançon, laquel l'on ne peut trover toute enterine[34] ne[35] autrement[36] qui en defaut.[37] Et por ce que je suis home de mon seignor le roy et tiens de lui tel fié que je ai par ma feme, dont je li ai fait homage et li dei servise de mon cors', ou, 'de[38] conpaignons', selonc ce qu'il en devra de servise, ou, 'franchement', s'ensi est,[39] 'laquel[40] mee espouse feme[41] n'en a[42] heirs prochains ne costiers ne lontains a qui le fié puisse ne doive[43] venir ne escheir que a mon seignor le roy ou[44] a ses heirs, ne mei ne ma dite feme ni avons ni ne[45] devons avoir en cestui dit fié[46] que la joiete[47] des biens a nostre vie, et por ce que a mon seignor le roy doit le dit fié venir et escheir[48] aprés le deces de ma dite[49] feme, je tres orendroit[50] en deget mei et ma dite[51] feme espouze de quey le dit[52] fié meut[53] hors[54] de tout le fié et le vos livre a vendre por la raançon de mon seignor parfaire et[55] aconplir. Et veuill que il soit vendu, se la cort l'esgarde ou conoist. Et se la court l'esgarde ou[56] conoisse que je plus en doive faire que se que je en[57] ai fait, je suis apareillé del faire por mon seignor aidier a delivrer et geter de prison.' La court doit lors, se cuit, conoistre ou esgarder que celuy a bien sa foy guardee vers son seignor, ne que nul ne l'en peut mais reter de sa foy, et que il doivent recevoir le dit fié[58] et faire crier et livrer au tiers jor come fié qui se vent contre l'assise.

---

[26] aprés] O: avant [27] faire les assembler . . . devisé] ABV lack [28] l'oiant de ceaus . . . assenblés] ABV lack [29] A adds: Biau; B: Beaus; V: Beau [30] V adds: bien [31] le roy qui est] ABV lack [32] A adds: le rei; B: le roi est [33] et de qui . . . delivrance] ABV: est venu [34] enterine] BOV: enterinement [35] ABV add: par enprunt (B: enpront; V: emprunt) ne [36] ne autrement] O: autrement ce [37] qui en defaut] ABV lack [38] O adds: compaignon ou de [39] dont je li . . . est] ABV lack [40] laquel] C: la [41] mee espouse feme] ABV lack [42] n'en a] B: n'a; C: ne as [43] doive] A: dee; BV: doie [44] a mon seignor le roy ou] AB: au rei (B: roi) et; V: au seignor et [45] ni ne] C: ni; O: ne ni [46] dite feme ni . . . fié] A: feme n'en avons ni ne devons aveir; B: feme ni avons ne ne devons avoir; V: feme n'en avons ne avoir ne devons [47] la joiete] A: la joye; B: l'issue [48] a mon seignor . . . escheir] AB: au roy deit (B: doit) cestui fié escheir (B: escheoir); V: au seignour doit escheir cestui fié [49] dite] ABV lack [50] tres orendroit] V: trais orendroit et [51] dite] ABV lack [52] quey le dit] O: qui le [53] espouze de quey . . . meut] ABV lack [54] hors] A: fors [55] parfaire et] AV lack; B: a [56] conoist. Et se . . . ou] C lacks [57] en] C lacks [58] Et veuill que . . . fié] ABV: et ensi (B: enssi; V: enci) doit (A: deit) livrer son fié a vendre et ceaus (A: ciaus) le doivent recevoir (A: deivent receveir)

Et se celui qui a et tient fié en ceste maniere ne le fait[59] enssi com il est desus devisé, et le seignor, aprés sa delivrance, s'en[60] vosist clamer a lui et[61] a sa court de celui qui enssi[62] li avroit[63] defailli de ce dont il[64] est[65] tenus de faire par l'assise dou roy Amauri, qui fu faite a Sur por la desconfiture qui fu des crestiens ou fait de Naples.[b] Si fu lors establi, ordené et asis que quant tel fait avendroit com est avant dit de prise de seignor, que tos ceaus qui avroient et tenroient tel maniere de fié com est desus dit[66] par leur feme le doivent ensi faire com est avant devisé[67] et livrer a vendre por la delivrance dou seignor. Et tos ceaus qui ne le feroient et avroient et tenroient en tel maniere fié fucent encheus vers le seignor de tel paine con vos orés aprés.[68] L'amende que le seignor[69] avroit et la paine que l'ome soufriroit[70] seroit[71] tel: que l'ome seroit forspaisé[72] toute[73] sa vie de tout le[74] reiaume dedens .vii. jors et perdra le dit fié que il n'avra enssi livré as homes de la court a vendre, et aussi feroit il autre fié .i. ou plusors, se il les avoit et tenoit, lui et ces heirs a tot[75] tens. Et il me senble que ce est droit et raison, por ce que ce est maniere de traïson aperte, car assés est clere chose a conoistre que ce soit traïson. Que se le seignor fust enssi pris et aresté, com est avant[76] dit, et le seignor venist a raançon motie a terme et jor nomé, et l'on ne peust trover la raançon dedens le dit terme ou ce qui en defaudreit, et aucun tenist tel maniere de fié et ne le livrast a vendre dedens le terme nomé, et sur ce les henemis dou seignor qui l'avroient et tenroient en lor poeir nel vosisent rendre por ochoison dou terme qui seroit pasé, et ensi le vosisent tenir por avoir greignor raançon, et celui qui avoit tel fié ou ceaus et ne le livrassent lors a vendre, bien les doit chascun tenir a traïtors, puis que il avroit ou avroient si malement failli vers lor seignor, et bien est traïson aparant.[77]

Mais se l'ome[78] faisoit[79] la maniere avant[80] dite dou fié livrer a vendre, et le fié fust vendu et le seignor delivré[81] de la prison et dou

---

[b] Nothing is known of a defeat at Nablus at the time of King Amaury.

---

[59] fait] A: faisseit; BV: faisoit [60] s'en] AB: se; V: se c'en [61] a lui et] V: de lui [62] enssi] AB lack [63] avroit] V: avoit [64] AB add: li [65] est] B: seroit [66] dit] O: devisé [67] devisé] O: dit [68] por la desconfiture . . . aprés] ABV lack [69] BV add: en [70] et la paine que l'ome soufriroit] ABV lack [71] seroit] C: est [72] forspaisé] C: paisé fors [73] toute] B lacks [74] de tout le] A: hors dou; B: dou; V: hors de tout le [75] tot] O: tous [76] avant] O: devant [77] dedens .vii. jors . . . aparant] ABV: et la feme aussi perdroit (V: auci perdroit tout) le fié. Si feroit (A: fereit) l'ome ce il aveit nul (B: avoit nul; V: avroit) autre fié de son conquest ou d'escheete [78] AB add: le [79] ABV add: en [80] avant] V: devant [81] delivré] C: delivrer

pooir de ses henemis,[82] le seignor est tenus de restorer le dit[83] fié a son home qui por sa delivrance[84] avra esté vendu ou restorer li le vaillant des rentes[85] dou fié chascun an tant come sa feme vivra. Ne le dit[86] fié ne doit estre refusé a vendre a nulle[87] maison de relegion n'a comune n'a yglise qui acheter le vueille. Et se aucun des avant dis[88] l'acheteit, la[89] condicion de la vente dou fié por tel besoin doit estre motie ou livrer dou fié, c'est asaveir que le fié doit estre livré dedens le tiers jor qu'il avra esté crié a vendre, et que se le seignor le veaut ravoir[90] dedens l'an et le jor, rendant ce qu'il fu vendu a celui qui l'acheta,[91] laissant et quitant lui totes les rentes[92] qu'il en avra eues et[93] receues. Et se l'an et le jor passe que le seignor[94] n'ait[95] le fié racheté,[96] il demore quitement et en pais a celui qui acheté l'avra,[97] que le seignor ne autre ne le peut ravoir ne recovrer.[98] Mais dedens l'an et le jor peut le seignor faire .iii. choses: l'une si est que il peut le fié dessus[99] dit acheter,[100] ou eschanger a autre sien[101] fié, ou vendre del[102] sien fié por celuy ravoir.[103] Et ces .iii. choses sont contre l'assise.[104] Quar por nule autre chose que por ces .iii. dessus dites[105] ne peut le seignor vendre riens de son fié ne eschanger[106] ne[107] autre fié[108] acheter qui[109] soit contre l'assise. Et la vente meimes qui est dou fié franc qui ne doit point de servise ne d'omage ne de redevance est contre l'assise. Quar nul fié ne se vent par l'assise que celui qui se vent por dete coneue en court ou a qui l'on la preuve.[110, 111]

---

[82] dou fié livrer . . . henemis] AB: et le seignor fust delivré; V: dou dit fié et delivroit le seignor [83] dit] ABV lack [84] por sa delivrance] A: ensi; B: enssi; V: enci [85] restorer li le vaillant des rentes] ABV: le vaillant de la rente [86] dit] ABV lack [87] refusé a vendre a nulle] A: vendu a; B: ven *(sic)* a; V: vendu en [88] C adds: de [89] la] C lacks [90] n'a comune n'a . . . ravoir] ABV: ne a home qui ne puisse fié acheter. Et se (A: ce) il le fust (V: feist), le seignor le peut recovrer (A: recouvrer) [91] l'acheta] V: l'a acheté [92] laissant et quitant . . . rentes] ABV: quitant li (V: lui) et laissant (A: laissant li; B: lessant) les biens [93] avra eues et] A: avreit; BV: avroit [94] le seignor] A: il [95] n'ait] B: n'a [96] racheté] C: acheté [97] acheté l'avra] A: l'acheta; B: l'achata; V: l'a acheté [98] peut ravoir ne recovrer] A: poreit rechater ne aveir que par la dreite assise de la vente des fiés; B: porroit avoir ne recovrer par la droite assise des ventes des fiez; V: poroit recovrer ne avoir que par la dite assise droite de la vente des fiés [99] dessus] B: devant [100] acheter] AV: racheter; B: rechater [101] sien] ABV lack [102] del] ABV: dou [103] ravoir] A lacks; B: recovrer [104] ABV add: tot aussi (V: tout auci) come est la vente dou fié [105] chose que por . . . dites] AB: assise que por ceste; V: assise ne pour ceste [106] eschanger] V: changier [107] ne] ABV: a [108] autre fié] AO: autrui fié; B: autre [109] C adds: ne [110] acheter qui ne . . . preuve] A: ne acheter fié; BV: ne fié acheter [111] ou a qui l'on la preuve] O lacks

***[217]** Coment seignor et home se doivent[1] entrequiter l'un l'autre de la foy qu'il s'entredoivent et rendre et quiter le fyé que l'ome tient do seignor.[2]

Quant seignor et home sont engrigné ou en bone volenté l'un vers l'autre, et il avient que l'ome qui[3] tient dou seignor fié de don qui doive servise de cors, et l'ome ne viaut plus tenir celui[4] fié por ce que il se sent gregié dou servise ou por ce que il viaut forspaiser et servir autre seignor hors[5] dou roiaume de Jerusalem,[6] se l'ome a le fié dou don dou[7] seignor, il le peut rendre[8] au seignor ou a l'eir dou seignor, et se il a le fié d'escheete il ne le peut rendre ne quiter au seignor ne a son heir por la tranlacion qui[9] devant a esté. Quar aussi bien sont heirs do fié ceaus qui sont aprés lui com il est,[10] sauve ce que il a et tient le fié por ce que il est plus prochain[11] et devant[12] les autres dont le fié meut. Mais se le seignor et l'ome[13] d'un acent[14] et d'une volenté s'acordent[15] a ce qu'il se veuillent entrequiter[16] de la foy dont il se sont promis et entredonés[17] l'un a l'autre, l'ome doit rendre et quiter au seignor[18] quanque il a et[19] tient de lui[20] en tel maniere que[21] le seignor et l'ome doivent priveement[22] apeler le chanblerlain dou roiaume ou celui qui est[23] en son leuc, et se le leu de la chanberlainie est vacant si doivent apeler celui qui tos jors est retenus a la parole dou seignor guarder,[24] et quant tout[25] ce faut, si doivent apeler[26] aucun des homes liges[27] dou seignor qui bien sache parole mostrer, et li doit le seignor comander et l'ome prier coment[28] il en plaine court doie deviser[29] la quitance de la foy

A: fols clxiv^{v}–clxv^{r} cap. 250; **B:** fols 200^{v}–201^{r} cap. 254; **C:** fols 206^{r}–207^{r} cap. 217; **O:** fols 287^{v}–289^{r}; **V:** fol. ccxxvii^{r-v} cap. 271; Beugnot, pp. 400–1, cap. 250.

[1] doivent] AB: pevent; V: peut [2] et rendre et . . . seignor] ABV lack [3] qui] O lacks [4] celui] V: son [5] hors] A: fors [6] de Jerusalem] ABV lack [7] don dou] V lacks [8] rendre] AV: rendre et quiter; B: quiter ou rendre [9] qui] O: que [10] il est] B: lui [11] prochain] A: preucheit [12] B adds: toz [13] BV add: sont [14] acent] O: acort [15] s'acordent] B: acordanz; V: et ci acordent [16] entrequiter] B: otrequiter [17] entredonés] A: entremis; B: entretenuz; V: entretenus [18] V adds: tout [19] a et] ABV lack [20] AB add: et [21] que] ABV: come vos orrés [22] priveement] V: premierement [23] est] ABV: sera [24] et se le . . . guarder] AB: et se il n'i (B: n'en i) a nul, celui qui acostumeement garde la parole dou rei (B: roy); V: ou celui qui acostumeement garde la parole dou seignor [25] tout] C: tuit [26] apeler] A: aveir; V lacks [27] liges] A lacks [28] coment] B: que [29] doie deviser] ABV: devise

dou seignor a l'ome et de l'ome au seignor,[30] par enssi que il doit avoir paine mise entre le seignor et l'ome qu'il ne repairont[31] de la quitance, ains[32] se conduront a quitance l'un vers l'autre, et otroierent le dit de celui qui la parole doit mostrer. Aprés ce qu'il[33] seront enssi[34] acordés, le seignor doit faire la court assenbler, et quant ele sera assenblee,[35] celui qui la parole doit mostrer doit dire en la presence dou seignor et de la court:[36] 'Seignors, vos qui estes homes[37] dou seignor de qui ceste court est,[38] je vos fais assaver que le[39] tel home', et le doit nomer, 'qui est nostre[40] per et home dou[41] seignor, ne le veaut plus estre,[42] ains rent au seignor[43] le[44] fié que il tient de lui et quite la foy que il li[45] doit, et le[46] seignor receit le fié et la quitance de la foi, et li quite[47] aussi tout ce dont il li est tenus et quanque[48] il li[49] peut et doit[50] quiter sauve sa foy et s'enor.' Et puis doit maintenant dire au seignor et a l'ome: 'Est il enssi con je ai si[51] retrait en la presence de la court?' Le seignor et l'ome doivent adonc[52] dire andeus[53] ensenble: 'Oil', por ce que l'un ne puisse l'autre prendre a point. Quar se l'un disoit 'oil' et l'autre, 'non', ensi avroit l'un pris l'autre a point et avroit sa foi blecee et seroit encheu de la poine qui en seroit[54] mise, si con il avint dou prince d'Antioche et de mesire Raoul de Thabarie.[a]

Et aucuns de nos grans maistres[55] dient[56] que l'un ne peut l'autre quiter par autrui, ne que l'on[57] peut conjurer son seignor[58] par autrui ne por autrui.[59] Et a moi senble que si peut, et dit por coi l'on le

---

[a] The mutual renunciation of fealty between Ralph of Tiberais and Pince Bohemond IV of Antioch dates to c. 1200. See 'L'estoire de Eracles empereur', *RHC Historiens Occidentaux*, 2, pp. 230–1; Philip of Novara, pp. 543–4, and below appendix 1.2.

---

[30] et de l'ome au seignor] C: 'au seigme *(sic)* au seignor' struck through. [31] repairont] O: repaireront [32] il doit avoir . . . ains] ABV: le seignor et l'ome (B: il) se doivent (A: deivent) acourder (B: aquiter; V: acorder) et pener que par la fei (B: foy; V: foi) qu'il s'entredoivent (A: s'entredeivent) qu'il [33] qu'il] AO: qu'il se; B: que se il se [34] enssi] V: entre [35] assenblee] A: ensemble [36] A adds: Biau; B: Beaus; V: Beau [37] homes] C: home [38] vos qui estes . . . est] ABV: qui si estes assemblés en la presence de mon seignor (B: dou seignor) de qui voz estes homes [39] le] BV lack [40] nostre] ABV: vostre [41] dou] AV: de mon [42] le veaut plus estre] A: viaut plus estre tenus a lui [43] rent au seignor] AB: li rent; V: rent [44] le] B: son [45] li] O lacks [46] le] AV: mon [47] quite] V: a quité [48] quanque] C: quant [49] li] AV lack [50] et doit] O: et i deit; V lacks [51] si] ABV lack [52] adonc] C: adont [53] andeus] A lacks; V: ambedeus [54] qui en seroit] A: qu'il avreit; BV: qui seroit; O: qui avroit esté [55] de nos grans maistres] B lacks [56] dient] AV: dit; B: veulent dire [57] ABV adds: ne [58] son seignor] V lacks [59] autrui ne por autrui] AV: autre; B: autrui que por soi

peut et doit faire. Car tot ausi[60] come l'on[61] fait homage et aliance de fey[62] par autrui qui l'omage devise, tout aussi peut l'on rendre le fié que l'on a et tient de don au seignor et[63] a l'eir dou seignor et quiter[64] la foi dont il li est tenus, car l'on n'a le fié que por le servise, et la foy est[65] en la premesse[66] et ou contenement et[67] en la devise de l'omage.

[60] ausi] B: enssi [61] l'on] ABV: l'ome [62] de fey] AV lack [63] et] ABV: ou [64] quiter] B: quite [65] est] B lacks [66] premesse] C: presence [67] ou contenement et] B lacks

***[218]** Coment et en quel maniere il n'i a point de bataille en chose qui monte a plus d'un marc d'argent, et coment et en quel maniere il peut avoir bataille des uns guarens as autres a l'usage do reiaume.[1] [a]

Se il avenist que aucun meist sus[2] .i. autre home que il li eust tolu aparaument de lui ou de son message devant gent aucune cantité d'avoir en or ou en argent ou en joiaus ou en monee, et celui de qui l'avoir avroit esté venist devant le seignor et se clamast de celui qui ce li avroit fait sans ofrir la preuve, et l'autre fust mandé querre et venist devant le seignor et deist ou feist dire par son conseill: 'Sire, le tel qui ci est', et nomer le, 'est ci venus devant vos con devant seignor en la presence de la court apareillé de dire a l'encontre de ce que celui qui de lui c'est clamé a dit ou vodra dire ou requerre a vos ou a lui', se le clamant fait redire sa clamor enssi com il est dessus dit sans nomer la preuve, et celui de qui l'on c'est clamé s'en viaut[3] deffendre, il n'i avra point de bataille. Quar il peut bien dire: 'Non place Deu', et desmentir le mot a mot de ce que celui li met sus, et que de ce a il bone guarantie que il a celui jor que celui dit ne a cele hore ne a cel point n'estoit il pas el leuc ne en la cité[4] ou le fait avint, et de ce a il bone garentie et preuve et[5] tes qui bien se conduiront par l'esgart de la[6] court a faire ce que il devront come celui qui est tot prest et aparillié. Et se enssi est dit et fait com il est dessus devisé, il n'i avra point de bataille se[7] l'autre ne l'eufre a prover par garans.

Et la maniere en quei il i peut avoir bataille des uns guarens as autres est tel con vos orrés aprés. Ce le clamant eufre en sa clamor a prover le fait par .ii. loiaus guarans de la loy de Rome ou de celui sur qui le fait avra esté mis, et l'autre s'en eufre a defendre par

---

C: fols 207v–209r cap. 218; **O:** fols 289r–291v; part edited in Edbury, *John of Ibelin*, p. 108 note 11.

---

[a] This chapter is lacking in ABV and in Beugnot's edition. A marginal note in O (fol. 289r) wrongly claims that it is taken from Philip of Novara.

---

[1] O adds: de Jerusalem [2] O adds: a [3] viaut] O: seit [4] el leuc ne en la cité] O: en cele cité ne en cel leuc [5] et] C lacks [6] la] C: sa [7] se] C: de

guarans de la loy dou clamant et l'autre partie sofrir le voille, enssi peut la bataille venir avant des uns guarens as autres se celui qui c'est clamé vient avant et eufre ses guarans. Adons celui de qui l'on cest clamés doit venir avant et rebuter, se il viaut, l'autre et ofrir les siens guarans et presenter en l'oure. Ceaus doivent dire au seignor en la presence de sa[8] cort: 'Sire, nos avons oi et entendu la clamor que le tel', et le noment, 'a faite de cestui qui ci est', et nomer le, 'por quei nos vos disons en verité que il ment. Et somes prest et apareillés de defendre celui sur qui il le mete sus qu'il n'i a colpes en ce que celui[9] li met sus. Et somes prest de prover que les guarans que il a amenés sont faus et desloiaus et loyés et qu'en eaus ne demore qu'il ne se parjurent. Et ce somes nos prest et appareillés de prover et mostrer lor de nostre cors contre les[10] lor et de rendre les mors ou recreans en une hore de jor tout ensi con la court esgardera et au jor que la court nos donra. Et vés en ci nos guages.' Et les tendent au seignor a genoils. 'Et vos prions et requerons que vos les recevés.'[11] Ce il avient lors que les guarens do clamant les en[12] veuillent desmentir et aler a l'encontre de lor dit et ofrir lor sairement et se metent a jurer, quant il se vodront agenoiller por fornir lor garantie, les autres guarans les en pevent ramir ains le sairement parfait, et se pevent atacher de bataille a iaus aussi bien come d'autre querele les uns garans as[13] autres. Ne i a ceaus de qui est la querele, c'est assaver le clamant et le defendant, ne s'atacheront de bataille en la maniere desus devisee fors les uns guarans as autres.

Et les guarans qui seront vencus doivent estre pendus tot ausi con por bataillle de murtre, et la greignor merci que le seignor en peut et doit avoir d'eaus si est de faire lor coper la lengue dont il voloient[14] motir le sairement et coper le poin destre de quei il voloient creanter et paumeer l'evangile por lor garentie enteriner et parfaire le sairement qu'il avoient fait. Et enssi doit il estre se les garans sont chevaliers. Mais se il sont gens de basse main, si doivent estre pendus sans nul autre[15] merci avoir. Et se il sont homes dou seignor, tos ensenble le[16] querelous et les guarans qui seront vencus, il doivent estre forspaisés de tot le reiaume a tos jors et perdre lor fiés a lor vie et doivent avoir respit de partir dou reiaume .vii. jors.

---

[8] sa] O: la [9] que celui] O: qui [10] les] C: le [11] recevés] O: receistes. Et [12] en] C lacks [13] as] O: contre les [14] dont il voloient] O: dom il voloit [15] nul autre] O: nule [16] le] O: les

Et bien deise pluisors autres choses en cest livre, mais trop i avroit de riote por quey je nel vueill faire ains me veuill prendre a dire et deviser toutes les choses dont je me suis peu ramenbrer et apencer et qui plus sont besoignables a savoir et user en la haute court dou reiaume de Jerusalem et de Chipre et conduire et delivrer les par droite forme de plait selonc ce que je ai oi et entendu et veu[17] user et delivrer et que a moi meimes senble que chascun en peut et doit dire et faire. Et aprés dirai la maniere dou coronement le roy dou reiaume de Jerusalem et l'ofice de ses ofisiaus dou dit reyaume et quei il sont tenus de faire le jor dou coronement et aprés par lor ofice. Et puis vos deviserai en ordene toutes les autres chozes si con je l'ais enpris a faire. Et puis vos deviserai les baronies, les seignories qui ont court et[18] coins et justise et[19] ou le roy dou reiaume de Jerusalem doit estre coroné et qui le corone,[20] et les sufraguacions et les servises qui sont et que l'on doit el dit roiaume et les aies que chascun deit quant besoing est en la terre et les chevaleries et les sergenteries par non et puis en some.[b]

[b] This chapter is clearly misplaced and belongs somewhere around cap. 85. It marks the end of the disucssion of the law and legal procedures, and the final paragraph outlines the material (caps 218–39) with which the book concludes.

[17] veu] C lacks [18] et] O lacks [19] et] C lacks [20] corone] O: doit coroner

***[219]** Ci dit ou le roy dou reiaume[1] de Jerusalem doit estre coroné, et qui le doit coroner.[a]

Le rey dou reyaume de Jerusalem ne tient son reiaume[2] que de Dieu, et il doit estre coroné en Jerusalem, s'ele est en mains de crestiens. Et quant ele n'i est, il[3] doit estre coroné a Sur. Et le patriarche doit coroner le roy,[4] se il[5] a patriarche el roiaume quant le roy se fait coroner.[6] Et se il n'a patriarche el roiaume,[7] l'arcevesque de Sur le doit coroner, por ce que il est le primat des arcevesques[8] do reiaume. Et s'il n'i a arcevesque a Sur, celui de Cesaire le doit coroner, et c'il n'i a arcevesque a Cesaire, celui de Nazereth le doit coroner.

A: fol. iii^{v} cap. 6; **B:** fols 35^{v}–36^{r} cap. 6; **C:** fol. 209^{r} cap. 219; **O:** fols 291^{v}–292^{r}; **V:** fol. ccxxxvi^{v} cap. 286; Beugnot, p. 29, cap. 6.

---

[a] In AB caps 219–20 come after cap. 5 above. For the coronation ritual in the Jerusalem, see H.E. Mayer, 'Das Pontifikale von Tyrus und die Krönung der lateinischen Könige von Jerusalem', *Dumbarton Oaks Papers*, 21 (1967), 141–232.

---

[1] dou reiaume] AB lack [2] reiaume] O: fié [3] n'i est, il] A: ne l'est, si; B: n'i est, si; V: n'est, si [4] doit coroner le roy] ABV: le doit coroner (V: courouner) [5] AV add: y [6] se il a . . . coroner] B lacks [7] n'a patriarche el roiaume] AB: n'i a patriarche; V: n'en y a patriarche [8] arcevesques] O: evesques

***[220]** Coment et en quel maniere le patriarche doit coroner le roy dou reiaume de Jerusalem, et[1] quel maniere de sairement l'un doit faire a l'autre, et quel servise sont tenus de faire les ofisiaus dou dit reiaume le jor dou coronement le roy par lor ofice.[a]

Le jor que[2] le patriarche corone le roy dou reiaume de Jerusalem,[3] la precesion li doit venir[4] a l'encontre. Et quant il est[5] a la porte dou mostier,[6] le patriarche, ou le perlat qui coroner le doit, li doit dire[7] pluisors orisons sur la teste, et il doit estre[8] a genoils, et les oficiaus dou dit reiaume de costé lui:[9]

CO:	**ABV:**
c'est assaveir le seneschal qui doit porter le septre, et le conestable qui doit porter le confanon,[10] et le mareschal qui doit mener le cheval dou roy, et le chanberlain qui doit porter la corone et l'espee et la pome et l'anel. Et quant le perlat a dite ses orisons, le roy se doit lever et pormetre se qui est usé o Sepulcre que il doit prometre. Et il meimes le doit lire en	et puis le rei se lieve et jure au patriarche un tel seirement:

A: fols iii^v^–v^r^ cap. 7; **B:** fols 36^r^–37^r^ cap. 7; **C:** fols 209^r^–211^r^ cap. 220; **O:** fols 292^r^–294^v^; **V:** fols ccxxxvi^v^–ccxxxviii^v^ cap. 287; Beugnot, pp. 29–31, cap. 7.

[a] Rubric in A: Coment l'on doit le roi coroner, et quel sairement il fait au patriarche et le patriarche a lui, et coment il doit torner dou sepulcre; B: Ci dit coment l'en doit le roi dou reaume de Jerusalem coroner, et quel maniere de serement il fait au patriarche, et ce que le patriarche li promet; V: Ci dit quel maniere de sarement fait le roy dou royaume de Jerusalem au patriarche quant il li met la corone au chief.

[1] O adds: en [2] Le jor que] ABV: Quant [3] dou reiaume de Jerusalem] ABV lack [4] doit venir] ABV: vient [5] Et quant il est] ABV lack [6] ABV adds: et [7] doit dire] ABV: dit [8] doit estre] ABV: est [9] dou dit reiaume de costé lui] ABV: li sont de costé [10] confanon] O: gonfanon

latin si con je le vos deviserai en francois por estre meaus entendu a ceaus qui le lirront et latin ne savront. Le roy dou reiaume de Jerusalem doit enssi dire:

'Je tel', et se doit nomer,[11] 'par digne[12] soufrance a coroner en[13] roy de Jerusalem, promet a toi mon seignor tel', et le doit nomer,[14] 'patriarche de Jerusalem[15] et a tes susesors canonement entrans, desous le tesmoing de Deu le tout puissant et de toute l'iglise et des perlas et de mes[16] barons qui ci environ[17] sont, que je de cest jor en avant serai ton feal et[18] aideor et defendeor de ta persone contre tos homes vivans el[19] reiaume de Jerusalem.[20] Les pocesions et les franchises de la sainte yglise de Jerusalem ma mere et[21] de totes les yglises apartenans[22] principaument a li,[23] lesqués pocesions et franchises[24] eles ont acostumé a avoir jadis es tens de bonseurous rois mes devanttiers et que eles aqueront justement ça en avant en mes[25] tens, maintendrai a eles et defendrai.[26] Les canoniques et les anciens proveliges et les deues leis[27] et les justises de ceaus et les ancienes costumes des franchises guarderai et maintendrai. Les persones ecclesiastes en[28] lor franchises guarderai.[29] As veves et as orfenins justise ferai. Les preveliges des bonseurous rois devanttiers[30] et les assises dou[31] roi Amauri et do roi Bauduin son fis et les ancienes costumes[32] dou reiaume de Jerusalem garderai. Et tot le peuple crestien do dit reiaume selonc les costumes ancienes et aprovees[33] de cest meimes reiaume et selonc les assises des devant dis rois en[34] lor drois et en lor justises guarderai, si con roi crestien et feal[35] le doit faire en son reiaume. Et totes les autres choses[36] desus dites guarderai feiaument. Enssi m'ait Dieu et ses saintes Deu evangiles.'[37]

---

[11] et se doit nomer] ABV lack [12] digne] C: dine [13] en] AV: a; B lacks [14] et le doit nomer] AV lack [15] promet a toi . . . Jerusalem] B: jure a toi patriarche [16] mes] C: tos les [17] ci environ] ABV: environ moi [18] et] ABV lack [19] el] B: en la; V: au [20] O adds: ma mere [21] et] V lacks [22] apartenans] O: apartenances [23] a li] V lacks [24] O adds: de la sainte yglise [25] mes] AV: mon [26] et defendrai] A lacks [27] leis] V lacks [28] en] V: et [29] guarderai] AB lack [30] rois devanttiers] A: reis mes devanciers; B: mes devantiers roys; V: mes devanciers [31] V adds: royaume et dou [32] costumes] AB: costumes et assises; V: assises et coustumes [33] aprovees] A: provees [34] devant dis rois en] V: avant dis roys et [35] et feal] AB lack; V: et feel de Dieu [36] choses] O lacks [37] Deu evangiles] A: evangiles de Dieu; BV: evangiles

CO:

Et puis aprés le perlat qui coroner le doit doit crier se que il porra:

ABV:

Et quant le devant dit rei a ce fait, le patriarche le lieve en piés et le prent par la main destre, et li promet en ceste maniere: 'Je t'aiderai la corone mise en ton chief justement a maintenir et[38] a defendre sauf m'ordre', c'il est d'ordre, et c'il est autre, 'la[39] sainte yglise de Rome.' Et ces choses dites, il le doit baissier en fei, et crier quanque il peut:[40]

'Entre vos qui si[41] estes assenblés: seignors, perlas, et[42] maistres, et ofisiaus dou roy, et[43] chevaliers, et homes liges, et autres[44] borgeis, et toute autre maniere de[45] peuple qui ci estes assenblés, nos somes ci[46] por coroner a roi[47] tel qui ci est', et le doit nomer.[48] 'Et volons que vos nos dites se il est droit heir dou reiaume de Jerusalem.'

CO:

Lors li doit l'on respondre 'oil'.[49] Puis redoit dire la segonde feis se il il doit estre roys et coroné dou reiaume de Jerusalem, et l'on li doit respondre 'oil'. Et puis redoit dire la tierce fois se il veulent que il le corone et se il doit estre coroné,[50] et il doivent respondre 'oil'. Et quant il a ensi par .iii. fois demandé, et il li ont respondu 'oil', lors

ABV:

et se deit dire par .iii. feis,[51] et l'on respont 'oil'. Et maintenant comensent *Te Deum laudamus*[52]

[38] Je t'aiderai la . . . et] V: Et je t'en aiderais. Et lors le met la corone au chief justement a maintenir et a sauver et [39] la] BV lack [40] quanque il peut] V lacks [41] si] ABV lack [42] et] AV lack [43] et ofisiaus dou Roy et] A: et barons; B: barons; V: et offeciaus barons [44] autres] AB lack [45] V adds: gens et dou [46] nos somes ci] B: et nos ausi [47] O adds: le [48] a roi tel . . . nomer] ABV: tel (B: le tel) a roi (A: rei) de Jerusalem [49] oil] C: oy [50] et se il doit estre coroné] O lacks [51] feis] V lacks [52] V adds: *te Dominum confitemur*

doivent comencer a chanter *Te Deum laudamus* et doivent entrer dedens le cuer tout enssi come il seront venus.

Et doit le Roy avoir un faudesteull tres devant l'autier et la se doit apuier desus en aflicions treusques a tant que le *Te Deum laudamus*[59] soit tot chanté, et quant il est tout chanté le perlat doit venir et li doit dire pluisors orisons desus la teste, et puis, quant il les a dites, le roy se doit aler seir en son siege, et l'on doit comencer la messe.

Et quant la messe est dite treusques aprés l'epistele,[66] .ii.[67] perlas doivent venir au roy, l'un a destre et l'autre a senestre, et le devent[68] mener treusques au faudesteull par devant l'autier, et la li doit dire le perlat aucune beneison, et puis aprés si[69] doit prendre le cresme et le doit oindre par desus le toup disant se qu'il y afiert des saumes de sainte yglise.

et s'en entrent dedens le cuer[53] o[54] ces barons qui portent sa corone et la pome et le seneschau porte le septre et le conestable[55] porte le gonfanon[56] et le rei est[57] vestu come diaque, la teste descoverte.[58] Et l'on a un faudestueill devant l'autier et la s'apuie le rei[60] en afflictions trusques[61] a tant que le *Te Deum laudamus*[62] soit chanté, et quant il est chanté[63] le patriarche ou le prelat qui le doit coroner vient et li dit pluissors orissons desuz la teste, et puis, quant il a ce dit, le rei s'en vait[64] seir en[65] son siege, et l'on comence la messe.

Et quant on a dit l'epistle et la sequence, .ii. prelas vienent au roi, et le meinent treusques[70] au faudesteull par devant l'autier, et la li dit celui qui le doit coroner beneissons et puis prent le cresme et l'oint par desus le toup dissant ce que est usé de dire et orissons et saumes.

---

[53] dedens le cuer] B: dedens; V: au cuer [54] o] V: aveuc [55] A adds: qui [56] gonfanon] V: confanon [57] est] V: doit estre [58] descoverte] V: deschevelee [59] *laudamus*] O lacks [60] la s'apuie le rei] V: il la s'apoie [61] treusques] BV: jusques [62] *laudamus*] A lacks [63] et quant il est chanté] V: lors [64] vait] B: va (here and elsewhere in this section) [65] en] A: sur [66] l'epistele] C: l'apistele [67] C adds: des [68] devent] O: doivent [69] si] O lacks [70] treusques] BV: jusques

Et aprés doit dire oreisons pluisors et li doit metre l'anel au deit qui senefie rey, et aprés l'anel l'espee qui senefie justise a defendre foy, et aprés la corone qui senefie la dignité,[71] et aprés le septre por chastier et defendre, et aprés la pome qui senefie la terre dou reiaume, et disant aucunes oreisons a chascune de ces choses, selonc l'usage de sainte yglise.

Et li met l'anel ou doit qui senefie roi, et aprés li seint l'espee qui senefie justise a defendre soi[72] et sainte yglise, et aprés la corone qui senefie la dignité, et aprés le septre por[73] chastier et defendre, et aprés la pome qui senefie la terre dou reaume, dissant toz jors ce qui est uzé en sainte yglise.

Et puis, quant tout ce est fait, le perlat qui le corone doit dire en latin: 'Vive le roy en bon prosperité!' Et ce doit il dire par .iii. fois hautement, et tos les autres perlas doivent ce meimes dire par .iii. fois aprés le perlat qui corone le roy.

Et puis, quant tot[75] ce est fait, le prelat qui le corone[76] et toz les autres dient en latin par .iii. fois: 'Vive le roy en bon prosperité!'

Puis aprés le perlat qui corone le roi doit prendre le roy par la main destre et li doit prometre en ceste maniere: 'Je t'aiderai,[74] la corone mise en ton chief, justement a maintenir et a defendre, sauf m'ordene'.

Aprés doit baiser le rei le perlat qui coroné l'a[77] en la bouche, et tos les perlas aprés. Et toutes les autres persones dou reaume de Jerusalem doivent faire feiauté au rei coroné[78] de guarder et sauver lui et ces heirs et toutes ces autres forteresces tant com il seront en son reiaume.

Et puis le rei baisse tos les prelaz

[71] dignité] C: dinité [72] soi] B: la foi [73] por] V: qui senfie [74] t'aiderai] C: t'ai [75] tot] B lacks [76] le corone] V: l'a coroné [77] qui coroné l'a] O lacks [78] coroné] C: come

Et puis doit le roi aler seeir[79] en son siege, et .ii. perlas le devent destreer treusques a son siege, l'un a destre et l'autre a senestre. Et aprés doivent chanter l'evangile et le parfait de la messe. Et au sacrement le roy doit oster sa corone. Et quant toute la messe est dite, le roy doit venir devant l'autier et se doit acomunier.[80]

et s'en vait seir[81] en son siege, et les[82] prelaz le destreent. Et l'on chante l'evangille et le parfait[83] de la messe. Et ou sacrement le roy oste sa corone. Et quant toute la messe est dite, le rei vient devant l'autier et s'acomenie.[84]

Et puis aprés le perlat qui coroné l'a doit prendre le gonfanon dou constable et le doit beneir et dire pluisors oreisons et beneir le d'aigüe beneite et metre[85] le en la main dou roy. Et puis le conestable le doit prendre de la main dou roy et se doivent retorner en l'ostel le roy tout en la maniere com il est[86] devisé.

Et aprés[87] le prelat prent le confanon[88] dou conestable et le beneist de l'aigüe beneite et le met en la main dou rei. Et le rei le livre au conestable et s'en retorne.[89]

Et quant le Roy est en l'ostel, si doit mangier, la corone sur la teste, tot ensi[90] atiré come il ist do mostrier tant com[91] il se doit aler reposer.

Et quant il est coroné en Jerusalem, si est coroné ou mostier dou[92] Sepulcre. Et vait au Temple Domini et la euffre sa corone sur l'autier ou fu offert nostre Seignor a Saint[93] Symeon. Et puis s'en[94] entre au Temple Salamon, qui est la maisson des templiers, et la sont mises les table, et il se assient au mangier, et les

[79] seeir] O lacks [80] acomunier] C: acomnier [81] vait seir] B: va [82] les] A: .ii. [83] le parfait] V: la proface [84] s'acomenie] B: se comenie; V: se comeine [85] metre] C: mete [86] O adds: dessus [87] aprés] B: puis aprés; V: puis [88] confanon] B: gonfanon (here and elsewhere in this section) [89] le rei le . . . retorne] V: constable le prent et s'en tourne [90] ensi] C: essi [91] com] O: que [92] mostier dou] V lacks [93] Saint] BV lack [94] s'en] V lacks

borgeis de Jerusalem servent cel jor les tables. Car ce est le servise qu'il doivent au rei.

Et quant il est coronés a Sur, il vait au chastel sur le cheval que l'on li mena devant covert,[95] et le mareschal par devant lui sur son cheval[96] portant le confanon, et toz les autres a pié. Et le conestable vait a pié devant le cheval dou rei areant[97] la gent. Le rei manive[98] la corone sur la teste. Le seneschal doit servir le rei[99] de toz ces mes, et le mareschal doit tenir le confanon devant le roi tant come il sera a table, et puis doit prendre le cheval dou conestable, et le conestable celui dou rei tot ensi covert, et le mareschal li vait devant portant[100] le confanon trusques[101] en sa herberge, car il est son home et li doit faire[102] homage.

[95] mena devant covert] V: meine [96] son cheval] B: le cheval dou conestable; V: le cheval dou conestable covert [97] dou rei areant] A: le rei veant [98] manive] B: manie [99] doit servir le rei] B: le doit servir [100] portant] A lacks [101] trusques] BV: jusques [102] doit faire] V: a fait

***[221]** Ce est assavoir l'ofice dou seneschal et la devise des chozes qu'il est tenus de faire le jor do coronement le roi et aprés.[a]

Le jor dou coronement[1] le seneschal peut et doit ordener le mangier dou jor et coment on servira celui jor en la maniere que[2] meaus[3] li semblera, se le roy ne li fait aucun especial comandement. Et celui jor meimes, si tost come le roy istra de sa chambre ou il sera vestu por aler au mostier, le seneschal doit tenir le septre et porter le devant lui jeusques dedens l'yglise et la tenir le jusques a tant[4] que il le preigne de sa main. Et si tost com il sera coroné, le seneschal doit aler avant a l'ostel et[5] faire ordener les choses qui li senbleront bien a faire. Et[6] ceaus qui porteront les escueles le rey et qui serviront a sa table de ce qui monte[7] au mangier, le seneschal peut ordener ceaus qui meillors li senbleront, se le rey ne li a[8] fait aucun[9] especial comandement. Ceaus qui serviront[10] par les tables dou[11] mangier, il les peut ordener et metre[12] tes com il li plaira. Quant le roi vodra mangier, le seneschal doit faire comander au chanberlain que il li porte l'aigüe a mains, et comander as autres par le paleis qu'il doignent l'aigüe quant le roi vodra laver.[13] Se il ne viaut tenir le septre en sa main[14] au mangier, il le doit bailler[15] au seneschal, et le seneschal le peut bailler a tenir devant le roy[16] a qui qui[17] li plaira,[18] tant come le roi[19] mangera, se le rei ne li en fait[20] aucun especial comandement. Le seneschau doit servir le cors le[21] roy le jor dou coronement de drecier devant lui tos ces mes. Et doit comander

---

A: fols clxvi^{r}–clxvii^{v} cap. 256; **B:** fols 207^{r}–208^{r} cap. 267; **C:** fols 211^{r}–213^{r} cap. 221; **O:** fols 294^{v}–297^{v}; **V:** fols ccxxxviii^{v}–ccxl^{r} cap. 288; Beugnot, pp. 407–9, cap. 256.

---

[a] Rubric in A: Nos voz dirons si aprés les offices (A rubrics (fol. 9^{r}) adds: des officiaus) dou reiaume de Jerusalem et aprés les servises. Et comenserons premierement a l'ofice dou seneschau; BV: Nos vos dirons ci aprés les offices des officiaus (V: offeciaus) dou reaume. (V: royaume. Et) Premierement dou seneschal (V: seneschau).

---

[1] AB add: dou rei (B: roy) qui est comensement (B: comencement) de toz (B: touz) les officiaus [2] que] C: qui [3] A adds: il [4] a tant] A lacks [5] et] B: por [6] B adds: doit ordener [7] monte] V: amonte [8] a] AV lack [9] aucun] V lacks [10] serviront] B: meill [11] dou] C: de [12] il les peut ordener et metre] B lacks [13] laver] A: mangier [14] en sa main] V lacks [15] bailler] V: doner [16] a tenir devant le roy] AB lack [17] qui] B: que; V: que il [18] plaira] B lacks [19] le roi] ABV: il [20] fait] A: faisseit; BV: faisoit [21] le] AB: dou

de[22] lever les tables[23] quant il li semblera tens et[24] faire li doner l'aigüe, si com il est desus[25] dit. Et quant le roy avra mangié, s'il ne viaut tenir le septre en sa main, le seneschal le doit tenir devant le roi et porter le devant[26] lui jusques en la[27] chambre ou il se vodra aler[28] despoiller de sa robe roial. Et puis doit le seneschal aler[29] mangier. Et toutes les escueles et les greaus en quei il avra servi le cors le[30] roy dou premier mes doivent estre soues, plaines de tel viande[31] con le cors le[32] roi avra esté servi celui jor, et il i doit mangier dedens.[33]

Et[34] as .iiii. festes anels de l'an ou as autres[35] solemnités ou[36] quant le roi veaut[37] porter[38] corone, le seneschau est tenus de drecier devant lui au mangier et d'ordener et de faire servir[39] en son ostel en la maniere[40] desus devisee.

Tos les baillis et les escrivains do roi dou reiaume de Jerusalem,[41] sauf ceaus de l'ostel le[42] roi,[43] doivent estre au comandement dou seneschal et respondre a lui por lui[44] de ces baillies et de ses acontes qu'il rendront,[45] et lor peut comander et recevoir lor acontes et metre les et oster et user en des choses desus[46] dites au meaus qu'il[47] li semblera au profit dou roi,[48] sauf[49] le comandement de lui[50] ou de ceaus qui tendront son leuc, et[51] se il ne[52] li font[53] aucuns especiaus comandemens.[54] Les rentes dou roy,[55] ques qu'eles soient dehors[56] ou dedens, quant il ou celui qui tendra[57] son leuc vodra qu'eles soient apautees, il les li[58] doit comander, et le seneschal les doit faire crier et multeplier au meaus que il porra. Et quant ce vendra au[59] livrer, se il ou celui qui tenra son leuc i veaut entendre que il soit fait par devant lui, il le[60] doit estre, et[61] se il ne veaut[62] ou ne peut entendre,[63] le seneschal en[64] peut faire le meaus que il savra. Et

[22] B adds: faire [23] C adds: et [24] et] C: de [25] desus] B: avant [26] le roi et porter le devant] B lacks [27] la] C: sa [28] aler] BV lack [29] aler] V lacks [30] cors le] AV: cors dou; B lacks [31] tel viande] A: tels viandes [32] le] ABV: dou [33] et il i doit mangier dedens] ABV lack [34] Et] A lacks; V: Et il y doit mangier [35] A adds: granz; V: grans [36] as autres solemnités ou] B lacks [37] veaut] AV: vodra; B: voudra [38] porter] O lacks [39] servir] A: servise [40] V adds: come est [41] dou reiaume de Jerusalem] ABV lack [42] le] C: dou [43] sauf ceaus de l'ostel dou roi] B lacks; V: sans ceaus de son ostel [44] por lui] C deletes; O lacks [45] rendront] ABV: tendront [46] desus] B: devant [47] qu'il] A: que; C: qui [48] dou roi] B lacks [49] sauf] V: sans [50] de lui] A: dou rei [51] et] ABV lack [52] ne] A lacks [53] font] B: fait [54] aucuns especiaus comandemens] ABV: aucun especiau comandement [55] dou roy] AB lack [56] dehors] A: defors [57] celui qui tendra] B: ceaus qui tendron<t> [58] les li] A: li; B: le; V: les [59] au] C: a [60] le] AV: y [61] et] C: ou [62] V adds: estre [63] entendre] A: estre; O: entendre que il soit fait par devant lui [64] en] C: l'en

encore soit ce que la chose se face par devant luy ou par devant celui qui sera en son leuc, quant ce vendra au livrer, le seneschal les[65] doit livrer par son ofice[66] par le comandement dou roy ou de celui qui tenra son leuc de tos les propres apaus do reiaume de Jerusalem[67] por ce que[68] l'on ne peut[69] estre de trop enginié,[70] que il sache[71] lor value de tot lor guaaing[72] que les apautors guaaigneront. En chascun apaut le seneschal doit avoir .ii. carobles franchement.

Les chasteaus et les fortereces dou roy dou reiaume de Jerusalem[73] le seneschal les peut et doit revisiter et faire lor avoir ce que besoing[74] lor i ert,[75] et changer et remuer sergens et toutes manieres d'offices[76] qui dedens les chasteaus[77] sont[78] ou dedens les fortereces[79] seront,[80] sauf le[81] cors des chastelains[82] ou[83] sauf le comandement dou roy ou de celui qui tenra son leuc, se il aucun propre comandement ne[84] fasoit. Et les devant dis chasteaus[85] devent estre obeissans a[86] son comandement, sauf le comandement dou roy ou de celui qui tenra son leuc.

Et le sairement de ces baillis et de ces escriveins le seneschal peut et doit recevoir por lui. Et au seneschal doivent estre tenu de ce qui monte[87] a son ofice tant con il seront es baillies et es escrivenages.

Se le roi ou celui qui tendra son leuc ne viaut ou ne peut entendre es plais, il les peut cometre[88] au seneschal, et le seneschal[89] y doit entendre[90] et[91] faire les delivrer par l'usage de la court. Se il avient que le roy ne soit ou reiaume ne home qui tieigne[92] son leuc, le seneschau peut et doit par son ofice estre en son leuc, sauf ost ou[93] chevauchee, ce est assaver de ce qui apartient a ces rentes et as plais et a la justise, et user en par les[94] cors dou reiaume selon l'usage sauf .iii. choses: les cors des homes liges chevaliers, et lor henors, et lor fiés. Et de ces .iii. choses et de toutes autres quereles ques qu'eles soient,[95] se le plait en fust comencié[96] devant le roy et

---

[65] les] V: le [66] se il ou . . . ofice] B lacks [67] reiaume de Jerusalem] A: reiaume; BV: roy; O: roy dou reyaume de Jerusalem [68] por ce que] C: por quei; V: que [69] peut] ABV: puisse; O: puist [70] AV add: et [71] que il sache] C: si que [72] tot lor guaaing] AB: toz les gaains [73] dou reiaume de Jerusalem] A: ou reiaume; BV lack [74] besoing] AV: mestier [75] i ert] V: est [76] d'offices] C: d'ofice [77] les chasteaus] V: chasteau [78] sont] ABV lack [79] les fortereces] V: forteresse [80] seront] B: sont [81] le] AB: les [82] des chatelains] B: dou castellains; V: dou chastelain [83] ou] B: et [84] ne] AV: en; B lacks; O: n'en [85] V adds: et chastelains [86] B adds: lui et en; V: lui ou a [87] monte] A: montera; B: affiert [88] cometre] V: comander [89] et le seneschal] B lacks [90] es plais, il . . . entendre] O lacks [91] y doit entendre et] V: doit entendre as plais et [92] tieigne] V: tient [93] ost ou] B: d'ost ou de [94] les] AB: le [95] soient] B: fussent [96] comencié] A lacks

entamé et ataché[97] de qui[98] en avant, celui plait, se le roy se partoit do pais sans ordener .i.[99] home en leuc de lui, celui plait poroit estre determiné devant le seneschal[100] par la court, ou se il i estoit et[101] il ne[102] poeit[103] entendre et il le vosist comander au seneschal.

Se le roi ou celui qui tenra[104] son leuc est en ost ou en chevauchee, et il i a tant de gent dont il[105] puisse avoir bataille a la conoissance de lui[106] ou de celui qui tenra son leuc, le seneschal la doit avoir. Et se il ne peut avoir la bataille, il doit estre en la bataille en coi le cors do roy ou[107] celui[108] qui tenra son leuc sera.[109] Dou guaaing que l'on fera en ost ou en cheuauchee, toute la part dou roy le seneschal la doit faire retenir[110] et guarder.

Les[111] asenemens qui se feront en la secrete le roi et les paies se doivent faire par le seneschal ou par son comandement.

---

[97] ataché] V: entaché [98] de qui] AO: d'enqui [99] .i.] OV: y [100] devant le seneschal] A lacks [101] i estoit et] V: n'i estoit ou [102] ne] ABO: n'i [103] poeit] V: peut [104] tenra] A: tendreit; BV: sera en [105] dont il] B: qu'il [106] de lui] B: dou roy [107] roy ou] O: seignor [108] celui] AV: de celui [109] sera] V lacks [110] retenir] A: receveir; BV: recevoir [111] Les] B: Touz les

***[222]** C'est assavoir[1] l'ofice dou conestable et la devise[2] des choses qu'il est tenus de faire le jor dou coronement le roi et aprés.[3]

Le jor dou coronement[4] le conestable doit venir au matin[5] en la heberge[6] dou roi, et le mareschal o lui[7] en sa[8] conpaignie, et faire porter le gonfanon roial devant lui. Et si tost come il sont[9] decendu a pié, le mareschal doit porter le gonfanon[10] devant lui[11] jusques a la porte de la chanbre en quey[12] le roi se vestira, et la se doit arester o tot le gonfanon. Et quant le roy istra hors[13] de la chanbre, le conestable doit prendre le gonfanon[14] do mareschal et aler devant le roi entre le cheval et ceaus qui portent[15] les autres ofices devant lui jusques au mostier, et tenir le devant le roy tant come il sera en[16] l'yglise,[17] et raporter le devant lui a l'issir jeusques a la porte dou mostier, et[18] la bailler le[19] au mareschal, et prendre le cheval le[20] roy et tenir le[21] par la raisne[22] et par l'estrier[23] tant que il soit monté. Et puis doit le conestable aler devant la chiere dou cheval, esreant[24] les .ii. qui le mainent[25] par le frain, et doit comander au mareschal par quel voie il ira. Et au dessendre dou roi doit tenir le cheval par la raisne[26] et par l'estrier[27] jeusques a tant que le roy soit[28] decendu.[29] Le cheval tout ensi atiré come il sera[30] doit estre dou conestable. Et entre le roy et le gonfanon doit aler le conestable jusques en la chanbre ou le roi devra entrer. Et aler en[31] son ostel celui jor il doit aler sur le cheval le roi tout enssi come il sera atiré quant il l'avra eu, et le mareschal devant lui portant le gonfanon jusques a son ostel.

Et doit faire[32] droit par l'usage[33] dou reiaume de Jerusalem a ceaus qui se clameront[34] por[35] lor sodees a luy, soient chevaliers ou

A: fols clxvii^{v}–clxviii^{v} cap. 257; **B:** fols 208^{r}–209^{v} cap. 268; **C:** fols 213^{r}–214^{r} cap. 222; **O:** fols 297^{v}–299^{v}; **V:** fols ccxl^{r}–ccxli^{v} cap. 289; Beugnot, pp. 409–11, cap. 257.

[1] C'est assavoir] A: Si dit quel est; B: Ci dit de; B rubrics (fol. 28^{r}) V: Ci dit [2] et la devise] V lacks [3] des choses qu'il . . . aprés] ABV lack [4] A adds: le rei; B: dou roy [5] au matin] B lacks [6] heberge] V: chambre [7] o lui] V lacks [8] sa] C: la [9] sont] AV: sera [10] Et si tost . . . gonfanon] B lacks [11] devant lui] AB lack [12] en quey] A: ou; B: en laquel [13] hors] A: fors [14] A adds: de la main [15] portent] B: porteront [16] en] V: devant [17] en l'yglise] O: au mostier [18] A adds: tenir le devant le rei tant come il y sera et [19] bailler le] B: le doit baillier [20] le] BO: dou [21] et tenir le] A: et tenir; B lacks [22] la raisne] AB: le frain; V: les regnes [23] l'estrier] B: l'estrief [24] esreant] A: dou rei areant; B: areant; V: errant [25] mainent] AV: menront; B: meinront [26] la raisne] A: les rennes; B: les reignes; V: les regnes [27] l'estrier] B: l'estrief [28] soit] B: sera [29] V adds: quant il sera descendu [30] sera] BV: est [31] aler en] B: s'en doit retorner a [32] faire] AOV: faire faire [33] l'usage] B: la rayson [34] V adds: par l'usage [35] por] C: de

sergens.[36] Et quant court est ensemble[37] por jugement ou por recors faire[38] ou por[39] conseill ou por avoiement[40] sans le roy ou sans celuy qui est[41] en son leuc, il doit et peut demander l'avis de chascun ou faire le demander au mareschal, se il veaut, et[42] peut destraindre chascun de dire ou[43] de soi aquiter si com il est usage, et peut comander a retraire l'esgart ou la conoissance ou le recort ou l'avoiement[44] auquel[45] que il vodra[46] de ceaus de la court.

Et quant le roi ou celui qui est[47] en son leuc est en ost ou en chevauchee, le conestable doit ordener[48] les batailles et totes les gens d'armes[49] et le chevaucher et l'aler et le retorner[50] par le comandement dou roy ou de celui qui tenra[51] son leuc. Et se le roy ou celui qui tenra[52] son leuc ne l'en fait[53] comandement, il en peut faire[54] a son sen. Il peut avoir .x. chevaliers aveuc soi en sa conpaignie, tes come il li plaira,[55] de totes les gens de l'ost ou de la chevauchee, sauf ceaus[56] de l'ostel le roy ou de la[57] bataille[58] ou de celui qui tenra[59] son leuc, et peut aler par les batailles deviser et ordener ce qui li semblera[60] bon sauf le comandement dou roy ou de celui qui tenra[61] son leuc[62] et revenir et estre en la bataille le roi de laquel il est. Et doit estre chevetaine aprés le roy et[63] sauf son comandement ou de celui qui tenra[64] son leuc. Et quant l'on devra[65] poindre,[66] il doit comander la pointe[67] au mareschal par le comandement dou roy ou de celui qui tenra[68] son leuc. Les chevaliers que le roy vodra[69] faire[70] retenir[71] en ost, le roi[72] li[73] doit comander, et il au mareschal, et[74] en porra[75] veir la mostre quant il[76] li[77] sera comandé ou quant il li sera[78] bon.[79] Se le roy n'est[80] en ost ou en chevauchee ne home en[81] leuc de lui,[82] le conestable peut et doit estre en leuc[83] do roy[84]

---

[36] A adds: ou escuiers; BV: ou escuers [37] ensemble] B: asemblee [38] faire] B lacks [39] V adds: conoissance ou pour [40] C adds: faire [41] est] V: sera [42] se il veaut, et] B: et se il veut il [43] ou] B: et [44] A adds: que la court a fait [45] auquel] C: a quel; V: ou quel [46] il vodra] B: li plaira [47] est] AV: sera [48] B adds: toutes [49] B adds: sont soute lui [50] l'aler et le retorner] B: le venir [51] tenra] A: sera en; BV: est en [52] tenra] AV: sera en; B; est en [53] l'en fait] A: li font; B: li font especiau; V: le font son [54] en peut faire] A: en fera; B: le fera; V: em peut faire ces volentés [55] plaira] A: plaire [56] ceaus] V lacks [57] la] ABV: sa [58] C adds: de lui [59] tenra] ABV: sera en [60] semblera] B: semble raison et [61] tenra] ABV: sera en [62] et peut aler . . . leuc] C lacks [63] et] BV lack [64] tenra] AB: sera en [65] l'on devra] B: on voudra; V: l'on vodra [66] poindre] C: prendre herberge [67] la pointe] V: a poindre [68] tenra] B: sera en [69] vodra] C: devra [70] faire] O lacks [71] retenir] V: tenir [72] AO add: les [73] le roi li] V: il [74] au mareschal, et] V: et le mareschal [75] en porra] A: peut [76] A adds: li plaira ou quant il [77] li] V lacks [78] sera] V: semblera [79] ou quant il li sera bon] A lacks; B: ou quant il li plaira [80] n'est] V: en est [81] en] C: o [82] leuc de lui] AV: son leuc [83] de lui, le . . . leuc] B lacks [84] en leuc do roy] V lacks

chevetaine[85] de toutes les gens de l'ost qui vivent d'armes et qui por fait[86] d'armes sont en l'ost,[87] et sur la justise d'eaus faisant la[88] faire par le conceill des homes le[89] roy, sans[90] le cors des homes liges le[91] roi. Et[92] il en areant peut ferir et[93] poucer[94] et bouter[95] de mace ou de baston tos ceaus qui sont desous[96] sa chevetainerie, sans[97] les chevaliers et les[98] homes liges, mais a ceaus peut il bien[99] ferir les chevaus et ocire desous eaus.[100] Des[101] chevaliers ou d'autres gens que le roi ou celui qui sera en[102] son leuc[103] li comandera a semondre de tel servise con ce sera, il les peut semondre ou faire semondre[104] au mareschal tes com il li plaira, se le roy ou celui qui tenra[105] son leuc ne les li motit.[106] Le conestable ne doit avoir point de bataille, se il ne plaist au roy ou a celui qui tenra[107] son leuc et[108] que il lor senble bon.[109] Il doit comander au mareschal de partir[110] le guaaing, et[111] quant le roy ou celui qui tenra[112] son leuc le li comandera, et peut estre au partir, se il li plaist. Le herbergier quant l'on chevauche, il le doit comander[113] au mareschal, quant il en avra[114] comandement dou roi ou de celui qui tenra[115] son leuc. Et si doit avoir l'omage dou mareschal, sauf le roy et les autres persones a cui il est tenus de foy, c'est assavoir de ce dont le fait[116] de la mareschausie est tenus a celui de la conestablie. Les defaus des servises de ceaus qui ne tienent[117] chevaliers ou sergens qui doivent servise,[118] il les doit recevoir en sa main por le roy ou faire le[119] recevoir au mareschal de tos ceaus de qui il sera sertefiés par le mareschal,[120] qui avront defailli de chevalier ou de sergent que il devront tenir.

---

[85] chevetaine] B lacks [86] fait] V: faire [87] l'ost] AB: ost [88] la] A: et [89] le] B: dou [90] sans] A: sauf [91] le] B: dou [92] C adds: quant [93] et] V: ou [94] poucer] C: poser [95] et bouter] A lacks; V: ou bouter [96] desous] AB: souz; V: de [97] sans] ABV: sauf [98] et les] ABV lack [99] bien] V lacks [100] et ocire desous eaus] A lacks [101] Des] BOV: De [102] en] C: a [103] leuc] A lacks [104] ou faire semondre] B lacks [105] tenra] AV: sera en; B: est en [106] les li motit] A: les li moutist; B: li motisse; V: les semont [107] tenra] A: sera en [108] et] C lacks [109] bon] A: besoin; B: besoing; V: besoign [110] de partir] A: a departi [111] et] ABV lack [112] tenra] ABV: sera en [113] Le herbergier quant . . . comander] A: Il deit comander de prendre herberge; B: Il doit comander de prendre herberge que l'on chevauche; V: Il doit comander quant l'on chevauche de prendre herberge [114] avra] V: n'a [115] tenra] AB: sera en [116] le fait] ABV: l'office [117] tienent] ABV: tendront [118] servise] BV: servises [119] le] BV: les [120] de tos ceaus . . . mareschal] A lacks

***[223]** Ce est assavoir[1] l'ofice dou mareschal et la devise des choses que il est tenus de faire par son office[2] le jor dou coronement le roy et aprés.[3]

Le jor dou coronement le roy[4] le mareschal doit venir au matin a[5] la herberge le roi en la conpaignie dou conestable[6] et faire porter le gonfanon royal[7] devant lui. Et si tost come il sera decendu a pié, il doit prendre le gonfanon[8] et porter le devant le conestable jusques a la porte de la chanbre en coi[9] le roi se vestira, et la se doit arester o[10] tout le gonfanon. Et si tost come il istra hors[11] de sa chanbre, il doit bailler le gonfanon au conestable, et doit aler tenir le cheval dou[12] roy par la resne et mener le jusques au mostier. Et quant le roy sera coroné et retorné[13] a la porte dou mostier por monter a cheval, il doit bailler au conestable le cheval dou roy et doit[14] prendre le gonfanon de la main dou conestable. Et quant le roy sera montés, le mareschal doit monter sur le cheval[15] dou conestable tout covert, et porter le gonfanon devant le roy a cheval. Et si tost come le roy[16] sera decendu, il doit descendre et porter le gonfanon devant lui, si con le conestable le[17] li ordenera, jusques au leuc ou il devra[18] mangier. Et tant con le roy mangera, il doit tenir le confanon devant lui. Et quant il avra mangié,[19] il doit porter le confanon devant lui jusques a[20] la chanbre ou il devra entrer por oster[21] ses vestimens roiaus. Et puis doit aler devant le conestable sur le cheval dou counestable tout enssi atiré come il est jusques a l'ostel dou conestable.[22] Et doit estre sien le cheval dou conestable.[23] Et quant le conestable sera[24] descendu en son ostel, le mareschal doit faire porter le confanon devant lui jusques a[25] son ostel.

A: fols clxviii^{v}–clxix^{v} cap. 258; **B:** fols 209^{v}–210^{v} cap. 269; **C:** fols 214^{r}–216^{r} cap. 223; **O:** fols 299^{v}–302^{v}; **V:** fols ccxli^{v}–ccxliii^{v} cap. 290; Beugnot, pp. 412–14, cap. 258.

---

[1] Ce est assavoir] A: Si aprés porés oyr; BV: Ci dit de [2] par son office] C reads: 'le jor par son ofice' struck through. [3] et la devise . . . aprés] AV lack; B: et la devise [4] le roy] V lacks [5] au matin a] V: en [6] au matin a . . . conestable] A: en la compaignie dou conestable en l'ostel le rei; B: en la compagnie dou conestable a la herberge dou roy [7] royal] C: le roy [8] B adds: roal devant lui [9] en coi] A: ou [10] o] BV: a [11] hors] A: fors [12] dou] AV: le [13] retorné] A: torné; V: issu [14] doit] BV lack [15] doit monter sur le cheval] C lacks [16] a cheval. Et . . . roy] B lacks [17] le] AB lack [18] devra] C: doit [19] mangié] B: mangier [20] a] BV: en [21] oster] B: desvestir [22] tout enssi atiré . . . conestable] V lacks [23] Et doit estre . . . conestable] ABV: Et doit (A: deit) estre sien le chevau (A: cheval); O lacks [24] le conestable sera] B: il [25] a] ABV: en

Et se il i[26] a contens dou seignor a l'escuier[27] ou de l'escuier au seignor,[28] sauf de sodees ou des choses[29] qui apartienent[30] a mort, il les doit determiner par l'usage. Les[31] sodeers, chevaliers ou sergens, qui le roy vodra faire retenir,[32] sauf ceaus de son hostel, le mareschal les doit retenir par le comandement le[33] roy ou de celui qui sera en son leuc ou dou conestable, et doit veir lor moustre et resevoir lor sairement et faire mostrer lor mostre au roi ou a celui qui sera en son leuc ou[34] au conestable, quant il la vorront veir.[35] Et doit avoir des[36] sos de chascun des sodeers chevaliers[37] dou rey .iiii. besanz sarasinas[38] l'an, sauf ceaus de son ostel. Lesquels[39] qui doivent avoir restor, soient chevaliers[40] homes liges ou sodeers, li doivent mostrer lor bestes, et il les doit faire reguarder et receveir les, c'est assavoir celes qui sont resnables a estre a restor selonc l'usage dou pais, et faire les escrire a son escrivein et en la grant secrete do roy. Et se le roy ou celui qui tenra[41] son leuc ou le conestable l'a comandé[42] a faire semondre chevaliers ou sergens, il les peut semondre[43] si come il li plaira, se il ne les[44] li motist[45] par non. Des sodeers que l'on[46] eufre au roy ou au conestable ou a luy a metre au[47] servise, il doit veir lor armeures[48] quant le roy ou le conestable ont receu[49] la persone et[50] resevoir le[51] harnes ou faire le comander a[52] amender se il y[53] a que[54] amender. Et se le roy ou selui qui tenra[55] son leuc ou le conestable le veullent veir devant eaus, faire le pevent. Le defaut de ceaus qui devront[56] retenir[57] chevaliers ou sergens et ne les retenront,[58] le mareschal les doit avoir en escrit et mostrer le fait[59] au roy ou[60] au conestable por[61] faire les cuillir.[62] Et se le conestable veaut, le mareschal les[63] doit cuillir ou faire les[64] cuillir[65] et faire les[66] bailler a luy ou a son comandement por le roy. Et se le conestable n'estoit

---

[26] i] AV lack [27] l'escuier] V: son escuer [28] au seignor] B: a l'ome; V: a son seignor [29] des choses] ABV: de chose [30] apartienent] A: aparteigne; BV: apartiegne; C: atienent [31] Les] ABV: des [32] retenir] C: tenir [33] le] ABV: dou [34] ou] C: et [35] la vorront veir] A: la vodront veyr; B: la voudront veoir; C: l'avront veu [36] des] CV: de [37] des sodeers chevaliers] A: sodeier; BV: sodeer [38] sarasinas] B lacks [39] Lesquels] ABV: Les chevaliers [40] chevaliers] ABV lack [41] tenra] V: sera en [42] l'a comandé] ABV: li comande [43] chevaliers ou sergens . . . semondre] V lacks [44] les] AB lack [45] motist] A: moutissent; V: motissent [46] l'on] C: l'en [47] au] AV: en; BO: ou [48] armeures] BV: armes [49] receu] B: veu [50] et] V: li doivent [51] le] C: les; V: leur [52] comander a] V lacks [53] y] C: li [54] il y a que] A: qu'il y a a [55] tenra] ABV: sera en [56] devront] B: doivent [57] retenir] ABV: tenir [58] retenront] AV: retienent; B: tinent [59] fait] AB lack [60] ou] BV: et [61] por] C: ou [62] cuillir] V: acuillir [63] les] C: le [64] les] A lacks [65] ou faire les cuillir] V lacks [66] les] AV lack

en son[67] reyaume, ou il n'en eust home establi en leuc de lui par le roy qui tenroit[68] son leuc,[69] le mareschal les peut cuillir[70] et recevoir par son ofice por le roy ou por celui qui tenra[71] son leuc. Et des clamors des sodeers, soient chevaliers ou sergens[72] ou escuiers, se le conestable n'est ou pais ou il n'en i a nul home establi por le conestable par le roi ou par persone qui tenist son leuc,[73] le mareschal en peut et doit faire droit par l'usage dou reiaume de Jerusalem,[74] aussi come le conestable feroit se il i estoit. Quant court est assenblee[75] por jugement[76] ou por conseill ou por aveement sans le roi ou sans celui qui est[77] en son leuc, le mareschal peut demander l'avis de chascun, se le conestable n'i est, et peut destraindre chascun[78] de dire ou de soi aquiter, si come il est usage, et peut comander a retraire l'esgart ou la conoissance ou le recort ou[79] l'aveement auquel[80] qu'il vodra de ceaus de[81] la court. Se le roy ou home[82] qui est en son leuc va[83] en ost ou en chevauchee ou en quelque autre leuc que ce soit en quey le confanon roial soit porté, se il i est et le mareschal i est,[84] il doit estre en son leuc en la bataille dou roy ou de celui qui tenra[85] son leuc et doit porter a point et a tos besoins le confanon roial, et doit poindre quant le roy ou celui qui tenra[86] son leuc[87] ou le conestable[88] le li[89] comanderont. Et quant le conestable n'est en la bataille dou roy, le mareschal doit estre en celle bataille en son leuc, jeusques a tant qu'il li covieigne a prendre le confanon, et de cele bataille ne se doit partir por aler en un[90] autre leu, se le roi ou celui qui tenra[91] son leuc ou le conestable ne l'en[92] font propre comandement.

Quant le roy ou celui qui tenra[93] son leuc ou le conestable[94] seront[95] en ost,[96] la justise dou peuple et des escuers[97] doit estre faite par le mareschal, faisant la par le roy ou par celui qui tenra[98] son

[67] en son] A: ou; V: au [68] tenroit] V: tendront [69] qui tenroit son leuc] A lacks [70] ou faire les . . . cuillir] B lacks [71] tenra] AB: sera en [72] sodeers, soient chevaliers ou sergens] B: soudees; V: chevaliers ou sergens sodeers [73] ou par persone . . . leuc] B lacks [74] reiaume de Jerusalem] ABV: pays [75] assenblee] AV: ensemble [76] jugement] A: jugier ou por recort faire; BV: jugement ou por recort faire [77] est] AV: sera [78] chascun] B lacks [79] le recort ou] A lacks [80] auquel] C: a quel [81] ceaus de] O lacks [82] home] B: celui [83] va] A: est; BV: vait [84] et le mareschal i est] AB: et le conestable n'i est (B: est mie); V: ou le constable y est [85] tenra] AB: sera en [86] tenra] BV: sera en [87] et doit porter . . . leuc] O lacks [88] ou le conestable] B lacks [89] le li] AB: li; V: le [90] un] A: nul; B lacks; V: nulle [91] tenra] ABV: sera en [92] l'en] ABV: li [93] tenra] ABV: sera en [94] ou le conestable] A lacks [95] seront] AB: sera [96] ABV add: ou en chevauchee (A: chevauchiee) [97] et des escuers] O lacks [98] tenra] AB: sera en

leuc, se il sont[99] present, et se il ne sont present[100] par le conseill dou conestable ou des autres homes dou[101] roy.

Quant l'on doit herbergier, si tost come le mareschal en[102] avra receu comandement[103] dou roy ou de celui qui sera en son leu ou dou conestable,[104] le mareschal doit comander a herbergier et faire partir les plases. Le guaaing que l'on fera en ost ou en chevauchee le mareschal les doit[105] partir quant il avra le comandement dou roy,[106] et doit[107] faire bailer la partie dou roi au seneschal. Et doit avoir le mareschal toutes les bestes groces qui sont[108] vaires dou guaaing, et doit avoir tos les chevaus rendus qui seront[109] au restor dou roy, sauf ceaus de son ostel. Et doit faire homage au conestable, sauf le roy et les autres persones a cui il est tenus de foi, ce est assaveir de ce[110] dont l'ofice de la mareschausie est tenus a celuy de la conestablie.

[99] sont] C: soit; V: y sont [100] et se il ne sont present] AV lack; B: ou [101] dou] AV: le [102] le mareschal en] AV: l'on; B: l'en [103] receu comandement] A: eu comandement; B: lacks [104] B adds: en comandement [105] les doit] ABV: le doit (A: deit) faire [106] A adds: ou de celui qui sera en son leuc [107] doit] ABV lack [108] sont] ABV: seront [109] rendus qui seront] B: qui sont renduz qui sont [110] V adds: qui afiert

***[224]** Ce est assavoir[1] l'ofice do chanberlain, et le devise[2] de ce qu'il est tenus de faire le jor do coronement le roy et aprés.[3]

Le jor dou coronement[4] le chanberlain doit venir au matin a[5] la herberge le roy et doit entrer en la[6] chanbre do roy et atirer tos les vestimens roiaus[7] que le roi doit vestir por[8] faire se[9] coroner. Et quant le roy vait[10] au mostier, le chanberlain doit aler aveuc[11] les autres[12] ofisiaus au devant dou[13] seneschal et doit porter l'espee[14] et la pome et l'anel et la corone et doit[15] entrer dedens le cuer dou mostier aveuc les autres ofisiaus[16] et tenir toutes ces choses treuques a tant que le roi les preigne.[17] Et quant le roi est coroné, il doit aler en l'ostel le roi[18] et faire apareiller ce que[19] besoin li sera por son ofice,[20] c'est assaver l'aigüe que il doit doner as mains le[21] roi quant il vodra[22] seir au[23] mangier. Et ce doit il faire quant le seneschal li comandera[24] avant mangier[25] et aprés. Et doit servir le roy a son mangier[26] de la[27] coupe, se le roy ne li en fait aucun especial comandement.[28] Et quant le roy avra mangié, il doit aler mangier aveuc[29] les autres oficiaus.[30] Et la coupe de quei il avra servi le roy doit estre soe, et doit boivre le jor dedens, et devant lui la doit tenir en la table ou il mangera.[31]

Et as .iiii. festes annels de l'an ou as autres[32] solemnités ou quant le roy vodra porter corone, le chanberlain est tenus de servir le de la coupe en la maniere desus devisee par son ofice.[33]

A: fols clxix^{v}–clxx^{r} cap. 259; **B:** fols 210^{v}–211^{r} cap. 270; **C:** fol. 216^{r-v} cap. 224; **O:** fols 302^{v}–303^{v}; **V:** fols ccxliii^{v}–ccxliv^{r} cap. 291; Beugnot, p. 414, cap. 259.

---

[1] Ce est assavoir] A: Si aprés voz dirons; A rubrics (fol. 9^{r}): Ci dit quels est; B: Si amprés vos deviserons; V: Ci aprés nos dirons [2] le devise] C lacks [3] et le devise . . . aprés] ABV lack [4] A adds: le rei; B: dou roy; O: le roy [5] a] ABV: en [6] herberge le roy . . . la] V lacks [7] V adds: en la chambre dou roy [8] por] C: de [9] se] BV: soi [10] vait] B: va [11] aveuc] A: o; B: devant [12] autres] V lacks [13] au devant dou] AV: devant le; B: et devant le [14] l'espee] C: le septre [15] la pome et . . . doit] ABV lack [16] dedens le cuer . . . ofisiaus] AB: o les autres officiaus ou cuer; V: o les offeciaus au cuer [17] toutes ces choses . . . preigne] ABV: l'espee (B: touz tens l'espee) tant que le roy (A: rei; V: roi) la preigne, et puis doit (A: deit) prendre les autres choses que les autres officiaus (V: offeciaus) tienent et doner les au roy (A: rei) [18] le roi] ABV lack [19] et faire apareiller ce que] B: por faire appareillier ce qui en [20] por son ofice] V lacks [21] le] ABV: dou [22] vodra] B: doit [23] seir au] ABV lack [24] ABV add: et [25] mangier] AV lack [26] a son mangier] ABV lack [27] la] AV: sa [28] se le roy . . . comandement] ABV lack [29] mangier aveuc] AV: o; B: ou [30] V adds: mangier [31] et devant lui . . . mangera] A lacks; BV: et tenir le devant lui a la table [32] de l'an ou as autres] ABV: et as granz (V: grans) [33] ou quant le . . . ofice] ABV: le deit (BV: doit) il ensi (B: enssi; V: enci) faire et servir come il est dessus dit (B: devant devisé)

Et quant aucun viaut faire homage au rey,[34] le chanberlain est tenus par son ofice[35] de deviser l'omage,[36] ou celui qu'il avra laissé[37] en son leuc se le chanberlain n'est ou n'i peut estre.[38] Et doit avoir le chanberlain les afublails de tos ceaus et toutes celes[39] qui font[40] homage[41] au roy ou a celui qui tenra son leuc.[42]

---

[34] au rey] ABV lack [35] par son ofice] ABV lack [36] V adds: o lui [37] qu'il avra laissé] ABV: qui sera [38] se le chanberlain n'est ou n'i peut estre] ABV lack [39] le chanberlain les . . . celes] ABV: toutes (a: totes) les despoilles (V: despoillees robes) de ceaus (A: ciaus); O: le chamberlain les affublails de tous ceaus ou de toutes [40] font] AB: feront [41] homage] AOV: l'omage [42] ou a celui qui tenra son leuc] ABV lack

***[225]** Ci dit quans chief seignors[1] il i a au reiaume de Jerusalem.[a]

Il y[2] a ou roiaume de Jerusalem .ii. chies seignors, l'un esperituel et l'autre temporel. Le patriarche de Jerusalem est le seignor esperituel, et le roy dou reiaume de Jerusalem est[3] le seignor temporel dou[4] dit roiaume.

A: fol. clxx[r] cap. 260; **B:** fol. 211[r] cap. 271; **C:** fol. 216[v] cap. 225; **O:** fol. 303[v]; **V:** fol. cclxxi[r] cap. 314; Beugnot, p. 415, cap. 260; Edbury, *John of Ibelin*, p. 110, cap. I (English trans. p. 191).

---

[a] Rubric in ABV: Ces (A rubrics (fol. 9[r]): Se; B: Ce) sont les servises dou reiaume (B: reaume; V: royaume) de Jerusalem, et les ayes que chascun doit faire (A: fait; A rubrics: deit faire) quant besoing est au dit reiaume, et les leus (A: les les) qui ont court et coins et justise, et toz (toz] B lacks; V: tous) les prelas dou dit reiaume, (B: reaume; V: royaume) et leur suffragans (B: lor sufragranz; V: les suffragans) devisarai ysi, les uns aprés les autres, tot par chapitle. (A rubrics (fol. 9v): deviserai si, l'un aprés l'autre par chapitle; B: deviserai je l'un amprés l'autre par chapistres; V: devisera ge ci l'un aprés l'autre tous par chapistles).

---

[1] seignors] C: seignor [2] y] A lacks [3] est] A lacks [4] dou] B: dou devant; V: au

***[226]** Ci dit quans sufragans a le patriarche de Jerusalem.[a]

Le patriarche de Jerusalem a .v. arcevesques[1] suffragans:[2]

l'arcevesque de Sur;
l'arcevesque de Cesaire;[3]
l'arcevesque de Bethssem[4] qui est dit de Nazeret;[5]
l'arcevesque de[6] Beisseret;[7]
l'arcevesque dou Babet[8] que les Greus[9] apelent Filadelfe qui au tens le roi Amauri fu translaté[10] au Crac et[11] est apelé arcevesque de La Pierre dou Desert.

Et si a[12] .iii.[13] evesques suffragans:

l'evesque de Saint Jorge[14] de Lidde;
l'evesque de Bethleem;
l'evesque d'Ebron[15] c'on dit de Saint Abraham.

Et si a[16] .vi. abbés et un prior suffragant:

l'abbé de Montecion;[17]
l'abbé de la Latine;
l'abbé do Temple[18] Domini;
l'abbé de Mont[19] Olivete;
l'abbé de Jozaphat.[20]

A: fol. clxx^{r} cap. 261; **B:** fol. 211^{r-v} cap. 272; **C:** fols 216^{v}–217^{r}; **O:** fols 303^{v}–304^{r}; **V:** fol. cclxxi^{r-v} cap. 315; Beugnot, pp. 415–16, cap. 261; Edbury, *John of Ibelin*, pp. 110–11, cap. II (English trans. p. 191).

---

[a] For a discussion of the material in caps 226–33, see Edbury, *John of Ibelin*, pp. 177–87.

---

[1] arcevesques] ABV lack [2] A adds: Ce est assaveir; BV: C'est asavoir (V: assavoir) [3] Cesaire] B: Cesarie; V: Cezaire [4] Bethssem] AB: Bessan; O: Bethcem; V: Besam [5] Nazeret] A: Nazereth; B: Nazareth; O: Nasareth; V: Nazarel [6] de] ABV: dou [7] Beisseret] A: Bessereth; B: Besseret; O: Beisscereth; V: Bisereh [8] Babet] A: Babbat; B: Babbast; OV: Babath [9] Greus] AB: Grex; C: gens; V: Gres [10] translaté] C: tranlaté [11] et] C lacks [12] si a] BV lack [13] .iii.] B: .iiii. [14] Jorge] B: Grege [15] d'Ebron] B: d'Ebbron [16] si a] BV lack [17] de Motecion] A: del Mont de Syon; BV: de Monte Syon [18] Temple] A: Templi [19] Mont] C: Monte [20] Jozaphat] A: Josafas; B: Josaphas; O: Josaphath; V: Jozaphas

Et ceaus[21] .v. portent mitre et croce et anel.

L'abbé de Saint Samuel[22] qui est de la Monjoie[23] qui porte croce et non mitre ne anel.

Et le prior do Sepulcre qui porte mitre et anel et non croce.

Et si a[24] .iii.[25] abeeces suffragans:

l'abeece de Nostre Dame[26] la Grant;
l'abeece de Sainte Anne;
l'abeece de Saint Ladre.

Et l'arcevesque des Ermins qui est el royaume a sufragans .ii.[27]
L'arcevesque des Jacopins.[28]
Et le maistre de Saint Ladre des meseaus.

---

[21] ceaus] AB: ces [22] Samuel] A: Samoel [23] Monjoie] C: Mongoie [24] si a] BV lack [25] .iii.] B: .iiii. [26] Dame] B: Dama [27] Et l'arcevesque des . . . .ii.] A: Et si a suffragant l'arcevesque des Ermins qui est ou reiaume; B: Et a suffraganz l'acevesques des Ermins qui est ou reaume de Jerusalem et; V: Et l'arcevesque des Ermins qui est el royaume au suffragans. [28] Jacopins] BOV: Jacobins

*[227] Ci dit quans sufragans a l'arcevesque de Sur.

L'arcevesque de Sur a .iiii.[1] evesques suffragans:

l'evesque de Barut;[2]
l'evesque de Saiete;[3]
l'evesque de Belinas;
l'evesque d'Acre.[4]

A: fol. clxx^{v} cap. 262; **B:** fol. 211^{v} cap. 273; **C:** fol. 217^{r}; **O:** fol. 304^{r-v}; **V:** fol. cclxxi^{v} cap. 316; Beugnot, p. 416, cap. 262; Edbury, *John of Ibelin*, p. 111, cap. III (English trans. p. 192).

---

[1] .iiii.] O: .iii. [2] Barut] AOV: Baruth [3] Saiete] A: Seete; B: Sayete [4] d'Acre] A: d'Accre

***[228]** Ci dit quans suffragans a l'arcevesque de Cesaire.

L'arcevesque de Cesaire si[1] a .i. sufragant: ce est assaveir[2] l'evesque dou Sabast.[3]

A: fol. clxx^{v} cap. 263; **B:** fol. 211^{v} cap. 274; **C:** fol. 217^{r}; **O:** fol. 304^{v}; **V:** fol. cclxxi^{v} cap. 317; Beugnot, p. 416, cap. 263; Edbury, *John of Ibelin*, p. 111, cap. IV (English trans. p. 192).

---

[1] si] ABV lack [2] ce est assaveir] ABV lack [3] Sabast] B: Sebast

***[229]** Ci dit quans suffragans a l'arcevesque de Becem.[1]

L'arcevesque de Bethcem[2] qui est dit de Nazereth[3] si[4] a .ii. suffragans: l'evesque de Tabarie[5] et le prior de Monte Tabor.[6]

A: fol. clxx^{v} cap. 264; **B:** fol. 211^{v} cap. 275; **C:** fol. 217^{r}; **O:** fol. 304^{v}; **V:** fol. cclxxi^{v} cap. 318; Beugnot, p. 416, cap. 264; Edbury, *John of Ibelin*, p. 112, cap. V (English trans. p. 192).

[1] Becem] AB: Bessan; O: Bethcem; V: Besam [2] Bethcem] AB: Bessan; C: Betheem; V: Besam [3] Nazereth] AB: Nazareth; O: Nazath; V: Nazarel [4] si] ABV lack [5] Tabarie] AOV: Thabarie [6] Tabor] B: Thabor; O: Thabour; V: Tabar

[230] Ci dit de[1] l'arcevesque de Beissereth.[2] [a]

L'arcevesque dou Beissereth[3] ne fu grant tens a en mains de latins,[4] et por ce ne set l'on[5] ses sufragans.

A: fol. clxx[v] cap. 265; **B:** fol. 211[v] cap. 276; **C:** fol. 217[r]; **O:** fol. 304[v]; **V:** fol. cclxxi[v] cap. 319; Beugnot, p. 416, cap. 265; Edbury, *John of Ibelin*, p. 112, cap. VI (English trans. p. 192).

[a] C lacks rubric.

[1] de] AB: quanz suffraganz a; V: quans suffragans a [2] de Beissereth] A: dou Besseret; B: dou Bessereth; O: de Beiscereth; V: de Bethserech [3] Beissereth] A: Bessereth; B: Besseret; O: Bescereth; V: Bethserech [4] latins] B: crestiens [5] l'on] AB: on

***[231]** Ci dit quans sufragans a l'arcevesque dou Babeth.[1]

L'arcevesque dou Babeth,[2] qui est dit[3] de La Pierre dou Desert, si[4] a .i. sufragant: l'evesque de Faraon[5] qui orés[6] est a Monte Synai.[7]

A: fol. clxx^{v} cap. 266; **B:** fol. 211^{v} cap. 277; **C:** fol. 217^{r}; **O:** fol. 304^{v}; **V:** fol. cclxxi^{v} cap. 320; Beugnot, p. 417, cap. 266; Edbury, *John of Ibelin*, p. 112, cap. VII (English trans. p. 192).

[1] Babeth] A: Babbat; B: Babast; O: Babath; V: Babbath [2] Babeth] A: Babbat; B: Babast; OV: Babath [3] dit] B lacks [4] si] ABV lack [5] de Faraon] AB: dou Faran; O: d<e> Faraan; V: dou Fran [6] orés] B lacks [7] Monte Synai] A: Mont Synay; BO: Monte Synay; V: Mont Sinay

***[232]** Ci dit quans sufragans a l'evesque[1] de Saint Jorge[2] de Lidde.[3]

L'evesque[4] de Saint Jorge[5] de Lidde[6] si[7] a .v. sufragans:

l'abbé de Saint Joseph[8] d'Arimatie[9] qui est orés[10] apelés Rantis;[11]
l'abbé de Saint Abacu[12] de Cancie;[13]
le prior de Saint Johan l'Evangeliste;
le prior de Sainte Caterine[14] de Mont Gisart;[15]
l'abbeece des .iii. Ombres.[16]

A: fol. clxx^{v} cap. 267; **B:** fol. 211^{v} cap. 278; **C:** fol. 217^{r-v}; **O:** fols 304^{v}–305^{r}; **V:** fol. cclxxi^{v} cap. 321; Beugnot, p. 417, cap. 267; Edbury, *John of Ibelin*, p. 113, cap. VIII (English trans. p. 192).

---

[1] l'evesque] BV rubrics (fol. 17^{v}): l'arcevesque [2] Jorge] B: George et [3] Lidde] V: Lide [4] L'evesque] O: L'arcevesque [5] Jorge] B: Gorge [6] Lidde] V: Lide [7] si] ABV lack [8] Joseph] C: Josep [9] d'Arimatie] A: d'Abarimatie; B: d'Arimathie; O: d'Armacie; V: de Barmatie [10] orés] B lacks [11] Rantis] O: Ratis [12] Abacu] A: Abaccu; B: Abacuch; OV: Abacuc [13] Cancie] AV: Cantie; B: Quantie [14] Caterine] ABV: Katerine [15] Mont Gisart] AOV: Mongisart [16] Ombres] B: Umbres; C: Onbres; V: Hombres

***[233]** Ci dit quans suffragans[1] a l'evesque d'Acre.[2]

L'evesque d'Acre[3] si[4] a .ii. suffragans: la Trinité[a] et les[5] Repenties.

A: fol. clxx^{v} cap. 268; **B:** fol. 211^{v} cap. 279; **C:** fol. 217^{v}; **O:** fol. 305^{r}; **V:** fol. cclxxi^{v} cap. 322; Beugnot, p. 417, cap. 268; Edbury, *John of Ibelin*, p. 113, cap. IX (English trans. p. 193).

---

[a] CO read 'La Latine' for 'la Trinité'. For reasons for preferring the reading found in ABV, see Edbury, *John of Ibelin*, p. 185 note 33.

---

[1] V adds: y [2] d'Acre] A: d'Accre [3] d'Acre] A: d'Accre [4] si] AB lack; V: y
[5] B adds: nonains des

[234] Ci dit quantes baronies il i[1] a o reiaume de Jerusalem.

Il y a ou reiaume de Jerusalem .iiii. baronies.[2]

L'une si est[3] le[4] conté de Japhe et d'Escalone et la seignorie de Rames et de Mirabel et de Ybelin.

L'autre si[5] est le[6] princé de Galilee.

La tierce si est[7] la seignorie de Saiete[8] et de Cesaire et de Bethcen.[9]

La quarte[10] si est[11] se dient les uns le[12] conté de Triple et les autres dient[13] la seignorie dou Crac[14] de Mon Real[15] et de Saint Abraham. Mais je croi meaus selonc ce que je ais oi dire a ceaus c'on tenoit a sages qui devant nos[16] ont esté[17] que le[18] conté de Triple soit[19] la quarte baronie[20] dou reiaume,[21] que ne soit la seignorie dou Crac[22] de Mon Real[23] et de Saint Abraham, et aveuc ce[24] le me senble il plus[25] por .ii. raisons. Quar il n'i a nule[26] des autres baronies do dit reiaume qui ne doive[27] servise de .c. chevaliers et qui n'ait conestable et mareschal, ce que nule des autres seignories dou dit reiame[28] n'a. Et le[29] conté de Triple a bien .c.[30] chevaliers et si[31] a conestable et mareschal, ne la seignorie dou Crac[32] de Mon Real[33] et de Saint Abraham n'est que de .lx.[34] chevaliers, ne je n'oi onques dire que il i eust conestable ne mareschal, por quei il ne me senble mie qu'ele soit des .iiii. baronies.

A: fols clxx[v]–clxxi[r] cap. 269 (part); **B:** fols 211[v]–212[r] cap. 280 (part); **C:** fol. 217[v]; **O:** fol. 305[r–v]; **V:** fols cclxxi[v]–cclxxii[r] cap. 323 (part); Beugnot, pp. 417–18, cap. 269 (part); Edbury, *John of Ibelin*, pp. 113–14, cap. X (English trans. p. 193).

---

[a] For a discussion of the material in caps 234–5, see Edbury, *John of Ibelin*, pp. 164–76.

[b] In this chapter only BO present 'conté' and 'princé' as feminine nouns.

---

[1] i] A rubrics (fol. 9[v])B lack [2] A adds: et pluisors autres seignories; BV: et plusors (V: plusours) autres segnories (V: seignories) qui ont cort (V: court) et coins et justise [3] L'une si est] ABV: Des (V: Les) baronies l'une est (A: est l'une) [4] le] BO: la [5] si] ABV lack [6] le] BO: la [7] La tierce si est] A: La tierce; BV: L'autre est [8] Saiete] A: Seete; B: Saete [9] Bethcen] AB: Bessan; C: Betheen; V: Besan [10] La quarte] BV: L'autre [11] si est] A lacks [12] le] BO: la [13] dient] A: se dient si est [14] ABO add: et [15] Mon Real] A: Mont Reau; B: Mont Royal; O: Mont Real [16] qui devant nos] V: que devant [17] ont esté] B: furent [18] le] BO: la [19] soit] A: seit miaus; V: si est [20] baronie] B: seignorie [21] B adds: meax [22] ABO add: et [23] Mon Real] A: Mont Reau; B: Mont Royal; O: Mont Real [24] aveuc ce] B: meax [25] plus] B lacks; C: meaus [26] nule] C: nules [27] doive] B: doie [28] dou dit reiame] A lacks; B: dou reaume [29] le] BO: la [30] .c.] V: .ii.c. [31] et si] C: qui [32] ABO add: et [33] Mon Real] AO: Mont Reau; B: Mont Royal; O: Mont Real [34] .lx.] B: .xl.

***[235]** Ci orés la hautesse et la franchise que les .iiii. baronies ont plus que les autres homes dou roiaume.[a]

La[1] hautesse et[2] la franchise que les .iiii. baronies ont plus que les autres homes dou[3] reiaume de Jerusalem[4] est tel que nul des seignors[5] de ces .iiii. baronies ne doit ne ne peut[6] estre par l'assise ou[7] l'usage de cest roiaume[8] jugé de son cors ne de s'ennor ne de son fié, c'est a entendre des chozes de sa baronie, que par ces pers, c'est l'un des dis barons[9] par les autres se il defendre s'en viaut.[b] Et aucunes gens dient que le conestable et le mareschal[10] [c] dou reiaume pevent et doivent juger o les[11] barons devant dis, et le plus dient que ne[12] font. Ne je n'oi onques dire certainement qu'il peusent[13] ne deusent aveuc eaus juger. Et[14] en[15] chascune des dites[16] baronies doit avoir conestable et mareschal. Et tos les autres homes dou chief seignor dou reiaume pevent[17] estre jugiés par les homes de la haute cort dou[18] reiaume et par ceaus des autres cors[19] qui ont faite la ligece au chief seignor par l'assise, fors que tant que home qui n'est chevalier et fis de chevalier et de dame[20] né en leal mariage ne peut franc home jugier des choses desus[21] devisees,[22] se les[23] frans homes[24] ne le veulent soufrir de lor gré. Et les barons pevent tos les autres[25] jugier de

---

A: fol. clxxi[r] cap. 269 (cont.); **B:** fol. 212[r–v] caps 280 (cont.)–281; **C:** fols 217[v]–218[r]; **O:** fols 305[v]–306[r]; **V:** fol. cclxxii[r–v] cap. 323 (cont.); Beugnot, pp. 418–19, cap. 269 (cont.); Edbury, *John of Ibelin*, pp. 114–15, cap. XI (English trans. pp. 193–4).

---

[a] ABV have no chapter division and no rubric.
[b] B begins a new chapter here with the rubric: Ci dit coment le conestable et le seneschal doivent estre au jugement o les autres barons.
[c] For possible reasons for preferring the 'seneschau' (as AB) to 'mareschal', see Edbury, *John of Ibelin*, p. 170.

---

[1] La] ABV: Et la [2] et] V: de [3] V adds: dit [4] de Jerusalem] ABV lack [5] des seignors] C: seignor [6] ne ne peut] A lacks [7] ou] B: ne; V: et [8] de cest roiaume] B: dou reaume de Jerusalem [9] l'un des dis barons] C: l'une des dites baronies [10] conestable et le mareschal] A: seneschau et le conestable; B: conestable et le seneschau [11] C adds: autres [12] ne] BO: non/0 [13] peusent] A: peust [14] Et] ABV lack [15] en] O lacks [16] dites] B: avant dites; V: .iiii. [17] pevent] B: puet [18] C adds: dit [19] dou reiaume et . . . cors] B lacks [20] et fis de . . . dame] A: et de bone renomee et; B: ne de bone renomee ne [21] desus] B: devant [22] devisees] A: dittes [23] des choses desus devisees, se les] O: mais qu'il soit home de court [24] les frans homes] B: le frans home [25] OV add: homes

toutes choses, et les frans homes les autres aussi fors[26] les[27] barons. Et de toutes autres quereles peut chacun chevalier[28] jugier, mais que il soit home[29] de court, se il n'a esté ataint ou prouvé d'aucun des crimes par quei on pert vois et respons en court.

[26] fors] V: fois [27] C adds: autres [28] peut chacun chevalier] B: pevent chavaliers
[29] soit home] B: soient homes

***[236]** Ces sont les leus qui ont cort et coins et justise au reiaume de Jerusalem.[a]

Tout premierement le chief seignor[1] a court et coins et justise de qui est la haute court, et il la peut tenir en tos les leus ou il la viaut tenir el dit[2] roiaume.

En Jerusalem a court de borgesie et justise.
Et a Naples a court de borgesie et justise.
Et a[3] Acre[4] a court de borgesie et justise.[5]
Et au Daron a court de borgesie et justise.[6]

Le conte[7] de Jafe et d'Escalone a court et coins et justise.

Et a Japhe a court de borgesie et justise.
Et a Escalone a cort de borgesie et justise.
Et le seignor de Rames a court et coins et justise.
Et a Rames a cort de borgesie et justise.[8]

Le seignor[9] de Ybelin a court et coins et justise.

Et a Ibelin a court de borgesie et justise.

Le prince[10] de Gualilee a cort et coins et justise.

Et a Tabarie a court de borgesie et justise.
Et au Safet, qui est de la princé de Gualilee, a court de borgesie et justise.

La seignorie[11] de Saiete et de Beaufort a cort et coins et justise.

Et a Saiete a court de borgesie et justise.
Et a Beaufort a cort de borgesie et justise.

A: fols clxxi[r]–clxxii[r] cap. 270; **B:** fols 212[v]–213[r] cap. 282; **C:** fols 218[r]–219[v]; **O:** fols 306[r]–307[r]; **V:** fols cclxxii[v]–cclxxiii[v] cap. 324; Beugnot, pp. 419–21, cap. 270; Edbury, *John of Ibelin*, pp. 115–18, cap. XII (English trans. pp. 194–5).

---

[a] For a discussion of the material in cap. 236, see Edbury, *John of Ibelin*, pp. 155–62.

---

[1] A adds: dou reiaume [2] el dit] A: ou; B: ou devant dit [3] Et a] A: Et en; BV: En [4] BV add: et au Daron [5] Et a Acre . . . justise] O lacks [6] Et au Daron . . . justise] ABV lack [7] Le conte] AO: La conté [8] Et le seignor de Rames . . . justise] A lacks [9] Le seignor] O: La seignorie [10] Le prince] O: La princé [11] La seignorie] ABV: Le seignor

Le seignor[12] de Cesaire a cort et coins et justize.

Et a Cesaire a court de borgesie et justise.

Le seignor[13] de Betcem[14 b] a cort et coins et justise.

Et a Betcem[15] a cort de borgesie et justise.[16]

Le seignor dou Crac[17] de Mont Real a court et coins et justize.

Et au Crac a court de borgesie et justise.
Et a Mont Real a court de borgesie et justise.[18]

La seignorie[19] de Saint Abraham a cort et coins et justise.

Et a Saint Abraham a cort de borgesie et justise.
Et a Gerico[20] a court de borgesie et justise.
Et a[21] Bethleem a court de borgesie et justise.[22]
Et a Bet Gibelin[23] a cort de borgesie et justise.

Le seignor[24] de la Blancheguarde a court et coins et justise.

Et a Guadres[25] a court de borgesie et justise.

L'evesque de Saint Jorge de Lidde[26] a court et coins et justise.

Et a Lidde a court de borgesie et justise.

Le seignor d'Arsur a cort[27] et coins et justise.

Et a Arsur a cort de borgesie et justise.
Et a saint Jorge[28] do Sabast a court de borgesie et justise.
Et au Merle a court de borgesie et justise.[29]
Et a Chastiau Pelerin a cort de borgesie et justise.[30]

---

[b] O is missing an unnumbered folio, and so lacks the text from here until later in this chapter.

---

[12] Le seignor] AB: La seignorie [13] Le seignor] A: La seignorie [14] Betcem] AV: Bessan; O: Bethcen [15] Betcem] A: Bessant; V: Bessan [16] Le seignor de Betcem . . . justise] B lacks [17] ABV add: et [18] Et au Crac . . . justise] ABV reverse the order of these two lines. [19] La seignorie] ABV: Le seignor [20] Et a Gerico] A: Et en Jerico; B: En Gerico; V: En Jericob [21] Et a] AV: Et en; B: En [22] Et a Gerico . . . justise] ABV reverse the order of these two lines. [23] Et a Bet Gibelin] A: Et en Bethgibelin; B: A Bethgibelin; V: A Gibelin [24] Le seignor] ABV: La seignorie [25] Guadres] AV: Gadres; B: Gardres [26] Jorge de Lidde] B: George; V: Jorge [27] a cort] V lacks [28] Jorge] A: Johan; B: George [29] V adds: est de la seignorie de Cesaire [30] V adds: est de la seignorie de Cesaire

Le seignor de Caifas[31] a cort et coins et justise.

Et a Caifas[32] a court de borgesie et justise.

Le seignor de Caimont a cort et coins et justise.

Et au Caimont a court de borgesie et justize.

L'arcevesque de Nazeret[33] a cort et coins et justise.

Et a Nazeret[34] a cort de borgesie et justise.

Le seignor[35] dou fié dou conte Jocelin a court et coins et justise.

Et au Chasteau do Roy qui est de celui fié a cort de borgesie et justise.

Le seignor[36] d'Escandelon a cort et coins et justise.

Et a Escandelon a cort[37] de borgesie et justise.

Le seignor[38] de Sur a[39] cort et coins et justise.

Et a Sur a court de borgesie et justise.

Le seignor dou Toron[c] et de Belinas et de l'Asebebe[40] et de Chasteau Neuf a cort et coins et justise.

Et au Toron a court de borgesie et justise.
Et a Chasteau Neuf a cort de borgesie et justise.
Et a Belinas[41] a court de borgesie et justise.

---

[c] In A this entry reads as follows:
La seignorie dou Thoron a cort et coins et justise.
Et au Thoron a court de borgesie et justise.
La seignorie de Belinas a court et coins et justise.
Et a Belinas a court de borgesie et justise.
La seignori<e> de l'Assebebe a court et coins et justise.
Et a l'Aseebebe a court de borgesie et justise.
Et a Chastiau Neuf a court de borgesie et justise.

---

[31] Caifas] AV: Cayphas; B: Chayphas [32] Caifas] AV: Cayphas; B: Chayphas [33] Nazeret] AB: Nazereth; V: Nazarel [34] Nazeret] A: Nazareth; B: Nazereth; V: Nazarel [35] Le seignor] AV: La seignorie [36] Le seignor] ABV: La seignorie [37] et coins et justise. Et a Escandelon a cort] B lacks [38] Le seignor] A: La seignorie [39] A adds: orrés; B: orés; V: oré [40] l'Asebebe] B: l'Asabele [41] Et a Chasteau . . . Belinas] BV: Et a Belinas et a Chastiau (V: au Chasteau) Neuf

Le seignor de Barut a court et coins[42] et justise.

Et a Barut a court de borgesie et justise.

Et il peut estre que il i ait[43] aucune autre seignorie au roiaume qui ait court et coins et justise et aucun autre leu[44] qui ait cort de borgesie[45] et justise,[d] mais je ne suis oré menbrant d'autres que de ceaus que je ai ores[46] devisé.

Si vos[47] deviserai aprés les servises que chascun des seignors des dis leus doivent[48] au chief seignor dou reiaume ains que la terre fust perdue, et les autres gens do dit reiaume, et les aides que les yglises et les religions et les gens des cités et des chasteaus dou dit reiaume[49] devoient[50] et faisoient au chief seignor[51] quant il aloient[52] a ost bani contre les henemis de la foi por defendre le[53] dit roiaume.

---

[d] End of lacuna in O.

---

[42] et coins] C: de borgesie [43] ait] B: a [44] qui ait court . . . leu] V lacks [45] qui ait court et coins . . . borgesie] B: de Jerusalem qui a court et coins [46] orés] C: or [47] vos] ABV lack [48] doivent] O: devoient [49] dou dit reiaume] B lacks [50] devoient] C: doivent [51] AB adds: dou reiaume [52] aloient] BV: aloit [53] B adds: devant

***[237]** Ci orés les servises que les baronies[1] doivent au chief seignor do reiaume de Jerusalem.[a, b]

La baronie de la conté[2] de Jafe et d'Escalone de qui[3] Rames et Mirabel et Ibelin sont doit[4] .c. chevaliers, et la devise:

De Jafe .xxv.[5]
D'Escalone .xxv.
De Rames et de Mirabel .xl.
Et de Ybelin .x.

La baronie de la princé[6] de Gualilee doit .c. chevaliers,[7] et la devise:

De la terre desa le flum Jordain .lx.[8]
Et de la terre dela le flum Jordain .xl.

La baronie de Saiete de qui Beaufort et Cesaire et Bethcem[9] sont doit[10] .c. chevaliers, et la devise:

De Saiete et de Beaufort .l.[11]
De Cesaire .xxv.
Et de Betcem[12] .xxv.[13 c]

La seignorie dou Crac et de Mont Real et de Saint Abraham doit .lx. chevaliers, et la devise:[14]

A: fol. clxxii[r–v] cap. 271 (part) ; **B:** fol. 213[r–v] cap. 283 (part); **C:** fols 219[v]–220[r]; **O:** fols 307[r]–308[r]; **V:** fols cclxxiii[v]–cclxxiv[r] cap. 325; Beugnot, pp. 422–3, cap. 271 (part) ; Edbury, *John of Ibelin*, pp. 118–20, cap. XIII (English trans. pp. 195–6).

---

[a] Rubric in ABV: Ce est le servise que les barons et les autres gens dou reiaume (B: reaume; V: royaume) de Jerusalem doivent (A: deivent) au chief seignor dou dit reiaume (B: dou reaume; V: dou dit royaume).

[b] For a discussion of the material in caps 237–9, see Edbury, *John of Ibelin*, pp. 127–54.

[c] There is what appears to be an unresolvable discrepancy here: O and apparently C (see note 13) give the figures as in the text while ABV have 60 knights for Sidon and Beaufort, 25 for Caesarea and 15 for Bethsan.

---

[1] les servises que les baronies] C: que les baronies le servise que il [2] de la conté] C: dou conté [3] qui] C: quei [4] sont doit] V: son droit [5] .xxv.] ABV: .xxv. chevaliers (and similarly throughout this chapter) [6] de la princé] C: dou prince [7] .c. chevaliers] C: cehvaliers .c. [8] .lx.] B: .xl. [9] Bethcem] AB: Bessan; O: Bethceem; V: Besam [10] doit] V: droit [11] .l.] ABV: .lx. [12] Betcem] AB: Bessan; O: Bethcem; V: Besam [13] .xxv.] ABV: .xv.; C: .xv. (with an erasure of an 'x'(?) immediately before) [14] et la devise] A: la devise; O lacks

Dou Crac[15] de Monreal .xl.
Et de Saint Abraham .xx.

La seignorie dou conte Jocelin doit .xxiiii.[16] [d] chevaliers, et la devise:

Le Chasteau do Roi[17] .iiii.
Saint Jorge .x.
La terre de sire Jofrei le Tor[18] .vi.
La terre sire Phelipe le[19] Rous[e] .ii.
La chamberlainé[20] .ii.

C'est le servise que les evesques dou reiaume de Jerusalem[21] doivent, et la devise:[22]

L'evesque de Saint Jorge[23] de Lidde doit .x. chevaliers.
L'arcevesque[24] de Nazereth[25] doit .vi.[26] chevaliers.

Le Toron et le Maron doivent[27] .xviii.[28] chevaliers:[29]

Le Toron .xv.
Et le Maron .iii.

De Belinas, de l'Asebebe,[30] de Chasteau Neuf, quel servise il doivent ne sai je dire[31] la sertaineté por ce que il ne furent grant piece[32] a en la main[33] des crestiens.

---

[d] The figure of 58 knights given by V is obtained by adding on the knights owed for the bishoprics and for Toron and Maron.

[e] Named as Philip 'Rufus' or 'Ruffus' in the Latin charters (*RRH*, 477, 517, 525, 608), the form 'Le Rous' (AB) seems preferable to 'de Rous' (CO).

---

[15] ABV add: et [16] .xxiiii.] V: .lviii. [17] O adds: chevaliers [18] Jofrei le Tor] B: Giefroi le Tort; V: Jofrei le Tour [19] le] CO: de; V lacks [20] chamberlainé] C: chanberlainé [21] de Jerusalem] O lacks [22] C'est le servise . . . devise] ABV lack [23] Jorge] B: George [24] L'arcevesque] CO: L'evesque [25] Nazereth] AO: Nazareth; B: Nazeret; V: Nazarel [26] doit .vi.] B: .x. [27] doivent] A: deit; BV: doit [28] .xviii.] B: .vi. [29] A adds: la devise; BV: et la devise [30] de l'Asebebe] A: et de l'Assebebe et; B: et de l'Asabele et; O: de l'Ascebebe; V: et l'Asebebe et [31] dire] A: mie; BV lack [32] piece] V: tens [33] la main] AB: mains

***[238]** Ce sont les servises que les cités dou reiaume de Jerusalem[1] doivent.[a]

Jerusalem[2] deit .xli.[3] [b] chevaliers,[4] et la devise:

Lorens de Francleuc .iiii. chevaliers.[5]
Ancel[6] Babin .v. chevaliers.
La feme Johan Comain[7] .iiii. chevaliers.
Beimont[8] le Bufle .iii.[9] chevaliers.
Henri des Mons .i. chevalier.
Nicole d'Artais[10] .i. chevalier.
Simon fis de Pierre l'Ermin[11] .ii. chevaliers.
André dou Temple .ii. chevaliers.
Pierre d'Antill[12] .i. chevalier.
Amauri[13] le fiz Arnal[14] .iii. chevaliers.
Baudin[15] de Saint Gile .iii. chevaliers.
Simon de Betleem[16] .i. chevalier.
Engerant[17] de Pinqueigni[18] .ii. chevaliers.
Dame Guile[19] la feme Joan de Valence[20] .i. chevalier.
Pierre le Neir .ii. chevaliers.
Fouque le Neir .i. chevalier.[21]

A: fols clxxii^{v}–clxxiii^{v} cap. 271 (cont.) ; **B:** fols 213^{v}–214^{r} cap. 283 (cont.); **C:** fols 220^{r}–221^{r}; **O:** fols 308^{r}–310^{r}; **V:** fols cclxxiv^{r}–cclxxv^{v} caps 326–9; Beugnot, pp. 423–6, cap. 271 (cont.) ; Edbury, *John of Ibelin*, pp. 120–4, cap. XIV (English trans. pp. 196–8).

---

[a] AB lack rubric. Rubric in V: Ce est le servise que la sainte cité de Jerusalem doit.

[b] V has a total of 43, the discrepancy being accounted for by giving five instead of three to Beimont le Bufle.

---

[1] dou reiaume de Jerusalem] O lacks [2] Jerusalem] V: La sainte cité de Jerusalem [3] .xli.] V: .xliii. [4] chevaliers] BC: chevalier [5] .iiii. chevaliers] O: chevaliers .iiii. (and similarly throughout this chapter) [6] Ancel] V: Anciau [7] Johan Comain] B: Jahan Coman; C: Joan Gomans; O: de Johan Comain; V: de Johan Amauri [8] Beimont] A: Reimont; BV: Raimont [9] .iii.] V: .v. [10] d'Artais] A: d'Arrais; B: d'Artois [11] l'Ermin] O: l'Ermine [12] d'Antill] V: d'Ancil [13] Amauri] C: Aumauri [14] Arnal] V: Arnaut [15] Baudin] AB: Baudoyn; O: Baudoin; V: Bauduin [16] Betleem] AV: Belleem; BO: Bethleem [17] Engerant] AV: Engeram; B: Enguerran; O: En Gerrant [18] Pinqueigni] AV: Pinquegni; B: Pinguigni [19] Dame Guile] A: Dame Gille; B: Dame Gile; V: Gille [20] Valence] C: Valente; V: Lavence [21] Fouque le Neir] B: Fouques le Noir (this entry appears directly after 'La dame de Cesaire' in the list of knights from Nablus)

Ancel[22] le Borgne[23] .i. chevalier.
Hue le Petit .i. chevalier.
Les anfans Robert de Pinqueigni[24] .ii. chevaliers.
Estase[25] Patric .i. chevalier.

Ci dit quans chevaliers deit la cité de Naples.[c]
Naples deit .lxxxv.[26] [d] chevaliers, et la devise:

Le visconte .x. chevaliers.
Renier Rohart[27] et sa mere .viii. chevaliers.
Joan Belarnier .v. chevaliers.
Eude[28] dou Merle .iiii. chevaliers.
La feme Hugue[29] de Mimars .iiii. chevaliers.
La feme Bauduin[30] le Prince .iii. chevaliers.
La feme Beimont[31].i. chevalier.
Joan de Saint Bertin .iii. chevaliers.[32]
Constantin le frere Beimont[33] .i. chevalier.
Guillaume[34] le Queu[e] .i. chevalier.[35]
Henri le fis de Gui Rais[36] .i. chevalier.
La feme Bauduin[37] de Paris .i. chevalier.
Ysac de la Pissine[38].i. chevalier.
Rogier l'Ahne[39] .i. chevalier.
Aubri[40] dou[41] Roy .ii. chevaliers.
Bernart Fouchier[42].i. chevalier.
Richart de Nazareth[43] .i. chevalier.[44]

---

[c] AB lack this rubric. V begins a new chapter with the rubric: Ce est servise que la cité de Naples deveit.

[d] ABO all give the total number of knights as 85, although the tally is in fact 83. C errs in giving the total as 80 but lists 83. V gives the total as 82 which is the correction addition for the entries in this manuscript (omitting Guillaume le Queu).

[e] 'Guillaume' (AB) seems preferable to 'Guile' or 'Gile' (CO) as a man of this name is known from the 1180s. See Edbury, *John of Ibelin*, p. 147.

---

[22] Ancel] V: Anciau [23] Borgne] C: Borgue [24] Pinquegni] AV: Pinquegni [25] Estase] B: Wistace [26] .lxxxv.] C: .lxxx. [27] Rohart] C: Richart [28] Eude] BV: Heude [29] Hugue] ABV: Hue [30] Bauduin] A: Baudoyn; BO: Baudoin [31] Beimont] B: Bermont [32] .iii. chevaliers] A: .i. chevalier [33] Beimont] A: Raimont [34] Guillaume] C: Guile; O: Gile [35] Guillaume le Queu .i. chevalier] V lacks [36] Gui Rais] B: Guirrais; O: Guy Ray; V: Gerars [37] Bauduin] AB: Baudoyn; O: Baudoin [38] Pissine] A: Pessine; C: Pisine [39] l'Ahne] BV: l'Asne; O: l'Agnei [40] Aubri] V: Auberin [41] dou] AB: de [42] Fouchier] V: Foucher [43] Nazareth] C: Nazereth; V: Nazarel [44] B places this entry later, immediately before Henry l'Aubalestrier

Raimont[45] Babin .i. chevalier.
Bauduin[46] de Rotrines .i. chevalier.
La feme Robert Salibe .i. chevalier.[47]
La feme de Michel le Grant[48] .i. chevalier.
Girart[49] Passerel .i. chevalier.
Baudoin[50] de Ybelin[51] por .ii. lignees de bedouins en reconoissance do fié[52] .iiii. chevaliers.
La dame de Cesaire .ii. chevaliers.
Henri l'Aubalestrier[53] .i. chevalier.
Gui de Naples. i. chevalier.
Arnaut[54] de Triple .i. chevalier.
Renaut de Soison[55] .i. chevalier.
Amauri de Landré[56] .i. chevalier
Phelipe de Nazereth[57] .i. chevalier.
Jorge[58] l'Escrivain .i. chevalier.
Sire Balian[59] de Ybelin por la terre que il tient a Naples .xv. chevaliers.
Simon de Darcian .ii. chevaliers.[60]

Ci dit quans chevaliers doit la seignorie d'Acre.[f]
La seignorie d'Acre doit[61] .lxxx.[g] chevaliers, et la devise:[62]

Le conestable .x. chevaliers.
Balian[63] le Chanberlain .vii.[64] chevaliers.
Reimont d'Escandelion .vii. chevaliers.
Paien[65] le sire de Caifas[66] .vii. chevaliers.[67]

---

[f] AB lack this rubric. V begins a new chapter with the rubric: Ce est servise que la cité d'Acre devoit au royaume de Jerusalem.

[g] ABCO all give the total as 80 knights, although in no manuscript does the tally match that figure. The best available readings would appear to point to a total of 77. V gives the total as 72 knights, but lists only 70.

---

[45] Raimont] B: Ramont; V: Beymont [46] Bauduin] A: Baudoyn; BO: Baudoin [47] C places this entry one line above. [48] le Grant] V: Legent [49] Girart] A: Berrart [50] Baudoin] AB: Baudoyn [51] de Ybelin] V: d'Iblin [52] en reconoissance do fié] ABV lack [53] l'Aubalestrier] B: l'Arbalestrier; V: l'Abalestrier [54] Arnaut] B: Hernaut; V: Ernaut [55] Soison] AO: Saisson; B: Soissons; V: Saissons [56] Landré] V: la Landré [57] Nazereth] A: Nazeret; O: Nazaret; V: Nazarel [58] Jorge] B: Gerge [59] Balian] A: Belleem; B: Belyan; O: Baudoin; V: Ballian [60] B lacks this entry; V places it one line above. [61] doit] B lacks [62] et la devise] A: la devise; C lacks [63] Balian] A: Belleem; B: Belian; C: Balcan; O: Belyan; V: Bellian [64] .vii.] B: .vi. [65] Paien] B: Paion; V: Paiem [66] Caifas] A: Kayphas; BO: Cayphas; V: Caiphas [67] A places entry one line above.

Phelipe le[68] Rous[69 h] .i. chevalier.
La feme de Eude[70] .ii. chevaliers.
Girart Espinal[71] .i. chevalier.
Dame Gile .iii. chevaliers[72]
Guillaume de Malenbec[73] .ii. chevaliers.
La feme de Guillaume d'Antioche .i. chevalier.
Gautier de Saint Denis .ii. chevaliers.
Raoul de Nazareth[74] .i. chevalier.
Simon des Molins .i. chevalier.
Robert[75] Tabour .i. chevalier.[76]
Simon de la Guerre .i. chevalier[77]
Rocelin[78] dou Conte .i. chevalier
Jordain de Terremonde .i. chevalier.
Michel de Monte[79] Sinay .i. chevalier.
Drue[80] le frere Gilebert de Flouri[81] .i. chevalier.
Gautier de la Blanchegarde[82] .ix. chevaliers.
le sire de[83] la Blanchegarde .viii. chevaliers.
Alart[84] de Brie .i. chevalier.[85]
La feme d'Adam Coste .i. chevalier.
Gautier le Bel .i. chevalier.
Eudde de la Mide[86] .i. chevalier.
Macé[87] le fiz Rohart[88] .i. chevalier.
Gile de Calevadri[89] .iiii. chevaliers.[90]
Le seneschal .iiii. chevaliers.
Quastrin[91] Benoit[92] .ii. chevaliers.

[h] See chapter 237 note d.

[68] le] CO: de; V lacks [69] Rous] C: Rons [70] de Eude] A: Hubbe; BV: de Hubbe [71] Espinal] O: Ospinal [72] Girart Espinal .i. . . . chevaliers] ABV lack [73] Malenbec] A: Mallenbec; C: Molenbec; V: Malembec [74] Nazareth] A: Nazereth; B: Nasereth; C: Nazerel; V: Nazaret [75] Robert] ABV: Rohart [76] ABV place this entry two lines above. [77] Simon de la Guerre .i. chevalier] ABV lack [78] Rocelin] AB: Jocelin; O: Roucelin; V: Joselin [79] Monte] ABV lack [80] Drue] AV: Dreue; B: Dreu [81] Flouri] A: Florri; BOV: Flori [82] Blanchegarde] V: Blancegarde [83] le sire de] A: ce est assaveir; B: et la devise: mesire de [84] Alart] A: Arnaut; B: Ernaut [85] le sire de . . . chevalier] V lacks [86] Mide] A: Nudde; B: Nude [87] Macé] AB: Gacé; V: Massé [88] Rohart] AB: Robert; V: de Robert [89] Calevadri] A: Collavardi; B: Calanadri; O: Calavadri; V: Kalavadri [90] .iiii. chevaliers] V: .i. chevalier [91] Quastrin] AV: Gozertin; B: Gosertin; O: Gasterin [92] Benoit] ABV: Bonet

Ernaut[93] de Difoille[94] .i. chevalier.
Le visconte .i. chevalier.
Johan Haran[95] .i. chevalier.
Johan Darain[96] .i. chevalier[97] pelerin.[98]

Ci dit quans chevaliers doit la cité[99] de Sur.[i]
La seignorie de Sur deit[100] .xxviii. chevaliers, et la devise:[101]

Les Veneciens .iii. chevaliers.[102]
Simon de Martini[103] .iii. chevaliers.[104]
La feme de Guillaume[105] le Grant[106].ii. chevaliers.
La feme de Gobert Vernier[107] .i. chevalier.
Fouque de Falendes[108] .ii. chevaliers
Ancel le fis de[109] Charle[110] .i. chevalier.
Girart[111] Gazel[112] .ii. chevaliers.
Henri de Maschelin[113] .i. chevalier.
Adam dou Cerne[114] .i. chevalier.
Denis le fis de[115] Jofrei[116] .i. chevalier.
Raoul le Bouteillier[117] .ii. chevaliers.
Rogier Savari[118] .vii. chevaliers
Simon des Molins[119] .i. chevalier.
Rogier le Gaste Bouteillier[120] .i. chevalier.

[i] AB lack this rubric. V begins a new chapter with the rubric: Ce est le servise que la cité de Sur doit au royaume de Jerusalem.

[93] Ernaut] AV: Arnaut; C: Ernaurt [94] Difoille] A: Difolle; BV: Difole; O: Clufoille [95] Haran] AB: Harenc; O: Harang; V: Areng [96] Darain] AV: de Rains; B: de Reins; O: Darrains [97] chevalier] O lacks [98] pelerin] AV lack [99] cité] O: seignorie [100] deit] B lacks [101] et la devise] A: la devise; C lacks [102] .iii. chevaliers] B: .i. chevalier [103] Martini] AO: Marcini; B: Marcim; V: Martem [104] .iii. chevaliers] B: .i. chevalier [105] Guillaume] V: Guille [106] le Grant] ABV lack [107] Vernier] ABV lack [108] Falendes] AV: la Falaisse; B: Falaise; O: Valence [109] de] ABV lack [110] Charle] V: Charie [111] Girart] ABV lack [112] Gazel] V: Guazel [113] Maschelin] ABV: Machelin; C: Maschelai [114] dou Cerne] ABV: d'Arsur; O: dou Serne [115] de] BOV lack [116] Jofrei] B: Giefroi; V: Jofer [117] Bouteillier] A: Boutillier; B: Boutellier; O: Bouteiller; V: Boutelier [118] Savari] ABV: Sauveri [119] des Molins] ABV: dou Molin [120] Gaste Bouteillier] A: Gast Botillier; B: Gast Boutellier; O: Guaste Boteiller; V: Gasc Botelier

Le Daron[121] deit .ii. chevaliers, et la devise:[122]

Girart[123] de Doai[124] .i. chevalier.
Renaut de Mont Gisart .i. chevalier.

La seignorie de Baruth[125] deit[126] .xxi. chevalier.

La some des chevaliers[127] si est .vi.c. et .lxxvii.[j]

---

[j] BCO agree in giving the final total as 677. A, presumably as the result of a scribal error, has 667. In fact the totals from the lordships (chapter 237) and the knights from the royal domain add up to 675, although the subtotals themselves are sometimes incorrect. V gives the final total as 666 which is an accurate sum of the subtotals in that manuscript.

---

[121] Le Daron] V: La seignorie dou Daron si [122] et la devise] A: la devise; C lacks [123] Girart] V: Gerhart [124] Doai] B: Douay; V: Douai [125] Baruth] C: Barut [126] deit] V lacks [127] A adds: dou reiaume de Jerusalem; V: desus dit

***[239]** Ce[1] sont les aies que les yglises et les borges[2] doivent quant il i a grant besoing[3] en la terre dou reiaume de Jerusalem.[4]

Le patriarche de Jerusalem doit sergens .v.c.[5]
Le chapitle dou Sepulcre doit[6] sergens .v.c.
Jozafas[7] doit sergens .c.l.
Montecion[8] deit sergens .c.l.
Mont[9] Olivete deit sergens .l.
Temple[10] Domini deit sergens .l.[11]
La Latine deit sergens .l.
L'evesque de Thabarie[12] deit sergens .c.
L'abé de Monte Tabor[13] deit sergens .c.
La cité de Jerusalem deit sergens .v.c.
La cité d'Acre deit sergens .v.c.
La cité de Sur deit sergens .c.
La cité de Naples deit sergens .iii.c.
La cité de Cesaire deit sergens .l.
L'evesque de Bethleem[14] deit sergens .ii.c.
Rames et Ybelin et Mirabel[15] doivent sergens .c.l.
L'evesque de Saint Jorge[16] doit sergens .ii.c.
Arsur deit sergens .l.
L'evesque dou Sabast[17] deit sergens .c.[18]
L'evesque d'Acre deit sergens .c.l.
L'evesque Saint Abraham deit sergens .l.
L'arcevesque de Sur deit sergens .c.l.
L'arcevesque de Nazereth[19] deit sergens .c.l.
L'evesque de Saiete deit sergens .l.
L'arcevesque de Cesaire doit sergens .l.[20]

A: fols clxxiii^{v}–clxxiv^{r} cap. 272; **B:** fol. 214^{r-v} cap. 284; **C:** fol. 221^{r-v}; **O:** fol. 310^{r-v}; **V:** fols cclxxv^{v} cap. 330; Beugnot, pp. 426–7, cap. 272; Edbury, *John of Ibelin*, pp. 124–6, cap. XV (English trans. pp. 199–200).

---

[1] Ce] AV: Ces [2] borges] AO: borgeis; B: borgois; V: bourgois [3] il i a grant besoing] A: le grant besoin est [4] A adds: Et ce est la devise [5] sergens .v.c.] B: .v.c. serjanz (and similarly throughout this chapter) [6] doit] B lacks here and in most subsequent entries. [7] Jozafas] AO: Josaphas; BV: Josaphat [8] Montecion] B: Monte Syon; V: Monte Sion [9] Mont] O: Monte [10] Temple] B: Templi; C: Tenple [11] .l.] V: .c.l. [12] Thabarie] C: Tabarie [13] Tabor] V: Chabor [14] Bethleem] C: Betleem; V: Belleem [15] Ybelin et Mirabel] C: Mirabel et Ybelin [16] Jorge] A: Jorge de Lidde; B: George [17] Sabast] B: Sebast [18] .c.] B: .c.l. [19] Nazereth] B: Naseret; O: Nasareth; V: Nazarel [20] L'arcevesque de Cesaire . . . .l.] C lacks

Escalone deit sergens .c.l.
Jafe deit sergens .c.[21]
Le Lion[22] deit[23] sergens .c.[24]
Le Gerin[25] deit sergens .xxv.
Caifas[26] deit sergens .l.
Tabarie deit sergens .cc.

La some des sergens[27] si est .v.m. et .c. et .lxxv.[28] [a]

[a] ABCO agree in giving the total as 5,175. The actual total of what would seem to be the best readings from these four manuscripts is 5,025. V's total is 5,075, which is a correct sum of the figures provided in that manuscript.

[21] Jafe deit sergens .c.] V lacks [22] Lion] A: Lyon; O: Lyion; V: Leion [23] deit] B: qui doit [24] B places this entry at the end of the chapter. [25] Le Gerin] C: Le Gerill; V: Le Legerin [26] Caifas] A: Kayphas; BO: Cayphas; V: Cayphais [27] A adds: dessuz diz; B: desus diz; V: dessus dit [28] B adds: serjans

APPENDIX 1—ADDITIONS UNIQUE TO MS C

MS C has been used as the basis for this edition on the grounds that it appears to be the manuscript which most nearly preserves John's original text. It does, however, contain two significant additions, neither of which are to be found in any of the other manuscripts. One is an insertion into chapter 53 which deals with the principle that 'force de turs ne tot saisine'; the other is a chapter lifted from Philip of Novara (cap. 73 of Beugnot's edition) describing the right of first holder of a fief to return his fief to his lord and the mutual renunciation of homage. Both contain clear autobiographical references, and for this reason these additions would seem to be the work of John himself.[1]

1.1. Insertion into chapter 53

This chapter illustrates a feature of Latin Syrian succession law applicable when property is recovered from Muslim occupation, and the insertion explains how it was that Margaret of Ibelin, the widowed lady of Caesarea, acquired the lordship of Ibelin when it was ceded to the Christians in 1241 in preference to her nephew, Balian lord of Beirut (1236–47). Margaret received Ibelin because she was the daughter of Balian of Ibelin (died c. 1193) who had been the last in seisin before Saladin's conquest of 1187, whereas Balian's namesake and grandson was a more distant kinsman, even though he was the descendant of Balian's eldest child and in the male line. Margaret is here named as the author's aunt, and Balian of Ibelin as the author's grandfather.

In the sentence immediately before the insertion, MS C twice speaks of 'le fis et la fille' instead of simply 'le fis', the reading found in all the other MSS. The reader is thereby alerted to the possibility that the claimant might be a woman and so prepared for Margaret of Caesarea's successful assertion of her rights.

---

[1] For further discussion, see introduction pp. 11–12.

> Que par l'assise ou l'usage dou reiaume de Jerusalem on ne peut requere et avoir le fié, que on dit qui li soit escheu, que par celui qui derainement en ait esté saisi et tenant con dou sien, et le fis *et la fille* est plus droit heir dou pere a heriter en ce dont il a eu derainement la saisine et la teneure que ne soit le fis *ou la fille* de son ainsné fis.

The presence of these alterations argues strongly against the possibility that the passage in question had been in the original text and had then been omitted from the ancestor of all the other manuscripts.

*[1.1]

Et par ceste meismes raison ot madame m'ante, la grant dame de Cesaire madame Marguerite, la seignorie d'Ybelin devant son nevou, mesire Belian d'Ybelin le seignor de Baruth, qui estet fis de son ainsné frere. Car monseignor Belian, mon aiol, pere de la dite dame de Cesaire, morut le derain crestien saisi et tenant d'Ybelin, ne depuis Ybelin ne fu en mains de crestiens jusques au tens dou conte Gautier.[a] Et adons le requist la devant dite dame de Cesaire come fille et dreit heir dou dit monseignor Belian, seignor d'Ybelin, et le dit seignor de Baruth requeret come fis de l'ainsné fis. Et leurs fu retrait le fait dou Daron, si com il est devant dit,[b] et par ce ot ele la saisine et la teneure d'Ybelin.

C: fol. 53^{r-v} cap. 52 (part); Beugnot, pp. 108–9 cap. 65 (part).

[a] A reference to Walter of Brienne (died c. 1244) who had had custody of Jaffa since the late 1230s.

[b] See above cap. 53.

1.2. Additional chapter from Philip of Novara

Directly after chapter 129 is a chapter lifted from Philip of Novara's treatise (cap. 73 of Beugnot's edition). In Philip's version of this passage there is mention of John of Jaffa, and in MS C the phrase concerned is recast into the first person, reading 'je meismes m'en entremis moult' for 'moult s'en entremist le conte de Jaffe'. References to John of Ibelin 'the Old Lord' of Beirut are emended to include the words 'mon oncle' and to John of Jaffa's mother who is now described as 'ma mere'.

The chapter is lacking from MS B' of Philip of Novara, but is present in both A' and M. John's text would appear to have greater affinity with M than A'. In A' the text of the chapter continues, but in M this chapter ends where John of Jaffa's text ends and the later material in A' is treated as a separate chapter. Also in one place John's text agrees with M in speaking of the lord of Beirut whereas A' speaks of the lord of Sidon (see note i).

The chapter deals with two separate issues: the mutual renunciation of homage which John deals with much later (cap. 217), and the rights of the first holder of a fief to return the fief to the grantor, a topic which is discussed at length in the chapter that follows (cap. 130).

*[1.2] Ci orrés des fiés que les seignors donent et que cil meismes a cui il les donent les rendent et quitent as seignors.

Nos avons tous jors oy dire et veu l'avons de pluisors que le conquereor dou fié le puet rendre et quiter au doneor en tel maniere que jamais il ne ses heirs ne recovreront celui fié. Et ensi avint de messire Raoul de Tabarie qui rendi et quita au prince un fié que il li avoit doné a Triple et dist que il voloit que chascun seust que il ne ses hoirs n'avroient droit en celui fié aprés ce que il qui estoit conquereor l'avoit rendu et quité au doneor.[a] Et dit l'on que le prince recut le fié et aprés dist a messire Raoul: 'Puis que vos m'avés quité le fié, quités moi la foi dont je vos sui tenus.' Et messire Raoul respondi: 'Je vos quit par si que vos quités moi.' Et le prince dist: 'Or vos ai je engignié, car celui qui avant quite se mesfait.' Et messire Raoul respondi: 'La promesse de la foi est ou contenement et en la devise de l'omage, et l'omage est por le fié, et puisque l'en quite le fié l'on puet bien quiter la foi qui est por le fié et toutes dettes puet l'on quiter, et se mesfait y a il est de vos. Quar vos avés reconeu que vos m'avés engignié, et si tost com home qui doit foi a autre le bee a engignier, il se mesfait en l'ore.' Le prince respondi paroles que je ne sai mie bien.

Aprés ce est avenu pluisors fois por les paroles devant dites et por autres que moult de gens se guardent de quiter avant. Et en Chypre meismes vi ge avenir au tel fait de plusors et nomeement d'un chevalier d'outremer qui avoit nom sire Menacier a qui le roi dona le Lumna[b] et il l'a rendi et quita puis au roi en plaine court et s'en ala hors de la terre. Aprés vint et en plaidea au roi en plaine court et fu pozé sur cort a recorder ce qui en avoit esté et esguarder ce qui en devoit estre. La court recorda que messire Menacier avoit rendu et quité le fié au roi et esguarda que lui et ses heirs l'avoient perdu a tousjors. Monseignor de Baruth mon oncle[c] fu a cel esguart

---

C: fols 105^{r}–106^{r} cap. 129. Cf Philip of Novara **A':** fols ccxxxviii^{r}–ccxxxix^{r}; **M:** fols 133^{v}–135^{v}; Beugnot, pp. 543–4 cap. 73 (part).

---

[a] See cap. 217 for a further reference to this incident concerning Ralph of Tiberias and Prince Bohemond IV which apparently dates to the 1200s.

[b] For 'le Lumna', the readings of A' ('Limniate') and M ('Lemenate') i.e. Limnatis (north of Limasssol) are probably to be preferred, although 'Lumna' could perhaps be a blundered reading for Limnia (near Salamis).

[c] Here and subsequently A'M lack 'mon oncle'.

et dist que ce avoit il oy et seu dou roi Aimeri[d] et de messire Raoul de Thabarie qui moult sorent d'us et d'assises et de raisons et moult furent soutils et sages de naturel sens et a lui meismes sembloit il bien raison que chascun puet rendre ce que l'on li avoit doné et dont la saisine n'estoit onc partie de lui. Et sans faille la maniere des dons des fiés est tel que le seignor done a lui et a ses heirs aprés lui et ensi est il en moult de preveliges, et se il n'est escrit si est il entendu. Quar en la vie dou conquereor n'a riens l'eir, mais puisque il est venu a aucun des heirs celui nel puet mie rendre. Car aussi bien sont heirs les autres qui vienent aprés lui com il est, sauf ce que il doit tenir por ce que il est premier, et puisque la saissine[e] est tranlatee a l'eir les autres heirs ne poent estre desherités se par autre assise ne le sont. Mais dou conquereor au doneor est il ensi jugié come il est dessus dit. Et ensi avint de maistre Ogier qui rendi et quita son fié au roi, et aprés y ot moult de prieres por recovrer le. Et je meismes m'en entremis moult, por ce que maistre Ogier avoit moult servi madame ma mere et moi[f] au tens des Longuebars, et par mi tout ce ne vost souffrir monseignor de Baruth mon oncle[g] que le roi rendist le fié a maistre Ogier ains li redona tout de noviau por ma priere.[h] Et monseignor de Baruth[i] disoit que le conquereor le puet ausi bien rendre et quiter a l'eir dou doneor come au doneor meismes puis que la premiere saisine n'estoit translatee ne partie dou conquereor, et je meismes entens[j] que monseignor de Baruth mon oncle[k] disoit raison. Mes je ne le vi onques avenir.[l]

---

[d] Following MS A' (cf. M: 'Hemenry') in preference to MS C: 'Amauri'.
[e] Following MS A' (cf. M: 'la saizine') in preference to MS C: 'l'assise'.
[f] For 'je meismes m'en . . . moi' A' reads: 'moult s'en entremist le conte de Jaffe pour ce que maitre Ogier aveit moult servi li et sa mere'; M: 'moult s'entremist le comte de Jaffe por ce que messire Roger avoit moult servy lui et sa mere'.
[g] See note c.
[h] For 'ma priere' A' reads 'la proiere dou conte'; M: 'le prierre du comte'.
[i] For 'Baruth' A', but not M, reads 'Saeste', i.e. Sidon.
[j] Here and in the next sentence the first person is repeated from Philip of Novara.
[k] See note c.
[l] Ogier's appeal evidently dates to the period between the civil war in Cyprus ('tens des Longuebars': 1229–33) and the death of the 'Old Lord' of Beirut in 1236. Menacier's case probably belongs to the same period.

APPENDIX 2—ADDITIONS UNIQUE TO MS O

The Oxford Bodleian: MS Selden Supra 69 (MS O) is closely related to MS C. Indeed, of all the medieval manuscripts of John's text, these two have the closest affinity. It does, however, contain one additional chapter not found in any other manuscript. This is inserted after chapter 32 and is taken from Philip of Novara (cap. 48 of Beugnot's edition). It is present in MSS A' and M but lacking in MS B'.

The reference to Saladin's capture of Jerusalem is an allusion to the doctrine of the *Letres dou Sepulcre*, a legal fiction not found in John's original text but incorporated from Philip of Novara into the *z* recension (see below appendix 3.1.1). It ought also to be noted that this insertion makes no attempt to mask the fact that Philip was writing with the procedures of the High Court of Cyprus, and not that of Jerusalem, in mind.

***[2.1]** Quant aucun dit que une choze est assise et l'autre la desdit, coment la doit prover et ques est la preuve.[a]

L'en[1] entens que celui qui dit que ce est assise doit dire que les assises sont ceues et provees par usage. Quar ce qui est usé en la court disant que ce est assise, et ce que l'on en a oy et entendu des sages homes qui jadis furent et qui asés sorent dou fait de la court, ce tient l'on por assise. Ne autrement ne peut l'on saver ne prover les assises, quar eles ne[2] furent en escrit ne en garde puis que Salahadin prist Jerusalem. Et celui qui dit que ce est assise ou autel fait ou senblant d'autel est usé come assise ou roiaume[3] de Chipre, ou l'on tient les us et les assises dou roiaume de Jerusalem, dont il requiert au seignor et a touz ceaus de la court qui la sont se il ont veu autel cas come celui est delivrer et user come assise, que il li delivrent cestui si come il li sont tenu. Et ce sil de la court qui la sont ne sont remenbrant qu'il aient[4] ce veu, il est prest dou prover tout enssi com la court esgardera que prover le doie. Qu'enssi est usé et fait en la court dou roiaume de Jerusalem et la court de Chipre, et, provant ce, il viaut et requiert qu'ensi soit fait soit assise ou usage, quar ausi bien a l'on juré les us et les costumes[5] come les assises. Or vos ai dit ce que le requerant peut dire, aprés vos dirai ce que a moi senble, sauf ce que je oye[6] meaus dire et je le coneuce, volentiers m'acorderoie. Se la court entent que ce soit usé ce con le requerant dit ele doit dire au seignor: 'Sire vos et nos avons juré de tenir les bons us et les assise dou roiau<me> de Jerusalem, et nos entendons que ce que le requerant dit est usé. Dont nos vos disons qu'ensi le devés[7] faire fornir.' Et se la court qui la est n'est clere qu'ensi soit, toutes voies por ce que le requerant a dit que il est prest de prover par l'une court ou par l'autre tout enssi con la court esgardera, la court doit dire au requerant: 'Vos avés ofert de prover ou par l'une court ou par l'autre. Coneue chose est que vos ne poés

---

O: fols 30r–31r. Cf Philip of Novara **A':** fols cclvir–cclviir cap. 81; **M:** fols 157v–159r; Beugnot, pp. 523–4 cap. 48.

---

[a] In sixteenth-century hand at the head of fol. 30r: Hoc capitulum non est autoris huius operis sed sumptum ex opere Philippi De Navara.

---

[1] L'en] A'M: Je [2] 'ne' interlined. A' lacks [3] A' adds: de Jerusalem et [4] aient] O: aieient [5] et les costumes] A' lacks [6] oye] O: ooye [7] devés] A': devons

amener la court dou roiaume de Jerusalem en nostre court prover vostre dit se ele ni vosist venir de son gré. Ne la nostre meimes ne poés vos acenbler por prover. Dont nos requerons au seignor qu'il esforce sa court au plus que il porra a tel jor, et quant nos serons ensemble se nos poons le fait delivrer nos le deliverons, et se nos n'en soumes cler et nos entendons que nos le puissons estre par la court dou roiaume de Jerusalem nos y manderons. Ne autrement ne nos senble que vostre preuve puise aler avant ne cheyr en autre droit.'

APPENDIX 3—THE 'Z' RECENSION

Between the mid-1260s when John finished the original version of his treatise (whence MSS C and O) and the completion of the Venice Marciana: MS fr. App. 20 (= 265) (MS A) in about 1290, the work was subjected to substantial revisions to produce a recension that Grandclaude dubbed '*z*'.[1] It was from this recension that MSS A, B (Paris BN: MS fr. 19026) and V (Rome Vatican: Cod. vat lat. 4789) are all ultimately derived. It has to be stressed from the outset that no manuscript copy of '*z*' exists, and that A, B and also V all represent further developments. (V presents particular problems as its text is clearly 'contaminated' by readings taken from a text related to CO.) Even so, by comparing AB and V with C and O, it is possible to gain a clear picture of the changes introduced in the course of these revisons.

Like MS C, MS A was a product of the Acre scriptorium, and has been dated to shortly before the city's destruction in 1291. MS B evidently dates to the fourteenth century and is likely to have been of Cypriot provenance, while MS V is thought to belong to the early fifteenth century. All three manuscripts have characteristics that distinguish them from C and O. There are countless instances in which MSS ABV or AB share readings which differ from those to be found in C and O, and occasionally their readings seem preferable.[2] There are seven instances in which some of the longer chapters in CO are split into two or more,[3] and two instances in which material that forms two chapters in CO is combined into one.[4] Several chapters have new rubrics.[5] Occasionally, as in chapters 216 and 220 there are significant alterations to the text. In a few instances the order

[1] Grandclaude, 'Classement sommaire', pp. 446–50, 475.

[2] For example, in cap. 172, where AB list surrendering one's city or fortress (*chastiau*) to the enemy as something meriting confiscation and disinheritance, CO speak of surrendering one's city or horse (*cheval*).

[3] Prologue and caps 1, 168, 175, 176, 178, 180.

[4] Caps 234–5, 237–8.

[5] Prologue and caps 1, 178, 201, 205, 209, 210, 211, 213, 214, 220, 221, 225, 237.

of chapters has been altered. By placing chapters 197–8 after chapter 203 and chapter 213 after chapter 184, the author of the '*z*' recension made a sensible rearrangement, but the decision to move the description of the coronation from its logical place near the end (caps 219–20) to a new position just before chapter 1 broke up the natural flow of the argument from the Prologue to the opening chapter as found in CO, and deprived the concluding chapters (221–39) of their coherence. Moving this material also entailed deleting chapter 218 and rewriting the end of the Prologue.[6] In CO the prologue comprises a well-rounded survey of the history of the legal system ending with a prayer and pious exhortations. In AB it is split into five chapters, with the result that the sense of unity is lost, while a passage taken from Philip of Novara describing the *Les Letres dou Sepulcre* is awkwardly inserted into the section dealing with the legal provision for the Syrian community in the kingdom.[7]

What is more, '*z*' contains twenty-one extra chapters, of which eleven were lifted or adapted from Philip of Novara,[8] while nine have not been identified as coming from any extant source.[9] The twenty-first chapter, which in MS A serves as the conclusion to the whole treatise, also contains some material from Philip of Novara.[10] The execution of some of these insertions, for example the three chapters that are stuck in after chapter 28, is clumsy in the extreme.[11]

In preparing these chapters for publication MS A has been taken as the base, but, on those occasions when the readings in MSS B and V agree with those found in the Philip of Novara manuscripts, they have been preferred.

[6] Below 3.1.2.
[7] Below 3.1.1.
[8] Below 3.2, 3.3, 3.5, 3.7, 3.8, 3.10, 3.11.
[9] Below 3.4, 3.6, 3.9, 3.12.
[10] Below 3.13.
[11] Below 3.2. For further discussion of the authorship and historical context of the 'z' recension, see above pp. 12–17, 21–3.

3.1. Insertions into the Prologue

3.1.1. *Les letres dou Sepulcre*

In the '*z*' recension, John's Prologue was split into five chapters, and this passage inserted into what now became chapter four (see Prologue note g). It is clearly based on part of Philip of Novara chapter 47 (present in MSS A' and M but not B'), but is adapted rather than copied verbatim. Other material from the same chapter is included in the chapter edited below as appendix 3.13.

The original version of John's treatise made no reference to the *Letres dou Sepulcre*, but it should be noted that an allusion to this doctrine found elsewhere in Philip's treatise is also to be found in the sole additional passage inserted into MS O (appendix 2.1).[1]

3.1.2. *The conclusion to the Prologue*

In '*z*' the original prologue is divided into five chapter, and the two chapters describing the coronation were re-positioned (caps 219, 220) directly after the end of the fifth chapter. In anticipation of this change, the end of prologue (= '*z*' cap. 5) is rewritten, and the passage edited here begins in mid sentence (see Prologue note i). In MS V caps 219 and 220 were put back in their original position, and that would seem to explain why that MS has a truncated version of the passage edited here (see apparatus note 4).

[1] For a discussion, see P.W. Edbury, 'Law and Custom in the Latin East: *Les Letres dou Sepulcre*', in *Intercultural Contacts in the Medieval Mediterranean*, ed. B. Arbel (= *Mediterranean Historical Review*, 10) (London, 1996), pp. 71–9. I no longer hold to the view expressed in this article that John himself was responsible for this insertion.

*[3.1.1]

Aprés ce que le Duc Godefroi et les autres qui aprés lui furent seignors et rois dou dit roiaume orrent les assises et les usages establis, et les .ii. dites cours si come il est avant dit,[1] lesquels assises et usages et[2] costumes estoient escrites chascune par soi de grant letres tornees, et la premiere letre dou comencement estoit enluminee d'or, et totes les rubriches estoient escrites[3] vermeilles. Et si estoient aussi bien les us et les[4] assises des borgeis come de la haute court. Et en chascune chartre avoit le seau et le seignau dou rei et dou patriarche aussi et dou visconte de Jerusalem. Et les apeloit on 'les Letres dou Sepulcre' porce qu'elles estoient ou Sepulcre en une grant huche. Et quant aucune fois avenoit que aucun debat estoit en la court d'aucune assise ou usage par quoi il covenist[5] que l'on veist[6] l'escrit, l'on en[7] ovroit la huche ou estoient celles letres a mains de[8] .ix. persones. Par estovoir covenoit que le rei i fust ou aucun de ces haus homes en leuc de lui, et .ii. de ces homes liges, et le patriarche ou le prior dou Sepulcre en leuc de lui, et .ii. chanoines, et le visconte de Jerusalem, et .ii. jurés de la court des borgeis. Et ensi estoient les dites assises et usages et costumes faites et gardees, et aprés ce le peuple des Suriens[9] vindrent . . .

A: fol. ii^{v} cap. 4 (part); **B:** fol. 34^{v} cap. 4 (part); **V:** fol. iii^{r-v} cap. 3 (part); Beugnot, pp. 25–6 cap. 4 (part). Cf Philip of Novara **A':** fols ccxxx^{v}–ccxxxi^{r} (part); **M:** fols 117^{r}–118^{v}; Beugnot, pp. 521–2 cap. 47 (part).

---

[1] il est avant dit] BV: est avant devisé [2] et usages et] A: usages [3] A adds: chascune par soi [4] us et les] A: unes et les autres [5] covenist] A: covenoit [6] veist] B: l'eust [7] en] A: n'en; B lacks [8] de] B: devant [9] Suriens] B: serjans; V: sergens

***[3.1.2]**

Et por ce que il me senble que ains que je parole en cest livre des assises et des usages ne des plais de la haute court dou dit roiaume, que je doie avant parler dou roi qui est chief seignor dou dit roiaume, et dire ou il doit estre coronés, et que il doit faire au patriarche ainz que il li met la corone[1] el chief et qu'il[2] le doie coroner, et, quant il li a mise la corone el chief, quei le patriarche li doit faire, et quei totes les genz dou roiaume aprés ce qu'il est coronés li doit faire.[3] Et quel qu'il ou le chief seignor dou dit roiaume[4] tot[5] ne sot il coronés,[6] les barons et les autres riches homes qui ont ou[7] roiaume court et coins et justise doivent estre, et quels les juges et les plaideors de leur cours, deviserai ge au comencement de mon livre ce que je ais enpris a dire dou rei et des avans dis.

A: fol. iii^{v} cap. 5 (part); **B:** fol. 35^{v} cap. 5 (part); **V:** fol. iv^{v} cap. 4 (part); Beugnot, p. 28 cap. 5 (part).

---

[1] corone] A: core [2] qu'il] B: qui [3] li doit faire] A lacks [4] et dire ou . . . roiaume] V lacks [5] dou dit roiaume tot] B: soit tout [6] B adds: et [7] BV add: dit

3.2. Insertion following chapter 28

These three chapters are drawn from Philip of Novara (cap. 11 of Beugnot's edition) and concern property disputes, and in particular the *assise de teueure* and the *assise de vente*. Whereas the text of the chapter is reproduced, here as elsewhere the rubrics are new. Two of the Philip of Novara MSS, A' and B', present the whole of this material as a single chapter without a break, but MS M has a new chapter beginning at 3.2.3.

***[3.2.1]** Si dit[1] que, se[2] la carelle est d'irritage qui est dedenz ville, coment l'on se deit defendre.

Et se il avient[3] que la carelle seit[4] d'irritage[5] dedenz ville close ou desclose, le fuiant peut respondre en tel maniere qu'il a celui irritage eu et tenus quitement et[6] en pais an et jor et plus, et por tant en[7] viaut demorer quittez et en pais[8] par l'assise de la teneure, se la court l'esgarde, et[9] mete son retenaill. Et se le clamant dit que ce est de son fié et que fié ne se peut vendre ne aliener que par l'assise des ventes ou[10] par partie de servise, c'il y a servise pluissors,[11] et de cestui irritage n'i[12] ot onques vente faite,[13] et por tant le viaut aveir, se la court l'esgarde, sauf[14] son retenaill, le fuiant respondra que chascun peut dire: 'Ce est de mon fié, et ce[15] ne se peut vendre que par l'assise'. Bien se gart qui l'alienera,[16] vendera ou donra, et la court qui le soufrira. Car l'assise est tote paree qui dit que por teneure d'an et de jor quitement et en pais a l'on desrainié tel maniere d'irritage come il[17] est dit devant. Et ce ciaus a qui l'on vent ou done ou aliene irritage dedenz ville ne pevent[18] pas saveir ce il est de fié ou non, celui qui le vent ou aliene s'en deit garder par la fei qu'il deit au seignor. Car ce qui est de fié ou de servise ne deit il[19] pas aliener franchement, ne la court ou il est aliené ne le deit soufrir, ce ce est de fié, por quei elle[20] le sache. Et ce il peut estre seu dedens an et jor,[21] bien peut estre rapelé, et por ce fait on la[22] seurté de garentir an et jor.[23] Bien est donc chose clere que ce l'an et le jor passe que l'irritage ne seit chalongié que l'assise de la teneure le delivre tot outre, ce celui qui a tenu l'irritage n'est parent de celui qui le requiert. Mais[24] le parenté brisse l'assise par tot mais que en .ii. leus tant soulement, ce est assaveir, quant celui qui

---

A: fols xviii^{v}–xix^{r} cap. 38; **B:** fol. 51^{r-v} cap. 39; **V:** fol. xxiv^{r}–xxv^{r} cap. 35; Beugnot, pp. 63–4, cap. 38. Cf. Philip of Novara **A':** fol. ccix^{r-v}; **B':** fol. 239^{r-v} cap. 9 (part); **M:** fols 79^{r}–80^{v}; Beugnot, p. 484 cap. 11 (part).

---

[1] Si dit] V lacks [2] que se] A rubric (fol. 1^{v}) V: quant [3] Et se il avient] V: Mais se il avient aucune fois [4] seit] B: est [5] V adds: qui soit [6] et] A lacks [7] en] A lacks [8] en pais] V: delivrés [9] et] B lacks [10] ou] V: nom pas [11] pluissors] V: de plusours chevaleries [12] cestui irritage n'i] V: cest heritage ne [13] V adds: pas l'assise ne dou par servise [14] sauf] V: et mete [15] ce] V: fié [16] A adds: ou [17] il] A lacks [18] pevent] AV: peut [19] il] A: l'on [20] elle] V: il [21] estre seu dedens an et jor] A: ce devant an et jor demander [22] on la] B: on; V: l'on [23] A adds: et [24] Mais] B: Car

a tenu l'irritage an et jor, l'a eu[25] d'escheete de son pere ou de sa mere qui en seit[26] mort saissi et tenant, et que il l'ait tenu devant sa mort an et jor veant et oiant celui qui orres le requiert. Aprés ce ne vaut riens le parenté[27] contre l'assise. Tot autretel est l'autre point, ce dient aucunes genz, mes je ne sui mie si bien membrant come de cestui.[28] Car ce celui qui tient irritage[29] an et jor voiant et oiant le pere ou la mere de celui qui le requiert,[30] ce l'irritage muet et escheit de celle part dont[31] le pere ou la mere dou requerant vint, et[32] celui ou celle a qui l'irritage peut escheir morust sanz ce qu'il le requeist ne eust,[33] le fiz ne peut riens aveir par parenteis contre[34] l'assise.

[25] eu] V: tenu [26] seit] V: sont [27] riens le parenté] A: le parenté neent [28] mes je ne . . . cestui] B: et bien le cuit; V: mais je ne sui mie si cler com de l'autre [29] irritage] B: l'eritage; V: l'eritage l'a tenu [30] A adds: et [31] dont] A: ou [32] et] A: ou [33] ne eust] V lacks [34] contre] B: encontre

***[3.2.2]** Si dit que por teneure que l'on face[1] de merme d'aage,[2] an ne li griege.[3]

Et ce il est chose[4] que celui ou celle[5] qui requiert l'irritage a esté merme d'aage en tant come l'autre l'a tenu, et il dedenz an et jor aprés ce qu'il fu en son dreit aage est venuz a sa[6] requeste, bien peut requerre,[7] et de tant de tens come il fu merme d'aage la teneure de son aversaire ne li griege.[8]

A: fol. xix^{r} cap. 39; **B:** fol. 51^{v} cap. 40; **V:** fol. xxv^{r} cap. 36; Beugnot, p. 65, cap. 39. Cf. Philip of Novara **A':** fols ccix^{v}–ccx^{r}; **B':** fol. 239^{v} cap. 9 (part); **M:** fol. 80^{v}; Beugnot, pp. 484–5 cap. 11 (part).

---

[1] B adds: d'eritage; V: de heritage [2] merme d'aage] A rubric (fol. 2^{r}) V: mermia [3] an ne li griege] B: ne li griege rienz; V lacks [4] Et ce il est chose] V: Mais se il avient [5] ou cele] AV lack [6] sa] A lacks [7] V adds: l'eritage [8] B adds: neent

***[3.2.3]** Si dit que por teneure que l'on face[1] de forspayssé ne li griege.[2]

Aussi[3] dit l'on que se[4] aucun home, ce il[5] est forspayscé, et il revient et il requiert aucun irritage que aucun autre ait tenu an et jor,[6] aucunes genz veulent dire que l'assise de la teneure ne li griege por ce qu'il esteit forspayscé, et que l'autre n'a[7] tenu[8] lui veant et oiant. Et[9] pluisors genz dient que la teneure vaut bien en celui point, et que por ce fu establie si longue espace come de an[10] et de jor, et que en tant de tens peut l'on bien venir d'outremer qui veut.[11] Et je ais oy dire[12] que ceste assise fu faite espessiaument por ciaus qui avoient les irritages ou reiaume de Jerusalem. Que[13] quant la terre estoit en mauvais point il aloient outremer, et l'on n'aveit qui defendist[14] la terre; et quant il savoient bones novelles, si[15] revenoient. Et por ce fu establi l'an et le jor. Et l'on dit que aucune feis le faisseit on des fiés meismes, et aprés demorra[16] et torna as irritages l'assise. Et ce celui qui estoit forspayscé en[17] viaut requerre esgart,[18] aveir le peut.[19]

A: fol. xix^{r} cap. 40; **B:** fol. 51^{v} cap. 41; **V:** fol. xxv^{r-v} cap. 37; Beugnot, p. 65, cap. 41. Cf. Philip of Novara **A':** fol. ccx^{r}; **B':** fol. 239^{v} cap. 9 (part); **M:** fols 80^{v}–81^{r}; Beugnot, p. 485 cap. 11 (part).

---

[1] Si dit que . . . face] B: Ci dit que por teneure que l'on face d'eritage; V: Ne (V rubric fol. 4^{r}: Se) i a pour teneure de heritage [2] B adds: riens [3] Aussi] V: Enci [4] B adds: il avient que [5] aucun home, ce il] V: celui qui requiert l'eritage [6] V adds: et [7] n'a] V: l'a [8] A adds: l'irritage [9] Et] BV lack [10] de an] V: l'an [11] veut] A: vodra [12] V adds: sovent [13] Que] B: Et; V: Car [14] defendist] V: deffendoit [15] si] A: il [16] A adds: des fiés [17] estoit forspayscé en] B: forpaisé est; V: forpaysa en [18] esgart] V: recort ou counoisance de court [19] peut] B: porra

3.3. Insertion following chapter 143 (or 142)

This chapter closely replicates chapter 30 in Beugnot's edition of Philip of Novara. In AB it is inserted after chapter 143, but in V it comes between chapters 142 and 143.

***[3.3]** Si dit dou fié que le seignor encombre, coment il deit[1] respondre.[a]

Se il avenist que Dieu feist son comandement d'aucun qui eust fié, et le seignor saissist le fié et le tenist un tenz sanz ce que nul le requeist, et aprés par tens ou tart le donast a aucun ou l'encombrast[2] en aucune maniere si que autre l'eust et[3] tenist en fié ou autrement, et il avenist par tens ou tart que aucun apartenant de celui de qui fu[4] le fié venist devant le seignor et le requeist[5] au seignor, et le seignor vosist dire[6] qu'il n'a ni ne tient le fié,[7] ne a lui ne[8] viaut[9] respondre por ce que il ne l'a ne[10] tient, que tant soulement qu'il li[11] fornira dreit, ce il s'en viaut clamer[12] de celui qui le tient, le requereor[13] peut respondre que il ne viaut ni ne deit requerre son fié que au seignor, car il a son fié enpeeschié et il le deit delivrer.[14] Ce il de ce se posent sur court, je cuit bien que la court esgardera que le seignor li deit respondre.

A: fols xci^{v}–xcii^{r} cap. 158; **B:** fol. 119^{v} cap. 158; **V:** fol. cxxi^{v} cap. 162; Beugnot, p. 238 cap. 158. Cf. Philip of Novara **A':** fol. ccxxii^{r}; **B':** fol. 258^{r-v} cap. 35; **M:** fols 97^{v}–98^{r}; Beugnot, p. 507 cap. 30.

---

[a] B lacks the rubric in the text, but it is present in the table of rubrics at fol. 22^{r}.

---

[1] encombre. coment il] B: done ou encombre coment il en [2] ou l'encombrast] B lacks [3] V adds: le [4] fu] V: fust [5] le requeist] AB: requeist le fié [6] dire] V: neer [7] le fié] V lacks [8] ne] B: n'en [9] V adds: il [10] ne] B: ne ne; V: ne ne le [11] li] AB: en [12] s'en viaut clamer] V: le veaut retenir [13] requereor] V: requerrant [14] A adds: Et

3.4. Insertion following chapter 149

This chapter is not identified as coming from any extant source.

***[3.4]** Coment l'on deit requerre a son seignor[1] son fié ou ce qui est de son fié.

Quant l'ome requiert au seignor chose,[2] se il ne[3] doute qu'il ne seit esloigniés au chief[4] de sa requeste, peut dire que ce qu'il a requis viaut il que le seignor li face, ce provant[5] come il a dit ou fait dire, se la court l'esgarde, et retenaill y seit toz jors.[6] Et ce il ensi le fait de la saissine, ce il la requiert,[7] faissant ce qu'il a offert de preuve[8] ou d'autre chose, son esgart premier requis irra avant par raisson.

A: fol. ci^{r} cap. 165; **B:** fol. 128^{v} cap. 165; **V:** fols cxxxiv^{v}–cxxxv^{r} cap. 170; Beugnot, p. 255 cap. 165.

---

[1] a son seignor] V lacks [2] chose] B lacks; V: son fié [3] ne] V lacks [4] ne seit esloigniés au chief] B: soit elloignié [5] ce provant] BV: por tant [6] et retenaill y seit toz jors] B: et mete son retenaill; V: sauf son retenaill [7] requiert] BV: requise [8] preuve] V: prover

3.5. Insertion following chapter 153

This chapter is adapted from the Philip of Novara (caps 20–22 in Beugnot's edition). The relationship is complex. MS B for the most part follows chapters 20–21 but lacks the material in chapter 22. A lacks most of chapter 21, but, in common with V, follows chapter 22 fairly closely. V divides the material into three chapters, but whereas the second of these divisions coincides with the beginning of Philip of Novara's chapter 22, the first does not coincide with the start of his chapter 21. None of the John of Ibelin texts have the rhymed couplet preserved by Philip in chapter 20 ('Ne doit mie garder l'aignel/Qui en doit avoir la pel.'), and the phrase found in B: 'couvoitise ne li feist faire de l'enfant la garde dou loup', which is repeated later in V, is not found in any of the manuscripts of Philip's text. The last sentences in V are not from Philip, and V continues with a unique additional chapter on the same topic edited below as appendix 7.5. Although B is generally closer to the MSS of Philip of Novara, A alone preserves Philip's phrase: 'endreit a une assise', and its reading: 'L'enfant deit estre en la garde dou plus preuchein de ces parens ou amis . . .' is closer to Philip than B's.

***[3.5]** Coment[1] quant pere ou mere muert[2] et il ont fié et[3] enfanz[4] mermes d'aage, qui doit avoir le baillage,[5] et qui doit guarder l'eir dou fié.[6]

Quant il avient chose[7] que[8] Dieu fait son comandement d'aucun ou d'aucune qui ait fié, se il a fiz ou fille de[9] leau mariage qui seit d'aage, il[10] se peut saissir dou fié sanz parler au seignor.[11] Car l'on dit[12] clerement que de ce dont pere ou[13] mere muert saissi et tenant come de la soe chose[14] fiz ou fille[15] demorre en tel saissine[16] come pere ou mere[17] aveit. Et se il avient que l'eir seit merme d'aage et aucun ou aucune qui li apartient[18] de la dont le fié muet vient avant[19] requerre le baillage si come il deit,

A	B	V
il le deit aveir dou fié. Mais l'enfant ne deit mie estre en sa garde, se le fié li peut escheir. Car en cest endreit a une assise qui dit que baill ne deit mie garder mermiau, et ce fu establi por ce que l'eir fust gardé de damage et de perill et le baill de honte et de pechié.	il l'a dou fié. Mais l'enfant ne doit mie estre en sa garde se le fié li puet escheoir, por ce que l'on doute que pechié ou couvoitise ne li feist faire de l'enfant la garde dou loup.	et .i. autre sien parent qui li apartiegne de l'autre partie si que a lui ne puisse le fié venir ne escheir, si doit avoir l'enfant en guarde et doit avoir son vivre couvenablement de son fié.

A: fols ciii^{v}–civ^{r} cap. 170; **B:** fol. 131^{r-v} cap. 170; **V:** cxxxviii^{v}–cxxxix^{r} caps 175–7; Beugnot, pp. 261–2, cap. 170. Cf. Philip of Novara **A':** fols ccxiv^{v}–ccxv^{r}; **B':** fols 242^{v}–243^{r} caps 15–16, fol. 254^{v} cap. 33; **M:** fols 87^{v}–89^{v}; Beugnot, pp. 495–8, caps 20–22.

[1] V adds: qui veaut fié requerre [2] muert] B: meurent [3] fié et] V lacks [4] B adds: qui sont [5] B adds: dou fié [6] doit guarder l'eir dou fié] V: l'enfant en garde [7] chose] V lacks [8] Quant il avient chose que] B: Et quant dame [9] de] V: né en [10] il] V si [11] V adds: pour quoi que il soit le droit heir a avoir celui fié si come il le contient en cestui livre [12] V adds: tout [13] ou] A: et [14] V adds: et [15] fiz ou fille] B: le fill ou la fille [16] A adds: et en tel teneure [17] V adds: tenoit et [18] apartient] BV: apartiegne [19] V adds: et

L'enfant deit estre en la garde dou plus preuchein de ces parens ou amis a qui le fié ne peut escheyr et deit aveir son vivre covenablement de son fié.

Et por ce doit estre l'enfant en la garde dou plus prochain parent ou ami a qui le fié ne puet escheoir. Et doit avoir son vivre couvenablement de son fié.

[Rubric] Coment il doit estre gardé se il est seignor de tere.

Et ce il est seignor de terre, par acort dou comun de ces homes deit estre gardé son cors et ces fortereces, et deit aveir son vivre honoreement et ces fortereces fornies covenablement des rentes de sa seignorie. Et quant l'eir dou vavassor est de l'aage de .xv. anz complis, il deit requerre son fié si come est devant dit.

Et se il est seignor de terre, par acort dou quemim de ses homes doit estre gardé son cors et ses fortereces, et doit avoir son vivre honorablement et les fortereces fornies couvenablement des rentes de la seignorie. Et quant l'oir dou vavassor est d'eage de .xv. anz compliz il ne doit mie requerre son fié a son baill, ainz doit offrir son homage a son seignor, et doit dire que, se le seignor ou son baill mescroit qu'il ne soit d'eage, il l'ofre a prover au seignor si come la cort esgardera ou conoistra qu'il prover

Et se il est seignor de terre par acort dou coumun de ces houmes doit estre guardé son cors et ces forteresces et doit avoir son vivre honorablement et les forteresces fornies couvenablement des rentes de la seignorie. Et cil a qui eschiet le bailliage ne doit guarder enfant, pour ce que ce l'eir moroit, il en seroit heir dou fié, et mescreu en seroit de la mort de l'enfant, et auci tost mauvaise couvoityse li feroit faire la guarde dou loup.

le doie. Et la preuve doit estre tele come vos avez oi autrefoiz desus come l'on doit prover eage. Et le seignor qui est tenu as deus, et doit garder le baill en son baillage jusques au parfait de .xv. anz, et doit metre l'oir en son heritage. Et quant il est d'eage, il doit recevoir la preuve de l'oir. Se il est mescreu ou se il le mescroit por son servise ou dou baill por son profit, l'oir le doit prover enssi come il est dit desus. Et se il n'est mescreu de l'eage, le seignor doit tantost recevoir son homage et li doit comander et abandoner qu'il voist a son heritage dont il est en saisine por son droit por ce que son pere ou sa mere en morut saisi et tenant. et il doit aler en son heritage. Son baill ne puet riens dire contre lui qui rienz vaille. Car l'oir ne se doit partir dou seignour.

Baillage ne peut nul aveir se le fié ne li peut escheir, fors que en une maniere: ce est se l'eir a pere ou mere, lequel qu'il ait des .ii., celui enporte le baillage devant toz les autres parenz par l'assise. Et est bien aparant que ce est assise, car dreit ne donast mie que celui qui n'ataint au conquereor dou fié eust le baillage et le proufit par devant ciaus qui li ataignent et a qui le fié peut escheir. Et le baillage de pere ou de mere est enterin, car il a le fié et l'enfant en garde por ce que l'escheete dou fié ne peut venir a lui.

[Rubric] Ci dit a qui le bailliage de fié doit escheir et a qui le doit requerre.

Bailliage ne doit nul avoir se le fié ne li peut escheir for ques en une sole maniere: se l'eir a pere ou mere, laquel que il ait des .ii. celui emporte le bailliage devant tous les autres par l'assise. Et bien est aparant que ce est assise, car droit ne donast mie que celui qui n'ataint au conquereor dou fié eust le bailliage et le proufit dou fié par devant ceaus qui li ateignent et a qui le fié peut escheir. Et le bailliage de mere ou de pere est enterin, car il l'a le fié et l'enfant en garde pour ce que l'escheete dou fié ne peut venir a lui. Et qui veaut avoir bailliage qui li soit escheu par l'assise, il doit amener ou aporter en la presence de la court ou il celui bailliage requiert l'enfant de par qui il le requiert. Et se il ne li amaine l'on ne li peut ne ne li doit par raison resoivre a baill ne metre le en saisine ne en teneure se l'on ne li veaut faire grace. Car se il estoit autrement trop de gent em poroient par se perdre lor raison et lor droit et estre desherité.

3.6. Insertion following chapter 174

These two chapters are not identified as coming from any extant source. In MSS A and B they are both located directly after chapter 174, but in V the chapter edited here as appendix 3.6.1 is lacking and appendix 3.6.2 is re-positioned to appear directly after the chapter edited below as appendix 7.10.2 and immediately before chapter 219.

There is apparently an allusion to 3.6.2 in John's discourse on the regency (below appendix 8.1 note c).

***[3.6.1]** Si devise[1] quel sairement deit faire le chief seignor[2] quant il entre premierement en sa seignorie avant que l'on li face homage.

Voz avés oy coment et quel sairement le chief seignor dou reiaume fait au patriarche quant il receit la corone,[a] et or orrés quel sairement il fait a ces homes avant qu'il li facent homage.[3] Il deit premierement jurer sur sainte evangilles de Dieu come crestien qu'il gardera et sauvera et aidera et defendera et maintendra[4] de tot son leau poer sainte yglise et veves et orfenines en leur dreit et en leur raisson par tot cestui reiaume. Et encores, par son dit sairement, tendra et fera tenir et acomplir et maintenir de tot son leau poeir les bons uz et les bones[5] costumes et les assises qui furent ordenees et faites ou dit reiaume ce est a entendre par tot le reiaume. Et encores, par son dit sairement, qu'il tendra et maintendra et fera tenir et maintenir les[6] dons et les preveliges que ces ancestres ont donés et fais[7] en cest reiaume. Et[8] se aucuns contens y eust es dons ou es preveliges qu'il ont donés et[9] fais, que voz ciaus contens ferés determiner par l'esgart ou la conoissance de sa[10] court. Et encores est tenu, par son dit sairement, de tenir[11] et de faire tenir et d'acomplir[12] justise.

A: fol. cxxiii[r–v] cap. 193; **B:** fol. 153[r] cap. 194; Beugnot, pp. 310–12 cap. 193.

[a] Below cap. 220. In AB cap. 220 is re-positioned earlier in the book, between the end of the prologue and chapter 1. The author of this chapter was evidently aware of this change.

[1] Si devise] A rubrics (fol. 6[v]) lacks [2] B adds: dou reaume [3] homage] B: l'omage [4] et maintendra] B lacks [5] les bones] B lacks [6] et maintendra et . . . les] B: et fera tenir [7] ancestres ont donés et fais] B: avantiers dounarent et fierent [8] B adds: que [9] donés et] B lacks [10] sa] B: vostre [11] B adds: et de maintenir [12] B adds: de tout son leau pooir

***[3.6.2]** Si devise[1] quel sairement deit faire baill quant il receit le baillage dou[2] reiaume, et coment il se deit contenir.

Quant[3] le reiaume escheit a baill et il entre[4] a tenir le baillage, il deit jurer et jure sur saintes evangilles[5] qu'il bien et leaument sauvera et aidera et[6] maintendra et defendera a tot son leau poeir contre totes riens qui vivre et morir puissent le dreit heir dou reiaume; et qu'il gardera et sauvera et[7] maintendra et defendera et fera garder et[8] sauver et[9] maintenir et defendre de tot son leau poeir le dit reiaume dont il est baill[10] au dreit heir et a ces heirs aprés lui; et qu'il tendra et maintendra et fera tenir et maintenir les dons et les preveliges que les dis reis et[11] ces ancestres ont donés et fais ou dit[12] reiaume, et,[13] se aucuns contens eust es dons ou es preveliges,[14] que il ciaus contens fera determiner par l'esgart ou la conoissance de la court dou dit reiaume, c'il en est requis en court; et qu'il menra et fera mener les homes dou dit reiaume par l'esgart ou la conoissance de la court dou dit reiaume;[15] et qu'il ne dessaissira ni[16] ne fera dessaissir aucun des homes dou dit reiaume de aucunes de leur teneures se ce n'est par l'esgart ou la conoissance de la dite[17] court; et qu'il au dit reiaume tendra et maintendra et fera tenir et maintenir justise; et qu'il tendra et maintendra et fera tenir et maintenir ou dit reiaume[18] les bons uz et les bones costumes et les assises que ces devansiers[19] firent et establirent; et qu'il[20] de totes les choses dessuz dittes, ensemble et de chascune par sei, il jure sur les saintes evangilles de Dieu de tenir et de garder et faire[21] acomplir come baill a bone fei sans aucune maniere d'engin tant come il tendra le baillage dou dreit heir dou reiaume; et qu'il a l'encontre ne venra[22] en aucune

---

A: fols cxxiii^{v}–ccxxiv^{r} cap. 194; **B:** fol. 153^{r-v} cap. 194; **V:** fol. ccxxxvi^{r-v} cap. 285; Beugnot, p. 312 cap. 194.

---

[1] Si devise] A rubrics (fol. 6^{v}) lacks [2] le baillage dou] A (but not A rubrics): baillage de [3] Quant] V: Et quant [4] entre] B: entendre [5] sur saintes evangilles] BV lack [6] et aidera et] B lacks [7] et sauvera et] B: sauvera [8] et] V lacks [9] garder et sauver et] B: garde sauver [10] baill] V: heir [11] et] B lacks [12] les dis reis . . . dit] V: ces avantdiciers ont fait au [13] B adds: que [14] A adds: qu'il donés et fais; V: que il l'ont fait [15] ou la conoissance . . . reiaume] V: de la court [16] ni] BV lack [17] dite] V lacks [18] tendra et maintendra et fera tenir et maintenir justise . . . reiaume] V lacks [19] devansiers] B: avantiers; V: avantdiciers [20] qu'il] B: que [21] et de garder et faire] B: de garder et faire et; V: et garder et faire garder et [22] a l'encontre ne venra] B: encontre n'en ira; V: a l'encontre n'en yra

chose ni ne soufrira a son poeir que autre[23] aille; et que les chastiaus et les fortereces qui sont dou dreit[24] heir dou reiaume seront en la garde et en la porveance des barons et des homes dou dit reiaume, et qu'il fera aveir[25] as chastelains que les avans[26] dis establiront le forment[27] des dis[28] chastiaus et des fortereces raisnablement en totes choses[29] par la conoissance des avanz dis ou de la plus grant partie.[30]

[23] BV add: y [24] dreit] B: dit [25] fera aveir] V: donra [26] avans] BV: devant [27] forment] BV: forniment [28] B adds: chastelains des [29] des dis chastiaus . . . choses] V lacks [30] BV add: d'eaus

3.7. Insertion following chapter 176

This chapter follows closely the material to be found in the second part of chapter 51 of Beugnot's edition of Philip of Novara. But unlike MS A', which is followed in Beugnot's prionted text, MSS B' and M both begin a new chapter at the point the chapter edited here starts.

***[3.7]** Encores dit coment les homes des homes dou chief seignor deivent faire a la requeste dou chief seignors et sans requeste por sauver[1] la foi de quei il li[2] sont tenus.[3]

Tot ce qui est[4] dessus escrit est ce[5] que l'on deit faire a la requeste et a la[6] semonce dou chief seignor. Et plus y a, ce il avient que le seignor de cui tienent lor fiés ciaus[7] qui ont fait la ligece porchace ou fait chose de quei il se[8] mesface vers le chief seignor, et ciaus qui ont faite la ligece se[9] pevent aparceveir, ja seit ce que le chief seignor le sache ou non, encores ne les en[10] ait il requis ne semons de riens, por ce qu'il se contient en la foi qu'il deivent le seignor garder et sauver contre totes riens qui vivre et morir puissent.[11] Il doivent dire et faire ce qui est dessus escrit, aussi bien come, se le chief seignor les en eust requis et semons, le deivent il[12] garnir au plus tost qu'il poront. Et se le seignor de cui il tienent[13] ne[14] fait la requeste dessus escrite[15] de ces homes, il deivent aler au chief seignor et servir le enterinement contre celui de qui il tienent. Et il lor[16] deit restorer bien et largement tot ce qu'il avront perdu por venir a lui et lor deit faire avoir leur fiés enterinement ce il sont en leuc ou il ait[17] pooir. Et se le seignor de qui il tienent ait forterece ou poeir tel qu'il peust[18] arester les fiés, le chief seignor lor deit restorer dedenz .xl. jors, et, se il ne le fait, les homes pevent retorner[19] au seignor de cui il tienent sans mesfaire[20] et servir le contre le chief seignor tant qu'il lor ait restoré lor fiés et lor pertes.[a]

Et se il avient que le chief seignor se doute d'aucun de ces riches homes qui ait chastel ou cité ou ville en quei il ait peuple d'armes,

---

A: fols cxxvi[v]–cxxvii[r] cap. 199; **B:** fol. 156[r–v] cap. 200; **V:** fols clxx[r]–clxxi[r] cap. 209; Beugnot, pp. 319–20 cap. 199. Cf. Philip of Novara **A':** fols ccxxxi[v]–ccxxxii[v] (part); **B':** fol. 262[r–v] caps 43–4; **M:** fols 121[v]–122[v]; Beugnot, pp. 526–7 cap. 51 (part).

---

[a] Philip of Novara MS B' begins a new chapter here.

---

[1] requeste por sauver] B: sa requeste por sauver et garantir [2] li] V lacks [3] B adds: par la ligece [4] B adds: ci [5] Tot ce qui est dessus escrit est ce] V: Tout soit ce que dessus est escrit [6] requeste et a la] V lacks [7] tienent lor fiés ciaus] B: ceaus tienent; V: tient ceaus [8] se] B lacks [9] se] B: s'en [10] en] A lacks [11] puissent] A: puisse [12] il] BV lack [13] A adds: lor fiés [14] ne] V n'a [15] dessus escrite] V lacks [16] lor] V lacks [17] A adds: force et [18] peust] V: puisse [19] retorner] B: recovrer [20] mesfaire] B: mesprandre

le seignor dou leuc est tenus par l'assise de faire tant que le peuple jure[21] feauté au chief seignor par celle condicion de requeste et de restor[22] et de tot ce[23] qui est dessuz devisié de ciaus qui ont faite la ligece. Et[24] quant ceste assise fu faite, ciaus de Seete[25] et de Biaufort[26] jurerent toz au rei Amauri quant la pais fu faite dou cotens qui estoit entr'iaus,[27] [b] et par l'assise fu la traitement de la pais.

Voz avés oy[28] les avantages que le chief seignor a en la ligece de ces homes. Aprés orrés l'eschange et l'avantage que les homes liges ont[29] encontre ce.

Le[c] rei otroia en l'establissement de l'assise[30] que toz ces homes liges qui tenoient de lui ou de ces homes, quels qu'il fucent, granz ou petis, fussent[31] tenus de fei l'un a l'autre de ce qui est dessus escrit, et que chascun d'iaus en peust requerre les autres come ces[32] pers. Et les homes en sont[33] tenus l'un a l'autre, aussi au plus petit come au plus grant, par quei il ne seit entechié[34] d'aucun des vices par quei l'on pert vois et respons[35] [d] en court.

---

[b] All the Philip of Novara MSS have readings approximating to that found in V at this point. The text refers to the *assise sur la ligece* enacted at the end of the dispute between King Amaury and Gerard, lord of Sidon and Beaufort. Cf. cap. 126.

[c] Philip of Novara MS M begins a new chapter here.

[d] Here again V's reading is supported by the Philip of Novara MSS.

---

[21] B adds: de faire [22] restor] A: restorer [23] et de tot ce] V lacks [24] Et] B lacks [25] Seete] B: Saete; V: Saiete [26] Baiufort] BV: Beaufort [27] quant la pais . . . entr'iaus] V: selonc ce que je ais entendu quant il ot guerre a mesire Girart de Sayete [28] Voz avés oy] A: si come voz avés oy et [29] ont] B lacks [30] de l'assise] V lacks [31] fussent] A: seent [32] ces] B lacks [33] en sont] V lacks [34] entechié] B: entagié [35] et respons] V lacks

3.8. Insertion following chapter 181

These two chapters closely follow the material to be found in Beugnot's edition of Philip of Novara chapters 37 and 39.

***[3.8.1]** Si devise[1] autre maniere de conjurement: quant aucun home est manassié, coment il deit[2] conjurer son seignor.[3]

Quant aucun[4] home est menassié ou en perill d'aucun contens qu'il a eu a[5] aucun[6] riche home ou povre, il deit[7] [a] venir devant le seignor et dire li: 'Sire, tel home[8] me menace', ou[9] 'je sui en tel perill, et je entens que je ais dreit et celui tort, et sui prest que[10] par voz qui estes mon seignor, ou par vostre court, ou par vostre comandement, ou par mise de bone gent, en soie a dreit tot ensi come vos comanderés.[11] Et ce faissant, je vos pri et requier et conjur come a[12] mon seignor par la fei que voz me devés que de ce me fassiés asseurer et me maintenés a dreit[13] selonc vostre poeir'. Et[14] [b] le seignor li deit respondre qu'il enquerra celui fait et le adressera, se il peut, ou par pars[15] ou par aucunes des manieres qu'il li a offertes.[16] Et se l'ome viaut ce faire que il li[17] a offert et l'autre est home dou seignor, il deit bien requerre[18] l'autre qu'il l'asseure et en receive dreit par aucunes des manieres dessus dittes, et li deit faire grant defence qu'il outre ce riens ne face.[19] Et se riens en[20] avenist[21] sur ce, il en deit faire curiousement[22] quanque il pora[23] par sa court. Et se il n'est son home, il deit maintenir celui qui est son[24] home et defendre le a[25] bone fei, ce il ne defaut de[26] ce qu'il a offert au comensement, ce il n'est plus tenus a celui a qui il a a faire que a lui.

A: fol. cxxxiii^{v} cap. 209; **B:** fols 163^{v}–164^{r} cap. 210; **V:** fol. clxxx^{r-v} cap. 219; Beugnot, pp. 334–5 cap. 209. Cf. Philip of Novara **A':** fol. ccxxvi^{r-v}; **B':** fol. 253^{r-v} cap. 30; **M:** fols 109^{v}–110^{r}; Beugnot, p. 514 cap. 37.

---

[a] All the Philip of Novara MSS, in common with V, read 'peut' or 'puet'.
[b] V's reading is supported by the Philip of Novara MSS.

---

[1] devise] V: orrés [2] deit] A rubrics (fol. 7^{r}) B: peut [3] B adds: se il est en doutance de son cors; V lacks: coment il deit conjurer son seignor [4] Quant aucun] V: Autre conjurement y a que l'ome peut faire au seignor quant .i. [5] a eu a] B: ait eu en [6] V adds: autre [7] deit] V: peut [8] V adds: ci [9] ou] V: et [10] que] B lacks [11] tot ensi come vos comanderés] V: et tout enci come vous comandement sera [12] a] B lacks [13] me maintenés a dreit] V: a droit maintenir [14] Et] V: Je entens que [15] pars] B: paiz; V: pais [16] li a offertes] B: a offrent [17] li] B lacks [18] requerre] A: requerra [19] qu'il outre ce riens ne face] V lacks [20] en] V lacks [21] avenist] B: avient [22] curiousement] B: counoissement [23] quanque il pora] A lacks [24] son] A lacks [25] a] B: en [26] de] A: de faire; V: a

***[3.8.2]** Se[1] le seignor ne fait tenir a son home esgart ou conoissance que la court a[2] fait ou defuit[3] a l'home de faire[4] ce qu'il li a requis en la court, coment celui[5] peut conjurer ces pers.[6]

Quant l'ome requiert au seignor escheete qui escheue li seit ou aucune autre requeste et en la fin de sa[7] parole en requiert esgart, et le seignor le delee en aucune maniere et ne se prent a l'esgart de l'ome qu'il a premier requis, et l'ome li requiert par pluisors feis, et le seignor sur ce par aucun point le defuit, l'ome peut bien requerre et conjurer ces pers qui sont en la court qu'il[8] doivent prier et requerre le seignor si destreiment[9] come il pevent et deivent qu'il li face aveir l'esgart qu'il[10] a[11] [a] premier requis et qu'il le maint raisnablement par sa court come son home et lor per. Et les homes liges en deivent requerre le seignor tot ensi come leur per les en a requis. Et ce il[12] a en la court poi d'omes liges, celui qui requiert peut aler hors[13] de la court et assembler les homes liges la ou il porra, et, se il ne les[14] peut assembler, il peut aler a chascun la ou il les[15] trovera et requerre luer et conjurer les[16] come ces pers qu'il veignent en[17] la court et prient et requierent au seignor qu'il escoute et entende sa requeste et le maint a dreit par l'esgart de sa court, et ce il[18] a requis esgart qu'il li face aveir son esgart premier requis ou li fornisse dreit par l'esgart de sa court. Et ces pers le deivent faire tot ensi sanz faille.[19] Et ce il avenist que le seignor ne les escoutast et par leur esgart ou par leur conoissance ne vosist fornir dreit a leur per ou li fausist[20] d'esgart, il pevent et deivent aussi bien gagier le[21]

A: fols cxxxiii^{v}–cxxxiv^{r} cap. 210; **B:** fol. 164^{r-v} cap. 211; **V:** fols clxxx^{v}–clxxxi^{r} cap. 220; Beugnot, p. 335 cap. 210. Cf Philip of Novara **A':** fol. ccxxvii^{r-v}; **B':** fols 253^{v}–254^{r} cap. 31; **M:** fols 112^{r}–113^{r}; Beugnot, p. 516 cap. 39.

---

[a] V's reading is supported by the Philip of Novara MSS.

---

[1] Se] BV: Et se [2] a] B: avra; V: ait [3] defuit] B: va defuiant [4] faire] V lacks [5] celui] A rubrics (fol. 7^{r}) il [6] B adds: por avoir l'esgart [7] sa] B: la [8] A adds: li [9] destreiment] B: destroitement; V: estroitement [10] B adds: li [11] qu'il a] V lacks [12] V adds: y [13] hors] A: fors [14] ne les] B: pouet ou nes [15] les] A: le [16] les] B lacks [17] en] B: a [18] BV add: li [19] faille] B: faillir [20] fausist] B: defausisis [21] le] V: leur

seignor de leur servise por ce[22] come il pevent por aucun esgart se il l'ont fait. Et se le seignor ne le tient et fornist, se leur per le[23] requiert que il ensi le facent, et que il,[24] de tot ce qu'il en avront veu et seu, se conteignent vers lui come vers leur per.

---

[22] V adds: que il est droit et assises de ce [23] se leur per le] B: a leur per ce qu'il li; V: se lor per lor [24] il] A: eaus

3.9. Insertion following chapter 199

This chapter is not identified as coming from any extant source.

***[3.9]** Quant[1] feme est semonce si come elle deit[2] de prendre baron et elle a passé aage, coment elle peut et deit la semonce refuser que ja le seignor n'avra amende de li[3] de defaut de servise.

Quant[4] le seignor semont ou fait semondre si come il deit feme de prendre baron quant elle a et tient fié qui deive[5] servise de cors et elle a passé aage,[6] et la semont ou fait semondre si come il est devant dit que on deit feme semondre de prendre baron,[7] elle deit venir devant le seignor[8] et demander conseill et puis faire[9] dire par son conseill: 'Sire, a ce que voz avés fait semondre[10] tel', et la nome,[11] 'dou servise que voz entendés qu'elle vos deit come[12] dame por le fié qu'elle a et tient de voz, a ce, sire,[13] vos respont elle[14] en tel maniere: qu'elle n'aquiaut vostre semonce, n'acuillir ne la viaut, se[15] court ne l'esgarde, et dit por quei: por ce que[16] elle entent a[17] estre quitte de son[18] servise qu'elle[19] deveit de son cors come[20] dame, et dit coment.'

'Tot premierement elle entent qu'il seit uz[21] ou costume ou assise ou[22] raisson ou reiaume de Jerusalem ou en cestui de Chipre,[23] que quant les genz qui servise deivent de leur cors ont passé .lx. anz d'aage qu'il sont quittes de celui servise. Et ce euffre elle bien[24] a prover tot ensi come la court esgardera ou[25] conoistra[26] que prover le dee, ne se n'est mie doute ains est chose certaine et manifeste que chascun a dit et toz jors a esté dit des sages qui ont esté et seu[27] des usages de la court et des anciens[28] qui plus sorent selonc la renomee d'iaus: que puis que l'on a .lx. anz d'aage passés que l'on est quitte dou servise de son cors. Et se il n'i a par aventure

A: fols cxlvi^{v}–cxlviii^{r} cap. 228; **B:** fols 179^{r}–180^{v} cap. 230; **V:** fols cxcix^{r}–cci^{r} cap. 243; Beugnot, pp. 362–4 cap. 228.

[1] Quant] A: Si dit quant [2] si come elle deit] A lacks, though present in table of rubrics (fol. 8^{r}) [3] de li] B: d'ele come; V: de elle [4] Quant] V: Se [5] deive] B: doit [6] si come il . . . aage] V: feme qui ait passé aage et elle ne veaut la semonce acuillir [7] et la semont . . . baron] BV lack [8] V adds: ou devant celui qui sera en son leuc [9] puis faire] B: faire et [10] V adds: madame [11] la nome] V: nomer la [12] come] V: de son cors come de [13] a ce sire] B lacks [14] V adds: et je pour elle [15] B adds: la [16] por ce que] B: quar; V: car [17] a] V lacks [18] de son] BV: dou [19] V adds: vous [20] V adds: de [21] uz] B: vois [22] ou cotume ou assise ou] V: et costume et [23] ou en cestui de Chipre] V lacks [24] bien] B lacks [25] esgardera ou] B lacks [26] ou conoistra] V lacks [27] a esté dite . . . seu] B: oi dire des sages qui ont; V: ais oy dire de sages qui ores sont [28] des anciens] V: ceaus qui furent et

en vie orres aucuns[29] qui aient veu tel maniere de cas avenir ne determiner[30] en leur tens, por ce ne se remue dreit ne l'usage ne l'assise qui fu jadis usé ou tens des proudes omes qui furent, et bien semble et deit sembler a chascun qui ce orra qu'il y a usage ou assise ou raisson de ce por quei persone qui a passé .lx. ans ne deit plus servir de son cors par destrece, se de son gré ne le fait.[31] Car il est bien chose certaine, ne ja ne se trovera que en cestui reiaume de Jerusalem ne en celui de Chipre[32] que nulle persone puis qu'elle eust[33] passé .lx. anz fust constrainte de servise de son cors outre son gré par nulle des seignories qui lors furent[34] la ou la persone s'en vosist defendre par aucunes des avant dittes raisons. Et bien mostre[35] tel', et la nome, 'qu'il est[36] ensi come elle a fait dire par le semblant cas. Car il est bien chose seue[37] corsablement[38] et pluisors feis est avenu que se un home qui a .lx. anz passés apelle ou il est apelés de chose ou il afierre bataille, qu'il se defende ou mostre[39] par champion, se de son gré ne le viaut faire de son cors. Et puis que son aage escuse son cors de bataille, donc est il bien semblant que miaus le deust[40] escuser dou servise. Et se euffre elle bien[41] a prover tot ensi come la court esgardera ou[42] conoistra qu'elle[43] prover[44] le dee, se aucun vosist dire qu'ensi ne fust. Et bien a l'on toz jors oy dire corsablement et aucune fois l'a l'on veu avenir que aucun chevalier, quant l'on[45] le semoneit de[46] servise de son cors et[47] il s'en voleit[48] escuser par ce qu'il aveit passé aage, que le seignor en aveit le cheval et les armes en eschange de son cors a son besoin totes les feis qu'il le[49] voleit semondre. Et se aucun vosist dire que non place Dieu ne[50] que son aage l'escusast, ne que le seignor eust[51] le cheval et les armes; se aucun deist ceste raisson, madame tel', et la nome,[52] 'direit que[53] non place Dieu que il[54] seit ensi, et bien[55] mostre par le semblant

[29] n'i a par . . . aucuns] B: en i a ores aucuns qui soient en vie [30] determiner] B: terminer [31] Et se il . . . fait] V lacks [32] que en cestui . . . Chipre] V lacks [33] qu'elle eust] V: que il ou elle ait [34] nulles des seignories qui lors furent] B: nul des seignors qui lors furent; V: nul seignor [35] mostre] B: demostre madame; V: mostre madame [36] la nome, 'qu'il est] B: la men, 'que ce doit estre; V: la nome, 'qui ci est que se doit estre [37] seue] B lacks [38] corsablement] V: couvenablement ou corsablement [39] se defende ou mostre] A: se defendent ou mostrent; B: s'en deffende; V: s'en deffent ou mostre [40] deust] B: doit il; V: doit elle [41] elle bien] V: bien a prover madame tel', et la nome, 'qui ci est [42] esgardera ou] BV lack [43] qu'elle] V: que [44] prover] B: mover [45] l'on] BV: le seignor [46] de] B: dou [47] B adds: se [48] voleit] V: veaut [49] le] V: les en [50] Dieu ne] B: a Dieu [51] eust] B: n'eust [52] et la nome] B lacks; V: qui ci est [53] que] B: et dit; V: et je pour lui que [54] il] V: ce [55] BV add: le

cas que ce ne devereit[56] ensi estre entendu. Car se il esteit ensi, donc ne sereit le chevalier escusé de son[57] servise que par l'essoine de son cors, et l'on[58] set bien certainement ne[59] en ce n'a il[60] nulle doute[61] que nul n'est[62] si juene ne si fort que c'il eust essoine[63] de son cors, qu'il ne s'escusast[64] bien dou servise, ne por ce ne donreit[65] il mie son cheval et ces[66] armes au seignor en eschange dou[67] servise, si come le vieill chevalier fait.[68] Car chascun peut bien saveir que raisson deit estre comune, et, puis que raisson est comune, se le vieill chevalier ne se peut escuser dou servise[69] vers son seignor par autre raisson que par le essoine de son cors, donc ne devereit aveir le seignor de lui son[70] chevau ne ces armes non[71] plus qu'il l'a dou juene si come je ai devant dit. Et[72] donc est il bien aparant que puis qu'il a le cheval et les armes dou vieill chevalier,[73] que il les a[74] par la raisson de l'aage qu'il a passé ne[75] mie par l'essoine ne par la febleté[76] de son cors. Et por une autre vive raisson doit l'on entendre que l'aage l'en escuse[77] dou servise, ne[78] mie selonc l'usage des essoines. Et puis que ce ne se conduit[79] selonc ledit usage, donc est il certaine chose qu'il sereit a la volenté dou seignor de faire le servise ou de prendre le cheval et les armes. Mais por ce semble il bien chose certaine que le seignor n'a[80] le cheval et[81] les armes dou vieill home[82] que por l'aage qu'il a passé ne[83] mie por l'essoine ne por la descheance de son cors.'

'Et encores[84] vos fait elle assaveir que, sauve seit vostre grace, elle n'entent que[85] voz la puissiés constraindre ne deés de prendre mari[86] selonc raisson, et dit coment.[87] Qu'il[88] est bien chose seue et veraie que mariage ne fu establi que por multeplier le ciecle[89] sanz pechié, et si est bien clere chose el tels qui court[90] orres et qui a ja[91] coru lonc tens a, que feme qui a .lx. anz passés a perdue la[92] porteure selonc nature, et puis que feme pert[93] porteure selonc nature, se

[56] devereit] B: doit [57] de son] V: dou [58] B adds: le [59] ne] V: que [60] il] V lacks [61] doute] B: doutance [62] n'est] V: n'en est [63] eust essoine] B: fust essoigniez; V: fust essoignés [64] s'escusast] V: s'en escusast [65] donreit] B: devroit [66] son cheval et ces] B: le cheval ne les [67] dou] V: de son [68] fait] B lacks [69] V adds: que il doit [70] son] BV: ne son [71] non] B: nens; V: neent [72] Et] BV lack [73] dou vieill chevalier] B lacks [74] que il les a] V: et que il laisa [75] ne] BV: non [76] par l'essoine ne par la febleté] V: pour essoigne ne pour feblece [77] l'en escuse] B: l'escuse [78] ne] BV: non [79] Et puis que . . . conduit] B: Que ce ne ce que on dit [80] n'a] B: ne; V: n'en a [81] et] B: ne [82] home] B: chavalier; V: chevalier [83] ne] BV: non [84] V adds: sire [85] que] B lacks [86] mari] B: baron [87] coment] V: pour quoi [88] Qu'il] BV: Il [89] ciecle] B: monde [90] court] B: est [91] ja] BV lack [92] a perdue la] V: si a perdu sa [93] V adds: sa

sereit bien contre dreit et[94] raisson de constraindre la de prendre baron outre son gré, et[95] sur que tot puis qu'elle viaut tenir chasteté a[96] garder[97] sei de pechié. Por quei, sire, madame tel[98] voz fait assaveir que elle a .lx. ans[99] passés et selonc nature[100] perdue[101] porteure, et si n'a[102] talant ne volenté de mari prendre et[103] a ferme propos de tenir chasteté[104] de son cors et garder sei de pechié.'

'Et[105] encores voz dit elle a[106] maniere de point de plait, que c'il esteit ensi que homes ou femes qui servise deivent de lor cors fussent toz jors tenus de faire le au seignor, ne vieillece ne febleté de cors por aage qu'il eussent[107] ne les en[108] peust escuser ne defendre, un mau[109] seignor poreit deseriter chascun ou chascune. Et especiaument semble il chose inpossible, car se sereit contre Dieu et contre raisson se seignor par destrece de servise peust marier les femes qui avroient .lxxx. ou .lxxxx. ou cent anz qui seroient si descheues come c'elles fucent[110] porries. Et[111] c'il estoit ensi, un mau[112] seignor poreit legierement deseriter ou raembre pluissors bones dames ou autres bones femes. Por quei l'on ne deit mie entendre que se puisse estre, ainz deit l'on creire[113] seinement que l'usage et la raisson seit tel[114] come l'on a devant dit.'[115]

'Por quei elle por totes les raissons qu'elle voz a[116] fait dire ou por aucunes d'elles entent que elle seit[117] quitte dou servise de son cors qu'elle vos deit por le fié qu'elle tient de vos,[118] ce est assaveir de mari prendre, ni[119] n'entent por chose que voz fachiés[120] dire ne orres ne autrefeis qu'elle ait a[121] acuillir vostre semonce, ne faire ne le viaut,[122] por les raissons que elle a faites dire se court ne l'esgarde. Et de ce se met elle en l'esgart de la court sauf son retenaill.'

Et je ne cuit que le seignor puisse chose dire par quei la court dee esgarder que elle puisse ne[123] dee sa semonce acuillir de prendre baron.[124]

---

[94] BV add: contre [95] B adds: en [96] a] V: et [97] chasteté a garder] B: chaste et tenir [98] sire, madame tel] B: sire, madame; V: elle [99] V adds: d'aage [100] B adds: a [101] V adds: sa [102] n'a] V: n'en a [103] V adds: si [104] chasteté] B: chaste; V: chaeste [105] Et] V lacks [106] a] B: en; V: et je pour li en [107] qu'il eussent] BV lack [108] en] B lacks [109] mau] V: mauvais [110] B adds: demi; V: la moitie [111] Et] BV lack [112] mau] V: mauvais [113] l'on creire] B: on entendre [114] seit tel] B: soient tex; V: si est tel [115] l'on a devant dit] V: la devant dite dame qui ci est requiert [116] voz a] B: a dites ou; V: vous en a [117] entent que elle seit] B: veut ele estre [118] por le fié . . . vos] V: come dame [119] ni] B: ne; V: et [120] fachiés] B: sachiés; V: aiés faite [121] ait a] B: doie [122] ne faire ne le viaut] B: ne ne la veull acuellir; V: ne acuillir ne la veaut [123] puisse ne] B lacks [124] elle puisse ne . . . baron] V: feme li doie tel maniere de servise puis que elle avra .lx. ans passés

3.10. Insertions following chapter 206

These two chapters are drawn from the material to be found in part of chapters 35 and 38 of Beugnot's edition of Philip of Novara.

MSS A and B insert these two chapters between chapters 206 and 207. In MS V the material comprising chapter 3.10.1 is the second part of a longer chapter (V cap. 255), the first part of which parallels the end of MS B chapter 240 and is edited below in appendix 5.2. The material in B chapter 240 is inserted after chapter 205, but in V chapters 254 and 255 the parallel material comes after chapter 206.

The chapter in MS V edited here as appendix 3.10.2 is inserted after chapter 207 and before chapter 208.

3.10.1

In both MS A' and MS M Philip of Novara's chapter begins in the same place as MS V chapter 255. (In MS B' it is part of a longer chapters which continues without a break at this point.) Towards the end of this chapter the texts diverge with all three manuscripts of Philip of Novara containing significantly more discussion.

3.10.2

Here MS AB and V have different versions of what in each case is clearly a separate paraphrase and rearrangement of the Philip of Novara's chapter. I have edited them in parallel together with Philip's version. The text of Philip's chapter is based on the readings in MS B' collated with MS A'. The seventeenth-century MS M has been also consulted.

The historical context of this chapter is the aftermath of the civil war in Cyprus. The siege of Kyrenia (Cherines) lasted from the summer of 1232 until the spring of 1233, and the surrender marked the end of the war. It comes a no surprise to find that the war had placed considerable strains on the royal finances. At this period John of Ibelin, lord of Beirut was the principal counsellor to the youthful King Henry I, and his intervention, ostensibly to prevent William Raymond and his associates from laying themselves open to charges of breach of faith, could well have been intended to prevent what was evidently a justifiable claim turning into a dispute that could have seriously damaged the crown.

It should be noted that both versions of the John of Jaffa text refer to John of Beirut as 'mon oncle', an indication that the adaptations of this chapter from Philip of Novara were the work of John himself. John of Jaffa also records his uncle appealing to the legal opinion of Aimery of Lusignan and Ralph of Tiberias in chapter 178.

***[3.10.1]** Si dit quel deit estre l'amende que l'ome deit faire au seignor quant il le destraint ou conjure autrement que il ne deit sans ce qu'il l'en ait[1] a faire.[a]

Quant home conjure ou destraint son seignor autrement qu'il ne deit, si li deit tel amende: qu'il[2] se[b] deit agenoillier devant le seignor[3] en la court: aveuc tant de ces amis come il porra trover illeuc, et li deit crier merci et dire[4] par la fei qu'il li deit, qu'il entendeit que il le peust faire resnablement, por ce que il entendeit[5] estre certain de la dette, et qu'il ne le fist selonc son essient a l'amermement de l'honor dou seignor,[6] et[7] adonc deit prier toz ces pers qu'il deivent prier au seignor qu'il li pardoint. Et[8] il li deivent prier, et il li deit pardoner ce qu'il le conjura avant qu'il l'eust requis en court sa dette pluisors feis sans semonce et sans conjurement. Mais ce il avient qu'il peust estre prové, si come il est dit dessus,[9] que l'ome seit paié de la quantité dont[10] il a conjuré son[11] seignor ou de partie, il perdra l'une partie por l'autre, se le seignor viaut. Et pis y a encores: car se il y[12] a en la court aucuns des homes dou seignor[13] qui vueille gregier celui, il li peut metre sus et dire que il est[14] fei mentie vers son seignor et[c] y avra bataille, se le seignor la viaut soufrir, si come est devant[15] dit, ou ce celui qui est apelé s'en set et viaut[16] defendre. Et por ce se deit chascun garder de riens requerre[17] au seignor, ce il n'en est[18] bien certain avant qu'il[19] requere riens au seignor,[20] ne destraigne ne conjure de sa fei.

A: fol. clvii^{r-v} cap. 238; **B:** fol. 193^{r} cap. 242; **V:** fols ccxv^{v}–ccxvi^{r} cap. 255 (part); Beugnot, pp. 382–3, cap. 238. Cf. Philip of Novara **A':** fol. ccxxv^{r-v} (part); **B':** fol. 251^{r-v} cap. 28 (part); **M:** fols 106^{v}–107^{r} (part); Beugnot, p. 512, cap. 35 (part).

---

[a] In V the material in the text is the second part of a longer chapter, and so there is no rubric.
[b] The Philip of Novara MSS approximate most closely to the reading of V.
[c] At this point the text edited here and the Philip of Novara MSS diverge.

---

[1] l'en ait] A rubrics (fol. 8^{v}) lacks; B: en ait [2] Quant home conjure . . . qu'il] B: L'amende que le seignor doit avoir de celui qui le destraint ou conjure autrement que il ne doit sanz ce que il en ait a faire, si est tele: que l'ome; V: L'amende que le seignor doit avoir, si come je entens, si est tel: que l'ome [3] le seignor] BV: lui [4] V adds: que [5] que il le . . . entendeit] A lacks [6] de l'honor dou seignor] B: dou seignor ne de son honor [7] et] BV lack [8] Et] V lacks [9] dessus] B: devant [10] dont] B: de quoi [11] son] V: le [12] y] B lacks [13] des homes dou seignor] B: de ses homes [14] et dire que il est] A: qu'il a sa [15] devant] B: avant [16] s'en set et viaut] B: ne s'en veut ou ne s'en set [17] requerre] V: querre [18] B adds: mout [19] B adds: en [20] ce il n'en . . . seignor] V lacks

***[3.10.2]** Si orrés coment je, qui ais fait cest livre, sos[1] certainement coment ces esconjuremens et ces destreces dessus dittes[2] se doivent faire[3] de l'home au seignor.[4] [a]

AB

Tout ce qui est dessus escrit des conjuremens que les homes font as seignors[5] dou fait de leur fiés, et la force des paroles dessus dittes, soz je et apris de mon seignor mon oncle le vieill seignor de Baruth.[6]

V

Voirs fu que je oy plusor fois dire a mon seignor mon oncle le viell seignor de Baruth et retraire les esconjuremens que les homes pevent et doivent faire a leur seignor pour la paie de leur fié tels com je les vos ais ci arierres retrais, et me disoit plusors fois que ce que il savoit, savoit il par le roy Heimeri et par mesire Raoul de Tabarie, et il meimes les retraist

Philip of Novara

Tout ce qui est[22] desus escrit des conjuremenz que les homes font es seignors dou fait de leurs fiez, et la force de toutes les paroles dessus[23] dites, devisa et dist le preudome monseignor de Baruth le vieill .ii. foiz, l'une amprés l'autre, en la ploine court devant le roy Henri ou grant palais et bas.[24] Et la out plusors plaideours qui tuit s'i acordarent et

A: fols clvii^{v}–clviii^{r} cap. 239; **B:** fol. 193^{r-v} cap. 243; **V:** fols ccxvi^{v}–ccxvii^{r} cap. 257; Beugnot, pp. 383–4, cap. 239. Cf Philip of Novara **A'**: fols ccxxvi^{v}–ccxxvii^{r}; **B'**: fol. 252^{r-v} cap. 28 (part); **M:** fols 110^{v}–112^{r}; Beugnot, pp. 515–16, cap. 38.

[a] Rubric in Philip of Novara A': Des conjurement que les homes font as seignours; M: Sy oreés le conjurment que messire Philippe Reymont fist au roi Henry de Chippre.

[1] sos] B: soi; V: soit [2] dessus dittes] B: desconditez [3] et ces destreces . . . faire] V: destrece ces desus dites [4] B adds: por le fait de lor fiez [5] as seignors] B: au seignor [6] Baruth] B: Barut [7] entendirent] B: entendoient [8] les] B lacks [9] Et] B lacks [10] vos honors] B: vostre honor [11] et] B: ne [12] Heymeri] B: Aimeri [13] Raou de Thabarie] B: Raul de Tabarie [14] dessus] B: devant [15] tuit] B lacks [16] l'aveit retrait] B: le recordoit et retraist [17] Il i fu mesire Guillaume Visconte] B: Mesire Guillaume Visconte y fu [18] Arneis] B: Erneis de Gibelet [19] Forson] B: Forsson [20] mersierent] B: mercia [21] moult] B lacks [22] B' adds: ci [23] dessus] B': devant [24] ou gran palais et bas] A' lacks

en Chipre en la presence de plusors sages.

distrent que il entendoient que tout enssi estoit veir[25] com il le retraist.[26] Et ces sont li tesmoing qui y furent: messire Guillaume Visconte; messire Hernois;[27] messire Renaut Forsson; messire Pol de Naples; sire Phelippe li Biau; sire Raimon de Conches,[b] qui estoit[28] mout sage borgois et qui venoit et plaideoit sovent en la haute court. Et je y fu et[29] l'oy et l'etendi tout enssi. Et plusors foiz le mis je puis de ce a raison, et mon seignor de Baruth meismes aussi mis je a raison d'aucuns poinz de ce, a qui Diex face merci. Et il m'en[30] dist et enseigna volentiers son avis. Et il[31] me sovient bien pour quoi ce avint: quar le roy et

[b] For these men, see Riley-Smith, *Feudal Nobility*, pp. 122–4.

[25] veir] B': verité [26] le retraist] A': ot retrait [27] Hernois] A': Herneis [28] estoit] A': estoient [29] et] A': qui [30] de ce a . . . m'en] A': mon seignor a raizon d'aucun de ces poins, et il qui Dieu face veraie merci [31] il] A' lacks

		les homes liges avoient juré a tenir les us et les assises dou reaume de Jerusalem, et le roy Henri[32] y estoit porve[33] et avoit mout despendu au siege de Cherines et devoit a ses homes qui ont les assises et a ceaus qui ont les estovoirs, et l'on li requeroit mout de dettes dou tens de sa mere. Et plusours genz qui avoient entendu que l'ome puet conjurer son seignor solonc l'usage dou reaume de Jerusalem de ce dont il est mermez de son fié[34] venoient en court et le conjuroient[35] et ne savoient coment.
Et avint en Chipre que aprés le siege de Cherines que le rei fu moult en dete et deveit moult a ces homes que de son tens que dou tens de sa mere, et moult de ciaus a qui il deveit entendirent[7] simplement que l'ome poeit conjurer son seignor de ce dont il esteit merme de son fié selonc l'usage dou reiaume de Jeruselem.	Car il avient aprés le siege de Cherines que le roy Henri devoit grant dete a ces homes, que des fiés que des estoviers.	
Et avint que la court fu pleniere et que grant partie de ciaus a qui le rei deveit lors vindrent devant le rei en la presence de sa court, et .i. d'iaus por toz conjura le rei et semonst por lui et por toz les[8] autres.	Si s'asemblerent une grant masse de ces homes, dont tout le plus estoient sergens. Poi y avoit de chevaliers. Si vindrent devant le roy en la court, et ot entreaus .i. chevalier qui avoit a nom mesire	A cele foiz avint que sire Guillaume Raimont vint devant le roy en la court et une grant amassee[36] de genz ou lui dont aucuns furent chevaliers et le plus serjanz qui avoient estovoirs a court.

[32] Henri] A' lacks [33] povre] B': pour ce [34] B' adds: il [35] le conjuroient] B': conjuroient le seignor [36] amassee] A': masse

	Guilliaume Raimont qui mout y avoit servi le roy si parla por tous les autres come celui qui acés poi savoit des assises et des husages de la court.	Sire Guillaume Raimont, qui cuida bien faire, conjura le roy et[37] semonst pour lui et pour les autres.
Et[9] mon seignor mon oncle, qui moult ameit lors les homes dou dit reiaume, si lor dist:	Et quant mon oncle vit et conut la simplece de lui et des autres, si se leva et dist:	Adonc se leva monseignor de Baruth[38] et dist:
'Biau seignors, le rei n'a talant de vos gregier ne prendre a point. Car sauve seit vos honors,[10] il semble que vos ne savés mie bien les uz et[11] les assises dou reiaume de Jerusalem, et por ce vos retrais ge volentiers en cest endreit ce que je entens et que je en ais oy et seu par le rei Heymeri,[12] qui moult en saveit, et par mesire Raou de Thabarie[13] et par autre pluissors sages. Et se je i faill ou je en ais riens oblié, il	'Mesire Guilliame, mon seignor le roy se peut mout loer de vous et de tous les autres, especiaument de vous qui mout l'avés servi, pour quoi il n'en a talant de vous prendre a point ne grever, car il semble bien que vous savés poi des assises et des husages dou royaume de Jerusalem. Et je qui mout me loe de vous et des autres vous retrairais volentiers en cestui endroit se que je entens.'	'Messire Guillaume, le roy se opuet[39] mout loer de vos et de touz les autres, et especiaument de vos qui l'avez enssi[40] come norri, et[41] il n'a talent de vos prendre a point ne de vos grever. Mais sauve soit[42] vostre honor, il[43] semble que vos ne savez mie bien les us ne[44] les assises dou reaume de Jerusalem, et je, qui me loe mout a Dieu et a tout le siecle[45] de vos et de touz les autres homes le roy, vos retraira

[37] A' adds: le [38] Baruth] A': Barut [39] le roy se opuet] A': mon seignor le rei se deit [40] enssi] A': aussi [41] et] B': pour quoi [42] soit] A' lacks [43] B' adds: me [44] ne] A': et [45] et a tout le siecle] B' lacks

a saiens pluisors sages homes qui y amenderont et diront ce qu'il entendront.'

Et lors retraist il en la pleniere court par .ii. feis l'une aprés l'autre ce qui est dessus[14] devisié. Et la ot pluissors plaideors qui tuit[15] s'i acorderent et distrent qu'il entendoient que tot ensi estoit come il l'aveit retrait.[16] Il i fu mesire Guillaume Visconte[17] et mesire Arneis[18] et mesire Renaut Forson[19] et mesire Pol de Naples et mesire Phelippe le Biau et sire Raimont

Lor retraist .ii. fois en la court l'une aprés l'autre ce qui est desus devisé. Et lors le dit Guilliaume et tous les autres l'en mercierent.

volentiers en cest endroit ce que je entens[46] et ce[47] que je ai oi et seu par le roy Haymeri[48] qui mout en savoit et par messire Raoul de Thabarie[49] et par autres plusors sages homes.[50] Et se je y faill ou ai riens oblié, il a ceenz plusours sages homes qui y amenderont et en diront ce qui il[51] entendent.'

Quant il out ce dit, sire Guillaume Raimont et toute la cort l'en mercierent mout, et sire Guillaume s'agenoilla devant lui, et il l'en leva mout cortoisement. Adonc avint en la pleine court par .ii. foiz, l'une amprés l'autre, dist tout[52] ce qui est desus devisé.[53]

[46] je entens] A': l'on en entent [47] ce] B' lacks [48] Haymeri] A': Aymeri [49] Raoul de Thabarie] A': Rau de Tabarie [50] homes] A': gens [51] B' adds: en [52] dist tout] B' lacks [53] A' adds: et dit

de Conches qui esteit moult sage borgeis et qui veneit souvent plaideer en la haute court. Et tote la court l'en mersierent[20] moult, et ciaus qui aveent conjuré le rei s'agenoillierent devant lui, et il les en releva moult[21] cortoissement.

3.11. Insertion following chapter 214

This chapter closely follows the material to be found in chapter 62 of Beugnot's edition of Philip of Novara. The chapter is lacking from Philip of Novara MS B'.

***[3.11]** Si dit coment l'on deit requerre devise[1] de terre, et coment le seignor deit comander a faire,[2] et coment ciaus a qui il la comande la deivent faire et dedens[3] quel termine.[4]

Quant aucun[5] viaut aveir devise de terre a son veissin,[6] il deit venir devant le seignor en la court et requerre la[7] selonc l'assise ou l'usage dou[8] reiaume de Jerusalem. Et que ce elle a esté faite, que elle seit porchaussiee. Et[9] ce elle n'a[10] esté faite, que elle le seit sauf son previlege[11] et le pris de son fié, et doit moutir les leus[12] de quei[13] il la requiert et sauf a cui il la requiert.[14] Et ce celui a qui l'on la requiert entent qu'il marchise au requereor des leus moutis, il deit otroier la devise et doit autresi dire et sauver[15] por sei meismes se que l'autre a dit et sauvé por sei. Mais ce il n'entent[16] qu'il marchisse a lui des leus moutis, il peut requerre et aveir respit resnable[17] por aler en sa terre enquerre et saveir de quei il marchist[18] a lui, et la devise deit estres des leus abitiés[19] de leur apartenances. Et le seignor ne deit soufrir que devise requise seit delee, se court[20] ne la respitast[21] en aucune maniere. Ne[22] baillage ne doaire ne deivent[23] devise. Le seignor y deit establir .iiii. de ces homes liges, et ciaus[24] .iiii. deivent jurer sur sainz que eaus[25] a[26] bone fei selonc leur conscience feront celle devise selonc l'assise ou l'usage dou reiaume de Jerusalem. Le seirement deit estre[27] fait en la presence dou seignor et de la court et des parties. Et se aucune des parties fust requise de venir en la court au seirement et n'i[28] venist, totes voies deivent jurer les deviseors, et ce deivent acorder d'estre sur la devise a un jor mouti, et deivent aveir parfaite la devise dedens .xl. jors dou jor qu'il l'ont

---

A: fols clxii^{r}–cxliii^{v} cap. 247; **B:** fols 198^{r}–199^{v} cap. 251; **V:** fols ccxxii^{v}–ccxxiv^{r} cap. 264; Beugnot, pp. 394–5 cap. 247. Cf Philip of Novara **A':** fols ccxxxiii^{v}–ccxxxv^{r}; **M:** fols 159^{r}–162^{r}; Beugnot, pp. 532–4, cap. 62.

---

[1] devise] B: partison; V: devise partison [2] A (but not A rubrics) adds: la [3] dedens] A rubric (fol. 9^{r}): a [4] termine] BV: terme [5] Quant aucun] V: Qui [6] de terre a son veissin] BV lack [7] la] BV: devise a son voisin [8] ou l'usage dou] V: et l'usage dou dit [9] BV add: que [10] n'a] A: n'en a [11] previlege] B: retenaill [12] doit moutir le leus] A: donc moutir le leuc [13] de quei] B: ou [14] et sauf a cui il la requiert] V lacks [15] autresi dire et sauver] V: auci dire et savoir [16] n'entent] B: entent [17] resnable] A: ce me semble [18] marchist] A: marchisse [19] abitiés] B: habitanz [20] court] B: recort [21] respitast] B: respitoit [22] Ne] V: Em [23] deivent] B: tient; V: doit estre [24] et ciaus] B: et cil; V: cil [25] sainz que eaus] B: la saintes evangiles de Dieu que il; V: sains que il [26] a] B: en [27] deit estre] B: est [28] n'i] V: ne

juree. Et le seignor lor deit doner escrivain et sergenz por assembler les genz de la contree, et les parties deivent jurer devant les deviseors qu'il n'ont doné luier ni[29] ne donront, ne chose faite ni[30] ne feront, ne porchassié ni[31] ne porchasseront, par eaus ne par autrui[32] n'ont consenti ne[33] consentiront chose par quei la devise ne peust estre faite bien et leaument sans aucune maniere d'engin ni de tort.

Les deviseors deivent venir en[34] la marche de la devise, et la deivent assembler les plus anciens de la contree et totes manieres de genz par cui il cuident estre assenés,[35] et lor deivent faire jurer qu'il diront et mostreront verité et se contendront[36] leaument ou fait de celle devise, ce il riens en sevent. Et[37] quant il avront ce juré, les deviseors deivent apeler chascun a une part[38] et deivent oyr son dit, se il riens en seit, et faire le dit escrire et requerre li destreitement coment il set ce qu'il dit. Et c'il[39] treuvent home de la lei de Rome qui dit qu'il seit[40] la devise et fu[41] au faire, et[42] il est tel que les deviseors li doignent fei, et lor semble par son dit et par les leus qu'il mostre qu'il face a croire, il le deivent sivre et[43] porchauchier la devise et boner la. Et c'il ne treuvent Franc de la lei de Rome, et il treuvent Suriens a cui il doignent fei, si come il est dit dessus,[44] il le deivent sivre. Et c'il ne treuvent Surien, et il treuvent Grec; et c'il ne treuvent Grec, et il treuvent aucun autre crestien de quelque generacion que il seit; ou[45] c'il ne treuvent crestien, et il treuvent Sarrazin qui jure selonc sa lei; et ce[46] il li donent fei, si come il[47] est dit dessuz,[48] sivre le deivent et porchauchier et boner la devise.

Et ce il ne treuvent devise qui ait[49] esté faite, les deviseors la deivent faire a[50] bone fei selonc leur consience tote novelle. Et la maniere de la novelle devise est tel, se me semble, qu'il deivent regarder les teneures des .ii. parties et enquerre des leus abités que les parties tienent, quels il furent ancienement et qu'il soleient tenir,[51] et ce il sont leus translatés[52] et remués d'une place a[53] autre, et se

[29] ni] BV lack [30] ne chose faite ni] B: ne n'ont chose faite; V: ne chose faite ne [31] ni] B: ne; V lacks [32] autrui] A: aucun de leur amis, ne de l'autrui; V: autrui de leur avoir ne de l'autrui [33] n'ont consenti ne] B: ne consenti n'ont ne ne; V: ne ne [34] en] V: a [35] assenés] V: avees [36] verité et se contendront] B lacks [37] Et] V lacks [38] part] V: partie [39] V adds: ne [40] dit qu'il seit] V: dient que il sevent [41] fu] V: que il furent [42] et] BV: se [43] le deivent sivre et] B: li doivent faire a [44] dit dessus] B: devant dit; V dessus [45] ou] B: et [46] ce] B lacks [47] il] BV lack [48] dit dessuz] B: devant dit [49] ne treuvent devise qui ait] B: treuvent que devise n'ait [50] a] B: en [51] quels il furent . . . tenir] B lacks [52] leus translatés] B: trois lances [53] a] B: en

le leuc de quei il sont remués estoit grant ou petit, et quels[54] apartenances il semble qu'il[55] deust et peust aveir, et se en[56] la teneure que les leus abités ont[57] orendreit raisnablement a gastines et murailles abatues qui par semblant quant les leus esteent abités deussent aveir[58] grant apartenances ou petites.

Et quant les[59] deviseors avront ce enquis[60] et regardé les leus et les places, il deivent parler a l'une partie et a l'autre, et, se il par assentement[61] les pevent acorder, il deivent marchier la devise la ou il sont assenti et boner la come devise novelle. Et ce il ne treuvent assentement, il la deivent faire selonc leur semblant tote novelle et boner la. Et[62] a ce faire deit l'on[63] apeler tant de[64] juene gent come l'on peut[65] aveir de[66] la contree, por aveir longue remembrance et garentie. Mais tot avant deivent estre les deviseors certefiés que les parties marchissent ensemble. Car ce il y a leuc gaste que l'on apelle chemin reau[a] qui est dou seignor,[67] l'on le[68] deit sauver au seignor tot premier;[69] et c'il y[70] a leuc d'autre persone[71] entre .ii. et que les parties ne[72] marchissent ensemble, de riens de ce ne peut estre devisé. Et c'il[73] avenist[74] que il y[75] eust discort entre le deviseors au porchauchier ou a faire la devise en tel maniere que les .ii. s'acordacent a[76] une chose et les autres .ii. a une autre,[77] le seignor i deit establir le quint, et des le comensement le[78] peut il metre, ce il viaut.

Et c'il avenist que aucune des parties mostrast son previlege ou le pris de son fié as deviseors au faire[79] la devise ou avant, sauver li deivent en fait ce il l'a sauvé[80] en dit quant il se mist en la devise. Et se l'autre[81] partie dit qu'il n'a[82] mie son previlege ne le pris de

---

[a] For 'chemin reau' the Philip of Novara MSS read 'vaselico' (MS A') or 'vassilice' (MS M). But note that only MS A has this phrase (See note 67).

---

[54] et quels] B: esquex [55] V adds: y [56] et se en] A: et que; V: en ce en [57] abités ont] A: abités sont; B: ont [58] semblant quant les . . . aveir] B: semblance devisent avoir esté quant lor leus estroient habitez; V: semblant deussent avoir quant les leus estoient abités [59] les] B lacks [60] enquis] B: enquis et il avront veu; V: veu et enquis [61] assentement] B: assemblamant [62] Et] BV lack [63] deit l'on] V: doivent [64] B adds: bon [65] peut] V: pora [66] de] B: en [67] que l'on apelle . . . seignor] B: ou terre qui soit estrainge dou signor ou de autrui; V: outre qui soit dou seignor [68] le] BV: la [69] premier] A: premierement [70] y] B lacks [71] d'autre persone] B: d'autres persones [72] ne] A lacks [73] V adds: y [74] avenist] B: avenoit [75] y] B lacks [76] a] V: en [77] une autre] B: autres [78] le] B: li; V: y [79] au faire] V: a faire de [80] ce il l'a sauvé] B: si il le sauva [81] l'autre] BV: la [82] n'a] V: n'en a

son fié apareillié et il en demande aucun court respit, aveir le deit[83] si court que la devise peust estre devisiee[84] dedens les .xl. jors dessuz moutis. Or voz ai devisiee l'assise et tot[85] ce que je entens que les seignors[86] et les parties et les deviseors deivent faire et dirre.

[83] A adds: et [84] devisiee] B: delivree; V: delivré [85] Or voz ai . . . tot] B: Et ce est [86] les seignors] B: le seignor

3.12. Insertions following chapter 217

In MS A this group of five chapters on the subject of serfs (*vilains*) is sandwiched between chapter 217 and chapter 221. In MSS B and V they follow some further additional material, edited below as appendices 5.3, 5.4 and 7.9, and come immediately before the chapter edited here as appendix 3.13. Whereas in MSS A and B the chapters follow in the same order, in MS V 3.12.3 follows 3.12.4.

These chapters have not been identified as coming from any extant source.

***[3.12.1]** Si dit coment l'on deit tenir[1] l'assise et l'establissement des vilains et des vilaines, et[2] coment l'on en deit user, et premier[3] coment l'on les deit[4] requerre.

Por ce que noz avons parlé des fiés des homes, est il bien[5] que noz devisons l'assise des vilains.[a] Se aucun demande[6] vilains ou vilaines par l'assise et celui a qui il les demande conut[7] qu'il[8] sont en sa terre, il les deit faire venir dedenz .viii. jors. Et ce celui[9] dit qu'il ne les a ne qu'il ne sont en sa terre, il deit jurer que c'il les peut aveir en sa terre ou[10] en son poeir qu'il les fera venir dedenz .xv. jors devant le seignor ou devant ciaus qui seront[11] establis a ce faire, dou jor[12] que il avra juré. Et se les .xv. jors passent et eaus[13] ne vienent, il est tenus par seirement que totes les feis qu'il les pora aveir[14] il meismes[15] les fera venir devant le seignor ou devant les devant[16] només.[17] Et ce il ne les fet venir et il peut estre coneus qu'il seient en sa terre, le seignor ou son comandement a poeir de prendre les[18] en sa terre et de rendre les sans plait a celui qui les requiert, et celui l'avra desrainié[19] et l'autre perdu.

A: fol. clxv[r] cap. 251; **B:** fols 203[v]–204[r] cap. 259; **V:** fol. ccxxxi[r–v] cap. 275; Beugnot, p. 403, cap. 251.

---

[a] V lacks the first sentence.

---

[1] Si dit coment l'on deit tenir] BV: Ci orrés [2] et] BV lack [3] premier] B lacks; V: premierement [4] B adds: et puet [5] est il bien] B: droiz est [6] demande] V: requiert a autre [7] par l'assise et . . . conut] V: et dit [8] conut qu'il] B: conoist qu'il [9] ce celui] V: deffendre les se il y entent d'avoir droit et se il [10] aveir en sa terre ou] B: trover en sa terre ne [11] seront] B: sont [12] ou devant ciaus . . . jor] V lacks [13] eaus] B: il [14] V adds: que [15] meismes] BV lack [16] les devant] B: ceaus qui sont desus [17] ou devant les devant només] V lacks [18] ou son comandment . . . les] V: les doit prendre [19] et celui l'avra desrainié] V: car il avra desraigné par l'assise

***[3.12.2]** Si dit quant les vilains s'enfuient ou partent de la terre de leur seignors, coment il les deivent[1] recouvrer.

AB

Se aucun vilain s'en vait[2] de la terre de son seignor ou fuie, et il apaute aucun apaut ou il a sodees, il deit torner en la terre de[3] son seignor dreiturier par la conoissance des enquereors. Et[4] en ceste assise toz ciaus qui avront delivré vilainz ou vilaines d'autrui poeir, il deivent doner por chascune[5] persone .ii. besanz a ciaus qui sont enquereors.

V

Se aucun vilain s'em part ou fuit de la terre de son seignor et vait en autre terre et il demore auci come par apaut ou sodees dou seignour, il doit torner en la terre de son seignor si tost come il le requera que celui qui l'a en sa terre ne le peut ne ne doit retenir par l'assise.

A: fol. clxv[r–v] cap. 252; **B:** fol. 204[r] cap. 260; **V:** fol. ccxxxi[v] cap. 276; Beugnot, p. 404, cap. 252.

---

[1] seignors, coment il les deivent] V: seignor coment il les doit [2] vait] B: va [3] de] B lacks [4] Et] B lacks [5] chascune] B: auchune

***[3.12.3]** Si dit quant les vilains se marient en autrui terre a autrui vilains[1] que ciaus de son seignor.[2]

Se aucune vilaine s'en vait d'un casau a[3] autre qui ne seit de[4] son seignor,[5] le seignor dou leu ou elle sera venue n'a poeir de li marier, et, se il la marie, il deit doner a son seignor une autre vilaine en eschange a la vaillance par la[6] conoissance de ciaus qui tienent l'assise.[7] [a] Et le seignor deit metre par les[8] contrees et par les seignories en chascun leu .iii. homes liges a tenir l'assise. Et se aucun des juges defaillent[9] ou il se remue de son leuc en autre leuc, l'on deit metre en son leuc un autre. Et deivent jurer ciaus qui sont establis a tenir l'assise en bone fei.

A: fol. clxv[v] cap. 253; **B:** fol. 204[r] cap. 261; **V:** fol. ccxxxii[r] cap. 278; Beugnot, pp. 404–5, cap. 253.

[a] V lacks the remainder of this chapter.

[1] autrui terre a autrui vilains] B: autre terre a autres vilains ou vilaines [2] en autrui terre . . . seignor] V: hors de la terre de leur seignor sans le comandement dou seignor de la vilaine [3] s'en vait d'un casau a] B: s'en va d'un casal en; V: vait de aucun cazal en [4] B adds: la terre de [5] V adds: et [6] vaillance par la] A lacks [7] ciaus qui tienent l'assise] V: bones gens sans faillir [8] deit metre par les] B: dit establir par [9] defaillent] B: defailloit

***[3.12.4]** Si dit quant les vilains se marient hors[1] de la terre de leur seignor sanz le comandement dou seignor de la vilaine.[2]

Se aucun vilain dou seignor ou de chevalier ou de dame veve ou d'autre[3] se marie a[4] vilaine de autre leu sanz le comandement dou seignor de la vilaine, le seignor dou vilain a cui sera mariee la vilaine estrange rendra au seignor de la vilaine une autre en[5] eschange a la vaillance et[6] de tel aage par conoissance de ciaus qui tienent l'assise.[7] Et ce il ne treuvent vilaine qui la vaille, il donra la meillor qu'il trovera[8] d'aage a[9] marier. Et se cil[10] qui sera marié a la vilaine estrange muert, le seignor dou vilain deit aveir son eschange, se la vilaine torne a son premier seignor. Et se la villaine est alee en la terre de l'autre,[11] son seignor a poeir de prendre la. Et ce son seignor i mete[12] defence, celui qui l'avra donee la deit garentir. Et se le seignor dou vilain dit au seignor de la vilaine qu'elle est mariee par son comandement, le seignor de la vilaine deit jurer sur saintes evangilles[13] que elle ne fu mariee par son comandement et ensi prendra[14] l'eschange. Et c'il ne veut jurer, le seignor dou vilain en est quittes et nul restor ne deit doner.

A: fol. clxv^{v} cap. 254; **B:** fol. 204^{r-v} cap. 262; **V:** fols ccxxxi^{v}–ccxxxii^{r} cap. 277; Beugnot, p. 405, cap. 254.

[1] hors] A (but not A rubric fol. 9^{r}): fors [2] la vilaine] B: qui la vilaine est [3] dou seignor ou . . . d'autre] V: de qui que se soit [4] a] V: ave<c> [5] en] B lacks [6] et] BV lack [7] ciaus qui tienent l'assise] V: bones gens [8] la meillor qu'il trovera] V: le meillor vilain qu'il avra [9] a] BV: de [10] se cil] B: se celui; V: c'il [11] de l'autre] B: d'autre seignor [12] mete] B: metoit [13] saintes evangilles] V: sainte evangile [14] prendra] B: perdra

***[3.12.5]** Si dit quel amende[1] deivent faire ciaus qui defaillent de dreit de vilains ou de[2] vilaines dessus[3] dittes.

AB	V
Quant aucun c'est clamé d'autre as juges qui tienent l'assise et il n'est present, les juges li deivent mander par leur letres qu'il veigne et mande le vilain ou[4] les vilains ou vilaines dedens un terme mouti, lequel terme il li[5] manderont escrit es letres selonc le leuc ou il sera.	Seaus qui requierent vilains ou vilaines doivent venir devant le seignor ou devant celui ou ceaus que il avra establi a ce faire, et ceaus doivent semondre celles persounes de qui l'on se clamera qui doivent venir devant eaus dedens .i. terme moti.
Et ce il ne vient dedens le dit terme, ou n'envee[6] les persones qui[7] seront requises, ou, c'il est essoignié,[8] il ne contremande son essoine si come il est devisié en cest livre que l'on deit son essoine[9] contremander, il deit perdre .c. besanz.	Et se il n'en y vienent dedens le dit terme, il doit paier une peine motie.
Et ce il nee qu'il n'a eues les letres ne[10] receues, il deit jurer sur sains qu'il n'a celles letres eues.[11] Et ce il ne le viaut jurer, il deit paier les .c. besanz dessus[12] dis. Et quant celui de qui l'on sera clamés sera enssi semons,[13] son seignor a qui il sera tenu d'omage et a qui il	Et se il le noie qu'il n'en ait esté semons, il doit jurer sur sains, et se il ne veaut jurer il paiera la peine si come est devant dit. Et se il est essoignés, il doit contremander s'essoigne. Et se il n'i vient et il envoie ceaus vilains ou vilaines que l'on li requiert dedens le dit

A: fols clxv^{v}–clxvi^{r} cap. 255; **B:** fols 204^{v}–205^{r} cap. 263; **V:** fol. ccxxxii^{r-v} cap. 279; Beugnot, p. 406, cap. 255.

[1] quel amende] B: queles amendes; V: ques amendes [2] defaillent de dreit . . . de] B: sont deffaillanz dou droit establi des vilains ou des [3] dessus] B: qui sont devant; B rubrics (fol. 27^{v}): devant [4] et mande le vilain ou] B: ou que il mande [5] li] B lacks [6] n'envee] B: ne voie [7] qui] B: que li [8] est essoignié] B: n'est essoignez et [9] son essoine] B lacks [10] eues les letres ne] B: les lettres [11] eues] B: receues [12] dessus] B: devant [13] sera enssi semons] A lacks

fera le servise li deit doner congie de venir devant les juges, et ce il n'i vient aprés le congie, il est encheu en la peine dessus ditte.

terme, il en est quite. Et quant il est enci semons, toutes semonces et toutes servises le delivrent se il n'a propre mandement dou chief seignor. Et puis que il sera venus devant ceaus qui sont establies a ce faire, il fera venir les vilains que l'on li requiert dedens .i. terme moti. Et se il ne les fait venir, il doit paier une peine motie.

Et ce il avient que celui vilain que l'on[14] requiert fuit, il deit jurer sur sains[15] que celui que l'on requiert[16] ne s'en foy par son comandement, et que totes les feis qu'il le pora aveir ou trover il le fera venir devant les juges.

Et se il dit que il sont fuis, il doit jurer sur sains que ceaus que l'on requiert ne son<t> fuis par son comandement et par son sens et que toutes les fois qu'il les pora trouver ne avoir a son comandement, il le fera venir devant les juges qui sont establis.

Et ce il ne viaut[17] jurer, il deit doner en eschange un autre vilain a la vaillance par la conoissance des juges. Et totes les feis que les juges manderont querre vilains ou vilaines por faire enqueste et il n'i[18] vienent dedenz le terme qui lor sera mis,[19] chascun deit paier .x. besanz d'amende.

Et se il ne veaut jurer il doit doner autres en eschange a la vaillance. Et se les vilains que l'on requiert vienent devant les juges et dient que il ne sont mie de celui qui les requiert et hom a besoign d'envoier quere autres vilains pour faire enqueste, il doivent venir dedens le terme que il lor sera mis. Et se il n'i vienent il doivent paier une peine motie.

---

[14] B adds: li [15] B adds: evangiles [16] que l'on requiert] B: vailain qui li est requis
[17] B adds: venir [18] n'i] B: ne [19] terme qui lor sera mis] B: dit terme

3.13. A CONCLUDING CHAPTER

In MS A this is the final chapter in John's treatise, coming directly after chapter 239. The rubric and the prayer at the end leave no doubt that it was intended as a conclusion to the whole work. However, in MSS B and V, where it has a different rubric, it is placed earlier and follows the chapter edited above as appendix 3.12.5.

The information on the royal succession and the length of the kings' reigns is correct. The inscription from the tomb of King Baldwin I (died 1118 and buried in the Holy Sepulchre) is of interest, not least because several other transcriptions have been preserved. They are, in chronological order:

- Theodericus (in the Holy Land in 1169 or 1172)[1]
- The 1309 recension of the *Lignages d'Outremer*[2]
- Nicolas de Martoni (in the Holy Land 1394–95)[3]
- Bernadino Amico (in the Holy Land in the 1590s; first published 1609)[4]
- Francesco Quaresmi (in the Holy Land in 1626; first published 1639)[5]
- Elzear Horn (1728)[6]

The readings given by these authorities vary, but it is immediately clear that a number of blunders have been introduced into the John of Ibelin manuscript-tradition. This is not the place to discuss the precise wording of the original inscription, except to note that the version in the early fourteenth-century version of the *Lignages* preserved in the same manuscript as the V text of John's treatise is clearly independent of the version found here.

---

[1] Theodericus, 'Libellus de Locis Sanctis', ed. R.B.C. Huygens in *Peregrinationes Tres: Saewulf, John of Würzburg, Theodericus*, Corpus Christianorum, Continuatio Mediaeualis 139 (Turnholt, 1994), p. 154.

[2] Vatican: MS. Codex Vaticanus latinus 4789 (i.e. MS V), fol. cclxxvi[v].

[3] 'Relation du pèlerinage à Jérusalem de Nicolas de Martoni, notaire italien (1394–1395)', ed. L. Le Grand, *Revue de l'Orient latin*, 3 (1895), p. 619.

[4] Bernardino Amico, *Plans of the Sacred Edifices of the Holy Land*, trans. T. Bellorini and E. Hoade with preface and notes by B. Bagatti (Jerusalem, 1953), p. 104.

[5] Francesco Quaresmi, *Historica, Theologica et Moralis Terrae Sanctae Elucidatio*, ed. C. de Tarvisio (Venice, 1880–81), vol. 2, p. 365.

[6] His drawing of the tomb, with a version of the inscription identical to Quaresmi's has been reproduced several times, for example in J. Folda, *The Art of the Crusaders in the Holy Land, 1098–1187* (Cambridge, 1995), p. 74.

The latter part of the chapter—King Aimery's knowledge of the law and his failed attempt to get Ralph of Tiberias to record the law for posterity—is loosely adapted from Philip of Novara chapter 47 and draws on material which comes straight after Philip's description of the *Letres dou Sepulcre* in the same chapter. It is noteworthy that the compiler of the '*z*' recension inserted Philip's account of the *Letres dou Sepulcre* into John's prologue (edited above at 3.1.1), and the theme of that account—the uncertainty about enacted law dating from before 1187—is now taken up again. The two sentences beginning 'Le rei Heymeri' are adapted from Philip's chapter 94, but it should be noted that in his treatise Philip does not allude to the *Livre dou Conquest*. It is generally agreed that the *Livre dou Conquest* is the Old French version of William of Tyre, but the story of King Amaury ransoming Aimery from Muslim captivity is not to be found there nor in any other source.

***[3.13]** Ce est le dereain chapitle de cest livre.[a]

Vos avés oy[1] dessus les assises et les usages dou reiaume de Jerusalem, lequels comensa premierement Godefrei du Buillon,[2] qui fu le premier roi de Jerusalem; mais il ne vost onques porter corrone[3] si come il se contient ou prelogue[4] de cest livre. Il ne regna que un an. Aprés lui regna Baudoyn[5] son frere .xviii. ans. Cil[6] fu le premier roi latin qui porta corrone ou reiaume de Jerusalem. Il trespassa en la terre[7] d'Egypte et fu porté en Jerusalem et mis souz Monte Calvaire[8] devant Golgatas[9] de pres son frere Godefrei.[10] Sur laquel sepulture sont escris ces vers:

Rex Baldoynus,[11] alter Iudas Machabeus,
spes patrie, vigor ecclesie, <virtus>[b] utriusque[12]
quem formidabant, cui dona[13] tributa ferebant[14]
Dam,[15] Cesar et Egyptus[c] [16] ac[17] homicida[18] Damascus.
Pro dolor in modico[19] clauditur hoc tumulo.[20] [d]

A: fol. clxxiv[r–v] cap. 273; **B:** fols 205[r]–206[r] cap. 264; **V:** fols ccxxxii[v]–ccxxxiv[r] cap. 280; Beugnot, pp. 428–30 cap. 273. Cf. Philip of Novara **A':** fols ccxxxi[r] (part), cclv[r] (part); **M:** fols 118[v]–119[r] (part), 181[v] (part); Beugnot, pp. 522–3 cap. 47 (part), pp. 569–70 cap. 94 (part).

---

[a] Rubric in B: Ci orrés en quel aage et de quant rois furent faites et ordeneez les assises que vos avez oiés en cest livre. Rubric in V: Ici orés en quel aage et de quans rois furent les assises que vous avés leues en cestui livre, et coment elles furent faites et ordenees.

[b] Supplied from Theodericus, Martoni, Amico and Quaresmi who agree in giving this reading.

[c] For 'Dam, Cesar et Egyptus', Theodericus and Quaresmi read: 'Cedar et Egyptus, Dan . . .' Their reading is probably to be preferred. The 1309 *Lignages* has 'Cedar, Dan, Egiptus . . .', Martoni 'Cedar Egyptus . . .', and Amico 'Cedar Aegypti, Dan . . .'.

[d] V here provides this translation of the Latin: Roi Bauduin, segont Judas Machabe, esperance dou pays, vigour de l'iglise, la vertu de tous, douquel fermissoient a cui treu rendoient et dons et presens portoient ceaus de Cesar et de Dam et Egipte Domas homecide. Allas, quel dolour! Em poi d'ore est sur lui close ceste sepulture.

---

[1] BV add: ci [2] Godefrei du Buillon] B: Godefroi de Boillon; V: le duc Guodeffroi de Buillon [3] V adds: d'or [4] prelogue] B: prologue; V: provelige [5] Baudoyn] B: Bauduyn; V: Bauduin [6] Cil] B: Celui [7] en la terre] V: au royaume [8] Calvaire] BV: Calvarie [9] Golgatas] BV: Golgata [10] Godefrei] B: Godefroy; V: Guodefroy [11] Baldoynus] V: Bauduinus [12] utriusque] V: virtutis quia [13] cui dona] A: cui danat; V: tridonat [14] ferebant] A: fedebant; V: faciebant [15] Dam] B: Nam [16] et Egyptus] A: et Egittus; V: Egiptus [17] ac] A: hac [18] homicida] B: homicidda [19] in modico] V lacks [20] hoc tumulo] A: hoc tumulto; V: hec tumulo

Aprés lui fu coronés Baudoyn de Borc[21] que l'on apeloit en surnon l'Aguillon, lequel regna .xiii.[22] anz en belle vie et en bone et a la mort se rendi chanoine dou Sepulcre. Aprés lui fu coronés Fouque[23] qui fu gendre dou dit Baudoyn,[24] lequel regna .xii. ans et morut devant Accre[25] a la chace d'un[26] lievre et fu portés en Jerusalem. Et[27] aprés lui regna Baudoyn[28] son fiz[29] .xx. ans. Et[30] aprés lui regna Amauri son frere .xi. anz. Et[31] aprés lui regna Baudoyn son fiz, le mezel, .xi. anz, et en sa vie fist il corroner[32] le petit rei qui avoit nom Baudoyn.[33] Fiz estoit dou marquis.

En l'aage des .vii. rois dessus[34] dis, qui fu .lxxxvi. anz, furent les assises faites et establies. Et[35] avant que la terre fust perdue en usoit l'on miaus que l'on ne peut orres faire.[36] Car noz les savons assés povrement, et ce[37] que noz en savons noz ne le savons que[38] par oyr dirre et par usage. Et nos tenons por assise ce que noz avons veu user come assise, dissant que l'on entent que tel[39] est celle assise, et[40] que l'on ne set ce elle est fornie[41] ou non. Mais l'on le dit[42] a nete conscience selonc son[43] entendement. Moult en pooient miaus user et ouvrer seurement ou reiaume de Jerusalem ainz que le terre fust[44] perdue la ou les assises estoient, si come il devise ou prelogue de cest livre, et aprés la terre perdu[45] fu tot perdu. Et veirs est que les anciens noz en[46] laissierent assés[47] de leur science. Le rei Heymeri de cuis noz trovons ou *Livre dou Conquest* que le rei Amauri rechata[48] de la prison de Domas,[49] qui estoit un povre vallet et gentishom, puis ot il toz les offices dou reiaume des la chamberlainie jusque a la conestablie, et puis fu il roi des .ii. reiaumes: premierement de Chipre et puis de Surie, et ambedeus les[50] gouverna bien et sagement jusque a la mort. Il[51] sot miaus les us[52] et les assises[53] que nul autre, se tesmoingnent ciaus qui le virent, et moult les avoit en memoire. Mais mesire Raou de Thabarie[54] estoit plus soutil de lui, si que

---

[21] Baudoyn de Borc] V: Bauduin dou Bourc [22] .xiii.] A: .xviii. [23] Fouque] B: Fouques [24] Baudoyn] B: Baudoin; V: Bauduin [25] Accre; V: Acre et [26] d'un] V: dou [27] Et] V lacks [28] Baudoyn] V: Bauduin [29] V adds: et regna [30] Et] BV lack [31] Et] BV lack [32] V adds: son fis [33] Baudoyn] V: Bauduin [34] dessus] B: devant [35] Et] V lacks [36] peut orres faire] BV: fait ores [37] ce] B lacks [38] que] B: fors [39] tel] B: cele [40] celle assise, et] V: et celle assise [41] fornie] V lacks [42] l'on le dit] B: on ne doit [43] son] V: nostre [44] fust] V: fu [45] aprés la terre perdu] B: a perdre la terre; V: a la terre perdue [46] en] BV lack [47] assés] B lacks [48] Amauri rechata] V: Heimeri fu racheté [49] la prison de Domas] B: prison [50] ambedeus les] V: au .ii. [51] Il] BV: Et [52] us] B: usages; V: husages [53] B adds: dou reaume de Jerusalem; V: dou royaume [54] Raou de Thabarie] B: Raul de Baruch; V: Raoul de Tabarie

le dit roi pria moult mesire Raou[55] ainz qu'il fust mau de lui qu'il vosist que entre eaus .ii. et autres .ii. vavassors feiscent escrire et renouveler les assises, et diseit le dit rei qu'il entendeit qu'il les recordereit moult bien si que[56] poi en faudreit. Mesire Raou respondi que de ce que il saveit ne fereit il ja son pareill nul borgeis ne nul bas[57] home letré.

Et[58] tot ce que je en ais dit et fait, se je en aucune chose ais failli or meseré,[59] je pri a toz ciaus qui le liront[60] qu'il prient Nostre Seignor qu'il par sa[61] mesericorde conduie les devans dis et moi meismes et toz crestiens a veraie repentance et a droite confession et a parfaite peneance[62] et a honorable fin. Amen.

[55] mesire Raou] B: le devant dit Raoul; V: le dit Raoul [56] que] B lacks [57] bas] V: sage [58] B adds: en; V: de [59] meseré] B: mespris [60] le liront] B: ce orront; V: ce oyront [61] V adds: douce [62] peneance] BV: penitence

APPENDIX 4—ADDITIONS UNIQUE TO MS A

The Venice Marciana: MS fr. App. 20 (= 265) was copied in Acre ca. 1290. This manuscript represents most closely the '*z*' recension as described in appendix 3, but it also contains a small amount of extra material, and it is this that is edited in this appendix.

4.1. Insertion following chapter 56

This chapter is something of a puzzle. It is not found in MS B, and so should probably not be considered part of the additional material that characterises the '*z*' recension. However, a version of the same chapter is present in the equivalent place in MS V. It is drawn from Philip of Novara (cap. 18 in Beugnot's edition). In the Philip of Novara manuscripts this chapter survives in two different forms: a short version represented by MSS A' and B' and a longer version represented by MS M. In the John of Ibelin manuscripts MS A reproduces the longer text while MS V has the shorter. But how and why the text should have been transmitted in this fashion is not clear.

Note the reference in MS A to John of Ibelin lord of Beirut as 'mon oncle'—a phrase not found in parallel passage in Philip of Novara MS M.

*[4.1] Coment on deit estre garni de prevelige ou de recort de court.

Celui qui[1] viaut requerre a son fié chose qui seit de fié, il deit estre garni de prevelige, c'il[2] peut, ou de recort de court. Le recort[3] peut estre en .ii. manieres: l'une si est dou don; l'autre si est se la court a veu celui[4] saissi et tenant de celui irritage et usant celui qui le requiert ou son ancestre come de son fié. Et ce ce est de l'ancestre et le seignor[5] vueille dire qu'il ne seit que[6] celui fu son ancestre, il esteut que le requerant preuve le parenteis. Et ce il le peut prover par .ii. leaus garens de la lei de Rome,[7] homes ou femes, bien baste. Et en garentie de parenteys ne d'aage n'a nul tornes de bataille de carelle qui seit de seignor a l'home ne de l'home au seignor.[8] Et les garens se sont mie tenus de dire: 'Nos savons que tel fu fiz de tel home', mais tant deivent dire sanz plus: 'Noz oymes et veymes que tel teneit por son fiz leau tel, et il teneit lui por son pere'. Et ensi se clamoient l'un l'autre.[9] Et qui est garni de tot ce qui est dessuz dit[10] peut requerre seurement ce qui est fié ou de fié, et,[11] ja ne seit il garni de ce,[12] se le seignor viaut errer en bone fei et il peut saveir[13] par gens anciens ou par vois comune ou par aucune renomee que l'irritage ait esté des ancestres dou requerant, et par longue teneure de mescreans ou de autres ennemis en ait esté longuement dessaissi le requerant ou ces ancestres, rendre li deit ce il ne viaut maligner.[a]

Et de tel endreit avint un grant escandle en Surie. Car il metent sus a monseignor mon oncle le vieill sire de Baruth qu'il fist un esgart en Surie quant l'empereor i fu dont tote la court se tint a lui, et dist par esgart que celui qui voleit requerre fié au seignor ne le poiet aveir c'il n'aveit prevelige ou recort de court. Mais le

---

A: fol. xxxviii^{r-v} cap. 69; **V:** fols lii^{v}–liii^{r} cap. 67; Beugnot, pp. 112–113 cap. 69. Cf. Philip of Novara **A':** fols ccxiii^{v}–ccxiv^{r}; **B':** fol. 241^{v} cap. 13; **M:** fols 83^{v}–84^{v}; Beugnot, pp. 492–3 cap. 18.

---

[a] Ms V and Philip of Novara MSS A' and B' end here.

---

[1] Celui qui] A: Qui [2] V adds: le [3] Le recort] A: La court [4] si est se . . . celui] V: se la court l'a veu [5] V adds: le [6] que] V: se [7] de la lei de Rome] V lacks [8] bien baste. Et . . . seignor] V: si com est desus dit en l'autre chapitre c'om doit prover preuve de parenté [9] clamoient l'un l'autre. Et] V: clament l'un a l'autre [10] dit] V: escrit [11] fié ou de fié, et] V: o fié ou est de fié [12] de ce] A lacks [13] errer en bone . . . saveir] V: ouvrer em bone foi se il peut ce prover

proudome s'en escondisseit moult et disseit bien que ensi ne fu il mie. Mais il avint sanz faille que la princece, mere dou prince Rupin, requist l'eritage dou Thoron et dist qu'il fu de ces ancestres et ce offri elle a prover tot ensi come la court esgardereit qu'elle prover le deust come celle qui en esteit bien garnie. Monseignor de Baruth esgarda sans faille et la court o lui que ce elle poeit prover le don ou la teneure par prevelige ou par recort de court et le parenteys par .ii. garenz si come est dit dessus que ce esteit assés; et veir dist il que ce esteit assés. Mais por ce ne dist il mie que, ce le seignor en poeit estre certefié en autre maniere, que rendre ne li deust.[b]

[b] Frederick II was in the East in 1228–29. He recovered the lordship of Toron from the Muslims by the Treaty of Jaffa and intended giving it to the Teutonic Knights, whereupon it was claimed by Alice of Armenia, a niece of Humphrey IV of Toron. See Riley-Smith, *Feudal Nobility*, pp. 171–2.

4.2. Insertion following chapter 115

This short chapter is an abridged version of the chapter which follows in MS A, edited above as chapter 116. There was clearly some confusion in the transmission of the text at this point, as at the corresponding place MS B gives chapter 116 twice.

***[4.2]** Coment celui vers qui l'on est plege dette peut celui qui li est ensi tenus mener par laquel de .ii. voies que il vodra.

Il avient aucune feis que l'on est plege dette, et celui a qui l'on est ensi tenus peut celui qui li est ensi tenus mener par laquel des .ii. voies qu'il le vodra mener: ou par la plegerie, ou par la detterie. Et ce il le meine par la deterie, il deit demander gage et faire le crier maintenant et livrer au tiers jor, car il n'i a point de quinsaine ne plus de terme que le tiers jor. Et ce il muert, l'on peut requerre a celui de ces heirs qui irrite en ces biens par la raisson de la deterie, ce que l'on ne poreit pas faire a l'heir de celui qui est plege sans plus. Et por ce fait il miaus receveir plege et dette que plege sans plus.

A: fols lxxvi^{v}–lxxvii^{r} cap. 129; Beugnot, p. 204 cap. 129.

4.3. A later medieval table of contents

In MS A John's law book ends at fol. clxxiv[v]. There then follows John's discourse on the Regency of the Kingdom of Jerusalem (edited below as appendix 8.1) which ends at fol. clxxvii[r]. Written on the remainder of that folio and on fol. clxxvii[v] is a summary table of contents. There are two scribal hands, both of which belong to the later middle ages, one on the recto and the other on the verso.

The list gives the chapter numbers as they appear in MS A. The numbers in this edition are added here in brackets.

The chief interest of this table is in showing which chapters someone in the later middle ages regarded as the most significant, and the idea that the treatise could be divided into four sections.

*[4.3]

A: fol. clxxvii^{r-v}; Beugnot, pp. 431–2.

[a] Change of hand.

[b] Should read: .ccliii.

[c] Cap. 225 begins the description of the ecclesiastical hierarchy. The services actually begin at cap. 237 (= 271 in MS A).

APPENDIX 5—THE 'z_1' RECENSION

After the '*z*' recension, characterised by additions and alterations common to MSS A, B, and V, there was a further round of changes which are evidenced by alterations common to MSS B and V. This new recension is designated 'z_1'.

The chief alterations made at this stage were the decision to move the final chapter to a point earlier in the text (discussed above at appendix 3.13) and the addition of the material edited below in this appendix. It is likely that it was also at this point in the development of the text that it was decided to place a version of the *Lignages d'Outremer* at the end of John's text and treat it as an integral part of it. MS B contains a version of the *Lignages d'Outremer* which, textual variants apart, is very similar to that found in MS A and is datable to c. 1268–1275.[1] The difference between them is that in MS B the *Lignages* follows directly after John's text with the chapter numbers (nos. 285–301) running on sequentially, whereas in MS A John's treatise and the *Lignages* are separated by other material. In MS V the later version of the *Lignages*, which M.-A. Nielen-Vandevoorde would date to 1309, has been placed at the end of the treatise, again with the chapter numbers (nos. 331–61) running sequentially.[2]

In this appendix I have used MS B as the base, preferring MS V only when the readings in B are manifestly corrupt or when V finds support is parallel passages in Philip of Novara or other authors.

---

[1] Nielen-Vandevoorde, 'Un livre méconnu', pp. 109–13, 118–19. [2] Nielen-Vandevoorde, 'Un livre méconnu', pp. 111, 112.

5.1. Insertion following chapter 196

MSS B and V each have different versions of the same material inserted at the same point. Two chapters further on, in the chapter edited above as appendix 3.9, there is another allusion to the rule that vassals no longer have to serve in person after the age of sixty, and it is possible that this material is included here as the editor of 'z_1' had realised that this convention had not hitherto been mentioned.

Note that the syntax of the first sentence in MS V is blundered.

***[5.1]** Quant l'ome a passé aage ou est maaigniez de mahaing apparent, quel servise il doit au seignor.[1]

B

Il est en l'assise[2] ou en l'usage dou reaume de Jerusalem que puis que l'ome a passé .xl.[3] anz de age ou que il soit mahaignié si que il ne puisse chevauchier ne armes porter il est quite dou servise de son cors et ne doit au seignor de servise que tenir hernois: c'est assavoir et armes que le seignor puet prendre ou faire prende en son besoing.

V

Il est assise et costume et husage que tous chevaliers, qui ont passé .lx. ans d'aage ou que il soit mahaignés de mehaign aparant, est quite dou servise de son cors, et, il s'en veaut escuser par ce que il a passé aage, le seignor en avra le cheval et les armes en eschange de son cors a son besoin toutes les fois que il en vodra semondre. Et se il est apellé ou il apelle de chose ou il a faire bataille que il ne s'en deffendra par champion se de son gré ne le veaut faire.

B: fol. 177v cap. 228; **V:** fol. cxcviir cap. 240; Beugnot, pp. 358–9, cap. 226 bis.

[1] quel servise il doit au seignor] V: doit estre quite dou servise [2] l'assise] B: l'asse [3] Evidently an error for .lx. as in MS V. See appendix 3.9 for confirmation that men aged over sixty were no longer required to serve in person. For other examples in which MS B reads '.xl.' for '.lx.' see cap. 234 n. 34, cap. 237 n. 9.

5.2. Insertion following chapter 205 (or 206)

In MS B this chapter is inserted between caps 205 and 206, but in MS V it comes after cap. 206. It closely follows the chapters from Philip of Novara edited by Beugnot as caps 32, 33, 34 and the first part of cap. 35. In B the chapter is presented as a single unit, but in V a second chapter begins at the point where Philip of Novara cap. 35 starts and it continues without a break to include the remainder of Philip's chapter—a passage which forms a separate chapter in MSS A and B and which is edited above as appendix 3.10.1.

***[5.2]** Ci amprés orrés[1] coment l'ome doit conjurer son seignor et de quoi, et, se il le faisoit[2] autrement qu'ensi com il est devisé, il le doit amender au seignor.

Se aucun des homes dou seignor[3] est merme de son fié ou de sa paie[4] ou d'autre[5] chose que le seignor ait et tiegne sanz esgart et[6] sanz conoissance de cort sans assise et sans usage,[7] il doit requerre a son seignor ce de quoi il est mermez de son fié amiablement.[8] Et se il por tant ne le puet avoir, il doit venir en la cort et requerre conseill et faire et dire par son conseill: 'Sire, tel qui ci est vos requiert, et je por lui, que vos le faciez paier de tel chose que vos li devez, ou de tel chose que vos avez, que il entent qui est de son fié et de tant entent il que il est merme de son fié. Et se vos ensi ne l'entendez, il vos prie et requiert come a son seignor que vos le faciez enquerre et esclarcir et li delivrez son fié.'[9] Se le seignor dit que il enquerra,[10] le conseill dou requereor doit dire: 'Sire,[11] quant comandez vos que il reviegne devans vos?' Le seignor sanz faille doit respondre a tel jor. Et ce le[12] jor est covenable l'ome le doit sofrir.

Et quant le jor sera passé ou venu,[13] il doit revenir[14] devant le seignor, se il n'est[15] paié, et doit requerre ou[16] faire requerre sa paie disant que le jor est passé. Se le seignor veut dire que il l'avoit oblié ou que il ne l'a[17] esclarci et il sur ce en demande[18] un cort respit, avoir le puet, et, se il passe le jor,[19] l'ome vient avant[20] en la cort et[21] puet faire dire: 'Sire, je vos ai requis ma paie ou tel chose qui est de mon fié amiablement, premierement hors de[22] cort et puis en cort par plusors foiz, et vos en avez eu plusors respiz, et de ce trai

---

B: fols 190^{r}–192^{r} cap. 240; **V:** fols ccxiv^{v}–ccxv^{v} caps 254, 255 (part). Cf. Philip of Novara **A':** fols ccxxiii^{r}–ccxxv^{r}; **B':** fols 249^{r}–251^{r} caps 27–8; **M:** fols 101^{v}–106^{v}; Beugnot, pp. 508–12, caps 32–4, 35 (part).

---

1 amprés orrés] B: orrés amprés 2 faisoit] V: fait 3 aucun des homes dou seignor] V: .i. home ou une feme 4 ou de sa paie] B lacks 5 d'autre] V: d'aucune autre 6 et] V: ou 7 sans assise et sans usage] B lacks 8 V adds: entre lui et lui 9 doit venir en . . . fié] V: li doit requerre en la court .ii. fois ou .iii. Et se il por tant ne le fait paier, il doit venir en la court et demander conseill a faire requerre par son conseill si come il est devisé en cestui livre. Et 10 enquerra] V: le quera 11 requereor doit dire: 'Sire] V: conquereor doit dire 12 tel jor. Et ce le] B: celui 13 ou venu] V lacks 14 revenir] B: venir 15 n'est] V: n'en est 16 requerre ou] V lacks 17 ne l'a] V: encor ne l'avoit 18 demande] B: requiert 19 passe le jor] V: le passe et 20 vient avant] B: puet revenir 21 et] V: il 22 hors de] V: dehor

je bien[23] la cort a garant.'[a] De qui en avant il puet bien conjurer et[24] semondre[b] le seignor si come vos orrez amprés. Et si covient que il die de sa bouche ce, et son conseill li puet dire belement mot a mot en l'oreille, quar nul ne puet conjurer son seignor par autrui que par soi meismes. Le requerant doit dire: 'Sire, je vos ai requis tel chose qui est de mon fié, et vos en ai deporté tant come je doi ou plus selonc mon entendement. Des ore ne vos en veull plus deporter, dont je vos pri et requier et semons et conjur come mon seignor en quanque je puis et doi que vos d'ui en quinz jors <ou de demain en quinze jors>[c] ou depuis demain en quinze jors m'aiez paié et delivré ce que je vos ai requis, et de ce trai je la cort a garant. Et se les trois quinzaines qui sont .xvii. jors passent sanz delivrance, il doit venir en la cort, et besoing li est que il i ait plusors de ceaus qui furent au començament et qui sachent que les trois quinzaines sont passees.

Adonc doit dire: 'Sire, je semons et conjurai et requis si come la cort l'entendi que vos m'eussiez delivré ce dont je sui merme de mon fié par les trois quinzaines qui sont passees, et vos ne l'avez <fait>.[d] Dont je vos pri et requier come mon seignor, et vos semons et conjure en quanque je puis et doi que vos de hui en quarante jors ou de demain en quarante jors ou depuis demain en .xl. jor. m'aiez paié ou delivré ce qui est de mon fié, et de ce trai je la cort a garant. Et se les trois quaranteines qui sont .xlii. jors passent sanz delivrance, le requerant puet venir en la cort et dire ou faire dire que por tant come il a requis et semons et conjuré son seignor de ce de quoi il est merme de son fié. Le seignor, si come il entent, est tenu de lui delivrer et veut que por tant le face se la cort l'esgarde ou conoist. Et se le seignor ne puet dire ou monstrer par raison a l'encontre ce por quoi il demore, la cort puet bien esgarder

[a] Philip of Novara MSS B' and M begin a new chapter here.
[b] V lacks an extended passage starting here, substituting the words: 'par les quinsaines et quarantaines qui sont devant devisees c'om doit son seignor semondre de avoir la paie de son fié ou ce qu'il li faut de son fie. Et se le seignor por tant ne le delivre, il le peut guagier et faire guagier a ces pers si come est devant devisé as autres chapistles.' The cross-references are to caps 178, 198, 204–5.
[c] Supplied on the basis of the readings in the Philip of Novara MSS.
[d] Supplied on the basis of the readings in the Philip of Novara MSS.

[23] vos en avez . . . trai je bien] V: de ce en trais [24] conjurer et] V lacks

ou conoistre que assez en a fait le requerant, et que sa paie ou sa delivrance de ce dont il est merme de son fié doit avoir sanz delai.[c]

Quant la cort avra esgardé, le requerant puet dire: 'Sire, puis que la cort a esgardé que je par usage ou par assise ai mené mon seignor a ce que je doi et de ce de quoi je sui merme de mon fié et que il me doit paier ou delivrer sanz delai, laquel chose il n'a ancore faite, dont je par l'asisse, se ele y est, ou par l'usage[25] le gaga dou servise que je li doi de cest fié, et de ce trai je la cort a garant.' Enssi puet l'ome gagier son seignor resnablement de son servise. Jusques a l'ore que il ait ce delivré il ne li fera servir de son[26] cors ne de conpaignons, se il le doit de celui fié, ne de hernois tenir, se il ne veut. Et quant il li rendra ce qu'il li doit de son fié, il covendra qu'il li reinde aussi bien la quantité dou tens que il le servoit se il peut avoir recort de cort de tot ce qui est devant dit. Mais por ce que le tens esloingne et cort oblie plus tost plusors choses que une soule, se il fait que sage, quant le trois quinzaines et les trois quarantaines seront passee et il vient a gagier son seignor de son servise, il li dira ou fera dire que por tant come en est avenu il veut gagier son seignor de son servise que il li doit de celui fié se la cort esgarde ou conoist que faire le doie ou puisse. Et se la cort fait esgart ou conoissance de ce legierement sera tenu et recordé se besoing est, et l'ome sera hors de perill. Et se le seignor demore un an et un jor amprés ce que son home l'avra gagié si resnablement come il est devant dit qu'il ne le delivre enterinement[27] de ce de quoi il est merme de son fié, il se puet se il veut forspaysier avec autre seignor en la terre ou il est ou en autre sanz mesfaire au seignor. Et couvendra en la fin que il soit aussi bien paiez dou tens que il n'a mie servi le seignor et que a servi a autrui ou pais ou dehors come dou tens qu'il a servi le seignor ainz qu'il le gagast dou servise.[f]

Et en ce puet avoir grant damage le seignor et l'ome grant profit, se il tient grant partie de son fié et est merme de poi. Et se il est mermez dou plus et l'ome ne veulle sievre ceste maniere qui est devant dite, il se puet prendre a l'autre qui est desouz devisee.

---

[c] Philip of Novara MS A' begins a new chapter here.
[f] Philip of Novara MS A' begins a new chapter here.

---

[25] l'usage (following the Philip of Novara MSS] B: l'assise [26] de son (following the Philip of Novara MSS)] B: se de [27] enterinement (following the Philip of Novara MSS)] B: delivrement

Tantost come l'esgart est fait le seignor li doit delivrer[28] son fié <de>[g] ce dont il est mermez sanz delay. Se le seignor ne le veut faire, il puet prier et requerre et semondre et conjurer ses pers que il constraignent le seignor que il tiegne ce que il ont esgardé que il face a lui qui est leur per ce que faire li doit por leur esgart. Et se le seignor ne le fait, il le doivent gagier de leur servises et ne le doivent jusques a tant que il ait forni parfaitement leur esgart.[h]

Et por la foy qui est entre seignor et home, l'ome ne doit faire riens de tot[29] ce qui est devant[30] dit se il n'entent certainement que il puet faire ce[31] loiaument. Et se le seignor entent que son home li requiert[32] raison et il a[33] pooir de l'amender, il ne doit noient soufrir ne atendre ce qui[34] est desus escrit[35] ainz le doit tantost delivrer por sa foy aquiter. Et se il n'a pooir dou delivrer,[36] il ne le doit noient encombrer par point de plait, ainz doit soufrir que l'ome parviegne a sa raison et a son profit par raison,[37] ou il doit querre fin se il la puet trouer. Mais au començament de la requeste, ainz qu'il soit semons ne conjuré, il se doit travaillier de savoir la quantité certainement. Et se l'ome li requiert outrage, il le[38] puet faire esclarrir en la cort: le seignor y avra henor et l'ome honte.

Et se il avenist que l'ome se astast de conjurer[39] le seignor avant que il l'eust requis si come est dit au començament ou avant[40] que la quantité fust[41] esclarcie se il ne fust demoré ou seignor[42] si come il est[43] devant[44] dit, le seignor se il veut et puet[45] clamer de l'ome a lui et a sa cort et dire que il entent que l'ome l'a[46] semons et conjuré autrement que il ne doit[47] come celui qui devaint ne l'avoit requis si come il deust et que il l'a conjuré de dette non coneue ne esclarcie ne par lui ne demore que ele ne le soit dont il[48] veut avoir tel raison come la cort esgardera[49] que avoir en doie. L'ome puet respondre que il l'a fait en bone foi come celui qui entent estre[50] certain que l'on li doit et puet dire que la dette de celui qui est

[g] Supplied on the basis of the readings in the Philip of Novara MSS.
[h] End of passage lacking in V.

[28] delivrer] B: delivvre [29] tot] V lacks [30] devant] V: desus [31] faire ce] V: tout ce faire [32] li requiert] B: le requiere [33] a] B lacks [34] V adds: en [35] dessus escrit] B: devant dit [36] n'a pooir dou delivrer] V: n'en a pooir de livrer ce [37] et a son profit par raison] V lacks [38] il le] B: si [39] conjurer] B: conjure [40] ou avant] B: ouant [41] fust] B lacks [42] ou seignor] V lacks [43] est] B lacks [44] devant] V: desus [45] V adds: tantost [46] l'a] V: l'en a [47] doit] B: deust [48] B adds: en [49] V adds: ou conoistra [50] estre] V: d'estre

fievé est tozjors provee. Et se le seignor veut dire qu'il entent[51] que l'ome est paié par bailli ou par apauteor le doit prover[52] par apodixes ou par garanz covenables, et, se la paie est faite devant le grant bailli de la secrete et devant les escrivans, c'est assez.[i]

Quant le seignor et l'ome averont dit ce qui est devant dit, se il se possent[53] sur cort en esgart ou en conoissance et il est enssi que l'ome ait semons et conjuré le seignor avant que il l'ait requis en cort par plusors foiz ce de quoi[54] il est merme de son fié si com il est dit au començament,[55] je entens que la cort dira que son conjurement est null et que de ce ne feront[56] il ja recort ne[57] esgart ne conoissance encontre le seignor jusques a tant que il l'ait[58] amendé au seignor et que il ait tot avant requis[59] sanz semondre et sanz conjurer[60] si come il doit.[61]

---

[i] V begins a new chapter with the rubric: 'Quant home conjure ou constraint ou semont son seignor autrement que il ne doit sans ce que il ne l'ait a faire, quel amende le seignor en doit avoir.' Philip of Novara MSS A' and M also begin a new chapter here.

---

[51] qu'il entent] B lacks [52] le doit prover] B lacks [53] ce qui est . . . possent] V: toutes leur raisons que il savront se il s'en oposent [54] de quoi] V: que [55] au començament] V: as autres chapistles [56] ne feront] B: feront; V: ne feroit [57] recort ne] V lacks [58] l'ait] V: ait [59] tot avant requis] V: requis avant [60] conjurer] V: conjurement [61] si come il doit] B: de sa foi

5.3. Insertions following chapter 217

These three chapters follow in sequence in both MS B and MS V, but, although the rubrics are similar, the texts of 5.3.1 and 5.3.2 differ significantly. In 5.3.1 it would seem that V gives a précis, perhaps an indication that the compiler of V was aware that much of the material had already appeared in chapter 61. In 5.3.2 the text appears to have been re-worked, although the information is basically the same.

Nothing is known of any antecedents for 5.3.1 and 5.3.2, but 5.3.3 is similar to chapters found in the 'B' version of Geoffrey Le Tor's treatise and in James of Ibelin. Appendix 5.3.1 deals with the topic discussed in chapter 218, a chapter found only in MSS C and O.

***[5.3.1]** Coment et en quel maniere il n'i a point de bataille en chose qui monte a plus d'un marc d'argent, et coment et en quel maniere il puet et doit avoir bataille des uns garanz as autres par l'assise.

B

Celui a qui on devra la dette doit venir en la cort et dire au seignor: 'Sire, je me claim a vos de tel', et le nomme, 'qui tel quantité de monoie me doit', et motisse la quantité, 'et, se il le noie, je sui prest que je li prove tout enssi come la cort esgardera que je prover li doie.' Se l'autre nee la dette, la cort doit esgarder que celui qui l'offre a prover le doit prover par deus loiaus garanz de la loi de Rome. Et lors celui doit demander jor d'amener ses garanz et le doit avoir si come est escrit <. . .> livre que on a le jor selonc le leu ou l'en les voche.

Et se celui de qui l'en s'est clamez s'en veut partir sainz bataille, il doit venir en la cort avant dou jor que son aversaire doit ses garanz amener et clamer se ou faire aucun autre clamer d'aucun de ceaus qu'il savra qui devront la garentie porter contre lui, et au claim li mete ou face metre aucun malfait et tel qu'il coviegne a

V

Se il avient que aucun se clame d'un autre de quarele de deniers qui monte plus d'un marc d'argent et l'euffre a prover si come la court esgardera ou conoistra que prover le doie, la court doit conoistre que il le doit prover par .ii. loyaus garens de la loi de Rome. Et si tost come il amene ces guarens a porter celle garentie l'apelleor, se il veaut geter .i. des guarens de celle garentie porter et passer s'ent sans bataille, il le peut geter en la manire avant dite coument l'on gete guarens de garentie a metre li sus une des choses qui devant sont devisees en cestui livre, par quoi l'on ne peut guarentie porter en la haute court, et offrir a prover ce que l'on li met sus si come la court esgardera ou conoistra que il le doie prover. Car autrement son dit ne vaudroit riens. Et ce face il ains qu'il face le serement si come il est devisé en cestui livre que hom le doit faire, et enci sera hors son cors de bataille. Et sera la

B: fol. 201^{r-v} cap. 255; **V:** fol. ccxxvi^{r-v} cap. 268; Beugnot, pp. 401–2 cap. 250 bis.

prover par garanz en qui il ait tornez de bataille et offre a prover ce que il li metra sus si come la cort esgardera. Ce croi que il le doit prover par deus loiaus garanz. Et quant la cort avra ce esgardé, vouche ses garanz si loins que il ait si lonc jor a ses garanz amener que le jor que la cort avra doné a son aversaire soit ainz passé. Et puis qu'il avra ce fait, se son aversaire amoine a son jor, celui a qui il avra mis sus le malfait et offert a prover par garanz et il veull porter garantie contre lui, quant son adversaire l'offrera a garant por la garantie porter, die li maintenant que il s'agenoillera por faire le sairement que garant doit faire: 'Tien toy', par non. Et puis dire au seignor: 'Sire, je ne veull que cestui soit receu a garant ne que il porte garantie contre moi tant qu'il se soit aleauté dou malfait que l'on li met sus et que l'on li a offert a prover par garanz en vostre cort si come vostre cort l'a esgardé. Car a home a qui a mis malfait sus et offert a prover par la cort si come a cestui ne doit porter garantie par l'assise ou l'usage dou reaume de Jerusalem tant qu'il se soit aleauté si come il doit dou malfait.' Et se mette en l'esgart de la cort. Le garant ne celui qui l'a amené ne porron<t> chose bataille des guarens, se celui qui ensi gete ose torner .i. des guarens qui garentiront contre lui. Et se il ne l'ose faire s'em pasera tout le fait sans bataille.

dire par quoi la garantie vaille, et enssi passera celui sanz bataille et son aversaire ne li avra mie prové la dette.[a]

Se il veut que la bataille soit des uns garanz as autres, si le face enssi: que quant celui qui a offert a prover la dette par garanz amenera ses garanz en la cort et il seront agenoilliez por le sairement faire, il le doit rebuter et dire que il n'est tel que il garantie puisse porter contre lui et l'offre a prover si come la cort esgardera ou conoistra qu'il prover le doie. Et la cort doit conoistre que il le doit prover par deus loiaus garanz de la loi de Rome. Le garant que l'on a enssi rebuté se doit aleauter et puet torner lequel que il veut des garanz qui portent cele garentie contre lui et combatre se a lui. Et enssi sera la bataille entre les garanz.

[a] This material is clearly related to that found in the opening section of cap. 61.

***[5.3.2]** Ci orrés coment celui de qui l'on se claime puet atraire a soi la preuve et tolir la[1] au requerant.

B

Un home vient en la cort devant le seignor et le dit: 'Sire, je me claim a vos de tel qui a tolu a mon home mon cheval ou ma mule que il pormenoit le tel jor entor la ville. Si vos pri et requier com a mon seignor que vos le doiez destraindre come il me rende mon cheval, et s'en passera briefment.' Le respondant dira au seignor et neera que il n'a le cheval pris et est chose que il ne porroit avoir faite en aucune maniere por quoi, quar au jor que celui dit que il perdi son cheval ou sa mule il estoit en tel leuc, et nomer un leu loins une jornee au plus, tot celui jor, et ce est il prest de prover tot enssi come la cort esgardera ou conoistra que prover le doie. Et enssi cherra la prove sur lui, non mie sur celui qui se claime.

V

Se il avient que .i. home se clame d'un autre et dit enci: 'Sire, je me clame a vous de tel et vous fais assavoir que .i. mien hom menoit mon cheval hors a chans et tel de qui je me clams le toli a mon home et l'en mena, por quoi je vous requier com a seignor que vous me faites rendre mon cheval.' A ce peut respondre le deffendeor que il le cheval n'en avoit pas pris, et ce est chose que il ne poroit avoir pris ne fait en nulle maniere, et disoit raison por quoi: 'Que au jour que tel', et le nome, 'dit que je pris son cheval, je estoie en tel leuc', et nome le leuc lointain, 'tout celui jour. Et se suis je aparaillé de prover tout ensi come la court esgardera que il prover le doie.' Et pour ce que il est assise et husage que l'euffre premiere offerte doit avant aler, et il doit prover ce que il a offert. Et le clamant ne pora chose dire qui li vaille a ce quoi le deffendeoir n'en ait la preve que il a premiere offerte.

B: fols 201v–202r cap. 256; **V:** fol. ccxxviv cap. 269; Beugnot, pp. 402–3 cap. 250 ter.

[1] la] B: le

***[5.3.3]** Ci[1] orrés quele est l'usage dou fait des douaires.[2]

L'usage des douaires par l'assise est tel: que quant l'ome meurt que[3] totes les[4] choses quelesque eles soient, muebles et estables, que l'on li treuve,[5] se il est chevalier, sa feme en doit avoit la motie, c'est asavoir puis que l'on a paié[6] la dette dou mort. Et la dette doit estre paiee dou mueble, et, se il ne fornist a paier la dete,[7] ce qui en faut l'oir en paie la motie et la feme l'autre motie. La feme ne puet riens faire de ce que ele a en douaire qui soit fié ou heritage, mais[8] que joyr des rentes sa vie. Et ceste assise est entendue des chavaliers.

B: fol. 202^{r} cap 257; **V:** fol. ccxxvi^{v} cap. 270. Cf Geoffrey Le Tor **B':** fol. 234^{r} cap. 16; Beugnot, p. 449 cap. 16; James of Ibelin **A':** fols cxc^{v}–cxci^{r}; **B':** fol. 230^{r}; Beugnot, p. 467 cap. 68.

---

[1] V adds: en droit [2] des douaires] V: douaires au royaume de Jerusalem [3] que] V lack [4] les] B: ses [5] V adds: si est [6] V adds: toute [7] a paier la dete] B: de [8] mais] V: fors

5.4. A further insertion following chapter 217

In MS B this chapter follows directly after 5.3.3, but in MS V the chapter from the *Livre au Roi* edited below as appendix 7.9 is placed between them. It follows closely the chapter from Philip of Novara that Beugnot edited as chapter 92 and which is found only in Philip of Novara MSS A' and M.

***[5.4]** Vos avés oi ci devant moult d'assises et ancores en orrés ci aprés, mais[1] vos orrés ci aucunes bones paroles ou il[2] a mout de biens.

Se il avient que aucun ait grace de soutil engin et[3] que il sache aucune chose de plait, ja soit ce que il ne l'aime[4] ne use volentiers, totes voies bien fait se il volentiers conseille et[5] loiaument povres et riches quant il vienent a lui. Et se il se treuve par aucune aventure a cort et que il soit[6] doné au conseill, que il conseille[7] bien et loiaument tant come il y sera. Et se il puet entendre ne[8] espier que il i doie avoir grant querele et deforz genz et il n'ait[9] pooir de soi ne de grant maintenemant d'autrui, eschive et fuie la cort tant come il porra. Et se il[10] covient par estovoir que il y[11] soit au conseill d'une des parties, si plaidoie cortoisement et loiaument totes voies.[12] Et se a la quereles afiert a dire vilaines paroles, il doit eschiver[13] a son pooir d'estre avantparlier. Et se il puet enssi passer le premier jornal, bon est, et l'autre foiz se il s'en puet garder ni reviegne mie, et, se il avient qu'il i reviegne, contiegne soi leaument que que il en doie avenir.

Et se il avient que tel plaideor ait seignor ou ami fort qui de volunté ou de sa conscience veulle conduire a esploit par plait ou par conseill de plaideor aucunes choses a tort, il doit desloer priveement et blasmer plusors foiz le tort. Et se il por tant ne[14] puet faire que le mal remaigne, se il unques puet querre aucune covenable essoigne, esloigne le fort. Quar se il demore pres de lui et desdit contralie sovent[15] sa volunté en sa presence, tost porra cheir en sa[16] hayne, et, se il otroie son gré, il en porra perdre premierement honor et amprés l'arme. Ce est dit por celui qui est feble. Mais riche home et puissant fait bien et[17] aumosne, se il vait[18] et use volentiers a[19] la cort. Et ja n'ait[20] il volenté d'estre plaideor, il puet faire mout des

---

B: fols 202^{r}–203^{v} cap. 258; **V:** fols ccxxix^{r}–ccxxxi^{r} cap. 274. Cf Philip of Novara **A':** fols ccl^{v}–cclii^{v}; **M:** fols 172^{r}–177^{r}; Beugnot, pp. 564–7 cap. 92.

---

[1] ci aprés mais] V: aprés [2] bones paroles ou il] V: paroles ou il y [3] Se il avient . . . et] V: Quant Dieu dont a home grace de avoir sens et soutil engin [4] l'aime] B: l'amai [5] et] V lacks [6] se il se . . . soit] V: quant il est a court et il est [7] que il conseille] V: il doit conseillier [8] puet ententre ne] V: entendre et [9] n'ait] V: n'en a [10] il] B lacks [11] y] B lacks [12] toutes voies] V lacks [13] B adds: la cort [14] V adds: le [15] et desdit contralie sovent] B: ou [16] sa] V lacks [17] et] V lacks [18] vait] B: va [19] a] B lacks [20] n'ait] V: n'en ait

biens, se il a bone foi[21] conseille et aide les desconseillez et les febles. Et se il siet au jugement, les autres i seront[22] et sont plus volentiers et jugent plus[23] baudement o lui. Quar tel oseroit parler ou mesdire dou jugement fait par fiebles genz qui n'oseroit[24] tentir[25] un sol mot se riches homes eussent[26] esté au jugement. Et les quereles des riches et des povres se delivrent plus tost quant les granz juges[27] et les puissanz veulent entendre a la delivrance. Quar les povres n'en osent partir tant come les riches i sont. Et grant honor est au seignor et a la cort et a toz ceaus qui[28] ont pooir quant la cort se descharge et droit[29] est pourseu[30] et quereles[31] sont delivrees, et avec l'onor est[32] ce grant aumosne. Quar sanz faille par les grant riches home et par les sages[33] covient que les granz faiz de cort et dehors cort se delivrent. Et mout est beneuré le pais et les genz qui y habitent, granz et petit, quant le chief seignor et les granz membres de la seignorie ont grace de naturel sens et de soutil[34] conoissance et ja soit ce que la grace est et meut de Nostre Seignor,[35] toute voie se doit l'on[36] pener et travaillier de porsivre la grace toz jors en amendament et aprendre por meaus ouvrer quanques l'on[37] puet de bien. Quar l'on dit en[38] preverbe: 'Diex done le beuf, mais non mie par[39] la corne'. Et en autre leu dit:[40] 'Qui se remeue, Dieus li aide'.

Entre les autres choses afiert[41] moult que les riches homes apreignent lettres, et, qui plus en savra, meax en vaudra. Quar il i a deus arz qui sont mout especiaus a savoir[42] ouvrer des deus plus glorioses branches de subtil conoissance: la premiere est sapience; la secunde est science. Et la grace de soutil conoissance est lor preciose souche.[43] L'art qui afiert[44] a sapience, si est devinité, quar sapience labore[45] toz jors et enseigne a laborer esperituelment, et l'art qui afert a science si est logique,[46] quar logique enseigne a parler soutilment des faiz terriens.[47] Et as livres des auctors meismes puet l'on moult aprendre des faiz dou secle. Et ceaus qui n'ont pooir ou volenté ou[48] lesir de demorer longuement en escole doivent au mains aprendre tant que il sachent lire et escrire, quar leur secré en devra estre miex

---

[21] a bone foi] B: aucune foiz [22] seront] V: sieent [23] volentiers et jugent plus] B lacks [24] n'oseroit] B: n'oseront [25] tentir] V: tenir [26] eussent] B: ont [27] juges] B: genz [28] B adds: sont et i [29] V adds: en [30] pourseu] B: coneu [31] V addss: en [32] est] B: sera [33] sages] B: riches [34] V adds: engin et [35] meut de Nostre Seignor] B: urent [36] l'on] B: on [37] l'on] B: lor [38] en] B: ou [39] mie par] V: pas [40] dit] V lacks [41] B adds: il [42] V adds: bien governer et [43] souche] B: chose [44] afiert] B: est aferable [45] labore] B: a laborer [46] logique] B: logue [47] terriens] B: terreines [48] n'ont pooir ou volenté ou] V: n'en ont pooir ne volenté ne

celé. Et ceaus qui en[49] sevent poi se[50] doivent reconforter en[51] la parole que Saint Pol dist: 'Ne voilliez savoir plus que il ne[52] covient, mais tant soulement ce que[53] baste.'[a] Et moralité tesmoigne que assez set d'escremie[54] qui[55] set veincre. Et certes assez set de sapience qui bien set la creance de Nostre Seignor Jhesu Crist et la tient, et qui sovent est remembrant de sa gloriose passion que il soufri[56] por nostre redemption et dou aut perdon que il establi as droiz repentanz et verais confes, faisanz parfaite penitence en cestui siecle ou en l'autre.

Et assez set de science qui[b] ententivement regarde et reverche les fais teriens qui sont present et ce qui semble qui en peut avenir. Car l'on dit: 'Qui de loins se garde,[57] de pres ce doit joir'. Et toutes fois doit l'on a bone foi trier et partir le bien dou mal et regarder son honor. Car profit hontous ne vient pas de bone sience. Et sur toutes choses se doit garder sience de fauser sapience. Car celui qui pour les temporelles choses pert les espirituelles et por ceste courte vie pert l'ame pardurable, certes il n'i a en lui sens ne soutille conoissance. Et en bone hore fu ne cil qui est seures de sapience et especiaument as fais terriens que les grans seignors ont, en court et hors court, sevent et pevent puiser et leur puis meimes l'aigue bone, douce et clere a leur besoign. Ce est que les grans seignors soient si sages d'eaus meimens que il puissent bien ouvrer par eaus. Car trop de choses leur covient a faire par estovoir sans conseill grant. Et si est il mout grant sens de faire et ouvrer par conseill, et le sage doit meaus demander conseill que le fol. Car le sage, se il[c] requiert conseill et l'on li done bon ou mavais, il bien savra[58] trier l'un de l'autre[d] et qui de plusors genz issent[59] plusors manieres de paroles. Et tel est sage qui n'est mie averti toz jors par soi quant il est soul de choisir le meillor. Et aucune foiz <avient que>[e] de la boche d'un simple ist aucune parole sage qui est profitable au conseill que l'on requiert.

---

[a] Romans 12:3.
[b] B lacks an extended passage beginning here. What follows is based on V which is parallelled by the Philip of Novara MSS.
[c] End of lacuna in B.
[d] V lacks the next sentences, substituting: 'Et le fol ne savra trier ne conoistre.'
[e] Supplied on the basis of the readings in Philip of Novara.

---

[49] en] V lacks [50] se] B: s'en [51] reconforter en] V: conforter a [52] V adds: vous [53] ce que] V: qui vos [54] d'escremie] B: d'escrivre [55] V adds: se [56] soufri] B: soufrir [57] se garde] V: regarde [58] savra] B: set [59] issent (following the Philip of Novara MSS] B: usent

Et se celui qui la dit ne conoist, le sage l'entent et la requiaut a son profit. Et ce n'est mie grant merveille, car[60] et sovent est avenu q'un asne ou .i. beuf marche en aventure si pres de la forme d'un lievre[61] ou dou leuc ou les perdriz sont qu'il les en fait voler et lever ausi tost come feroit .i. brachet qui les sentist et queist.[f] Et par plusors manieres de raison fait bon avoir conseill devant l'euvre et que l'on gart toutes voies a qui l'en se conseille, se ce est chose qui face a celer.

Por toutes les[62] raisons devant dites et por mout d'autres est il grant joie et[63] grant profit et grant honor que home de pooir soit sage et soutil. Et tot autant de mal et de honte et de perill est il quant[64] il est fol et nice. Quar se il s'en bat ou fait mal ou desleauté, il ne s'en savra garder. Et se il est desleau, il ne sera mie soul. Car si tost come males genz et desloiaus conoissent riche home fol[65] et nice, il vienent a lui a cenz et a milliers et caschun i a son coup. Et se il treuvent aucun preudome pres de lui,[66] il le sevent bien hoster, et le fol ne le set retenir.[67] Desloiau dote toz jors que preudome ne soit pres de son seignor,[68] por ce que il meismes ne perde leuc, et desloiau ne puet amer[69] leaument seignor ne autre et ne li[70] chaut se le seignor pert les bons serviours,[71] et desloiaus losengiers aprochent volentiers et seurement[72] riche home fol ou nice.[g] Deus manieres y a de losengiers. Les mains mauvas sont ceaus qui dient voluntiers a plaisir a riches homes et s'acordent voluntiers a ce qu'il dient et loient ce que il aiment et les tienent pres en toutes guisses; neis les sages homes et riches sont sovent serviz de tex losenges et aiment plus losenges que rampones. Mais les tres mauvais losengeors losengent les fos homes riches de trop perillouses losenges et les enflent si que il devienent ydropiques, disant leur: 'Sire, vos estes si riches si puissant et sage et vaillant por touz vaincre'. Ne soufrez celui ne cel autre. Deus manieres d'idropesie y a: l'une est a morir, et l'autre

[f] End of lacuna in V.
[g] V lacks the next sentences.

[60] car (following the Philip of Novara MSS] B: et [61] lievre (following the Philip of Novara MSS] B: livre [62] les] B lacks [63] est il grant joie et] V: en grant joie et en [64] de mal et . . . quant] B lacks [65] conoissent riche home fol] B: conoissement aucun fol riche home [66] lui] B: leur [67] retenir] B: tenir [68] B adds: et [69] amer] B: avoir [70] V adds: en [71] les bons serviours] B: toz ses bons et loiaus conseillors [72] seurement] V: servent

a languir une piece et morir toutes voies. Cele dont le fol nice meurt maintenant, si est quant il par desloiaus losengiers enprent hastivement si grant fait perillous et mauvais de quoi il est tantost destruit. Et cele de quoi il languist une pece, si est quant il se travaille longuement de croire les foles losenges et enflent touz jors tant que a la fin crieve et perist de ce meismes.[h] Et ce et pis puet dou puissant avenir, se il est fol et nice. Mais dou puissant soutill et conoissant, se il avenist que il fust malicious et vousist mal ouvrer en aucune chose,[73] toutes voies il en avroit honte et s'en savroit garder se il vosist,[74] et se il mesfaisoit, il le savroit amender et toz jors cuideroit[75] que un autre soutil s'en preist garde et coneust[76] son mesfait. Et por ce et por autre[77] raisons doit on mout voloir que le[78] puissant soit sage et soutil.

Mais a tant lairons de cest endroit et tornerons dirons des assises des vilains.[i]

[h] End of lacuna in V.
[i] This final sentence is lacking in V. It introduces the material which follows in both B and V and which is edited above as appendix 3.12.

[73] aucune chose] B: aucunes choses [74] vosist] B: voloit [75] cuideroit] V: cuideront [76] coneust] B: coneus [77] autre] V: toutes autres [78] le] B lacks

5.5. Insertions following 3.13

In MS A the chapter edited above as appendix 3.13 forms the final chapter of the treatise, but in MSS B and V it is re-positioned earlier. In both B and V it is followed immediately by the two chapters edited here.

Both chapter are taken from *Li Livres dou Tresor* by Brunetto Latini where they form chapters 75 and 74 respectively.[1] These are the only insertions into John of Ibelin's treatise so far identified as coming from a literary text not composed in the East. However, it may be of interest that one thirteenth-century manuscript of Brunetto's text also contains Philip of Novara's *Les quatre âges de l'homme*.[2] What the redactor has done is to adapt Brunetto's text so that applies to the relations between the lord and his vassals in a feudal context rather than to relations between the lord and the citizens in the civic context that the original author was addressing. Thus in the opening sentence of 5.5.1 where our manuscripts read 'homes' or 'homes liges', Brunetto had written 'citeins'; references that relate specifically to urban conditions are deleted from clauses 1, 2, and 5, and Brunetto's concluding passage is almost entirely discarded. In 5.5.2 we find 'genz' and 'homes' in MS B where MB V and Brunetto have 'villes' and 'subgés' or 'subtés' (see apparatus notes 4 and 15). Elsewhere B and V both read 'homes', 'dou pays' and 'sa seignorie' where Brunetto has respectively 'borgois', de la vile' and 'son office' (see apparatus notes 11, 16 and 21).

MS B and MS V differ significantly in cap. 5.5.1. MS B is closer to Brunetto's text in that it follows his twelve headings—MS V omits nos. 2 and 11– but in a number of places V preserves readings that are closer to Brunetto's. In preparing chapter 5.5.2 for publication, the text of B has normally been followed except where Brunetto and MS V agree on a different reading.

[1] *Li Livres dou Tresor de Brunetto Latini*, ed. F.J. Carmody (Berkeley/Los Angeles, 1948), pp. 392–5. [2] Philip of Novara, *Les quatre âges de l'homme*, ed. M. de Fréville (Paris, 1888), p. xiv.

***[5.5.1]** Ci dit quel home doit estre seignor et governeor dou pais et dou pueple.

B

Por ce que le seignor est aussi come le chieff de ses homes et que touz homes desirent a avoir saine <teste>, por ce que, quant le chief est dehaitiez, tres tout membres en sont malades. Por ce se doit celui qui est seignor estudier et considerer que il soit tel governeor que conduie ses homes et son pueple a bone fin selonc droit et justise. Et a droit esgarder roy devroit conssire de .xii. choses:

La premiere est que Aristote dist que par longue preuve de maintes choses doivent li home sage, et longue preuve ne puet nus avoir se par longue vie non. Donques pert il que juenes hons ne puet estre sage, ja soit ce que il puisse avoir bon engin de savoir.[a] Et por ce dit Salemon que mal est a la terre qui a jeune roy.[b] Et ne por quant l'on puet bien estre de grant aage et de petit de sens, quar autant est on jeune de sens come d'aage.

V

Pour ce que le seignor est autreci come le chief des homes liges et dou peuple et que tous homes desirent a avoir saine teste, car, quant le chief est dehaities, tous les membres en sont malades. Pour ce doivent tous jours prier a Jhesu Crist que il leur doint tel seignor qui les conduist a bone fin selonc le droit et selonc justize dou bon seignor et parfait. Doit avoir en celui .x. choses:

La premiere est que Aristote dit que nul ne peut estre parfaite se il n'en a mout veu, ne nul ne peut mout aveir veu se il n'a mout vescu. Et pour ce dit Aristote que il est grant perill de avoir jeune seignor.[a] Et Salomon dit que male est en la terre qui a jeune roy.[b]

B: fol. 206^{r-v} cap. 265; **V:** fol. ccxxxiv^{r-v} cap. 281. Cf Brunetto Latini, ed. Carmody, pp. 393–5 cap. 75.

[a] *Nicomachean Ethics*, I.3.

[b] Ecclesiastes 10:16.

La secunde est que il ne garde mie a la puissance de soi ne de son lignage tant come a la noblece de son ceur et a l'eneur de ses meurs et a la valeur de ses ancestres, si que son pais soit honoré por lui, non mie lui por son pais.	
La tierce est qu'il ayme justise. Qua Tulles dit que sens sanz justise n'est mie sens mais malice, ne nul ne puet valoir sanz justise.[c]	La segonde si est que il aime justises. Car Tuilles dit que sens sans justize n'en est pas sens mais malice, ne nus ne peut valoir sans justise.[c]
La quarte est que il ait bon engin et soutil entendement a conoistre toute la verité des choses et a entendre et savoir legierement ce qui covient et aparcevoir la raisons de ses choses. Quar ce est layde chose a estre deceuz par povreté de conoissance.	La tierce est que il ait bon engin et soutill entendement a conoistre toute la verité des choses et a entendre et savoir legierement ce que il couvient et aparcevoir la raison des choses. Car ce est laide chose a estre deceus pour povre conoissance.
La quinte est que il soit fort et estable et de grant courage, non mie de movés et de vaine glorie, et que il ne croie mie legieremet a totes choses.	La quart si est que il soit fort et estable et de grant corage, non mie d'enuie et de vaine gloire, et que il ne croie pas legierement a toutes choses. Et nus n'en est tenus a prodome par sa dignité mais par ces heuvres.[d]
La sixte si est que il ne soit mie covoiteus d'argent ne de ses autres volentez. Car ce sont .ii. choses qui tost le geteroient de sa cheere, et il est mout	La quinte si est que il ne soit couvoitous de monoie ne de ces autres volentés. Car ces sont .ii. choses qui tost le geteront de sa chaiere, et il est mout

[c] Cf Cicero, *De officiis*, I.20–41 *passim*.
[d] This sentence, missing in B is present in Brunetto Latini's text.

desonorable chose que il ne se laisse ploier pour paor soit deue que il soit deteus par deniers, et que il soit veincu par ses voluntez. Mais mout doit home garder que il ne soit mie trop desirrans de degnitez avoir, quar maintes foiz vaut meax a lassier les que prendre.	deshenorable chose que celui qui ne si laisse ploer pour paour soit despecies par deniers, et qui ne se laisse veincre a grant travaills que il soit veincus par ces volentés.
La septime est que il soit tres bon parleor, quar il affiert mout a seignor qu'il parole meas que les autres por ce que le monde tient a plus sage celui qui plus sagement dit, meismement se il est juenes hons. Mais sour toutes choses covient il a garder que il ne parole trop, por ce que eu trop dire ne defaut pechie.	La siste si est que il soit tres bons parleours, car il afiert au seignor que il parole meaus que li autres pour ce que li mondes tient a plus sage celui qui plus sagement parle.
L'uitisme est que il ne soit desmesurez en despendre ne en gaster le sien, quar tout home qui ce fait il le covient cheoir a ravine et a lairecin, et ne por quant il ne doit mie eschiver ses vices en tel maniere qu'il en soit eschars ne avers, quar ce est la chose qui plus honist vilment cors de seignor.	La setime est que il ne soit desmesurés em despendre ne en gaster ces choses, car tout home qui se fait chiet en rapine et en larecin, et ne por quant il ne doit pas eschiver ces vices en tel maniere que il en soit chars et aveirs, car ce est laide chose et qui plus vilement honist cors de seignor.
La novisme est qu'il ne soit trop corouçables et que il ne dure trop en sa ire et en son mautalent, quar ire qui habite en seignorie est resemblable a foudre qui ne laisse conoistre la verité ne droit jugement doner.	La huitime est que il ne soit trop coursable et que il ne dure trop en sa ire et en son maltalant, car yre qui abite en seignorie est semblance a foudre qui ne laisse conoistre verité ne droit jugement doner
La disme que il soit riches et mananz, quar, se il est riches et mananz on n'a gardé de ce	La nouvime est que il soit riches et manans, car, se il est garnis d'autres vertus, ce est

quar se il est garniz d'autres vertuz, se est semblant qu'il ne soit corrompuz par deniers.[1] Et ne por quant je loe plus bon povre que mauvais riche.

L'onzime est qu'il n'ait lors autre seignorie, quar il n'est mie creable que nul home soit soufisant a .ii. choses de si grant pesantor come governement de genz est.

La douzime est la somme de toutes choses que il ait droite foy a Dieu et as homes, quar sanz droiture n'iert la droituiture gardee.

Cestes et autres vertuz doivent avoir toz seignors.

semblant que il ne soit corompus par deniers. Et ne pour quant je loe plus bon povre que mavais riche.

La disime est la soume de toutes choses, ce est que il ait droite foi a Dieu et as homes, car sans foi et sans loyauté n'en est ja droiture guardee.

Sens et bones vertus doivent seignor avoir.

[1] deniers (following Brunetto Latini)] B: dedenz

***[5.5.2]** Ci dit des seignories dou reaume[1] et de ses piliers.

Toutes seignories et toutes degnitez nos sont baillies par le Souvrains Pere,[2] qui entre les sainz establissement des choses dou siecle vostrent[3] que le governement des villes[4] fust fermez de troiz piliers: ce est de justise, de[5] reverence et d'amor.

Justise doit estre ou seignor si[6] establement fermee dedenz son ceur que il doins a chascun[7] son droit, ne que[8] il ne soit ploiez a destre ne a senestre. Quar Salemon dit que justes roys n'avra[9] ja mescheance.[10] [a]

Reverence doit estre en ses homes[11] et en ses subjez, quar ce est la soule chose ou munde qui poursit[12] merites de foy et qui sormonte touz sacrefices. Por ce dist li apostres: 'Henorez, fait il,[13] vostre seignor.'[b]

Amour doit estre en l'un et en l'autre,[14] quar li sires doit amer ses subgés[15] de grant ceur et de clere foy et veillier de jor et de nuit au comun profit dou pays[16] et de touz[17] ses homes. Tout autressi doivent il[18] amer leur seignor a droit cuer et a veraie entencion de doner li conseill et ayde[19] a maintenir sa seignorie.[20] Quar a ce que[21] il n'est que .i. soul home entreaus il[22] ne povroit riens faire se par eaus non.

Mais a tant vos lairons ester de ce et vos dirons des offices et des servises dou reaume.[c]

B: fols 206v–207r cap. 266; **V:** fols ccxxxivv–ccxxxvr cap. 292. Cf Brunetto Latini, ed. Carmody, pp. 392–3 cap. 74.

---

[a] Cf. Proverbs 10:30, 12.21 or 20:28.

[b] 2 Peter 2:17.

[c] This last sentence (found only in B) is not taken from Brunetto Latini but introduces the description of the grand offices of state and other material that follows immediately (caps 221–39). V reads: 'Mais a tant vous lairais a parler de ce et vous dirais coment le chief seignour se doit couroner et quel sarement il doit faire a ces homes et a patriarche de Jerusalem.' Here the reference is to the material in caps 218–19, which in V follows after the insertions edited as appendices 7.10.1, 7.10.2, and 3.6.2. (In B caps 218–19 are re-positioned to near the start of the whole work.)

---

[1] des seignories dou reaume] V: de seignorie [2] le sourvrains pere] B: les sainz peres [3] vostrent] B lacks [4] villes] B: genz [5] de] V: et [6] si] B lacks [7] doins a chascun] V: doit a chascun doner [8] que] B: quel [9] n'avra] V: n'en avra [10] ja mescheance] B: jamais cheance [11] homes] Brunetto Latini: borgois [12] porsit] B: sormonte plus les [13] fait il] B lacks [14] B adds: partie [15] subgés] B: homes [16] dou pays] Brunetto Latini: de la ville [17] dou pays et de touz] V: de [18] autressi doivent il] V: auci doivent [19] ayde] V: ayder li [20] sa seignorie] Brunetto Latini: son office [21] a ce que] V lacks [22] il] V: si

APPENDIX 6—ADDITIONS UNIQUE TO MS B

MS B contains three further chapters which are edited here.

6.1. Insertion into chapter 1

In MSS ABV chapter one of John's treatise is divided into three separate chapters, and in MS B the chapter edited here is placed after the first of the three. It is taken, with some alterations, from the *Livre des Assises de la cour des bourgeois* chapter 2.

***[6.1]** Ci dit que doit avoir en soi le seignor qui veut faire droit et dire droit a toutes genz.

Ancor dit ci quique veut droit enquerre et faire justise sur toutes riens doit Dieu crembre et amer. Car nul home ne puet Deu creimbre ne amer se il n'a foy, et se il a foy donques avra il verité et justise en soi. Car ce dit l'escripture en la loi: 'Fideli omnia oportantur in bonum'.[a] Ce est: 'a feel home toutes choses euvre en bien.' Donques qui a autre veut faire justise, la paor Dieu et s'amor doit toz jors en soi avoir, et ensi porra enquerre verité et faire a autrui justise et droit. Et mout covient a estre bien enseigné celui qui autrui mesfait veut juger. Car il doit bien savoir que tout en tel maniere com il jugera les autres, sera il jugé. Car ce dit l'evangile: 'Quocunque enim judicio judicabitis, judicabimini',[b] et Davit dit: 'Justicia Dei manet in seculum seculi.'[c]

B: fol. 37^{r-v} cap. 9. Cf 'Livre des Assises de la cour des bourgeois', *RHC Lois*, 2, p. 20, cap. 2.

---

[a] Romans 8:28.

[b] Matthew 7:1–2.

[c] Psalm 111:3. This last quotation is from the *Livre des Assises de la cour des bourgeois*, cap. 1.

6.2. Insertion following chapter 159

MS B places this chapter after cap. 159 where it fits reasonably well into the surrounding context. There is a related version of the same text in MS V, but there it is positioned much later, coming immediately before cap. 215, and lacking the same contextual justification. As the parallel versions below make clear, V's text only partially follows B's, and, even when the two versions do approximate, there are many variant readings. The opening sentence of V is drawn from Philip of Novara cap. 30 (p. 507 in Beugnot's edition). These divergences and the contrasting locations of the chapter point to the conclusion that its presence in these manuscripts is not the work of the 'z_1' redactor, but that the texts were added separately.

***[6.2]** Ci dit que se vos avez a requerre au seignor aucune chose qui escheue vos soit, et vos avez preuve vaillable contre le seignor, et le seignor vos en veut faire grace, ne la recevez pas ainz le provez si come cort esgardera que prover le doiez.[a]

B	**V**
Se il avient que fié vos soit escheu de par aucun vostre parent ou parente qui en soit mort saisi et tenant et vos voulez cele escheete avoir, vos la devez requerre si com il est devisé en cest livre que l'on doit escheete requerre, et offrir a prover la parenté.[b] Et se il avient que maintenant, ou aprés un espace de tenz, le seignor, droit hoir ou baill, quelque il soit, vos souffroit a avoir la saisine et la teneure que vos li avriés requis en la cort et offert a prover sanz esgart et sanç conoissance de court et sanç preuve que vos feissiés, ne le faites. Car vos ou vos hoyrs en povriez estre travailliez en aucun tenz, et ensi le povrés vos entendre que l'oir dou seignor ou dou baill qui ceste saisine vos avroit soufferte a avoir le povroit requerre a vos	

B: fols 136^{r}–137^{v} cap. 177; Beugnot, pp. 277–9, cap. 176 bis. Cf **V:** fols ccxxiv^{r}–ccxxv^{v} cap. 266.

[a] Rubric in V: Quant l'on ressoit fié qui li est escheu, lequel fié l'on a requis au seignor et offert a prover par l'esgart de la court et l'on ne le preuve ains le ressoit par grace, coment il em peut estre travaillés.

[b] Above caps 137–47 *passim.*

ou a vos hoyrs en tel maniere en sa court:	
	Se il avenist que Dieus feist son comandement de aucun qui eust fié, et le seignor saisist le fié et le tenist .i. tens sans ce que nus le requeist, et aprés par tens ou tart venist avant le plus droit heir a avoir le dit fié et le requeist au seignor et offrist a prover le parenté et la teneure de son ancestre, et le seignor le deffendist ou deleast, et aprés une espace de tens le seignor le meist en saisine sans recevoir la preuve que il avroit offert, l'eir dou seignor a lui ou a son heir ou le seignor a son heir les em poroit mout travaillier. Et en ceste maniere poroit dire:
'Vos, tel, qui avés ore et tenez cel fié, lequel fié je entent qui est de mon droit, por quoi je requier a avoir la saisine, et, quant je serai en la saisine, je offre bien de faire ce que je devrai par la cort, se vos le me requerés.	'Vous, tel, avés hores et tenés tel fié, lequel je entens qui est de mon droit, pour que je requiert a avoir la sassine, et, quant je serais en la saisine, je vous euffre bien de faire ce que je devrais par ma court, se vous me requerés.
Et la raison por quoi je requier la saisine si est tele: que au tenz de mon ancestre ou de mon baill cestui fié echei par la mort de tel, qui fu mort sanz hoyr qui fust descendu de lui, si que mon ancestre ou mon baill out la saisine et la teneure de cestui fié por son droit,	Et la raison pour quoi je requier la saisine si est tel: de mon ancestre cestui fié li eschei par la mort de tel', et le nome, 'qui fu mort sans heir qui de lui fust desendu,
et fu bien voir que vostre ancestre vint en la presence de mon ancestre et requist la	et fu bien voir que vostre ancestre tel vint en la presence dou mien et requist l'escheete

saisine de l'escheete de cestui fié et dist ses raisons teles come il vost, coment il estoit droit hoir a avoir le, et offri aucune foiz a prover le parenté de la ou il le requeroit. Et aprés ce que mon ancestre ou mon baill out tenu une espace de tens cel fié, il fu de sa volenté qu'il mist ou souffri celui a metre en saisine et en teneure dou dit fié, sanz ce que vostre ancestre provast ne mostrast en la court enssi come il dut qu'il fust hoir a avoir cestui heritage.

Et puis qu'il le firent de leur volenté ou par negligence, ou se mon baill le fist par grace, il est bien chose certaine que je ne sui mie tenuz de tenir les graces que mon baill fist. Et ce sui je prest de prover par le recort de la cort, se l'on mescroit qu'il enssi ne fust. Et ce faisant, je requier a avoir la saisine, se la cort l'esgarde, et de ce me met je en l'esgart de la cort sauf mon retenaill.'

A ce povrés vos respondre en tel maniere: 'Sire, je ai entendu ce que vos a pleu a dire et a retraire en la presence de vostre cort, et, se vostre plaisir est, je

de cestui fié et dist ces raisons si come il vost, et coment il estoit droit heir a avoir le, et offri aucune fois a prover le parenté de la ou il requiert. Et aprés ce que mon ancestre l'ot tenu une espace de tens, il par grace mist en saisine vostre ancestre, sans ce que il provast ne mostrast en la court si come il dut que il estoit droit heir a avoir cestui heritage et sans don que mon ancestre li en feist en court.

Et puis que il l'ot sans preuve et sans don, je n'entens que teneure que vostre ancestre ne vous en aiés vous vaille ne a moi griege, que je n'en aie la saisine se la court l'esgarde et sauf mon retenaill.'

Et a ce peut l'om respondre en tel maniere:

dirai et mostrerai tot avant, et puis respondrai as paroles que vos avez ditez. Je mostrerai tout premier le privilege dou donatif et le feroie lire, et puis proveroie si come la cort esgarderoit le parenté venant tresques a mon ancestre. Et que tot ce que je di soit pure verité, fu bien apareillié mon ancestre et garni de prover tout, quant il requist la saisine dou fié, se il en fust mescreu.

'Sire, ce fié que mon ancestre tint et que je tiens encor et que vos requerés fu doné a nos ancestres et ce suis je aparaillés de prover par la prevelige dou dontatif et de tout ce fu aparaillé de prover mon ancestre le don et le parenté et la teneure se il en fust mescreu.

Mais vos savés que riens ne sauve ne ne garit le seignor vers l'ome, ne l'ome vers le seignor, que la foi qui conoist la droiture ou de son seignor ou de son home; il ne li mette ne delay ne empeeschement qui le veut faire de nete conscience et de pure si come la foy doit estre tenue. Et se mon ancestre vint avant et requist l'escheete qui escheue li estoit et reconta le parenté dont il estoit descendu et l'offri a prover se il en estoit mescreu, et vostre ancestre, come seignor de nete conscience, et par le bon conseill que il avoit et usoit, fu

Mais vous savés que nulle riens ne sauve ne ne garde le seignor vers l'ome, ne l'ome vers le seignour, que la foi que il conut la droiture de son seignor ou de son home; il ne li mete ne delai ne empeeschement qui le veaut faire de nete consience et de pure si come la foi doit estre tenue. Et se mon ancestre vient avant et requist l'escheete qui escheue li estoit et reconta le parenté dont il estoit desendu et l'offri a prover se il en fust mescreu, et vostre ancestre, come seignor de nete consience, et par conseill fu certefié que mon ancestre disoit voir et certefié que mon ancestre disoit voir et requeroit droit, et il de bonté et de loiauté de lui ne vout la chose enpeeschier ne encombrer ainz la vout delivrer come la chose dont il estoit certain, et espargnoit la court de travaill de faire cognoissance de ce dont il ne covenoit, on de doit mie por ce entendre que vostre ancestre feist grace au mien, ainz doit l'on entendre qu'il fist ce que il dut et garda son honor et sa conscience.

Car quant on requiert aucune chose que l'en a usé a soue, l'on doit toz jours au daesrain, se l'on estoit mescreu, que enssi ne fust que on l'offre bien a prover si come la cort conoistra que faire le doive. Et se l'on est mescreu, bien fait a conoistre la maniere de la preve a la cort. Et se l'on ne l'est, quel conoissance ne quel preuve y covient il? Certes nule. Et por ce doit l'on entendre, que puis que mon ancestre requist l'escheete et son droit et offri a prover le parenté se il fust mescreu, et que la verité estoit si clere et si palese, come chascun set et conoist, et vostre ancestre, por s'enour et por sa conscience sauver ne vout deleer ne empeschier ne la cort travaillier dou droit de mon ancestre, puis qu'il fu certifié, on doit entendre qu'il fist ce que il dut, mais non mie qu'il feist grace

requeroit droit, et il de bonté et le loyauté de li ne vost la chose emcombrer ne empescheir ains la vost delivrer come de chose dont il estoit certefié et esparaignoit la court de travaill de faire la conoissance de ce dont il ne covenoit, l'on ne doit mie pour ce entendre que le seignor feist grace a mon ancestre, ains doit l'on entendre que il fist ce que il dut et garda son honor et sa consience.

Car quant l'on requiert aucune chose que l'on a voé a soue, l'on dit tous jours au derain se l'on en estoit mescreu, qu'enci ne fust home euffre bien a prover le si come la court conoistra que faire le doie. Et se l'on en est mescreu, bien fait ou conoistre a la court la maniere de la preuve. Et se l'on ne l'est, quel conoissance ne quel preuve il covient il? Certes nule. Et por ce doit l'on entendre, que puis que mon ancestre requist c'escheete et son droit et offri a prover le parenté se il en fust mescreu, et que la verité est si clere et si paleise, come chascun seit et conut, et le seignor, por son honor et por sa consience sauver ne vost deleer ne empeeschier ne la court travaillier dou droit de mon ancestre, puis que il estoit certefié, l'on doit entendre que il fist ce que il dut, mais non

a mon ancestre de chosc si palese et si certaine come ceste est.	mie que il feist grace au mon ancestre de chose si palese et si certaine come ceste est.
Et de ce que l'on savoit que mon ancestre estoit garni, se il fust mescreu de quanque mestier li estoit, l'on ne doit mie dire que la saisine fust de grace. Et por toutes les raisons que je ai ditez, ou por aucunes d'elles, je n'entent que vos doiez avoir la saisine de ce que vos requerés, ainz doi je demorer en ma saisine et en ma teneure, fornissant par vostre court droit a vos et a tot autre qui riens me voudra demander.	Et de ce que l'on savoit que mon ancestre en estoit garni, se il en fust mescreu de quanque mestier li estoit, hom ne doit mie dire que la saisine fust grace. Et pour toutes les raisons que je ais dit, ou par aucunes d'elles, je n'entens[1] que vous doiés avoir la saisine de ce que vous requerés, ains doie demourer en ma saisine et en ma teneure, et fornissant par vostre court droit a vous ou a nulle autre persone qui de rien me savra ne vodra demander.
Et por tant come je ai dit, veull je demorer quites et en pais se la court l'esgarde, et de ce me met je en l'esgart de la cort sauf mon retenaill.'	Et de ce me met je en l'esgart de la court sauf mon retenaill.'
Et ce que la court doit esgarder, ne que l'on puet aprés tout ce dire, n'en dirai je ores plus, mais por traire se hors de tout cest perill, ne se devroit nul metre en saisine sanz preuve de parenté ne sanz esgart ne conoissance de court.	
	Et a ce doit avoir esgart, et aprés l'esgart peut chascun dire por retenaill que il a sauvé si em peut estre l'ome mout travaillés par ce.

[1] n'entens] V: entens

6.3. Insertion before chapter 204

In MS B this chapter follows directly after cap. 198 and immediately before cap. 204 (In MSS ABV the order of the chapters at this point differs significantly from that in CO.)

***[6.3]** Se celui qui aliene tout son fié ou partie de son fié sanz l'otroi et le congie de son seignor, que en doit estre.

Qui aliene tot son fié ou partie de son fié sanz l'otroi de son seignor et autrement que par l'assise ou l'usage dou reaume de Jerusalem et le met en mains de genz d'iglise ou de relegion ou de comunes, le seignor de qui il tient celui fié puet prendre et avoir ce que il a aliené et tenir et user come de soue chose. Quar le seignor dou fié qui l'a tout ou partie aliené sanz assise et sanz usage et sanz otroi dou seignor de qui il tient le fié est encheu par la faute que il a faite vers son seignor de perdre a toz jors mais a lui et a ses hoirs ce que il a aliené dou dit fié. Et le seignor de qui il le tenoit le puet et doit avoir en fié, a lui et a ses hoirs, come la soue propre chose.

B: fol. 185^r cap. 237; Beugnot, p. 372, cap. 234 bis.

APPENDIX 7—ADDITIONS UNIQUE TO MS V

Manuscript V contains the official version of John's text prepared in Cyprus in the aftermath of the murder of King Peter I in 1369. It begins with an extended prologue (appendix 7.1) which describes the meeting of the High Court of Cyprus on the day following the king's death. There were two main items for discussion: the appointment of a regent to act until Peter's son came of age, and the drawing up of an ordinance, or *remède*, designed to correct the abuses that had characterised the later stages of Peter's rule. In an attempt to reassert the traditional rights of the vassals, it was agreed that, among other provisions, a text of John of Ibelin's treatise should be kept in Nicosia cathedral as a work of reference for the High Court. The presence of this prologue, and also of the *remède* drawn up in 1369 (appendix 7.11.19), leaves no doubt that MS V is indeed a copy of the version of John's treatise prepared in response to this decision.

In presenting the material unique to MS V, a distinction has to be drawn between those sections that were added in 1369—the prologue and a contiguous block of material edited below as appendix 7.11—and other chapters which may well have been already present in the manuscripts employed by the 1369 redactors but which are not otherwise extant. The precise nature of the manuscripts the redactors used is not altogether clear, but there is no particular reason to think that they used any of the existing manuscripts. It would seem that they relied heavily on a text which most closely resembled the version found in MS B, and that they 'corrected' it from readings found in a manuscript related to MSS C and O. That would explain why MS V from time to time preserves variant readings that agree with CO against AB. Like MS B, MS V has a version of the *Lignages d'Outremer* added at the end with the chapters numbered sequentially, but this version is later—from internal evidence it would appear to date to about 1309—and is completely rewritten. The compilers of the 1369 text made no attempt to update this version of the *Lignages* to 1369, and its presence would seem to indicate that the manuscript they were using contained a text that dated from around the end of the first decade of the fourteenth century. The material in appendix 7.11 was added in 1369—besides the *remède*, there are other texts from the fourteenth century including a description of the decision to accept Hugh IV as king of Cyprus in 1324 alluded to in the 1369 prologue—and the prologue explicitly states that such texts had indeed been added. However, we cannot know how much of the other material found only in MS V was introduced at the same time—maybe the chapter from James of Ibelin that forms appendix 7.10—and how much was simply copied from the manuscripts of John's treatise at the redactors' disposal.

7.1. The 1369 Prologue

The murder of King Peter I of Cyprus in a palace *coup d'état* in January 1369 resulted in the accession of his thirteen-year-old son, Peter II (1369–82). The murder had been perpetrated by members of well-established noble families with the apparent connivance of the king's own brothers, and in the aftermath of the murder it was these same people who took control. The king's eldest surviving brother, John prince of Antioch, became regent, and there was an immediate backlash against Peter's foreign favourites. The 1369 prologue describes the meeting of the High Court the day after the murder by way of explaining how the revised version of John's treatise had come into being. The nobles clearly regarded it as a repository of good custom that would serve to defend them against any unjust behaviour by a future king, and, in what has to be seen as a conscious echo of the belief that the supposed twelfth-century *Letres dou Sepulcre* had been kept in a locked chest in the Holy Sepulchre in Jerusalem, it was agreed that an 'official' version of John's text should be kept for reference locked in Nicosia cathedral. The prologue further explains that no action was taken on the initial decision until the following November when a committee of sixteen nobles was appointed to attend to it. It should be noted that the committee included Peter's other brother, James of Lusignan (the future King James I of Cyprus), and the three men, Philip of Ibelin, lord of Arsur, Henry of Gibelet and John of Gaurelles, who were the actual regicides.

*[7.1]

En l'incarnacion nostre Seignor .m. .ccc. .lxviii. de Crist, a .xvi. jours dou mois de jenvier de la dite annee,[a] Dieus fist son comandement dou roy Piere, quinzime roy latin de Jerusalem et roy de Chipre. Et en celui meismes jour la coumunauté des homes liges s'asemblerent en l'ostel dou roy a Nicossie, et par coumun acourt de tous ensemble ordenerent leuctenant dou seneschau dou royaume de Chipre messire Phelipe de Ybelin sire d'Arsur, pour ce que le seneschau de Chipre estoit apsent.[b] Et faissant ce, la coumunaté des homes liges, pour ce que le roy Pierre laissa un fis merme d'aage et estoit present en la court, c'est assaver Piere de Leseigniau conte de Triple,[c] les dis homes liges furent d'une part pour veir ce que eaus avoient a faire, et estant regarderent sur .ii. poins: l'un sur le bailliage dou dit Pierre—qui devoit tenir les royaumes en jusques a parfait aage dou dit Pierre; l'autre pour les novelletés et plusors choses que au tens passé se faissoient sans l'assent et otroi des homes liges, lesquels estoient encontre les assises et husages et auci o grant damage de homes liges et a la coumunauté dou peuple, pour ce que les dites assises et husages dou royame ne se tenoient enci come elles furent ordenés et establiés par Guodeffroi de Buillon, premier roy de Jerusalem, et des homes liges et jurés et les autres roys et homes liges que aprés lui ont esté, les uns aprés les autres.

O premier point dou bailliage, aprés grant debat qui fu debatu, et regardant les homes liges la requeste que le roy Hugue, quartosime roy des latins de Jerusalem et roy de Chipre, requist les dis royaumes par la mort dou roy Henri son oncle et les ot par la conoissance de la court avant des seurs dou dit roy Henri, c'est assaver Aalis et Helvis de Lezeigniau,[d] par les aleguacions que le dit roy Hugue alega

---

V: fols 19r–22r; Beugnot, pp. 3–6. English translation in Guillaume de Machaut, *The Capture of Alexandria*, trans. J. Shirely and P. Edbury (Aldershot, 2001), pp. 202–6.

---

[a] I.e. 16 January 1369 (n.s.).

[b] The seneschal was James of Lusignan, Peter I's youngest brother who was then in Famagusta.

[c] Peter II (1369–82).

[d] In 1324 Hugh IV became king of Cyprus in preference to his aunts, Alice and Helvis, who arguable were closer relatives of the deceased king, Henry II. See below appendix 7.11.17

et par les cas semblables que il mostra que au royaume de Jerusalem avint le cas, et pour les perils et autres qui poroient avenir, les dis homes liges counurent que le bailliage des dis royaumes doit avoir et tenir en jusques au parfait aage dou dit Pierre monseignor Johan de Leseigniau, prince d'Antioche et conestable dou royaume de Chipre, son oncle, qui seroit heir des dis royaumes par la mort dou dit roy Pierre son frere, qui derainement en morut saisi et tenant, se le dit Pierre son fis ne fust esté, faissant le serement uzé et les choses qui furent ordenees.

O segont point com est avant dit, fu ordené et couneu pour ce que plusors s'entremistrent et firent livres des assises, et les uns les entendeent en une maniere et les autres en une autre, ordenerent de faire porter tous les anciens livres des assises que le viel conte de Jaffe a fait, et coreger les en la presence de la court, et trover le plus verai de tous, et faire le escrire, et joindre les autres chapistles des ordinances qui ont esté fais au dit livre et la conoissance qui fu faite par les houmes liges pour le roy Hugue et autres assises et ordinances qui furent fais par les seignors roys et homes liges de la court au tens passé, et metre le dit livre o tresor de la mere yglise de Nicossie dedens une huche en la garde de .iiii. homes liges, seelé de lor ceaus, l'un en leuc dou seignor et les autres .iii. court. Et quant aucun cas venra a la court que les houmes seront enserés, que le seignor puisse mander faire ouvrir par .iiii. homes de la court, et faire porter le dit livre pour esclersir le dit cas celon qui estoit usé au royaume de Jerusalem.

Et ce faisant, la coumunauté des homes liges furent en la presence de monseignor Johan de Lezeigniau, prince d'Antioche et conestable dou dit royaume, frere dou dit roy Pierre, et le tricoplir dou dit royaume de Chipre, messire Jaque de Nores, pour la coumunauté des houmes liges, en la presence de l'arcevesque de Nicossie et des autres perlas et autres qui present furent, et auci estoient le dit Pierre conte de Triple present en la court qui estoit merme d'aage.

Et le dit tricoplier dist au sus dit monseignor Johan de Lezeigniau: 'Sire, il est ensi que regardant la coumunauté des homes qui si sont present, que Dieus en a fait son comandement de nostre seignor le roy Piere, vostre frere, et a laissé .i. fis, c'est assaver Pierre de Lezeignau, conte de Triple, qui est merme d'aage et present en la court. Il ont esté d'une part et ont regardé et couneu que vous estes le droit heir a avoir et tenir les royaumes de Jerusalem et de Chipre pour le bailliage de monseignour Pierre de Lezeigniau, conte de

Triple, fis de vostre frere le sus dit roy et vostre nevon, qui est merme d'aage, en jusques a son parfait aage, et veullent et vous prient et requerent que vous requerrés le dit bailliage, qui est de vostre droit et a vous monte d'avoir et tenir en jusques a parfait aage de vostre nevon, et avoir le poiés toutefois que requerre le vodrés, faisant nous le serrement usé que en tel cas le requierent selon les assises, et par vostre dit serement garder et tenir et maintenir le<s> ordenances qui ont esté ordenees et faites et couneues en ce jour et les conoissances et assises qui ont esté faites par les seignors rois et hommes liges de la court, lesquels se doivent metre au livre. Et faisant nous les dis seremens, requerrés la dit bailliage, et nos vous recevrons au baill et nostre seignor en jusques que le dit Pierre vostre nevou soit en son age.'

Et sur ce le dit monseignor le prince respondi et dist: 'Seignors, nos avons oy et entendu les paroles que le tricoplier de Chipre nous a retrait par vous autres, et nos vous mercions de la bone volenté que entre vous autres avés envers nous. Et de ce que entre vous autres volés que nous deons requerre le bailliage des dis royaumes qui sont de nostre droit d'aver et tenir jusques au parfait aage de nostre nevou le conte de Triple, sachés, seignours, qui n'en a[1] que nous puissons faire pour vous que nous ne feyssiens volentiers pour vous. Mais pour requerre le dit bailliage, nous ne sentons tant de vertu en nous que nous puissens reger les dis royaumes enci com il couvendroit, et vous prions que il ne vous desplaise dou respons que nous vous faisons.' Et dist acés d'autres raisons pour soi deffendre de non entrer au dit bailliage.

Et sur ce la coumunauté des homes liges li respondirent et distrent que pour escuse que il s'escusoit a eaus ne lor sembloit ni ne voloient que il deust demourer a requerre ce que il estoit de son droit et sien, et qu'il estoit par eaus couneu, et li prioient et requeroient que il le deust requerre et faire, car eaus ne voloient ne n'entendoient que autre deust avoir son droit, et auci pour le profit de nostre mermeau et des homes liges et dou peuple et l'avancement dou pais et de la regalle par son sens et sa bonté et sa loyauté, et que tous biens avendroient et seroient au royaume par son regement.

Et regardant monseignor le prince et oyant les paroles et raisons des homes liges otrea a faire ce que eaus en avoient fait et couneu

[1] chose] interlined in later hand

et dit et requist le dit bailliage des dis royaumes o leuctenant de seneschau de Chipre par messire Thomas de Montolif l'auditor,[c] et l'ot, et fist le serement uzé que baill doit faire selon que a l'assise contient, et auci jura de maintenir et garder et faire les ordenances qui furent faites com dessus est dit. Et en celle oure en la presence des sus dis perlas et estant son nevon present ressut la seignorie dou bailliage, et les homes liges li firent les homages et ligesses que chascun devoit, et furent tous autres seremens fais par les autres selon que use a esté.

Et pour les grans fais servises et ordenances qui furent a faire por le royaume l'ordenance dou livre demoura jusques a .xvi. jours de novembre aprés qui fu en l'an de .ccc. .lxix. de Crist. Et adons monseignor le baill, pour son serement garder et maintenir, fist assembler la coumunauté des houmes liges et lor fist dire par messire Thomas de Montholif l'auditor que a eaus n'estoit selé que, faisant Dieu son comandement dou roy Pierre, que Dieus asoille, la coumunauté des homes lieges firent plusors ordenances pour le coumun profit de tous et dou pais, lesquels furent jurés par monseignor le bail et la coumunauté des homes liges. Et en les dites ordenances est qu'il se puisse trover un le plus verai livre des assises, c'est asavoir dou conte de Jaffe, et regarder le par le seignor et les homes et coreger le et metre le au tresor de l'yglise en une huche et estre a la garde de l'iglise et souce le seau de .iiii. houmes de la court, et quant aucun cas venra a la court que les homes seront enserés que le seignor doie mander faire ouvrir par .iiii. homes et faire porter le dit livre por esclersir le dis cas selon qu'il estoit usé au royaume de Jerusalem. Et aprés ce que monseignor le baill ot dit, la comunauté des homes liges furent d'une part et ordenerent pour ce que la dite besoigne est de grant fait et couvenoit de faire ce a droit. Et pour ce que il estoient acés lor sembla qui ne se feroit a point par tous ensemble, et s'acorderent et ordenerent que le dit livre et besoigne se feist par .xvi. homes liges de la court en la presence de monseignor le baill, lesquels furent les aprés ci devisés:

messire Jaque de Lezeigniau, seneschau de Chipre
messire Phelippe de Ybelin, sire d'Arsur
sire Johan dou Morf, conte de Rohais

---

[c] Thomas of Montolif is here acting as counsel to the prince. As auditor, his role seems to have been scrutinizing petitions to the crown.

sire Thomas de Montolif, l'auditor
sire Symon Tenouris, mareschau de Jerusalem
sire Mathé de Plessié, boutellier de Jerusalem
sire Reymon Babin, boutellier de Chipre
sire Thomas d'Antioche
sire Johan de Montolif
sire Jaque Beduin l'ehné[2]
sire Johan de Giblet, fis sire Guilliaume
sire Thomas de Montolif l'ehné
sire Henri de Giblet
sire Johan de Guaurelle
sire Jaque de Bon
sire Reinier le Petit

Et en celle houre fu retrait se que les homes ordenerent en la presence de monseignor le baill, et monseignor le baill otrea ce que les homes lieges avoient fait. Et sur ce monseignor le baill fist recouvrer la plus grant partie de livres des assises les plus verais que le conte ot fait en la presence des avans noumés furent coregés. Et ehlurent le plus verai livre des assises et fu contre escrit et mis les ordenances sus dites que les homes liges ont fait et la conoissance que fu faite pour le roy Hugue et les autres assises et autres qui furent fais au tens passé, lequel livre et ordenences et conoissances et assises le dit monseignor le baill jura, et les homes liges ausi jurerent avant que monseignor le baill ne ressut le dit bailliage com devant est dit.

Et ce est fait pour le coumun proufit dou seignour et des homes liges et de tout le peut de tenir et maintenir ce qui a esté fait et juger selon que ordené fu et doivent auci jurer les seignors par la maniere avant qui ne resevent la seignorie enci com il vendront les uns aprés les autres, et auci les homes liges. Et fu mis le dit livre o tresor de la dite yglise dedens la huche ceelé des .iiii. ceaus come est devant dit.[f]

[f] The manuscript has four full-page coats of arms (fols 22^{v}–24^{r}), between the end of the 1369 prologue and the beginning John's own prologue at fol. i^{r}.

[2] In central margin: l'ainsné

7.2. Insertion following chapter 51

The reference in the first line to 'mon seignor mon oncle' suggests that this chapter is by John of Jaffa himself and that he is speaking of his uncle and namesake, John of Ibelin lord of Beirut. Maybe John was the author, but the fact that it is only to be found in a single, late manuscript of his work means that some doubt must remain.

***[7.2]** Ci dit que chascun sage doit mout eschiver plait a som pooir, et ssur que tout a son seignor plus que au autres.

Voirs est que maintes fois j'ais oy dire et entendu de mon seignor mon oncle et des autres saiges, et maintes fois ais esté en court ou je ai veu et oy, par quoi je puis dire souvent que mout sont perillous et font a eschiver les plais, et sur que tout ceaus qui sont entre seignor et houme, car entreaus est la foi. Et mout doit chascun espurgier et neteer sa consience, et bien garder que par lui ne soit la foi bleciee ne empiree. Et sertes par mon conseill je lo que chascun laisse avant de sa raison que il soit riotous ne querillos, car mout de maus em poroit avenir d'estre le. Car grant vertu est soffrance, et l'on dit en .i. proverbe tous jours dit l'on que li bon souffrant sont de lor fait a la fin venqueour. Car si com je ai dit en aucune part, l'on n'en est mie part tout bien guarni de conseill. Et se l'on l'est, si n'est l'on mie toutes les fois bien entendu ne bien jugiés, pour quoi l'om pert aucune fois sa quarele par nonsachance; si en n'est l'on mout de fois mescreu et ahonti. Et pour ce se doit chascun mout pourveir et bien conseiller avant que il coumence a plaideer pour savoir a quel fin il em pora venir de sa quarele, et se il avient aucune fois qui li soit honorable et proufitable ne soit mie cruel ne dehdeignable. Car bon fait les perills dessus dit eschiver.

V: fols xlvii^{v}–xlviii^{r}; Beugnot, p. 103, cap. 63 bis.

7.3. Insertion following chapter 66

The rubric to this chapter is virtually identical to the rubric to chapter 66, and the wording and content of the chapter is similar.

***[7.3]** Ou qui devant gent counoist que il a acune persoune doit dette ou que il est som plege ou que il ait autres couvenans, et celui a qui il dit qu'il est d'aucune des dites choses tenus n'est la present, se la dite counoissance li doit valoir.

Se home ou feme dit ou counoist devant gent: 'Je doi a tel', et le nome et die combien, ou die: 'Je sui plege vers tel de tel chose', et le nome et die de quoi, ou: 'Je ai tel couvenans', et les motise, et celui a qui il dit que il doit la dette otroie que il est plege ou a qui il a les couvenans n'est la present, ceaus qui li avront ce oy dire ne poront porter guarentie de tel dit qui li vaille a celui que il dit a qui il devoit la dette, ou de qui il dist que il estoit pleges, ne a celui a qui il dist que il avoit les couvenans, pour ce que il couvient par la dite assise ou l'usage que les guarens dient a la guarentie porter que il furent a leuc et en la place ou il oyrent a tel counoistre et a tel qui estoit present que il devoit tel chose ou que il estoit som plege de tel chose, ou que il avoit couvenans, et les noment et motissent la dete ou la plegerie ou les couvenans, que autrement ne vaudroit la guarentie par l'assise ou l'usage dou royaume de Jerusalem.

V: fol. lxi^{r-v} cap. 78; Beugnot, p. 128 note.

7.4. Insertion following chapter 114

This chapter largely repeats the material found in chapter 116.

***[7.4]** Coument plege et dete est plus fort que plegerie n'est et plus perelious au plege.

Se .i. houme est plege et dette a .i. autre, celui a qui il est plege et dette peut celui qui enci li est tenus mener par laquel des .ii. manieres que il veaut mener. Par celle de la plegerie il doit dire si come est avant dit de la plegerie. Et se il le veaut mener par la deraine, il conduira le clain en la maniere aprés devisee, et les biens de celui et de ses heirs en sont tenus aprés son deseit.

V: fol. ciii[r] cap. 131; Beugnot, p. 203 cap. 127 bis.

7.5. Insertion following chapter edited as appendix 3.5

In appendix 3.5, MSS A, B and V all give different versions of the same material, to a greater or lesser extent drawn from caps 20–22 of Philip of Novara. MS V uniquely ends with some material not found in Philip's text, and the chapter edited here continues the discussion.

***[7.5]** Ci esclersise le fait par quel raison l'om peut demander bailliage.

Car ce aucun venist en court et deist: 'Tel ot de moi .i. enfant, lequel enfant est vif, et je requier som bailliage come cil qui som pere ou sa mere sui', et l'enfant ne fust en la court present au jour et a l'oure que l'on requiert le bailliage pour lui, le seignor et la court ne seront pas certains par tel maniere de dit que enfant y eust. Car encor amenast l'enfant l'en a court de par qui l'on requeist le bailliage, si couvendroit il que il offrist a prover, si come court esguarderoit ou conoistroit que prover le deust, que celui ou celle de qui l'on diroit que l'escheete seroit venue a celui enfant l'eust tenu a son fis ou a sa fille ou a son parent et prover le se il fust qui contredeist ou mescreist. Car trop seroit contre toutes manieres de droit et d'assise, qui autrement recevroit houme ou feme a baill, ne ne li souffriroit bailliage avoir. Car s'ensi n'estoit, l'on em poroit requerre bailliage et avoir pour enfant sans ce que l'on l'eust onques eu. Et se l'on l'eust eu et il fust mort, si le poroit l'on por le mort requerre et avoir, et par ce seroient les freres et les seurs ou les autres parens a qui aucune des dites choses seroient escheues deshe-rités, et seroit tort apert et contre raison et droit.

V: fol. cxxxix^{r-v} cap. 178; Beugnot, p. 263 cap. 170 bis.

7.6. Insertion following chapter 155

***[7.6]** Coment nul ne peut avoir escheete qui escheue li soit, s'il ne se saisit persounament.

Il est us et coustume et husage au royaume de Jerusalem que ce aucun a droit en aucune chose qui escheue li soit et dont il soit le plus droit heir aparant, se il ne vient au dit royaume et ne requiert c'escheete si come il doit et la ou il doit, que l'on n'est pas tenus de respondre ne de rendre l'escheete a autre que pour lui la requiere, puis que celui a qui l'escheete sera escheue n'avra esté au pays ne en la presence de la court ou l'on doit l'escheete requere ne ne l'avra requise si come il doit ne ne sera mis personament en saisine de l'escheete qui li sera escheue de som pere ou de sa mere. Et que se .i. des autres heirs de celle part dont l'escheete meut vient em presente de la court ou l'on celle escheete doit requerre et la requiert si come le plus droit heir aparant qui la en court soit et l'euffre a prover, se il est nul qui le mescree qu'il en doit avoir la saisine, et l'autre non, et em peut user come de son[1] droit tant que autre soit venus en court qui ait prové en la court si come il doit que il en soit plus droit heir que celui qui enci l'a et tient. Et enci le tient et doit avoir et autrement non.

V: fol. cxli^{v}, cap 181; Beugnot, p. 267 cap. 172 bis.

[1] son] MS: sont

7.7. Insertion following chapter 195

***[7.7]** Coment le seignor peut faire semondre ces homes de venir a court et destraindre d'estre y tant come la court se tera lors.

Se seignor fait semondre ces homes par banier ou par .iii. de ces homes d'aler a court et il n'i viegnent, il sont defaillis dou servise s'il ne sont essoignés et que il fasent assavoir leur essoigne as .iii. homes ou a banier. Et se il vont en la court par la semonce dessus dite, celui qui se partira de la court dou seignor sans congie tant come elle s'en tera a celle fois sera deffaillant de servise, car ce est .i. propre servise que tous ceaus qui doivent servise au seignor de leur cors li doivent. Et se il sel servise ne li deussent et les autres servises qui sont devant devisé en cestui livre, il ne poroit tenir court ne faire droit ne justise a ceaus qui la li requeroient; pour ce sont les dis servises establis que il puissent ces homes destraindre de venir a court et de demorer y et des devant dites choses faire por les plais et les quareles oyr et juger, car court ne vaudroit ne plais se le seignor ne pooit ces homes destraindre d'estre y et faire en la court les avant dites choses, que le seignor ne peut jugement faire ne estre a jugement. Et se le seignor semont ou fait semondre aucun de ces homes de servise que il li doit, et il le fait en la maniere avant dite, et il en deffaut, et le seignor n'en veaut aver droit, il le doit faire en la maniere avant dite.

V: fols cxcv^{v}–cxcvi^{r} cap. 238.

7.8. Insertion following chapter edited as appendix 3.11

Of the two chapters inserted at this point, the first (7.8.1) appears to be related to James of Ibelin chapter 62 (p. 467) where, although there are distinct similarities in phraseology, the material is cast in the first person. The second chapter (7.8.2) is related to the chapter found only in MS B and is edited above in parallel to the text given by that manuscript as appendix 6.2. In MS V it is followed by cap. 215.

***[7.8.1]** Quant fié eschet a home ou a feme et il le requiert au seignor, il le doit recevoir par la preuve dou parenté ains que par grace.

Qui requiert au seignor fié que il tiegne, lequel fié li est escheu, il doit offrir a prover le parenté et la teneure de celui de par qui il le requiert tout enci come la court esgardera que il prover le doie; et il l'ait preves valables a ce prover, il le doit prover et non recevoir le par grace. Car qui l'a par preuve contre le seignor par esgart de la court, il ne respondra a nul home qui rien li demandast en celui fié, se il ne le demande de par celui de par qui il avroit fait la preuve.

7.8.2 The text of this chapter is printed above at appendix 6.2 in parallel to a similar chapter found only in a different context in MS B.

V: fol. ccxxiv^{r} cap. 265.

7.9. Insertion following appendix 5.3

This chapter is sandwiched between the chapters edited above as appendices 5.3.3 and 5.4. It is a somewhat abbreviated version of *Livre au Roi* cap. 21.

***[7.9]** Ci dit dou chevalier patalin de qui doit estre le fié et que l'on doit faire de lui.

Se il avient par aucune male noriture ou par aucun mal enseignement que .i. chevalier soit patalin ou mescreant en Jhesu Crist et il em peut estre ataint ou prové par veue de ces voisins ou par sa reconoissance ou par ces compaignons qui revienent a la droite foi et l'encusent, ces pers le doivent jugier a arder, et tout quanque il a escheit au seignor par droit tant y a. Que se celui fié que il deservoit movoit de par la feme qui est de droite foi, elle doit avoir tout son fié enterinement, que pour la mauvaisté dou baron ne doit mie perdre sa feme de par qui meut la featé dou fié et en doit faire le servise que le fié doit, et aprés sa mort si doit escheir a son ainsné fis ou a ces filles si come fié peut escheir, soient enfans dou patalin ou d'autre baron, mais que il soient de droite foi. Et se le fié meut de par le baron patalin, tout le fié doit estre dou seignor, et la feme en doit avoir son douaire, et, se il a nul enfant, il en sont desherités de celui fié et de tous ces biens.

V: fols ccxxviii^{v}–ccxxix^{r} cap. 273. Cf. *Livre au Roi*, ed. Beugnot, p. 620 cap. 21; ed Greilsammer, pp. 195–9 cap. 21.

7.10. Insertion following appendix 5.5

These two chapters are derived from chapter one of the treatise by James of Ibelin. In MS V they come directly after the two chapters taken from Brunetto Latini edited above as appendix 5.5. MS V then has the chapter edited as appendix 3.6.2 and this is followed by caps. 219 and 220 which describe the coronation.

Beugnot, who seems not to have realised that it originated with James of Ibelin, printed the first of these chapters (7.10.1) as chapter one of his 'Documents relatifs à la successibilité au trône et à régence', but omitted the second.

***[7.10.1]** Ci dit coment l'eir costeer a qui escheit le royaume le doit requere as homes dou royame de Jerusalem.

Quant le royaume de Jerusalem escheit a aucun heir costeer, mais que il soit droit heir a avoir le dit royaume, il doit asembler le plus et le meaus de ces homes liges dou royaume et leur doit faire assavoir coment le dit roiaume li est escheu et raconter coment et par quel raison, por ce que il y avra espoir aucuns qui ne le savront mie devant ce que il avront oy de lui, et puis requere leur en generau coment il li facent come a seignor et a droit heir ce que il li doivent pour fiés: tout premierement les homages et les autres redevances, et aprés les servises si come chascun les doit, et il euffre bien tout premier a eaus quanque le seignor doit faire quant il entre et ress-soit tel seignorie.

Les homes doivent tuit aler a une part et recorder se que le seignor lor a requis et offert, et, c'il sont certains qu'il soit droit heir enci come il s'en avoue, il doivent maintenant venir devant le seignor et dire li: 'Sire, nos conoissons bien que vous estes tel come vous nos avés dit et somes prest et aparaillés maintenant de faire ce que vous avés requis, faissant vous premier si come vous l'en avés offert ce que vous devés.'

V: fol. ccxlv^{r-v} cap. 283; 'Documents relatifs à la successibilité au trône et à régence', p. 397 cap. 1. Cf James of Ibelin, pp. 453–4 cap. 1 (part).

***[7.10.2]** Ci orrés ques est le sarement que le chief seignor fait a ces homes avant que il li facent homage, ne que il ne ressoivent a seignor.

Lors doit estre aportee l'evangile, et le seignor se doit agenoiller et metre la paume destre dessus, et .i. des homes doit deviser et dire enci: 'Sire, vous jurés sur les saintes evangiles de Dieu come crestien que vous garderés et sauverés et ayderés et maintendrés et deffendrés de tout vostre loyal pooir sainte yglise, veves et orfenins en leur raisons et en leur droiture par cestui royaume. Et encores par vostre dit serement tendrés et ferés tenir et acomplir et maintenir de tout son loyal pooir les bons hus et les bones coustumes et les assises qui furent ordenees et faites au dit royaume, ce est a entendre par tout le royaume. Et encor par vostre dit serement que vous tendrés et ferés tenir et maintenir les dons et les preveliges que vous avantdiciers ont dounés et fais en cestui royaume. Et se aucun contens y eust as dons ou as preveliges que il l'ont fais que vous ceaus contens ferés determiner par l'esgart ou la conoissance de vostre court. Et encores estes tenus par vostre dit serement de tenir et maintenir et faire tenir et de acomplir de tout vostre loyal pooir justize.' Et aprés ce que ces desus dites choses seront complies, le seignor se doit seir, et les homes, l'un aprés l'autre, li doivent faire homage si come est devisé en cestui livre.[a]

V: fols ccxlv^{v}–ccxlvi^{r} cap. 284. Cf James of Ibelin, p. 454 cap. 1 (part).

---

[a] Above cap. 175. James of Ibelin continues with a description of the vassals' oath of homage.

7.11. Insertions made in 1369 following chapter 224

The 1369 prologue (appendix 7.1) made it clear that additional material including a description of King Hugh IV of Cyprus's claim to the throne in 1324 had been incorporated into the new version of John's treatise. In fact this particular chapter comes towards the end of a substantial block of twenty-two chapters concerned with constitutional precedent stretching back to the regency disputes of the 1260s that are inserted into John's text between chapters 224 and 225. Beugnot included all this material in his edition of the *Lois*, but he broke it up with the result that it has not been possible to see this assemblage as a whole. It comprises:

1. A detailed account of the disputes over the regency of Jerusalem in the 1260s (7.11.1–7.11.15)[1]
2. The text of an ordinance issued by King Henry II of Cyprus in January 1311 dealing with legal problems resulting from his brother's usurpation which had ended the previous year (7.11.16)[2]
3. The arguments put forward at the time of King Hugh IV's accession in 1324 (7.11.17)[3]
4. An *assise* issued by the king in 1355 which from other evidence may in fact have been the reissue of an enactment dating to the 1310s (here split into four chapters) (7.11.18)[4]
5. The text of the *remède* drawn up in January 1369 in the aftermath of Peter I's death which, like the 1369 prologue, records among other things the decision to find the best version of John's treatise, "correct" it and place it in a chest in the cathedral treasury. (7.11.19)[5]

The material is inserted into the text after John's description of the coronation and the duties of the officers of state (caps 219–24) and before his description of the ecclesiastical hierarchy, the status of the barons, and his lists of the lords with rights of *cour et coins et justise* and of the service owed the crown on the eve of Hattin (caps 225–39). It is thus placed with the material that John himself had assembled that bears on the constitution and government of the kingdom.

[1] 'Documents relatifs à la successibilité', caps 3–17, pp. 401–19; Edbury, 'Disputed Regency', pp. 21–47. [2] 'Bans et Ordonnances des rois de Chypre', *RHC Lois*, 2, no. 25, pp. 368–70. [3] 'Documents relatifs à la successibilité', cap. 18, pp. 419–22. [4] 'Bans et Ordonnances', no. 31, pp. 373–7. [5] 'Bans et Ordonnances', no. 33, pp. 378–9.

7.11.1–7.11.15

I have discussed the regency disputes of the 1260s at length elsewhere.[1] The first nine of these chapters relate to a dispute between the cousins Hugh of Antioch-Lusignan (later King Hugh III) and Hugh of Brienne over who should be regent for their other cousin, King Hugh II of Cyprus, who in his turn was titular regent of Jerusalem for the absentee Conrad V of Hohenstaufen. This section, which is easily the best example of legal debate to have survived form the Latin East, can be dated to 1264, 1265 or 1266. Chapters 10–15 record the dispute between Hugh of Antioch-Lusignan and his kinswoman, Maria of Antioch, for the regency of Jerusalem on behalf of Conrad V now that Hugh II had died. Maria later sold her rights to the king of Sicily, Charles I of Anjou, and it is likely that the notarised copy of these texts mentioned in appendix 7.11.15 was used in an attempt to discredit Maria's claim to the throne of Jerusalem. It would also seem that these texts were used at the time of King Hugh IV's accession in 1324 to provide some of the precedent required as justification for discounting any rights Hugh's aunts may have had to succeed (appendix 7.11.17).

[1] Edbury, 'Disputed Regency', pp. 1–19.

***[7.11.1]** Ces sont les erremens dou roi Huge[a] et dou conte de Braine[b] sur le fait dou bailliage dou royaume de Jerusalem, et tout premier ce est le dit dou roy Hugue.

'Seignors, il est chose certaine que la royne Aalis,[c] m'ayole, fu dame de ce royaume, et l'ot et tint et en usa come dame, et morut saisie et tenant come de son droit. Et quant Dieu ot fait son comandement de li, ce royaume eschei a mon oncle, le roy Henri,[d] qui fu son fis, si l'ot et tint et usa come seignor, et morut saisi et tenant come de son droit. Et quant Dieu ot fait son comandement de lui, ce royaume eschei a mon seignor Hugue,[e] son fis, vostre petit seignor, que Dieu creisse en bien, et ce mon dit oncle n'eust heu heir de sa feme espouse lors qu'i<l> morut, fust escheu ce royaume a madame ma mere[f] com a son droit heir. Mais pour ce que il eschei au dit Hugue, la royne Plaisance,[g] sa mere, pour ce qu'il estoit merme d'aage, ot le bailliage de ce royaume par l'usage dou dit royame pour le droit de son dit fis. Et quant Dieu fist son comandement de la dite royne Plaisance, le dit bailliage vint a madame ma mere, qui fu fille de la royne Aalis et seur dou roy Henri et ante dou dit Hugue, come a celle a qui ce royaume fust escheu com a plus droit heir dou dit Hugue c'il fust mesavenu de lui. Et la raison en est clere, car il est us ou costume ou assise en ce royaume quant heir merme d'aage n'a pere ou mere qui puisse tenir son bailliage, que

---

V: fols ccxliv[r]–ccxlv[r] cap. 292; 'Documents relatifs à la successibilité au trône et à régence', pp. 401–2 cap. 3; Edbury, 'Disputed Regency', pp. 21–3 cap. 1.

---

[a] Hugh of Antioch-Lusignan, regent of Cyprus (1261–67), regent of Jerusalem (1264/66–69), king of Cyprus (as Hugh III, 1267–84), king of Jerusalem (1269–84).

[b] Hugh, count of Brienne (1261–96), count of Lecce (1271–96).

[c] Alice of Champagne, wife of King Hugh I of Cyprus, regent of Jerusalem (1243–46), died 1246.

[d] Henry I, king of Cyprus (1218–54), regent of Jerusalem (1246–54). For the date of his death as 1254 and not 1253 as usually stated, see P.W. Edbury, 'Redating the Death of King Henry I of Cyprus?', in *Dei Gesta Per Francos: Etudes sur les croisades dédiées à Jean Richard*, ed. M. Balard, B.Z. Kedar, J. Riley-Smith (Aldershot, 2001), pp. 339–48.

[e] Hugh II, king of Cyprus (1254–67), titular regent of Jerusalem (1258–67).

[f] Isabella of Lusignan, daughter of Hugh I of Cyprus and Alice of Champagne, regent of Jerusalem (1263–64), died 1264.

[g] Plaisance, daughter of Bohemond V of Antioch, third wife of Henry I, regent of Cyprus (1254–61), regent of Jerusalem (on behalf of her son, 1258–61), died 1261.

le plus droit heir et le plus prochain de ces parens, qui sont en vie, a qui c'escheete doie escheir, a la garde et le bailliage de ces biens devant tous autres gens quant il les requiert, et avoir les doit, car il avroit l'eritage ce il escheoit. Et pour ce madame ma mere, qui estoit le plus droit heir et la plus prochaine de parenté dou dit Hugue a avoir <l'e>scheete de ce royaume, requist li et monseignor mon pere[h] le bailliage de ce royaume et l'orent et tindrent et en userent tant come elle vesqui com de leur droit. Et puis que Dieu ot fait son comandement de li, je, qui sui son fis et son droit heir et cousin germain dou dit Hugue, sui venus en ce royame com en mon droit.'

'Et vous fais assavoir que je sui le plus droit heir et le plus prochain parent dou monseignor Huge, mon cousin, a avoir et tenir le bailliage de ce royaume, qui est sien, jusques a son parfait aage, et di coment: car je entens que il est us ou coustume ou raison en ce royaume que, quant aucune escheete d'eritage ou de bailliage <eschiet> a plusors parens qui sont en .i. degré de parenté a celui ou a celle de par cui l'escheete leur vient, de celle part dont elle muet, que l'ainsné de ceaus qui sont en vie l'a pardevant les mainsnés, ce il la requiert. Et ce est clere chose, que enci doie estre, car par l'assise ne l'usage de ce royaume fié ne seignorie qui eschee ne se part entre freres ne entre autres parens masles ains le doit tout avoir l'un d'eaus, c'est assavoir l'ainsné de ceaus qui sont en vie devant tous les autres parens, se il le requiert; que trop seroit fort chose et estrange, que de ceaus qui sont en .i. degré de parenté le mainsné heritast devant l'ainsné l'a ou l'ainsné le requeist, ne onques n'avint en ce royaume, ne i avendra se Dieu plaist, que seroit contre l'assise et l'usage de ce royaume et tort apert. Et je di que je sui l'ainsné de tous les parens qui sont en vie de monseignor Hugue, mon dit cousin, a qui l'eschecte de ce royaume peut escheir, qui soient desendus a nostre dite ayole, et pour ce est il clere chose selonc raison ou l'usage de ce royaume que je sui son plus prochain parent et son plus droit heir, si com je ai devant dit, a avoir son bailliage de ce royaume. Que fis ou fille demore en saisine ou en teneure de ce dont son pere ou sa mere meurt saisi et tenant com de son droit. Et puis que enci est, dont est il clere chose a conoistre a chascun, que ce bailliage est mon droit par les raisons que je ai dites: que acés est clere chose et seue que madame ma mere morut saisie et tenant de ce

[h] Henry of Antioch, a younger son of Prince Bohemond IV, died 1276.

bailliage com de son droit, et que je sui l'ainsné des parens dou mon cousin si com je ai dit.'

'Pour quoi je doi avoir le bailliage de ce royaume devant tous autres, com celui qui sui le plus droit heir dou dit Hugue a avoir c'escheete, si le veulle avoir, et pour toutes les raisons que je ais dites, ou pour aucunes d'elles, se vous conoissés que je avoir le doie; et ce vous conoissés que je le doie avoir, je en euffre a faire ce que je doi com baill, faisant l'on a moi ce que l'on doit com a baill.'

***[7.11.2]** Ce est le dit dou conte de Braine aprés ce que le baill[a] a fait sa requeste.

'A ce que vous dites que la royne Aalis fu vostre ayole et le roy Henri vostre oncle et monseignor Hugue son fis, que Dieu face preudome, vostre cousin germain, et que vous estes le plus droit heir dou dit Hugue a avoir le bailliage de ce royaume par les raisons que vous avés dites, je di que non estes ains le sui je; qu'ausi fu la royne Aalis m'ayole et le dit roi mon oncle, com il furent vos, et le dit Hugue mon cousin come vostre. Et quant la royne Aalis, nostre dite ayole, morut et la seignorie de ce royaume eschei a ces enfans, ma mere[b] et la vostre et le roy Henri, nostre oncle, et ma mere, qui estoit ainsnee de ces enfans, eust heu l'escheete devant ces autres enfans, pour ce qu'elle estoit l'ainsnee, ce ne fust qu'en cest royaume heritent les fis devant les filles; et pour ce ot le dit roi, nostre oncle, l'eritage par devant ma mere. Et il est usage en ce royaume que le fis et la fille demore el point de son pere et de sa mere, quant il meurt, a avoir leur drois et leur escheetes mais que de bailliage. Et puis que enci est, je, qui sui fis de la contesse Marie qui fu ainsnee de vostre mere, doi avoir le baillage de ce royaume devant vous auci com ma mere l'eust devant la vostre, ce elles vesquissent, come celui qui sui demorés el point de ma mere avoir ces drois et ces escheetes si come je ai devant dit. Et qu'il soit voir que fis ne fille ne demore en tel saisine ne en tel teneure come vous dites dou bailliage, il est chose seue que bailliage n'echiet ne ne peut escheir au fis ne a la fille de celui qui a tenu le bailliage, s'il y a plus prochain parens ou plus droit heir de lui a l'eir de par qui l'on tient le bailliage de celle part dont l'eritage meut; que ce le roi, nostre oncle, et nos meres eussent eu une seur mainsnee de vostre mere, il n'est pas doute que elle n'eust eu le bailliage de nostre dit cousin devant nous come selle qui seroit plus prochain de lui que vous estes. Dont je di que vous ne devés pas avoir ce bailliage par ce que vous

V: fols ccxlv^r–ccxlvii^r cap. 293; 'Documents relatifs à la successibilité au trône et à régence', pp. 403–4 cap. 4; Edbury, 'Disputed Regency', pp. 23–5 cap. 2.

[a] I.e. Hugh of Antioch-Lusignan, so-called because he was already regent of Cyprus
[b] Maria of Lusignan, wife of Count Walter IV of Brienne

dites que vous demorés en tel saisine et en tel teneure come vostre mere avoit dou dit bailliage.'

'Et a ce que vous dites que il est us ou costume ou assise en ce royaume, que, quant il y a plusors parens qui apartienent a home ne a feme en .i. degré et il meurt, que c'escheete eschiet et vient a l'ainsnee de ces plus prochains parens qui sont en vie qui li apartienent en .i. degré de celle part dont l'eritage meut, et que vous estes l'ainsné des plus prochains parens dou monseignor Hugue, qui fu fis dou roy Henri, qui soient desendus de nostre dite ayole, et que, par l'assise ou l'usage de ce royaume ou par raison, vendroit a vous l'escheete de ce royaume, se Dieu faisoit son comandement dou dit Hugue sans heir que il eust de sa feme espouse, et que vous, par les raisons que vous avés dites, devés avoir le dit bailliage, je di que non devés et di coment: car vostre ainsneesce en ce cas ne vous doit valoir contre moi, pour ce que il est chose seue que madame ma mere fu ainsnee de la vostre et fu heir de la royne Aalis a avoir l'escheete de ce royaume devant vostre mere, et la premiere ainsneesce doit avant aler et doit estre premiere contee, et a celle se doit on prendre et tenir. Et puis que enci est, je di que je doi avoir le bailliage des biens de nostre dit cousin par ainsneesce de madame ma mere com celui qui sui son heir et demores en son point a avoir ces raisons et ces escheetes.'

'Et a ce que vous volés que l'assise ou l'usage de ce royaume vous vaille a avoir le bailliage pour ce que vous estes ainsné de moi, je di que ce ne vous ne doit valoir que assise ou usage y a de ce peut estre que ce est des freres et des seurs, ne, je n'entens que, par us ou costume ou assise[1] de ce royaume, gens qui sont en tel cas com nous soumes, que l'ainsné le puisse ne doie avoir devant le mainsné, ne que esgart ne conoissance de court en fu onques fait en ce royaume que il l'eust ou deust avoir par l'assise ou l'usage de ce royaume; mais el royaume de Chipre, ou l'on a juré a tenir les us et les costumes et les assises de ce royaume, avint le contraire de ce que vous dites. Que par celle haute court fu esgardé que sire Oste Beduin, qui estoit mainsné de sire Thomas de Malandre qui estoit son cousin germain si com nous soumes, eust le fié de sire Thomas Beduin, leur ayol, devant le dit Thomas de Malandre qui estoit ainsné de lui, pour ce que le dit Oste fu fis de l'ainsné des enfans

[1] MS: assisise

de sire Thomas Beduin, ne ne demora qu'il ne l'eust pour ce que le dit Thomas de Malandre estoit ainsné de lui.[c] Ne nul ne doit entendre que la dite court, ou il a tant de preudes homes et de sages, eust ce esgardé qu'elle esgarda, c'ele entendist que l'esgart qu'elle fist fust contre l'assise ou l'usage dou ce royaume; ne par defaute de bieu plaidoier ne doit nul entendre que le dit Thomas de Malandre le perdist, puis que il l'ot a son conseill sire Phelipe de Nevaire, que l'on tient au meillour plaideour de sa mer.[d] Et fort chose est a croire, que il ait usage en ce royaume qui soit contraire a l'usage de France; que ceaus qui les y establirent ou conquest de la tere furent franceis, et au royame de France est usage que le fis de l'ainsné ou de l'ainsnee a l'eritage devant le fis dou mainsné ou de la mainsnee soit ainsné dou fis dou l'ainsné ou de l'ainsnee.'

'Et a ce que vous dites que fié ne seignorie ne se part en ce royaume entre freres ne entre autres parens masles, et que l'ainsné le doit avoir devant le mainsné, par celle raison ne devés vous avoir le bailliage de ce royaume devant moy, ains le doi je avoir devant vous, que il est chose certaine que ma mere fu ainsnee de la vostre et plus droit heir de la royne Aalis sa mere que la vostre. Et puis que elle fu ainsnee, et puis que a la premiere ainsneece se doit on prendre, si come je ai devant dit, il est bien clere chose que je sui plus prochain parent de vostre dit cousin et le plus droit heir de vous a avoir le bailliage de ces biens, et que la raison est moie et non vostre.'

'Et pour toutes les raisons que je ai dites, ou pour aucunes d'elles, di je que le bailliage de ce royaume et que la raison en est moie et non vostre, et que c'est mon droit, et le doi avoir devant vous; si le veull avoir se les homes de la haute court de ce royaume conoissent que je avoir le doie, et, se il conoissent que je avoir le doie, je euffre a faire ce que je doi com baill, faisant l'on a moi ce que l'on doit com a baill.'

---

[c] A Thomas Beduin witnessed a treaty between the Cypriots and the Genoese in 1232. *RRH*, no. 1049 (wrongly dated to 1233). The others are not otherwise known.

[d] Philip of Novara, the Cypriot jurist and politician. The use of the present tense (*tient*) indicates that he was still alive at the time of this hearing.

***[7.11.3]** Ce est le segont dit dou baill a premiere dit dou conte.

'A ce que vos dites que le bailliage de ce royaume est vostre droit et non le mien, pour ce que quant la royne Aalis, nostre ayole, morut ce royaume eschei a ces enfans, vostre mere et la moie et le roy Henri nostre oncle, et que vostre mere, qui estoit l'ainsné de la dite royne, eust eu c'escheete devant ces autres enfans pour ce que elle estoit l'ainsnee, se ne fust ce que en ce royaume heritent les fis devant les filles, voirs est que ce royaume eschei au roy Henri, nostre oncle, par la mort de nostre dite ayole com a celui qui son droit heir estoit, et il vint en ce royaume, et l'ot et tint et usa come seignor jusques a sa mort com de son drot. Mais a vostre mere n'eschei riens qui valoir vous doie de chose qui escheir li peust de par sa mere, com celle qui n'ot onques saisine ne teneure ne avoir ne la peust devant le dit roy, et c'est aparant. Car puis que le dit roy, nostre oncle, en fu saisi et tenant, si com est desus dit, se vostre mere peust demander aucune raison en ce royaume par l'escheete que vous dites qui li eschei de par sa mere, elle le perdi par la teneure dou dit roi, et que ce soit voirs il est cler a conoistre que ce elle le hust survescu, ce que elle ne fist mie, et il fust mort sans heirs de sa feme espouse, et elle vosist requere la seignorie de ce royaume et avoir, il couvenist que elle la requeist de par le dit roi, son frere, et non pas par la dite royne, sa mere, pour ce que il en morut derainement saisi et tenant come de son droit. Car il est us ou coustume ou assise en ce royaume que l'on doit requere escheete de par le derain saisi et tenant, et non de par autre qui valoir li doie; que ce il la requiert de par autre, l'on ne li est tenus de respondre. Ne a vostre mere n'eschei riens, ne ne peut escheir, de ce royaume de par le roy, nostre oncle, pour ce qu'elle morut avant de lui; qu'a mort n'a morte ne peut riens escheir, pour quoi vostre mere n'ot ne ne pot avoir droit en l'escheete dou roi, nostre oncle. Et puis que elle ne ot ne ne pot avoir droit, vous ne le poés ne le devés avoir de par lui, et puis que vous ne l'avés ne poiés avoir de par lui, donc di je que ainsneesce ne vous peut ne ne doit riens valoir a avoir le bailliage ne l'escheete de ce royaume devant moi, qui sui devant vous.'

V: fols ccxlvii^{r}–ccxlix^{v} cap. 294; 'Documents relatifs à la successibilité au trône et à régence', pp. 405–7 cap. 5; Edbury, 'Disputed Regency', pp. 26–9 cap. 3.

'Et a ce que vous dites que vous volés que l'assise ne l'usage de ce royaume <ne> me doie valoir a avoir le dit bailliage, pour ce que je sui ainsnés de vous, je di que si doie et veull que l'assise ou l'usage de ce royaume ou raison me vaille et doie valoir a avoir le dit bailliage. Car il est clere chose et aperte que ce royaume est escheu par la mort de nostre dit oncle a son dit fis, Hugue nostre dit cousin, et que aucun doit avor par assise ou par usage de ce royaume ou par raison le bailliage de ces biens, donc le doit avoir celui qui plus grant raison y a devant les autres, se il le requiert. Et je ai plus grant raison et plus grant droit que les autres qui aucune maniere de droit et de raison y pevent demander come celui qui sui l'ainsné de tous les parens de nostre dit oncle qui derainement morut saisi et tenant et de nostre dit cousin a qui ce royaume est escheu, si com je ai dit, que de nostre dit ayole sont desendus. Car par l'assise ou l'usage de ce royaume, fié ne signorie ne se part ne ne doit partir entre heirs masles, ains le doit avoir l'un d'eaus donc est il cler a conoistre que ensi doie estre com je ai dit; que trop seroit fort chose et estrange et tort apert, que de ceaus qui sont en .i. degré de parenté le mainsné heritast devant l'ainsné la ou l'ainsné le requist, ne onques n'avint ne ya ne vendra, ce Dieu plaist, que ce seroit contre l'usage et l'assise de ce royaume et tort apert. Car en ce royaume ne fit onques use, ne raison ne le done, que le mainsné des parens qui sont en .i. degré eust heritage ne le bailliage devant l'ainsné, quant il le requiert, auci des autres parens com des freres, ne il ne se trovera ja que le mainsné heritast devant l'ainsné la ou l'aisné le requeist, donc est il clere chose que je <qui> sui ainsné de vous doi avoir le bailliage de ce royaume devant vous.'

'Et a ce que vous dites que esgart ne conoissance de court ne fu onques fait en ce royaume, que l'ainsné de ceaus qui sont en tel cas come nous soumes eust l'eritage ne le bailliage devant les mainsné, se enci est com vous dites, il n'est demoré que por ce que debat de tel cas ne vint onques en court; et de choses si cleres et si usees com cest est n'est mestier de metre s'en sur court a faire ent esgart ne conoissance, que ce seroit viseuce et tenu abusion auci com se l'on le faisoit des freres. Et a se que vous dites que le contraire de ce fu fait en Chipre, ou l'on a juré de tenir les us et coustumes et les assises dou royaume de Jerusalem, et esgardé par la haute court dou fait de sire Oste Beduin et de sire Thomas de Malandre, esgart n'est pas assise ne ne doit estre tenus com assise; que court ne peut faire esgart que de paroles de quoi l'on se met en esgart, et plaideer peut faillir et faut souvent, que mout meillour plaideour de sire Phelippe de Nevaire a l'on veu souvent faillir a dire ce que mestier li estoit en plait, et il est chose certaine que mesire Phelipe de Nevaire failli lors a bien plaideer, et que ce qui lors en fu fait par esgart fu par la defaute de ce que l'on ne dist pas tout ce que mestier y fu si com il a esté aparant. Que la ou les homes de la haute court de Chipre furent assemblés plus esforceement que l'on ne les vit piesa et messire Phelippe aveuc eaus, j'os le bailliage dou royaume de Chipre par leur conoissance com le plus droit heir dou fis dou roi, nostre dit oncle, a avoir son bailliage sauve madame ma mere se elle le requeist; et ce fu fait vostre oyant et vostre veyant, qui estiés en vostre parfait aage, sans droit que vous y demandiciés ne sans chalonge ne debat que nous y meyssiens. Pour quoi je dis que ledit esgart ne vous doit valoir, mais a moi doit valoir la dite conoissance qu'elle fu fait par toute la coumunauté des houmes de la dite court de Chipre, vostre oyant[1] et vostre veyant; ne le fait de sire Oste Beduin ne de sire Thomas de Malandre ne fu pas en tel cas com le nostre, ne le dit esgart qui en fu fait ne vous doit valoir.'

'Et a ce que vous dites que les usages de ce pais furent pris et estrais des usages dou royaume de France et que par l'usage de France le fis de l'ainsné encor soit il mainsné emporte l'eritage quant il eschiet devant l'ainsné quant il sont en tel cas com nos soumus, je ne sai que il soit ensi com vous dites, et, tout le fust il, ne requier je riens par l'usage dou France, mais par l'usage de ce royaume le requier je, les quels doivent estre tenus et maintenus en ce royaume; ne en ce royaume n'est pas l'usage tel com vous dites qu'il est en France, ains est tout le contraire. Et bien est aparant par les raisons que je ais dit, et pour ce que la dame de Thabarie et de madame Eschive de Thabarie, qui sont en tel degré de parenté come nos soumes et leur fait semblant au nostre, fu que la dame de Thabarie ot la seignorie de Thabarie devant madame Eschive, pour ce que elle estoit ainsnee de li, ne ne demora que elle ne l'eust, pour ce que elle fu fille dou mainsné, et ce fu pour ce qu'elles ne puissent riens requerre ne avoir de par leur peres, qui onques ne furent saissis ne tenans, ains l'ot de par madame Eschive leur ayole, qui derainement

[1] MS: voyant

fu saisie et tenant.[a] De par celle meysme maniere ot sire Gautier de Flouri[b] la mareschaucie de Thabarie devant sire Helies Charles, et a Sayete avint il auci dou fait qui fu de sire Hugue de Masaire.[c] Ne onques le contraire de ce n'avint en ce royaume pour quoi il est clere chose que l'usage de ce royaume n'est pas tel com vos dites que celui de France est.'

'Et pour toutes les raisons que je ai ore et autre fois dit, ou por aucune d'elles, di je que le bailliage de ce royaume est mon droit et non le vostre, si le veull avoir, se les homes de la haute court de ce royaume conoissent que je avoir le doie, et, se il conoissent que je avoir le doie, je euffre a faire ce que je doie come baill, faisant l'on a moi ce que l'on doit com a baill.'

---

[a] Tiberias, lost by the Christians in 1187 and recovered in 1241, was disputed by two cousins each named Eschiva, granddaughters of Eschiva of Bures, who had seisin at the time of the Muslim conquest in 1187.

[b] Cross in margin and the words 'ci dit de le maresal de Flury' at the head of the page in a fifteenth-century hand. The Fleury family owned the manuscript in the fifteenth century.

[c] For references to these people, see Edbury, 'Disputed Regency', p. 12 n. 47.

***[7.11.4]** Ce est le segont dit dou conte au segont dit dou baill.

'Vous avés entendu coment j'ai dit que ma mere fu ainsnee de la vostre et coment elle fu droit heir de nostre dit ayole, la royne Aalis, et de nostre dit oncle, le roy Henri, devant vostre mere come celle qui estoit ainsnee de vostre mere, et par quel raison vostre ainsneesce ne doit valoir contre moi, et coment l'ainsneesce ma mere doit valoir contre vos, et coment la premiere ainsneesce doit avoir aler, et que celle ce doit on prendre et tenir, et coment je sui demourés el point de ma mere a avoir ces raisons et ces escheetes, et par quel raison la teneure de vostre mere dou bailliage, que elle tient, de ce royaume ne vos doit valoir, et par quel raison je sui plus droit heir de vous a avoir le bailliage de ce royame par devant vous. Et a ce que vous dites que il ne me doit valoir, ce que ma mere fu droit heir devant la vostre de la royne Aalis, nostre ayole, et de nostre oncle, le roy Henri, ne que l'ainsneesce de ma mere ne me doit valoir, ne qu'a celle ne se doit l'on tenir, je dis que si fait par les raisons que j'ais autre fois dites. Et se il estoit enci com vous dites, ce ne me doit pas ennuire par raison, car la en vie de vostre mere ne li eschei riens de ma dite ayole ne par mon dit oncle qui valoir vos doie, com celle qui riens ne tint ne ot en ce royaume de heritage qui escheu li fust de par eaus, si com il est aparant que mon seignor Hugue, qui est desendus de nostre ayole, est en vie, a qui ce royaume eschei par la mort de nostre dit oncle; et puis que enci est que <a> vostre mere, tant come elle vesqui, n'eschei riens d'eritage de par nostre dite ayole ne de nostre oncle qu'elle tenist ne heust come le sien, donc di je que tout auci com ma mere heust eu la seignorie de ce royaume devant la vostre, se il fust mesavenu de nostre dit oncle sans heir de c'espouse, la doi je avoir, se il mesavenoit de nostre dit cousin sans heir que il eust de sa feme espouse; et puis que enci est, il est cler a conoistre que je doi avoir le bailliage de ce royaume devant vous. Et a ce que vous dites que bailliage de ce royaume est esceu, et que aucun le doit avoir, et que celui qui plus grant raison y a le doit avoir, ce est voirs, et je, qui plus grant raison y a de vous par les raisons que je ai dites ores et autrefoit, le doi avoir devant vous, ne vostre ainsneesce ne vos doit valoir en ce

---

V: fols ccxlix^{v}–ccli^{v} cap. 295; 'Documents relatifs à la successibilité au trône et à régence', pp. 407–9 cap. 6; Edbury, 'Disputed Regency', pp. 29–32 cap. 4.

cas; mais celle de ma mere me doit valoir par les raisons que je ai avant dites, ne ne doit demourer que elle ne me vaille pour chose que vous aiés dite qui soit assise ou usage en ce royaume ou raison que fié ne seignorie ne se part.'

'Et a ce que vous dites qu'il ne fu onques usé en ce royame, ne raison ne le done, que le mainsné heritast devant l'ainsné qui sont en .i. degré auci bien d'autres com de freres, se il estoit si com vous dites, ce que je n'entens pas, ne fu il onques usé en ce royaume que l'ainsné des parens qui sont en .i. degré, autres que freres ou seurs, eust heritage ne bailliage devant le mainsné de l'ainsné par esgart ne par conoissance de court. Et se la dame de Thabarie ou sire Gautir de Flouri[a] ou autres l'ont eu si com vous dites, ce n'a esté par droit ne par esgart ne par conoissance de court, ains a esté par ce que ceaus qui raison y avoient se sont soufeis de venir en court et de demander leur raison; pour quoi di je que ce ne vous vaut, ne valoir ne vous doit, n'a moi ennuire que je n'aie par devant vous le bailliage de ce royaume com celui qui suis plus droit heir de vous a avoir le par devant vous par les raisons que je ai dit.'

'Et a ce que vous dites que esgart qui fu fait en Chipre de sire Oste Beduin et de sire Thomas de Malandre <ne> me vaille, et que vous volés que la conoissance qui fu faite en Chipre dou bailliage, que vous eustes, vous vaille a avoir cestui bailliage, je di que le dit esgart me doit valoir, mais a vous ne doit valoir la dite conoissance, et di raison pour quoi: car le fait de sire Oste Beduin et de sire Thomas de Malandre, qui requeroient l'escheete de leur ayole, fu debatue en court par les parties longuement, et aprés fu esgardé que la raison estoit de sire Oste Beduin, et encor fust il mainsné dou dit Thomas, pour ce que il estoit fis de l'ainsné des enfans de son ayol. Et quant vous requeistes le bailliage de Chipre, il est chose seue que je ne le debati ne en court, ne mis pour debatre, le que je m'en souffri que l'onour de madame m'ante, vostre mere, qui nouri m'avoit, que je doutai qu'elle ne me seust mau gré; ne celle conoissance, qui adonc fu faite, ne vous doit valoir ne a moi ennuire, et, ce la court connut ce que vous dites, celle conoissance ne vos doit valoir contre moi a avoir le bailliage de ce royaume par les raisons que je ai dites, ains doit valoir a moi l'esgart qui fu de sire Oste Beduin et de sire Thomas de Malandre, si come je ai devant dit.'

---

[a] Cross in margin.

'Et a ce que vous dites que vous volés requere le bailliage par l'usage de ce royaume et non pas par celui de France, vous avés entendu que je ai dit autrefois, qu'il ne fu onques esgardé ne coneu en ce royaume que l'ainsné de ceaus qui sont en .i. degré autres que freres, fis de la mainsneece, heust heritage ou bailliage devant le mainsné fis de l'ainsnee, et que les usages de ce pais furent pris et etrais de ceaus de France au conquest de ce roiaume. Et puis que vous dites que dou mainsné fis de l'ainsné ne fu onques fait esgart ne conoissance en court, et je di que l'ainsné fis de la mainsnee[1] ne fu onques fait esgart ne conoissance de court en ce royaume, dont je di com se doit prendre as usages de France; et je ai dit autre fois que l'usage de France est, et encor je di; et que il soit voirs, ce que je di autrefois est avenu en ce royaume, qui n'avoit esté debatu ne coneu par esgart ne par conoissance de court, de quoi l'on estoit enseré que l'on se travailloit de savoir la verité de l'usage de France et par sel usage l'on deliveroit le fait en ce royaume, et se est chose aperte et seue. Car quant messire Henri le Bufle fu mort et ces filles furent en debat de l'escheete de leur pere, l'on s'en acerteni par l'usage de France et atendi l'on plus d'un an le conte de Sansuerre pour savoir quel usage estoit en France de tel cas, et par l'usage qui fu delivree celle quarele si com est apaant que encor court en ce royaume.'[b]

'Pour quoi par ceste raison et por toutes les autres que je ai dites ores et autres fois ou par aucune d'elles, je veull avoir le bailliage de ce royaume par devant vous com celui qui sui le plus droit heir de nostre dit cousin a avoir c'escheete, se les homes de la haute court qui si sont assemblés conoissent que je le doi avoir. Et ce il counoissent que je avoir le doie, je euffre a faire ce que je doie com baill, faisant l'on a moi ce que l'on doit com a baill.'

[b] There appears to be a blunder in the transmission of the text at this point. Henry le Bufle died sometime in the late 1160s and Count Stephen of Sancerre was in the East in 1171. This case was also mentioned by Philip of Novara. See Edbury 'Philip of Novara', p. 559 note 23.

[1] MS: l'ainsnee

***[7.11.5]** Ce est le tiers dit dou baill au segont dit[1] dou cont.

'Vous avés entendu coument j'ais autrefois dit, et encor di, que riens n'eschei a vostre mere de par nostre dite ayole, la royne Aalis, qui valoir vous doie, ne ne par nostre dit oncle, le roi Henri, n'eschei riens a vostre mere n'escheu ne pot que elle morut avant de lui, n'a mort n'a morte ne peut riens escheir, et par quel raison l'ainsneesce de vostre mere ne vous doit valoir a avoir le bailliage de ce royaume pour nostre dit cousin. Et a ce que vous dites que vous n'entendés que ce que je ais dit fust onques usé en ce royaume, ne raison ne done que le fis dou mainsné, quant il est ainsné, heritast devant le fis de l'ainsné ce il est mainsné de lui, ausi bien des parens qui sont en .i. degré taignans a celui de qui l'escheete leur est venue de la ou elle meut com des freres, se vous ne l'e<n>tendes, pour ce ne remaint il mie qu'il ne soit et doie estre si com je ais dit, et di pourquoi. Car il est chose manifeste que, quant on meurt et il y a .ii. fis, que autant li ataint l'un de parenté com l'autre, et que auci devroit avoir part el fié et en la seignorie le mainsné com l'ainsné, se l'usage de ce royaume ne li toloit, qui est tel que l'ainsné l'a tout. Et par celle meisme maniere et par tel raison il est clere chose et aperte que, se .i. home a .ii. fis et il meurent ains de lui sans avoir aucune teneure des biens de lor pere et chascun de ceaus ait fis, que son fié et sa seignorie eschiet as fis des fis et puis que il eschiet a ceaus, donc le doit avoir l'ainsné devant le mainsné; car auci bien sont il en .i. cas l'un devers l'autre a avoir l'eritage de leur ayol com leur peres, c'il eussent survescu leur pere, car l'usage de ce royaume est que l'on doit requerre s'escheete de par le derain saisi et tenant, dou di je que les dis cousins de par leur pere ne peuent riens requerre, qui onques n'en orent teneure ne raison qu'il avoir puissent, ce il eussent survescu leur pere, <et> a leur enfans ne leur doit riens valoir. Pour quoi je di que l'ainsneesce de vostre mere ne vous doit valoir, con celle qui morut ains nostre dit oncle, son frere; et puis com ne doit requere escheete fors de par le derain saisi, et que fié ne seignorie ne se doit partir, si com j'ais autrefois dit, il convient

V: fols ccli^{v}–ccliii^{v} cap. 296; 'Documents relatifs à la successibilité au trône et à régence', pp. 409–10 cap. 7; Edbury, 'Disputed Regency', pp. 32–4 cap. 5.

[1] Following table of rubrics (fol. 16^{v})

que l'un des .ii. qui sont en .i. degré l'ait, et puis qu'il convient que l'un l'ait, il est bien droit et raison que l'ainsné l'ait devant le mainsné; et enci a tous jours esté usé ne onques en ce royaume n'avint le contraire, pour quoi je di qui est clere chose que je qui sui ainsnés de vous doi avoir ce bailliage devant vous qui estes le mainsné.'

'Et a ce que vous dites que il ne fu onques usé par esgart ne par conoissance de court, que l'ainsné fis dou mainsné ou de la mainsnee heritast devant le mainsné fis de l'ainsné ou de l'ainsnee,[2] je di que ce il n'a esté fait par esguart ne par conoissance de court ce ne me doit nuire, qui n'est demouré que par ce que tel cas ne vint onques en court. Que quant tel cas sont avenus, ceaus qui estoient certains que il n'i avoient droit et que ce il venoient en court qu'il le perderoient par esgart de court, si n'avroient honour ne profit et venir ysi s'en soit soufers. Que fort chose est a croire que, ce il cuidassent desrainier par court, que ces que je ais només se fussent soufert de venir en court requere leur raison et de si grans fais come ceaus estoient, ce le contraire de ce que je ais dit ne fu onques en ce royaume esgardé ne coneu ne fait en court ne dehors court. Ne le fait de la dame de Thabarie et de madame Eschive, sa cousine, ne fu pas par souffrance ains fu acertainé par les plus sages homes qui desa mere fussent au jour, et il en y avoit plus lors qu'il n'a ore, que ceaus qui ores sont y estoient et plusors autres qui sont puis mors, et par tous fu dit et conseillé au seignor de Sur, leur oncle,[a] sur qui elles c'estoient mises que droit et la raison en estoit de la dame de Thabarie, pour ce que elle estoit ainsnee de madame Eschive qui estoit fille de l'ainsné. Et par les raisons que je ai dites di je que raison et ce, qui a estée fait et usé en ce royaume de tel cas com le nostre est, me doit valoir a avoir le bailliage de ce royaume devant vous, car chose acertenee par tant de gens doit porter plus grant force et estre meaus tenue que esgart et conoissance que l'on pert souvent par ce que le plait est mal plaidee.'

'Et encor di je que la conoissance qui fu faite en Chipre de mon bailliage, me doit meaus valoir qu'a vous l'esgart qui fu fait de sire

---

[a] Philip of Monfort, lord of Tyre, 1246–70. The two Eschivas were the daughters of two brothers, Oste and Ralph of Tiberias, who had married two sisters, the daughters of Helvis of Ibelin and Reynald of Sidon. Philip was the son of Helvis of Ibelin by a later marriage.

---

[2] MS: mainsné ou de la mainsnee

Oste Beduin et de sire Thomas de Malandre, par les raisons que je ais dites. Et a ce que vous dites que vous volés come se preigne a l'usage de France pour aucunes raisons que vous avés dites, et pour ce meismes que vous dites que l'on atendi le conte de Sanseure .i. an et plus pour acertener le fait de messire Henri le Bufle, de quoi l'on se trovoit ensere, et qu'encor court en ce royaume ce que adonc fu establi tout fust il ensi com vous dites, di je que ce cas n'est pas semblant a celui, car tel cas com celui des seurs fu adonc n'estoit onques avenu en ce royaume, ne de cestui cas en quoi vous et moi soumes ne peut l'on dire qu'il ne soit avenu en ce royaume plusors fois ne que l'on se soit onques trové enserre, quant il avint que l'on a veu tous jours user en ce royaume que l'ainsné fis dou mainsné ou de la mainsnee a l'eritage devant le mainsné fis de l'ainsné ou de l'ainsnee, se il le requiert, quant il sont en .i. degré de parenté de celle part dont l'escheete meut, si com il a esté aparant de plusors si com je[3] l'ai autre fois dit. Et aucune fois est avenu que court estoit enseree d'aucunes choses, et que l'une court mandoit demander conseill a l'autre court, ne celle qui demandoit conseill n'estoit pas pour ce tenue de tenir le conseill ne l'usages des autres cours a qui elle demandoit conseill, se il ne li sembloit bon, et mout de fois est avenu que la court de ce royaume a mandé requere conseill en Chipre, en Antioche, a Triple et en autres leucs de quels le plus n'ont pas tel usage com il y a en ce royaume, que l'on fust tenus de tenir les usages de celui pais de toutes les autres choses qui en ce royaume avendroient, et tout soit ce com ait aucune fois demandé conseill as autres cours n'est l'on pas tenus de croire leur conseill de tenir leur usage se il ne leur semble bon.'

'Et pour toutes les raisons que je ai dites ore et autre fois, ou par aucunes d'elles, di je que je doi avoir le bailliage de ce royaume et avoir le veull devant vous com le plus droit heir de nostre cousin a avoir c'escheete, ne pour chose que vous aiés dite ore et autre fois, je ne veull qu'il demeure que je n'aie le dit bailliage, se les homes de ceste court conoissent que je avoir le doie, et se il conoissent que je le doi avoir, je en euffre a faire ce que j'en doi com baill, faisant l'on a moi ce que l'on doit com a baill.'

[3] MS: le

***[7.11.6]** Ce est le tiers dit dou conte au tiers dit dou baill.

'Vous avés entendu coment j'ai plusors fois dit, et encor di que <de par> la royne Aalis, nostre dite ayole, eschei ce royaume a ces enfans, et que ma mere fu l'ainsnee de ces enfans et fu plus droit heir de lui, que vostre mere ne fu, a avoir l'escheete de ce royaume, et coment je sui par les raisons que je ais dites demorés el point de ma mere a avoir ces drois et ces escheetes, et coment et pour quel raison je sui plus droit heir de vous a avoir le bailliage de ce royaume. Et a ce que vous dites que quant .i. home meurt qui a .ii. fis, que autant li taint de parenté l'un com l'autre, et que auci devroit part avoir el fié, et en la seignorie le mainsné ne con l'ainsné, se l'usage de ce royaume ne li tolloit, qui est tel que l'ainsné la tout; et que par celle meisme raison se .i. hom a .ii. fis et il meurt sans avoir aucune teneure de ces biens, et chascun d'eaus a fis que, l'escheete dou pere des .ii. freres eschiet as fis des fis; et que puis qui leur eschei l'ainsné le doit avoir devant le mainsné, je di que ce est voirs ce il est fis de l'ainsné, mais ce il est fis dou mainsné, je di que il ne le doit pas avoir. Et a ce que vous dites que il est husage en ce royaume con doit requere c'escheete de par le derain saisi et tenant, je n'entens que l'usage de ce soit tel com vos dites, que la court de ce royaume en fist onques esgart ne conoissance que l'usage fust tel com vous avés dit, ne en tel cas com nos somes ce ne vous doit valoir; car trop est clere chose et manifeste que ma mere fu plus droit heir que la vostre de nostre dite ayole et de nostre dit oncle, et ce vostre mere survesqui la moie et ot le bailliage de ce royaume, ce ne me doit nuire, que j'ai autre fois dit et encor di, que bailliage n'eschiet pas de baill a baill quant il y a plus prochein parent ou plus droit heir de celui ou de celle por cui l'on tient le bailliage; ne vostre <mere> en sa vie n'aquist riens des biens de nostre dite ayole ne de nostre dit oncle a heritage qui valoir vous doie. Et bien est clere chose, que puis que ensi fu que vostre mere morut sans avoir teneure d'aucune chose qui escheir li peust a heritage de nostre dite ayole ne de nostre dit oncle, que tout auci com ma mere fu leur droit heir devant la vostre, que je le doi estre et sui devant vous, pour ce que je sui son fis, qu'elle estoit ainsnee de vostre mere, et

---

V: fols ccliii^{v}–cclv^{v} cap. 297; 'Documents relatifs à la successibilité au trône et à régence', pp. 410–12 cap. 8; Edbury, 'Disputed Regency', pp. 35–7 cap. 6.

que je sui demorés par l'usage de ce royaume el point ou ma mere estoit quant elle morut a avoir ces raison et ces escheetes; pour quoi je di que encor fust ce que gent, qui fussent en tel cas com nos somes, covenist a requerre de par le derain saisi et tenant, ce que je n'entent pas, suis je et doi estre droit heir de nostre dit oncle et de son dit fis par devant vous, pour ce que ma mere fu droit heir devant la vostre de nostre dit oncle, qui estoit ainsnee de la vostre. Et trop seroit estrange chose et contre toutes manieres des drois et des raisons que vous, qui estes fis de celle de la quel ma mere estoit plus droit heir dou dit roy, nostre oncle, par devant vostre mere, deuciés avoir le bailliage ne l'eritage de chose qui fust escheue de nostre dit oncle et qui est de nostre dit cousin par devant moi, qui suis fis de celle qui de nostre dit oncle estoit plus droit heir par devant la vostre, et le fust de nostre dit cousin c'elles vesquissent.'

'Et a ce que plusors gens en ce royaume qui estoient ainsnés et fis de mainsnés ont herité et <eu> leur escheetes devant les mainsnés fis des ainsnés qui estoient en tel cas com nous somes, vous avés entendu coment j'ai dit autre fois par quels ce ne me doit nuire n'a vous valoir, car se aucune personne se veaut souffrir de requerre et d'avoir sa raison, celle soffrance ne doit pas tolir la raison de celui ou de celle qui la veaut avoir et la requiert. Et de ce que vous dites que le fait de la dame de Thabarie et de madame Eschive, sa cousine, fu mis sur le seignor de Sur a acertenir de cui la raison estoit et qu'il fu acertené par les plus sages gens de ce pais, ce n'en sais je, et tout fust il enci ce ne me doit mie ennuire ne a vous ayder. Car mout de fois avient que l'on quiert aucune chose a aucune gens, que ceaus a qui l'on le requiert ne sont mie bien voyans cler de la raison, et mout de fois semble as gens c'une chose soit raison que a ceaus meismes semble puis le contraire quant il oient la raison d'une part et d'autre; ne tel maniere d'enqueste n'est pas esgart ne conoissance ne ne la doit on tenir a usage ne a assise; et parmi tout ce est il chose seue et certaine que, ce que le seignor de Sur fist de celui fait, qu'il le fist par l'assent des parties, ne null peut meaus laisser sa raison, que celui de qui elle est. Ne se que madame Eschive, ne les autres que vous dites qui en tel cas furent, se laisserent de requere et d'avoir leur raison, me doie tourner a damage, ains vell avoir le bailliage de ce royaume par devant vous, com celui qui sui le plus droit heir de nostre dit cousin, que vous n'estes, a avoir c'escheete par devant vous, s'elle escheoit par les raisons que je ai dites. Et a ce que vous m'avés porté une maniere d'example, que s'une court demande[1] conseill a autre des choses dont elle se treut enseree, et que por ce n'est mie celle court qui demande conseill tenue de croire le conseill ne tenir l'usage de l'autre c'il ne li semble bon, et que la court de ce royaume a plusors fois requis conseill a plusors cours, ne que por ce n'est elle pas tenue de tenir les usages de celles cours, je di que ceste comparison n'est pas couminau et di coment: que chose est seue quant Anthioche fu conquise par crestiens, que Boemont[a] en fu seignor que j'entens qui fu de Puille, et peut estre quant il en fu seignor qu'il y mist les usages tels com il vost, et auci le conte de Toulouse, qui fu seignor de Triple,[b] et auci firent les autres qui furent seignors des autres <seignories> quant elles furent conquises; et le royaume de Jerusalem soit l'on bien que fransois conquisterent, et qu'il pristerent et traisterent les usages de ce royaume de ceaus de France, pour quoi je di que de cestui cas se doit l'on prendre a l'usage de France, ne qu'il doit demourer por chose que vous aiés dite com ne si preigne.'

'Et por toutes les raisons que je ai dites ore et autre fois, ou pour aucunes d'elles, veull je avoir li dit bailliage, se les homes de la haute court de ce royaume conoissent que je avoir le doie; et c'il conoissent que je le doi avoir, je en euffre a faire ce que je doi come baill, faisant l'on a moi ce que l'on doit come a baill.'

[a] Bohemond of Taranto, prince of Antioch, 1098–1104; died 1111.
[b] Raymond of St Gilles, count (as Raymond IV) of Toulouse (1088–1105), first count of Tripoli.

[1] MS: devant

***[7.11.7]** Ce est le quart dit dou bail au tiers dit dou conte.

'J'ais mout de paroles dites et plusors raisons monstrees les qu'elles vous et les homes de la court avés entendues qu'il n'est mestier que je redie, et pour le fait abergier je mostre brefement par une raison coment je sui plus droit heir de vous a avoir ce bailliage et l'eritage de ce royaume c'il mesavenoit de nostre dit cousin a qui Dieu doint bone vie. Il est certaine chose qu'il nos couvient a requerre ce bailliage, se nous le volons avoir, de par celui a qui l'eritage de ce royaume est escheu com a droit heir, ce est mon seignor Hugue, le fis de nostre dit oncle, a qui ce royaume eschei de par nostre dit oncle qui derainement morut saisi et tenant com de son droit. Et pour ce devons nous requerre cest bailliage de par nostre dit cousin, qu'il est assise ou l'usage en ce royaume que, quant fié ou seignorie eschiet a enfant merme d'aage et il n'a pere ne mere, que celui ou celle qui est son plus drot heir a avoir celle escheete devant tous autres se l'enfant merme d'aage moroit doit avoir le bailliage dou dit fié ou de la devant dit seignorie devant tous ces autres parens, et l'a si la requiert; et il est voirs que la seignorie de ce royaume eschei a nostre dit cousin par la mort de nostre dit oncle, et que madame ma mere ot et tint le bailliage de ce royaume et en morut saisie et tenant com le plus droit heir de nostre dit cousin a avoir c'escheete. Et il est certaine chose et veraie qu'a vostre mere n'eschei heritage ne bailliage de ce royaume ne aucun autre chose de par nostre dit oncle n'escheir ne li pot, pour ce que elle morut lonc tens avant de lui, qu'a mort n'a morte ne peut riens escheir, si com j'ais autre fois dit; ne de par nostre dit cousin ne li poroit riens escheir, com a celle qui ne fu onques heir dou dit Huge n'estre ne le pot, pour ce qu'elle morut lonc tens ains qu'il fust nés ne engendrés, ne que son pere eust espousee la royne Plaisance, sa mere. Et puis que de par nostre dit oncle ne li eschei aucune chose ne escheir ne li pot pour les raisons que je ai dites, ne qu'elle ne fu onques heir de nostre dit cousin si com j'ais avant dit, donc est il clere chose qu'elle n'ot ne pot avoir aucun droit en ce royaume, et puis qu'elle ne l'ot ne avoir ne le post, vous de par lui ne l'avés ne avoir ne poés. Et puis que de par li ne l'aves ne ne poés avoir s'a<i>nsneesce ne vous

V: fols cclv[v]–cclvi[v] cap. 298; 'Documents relatifs à la successibilité au trône et à régence', pp. 412–13 cap. 9; Edbury, 'Disputed Regency', pp. 37–9 cap. 7.

vaut ne ne peut valoir a avoir l'eschecte ne le bailliage de ce royaume devant moi; et ce je de par ma mere qui survesqui la vostre et nostre dit oncle et qui ot le bailliage de ce royaume si com j'ais autre fois dit, ne puis requerre ne avoir droit el dit bailliage par les raisons que vous dites, donc est il certaine chose que vous ne le poiés requerre ne avoir de par vostre mere par les raisons que je ai dites; et ce nous de par nos meres ne le poons requerre n'avoir, donc covient il, se nos le volons avoir, que nous le requerons de par nostre dit cousin si com j'ai autre fois dit. Et puis que de par lui le nous covient a requerre, je die que je le doi meaus avoir de vous que je suis ainsnés de vous; que par raison que vous dites que vostre mere heust eu l'eritage et le bailliage de ce royaume devant la moie, se elles vesquissent et il leur fust escheu por ce que vostre mere fu ainsnee de la moie, di je que par celle meisme raison le doi je avoir devant vous, puis que il nos est escheu, que je sui ainsné de vous. Et je vous ais autre fois dit et di encor que je ne sai que les usages de France sont, et tout fust l'usage de France tel com vous avés dit, ce que je n'entens mie, je ne requier ne ne doi requere le bailliage de ce royaume par autre usage que par celui de ce royaume: par lesquels usages je le doi avoir pour toutes les raisons que je ais dites, ne ne veull qu'il demore pour chose que vous aiés dit ne diés, que je ne l'aie devant vous.'

'Pour toutes les <raisons> que j'ai dites ores et autre fois, ou par aucun d'elles, ce les homes de la haute court de ce royaume qui si sont conoissent que je le doi avoir, et de ce me met je en leur counoissances, et c'il conoissent que je le doi avoir, je en euffre a faire ce que je doi com baill, faisant l'on a moi ce que l'on doit com a baill.'

***[7.11.8]** Ce est le quart dit dou conte au quart dit dou baill.

'Ja soit ce que je aie plusors fois dit et mostre clerement par quels raisons je sui le plus droit heir de vous a avoir le bailliage de ce royaume, com celui qui sui le plus droit heir de vous de nostre dit cousin,[1] a qui ce royaume est escheu par la mort de nostre dit oncle, qui derainement en morut saisi et tenant, por aberger le fait <et> eschiver riote je dirai as plus courtes paroles que je porai ce que besoign m'est a avoir ce bailliage par devant vous qui est mon droit. Il est chose certaine que ce royaume eschei de par la royne Aalis, nostre ayole, a ces enfans, et que ma mere fu l'ainsnee[2] de ces enfans et son plus droit heir devant la vostre, et puis que ce royaume eschei de par nostre dite ayole a ces enfans et que ma mere fu son plus droit heir devant la vostre, je sui plus droit heir de vous a avoir ce bailliage. Car par forme de droit et de raison nous nous devons prendre a nostre dite ayole, dont l'eritage nous est escheu, par droit ligne desendant; et ce nos devons requerre ne avoir le bailliage de ce royaume par la droite ligne desendant de nostre dite ayole par les raisons que je ai dites, et il le nous couvient a requere de par nostre dit cousin, a qui ce royaume est escheu par la mort de nostre dit oncle qui derainement morut saisi et tenant, je di que je sui plus droit heir de nostre dit cousin que vous n'estes a avoir c'escheete de ce royaume, c'il estoit mesavenu de lui, dont Dieu l'en gart, pour quoi je doi avoir le bailliage de ce royaume par devant vous. Et clere chose est et certaine, que nous ne poons avoir raison que par nos meres qui furent seurs germaines de nostre dit oncle et antes de nostre dit cousin, et puis que nous n'i avons raison ne ne poons a avoir que par nos meres, et ma mere fu ainsnee[3] de la vostre et plus droit heir de nostre dit oncle et de nostre dit cousin que la vostre, se elles vesquissent, dont sui je plus droit heir de vous a avoir ce bailliage, com celui qui sui fis de celle qui l'eust eu devant la vostre. Et a ce que vous avés dit et dites que ma mere morut ains la vostre, et que pour ce a vostre mere vint ou pot venir la raison d'avoir l'escheete de nostre dit oncle a heritage c'il fust mesavenu

---

V: fols cclvi^v^–cclviii^v^ cap. 299; 'Documents relatifs à la successibilité au trône et à régence', pp. 413–14 cap. 10; Edbury, 'Disputed Regency', pp. 39–41 cap. 8.

---

[1] MS: oncle [2] MS: l'ainsné [3] MS: ainsné

de lui sans heir de c'espouse, ce ne vous vaut ne ne doit valoir ne a moi ennuire, que a vostre mere en sa vie n'eschei riens de nostre dit oncle a heritage. Et puis qu'elle en sa vie n'aquist la raison qui li vint ou pot venir, pour ce qu'elle survesqui ma mere com celle a qui n'eschei riens de nostre dit oncle a heritage, si com j'ais dit, ne riens n'en ot ne tint qui valoir vous doie, di je que par celle meisme raison l'escheete de nostre dit oncle est revenue a moi par devant vous tout auci com elle estoit de ma mere par devant la vostre. Car nos soumes demourés el point de nos meres a avoir tel raison chascun l'un devant l'autre, com nos meres eussent, c'elle[4] vesquissent l'une devant l'autre, ne il n'est pas doute que ma mere ne l'eust devant la vostre, dont la doi je avoir devant vous; que estrange chose seroit et tort manifest ce vous, qui estes fis de celle de laquel ma mere estoit plus droit heir a avoir l'escheete de nostre dit ayole et de nostre dit oncle et de nostre cousin, si com j'ai dit, <deuciés l'avoir par devant moi>;[5] ne je n'entens que de gens, qui soient en tel cas com nos somes, il avenist onques par esgart ne par conoissances de court ne par raison ce que vous avés dit qui est plusors fois avenu et fait en ce royaume, ne il n'avendra, ja se Dieu plaist, car se seroit contre toutes manieres de drois et de raisons et tort manifest et apert. Et pour ces raisons et pour toutes les autres que je ai dites ores et autre fois, je di que vous ne devés avoir le bailliage de ce royaume par devant moy, ains le doi avoir par devant vous come celui qui sui plus droit heir de vous dou fis dou roy nostre dit oncle a avoir c'escheete, c'il mesavenoit de lui sans heir de c'espouse, dont Dieu l'en gart, ne ne veull pour chose que vous aiés dites ore et autre fois, qu'il demeure que je n'aie[6] le dit bailliage par devant vous, si le veull avoir se les homes de la haute court conoissent que je avoir le doie. Ne pour ce que vous dites que vous n'entendés que l'usage de Franche est tel com j'ais dit, et que tout fust il tel que vous ne requerés que par l'usage de ce royaume, je ai dit et encor di que il est chose certaine que l'usage de France est tel com j'ai dit, et que il fu mis et establi au conquest de la terre en ce royaume; et je n'entens que puis que cest usage fu establi, qu'il eust autre establi au conquest de la terre en ce royaume, et je

[4] MS: de c'elle [5] There is clearly a phrase missing here. This reconstruction is based on the wording of the parallel passage in Hugh of Brienne's previous speech (7.11.6). [6] MS: n'age

ne croi quc il eust autre establi par le seignor ne par les homes, qu'il le cassast ne qui contraire li fust; por qui je veull que cel usage me vaille et doit valoir pour les raisons que j'ai dites ores et autre fois, se la court conoist que valoir me doie.'

'Si vell avoir le bailliage de ce royaume par devant vous pour toutes les raisons que je ai dite ores et autre fois ou par aucunes d'elles, se les homes de la haute court de ce royaume conoissent que je avoir le doie, si me met je en leur conoissance; et c'il conoissent que je le doi avoir, je en euffre a faire ce que je doi com a baill faisant, l'on a moi se que l'on doit com a bail.'

***[7.11.9]** Ce est la maniere coment la haute cour dou royaume de Jerusalem connut par l'assise dou dit royaume que le bailliage de Jerusalem montoit au baill por ce que il estoit ainsné dou son cousin, le conte dou Braine, et coument li firent les homages.

Aprés cest aleguacion la court dou royaume et messire Joffré de Sargines[a] et le legat[b] et les maistres et les comunes et les frairies s'acorderent que le baill eust le bailliage dou royaume avant que le conte de Braine, et tous les chevaliers homes liges furent d'une part et conurent par l'assise dou royame de Jerusalem que le bailliage montoit au dit baill pour ce qu'il estoit ainsnés dou conte de braine. Et lors messire Goffroi de Sargines se despoula et ala premiers et fist homage au baill, et puis tous les homes et bourgois et fraires. Et ensi ot le roy Hugue le baillage dou royaume de Chipre et puis celui de Jerusalem, et tint le bailliage tant que le petit roy trespassa de ce ciecle,[c] et puis se fist coroner dou royaume de Chipre. Mais entre ces faites vint damoisele Marie[d] et requist le bailliage dou royaume de Jerusalem et dist aucunes choses que vous orés ci aprés.

V: fol. cclviii^{v} cap. 300; 'Documents relatifs à la successibilité au trône et à régence', pp. 414–15 cap. 11; Edbury, 'Disputed Regency', pp. 41–2 cap. 9.

---

[a] Geoffrey of Sergines was the seneschal of Jerusalem and commander of the French garrison in Acre from 1254 until his death in 1269. He acted as regent of the kingdom 1259–63.

[b] William, former bishop of Agen (1247–62), was papal legate in the East and patriarch of Jerusalem, 1262–70.

[c] Hugh II died in 1267.

[d] Maria of Antioch, daughter of Prince Bohemond IV of Antioch and Melisende of Lusignan; died 1307.

***[7.11.10]** Ce est la maniere coment les homes de la haute court de Chipre[1] resurent au seignor le sus dit baill, et fu coroné dou dit royaume aprés la mort dou roy Huge, qui estoit mermeaus, qui tenoit son bailliage.

Quant Dieu fist son comandement de Hugue, le petit roy qui fu fis dou roy Henri et de royne Plaisance, le roy Hugue qui tenoit son bailliage adonc pour ce que elle estoit mermeaus, ala avant et requist as houmes de la seignorie, et les homes le resurent a seignor et fu coronés.

Et aprés avint en Acre a requere le royaume de Jerusalem as homes et a la gent d'Acre, le legat et les gens de religion et le maistre dou temple et de l'ospital et des alemans[a] et le consle de Pise et le baill de Veneise[b] et les frairies et tous les homes d'Acre que la se troverent et <le> desus nomé roy dist as homes de la haute court de Jerusalem qui la estoient assemblés en la presence des dessus només.

V: fols cclviii^{v}–cclix^{r} cap. 301; 'Documents relatifs à la successibilité au trône et à régence', p. 415 cap. 12; Edbury, 'Disputed Regency', p. 42 cap. 10.

---

[a] Respectively: Thomas Berard (1256–73), Hugh Revel (1257–74) and Anno of Sangerhausen (1257–74).
[b] Michele Doro.

---

[1] MS: Jerusalem

***[7.11.11]** Ce est la maniere coment le sus dit baill asembla la haute court dou royaume de Jerusalem et leur requist le dit royame com droit heir, et coument la dite court conut que il estoit le droit heir et li offrirent leur homages.

'Seignors vous savés bien si com nos vous le deymes autre fois en la presence dou patriarche, qui adonc estoit, si a le plus de vous autres qui si estes asemblés, que, quant vous nos feistes assavoir le pereillous estat ou le royame estoit, nous en alames a plus tost que nos poemes. Et nostre venue fu pour .ii. choses: l'une pour le grant besoign de ce royaume, et l'autre pour entrer raison de ce royaume qui escheu nous estoit. Et nous deymes adonc que nos aviens aucunes autres choses a dire et requerre, que nous ne voliens lors dire ne requerre jusques a tant que le leuc et point fust. Et or nous semble quel soit leuc et tens de dire. Car le seignor de Sur et dou Thouron[a] sont ores ci, qui n'estoient adonc, pour qui nous vous faissons assavoir qu'il ne nous couvient pas ores a retraire que nous soumes ne d'ou soumes venus ne de quel gens estrais, car nos entendons bien que asses est seu et coneu a entre vous. Et si savés coment ce royaume, dou quel nous tenons le bailliage, nous est <es>cheus a heritage par la mort dou monseignor Huguet, mon cousin, que Dieus pardoint, qui merme d'aage estoit. Et quel royaume, puis que nous venimes, nous soumes entrés et avons usé et usons com de nostre droit, pour qui vous nous[1] faites le homages et les redevances et les servises si com l'on doit a faire a seignor de ce royaume, et nous somes prest de faire vers vous se que nous devons.'

Et quant le roy ot ce retrait, les devant dis homes de royaume alerent d'une part et au chief d'une piesse se retournerent et firent dire par la coumunauté et par l'otroi d'eaus tous par un d'eaus, c'est

---

V: fol. cclix^{r-v} cap. 302; 'Documents relatifs à la successibilité au trône et à régence', pp. 415–16 cap. 13; Edbury, 'Disputed Regency', pp. 42–3 cap. 11.

---

[a] Respectively Philip of Montfort and his son John of Montfort who succeeded his father as lord of Tyre in 1270 and died in 1283. John had inherited Toron from his mother.

---

[1] MS: vous nous

assavoir par sire Jaque Vidan,[b] que, selon clere requeste que le roy lor avoit fait, il estoient tout aparaillés de faire li leur homages et leur redevances et servises, si com l'on estoit usé de faire au seignors dou dit royaume.

[b] For James Vidan or Vidal, see Riley-Smith, *Feudal Nobility*, p. 37.

***[7.11.12]** Ce est coment damoissele Marie, fille de messire Beamont,[a] fist lire .i. chartre par .i. clerc en la presence de la haute court de Jerusalem, faissant lor assavoir que elle estoit plus droit heir a[1] avoir le dit royaume que le baill n'estoit, pour ce que elle estoit desendue de l'ainsnee[2] seur de la mere de sus dit baill.[b]

'Par devant vous, monseignor Hugue de Leisegniau par la grace de Dieu roy de Chipre, je, damoissele Marie, sui venue par devant vous, seignors, par les religions et homes liges de la haute court dou royame de Jerusalem, et vous fais assavoir com se fu chose que la royne Yzabeau[c] fu dame et droit heir dou royaume de Jerusalem; si ot plusors filles: l'une des filles fu la royne Marie,[d] qui fu filles dou marques,[e] et espouse le roy Johan;[f] de ceste Marie fu nee Yzabel, espouse de l'empereor Fedric;[g] de ceste Yzabel fu nés le roy Conras,[h] pere de Conradin;[i] l'autre de<s> avant dites filles fu la royne Aalis, que la devant dite Yzabeau ot dou conte Henri de Champaigne;[j] de la devant dite Aalis fu nés ly rois Henri de Chipre et dou roy Henri de Chipre fu nés Huguet qui morut avant son aage; l'autre fille de la royne fu madame Melissent, princesse d'Antioche, fille dou roy Heimeri de Lesignau,[k] qui fu ma mere, si com chascun set. Por laquel chose je vous pri et requier et conjuir, si com vos estes tenus

---

V: fols cclix^{v}–cclx^{v} cap. 303; 'Documents relatifs à la successibilité au trône et à régence', pp. 416–17 cap. 14; Edbury, 'Disputed Regency', pp. 43–4 cap. 12.

---

[a] Prince Bohemond IV of Antioch, 1201–33.
[b] The final statement in the rubric is erroneous. However, all the genealogical details given in the body of this chapter are correct.
[c] Isabella I, queen of Jerusalem, 1190–1205.
[d] Maria of Montferrat, queen of Jerusalem, 1205–1212.
[e] Conrad of Montferrat, died 1192.
[f] John of Brienne, king of Jerusalem, 1210–25; died 1237.
[g] Isabella II, queen of Jerusalem (died 1228), married the emperor Frederick II in 1225.
[h] Conrad IV of Hohenstaufen, titular king of Jerusalem (1228–54).
[i] Conrad V (Conradin) of Hohenstaufen, executed 1268.
[j] Alice of Champagne (died 1246) was the daughter of Isabella I and Henry of Champagne (died 1197). She married King Hugh I of Cyprus (1205–18).
[k] Melisende was the daughter of Isabella I by her fourth husband, Aimery of Lusignan. She married Bohemond IV of Antioch.

---

[1] Following table of rubrics (fol. 17^{r}). [2] Following table of rubrics (fol. 17^{r}).

de garder et sauver et maintenir chascun en son drot par les us ou coustume dou royaume de Jerusalem, com cele qui sui le plus prochain heir dou royaume et le plus aparant et fille de la fille de la royne Yzabel et la plus prochaine de la royne Yzabel, mere dou roy Conras, la deraine saisie dou royaume de Jerusalem, a qui vous estes tenus de sauver ces heirs par vous fois, et com celle, que madame ma mere survesqui toutes ces seurs, que vous en saisine et en teneure me metés de la seignorie de Jerusalem, et me faites homage et redevance come a dame et a plus aparant heir qui soit ores en ce royame de Jerusalem. Et je sui aparaillé et bien le vous euffre tout se que les seignors et les dames doivent faire a leur homes, selonc se que les autres seignors dou dit royaume ont fait et usé de faire.'

Quant le clerc ot leu la chartre, le desus nomé roy demanda a la damoysele ce que le clerc ot leu et dit l'avoit dit pour elle, et elle respondi que 'oil'. Tantost le desus nomé roy dist.

***[7.11.13]** Ce est le respons que le sus dit baill fist contre la requeste[1] de la sus dite damoisele Marie.

'Dame, nos vous responderons pour ce que aucunes choses atouchent a nous de ce que vous avés fait dire, et les homes vous feront tel respons com il lor semblera que a eaus apartient.

'Sachés, dame, que nous vodriens que vous eussiés bien et honor, pour ce que vous m'apartenés de si pres com chascun seit, et se qui seroit de vostre raison, Dieus le seit, que vodriens que vous l'eussiés, et qu'il vous fust gardé par tens. Et pour ce que nous vodriens que chascun seust coment l'on vous forsconseille, nos esclersirons devant toute ceste gent aucune chose que vous nous deymes arseres devant le maistre dou temple et le sire de Sur <et> devant plusors autres gens, tout soit ce que nos avons yroient a plaidoier a vous, ne vous n'estes en point que vous le puissiés faire par plusors raisons. Et ce nous ne fuissiens au pais et il ne eust nul autre heir et vous feyssiés as homes tel requeste com vous leur faites, si s'en passeroient il legierement; toutes voies se que nos dirons sera pour esclersir les gens se que vos nous deymes.'

'Sachés, dame, que nos volons que chascun sache que, selonc l'usage de ce royame, qui veaut requerre escheete ou heritage il couvient qu'il le requiert de par celui ou de par celle qui en a eu la deraine saisine, c'il est de celui lignage, et asses est seu et debatu qui est ensi, et si autrement seroit grant tort seroit et grant perill en par plusors manieres, car nulle saisine ne teneure ne vaudroit riens, et les heirs costiers deseriteroient souvent les drois heirs desendans de la souche, et autres maus a ces se poroient faire; et puis que requere couvient par raison et par usage de par ceaus qui ont esté derainement saisi. Car si fu mon oncle, le roy Henri, et son fis de tel maniere de teneure et de saisine come heir merme peut estre saisi, et que je ne soie lor plus prochain et lor plus droit heir nul ne le peut contredire ne debatre; et se vos volés requerre de par le roy Conrat, nos vous disons que le roy Conrat est en son aage, et l'on seit bien que le bailliage ne se peut requerre que par soi meymes

V: fols cclx^{v}–cclxi^{v} cap. 304; 'Documents relatifs à la successibilité au trône et à régence', pp. 417–18 cap. 15; Edbury, 'Disputed Regency', pp. 45–6 cap. 13.

[1] Following table of rubrics (fol. 17^{r}).

de par le derain saisi. Et vous entendés a requerre de par le roy Conrat, que on seit bien que onques ne fu saisi, et que se il fust present il li couvendroit requerre de par le derain saisi et non mie de par lui. Et celui meismes li covendroit requerre de par autrui, c'est assavoir de par le derain saisi, donc est il bien clere chose que vous, ne autre, ne poiés requerre de par lui, et ne pour quant ces choses ne disons nous mie pour fourme de plait, car elles ne nous ont besoign. Et sachés, nos volons bien que chascun sache que, se les homes de ce royaume entendent que vous n'aves nulle raison, que il la vous sauvent se vous l'avés et tenés en sont par droit et selonc l'usage de ce royaume, et bien l'ont fait tout jours des heirs que il entendent que avoient raison, tout sans ce que il fussent present, ne que nul ne requist de par eaus, si com est aparant de Conrat et de ces heirs; et ce il entendissent que vous ou vostre mere ou autre eusiés droit, il l'eussent sauve com il firent a eaus.'

Et quant le desus nomé roy ot ce dit, les homes liges dou royaume alerent ensemble pour faire respons a la desus nomee damoisele des choses que elle avoit dites, et sur ce la dite damoysele s'en parti sans oyr respons.

***[7.11.14]** Ce est la maniere coment les homes de la haute court vindrent en presence dou dit roy et li firent savoir coment il estoient venus faire respons a la sus dite damoysele Marie sur la requeste que elle lor fist, et troverent que elle estoit partie de la, et li manderent par .iii. homes que ce elle voloit atendre li feroient respons de ce que elle a requis.

Adonc les homes liges revindrent devant le roy, et parla par la comunaté de tous sire Jaque Vidan, et dist au desus dit roy en tel maniere: 'Sire, les houmes liges de ce royaume qui si sont estoient a une part pour faire respons a damoysselle Marie d'aucunes paroles que elle avoit dites et fait dire n'a pas granment en la presence de vous <et> de ces seignors qui si sont; de qui il voloient faire respons de ce que a ceaus montoit, et sur ce il entendirent qu'elle sen aloit hors de se gens; si manderent par .iii. homes se elle voloit atendre qui li feroient respons a ce que elle avoit requis et dit, et elle ne vost riens atendre, ains s'en ala; dont les homes de la seignorie qui si sont vous dient que pour chose que il aient oye jusques, il ne se beent riens a retraire de ce faire qu'il vous ont offert a faire, faisant vous a eaus de qu'il vos ont requis, se vous de vostre volenté ne vous en volés arester.

V: fol. cclxi^{v} cap. 305; 'Documents relatifs à la successibilité au trône et à régence', p. 418 cap. 16; Edbury, 'Disputed Regency', p. 46 cap. 14.

*[7.11.15] Ce est le repons que le sus dit roy fist as homes de la sus dite court, que nulle chose n'estoit dite ou faite que il deust arester de non faire envers eaus ce que il doit, et que il feissent vers lui se que eaus faire devoient.

Si que le desus nomé roy lor respondi et dist que chose n'estoit dite ne faite dont il deust arester, et qu'il estoit prest et aparaillé de faire ce que il lor avoit autre fois dit a faire vers eaus se que il devroit, et que il feissent vers lui se que il faire devroient, si com il avoient dit; si que le desus nome Jaque Vidan li paroffri un escrit en qui se contenoit la tenour dou serement que il disoient que les seignors dou dit royaume estoient usé de faire et devreent faire. Et il tout ensi le jura com il contenoit en celle escrit, et tantost com il ot se fait les homes liges, qui la estoient, dou dit royaume de Jerusalem, li firent homage et tout premierement messire Goffrei et le sire de Sur et le sire dou Thouron et tout le remenant de homes qui la se troverent; et puis aprés resut les homages des autres qui li estoient tenus a faire; et aprés ressut le serement des frairies et de tous les autres que serement li devoient; et tint le royaume dou Jerusalem quites et em pais, et fu coronés a Sur, la ou les roys de royaumes se coronent; et fist tant par son sens que temple et ospitau et sire Goffrey de Sargines et toutes manieres des gens l'obeyssoient et servoient come au seignor.

Et tant pourchassa et fist vers le legat et vers tote la gent de religion, qui li firent une lettre ouverte, seelees de leurs seaus, de trestous leur eremens qui sont desus escris,[a] et coment le royaume li eschut par l'usage, et coment il le requist as homes come son droit, et il li firent homage com a droit heir, et que plus droit heir ne avoit, ne le conte de Braine ne damoisele Marie, et en tel maniere ot et tint le dit roy les .ii. royaumes quites et en pais com de son droit et sa raison par l'assise et l'usage dou royaume de Jerusalem et de Chipre.

V: fols cclxi^{v}–cclxii^{v} cap. 306; 'Documents relatifs à la successibilité au trône et à régence', pp. 418–19 cap. 17; Edbury, 'Disputed Regency', pp. 46–7 cap. 15.

---

[a] i.e. all the material in appendix 7.11.1–7.11.15.

7.11.16

In 1306 King Henry II of Cyprus (1285–1324) was removed from power in a bloodless coup, and his brother Amaury, the titular lord of Tyre, seized power. What to do with Henry proved problematic, and eventually, in February 1310, Amaury had his brother taken to Cilician Armenia where he was held prisoner. Then in June of that year Amaury was murdered, and the king's restoration followed in August. So far as Henry was concerned, his brother's regime had lacked legality, and so the question of the validity of the various governmental actions that dated from the period of his rule needed to be addressed. The *assise* of January 1311 edited here was intended to sort out these problems.

***[7.11.16]** Ce est la maniere dou remede qui fu fait par le roy Henri et ses homes des choses qui ont esté faites au tens dou sire de Sur a ce que la gent ne soient perdans, lequel fu fait a mois de jenvier de .iii^{c}. et .x. de Crist.[a]

Premierement, que toutes les dettes, couvenances et fins qui ont esté faites devant le sire de Sur et les homes le roy, selles qui seront requises, seront conducés par les homes de court come garens, et si n'i avra point tourne de bataille, ou par autre maniere selonc l'usage. Et qui ensi le provera, avra asses prové. Et par les susdites manieres se proveront les paies.

Et les detes qui seront couneues par devant l'auditour et seront requises, se il ne pevent prover par garens, l'auditour et l'escrivain seront auci guarens com les autres ou les guarens qui seront en la chartre et qui faudront as guarens, <et> la chartre et le cartulaire seront guarentie. Et se il n'i a guarentie que le cartulaire, la chose se doit presenter devant le roi pour avoir conseill. Et par la susdite maniere se proveront les paies.

Et des dettes qui sont couneues par devant la segrete et seront requises, si se condueront par la guarentie de celui qui estoit bailli de la segrete et par les escrivains et les escris de leur livres. Et par la susdite maniere se proveront les paies et toutes les autres choses que a la secrete sont atachés, que par la segrete se doivent conduire.

Et se il avenoit que detes fussent requises lequels ne fussent couneues as susdis leus et que l'on les vosist prover par guarens, que celle guarentie se conduze a l'usage dou royaume.

Et des paies des assenés se doivent prover par celui qui estoit bailli de la segrete et par les escrivains et par leur livres, et se aucun fust esté assené ou eust assené en la segrete autre qui se doit condure par la susdite maniere et les coumers auci.

Et des dons que gens averont fait a leur mort de meubles, que cel don se doie prover par guarens, et vaudra a tant come se il fust doné par court, et que il n'i a point de tournes.

V: fols cclxii^{v}–cclxiii^{v} cap. 307; 'Bans et Ordonnances des rois de Chypre', pp. 368–70 cap. 25.

---

[a] i.e. January 1311 (n.s.).

Et les fiés et rentes qui furent prises par raison de la seignorie par defaute d'eir par l'usage ne pevent riens demander.

Et tous ceaus qui ont esté semons pour le servise dou pais et n'en alerent et leur fiés furent arestés, ne pevent requere amende.

Des dons et ventes et eschanges et apaus qui touchent en la haute court et en la segrete, les quels ont deniers douné, doivent recouvrer leur deniers et doivent rendre le surplus qu'il avront resseu, acuillant les mecions qu'il avront faites et les bastimens, et se pour tant se qui se trovera par conseill, se il doivent avoir amende nulle pour leur deniers

Et tous ceaus qui avront vendu eschange, apaute <ou> doune doivent venir devant le roy requerre les saisines, et le roy doit faire venir les parties et faire rendre le leur et as autres leur deniers dedens .vii. jours, par l'usage.

Dou fait de la taille dou tens passé, tout la doivent paier, sauve la saison de ceaus qui estoient arestés, et qui estoient hors dou pays et en confines.

Et des devises, le roi doit ordener gent d'aler lever les bones qui furent mises au tens passé et comander que chascun soit en son usage.

Des enquestes qui furent au tens passé, chascun le doit faire savoir a roy quant il vodront recouvrer le leur, a ce que il aient leur raison.

Et se il li a chose oblié en la quelle doit estre mis remede, elle doit estre esclersie par le roy et ces homes, ou par la plus grant partie qui au jour se troveront des ordenés, et de ce metre les homes en raison.

Et pour ce que les choses desus escrites soient fermes et estables, se doivent faire .ii. chartres: l'une sera o poier dou roy et l'autre o poier des homes, a ce que se debat fust, que la chose fust esclersie par les chartres.

Et les fins qui furent faites des servise ne pevent riens requere amende.

Et des defaus et des fins qui furent prises en celui tens, le roy ne peut riens requere ne autre pour lui.

7.11.17

King Henry II died childless in March 1324. The question of the succession must have been thought out well in advance, and the throne passed to his nephew, Hugh IV (1324–59), without, so far as is known, any difficulty. The problem, however, was that Hugh, the son of Henry's brother Guy who had died in about 1300, was not strictly speaking Henry's closest heir. Henry was survived by two sisters, Alice and Helvis. Helvis was unmarried, and Alice's husband had been a leading supporter of the usurper, Amaury of Tyre, and had died a prisoner in Kyrenia castle in 1316. Although under normal circumstances a sister was considered a closer heir than a nephew, here in 1324 it was argued—tendentiously—that the rules for the royal succession were different. Even if Hugh's two aunts had waived their rights to the throne—and the prospect of the rule of an ageing unmarried woman was something that few would have welcomed—it was important for Hugh to have his right to rule clearly established and universally recognised, not least because Henry II had had other nephews, the exiled sons of his brother and adversary, Amaury of Tyre.

***[7.11.17]** Coment mesire Hugue de Leseigniau,[a] constable dou royaume de Chipre, a requis le royame de Chipre au mesire Gui d'Iblin, leuc tenant dou seneschau,[b] et l'ot par la conoissance de la court.

Con ce soit chose que en l'incarnacion Nostre Seignor .M.CCC.xxiv. de Crist au .ii. jours dou mois d'avrill, que le roy Henri de Jerusalem, treszime des latins, trespassa de ce siecle, le samedi derain jour de mars de la dite annee; et quant ce vint le dit lundi a .ii. jours d'avrill aprés vint mesire Hugue de Lezeigniau, nevou dou desus dit roy, c'est assavoir fis de son fre<re>, monseignor Gui de Lezeigniau de bone memoire,[c] en[1] la presence de la coumunaté des homes liges dou dit royaume de Chipre, et fist dire par sire Bartholemé de Montolif le coment il n'estoit pas chose celee as homes dou royaume le coment Dieu avoit fait son comandement de son seignor et son oncle le dit roy, pour quoi il entendoit, selonc les husages dou royaume de Jerusalem et de ceaus de Chipre, avoir gregnour raison et l'escheete dou royaume que nulle persone de ces parens qui demourés estoient aprés lui, pour quoi il prioit et requeroit les homes dou royaume que il deussent metre le fait de la court en tel estat que il puist requere le droit et la raison que il entendoit avoir; car il ne veet que il eust seneschal au jour, devant que il peust requere sa raison selonc l'usage dou dit royaume. Les homes furent d'une part, et leur sembla que selonc l'usage il deveent ordener home qui tenist leuc dou seneschau pour oyr ce que le dit messire Hugue vosist requerre et demander de la dite escheete. Et par le coumun ascent de tous ehleu mesire Gui d'Iblin lequel tint la court plaigniere.

V: fols cclxiii[v]–cclxvi[v] cap. 308; 'Documents relatifs à la successibilité au trône et à régence', pp. 419–22 cap. 18.

---

[a] Hugh had been appointed constable of Cyprus by 1318.

[b] As John of Ibelin's account (cap. 221) made clear, in the absence of the king, the seneschal presided in the High Court. It was thus appropriate that the he should preside over the meeting of the Court at which a new king was received. (For the same procedure in 1369 see appendix 7.11.1.) Guy of Ibelin was the son of Philip of Ibelin, the maternal uncle of King Henry II and seneschal of Cyprus until his death in 1318; in due course Guy came to occupy that office in his own right.

[c] Guy of Lusignan had died ca. 1300.

---

[1] MS: et

Et le dit monseignour Hugue de Lezeigniau vint en la presence dou dit leuc tenant dou seneschau, et ce paia de conseill, et fist dire le coment n'estoit pas chose celee la mort dou roy Henri son seignor et son oncle, par la cui mort il entendoit que le royaume de Chipre li estoit escheu com a son heir. Et pour ce espoir que le dit roy avoit seurs en vie, et que aucunes simples gens poroient cuider qu'elles eusset gregnour <raison> en l'escheete dou dit royaume que lui, pour ce que elles estoient seurs dou dit roi et il estoit son nevou, il fist dire et declarer en la court l'usage de cestui cas, de ce que avoit esté use au royaume de Jerusalem et en celui de Chipre, c'est assavor au quel des parens des roys poroit et devoit escheir le royaume quant moroit, lesquels usages estoient au coumun cors des escheetes des fiés, ains ce devoit juger l'escheete dou royaume selonc l'usage dou contraire.

Et pour ce que l'on seust que il estoit usage de ce en ce cas, le dit monseignor Hugue fist dire le coment il estoit clere chose et manifeste par les ansienes escritures, coment le roy Bauduin de Jerusalem de bone memoire, quant il fu si surpris de la dite maladie et conut que il estoit pres de sa fin, veant ces heirs qui aprés lui estoient, c'est assavoir .iii. seurs et .i. petit nevou, il, counoissant la raison de son petit nevou qui estoit de .v. ans d'aage, le fist coroner, a ce que il fust plus seur que raison ne li fust empeeschee.[d] Et que por ce que l'on avoit seu de ce que celui prodome fist en sa fin, poient home clerement prizunier que les nevous, pour ce que il sont mahles, heritent au royaume avant des seurs, pour ce que elles sont femelles.

Encor avint de cestui cas plus prochain, puis ce que quant le roy Henri le Gras morut, il laissa aprés lui .i. fis mermiau et une soue seur qui ot a nome madame Yzabeau de Lezeigniau et .ii. siens nevous, c'est assavoir monseignour Hugue de Lezeigniau et monseignor Hugue conte de Braine. Et selonc l'usage de <ce royaume> la roine Plaisance, espouse dou dit roy Henri le Gras et mere dou mermeau que le dit roy laissa, ot et tint le bailliage de son fis selonc l'usage que les meres ou les peres doivent avoir avant toutes persones. Et quant elle ot tenu le dit bailliage une espace de tens, elle morut, estant encour son dit fis merme d'aage, et sur ce le bailliage

[d] King Baldwin IV of Jerusalem (1174–85) had his nephew, Baldwin V (1185–6), crowned in 1183 during his own lifetime, thereby passing over the king's two (not three) sisters, Sybilla and Isabella.

dou dit royaume vaqua, lequel par raison devoit escheir a un des .iii. parens dou dit roy Henri le Gras desus nomé, c'est assavoir ou a madame Yzabeau de Lezeigniau, seur dou dit roy Henri Gras, ou a messire Hugue de Lesiengniau, son nevou, ou a messire Hugue conte de Braine, son autre nevou. Et par la conoissance que ceaus prodes homes qui lors estoient houmes dou dit royaume firent, fu coneu que monseignor Hugue de Lezeigniau avoit gregnour raison en l'escheete dou dit royaume, que non avoit madame Yzabeau, seur dou dit roy, por ce que il estoit home et elle feme. Et que encor avoit le dit monseignor Hugue de Leseigniau gregnor raison au dit royaume que le conte de Braine, pour ce que il estoit ainsné dou dit conte. Et pour celle conoissance ot le dit monseignor Hugue de Leseigniau l'escheete dou dit bailliage com celui qui est heir le plus prochain a avoir l'escheete dou dit royaume, et par celle counoissance se demostre clerement que en l'escheete dou royaume heritent avant les heirs mahles que les femelles, encor ne soient il si prochains de parencé au derain saisi, et que en cestui propre cas ou autre esté l'escheete dou roy Henri le Gras entre sa seur et ces nevons estoit ores venu le cas sans nulle comparison l'escheete de cestui nostre seignor Henri qui ores est mort entre ces seurs et son dit nevon. Car tout auci come quant le roy Henri le Gras morut et laissa aprés lui seurs et nevous poiet escheir son royaume tout ensi. Cestui roi Henri a laissé seurs et nevon, et par la conoissance que lors fu faite par messire Hugue de Lezeigniau, son ayol, entendoit il que les houmes devroient estre bien clers de faire ceste conoissance de l'escheete qui requiert ores.

N'en pour enques encor disoit il que il voloit faire plus clers les homes dou royaume de cest usage, et faisoit dire ensi que il n'estoit pas chose celee dou plait qui avoit esté entre madamoisele Marie et le dit mesire Hugue de Leseigniau sur l'escheete qui leur eschut par la mort dou Conradin, leur cousin, dou royaume de Jerusalem: par lequel parenté que eaus .ii. avoient au dit Conradin, la dite madamoisele Marie estoit plus prochaine de lui de .i. degré, car celle estoit cousine germaine dou dit Conradin, et le roy Hugue estoit au dit Conradin en tiers degré. Mais ja pour ce que la dite damoysele Marie estoit plus prochaine dou dit Conradin de .i. degré, que n'estoit le roy Hugue, ne demora que la conoissance ne fu faite par la court dou royaume de Jerusalem, qui lors fu faite en la cité d'Acre, que le roy Hugue estoit plus droit heir a avoir le dit royaume de Jerusalem que n'en estoit madamoisele Marie, et que par celle conoissance que lors fu faite est clere demonstracion que l'usage dou royame de Jerusalem est tel que les heirs mahles, encores soient les femelles plus prochaines dou derain saisi, heritent au royaume avant que les heirs femelles qui plus prochaines sont.

Et pour toutes les raisons et cleres demonstrances que monseignor Hugue faisoit dire, il entendoit que selonc l'usage de Jerusalem et de celui de Chipre, que il estoit plus droit heir a avoir l'escheete dou royame de Chipre avant que nul autre persone que en vie fust, com celui qui estoit nevon de cestui nostre seignor le roy Henri, qui ores est mort, c'est assavoir fis de son frere messire Gui de Lezeigniau, et desendu et venu de celle part dont le dit royaume meut. Et se il eust nul qui mescreust qu'il n'en estoit tel com il se faisoit et apartenist au roy Henri en tel degré com est sus dit, et que le dit roy Henri ne le tenist et avouast a son nevou loyal, et a lui oncle, et de celle part dont le royaume meut, aparaillié estoit de prover le tout enci come court conoistroit ou esgarderoit que prover le deust, et ce provant et faisant a sainte yglise et as homes ce que il devoit faire selonc usage que les seignor sont[2] usés de faire, quant il doivent entrer en la seignorie, et entendoit et voloit que le dite mesire Gui, tenant leuc dou seneschau, le deust metre en la saisine dou dit royaume, se la court le conoissoit, et li requist que il li deust faire avoir la conoissance de la court.

Sur ce le dit tenant leuc dou seneschau comanda a la court qu'elle deust conoistre ce que il en avoit a faire selonc sa requeste par l'usage. La conoissance de la court est tel que, provant monseignor Hugue de Lezeigniau ce que il a offert a prover, et faisant a sainte yglise et as homes ce que il doit faire quant les rois doivent entrer en la seignorie selon l'usage, 'vous, sire, avés a faire sa requeste'.

Et quant c'en vint le dit jour que la dite conoissance fu retraite au dit monseignor Gui d'Iblin, tenant leuc dou seneschau en Chipre, le dit monseignor Hugue de Lezeigniau fist dire par son conseill sire Bertelemé dou Montolif au leuc tenant de seneschau coment il avoit oy retraire la dite conoissan<ce> que les homes dou royaume avoient fait sur la requeste qu'il fist; en laquelle conoissance contenoit que, provant ce que il avoit offert a prover de son lignage, que le dit tenant leuc dou seneschau avoit a faire sa requeste, pour quoi il li fist dire que guarens estoient aparaillés de prover le parenté qui estoit

[2] MS: son

entre lui et son seignor son oncle, le roy Henri, qui mort estoit. Et maintenant le dit tenant leuc dou seneschau ressut la preuve selonc l'usage. Et puis que la dite preuve fu faite, le dit monseignor Hugue de Leseigniau fist offrir par son dit conseill as homes dou royaume que il estoit aparaillés de faire a sainte yglise et as homes ce que il estoit tenu de faire selonc l'usage avant que les seignors entrent en la seignorie. Et la maintenant le dit monseignor Hugue s'agenoilla et jura sur les saintes Dieus evangiles, en la main de frere Johan, l'arcevesque de Nicossie,[e] le serement qui est usé que les roys font avant ce que il entrent en la seignorie dou royaume. Et quant il ot fait, il fist requere au dit tenant leuc dou seneschau que il le deust metre en la saisine dou dit royaume selonc la conoissance de la court. Et le maintenant le dit tenant leuc dou seneschau, en presence de la court, le saisi dou dit royaume par une verge. Et aprés fist requerre as homes dou royaume que il li deussent faire ce que il doivent, et le maintenant li firent homages tous ceaus qui se troverent, c'est assavoir come grant partie d'eaus.

[e] John of Conti OP, archbishop of Nicosia (1312–32).

7.11.18

The *assise* issued by Hugh IV in 1355 is in four parts, and the compilers of the 1369 version of the treatise opted to give each section its own chapter number. There are two other versions of this *assise*. One, copied at the end of the fourteenth-century section of MS A (fols ccclxii^{r}–ccclxiv^{v}), is also dated 1355. The other, found in the Munich: Bayerische Staatsbibliothek: Codex Gallus 51, where it is specified that the *assise* was issued by King Henry (II) in 1312 and was to be in force until February 1316 (i.e. 1317 n.s.). It would seem therefore that Hugh IV has reissued an earlier piece of legislation.

***[7.11.18.1]** Ce est l'assise qui fu ordené[1] et juré par le roy Hugue et ces homes a .xvi. jours de may, l'an de .M.CCC.lv. de Crist.

L'assise des oizeaus et des chiens et de chevacheures perdues.

Ceaus qui les troveront ne souffriront que eaus ne leur mehnees ne leur vilains les tienent depuis que il le<s> saveront, et dedens .xv. jours il les facent enveer en la cité plus prochain ou il seront trovés; et celui de qui sera l'oizeau ou le chien ou la chevacheure paiera le despens que l'on avra fait de mander en la vile, jusques a tant que il sera rendu, et se donra pour la troveure d'estoir ou pour facon formé .ii. bezans, et pour le tresiau .i. bezant, et pour l'espervir .i. bezant, et pour levrier ou brachet .i. bezant, et pour cheval .v. bezans, et pour ronssin ou mull ou mulle .iii. bezans, et pour ahne .i. bezans.

Et se il avenoit que aucun chevalier fust mescreu ou autre home lige d'avoir tel oiseau ou chien ou beste, il jurera de non, ou il paiera la value de l'oiseau ou dou chien ou de la beste, laquele value doit estre prisee par ceaus que l'on cuidera que meaus conoissent l'oseau ou le chien ou la chevacheure, et paiera de painne pour l'estoir ou facon formé .c. bezans, et pour le treseau .l. bezans, et pour le chien .i. marc d'argent, et pour l'espervier ou esmerlion .x. bezans, et de la chevacheure .iii.c. bezans, et de ahne ou de beuf .xxv. bezans.

Et se il avenoit que aucun home lige neast la chose et feist le serement et fust puis ataint de la chose, il paiera a seignor de la chose la value au double, et paiera de paine mil bezans.

Et celui qui sera mescreu d'avoir celé ou emblé des devant dites choses, ce il n'est chevalier ou home lige, le roi fera faire enqueste, et se il est ataint par l'enqueste, il sera a la merci dou roi de paier la value au double et la paine devant dite et de estre justizé ou d'autre laresin. Et se il est fis ou frere ou parent prochain <de> chevalier, il paiera la value de la peine et si avra la honte.

V: fols cclxvi^{v}–cclxvii^{r} cap. 309; 'Bans et Ordonnances des rois de Chypre', pp. 373–4 cap. 31,1.

---

[1] MS: ordenee

***[7.11.18.2]** L'assise des esclas et des esclaves.

Les esclas ou les esclaves qui s'enfuiront et veront au poier de aucun ou de aucune persone, si tost come il saveront l'aresteront et le manderont as sités plus porchaines de la ou sera trové, si come est avant dit, a ceaus qui seront establis de resever. Et le seignor de l'esclaf ou de l'esclave doit rendre en generau les mencions que l'on avra faites jusques a tant que il sera mené en la vile. Et quant l'on menra la chose perdue en la sité et livre a celui qui sera ordené, celui est tenus de rendre les mencions et les choses ordenees, si come est desus devisé. Et le seignor de l'esclaf donra pour la troveure de l'ome .iv. bezans, et por le garson .ii., et pour la feme grant .iii. bezans, et pour la garce .ii. bezans. Et ce chevalier ou home lige est mescreu d'avoir celé ou fortrait ou pacé par sa terre ou forvee aucun des avant dites persounes, ou il jurera de non, ou il paiera la value de l'esclaf ou de l'esclave. <. . .>[1] sera .c. bezans; et se il est autre que home lige, il emportera autel paine com est desus devisé a chapistle devant dit des chiens et oseaus.

V: fol. cclxvii[v] cap. 310; 'Bans et Ordonnances des rois de Chypre', pp. 374–5 cap. 31,2.

[1] Evidently a phrase has been omitted—possibly a homeoteleuton ('et la value de l'esclaf ou de l'eslave sera . . .')

***[7.11.18.3]** L'assise des vilains et des vilaines fuitives.

Tous les vilains et vilaines estranges, qui veront de si en avant ou qui seront en la terre dou roy ou d'aucun home lige ou d'aucune feme lige ou autre qui ait terre, dedens quinse jours puis que il seront venus, les doit on ausi mander as sités plus prochaines au poier de ceaus qui seront ordenés, si come il est dit en l'autre chapistle. Et ce le vilain n'en a letres ou bone garentie que il vait en aucun servise ou a comandement de son seignor, et celui ou celle qui ne les mandera et pora estre prové par enqueste que les vilains ou les vilaines aient esté en la terre de celui qui ne les avra mandé puis les .xv. jours, il paiera de painne, c'est assavoir dou vilain .ii.c. bezans, et de la vilaine .c. bezans, et de garson ou de garce .l. bezans, et au seignor de qui sera le vilain, dou vilain .ii.c. bezans, et de la vilaine .c. bezans, et dou garson ou de garce .l. bezans.

Et se la defaute est dou seignor de la terre, il doit paier la painne, et se la defaute est de son bailli ou de son juré ou de la gent de son cazal a qui il avra eschargé se fait, il doivent paier la dite painne, se il ont le poier; et se il n'en ont le poier, leur seignor les doit livrer a seignor come ceaus qu'il sont encheus en sa merci.

En .iii. saisons nul ne doit arester les dis vilains et vilaines, c'est assavoir au tens de seailles, les quels coumensent de l'entrant d'avrill et definent par tout jugn; et l'autre saison est as vendenges, qui comensent de l'entrant de setembre et durent par tout huitouvre; et l'autre au labour des vignes, qui comensent de l'entrant de mars et definent par tout avrill; c'est assavoir par tous les leus ou il y a seailles ou vignobles en tel maniere que se le seignor de ceaus vilains ou vilaines les mandent querre, que l'on ne les doit arester ne garentir pour l'eschaison de la painne que lors ne court.

Et de ceaus qui s'avouent pour frangomates ou esclas franchis, il doivent porter letres seelees dou visconte ou dou bailli de la contree en quoi il sont, coment il sont frans, a ce que l'on ne les puisse arester.

V: fols cclxvii^{v}–cclxviii^{r} cap. 311; 'Bans et Ordonnances des rois de Chypre', p. 375 cap. 31,3.

***[7.11.18.4]** L'assise des larons dou bestiaill.

Le roy doit metre en .v. leus de Chipre, c'est assavoir a Nicossie, a Baphe, a Limeson, au Chief, et a Famagust, en chascune des ses leus .ii. de ces homes dignes de foi, lesquels doivent jurer sur les saintes evangiles de Dieu que en[1] bone foi et sans nul mal engin, ne pour amisté ne pour haine, que il ne doivent laisser de dire voir et faire droit. Il doivent enquerre selonc leur consience tous ceaus que il troveront qui ont emblé bestes menues ou pors, et a la premiere fois il li feront tailler le nes, et a la segonde fois tailler le pié, et a la tierce fois pendre. Et ceaus que il troveront que il averont emblé beufs ou chevacheure ou ahnes, a la premiere fois il doivent tailler le pié, et a la segonde fois pendre. Et se il a emblé des bestes menues ou de pors tant que il soit de la value de .xxv. bezans, il doit avoir le pié taillé et a la segonde fois pendre.

Et les juges qui sont establis as leus devant nomées doivent mander au seignor de celui a qui l'on met le larecin sus, <que il, dou jor que il avera receu leur lettres en quinze jours, doit enveer cel home ou ceaus a qui l'on met le larecin sus;>[2] et se il ne les envee, il doit venir en sa propre persone, se il n'en a essoigne de son cors, dou quel essoigne, se il a esté ensoigné, il doit estre creu par son serement. Aprés doit jurer que tel home ou ceaus qui seront esté requis ne sont en son pooir, ne il ne les a fait fuïr ne son comandement, et que toutes les fois que il les pora trover il les fera venir devant eaus. Et se il avenoit que il ne les envoyast dedens le terme qui est nomé, puis que il avront esté requis, ne il n'en alast pour soi espurger par son serement, il doit paier de paine .c. bezans, et de ceaus que l'on se clame dou laresin sont encheus, et les juges ont poier de prendre les en quelque part que il les truissent et faire la justize com celui qui est encheu en la consience des juges et tel que l'on ne doie justize faire, et regardant a ce qu'il em porent savoir ou cuider veraiement par enqueste ou par oyr dire de gens digne de foi, que il a fait le laresin en maniere que l'on ne doit faire justize.

V: fols cclxviii[r]–cclxix[v] cap. 312; 'Bans et Ordonnances des rois de Chypre', pp. 376–7 cap. 31,4.

---

[1] MS: in [2] A homeoteleuton in both MS V and MS A. Following Munich Cod. Gall. 51.

Et se aucun vilain ou esclaf emble de son seignor ou de ses vilains, le seignor le peut faire quiter ou faire les mener devant les juges, et les juges doivent faire justize devant nomee. Et se les juges mandent a aucun fenier ou a son bailli pour ces vilains ou pour ces homes, il doit envoier celles persones qui seront requises pour enquere dedens .viii. jors que il leur seront requis et qu'il avront receu le comandement. Et se il ne les envoient dedens le terme que il paieront pour chascune persone .x. bezans, et chascune fois que il les requeront et ne les envoient, il paieront por chascune persoune .x. bezans. Et celui qui avra perdu le sien, les doit recovrer dou laron, se il ont de quoi, et se il n'en a de quoi il doivent livrer le laron a celui qui avra perdu le sien, se il ne doit estre pendu et doit estre en son poier tant que son seignor le delivre. Et se le fenier ou le bailli nee que il n'en a resseu les letres, se il ne veaut jurer, il doit paier .c. bezans. Et qui avra emblé bestes menues ou pors le vaillant de .i. beuf, l'on doit faire de lui justize com de celui qui a emblé .i. beuf

Et tous les vilains ou vilaines et esclas ou esclaves et toute maniere de bestials et chiens <et> oizeaus, qui sont en la terre ou au poier des avant només, doivent estre en la maniere et en la paine desus devisee.

Et tous les bezans que l'on resevoir de ceaus qui seron<t> encheus as paines de devant devisees dovient estre mis en la taille.

Et quant l'on avra mené aucun vilain ou vilaine ou esclaf[3] ou beste ou chien ou oizeau ou autre a aucun des ordenés, et ne sera de son dioce, il le doit faire savoir a celui qui sera plus prochain de lui que une tel chose n'i a esté menee le tel jour qui est de tel, a se que celui le face savoir as autres par quoi le seignor de la chose le puisse savoir, et toutes les mensions que l'on avra faites le seignor de la chose les doit paier.

Et tout cest ordenement des vilains et des vilaines et des esclas et de esclaves et de bestes et de chie<n>s et de oizeaus et autres est pour ceaus qui ont terres et pour ceaus qui n'en ont terre.

Et se il y a riens a amender, que il se puisse faire par le roy et par ces homes.

---

[3] MS: ensclaf

7.11.19

The *remède* issued on the day of King Peter I's murder has to read in conjunction with the prologue to the 1369 version of John's treatise (appendix 7.11.1), and is alluded to in that text. Most of the provisions can be linked directly to what were considered Peter's abuse of royal authority.

***[7.11.19]** Ce est l'ordenance et remede que il a esté par l'asent des houmes par court le mardi a .xvi. jours de jenvier, l'an de .M.iiic.lxviii. de Crist,[a] lequel remede se doit joindre au livre des assises.

Tout premierement, que l'office des enquestes soit de tout abatue, et que il ne puisse metre nul nouvel husage de nul office, se il n'en est par l'asent et la volenté des homes, ne nulle cabele ne nulle condamnacion, se il n'en est par l'asent des homes ou la plus grant partie; et faire abatre tous les droitures et apaus que les maistres des enquestes et autres ont mis ou usé sans l'asent des homes.

Le segont, que la mise qui fu ordenee pour le Smirne pour les galees soit abatue, con se soit chose que l'alié de Smirne est desfaite,[b] et la taile soit ordenee pour la gent d'armes et le tarsenal et la zardehané[c] de Famaguste, et qu'il ne puisse estre desturbié en autre place; et que l'escrivain de la taille puisse rendre aconte chascun an a .ii. chevaliers que le seignor ordenera; et que la reguale et toute maniere de gent puissent paier la taille, et ne doit durer que le tens qui est ordené.

Le tiers, que la mise dou focé de Nicossie se puisse metre o servise dou focé et des murs par la maniere qui fu comensé, et non en autre part, en tant qui soit parfait.

Le quart, que les homes soient tenus et maintenus en leur franchises et drois et preveliges selonc l'assise, et que null ne soit tenus de aler par comandement, sauve ce que l'on est tenus par l'assise.

V: fols cclxix[v]–cclxxi[r] cap. 313; 'Bans et Ordonnances des rois de Chypre', pp. 378–9 cap. 33. English translation in Guillaume de Machaut, *The Capture of Alexandria*, pp. 206–8.

---

[a] I.e. 16 January 1369 (n.s.). This was the date of Peter I's murder. For an analysis, see J. Richard, 'La révolution de 1369 dans le royaume de Chypre', *Bibliothèque de l'Ecole des chartes*, 110 (1952), pp. 108–23; cf. P.W. Edbury, 'The Murder of King Peter I of Cyprus (1359–1369)', *Journal of Medieval History*, 6 (1980), pp. 227–9.

[b] Smyrna had been captured from the Turks in 1344, and the kings of Cyprus had been partly responsible for maintaining galleys for its defence.

[c] Otherwise *zardkhané*—'magasin aux cottes de mailles'. I thank Professor J. Richard for his advice on this term.

Le quint, que le seignour ne puisse metre main ne faire metre main as ses homes ne a leur femes ne a leur enfans ne a leur biens, se il n'en est par esgart ou par conoissance de court.[d]

Le sist, que le seignor puisse tenir court une fois le mois et plus, se a lui plaist; et se il ne peut, que il puisse ordener autre en leuc de lui a tenir court et escouter la gent.

Le septime, que le seignor ne puisse esforcier nulle feme lige de marier, se c'est assavoir celles qui doivent servise de cors celonc l'assise, se il n'en est a persone per a elle et de son baron, et par l'asent de ces plus prochains parens; et qu'il ne la puisse mener a autre que avoir droit de son fié selonc l'assise par esgart et par conoissance de court; et que ce elle est veve que elle aie espace de .i. an depuis que son baron morut a faire son deull celonc l'assise.

Le huitime, que il se puisse trover .i. le plus verai livre des assises, c'est assavoir dou conte de Japhe, et regarder le par le seignour et les homes, et coreger le, et metre le au trezor de l'iglise en aucune huche, et estre a la garde de l'iglise et soute le seel de .iv. homes de la cort. Et quant aucun cas verra a la court que les homes seront enserés, qu'il puissent mander faire ouvrir par les dis homes, ou la plus grant partie, et faire porter le dit livre pour esclersir le dit cas, selonc ce qui est usé a royaume de Jerusalem.[e]

Le nouvime, que les salines se puissent remetre en leur premier estat dou tens dou roy Hugue, sauve ce qui est eschangé et fait par court.

Le disime, que le seignor ne puisse prendre guerre, ne faire pais, ne mander querre ne resevor gent d'armes de .c. persones en amont, se il n'en est par l'asent et conseill de tous les homes ou la plus grant partie.

Le onzime, qui touche a la conestablie, que null sodeer qui parte de son seignor ou que son seignor le congee, et que il ne vient dedens le terme de .iii. mois, se il est au pais, de venir requerre par devant le conestable au son seignor qui li doit, et, se il est hors dou pais, .i. an, que ce le dit terme passe que il ne soit plus escouté.

---

[d] Inserted in bottom margin: 'Save que se acun des anfans des homes liges, qui ne fust home lige, feist acun otrage ou enuire ou chose non deue, que sertefiant se, le seignor doit metre main sur luy et punir selon la defaute qui fera, et selon son estat, et autrement non.' It is not clear whether this passage was part of the original text or not.

[e] An allusion to the *Letres dou Sepulcre*. See above appendix 3.1.1.

Le douzime, que quant aucun fait nouveleté de terre ou de aigue ou de autre, et que enqueste se fait, et se treut par l'enqueste que noveleté a esté faite, que celui qui avra fait la nouvelleté doie paier au l'autre partie le damage pour le pris que le seignor ordenera par ces homes mandant veir le damage.

Le trezime, que les homes puissent jurer l'un a l'autre ores et toutesfois que l'ome fait la feauté que l'un soit tenu a l'autre de ayder et conseiller a leur raison, gardant les drois et les raisons et honor dou seignor quant aucun sera hotragé hors de assise et de usage.

APPENDIX 8—JOHN OF IBELIN'S DISCOURSE ON THE REGENCY

Apart from his treatise, John wrote one other work that has survived, an account of the rules governing the regency (or *bailliage*) of the kingdom of Jerusalem. The only extant copy is in MS A where it follows directly after the conluding chapter (above appendix 3.13), 'le dereain chapitle de cest livre'. The compiler of MS A evidently regarded it as a separate work, even though the rubric refers to John's account of the coronation (above caps 219–20), and in the text there is what appears to be a cross reference to the *bailli's* oath, presumably the chapter edited here as appendix 3.6.2.

John's description of the rules governing the *bailliage* turns into a highly partisan account of the history of the regency arrangements since the marriage of Queen Isabella II to the Emperor Frederick II of Hohenstaufen in 1225. Since then the kingdom of Jerusalem had had an absentee monarchy, and conseqently authority had had to be exercised by a series of regents. Most of them held power in defiance of the Hohenstaufen, and what John has done is to compose an *apologia*, seeking to give their decidedly questionable rights to rule a semblance of legality.[1]

[1] The best discussion of this subject remains Riley-Smith, *Feudal Nobility*, cap. 8.

***[8.1]** Voz avés oy devant coment on deit coroner le rei,[a] c'est assaveir quant il est d'aage aprés la mort de son pere ou de sa mere ou de celui qui a le reiaume par irritage. Et or orrés quant les enfanz demorrent merme d'aage que l'on deit dire et faire.

Quant il avient que Dieu fait son comandement dou roi qui a le reiaume par irritage, la royne deit aveir le baillage jusques a l'aage de ces enfans; ne chose qu'il facent ne vaut que tant come le baillage dure, se il n'est <par> esgart ou conoissance ou recort de court. Et quant Dieu fait son comandement dou roi ou de la reyne, ou que le rei seit en prisson, et les enfanz seient mermes d'aage ou fors dou pays et il a parent ou parente qui li ateint de la ou le fié muet, le plus preuchein, seit home ou feme, deit aveir et tenir le baillage jusques a l'aage des enfans. Ne riens qu'il donent n'est valable, que tant come le bailage dure. Et qui defaut de faire homage <au baill un an>[b] et un jor, ou feme se marie sanz son congie, il ne perdent leur fiés, fors tant come le baillage dure, ce est assaveir de pere ou de mere ou de parent de la ou le fié muet, por ce que l'on est tenus de faire homage a ciaus sauve le dreit heir. Et la raisson por quei si est: por ce qu'il n'i ait plait a celui qui tendra le baillage, et que les homes seient quittes a lui piestant que l'eir sera d'aage ou qu'il veigne a son reiaume. Ne l'on n'en apelle baill que ciaus a qui le reiaume peut escheir, et pere et mere est baill, et toz ciaus qui sont sur le fait de la seignorie sont baillis, et deivent jurer[1] as homes liges le sairement avant dit.[c] Ne nul des homes <. . .> de faire lor homage par l'assise ne par l'usage en nulle maniere, mais il pevent bien faire homage au mermiau ce il lor plaist, et se il ne veulent, il ne sont riens tenus de faire le. Car il sereient tenus au seignor de fei, et le seignor qui sereit merme ne sereit de riens tenus a eaus. Et por ce

---

A: fols clxxiv[v]–clxxvii[r]; 'Documents relatifs à la successibilité au trône et à régence', pp. 397–401 cap. 2.

---

[a] Above caps 219–20.
[b] Folio damaged.
[c] Above appendix 3.6.2.

---

[1] MS: jures

fait on homage de ces mains entre les mains de son seignor, que le seignor et les homes otreient en la presence de la court les paroles que l'on dit a l'homage faire et receveir la fei. Et por ce que l'omage est fei, est il raisson que le seignor et l'ome l'otreient en la presence de la court; que la court tesmoigne et juge del seignor a l'home et de l'home au seignor.

Et quant il n'i a parent ou parente qui atient as enfanz de la ou le reiaume muet, les homes dou reiaume se deivent assembler, ou la greignor partie d'iaus, et esli<re> un d'iaus, celui qui lor semblera qui seit plus proufitable, et la ou le plus des homes s'acorderont a estre sur le fait de la seignorie por faire et tenir dreit a la gent et assembler court et faire esgart ou conoissance a ciaus qui li requeront, et sera valable ce qui se fera devant lui, sauve de .iii. choses de quei on ne deit respondre senon devant son seignor qui est a eaus tenus de fei et eaus a lui, ce est assaveir: de son cors et de son fié et de son honor.

Et ensi est il en l'assise et en l'usage dou reiaume de Jerusalem, si come je l'ais oy retraire as anciens. Quant le rei Baudoyn fu pris vers la terre d'Antioche des ennemis de la fei, les homes dou reiaume s'assemblerent et eslurent sur le fait de la seignorie mesire Estace Garnier, qui esteit seignor de Seete et de Cesaire. Et le dit Estace la ressut, et en ouvra moult bien a l'honor de Dieu et au proufit de la Sainte Terre. Car par le conseill des proudesomes dou reiaume et o l'aye des Veneciens ala il assegier la cité de Sur qui encores esteit de Sarazins, et rechatata le rei.[d]

Et ce vi ge au tens de l'empereor Federic, que quant il man<da> querre por espouser ma cosine, la juene royne Ysabel, elle fu coronee a Sur, et toz les homes li firent homage, et mon cosin mesire Belleem, le[2] seignor de Seete,[e] et pluisors des homes liges la menerent.[f]

[d] King Baldwin II of Jerusalem (1118–31) was the prisoner of Balak, ruler of Aleppo, from April 1123 until August 1124. It was during this period that the forces of the kingdom of Jerusalem in conjunction with a Venetian fleet commanded in person by the doge laid siege to Tyre which surrendered on 7 July 1124. Eustace Grenier, the lord of Sidon and Caesarea, died in June 1123.

[e] Balian lord of Sidon was the son of John of Jaffa's father's sister.

[f] Isabella II (Isabella of Brienne) was crowned as queen of Jerusalem and married by proxy to Frederick II at Tyre in the late summer of 1225. Balian of Sidon was a member of the party that conducted her to Italy. She and John of Jaffa shared a common ancestor in Maria Comnena.

[2] MS: et le

Et quant il retornerent, l'empereor manda le conte Thomas[g] por estre en son leuc sur le fait de la seignorie, et i fu tant que Dieu fist son comandement de l'empereris devant ditte. Et elle laissa son fiz le rei Conrat d'un an.[h] Quant on oy la mort de la ditte empereris, les homes liges s'assemblerent et eslurent mon oncle, le vieill seignor de Baruth,[i] et mon cosin, le seignor de Seete, a estre sur le fait de la seignorie jusques a la venue de l'empereor. Mon oncle dist qu'il n'i sereit pas, et on vost metre mesire Johan, le seignor de Cesaire,[j] et il dist qu'il ne poeit estre, por ce qu'il esteit <. . . . .>pre.[k] Et adonc esluerent il a <estre> aveuc le seignor de Seete le conestable, mesire Eudde de Monbeliart,[l] et furent jusques a la venue de l'empereor.

Et quant l'empereor s'en retorna,[m] il laissa en son leuc le seignor de Seete et mesire Garnier l'Aleman. Mesire Garnier l'Alemen fu un poi de tens et se rendi frere dou Temple,[n] et le conestable fu en son leuc. Aprés avint que l'empereor manda un evesque en cest pays et letres au seignor de Seete et au conestable comandant, coment mesire Phelippe de Maugastiau fust sur le fait de la seignorie. Le seignor de Seete et le conestable assemblerent les homes liges a Sainte Cruis,[o] et y esteit le patriache Girot,[p] et firent lire les letres, es quels conteneit le comandement devant dit de l'empereor. Mon cosin, mesire Johan le seignor de Cesaire, si vint la et dist la parole por les homes liges, car le seignor de Baruth et noz toz estemes en Chypre, et dist coment l'empereor et le conestable et le seignor de Seete, qui la estoient, avoient juré quant il demorerent en son leuc de tenir les assises et les bonz uz et les bones costumes dou reiaume

[g] Thomas of Aquino, count of Acerra, was Frederick's regent in the kingdom of Jerusalem, 1226–28.

[h] Isabella died on 8 May 1228, shortly after giving birth to Conrad.

[i] John of Ibelin, lord of Beirut (died 1236), the elder brother of John of Jaffa's father, Philip of Ibelin.

[j] Not yet lord of Caesarea as his father, Walter (died 1229) was still alive. John died c. 1240.

[k] Folio damaged.

[l] Odo of Montbéliard, the constable of Jerusalem, was the nephew of Walter of Montbéliard who had come to the East at the time of the Fourth Crusade.

[m] Frederick II was in the East from September 1228 until May 1229.

[n] Garnier l'Aleman (Werner of Egisheim) appears to have joined the Templars in about 1233 and had died before the end of 1237.

[o] Acre cathedral.

[p] Gerald of Lausanne, patriarch of Jerusalem 1225–39.

de Jerusalem, et que lui meismes et toz les autres homes en estoient tenus par leur feis, et espessiaument ciaus qui tenoient les seignories en estoient tenus par leur feis et par leur seirement de tenir et de maintenir les assises et les bons uz et les bones costumes dou dit reiaume, et que ce que l'empereor mandeit esteit a l'encontre de ces assises et de ces usages, por ce qu'il voleit desfaire par letres ce qu'il aveit fait devant court, et que ceste chose ne poeient il faire ne soufrir por les raissons devant dittes. Si que y ot si grant remor que la campane dou comun sona, et l'evesque s'en parti, et le seignor de Seete et le conestable demorerent ensi come il estoient sur le fait de la seignorie.[q] Le seignor de Seete morut,[r] et le conestable demorra sur le fait de la seignorie.

Et aprés ce, quant le rei Conrat fu d'aage,[s] il manda letres et messages por metre home en son leuc, si que les homes liges s'assemblerent, et i fu l'arcevesque Estorgue de Nicossie,[t] qui au jor estoit vicaire dou patriarche, et distrent ensi: que ce il plaisseit au rei Conrart de venir en sa seignorie, qu'il le recevereient come leur dreiturier seignor; car l'assise et l'usage dou dit reiaume esteit tel, que por letres ne por messages ne pooient il faire vers lui ce qu'il devoient; car ce sereit contre leur seirement et contre leur leauté, ce qu'il esteient certains de lui qui estoit leur seignor et deveit estre tenu a eaus de fei ne vodrent mie faire qu'il fausicent de nulle chose qui fust contre l'assise ou l'usage dou dit reiaume, lequel il meismes est tenus de tenir et de faire tenir; et por ce qu'il lor sembloit qu'il ne savoit mie bien le dit usage, le li faisseient il assaveir, mais qu'il gardereent le reiaume selonc lor ussage jusques il li plaireit de venir.

Et quant le rei Conrat fu d'aage, les homes s'assemblerent et vindrent chés l'arcevesque Estogue de Nicossie, qui au jor esteit vicaire de Nicossie[u] si come je voz ai devant dit, et distrent coment le rei Conrat leur seignor esteit d'aage et puis qu'il esteit en son aage, que l'empereor Federic son pere n'esteit plus baill de cest pays. Car l'assise et l'usage dou reiaume de Jerusalem est tel, et aussi celui de Chypre, que puis que le dreit heir est en son aage que pere et mere

[q] There events occurred in late 1232 or early 1233.

[r] In 1239.

[s] In 1242, although Conrad was only fourteen at the time. See Edbury, *John of Ibelin*, p. 70.

[t] Eustorgue of Montaigu, archbishop of Nicosia 1217–50.

[u] Correction in margin: dou patriarche

pert le baillage. Et por ce l'aveit perdu lempereor Federic. Et qu'il voleient metre home sur le fait de la seignorie, si come il esteit uzé de faire. Et por ce que mesire Belleem, le seignor de Seete, esteit mort, eslurent il le conestable, mesire Eudde de Monbeliart, sur le fait de la seignorie, car mon cosin, le sire de Cesaire, ne mei n'en y vomes estre por aucunes raissons.

Et quant ma cosine, la royne Aalis, sot que l'empereor aveit perdu le baillage par l'aage de son fiz, elle fist assembler toz les homes liges qu'elle post aveir, et ala chés le devant dit arcevesque, et i fu le maistre dou Temple, frere Armant de Pierregort,[v] et le concelle de Gene, et le baill de Veneisse,[w] et requist le reiaume de Jerusalem de par sa niece, l'emperis Ysabel, come le plus dreit heir aparant requerant en la court, et disseit que puis que son nevou le rei Conrat esteit d'aage et il ne veneit en persone entrer en son reiaume, que le plus preuchein heir i deveit entrer, et que elle esteit le plus preuchein heir de la ou le reiaume moveit, et que ce esteit elle prest de prover tot ensi come la court esgardereit ou conoistreit que prover le deust, et por ce lor prioit elle et requereit que letres ne messages que le rei Conrat aveit mandé ou mandast ne deussent acuillir, que se sereit contre l'assise et l'usage dou dit reiaume, dou quel il ne pooient en nulle maniere aler a l'encontre. Les homes liges orrent conseill et s'acorderent toz de receveir la royne Aalis, sauve le conestable qui ne voleit que l'on la receust tant que l'on mandast au rei Conrat qu'il venist ou que l'on receveit s'ante. Le seignor de Baruth[x] et mei et les autres deymes que l'on ne li aveit pas a mander, et ensi entra la reyne Aalis en la seignorie et li fist l'on homage come au plus dreit heir aparant et requerant en la court, sauve le rei Conrant. Et furent rapelés toz les dons que l'empereor aveit fait, et mesire Reymont de Gibelet meismes fu fors de la seneschausie. Car nulle chose n'est valable qui se fait hors d'assise ou d'usage, et por ce furent il rapelés.

Et la ditte royne manda en Chypre a son fiz, le roi Henri, et a noz parens qui vindrent premier. Et lors le seignor de Baruth et le seignor dou Thoron, mesire Phelippe de Monfort, et le seignor Arsur, mesire Johan de Ybelin, et mei et la chevalerie d'Accre alames par

[v] Armand of Périgord, c. 1232–c. 1245.
[w] Marsilio Zorzi.
[x] Balian of Ibelin, lord of Beirut 1236–47.

terre aveuc mesire Raou de Saisson, espous de la ditte royne, prendre Sur de mesire Ytier Filangier,[y] qui y estoit de par l'empereor, et la preymes.[z] Et les homes liges la donerent en garde au seignor de Baruth et le chastiau d'Accre au seignor dou Thoron et a mesire Nicolle Antiaume, por ce que les homes liges deivent garder les fortereces dou reiaume quant les heirs sont mermes d'aage ou quant il sont hors dou pays et il ne sont entrés en leur reiaume si come il deivent. Ne ne soufrimes mie que le dit Raou de Saisson les eust en son poeir, por aucuns perill qui peussent avenir, si come il avint dou fait de la Moré[3] as enfanz dou Champeneis, de sire Jofrei de Villehardoin en cui mains elle demorra.[aa]

Et puis la mort dou rei Henri avint aussi que les homes liges mistrent le seignor d'Arsur sur le fait de la seignorie, et puis i fuis ge par eaus. Si os a besoignier a Japhe contre les ennemis de la fei. Si remeimes noz le seignor d'Arsur sur le fait de la seignorie, et il y demora jusques a tant que la royne Plaissence et son fiz vint en Accre et requist le baillage et l'ot, et quant elle s'en parti, elle laissa le seignor d'Arsur en son leuc.[bb]

Or avés oy coment les homes liges deivent faire baill quant les heirs sont mermes d'aage, ou quant il sont fors dou pays et il ne sont encores entrés en leur reiaume si come il deivent.

---

[y] Lotario Filangieri

[z] Tyre was taken by the anti-Hohenstaufen coalition in July 1242.

[aa] A reference to the Geoffrey of Villehardouin, a nephew of his namesake the historian, who in 1209–10 seems to have used chicanery to supplant the heirs of the William of Champlitte and take control of the principality of the Morea.

[bb] John omits to mention that on the death of Alice of Champagne in 1246, the regency passed to King Henry of Cyprus. For much of his period of office, Henry delegated the government in Acre in John of Ibelin, lord of Arsur. On Henry's death, no one seems to have claimed the regency until 1258 when his widow, Plaisance of Antioch, claimed it on behalf of her infant son, Hugh II. In the meantime John of Jaffa (1254–6) and John of Arsur (1256–8) held office as the appointees of the vassals. Having asserted her rights and those of her son in 1258, Plaisance retired to Cyprus, leaving John of Arsur, who died later that same year, as her deputy.

---

[3] MS: mere

BIBLIOGRAPHY

1. Previous editions of John of Ibelin

(i) *French*

Thaumas de La Thaumassière, G., *Coustumes de Beauvoisis, par Messire Philippes de Beaumanoir Bailly de Clermont en Beauvoisis. Assises et bons usages du royaume de Jerusalem, par Messire Jean d'Ibelin comte de Japhe et d'Ascalon, sire de Rames et de Baruth. Et autres anciennes coutumes le tout tiré des Manucripts* (Bourges, 1690).
'Livre de Jean d'Ibelin', *RHC Lois*, 1, pp. 1–432.

(ii) *Italian*

L'Alta Corte, le Assise, et buone usanze del Reame de Hyerusalem (Venice, 1535), fols 1–74v.
Canciani, P. (ed.), *Barbarorum leges antiquae* (Venice, 1792), 5, pp. 133–296.

2. Other legal writings from the Latin East

'Abrégé du Livre des Assise de la Cour des Bourgeois', *RHC Lois*, 2, pp. 227–52.
Assises d'Antioche, reproduites en françois, ed. L.M. Alishan (Venice, 1876). Another version translated into Russian: 'Armianskii perevod "Antiokhiiskikh Assiz"', trans. A.A. Papovian, *Vestnik Matenadarana*, 4 (Erevan, 1958), pp. 331–75.
'Bans et Ordonnances des rois de Chypre', *RHC Lois*, 2, pp. 353–79.
'La Clef des Assises de la Haute Cour du royaume de Jérusalem et de Chypre', *RHC Lois*, 1, pp. 573–600.
'De la bataille por murtre', *RHC Lois*, 2, pp. 327, 329, 331, 333, 335.
'Document relatif au service militaire', *RHC Lois*, 2, pp. 423–34.
'Documents relatifs à la successibilité au trône et à la régence', *RHC Lois*, 2, pp. 393–422.
Edbury, P.W., 'The Disputed Regency of the Kingdom of Jerusalem, 1264/6 and 1268', *Camden Miscellany*, 27 (= Camden Fourth Series, 22, 1979), pp. 1–47. (Reprinted in *Kingdoms of the Crusaders* V)
'Formules', *RHC Lois*, 2, pp. 381–9.
Geoffrey Le Tor, 'Livre', *RHC Lois*, 1, pp. 433–50.
James of Ibelin, 'Livre', *RHC Lois*, 1, pp. 451–68.
'Les Lignages d'Outremer', *RHC Lois*, 2, pp. 435–74.
'Livre des Assises de la Cour de Bourgeois', *RHC Lois*, 2, pp. 3–226. (Medieval Greek version: *Ἀσσίζαι του Βασιλείου των Ιεροσολύμων και της Κύπρου*, ed. C. Sathas in *Μεσαιωνική Βιβλιοθηκή*, 6 (Venice, 1877), pp. 3–497; English translation from the Greek by N. Coureas, *The Assizes of the Lusignan Kingdom of Cyprus* (Nicosia, 2002).)
Le Livre au Roi, ed. M. Greilsammer, Documents relatifs à l'histoire des croisades 17 (Paris, 1995) (also in *RHC Lois*, 1, pp. 601–44).
Philip of Novara, 'Livre de forme de plait', *RHC Lois*, 1, pp. 469–71.

3. Other primary sources

Brunetto Latini, *Li Livres dou Tresor*, ed. Francis J. Carmody (Berkeley and Los Angeles, 1948).
'Chronique d'Amadi', ed. R. de Mas Latrie in *Chroniques d'Amadi et de Strambaldi* (Paris, 1891–93), vol. 1.
'L'estoire de Eracles empereur', *RHC Historiens Occidentaux*, 2.
Guillaume de Machaut, *The Capture of Alexandria*, trans. J. Shirley and P.W. Edbury (Aldershot, 2001).
Philip of Novara, *Les quatre âges de l'homme*, ed. M. de Fréville (Paris, 1888).
Smbat, *La Chronique attribuée au Connétable Smbat*, trans. G. Dédéyan, Documents relatifs à l'histoire des croisades 13 (Paris, 1980).

4. Secondary Works

Brayer, E., 'Un manuel de confession en ancien français conservé dans un manuscrit de Catane (Bibl. Ventimilians, 42)', *Mélanges d'archéologie et d'histoire*, 59 (1947), pp. 155–98.
Brayer, E., P. Lemerle and V. Laurent, 'Le Vaticanus latinus 4789. Histoire et alliances des Cantacuzènes aux XIVe–XVe siècles', *Revue des Etudes byzantines*, 9 (1951), pp. 47–105.
Charles-Gaffiot, J. (ed.), *La France aux portes de l'Orient; Chypre XIIème–XVème siècle* (Paris, 1991).
Edbury, P.W., 'The Ibelin Counts of Jaffa: a Previously Unknown Passage from the "Lignages d'Outremer"', *English Historical Review*, 89 (1974), pp. 604–10. (Reprinted in *Kingdoms of the Crusaders* VI).
——, 'The Murder of King Peter I of Cyprus (1359–1369)', *Journal of Medieval History*, 6 (1980), pp. 219–33. (Reprinted in *Kingdoms of the Crusaders* XIII).
——, 'Law and Custom in the Latin East: *Les Letres dou Sepulcre*', in *Intercultural Contacts in the Medieval Mediterranean*, ed. B. Arbel (= *Mediterranean Historical Review*, 10) (London, 1996), pp. 71–9. (Reprinted in *Kingdoms of the Crusaders* IX).
——, *John of Ibelin and the Kingdom of Jerusalem* (Woodbridge, 1997).
——, 'John of Jaffa and the kingdom of Cyprus', *Επετηρίδα του Κέντρου Επιστημονικών*, 23 (Nicosia, 1997), pp. 15–26. (Reprinted in *Kingdoms of the Crusaders* VIII)
——, 'The *Livre des Assises* by John of Jaffa: The Development and Transmission of the Text', in *The Crusades and Their Sources: Essays Presented to Bernard Hamilton*, ed. J. France and W.G. Zajac (Aldershot, 1998), pp. 169–79.
——, *Kingdoms of the Crusaders: From Jerusalem to Cyprus* (Aldershot, 1999).
——, 'Philip of Novara and the *Livre de forme de plait*', in *Πρακτικά του Τρίτου Διεθνούς Κυπρολογικού Συνεδρίου (Λευκωσία 16–20 Απρίλιου 1996)*, vol. 2, ed. A. Papageorgiou (Nicosia, 2001), pp. 555–69.
——, 'Redating the Death of King Henry I of Cyprus?', in *Dei Gesta Per Francos: Etudes sur les croisades dédiées à Jean Richard*, ed. M. Balard, B.Z. Kedar, J. Riley-Smith (Aldershot, 2001), pp. 339–48.
Folda, J., *The Art of the Crusaders in the Holy Land, 1098–1187* (Cambridge, 1995).
——, 'The Hospitaller Master in Paris and Acre: Some Reconsiderations in Light of New Evidence', *Journal of the Walters Art Gallery*, 54 (1996), pp. 51–9, 269–72.
Folda, J., and P.W. Edbury, 'Two Thirteenth-Century Manuscripts of Crusader Legal Texts from Saint-Jean d'Acre', *Journal of the Warburg and Courtauld Institutes* 57 (1994), pp. 243–54.
Grandclaude, M., *Étude critique sur les Livres des Assises de Jérusalem* (Paris, 1923).
——, 'Classement sommaire des manuscrits des principaux livres des assises de Jérusalem', *Revue historique de droit français et étranger* ser. 4, 5 (1926), pp. 418–75.

Grivaud, G., 'Ο πνευματικός Βίος και η γραμματολογία κατά την περίοδο τησ Φραγκρατίας, in *Ιστορία της Κύπρου*, ed Th. Papadopoullos, vol. 5 (Nicosia, 1996), pp. 863–120.

Hiestand, R., 'Die Herren von Sidon und die Thronfolgekrise des Jahres 1163 im Königreich Jerusalem', in *Montjoie. Studies in Crusade History in Honour of Hans Eberhard Mayer*, ed. B.Z. Kedar, J. Riley-Smith and R. Hiestand (Aldershot, 1997), pp. 77–90.

Hunt, D. and I. (eds.), *Caterina Cornaro: Queen of Cyprus* (London, 1989).

Mayer, H.E., 'Das Pontifikale von Tyrus und die Krönung der lateinischen Könige von Jerusalem', *Dumbarton Oaks Papers*, 221 (1967), 141–232.

Nielen-Vandevoorde, M.-A., 'Un livre méconnu des *Assises de Jérusalem*: Les *Lignages d'Outremer*', *Bibliothèque de l'Ecole des chartes*, 153 (1995), pp. 103–30.

Prawer, J., *Crusader Institutions* (Oxford, 1980).

Recoura, G., 'Notes sur six manuscrits inédits ou peu connus des Assises de Jérusalem', *Mélanges d'archéologie et d'histoire de l'École française de Rome*, 42 (1925), pp. 147–66.

Richard, J., 'La révolution de 1369 dans le royaume de Chypre', *Bibliothèque de l'Ecole des chartes*, 110 (1952), pp. 108–23. (Reprinted in *Orient et Occident au Moyen Age* XVI).

——, 'Les Listes de seigneuries dans "Le livre de Jean d'Ibelin". Recherches sur l'Assebebe et Mimars', *Revue historique de droit français et étranger*, ser 4, 32 (1954), pp. 563–77. (Reprinted in *Les relations entre l'Orient et l'Occident*).

——, *Chypre sous les Lusignans: Documents chypriotes des archives du Vatican (XIVe et XVe siècles)* (Paris, 1962).

——, *Orient et Occident au Moyen Age: contacts et relations (XIIe–XVe s.)* (London, 1976).

——, *Les relations entre l'Orient et l'Occident au Moyen Age* (London, 1977).

——, 'Freedom and Servitude in Cyprus and Rhodes: An Assize Dating from 1396', in *Intercultural Contacts in the Medieval Mediterranean*, ed. B. Arbel (= *Mediterranean Historical Review*, 10) (London, 1996), pp. 272–83.

Riley-Smith, J., *The Feudal Nobility and the Kingdom of Jerusalem, 1174–1277* (London and Basingstoke, 1973).

Röhricht, R., *Regesta Regni Hierosolymitani (1097–1291)* (Innsbruck, 1893; supplement 1904).

Rüdt de Collenberg, W.-H., 'L'Heraldique de Chypre', *Cahiers d'Heraldique*, 3 (1977), pp. 86–157.

INDEX NOMINUM

INDEX RERUM